T0286928

THE ROUGH GUIDE TO
MOROCCO

ROUGH
GUIDES

This thirteenth edition updated by
Stuart Butler

Contents

Introduction to
Morocco

For Westerners, Morocco holds an immediate and enduring fascination. Though just an hour's ride on the ferry from Spain, it seems at once very far from Europe, with a culture – Islamic and deeply traditional – that is almost wholly unfamiliar. Throughout the country, despite the years of French and Spanish colonial rule and the presence of modern and cosmopolitan cities like Rabat and Casablanca, a more distant past constantly makes its presence felt. Fez, perhaps the most beautiful of all Arab cities, maintains a life still rooted in medieval times, when a Moroccan kingdom stretched from Senegal to northern Spain, while in the mountains of the Atlas and the Rif, it's still possible to draw up tribal maps of the Berber population. As a backdrop to all this, the country's physical make-up is extraordinary: from the Mediterranean coast, through four mountain ranges, to the empty sand and scrub of the Sahara.

Across much of Morocco, the legacy of **colonial occupation** is still felt in many aspects of daily life. The **Spanish zone** contained Tetouan and the Rif, the Mediterranean and the northern Atlantic coasts, Sidi Ifni and the Tarfaya Strip; the **French zone** the plains and the main cities (Fez, Marrakesh, Casablanca and Rabat), as well as the Atlas. And while Ceuta and Melilla are still the territory of Spain, it is the French – who ruled their "protectorate" more closely – who had the most lasting effect on Moroccan culture, Europeanizing the cities to a strong degree and firmly imposing their language, which is spoken today by all educated Moroccans (after Moroccan Arabic or one of the three local Berber languages).

This blend of the exotic and the familiar, the diversity of landscapes, the contrasts between Ville Nouvelle and ancient Medina, all add up to make Morocco an intense and rewarding experience, and a country that is ideally suited to independent travel – with enough time, you can cover a whole range of **activities**, from hiking in the Atlas and sandboarding in the Sahara to getting lost in the back alleys of Fez and Marrakesh. It can be hard at times to come to terms with the privilege of your position as a tourist in a country with severe poverty, and there is, too, occasional hassle from unofficial guides, but Morocco is essentially a **safe** and **politically stable** place to visit: the death in 1999 of King Hassan II, the Arab world's longest-serving leader, was followed by an easy transition to his son, Mohammed VI, and the country pretty much carried on as normal while the Arab Spring uprisings toppled governments in nearby Libya, Tunisia and Egypt. Indeed, your enduring impressions are likely to be overwhelmingly positive, shaped by encounters with Morocco's powerful tradition of hospitality, generosity and openness. This is a country people return to again and again.

Where to go

Geographically, the country divides into four basic zones: the coast (Mediterranean and Atlantic); the great cities of the plains; the Rif and Atlas mountains; and the oases and desert of the pre- and fully fledged Sahara. With two or three weeks – even two or three months – you can't expect to cover all of this, though it's easy enough (and highly recommended) to take in something of each aspect.

Broadly speaking, **the coast** is best enjoyed in the north at **Tangier** – still shaped by its old "international" port status despite undergoing considerable renovation – **Asilah** and **Larache**, and in the south at **El Jadida**, **Essaouira**, perhaps the most easy-going resort, or remote **Sidi Ifni**. **Agadir**, the main package-tour resort, is a functional enough base for exploration.

Inland, where the real interest of Morocco lies, the outstanding cities are **Fez** and **Marrakesh**. The great imperial capitals of the country's various dynasties, they are almost unique in the Arab world for the chance they offer (particularly in the former) to witness city life that, in patterns and appearance, remains in large part medieval. For monuments, Fez is the highlight, though Marrakesh is for most visitors the more enjoyable.

FACT FILE

- Morocco's **area** of 446,550 square kilometres (722,550 sq km including the Western Sahara) makes it slightly smaller than France or Spain, slightly larger than California. The population of just under 34 million compares with just eight million at independence in 1956.
- Nearly 99 percent of Moroccans are **Muslim**, with 1 percent **Christian** and a tiny minority (an estimated 6000 people) **Jewish**. The literacy rate is 68.5 percent (78.6 percent for men, 58.8 percent for women).
- The **main languages** are Arabic, Berber (Tarfit, Tamazight and Tashelhaït) and French. Spanish is still widely spoken in the north, and English is increasingly spoken by young people, especially in tourist areas.
- Morocco gained **independence** from French and Spanish rule on March 2, 1956. The head of state is **King Mohammed VI**, who succeeded his father Hassan II on July 30, 1999. The government is chosen from an **elected legislature** and is currently run by Prime Minister Saadeddine Othmani of the moderate Islamist PJD (Party of Justice and Development). The main opposition parties are the Istiqlal (Independence) Party, Morocco's oldest political group, and the RNI (National Rally of Independents).
- Such is the importance of **date palms** in the Moroccan south that oases are traditionally measured by the number of their palms rather than their population, and it was once illegal to sell a date tree, a historically vital source of food.
- Despite the beauty of **zellij** work in medersas and fountains across the country, it is thought that there is at least one flaw in every mosaic due to the Islamic belief that only Allah can create perfection.

Canary Islands (Sp.)

ATLANTIC
OCEAN

Goulimine
Tarfaya
Tan Tan
Border
Closed
Tindouf
Laayoune
Boujdour
Boukra
Smara

Dakhla

S A H A R A

Bir Mogrein

MAURITANIA

0   200
kilometres

Nouadibhou

Choum

ATLANTIC
OCEAN

Kenitra
Salé
RABAT

Mohammedia
Casablanca

Azemmour
El Jadida
Berrechid
Settat
Oued
Zem

Oued Oum er Rbia
Khouribga

Oualidia

Beni Mellal
Kasb
Tad

Safi

Benguerir

Oued Tensift

Azilal

Demnate
Jebel M'Goun
(4071m)

Essaouira
Chichaoua

Marrakesh

Boumaln
du Dadès

Tizi n'Tichka
(2260m)

Asni
Jebel
Toubkal
(4167m)

Oued Dadès

N'Kou

Tin Mal
Tizi n'Test
(2092m)

HIGH

Ouarzazate

ATLAS

JEBE

Agdz

Taroudant
Jebel Siroua
(3304m)

Tazenakht

Oued Dr

Zago

Agadir
Inezgane
Oued Souss
Taliouine

Foum Zguid

Tiznit
Tafraoute

ATLAS

Tata

Sidi
Ifni
ANTI
Akka

ALGERIA
(BORDERS
CLOSED)

Bou Izakarn
Foum
el Hassan

Goulimine

Tan Tan & Laayoune
SEE INSET FOR CONTINUATION
Tindouf

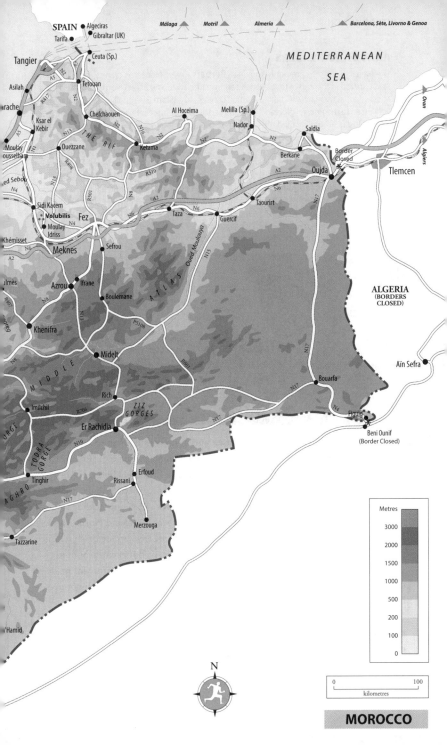

ARABS AND BERBERS

The Amazigh – more commonly known as **Berbers** – were Morocco's original inhabitants. The Arabs arrived at the end of the seventh century, after sweeping across North Africa and the Middle East in the name of their revolutionary ideology, **Islam**. Eventually, nearly all the Berbers converted to the new religion and were immediately accepted as fellow Muslims by the Arabs. When Muslim armies invaded the Iberian peninsula from Morocco, the bulk of the troops were Berbers, and the two ethnic groups pretty much assimilated. Today, most Moroccans can claim both Arab and Berber ancestors, though a few (especially Shereefs, who trace their ancestry back to the Prophet Mohammed, and have the title "Moulay") claim to be "pure" Arabs. In the Rif and Atlas mountains, and in the Souss Valley, though, groups of pure Berbers remain, and retain their **ancient languages** (Tarifit, spoken by about 1.5m people in the Rif; Tamazight, spoken by over 3m people in the Atlas; and Tashelhaït, spoken by around 4m people in the Souss Valley region). In recent years, there has been a resurgence in Berber pride (often symbolized by the Berber letter ⵣ); TV programmes are now broadcast in Berber languages, and they are even taught in schools, but the country's majority language remains Arabic.

Travel in the **south** is, on the whole, easier and more relaxing than in the sometimes frenetic north. This is certainly true of the **mountain ranges**, where the **Rif** can feel disturbingly anarchic, while the southerly **Atlas ranges** (Middle, High and Anti-) that cut right across the interior are both beautiful and accessible. Hiking in the **High Atlas**, following old mule paths through mud-brick villages or tackling some of the area's impressive peaks, is increasingly popular, especially around North Africa's highest mountain, **Jebel Toubkal**, though more and more trekkers are being tempted east by the quieter trails that cut through the beguiling Aït Bouguemez. Summer treks are possible at all levels of experience and altitude, and despite inroads made by commercialization, the vast majority of the area remains essentially "undiscovered" – like the Alps must have been in the nineteenth century.

Equally exploratory in mood are the great **southern routes** beyond the Atlas, amid the **oases** of the pre-Sahara. Major routes here can be travelled by bus, minor ones by rented car or local taxi; the really remote ones by 4WD vehicles or by getting lifts on local *camions* (trucks), sharing space with market produce and livestock. The oases, around **Skoura**, **Tinghir**, **Zagora** and **Erfoud**, or (for the committed) **Tata**, are classic images of the Arab world, vast palmeries stretching into desert horizons. Equally

memorable is the architecture that they share with the Atlas – bizarre and fabulous *pisé* (mud) **kasbahs** and **ksour**, with Gothic-looking turrets and multi-patterned walls.

Further south, you can follow a route through the **Western Sahara** all the way down to Dakhla, just 22km short of the Tropic of Cancer, where the weather is scorching even in midwinter.

When to go

As far as the **climate** goes, it is better to visit the south – or at least the desert routes – outside midsummer, when for most of the day it's far too hot for casual exploration, especially if you're dependent on public transport. However, temperatures in July and August – the hottest months – reach an ideal level on the coast, although resorts often get overrun with Moroccan tourists flocking here to escape the inland heat.

Spring, which comes late by European standards (around April and May), is perhaps the best overall time, with a summer climate in the south and in the mountains, as well as on the Mediterranean and Atlantic coasts. Relatively moderate conditions also permeate the country in early **autumn** (September and October), another optimal time to travel. **Winter** can be perfect by day in the south, though desert nights can get very cold – a major consideration if you're staying in the cheaper hotels, which rarely have heating. If you're planning to **hike in the mountains**, it's best to keep to the months from April to October unless you have some experience of snow conditions.

Weather apart, the **Islamic religious calendar** and its related festivals will have the most seasonal effect on your travel. The most important factor is **Ramadan**, the month of daytime fasting (see page 44); this can be a problem for transport, and especially hiking, though the festive evenings do much to compensate.

AVERAGE MONTHLY TEMPERATURES AND RAINFALL

	Jan	Feb	Mar	Apr	May	Jun	Jul	Aug	Sep	Oct	Nov	Dec
TANGIER												
Max/min °C	16/7	16/7	18/9	19/11	22/12	26/12	28/18	28/18	26/17	23/14	18/11	16/8
Rain (mm)	103	98	71	62	37	16	2	2	14	65	134	129
FEZ												
Max/min °C	15/4	16/5	18/6	20/8	25/10	28/13	34/17	34/17	30/15	25/11	19/8	16/5
Rain (mm)	72	100	93	87	53	24	3	3	17	62	89	85
MARRAKESH												
Max/min °C	18/4	20/6	23/9	26/11	29/14	33/17	38/19	38/20	33/17	28/14	23/9	19/6
Rain (mm)	25	28	33	31	15	8	3	3	10	23	31	31
LAAYOUNE												
Max/min °C	22/10	23/11	24/12	24/14	26/15	27/17	29/18	30/19	29/18	28/17	25/16	21/10
Rain (mm)	3	2	1	1	0	1	0	0	0	4	7	8

Author picks

Our authors have haggled in the souks and camped in the desert, clocked up hundreds of kilometres aboard buses and on mules, and generally consumed more mint tea than can possibly be good for them. Here are a few of their favourite things…

Helping Hands in the Happy Valley Shop at truly fair-trade associations in the Aït Bouguemez valley by visiting Anou-certified cooperatives, where artisans in remote regions sell their work directly to customers (see page 221).

Take the tram Modern tramway networks have been constructed in Rabat (see page 245) and Casablanca (see page 262), offering an easier way to get to the sights while rubbing shoulders with the locals.

The sound of the muezzin The call to prayer (see page 513) is one of the most evocative sounds in Morocco, whether it's sweeping across the rooftops of an imperial city or echoing through a mountain village.

Stargaze in the Sahara Head to North Africa's first private observatory, *Kasbah Hotel SaharaSky* (see page 383), for an unforgettable evening of rooftop stargazing and venture onwards into the Erg Chigaga to camp in one-million-star accommodation (see page 382).

Surfing in Taghazout A line-up of good right-hand breaks have made this friendly, easy-going little fishing village Morocco's top surf spot (see page 432).

The painted rocks of Tafraout Out in the middle of nowhere, tiny Tafraout is surrounded by some of Morocco's most jaw-dropping scenery, including an incongruous collection of blue-painted boulders that make it seem as though the sky has somehow leaked into the ground (see page 450).

Middle Earth in the Middle Atlas The charming town of Bhalil (see page 205) in the Middle Atlas has hillsides pocked with cave houses where you can share mint tea and *msimmen* pancakes with Berber families.

> Our author recommendations don't end here. We've flagged up our favourite places – a perfectly sited hotel, an atmospheric café, a special restaurant – throughout the Guide, highlighted with the ★ symbol.

SURFERS AT TAGHAZOUT
ART DECO ARCHITECTURE, SIDI IFNI

25

things not to miss

It's not possible to see everything that Morocco has to offer in one trip – and we don't suggest you try. What follows is a selective and subjective taste of the country's highlights, in no particular order: fascinating cities, Roman ruins, mountain hikes and stunning buildings. All entries have a page reference to take you straight into the Guide, where you can find out more. Coloured numbers refer to chapters in the Guide section.

1 CHEFCHAOUEN
See page 112
Simply the most beautiful small town in Morocco, its blue-washed walls enclosed by mountains.

2 KOUTOUBIA MOSQUE
See page 296
The symbol of Marrakesh, the Koutoubia's twelfth-century minaret is visible for miles around the city.

3 CAMEL TREKKING
See pages 379, 383 and 410
Venture into the Sahara on a camel trek from Zagora, M'Hamid or Merzouga.

4 ATLAS PASSES
See pages 357 and 364
The nerve-shredding Tizi n'Test and the higher Tizi n'Tichka wend up over the Atlas mountains, providing breathtaking views along the way.

5 CASCADES D'OUZOUD
See page 219
The most dramatic of the country's waterfalls, with overhanging cafés, and a thunderous sheet of water that plunges into the pools below.

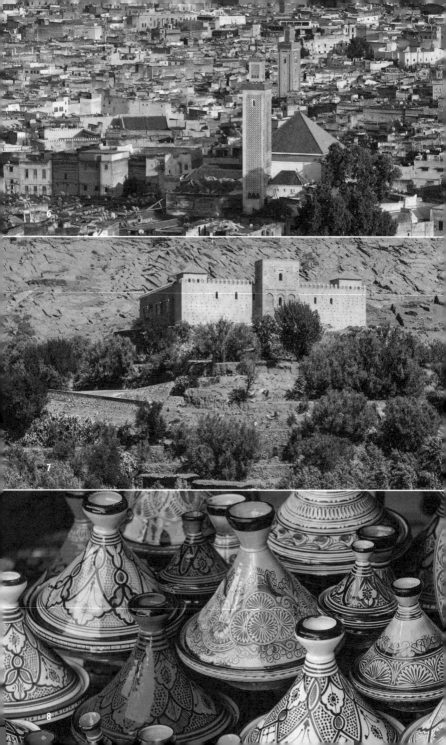

6 FEZ
See page 154
The most complete medieval city in the Arab world, Fez's labyrinthine streets conceal ancient souks and iconic monuments, none more so than the exquisitely decorated Medersa Bou Inania.

7 TIN MAL MOSQUE
See page 355
This great Almohad building stands isolated in an Atlas river valley.

8 CRAFTS
See page 51
From carpets and carpentry to leatherwork and ceramics, Morocco's craft tradition is extraordinarily vibrant, and on magnificent show in its souks.

9 BAB OUDAÏA, RABAT
See page 239
The most beautiful gate of the medieval Moorish world.

10 TEA
See page 42
"Whisky Marocain" (mint tea) is the accompaniment to any discussion or transaction.

11 TELOUET
See page 365
An evocative relic of the time when the infamous Glaoui clan ruled over the Atlas and Marrakesh.

12 JEMAA EL FNA, MARRAKESH
See page 294
Musicians, acrobats and storytellers converge each night on this spellbinding city square.

13 TODRA GORGE
See page 397
Take a walk (or a climb) in the majestic Todra Gorge, with its towering 300m canyon walls.

14 BARBARY MACAQUES
See page 211
Troupes of these endangered "apes" inhabit the cedar forests of the Middle Atlas.

15 SIDI IFNI
See page 463
This old Spanish colonial town retains a seductive array of Art Deco buildings.

13

14

15

18

19

20

21

22

23

21 KASBAHS AND OASES
See page 364 and 360
Morocco's southern oases are dotted with crumbling kasbahs and traditional Berber villages.

22 IMILCHIL MOUSSEM
See page 217
The Moroccan cultural calendar is packed with festivals but few can match the largesse of Imilchil's three-day "Marriage Festival".

23 MAJORELLE GARDEN & YSL MUSEUM, MARRAKESH
See page 312
A lovely, mature botanical garden, once owned by Yves Saint-Laurent, with a museum dedicated to his work next door.

24 RIADS
See page 39
These renovated old mansions, centred on a courtyard and often full of stylish designer touches, provide a tranquil retreat from the outside world.

25 TREKKING IN THE ATLAS
See page 346
The High Atlas offer fantastic trekking opportunities, from day walks in the Toubkal Massif to expeditions through isolated valleys.

Itineraries

The following itineraries will take you right across Morocco, from the Medinas of Marrakesh and Fez to longer trips into the mountains and the desert beyond. With bustling souks and showpiece squares, vast palmeries and dizzying gorges, there is something for everyone.

A SHORT BREAK IN MARRAKESH

DAY ONE

Koutoubia Minaret Marvel at tthis twelfth-century, 70m-high tower. See page 296

Jemaa el Fna Head to the famous central square, a feast for the senses. See page 294

Souks Shop for rugs and carpets in La Criée Berbère, or watch the dyers at work in Souk des Teinturiers. See page 298

Dinner Packed come nightfall, the food stalls of Jemaa el Fna serve up couscous, fried fish, and plenty more besides. See page 320

DAY TWO

Ben Youssef Medersa A textbook study in zellij, stucco and carved cedar wood. See page 301

El Badi Palace It may now lay in ruins, but this palace is still a magnificent sight. See page 307

Majorelle Garden and YSL Museum Head to Yves Saint-Laurent's (ticketed) tranquil garden and museum. See page 312

Dinner Book ahead for *Le Tobsil*, an intimate palace restaurant. See page 323

A SHORT BREAK IN FEZ

DAY ONE

Medersa Bou Inania Arguably the finest building in Morocco, and a dazzling testament to the craftsmen of medieval Fez. See page 159

Talâa Kebira Journey through the Medina past *fondouks* and mosques and souks specializing in everything from brass to henna. See page 163

Dinner Sample the famous camel burger at hip little *Café Clock*. See page 180

DAY TWO

Nejjarine and Seffarine Take in the sights of Place en Nejjarine before some people watching on Place Seffarine. See pages 165 and 168

Tanneries A surreal scene: men standing knee-deep in vats of coloured dyes, soaking leather skins red, yellow, blue and black. See page 168

Fez el Jedid Home to the synagogues, cemeteries and overhanging houses that make up Morocco's original Jewish district. See page 171

Dinner Tuck into lovingly-cooked tagines in a family home at Dar Hatim. See page 180

Create your own itinerary with Rough Guides. Whether you're after adventure or a family-friendly holiday, we have a trip for you, with all the activities you enjoy doing and the sights you want to see. All our trips are devised by local experts who get the most out of the destination. Visit **www.roughguides.com/trips** to chat with one of our travel agents.

THE GRAND TOUR

Factor in 3 weeks to cover this epic route of Morocco's finest sights.

❶ **Tangier** Take a breather in one of the Petit Socco's historic cafés. See page 68

❷ **Chefchaouen** A laidback and picturesque antidote to Tangier's bustle. See page 112

❸ **Meknes** Wander Moulay Ismail's monumental Ville Impériale before exploring the Roman ruins at nearby Volubilis. See page 184

❹ **Fez** Getting lost somewhere amid the souks and tanneries of Fez el Bali is a quintessential Moroccan experience. See page 154

❺ **Merzouga** The Erg Chebbi dunes make a memorable first sight of the Sahara. See page 409

❻ **Aït Benhaddou** The mother of all kasbahs, and one you won't forget in a hurry. See page 366

❼ **The High Atlas** The best trekking in the country, along rutted mule tracks and through ancient Berber villages. See page 332

❽ **Marrakesh** Barter for babouches and revel in the theatre of the Jemaa el Fna. See page 288

❾ **Essaouira** A fish supper is the perfect end to the day in this coastal town. See page 275

OUTDOOR ACTIVITIES

Allow 2 weeks to tick off all of these, plus another week to recover.

❶ **Kitesurfing in Essaouira** Simply the best place in the country to try your hand at kitesurfing. See page 285

❷ **Surfing near Taghazout** Ride Killers, Anchor Point and other challenging breaks at this relaxed surfers' hangout. See page 432

❸ **Hiking in the High Atlas** A wealth of scenic routes cut across the Toubkal Massif. See page 339

❹ **Skiing at Oukaïmeden** Hitting the slopes at Oukaïmeden is worth it for the novelty value alone. See page 337

❺ **Camel trekking in the Erg Chigaga** M'Hamid is the jumping-off point for camel trips into this remote section of the Sahara. See page 410

❻ **Climbing in the Todra Gorge** You could spend days scaling the rocky walls of this dramatic mountain gorge. See page 397

❼ **Sandboarding in the Erg Chebbi** A surreal contrast to Oukaïmeden, though carving down the Grand Dune de Merzouga is just as memorable. See page 411

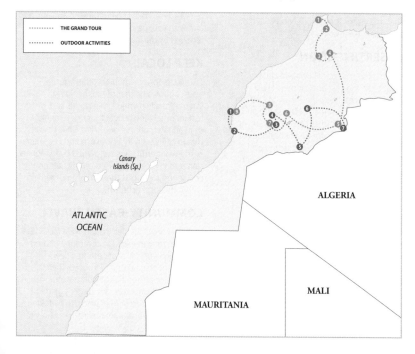

Sustainable travel

Morocco faces many environmental and social challenges, but with just a little planning it's easy to avoid contributing to these and enjoying a sustainable holiday.

Morocco might be a shade away from Europe, but culturally, economically and environmentally life here is very different to the lifestyle you might be used too. The country faces many environmental and social challenges, including the impact of global warming, increasing desertification and the battle between traditional culture and a new way of looking at the world. It's important that any visitor is respectful and aware of these challenges.

DESERTIFICATION

Water-, and the lack of it, is without a doubt, the biggest environmental issue Morocco faces. The Sahara and pre-Sahara occupies great swathes of the south and east of Morocco, but as Morocco heats up, dries up and the water table continues to fall, the desert sands march further and further north. Do your bit to save water by reducing how long you spend in the shower (or avoid showering everyday) and avoid actively choosing a hotel because it has a swimming pool. Golf courses are very thirsty so for environmental reasons it's better to avoid a golf holiday in Morocco. One of the biggest causes of expanding desertification in Morocco is not totally climate related but is due to overgrazing by livestock – and in particular goats. While goat is a popular meat in Morocco, the more goat you eat the more goats that are reared, so consider opting for chicken which is more environmentally sound.

SOCIAL CHANGE

Morocco is the midst of great cultural change. Older, rural generations in particular are likely to have a very different outlook on life to young, middle class urban dwellers. It's important for you – as a visitor – to be aware of and respect local cultural standards regarding dress and behaviour. For example, walking around a remote desert oasis half undressed and arm and arm with your partner is not likely to be well-received by the local population.

KEEP LOCAL

Try and keep your money within your host community. That means avoiding internationally owned chain hotels and restaurants. Using a local tour operator rather than an international one. And, being aware that in cities such as Marrakech and Fez, many of the wonderful riads are owned by foreigners rather than locals, and accordingly the money you spend staying at these might not remain within the local economy.

COMMUNITY-BASED TRAVEL

Nobody knows the destination like a local does and so getting involved in community-based tourism is a good way of getting a deeper cultural understanding of Morocco. There are lots of opportunities for cultural tourism. These range from taking an insider's guided walking tour of Fez or Marrakech, to partaking in a cookery course, learning first-hand how to

EXOLORING THE DESERT IN FIGUIG

weave a rug in Marrakech or opting to sleep in a village homestay. Actively seeking out community-based travel experiences provides you with great memories and gives local people with an additional income.

OVERLAND TO MOROCCO

By now we are all aware that air travel is a major contributor to the greenhouse gases that hasten global warming (of which Morocco is particularly vulnerable). Most visitors to Morocco arrive by air but, with just a few extra days at your disposal, it's possible to travel from anywhere in Europe to Morocco by train, bus and ferry. It's better for the environment and it promises to be quite an adventure. Once in Morocco, forgo the hire car and stick with public transport. Good quality and fast trains link almost all of the major cities while buses go frequently to pretty much every small town and village in the country. This makes travelling by public transport easy, cheap and better for the planet.

UNDER TOURISM

There are certain key tourism honey pots in Morocco such as Marrakech, Fez and Essaouira, where increasing numbers of visitors are leading to over tourism. To both spread the tourist dollar around the nation and ensure a more

pleasant holiday for yourself, consider avoiding these places. Instead of Marrakech head to the 'mini-Marrakech' of Taroudant and swap Meknes for Fez. When it comes to the seaside town of Essaouira, there are thousands of kilometres of Atlantic and Mediterranean coastline that rarely see a foreign tourist. If you're looking for a desert experience, then skip the masses at Merzouga and instead venture out to fascinating Figuig.

BABOUCHES

Basics

Getting there

The simplest way to get to Morocco is, of course, to fly. Alternatively, you could fly to France, Spain or Gibraltar and pick up a ferry there; or, from Britain or Ireland, you could go all the way by land and sea.

Fares usually depend on the **season**, the highest being at Christmas and the New Year, and at the peak of summer in July and August, when seats can also be scarce. Flying at weekends may cost more than midweek.

You can often cut costs by going through an **online or discount flight agent**. The cheapest tickets will be subject to restrictions such as fixed dates, and some may require advance purchase.

Note that, if you have to change planes en route, tight connections can make baggage loss more likely, and if your **baggage goes astray** in transit, you cannot have it delivered to your hotel in Morocco and you will have to go back to the airport to pick it up in person when it does arrive.

Flights from the UK and Ireland

Royal Air Maroc (RAM; ⓦroyalairmaroc.com) runs **direct scheduled flights** daily from Heathrow to Casablanca, and British Airways (ⓦbritishairways. com) flies from Gatwick to Marrakesh. From Dublin, Aer Lingus (ⓦaerlingus.com) sometimes has winter flights to Agadir. In addition to these, there are no-frills flights to Marrakesh, Fez, Agadir and other destinations from various UK airports with EasyJet (ⓦeasyjet. com) and Ryanair (ⓦryanair.com). Tui (ⓦtui.co.uk) serves Marrakesh and Agadir from Gatwick and Manchester, Marrakesh also from Birmingham. Flights typically take around three and a half hours.

In addition to these, there are **charter flights** run by tour operators such as First Choice (ⓦfirstchoice. co.uk) from Britain or Sunway (ⓦsunway.ie) from Ireland. Flights are usually from Gatwick, Manchester or Dublin, but occasionally other British and Irish airports, to Agadir and sometimes Marrakesh, although they do not necessarily fly all year and are not especially cheaper than scheduled services; they may also limit you to a two-week stay.

Otherwise, you can get an **indirect flight** to Morocco from most British or Irish airports via London or a European city such as Paris or Amsterdam. From Casablanca, it's possible to take a connecting flight to most other Moroccan airports. The Spanish enclave of Melilla is served by Iberia (ⓦiberia.com) via Madrid.

A return flight from London to Casablanca with RAM are quite reasonable, depending on the specific flights you choose, and how early you book. Fares on flights with the no-frills airlines depend on demand, the earlier you book, the lower the price will be, and of course you pay extra for checked-in baggage. A no-frills flight from Ireland will be similar, depending on the time of year and the popularity of the flight.

It is also possible, and often cheaper, to take a **flight to Málaga or Gibraltar**, where you can either get a ferry directly across the Straits, or take a bus to Algeciras for more frequent ferries from there (see page 30). Airlines such as EasyJet and Ryanair run low-cost flights to Málaga from several British and Irish airports. From Gibraltar you'd have to walk across the border to La Linea for the bus. From Málaga airport, there are buses to Algeciras (2hr), but you may have to change at Marbella (see ⓦportillo.avanzabus. com for details).

Flights from the US and Canada

Royal Air Maroc (RAM; ⓦroyalairmaroc.com) run nonstop flights to Casablanca from New York and Montreal (flight time 7hr 30min). Air Canada (ⓦaircanada.com) also fly from Montreal. The alternative is to take an **indirect flight** with a European carrier, changing planes at their European hub. Those serving Casablanca include Air France (ⓦairfrance. com) and Alitalia (ⓦalitalia.com), while Lufthansa (ⓦlufthansa.com) serve Marrakesh, and Iberia (ⓦiberia.com) fly to Casablanca, Marrakesh, Rabat, Tangier and the Spanish enclave of Melilla. If you're flying from elsewhere in North America, you can take a connecting flight to New York or Montreal and continue from there on RAM or Air Canada, or buy a through ticket via Europe with a European airline, or with a US airline such as American (ⓦaa.com) or Delta (ⓦdelta.com) in conjunction with a European carrier.

From New York, you can expect to pay (including tax) US$1000 in high season, or approximately half that in low season for the cheapest flight to Casablanca. From Montreal, the fare will be more. Getting to Morocco from the west coast (i.e. LA or Vancouver) will obviously cost more.

Flights from Australia, New Zealand and South Africa

There are no direct flights from Australia, New Zealand or South Africa to Morocco. **From Australasia**, you will need to change planes in Europe or the Middle East. Emirates (ⓦemirates.com) or Etihad (ⓦetiha-dairways.com) via the UAE are often the most conven-

A BETTER KIND OF TRAVEL

At Rough Guides we are passionately committed to travel. We believe it helps us understand the world we live in and the people we share it with – and of course tourism is vital to many developing economies. But the scale of modern tourism has also damaged some places irreparably, and climate change is accelerated by most forms of transport, especially flying. We encourage all our authors to consider the carbon footprint of the journeys they make in the course of researching our guides.

ient airlines, with Emirates in particular offering a decent choice of Australian and New Zealand airports to depart from. Alternatively, you can also fly with a European airline such as Air France (W airfrance.com), or buy a through ticket with Qantas (W qantas.com) or Air New Zealand (W airnz.co.nz) in conjunction with their partners in Europe, which has the advantage of offering a wider choice of departure airports. The cheapest through tickets may require two changes of plane en route.

Flying **from South Africa**, you could fly with an operator such as Emirates (W emirates.com) via Dubai, Egyptair (W egyptair.com) via Cairo, or Air France (W airfrance.com) via Paris. The most direct route, however, is to fly SAA (W flysaa.com) to Lagos or Dakar, changing there onto a Royal Air Maroc (W royalairmaroc.com) flight to Casablanca.

By rail from the UK and Ireland

London to Morocco **by train and ferry** via Paris, Madrid and Algeciras, takes 36hr at full pelt, and will usually cost rather more than a flight. The journey from London to Algeciras costs upwards of £140; details can be found on the Man in Seat 61 website (W seat61.com/Morocco.htm). Tickets for the London to Paris stage are available online from Eurostar (W eurostar.com), for Paris–Madrid from Loco2 (W loco2.com), and for Madrid to Algeciras from the Spanish railway company RENFE (W renfe.com); be aware that seat reservation is compulsory, so it's advisable to book all your connections in advance, or you may not be able to get on your preferred train.

By bus from the UK and Ireland

There are **bus services** with Eurolines (W eurolines.com) from London's Victoria Coach Station to Algeciras for the boat to Tanger-Med, but they aren't an attractive option. It's a gruelling 36hr journey, including a change of bus in Paris and another in Spain, but it's one of the cheapest ways to get there. Connections from elsewhere in Britain and Ireland can involve long stopovers in London.

By car from the UK and Ireland

Driving to Morocco, allow a minimum of four days from London or southern England, and five days from Scotland or Ireland. The most direct **route** is: London–Channel Tunnel–Calais–Paris–Tours–Bordeaux–Bayonne–San Sebastián (Donostia)–Madrid–Granada–Málaga–Algeciras. French and Spanish motorways charge hefty tolls, but routes that avoid them are much slower. From Ireland, you can cut out Britain by taking a ferry to France with Brittany Ferries (W brittany-ferries.co.uk) or Irish Ferries (W irishferries.com). From Britain, you can cut out the French section of the route by taking a direct ferry to northern Spain with Brittany Ferries. Otherwise, you can cut out Spain by taking a ferry to Morocco from Sète in France (see page 30).

Entering Morocco by ferry

Leaving Europe for Morocco proper (not Ceuta or Melilla), you have to go through passport control before boarding the **ferry**. On some ferries to Tanger-Med, you have to obtain a **disembarkation form** from the purser's office, fill it in, and submit it with your passport for stamping to a **Moroccan immigration** official on the boat. Announcements to this effect are not always made in English, but if you don't have a stamp, you'll have to wait until everyone else has cleared frontier and customs controls before being attended to. When disembarking, show your newly acquired stamp to a Moroccan policeman at the exit.

Most ferries to **Tangier** dock at the new port of Tanger-Med (see page 81), 40km east of Tangier itself, to which it is connected by local bus, taxis (including shared ones) and a couple of daily trains. Only the catamaran from Tarifa (see page 30) drops you at Tangier's old port, from which you can walk straight into town.

Returning from Morocco to Spain, you need to collect an embarkation form and departure card at the ferry port and have these stamped by the port police prior to boarding your ferry.

Vehicle red tape

Taking a vehicle to Morocco you must take out insurance; the best way to do this is to get **Green Card Insurance** covering Morocco before you leave (it speeds things up on arrival if the reference to Morocco is prominent and in French). Failing that, you can obtain insurance from Assurance Frontière at the border or port of entry (see page 35). You will also need your vehicle registration document – which must be in your name or accompanied by a letter from the registered owner. Trailer caravans, as well as the vehicle itself, need **temporary importation documents (D16 ter)**, which are obtainable at the frontier (or on the ferry, if not travelling to Ceuta or Melilla) for no charge, or can be applied for online at Ⓦ www.douane.gov.ma/d16ter/formAT.jsf. Information on driving in Morocco can be found under "Getting Around" (see page 33), as can information on legal requirements for driving (see page 33).

AGENTS AND OPERATORS

Best of Morocco Morocco Ⓦ morocco-travel.com. Hotels, riads, and upmarket "designer" trekking, culinary tours, birdwatching and other specialist options.

Compass Odyssey Ⓦ compassodyssey.net. Family-owned tour operator/agency offering affordable customized itineraries within Morocco, plus one or two annual group tours led by Rough Guide contributor Darren Humphrys.

Journey Beyond Travel Ⓦ journeybeyondtravel.com. Specialists in sustainable travel in Morocco, with sightseeing, trekking and other tours tailored to individual needs and supporting local projects.

Morocco Explored Canada Ⓦ moroccoexplored.com. Specialists in tailor-made tours, including hiking, camel treks and 4WD off-roading.

Naturally Morocco Ltd UK Ⓦ naturallymorocco.co.uk. Ecologically oriented tours of Morocco, with vegetarian or vegan food if desired and a variety of tours including adventure sports and even Moroccan cookery lessons.

North South Travel UK ☎ 01245 608291, Ⓦ northsouthtravel. co.uk. Friendly, competitive travel agency, offering discounted fares worldwide. Profits are used to support projects in the developing world, especially the promotion of sustainable tourism.

Surf Maroc Ⓦ surfmaroc.com. Surfing holidays based at Taghazout, including lessons for beginners and more advanced surfers.

Trailfinders Ⓦ trailfinders.com. One of the best-informed and most efficient agents for independent travellers in the British Isles.

Travel Cuts Canada Ⓦ travelcuts.com. Canadian youth and student travel firm.

USIT Ⓦ usit.ie. Ireland's main youth and student travel specialists.

Getting around

Moroccan public transport is, on the whole, pretty good, with a rail network linking the main towns of the north, the coast and Marrakesh, and plenty of buses and collective taxis. Renting a car can open up routes that are time-consuming or difficult on local transport.

By plane

Royal Air Maroc (RAM; Ⓦ royalairmaroc.com) operates **domestic flights** from its Casablanca hub to major cities nationwide. You will usually have to change planes at Casablanca in order to travel between any other two points, unless both are stops on a single Casa-bound flight (Dakhla to Laayoune, for example). In general, flying is not really worthwhile except for long-distance routes such as to Laayoune or Dakhla in the Western Sahara, when they can save you a lot of time. A one-way ticket from Casablanca to Laayoune, for example, would set you back 787dh (£64/$84) and take an hour and three quarters (plus journey time to the airport, check-in time and potential delays), compared to nineteen hours by bus. Casa to Dakhla – 987dh (£80/$105) one way on RAM – would take you two hours and twenty minutes by air compared to 28 hours by bus.

Information on Morocco's airports, including daily departure lists for some of them, can be found on the website of the Office National des Aéroports at Ⓦ onda.ma. You should confirm flights 72 hours before departure. Student and under-26 youth **discounts** of 25 percent are available on RAM domestic flights, but only if the ticket is bought in advance from one of its offices.

By train

Trains cover a limited network of routes, but for travel between the major cities they are easily the best option, comfortable and fairly fast, but sometimes subject to delays.

There are two main lines: from Tangier in the north down to Marrakesh, and from Oujda in the northeast, also to Marrakesh, joining with the Tangier line at Sidi Kacem. Branch lines serve Nador, El Jadida, Safi, Oued Zem and Casablanca airport. A high-speed line (LGV) from Tangier to Casablanca means the journey time between the two cities to just over two hours. Eventually the high speed line will extend to Marrakesh.

Aside from that, schedules change very little from year to year, but it's wise to check times in advance at stations. **Timetables** are displayed at major train stations, and any station ticket office will print you off a mini timetable of services between any two stations. You can also check schedules (*horaires*) and

FERRY ROUTES

Taking a ferry to Morocco is undoubtedly a romantic way to arrive. All departures are subject to **weather conditions**. For detailed schedules and prices, contact the operators, or their UK agents: Southern Ferries (🔘 southernferries.co.uk) are agents for Trasmediterranea, GNV and SNCM; Viamare (🔘 viamare.com) are agents for Trasmediterranea, Baleària, Grimaldi and GNV.

Most passenger **tickets** can be bought at boat stations on departure, but for vehicles, especially at times of high demand, and for departures out of Sète, it is best to **book in advance** – for vehicles on ferries out of Sète, make that well in advance. Operators and routes change yearly, and sometimes at short notice; the list at 🔘 directferries.co.uk/morocco.htm should be up to date, but it's always worth checking by phone before departure.

ALGECIRAS

Tickets can be bought in Algeciras from any travel agent (there are dozens along the seafront and on the approach roads to the town) or at the boat station. Boats regularly depart thirty minutes to an hour late, and the next to leave may not necessarily be the first to arrive, since fast ferries frequently overtake slow boats on the crossing. Ferries from Livorno, Genoa and Sète to Tanger-Med stop at Barcelona en route.

Algeciras–Ceuta Trasmediterranea, Baleària and FRS. 12–22 daily (1hr–1hr 30min).
Algeciras–Tanger-Med Trasmediterranea, Baleària, FRS and Inter Shipping. 16–22 daily (1hr 30min–2hr).

TARIFA

Free shuttle buses are available from Algeciras if you buy your ticket there.
Tarifa–Tangier FRS and Inter Shipping. 12 daily (1hr).

GIBRALTAR

Gibraltar–Tanger-Med FRS. Weekly (1hr 30min).

MOTRIL

Shuttle buses available from Málaga; book in advance with Armas.
Motril–Melilla FRS. 6 weekly (5hr).
Motril–Nador Armas. 6 weekly (5hr).
Motril–Al Hoceima Armas. 5 weekly (5hr).

MÁLAGA

Málaga–Melilla Trasmediterranea, Baleària. 5–9 weekly (6hr 30min–9hr).

ALMERÍA

Almería–Melilla Trasmediterranea, Armas, Baleària. 5–7 weekly (6hr–8hr 30min).
Almería–Nador Trasmediterranea. 1–2 daily (6–8hr).

BARCELONA

Barcelona–Tanger-Med Grimaldi, GNV. 4 weekly (32hr).
Barcelona–Nador GNV. 1 weekly (32hr).

SÈTE

Booking well in advance is essential for Sète ferries. Prices on this route sometimes go up steeply in summer.
Sète–Tanger-Med GNV. 3 weekly (40–45hr).
Sète–Nador GNV. 1 weekly (29hr).

GENOA

Genoa–Tanger-Med GNV. 2 weekly (48hr 30min).

SAVONA

Savona–Tanger-Med Grimaldi. Weekly (60hr).

FERRY OPERATORS

Armas 🔘 www.navieraarmas.com
Baleària 🔘 balearia.com.
FRS (Ferrys Rápidos del Sur) 🔘 frs.es
Grimaldi Lines 🔘 www.grimaldi-lines.com
GNV (Grandi Navi Veloci) 🔘 gnv.it
Inter Shipping 🔘 intershipping.es
Trasmediterranea 🔘 trasmediterranea.es

fares (*tarifs*) and buy tickets on the ONCF website at 🔘 www.oncf.ma. Except for sleeper services, tickets do not need to be booked in advance; you can just turn up at the station and buy one. There are two **classes** of tickets – first and second. **Costs** for a second-class ticket are slightly more than what you'd pay for buses; on certain "express" services ("express" refers to the level of comfort rather than the speed), they are around thirty percent higher. In addition, there are **couchettes** (690dh) available on the Tangier–Marrakesh and Casablanca–Oujda night trains – worth the money for both the comfort and

FARES

For **comparison**, between Casablanca and Marrakesh, a train will take three and a quarter hours. A CTM bus will take three and a half hours, while an ordinary bus will take around four hours. A shared *grand taxi* (if you can find one) will take just under two hours. The plane takes forty-minutes plus a lot of waiting around at airports.

the security, as couchette passengers are in their own locked carriage with a guard. Most **stations** are located reasonably close to the modern city centres. Note that they do not have **left-luggage** facilities.

By bus

Bus travel is generally only marginally cheaper than taking a shared *grand taxi* (see page 32, and around thirty percent slower, but also safer and more comfortable, though on some older buses leg room is limited, and for anyone approaching six feet or more in height, long journeys can be rather an endurance test. Many long-distance buses run **at night** when they are both quicker and cooler. Most are fitted with reading lights but they are invariably turned off, so you will not be able to read on buses after dark. Also note that the rate of accidents involving night buses is quite high, especially on busy routes.

Travelling during the day, especially in summer, it pays to sit on the side **away from the sun**. Travelling from north to south, this means sitting on the right in the morning, on the left in the afternoon, vice versa if going the other way. Travelling from east to west, sit on the right, or on the left if going from west to east. In fact, Moroccan passengers often pull down the blinds and shut the windows, which can block out the scenery and make the journey rather claustrophobic. Note too, especially on rural services, that some passengers may be unused to road travel, resulting in travel sickness and vomiting.

CTM and private lines

Buses run by **CTM** (the national company; ⓦctm. ma) are faster and more reliable than private services, with numbered seats and fixed departure schedules, which can be checked online. CTM services usually have reading lights, though you may have to ask the driver to turn those on. Some of the **larger private company** buses, such as SATAS (which operates widely in the south) and Trans Ghazala (which runs in the north) are of a similar standard, but many other private companies are tiny outfits, with a single bus which leaves only when the driver considers it sufficiently full. On the other hand, such private buses are much more likely to stop for you if you flag them

down on the open road, whereas CTM services will only pick up and set down at official stops.

Bus terminals

Most towns have a main **bus station** (*gare routière*), often on the edge of town. CTM buses usually leave from the company's office, which may be quite a way from the main bus station, though in several places CTM and the private companies share a single terminal, and in some cases the CTM bus will call at the main bus station when departing a city, though not when arriving.

Bus stations usually have a number of ticket windows, one for each of the companies operating out of it. There is occasionally a departures board, but it may be out of date and in Arabic only, so you should always check departure times at the appropriate window. Bus conductors or ticket sellers may be calling out destinations in the bus station in any case, or may greet you as you come in by asking where you want to go. On the more popular trips (and especially with CTM services, which often run just once a day in the south), it's worth trying to buy **tickets in advance**, though this may not always be possible on smaller private-line services.

You may occasionally have problems getting tickets at **small towns** along major routes, where buses can arrive and leave already full. It's sometimes possible to get round this by taking a local bus or a *grand taxi* for the next section of the trip (until the bus you want empties a little), or by waiting for a bus that actually starts from the town you're in. Overall, the best policy is to arrive at a bus station early in the day (ideally 5.30–6am).

On private-line buses, you generally pay for your **baggage** to be loaded into the hold (or onto the roof). The standard fee is 5dh, but this may be forgone on short hops. Note that you only pay to have your baggage loaded, not to have it unloaded on arrival, whatever anybody may say. On CTM, SATAS and Supratours buses your luggage is weighed and you are issued with a receipt for the baggage charge (usually 5–10dh, depending on weight and distance – allow time for this procedure). On arrival, porters with wheeled box-carts (*chariots*) may offer their services, but always agree a price before engaging one.

Supratours buses

An additional service, on certain major routes, is the **Supratours express buses** run as feeder services by the train company, **ONCF**. These are fast and very comfortable, and run from Tetouan, Essaouira, Agadir and the Western Sahara to connect with rail services from Oujda, Tangier and Marrakesh. Timetables and fares for Supratours buses can be found along with those for trains on the ONCF website (**W** www.oncf. ma) and on their own site at **W** www.supratours. ma. Supratours services compare, in both time and cost, with CTM buses. They do not use the main bus stations, but depart from outside their own town-centre offices (detailed in the relevant chapters). Through tickets to and from connecting rail stations are available (Essaouira through to Fez, for example), and travellers with rail tickets for connecting services have priority. It's best to book tickets in advance if possible.

By shared taxi

Shared *grands taxis* are one of the best features of Moroccan transport. They operate on a wide variety of routes, are much quicker than buses (usually quicker than trains, too), and fares vary from slightly more than the bus to around twice as much.

The taxis are usually big Peugeot or Mercedes cars carrying **six passengers** (Peugeots are less common but have a slightly less cramped seating arrangement). Most business is along **specific routes**, and the most popular routes have more or less continuous departures throughout the day. You just show up at the terminal (locations are detailed in the Guide) and ask for a place to a specific destination. The best time to arrive is **early morning** (6–8am), when a lot of people are travelling and taxis fill up quickly; lunchtime, on the other hand, is a bad time to turn up, as fewer people will be travelling, and the taxi will take

longer to get full. As soon as six (or, if you're willing to pay extra, four or five) people are assembled, the taxi sets off. Make sure, when asking about *grands taxis*, that it is clear you only want a place (*une place* in French, *plassa* in Arabic, or hold up one finger) in a shared taxi (*taxi collectif*), as drivers often "presume" that a tourist will want to charter the whole taxi (see below), which means paying for all six places. Women travelling alone may wish to pay for two places and get the front seat to themselves rather than be squashed up against male passengers.

Picking up a shared taxi on the road is more problematic, as they will only stop if they have a place free (if a passenger has already alighted). To **hail a taxi** on the open road, hold up one, two or more fingers to indicate how many places you need.

Fares for set routes are fixed, and drivers do not usually try to overcharge tourists for a place (though occasionally they try to charge for baggage, which usually travels free of charge). If you think that you are being overcharged, ask the other passengers, or check the price with your hotel before leaving. Occasionally, five passengers may agree to split the cost of the last place to hasten departure, or one passenger may agree to pay for two places. You pay the full fare for the journey even if travelling only part of the way.

If you want to take a **non-standard route**, or an excursion, or just to have the taxi to yourself, it is possible to charter a whole grand taxi (*une course* in French, *corsa* in Arabic). In theory this should be exactly six times the price of a place in a shared taxi if the route has a set fare, but you'll often have to bargain hard to get that. Hotels can sometimes be useful in helping to charter *grands taxis*.

Some people consider shared taxis **dangerous**. It is certainly true that they are prone to practices such as speeding, and overtaking on blind curves or the brows of hills, and that they have more than their fair

POLICE CHECKPOINTS

There are **police checkpoints** on roads throughout the country. European cars, or rental cars, are usually waved through. Buses (other than CTM services) are more likely to be stopped, but usually only briefly. Sometimes the police may ask to check your passport or (if driving) licence, often only because they want to relieve their boredom with a chat. Nonetheless, you should always have your **passport** with you if travelling between towns – even on day-trips.

Checkpoints in the **Western Sahara** are more thorough, and for foreigners they can involve a considerable amount of form-filling and delay (see page 480).

In the **Rif mountains**, especially around Ketama, police may stop vehicles to search for cannabis. Buses are usually delayed more than *grands taxis* at such checkpoints, and passengers may be searched individually. There are also sometimes lengthy checks for duty-free contraband on buses from Nador to Fez.

share of accidents. Drivers may work all day and into the night, and it seems a large number of **accidents** involve them falling asleep at the wheel while driving at night, so you may wish to avoid using them for night-time journeys, especially on busy roads. Note also that with the seating arrangements, it is not usually possible to wear a seat belt, though if you pay for two places, you can get the front seat to yourself and put the belt on.

Trucks and hitching

In the countryside, where buses may be sporadic or even non-existent, it is standard practice for **vans** and **lorries** (*camions*), **pick-up trucks** (*camionettes*) and **transit-vans** (*transits*) to carry passengers for a charge. You may be asked to pay a little more than the locals, and you may be expected to bargain over the price – but it's straightforward enough.

In parts of the **Atlas**, local people run more or less scheduled truck or transit services, generally to coincide with the pattern of local souks. If you plan on traversing any of the more ambitious Atlas *pistes*, you'll probably be dependent on these vehicles, unless you walk.

Hitching

Hitchhiking is not big in Morocco, but you may resort to it on routes where transport is scarce. Fellow tourists may pick you up, and Moroccans may carry you for free, but usually you pay, around the same as a bus or *grand taxi* fare. This is especially the case in country areas, where local rides can operate in much the same way as truck taxis. As a rule, however, hitching is not really safe, and it is definitely not advisable for women travelling alone. We have heard of (Moroccan) hitchhikers being robbed on the N12 Tata–Bou Izakarn road, and it probably happens elsewhere too.

By car

There are few real problems **driving** in Morocco, but **accident rates** are high, largely because motorists routinely ignore traffic regulations and drive aggressively and dangerously (most people pay *baksheesh* for their licence). Do not expect other drivers to indicate or observe lane discipline, beware when coming up to blind curves or hills where vehicles coming in the other direction may be trying to overtake without full view of the road ahead, treat all pedestrians with the suspicion that they will cross in front of you, and all cyclists with the idea that they may suddenly swerve into the middle of the road. All this makes driving a

---

DRIVING REQUIREMENTS

The **minimum age** for driving in Morocco is 21 years. EU, North American and Australasian **driving licences** are recognized and valid in Morocco, though an **International Driving Licence**, with its French translations (available from the AA or equivalent motoring organizations) is a worthwhile investment, especially if your domestic licence doesn't have a photograph on it (Moroccan police will find that strange). You must **carry your driving licence and passport** at all times. You **drive on the right.**

---

particularly hair-raising experience in towns, and even experienced drivers may find city driving quite stressful. The difficulty of finding places in cities due to lack of street signs adds to the problem. Be particularly wary about driving **after dark**, as it is legal to drive up to 20km/h without lights, which allows all cyclists and mopeds to wander at will; donkeys, goats and sheep do not carry lights, either.

However, with those caveats in mind, daytime and certainly long-distance driving can be as good as anywhere. Good road surfaces, long straight roads, and little traffic between inhabited areas allow for high average speeds. The usual **speed limit** outside towns is 40km/h (25mph) in built-up areas, 100km/h (62mph) on ordinary roads, and 120km/h (75mph) on motorways. There are on-the-spot fines for speeding, and oncoming motorists flashing their headlights at you may well be warning you to slow down for a police check ahead (radar speed traps are common).

The rule of giving priority to traffic from the right is observed at **roundabouts and junctions** – meaning that cars coming onto a roundabout have priority over those already on it.

By law, drivers and passengers are required to wear **seat belts**. Almost no one does, but if you follow suit and are stopped by the police, you may have a small (possibly unofficial) fine extracted. Given Morocco's high road accident rate, it is foolhardy not to wear a seat belt anyway.

Piste and off-piste driving

On the **pistes** (rough, unpaved tracks in the mountains or desert), there are special problems. Here you do need a good deal of driving and mechanical confidence – and if you don't feel your car is up to it, don't drive on these routes. Obviously, a **4WD** vehicle is best suited to these surfaces, but most *pistes* are passable, with care, in an ordinary small car, though it's worth asking local advice first. On **mountain roads**, beware of gravel, which can be a real danger on the frequent hairpin bends, and, in spring, flash floods caused by melting snow. The six-volume series, *Pistes du Maroc* (Gandini), are invaluable guides for anyone planning on driving on *pistes*; they are available in major Moroccan bookshops or online (**Ⓦ** extrem-sud. com/guides.php).

Driving a 4WD can be an exciting way of exploring the mountains and desert, off-tarmac, or even **off-piste**. Some companies lay on vehicles, driver and mess tent, organize food and cooking and will go wherever requested. For economical and practical reasons, the optimum group size is five or eleven people, so you'll probably find yourself exploring with strangers.

Car rental

Car rental starts at around 3000dh (£250/$320) per week or 500dh (£40/$55) a day (there's usually a three-day minimum) for a basic car with unlimited mileage and insurance cover. You will be expected to leave credit card details, and fuel prices are high (see below). Having a car pays obvious dividends if you are pushed for time, especially in the **south**, where buses and taxis may be sparse, but chartering a *grand taxi* and agreeing a daily rate will not cost that much more.

Many visitors rent a car in Casablanca, Marrakesh or Agadir, but it may work out cheaper to **arrange car rental in advance** through the travel company who arranges your flight. With international franchises such as Hertz, Budget, Europcar and Avis, you can book from home by phone or online. Local **car rental firms** are listed in city "Arrival and Departure" sections in the Guide. Deals to go for are unlimited mileage and daily/weekly rates; paying by the kilometre -invariably works out more expensive. Local firms have the advantage that the price is more likely to be negotiable, though you should check the condition of the vehicle carefully. Many hotels can arrange car rental at reasonable rates.

Before setting out, make sure the car comes with a spare tyre, a toolkit and full documentation – including **insurance** cover, which is compulsory issue with all rentals. It's a good idea to get full insurance to avoid charges for bumps and scratches. Most car rental agreements prohibit use of the car on unsurfaced roads, and you will be liable for any damage sustained if you do drive off-tarmac.

Equipment

Whether you rent a car or drive your own, always make sure you're carrying a **spare tyre** in good condition (plus a jack and tools). Flat tyres occur very frequently, even on fairly major roads, and you can often be in for a long wait until someone drives along with a possible replacement. Carrying an **emergency windscreen** is also useful, especially if driving your own car for a long period of time. There are lots of loose stones on the hard shoulders of single-lane roads and they can fly all over the place. If you're not mechanically minded, be sure to bring

DISTANCE CHART (KILOMETRES BY ROAD)

	Ag	Al H	Casa	Dakh	Er Rach	Ess	Fez	Figuig
Agadir	–	1037	511	1208	773	173	756	1151
Al Hoceima	1037	–	570	2245	637	940	281	773
Casablanca	511	570	–	1719	557	351	289	935
Dakhla	1208	2245	1719	–	1981	1381	1964	2359
Er Rachidia	773	637	557	1981	–	676	350	378
Essaouira	173	940	351	1381	676	–	640	1054
Fez	756	281	289	1964	350	640	–	706
Figuig	1151	773	935	2359	378	1054	706	–
Laayoune	694	1731	1205	514	1467	867	1450	1845
Marrakesh	273	764	238	1481	500	176	483	878
Meknes	740	341	229	1948	328	580	60	706
Nador	1063	280	596	2271	554	947	307	525
Oujda	1076	397	609	2284	564	960	320	386
Ouarzazate	375	927	442	1483	296	380	646	674
Rabat	602	479	91	1810	466	442	198	1199
Tangier	880	323	341	2088	595	692	303	1457
Tetouan	873	273	362	2081	595	713	276	1478

a car **maintenance manual** – a useful item, too, for anyone planning to rent a vehicle.

Fuel and breakdowns

Filling stations can be few and far between in rural areas: always fill your tank to the limit. Unleaded fuel is available in most places nowadays, but it's always worth filling up when you have the chance as supplies can be sporadic. **Fuel prices** are generally lower than in Western Europe. In the Saharan provinces (basically the Western Sahara), fuel is subsidized, and costs about a third less. Fuel in the duty-free Spanish enclaves of Ceuta and Melilla is cheaper than it is on the Spanish mainland, but slightly more for petrol than in Morocco proper.

Moroccan mechanics are usually excellent at coping with **breakdowns** and all medium-sized towns have garages (most with an extensive range of spare parts for most French cars, and usually for Fiats too). However, if you break down miles from anywhere you'll probably end up paying a fortune to get a truck to tow you to the nearest town.

If you are driving your **own vehicle**, there is also the problem of having to re-export any car that you bring into the country (even a wreck). You can't just write off a car: you'll have to take it out of Morocco with you.

Vehicle insurance

Insurance must by law be sold along with all rental agreements. Driving your own vehicle, you should obtain Green Card cover from your insurers. If you don't have it on arrival, you can buy it from Assurance Frontière for a car or camper van, at Tangier port, Nador port, or the land frontiers at Ceuta and Melilla, or on line (for example at Ⓦatel.fr/assurance-frontiere-maroc.html), or contact the Fédération Marocaine des Sociétés d'Assurances et de Réassurance (FMSAR; Ⓦbcma.org.ma).

Parking

Parking in almost any town, you will find a **gardien de voitures**, usually licensed by local authorities to look after cars, and claiming a couple of dirhams by way of parking fees. Alternatively, most of the larger hotels in the Ville Nouvelle quarters of cities have parking spaces (and occasionally garaging). It's always worth paying for a *gardien* or parking in a garage, as new and well-looked-after cars attract a certain level of vandalism. Red-and-white-striped kerbs mean no parking is allowed.

By motorbike

Morocco has all the major attractions sought by **motorbike** enthusiasts, but if you've never taken a bike abroad before, seriously consider going with a group. H-C Travel in the UK (Ⓦwww.hctravel.com), Moto Adventures in Andorra (Ⓦmotoaventures.com) and Wilderness Wheels in Ouarzazate (Ⓦwildernesswheels.com) provide off-road and trailbiking packages. Taking your own bike is subject to the same bureaucracy as taking a car (see page 29). One way of avoiding that is to **rent a motorbike** in Morocco

Laay	Mar	Mek	Nad	Ouj	Ouarz	Rab	Tan	Tet
694	273	740	1063	1076	375	602	880	873
1731	764	341	280	397	927	479	323	273
1205	238	229	596	609	442	91	341	362
514	1481	1948	2271	2284	1483	1810	2088	2081
1467	500	328	554	564	296	466	595	595
867	176	580	947	960	380	442	692	713
1450	483	60	307	320	646	198	303	276
1845	878	706	525	386	674	1199	1457	1478
–	967	1434	1757	1770	1069	1296	1574	1567
967	–	467	790	803	204	321	579	600
1434	467	–	363	380	652	138	267	267
1757	790	363	–	139	840	501	597	547
1770	803	380	139	–	850	518	714	664
1069	204	652	840	850	–	528	783	804
1296	321	138	501	518	528	–	250	271
1574	579	267	597	714	783	250	–	58
1567	600	267	547	664	804	271	58	–

(see pages 316 and 425). So far as road conditions are concerned, our comments on driving (see page 33) also apply to motorbikes.

Taking your own bike

If you take your own motorbike, you will need **special insurance**. Most companies, especially those based outside Europe, will not cover motorcycling as part of a holiday overseas, particularly when off-road riding is contemplated or inevitable (as it often is in Morocco). You'll have to shop around and remember to take the policy with you, together with your bike registration certificate, biker's licence and International Driving Permit. Even large insurance companies don't give clear answers about "**Green Cards**" for motorcycling in Morocco and do not understand that you may encounter up to a dozen police checks a day.

When **entering Morocco**, try to arrive as early in the day as possible. If you are a lone traveller and speak neither Arabic nor French, you may be left queuing until those without queries have been dealt with. If the office then closes, you may have to return the next morning. In these circumstances, it might be worth investing in a tout who, for a fee, will take your papers to a friendly officer. It's also worth picking up a couple of (free) extra **immigration forms** for the return journey.

What to take and when to go

If possible, don't take a model of a bike likely to be unfamiliar in Morocco. It's worth carrying cables and levers, inner tubes, puncture repair kit, tyre levers, pump, fuses, plugs, chain, washable air filter, cable ties, good tape and a toolkit. For riding **off-road**, take knobbly tyres and rim locks, brush guards, metal number plate and bashplate. In **winter**, take tough fabric outer clothing. In **summer**, carry lighter-weight clothing, woollen jumpers and waterproofs. Drying out leathers takes a long time. In the south, the heat in summer can be overwhelming, making travelling a less enjoyable experience.

By bicycle

Cycling – and particularly **mountain biking** in the Atlas (see page 353) and other areas – is becoming an increasingly popular pursuit for Western travellers to Morocco. The country's regular roads are well maintained and by European standards very quiet, while the extensive network of **pistes** – dirt tracks – makes for exciting mountain-bike terrain, leading you into areas otherwise accessible only to trekkers or four-wheel-drive expeditions.

Regular roads are generally surfaced (*goudronné* or *revêtue*) but narrow, and you will often have to get off the tarmac to make way for traffic. Beware also of open land-drains close to the roadsides, and loose gravel on the bends.

Cycling on **pistes**, mountain bikes come into their own with their "tractor" tyres and wide, stabilizing handlebars. There are few *pistes* that could be recommended on a regular tourer. By contrast, some intrepid mountain bikers cover footpaths in the High Atlas, though for the less than super-fit this is extremely heavy going. Better, on the whole, to stick to established *pistes* – many of which are covered by local trucks, which you can pay for a ride in if your legs (or your bike) give out.

Getting your bike to Morocco

Many **airlines** carry bikes free of charge, so long as they don't push your baggage allowance over the weight limit, but the no-frills airlines will charge you. When buying a ticket, register your intention of taking your bike and check out the airline's conditions. They will generally require you to invert the handlebars, remove the pedals, and deflate the tyres; some provide or sell a cardboard **box** to enclose the bike, as protection for other passengers' luggage as much as for the bike; you are, however, unlikely to be offered a box for the return journey. A useful alternative, offering little protection but at least ensuring nothing gets lost, is to customize an industrial nylon sack, adding a drawstring at the neck.

If you plan to cross over **by ferry to Morocco**, things couldn't be simpler. You ride on with the motor vehicles (thus avoiding the long queues of foot passengers) and the bike is secured during the voyage. At the time of writing, bicycles travel for free on most ferries other than the runs from Tarifa and Motril.

Bikes and local transport

Cycling around Morocco, you can make use of local transport to supplement your own wheels. **Buses** will generally carry bikes on the roof. CTM usually charges around 15dh per bike – make sure you get a ticket. On other lines it's very much up to you to negotiate with the driver and/or baggage porter (who will probably expect at least 10dh). If you're riding and exhausted, you can usually flag down private-line buses (but not usually CTM services) on the road.

Some *grands taxis* also agree to carry bikes, if they have space on a rack. You may have to pay for this, but of course you can haggle. In mountain or desert areas, you can have your bike carried with you on **truck or transit services** (see page 33). Prices for this are negotiable, but should not exceed your own passenger fare.

Bikes are carried on **trains** for a modest handling fee, though it's not really worth the hassle. They have to be registered in advance as baggage and won't necessarily travel on the same train as you (though they will usually turn up within a day).

Accommodation

Accommodation doesn't present any special problems. The cheaper **hotels** will almost always let you keep your bike in your room – and others will find a disused basement or office for storage. It's almost essential to do this, as much to deter unwelcome tampering as theft, especially if you have a curiosity-inviting mountain bike. At **campsites**, there's usually a *gardien* on hand to keep an eye on your bike, or he might stow it away in his chalet.

ROUTES

Rewarding areas for cycling include:

Tizi n'Test (High Atlas) Asni to Ijoukak, and an excursion to Tin Mal.

Asni to Setti Fatma (High Atlas: Ourika Valley) And beyond, if you have a mountain bike.

Northern and Western Middle Atlas Good routes on the well-watered side.

Jebel Saghro and Jebel Bani A choice of decent east–west Anti-Atlas routes.

Southern oasis routes In summer it wouldn't be a good idea to go much beyond the Atlas, though given cooler winter temperatures, rewarding long routes exist in the southern oasis routes, such as Ouarzazate to Zagora or Ouarzazate to Tinghir, and the desert routes down to Er Rachidia, Erfoud and Rissani.

Repairs

Most towns have **repair shops** in their Medina quarters, used to servicing local bicycles and mopeds. They may not have spare parts for your make of bike, but can usually sort out some kind of temporary solution. It is worth bringing **spare spokes** (and tools) with you, plus **brake blocks** and **cable**, as the mountain descents can take it out on a bike. **Tyres** and **tubes** can generally be found for tourers, though if you have anything fancy, best bring at least one spare, too.

Obviously, before setting out, you should make sure that your brakes are in good order, renew bearings, etc, and ensure that you have decent quality (and condition) tyres.

Problems and rewards

All over Morocco, and particularly in rural areas, there are stray, wild and semi-cared-for **dogs**. A cyclist pedalling past with feet and wheels spinning seems to send at least half of them into a frenzied state. Normally, cycling in an equally frenzied state is the best defence, but on steep ascents and off-road this isn't always possible. In these -situations, keep the bike between you and the dog, and use your pump or a shower from your water bottle as defence. If you do get bitten, a rabies inoculation is advisable.

Another factor to be prepared for is your suscep-tibility to the unwanted attentions of local people. Small **children** will often stand in the road to hinder your progress, or even chase after you in gangs and throw stones. Your attitude is important: be friendly, smile, and maintain strong eye contact. On no account attempt to mete out your own -discipline: small children always have big brothers.

The heat and the long stretches of dead straight road across arid, featureless plains – the main routes to (or beyond) the mountain ranges – can all too easily drain your energy. Additionally, public **water** is very rare – there are few roadside watering places, and towns and villages can be a long way apart.

Despite all this, cycling in Morocco can be an extremely rewarding experience; as one of our readers once put it: "I felt an extra intimacy with the country by staying close to it, rather than viewing it from car or bus windows. And I experienced unrivalled generosity, from cups of tea offered by policemen at roadside checkpoints to a full-blown breakfast banquet from a farming family whose dog had savaged my leg. People went out of their way to give me advice, food, drink and lifts, and not once did I feel seriously threatened. Lastly, the exhilaration I felt on some of the mountain descents, above all the Tizi n'Test in the High Atlas, will remain with me forever. I was not an experienced cycle tourer when I arrived in Morocco, but the grandeur of the scenery helped carry me over the passes".

City transport

You'll spend most time exploring Moroccan cities **on foot**. The alleys of the old Medina quarters, where the sights and souks are, will rarely accommodate more than a donkey. In the newer quarters, you may want to make use of city **taxis** and occasion-ally a **bus**. Be aware that pedestrian crossings don't count for very much, except perhaps at junctions "controlled" by traffic lights. And even then, bikes and mopeds pay scant attention to traffic lights showing red.

Petits taxis carry up to three passengers and (unlike *grands taxis*; see page 32) can only operate within city limits. All *petits taxis* should have meters, and you should insist that they use them. Failing that, you will need to bargain for a price – either before you get in (wise to start off with) or by simply presenting the regular fare when you get out. If you are a lone passenger, your taxi driver may pick up one or two additional passengers en route, each of whom will pay the full fare for their journey, as of course will you. This is standard practice.

Don't be afraid to argue with the driver if you feel you're being unreasonably overcharged. During the daytime, you should pay what is on the meter. After 8pm, standard fares rise by fifty percent. Tips are not expected, but of course always appreciated. Taxis from airports usually run at special rates agreed among the drivers, in which case they will not agree to use the meter.

Accommodation

Hotels in Morocco are cheap, good value, and usually pretty easy to find. There can be a shortage of places in the major cities and resorts (Tangier, Fez, Marrakesh and Agadir) in August, and in Rabat or Casablanca when there's a big conference on. At other times, you should be able to pick from a wide range of accommodation.

In winter, one thing worth checking for in a hotel is **heating** – nights can get cold, even in the south (and especially in the desert), and since bedding is not always adequate, a hotel with heating can be a boon. It's always, in any case, a good idea to ask to see your room before you check in.

Prices quoted for hotels in the Guide (at the end of reviews) are for the cheapest double room or dorm bed in high season, and are for the room only, unless we specify BB for bed and breakfast, HB for half-board,

or FB for full board. Camping prices are for a pitch and two people.

Unclassified hotels

Unclassified (**non-classé**) hotels are often in the older parts of cities – the walled Medinas – and are almost always the cheapest accommodation options. They have the additional advantage of being at the heart of things: where you'll want to spend most of your time, and where all the sights and markets are concentrated. The disadvantages are that the Medinas can at first appear daunting – with their mazes of narrow lanes and blind alleys – and that the hotels themselves can be, at worst, dirty flea traps with tiny, windowless cells and half-washed sheets. At their best, if well kept, they're fine, in traditional buildings with whitewashed rooms round a central patio.

One other minus point for unclassified Medina hotels is that they sometimes have a problem with **water**. Most of the Medinas remain substantially unmodernized, and some cheap hotels don't have hot water and only have squat toilets. On the plus side, there is usually a hammam (Turkish bath; see page 39) nearby.

Classified hotels

Classified (**classé**) hotels are most likely to be found in a town's Ville Nouvelle – the "new" or administrative quarter. They are allowed, regardless of **star-rating**, to set their own prices – and to vary them according to season and demand. Prices should be on display at reception.

For Western-style standards of comfort, you need to look, on the whole, at **four-star hotels**, but even here, you are advised to check what's on offer. The plumbing, heating and lighting are sometimes unreliable; restaurants are often closed and swimming pools empty. Hotels in this price category are particularly likely to offer discounted and promotional rates off-season, and will almost always be cheaper if booked through a travel agent online or abroad than at the "rack rates" offered to travellers who just turn up. One safe but boring option at this level is the Ibis Moussafir chain (**W**ibishotel.com), whose hotels are often next to train stations, rather characterless and generally all identical, but comfortable, efficient and good value.

Hotels accorded the **five-star-luxury rating**, can sometimes be very stylish, whether in a historic conversion (most famously the *Hôtel la Mamounia* in Marrakesh; see page 297, and the *Palais Jamaï* in

---

ACCOMMODATION PRICE GUIDE

Room prices are based on a double room in high season, excluding breakfast unless otherwise stated.

€ = below DH500
€€ = Dh501-1000
€€€ = DH 10001-1500
€€€€ = DH1501 and above

HAMMAMS

The absence of hot showers in some of the cheapest Medina hotels is not such a disaster. Throughout all the Medina quarters, you'll find local **hammams**. A hammam is a Turkish-style steam bath, with a succession of rooms from cool to hot, and endless supplies of hot and cold water, which you fetch in buckets. The usual procedure is to find a piece of floor space in the hot room, surround it with as many buckets of water as you feel you need, and lie in the heat to sweat out the dirt from your pores before scrubbing it off. A plastic bowl is useful for scooping the water from the buckets to wash with. You can also order a **massage**, in which you will be allowed to sweat, pulled about a bit to relax your muscles, and then rigorously scrubbed with a rough flannel glove (*kiis*). Alternatively, buy a *kiis* and do it yourself. For many Moroccan women, who would not drink in a café or bar, the hammam is a social gathering place, in which tourists are made very welcome too. Indeed, hammams turn out to be a highlight for many women travellers, and an excellent way to make contact with Moroccan women.

Several hammams are detailed in the text, but the best way of finding one is always to ask at the hotel where you're staying. You will often, in fact, need to be led to a hammam, since they are usually unmarked and can be **hard to find**. In some towns, you find a separate hammam for women and men; at others the same establishment offers different hours for each sex – usually mornings and evenings for men, afternoons (typically noon to 6pm) for women.

For both sexes, there's more **modesty** than you might perhaps expect: it's customary for men (always) and women (generally, though bare breasts are acceptable) to bathe in swimming costume (or underwear), and to undress facing the wall. Women may be also surprised to find their Moroccan counterparts completely shaven and may (in good humour) be offered this service; there's no embarrassment in declining.

Finally, don't forget to bring **soap and shampoo** (though these are sometimes sold at hammams), and a **towel** (these are sometimes rented, but may not always be as clean as you'd like). Moroccans often bring a plastic mat to sit on, too, as the floors can get a bit clogged. Mats can be bought easily enough in any town. Most Moroccans use a pasty, olive oil-based soap (*sabon bildi*), sold by weight in Medina shops. On sale at the same shops, you'll find *kiis* flannel gloves, a fine mud (*ghasoul*), used by some instead of shampoo, pumice stones (*hazra*) for removing dead skin, and alum (*chebba*), used as an antiperspirant and to stop shaving cuts from bleeding.

Fez) or in a modern building with a splendid pool and all the international creature comforts, but most Moroccan five-star hotels – particularly those catering for tour groups – are more like four-stars elsewhere, and service is frequently amateurish by Western standards.

In the Spanish enclaves of **Ceuta and Melilla**, accommodation at the lower end of the spectrum costs about twice as much as it does in Morocco proper. At the top end of the scale, prices tend to be much the same as they are in Morocco.

Riads

Morocco's trendiest accommodation option is in a **riad** or **maison d'hôte**. Strictly speaking, a riad is a house built around a patio garden – in fact, the word riad correctly refers to the garden rather than the house – while *maison d'hôte* is French for "guest house". The two terms are both used, to some extent interchangeably, for a residential house done up to rent out to tourists, but a riad is generally more stylish and expensive, while a *maison d'hôte* is likely to be more homely. In a riad, it is often possible to rent the whole house.

The riad craze started in Marrakesh, and quickly spread to Fez and Essaouira. Since then it has gone nationwide and almost every town with tourists now has riads too. Even the Atlas mountains and the southern oases are dotted with them.

Most riads are eighteenth- or nineteenth-century **Medina townhouses** which have been bought and refurbished by Europeans or prosperous Moroccans (often Moroccans who have been living in Europe). Some of them are very stylishly done out, most have roof terraces, some have plunge pools or jacuzzis, pretty much all offer en suite rooms, and breakfast is usually included in the room price. The best riads have a landlord or landlady who is constantly in attendance and stamps their own individual personality on the place, but many riads nowadays are really just boutique hotels, and can be quite impersonal.

The popularity of riads has also attracted a fair few **amateur property developers**, some of whom invest minimum money in the hope of maximum returns. Therefore, before you take a riad, even more than with a hotel, it is always best to give it a preliminary once-over. Riads may be more expensive than hotels with a similar level of comfort, but at the top of the market, they can be a lot classier than a run-of-the-mill five-star hotel.

Hostels

Morocco has seven *Auberges de Jeunesse* run by its YHA, the Fédération Royale Marocaine des Auberges de Jeunesse. Most are clean and reasonably well run, and most have private rooms too. Hostelling International (HI) membership cards are not usually required but you may have to pay a little extra if you do not have one. The hostels are located at Asni, Casablanca, Essaouira, Fez, Marrakesh, Martil, Meknes, Ouarzazate, and Rabat, and at Laayoune in the Western Sahara. Most are reviewed in the relevant sections of the Guide. Further information on Moroccan youth hostels can be found on the Hostelling International website at ⓦ hihostels.com.

Refuges and gîtes d'étape

In the Jebel Toubkal area of the High Atlas mountains, the Club Alpin Français (CAF; ⓦ ffcam.fr) maintain two huts, or refuges (at Oukaïmeden, Tazaghart and Toubkal) equipped for mountaineers and trekkers. These provide bunks or bedshelves for sleeping, with discounts for members of CAF or its affiliates. They also provide meals and/or cooking facilities.

Also in trekking areas, a number of locals offer rooms in their houses: such places are known as **gîtes d'étape**.

Camping

Campsites are to be found at intervals along much of the developed Moroccan coast and in most towns or cities of any size. They vary in price and facilities; cheap sites may have quite **basic washing and toilet facilities**, and often charge 10dh or so for a **hot shower**. More upmarket places may offer better facilities and even **swimming pools**, and cost about twice as much, sometimes more. Comprehensive, and often highly critical reviews of Morocco's campsites,

in French, can be found in Émile Verhooste and Pascal Samson's annual *Campings du Maroc* (published by Extrem'sud), which is sometimes available at Moroccan campsites and bookshops.

Campsites don't tend to provide much **security**, and you should never leave valuables unattended. This obviously applies even more when camping outside official sites; if you want to do this, it's wise to ask at a house if you can pitch your tent alongside – you'll usually get a hospitable response. If you're trekking in the Atlas, it is often possible to pay someone to act as a *gardien* for your tent. In the south especially, and particularly in the winter, campsites are not much used by backpackers with tents, but rather by retired Europeans in camper vans seeking the sun.

If travelling in a **camper van**, you can often park up somewhere with a *gardien*, who will keep an eye on things for a small tip. Failing that, you may be able to park outside a police station (*commissariat*). In the north of the country, at Larache, Kenitra and Malabata (near Tangier), there are *Aires de Repos*, which are rest areas for tourist coaches, with toilets, showers, a restaurant and *gardien*. There's no fee for parking your camper here or using the facilities, but it is usual to pay a contribution of around 20dh to the *gardien* if you stay overnight.

Food and drink

Basic Moroccan meals may begin with a thick, very filling soup – most often the spicy, bean and pasta harira. Alternatively, you might start with a salad (often very finely chopped), or have this as a side dish with your main course, typically a plateful of kebabs – either brochettes (small pieces of lamb on a skewer) or kefta, (minced lamb). A few hole-in-the wall places specialize in soup, which they sell by the bowlful all day long – such places are usually indicated by a pile of soup bowls at the front. As well as harira, and especially for breakfast, some places sell a thick pea soup called bisara, topped with olive oil.

Another dish you'll find everywhere is a **tajine**, essentially a stew, steam-cooked slowly in an earthenware dish with a conical earthenware lid (see box below). Classic tajines include lamb or mutton with prunes and almonds, or chicken with olives and lemon. Less often, you may get a fish or vegetable tajine, or a tajine of meatballs topped with eggs.

Kebabs and tajines are usually cheap and cheerful at hole-in-the-wall places in the Medina, which typically have just two or three tables. You are not expected to bargain for cooked food, but **prices** may be higher in such places if you don't ask how much items cost before you order them. There is often no menu – or just a board written in Arabic only. Restaurants are typically open noon to 3pm for lunch and 7 to 11pm for dinner, though cheaper places may be open in the morning and between times too.

If you're looking for **breakfast or a snack**, you can buy a half-baguette – plus butter and jam, cheese or eggs, if you want – from many bread or grocery stores, and take it into a café to order a coffee. Many cafés, even those which serve no other food, may offer a breakfast of bread, butter and jam (which is also what you'll get in most hotels), or maybe an omelette. Some places also offer soup, such as *harira*, with bread, and others have stalls outside selling by weight traditional griddle breads such as *harsha* (quite heavy with a gritty crust), *melaoui* or *msimmen* (sprinkled with oil, rolled out thin, folded over and rolled out again several times, like an Indian *paratha*) and *baghira* (full of holes like a very thin English crumpet). If that is not sufficient, supplementary foods you could buy include dates or olives, yoghurt, or soft white cheese (*ejben*).

Street food includes small kebabs or spicy merguez sausages cooked at roadside stalls (make sure the sausages are well done), peanuts, sunflower seeds or roasted chickpeas sold at peanut stands, and *sfenj* (doughnut-shaped fritters), sold from little shops, particularly in the morning.

Restaurant meals

Restaurants usually offer **fish**, particularly on the coast, lamb (*agneau*) or mutton (*mouton*), usually

in a tajine, and **chicken** (*poulet*), either spit-roasted (*rôti*) or in a tajine with lemon and olives (*poulet aux olives et citron*). You will sometimes find **pastilla**, too, a succulent pigeon or chicken pie, prepared with filo pastry dusted with sugar and cinnamon; it is a particular speciality of Fez.

And, of course, there's **couscous**, the most famous Moroccan dish; Berber in origin, it's a huge bowl of steamed semolina piled high with vegetables and mutton, chicken, or occasionally fish. Restaurant couscous can be disappointing as there is no real tradition of going out to eat in Morocco, and this is a dish that's traditionally prepared at home, especially on Friday or for a special occasion.

At festivals, which are always good for interesting food, and at the most expensive tourist restaurants, you may also come across **mechoui** – roast lamb, which may even take the form of a whole sheep roasted on a spit. In Marrakesh particularly, another speciality is **tanjia**, which is jugged beef or lamb, cooked very slowly in the embers of a hammam furnace.

Dessert may consist of a pastry, or a crème caramel, or possibly yoghurt, which is often – even in cheap places – the restaurant's own. Otherwise, you may get fruit, either an orange, or perhaps a fruit salad.

TAJINES

Like paella or casserole, the word **tajine** strictly refers to a vessel rather than to the food cooked in it. A tajine is a heavy ceramic plate covered with a conical lid of the same material. The prettiest tajines, decorated in all sorts of colours and designs, come from Safi (see page 272), but the best tajines for actual use are plain reddish-brown in colour, and come from Salé (see page 248). The food in a tajine is arranged with the **meat** in the middle and the **vegetables** piled up around it. Then the lid is put on, and the tajine is left to cook slowly over a low light, or better still, over a charcoal stove (*kanoun*), usually one made specifically for the tajine and sold with it. The classic tajines combine meat with fruit and spices. Chicken is traditionally cooked in a tajine with green olives and lemons preserved in brine. Lamb or beef are often cooked with prunes and almonds. When eating a tajine, you start on the outside with the vegetables, and work your way to the meat at the heart of the dish, scooping up the food with bread.

Eating Moroccan style

Eating in local cafés, or if **invited to a home**, you may find yourself using your hands rather than a knife and fork. Muslims eat only with the **right hand** (the left is used for the toilet), and you should do likewise. Hold the bread between the fingers and use your thumb as a scoop; it's often easier to discard the soft centre of the bread and to use the crust only – as you will see many Moroccans do. Eating from a **communal plate** at someone's home, it is polite to take only what is immediately in front of you, unless specifically offered a piece of meat by the host.

Vegetarian eating

Vegetarianism is met with little comprehension in most of Morocco, though restaurants in some places are becoming aware that tourists may be vegetarian, and many places do now offer a meat-free tajine or couscous. In Marrakesh there is even a vegetarian restaurant (see page 322), and pizzas are usually available in large towns. Otherwise, aside from omelettes and sandwiches, menus don't present very obvious choices. *Bisara* (pea soup), a common breakfast dish, should be meat-free, but *harira* (bean soup) may or may not be made with meat stock, while most foods are cooked in animal fats. It is possible to say "I'm a vegetarian" ("*Ana nabaati*" in Arabic, or "*Je suis vegetarien/vegetarienne*" in French), but you may not be understood; to reinforce the point, you could perhaps add "*La akulu lehoum (wala hout)*" in Arabic, or "*Je ne mange aucune sorte de viande (ni poisson)*", both of which mean "I don't eat any kind of meat (or fish)".

If you are a very strict vegetarian or vegan, it may be worth bringing some **basic provisions** (such as yeast extract, peanut butter and veggie stock cubes) and a small camping gas stove and pan – canisters are cheap though quite hard to find (Carrefour hypermarkets usually have them, as do the DIY chain Mr Bricolage), and some cheap hotels allow guests to cook in their rooms.

The most difficult situations are those in which you are invited to eat at someone's house. You may find people give you meat when you have specifically asked for vegetables because they don't understand that you object to eating meat, and you may decide that it's more important not to offend someone showing you kindness than to be strict about your abstinence. Picking out vegetables and leaving the meat from a tajine won't offend your hosts, but declining the dish altogether may end up with the mother/sister/wife in the kitchen getting the flak.

Fruit

Morocco is surprisingly rich in seasonal **fruits**. In addition to the various kinds of **dates** – sold all year but at their best fresh from the October harvests – there are grapes, melons, strawberries, peaches and figs, all of which should be washed before eaten. Or for a real thirst-quencher (and a good cure for a bad stomach), you can have quantities of **prickly pear** (cactus fruit), peeled for you in the street for a couple of dirhams in season (winter).

Tea, coffee and soft drinks

The national drink is **mint tea** (*atay deeyal naanaa* in Arabic, *thé à la menthe* in French, "Whisky Marocain" as locals boast), Chinese gunpowder green tea flavoured with sprigs of mint (*naanaa* in Arabic: the gift of Allah) and sweetened with a large amount of sugar, often from a sugar loaf (you can ask for it with little or no sugar – *shweeya soukar* or *ble soukar*). In winter, Moroccans often add bitter wormwood (*chiba* in Arabic, *absinthe* in French), to their tea "to keep out the cold". You can also get **black tea** (*atai ahmar* in Arabic, *thé rouge* in French, literally meaning "red tea") – inevitably made with the ubiquitous Lipton's tea bags, a brand fondly believed by Moroccans to be typically English. The main **herbal infusion** is verbena (*verveine* or *louiza*).

Also common at cafés and street stalls are a range of wonderful freshly squeezed **juices**: orange juice (*jus d'orange* in French, *'asir burtuqal* in Arabic – if you don't want sugar in it, you'll need to say so) almond milk (*jus d'amande* or *'asir louze*), banana "juice", meaning milk shake (*jus des bananes* or *'asir mooz*) and apple milk shake (*jus de pomme* or *'asir tufah*). Also common is *'asir panaché*, a mixed fruit milk shake often featuring raisins. *Leben* – soured milk – is tastier than it sounds, and does wonders for an upset stomach.

Moroccan tap **water** is usually chlorinated and safe to drink, but tourists generally prefer to stick to bottled water. Mineral water is usually referred to by brand name, ubiquitously the still Sidi Harazem or Sidi Ali (some people claim to be able to tell one from the other), or the naturally sparkling Oulmès. The Coca-Cola company markets filtered, processed non-mineral water in bottles under the brand name Ciel. **Coffee** (*café*) is best in French-style cafés – either *noir* (black), *cassé* (with a drop of milk), or *au lait* (with a lot of milk). Instant coffee is known, like teabag tea, after its brand – in this case Nescafé.

Lastly, do not take risks with **milk**: buy it fresh and drink it fresh. If it smells remotely off, don't touch it or you may end up unwell.

Wine and beer

As an Islamic nation, Morocco gives **drinking alcohol** a low profile, and it is not generally possible to buy it in city Medinas. Ordinary **bars** are very much all-male preserves, in which women may feel quite uncomfortable (bartenders may occasionally be female, but any female Moroccan customers are likely to be on the game), but upmarket bars – especially in Marrakesh or Casablanca or in tourist hotels – are usually fine however.

Moroccan **wines** can be palatable enough, if a little heavy for drinking without a meal. The best is the pinkish red Clairet de Meknès, made purposefully light in French claret style. Beauvallon is another good one, but usually reserved for export. Other varieties worth trying include the strong red Cabernet, and Ksar, Guerrouane and Siraoua, which are also red, the rosé Gris de Boulaouane and the dry white Spécial Coquillages.

Those Moroccans who drink in bars tend to stick to **beer**, usually the local Stork or Flag. Flag from Fez is held by many to be superior to the version brewed in Casablanca (the label will tell you which it is). The most popular foreign brand is Heineken, which is made under licence in Morocco.

The media

British dailies and the *International Herald Tribune* are available at some newsstands in city centres and tourist resorts.

Newspapers and magazines

The **Moroccan press** has a range of papers in French and Arabic, but news coverage, especially of international news, is weak. Of the **French-language** papers, the most accessible is the pro-government daily, *Le Matin* (🌐lematin.ma). Others include *L'Opinion* (Istiqlal party; 🌐lopinion.ma), *Maroc Soir* (pro-government evening daily), *L'Economiste*, (independent but generally pro-government; 🌐leconomiste.com), and *Al Bayane* (Communist; 🌐albayane.press.ma). Periodicals include *Maroc-Hebdo* (🌐maroc-hebdo.press.ma), *La Vie Eco* (🌐lavieeco.com), and the Time/Newsweek-style news magazine *Tel-Quel* (🌐telquel.ma). The most widely read **Arabic** daily newspapers are *Al Akhbar*, *Al Massae*, which is sufficiently independent for its director to have served time for criticizing the establishment, and *Assabah*, the sister paper to *L'Economiste*. In addition to these, Morocco has a number of football magazines, women's magazines and other publications in French, as well as the excellent Francophone African news magazine, *Jeune Afrique* (🌐jeuneafrique.com).

Morocco also has a large and constantly changing selection of **online newspapers**, including a few in English. You'll find a list with links, though not all up-to-date, at 🌐onlinenewspapers.com/morocco.htm. The main online paper in English is the *Moroccan Times* (🌐themoroccantimes.com), an English-language equivalent of Morocco's pro-government French-language press, which is really more like propaganda than news.

Radio

The **BBC** have cut World Service short-wave -broadcasts to North Africa, but with a deft twiddle of the dial you may be able to pick up short-wave broadcasts for West Africa, or MW broadcasts to Europe; programme listings can be found online at 🌐bbc.co.uk/worldservice. The **Voice of America** varies its frequencies through the day, but can often be found on 909KHz, 13,590KHz or 15,580KHz – see 🌐voanews.com for up-to-date frequency and programme listings.

Television

Most of the pricier hotels receive **satellite TV** – CNN, the French TV5, and occasionally UK Sky channels. In the north of the country you can also get Spanish TV stations and, in Tangier, English-language **Gibraltar TV**. The independent Qatari news channel Al Jazeera is a major source of news for people in Morocco (many cafés show it), and you may even be able to get it in English if you have access to cable or satellite, but it is unfortunately not obtainable on terrestrial TV.

Morocco's own two TV channels broadcast in Arabic, but include some French programmes – plus news bulletins in Arabic, French, Spanish and, more recently, Berber.

Festivals

Morocco abounds in holidays and festivals, both national and local, and coming across one can be the most enjoyable experience of travel in the country – with the chance to witness music and dance, as well as special regional foods and market souks. Perhaps surprisingly, this includes Ramadan, when practising Muslims, including most Moroccans, fast from sunrise to sunset for a month, but when nights are good times to hear music and share in hospitality.

RAMADAN AND ISLAMIC HOLIDAYS

FÊTES NATIONALES

Secular public holidays are tied to Western calendar dates. The largest secular holiday is the **Feast of the Throne**, a colourful affair, celebrated throughout Morocco, with fireworks, parades and music over two to three days.

January 1 **New Year's Day**
January 11 **Anniversary of Istiqlal Manifesto** (see page 505)
May 1 **Labour Day**
July 30 **Feast of the Throne**
August 14 **Allegiance Day**
August 20 **King and People's Revolution Day**
August 21 **King's Birthday and Youth Day**
November 6 **Anniversary of the Green March** (see page 507)
November 18 **Independence Day**

RELIGIOUS HOLIDAYS

Aïd el Kebir (see page 45) and **Aïd es Seghir** (see page 45) are marked by a two-day public holiday, announced or ratified by the king on TV and radio the preceding day. **Mouloud** is a one-day holiday. On these, and on the secular *fêtes nationales* listed above, all banks, post offices and most shops are closed; transport is reduced, too, but never stops completely.

Islamic religious holidays are calculated on the **lunar calendar**, so their dates rotate throughout the seasons (as does Ramadan's), losing about eleven days a year against the Western (Gregorian) calendar. Exact dates in the lunar calendar are impossible to predict – they are set by the Islamic authorities in Fez – but approximate dates for the next few years are:

	2025	2026	2027
1st day of Ramadan	28 Feb	17 Feb	7 Feb
Aïd es Seghir	31 March	20 March	9 March
Aïd el Kebir	5 June	26 May	15 May
Moharem	26 June	16 June	6 June
Mouloud	4 Sept	25 Aug	15 Aug

Ramadan

Ramadan, the ninth month of the Islamic calendar, commemorates the first revelation of the Koran to Mohammed. Most people observe the fast; indeed Moroccans are forbidden by law from publicly disrespecting it, and a few people are jailed for this each year.

The **fast** involves abstention from food, drink, smoking and sex during daylight throughout the month. Most local cafés and restaurants close during the day, and many close up altogether and take a month's holiday. Smokers in particular get edgy towards the month's end, and it is in some respects an unsatisfactory time to travel: efficiency drops, drivers fall asleep at the wheel (hence airline pilots are excused fasting), and guides and muleteers are unwilling to go off on treks, and when the fast ends at sunset, almost regardless of what they are doing, everybody stops to eat. The month-long closure of so

many eating places can also make life difficult if you are dependent on restaurants.

But there is compensation in witnessing and becoming absorbed into the pattern of the fast. At **sunset**, signalled by the sounding of a siren, by the lighting of lamps on minarets, and in some places by a cannon shot, an amazing calm and sense of wellbeing fall on the streets. The fast is traditionally broken with a bowl of *harira* and some dates, a combination provided by many cafés and restaurants exactly at sunset. You will also see almsgiving (*zakat*) extended to offering *harira* to the poor and homeless.

After breaking their fast, everyone – in the cities at least – gets down to a night of celebration and **entertainment**. This takes different forms. If you can spend some time in Marrakesh during the month, you'll find the Jemaa el Fna square at its most active, with troupes of musicians, dancers and acrobats coming into the city for the occasion. In Rabat and

Fez, there seem to be continuous promenades, with cafés and stalls staying open until 3am. Urban cafés provide venues for live music and singing, too, and in the southern towns and Berber villages you will often come across the ritualized *ahouaches* and *haidus* – circular, trance-like dances often involving whole communities.

If you are a **non-Muslim** outsider you are not expected to observe Ramadan, but you should be sensitive about breaking the fast (particularly smoking) in public. In fact, the best way to experience Ramadan – and to benefit from its naturally purifying rhythms – is to enter into it. You may lack the faith to go without an occasional glass of water, and you'll probably have breakfast later than sunrise (it's often wise to buy supplies the night before), but it might be worth an attempt.

Other Islamic holidays

Ramadan ends with the feast of **Aïd es Seghir** or **Aïd el Fitr**, a climax to the month's night-time festivities. Even more important is **Aïd el Kebir**, which celebrates the willingness of Abraham to obey God by sacrificing his son (Isaac in the Old Testament, but believed by Muslims to be his older son Ishmael). Aïd el Kebir is followed, about two months later, by **Moharem**, the Muslim New Year.

Both *aïds* are traditional family gatherings. At Aïd el Kebir, every household that can afford it will slaughter a sheep. You see them tethered everywhere, often on rooftops, for weeks prior to the event; after the feast, their skins can be seen being cured on the streets. On both *aïd* days, shops and restaurants close and buses don't run; on the following day, all transport is packed, as people return to the cities from their family homes.

The fourth main religious holiday is the **Mouloud**, the Prophet's birthday. This is widely observed, with a large number of moussems timed to take place in the weeks around it, and two particularly important moussems at Meknes (see page 194) and Salé (see page 248). There is also a music festival, **Ashorou**, which is held thirty days after Aïd el Kebir, when people gather to play whatever traditional instrument they feel capable of wielding, and the streets are full of music.

Moussems and ammougars

Moussems – or **ammougars** – festivals held in honour of saints or *marabouts*, are local and predominantly rural affairs, and form the main religious and social celebrations of the year for most Moroccans, along with Aïd es Seghir and Aïd el Kebir.

Some of the smaller *moussems* amount to no more than a market day with religious overtones; others are essentially harvest festivals, celebrating a pause in agricultural labour after a crop has been successfully brought in, but a number have developed into substantial occasions – akin to Spanish fiestas – and a few have acquired national significance. If you are lucky enough to be here for one of the major events, you'll get the chance to witness Moroccan popular culture at its richest, with horseriding, music, singing and dancing, and of course eating.

There are enormous numbers of *moussems*. An idea of quite how many can be gathered from the frequency with which, travelling about the countryside, you

MOUSSEM CALENDAR

February	**Tafraoute** Moussem to celebrate the almond harvest (see page 450).
May	**Moulay Bousselham** Moussem of Marabout Moulay Bousselham (see page 97).
	Berkane Harvest moussem for clementines (see page 139).
	El Kelâa M'Gouna Rose festival to celebrate the new crop (see page 387).
June	**Tan Tan** Moussem of Sidi Mohammed Ma el Ainin (see page 474).
July	**Beni Arouss** Moussem of Moulay Abdessalem Ben Mchich (see page 109).
	Sefrou Fête des Cerises (see page 203).
August	**Setti Fatma** Moussem of Setti Fatma (see page 335).
	Sefrou Moussem of Sidi Lahcen el Youssi (see page 203).
	Tiznit Moussem of Sidi Ahmed ou Moussa (see page 458).
	Immouzer Honey moussem (see page 433).
September	**Moulay Idriss** Moussem of Moulay Idriss (see page 182).
	Imilchil Marriage moussem (see page 216).
	Fez Moussem of Moulay Idriss II (see page 154).
November	**Erfoud** Festival of Dates (see page 404).
December	**Rafsaï** Olive Festival (see page 142).

see *koubbas* – the square, white-domed buildings covering a saint's tomb. Each of these is a potential focal point of a *moussem*, and any one region or town may have twenty to thirty annual *moussems*. Establishing when they take place, however, can be difficult for outsiders; most local people find out by word of mouth at the weekly souks. Some are held around religious occasions such as **Mouloud** (see page 45), which change date each year according to the lunar calendar; others follow the solar calendar (see page 44).

The **accommodation** situation will depend on whether the *moussem* is in the town or countryside. In the country, the simplest solution is to take a tent and camp – there is usually no objection to anyone camping wherever they please during a *moussem*.

Aims and functions

The ostensible **aim** of the *moussem* is religious: to obtain blessing, or **baraka**, from the saint and/or to thank God for the harvest. But the social and cultural dimensions are equally important. *Moussems* provide an opportunity for country people to escape the monotony of their hard-working lives in several days of festivities, and they may provide the year's single opportunity for friends or families from different villages to meet. Harvest and farming problems are discussed, as well as family matters – marriage in particular – as people get the chance to sing, dance, eat and pray together.

Music and singing are always major components of a *moussem* and locals will often bring tape recorders to provide sounds for the rest of the year. Sufi brotherhoods have a big presence, and each bring their own distinct style of music, dancing and dress.

Moussems also operate as **fairs**, or markets, attracting people from a much wider area than the souk and giving a welcome injection of cash into the local economy, with traders and entertainers doing good business, and householders renting out rooms.

At the **spiritual level**, people seek to improve their standing with God through prayer, as well as the less orthodox channels of popular belief. Central to this is *baraka*, good fortune, which can be obtained by intercession of the saint. Financial contributions are made and these are used to buy a gift, or *hedia*, usually a large carpet, which is then taken in procession to the saint's tomb; it is deposited there for the local *shereefian* families, the descendants of the saint, to dispose of as they wish. Country people may seek to obtain *baraka* by attaching a garment or tissue to the saint's tomb and leaving it overnight to take home after the festival.

The procession taking the gift to the tomb is the high point of the more **religious** *moussems*, such as that of **Moulay Idriss** in Fez, where an enormous carpet is carried above the heads of the Sufi **brotherhoods**, each playing its own hypnotic music. Spectators and participants, giving themselves up to the music, may go into a trance. If you witness such events, it is best to keep a low profile so as not to interfere with people trying to attain a trance-like state, and certainly don't take photographs.

Release through trance probably has a therapeutic aspect, and indeed some *moussems* are specifically concerned with **cures** of physical and psychiatric disorders. The saint's tomb is usually located near a freshwater spring, and the cure can simply be bathing in and drinking the water. Those suffering from physical ailments may also be treated at the *moussem* with herbal remedies, or by recitation of verses from the Koran. Koranic verses may also be written and placed in tiny receptacles fastened near the affected parts.

Sports and outdoor activities

Morocco offers magnificent trekking opportunities, impressive golf facilities, a couple of ski resorts (plus some adventurous off-piste skiing) and excellent fishing. The national sporting obsession is football; enthusiasts can join in any number of beach kick-about games, or watch local league and cup matches.

Trekking

Trekking is among the very best things Morocco has to offer. The High Atlas is one of the most rewarding mountain ranges in the world, and one of the least spoilt. A number of **long-distance Atlas routes** can be followed – even a "Grand Traverse" of the full range, but most people stick to **shorter treks** in the **Jebel Toubkal** area (best in spring or autumn; conditions can be treacherous in winter; see page 346). Other promising areas include the **Jebel Sirwa** (see page 441), the **Western High Atlas** (see page 357), and, in winter the **Jebel Saghro** (see page 392) and **Tafraoute** region of the Anti-Atlas (see page 450). The **Middle Atlas** has much attractive walking too, in such places as **Tazzeka** (Taza; see page 146), and around **Azrou** (see page 209). General **trekking practicalities** are discussed in the High Atlas section of the Guide (see page 346).

Skiing

Morocco doesn't immediately spring to mind as a skiing destination, but the High Atlas mountains are reliably snow-covered from late January to early April, with good skiing at **Oukaïmeden** (see page 337).

Off-piste skiing is popular, particularly in the **Toubkal massif**. Most off-piste activity is ski mountaineering, but skinny skis (*langlauf*) are good in the Middle Atlas if there is snow, in which case the Azilal–Bou Goumez–Ighil Mgoun area is possible. **Snowboarding** is also gaining in popularity at Moroccan resorts.

Horseriding

The established base for **horseriding holidays** is *Domaine de la Roseraie* at **Ouirgane** (see page 352), which runs trekking tours into the **High Atlas** (bring your own helmet). Another stable offering horseriding is Amodou Cheval near Agadir (W amodoucheval. com). A number of operators offer **horse and camel treks**, including Best of Morocco (see page 29).

Fishing

Morocco has an immense Atlantic (and small Mediterranean) coastline, with opportunities to arrange **boat trips** at Safi, Essaouira, Moulay Bousselham (near Asilah), Boujdour, Dakhla and elsewhere.

Inland, the **Middle Atlas** shelters beautiful **lakes** and **rivers**, many of them well stocked with trout. Good bases include Azrou (near the Aghmas lakes), Ifrane (near Zerrrouka), Khenifra (the Oum er Rbia River) and Ouirgane (the Nfis River). Pike are also to be found in some Middle Atlas lakes (such as Aguelmame Azizgza, near Khenifra), and a few of the huge artificial barrages, like Bin el Ouidaine (near Beni Mellal), are said to contain enormous bass.

For all fishing in the country, you need to take your own **equipment**. For coarse or fly-fishing you need a **permit** from the Administration des Eaux et Fôrets at: 11 Rue Moulay Abdelaziz, Rabat (T 0537 762694); 25 Bd Roudani, Casablanca (T 0522 271598); or any regional office. For trout fishing, you are limited to the hours between 6am and noon; the season varies slightly from year to year, but usually runs April–September.

Watersports and swimming

Agadir offers opportunities for **sailing**, **yachting**, **windsurfing** and **diving**, while Taghazout, just to its north, has become something of a **surfing** village, with board rental and board repair shops and some great surfing sites (see page 432). There are lesser surfing centres at Sidi Ifni, Mirhleft, Kenitra, Bouznika Plage (between Rabat and Casablanca), El Jadida, Safi, and even Rabat. With your own transport, you could scout out remote places all the way down the coast. When they're working, all breaks can be busy in peak season (Oct–Feb), when deep lows come barrelling east across the mid-Atlantic. Wet suit-wise, a good 3mm will cover winter months (although a thermal rash vest keeps things snug in Jan) and it's also worth bringing booties, unless you enjoy digging urchin spines out of your feet.

For **windsurfing**, the prime destination is Essaouira, which draws devotees year-round. Online **weather information** for surfers and windsurfers can be found at W windguru.com/int. Another increasingly popular windsurfing destination is Dakhla in the Western Sahara, and both Dakhla and Essaouira are good for **kitesurfing** as well.

ANIMAL WELFARE

Animals – and especially pack animals – have a tough life in Morocco. The **Society for the Protection of Animals Abroad** (SPANA; W spana.org and W spana.org.ma), works across Africa to improve conditions for working donkeys and horses, replacing painful, old-style bits, employing local vets and technicians and running animal clinics. There are SPANA centres in Casablanca, Marrakesh (see page 328), Khémisset, Had Ouled Frej (near El Jadida) and Chémaia (near Marrakesh); they also manage the birdwatching reserve at Sidi Bourhaba near Kenitra. All of these can be contacted or visited if you are interested or are concerned about animals you come across. The best initial contact address in Morocco is SPANA's administrative office in Harhoura (T 0537 747209), 14km south of Rabat.

Endangered species in Morocco include **Barbary Macaque**, "ape" monkeys (see page 211), whose existence is threatened by habitat loss, as well as by illegal poaching and trafficking. Sadly, tourists in Marrakesh may unwittingly contribute to this trade by paying to have photos taken with monkeys (see page 297). Paying snake charmers similarly contributes to cruelty and the removal of **snakes** from the wild.

The Atlantic can be very exposed, with crashing waves, and surfers, windsurfers and **swimmers** alike should beware of strong undertows. Inland, most towns of any size have a municipal **swimming pool**, but women especially should note that they tend to be the preserve of teenage boys. In the south, you'll be dependent on campsite pools or on those at the luxury hotels (which often allow outsiders to swim, either for a fee or if you buy drinks or a meal).

The High and Middle Atlas have also become a popular destination for **whitewater rafting** and **kayaking** enthusiasts. One holiday firm specializing in these sports is Water by Nature (⦿ waterbynature.com).

Golf

The British opened a **golf course** in Tangier as far back as 1917. We list a number of golf courses in the relevant city or town Directories of this guide, including: an international-level course at Rabat (see page 248), eighteen-hole courses at Mohammedia (see page 254), Marrakesh (see page 327), Tangier (see page 87), Cabo Negro (near Mdiq; see page 111), Melilla (see page 136); Saïdia (see page 137), Larache (see page 95), El Jadida (see page 271), Essaouira (see page 284), Agadir (see page 424), Fez (see page 184) and Ben Slimane (Royal Golf, Av des FAR, BP 83, Ben Slimaneand nine-hole courses at Meknes (see page 196), Ouarzazate and Bouznika (near Mohammedia, Route Secondaire de Bouznika Plage, Km22). Further information on courses can be found online at ⦿ golf-today.co.uk/clubhouse/coursedir/world/morocco. Several tour operators (including Best of Morocco; see page 29) offer Moroccan golfing holidays.

Football (soccer)

Football is Morocco's most popular spectator sport by a long chalk, and foreign clubs – particularly Barcelona and Real Madrid – are widely followed here, with **matches** commonly shown on live TV in cafés. Morocco's national side has made the **World Cup finals** on five occasions, and was the first African team to reach the finals (in 1970), and the first to progress beyond the group stage (in 1986). Morocco has won the **African Nations Cup** only once (in 1976), but reached the final in 2004, and was due to host the tournament in 2015, but had to withdraw due to fears over an ebola outbreak in West Africa. Moroccan teams have been very successful in African club competitions. Raja Casablanca have won the African Champions League three times, and Wydad Casablanca have also won three times, most recently in 2022. Moroccan clubs have also done well in the CAF Confederation Cup (equivalent to Europe's UEFA Cup), which was won by FAR Rabat in 2005, FUS Rabat in 2010, and MAS Fez in 2011.

Moroccan clubs compete in an annual **league** and the (knockout) **Throne Cup**. For a long time there was just one full-time professional team, **FAR** (the army), but the 1990s saw the introduction of sponsorship and a number of semi-professional sides, whose big names include **Wydad** (WAC) and **Raja**, the two big Casablanca teams, plus **FUS** from Rabat, **MAS** from Fez and **Hassania** from Agadir. The result is a fairly high standard of skill in the Moroccan league, but unfortunately Moroccan clubs are unable to afford the money commanded by top players in Europe, with the result that the best Moroccan players end up in European clubs.

Other sports

Morocco has two **marathons**: the Marrakesh Marathon (see page 327) and the even more gruelling Marathon des Sables (see page 385).

Most four-star and five-star hotels (especially in Agadir and Marrakesh) have **tennis** courts, though equipment, if available, is not often up to much, so you're advised to bring your own racket and balls.

Paragliding is increasingly popular in the south of Morocco, around Tafraoute and Mirhleft in particular, where there are thermals even during winter. Paragliding, hang-gliding and paramotoring trips, with instructors, are offered by Passion Paragliding (⦿ passionparagliding.com). Note that in order to paraglide in Morocco, you need to obtain official authorization before your trip.

Also popular in the south is **rock climbing**, particularly in the region around Tafraoute, and at Todra Gorge, where Rock & Sun (⦿ rockandsun.com) offer packages. Claude Davies's comprehensive *Climbing in the Moroccan Anti-Atlas: Tafroute and Jebel El Kest* (published by Cicerone Press, 2004) has marked-up photos and detailed descriptions of Anti-Atlas ascents.

Culture and etiquette

Moroccans are extremely hospitable and very tolerant. Though most people are religious, they are generally easy-going, and most young Moroccan women don't wear a veil, though they may well wear a headscarf. Nonetheless, you should try not to affront people's religious beliefs,

especially those of older, more conservative people, by, for example, wearing skimpy clothes, kissing and cuddling in public, or eating or smoking in the street during Ramadan.

Clothes are particularly important: many Moroccans, especially in rural areas, may be offended by clothes that do not fully cover parts of the body considered "private", including both legs and shoulders, especially for women. It is true that in cities Moroccan women wear short-sleeved tops and knee-length skirts (and may suffer more harassment as a result), and men may wear sleeveless T-shirts and above-the-knee shorts. However, the strict Muslim idea of "**modest dress**" (such as would be acceptable in a mosque, for example) requires women to be covered from wrist to ankle, and men from over the shoulder to below the knee. In rural areas at least, it is a good idea to follow these codes, and definitely a bad idea for women to wear shorts or skirts above the knee, or for members of either sex to wear sleeveless T-shirts or very short shorts. The best guide is to note how Moroccans dress locally.

When **invited to a home**, you normally take your shoes off before entering the reception rooms – follow your host's lead. It is customary to take a gift: sweet pastries or tea and sugar are always -acceptable, and you might even take meat (by arrangement – a chicken from the countryside for example, still alive of course) to a poorer home.

Tipping

You're expected to **tip** – among others – waiters in cafés (1–2dh per person) and restaurants (5dh or so in moderate places, 10–15 percent in upmarket places); museum and monument curators (3–5dh); *gardiens de voitures* (5dh; see page 35); filling station attendants (3–5dh); and porters who load your baggage onto buses (5dh). Taxi drivers do not expect a tip, but always appreciate one.

Mosques

Without a doubt, one of the major disappointments of travelling in Morocco if you are not Muslim is not being allowed into its **mosques**. The only exceptions are the partially restored Almohad structure of **Tin Mal in the High Atlas** (see page 355), the similarly disused **Great Mosque at Smara** in the Western Sahara (see page 485), the courtyard of the sanctuary-mosque of **Moulay Ismail in Meknes** (see page 187) and the **Hassan II Mosque in Casablanca** (see page 260). Elsewhere, if you are not a believer,

you'll have to be content with an occasional glimpse through open doors, and even in this you should be sensitive: people don't seem to mind tourists peering into the **Kairaouine Mosque in Fez** (the country's most important religious building), but in the country you should never approach a shrine too closely.

This rule applies equally to the numerous white-washed **koubbas** – the tombs of *marabouts*, or local saints (usually domed: *koubba* actually means "dome") – and the "monastic" **zaouias** of the various Sufi brotherhoods. It is a good idea, too, to avoid walking through **graveyards**, as these also are regarded as sacred places.

Women in Morocco

There is no doubt that, for **women** especially, travelling in Morocco is a very different experience from travelling in a western country. One of the reasons for this is that the separate roles of the sexes are much more defined than they are in the west, and sexual mores much stricter. In villages and small towns, and even in the Medinas of large cities, some older women still wear the **veil**, and respectable women **don't smoke or drink** in bars, with some people still taking the attitude that any woman who does cannot therefore be respectable.

It should be said, however, that such ideas are fast disappearing among the urban youth, and you will nowadays find Moroccan women drinking in the more sophisticated bars, and even more often in cafés, formerly an all-male preserve. In the Villes Nouvelles of large cities, and especially in the Casa–Rabat–El Jadida area, and in Marrakesh, you'll see most women without a veil or even a headscarf. You'll also see young people of both sexes hanging out together, though you can be sure that opportunities for premarital sex are kept to a minimum. Even in traditional Moroccan societies, mountain Berber women, who do most of the hard work, play a much more open role in society, and rarely use a veil.

Sexual harassment

Different women seem to have vastly different experiences of **sexual harassment** in Morocco. Some travellers find it persistent and bothersome, while others have little or no trouble with it at all. Many women compare Morocco favourably with Spain and other parts of southern Europe, but there is no doubt that, in general, harassment of tourists here is more persistent than it is in northern Europe or the English-speaking world.

Harassment will usually consist of men trying to chat you up or even asking directly for sex, and it can be constant and sometimes intimidating. In part this is to do with Moroccan men's misunderstanding of Western culture and sexual attitudes, and the fact that some think they can get away with taking liberties with tourists that no Moroccan woman would tolerate.

The obvious **strategies** for getting rid of unwanted attention are the same ones that you would use at home: appear confident and assured and you will avoid a lot of trouble. Making it clear that you have the same standards as your Moroccan counterparts will usually deter all but the most insistent of men. No Moroccan woman would tolerate being groped in the street for example, though they may often have to put up with catcalls and unwanted comments. Traditionally, Moroccan women are coy and aloof, and uninhibited friendliness – especially any kind of physical contact between sexes – may be seen as a come-on, so being polite but formal when talking to men will diminish the chances of misinterpretation. The negative side to this approach is that it can also make it harder for you to get to know people, but after you've been in the country for a while, you will probably develop a feel for the sort of men with whom this tactic is necessary. It's also wise not to **smoke** in public, as some men still seem to think this indicates that you are available for sex.

How you **dress** is another thing that may reduce harassment. Wearing "modest" clothes (long sleeves, long skirts, baggy rather than tight clothes) will give an impression of respectability. Wearing a headscarf to cover your hair and ears will give this impression even more. One reader told us she felt a headscarf was "the single most important item of dress", adding that you can pull it over your face as a veil if unwanted male attention makes you feel uncomfortable. Indeed, Western liberals often forget that the purpose of wearing a veil is to protect women rather than to oppress them. However, you will notice that many Moroccan women totally ignore the traditional dress code, and do not suffer excessive harassment as a result. As for immodestly dressed women being taken for prostitutes, the fact is that actual sex workers in Morocco are often veiled from head to foot, as much to disguise their identities as anything else.

Other strategies to steer clear of trouble include avoiding eye contact, mentioning a husband who is nearby, and, if travelling with a boyfriend or just with a male friend, giving the impression that he is your husband. You should also avoid physical contact with Moroccan men, even in a manner that would not be considered sexual at home, since it could easily be misunderstood. If a Moroccan man touches *you*, on the other hand, he has definitely crossed the line, and you should not be afraid to **make a scene**. Shouting "*shooma!*" ("shame on you!") is likely to result in bystanders intervening on your behalf, and a very uncomfortable situation for your assailant.

It is often said that women are second-class citizens in Islamic countries, though educated Muslim women are usually keen to point out that this is a misinterpretation of Islam. While sex equality has a long way to go in Morocco, in some ways, at least in theory, the sexes are not as unequal as they seem. Men traditionally rule in the street, which is their domain, the woman's being the home. One result is that Moroccan women will receive their friends at home rather than meet them in, say, a café (although this is slowly changing) and this can make it difficult for you to get to know Moroccan women. One place where you *can* meet up with them is the hammam (see page 39). It may also be that if you are travelling with a man, Moroccan men will address him rather than you – but this is out of respect for you, not disrespect, and you will not be ignored if you join in the conversation. In any case, however interpreted, Islam most certainly does not condone sexual harassment, and nor do any respectable Moroccans. Being aware of that fact will make it seem a lot less threatening.

Shopping

Souks (markets) are a major feature of Moroccan life, and among the country's greatest attractions. They are found everywhere: every town has a souk area, large cities like Fez and Marrakesh have labyrinths of individual souks (each filling a street or square and devoted to one particular craft), and in the countryside there are hundreds of weekly souks, on a different day in each village of the region.

When buying **souvenirs** in Morocco, it's worth considering how you are going to get them home, and you shouldn't take too literally the claims of shopkeepers about their goods, especially if they tell you that something is "very old" – *trafika* (phoney merchandise) abounds, and there are all sorts of imitation fossils and antiques about.

Souk days

Some villages are named after **their market days**, so it's easy to see when they're held. The souk days are:

Souk el Had – Sunday (literally, "first market")
Souk el Tnine – Monday market
Souk el Tleta – Tuesday market

Souk el Arba – Wednesday market
Souk el Khamees – Thursday market
Souk es Sebt – Saturday market

There are very few village markets on **Friday** (el Jemaa – the "assembly", when the main prayers are held in the mosques), and even in the cities, souks are largely closed on Friday mornings and very subdued for the rest of the day.

Village souks usually begin on the afternoon preceding the souk day, as people travel from across the region; those who live nearer set out early in the morning of the souk day, but the souk itself is often over by noon and people disperse in the afternoon. You should therefore arrange to arrive by mid-morning at the latest.

Craft traditions

Moroccan **craft** traditions are very much alive, but finding pieces of real quality is not that easy. For a good price, it's always worth getting as close to the source of the goods as possible, and steering clear of tourist centres. **Tangier**, **Casablanca** and **Agadir**, with no workshops of their own, are generally poor bets, for example, while **Fez** and **Marrakesh** have a good range but high prices. In places like Fez and Marrakesh, different parts of the Medina produce specific goods, from furniture to ironwork to sandals to musical instruments. Jewellery and carpets tend to come in from the countryside, where each region – each village even – has its own style and its own techniques. Shopping in a big city, you'll have a wide range to choose from, but there's a very special pleasure in tracking the souvenir you want down to the place where it's made, and even seeing the artisans at work making it. A good way to get an idea of standards and quality is to visit **craft museums**: there are useful ones in Fez (see page 159), Meknes (see page 185), Rabat (see page 239), Agadir (see page 423) and Marrakesh (see page 301).

Carpets, rugs and blankets

Morocco produces some lovely **carpets** in wonderful warm colours – saffron yellow, cochineal red, antimony black – that look great in any living space. Nowadays most carpets are coloured with synthetic dyes, but their inspiration remains the natural dyes with which they were traditionally made. The most expensive carpets are hand-knotted, but there are also **kilims** (woven rugs).

Knotted carpets are not cheap – you can pay around €1400/£1250/$1600 and more for the finer Arab designs in Fez or Rabat – but rugs and kilims come in at more reasonable prices, and you can buy a range of strong, well-designed weaves for €40–60/£35–55/$45–70. Most of these kilims will be of Berber origin and the most interesting ones usually come from the High and Middle Atlas. You'll find a big selection in Marrakesh, but if you're looking seriously, try to get to the town souk in Midelt or the weekly markets in Azrou and other villages in the region. One of the best ways to find carpets is to wander around villages or parts of town where they are made, listen for the telltale sound of the loom in use, and ask at the weavers' homes if they have any carpets for sale.

On a simpler and cheaper level, the Berber **blankets** (foutahs, or couvertures) are imaginative, and often very striking with bands of reds and blacks; for these, Tetouan and Chefchaouen, on the edge of the Rif, are promising.

Ceramics

Pottery is colourful if fairly crudely made on the whole, though the blue-and-white designs of Fez and the multicoloured pots of Chefchaouen (both produced largely for the tourist trade) are highly attractive. The essentially domestic pottery of Safi – Morocco's major pottery centre – is worth a look, too, with its colourful plates, tajines and garden pots. Safi tajines are nice to look at, but for practical use, the best are those produced by the Oulja pottery at Salé, near Rabat, in plain red-brown earthenware.

Jewellery

Arabic-style **gold jewellery** tends to be a bit fussy for Western tastes, but **silver** is another story. In the south particularly, you can pick up some fabulous Berber necklaces and bracelets, always very chunky, and characterized by bold combinations of semiprecious (and sometimes plastic) stones and beads. Women in the Atlas and the Souss Valley regions in particular often wear chunky silver bracelets, belts embellished with old silver coins, or heavy necklaces with big beads of amber, coral and carnelian. Silver brooches are used to fasten garments, and many of the symbols found in Moroccan jewellery, such as the "hand of Fatima" and the five-pointed star, are there to guard against the evil eye. Essaouira, Marrakesh and Tiznit have particularly good jewellery souks.

Wood

Marquetry is one of the few crafts where you'll see genuinely old pieces – inlaid tables and shelves – though the most easily exportable objects are boxes. The big centre for marquetry is Essaouira, where cedar or thuya wood is beautifully inlaid with orange-tree wood and other light-coloured woods to make trays, chess and backgammon sets, even plates and bowls, and you can visit the workshops where they are made.

Fez, Meknes, Tetouan and Marrakesh also have souks specializing in carpentry, which produce not only furniture, but also chests, sculptures, and kitchen utensils such as the little ladles made from citrus wood that are used to eat *harira* soup.

Clothes

Moroccan clothes are easy to purchase, and though Westerners – men at least – who try to imitate Moroccan styles by wearing the cotton or wool *jellaba* (a hooded outer garment) tend to look a little silly in the street, they do make good nightgowns. Some of the cloth on sale is exquisite in itself, and walking through the dyers' souks is an inspiration. Women will find some sumptuous gowns if they look in the right places – Marrakesh in particular has shops selling beautiful dresses, kaftans, *gandoras* (sleeveless kaftans) and tunics. Brightly coloured knitted caps are more likely to appeal to men, and there are plenty of inexpensive multicoloured silk scarves on offer too. Even ordinary jackets and trousers are often on sale in the souks at bargain prices.

Leatherware

Moroccan leather is famously soft and luxurious. In towns like Fez, Marrakesh and Taroudant you can even visit the tanneries to see it being cured. It comes in a myriad of forms from belts, bags and clothing to pouffes and even book covers, but Morocco's best-known leather item is the **babouche**, or slipper. Classic Moroccan *babouches*, open at the heel, are immensely comfortable, and produced in yellow (the usual colour), white, red (for women) and occasionally grey or black. A good pair – and quality varies enormously – can cost anything between 50dh (€4.55/£4.10/$5.35) and 250dh (€22.65/£20.35/$26.65). Marrakesh and Tafraoute are especially good for *babouches*.

Minerals and fossils

You'll see a variety of **semiprecious stones** on sale throughout Morocco, and in the High Atlas they are often aggressively hawked on the roadsides. If you're lucky enough to be offered genuine amethyst or quartz, prices can be bargained to very tempting levels. Be warned, however, that all that glitters is not necessarily the real thing. Too often, if you wet the stone and rub, you'll find traces of dye on your fingers.

Fossils too (see page 413) are widely sold in Morocco, and can be as beautiful as they are fascinating. The fossil-rich black marble of the Erfoud region, for example, is sold in the form of anything from ashtrays to table-tops. But again, things aren't always what they seem, and a lot of fossils – probably most of those on sale, in fact – are fakes, some of them quite sophisticated. This is particularly true of any black or brown fossil on a grey background.

Foodstuffs

Some Moroccan **food products** would be hard to find at home, and make excellent and inexpensive gifts or souvenirs (assuming your country's customs allow their importation). Locally produced **olive oil** can be excellent, with a distinctive strong flavour, and in the Souss Valley there's delicious sweet **argan oil** too (see page 433). Olives themselves come in numerous varieties, and there are also almonds, walnuts and spices available, notably **saffron** from Taliouine, and the spice mix known as Ras el Hanout. A jar of lemons preserved in brine is useful if you want to try your hand at making a tajine back home.

Bargaining

Whatever you buy, other than groceries, you'll be expected to **bargain**. There are no hard and fast rules – it is really a question of paying what something is worth to you – but there are a few general points to keep in mind.

First, don't worry about **initial prices**. These are simply a device to test your limits. Don't think that you need to pay a specific fraction of the first asking price: some sellers start near their lowest price, while others will make a deal for as little as a tenth of the initial price.

Second, have in mind a figure that you want to pay, and a maximum above which you will not go. If your maximum and the shopkeeper's minimum don't meet, then you don't have a deal, but it's no problem.

Third, **don't ever let a figure pass your lips** that you aren't prepared to pay – nor start bargaining for something you have absolutely no intention of buying – there's no better way to create bad feelings.

Fourth, **take your time**. If the deal is a serious one (for a rug, say), you'll probably want to sit down over tea with the vendor, and for two cups you'll talk about anything but the rug and the price. If negotiations do not seem to be going well, it often helps to have a friend on hand who seems – and may well be – less interested in the purchase than you and can assist in extricating you from a -particularly hard sell.

Fifth, remember that even if you're **paying more than local people**, it doesn't necessarily mean you're being "ripped off". As a Westerner, your earning power is well above that of most Moroccans and it's rather mean to force traders down to their lowest possible price just for the sake of it.

The final and most golden rule of all is never to go shopping with a **guide** or a hustler. Any shop that a guide steers you into will pay them a commission, added to your bill of course, while hustlers often pick up tourists with the specific aim of leading you to places that (even if you've agreed to go in "just to look") will subject you to a lengthy high-pressure hard-sell.

An approximate idea of what you should be paying for handicrafts can be gained from checking the **fixed prices** in the state- or cooperative-run Ensembles Artisanals, which are slightly higher than could be bargained for elsewhere.

Travelling with children

Travelling with small children, you may well find that people will frequently come up to admire them, to compliment you on them and to caress them, which may be uncomfortable for shyer offspring. In Moroccan families, children stay up late until they fall asleep and are spoiled rotten by older family members. The streets are pretty safe and even quite young children walk to school unaccompanied or play in the street unsupervised.

As a **parent**, however, you will encounter one or two difficulties. For example, you won't find baby changing rooms in airports, hotels or restaurants, and will have to be discreet if breastfeeding – find a quiet corner and shield infant and breast from view with a light cloth over your shoulder. Beach resort and package tour hotels may have facilities such as playgrounds, children's pools and a babysitting service, but mid-range city hotels are far less likely to cater for children, though many allow children to share their parents' room for free.

You may want to try a holiday with Club Med (<0xE2><0x93><0xA6> club med.com), whose purpose-built holiday resorts at Agadir, Marrakesh and near Tangier feature kids' club, entertainment and sports facilities on site. **Attractions** that should appeal to small people include Magic Park in Salé, Oasiria in Marrakesh (see page 328), and the tourist train in Agadir (see page 421).

Disposable nappies (diapers) are available at larger supermarkets, and sometimes city-pharma-cies, at prices similar to what you pay at home, but off the beaten track, you may need to stock up, or take washables. You may also want to take along some **dried baby food**; any café can supply hot water.

On **buses and grands taxis**, children small enough to share your seat will usually travel free, but older kids pay the full adult fare. On trains, travel is free for under-fours, and half price for four- to eleven-year-olds.

Among **hazards** that you'll need to bear in mind are traffic and stray animals. Dogs can be fierce in Morocco, and can also carry rabies, and there are a lot of feral cats and dogs about. Children (especially young ones) are also more susceptible than adults to heatstroke and dehydration, and should always wear a sunhat, and have high-factor sunscreen applied to exposed skin. If swimming at a beach resort, they should do so in a T-shirt, certainly for the first few days. The other thing that children are very susceptible to is an upset tummy. Bear in mind that anti-diarrhoeal drugs should generally not be given to young children; read the literature provided with the medication or consult a doctor for guidance on child dosages.

Note that children travelling to Morocco should have their own **passport** and may not travel on that of their parents.

Travel essentials

Accessible Travel

Facilities for people with **disabilities** are little developed in Morocco, and, although families are usually very supportive, many disabled Moroccans are reduced to begging. Despite this, able-bodied Moroccans are, in general, far more used to mixing with disabled people than their Western counter-parts, and are much more likely to offer help without embarrassment if you need it.

Blindness is more common than in the West, and sighted Moroccans are generally used to helping blind and visually impaired people find their way around and get on and off public transport at the right stop.

There is little in the way of **wheelchair access** to most premises. In the street, the Ville Nouvelle districts are generally easier to negotiate than the often crowded Medinas, but don't expect kerb ramps at road crossings or other such concessions to wheelchair users. Medina areas in cities like Rabat and even Marrakesh should not be too hard to negotiate at quiet times of day, but in Fez and Tangier, where the streets are steep and interspersed with steps, you would need at least one helper and a well-planned route to get around.

Bus and train travel will be difficult because of the steps that have to be negotiated, but **grands taxis** are a more feasible mode of transport if you can stake a claim on the front seat (maybe paying for two places to get the whole of it) – if you don't have a helper travelling with you, and you require assistance, the driver or other passengers will almost certainly be happy to help you get in and out.

Accommodation at the lower end of the market is unlikely to be very accessible. Cheap city hotels tend to have small doorways and steep, narrow staircases, and often no elevator, though many will have ground-floor rooms. Beach hotels are more able to cater for visitors with mobility difficulties. Some package hotels, especially in Agadir, now cater for wheelchair-users, although a place with ramps, for example, may not necessarily have accessible toilets. However, new five-star hotels usually have a couple of rooms specifically adapted for wheelchairs. These need to be booked well in advance, and it does mean you are largely confined to expensive places, but it is at least a start.

You'll probably find a **package tour** much easier than fully independent travel, but contact any tour operator to check they can meet your exact needs before making a booking. It's also important to ensure you are covered by any **insurance** policy you take out (see page 60).

Hotels with rooms specially adapted for wheelchair users include the *Mövenpick* in Tangier (see page 83), the *Tryp* in Melilla (see page 135), the *Sofitel*

GUIDES, HUSTLERS, CONMEN AND KIDS

Armed with this book, you shouldn't need a guide, but some people like to hire one to negotiate the Medinas of larger cities. **Official guides**, identified by a large, brass "sheriff's badge", can be engaged through tourist offices or large hotels. They charge around 200–300dh a day, plus sustenance. The rate is for the guide's time, and can be shared by a group (though you'd then be expected to give a good tip).

Young Moroccans may also offer their services as **unofficial guides**, which is illegal, and subject to occasional police clampdowns. Be very careful in making use of unofficial guides. Some are indeed genuine, usually unemployed youths hoping to make a few dirhams by showing tourists around, and they should be cheaper than official guides, less formal, offer a more street-level view, and perhaps show you things that official guides would not – indeed, many tourists end up making lasting friendships with people who've approached them as unofficial guides – but some will be aiming only to get you into shops or hotels which pay them commission, or they may be confidence tricksters. If you do decide to hire an unofficial guide, be sure to **fix the rate** in advance (make it clear that you know the official rates), as well as the **itinerary** (so that it does not include shops, for example – this also applies to official guides).

In general, never agree to a guide showing you to a **hotel**, and never go **shopping** with a guide, official or otherwise, as they will only take you to places which pay them a commission, meaning a higher bill for you – often as much as fifty percent higher. Hotels that pay commission to guides for bringing tourists to them are also likely to be dubious in other ways. On the other hand, letting someone guide you to a **café** or **restaurant** won't increase the price of a meal (although waiters may make a small tip to the guide).

CONMEN AND SCAMS

Hustlers and conmen have been largely cleaned off the streets, and those who remain are less persistent, but tourists are the obvious target for them. It's important not to treat every Moroccan who approaches you as a hustler – many (though not usually in tourist hot spots) are just trying to be friendly. However, forewarned is forearmed, so a few notes on the **most common scams** follow:

• Most hustlers (and guides, official or not) hope to earn money by steering you, sometimes with the most amazing deviousness, into shops that will pay them a commission, most commonly **carpet shops** where you will be subjected to hours of hard-sell. Never be afraid to walk away from such a situation, even if (as is quite likely) you are then subjected to abuse, and never buy anything from a shop that you are taken to by a guide or hustler.

(see page 246) and *Riad el Maâti* in Rabat (see page 246), the *Hyatt Regency* in Casablanca (see page 262), *Le Médina* in Essaouira (see page 282), the *Borj Biramane* in Icht (see page 448), and the *Atlas Medina* and *Ryad Mogador Menara* among other Hivernage hotels in Marrakesh (see page 319). The Ibis Moussafir chain (**ⓦ**ibis.accorhotels.com) has adapted rooms at several of its hotels, including those in Tangier, Fnideq, Meknes, Casablanca, El Jadida, Essaouira and Ouarzazate. *Auberge Camping Toubkal* in Talioune (see 426) also has rooms adapted for wheelchair users. Some other hotels, such as the *Royal Atlas* in Agadir (see page 426), claim to be accessible, and to cater for wheelchair users, but do not have specially adapted rooms. Obviously, you should always call ahead to check whether any particular hotel can meet your specific needs.

Costs

Costs for food, accommodation and travel in Morocco are similar to mainland Europe. If you stay in the cheaper hotels (or camp out), eat local food, and share expenses and rooms with another person, you can make it more budget friendly.

Accommodation costs range from low in a basic hotel to the sky's the limit in a luxury hotel or riad. The price of a **meal** reflects a similar span with a sandwich being the cheapest option for lunch. **Alcohol** compares unfavourably with Western prices.

Inevitably, **resorts** and larger **cities** (Marrakesh especially) are more expensive than small towns with few tourists, but in **remote parts** of the country (including trekking regions in the High Atlas), where goods have to be brought in from some distance, prices for provisions can be high.

- If a hustler guides you into the Medina till you have no idea where you are, and then demands a large fee to take you back out, don't be afraid to appeal to people in the street, and if you feel genuinely menaced or harassed, threaten to go to the **police**: hustlers tend to vanish fast at the prospect of police involvement.
- Hustlers may attach themselves to you using the excuse of a letter ("Could you help translate or write one?"), or by pretending to be someone you have met but forgotten – so if someone you don't remember says, "Hey, remember me?" it's probably a hustler trying to practise some scam on you. Another trick is to tell you that a site that you are on your way to visit is closed and that they can show you something else instead, or they may tell you that there is a Berber market taking place and this is the only day of the week to see it. If you **ignore** these people or turn them down, they may accuse you of being paranoid, angry or racist – and such an accusation is a sure sign that you were right.
- **Con merchants**, working alone or in couples, may befriend tourists, and then, after a day or two, tell some sad tale about needing money to get a passport or for a sick relative, or some such.
- On trains, especially at Tangier, hustlers sometimes pose as porters or **railway staff**, demanding an extortionate fee for carrying baggage or payment of supplements. Genuine rail staff wear beige overalls and have ID cards, which, if suspicious, you should ask to see.
- Drivers should beware of **hitchhiking hustlers**, who spend all day hitching between a pair of towns and can get quite obnoxious in their demands for money when you approach one or other destination. Alternatively, they may wish to thank you for the lift by taking you home for a cup of tea – except that "home" turns out to be a carpet shop, where you are then subjected to hours of hard-sell. A variation on this is the fake breakdown, where people on the road flag down passing tourists and ask them to take a note to a "mechanic", who turns out to be a carpet salesman. This one is particularly common on the road from Erfoud to Merzouga, where most of the motorists are tourists.

DEALING WITH CHILDREN

In the countryside especially, children may demand a dirham, *un cadeau* (present) or *un stylo* (a pen/pencil). Working out your own strategy is all part of the game, but be sure to keep good humour: smile and laugh, or kids can make a serious nuisance of themselves. Faced with **begging from children**, we recommend not obliging, as this ties them to a begging mentality, and encourages them to harass other visitors.

Beyond accommodation and food, your major outlay will be for **transport** – expensive if you're renting a car (don't forget you will have to pay extra for fuel) or travelling by taxi, but reasonable if you use the local trains, buses and shared taxis (see page 31).

Youth/student ID cards can save you a small amount of money, entitling you to cheaper entry at some museums and other sights, and a small discount on some ferry tickets and domestic airfares. They're not worth going out of your way to get, but if you have one you may as well bring it along.

In the Spanish enclaves of Ceuta and Melilla, prices for most things are slightly higher than in mainland Spain (except that there is no duty on alcohol, tobacco and electronic goods, and around twice as expensive as in Morocco proper.

Hidden costs

You'll probably end up buying a few **souvenirs**. Rugs, carpets, leather, woodwork, pottery and jewellery are all outstanding – and few travellers leave without something.

Harder to come to terms with is the fact that you'll be confronting real **poverty**. As a tourist, you're not going to solve any problems, but even small **tips** can make a lot of difference. For Moroccans, giving alms to **beggars** is natural, and a requirement of Islam, especially since there is no social security here, so for tourists, rich by definition, local poverty demands at least some response. Do not, however, dispense money indiscriminately to **children**, which encourages pestering and promotes a dependence on begging.

Crime and personal safety

Keep your **luggage and money** secure. Morocco does not have a high crime rate, but it is obviously unwise to carry large sums of cash or valuables on your person – especially in Casablanca and Tangier, and to a lesser extent Fez and Marrakesh. Mugging as such is pretty rare; those who fall victim to theft usually have things taken by stealth, or are subject to some kind of scam (see page 54). Be especially vigilant at transport stations (new arrivals are favourite targets, and just before departure is a favourite time to strike) and in crowded situations where pickpockets may operate. Credit card fraud is also relatively common, so don't let the plastic out of your sight while using it, and keep an eye out when withdrawing money from ATMs.

Hotels, generally, are secure and useful for depositing money before setting out to explore; larger ones will keep valuables at reception, and some rooms will have safes. **Campsites** are considerably less secure, and many campers advise using a **money belt**, even when sleeping. If you do decide on a money belt (and many people spend time quite happily without), cotton is preferable to nylon, which can irritate in the heat.

The police

There are two main types of Moroccan **police**: the *Gendarmerie* (who wear grey uniforms and man the checkpoints on main roads, at junctions and the entry to towns), and the Police (*Sûreté*), who wear navy-blue uniforms or plain clothes. Either may demand to see your passport (and/or driving papers). It is obligatory to carry official ID (in practice a passport), though you should not have any problems if you leave yours in a hotel safe while wandering around town, especially if you carry a photocopy of the important pages. You are unlikely to have any contact with the green-uniformed *Force Auxiliaire*, a backup force who wear berets and look more like the army.

The *gendarmes* have jurisdiction outside built-up areas, the police, within towns. Both are usually polite and helpful to visitors, and there is a *Brigade Touristique* in cities such as Marrakesh and Fez, specifically set up to protect tourists.

If you do need to **report a theft**, try to take along a fluent French- or Arabic-speaker if your own French and Arabic are not too hot. You may only be given a scrap of paper with an official stamp to show your insurance company, who then have to apply themselves to a particular police station for a report (in Arabic). If you cannot prove that a theft has taken place, the police may decline to make any report, especially if the theft is of money only. They will always give you a report, however, if you have lost any official document (passport, driving licence, etc).

Kif and hashish

The smoking of **kif** (marijuana) and **hashish** (cannabis resin) has long been a regular pastime of Moroccans and tourists alike, but it is nonetheless illegal, and large fines (plus prison sentences for substantial amounts) do get levied for possession. If you are arrested for cannabis, the police may expect to be paid off, and this should be done as quickly as possible while the minimum number of officers are involved (but offer it discreetly, and never refer to it as a bribe or even a *cadeau*). Consulates are notoriously unsympathetic to drug offenders, but they can help with technical problems and find you legal representation.

Obviously, the best way to avoid trouble is to keep well clear – above all, of the *kif*-growing region of **Ketama** in the Rif mountains (see page 127) – and always reply to hustlers by saying you don't smoke. If you are going to indulge, be very careful who you buy it from (definitely do not buy it from touts or hustlers), and above all do not try to take any out of the country, even to Spain, where attitudes to possession are relaxed but much harsher for importing. Searches at Algeciras and Málaga can be very thorough, with sniffer dogs, which also operate at Moroccan ports and airports, and you'll get sometimes as many as four checks if travelling to Spain via Ceuta or Melilla.

Electricity

The supply is **220v 50Hz**. Sockets have two round pins, as in Continental Europe. You should be able to find adaptors in Morocco that will take North American plugs (but North American appliances may need a transformer, unless multi-voltage). Adaptors for British and Australasian plugs will need to be brought from home.

Entry requirements

If you hold a full passport from the UK, Ireland, the US, Canada, Australia, New Zealand or any EU country, you don't need a **visa** to enter Morocco as a tourist for up to **ninety days**. In principle, and especially if you have an onward or return ticket, your passport need only be valid for the duration of your stay, but it's just possible that border officials at obscure crossings may think it needs to be valid for **six months** beyond your date of entry (which was formerly the rule), and it's always worth double-checking your visa require-ments before departure, as the situation can change. South African citizens are among those who need a visa; applications should be made to the Moroccan embassy or consulate in your country of residence (South Africans should be able to get one in London), with three passport photos, and a form that you can download from the websites of some Moroccan consulates (for example, London's at Ⓦwww. consulate.ma).

Entry formalities are fairly straightforward, though you will have to fill in a form stating personal details, purpose of visit and your profession. In the past, Moroccan authorities have shown an occasional reluctance to allow in those who categorize themselves as "journalist"; an alternative profession on the form might be wise.

Customs regulations

You can bring in, without charge: one litre of spirits and one of wine; 200 cigarettes, 25 cigars or 250g of tobacco; 150ml of perfume and 250ml of eau de toilette; jewellery, camera, phone and laptop for personal use; gifts worth up to 2000dh. **Prohibited**

goods include arms and ammunition (except for hunting), controlled drugs, and printed, audio or video media containing material deemed "immoral, sexual or offensive".

It's just possible that items such as **electronic equipment and video cameras** may be entered on your passport. If you then lose them during your visit, they will be assumed "sold" when you come to leave and (unless you have police documentation of theft) you will have to pay one hundred percent duty. All goods entered on your passport should be "cleared" when leaving to prevent problems on future trips. Vehicles need a Green Card (see page 29).

Carrying ID

It is in theory obligatory in Morocco to **carry official ID** at all times. In practice, a photocopy of the important pages of your passport will do, so long as the real thing is in your hotel in the same town. When travelling between towns, you should always have your passport on you.

Visa extensions

To **extend your stay** in Morocco you should – officially – apply to the Bureau des Étrangers in the nearest main town for a residence permit (see below). This is, however, a very complicated procedure and it is usually possible to get round the bureaucracy by simply leaving the country for a brief time when your three months are up. If you decide to do this – and it is not fool proof – it is best to make a trip of at least a few days outside Morocco. Spain is the obvious choice and some people just go to Ceuta or Melilla; the more cautious re-enter the country at a different post. If you are unlucky, you may be turned back and asked to get a **re-entry visa**. These can be obtained from any Moroccan consulate abroad (see opposite).

Extending a stay officially involves opening a bank account in Morocco (a couple of days' procedure in itself) and obtaining an *Attestation de Résidence* from your hotel, campsite or landlord. You will need a minimum of 20,000dh (€1850/£1650/$2100) in your account.

You then need to go to the **Bureau des Étrangers** in the central police station of a large town at least twenty days before your time is up, equipped with: your passport and two photocopies of its main pages and entry stamp; four (or sometimes eight) passport photos; two copies of the *Attestation de Résidence*; and two copies of your bank statement (*Compte de Banque*). If the police are not too busy they'll give you a form to fill out in triplicate and, some weeks later, you should receive a plastic-coated permit with your photo laminated in.

Foreign embassies and consulates in Morocco

Foreign embassies and consulates in Morocco are detailed in the "Directory" sections for Rabat (see page 248), Casablanca (see page 265) and Agadir (see page 429). Foreign representation in Morocco is detailed on the Moroccan Foreign Ministry's website at Ⓦ www.diplomatie.ma/en (in "Diplomatic and Consular Corps in Morocco" under "Embassies").

Ireland has honorary consuls in Casablanca (see page 265) and Agadir (see page 429), but no embassy. New Zealanders are covered by their embassy in Cairo (Ⓣ 00 202 91 523 0226), but can use UK consular facilities in Morocco. Australians are covered by their embassy in Paris (Ⓣ 00 33 1 4059 3300), but can use Canadian consular facilities in Morocco.

Health

For minor health complaints, a visit to a **pharmacy** is likely to be sufficient. Moroccan pharmacists are well trained and dispense a wide range of drugs, including many available only on prescription in the West. If pharmacists feel you need a full diagnosis, they can recommend a doctor – sometimes working on the premises. Addresses of English- and French-speaking doctors can also be obtained from consulates and large hotels.

If you need **hospital treatment**, contact your consulate at once and follow its advice. If you are near a major city, reasonable treatment may be available locally. State hospitals are usually OK for minor injuries, but for anything serious, a private clinic is generally preferable. Depending on your condition, repatriation may be the best course of action.

The latest advice on health in Morocco can be found on the US government's travel health website at Ⓦ cdc.gov/travel.

Inoculations

No **inoculations** are required but you should always be up to date with polio and tetanus. Those intending to stay a long time in the country, especially if working with animals or in the healthcare field, are also advised to consider vaccinations against typhoid, TB, hepatitis A and B, diphtheria and rabies, though these are not worth your while if just going on holiday.

A very low level of **malaria** does exist in the form of occasional cases between May and October in the region to the north of Beni Mellal and Khenifra, between Chefchaouen and Larache, and in the province of Taza, but local strains are not life-threatening and malaria pills are not normally considered necessary unless you actually fall ill with it (in which case they are easy enough to get at any pharmacy). More importantly, avoid bites; use mosquito repellent on all exposed areas of skin, especially feet, and particularly around dusk. Repellents containing DEET or icaridin or PMD (such as the British brand Incognito) are usually recommended for adults but not available in Morocco.

Water and health hazards

Tap water in most of Morocco is generally safe to drink, though in the far south and Western Sahara it's best to stick to bottled mineral water.

A more serious problem in the south is that many of the **river valleys and oases** are infected with **bilharzia**, also known as **schistosomiasis**, caused by a tiny fluke worm that lives part of its life cycle in a freshwater snail, and the other part in the blood and internal organs of a human or other mammal which bathes in or drinks the water. The snails only live in stagnant water, but the flukes may be swept downstream. Staying clear of slow-flowing rivers and oasis water is the best way to avoid it. If infected while bathing, you'll probably get a slightly itchy rash an hour or two later where the flukes have entered the skin. Later symptoms may take several months to appear, and are typified by abdominal pains, and blood in faeces or even urine. If you suspect that you might have it, seek medical help. Bilharzia is easily cured, but can cause permanent intestinal damage if untreated. Care should be taken, too, in drinking water from **mountain streams**. In areas where there is livestock upstream **giardiasis** may be prevalent and is a common cause of travellers' diarrhoea. Other symptoms include nausea, weight loss and fatigue which usually last no more than two weeks and settle without treatment. If they continue for longer, then a course of **metronidazole** (Flagyl) generally leads to effective eradication, but always finish the course, even after symptoms have gone, and even though this antibiotic will probably make you feel nauseous and precludes consumption of alcohol. Using iodine water purification tablets, a hand-held ultraviolet purification system such as SteriPEN or boiling any drinking or cooking water if it's from dubious sources (remember that you'll have to boil it for longer at high altitudes, where the boiling point is lower) is the simplest way to avoid putting yourself at risk from either of these illnesses.

Diarrhoea

At some stage in your Moroccan travels, it is likely that you will get **diarrhoea**. As a first stage of treatment it's best simply to adapt your diet. Plain boiled rice and vegetables are your safest bet, while yoghurt is an effective stomach settler and prickly pears (widely available in summer) are good too, as are bananas, but other fruit is best avoided, along with greasy food, dairy products (except yoghurt), caffeine and alcohol. If you have diarrhoea, it's important to replace the body fluids and salts lost through dehydration (this is especially the case with children); dissolving **oral rehydration salts** (sels de réhydratation orale in French) in water will help. These are available at any pharmacy, but if you can't get any, a teaspoon of salt plus eight of sugar per litre of water makes a reasonable substitute. Water (at least two litres per adult daily) should be drunk constantly throughout the day, rather than all in one go.

If symptoms persist for several days – especially if you get painful cramps, or if blood or mucus appear in your stools – you could have something more serious (see opposite) and should seek medical advice.

Other hazards

There are few natural hazards in northern Morocco, where wildlife is not very different from that of Mediterranean Europe. If you venture into the Sahara, however, be aware of the very real dangers of a bite from a **snake** or **scorpion**. Several of the Saharan snakes are deadly. Bites should be treated as medical emergencies.

Certain scorpions are very dangerous; their sting can be fatal if not treated. Avoid going barefoot or in flip-flops (thongs) in the bush, or turning over stones. In the desert, shake out your shoes before putting them on in the morning. All scorpions sting, which can be extremely painful, especially if you are allergic, but not many are life-threatening. Most snakes are non-venomous and, again, few are life-threatening, but one or two species can be dangerous, most notably the horned viper.

If you do get **bitten** by a snake or stung by a scorpion, don't panic – even in the case of life-threatening species, actual fatalities are rare, and you should be in no danger if treated in a reasonable time. Sucking out the poison only works in movies, and tourniquets are dangerous and ill-advised. The important thing is to relax, try not to move the affected part of your body, and seek medical help as quickly as possible. Try to remember what the creature looked like, and if it's possible to kill or catch it without danger, then do so, so that you can show it to doctors or paramedics.

Never underestimate Morocco's **heat**, especially in the south. A hat – preferably light in both weight and colour – is an essential precaution and, especially if you have very fair skin, you should also take sunblock cream with a very high screening factor, as the sun really is higher (and therefore stronger) in Morocco than in northern latitudes. Resulting problems include **dehydration** – make sure that you're drinking enough (irregular urination such as only once a day is a danger sign) – and **heatstroke**, which is potentially fatal. Signs of heatstroke are a very high body temperature without a feeling of fever, but accompanied by headaches, nausea and/or disorientation. Lowering body temperature, with a tepid shower or bath, for example, is the first step in treatment, after which medical help should be sought.

Contraceptives and tampons

Poor quality and rather unreliable **condoms** (préservatifs) can be bought in most pharmacies, and so can the **pill** (officially by prescription, but this isn't essential).

Tampons can be bought at general stores, not pharmacies, in most Moroccan cities. Don't expect to find them in rural or mountain areas.

Insurance

It's frankly reckless to travel without **insurance cover**. Home insurance policies occasionally cover your possessions when overseas, and some private medical schemes include cover when abroad. Bank and credit cards often have certain levels of medical or other insurance included and you may automatically get travel insurance if you use a major credit card to pay for your trip. Otherwise, you should contact a specialist travel insurance company. A typical travel insurance policy usually provides cover for the loss of baggage, tickets and – up to a certain limit – cash or cheques, as well as cancellation or curtailment of your journey. Most of them exclude so-called dangerous sports unless an extra premium is paid: in Morocco this could include mountaineering, skiing, water rafting or paragliding. Read the small print and benefits tables of prospective policies carefully; coverage can vary wildly for roughly similar premiums. Many policies can be chopped and changed to exclude coverage you don't need. For medical coverage, check whether benefits will be paid as treatment proceeds or only after returning home, and whether there is a 24-hour medical emergency number. When securing baggage cover, make sure that the per-article limit will cover your most valuable possession. If you need to make a **claim**, you should keep receipts for medicines and medical treatment, and in the event you have anything stolen, you must obtain an official statement from the police (called a papier de déclaration).

Internet

Cybercafés are almost non-existent nowadays, but 4and 5G phone signal is universal in all urban areas except some remote villages where 3G might be all you get. Almost every hotel offers free wi-fi.

Laundry

In the larger towns, **laundrettes** will take in clothes and wash them overnight, but you'll usually find it easier to ask at hotels – even in cheap hotels without an official laundry service, the cleaning lady will almost certainly be glad to make a few extra dirhams by taking in a bit of washing.

Left luggage

Train stations do not have **left-luggage** (baggage deposit) facilities, but major bus stations, CTM offices and ferry stations usually do. Where no left-luggage facilities are available, café proprietors may agree to look after baggage for you, sometimes for a small fee, but more often for free in out-of-the-way places.

LGBTQ+ travellers

As a result of sexual segregation, **male homosexuality** is relatively common in Morocco, although this is rarely admitted. Few Moroccans will declare themselves gay – which has connotations of femininity and weakness; the idea of being a passive partner is virtually taboo, while a dominant partner may well not consider himself to be indulging in a homosexual act. Private realities, however, are rather different from public show (on which subject, note that Moroccan men of all ages often walk hand in hand in public – a habit that has nothing to do with homosexuality and is simply a sign of friendship).

Gay sex is **illegal** under Moroccan law. Article 489 of the Moroccan penal code prohibits any "shameless or unnatural act" with a person of the same sex and allows for imprisonment of six months to three years, plus a fine. There are also various provisions in the penal code for more serious offences, with correspondingly higher penalties in cases involving, for example, corruption of minors (under-18s). The International Gay and Lesbian Human Rights Commission post the latest Moroccan gay rights news at ⓦiglhrc.org/region/morocco. There's some information on gay-friendly spots in Morocco in French on the Gay Voyageur website at ⓦgayvoyageur.com/maroc.

Tangier's days as a gay resort are long gone but a tourist-oriented gay scene does seem to be emerging, discreetly, in Marrakesh (see page 325), and to a lesser extent Agadir, though pressure from religious fundamentalists makes it difficult for the authorities to ease up, even if they wanted to, and arrests of tourists for having gay sex are not unknown. A British tourist and his alleged gay lover were arrested in Marrakesh in 2014 and only released after the story caused outrage in the international press. Discretion is always advisable. There's little public perception of **lesbianism** in Morocco, and as a Western visitor, your chances of making contact with Moroccan lesbians are small. Moroccan women are under extreme pressure to marry and bear children, and anyone resisting such pressure is likely to have a very hard time of it. In 2016 two teenage girls in Marrakesh were arrested after the mother of one of them reported the pair to the police just for kissing; they were only released after the case caused a worldwide scandal. Nonetheless, awareness is slowly growing.

Living in Morocco

Your best chance of paid work in Morocco is **teaching English**. The schools listed here will require reasonable spoken French and an EFL qualification, and usually do their recruiting at home, but they sometimes advertise jobs online, and they may be able to direct you to smaller schools in Casablanca, Rabat and other Moroccan towns.

It is also possible to **volunteer** for a work camp, most of which are open to anyone over eighteen. You pay travel costs but generally receive free accommodation (though bring a sleeping bag) and meals.

ENGLISH SCHOOLS

American Language Center 1 Pl de la Fraternité, Casablanca Ⓦ aca.org.ma. Also in Agadir, Fez, Kenitra, Marrakesh, Meknes, Mohammedia, Oujda, Rabat, Tangier and Tetouan.
The American School 1 bis Rue el Amir Abdelkader, Agdal, Rabat Ⓦ ras.ma; Route de la Mecque, Lotissement Ougoug, Quartier Californie, Casablanca Ⓦ www.cas.ac.ma; BP 6195, Km9, Route de Ouarzazate, Marrakesh Ⓦ asm.ac.ma; 149 Rue Christophe Colombe, Tangier Ⓦ ast.ma.
British Council 11 Av Allal Ben Abdellah, 5th floor, Rabat; 87 Av Nador, Polo, Casablanca; Ⓦ britishcouncil.ma.

WORK PLACEMENT CAMPS

Chantiers Jeunesse Maroc (CJM) BP 1351, 10000 Rabat Ⓦ cjmfes.wordpress.com.
Chantiers Sociaux Marocains (CSM) BP 456, 10001 Rabat Ⓦ csm.0fees.net.
Service Volontaire International (SVI) Ⓦ servicevolontaire. org. A Franco-Belgian organisation that recruits volunteers for the Moroccan organizations Chantiers Sociaux Marocains (CSM), Chantiers des Jeunes Volontaires (CJV) and Chantiers Jeunesse Maroc (CJM).
One World 365 Ⓦ sciint.org; UK Ⓦ oneworld365.org/travel/ morocco. Directory listing a number of different opportunities for volunteering in Morocco.
SCI/IVS Ⓦ sciint.org; US Ⓦ volunteersciusa.org; Great Britain, Ⓦ ivsgb.org; Ireland (Republic and North) Ⓦ vsi.ie; Australia Ⓦ www.ivp.org.au. Recruits work camp volunteers.
Volunteering Solutions (VolSol) Ⓦ volunteeringsolutions.com; Volunteering placements, mostly in Rabat.

Mail

Letters between Morocco and Western Europe generally take around a week to ten days, and around two weeks for North America or -Australasia. There are postboxes at every post office (Ⓦ poste.ma) and on the wayside; they seem to get emptied fairly efficiently, even in out-of-the-way places.

Stamps can sometimes be bought alongside postcards, or from some *tabacs* as well as at the post office, where there is often a dedicated counter (labelled *timbres*). At major post offices, there is a separate window for **parcels**, where the officials will want to examine the goods you are sending. Always take them unwrapped; there is usually someone to supply wrapping paper, string and tape.

Post office hours are typically Monday to Friday 8am–4.15pm; larger offices may stay open later and on Saturday mornings for stamps, money changing and money transfer, but not for parcels or poste restante. Where opening hours differ from the norm, we have stated the times in the relevant sections of the Guide. During Ramadan, offices open Monday to Friday 9am–3pm.

Poste restante

Receiving letters **poste restante** (general delivery) can be a bit of a lottery, as Moroccan post office workers don't always file letters under the name you might expect. Ask for all your initials to be checked (including "M" for Mr or Ms, etc) and, if you're half-expecting anything, suggest other letters as well. To pick up your mail you need your passport. To have mail sent to you, it should be addressed (preferably with your surname underlined) to Poste Restante at the central post office of any major city.

Maps

The **maps of Moroccan towns** in this book should be sufficient for most needs, though commercial plans of greater Rabat or Casablanca may be useful if you need to visit the suburbs, and detailed maps of the Medinas in Marrakesh and Fez may help to navigate tortuous Medina alleyways.

Reasonable **road maps** are sometimes available at ONMT tourist offices, and these are adequate if you are not driving or going far off the beaten track. The best is Reise-Know-How's, on a scale of 1:1,000,000 (1cm to 1km), printed on waterproof, tear-proof plastic. Among the alternatives, good choices include Marco Polo or IGN's 1:800,000 map, with the Western Sahara on a 1:2,500,000 inset, Freytag-Berndt's, on 1:800,000, with the Western Sahara on 1:2,000,000, and Michelin's *Morocco* map (#742), on 1:1,000,000. Maps (or guidebooks) which do not show the Western Sahara as part of Morocco are banned and liable to confiscation.

Trekking maps and guides

Topographical maps used by trekkers, climbers, skiers, etc (1:50,000 and 1:100,000) are difficult to find in Morocco. You may have to go in person to the Division de la Cartographie, Avenue Hassan II, Km4, Rabat (near the *gare routière* bus station, ask for *Résidence Oum Kaltoum*); for some maps, you have to show your passport and submit an order which *may* then be available for collection two working days later – if the request is approved, which is far from certain, although maps of Toubkal and some others will be

EMERGENCY NUMBERS

Fire ☎ 15
Police (in towns) ☎ 19
Gendarmes (police force with jurisdiction outside towns) ☎ 177

served over the counter. However, if you are planning to go trekking, it is best to try and get maps through a **specialist map outlet** before you leave home. Look for 1:100,000 (and if you're lucky 1:50,000) maps of the Atlas and other mountain areas. Stanfords in London (online orders worldwide at ⓦ stanfords.co.uk) has several trekking maps covering the High Atlas and in particular the Jebel Toubkal area.

More **detailed trekking guidebooks** exist in both English and French, but are not always easily available. The most useful are Hamish Brown's *The High Atlas: Treks and Climbs on Morocco's Biggest and Best Mountains* (Cicerone Press, 2012), and Walks and Scrambles in the Moroccan Anti-Atlas by David Wood (Cicerone Press, 2018) and the now dated Robin Collomb's *Atlas Mountains* (West Col, 1980), Michael Peyron's *Grand Atlas Traverse* (2 vols, West Col, 1990), Karl Smith's *Atlas Mountains: A Walker's Guide* (Cicerone Press, 1998), and Alan Palmer's *Moroccan Atlas the Trekking Guide* (2nd edition, Trailblazer, 2014). Also handy if you can get it is West Col's map guide to the Mgoun Massif at 1:100,000, which covers a wide region, second only to Toubkal in popularity. For climbing, Jean Dresch and Jacques de Lépiney's 1942 *Le Massif du Toubkal*, (republished by Éditions Belvisi, Casablanca), is useful but hard to find.

Money

Though the easiest way to carry your money is in the form of plastic, it is a good idea to also carry at least a couple of days' survival money in cash, and maybe some travellers' cheques as an emergency backup.

Morocco's basic unit of **currency** is the **dirham** (dh). The dirham is not quoted on international money markets, a rate being set instead by the Moroccan governmentAs with all currencies there are fluctuations, but the dirham has roughly held its own against Western currencies over the last few years. A dirham is divided into 100 **centimes**, and you may find prices written or expressed in centimes rather than dirhams. Confusingly, centimes may also be referred to as **francs** or, in former Spanish zones of the country, as **pesetas**. You may also hear prices quoted in **rials**, or *reales*. In most parts of the country a dirham is -considered to be twenty rials, though in Tangier and

the Rif there are just two rials to the dirham. Coins of 10, 20 and 50 centimes, and 1, 5 and 10 dirhams are in circulation, along with notes of 20, 50, 100 and 200 dirhams.

In Algeciras, you can buy dirhams at poor rates from **travel agents** opposite the port entrance, and at slightly better rates from those inside the ferry terminal. You can also buy dirhams at similar rates from agents near the ferry terminals in Ceuta and Melilla. In Gibraltar, **moneychangers** will usually give you a very slightly better rate than in Morocco itself. When you're nearing the end of your stay, it's best to get down to as little Moroccan money as possible. You can change back dirhams at the airport on departure (you can't use them in duty-free shops), but you may be asked to produce bank exchange receipts – and you can change back only fifty percent of sums detailed on these. You'll probably be offered re-exchange into euros only. You can also change dirhams (at bad rates) into euros in Ceuta, Melilla and Algeciras, and into sterling in Gibraltar. It is illegal to import or export more than 2000dh.

Banks and exchange

English pounds and US and Canadian dollars can all be changed at banks, large hotels and forex (foreign exchange) bureaux, but by far the most widely accepted foreign currency is the **euro**, which many people will accept in lieu of dirhamsGibraltarian banknotes are accepted for exchange at a very slightly lower rate than English ones, but Scottish and Northern Irish notes are not negotiable in Morocco, and nor are Australian and New Zealand dollars, South African rand, Algerian dinars or Mauritanian ouguiya, though you should be able to change CFAs. Moroccan bank clerks may balk at changing banknotes with numbers scrawled on them by their counterparts abroad, so change any such notes for clean ones before leaving home.

BMCE tends to be the best **bank** for money changing. Usually at banks, you fill in forms at one desk, then join a second queue for the cashier, and you'll usually need to show your passport as proof of identity. Standard banking hours for most of the year are Monday to Friday 8.15am to 3.45pm, but some BMCE branches open Mon–Fri 9.15am–5.45pm. During Ramadan (see page 44), banks typically open from 9.30am to 2pm. BMCE and some other banks sometimes have a separate bureau de change open longer hours and at weekends, and there are now private foreign exchange bureaux in most major cities and tourist destinations, which open longer hours (often on Sundays), change money with no fuss or bureaucracy, and don't usually charge commission. Many post offices and hotels will change cash.

There is a **small currency black market** but you are recommended not to use it: changing money on the street is illegal and subject to all the usual scams, and the rate is not particularly preferential.

Credit and debit cards

Credit and debit cards on the Visa, Mastercard, Cirrus and Plus networks can be used to withdraw cash from **ATMs** at many banks, but not the ones outside post offices. Otherwise, banks may advance cash against Visa or Mastercard. By using ATMs, you get trade exchange rates, which are better than those charged by banks for changing cash, but your card issuer may add a transaction fee, sometimes hefty. There is a daily limit on ATM cash withdrawals, typically 4000dh.

You can pay directly with plastic (usually with Mastercard, Visa or American Express, though the latter cannot be used in ATMs) in upmarket hotels, restaurants and tourist shops.

Prepaid cards and money wiring

Travellers' cheques are no longer negotiable in Morocco. They have been superseded by **prepaid cards**, such as those issued by Visa, which you can load up with credit before you leave home and use in ATMs like a debit card. For wiring money, **Western Union** is represented at every post office. Money-Gram's local agents include branches of Crédit du Maroc and Banque Centrale Populaire.

Opening hours

Opening hours follow a reasonably consistent pattern: banks Mon–Fri 8.15am–3.45pm; museums daily except Tues 9am–noon & 3–6pm; offices Mon–Thurs 8.30am–noon & 2.30–6.30pm, Fri 8.30–11.30am & 3–6.30pm; Ville Nouvelle shops Mon–Sat 8.30am–noon & 2–6.30pm; Medina shops Sat–Thurs 9am–6pm, Fri 9am–1pm. Note, however, that these hours will vary during Ramadan (see page 44), when banks, for example, open 9.30am to 2pm, and everything will close before nightfall, when those observing the fast – which is to say, nearly everybody – have to stop and eat.

Phones

Téléboutique are common everywhere. Some use coins – 5dh and 10dh coins are best for foreign calls (you'll probably need at least 20dh) – others give you a card and charge you for the units used. International calls from a hotel are pricey and may be charged in three-minute increments, so that if you go one second over, you're charged for the next period.

Morocco has almost universal **mobile phone** coverage. Depending on how long you are spending in Morocco, it may be worth signing up with Maroc Télécom or Meditel, using their SIM card and getting a Moroccan number. Sim cards with data packs can be bought from most big airports on arrival. You normally have to show your passport in order to get a local SIM card but the process is normally quick and easy. Getting one from a mobile phone shop in a city is also possible but normally takes a little longer.

Instead of a dialling tone, Moroccan phones have a voice telling you in French and Arabic to dial the number. When calling a Moroccan number, the **ringing tone** consists of one-and-a-half-second

CONVERTING PHONE NUMBERS

Because Maroc Telecom changes all the phone numbers every few years, it's not at all unlikely that phone numbers you may have (even from current websites) may be out of date, but they should be easy to convert using this table.

	pre-2002	2002	2006	since 2009
Casablanca region	☎02 000000	☎022 000000	☎022 000000	☎0522 000000
El Jadida region	☎03 000000	☎023 000000	☎023 000000	☎0523 000000
Marrakesh region	☎04 000000	☎044 000000	☎024 000000	☎0524 000000
Fez/Meknes region	☎05 000000	☎055 000000	☎035 000000	☎0535 000000
Oujda region	☎06 000000	☎056 000000	☎036 000000	☎0536 000000
Rabat region	☎07 000000	☎037 000000	☎037 000000	☎0537 000000
Agadir region	☎08 000000	☎048 000000	☎028 000000	☎0528 000000
Tangier region	☎09 000000	☎039 000000	☎039 000000	☎0539 000000
old mobiles	☎01 000000	☎061 000000	☎061 000000	☎0661 000000
newer mobiles	–	–	☎0xx 000000	☎06xx 000000

bursts of tone, separated by a three-and-a-half-second silence. The **engaged tone** is a series of short tones (pip-pip-pip-pip), as in most other parts of the world. A short series of very rapid pips may also indicate that your call is being connected.

Phone numbers

Maroc Télécom seem to change all their numbers every few years. Moroccan numbers are now ten-digit, and all ten digits must be dialled, even locally. All mobile numbers now begin with 06, all ordinary landline numbers with 05. If the number you have doesn't start with either of these, you'll need to convert it (see box, page 63).

The Spanish enclaves of **Ceuta and Melilla** have nine-digit numbers, incorporating the former area codes (956 for Ceuta, 952 for Melilla), and all nine digits must be dialled, even locally. To call from mainland Spain, you'll only need to dial the nine-digit number. Calling Ceuta or Melilla from abroad, or from Morocco proper, dial the international access code (00 from Morocco), then 34, then the whole nine-digit number. To call Morocco from Ceuta or Melilla, dial 00 212, then the last nine digits of the number, omitting the initial zero.

International calls

To **call Morocco from abroad**, you dial the international access code (00 from Britain, Ireland, Spain and New Zealand; 0011 from Australia; 011 from the US and most of Canada), 09 from South Africa, then the country code (212), then the last nine digits of the number, omitting the initial zero. To **call Ceuta or Melilla**, dial the international access code, then 34, then all nine digits of the number, beginning with 956 for Ceuta, 952 for Melilla.

To make an **international call** from Morocco, Ceuta or Melilla, dial 00, followed by the country code (1 for North America, 44 for the UK, etc), the area code (omitting the initial zero which prefixes area codes in most countries outside North America) and the subscriber number. To **reverse call charges**, a good policy is to phone someone briefly and get them to ring you back, as collect (reverse charge) calls are hard to arrange.

Photography

Photography needs to be undertaken with care. If you are obviously taking a photograph of someone, ask their permission – especially in the more remote, rural regions where you can cause genuine offence. In Marrakesh's Jemaa el Fna, taking even quite general shots of the scene may cause somebody in the shot to demand money from you, sometimes quite aggressively. Also note that it is illegal to take photographs of anything considered strategic, such as an airport or a police station, so be careful where you point your camera – if in doubt, ask. On a more positive front, taking a photograph of someone you've struck up a friendship with and sending it on to them, or exchanging photographs, is often appreciated.

Time

Morocco is on Central European Time (CET). Ceuta and Melilla keep Spanish time, which is GMT+1 in winter and GMT+2 in summer. The difference should be borne in mind if you're coming from Morocco to catch ferries out of Ceuta or Melilla, or trains out of Algeciras.

Tourist information

Morocco's national tourist board, the **Office National Marocain de Tourisme** (ONMT; Ⓦvisitmorocco. com) maintains general information offices in several Western capitals, where you can pick up pamphlets on the main Moroccan cities and resorts, and a few items on cultural themes.

In Morocco itself, you'll find an **ONMT** office (*délégation de tourisme*) or a locally run office called a **Syndicat d'Initiative** bureau in all towns of any size or interest – often both (addresses detailed in the Guide). They can of course answer queries, though the *délégation*'s main function is promoting tourism

---

INTERNATIONAL DIALLING CODES

	From Morocco, Ceuta or Melilla	To Morocco	To Ceuta or Melilla
UK	☎00 44	☎00 212	☎00 34
Ireland	☎00 353	☎00 212	☎00 34
US and Canada	☎001	☎011 212	☎011 34
Australia	☎00 61	☎0011 212	☎0011 34
New Zealand	☎00 64	☎00 212	☎00 34
South Africa	☎00 27	☎09 212	☎09 34

and gathering statistics. Both offices should also be able to put you in touch with an officially recognized guide.

In addition, there is quite a bit of information available online, and plenty of books on Morocco (see page 533). The Maghreb Society, based in the UK at the Maghreb Bookshop, 45 Burton St, London WC1H 9AL (☎ 020 7388 1840, ⓦ maghrebreview.com), publishes the *Maghreb Review*, the most important English-language journal on the Maghrebian countries.

ONMT OFFICES ABROAD

Spain c/Ventura Rodriguez 24, first floor, left, 28008 Madrid ⓦ turismomarruecos.com.

UK 205 Regent St, London W1B 4HB, ⓦ visitmorocco.com.
US 104 W 40th St, Suite 1820, New York, NY 10018 ⓦ visitmorocco.com.

GOVERNMENT TRAVEL ADVISORIES

Australian Department of Foreign Affairs ⓦ martraveller.gov. au/countries/africa/north/pages/morocco.aspx.
British Foreign & Commonwealth Office ⓦ gov.uk/foreign-travel-advice/morocco.
Canadian Department of Foreign Affairs ⓦ travel.gc.ca/destinations/morocco.
US State Department ⓦ travel.state.gov/content/travel/en/international-travel.html.

Tangier, Tetouan and the northwest

MOULAY BOUSSELHAM

1

Tangier, Tetouan and the northwest

At first glance, it would appear that Morocco's northwest corner has everything a traveller could want. Bordered on one side by sweeping expanses of near-deserted coastline washed by both Atlantic and Mediterranean waters, and on the other by the wild, rugged Rif mountain range that defines the physical boundary between Europe and Africa, this part of the country is home to a number of ancient, walled Medinas that remain mainly non-touristy and begging to be explored. As idyllic as it may sound, in reality the region has often been the country's ugly duckling and, especially in the latter half of the twentieth century, was virtually ignored by both king and state.

The reasons for this cold shoulder were historical and twofold – Tangier's reputation for European-influenced vice and extravagance, and two assassination attempts on the king (Hassan II, the current king's late father) that were widely believed to have emanated from within the largely lawless interior of the Rif mountains. This is all firmly in the past now, however. As a young prince, King Mohammed VI enjoyed many a summer holiday here jetskiing and hiking, and since the death of his father in 1999 he has steadily opened the country's (and foreign investors') eyes to the northwest's obvious charm and attraction, both in its natural beauty and close proximity to Europe.

Nowhere is this progress more visible than in **Tangier**. Once seedy from its days as a centre of international espionage and haven for gay Europeans and dodgy banks, the city has reinvented itself over the past 20 years as a vibrant, accessible and modern Mediterranean beach resort. South of Tangier along the Atlantic coast are the seaside resorts of Asilah and Larache, both of which offer wonderful, aimless meanderings within their compact whitewashed Medinas. **Asilah** is a relaxed and low-key town, well known for its international arts festival, while **Larache** is similarly attractive, and close to the ancient Carthaginian-Roman site of **Lixus**. A more distinctively Moroccan resort is **Moulay Bousselham**, south of Larache, with its windswept Atlantic beach and abundance of birdlife.

The Spanish enclave of **Ceuta** was a possession too valuable for the Spanish to hand back to Morocco upon the latter's independence in 1956, and makes a pleasant change of pace when coming from the relatively haphazard and chaotic Moroccan side of the border. In the shadow of the Rif mountains, **Tetouan** has a proud Andalusian-Moroccan heritage and offers up yet another fascinating, authentic Medina while its nearby beaches are popular with both locals and visitors. South of Tetouan is the mountain town of **Chefchaouen** – a small-scale and enjoyably laidback place with perhaps the most photographed Medina of them all.

Northern Morocco has an especially quirky **colonial history**, having been divided into three separate zones. Tetouan was the administrative capital of the Spanish zone; the French zone began at Souk el Arba du Gharb, the edge of rich agricultural plains sprawling southward; while Tangier experienced International Rule under a group of foreign legations. Subsequently, although French is the official second language (after Arabic) throughout Morocco, older people in much of the northwest are equally, or more, fluent in Spanish – a basic knowledge of which can prove useful.

Tangier

At the meeting point of two seas as well as two continents, **TANGIER**'s strategic location has made it a highly sought-after locale since ancient times. Founded by Mediterranean trading nations, ruled by empirical Romans, and squabbled over by European powers

ANCIENT LIXUS

Highlights

❶ Tangier's café squares Sit with the ghosts of French spies and British secret agents as you wile away the hours over a mint tea or espresso. See page 78

❷ The Caves of Hercules Look out to sea from this grotto in the cliffs, through a cave window shaped like Africa. See page 87

❸ Asilah A laidback beach resort with an intimate pastel-washed Medina, an international arts festival, and the palace of an old bandit chief. See page 89

❹ Ancient Lixus Extensive Roman ruins in a fine setting, which you'll have pretty much to yourself to explore. See page 95

❺ Moulay Bousselham Wander the expansive windswept Atlantic beach and take a boat ride on the nearby lagoon, home to diverse birdlife and pink flamingos. See page 97

❻ Ceuta A Spanish enclave with a couple of forts and no less than three army museums – not to mention good beer, tapas and shops full of duty-free booze. See page 98

❼ Chefchaouen One of the prettiest and friendliest towns in Morocco, up in the Rif mountains, with a Medina full of pastel-blue houses. See page 112

HIGHLIGHTS ARE MARKED ON THE MAP ON PAGE 70

1

before finally returning to the Moroccan nation in 1956, it's perhaps no surprise that the city defies comparison with any other in Morocco.

For the first half of the twentieth century, Tangier was an international city with its own laws and administration, plus an eclectic community of exiles, expatriates and refugees. It was home, at various times, to Spanish and Central European refugees, Moroccan nationalists and – drawn by loose tax laws and free-port status – to over seventy banks and four thousand companies, many of them dealing in currency transactions forbidden in their own countries. Writers were also attracted to the city, including the American novelist **Paul Bowles** who called it his "dream city" and lived here for 52 years, and **William Burroughs** who spent most of the 1950s here. Tangier

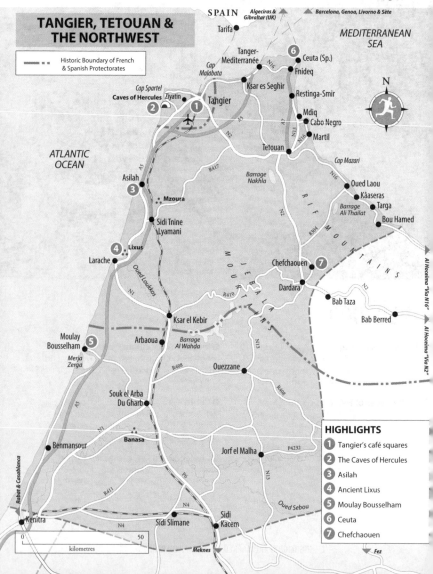

TANGIER, TETOUAN & THE NORTHWEST

- - - - — Historic Boundary of French & Spanish Protectorates

SPAIN
Algeciras & Gibraltar (UK)
Tarifa
Barcelona, Genoa, Livorno & Sète

MEDITERRANEAN SEA

Cap Malabata
Tanger-Mediterranée
Ceuta (Sp.)
Fnideq
Ksar es Seghir
Restinga-Smir

Cap Spartel
Caves of Hercules Ziyatin
Tangier
Mdiq
Cabo Negro
Martil

ATLANTIC OCEAN

Tetouan
Cap Mazari

Asilah
Barrage Nakhla
Oued Laou
Kâaseras
Targa
Bou Hamed

Mzoura
Sidi Tnine Lyamani
Lixus
Larache
Chefchaouen
Dardara
Bab Taza
Al Hoceïma "Via N16"
Al Hoceïma "Via N2"

Oued Loukkos
Ksar el Kebir
Bab Berred

Moulay Bousselham
Arbaoua
Barrage Al Wahda
Merja Zerga
Ouezzane

Souk el Arba Du Gharb

Banasa
Benmansour
Jorf el Malha

Kenitra
Sidi Slimane
Sidi Kacem

Rabat & Casablanca

0   50
kilometres

Meknes
Fez

HIGHLIGHTS

1. Tangier's café squares
2. The Caves of Hercules
3. Asilah
4. Ancient Lixus
5. Moulay Bousselham
6. Ceuta
7. Chefchaouen

TANGIER'S HUSTLERS

Faux guides ("false guides") are petty crooks who attach themselves to new-in-town tourists, usually claiming to be "guiding" you and therefore due payment, or just steering you into hotels or shops where they receive a commission (added to your bill, naturally). At one time, Tangier's *faux guides* were particularly heavy; nowadays they have largely been cleaned out of town thanks to a **nationwide police crackdown**, though you may still experience some hustling when arriving at the *gare routière* or Tanger Med port. Generally speaking, *faux guides* now limit their activities to encouraging you to visit the shops that employ them – though if they can hustle you into a hotel that will pay them commission, they will do that too (the price of a room will be higher than it should be to cover this commission). Some may also insist that you will need help buying train and ferry tickets (which you don't) or try to sell you *kif* (cannabis).

There are a number of approaches you will soon learn to recognize: a favourite is trying to guess your nationality, or asking "Are you lost?" or "What are you looking for?" If you ignore them or turn down their advances, they will sometimes accuse you of being angry or "paranoid". The best way to get rid of them is to **ignore them completely** or explain politely (while never slackening your pace) that you are alright and don't need any help. As a last resort – and it should not come to this – you can dive into a café or even threaten to go to the **police** if necessary (the Brigade Touristique are based in the former Gare de Ville train station at the entrance to Tanger Ville port, and there is also a police post in the kasbah). Bear in mind that local residents, as well as the law, are on your side.

was also the world's first and most famous **gay resort**, favoured by the likes of Tennessee Williams, Joe Orton and Kenneth Williams. In the words of the English academic Andrew Hussey, Tangier was a "utopia of dangerous, unknown pleasures".

Rooted in an enduring eccentricity, Tangier's charm is undeniable. Until fairly recently, the city's tourism future didn't look too rosy, having, over the years, gained a reputation as somewhere to avoid due to continuing reports of a large population of hustlers and unsavoury characters known to prey on foreign arrivals. King Mohammed VI, however, has provided much of the impetus for Tangier to re-invent itself under a flurry of renovation and building projects. These include the recent remodelling of the port area, which now has a newly-vamped cruise ship jetty and terminal (they often dock here on their way from the Atlantic to the Mediterranean) as well as an additional 1400 berth yacht marina called Tanja Marina Bay. Restaurateurs, hoteliers and even boutique owners have also done much to enhance the city for Tangerines, expat residents and visitors.

Brief history

Tangier was known in ancient times as Tingis, which is Amazigh (Berber) for a marsh and reveals the site's Berber origins. It was colonized around the seventh century BC by the **Phoenicians**, a seafaring people from what is now Lebanon, and in 42 AD, the **Romans** made Tingis the capital of their newly created province of Mauretania Tingitania (roughly the north of modern Morocco). In 429 AD, with the collapse of the Roman Empire's western half, Tangier was taken by the Vandals, after which point things become a bit hazy. It seems to have been regained a century or so later by the Roman Empire's resurgent eastern half in the form of the **Byzantines**, before falling to Spain's rulers, the **Visigoths**, in the early seventh century.

Andalusian and European Influence

In 707, Tangier was taken by the **Arabs**, who used it as a base for their invasion of the Iberian Peninsula four years later. However, with the Christian reconquest of Spain and Portugal from the eleventh to fifteenth centuries, Tangier was itself vulnerable to attack from across the Straits, and eventually fell to the **Portuguese** in 1471. In 1661, they gave it to the **British** (along with Bombay) as part of Princess Catherine of Braganza's

1

Le Vieille Montagne & **2**

Le Vieille Montagne & Cap Spartel

Hospital Mohammed

ROUTE DE LA PLAGE MERCALA

Dar el Mendoub

AVENUE HADJ MOHAMED TAZI

RUE HASSANI

AVENUE DES USA

Stade Marshan

School

Punic Tombs

RUE DE MARSHAN

Bab el Kasbah

Dar el Makhzen

AVENUE F. ROOSEVELT

Italian Consulate

2

KASBAH

LA MARSHAN

RUE AL KORTOBI

RUE DE LA KASBAH

RUE DU DR CENATRO

Tomb of Ibn Battutah

Bab Gzenaya

RUE D'ITALIE

RUE HASSAN I

Mendoubia Gardens

AVENUE SIDI MOHAMMED BEN ABDALLAH

RUE ARRAKIA

GRAND SOCCO

RUE DE LA LIBERTÉ

Cinema Rif

St. Andrew's Church

AVENUE HASSAN II

RUE IBN ZAIDOUN

SIDI BOUABID

Galerie d'Art Contemporain

BOULEVARD D'ANGLETERRE

RUE DE RUSSIE

French Consulate

(RUE EL HOURIA)

RUE DE HOLLANDE

AVENUE

RUE IBN ZAIDOUN

RUE

PLACE KOWEIT

Mosque Mohammed V

RUE DE BELGIQUE

1

PLACE DE FRANCE

RUE SIDI BOUABID

SIDI MOHAMMED

RUE DU MEXIQUE

RUE DE HOLLANDE

RUE S. PEPYS

RUE DE FES

Spanish Consulate

BOULEVARD D'ANGLETERRE

Instituto Cervantes de Tangier

BEN

Hôpital Espagnol

RUE GANDHI

RUE MAHATMA

PLACE OUED EL MAKHAZINE

RUE EMSALLAH

RUE DE COLOMBIA

RUE DE COLOMBIA

RUE

ABDALLAH

0   200
metres

Airport & Asilah ▼   Airport & Asilah ▼

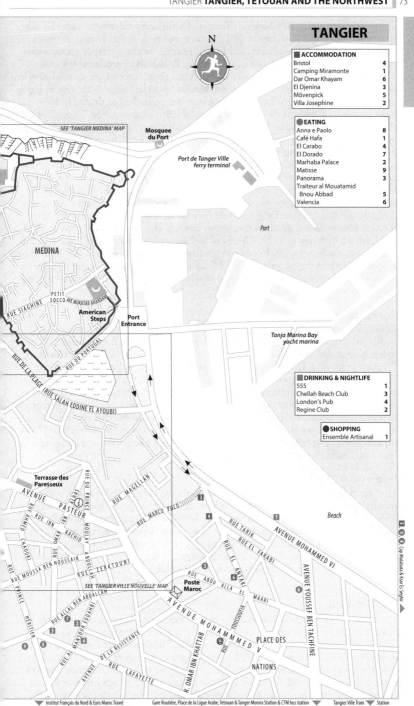

TANGIER

■ ACCOMMODATION

Bristol	4
Camping Miramonte	1
Dar Omar Khayam	6
El Djenina	3
Mövenpick	5
Villa Josephine	2

● EATING

Anna e Paolo	8
Café Hafa	1
El Carabo	4
El Dorado	7
Marhaba Palace	2
Matisse	9
Panorama	3
Traiteur al Mouatamid Bnou Abbad	5
Valencia	6

■ DRINKING & NIGHTLIFE

555	1
Chellah Beach Club	3
London's Pub	4
Regine Club	2

● SHOPPING

Ensemble Artisanal	1

SEE 'TANGIER MEDINA' MAP

Mosquee du Port

Port de Tanger Ville ferry terminal

Port

MEDINA

PETIT SOCCO AVE MOKHTAB AHARDANE

RUE SIAGHINE

American Steps

Port Entrance

RUE DU PORTUGAL

RUE DE LA PLAGE (RUE SALAH EDDINE EL AYOUBI)

Tanja Marina Bay yacht marina

Terrasse des Paresseux

AVENUE PASTEUR

RUE DU PRINCE MOULAY ABDULLAH

RUE MAGELLAN

RUE MARCO POLO

RUE TARIK

AVENUE MOHAMMED VI

Beach

RUE AHMED CHAOUKI

RUE IBN RACHID

RUE AL MANSOUR EDDAHBI

RUE MOUSSA BEN NOUSSAIR

RUE ZERKTOUNT

RUE EL FARABI

RUE EL ANTAKI

RUE ABOU ALLA EL MAARI

AVENUE YOUSSEF BEN TACHFINE

SEE 'TANGIER VILLE NOUVELLE' MAP

Poste Maroc

RUE PRINCE HERITIER

RUE ALLAL BEN ABDALLAH

AVENUE DE LA RESISTANCE

R. OMAR IBN KHATTAB

AVENUE MOHAMMED V

PLACE DES NATIONS

RUE LAFAYETTE

Cap Malabata & Ksar Es Seghir

1

dowry on her wedding to Charles II. Tangier's Portuguese residents, accusing British troops of looting and rape, abandoned the town, but new settlers arrived, many of them Jewish refugees from Spain, and Britain granted the city a charter guaranteeing freedom of religion, trade and immigration. The British also introduced **tea**, now Morocco's national drink. Under virtually constant siege, however, they found Tangier an expensive and unrewarding possession. **Moulay Ismail** laid siege to the city in 1678, and in 1680, England's parliament refused any further funding to defend it. Four years later, unable to withstand the siege any longer, the British abandoned Tangier. The city then remained in Moroccan hands until the twentieth century, growing in importance as a port – one of its exports, mandarins, even took their name from the city, being known in Europe as **Tangerines**.

Tangier's strategic position made it a coveted prize for all the colonial powers at the end of the nineteenth century. European representatives started insinuating themselves into the administration of the city, taking control of vital parts of the infrastructure, and when France and Spain decided to carve up Morocco between them (see page 504), Britain insisted that Tangier should become an **International Zone**, with all Western powers having an equal measure of control. This was agreed as early as 1905, and finalized by treaty in 1923. An area of 380 square kilometres, with some 150,000 inhabitants, the International Zone was governed by a Legislative Assembly headed by a representative of the sultan called the Mendoub. While legislative power rested with the assembly – consisting of 27 members of whom eighteen were European – the real power was held by a French governor.

Morocco takes control

At the International Zone's peak in the early 1950s, Tangier's foreign communities numbered sixty thousand – then nearly half the population. As for the other half, pro-independence demonstrations in 1952 and 1953 made it abundantly clear that most Tanjawis (natives of Tangier) wanted to be part of a united, independent Morocco. When they gained their wish in 1956, Tangier lost its special status, and almost overnight, the finance and banking businesses shifted their operations to Spain and Switzerland. The expatriate communities dwindled too as the new national government imposed bureaucratic controls and instituted a "clean-up" of the city. Brothels – previously numbering almost a hundred – were banned, and in the early 1960s "**The Great Scandal**" erupted, sparked by a number of paedophile convictions and escalating into a wholesale closure of the once outrageous gay bars.

Tangier today

After a period of significant decline, the early 2000s saw Tangier reborn as one of the country's premier **beach holiday resorts** as both the Moroccan government and foreign investors directed more interest (and more funds) towards the city and its future. Marketed mainly towards the domestic market as well as day-tripping Spaniards, Tangier's regeneration shows no sign of fading. As well as the redevelopment of the old port and its glitzy marina, much of the Medina has been restored, and many of the city's main streets and boulevards have new palm trees as part of a city-wide beautification project.

The Medina

The layout within Tangier's **Medina**, like most throughout Morocco, was never planned in advance. As the need arose, a labyrinth of streets and small squares emerged that eventually became the various quarters there today. The **Grand Socco** offers the most straightforward approach to the Medina. This is a busy transport hub and a good place to watch the chaos of traffic, carts, and people go about their daily routines. The **arch** at the northern corner of the square opens onto Rue d'Italie, which becomes Rue de la Kasbah, the northern entrance to the **kasbah** quarter. Through an opening on the right-hand side of the square is **Rue es Siaghin**, off which are most of the souks and at the end of which is the **Petit Socco** (see page 76), the Medina's small, main square. An alternative approach to the Medina is from the **seafront**: follow the American steps, west of the port, up from Avenue Mohammed VI, walk round by the Grand Mosque, and Rue des Postes (Rue Mokhtar Ahardane) will lead you into the Petit Socco.

Rue es Siaghin

Rue es Siaghin – Silversmiths' Street – connects Grand Socco with the smaller Petit Socco, and was Tangier's main thoroughfare into the 1930s. Many of the buildings along here were constructed by Europeans in the late 1800s, with windows and balconies looking out onto the street rather than the traditional inward-looking Medina architecture. Most of the silversmiths have since been replaced by bureaux de change and souvenir shops, but it's a pleasant enough access road.

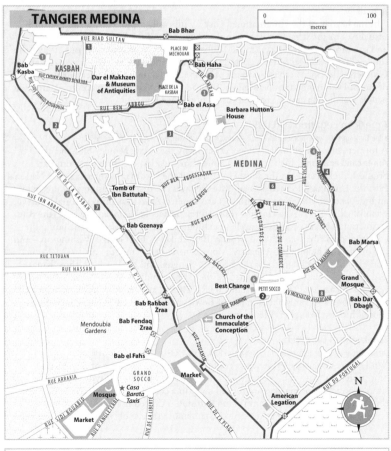

ACCOMMODATION					EATING				SHOPPING	
Continental	4	Dar Nour	2	Riad Jamila	5	A L'anglaise	5	El Morocco Club	1	Boutique Majid	1
Dar Chams Tanja	3	Dar Rif	6	La Tangerina	1	Café Baba	3	Le Salon Bleu	2	Volubilis Boutique	2
Dar Kasbah	7	Mamora	8			Café Tingis	6	Rif Kabdani	4		

1

Church of the Immaculate Conception
Rue es Siaghin

The **Church of the Immaculate Conception**, halfway along Rue es Siaghin, was built in 1880 by a Franciscan missionary, Father José Lerchundi and is the only church in Morocco found within the walls of a Medina. No longer used for services, the building is occupied by Mother Teresa's Missionaries of Charity. The area behind here was formerly the **Mellah**, or Jewish quarter, centred around Rue des Synagogues.

The Petit Socco

Looking at it today, the **Petit Socco**, or Zoco Chico (Little Market), seems too small ever to have served such a purpose, though up until the nineteenth century the square was almost twice its present size, and it was only at the beginning of the twentieth century that the hotels and cafés were built. Up until the 1930s, when the focus moved to the Ville Nouvelle, this was the true heart of Tangier, and a broad mix of people – Christians, Jews and Muslims, Moroccans, Europeans and Americans – would gather here daily.

In the heyday of the "International City", with easily exploited Arab and Spanish sexuality a major attraction, it was in the **alleys** behind the Socco that the straight and gay brothels were concentrated. William Burroughs used to hang out around the square: "I get averages of ten very attractive propositions a day", he wrote to Allen Ginsberg. The Socco cafés lost much of their appeal at independence, when the sale of alcohol was banned in the Medina, but they remain diverting places to sit around, people watch, talk and get some measure of the Medina.

American Legation (TALIM)

8 Rue d'Amérique • Closed on Moroccan public hols • Charge; guided tour charge • ⊛ legation.ipower.com/blog

A former palace given to the US government by the sultan Moulay Slimane, the **American Legation** (officially Tangier American Legation Institute for Moroccan Studies), tucked away in the southern corner of the Medina, is America's only National Historic Landmark located abroad. Morocco was the first overseas power to recognize an independent United States and this was the first American ambassadorial residence, established in 1777. A fascinating three-storey **palace**, bridging an alleyway (the Rue d'Amérique) below, it houses excellent exhibits on the city's history – including the correspondence between Sultan Moulay Ben Abdallah and George Washington – and has displays of **paintings** by, mainly, Moroccan-resident American artists. Malcolm Forbes's military miniatures of the Battle of Songhai and the Battle of Three Kings are also on display having been donated by the Forbes family when the Forbes Museum was closed (see page 79). Downstairs, by the **library**, are a couple of rooms dedicated to Paul Bowles features photographs of Bowles and his contemporaries, including a shot of him by Beat poet Allen Ginsberg.

Tomb of Ibn Battutah

Cnr Rue Ibn Batouta & Rue Gzenaya, Quartier Jnan Kaptan • Daily, no set times • Free; caretaker donation suggested

While there's no actual evidence to confirm or deny the existence of the remains of explorer Ibn Battutah (see page 77), they are said to lie in this typically small, simple, nondescript mausoleum tucked away in a corner of Tangier's Medina. Inside the serene mausoleum, the **Tomb of Ibn Battutah** is draped in the colour of Islam (green) and watched over by a caretaker; remember to take off your shoes as you enter.

The kasbah

The **kasbah**, walled off from the Medina on the highest rise of the coast, has been the city's palace and administrative quarter since Roman times. It was the Brits who destroyed the city's medieval fortifications, including a great upper castle which covered

IBN BATTUTAH

Abu Abdallah Muhammad Ibn Abdallah Ibn Muhammad Ibn Ibrahim Ibn Battutah al-Lawati al-Tanji, better known simply as **Ibn Battutah**, was born in Tangier in 1304. At the age of 21 he went on a **pilgrimage** to Makkah (Mecca), a journey that stretched out to nearly **thirty years** as he explored much of the then-known **Islamic world**. Travelling alone and three times as far (in distance) as the more famous Middle Ages explorer Marco Polo, who died shortly before Ibn Battutah started his journey, Battutah visited the coasts of East and North Africa, the Middle East, India, China and travelled across the Sahara to Mali. He mostly worked for his passage and was sometimes employed as a judge and ambassador by several of the rulers he visited. In 1354 he returned to Morocco and related his travels to the Sultan. A Granadian scribe later wrote down Ibn Battutah's stories in **El Rihla** (*"The Travels"*), considered to be one of the all-time great travelogues and an invaluable literary account of the Islamic world as it was. Ibn Battutah died in 1377 and his remains are (possibly) in a modest mausoleum in Tangier's Medina (see page 76). For more on the "world's first backpacker", read *Travels with a Tangerine: A Journey in the Footnotes of Ibn Battuta* by British travel writer Tim Mackintosh-Smith (ⓦmackintosh-smith.com).

the entire site of the present-day kasbah. It is a strange, somewhat sparse area of walled compounds, occasional colonnades, and a number of luxurious villas built in the 1920s, when this became one of the Mediterranean's choicest residential sites.

The eccentric Woolworths heiress, Barbara Hutton, moved into the kasbah quarter in 1947, reputedly outbidding General Franco for her mini palace, Sidi Hosni. Her parties were legendary – including a ball where thirty Reguibat racing camels and their drivers were brought a thousand miles from the Sahara to form a guard of honour.

Most visitors approach the kasbah from the Medina through **Bab Haha**. There are touts here who will offer to give you a guided tour but this is unnecessary as the kasbah is small and signs point the way. Another approach is **Bab el Assa**, featured in the 1912 painting *La porte de la Kasbah* by the French artist, Henri Matisse. Just inside this gate is the Seqaya Bab el Assa, one of the largest and most beautiful fountains of the Medina featuring exquisite zellij mosaic tiling and an ornamental wooden roof. The kasbah's main point of interest is the former **Dar el Makhzen**, or Sultanate Palace (see below). It stands to the rear of a formal court, or *mechouar*, where the town's pashas held public audience and gave judgment well into the twentieth century.

Museum of Antiquities
Dar el Makhzen, Pl de la Kasbah • Charge

The **Dar el Makhzen** – built, like the Medina's Grand Mosque, in the seventeenth century by Moulay Ismail – last saw royal use in 1912, as the residence of the sultan Moulay Hafid and his entourage of 168, who was exiled to Tangier after his forced abdication by the French. The ground floor kitchens and first floor apartments are home to the **Museum of Antiquities**, often just called the Kasbah Museum. The rooms are centred on two interior courtyards, each with rich arabesques, painted wooden ceilings and marble fountains. Some of the flanking columns are of Roman origin, particularly well suited to the small display of **mosaics** and finds from Volubilis (see page 197). In the rooms are well-presented artefacts discovered in and around Tangier, with origins dating from the Palaeolithic era up until Portuguese occupation. Other exhibits include a map depicting international trade routes, a section dedicated to the Islamization of Tangier, an interesting room concerned with Roman religion and funeral rites, and other rooms are devoted to Moroccan arts including silks and ceramics from Fes.

Opposite the museum's entrance, and off the main interior courtyard, are the herb- and shrub-lined palace **gardens**, shaded by jacaranda trees.

Ville Nouvelle

Sprawling westwards and southwards from the ancient Medina is the European-built **Ville Nouvelle**. Much of its architecture and layout, especially immediately outside the Medina, is of Spanish origin, reflecting the influence of the city's large Spanish population during the nineteenth and early twentieth centuries.

Grand Socco

The **Grand Socco** is the obvious place to start a ramble around the town. Its name, like so many in Tangier, is a French–Spanish hybrid, proclaiming its origins as the main market square. The markets have since long gone, but the square remains a meeting place and its cafés make good spots to soak up the city's life. The Grand Socco's official but little-used name, **Place du 9 Avril 1947**, commemorates the visit of Sultan Mohammed V to the city on that date – an occasion when, for the first time and at some personal risk, he identified himself with the struggle for Moroccan independence.

A memorial to this event (in Arabic) is to be found amid the **Mendoubia Gardens**, flanking the northwest side of the square, which enclose the former offices of the

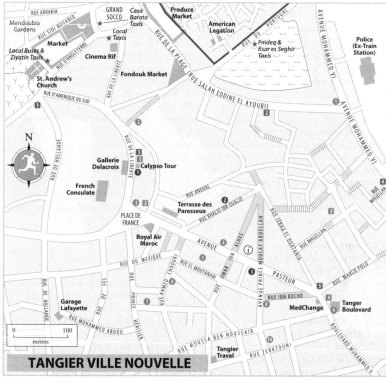

TANGIER VILLE NOUVELLE

■ ACCOMMODATION		● EATING					■ DRINKING & NIGHTLIFE		● SHOPPING	
Biarritz	4	Africa		La Pagode	7		Caid's Bar	1	Galerie Tindouf	1
Le Grand Hôtel Villa		Café Metropole	4	Le Saveur de Poisson	2		Le Coeur de Tanger	2	Les Insolites	2
de France	1	Café Porte	8	Rahmouni	10		Number One	4	Librairie	
El Minzah	3	Eric's Hamburger Shop	5	San Remo	6		The Tangerinn Pub	3	des Colonnes	3
Pension Miami	2	Gran Café de Paris	3	Terrasse Boulevard	9					
Rembrandt	5									

MALCOLM FORBES: TANGIER'S LAST TYCOON

The American publishing tycoon **Malcolm Forbes** bought the **Dar el Mendoub**, on Rue Mohammed Tazi in La Marshan, in 1970. His reason, ostensibly at least, was the acquisition of a base for launching and publishing an Arab-language version of *Forbes Magazine* – the "millionaires' journal". For the next two decades, until his death in 1990, he was a regular visitor to the city, and it was at Dar el Mendoub that he decided to host his last great extravagance, his **seventieth birthday party**, in 1989.

This was the grandest social occasion Tangier had seen since the days of Woolworths heiress Barbara Hutton (see page 77). Spending an estimated $2.5m, he brought in his friend **Elizabeth Taylor** as co-host and chartered a 747, a DC-8 and Concorde to fly in eight hundred of the world's rich and famous from New York and London. The party entertainment was on an equally imperial scale, including six hundred drummers, acrobats and dancers, and a *fantasia* – a cavalry charge which ends with the firing of muskets into the air – by three hundred Berber horsemen.

Forbes's party was a mixed **public relations exercise**, with even the gossip press feeling qualms about such a display of American affluence in a country like Morocco. However, Forbes most likely considered the party a success, for his guests included not just the celebrity rich – Gianni Agnelli, Robert Maxwell, Barbara Walters, Henry Kissinger – but half a dozen US state governors and the chief executives or presidents of scores of multinational corporations likely to advertise in his magazine. And, of course, it was tax deductible.

For a while Forbes opened part of Dar el Mendoub as a museum to display his curious collection of 119,000 lead soldiers, but after his death, his children sold the property to the government and it is now used as a VIP residence for royal and state guests.

Mendoub – the sultan's representative during the international years – and now home to the local Chamber of Commerce. Here there's also a spectacular banyan tree, said to be over 800 years old. Essentially now an open grassed area, the gardens are popular with local families who enjoy the small playground.

Place de France

In **Place de France**, south and uphill of the Grand Socco, the **cafés** are the main attraction – and at their best in the late afternoon and early evening, when an interesting mix of local and expatriate regulars turn out to watch and be watched. The seats to choose are outside the 1920s *Gran Café de Paris* (see page 84), a legendary **rendezvous** throughout the years of the International Zone. During World War II, this was notorious as a centre of deal making and intrigue between agents from Britain, America, Germany, Italy and Japan. Later the emphasis shifted to Morocco's own politics: the first nationalist paper, *La Voix du Maroc*, surfaced at the café, and the nationalist leader Allal el Fassi, exiled in Tangier from the French-occupied zone, set up his Istiqlal party headquarters nearby.

Terrasse des Paresseux

Just to the east of Place de France is a wide terrace-belvedere looking out over the Straits to Spain. Officially titled Place de Faro but known as **Terrasse des Paresseux** ("terrace of the lazy"), it's a great spot for people watching, and on a clear day the pay-for-use telescopes (1dh) afford a good view of the Spanish port of Tarifa.

St Andrew's Church

Bv d'Angleterre • Sun service 8.30am & 11am • At other times knock on the door and the caretaker will give you a tour • Donation expected

The nineteenth-century Anglican **Church of St Andrew** is one of the city's odder sights in its fusion of Moorish decoration, English country churchyard and flapping Scottish flag – the cross of St Andrew, to whom the church is dedicated (though, being an English church, they sometimes fly the cross of St George instead). The regular

1

congregation has fallen considerably but the church is still used for a Sunday morning service, when the numbers swell with worshippers from West African countries en route (hopefully) to a better life in Europe.

In the strangely serene graveyard, among the laments of early deaths from malaria, you come upon the tomb of **Walter Harris** (see page 533), the most brilliant of the chroniclers of "Old Morocco" in the closing decades of the nineteenth century and the beginning of the twentieth. Also buried here is **Dean** of *Dean's Bar* ("Missed by all and sundry"), a former London cocaine dealer (real name Don Kimfull) who tended the bar in the *El Minzah* hotel before opening his own place in 1937, and worked as a spy for British intelligence in Tangier during World War II; and **Caid Sir Harry Maclean**, the Scottish military adviser to Sultan Moulay Abd el Aziz at the turn of the twentieth century. Inside the church another Briton is commemorated, **Emily Keane**, who married the Shereef of Ouezzane in 1877 – at the time one of the most holy towns of the country (see page 84). Also look out for the Lord's Prayer engraved in exquisite Arabic calligraphy on an archway behind the altar.

La Marshan

To the west of the kasbah is **La Marshan**, an upmarket 1840s residential district that offers a pleasant meander through its rich spread of villas, consulates and royal properties. Here you'll also find *Café Hafa* (see page 84).

The beach

Tangier's **beach** is a pleasant place to escape the city streets. It's especially good for a daytime stroll, either on the beach itself or along the 3km-long promenade that runs between the sand and Avenue Mohammed VI. Lining the promenade is a string of cafés, some of which offer a place to change into/out of your beach wear as well as showers, deckchairs, food and drink. Swimming here is unfortunately not a good idea though as the water isn't very clean. *The Sun Beach* (99 Av Mohammed VI) is where Tennessee Williams wrote a first draft of *Cat on a Hot Tin Roof*, though renovations have stripped it of its original character. The promenade is quite safe at night, but it's advisable to avoid walking on the beach in the evenings.

ARRIVAL AND DEPARTURE   **TANGIER**

Tangier is one of the major transport hubs in Morocco. Travelling on into Morocco from Tangier is simplest either by **train** (the lines run from Meknes–Fez–Oujda or Rabat–Casablanca–Marrakesh; all trains stop at Asilah en route), or, if you are heading east to Tetouan, by **bus** or shared **grand taxi**.

private transfer with your Tangier accommodation, the only other transport option from the airport is to walk 2km to the main road, where you can pick up bus #9, which goes to Rue de Fez in town. To get to the airport from Tangier, most hotels will be able to organize a transfer for you, or you can rent a *grand taxi* from the Grand Socco.

BY PLANE

Tangier Ibn Battouta Airport (ⓦonda.ma/en) is off the N1 road 15km west of the city. It is served by a number of international airlines, many of them budget operators from Europe, and flights from Casablanca by RAM. On departure, be prepared for slow queues at immigration before flights to Europe. There are four banks/bureaux de change plus a couple of ATMs, cafés and shops. Car rental is also available here (see page 82). Royal Air Maroc have an office at 1 Pl de France, Ville Nouvelle (ⓦroyalairmaroc.com). Cream/ beige *grands taxis* line up outside the terminal; there is a notice board listing set prices at the terminal's exit and another at the taxi rank itself. Other than pre-organizing a

BY TRAIN

The first stage of the country's grand development of a 1500km high-speed rail (HSR) network is currently under construction between Tangier and Casablanca. Work began in 2011 and the section between Tangier and Kenitra (47km northeast of Rabat) is now complete. Work continues on the Casablanca to Kenitra sectionEven with a change in Kenitra it can take just under two hours to travel from Tanger to Rabat.Tangier's main train station, Tanger Ville, is 2km east of the Medina on the continuation of Av Mohammed V, and only 300m or so off the eastern end of the beach. The station was completely rebuilt in 2018 and has ATMs, cafés and shops. The best way to reach the station is by *petit taxi* (20dh

1

or so); it is also served by bus #16 from the bus station but not by any buses from the city centre. A convenient service from Tangier is the night train to Marrakesh, departing at 9.40pm and arriving at 8.10am; it's regularly full, so book ahead at any train station or Supratours office if possible.

Destinations Asilah (12 daily; 40min); Casablanca Voyageurs (8 direct daily; 4hr 40min–6hr 20min & 2 connecting daily; 7–8hr); Fez (4 direct & 1 connecting daily; 4hr 30min–5hr 10min); Marrakesh (1 direct overnight & 9 connecting daily; 8hr 30min–10hr 30min); Meknes (4 direct & 1 connecting daily; 4hr–4hr 15min); Rabat (8 direct & 3 connecting daily; 3hr 35min–5hr 30min); Souk el Arba du Gharb (11 daily; 2hr).

BY BUS

The *gare routière* is 2km south of the Ville Nouvelle on Pl Al Jamia al Arabia;a 15min walk from the centre or around 20dh in a *petit taxi*. With the exception of CTM, all long-distance buses operate from here including Supratours. The CTM *Gare Voyageurs* bus station is on Route de Tetouan (N2), approximately 5km south of the city centre. However, CTM has a ticket office in the *gare routière* from where they will transfer you to their bus station on a free shuttle bus.

Destinations Al Hoceima (1 CTM & over 5 others daily; 8–9hr); Asilah (No CTM services; over 10 others daily; 45min); Casablanca (4 CTM & over 10 others daily; 5hr 30min–6hr 30min); Chefchaouen (1 CTM & over 10 others daily, ask for a direct *sans détour* service; 3hr); Fez (3 CTM & 5 others daily; 6–8hr); Fnideq (for Ceuta; no CTM services; over 10 others daily; 2hr); Larache (3 CTM & over 10 others daily; 1hr 30min–2hr); Marrakesh (1 CTM & over 5 others daily; 9hr 30min); Meknes (2 CTM & 9 others daily; 4hr 30min–5hr 30min); Nador (2 CTM & over 5 others daily; 10–11hr); Rabat (4 CTM & over 10 others daily; 4–5hr); Tetouan (4 CTM & over 20 others daily; 1hr–1hr 30min).

BY GRAND TAXI

Grands taxis mostly operate from the *gare routière* and its immediate surrounds. From the rank in the *gare routière*, grands taxis run to/from Tanger Med port, Chefchaouen, Tetouan and Fnideq. Occasionally you may find a taxi direct to the Ceuta border, 2km beyond Fnideq. *Grands taxis* running to the Malabata beaches and Ksar es Seghir are parked along Av Moulay Idriss I, opposite the main bus exit. It's also possible to pick up *grands taxis* to Fnideq and Ksar es Seghir from Rue du Portugal, off Rue de la Plage at the southernmost corner of the Medina. For destinations in the immediate vicinity of Tangier, you may need to charter a *grand taxi* at the rank on the Grand Socco, though it's possible to get to places like the Caves of Hercules or Cap Malabata by shared *grand taxi* or city bus (see page 82).

Traffic can sometimes be gridlocked around the *gare routière*, thus lengthening the travel times listed below.

Destinations Asilah (1hr); Chefchaouen (2hr); Fnideq (for Ceuta; 1hr); Ksar es Seghir (30min); Tanger Med port (1hr); Tetouan (1hr).

BY FERRY

Morocco lies just a short 14km from Spain and fast hydrofoils can take just 30 (choppy) minutes to cross. Ferries for Tarifa in Spain arrive and depart from the old port, Tanger Ville. All other ferries run to and from Tanger Med Gare Maritime, some 40km northeast of the city. Reservations are useful at the end of the Easter week and during the first and last weeks of Aug. Full details of routes can be found in "Basics" (see page 30); be aware, too, that immigration formalities (see page 57) take place as you are sailing to Morocco, except when you are sailing from Tarifa where immigration is performed in the terminal building prior to embarkation. Departing Morocco, each passenger needs an embarkation form and departure card, which must be stamped by the port police prior to boarding. At both ports, all passengers must clear a security check, so allow plenty of time for this. Tickets and timetables can be obtained from any travel agent in Tangier or from the ferry companies themselves (see page 30). Remember to scrutinize timetables carefully as Spain is one hour ahead of Morocco local time.

Tanger Med Gare Maritime ⓦtangermed-passagers. com. Ticket booths for all the ferry companies (see page 30), plus banks, bureaux de change, ATMs and cafés are in the port terminal building and wi-fi is available. Transport options between the city and port include by train (7.15am, 2.50pm & 6pm from Tanger Ville; 9.45am, 11am & 5.35pm from Tanger Med; 1hr; 32dh, but check the ONCF website ⓦoncf.ma for the up-to-date schedule); there is a free 10-minute shuttle bus for the 3km between Tanger Med train station and the ferry terminal. Bus # I-3 (a capital 'i', not an L or 1) runs every hour (5.30am–10pm from Tanger Ville train station; 6.15am-11.15pm from Tanger Med Gare Maritime; 1hr10min; 7dh). *Grand taxis* take about 1hr.

Destinations Algeciras (22-24 daily; 30min fast ferry, 1hr 30min–2hr slower ferries); Barcelona (1 daily; 24–27hr); Genoa via Barcelona (2 weekly; 48–50 hr); Gibraltar (weekly, 1hr 30min–2hr); Sète (3 weekly; 35hr).

Port de Tanger Ville Av Mohammed VI ⓦtangerport. com. All hydrofoil "fast" ferries to/from Tarifa operate from the old port where the ferry terminal has been modernised and renovated. There are bureaux de change, ATMs and cafés. It's a relatively short – though at times uphill – 20min walk into the centre from the port or a short ride by *petit taxi* (expect exorbitant rates).

INFORMATION

Tourist information The tourist office, ONMT Délégation de Tourisme, is at 29 Av Pasteur (Mon–Fri 8.30am–4.30pm; ☏0539 948050); official guides can be hired here.

1

GETTING AROUND

By bus City buses are not much use to tourists. The most useful route is #2, which runs from St Andrew's Church in the Grand Socco to Ziyatin and on to the village of Jabila, not far from the Caves of Hercules. Route #9 goes from Rue de Fez along the Rabat road to the airport turn-off, some 2km from the airport itself. Route #16 connects the train station and the bus station, and runs on to Cape Malabata, but does not serve the city centre.

By grand taxi *Grands taxis* (large cream/beige Mercedes) are permitted to carry up to six passengers.

By petit taxi Small blue/green *petits taxis* (which carry just three passengers) can be flagged down around the town.

By car While Tangier's traffic is rarely gridlocked and a car can be handy for day-trips within the region, the city itself is small enough to explore on foot. Agencies include Amine Car, 43 Av Mohammed V (w aminecar.pro.ma); Avis, airport (w avis.com); Estrella Car, 1 Rue Allal Ben Abdellah (w rentcartanger.com); Europcar, 87 Bd Mohammed V (and airport (w europcar.com).

ACCOMMODATION

Tangier has a wide range of hotels and *pensions*, and finding a room is rarely much of a problem. The city does, however, get crowded during July and Aug, when many Moroccan families holiday here. Cheaper places hike up their prices at this time of year, and you'll often get a better deal at one of the mid-range hotels.

MEDINA, SEE MAP PAGE 75

Continental 36 Rue Dar Baroud ☎0539 931024. Commanding a great view over the port and Straits, the *Continental* opened in 1870, with Queen Victoria's son Alfred its first official guest. Today, the hotel has a somewhat faded grandeur but it's still comfortable enough and the service is good. Ask to see a selection of rooms before checking in. The multistorey hotel is alcohol-free and there's no lift, but porters are always available. BB €

★ **Dar Chams Tanja** 2–4 Rue Jnan Kabtan, Bab el Assa w darchamstanja.com. One of the best *maisons d'hôte* in the Medina, with hands-on multilingual owners. Surprisingly spacious inside, the large uncluttered rooms all have a/c and satellite TV, and some enjoy glorious port and bay views. There's a floor dedicated to wellness, offering a hammam, separate massage room, and a chill-out room to savour the experience. Meals can be taken formally in the dining room or casually up on the roof terrace. BB €€€

Dar Kasbah 12 Rue de la Kasbah w dar-kasbah.com. Located just outside the Medina near Bab Gzenaya in a striking European-built former 19th-century telegraph office, this place has airy single, double and quad rooms with antique furniture, wooden floors and nice modern artwork, some with sea views, and oozes with character. There's a lounge, rooftop terrace and courtyard restaurant. €€

Dar Nour 20 Rue Gourna, in the kasbah, off Rue Sidi Ahmed Boukouja w darnour.com. A perennially popular *maison d'hôte* run by an attentive English-speaking French trio who have created ten individually styled rooms and suites in what was once five small houses. There are a number of communal areas, including little nooks and crannies perfect for a spot of quiet reading, interesting *objets d'art* throughout, and a well-stocked library. Literally topping it all off are three terraces with sweeping views of the Medina and Straits – a favourite spot for evening cocktails. BB €€

Dar Rif 17 Rue Mohamed Bergach ☎0539 939497. This friendly small B&B with traditional colorful décor is on the same street as Dar Jameel (see 84), both a five-minute walk away from Grand Socco. Not all rooms have much natural light but are comfortable and en suite and there are views of the port from the roof terrace. Generous breakfasts and will give you a packed one if having an early start. Also runs the Rif Kebdani restaurant (see page 84) 100m away. BB €

Mamora 19 Av Mokhtar Ahrdan ☎0539 934105. A little bit sterile but centrally located in the heart of the Medina and with very friendly, helpful staff. The fourteen clean, pleasant rooms are spacious and have satellite TV and good views, but the bathrooms are small and hot water can be a bit sporadic. Avoid the ones overlooking the Grand Mosque as the calls to prayer can be noisy. €€

★ **Riad Jamila** 6 Rue Mohammed Bergach ☎0539 334680. Set on five levels but with only eight a/c rooms arranged around an ornate central courtyard. Beautifully decorated with mosaic tiled walls, traditional furnishings and colourful fabrics, this leans towards boutique-style but is surprisingly well-priced. Some rooms have four-poster beds and views of the Straits. Breakfast is taken in a rooftop sunroom. BB €€

★ **La Tangerina** 19 Riad Sultan, in the kasbah w latangerina.com. Pared-down Mediterranean elegance, stylishly composed interiors, an ambience of simple luxury and an outstanding terrace overlooking the Straits continue to rate this well-run guesthouse as one of Tangier's best. The rooms are arranged around a courtyard and cover a range of budgets while the attentive service and delicious cuisine are first-class. BB €€€

VILLE NOUVELLE AND SEAFRONT, SEE MAPS PAGES 72 AND 78

It's a steep climb from the port or bus station to the Ville Nouvelle, so you may want to grab a taxi if carrying heavy luggage.

Biarritz 104 Av Mohammed VI ☎0539 932473. A family-run protectorate-era budget hotel within a short (and flat) walk from the port's gates. A marbled staircase leads to comfortable en suite rooms, some with a balcony, some triples, and a fair bit of old-fashioned charm. Ask for a room away from the busy road. €

Bristol 14 Rue el Antaki ☎0539 944347. Situated 100m uphill from the beach, this is a good bet, with large brightly coloured rooms with TVs and compact bathrooms. Rooms on the upper floors – accessed by an antique elevator – miss most of the noise from the street-level restaurant-bar. €

Camping Miramonte Marshan ☎0539 423322, Ⓦ campingmiramonte.com. This is one of the best campsites on the Atlantic coast, but unfortunately access for camper vans is a little difficult. There are well-maintained grounds that include electrified sites, ablutions with hot water, motel-style rooms, self-contained bungalows, two restaurants, two swimming pools and a bar. Gets pretty busy and noisy in Aug. It's best accessed by the oceanside road that links the port with the city's Marshan neighbourhood (see page 80). Camping €, rooms €, bungalow €€

Dar Omar Khayam 26 Rue el Antaki Ⓦ daromarkhayam. com. This former convent is a popular stalwart of Tangier's budget accommodations. You can opt for cell-like singles with shared bathrooms or splash out on en suite doubles with a/c. Rooms at the rear are quieter. Breakfast is taken in the pleasant courtyard garden. BB €

El Djenina 8 Rue el Antaki Ⓦ hoteleldjenina.com. Though the bland but modern rooms are a little on the small side, they are all en suite with TV and always sparkling clean. It's well managed and only a short walk from the beach. €

Le Grand Hôtel Villa de France Cnr Rue de Hollande & Bv d'Angleterre ☎0539 333111. Built in the late 18th century but completely restored, this hotel looks out over St Andrew's Church and beyond to the ocean; this was the view from room 35 (refurbished to its past glory as a pseudo-museum), where French impressionist Henri Matisse painted his famous *Vue de la fenêtre à Tanger* (*View from a Window in Tangier*) in 1912. There's a range of rooms and suites available, most with a distant sea view, plus a fine-dining restaurant, piano bar and expansive gardens. While the refurbished decor leans a bit too much to kitsch Orientalism,

the overall ambiance is still one of grandness. BB €€

El Minzah 85 Rue el Houria (Rue de la Liberté) Ⓦ leroyal.com/en/AFRICA. Built in 1930, this remains one of Morocco's most prestigious hotels, with a wonderful garden, a huge pool overlooking the sea and town, several (pricey) restaurants and bars, and a spa with hammam and gym. The slightly faded grandeur rooms are still worth the price for the hotel's nostalgic atmosphere. BB €€€

Mövenpick Av Mohammed VI ☎0539 329300, Ⓦ movenpick.com. Consistently one of Tangier's better deluxe hotels, 3km east of town on the road to Malabata, with all the facilities you'd expect from this Swiss chain – three restaurants, a pool, health club, sauna and casino. There's an array of room options (two of which have been adapted for wheelchair users) mostly offering splendid sea views. €€€€

Pension Miami 126 Rue de la Plage ☎0539 932900. Beautifully tiled old Spanish townhouse said to be over 110 years old. One of many very cheap hotels around Rue de la Plage with clean rooms, some with balconies, squat toilets on each corridor and two hot showers downstairs. Friendly reception staff. €

Rembrandt Cnr Avs Pasteur and Mohammed V Ⓦ rembrandthotel.ma. One of the city's better value hotels, exuding a 1950s feel while still offering modern, spacious rooms (ask for a sea view) with all the mod cons. Downstairs there's an average restaurant, a shaded poolside café and a sultry piano-lounge bar. The service is usually good and there's free parking. BB €

OUT OF TOWN, SEE MAP PAGE 72

Villa Josephine 231 Rue de la Montagne, Sidi Masmoudi Ⓦ villajosephine-tanger.com. Resplendent in antiques, oak panelling and Moroccan carpets, the villa has ten opulent suites – five with private balconies or terraces overlooking the sea. Built in the 1920s by Walter Harris (see page 533) and a former summer residence of Pasha el Glaoui (see page 304) the estate is in impeccable condition. There's also a colonial-esque bar and a very good restaurant (non-guests welcome) offering daytime snacks and a French-inspired dinner menu served either inside the classy restaurant or on the outdoor poolside terrace with fantastic Straits views. €€€€

EATING

SEE MAPS PAGES 75 AND 78

Tangier is certainly no culinary hot spot, but the city's continuing rejuvenation has encouraged a general rise in the standard and variety available, plus there's now a wealth of attractive cafés and patisseries too. Most top-end restaurants serve alcohol.

A L'anglaise 37 Rue de la Kasbah ☎0635 186766. This hole-in-the-wall pavement café-restaurant is in the female owner-manager's house, which perhaps explains the warm atmosphere, eclectic furnishings and excellent

home-cooked dishes. The blackboard menu covers most traditional dishes, including pastilla, while the breakfast spread is a renowned tummy stretcher. Try and get a table on the lovely upstairs terrace. No alcohol. €€

Marhaba Palace 26 Palais Ahannar, just outside the Medina ☎0539 937927. One of a number of "palaces" catering to tourists, this one rates highly due to its warm ambience, unobtrusive musicians and good Moroccan food. The interior is indeed palatial in style with faux-zellij tiling,

1

antiques and colourful furniture. Set menus from €€€

★ **El Morocco Club** Place du Tabor, Kasbah ⊕ elmorocco club.ma. This French-owned Kasbah landmark is open for breakfasts and light meals in the terrace café, and lunch and dinner in the fine dining restaurant with its beautifully decorated rooms. Great for a treat, the evening menu might feature the likes of foie gras with rose-flavoured tomatoes, sardines with chermoula sauce or seafood couscous (mains €€). Plus there are gooey desserts and an extensive wine list. The piano bar is open from 7.30pm; look out for the photographs of Tangier's famous writers on the walls. €€€

Le Salon Bleu 71 Rue Amrah ☎ 0539 371618. There are tremendous views over the Straights (to Tarifa in Spain on a clear day) from the rooftop cushioned terraces of *Le Salon Bleu*, which make it a great place for (non-alcoholic) sundowners - try the fresh watermelon or lemon juice. The restaurant offers two fixed priced menus or you can order a la carte, and the grilled fish and tajines are particularly good. €€

Rif Kabdani 14 Rue Dar Baroud ☎ 0539 371760. In a handy location close to the *Hotel Continental*, and with cosy nooks and traditional decor, this offers a menu of Moroccan standards that out-tastes much of its fancier and more expensive competition. The complimentary tapas and mint tea are a bonus, as are the typically French-style desserts like lemon tart or strawberry panna cotta and attentive service. No alcohol. €

VILLE NOUVELLE AND SEAFRONT

Africa 83 Rue Salah Eddine Ayoubi ☎ 0539 935436. A simply decorated and peaceful dining room known for its excellent-value four-course set menu. There's also a la carte standards such as lamb tajine and beef couscous. €

Anna e Paolo 77 Av Prince Héritier ☎ 0539 944617. Managed by Anna and Paolo themselves, this is quite simply the best Italian food in Tangier. The dark interior is decorated with pictures of old Italy and the menu bows to tradition with a host of authentic pizza, pasta (the ravioli *neri* is recommended), meat and seafood dishes. €€

El Dorado 21 Rue Allal Ben Abdallah. A stalwart of Tangier's restaurant scene with a dependable Moroccan-Spanish menu that also includes a good selection of seafood dishes. Try their couscous on Fri or the good-value paella on Sun. You can dine alfresco at the back. €€

Eric's Hamburger Shop Arcade Mentoubi, between Av Pasteur and Rue el Moutanabi. It doesn't get much simpler than this: *Eric's* has been open 24/7 since 1968 and succeeds because it doesn't claim to be anything other than a cheap diner. There's a row of wooden stools lined up against the stainless steel counter, and the menu consists of four hamburgers and four hot dogs. Close to some of the city's seedier nightclubs, it's immensely more attractive at midnight than midday. No alcohol. €

★ **Le Saveur de Poisson** 2 Escalier Waller ☎ 0539

336326. On the stairs leading to the medina, this friendly family-run restaurant has just one room, cluttered with paintings, and an adjoining kitchen, and is often packed with in-the-know locals. There's just a single five- to six course *menu du jour* dominated by seafood from the adjacent market, eaten with wooden cutlery on clay plates. Count on dishes like squid baked with coriander, cumin-scented plaice or *merlan* (whiting) pan-fried in butter with garlic, onions and spinach. Their in-house fruit punch is brewed daily in a big vat in the kitchen. No alcohol. Closed during Ramadan. €€€

San Remo 15 Rue Ahmed Chaouki ☎ 0539 938451. This popular restaurant serves up credible, good-value Mediterranean cooking, including a dependable selection of seafood and meat grills. There's also a good choice of pizzas, available either in-house or from their cheaper pizzeria across the road. €€

Valencia 6 Av Youssef Ben Tachfine ☎ 0539 945146. A simply furnished fish restaurant, very popular with both locals and tourists. The straightforward menu includes a variety of *friture* (fried) or *grillé* (grilled) dishes, with *calamars* (calamari), *merlan* (whiting) and sole the most prevalent. No alcohol. €€

CAFÉS

Café Baba Rue Zaitouni; ☎ 0539 309943. Very smoky and slightly edgy, this legendary hole in the wall café has been going strong since 1941. In the late-1940s, American socialite Barbara Hutton used to drink tea on the balcony, but perhaps the most famous image on its wall of photographs of celebrity visitors is the one of Keith Richards lighting up a kif pipe at one of Cafe Baba's tables (he sent it to them himself). The mint tea is still good.

Café Hafa Off Av Hadj Mohamed Tazi, La Marshan. A ramshackle affair and popular locals' café that dates back to 1921, with steep terraces hugging a cliffside looking directly out to the Straits. While the service can be overly casual, the mint tea is good and the views sublime.

Café Metropole 27 Av Pasteur. The *Metropole* serves one of the best *cafés au lait* in town; pastries can be bought across the road at *Pâtisserie Le Petit Prince* and consumed at your table.

Café Porte Cnr Av Prince Moulay Abdellah and Rue Ibn Rochd ☎ 0661 163644. A 1950s café, the *Porte* is popular with a young crowd who come for the ice-cream selection and free wi-fi. There's also a decent menu offering breakfast and light meals.

Café Tingis Petit Socco. A favourite haunt of Tennessee Williams and Paul Bowles, this traditional high-ceilinged café remains full of charm and character. A raised terrace looks down upon the Petit Socco and is the best spot in the Medina for people watching. The café's sole concession to the twenty-first century is a flat-screen TV showing football matches.

1

★**Gran Café de Paris** Pl de France. Tangier's most famous café from its conspiratorial past (see page 79). There are two levels of seating inside, including the original 1920s section with studded leather seats. Outside there's the standard line of chairs for people watching. It's still a staple meeting place for expats and usually a good place to track down English newspapers in the morning and get a coffee and pastry.

Matisse Residence Nasser, 53 Rue Allal Ben Abdallah ☎0539 340050. A classy, French-owned patisserie that offers a good selection of pastries, biscuits and deliciously creamy gâteaux (eat in or take away), as well as artisan bread and even a few bottles of wine.

Panorama 6 Av Mohammed VI ☎0539 946331. A modern café located on the seafront with magnificent ocean views from the deck. The service though is slow and the food (from sandwiches to steaks; mains€) a little uninteresting, but it's a good stop for a coffee and pastry on a walk along the promenade. Useful for train travellers too, as it's right next to Tanger Ville train station and opens early.

Rahmouni 35 Av Prince Moulay Abdellah ☎0539 940787. A well-established family-run patisserie franchise – there's another branch in Tetouan – renowned for its high quality, reasonably priced biscuits and cakes and sweet and savoury pastries.

Terrasse Boulevard Tanger Bd Complex, 23 Av Mohammed V ☎0553 036848. This café has magical views of the port and Straits, and is comfortable at any time of the year thanks to ceiling-high glass windbreakers and a covered roof. If you want more than a coffee, they have a pretty good menu of light meals, as well as milkshakes and fresh juices.

Traiteur al Mouatamid Bnou Abbad 16 Rue al Mouatamid Ibn Abadd ☎0539 341725. Popular with local Tanjawis catering for a party or celebration, this patisserie offers tray upon tray of sweet biscuits (€/100g) and pastries within a stunning Moroccan zellij (mosaics) interior.

DRINKING AND NIGHTLIFE

SEE MAPS PAGES 72 AND 78

The choice of bars and clubs in Tangier is fairly limited, and many are either stuck in a time warp or are the domain of hard drinking, heavy smoking Moroccan men. Additionally, the famous beach bars along Avenue Mohammed V1 have all been demolished to make way for the new marina. Nonetheless new places are popping up too as the city reinvents itself and young Tangerines (male and female) demand fashionable places to socialise, although some tend to be grossly expensive. Be careful leaving late at night as the streets can be none too safe; best to ask the staff to call a taxi.

555 Av Mohammed VI, opposite the Atlas Rif Hotel ⓦbeachclub555.com. This massive modern European-style nightclub that can accommodate 1500 serves up body-thumping dance mixes until dawn - don't even think about arriving until after midnight. Often hosts international DJs and groups can book a VIP table with a bottle of alcohol. Both the entrance fee and the drinks are expensive, but Ladies Night (free entry and drinks) is every Fri.

Caid's Bar Hôtel el Minzah, 85 Rue de la Liberté ☎0539 333444. Classy establishment that oozes nostalgia for Tangier's International Zone days. There's a pianist tinkling away most nights, while over the bar is the centrepiece of the ritzy decor, a grand painting of Caid Sir Harry Maclean, former commander in chief of the sultan's army (see page 80). During the day you can sit by the swimming pool.

★**Chellah Beach Club** Chellah Hôtel, 47-49 Rue Allal Ben Abdellah ☎0539 321002. This was a beachside bar, and while it has kept its name, because of the new marina it has moved into the Chellah Hôtel in Ville Nouvelle. Nonetheless it remains an especially popular bar with both locals and expats thanks to its fun atmosphere and lack of pretension. The music (live and DJs), ranges from jazz and flamenco, to Moroccan Gnaoua.

Le Coeur de Tanger 1 Rue Annoual, Pl de France. Large easy-going bar upstairs from *Gran Café de Paris* (see page 85); the entrance is down a side street. It has a balcony overlooking the action in Place de France, the beer, wine and other drinks are reasonably priced, and there's a good mix of young locals and visitors as hotels often steer people here looking for a drink. A bonus is the free tapas that do the rounds.

London's Pub 15 Rue Al Mansour Eddahbi ☎0539 942094. As the name suggests, modelled on a typical English pub with a wood-panelled interior and long bar, popular with groups of young middle-class Moroccans after work or to watch the football and for the novelty of cold pints of Moroccan beer on tap (rarely seen). Little plates of complimentary tapas are brought around, and there's a decent dinner menu.

Number One 1 Av Mohamed V ☎0539 941674. This cosy little bar has funky kitsch décor, loads of interesting photos and newspaper articles on the walls, chilled music, and a tapas restaurant in the room next door. The draft beer is cold, and it also has a good, if not expensive, selection of wines and spirits.

The Tangerinn Pub 16 Rue Magellan, below the Hôtel el Muniria ☎0613 321594. One of Tangier's last surviving International Zone relics – there's a faded framed picture of Jack Kerouac on the wall – the *Tangerinn* is more reminiscent of a private club but without the dress standards. The clientele nowadays is mostly local (both male and female), the music is often loud and the service pretty good.

Regine Club 8 Rue al Mansour Eddahbi ☎0675 031247. Mainstream club firmly stuck in the 1980s with mirror balls

1

TANGIER'S ART GALLERIES

There's a vibrant **art scene** in Tangier, with at least two or three **exhibitions** on at any given time. Up-to-date **listings** and information on various small galleries can be found in the window of Bab el Fen, a well-stocked art supply shop at 25 Rue Ibn Rochd, opposite the *Rembrandt Hotel*.

Galerie d'Art Contemporain Mohamed Drissi 52 Bv d'Angleterre, Ville Nouvelle ☎ 0539 936073. Located in the former British Consulate built in 1898 and surrounded by a magnificent garden, with a number of rooms hosting contemporary works by mainly Moroccan and European artists. Admission 10dh.

Galerie Delacroix 86 Rue de la Liberté, Ville Nouvelle ☎ 0539 941054. The gallery for Tangier's

Institut Français du Nord (see page 85), with regular exhibitions by Moroccan artists, and sometimes non-Moroccans residing in Tangier.

★ **Medina Art Gallery** 30 Av Abou Chouabib Doukali, Ville Nouvelle ⓦ medinagallery.com. Founded in 1999 by local artists Saïd Kadiri and Omar Salhi, this gallery aims to discover new local talent and refocus attention on some of the past Moroccan masters, such as Mohamed Hamri.

Volubilis Art Gallery 6 Sidi Boukouja, Kasbah ☎ 0539 333875. This little gallery has regular exhibitions of mainly Moroccan artists, including owner Mohamed Raïss El Fenni.

and padded booth seating. It's larger and a little cheaper than most, and is especially fun after midnight. Happy hour

2-for-1 drinks Mon 11pm–1am. Free admission.

FESTIVALS AND ENTERTAINMENT

The city's possibilities for films, theatre, the occasional concert and, at the right time of year, festivals are refreshingly varied nowadays.

American Legation (TALIM) 8 Rue d'Amérique, Medina ⓦ legation.org. The American Legation (see page 76) often hosts free cultural events such as live performances, book launches and discussions on a range of themes, such as North African art, military history and languages.

Cinema Rif Grand Socco ⓦ cinemathequedetanger. com. This renovated 1930s Art Deco landmark has nightly showings of new releases, documentaries and classics, plus regular week-long film festivals, including the Mediterranean Short Film Festival of Tangier (ⓦ ccm.ma). Check beforehand if the film is dubbed into Arabic.

Institut Français du Nord 1 Rue Hassan Ibn Ouazzane,

Ville Nouvelle ⓦ if-maroc.org/tanger. The cultural arm of the French government presents a weekly programme of events that includes art & literary functions, as well as films and live performances from its 170-seater theatre.

Instituto Cervantes de Tanger 99 Av Sidi Mohammed Ben Abdallah, Ville Nouvelle ⓦ tanger.cervantes.es. Like its French counterpart, this branch of Spain's cultural arm is enthusiastically involved in Tangier's social scene, providing a weekly programme of film screenings, discussions, concerts and general cultural exchange.

TanJazz ⓦ tanjazz.org. Highly regarded jazz festival, attracting quality artists from Europe, the Americas, Africa as well as the odd performer from Asia and Australia, which takes place in a number of venues over four days in Sept.

SHOPPING

SEE MAPS PAGES 72, 75 AND 78

The vast majority of craftwork found in the city's market stalls and stores are produced elsewhere in Morocco, something worth considering if you're travelling further into the country.

Boutique Majid 66 Rue Almohades, Medina ⓦ boutique majid.com. A decades-old antique and souvenir emporium selling rugs, jewellery, pottery, wood and metal crafts, textiles and silk embroideries and clothing. Majid himself might be on hand with his entertaining stories about celebrity visitors.

Ensemble Artisanal Cnr Rue Belgique & Rue M'sallah (left-hand side, going west from the Pl de France). A government-run centre that both produces and sells Moroccan crafts, such as *zellij* (mosaics), woodwork and book binding. There's virtually no haggling which often relates to higher prices than what you might get elsewhere,

but without the stress. It's recently renovated and is a pleasure to stroll around and browse.

★ **Galerie Tindouf** 72 Rue de la Liberté, opposite Galerie Delacroix ⓦ galerietindouf.com. One of the better-quality junk/antique shops, with a good array of hand-embroidered cushions and throws, carpets, Moroccan lamps and ceramics from both Fez and Salé.

Les Insolites 28 Rue Khalid Ibn Oualid, off Av Pasteur. The hippest bookstore in Tangier with friendly French owners, showcasing Moroccan and North African contemporary writers alongside classics from Paul Bowles, William Burroughs, Tennessee Williams and the like. There's also an excellent choice of modern art for sale and light lunches and tea can be taken at the pavement tables.

Librairie des Colonnes 54 Av Pasteur ⓦ librairie-des-colonnes.com. Tangier's premier bookshop with a selection of souvenir coffee table books as well as English-language classics.

Volubilis Boutique 15 Petit Socco, Medina. Shop for

the artist and designer Mohamed Raiss el Fenni, with an interesting mix of traditional Moroccan and Western clothing and accessories on offer, as well as paintings.

DIRECTORY

Banks and exchange Most banks, as well as a number of private bureaux de change, are grouped along Av Pasteur and Av Mohammed V. BMCE has branches at 21 Av Pasteur and in the Grand Socco, both with ATMs, and SGMB also has a Grand Socco branch with ATM. MedChange at 5 Av Mohammed V, near the junction with Av Pasteur opens 9am–10pm daily, as does Best Change at 91 Rue Siaghine, off the Petit Socco in the Medina.

Golf Royal Country Club of Tangier, Route de Boubana ⓦ royalgolfdetanger.com. 18-holes, open daily except Mon 7am-8pm, clubs, caddies and carts can be hired.

Hospitals Clinique Assalam, 10 Av de la Paix, off Av Moulay Youssef to the west of the *gare routière* (ⓦ cliniqueassalam. com), is regarded as the best private clinic in Tangier for medical emergencies. Closer to the city centre is Hôpital Espagnol ☎ 0539 931018 on Rue de l'Hôpital Espagnol near Pl Oued el Makhazine. For a private ambulance, call ☎ 0539 954040 or ☎ 0539 946976.

Internet access Almost all hotels offer Wi-Fi, as do many cafés.

Pharmacies There are several English-speaking pharmacies on Pl de France and along Av Pasteur. They are generally open Mon-Fri 9am-1pm & 4-8pm, Sat 9am-1pm. A roster of all-night and weekend pharmacies is displayed in every *pharmacie* window. Pharmacists can also recommend local doctors.

Police There are several police posts around the city including one on the Grand Socco and in the kasbah. Emergency ☎ 19.

Post office The main Poste Maroc office is at 33 Bd Mohammed V and has a poste restante service (Mon–Fri 8am–6pm, Sat 8am–noon).

Travel agencies The following can organize ferry tickets and other transport, as well as local tours. Calypso Tour, 71 bis Rue de la Liberté (ⓦ calypsotanger.com); Euro Maroc Travel, 67 Av la Résistance (ⓦ euromaroctravel.com); Tangier Travel, 40 Rue Zerktouni (ⓦ tangiertravel.ma).

The Caves of Hercules

16km outside Tangier and 5km south of Cap Spartel • Charge

To the south of **Cap Spartel**, Africa's most northwesterly promontory, begins the vast and wild Atlantic, known locally as Robinson Plage. It is broken only by a rocky spit, 5km from the Cape, which is home to the **Caves of Hercules** (Les Grottes d'Hercule), something of a symbol for Tangier, with their strange sea window shaped like a map of Africa. The name, like Hercules' legendary founding of Tangier, is purely fanciful, but the caves make an attractive excursion from Tangier. Natural formations, which were occupied in prehistoric times, the caves are most striking for a man-made addition – thousands of disc-shaped erosions created by centuries of **quarrying** for millstones. There were still people cutting stones here for a living until the 1920s, but by that time their place was beginning to be taken by professional guides and discreet sex hustlers; it must have made an exotic brothel. The caves are a couple of minutes' walk downhill from the Hotel Le Mirage (below) and are accessed by descending a narrow set of stairs that can at times be slippery from the ocean mist.

If you feel like staying by the sea for a few days, the **beach** here can be a pleasant base (see below); outside of July and August only stray groups of visitors share the long surf beaches. Take care with currents, however, which can be very dangerous even near the shore.

ARRIVAL AND DEPARTURE

CAVES OF HERCULES

By bus On summer weekends, the #2 bus runs here from St Andrew's Church by the Grand Socco in Tangier (daily 9am, 11am & 4pm; 45min); at other times it runs to the nearby village of Jabila, a long walk from the caves – you're better off alighting before then, at Ziyatin on the old airport road, from where there are connecting taxis to the caves.

By grand taxi You can charter a *grand taxi* from the

Grand Socco or get to Ziyatin in shared *grands taxis* from St Andrew's Church. For the return journey to Tangier there are *grands taxis* by the caves themselves, and there's another taxi rank by the Hotel Le Mirage itself, opposite Camping Achakar.

By car The caves are a 15min drive from Tangier, travelling west of the city via the plush residential quarter of La Vieille

1

Montagne and Cap Spartel. You can make a round trip by continuing along the coast road, then take either the minor road through Jabila or the faster main road (N1) back to Tangier.

ACCOMMODATION AND EATING

Camping Achakar ☎ 0612 249727. Close to the caves, this pleasant, well-wooded campsite has grass pitches and twelve bungalows that sleep four. Showers are clean but usually cold, and there's a café, restaurant, small shop and children's playground. Camping €, bungalow €

Le Mirage ⓦ lemirage.com. This upmarket clifftop complex of luxury bungalows and villas is a two-minute walk from the caves and has full facilities including a swimming pool. The restaurant and piano bar are open to non-residents and make a very pleasant, albeit expensive, day-trip lunch stop. BB €€€

East of Tangier

The best beaches in the immediate vicinity of Tangier are to be found at **Cap Malabata**, where much wealthy villa development has been taking place, but long open swathes of sandy beach can still be found. Beyond here, **Ksar es Seghir** offers a pleasant day by the sea, or a stop on the coast road to Ceuta. Inaugurated in 2007, the **Tanger Med port complex** near the village of Dalia, 20km from Ceuta, is still being expanded and together with a new road and rail network, has transformed the rugged coastline into a busy trade hub.

Cap Malabata

Bus #15 or #16 (every 45min; 5.30am–10pm) from the Grand Socco in Tangier, or *grand taxi* from Av Moulay Idriss I, opposite the *gare routière* main exit

The bay east of Tangier is flanked by long stretches of beach and a chain of elderly villas and newer apartment blocks until you reach **Cap Malabata**, which has a couple of intermittently open hotels and some attractive stretches of beach. Further on, an old Portuguese fort on an outcrop makes a good destination for coastal walks.

Ksar es Seghir

Buses travelling between Tangier and Fnideq (1hr; see page 81) stop at the junction in the centre of town; shared *grands taxis* depart from Tangier's Rue de Portugal

The formerly picturesque little fishing port of **KSAR ES SEGHIR** has grown a little ugly in recent years, with a modern breakwater constructed at its western entrance and the autoroute from the Tanger Med port towering over the village to its south. Although it continues to attract a fair number of Moroccan beach campers in summer, it now sees few European visitors. Just across the river from the town centre lie the remains of a **medieval Islamic town** and **Portuguese fortress** (there's a plan of the site posted up by the west side of the bridge). Ksar es Seghir has been of specific interest to archaeologists, being positioned at the meeting point of three distinct terrains: the Habt (Atlantic lowlands), Jabala (sandstone hills), and the Rif mountains.

ACCOMMODATION AND EATING

Diamant Bleu At the western entrance to town; often closed Jan, Feb, Nov & Dec. With a nice view of the coast, this restaurant offers a Moroccan and Mediterranean menu, specializing in seafood. €€

Ksar al Majaz N16 Hwy, 3km from the Tanger Med port ☎ 0539 593647. Block-type hotel built to take advantage of passing trade from the new port. Lacking any real character, the modern rooms are nonetheless comfortable

and good value and there's a seasonal outdoor pool and sun terrace. There are a number of café-restaurants close by. €€

Saif Tarifa Beach On the N16 or old coastal road, 18km from Tangier, 12km before town ⓦ saifhotels.com. A smart modern place with comfortable and spacious en suite rooms and suites overlooking the sea, a good-sized pool and terrace next to the beach, and a restaurant serving Moroccan staples and seafood. €€

Asilah

The first town south of Tangier – and first stop on the train line – **ASILAH** (sometimes spelt Assilah) is one of the most elegant of the old Portuguese Atlantic ports, small, clean and easy to navigate. First impressions are of wonderful square stone ramparts, flanked by palms, and an outstanding beach – an immense sweep of sand stretching to the north halfway to Tangier. The town's **Medina** is one of the most attractive in the country, colourwashed in pastel shades, and with a series of murals painted for the town's **International Cultural Festival** (3–4 weeks in Aug; ⓦc-assilah.com), which attracts performers from around the world with a programme of art, dance, film, music and poetry.

Before the tourists and the International Festival, Asilah was just a small fishing port, quietly stagnating after the indifference of Spanish colonial administration. Whitewashed and cleaned up, it now has a prosperous feel to it, with a new Grand Mosque, wide paved seaside promenade and swish property developments. There's a villagers' **market**, at its liveliest on Thursday and Sunday, held on Avenue Moulay Ismail below the *grand taxi* stand. As with Tangier, the **beach** is the main focus of life in summer. The most popular stretches are to the north of the town, out towards the train station. For more isolated strands, walk south, past the Medina ramparts.

The Medina

The **Medina**'s circuit of towers and **ramparts** – built by the Portuguese military architect Botacca in the sixteenth century – are pleasant to wander around. They include two main gates: **Bab el Homar**, on Avenue Hassan II, and **Bab el Kasba**. If you enter by the latter, you pass the **Grand Mosque** and the **Centre Hassan II des Rencontres Internationales**, formerly a Spanish army barracks and now an arts venue and accommodation centre for the festival, with a cool open courtyard.

Further on is a small square overlooked by the "red tower", **El Hamra**, used for exhibitions. Turn right past here, along a tiny network of streets, and down towards the platform overlooking the sea, and you'll come upon at least a half-dozen **murals** painted (and subsequently repainted) during the festival; they form an intriguing mix of fantasy-representational art and geometric designs. Keep an eye out for the small **art galleries** of local artists which are scattered around the Medina.

Palais de Raisuli

Rue Sidi Ahmed Ben Mansour • Other than during the International Cultural Festival, it's not officially open to visitors but if you're interested, knock or enlist the help of a local and you may strike lucky with the caretaker

The town's focal sight, the **Palais de Raisuli**, overhangs the sea ramparts towards the far end of the Medina, away from the beach. Built in 1909 with forced tribal labour by **Moulay Ahmed er Raisuli**, a local bandit, the interior is worth seeing, if you can gain access (see above). One of the strangest figures to emerge from what was a bizarre period of Moroccan government, he began his career as a cattle rustler, achieved notoriety with a series of kidnappings and ransoms (including the British writer Walter Harris and a Greek-American millionaire, Perdicaris, who was bailed out by Teddy Roosevelt), and was eventually appointed governor over practically all the tribes of northwest Morocco. Harris described his captivity in *Morocco That Was* as an "anxious time", made more so by being confined in a small room with a headless corpse. Despite this, captor and captive formed a friendship, Harris finding Raisuli a "mysterious personage, half-saint, half-blackguard", and often entertaining him later in Tangier.

Another British writer, Rosita Forbes, visited Raisuli in his palace in 1924. Raisuli told Forbes that he made murderers walk to their death from the palace windows – a 27-metre drop to the rocks. One man, he said, had turned back to him, saying, "Thy justice is great, Sidi, but these stones are more merciful".

1

Church of San Bartolome

Cnr Av Mohammed V and Av Prince Héritier Sidi Mohamed • No set visiting hours; Mass Sun 11am • Ring the bell by the door alongside the church

The **Church of San Bartolome** was built in 1925 by Franciscan priests from Galicia, in northwest Spain. The cool and airy colonial-Spanish-style interior is complemented by the nuns' own small chapel in Moorish style, with prayers common to Islam and

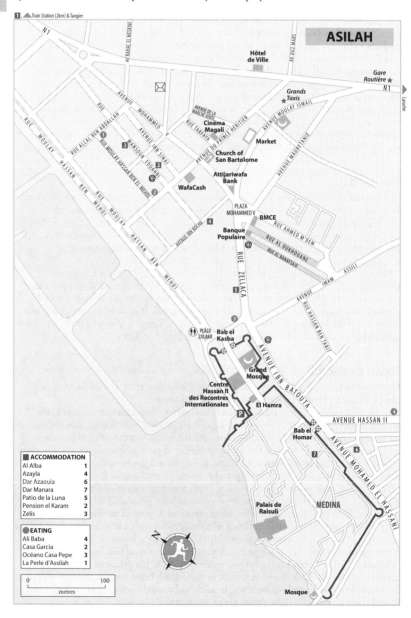

ASILAH

ACCOMMODATION

Al Alba	1
Azayla	4
Dar Azaouia	6
Dar Manara	7
Patio de la Luna	5
Pension el Karam	2
Zelis	3

EATING

Ali Baba	4
Casa Garcia	2
Océano Casa Pepe	3
La Perle d'Assilah	1

0   100
metres

Christianity carved in Arabic. One of the few church bells allowed to be used in Morocco is rung for Sunday Mass, and the sisters, from a teaching order founded by Mary Ward in Yorkshire in 1585, train local girls in dressmaking, embroidery and literacy.

1

ARRIVAL AND DEPARTURE

ASILAH

Tangier Ibn Battouta Airport is about halfway between Tangier and Asilah on the N1 highway. Buses and trains don't stop there, so from Asilah catch a Tangier-bound *grand taxi* and ask to be dropped off at the airport on the way.

By train The train station is located 2km north of the town; *Grands and petit taxis* meet arrivals or It's a straightforward 15min walk into town. Book ahead if you're planning on catching the overnight couchette service to Marrakesh, which departs Asilah at about 10.45pm.

Destinations Casablanca Voyageurs (8 direct & 2 connecting daily; 4hr–5hr 30min); Fez (4 direct & 1 connecting daily; 3hr 40min–4hr 10min); Marrakesh (1 direct & 9 connecting daily; 8hr–9hr 30min); Meknes (4 direct & 1 connecting daily; 3hr–

3hr 30min); Oujda (1 direct & 1 connecting daily; 10–11hr); Rabat (8 direct & 3 connecting daily; 3–4hr); Souk el Arba du Gharb (11 direct daily; 1hr 15min); Tangier (12 direct daily; 40min); Taza (1 direct & 3 connecting daily; 6hr 20min–7hr).

By bus Buses arrive at the *gare routière* opposite the Shell petrol station on the Tangier–Larache (N1) road. From here it's a short walk across the N1 and down Av Moulay Ismail to the central Plaza Mohammed V. Note that CTM doesn't stop at Asilah; Larache (over 20 daily; 1hr); Tangier (over 20 daily; 1hr); Tetouan (4 daily; 1hr 25min).

By grand taxi *Grands taxis* park just north of Plaza Mohammed V on Av Moulay Ismail and others operate from the bus station.

ACCOMMODATION

SEE MAP PAGE 90

Accommodation in Asilah once used to mostly consist of bland, multistorey hotels or cheap *pensions* but a number of good quality, intimate **guesthouses** have now opened up too. From May to Sept (especially on a weekend or during the International Cultural Moussem), reservations are recommended. **Camper vans** are usually allowed to park for the night in an open parking area just outside the Medina wall at the end of Rue Moulay Hassan Ben Mehdi – tip the *gardien* 20dh. Note that recently there has been a marked increase in **touts** preying on travellers arriving at the Medina – their ploy is to advise you that your chosen guesthouse is fully booked or closed, in their intent to then lead you to alternative accommodation.

★ **Al Alba** 35 Lot Nakhil ☎0539 429190 ⓦhotelalalba. com. A comfortable riad about 1km north of the centre with traditional Moroccan décor and deservedly popular thanks to great service and good facilities including a hammam, lovely tea room with relaxing couches, and excellent restaurant (open to non-guests). The 10 spotless rooms are decked out in a pleasing blue, white and gold, have a/c, heating and TV, and some can sleep three. BB €€

Azayla 20 Av Ibn Rochd ☎0539 416717. A simple but centrally located hotel and easy to find, with clean and spacious en suite rooms with powerful showers and a/c, some with balconies and sea views. The English-speaking reception staff are very helpful. No breakfast but close to cafés, and parking is available on the street out front. €€

Dar Azaouia Rue 6 n° 18, Quartier Moulay Idriss (near Bab el Homar), ⓦdarazaouia-asilah.com. Located just outside the Medina in the old Jewish quarter, *Dar Azaouia*

has just four rooms making it feel homely and inviting. Each is individually styled with antiques and Moroccan textiles and have large bathrooms and a fireplace. A split-level rooftop terrace is the setting for a delicious breakfast or dinner cooked by the Belgium owner. BB €€

Dar Manara 23 Rue M`Jimma ☎0539 416964, ⓦasilah-darmanara.com. Lovely, bright Medina guesthouse known for its friendly and personalized service. Five small but comfortable rooms with private bathrooms are spread over three floors that open inwards to a serene central courtyard perfect for long mint teas and a good book. BB €

Patio de la Luna 12 Rue Zellaca ☎0539 416074. A small house, beautifully converted into a tastefully decorated guesthouse, with simple, rustic double and triple rooms overlooking a peaceful patio-garden. There's also a sunny rooftop terrace and friendly, Spanish-speaking management. €€

Pension el Karam 40 Rue Mansour Eddahbi ☎0539 417626. A small, homely *pension* close to the seafront but a little way from the Medina. Rooms are all ground level, opening onto a pleasant, open courtyard. Shared bathrooms. €

Zelis 10 Rue Mansour Eddahbi ☎0539 417029. Asilah's only "skyscraper" and still one of the better hotels in town, but not especially attractive and a little dated. Often used by tour groups, with bright, airy rooms, some of which have ocean views. There's a swimming pool and buffet breakfast is passable in the restaurant, but there are better places for dinner. BB €€

EATING

SEE MAP PAGE 90

Dining in Asilah has an obvious lean towards fresh **seafood**, and a number of the town's restaurants are frequently

visited by regulars from Tangier, Rabat and Casablanca.
Ali Baba 153 Av Hassan II ⓦrestaurantalibaba.com.

1

About 150m south of the Medina, this doesn't look much from outside but offers sunny pavement tables, attentive service, and is very good value considering the generous portions. The menu includes tajines, brochettes and pizza, along with plenty of seafood options including a platter for two. No alcohol. €€

Casa Garcia Cnr Av du Prince Héritier and Rue Moulay Hassan ben el-Mehdi ☎ 0601 431810. Popular restaurant with tables inside and out on a balcony terrace. Regulars compliment the consistently high standard of the dishes, such as delicious seafood tajine, Spanish paella and fish tapas washed down with Moroccan rosé. It can get pretty busy at times; book ahead on Sun. €€€

Océano Casa Pepe 22 Pl Zalaka (opposite Bab Kasbah, the medina's walled garden) ☎ 0539 417395. An Asilah institution, this is one of the more formal dining options in town. Seafood dishes make up most of the menu, including a house paella as well as the Asilah speciality of marinated white anchovies. There's seating inside and out, black-tied waiters and a wine list dominated by Spanish vineyards. €€€

★ **La Perle d'Assilah** Cnr Rue Allal Ben Abdallah and Av Melilla ☎ 0539 418758. This classy, friendly restaurant is owner-managed by Moroccan-Irish couple Lahcen and Helen Iouani, Lahcen doubling as head chef. Outdoor tables are shielded by glass windbreakers, while the wood-panelled and spacious interior creates an intimate dining area. The menu includes a variety of seafood, meat and vegetarian choices, as well as good-value set menus, plus there's also a decent wine list. €€

DIRECTORY

Banks Banque Populaire, BMCE, Crédit Agricole and Attijariwafa Bank all have branches with ATMs on Plaza Mohammed V. There's a WafaCash bureau de change on Av du Prince Héritier.

Larache

LARACHE is a relaxed, easy-going town, its summer visitors primarily Moroccan tourists who come to enjoy the beaches to the north of the estuary of Oued Loukkos. You'll see as many women around as men – a reassuring feeling for women travellers looking for a low-key spot to bathe. Nearby, and accessible, are the ruins of **ancient Lixus**, legendary site of the Gardens of the Hesperides.

Larache was the main port of the northern **Spanish zone** and still bears much of its former stamp. There are faded old Spanish hotels, Spanish-run restaurants and Spanish bars, even an active Spanish cathedral for the small colony who still work at the docks. In its heyday it was quite a metropolis, publishing its own Spanish newspaper and journal, and drawing a cosmopolitan population that included the French writer Jean Genet, who spent the last decade of his life here and is buried in the old Spanish cemetery found to the southwest of town.

Before its colonization in 1911, Larache was a small **trading port**. Its activities limited by dangerous offshore sand bars, the port-town eked out a living by building pirate ships made of wood from the nearby Forest of Mamora for the "Barbary Corsairs" of Salé and Rabat.

Downtown Larache remains delightfully compact and has a lovely relaxed atmosphere, largely bereft of any hustle or hassle, despite the construction of the LIXUS Beach Resort Hôtel, a golf and marina resort to the north of the estuary. A true hybrid of its Andalusian-Arabic heritage, this is a town where paella is served alongside tajine, and where the evening *paseo* (promenade) is interrupted by melodic *meuzzins* (calls to prayer).

Place de la Libération

The town's circular main square, **Place de la Libération**, is still often identified by its original name, Plaza de España. Set just back from the sea and centred around a fountain within well-kept gardens and impressive palm trees, the plaza is encircled by many striking examples of Spanish colonial architecture, best appreciated by one of the cheap and cheerful cafés underneath the section known simply as "the Arches".

Iglesia de Nuestra Señora del Pilar

Av Mohamed V, just south of Place de la Libération • Mass Sun 11am

Built in the 1920s and designed by Spanish architects, the **Iglesia de Nuestra Señora del Pilar** (Our Lady of the Pillar) cathedral is another architectural reminder of Larache's Andalusian relationship. Its exterior is not unlike a mosque, while the interior is very much that of a traditional Catholic cathedral. Mass is still given every Sunday.

The Medina

A high Hispano-Moorish archway on Place de la Libération, **Bab el Khemis**, leads into the **Medina**, a surprisingly compact wedge of alleys and stairways leading down towards the port and up to Plaza Dar el Majzen. The colonnaded market square, Zoco de la Alcaiceria, just inside the archway, was built by the Spanish in the seventeenth century.

Though lacking in actual sights, wandering through the Medina's blue- and whitewashed streets is a wonderful opportunity to absorb and view everyday Medina life without the niggling concern of getting lost or being pressured to buy something. At the high, eastern edge of the Medina are the small twin plazas of **al Anuar** and **Dar el Majzen**. Separated by a small archway and mosque that defines the Medina's outer wall, this is a great spot to view midday prayers, especially on a Friday, when worshippers spill out onto a shaded, matted area on Plaza al Anuar. On Plaza Dar el Majzen is the **Château de la Cigogne** (House of the Stork), a grand two-storey colonial mansion that has been renovated and now houses a music school. Standing guard over the plaza is

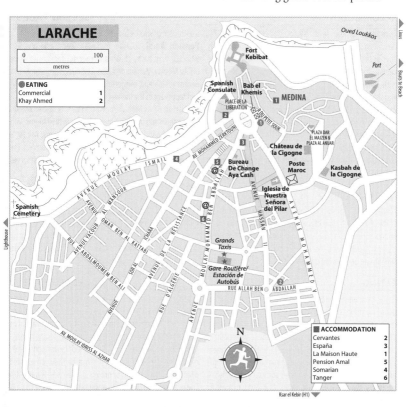

1

a hulking, three-sided fortress, the **Kasbah de la Cigogne**, dating back to the original Spanish occupation in the seventeenth century.

The beach

Bus #4 from the port (June–Aug only, every 20min; 45min), though some buses start from Plaza Dar el Majzen, or you can get a *grand taxi*) or a fishing boat, which shuttle across to the opposite bank, from where it's a short but hot walk over to the beach

The shore below Avenue Moulay Ismail is wild and rocky; cross the estuary of the Oued Loukkos, however, and you'll find a popular sandy **beach** sheltered by trees and flanked by a handful of café-restaurants during summer. Further along the beach, you'll come to the Lixus Beach Resort Hôtel; a vast property on 12 acres with 253 rooms, a golf course, spa, and restaurant. Non-guests are permitted to visit to use the facilities (ⓦlixusbeachresort.com).

ARRIVAL AND DEPARTURE   LARACHE

By bus Long-distance buses, including CTM, use the town bus station (*estación de autobús*) just off Av Moulay Mohammed Ben Abdallah. The bus station is a straightforward 400m walk from Pl de la Libération, down Av Moulay Mohammed Ben Abdallah.
Destinations Asilah (over 20 daily; 1hr); Casablanca (1 CTM & 5 others daily; 4–5hr); Fez (2 CTM & 2 others daily; 4–5hr); Ksar el Kebir (over 5 daily; 45min); Meknes (2 CTM

& 3 others daily; 3–4hr); Rabat (2 CTM & over 10 others daily; 2hr 30min–3hr 30min); Souk el Arba du Gharb (over 10 daily; 1hr); Tangier (3 CTM & over 10 others daily; 1hr 30min–2hr).
By grand taxi *Grands taxis* operate from outside the bus station.
Destinations Asilah (1hr); Ksar el Kebir (30min); Moulay Bousselham (1hr); Souk el Arba du Gharb (45min).

ACCOMMODATION   SEE MAP PAGE 93

Cervantes 3 Rue Tarik Ibnou Ziad ☎0539 910874. *Cervantes*, just off Pl de la Libération, was built in the early days of the Spanish Protectorate – don't be put off by the peeling exterior paintwork. This is a friendly little place, with comfortable enough rooms (some with a sea view) and shared hot showers. €̄
España Pl de la Libération; entrance at 6 Av Hassan II ⓦhotelespanalarache.com. This was the *Gran Hotel* in Spanish days, and there's still a touch of elegance about the place today. An ornate, carpeted staircase leads from an impressive reception area to a range of large en suite rooms with a/c and TV. A selection of cafés close by makes up for the lack of an in-house restaurant. €̄€̄
★ **La Maison Haute** 6 Derb Ben Thami ⓦlamaison haute.free.fr. This small traditional house in the heart of the Medina is full of colour, authentic furniture and antiques, has a family-home atmosphere and excellent views of town from the roof terrace where breakfast is served. The doubles are en suite, while the triple room uses

a bathroom down the hall. BB €̄
Pension Amal 10 Rue Abdallah Ben Yasin ☎0539 912788. Very basic, cheap and cheerful family-run place off Av Moulay Mohammed Ben Abdallah, with simple but decent rooms and comfortable beds. Hot showers (12dh) and toilets are in the hallways. €̄
Somarian 68 Av Mohammed Zerktouni ☎0648 388898. This Spanish-run modern hotel offers large tiled rooms with a/c, TV and good water pressure in the showers. Ask for a sea view if possible, rather than a room overlooking the central covered market. Decent restaurant too, which serves alcohol. Parking is available on the street outside. €̄€̄
Tanger Cnr Av Moulay Mohammed Ben Abdallah and Rue Tanger ⓦhoteltanger.business.site. This family-run hotel has large, bright rooms, some en suite though those with shared facilities are particularly good value. Spread over three floors, there's no lift but the friendly management are on hand to assist with luggage. There are good views from the rooftop terrace. €̄

EATING   SEE MAP PAGE 93

There are plenty of reasonably priced places around Place de la Libération, and leading off from here south, along the main pedestrian road, Avenue Hassan II.
Commercial Pl de la Libération. This old restaurant is pretty basic inside but has a good location on the main square. It's popular with the locals, who come for its simple and cheap dishes such as paella and portions of fried fish. €̄
★ **Khay Ahmed** 1 Av Salah Eddin Al Ayoubi, just off Av

Hassan II near Banque Populaire ☎0661 379362. This multi-floored setup is always busy with locals, yet service is fast and friendly and it is worth the 10-minute walk from Place de la Libération. It offers up the usual Mediterranean-Moroccan standards, plus charcoaled lamb and steak, or simply select a fillet of line fish from their refrigerated display and have it fried or grilled just the way you like. On Friday afternoons they serve traditional couscous. €̄

DIRECTORY

Banks and exchange Banque Populaire, Crédit Agricole and Crédit Immobilier et Hôtelier (CIH) are all on Av Mohammed V, just south of Pl de la Libération. Bureau De Change Aya Cash, 25 Av Moulay Mohammed Ben Abdallah (Mon–Fri 10.30am–10pm, Sat 10.30am–7pm, Sun 10.30am–2pm).

Consulate Spain, 1 Rue de Casablanca (Mon–Fri 8am–2pm; ☎ 0539 15392).

Golf Port Lixus Resort Golf Club, north of Oued Loukkos, turn off at Lixus ruins (18 holes; ☎ 0539 500782).

Ancient Lixus

Ancient Lixus is one of the oldest – and most continuously – inhabited sites in Morocco. It had been settled in prehistoric times, long before the arrival of Phoenician colonists around 1000 BC, under whom it is thought to have become the first **trading post** of North Africa. Later, it was in turn an important Carthaginian and Roman city, and was deserted only in the fifth century AD, two hundred years after Diocletian had withdrawn the empire's patronage. There are remains of a **church** from this period, and Arabic coins have also been found.

As an **archeological site**, then, Lixus is certainly significant, and its legendary associations with Hercules add an element of mythic allure. The ruins lie upon and below the summit of a low hill on the far side of the Oued Loukkos estuary, at the crossroads of the main Larache–Tangier road and the narrow lane to Larache beach. A track, worth climbing for the panoramic view alone, wends up to the amphitheatre area, where there are mosaics. The ruins are interesting rather than impressive, and only around a quarter of the site has been excavated.

The site

While there is a visitor centre, the **site** is not effectively enclosed and therefore always open and accessible. There's a useful map board by the roadside at the entrance, but there is no interpretive signage within the site itself. On random days there is a self-appointed French-speaking *gardien* who is eager to show visitors the main points of interest for a tip. The **Lower Town**, spreading back from the modern road, consists largely of the ruins of factories for the production of salt – still being panned nearby – and *garum* fish sauce. The factories seem to have been developed in the early years of the first century AD and they remained in operation until the Roman withdrawal.

A track, some 100m down the road to Tangier, leads up to the Acropolis (upper town), passing on its way eight rows of the Roman **theatre** and **amphitheatre**, unusually combined into a single structure. Its deep, circular arena was adapted for circus games and the gladiatorial slaughter of animals. Morocco, which Herodotus knew as "the wild-beast country", was the major source for these Roman *venations* (controlled hunts), and local colonists must have grown rich from the trade. Until 1998, the **baths** built into the side of the theatre featured a remarkable **mosaic** depicting Neptune's head on the body of a lobster; unfortunately, the mosaic was irreparably damaged when the *gardien*'s son tried to dig it up to sell, and just about a third of it remains.

Climbing above the baths and theatre, you pass through ramparts to the main fortifications of the **Acropolis** – a somewhat confused network of walls and foundations – and **temple sanctuaries**, including an early Christian basilica and a number of pre-Roman buildings. The most considerable of the sanctuaries, with their underground cisterns and porticoed priests' quarters, were apparently rebuilt in the first century AD, but even then retained Phoenician elements in their design.

ARRIVAL AND DEPARTURE   **ANCIENT LIXUS**

By bus and grand taxi From Larache port, bus #4 (June–Aug only, every 20 min) and bus #5 (5 daily) will both drop off at the ruins (35min); bus #4 continues on to the beach; alternatively, charter a *grand taxi* but be sure to agree on

1

WETLAND WILDLIFE

Adjoining the Moulay Bousselham lagoon is a large wetland area known as **Merja Zerga** ("Blue Lake"). The lagoon's periphery is used for grazing by nomadic herds of sheep, cattle and goats, and the lagoon itself is a Ramsar-listed Wetland of International Importance, and is one of the largest of its kind in Morocco.

The huge extent of the site ensures rewarding **birdwatching** at all times of the year. There are large numbers of waders, including a large colony of flamingos, plus little-ringed plovers, black-winged stilts and black-tailed godwits.

For serious birdwatchers, it is the **gulls and terns** that roost on the central islands which are worthy of the closest inspection, as, among the flocks of lesser black-backed gull and black tern, it is possible to find rarer species such as **Caspian tern**. The adjacent grassland is probably the best place in Morocco to see pairs of North African **marsh owl**, which usually appear hunting above the tall grasses shortly after sunset. Marsh harrier and osprey can also sometimes be spotted. One bird you'll certainly see wintering here, usually around cattle (and sometimes sitting on their backs), is the **cattle egret**. For rarity-spotters, the current grail is the lesser crested tern and its cousin the royal tern, both immigrants from Mauretania during spring and summer.

English-speaking local ornithologist Hassan Dalil (☏ 0668 434110) is easily the best guide in the region, and can be contacted directly or via the *Café Milano* in Moulay Bousselham, which also keeps a **bird log**. Beware of copycat guides purporting to be "the" Hassan. The tours are best taken in early morning or at dusk, depending on the tides; the boat isn't shaded so bring along a hat, protective clothing, sunscreen and water.

a collection time from the ruins and only pay once you're back in town.

On foot It's a 4–5km walk to the ruins from both Larache

beach or town. Currently lacking any great signage, the entrance to the site is on the corner of the Larache–Asilah road and a minor road signposted as "Plage Ras Rmel".

Ksar el Kebir

As its name – in Arabic, "the Great Enclosure" – suggests, **KSAR EL KEBIR**, an eleventh-century Arab power base 36km southeast of Larache, was once a place of some importance. It was 12km north of here where, in August 1578, the Portuguese fought the disastrous **Battle of the Three Kings**, the most dramatic and devastating in their nation's history – a power struggle disguised as a crusade, which saw the death or capture of virtually the entire nobility and which ultimately resulted in 62 years of Spanish rule.

The town fell into decline in the seventeenth century, after a local chief incurred the wrath of Moulay Ismail, though its fortunes were revived to some extent under the Spanish protectorate, when it served as a major barracks.

The **Sunday souk** is held right by the *gare routière* and Moulay el Mehdi station. On any morning of the week, however, there are lively souks around the main *kissaria* (covered market) of the old town – in the quarter known as Bab el Oued (Gate of the River). Beyond Ksar el Kebir, a decaying customs post at **Arbaoua** marks the old colonial frontier between the Spanish and French zones.

ARRIVAL AND DEPARTURE

By train The easiest way to get to Ksar el Kebir is by train, either on a direct service or via Casa Voyageurs or Sidi Kacem stations. Ksar el Kebir station is way out on the northern edge of town; for the town centre, get off at Moulay el Mehdi station, one stop south.

Destinations Asilah (12 daily; 40min–1hr); Casablanca Voyageurs (8 direct & 3 connecting daily; 3hr 30min–5hr); Rabat (8 direct & 3 connecting daily; 2hr 25min–4hr); Sidi Kacem (5 direct daily; 1hr 30min) Tangier (12 direct daily; 1hr 30min).

By bus The *gare routière* is next to Moulay el Mehdi station. However, as the motorway bypasses the town, few long-distance buses come here.

Destinations Larache (over 5 daily; 45min); Moulay Bousselham (5 daily; 35min).

By grand taxi *Grands taxis* from Larache operate to and from a station just across the tracks from the *gare routière*, and those from Souk el Arba du Gharb operate from one 500m further south.

Destinations Larache (30min); Moulay Bousselham (30min); Souk el Arba du Gharb (30min).

ACCOMMODATION AND EATING

There are a number of hotels and basic places to eat located on or near the town square; head south from the Moulay el Mehdi station and turn right after 300m.

Ksar al Yamama 8 Bd Hassan II ☎ 0539 907960. A good-value place, with nice, large, airy rooms, some en suite with a bathtub, and some with balconies overlooking the town square. No wi-fi. €

Moulay Bousselham

MOULAY BOUSSELHAM, 55km from Ksar el Kebir, is a very low-key resort, popular almost exclusively with Moroccans. It comprises little more than a single street, crowded with grill-cafés and sloping down to the sea at the side of a broad lagoon and wetland area, known as **Merja Zerga**. This is one of northern Morocco's prime **birdwatching** locations (see page 96), and avid birdwatchers from all over the world come here to see the lagoon's flamingo and other bird colonies.

The **beach** itself is sheltered by cliffs – rare along the Atlantic – and has an abrupt drop-off, which creates a continual crash of breaking waves. While a lot of fun for swimming as well as beginner surfers, the currents can at times be quite strong and only the most confident of swimmers should venture out past the breakers. In summer, a section of the beach is patrolled by lifeguards.

For Moroccans, the village is part summer resort, part pilgrimage centre. The village's namesake saint, **Marabout Moulay Bousselham**, was a tenth-century Egyptian whose remains are housed in a *koubba* prominently positioned above the settlement. In July this sees one of the largest **moussems** in the region.

ARRIVAL AND DEPARTURE   MOULAY BOUSSELHAM

By bus Buses stop at a car park at the entrance to the village. From here it's a short, slightly uphill walk to the village centre or a similar distance but slightly downhill to the two camping sites. Note that CTM buses do not come here.

Destinations Ksar el Kebir (5 daily; 35min); Souk el Arbaa du Gharb (4 daily; 40min). You will need to change buses at either one of these to get to Larache.

By grand taxi *Grands taxis* stop at the same spot as the buses, though it's worth asking the driver to drop you off in the village centre or even at your accommodation. The frequency of services increases greatly during the summer holiday season.

Destinations Ksar el Kebir (20min); Larache (1hr); Souk el Arba du Gharb (30min).

ACCOMMODATION AND EATING

Most Moroccan families either camp or rent houses so there's not much choice of accommodation. During the summer try and book in advance. In the village centre is a line of **grill-cafés**; indistinguishable from each other – they will all fix you a large, great value mixed platter of freshly fried fish. Another interesting alternative is to go to

---

MOUSSEM OF MOULAY BOUSSELHAM

The **Moussem of Moulay Bousselham** is held annually in mid-July. The village, already bursting at the seams at this time of the year, overflows with pilgrims dressed in white who come to pay homage to the saint by visiting the *koubba*. A **fantasia** – a traditional cavalry charge culminating in firing of muskets in the air – also usually takes place during the festival, on a level field between the village and the autoroute.

MOROCCO-SPAIN BORDER FENCE

Over the last few decades, the economies on both sides of Ceuta's **border** seemed to benefit from the enclave, spurred on by the city's duty-free status. However, the border is also the frontier between Africa and Europe, and inevitably the EU became increasingly concerned about traffic in **drugs** and **illegal immigrants**, financing in 2005 a £15m ($22m) hi-tech "wall" with a double fence, CCTV, regular watch towers and movement sensors along the 8km boundary.

The money to be made from outflanking these defences has attracted hi-tech smugglers trading in hash and hard drugs. But in recent years it has been the storming and scaling of the six-metre-high **border fence** by migrants that has been more newsworthy. It has become a regular occurrence that groups of up to six hundred men – desperate refugees from as far south as Liberia and Rwanda and some disadvantaged Moroccans – simultaneously rush the Moroccan border guards and ascend the fence. There have been incidences where these men have used sticks, stones and petrol bombs as defence weapons and, equally, that the Moroccans and Spanish guards have resorted to using rubber bullets. While some migrants get stopped, often between the double barriers or stuck on top, others to do manage to climb over into Spanish Ceuta. They then continue to go over to mainland Spain by night, often in small boats unsuited to the short but difficult crossing. The same has been happening at the sister city of Melilla, and in 2018, Spain surpassed both Italy and Greece as the number one destination for migrants crossing the Mediterranean by boat.

the market and buy your own fish and take it to one of the vendors to be grilled for a small charge.

Camping Caravaning International 500m east of town on the lagoon ☎0537 432477. This large, grassy, shaded but ageing campsite remains ever popular due to its lagoon-side location. It can get very busy during summer, when both the ablutions and mosquitoes are a worry. It has a restaurant and takeaway and vendors sell fresh fish at the gate. Price includes an electric point. €̄

Flamants-Loisirs 1km east of town, signposted opposite the post office ⓦcampingmaroc1.com. The better of the town's two campsites, set away from the village in a relatively secure lot overlooking the lagoon from up high. There's lots of shady camping sites and basic ablutions with hot water, as well as an on-site restaurant, small grocery shop and large swimming pool (summer only). Price includes an electric point. €̄

Le Lagon Main road, village centre ☎0537 432650. An ageing, crumbling, overpriced 80s-era hotel with fantastic views over the lagoon – its one and only attribute. Rooms are en suite and some also have TV. €̄

La Maison des Oiseaux About 2km east of town; phone ahead for directions ⓦmoulay.bousselham. free.fr. The "house of the birds", down by the lagoon, is a whitewashed villa with a pleasant garden, though the homely atmosphere of times gone by seems to have disappeared. There's a variety of rooms, including some family suites that sleep up to six adults. BB €̄

★ **Vila Bea** 41 Rue de Mer ⓦvilabea.com. Easily the village's best accommodation, this charming French-owned guesthouse overlooks the Atlantic. The spacious rooms boast quality furnishings and some have views over the welcoming infinity pool to the ocean. An in-house restaurant offers sumptuous breakfasts and fine seafood dinners. BB €̄€̄€̄

Villa Nora At the far northern end of town, about 1.5km from the centre ☎0537 432071. This British-owned, friendly guesthouse overlooks the beach and the Atlantic rollers, offering rooms that are small but comfortable, with a shared bathroom. The service is still commendable and meals can be arranged, but many of the furnishings are in need of repair and the overall standard seems to have dropped of late. BB €̄€̄

DIRECTORY

Banks Attijariwafa, Banque Populaire and Crédit Agricole are all located at the entrance to the village; all have ATMs.

Post office At the entrance to the village, close to the banks.

Ceuta

A Spanish enclave since the sixteenth century, **CEUTA** (Sebta in Arabic) is a curious political anomaly. Along with Melilla, east along the coast, it was retained by Spain after Moroccan independence in 1956 and today functions largely as a military base, its economy bolstered by a limited duty-free status. It has been an **autonomous city**, with a large measure of internal self-government for its eighty-five thousand inhabitants, since 1995. The city makes for an attractive stop when en route either to or from Morocco with its relaxed European atmosphere, pristine squares, tapas bars, coastal walks and pleasant accommodation options. Note that the euro is the only accepted currency (see page 101) and Ceuta runs on Spanish time (see page 64).

Plaza de Nuestra Señora de Africa

The most attractive part of Ceuta is within several hundred metres of the ferry terminal, where the **Plaza Nuestra Señora de Africa** is flanked by a pair of Baroque churches, **Nuestra Señora de Africa** (Our Lady of Africa; open most days) and the **cathedral** (usually locked). Bordering the square, to the west, are the most impressive remainders of the city walls – the walled moat of **Foso de San Felipe** and the adjacent **Muralla Real** (Royal Walls). The oldest sections of the fortifications were built by the Byzantines.

Museo de Ceuta

30 Paseo del Revellín · Free · ☎ 956 511398

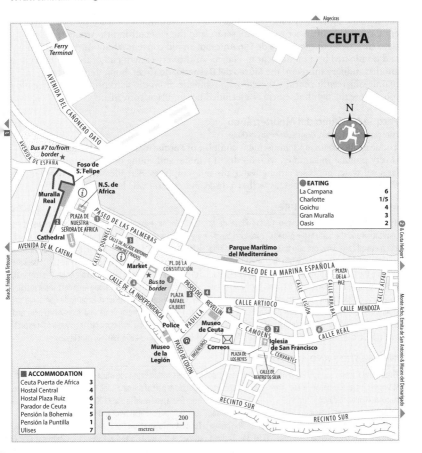

1

To the east of Plaza de la Constitución, an oldish quarter rambles up from the bottom of the long **Paseo del Revellín**. There's an interesting little municipal museum here, the **Museo de Ceuta**, displaying archeological finds from Stone Age and Roman times through to the Islamic era, well laid out and with good explanations, but in Spanish only. There is also a section dedicated to contemporary art exhibitions on the ground floor.

Museo de la Legión

1 Paseo de Colón • Free

On the southern flank of the city centre, the **Museo de la Legión** offers an interesting glimpse of Spanish–African military history. Relatively small in size, its four exhibition rooms are crammed with uniforms, weapons and paraphernalia of the infamous Spanish Foreign Legion. Opposite the museum is a statue of a *legionario* accompanied by a Barbary sheep, just one of many mascots that the Ceuta regiment has had over the years.

The peninsula

A round circuit of the **peninsula** makes for a pleasant day-trip if the weather is fine. Start by heading east (and uphill) on Recinto Sur; as the buildings gradually disappear from view, the land swells into a rounded, pine-covered slope offering fine views out to the Rock of Gibraltar. Known as **Monte Acho**, the summit is crowned by a Byzantine-era fort that is still an active military setup, and therefore off-limits. Around midway, signs direct you to the **Ermita de San Antonio**, an old convent rebuilt during the 1960s and dominated by a monument to Franco. At the very eastern end of the peninsula is another military museum, the **Museo del Desnarigado** (free), housed in a fort that is mainly nineteenth-century, though with remnants from the sixteenth and seventeenth too. Below the lighthouse here is a secluded beach, Playa Torrecilla.

Parque Marítimo del Mediterráneo

Paseo de la Marina Española, Ⓦ parquemaritimo.es • Charge

The seafront leisure and amusement complex of **Parque Marítimo del Mediterráneo** is very popular in summer, with hordes of families and young people enjoying three large saltwater pools set among waterfalls and sculptures. A replica Muralla Real houses restaurants, bars and cafés, as well as a disco and casino come late.

ARRIVAL AND DEPARTURE · CEUTA

By bus & taxi Running between Ceuta's Plaza de la Consitutíon and the border (see page 101) are local bus #7 and metered taxis. Taxis can also be usually found waiting outside Ceuta's ferry terminal, while the closest bus stop is opposite the *Muralla Real* (Royal Walls) on Avda de España.
By ferry The ferry terminal is a short walk northwest of the town centre. Aside from Semana Santa and the last week in Aug, it's usually possible for foot passengers to board a ferry for Algeciras within a couple of hours of arriving at the port (15–20 daily; 1hr–1hr 30min for standard ferry and 45min for more expensive hydrofoil). Timetables and fares are on the websites. They also transport cars; book ahead, which you can do online. Ticketing offices for Acciona Trasmediterránea (Ⓦ trasmediterranea.es), Balearia (Ⓦ balearia.com) and FRS (Ⓦ frs.es) are inside the terminal, and there are ticket agencies along Avda del Cañonero Dato.
By helicopter Ceuta Heliport is on Avda Compañía del Mar. Flights go between Ceuta and Algeciras (7min) and Málaga (35min) for a lot less money than you might expect. Helity (Spain ☎ +34 856 590146, Ⓦ helity.es).

INFORMATION AND ACTIVITIES

Time Ceuta works to Spanish time, an hour ahead of Morocco (2hr ahead between the times when Europe and Morocco change to daylight saving).
Telephone When phoning Ceuta from Morocco (or anywhere else outside Spain), you must prefix phone numbers with the international code (☎ 00 34). Dialling numbers within Ceuta you must include the old local code (☎ 956) as part of the nine-digit number. To phone Morocco from Ceuta, you need to dial ☎ 00 212, followed by the local code (minus the initial zero) and number.
Tourist Information The tourist office is under the traffic flyover at the western end of Paseo de las Palmeras ☎ 956

1

506275). The website of private company Servicios Turísticos De Ceuta has excellent information in English (w ceuta.si) **Kayak tours** Ceuta Kayak (w ceutakayak.es) offers a number of guided paddles around the Ceuta coastline as well as a very interesting circuit that explores the waterside fortifications of the Muralla Real.

ACCOMMODATION SEE MAP PAGE 99

It's advisable to book ahead throughout the year, but especially during the main festivals: Carnival (Feb), Holy Week (Easter), the Fiesta de Nuestra Señora de Monte Carmel (July 16), and the Fiesta de Nuestra Señora de Africa (Aug 5).

Ceuta Puerta de Africa Calle de Alcalde Antonio L. Sánchez Prados w ceutapuertadeafrica.com. Modern, large three-star chain hotel centred around a gleaming white atrium, offering a hundred and twenty rooms with all the mod cons. The breakfast buffet is extensive but the in-house restaurant isn't as good. Underground parking is available (charge). BB €€

Hostal Central Paseo del Revellín 15, first floor w hostalesceuta.com. One of the cleaner and more modern of the city's cheap hotels, in a good, central location, offering small but comfortable en-suite rooms complete with TV and fridge. Single rooms available (€). €€

★ **Hostal Plaza Ruiz** Plaza Teniente Ruiz 3, second floor w hostalplazaruizceuta.com. Located opposite the Museo de Ceuta, this reliable option offers similar but slightly larger rooms than its sister hotel down the road, *Hostal Central* (see above), some of which benefit from wrought-iron balconies overlooking the plaza below. Triples (€€) and quads (€€) also available. €€

Parador de Ceuta Pl Nuestra Señora de Africa 15 w parador.es. Formerly the *Gran Hotel La Muralla* and set into the Muralla Real, Ceuta's grand old dame retains a certain colonial charm. Rooms, some with balcony, are looking a little tired but offer great views of the verdant garden and swimming pool or across a car park to the Mediterranean. BB €€

Pensión la Bohemia Paseo del Revellín 12, first floor ☎ 956 510615. Best deal among the cheapies, this clean and comfortable *pensión* is centred around a pleasant interior courtyard. Most of the rooms lack outside windows but all come with fan and TV; bathrooms, with hot water, are shared. The *pensión* can be difficult to locate as trees sometimes obscure the blue sign. €

Pensión la Puntilla Carretera de Servicio la Puntilla 28 w pensionlapuntilla.com. Despite looking a little

CROSSING THE BORDER AT CEUTA

Since the Algeciras–Ceuta ferries and hydrofoils are quicker than those to Tangier (and the ferries significantly cheaper for cars or motorbikes), Ceuta is a popular **point of entry and exit** to Morocco. There is no customs/passport check at the port as the *frontera* (border; open 24hr) is 3km out of town and a further 2km from the Moroccan town of Fnideq (see page 109).

   At the border, which is well signposted from the port and vice versa, formalities for entering and leaving Spain are brief. On the **Moroccan side**, the procedure can be time-consuming, especially for drivers. Each passport holder needs an immigration form (yellow or photocopied white) and, if you have a car, an additional green form; these are available – though you have to ask for them – from the officials sitting inside the small immigration posts. The car form requires inconvenient details such as chassis number and date of registration. If you despair of getting a form and having it processed, you can always enlist one of the innumerable touts for asmall fee; ignore their standard scam of trying to charge you for immigration forms, which are free. The whole business can take ten minutes on a good day, an hour or two on a bad one, and the noise and chaos can be a bit unsettling. Just try to keep a steady head and if you are in doubt as to where and what you should do, ask one of the (sometimes over-stressed) officials for assistance or directions.

   Coming from Ceuta into Morocco, try to arrive early in the day so that you have plenty of time to move on to Tetouan or Tangier – and possibly beyond. Once across and into Morocco proper, you can take a shared **grand taxi** to Fnideq (see page 109), 2km away , where you'll find connecting bus and taxi services to **Tetouan** or **Tangier**. When travelling to Fnideq by bus from Tangier, services that travel via Ksar el Seghir will drop you at the border post, whereas the services that travel via Tetouan terminate at Fnideq's *gare routière*. You can also book your own *grand taxi* from the border to Tangieror Tetouan. On the Moroccan side of the border is an Attijariwafa **bureau de change**, and on the Spanish side there are a couple of travel agencies that will change Moroccan dirhams into euros.

1

worn, this is still one of the best and most welcoming places among a number of small, cheap lodgings in this area. Bathrooms with hot water are shared, and there's a small kitchen. It's a bit far from the sites, but walking distance from the port, which is handy if you're taking an early ferry. €

Ulises Calle Camoens 5 ⊕hotelulises.com. One of the best hotels in town, all 124 rooms sport a contemporary look with wood-panelled floors and works of art adorning the walls; those on the higher floors offer unobstructed sea views from balconies and the least street noise. A swimming pool operates inn summer. BB €€

EATING AND DRINKING
SEE MAP PAGE 99

Ceuta's main concentration of restaurants is around the Plaza de la Constitución. For tapas bars, check the smaller streets off Calle Camoens. All of the below recommendations serve alcohol.

La Campana Calle Real 13 ☎956 514395. A pasteleria with a reasonable set menu (though not much choice for non-pork eaters), plus tapas, spaghetti, sandwiches, beer and wine from the barrel. €

★ **Charlotte** Plaza de los Reyes, Calle Cameons. This popular and inviting café-tapas bar overlooks a busy plaza and offers a varied menu of breakfasts and light dishes. There's also plenty of beers, wine and cocktails to choose from, and a great range of leaf teas served in heavy clay teapots. A second café is located down at Paseo de las Palmeras 10 (same opening hours). €

Goichu Calle Independencia 15 ⊕goichu.com.com. One of the best places to eat in town, although pricey, it is

in a wonderful location overlooking La Ribera Beach and with both indoor and covered outdoor seating. It offers an innovative menu that mixes the food of the Basque Country with hints of Japan. €€€€

Gran Muralla Plaza de la Constitución 4. A popular, long-established Chinese restaurant with sweeping views over the harbour. The extensive menu (in English) offers the usual standard dishes, including some good seafood choices, as well as sushi. €€

★ **Oasis** Urb San Antonio 89 ☎956 515925. It's worth taking a taxi (15min) out to this pleasant spot high up in the hills overlooking the sea on the outskirts of town for views of the Rock of Gibralter on a clear day. The menu features tasty Moroccon lamb, chicken, fish and vegetable tajines as well as Spanish seafood dishes. Wine, beer and traditional teas compliment a leisurely meal. €€

DIRECTORY

Banks and exchange Only the euro is used in Ceuta. Currency exchange is available on the Spanish side of the border and at most banks on Paseo del Revellin in Ceuta. There is a *telebanco* (ATM) on the ground floor of the ferry terminal.

Police Paseo de Colón, next door to the Museo de la Legión (see page 100).

Tetouan

Approaching **TETOUAN** from the landward side it looks strikingly beautiful, poised atop the slope of an enormous valley against a dark mass of rock. Its name (pronounced Tet-tá-wan) means "open your eyes" in Berber, an apparent reference to the town's hasty construction by Andalusian refugees in the fifteenth century.

The city has shaken off its bad reputation for conmen and hustlers of the early noughties, and, thanks to both Moroccan and European **investment**, the past few years have seen Tetouan almost **reborn** again – in particular, the once-neglected Spanish Medina is now looked upon affectionately as one of the most "untouched" in the country. Tetouan has remained a **popular Moroccan resort** that attracts huge numbers of Moroccan families in the summer, who flock to the nearby beaches to escape the heat.

Brief history

Two cities rose and fell in the vicinity of Tetouan before the present-day city was built. **Tamuda**, the scant ruins of which can still be seen on the south side of Oued Martil, 4km southeast of town, was founded by the Berber Mauritanians in the third century BC, and razed by the Romans in 42 AD; and the original Tetouan, built by the Merenids in 1307, on the same site as today's Medina, destroyed by a Castilian raiding party in 1399. The present town was established in 1484 by Muslims and Jews fleeing the Christian reconquest of Andalusia in southern Spain. Jewish merchants – able to pass relatively freely between Muslim North Africa and Christian Europe – brought prosperity to the city, and ramparts were put up in the seventeenth century under Moulay Ismail.

Tetouan has since been occupied twice by the Spanish. It was seized briefly, as a supposed threat to Ceuta, from 1859 to 1862, a period which saw the **Medina** converted to a town of almost European appearance, complete with street lighting. Then, in 1913 a more serious, colonial occupation began. Tetouan served first as a military garrison for the subjugation of the Rif, later as the capital of the **Spanish Protectorate Zone**. As such it almost doubled in size to handle the region's trade and administration, and it was here in 1936 that **General Franco** declared his military coup against Spain's elected Liberal–Socialist coalition government, thus igniting the Spanish Civil War.

For Tetouan's Moroccan population, there was little progress during the colonial period. Spanish administration retained a purely military character and only a handful of schools were opened throughout the entire zone. This legacy had effects well beyond independence in 1956, and the town, alongside its Rif hinterland, adapted with difficulty to the new nation – it was at the centre of anti-government rioting as recently as 1984. Aware of this undercurrent, King **Mohammed VI** made it his business to visit the former Spanish protectorate almost as soon as he ascended the throne in 1999, a gesture that helped to give Tetouan and its region a much stronger sense of nationhood than it had under the previous monarch.

Place Hassan II

Tetouan's old meeting place and former market square, **Place Hassan II** joins the Medina with the Spanish Ville Nouvelle, El Ensanche. It's also where the **Royal Palace** (built on the site of the old Spanish consulate) stands, incorporating parts of a nineteenth-century Caliphal Palace that once stood beside it. Much of the square is roped off for security reasons, but it's usually OK to take a picture of the palace from the perimeter. You'll know when the king is in residence by the number of soldiers and police here. Facing the palace, the laneway to the right off Place Hassan II is Rue al Qods, the main street of the **Mellah**, the old Jewish quarter that was created as late as 1807.

The Medina

The **Medina** dates back to the fifteenth century, following the mass migration to North Africa of persecuted Muslims and Jews from Andalusian Spain. The refugees brought with them the most refined sophistication of Moorish Andalusia, reflected in the **architecture** of the UNESCO heritage-listed Medina, and even their houses, with tiled lintels and wrought-iron balconies, seem much more akin to the old Arab quarters of Cordoba and Seville than those of Moroccan towns. Largely **hassle-free**, the Medina can be a delight to explore; meander into the Medina's heart and you'll be immersed into ancient Medina life – no traffic, children playing games, women chatting over chores, and men chatting over coffee.

Bab er Rouah, on the southern flank of the Royal Palace, is the main gateway into the Medina from Place Hassan II. Immediately through the gate is **Rue Terrafin**, a relatively wide lane with overhead terracing and a string of **jewellery shops** that (with its continuations) cuts straight across to the east gate, **Bab el Okla**. Along the way a series of alleys give access to most of the town's **food and craft souks**. The **Souk el Houts**, a small shaded square directly behind the grounds of the Royal Palace is a good point of reference, being a central point between the northern and southern halves of the Medina. Another trick for orientation is to look at the longer central stones running down the middle of the cobblestoned streets. If they are three wide it means that it

1

is a main street leading to one of the medina's seven gates; two wide, a thoroughfare leading to a main street; and one wide, a residential alleyway or a dead end.

Guersa el Kebira

From the north side of the Souk el Houts, two lanes wind up through a mass of alleys, souks and passageways towards Bab Sebta. Following the one on the right (east) for

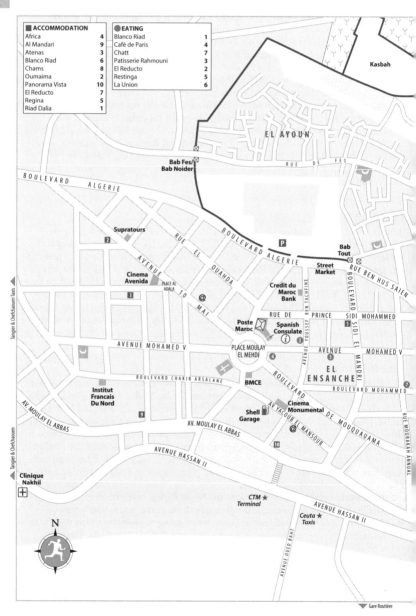

■ ACCOMMODATION	
Africa	4
Al Mandari	9
Atenas	3
Blanco Riad	6
Chams	8
Oumaima	2
Panorama Vista	10
El Reducto	7
Regina	5
Riad Dalia	1

● EATING	
Blanco Riad	1
Café de Paris	4
Chatt	7
Patisserie Rahmouni	3
El Reducto	2
Restinga	5
La Union	6

about twenty metres, you'll see an opening to another small square. This is the **Guersa el Kebira**, essentially a cloth and textile souk, where a number of stalls sell the town's highly characteristic *foutahs* – strong and brilliantly striped lengths of rug-like cotton, worn as a cloak and skirt by the Jebali and Riffian women.

Leaving the Guersa at its top right-hand corner, you should emerge more or less on **Place de l'Oussa**, another beautiful little square, easily recognized by an ornate, tiled

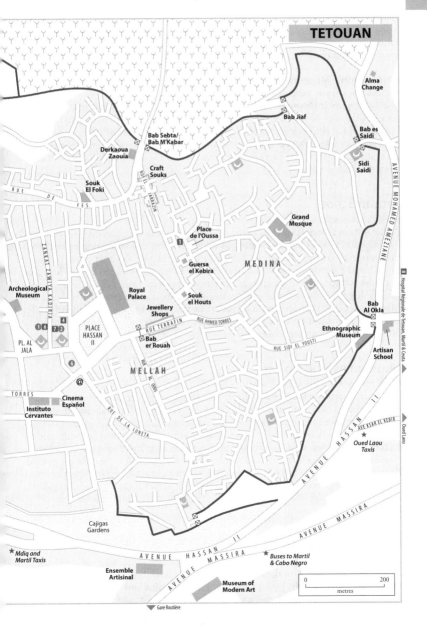

TETOUAN

Alma
Change

Bab Jiaf

Bab es
Saidi

Bab Sebta/
Bab M'Kabar

Derkaoua
Zaouia

Sidi
Saidi

Craft
Souks

Souk
El Foki

RUE   DE   FES

Grand
Mosque

Place
de l'Oussa

MEDINA

Guersa
el Kebira

Archeological
Museum

ZANKAT ZAWYA KADIRA

Royal
Palace

Souk
el Houts

Jewellery
Shops

RUE TERRAFIN

RUE AHMED TORRES

Bab
Al Okla

PLACE
HASSAN
II

Bab
er Rouah

Ethnographic
Museum

PL. AL
JALA

RUE SIDI EL YOUSTI

Artisan
School

MELLAH

TORRES

Cinema
Español

Instituto
Cervantes

RUE DE LA LUNETA

AVENUE   HASSAN   II

AVE KSAR EL KEBIR

Oued Laou
Taxis

AVENUE MASSIRA

Cajigas
Gardens

Mdiq and
Martil Taxis

AVENUE   HASSAN   II

AVENUE   MASSIRA

Buses to Martil
& Cabo Negro

Ensemble
Artisinal

Museum of
Modern Art

0   200
metres

AVENUE MOHAMED AMEZIANE

Hospital Régionale de Tetouan, Martil & Ceuta

Oued Laou

Gare Routière

1

fountain and trellises of vines. Along one of its sides is an imposing nineteenth-century **Xharia**, or almshouse; on another is a craft shop, elegantly tiled and with good views over the quarter from its roof.

Craft souks

Most of the specific **craft souks** lie beyond Place de l'Oussa, heading up towards Bab Sebta. Among them are copper and brass workers, renowned makers of *babouches* (pointed leather slippers), and carpenters specializing in elaborately carved and painted wood. Most of the shops along the central lane here – **Rue el Jarrazin** – focus on the tourist trade, while the souks themselves remain refreshingly traditional and don't see much tourist traffic.

Ethnographic Museum

Bab al Okla • Charge • ⓦ maroc.net/museums

The **Ethnographic Museum** is housed in a former arms bastion of the nineteenth-century Alaouite sultan Moulay Abderrahman. Themed around the everyday but staunchly private elements of Moroccan life, the museum's exhibits include exquisitely detailed **traditional costumes** (wedding gowns, for example) as well as a decorative funeral coffin. There's also a great view of the surrounding countryside from the roof terrace.

Artisan School

Opposite Bab el Okla, outside the Medina • Charge

At the **Artisan School** (École des Métiers) you can see master craftsmen (*maâlem*) watch over apprentices working at new **designs** in the old ways, essentially unmodified since the fourteenth century. This is the only arts program in Morocco that offers a diploma to students. Ranging in trades from metalwork and wood turning to embroidery, many of the **workshops** have items for sale. Perhaps owing to its Andalusian heritage, Tetouan actually has a slightly different zellij (enamelled tile mosaics) technique to other Moroccan cities – the tiles are cut before rather than after being fired. A slightly easier process, it is frowned upon by the craftsmen of Fez, whose own pieces are more brittle, but brighter in colour and closer fitting.

Museum of Modern Art

Cnr Av Hassan II and Av Massira • Free • ☎ 0666 046081

Tetouan's **Museum of Modern Art** (Centro de Arte Moderno de Tetuán) is located in the city's renovated old train station (1918), and the green and white building looks half castle, half mosque but is now all sleek and modern inside. The main entrance is from the rear of the building, and visitors are welcomed to a large sunlit space with welded **figurative sculptures**, while to the right is a colonnaded gallery displaying traditional classics from painters such as Mohamed Serguini and others. A second, larger ground-floor gallery is dedicated to contemporary works from a number of leading Moroccan artists, including Tetouan-based Hassan Echair and Safaa Erruas. The upstairs gallery exhibits a wide range of works – abstract, impressionist and contemporary – by **Moroccan artists**.

Ensemble Artisanal

Av Hassan II

The **Ensemble Artisanal** on the main road below the town has a wide range of **handicrafts** for sale on the ground floor, which are worth a look if you're planning to make purchases in the souks and want to assess prices and quality first. However, the

1

main points of interest are upstairs, where you will find a fascinating array of carpet and embroidery **workshops**, and outside the building, where there are metalwork, basketry and musical instrument artisans at work. This is a unique opportunity to get up close to the craftsmen and -women and their work without feeling pressured into buying anything.

Archeological Museum

2 Rue Ben Hussaien, off Pl al Jala • Charge • ⓦ maroc.net/museums

The **Archeological Museum** was founded during the Spanish protectorate and, unsurprisingly, features exhibits from that zone of influence, including rock carvings from the Western Sahara. Highlights, as so often in North Africa, are the **Roman mosaics**, mostly gathered from Lixus and the oft-plundered Volubilis. Other than these, the most interesting exhibits are concerned with the ancient stone circle at **Mzoura**, near Asilah, including a model and aerial photographs. The signage is all in French, Spanish and Arabic.

El Ensanche

The Spaniards left an attractive architectural legacy behind in Tetouan, largely in the Spanish quarter, **El Ensanche** ("the widening"). Directly west of the Medina's walls, this neighbourhood of wide *avenidas* and tall colonial buildings was the Spanish version of the French Ville Nouvelle. Upon independence, however, El Ensanche faded into a derelict obscurity following decades of little development or investment by the state. In recent years, however, the quarter has benefited greatly from the renewed interest and investment in Tetouan and El Ensanche is once again looking proud and grand. Boulevard Mohammed V, the cobblestoned pedestrian avenue that meanders between Place Moulay el Mehdi and Place al Jala, looks more like a street in Barcelona these days with some interesting examples of Spanish colonial and 1920s Art Deco architecture. At sunset, it's very popular for a stroll and to have coffee or ice cream.

ARRIVAL AND INFORMATION · TETOUAN

By bus Besides CTM, all buses serve Tetouan's *gare routière*, 1km south of the city; *petits taxis* are usually parked out the front of the building. Ticket booths are on the ground floor, and Supratours also have an office in the Ville Nouvelle, on Bd 10 Mai. CTM buses (ticket office daily 4am–midnight) use their own separate station, more conveniently located just below the Medina on Av Hassan II.

Destinations Al Hoceima (2 CTM & over 5 others daily; 8hr); Casablanca (5 CTM & over 10 others daily; 6–7hr); Chefchaouen (5 CTM & over 10 others daily; 1–2hr); Fez (4 CTM & over 10 others daily; 6hr); Fnideq (for Ceuta; 1 CTM & over 10 others daily; 1hr); Larache (2 CTM & over 5 daily; 2–3hr); Marrakesh (1 CTM & over 5 others daily; 9–10hr); Nador (2 CTM & over 5 others daily; 13hr); Oued Laou (5 daily;

1hr 30min); Rabat (5 CTM & over 10 others daily; 5–6hr); Tangier (4 CTM & over 20 others daily; 1hr–1hr 30min).

By grand taxi Collective *grands taxis* for Tangier and Chefchaouen arrive and depart from Av Khaled Ibnou el Oualid, west of town, a 20min walk or short *petit taxi* ride. *Grands taxis* to Fnideq (Ceuta border), Mdiq, Martil and Cabo Negro leave from Av Hassan II; those for Oued Laou leave from the beginning of Av Ksar el Kebir, which is the Oued Laou turn-off from Av Hassan II, not far from Bab el Okla.

Destinations Chefchaouen (1hr); Fnideq (for Ceuta; 20min); Martil (15min); Mdiq (20min); Oued Laou (1hr); Tangier (1hr).

Tourist information 30 Bd Mohammed V ☎ 0539 961915; official guides can be enlisted here.

ACCOMMODATION · SEE MAP PAGE 104

MEDINA

★ **Africa** 17 Kaid Ahmed ☎ 0539 701520. Popular with ultra-budget travellers, this spotless guesthouse near the Royal Palace and the riads below is in a typical medina house

with arches and mosaics and is run by affable Nordin who will ply guests with mint tea and tell his tales. Four doubles, and other rooms accommodate up to four (including single travellers; 80dh), good shared bathrooms with hot water,

1

and magnificent medina views from the rooftop terrace. €

Blanco Riad 25 Zankat Zawiya Kadiria ⓦ blancoriad. com. This former Spanish Consulate, in an arched lane off Bd Mohammed V, is surprisingly spacious with a central courtyard and separate paved garden area. The eight rooms and one suite range in style from small and minimalistic to grand and exquisitely Andalusian. There's also a hammam and great restaurant (see page 108). BB €€

★ **El Reducto** 38 Zankat Zawiya Kadiria ⓦ elreducto. com. Tetouan's most upmarket accommodation, this small riad was the home of the city's Grand Vizier in the 1940s, and was lovingly brought back to life in 2006 by the current owner. Six suites, each individually furnished in the Andalusian style, overlook a central courtyard and an excellent restaurant (see page 108). Book ahead. BB €

Riad Dalia 25 Pl el Ouessaa ☎ 0539 964318. This older riad once housed the Dutch Consul-General. A quirky combination of palatial and antique (though they're in danger of becoming tired), the seven rooms range from very large and luxurious to tiny, with a shared bathroom. This range in room types (and costs) attracts a welcoming mix of travellers. There's a great roof terrace and an in-house restaurant. BB €

EL ENSANCHE

Al Mandari Av Moulay Abbas 108 ⓦ hotelalmandari. ma. This fairly new offering has 32 spacious, light-filled rooms on four storeys with a/c, TV and coffee machines, some with balconies and singles and triples available. The restaurant on the first floor has great views of the mountains around Tetouan and offers a good-value

Moroccan and Italian menu. BB €€

Atenas 7 Bd Allal Ben Abdellah ⓦ hotelatenas.ma. This modern hotel is a class above anything else in this part of town, with eighty large rooms over four floors, all en suite with satellite TV, a small fridge and balcony, and some small but good-value triples (815dh). There's a restaurant and covered parking. BB €€

Oumaima Av 10 Mai ☎ 0539 963473. This ageing hotel is central and functional but a little soulless. The rooms are on the small side but are all en suite with TV. The ground-floor café does a nice breakfast. €

Panorama Vista Av Moulay el Abbas ☎ 0539 964970. In a handy location close to the CTM bus station and with indeed a lovely panoramic view from the mountain-facing rooms, this three-star hotel offers 63 dated but clean rooms with small en suites. Parking is chargeable and there's a restaurant 150m away for supper. BB €€

Regina 8 Rue Sidi Mandri ⓦ hotelreginamaroc.com. This ageing, budget hotel still offers very good value for money. The large, bright rooms have colourful, Riffian fabrics on the beds and clean bathrooms with constant hot water. A ground-floor café serves breakfast. €

OUT OF TOWN

Chams Rue Abdelkhalek Torres ⓦ hotel-chams.com. This three-storey, modern hotel is 3km out of town and perhaps only worth it if you have your own transport. The en-suite rooms are all very comfortable with a/c and satellite TV, and there's a good-sized swimming pool and in-house restaurant. Large discounts out of season. BB €€€

EATING

SEE MAP PAGE 104

RESTAURANTS

MEDINA

Blanco Riad 25 Zankat Zawiya Kadiria ⓦ blancoriad. com. Serving the best cuisine in the city, this riad's (see page 108) restaurant offers tables inside a traditional indoor courtyard of whitewashed walls studded with exquisite zellij tiling, or in a peaceful, sunny stone-paved outdoor garden. The menu – traditional Moroccan with a contemporary Mediterranean twist – is incredibly inventive; think seafood pastilla or goat and caramelized fig tajine. €€

El Reducto 38 Zankat Zawiya Kadiria ⓦ elreducto. com. The menu (in Spanish; ask for a translation) at this stylish restaurant in a riad (see page 108) takes inspiration from Tetouan's Spanish and Moroccan heritage; try their signature dolmas or *kefta* tajine. Choose to dine on the cosy, traditionally decorated ground-floor courtyard or flop back on loungers under a rooftop tent. It's also one of the few places that serves wine and spirits. €€

EL ENSANCHE

★ **Restinga** 21 Av Mohammed V. Eat indoors or in the leafy courtyard at this very pleasant restaurant serving tajine, couscous and fried fish every day since 1968. Popular with locals for a midday meal, the service is attentive, with some English-speaking staff. Beer and wine are available. €

La Union 1 Pasaje Achaach. Popular with locals, this budget place serves up standard Moroccan fare, including *harira*, brochettes and a reasonable meat tajine. To find it, go through the arcades opposite Cinema Español. No alcohol. €

CAFÉS

EL ENSANCHE

Café de Paris Pl Moulay el Mehdi. A large café on the main square, which has become quite a fashionable and relatively female-friendly hangout. Besides great coffee and mint tea, there are also fresh pastries and some delicious gateaux on offer.

Chatt Rue Mourakah Annual. A small and popular diner that's been serving up fast (and cheap) snack food for years. The wall-mounted menu offers pretty much everything

you'd need for breakfast (pastries, fresh orange juice), plus tea, coffee, burgers, omelettes and snacks (mains €).
Patisserie Rahmouni Bd Youssef Ben Tachfine. Clean, modern café-patisserie with a good selection of breakfast and tea delights, such as chocolate doughnuts, croissants, *baghrir* (Moroccan crumpet), and plenty of cakes and biscuits, purchased by weight. There's also ice cream, coffee and tea, plus tables with waiter service.

ENTERTAINMENT

Cinema Avenida Pl al Adala. Shows current release movies, including the odd Hollywood flick, though it will always be dubbed.
Cinema Español Bd Mohammed Torres. Mainly shows "*L'histoire et la géographie*" (a double bill of Bollywood and kung fu).
Institut Français du Nord 13 Bd Chakib Arsalane ⓦif-maroc.org/tetouan. The cultural arm of the French government, the Tetouan branch is quite active and often presents cultural events such as exhibitions, films and live performances.
Instituto Cervantes 93 Bd Mohammed Torres ⓦtetuan.cervantes.es. Like its French counterpart, this branch of Spain's cultural organization provides a weekly programme of film screenings, discussions, concerts and general cultural exchange.

DIRECTORY

Banks and exchange Attijariwafa Bank, BMCI and Société Général Bank are all on Bd Sidi el Manri. Alma Change is on Av Mohamed Ameziane close to the Bab es Saida gate to the medina.
Hospitals Clinique Nakhil, 74 Av Hassan II (☎0539 962600, ⓦcliniquenakhil.com); Hospital Régionale De Tetouan, Av Abdelkhalek Torres (about 2km from the city centre; ☎0535 998750).

The Tetouan coast: Fnideq to Oued Laou

Despite the numbers of tourists passing through, Tetouan is above all a resort for Moroccans, rich and poor alike – a character very much in evidence on the extensive **beaches** to the east of the town. Throughout the summer, whole villages of family tents appear at **Martil**, **Mdiq** and, particularly, around **Restinga-Smir** and **Fnideq**, further north. **Oued Laou**, 40km southeast of Tetouan, is the destination of a younger, more alternative crowd. The general increase of investment in the region has encompassed this section of the coast, with the appearance of beachside promenades (*corniches*) as well as new hotels and all-inclusive resorts with private mini-marinas.

Fnideq

Fnideq, sometimes called by its Spanish name Castillejos, has little to recommend it, especially compared with Mdiq and Martil further along the coast. However, it has seen some development of late, including a **beachside promenade** between here and the beach at Restinga-Smir, and there's a couple of good hotels; if you're arriving late in the day on your way to or from Ceuta, it makes a decent stopover.

TETOUAN'S FESTIVALS

Tetouan's International Mediterranean Film Festival (Festival International du Cinéma Méditerranéen; ⓦfestivaltetouan.org), takes place around the end of March each year. Established in 1985 by a group of Tetouan-based film lovers and originally called "Rencontres Cinématographiques de Tétouan" (Tetouan Film Encounters), the week-long festival has since become truly Mediterranean and features a diverse offering of over eighty films from all over the region.

The **moussem of Moulay Abdessalem Ben Mchich** is a very religious, traditional occasion with a large number of Riffian tribesmen in attendance. It's usually held on 1 July at the saint's *marabout*, or tomb on a flat mountain-top near the village of Beni Arouss, about halfway between Tetouan and Chefchaouen off the N2. Contact the Tourist Information Office in Tetouan (see page 107) for more information.

1

By bus Fnideq's *gare routière* is in the centre of the town, set a couple of blocks back from the seafront highway. *Grands taxis* ply the route from the station to the Ceuta border, about 3km away (7dh).

Destinations Casablanca (1 CTM & 2 others daily; 6hr); Martil (6–10 daily; 30min); Mdiq (6–10 daily; 20 min); Rabat (1 CTM & 2 others daily; 4hr 30min); Tangier (10 daily; 2hr); Tetouan (1 CTM & over 10 others daily; 1hr).

By grand taxi *Grands taxis* gather at both the bus station and a separate taxi rank at the northern (Ceuta) end of town. They depart for the Ceuta border (5min; see page 101) throughout the day, though the wait is a little longer during the night, and similarly for Tetouan (35min) via Restinga-Smir, Mdiq (15min) and Martil (25min). There are also irregular runs to Tangier (1hr), travelling directly past the Tanger Med port.

ACCOMMODATION AND EATING

La Corniche Av Hassan II, southern end of town towards Restinga-Smir ☎ 0539 976163. The best of Fnideq's hotels, with modern, comfortable rooms, some with sea views and balconies. There's also a classy sea-facing café-restaurant, which offers light meals like omelettes, pizzas and salads (€), and usefully an underground carpark. BB €€
Senator Route de Ceuta, northern end of town ☎ 0539 677777. This smart white block is a former Ibis hotel and

has good facilities including a large pool with pleasant sun terrace and a decent restaurant. The 101 rooms have recently been refurbished and are very comfortable with TV and a/c, though note that those facing the sea also face the busy Av Hassan II road. Note that entry is via the parallel Route de Ceuta which joins Av Hassan II at a roundabout 250 m north of the hotel. Parking is extra. BB €€

Mdiq

Mdiq is a lovely coastal town and an active fishing port. A popular promenade overlooks the town beach (which gets better the further north you go) while a vibrant **café-restaurant quarter** lies one block back. The small port has recently been redeveloped and split into roughly two halves; one side retains the fishing industry while the other is now an **upmarket marina with a yacht club** There are a handful of nice places to stay and plenty of seafood to eat, which only adds weight to the town's honest claim of being the best of Morocco's northwestern coastal resorts.

By bus and grand taxi Mdiq is on the bus and *grand taxi* route between Fnideq and Tetouan, with both forms of transport operating from a large open stand at the northern entrance to the town, a 5–10min walk from all the action.

The frequency of services increases July–Aug.
Destinations Fnideq (for Ceuta; 15–20min); Martil (10–15min); Tangier (via Fnideq or Tetouan; 1hr 30min to 2hr); Tetouan (15–25min).

ACCOMMODATION

Badis Cnr Av Lalla Nezha and Av Casablanca, northern end of town ☎ 0539 663030. Three floors of small but modern rooms with TV, some sleeping up to four comfortably and others with sea views. However, the main road down below can be noisy with traffic in season. A ground-floor café serves a decent breakfast of pastries and eggs. BB €€
Golden Beach Av Lalla Nehza 84, on the beachside corniche at the northern entrance to town ☎ 0539 975077. This large resort-style hotel has long been one of the best along this coast. The sea is so close that rooms with a

sea view feel like they're literally in the water. Besides a very decent restaurant, there's a large swimming pool, a bar and a nightclub, which can get pretty loud during the summer holidays; request a room away from it during this time. BB €€
Zain Av Omar Ibn Abdelazziz, centre of town ☎ 0539 664995. This modern and comfortable hotel is a five-minute walk from Av Lalla Nezha and the beach, which makes it quieter than most, with four floors of bright and airy en suites with TV, microwaves, fridges, and excellent walk-in showers. No breakfast but plenty of cafés nearby. €

EATING

Besides the beachside eating options listed below, there's a bevy of cafés and cheap restaurants gathered along a couple of **pedestrianized streets** just one block back from the beach. During the season, this area has a great atmosphere throughout the day and into the night.

Cafe Blue Sky Av Lalla Nehza ⓦ cafe-blue-sky.negocio. site. Overlooking the beach next to *Las Olas* below, this family-friendly spot with an oceanfront terrace that is very popular during the summer season. It offers an impressive and reasonably priced menu of anything from sandwiches,

pizzas and tacos to paella and grilled fish and calamari. A good coffee or ice-cream stop, too. €€
Las Olas Corniche car park, Av Lalla Nezha ☎0539 664433. This beachfront landmark, resembling a lighthouse,

offers fantastic views as well as a decent menu. More of a café downstairs and restaurant upstairs, the a la carte menu offers good variety, with some Italian and Moroccan standards accompanying the seafood. €€

DIRECTORY

Banks Attijariwafa Bank, Banque Populaire BMCE and Crédit Agricole (all with ATMs) are all on Av Lalla Nehza.
Golf Royal Golf of Cabo Negro, Route de Martil, located between Martil and Mdiq �🌐golfcabonegro.com. 18 holes;

clubs, caddies and carts can be hired.
Post office Poste Maroc is on Av Abdelkarim el Khatabi, opposite the bus and *grand taxi* stand.

Martil

Martil, only 10km or a 15-minute drive from the centre of Tetouan and essentially the city's beach, was its port as well until the river between the two silted up. Today it is a modern **seaside town** which takes on a resort-like feel in summer when Moroccan families flood the beach to escape the heat. The **beach**, stretching all the way around to the headland of Cabo Negro, is an 8km stretch of fine, yellow sand that is long enough to remain uncrowded, despite its summer popularity and colonization by Club Med and other tourist complexes.

ARRIVAL AND DEPARTURE   MARTIL

By bus and grand taxi Martil is on the bus and *grand taxi* route between Fnideq and Tetouan, with the frequency of services increasing July–Aug. Buses operate from a large water tower located five streets back from the southern end of the beachside corniche, while *grands taxis* can be found

opposite the Mohammed V Mosque off Av Moulay el Hassan II (the N16 highway to Tetouan).
Destinations Fnideq (for Ceuta; 25–35min); Mdiq (10–15min); Tangier (via Fnideq or Tetouan; 1hr 40min to 2hr 15min); Tetouan (10–15min).

ACCOMMODATION AND EATING

Besides the hotel restaurants below, there's a string of café-restaurants on the land side of the beachfront promenade.
Etoile de la Mer Av Moulay el Hassan II, southern end of the beachfront ☎0539 979058. One block from the beach and close to the *grand taxi* rank, with clean and colourful en suite rooms, some with sea views, although hot water is intermittent. The in-house restaurant (open to non-guests) serves up good breakfasts and some seafood dishes and has pleasant pavement tables. BB €
Hacienda Route de Cabo Negro �🌐haciendamartil. com. A 10-minute walk from Martil's beach, this sprawling, friendly hacienda offers a surprising number of spacious, though slightly dated rooms (some sleep four comfortably),

as well as large bungalows with equipped kitchen. There's a lovely swimming pool surrounded by a leafy garden, and a good in-house licensed restaurant that's open to non-guests. BB €€€
Suites Hôtel Omeya Av Lalla Hasna Corniche ☎0539 688888. Easily the best hotel in town, with a range of modern rooms and suites, all with a sizeable balcony and great sea views. The restaurant specializes in seafood and Moroccan standards, while a street-front café is a good spot for a quick coffee or lunch. There's also a second-floor piano-lounge-cum-bar with live (and loud) music most weekends; ask for a room on one of the higher floors. Rates include breakfast and dinner. €€€

Oued Laou

Travelling southeast from Tetouan, the coastline almost immediately changes and you come under the shadow of the **Rif**. The coastal highway (N16) continues to follow the coast while also hugging the foothills of the Rif; it's a stunning drive. Though experiencing something of a construction boom since the N16 was paved in 2012, **Oued Laou** – named after the River Laou that reaches the ocean here from its source in the Rif mountains near Chefchaouen – is still quieter than the more popular beach towns closer to Tetouan. It's not an especially pretty place (Riffian villages tend to look spread out and lack any core) but it has a near-deserted beach, which extends for miles on each side, particularly to the southeast, where the river has created a wide, fertile bay

1

down to **Kâaseras**, 8km distant. There's not much to do other than relax, read, swim and watch the fishermen hauling in their nets of seabream, anchovies and sardines – not an altogether terrible itinerary. On Tuesdays there is a **souk** held in Oued Laou's main square, which draws villagers from all over the valley.

ARRIVAL AND DEPARTURE

OUED LAOU

By bus and grand taxi Buses and *grands taxis* operate from the old village square, one block back from the beach, opposite the mosque.
Destinations (bus) Chefchaouen (daily; 1hr 30min); El

Jebha via Kâaseras (daily; 5hr); Tetouan (3 daily; 2hr).
Destinations (grand taxi) Dar Ackoubaa (for connecting taxis to Chefchaouen and Tetouan; 20min); Kâaseras (20min).

ACCOMMODATION

Mare Norstrum 4km north of Oued Laou, signposted off the N16 ☎ 0677 628287. The Tetouan coast's one true luxury option, situated on a cliff overlooking a secluded bay. The ten large bungalows with four-poster beds all offer sea views from good-sized balconies, and there's a good restaurant and a stunning infinity pool; however, it's a bit of

trek down to the beach and back up. BB €€€
Oued Laou 8 Bd Massira ☎ 0648 064435. This basic but friendly hotel is one block from the beach in a cul-de-sac bordering the village's new square and corniche. It is open year-round and has simple yet clean and sunny rooms, with shared toilets and bathrooms. €

EATING AND DRINKING

Aramar 2 Bd Massira ☎ 0539 569854. The best of a number of beachfront restaurants. While fresh fish is the house speciality (the fishing boats are right out front), there's also a pretty good menu offering Moroccan standards such as tajines, brochettes and *harira* soup. €
Café Picasso Picasso beach, 3km north of village

centre ☎ 0661 459865. Built into the rock and made from driftwood and reeds, *Café Picasso* is like something out of *Robinson Crusoe*. This is a great place to relax and in the summer months the owner cooks up tajines on the beach, and they serve (usually warm) beer. €

Chefchaouen

An isolated refuge for over four hundred years before absorption in the 1920s into the Spanish Protectorate, **CHEFCHAOUEN** (pronounced "shef-**sha**-wen", sometimes abbreviated to Chaouen) remains today somewhat aloof from the goings-on in the rest of the country. Visiting Chefchaouen requires venturing into the rugged **Rif mountains** and it almost feels by chance that one comes upon the town, still hidden beneath the towering peaks from which it takes its name. The setting, like much of the Rif, is largely rural and the bright lights and bustling noise of cities less than half a day's drive away are soon forgotten. That's not to say that Chefchaouen is completely isolated, for the town has long been a stop on the backpacker circuit – thanks in part to the easy availability of the Rif's *kif* – and it has also now become popular with mainstream tourists, who are arriving in increasing numbers to wander the town's blue-washed Medina, surely the prettiest in the country.

While the increase in visitors has inevitably led to a slight rise in hassle, local attitudes are still very relaxed, and the Medina *pensions* are among the friendliest and cheapest around.

Brief history

Chefchaouen translates to "watch the horns" in Berber, in reference to the mountain that is split in two by the slope on which the town lies. The region hereabouts has forever been sacred to Muslims due to the presence of the tomb of **Moulay Abdessalam Ben Mchich** – patron saint of the Jebali Riffian tribesmen – and over the centuries has acquired a considerable reputation for pilgrimage and *marabouts* – "saints", believed to hold supernatural powers. An isolated location, it was the perfect base in 1471 for one of Moulay Abdessalam's *shereefian* (descendant of the Prophet) followers, Hassan Ben Mohamed el Alami, known as **Abu Youma**, to launch secret attacks on the Portuguese in their coastal enclaves of Asilah, Tangier, Ceuta and Ksar es Seghir. Abu Youma

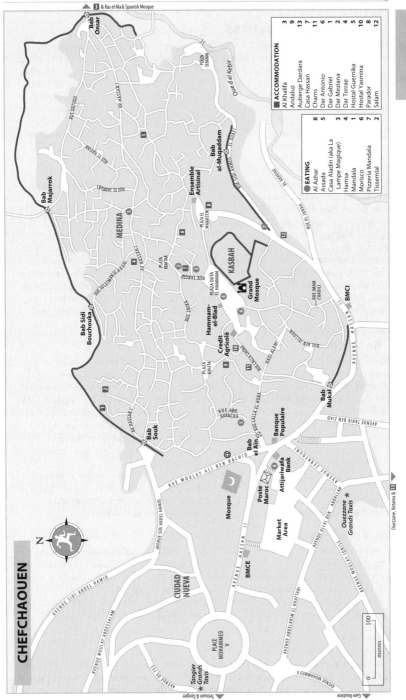

CHEFCHAOUEN

ACCOMMODATION	
Al Khalifa	3
Andaluz	9
Auberge Dardara	13
Casa Hassan	7
Chams	11
Dar Antonio	6
Dar Gabriel	1
Dar Meziana	4
Dar Terrae	4
Hostal Guernika	5
Hostal Yasmina	10
Parador	8
Salam	12

● EATING	
Al Azhar	8
Assada	5
Casa Aladin (aka La Lampe Magique)	3
Hamsa	4
Mandala	1
Morisco	6
Pizzeria Mandala	7
Tissemlal	2

1

NO ENTRY FOR CHRISTIANS

Until the arrival of Spanish troops in 1920, Chefchaouen had been visited by just three Westerners. Two were missionary explorers: **Charles de Foucauld**, a Frenchman who spent just an hour in the town in 1883, disguised as a Jewish rabbi, and **William Summers**, an American who was poisoned by the townsfolk here in 1892. The third, in 1889, was the British journalist **Walter Harris** (see page 533), whose main impulse, as described in his book, *Land of an African Sultan*, was "the very fact that there existed within thirty hours' ride of Tangier a city in which it was considered an utter impossibility for a Christian to enter". Thankfully, Chefchaouen today is more welcoming towards outsiders, and a number of the Medina's newer guesthouses now include owners hailing from Britain, Italy and the former Christian enemy, Spain.

perished in one of these raids and his cousin, Ali Ben Rachid moved the settlement to its current site on the other side of the river.

In the ensuing decades, as the population was boosted by Muslim and Jewish refugees from Spain, Chefchaouen grew increasingly **anti-Christian** and autonomous. For a time, it was the centre of a semi-independent emirate, exerting control over much of the northwest, in alliance with the Wattasid sultans of Fez. Later, however, it became an almost completely isolated backwater. When the Spanish arrived in 1920, they were astonished to find the Jews here speaking medieval Castilian, a language that hadn't been heard on the Iberian peninsula for four hundred years. In 1924 the Spanish were repelled back to the coast by the Riffian rebel leader Abd el Krim el Khattabi (see page 124), but two years later they retook Chefchaouen and held it until the end of the Protectorate in 1956.

The Medina

Chefchaouen's **Medina** is small when compared to others in Morocco, and it is undoubtedly a place to enjoy exploring at random. The architecture has a strong Andalusian character, reflecting the city's history: Sultan Mohammed Ben Abdallah (Mohammed III) ordered the Jewish families to move into the Medina around 1760, their **Mellah** taking in the area that today encompasses the southern quarter between the kasbah and Bab el Aïn. Here they built their whitewashed ochre houses with small balconies, tiled roofs and Andalusian-style courtyards. It's from this time that Chefchaouen's famous shades of **blue** arose, the Jews adding indigo into the whitewash to contrast the Mellah against the traditional green of Islam.

The main gateway to the Medina is **Bab el Aïn**, a tiny arched entrance at the junction of Avenue Hassan II with Rue Moulay Ali Ben Rachid. Through the gate a clearly dominant lane winds up through the Medina to the main square, **Plaza Outa el Hammam** and beyond to a second, smaller square, **Plaza el Makhzen.**

Plaza Outa el Hammam

Considering the compact layout of the Medina, **Plaza Outa el Hammam** is surprisingly large. It takes its name from the number of public hammams that used to be located on or around the plaza – one still exists and is tourist-friendly (see page 117). Watching over the plaza's daily proceedings is Jamae Kebir, the **Grand Mosque**. Chefchaouen's oldest and largest mosque, it was built in 1560 by Moulay Mohamed, son of the town's founding father Ali Ben Rachid; its octagonal minaret was added to the mosque in the 1700s.

The kasbah

Plaza Outa el Hammam • Charge for museum

The town's **kasbah**, a quiet ruin with shady gardens, was built by Ali Ben Rachid in 1471, when he moved the original settlement from across the other side of the Ras el Ma River. Inside, and immediately to the right, in the first of its compounds, are the old town prison cells, where Abd el Krim (see page 124) was imprisoned after his surrender in nearby Targuist in 1926. Four years earlier, he had driven the Spanish from the town, a retreat that saw the loss of several thousand of their troops. Also within the kasbah is a small **art gallery** exhibiting works from local artists, and an **Ethnographic Museum** housing musical instruments, ancient weapons, tapestries and carpets, as well as interesting photos of old Chefchaouen. It's also worth climbing the tower for the broad view of the town and taking a stroll through the beautiful grounds.

Plaza el Makhzen
Ensemble Artisanal

Plaza el Makhzen – the colonial-era "government square" – is an elegant clearing with an old fountain and flanked by souvenir stalls. It's home to the **Ensemble Artisanal**, where a few craftworkers can be seen producing the town's signature brightly coloured rugs and thick woollen jumpers.

Ras el Ma
Just outside Bab Onsar – dating back to the early 1500s and the Medina's easternmost exit – **Ras el Ma** (head of the water) is where the Oued el Kebir bursts from a sheer cliff-face to cascade down the mountain slope. Riffian women do their **laundry** here, at a number of modern, concrete washhouses complete with diverted water channels and built-in washboards. A good view of the river and surrounding area can be enjoyed from **Plaza Sebanin**, from where a small bridge leads to a compact residential quarter on the other side. Along the far side of the river are narrow canals that used to carry water to power **flourmills**. The mill houses are now a couple of pleasant, shaded riverside cafés, and while another is still intact, it's unused.

Spanish Mosque
Over to the east of the town, an enjoyable, though uphill thirty-minute walk from Bab Onsar brings you to the "**Spanish Mosque**". Built by the Spanish in the early 1920s, the mosque itself has never been used and was derelict up until 2010, when it was restored, again by the Spanish. Set on a hilltop with sweeping views of both the Medina and the surrounding countryside, it's a popular meeting point for young locals. Alongside the path to the mosque are some spectacular **rock-climbing pitches** (see page 124), and in the limestone hills behind, there are active **cave systems** – the source of local springs.

ARRIVAL AND DEPARTURE	CHEFCHAOUEN

By bus The *gare routière* is 1.5km southwest (and downhill) from the town centre – about a 15min walk. Alternatively catch a *petit taxi* (unmetered) to/from Bab el Aïn (the main gate to the Medina) or to the main taxi drop off point inside

---

HIKES AROUND CHEFCHAOUEN

For a short, but uphill, 1.5km walk from the Medina's Bab Onsar, follow the easily found trail to the *Hotel Atlas* (one of the town's largest buildings, you can't miss it). As you get higher there's a great view over Chefchaouen and the Rif Mountains from the north. A good **day's hike** from Chefchaouen is to head east, up over the mountains behind. As you look at the "two horns" from town, there is a path winding along the side of the mountain on your left. A four-hour (or more) hike will take you up to the other side, where a vast valley opens up, and if you walk further, you'll see the sea. The valley, as even casual exploration will show, is full of small farms cultivating *kif* – as they have done for years. Walking here, you may occasionally be stopped by the military, which is cracking down on foreign involvement in the crop. For more ambitious hikes – and there are some wonderful paths in the area – ask at the *pensions* about hiring a **guide**. Someone knowledgeable can usually be found to accompany you for a small fee.

1

THE R410

If you have your own transport and wish to head towards the west coast from Chefchaouen, an alternative route to the N13 is the **R410 to Ksar el Kebir** and is a highly recommended scenic route and a short cut. After heading south from Chefchaouen, the road is signed off the N13 on your right about 2km after Derdara (11km from Chefchaouen). The route wends its way through wooded high country following the Oued Loukkos to the Barrage Oued el Makhazine reservoir, where there are magnificent vistas, and on to Ksar el Kebir.

the Medina at Plaza el Makhzen. Some waiting outside the bus station will try to charge arriving tourists a higher fee – ignore them and walk down the street a bit and flag one down. CTM & most other companies start their Chefchaouen routes elsewhere, so buses can arrive full, with no space. It's best to book a ticket in advance, or at least arrive at the station early.

Destinations Al Hoceima (3 CTM daily; 6–7hr); Casablanca (1 CTM & 1–2 others daily; 6hr); Fez (4 CTM & over 5 others daily; 4hr 30min); Rabat (1 CTM & 2 others daily; 5hr); Tangier (1 CTM & over 10 others daily, ask for a direct *sans détour* service; 3hr); Tetouan (5 CTM & over 10 others daily; 1–2hr).

By grand taxi *Grands taxis* for Bab Berred (connecting there for Issaguen Ketama and points east) operate from around the junction of Av Allal Ben Abdallah and Av Zerktouni. Tangier and Tetouan services operate from Av Jamal Dine el Afghani, off the west side of Pl Mohammed V.

Destinations Bab Berred (50min); Tangier (2hr); Tetouan (1hr).

ACCOMMODATION

SEE MAP PAGE 113

Chefchaouen can get bitterly cold during winter and all of those listed proclaim to have hot water, though few will have any room heating other than plenty of blankets. Although it gets busy in the summer months and booking is advisable, if you are arriving on spec at any time of year, it's well worth asking for a discount on rack rates.

MEDINA

Andaluz 1 Rue Sidi Hmed El Bouhali ☎0539 986034. Small, functional *pension* with friendly management, signposted off to the left at the near end of Plaza Outa el Hammam. Rooms face an inner courtyard and have shared showers; there's a kitchen and a nice rooftop terrace, with a handy tub for doing your laundry. €

★ **Casa Hassan** 22 Rue Targui ⓦcasahassan.com. Located 100m from Plaza Outa el Hammam, the eight en suite, a/c and heated rooms in this stylish guesthouse feature traditional furnishings and artwork from local artists. Breakfast is served where you choose - the courtyard with its fountain, the rooftop terrace or in your room. There's also a hammam, lounge with fireplace and the excellent Tissemlal restaurant. HB €€

Chams 22 Rue Lalla el Hora ☎0539 987784. A good compromise of *pension* price and hotel comfort, this centrally located place has large, modern rooms (en suite or shared bath), a dining area and a very pleasant terrace. Eight of the sixteen rooms are singles. BB €

★ **Dar Antonio** 36 Calle Garmata ☎0539 989997. This cosy guesthouse was personally restored and imaginatively decorated by the hands-on owner-manager. The seven rooms sleep from one to four and each is unique, colourful and warm, and there's even one with a working fireplace. There's a kitchen, two shared bathrooms, courtyard and rooftop terrace. €€

Dar Gabriel Derb Cadi Ben Maimoun, Bab Souk ☎0539 989244. British-owned and Moroccan-managed, this is one of the better guesthouses in the Medina. The compact (though not poky) rooms are all simply but thoughtfully furnished, while the common areas include a dining room with fireplace, and a three-tiered rooftop terrace. BB €€

Dar Meziana 7 Rue Zagdud, Bab Souk ⓦriadmeziana. com. One of the Medina's most luxurious guesthouses, with three floors of compact, tastefully decorated en suite and a/c rooms and suites overlooking an open-plan courtyard and kitchen. Comfortable common areas, as well as great panoramic views from the terrace, plus a hammam. HB €€

Dar Terrae Av Hassan I, Quartier Andalous ⓦdarterrae. com. One of Chefchaouen's earliest Medina riads, this charming old Andalusian-style house has a great homely atmosphere. The six cheerful rooms are all tastefully furnished, reflecting the Italian owner's taste, and though not all are en suite and only some have a fireplace, each has its own terrace. BB €€

Hostal Guernika 49 Rue Onsar ☎0539 987434. This old house, in the higher quarter of the Medina, towards Bab Onsar, has been superbly converted by its Basque owner. Life here revolves around the central fireplace and small library in winter, and the rooftop terrace in summer. The rooms are all en suite; ask for a mountain view. Extra charge for a room heater. Breakfast available. €

Hostal Yasmina 12 Rue Lalla el Hora ☎0539 883118. Small, bright and clean with just six modern rooms; the back four face inward with no outside windows. It's very conveniently located, just off Plaza Outa el Hammam, and a very pleasant little place to stay. There are shared hot showers, and during summer – when you should book ahead – guests are welcome to sleep on the rooftop terrace. €

1

OUTSIDE THE MEDINA

Al Khalifa Av Ras el Ma ⓦ hotel-alkhalifa.com. Close to Ras el Ma and a 5min stroll from Bab Onsar, this two-star offering has modern, spacious en suite rooms with sweeping Medina and mountain views from large arched windows. Breakfast can be taken in a large salon inside or at a shaded table outside. Attentive service. Parking. BB €€

Parador Pl el Makhzen ⓦ hotel-parador.com. This former Spanish "grand hotel" is in a great location on the edge of the Medina in the ciudad nueva (new town), and offers an adjoining car park. Popular with both independent travellers and tour groups, there are stunning mountain vistas from a poolside terrace and bar. The 56 rooms and suites are comfortable and have TV and a/c, and they're also heated in winter. €€€

Salam 39 Av Hassan II ☎ 0539 986239. A cheap, friendly place also in the ciudad nueva and a favourite with backpackers who don't want to be in the Medina. The high-ceilinged rooms are very basic, and bathrooms are shared although hot water is not to be relied on. The back rooms as well as a shady roof terrace overlook the valley. €

OUT OF TOWN

Auberge Dardara 11km from Chefchaouen at the junction of the N2 to Al Hoceima and P28 to Ouezzane ⓦ aubergedardara. Guests, including King Mohammed VI when he was prince, come here to experience a unique blend of rustic getaway and agri-tourism. The brainchild of local resident El Hababi Jaber ("Jabba"), the *Auberge* has twelve comfortable rooms. The restaurant serves fresh, hearty food. €€€

EATING

SEE MAP PAGE 113

While not offering any great culinary experience, Plaza Outa el Hammam is Chefchaouen's prime spot for a meal day or night. There are about a dozen restaurants on the plaza, all with outdoor tables for prime people watching. Note if you're travelling during Ramadan, you'll be asked to dine indoors out of respect for local people. One of the few places selling alcohol in Chefchaouen is *Hôtel Parador*.

MEDINA

Assada Rue Abi Khancha, just north of Bab el Aïn ☎ 619-569778. Extending across the lane and above to an open rooftop terrace, this has long been a favourite of locals and travellers alike. Very friendly service and food all day from breakfast through to a tajine for dinner or a Fri couscous. Also does excellent fruit juice shakes. €

Casa Aladin (aka La Lampe Magique) 17 Rue Targui ☎ 0539 989071. Just north of Plaza Outa el Hammam, with two floors and a terrace, and beautifully done out in *Arabian Nights* style as its name suggests. Expect great tajines, couscous (including vegetarian) and other staple fare. €€

Hamsa 32 Place Outa El Hamam ⓦ hamsachaouen. wixsite.com/akhawat. A child-friendly typical Moroccan restaurant offering a simple menu but it does a great breakfast, lunch or dinner with a view. Vegan and vegetarian options. Try to get a seat on the terrace. €€

★ **Mandala** Av Hassan I, Quartier Andalous ☎ 0654 614449. Not to be confused with the pizzeria of the same name, this *Mandala* is quite different. Consisting of a ground-level restaurant and second-floor lounge area, the three major cultural influences of journeyman-owner Giani "Gigi" Uigi – Italian, Indian and Moroccan – are all evident in the varied menu, ambience, and the many available *kif* pipes. Come here with time to spare, even just for a *chai*, a game of backgammon and some relaxing world music. €€

Morisco Plaza Outa el Hammam ☎ 0539 882323. This is one of the best places on the plaza for a casual meal and it also has a terrace on the second floor with great views of the Kasbah and mosque. Apart from sandwiches, pizzas and grilled fish, local specialities include breakfast of goat's cheese, eggs and olive oil, harira soup, and goat or anchovy tajine. €€

Tissemlal Casa Hassan, 22 Rue Targui ⓦ casahassan. com. A long-standing and popular restaurant, with a choice between tables on the ground floor with a fireplace and an upstairs roof terrace. Serving only a set menu with a small selection of starters and a good choice of mains including a few tajines, *grillés*, fish and couscous dishes. The atmosphere is welcoming and the is standard good. €€

CIUDAD NUEVA (NEW TOWN)

Al Azhar At the bottom of the steps on Av Moulay Idriss. Popular local snack restaurant with good food and service. Fast and cheap, with a choice of brochettes, tajines, grilled chicken, sandwiches and omelettes. €

Pizzeria Mandala Cnr Av Hassan II and Rue Sidi Ahmed el Ouafi ⓦ pizzeriamandala.com. This intimate Italian restaurant is popular with locals. As well as pizzas, the menu offers numerous pasta and meat dishes, as well as some great salads, desserts and ice cream. Takeaway & delivery. €

DIRECTORY

Banks and exchange Banque Populaire and Attijariwafa Bank (with ATMs) are both on Av Hassan II, opposite Bab el Aïn. A BMCI bureau de change (with ATM) is on Av Hassan II. Crédit Agricole, with a bureau de change, is on Plaza Outa el Hammam.

Hammam Dating to 1549, Hammam-el-Blad is the only hammam left on Plaza Outa el Hammam and is near *Pension la Castellana*. Note there are cheaper, less historic, options around the Medina – ask at the *pensions* for recommendations.

Internet Almost all accommodation offers wi-fi.

Post office Av Hassan II, opposite the mosque.

The Medi-terranean coast and the Rif

THE COAST NEAR AL HOCEIMA

The Mediterranean coast and the Rif

Morocco's Mediterranean coast extends for nearly 500km, from the Spanish enclave of Ceuta east to Saïdia on the Algerian border. Much of it lies in the shadow of the Rif mountains, which restrict access to the sea to a very few points. Despite a rash of stalled tourism developments dotted along the coast, such beaches as there are here remain mostly low-key and charming; for a seaside stop head for the fishing harbour and holiday resort of Al Hoceima, or to the lively summer resort of Saïdia on the country's (closed) border with Algeria. To the east of the Rif is Oujda, a pleasant, relaxed city within a day's travel from the scenic Zegzel Gorge, and there are further gorges cutting into the Middle Atlas, near the once-important trading centre of Taza. Between Al Hoceima and Oujda is the Spanish enclave of Melilla, an attractive town offering an authentic slice of Spanish life; the dunes and lagoons spreading around nearby Nador are among the richest birdwatching sites in Morocco.

The **Rif mountains** themselves are even less on the tourist trail than the coast – and it's easy to see why. A vast, limestone mass, over 300km long, up to 2500m in height, and with forests of towering oak and cedar, the Rif is the natural boundary between Europe and Africa. Traditionally isolated from central government and the authorities, and with an infamous economy based almost solely on the cultivation of cannabis, or *kif* (see page 127), the Rif is also considered the most wild and remote of Morocco's mountain ranges. For some dramatic Riffian **scenery**, travel between Chefchaouen and Fez, via Issaguen (Ketama) or between Al Hoceima/Nador and Taza, via Aknoul.

Chefchaouen to Al Hoceima

One of Morocco's most memorable journeys is the 210km **mountain road** (the N2) from **Chefchaouen** (see page 112) to **Al Hoceima** which weaves along high on the crests of the Rif mountains. Snow may occasionally block the road in winter but snowploughs soon restore the flow of traffic. The views for most of the year are simply spectacular. Paul Bowles describes the route well in "The Rif, to Music" chapter of *Their Heads Are Green* (see page 533) – "mountains covered with olive trees, with oak trees, with bushes, and finally with giant cedars".

The road from Chefchaouen sweeps steadily upwards through attractive countryside with olive farms, cork oaks and flowery hedgerows to reach the village of **Bab Taza**, where, suddenly, the feeling of being at altitude kicks in. Beyond **Khamis Medik**, the road runs through woods of various oak species with the richest cultivation in the Rif on the impressively deep slopes below, dotted with farms and the expensive and isolated villas that are testimony to the wealth generated by the cannabis trade. The road reaches its highest level at **Bab Besen** (1600m) where the landscape is covered in magnificent cedar forests.

Issaguen (Ketama)

Issaguen (usually marked on maps simply as "Ketama", though that is the name of the region, not the village) sits at the heart of *kif* country, and although hassle has toned

Highlights

❶ Chefchaouen to Al Hoceima The scenic and sometimes vertiginous drive along the northern slopes of the Rif is simply spectacular. See page 120

❷ Al Hoceima National Park The largest protected area on Morocco's Mediterranean coast, with deserted coves, rewarding hikes and a few sleepy fishing hamlets. See page 125

❸ Melilla This sophisticated Spanish enclave boasts a wealth of Art Nouveau buildings and an imposing fortress-like Medina, perfect for touring after tapas. See page 131

❹ Saïdia Close to the Algerian border, this enjoyable beach resort comes alive in summer, hosting a *raï* music and popular arts festival in May. See page 137

❺ Zegzel Gorge Fantastic hiking through dramatic limestone cliffs, terraced fruit groves and magnificent cedar-and-oak forests. See page 140

❻ Cirque du Jebel Tazzeka This classic car-driver's route offers stupendous views of both the Rif and Atlas ranges and passes by the massive Friouato Caves. See page 145

HIGHLIGHTS ARE MARKED ON THE MAP ON PAGE 122

down somewhat in recent years, it still has a rather lawless and menacing edge; if you choose to stop in or around the town your presence may gain the attention of the local *kif* sellers.

The village itself is not much of a place and only worth stopping at if you have to change *grands taxis* or want to check out the Thursday souk. **Driving** through the Ketama area is perfectly possible and immensely picturesque and enjoyable. However, common sense applies; drive only in daylight, don't stop for hitchhikers or people who appear to be asking for help, and never stop if a car pulls over to the side of your vehicle – local sellers sometimes try to pressurize drivers into buying low-grade hash.

ARRIVAL AND DEPARTURE ISSAGUEN (KETAMA)

By grand taxi *Grands taxis* congregate on the main road. Services operate throughout the day, and increase in frequency during the *kif* harvest season (July and Aug).

Destinations Al Hoceima (2hr 30min); Bab Berred (45min); Chefchaouen (2hr); Taounate (1hr 20min); Targuist (45min).

ACCOMMODATION AND EATING

With a reputation that certainly precedes itself, Issaguen sees little tourist traffic. Other than the hotel listed here,

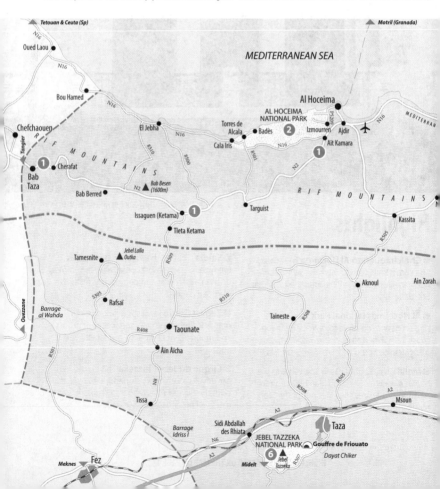

there are a few scruffy hotels and café-restaurants lining the main road through town.

Tidghine R509 highway ☎ 0539 813132. An old Spanish *parador* just south of the junction and a surprisingly good hotel despite the lack of any recent investment in upkeep or refurbishment efforts. Rooms are all en suite with TV, and there is heating in winter. There's a fairly decent in-house restaurant and bar on site too, as well as a swimming pool. BB €

Targuist

East from Issaguen (Ketama), the cedar forests give way to a more barren, stony landscape. The road continues to wend down the southern flank of the hills then twists down to bypass **Targuist**. The town itself is a new conglomeration of ugly buildings and far removed from being the site of Abd el Krim's headquarters (see page 124). There are a few basic hotels and a lively Saturday souk, but no real reason to stay.

The sea finally comes into view just 46km before the village of Ajdir, and that distance descends the flank of a single long ridge; rather an anti-climax if it wasn't for the payoff of reaching the coast.

2

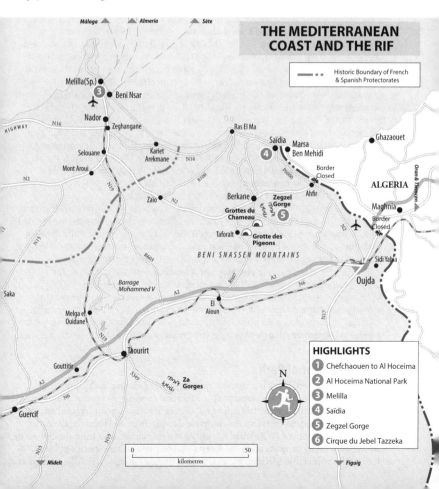

THE MEDITERRANEAN COAST AND THE RIF

— ·· — Historic Boundary of French & Spanish Protectorates

Málaga Almería Sète

Melilla(Sp.)
3
Beni Nsar

Nador
Zeghangane

HIGHWAY N16

Selouane
Kariet Arekmane N16

Mont Aroui

N2

Ras El Ma

Saïdia Marsa
4 Ben Mehidi

Ghazaouet

Zaio N2

Berkane Zegzel Gorge
Grottes du Chameau **5**

Border Closed

Ahfir

ALGERIA

Maghnia
Border Closed

Taforalt Grotte des Pigeons

BENI SNASSEN MOUNTAINS

Oran & Tlemcen

Sidi Yahia

N15

Barrage Mohammed V

Saka

Melga el Ouidane

Taourirt

El Aioun

A2 Oujda

N17

N6

Gouttitir

A2
N6

Za Gorges

N

Guercif

N15

Midelt kilometres

Figuig

0 50

HIGHLIGHTS

1 Chefchaouen to Al Hoceima
2 Al Hoceima National Park
3 Melilla
4 Saïdia
5 Zegzel Gorge
6 Cirque du Jebel Tazzeka

2

ABD EL KRIM AND THE REPUBLIC OF THE RIF

Until the establishment of the Spanish Protectorate in 1912, the **tribes of the Rif** existed outside government control. They were subdued temporarily by *harkas*, the burning raids with which sultans asserted their authority, and for a longer period under Moulay Ismail; but for the most part, bore out their own name of **Imazighen**, or "Free Ones".

Closed to outside influence, the tribes developed an **isolated** and self-contained way of life. The Riffian soil, stony and infertile, produced constant problems with food supplies, and it was only through a complex system of alliances (*liffs*) that outright wars were avoided. Unique in Morocco, the Riffian villages are scattered communities, their houses hedged and set apart, and where each family maintained a pillbox tower to spy on and fight off enemies. They were different, too, in their religion: the *salat*, the prayers said five times daily – one of the central tenets of Islam – was not observed. *Djinns*, supernatural fire spirits, were widely accredited, and great reliance was placed on the intercession of local *marabouts*.

It was an unlikely ground for significant and organized rebellion, yet for over five years (1921–27) the tribes forced the Spanish to withdraw from the mountains. Several times they defeated whole Spanish armies; first and most memorably at **Annoual** in 1921 (see page 504). It was only through the intervention of France, and the joint commitment of nearly half a million troops, that the Europeans won eventual victory.

In the intervening years, **Abd el Krim el Khattabi**, the leader of the revolt, was able to declare a **Republic of the Rif** and established much of the apparatus of a modern state. Well educated, and confident of the Rif's mineral reserves, he and his brother, Mohammed, manipulated the *liff* system to forge an extraordinary unity among the tribes. Impressively, the brothers managed to impose a series of social reforms – including the destruction of family pillboxes and the banning of *kif* – which allowed the operation of a fairly broad administrative system. It was the first nationalist movement in colonial North Africa, and although the Spanish were ready to quit the zone in 1925, it was politically impossible for the French to allow that. Defeat for the Riffians – and the capture of Abd el Krim at Targuist – brought a virtual halt to social progress and reform. The **Spanish** took over the administration en bloc but there was no road-building programme nor any of the other "civilizing benefits" introduced in the French zone. Many of the Riffian warriors were recruited into Spain's own armies, allowing General Franco to build up a power base in Morocco. It was with **Riffian troops** that he invaded Andalusia in 1936, and it was probably their contribution that ensured the Fascist victory in the Spanish Civil War.

When, in April 1957, the Spanish finally surrendered their protectorate, the Berbers of the former Spanish zone found themselves largely excluded from government. Administrators were imposed on them from Fez and Casablanca, and in October 1958, the Rif's most important tribe, the **Beni Urriaguel**, rose in open **rebellion**. The mutiny was soon put down, but necessitated the landing at Al Hoceima of then Crown Prince Hassan and some two-thirds of the Moroccan army.

The Rif is still perhaps the most **unstable** part of Morocco, remaining conscious of its under-representation in government and its historical underdevelopment. However, King Mohammed VI seems sympathetic to this situation and over the past decade the region has witnessed substantial school-building programmes, improved road, air and ferry accessibility, large agricultural projects in the plains south of Nador and Al Hoceima, and continues to see an increase in **tourism development** along its coast, mainly in the form of large resort complexes.

Hoceima National Park

The **Al Hoceima National Park** is a fantastic spot for walking, diving, rock climbing and mountain biking. Declared a national park in 2004 and covering 485 square kilometres, which includes a marine area of 190 square kilometres, it is the largest protected area on Morocco's Mediterranean coastline. An enjoyable day-trip from Al Hoceima, the park's eastern border – the tarred P5209 road – is only a fifteen-minute drive from the city centre.

The majestic **rocky canyons and pine forests** harbour several rare species of birds, including the vulnerable Mediterranean osprey (*Pandion haliaetus*), reptiles, jackals and wild boar. As well as three accessible bird hides, 30km of well-marked tracks crisscross the park, most negotiable by a **tourist vehicle** (see below), and you can also scramble down to a few isolated beaches where you may be lucky enough to spot dolphins. A few **Berber settlements** are dotted around the park, where you can see traditional crafts such as pottery and basket weaving in action.

Cala Iris
60km west of Al Hoceima

At the village of **Cala Iris** you'll find a long, narrow beach with a natural breakwater, formed by a sand spit that runs out to one of two islets in the bay (accessible on foot at low tide). Although technically within the national park's boundaries, a massive **tourism development** has been earmarked for the village; however, at the time of writing much of the construction was stalled, leaving this spot not quite undiscovered, but not quite developed. Cala Iris still manages to offer a little charm, with a couple of sleepy cafés by the small fishing harbour at the western end of the beach.

Torres de Alcala
5km east of Cala Iris

The simple, whitewashed hamlet of **Torres de Alcala** lies 250m from a small, pebbly **beach** framed by cliffs. On the western headland is a deserted **fort**, probably Spanish, with stunning views along the Mediterranean coast. There's just a bakery, the smallest of shops and a tiny café on the beach – it's about as laidback as you can get.

Badès
10km east of Cala Iris

Badès (also known as Badis), was the main port of Fez from the fourteenth to the early sixteenth century, and used for trade with the western Mediterranean states, in particular Venice. **Ruins** from that era look over a river mouth and sandy bay, where a nondescript blue line on the beach marks the somewhat bizarre international border with Spain and one of its *plazas de soberanía* ("places of sovereignty"), Peñon de Vélez de la Gomera. It's guarded on both sides and the taking of pictures is not welcomed.

ARRIVAL AND TOURS   AL HOCEIMA NATIONAL PARK

By grand taxi *Grands taxis* for Cala Iris (via Torres de Alcala) depart from Al Hoceima, west of Av Mohammed V on Rue Raya al Maghriba. A chartered taxi will cost around 200dh for the return trip. Some *transits* travel irregularly along the winding dirt road between Torres de Alcala and Badès (1–2 daily, more frequently in summer).

Tours *Hotel Villa Florido* in Al Hoceima (40 Pl du Rif; ⓦ florido.alhoceima.com) offers a number of day-trips into the park, including a full day "safari" with some hiking, swimming and a visit to a local village.

ACCOMMODATION

There are a number of **gîtes** available to rent, sleeping two to twelve people, each with a kitchen and hot water (from 150dh/per person); contact *Hotel Villa Florido* in Al Hoceima (see above).
Amis de Cala Iris Cala Iris ⓦ amisdecalairis.com. Above the western end of Cala Iris beach, this basic but friendly campsite also offers a number of self-catering chalets and apartments as well as *caidal* (Bedouin-style) tents and caravans. A restaurant operates during the summer months, but call ahead out of season to make sure it's open. No wi-fi. Camping €̄, tents/caravans €̄, chalets/apartments €̄€̄

Al Hoceima

Coming from the Rif, **AL HOCEIMA** can be a bit of a shock. It may not be quite the "exclusive international resort" the tourist board claims, but it is truly Mediterranean and has developed enough to have little in common with the farming hamlets and tribal markets of the surrounding mountains. Relaxed and friendly throughout the year, Al Hoceima (from the Spanish *alhucemas*, meaning lavender) is at its best in late spring or September, when the beaches are quiet and not so crowded under the midsummer weight of Moroccan families and French and German tourists.

Al Hoceima was developed by the Spanish after their counteroffensive in the Rif in 1925 (see page 124), and was known by them as **Villa Sanjuro**. The name commemorated the Spanish general José Sanjuro, who landed in the bay, under the cover of Spanish and French warships, with an expeditionary force. Coincidentally, it was at Al Hoceima, too, that then Crown Prince Hassan led Moroccan forces to quell the Riffians' revolt in 1958, following independence.

Al Hoceima's compact size is one of its charms. Until the 1950s, it consisted of just a small fishing port to the north of the bay, and a fringe of white houses atop the barren cliffs to the south. At the heart of this older quarter is the atmospheric **Place du Rif**, enclosed by café-restaurants and *pensions*.

Spanish College

Pl Mohammed VI

Names aside, the Spanish left little to distinguish their occupation. The only notable architectural feature is the attractive **Spanish College** (Colegio Español de Alhucema),

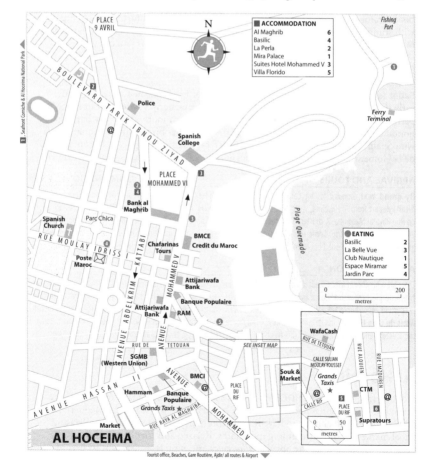

KIF IN MOROCCO

Although many of the Riffian tribes in the **mountains** had always smoked **kif**, it was the Spanish who really encouraged its cultivation – probably as an effort to keep the peace. This situation was apparently accepted when Mohammed V came to power, though the reasons for his acceptance of the status quo aren't obvious. There is a story, probably apocryphal, that when he visited Ketama in 1957, he accepted a bouquet of cannabis as a symbolic gift.

In the early 1970s the Rif became the centre of a significant **drug industry**, exporting to Europe and America. This sudden growth was accounted for by the introduction, by an American dealer, of techniques for producing hash resin. Overnight, the Riffians had access to a compact and easily exportable product, as well as a burgeoning world market for dope. Inevitably, big business was quick to follow, and today it's estimated that Morocco produces anywhere from one third to almost half of all hashish sold around the world, supplying the vast majority of Europe's demand. As such it provides the economic base for much of the country's north and a living for some one hundred thousand households. That said, the trade has brought little overall wealth to the region, with farmers saying a kilogram of *kif* sells for just $8, and they earn about $3000–4000 a year. The government, with help from EU and US grants, tried to reduce cultivation by introducing other crops such as olives, figs and almonds, but these efforts largely failed due to drought and infertile soil, and most farmers have since turned back to growing the hardy weed-like cannabis plant. Recently, there's been a steady increase in the number of police-supervised **clearing of crops**, many of which have been well publicized, no doubt to please Morocco's European neighbours. A dark undercurrent of **corruption** pervades these clear-up acts: those farmers who can't, or won't, pay a bribe are targeted and even jailed. The bare fact remains, however, that farmers earn immeasurably more from cannabis than they would from growing legal crops.

Some (non-government) experts are saying that the eradication cause is a lost one, and believe it's better to encourage farmers to rotate cannabis with other crops to avoid ruining their land with overuse of chemical fertilizers – whatever European hippies might like to think, cannabis grown in the Rif is anything but "organic" – rather than waste resources on trying to stop the industry altogether. Under UN drug conventions, marijuana can be legally grown for industrial and medical uses. In what is to date Morocco's most high-level acceptance of the situation, in 2014, the opposition Party of Authenticity and Modernity that was founded by a close associate of the king, and the Istiqlal (Independence) Party, Morocco's oldest political party, joined together to present to parliament a **draft bill** that would keep consumption illegal but **legalize production**. Under the draft legislation, the entire crop would go to a state agency that would use it to produce new cannabis-based medications that have been developed to aid sufferers of cancer and multiple sclerosis, as well as for industrial uses such as textiles, paper and fibreboard. The two parties say that factories would be set up in the Rif region to process the plant and provide jobs, and the state-driven industry would prevent cannabis from being turned into hash and going to the smugglers. The draft bill has received some high-profile backing, including the ministers of health and higher education, who have supported the idea of using marijuana for scientific research. However, the Islamist-led government and the palace have remained silent, with few wanting to break a deep-rooted taboo against illegal drugs. The growers themselves have expressed suspicion about the ground-breaking plan, stating concerns of a possible fall in the already low price for their crop, and fears that legalization would only benefit a select few wealthy estates that boast vast acreage and the latest agricultural technology.

However it's worth noting here that Moroccan law still forbids the cultivation, production, sale, purchase, possession and smoking of cannabis (see page 56). These laws are enforced on occasion with some vigour, so don't be seduced by the locals: police roadblocks are frequent, informers common. Cannabis in the Rif is obviously big business and potentially **dangerous** for casual visitors to get mixed up in.

overlooking Place Mohammed VI, which, until 1956, was the provincial headquarters of the Misión Cultural Española in Morocco. An attractive colonial villa, it is distinguishable by its exterior blue-and-white *azulejo* tiles, common throughout parts of the Iberian peninsula. In addition to offering Spanish Baccalaureate-level education, the college sometimes hosts live cultural events as well as art and craft exhibitions.

Peñon de Alhucemas

From some vantage points just south of the city centre, such as the beaches of Asfiha and Izly, you get a view of the **Peñon de Alhucemas**, another of the Spanish *plazas de soberanía* ("places of sovereignty") off this coast (and a former penitentiary). Housing a garrison of sixty soldiers and off-limits to visitors, the rocky outcrop is topped with sugar-white houses, a church and tower. The Spanish took it in 1673 and have held it ever since – a perennial source of dispute between Morocco and Spain.

Beaches

For many visitors, Al Hoceima's **beaches** are its main drawcard; unfortunately, rubbish can be a problem throughout the year. The most central, **Plage Quemado**, set in a protected bay and a bit of a downhill hike from the town centre, has a stunning setting, despite a towering chain hotel recently constructed right on the beach. There are also some nice beaches to the southeast – **Cala Bonita** is the first, down an unmarked road 1km out of town, with pedaloes and a couple of cafés. Three kilometres from town is **Plage Izly**, a long shingle beach, and another 2km will bring you to the twin beaches of **Asfiha** and **Souani**, both long black sandy beaches separated by the mouth of the Oued Ghis. Souani is the easier to access of the two, and offers pleasant cafés and good sun loungers, though it's earmarked for major development.

ARRIVAL, INFORMATION AND TOURS — AL HOCEIMA

By plane Al Charif al Idrissi Airport (@ onda.ma/en) is 17km southeast of Al Hoceima, just before the village of Imzouren. The airport largely caters for flights from Amsterdam and Brussels, plus charter flights from Charleroi in Belgium and Rotterdam in Holland during summer. *Grands taxis* are found directly outside the terminal building, charging 175dh/vehicle (1–6 passengers) for the 15min drive into Al Hoceima. Royal Air Maroc have an office on the corner of Av Hassan II and Av Mohammed V @ royalairmaroc.com.
Destination Casablanca (4 weekly; 2hr 30min).

By bus The bus station is 2km south of the city centre; all of the bus companies have ticket booths here. Blue and yellow *petits taxis* are sometimes waiting outside the station, otherwise just hail one from the busy main road opposite; it's an inexpensive ride into town. CTM and Supratours have offices on Pl du Rif, although their buses don't call here. Destinations Aknoul (daily; 1hr 30min); Bab Berred (2 CTM & 23 others daily; 4hr 30min); Chefchaouen (3 CTM daily; 6–7hr); Issaguen/Ketama (2 CTM & 5 others daily; 4–5hr); Nador (2 CTM & over 5 others daily; 3–4hr); Rabat (2 CTM daily; 9–10hr); Tangier (1 CTM & over 5 others daily; 8–9hr); Taza (2 CTM daily; 4hr); Tetouan (2 CTM and over 5 others daily; 8hr).

By grand taxi Most *grands taxis* gather in and around Pl du Rif, other than those from Imzouren and Cala Iris, which congregate west of Av Mohammed V on Rue Raya al Maghriba. Destinations Cala Iris (45min); Fez (occasionally; 4hr); Issaguen/Ketama (2hr); Kassita (1hr); Nador (2hr 15min–3hr); Oujda (5hr 30min); Targuist (1hr 30min); Taza (4hr 30min).

By ferry The small ferry terminal is between Plage Quemado and the fishing port. Armas (@ navieraarmas. com) offers summer crossings to Granada.
Destination Motril, Granada (May–Sept 1–2 weekly; 5hr).

Tourist information and tours The official tourist office is on Bd al Hamra, Cala Bonita, 1km south of the town centre (@ 0539 981185). Chafarinas Tours, centrally located at 109 Bd Mohammed V (@ rifitours.tripod.com), can also help with travel information, plus they organize walking tours and pony trekking in the Rif mountains.

ACCOMMODATION — SEE MAP PAGE 126

Outside of June–Aug, most places will offer sizeable discounts; during the summer months prices are higher and it's advisable to book ahead.

Al Maghrib 23 Rue Imzouren @ 0612 245699. This clean and friendly cheapie is located on a busy side street off Pl du Rif, surrounded by plenty of cafés offering cheap breakfasts.

Spread out over a number of floors accessed by a narrow staircase, the large, tiled rooms (no heating in winter) come with comfortable beds, hand basins and balconies. The spotless bathrooms are shared and have hot water. €

Basilic 131 Av Abdelkrim Kattabi ☎ 0539 980083. This stylish yet affordable hotel has a touch of luxury about it, and the large, chocolate-beige rooms have wooden floors and include a separate sitting area and modern bathroom; some have sea-view balconies – though the accompanying street noise can be a negative. €€

La Perla Boulevard Tarik Ibnou Ziyad ⦿ hotellaperla. ma. Friendly mid-range hotel offering bland albeit functional and spacious en-suite tiled rooms. Overlooking a busy street and with a first-floor restaurant and popular ground-floor café, it's best to request a room at the back. Street parking with overnight security guards. BB €

Mira Palace Hay Mirador Espace Mirador ⦿ hotel-mirapalace.com. About 2km west of Place Mohammed VI, and set in spacious grounds with car park, large pool, decent restaurant and rooftop bar, this is one of the more peaceful options in Al Hoceima and has fantastic sea views from its elevated hillside position. The 30-odd rooms are comfortable and contemporary with a/c, TV and solid furnishings; upgrades will get you a balcony and/or spacious sitting area. BB. €€

Suites Hotel Mohammed V Pl Mohammed VI ☎ 0539 982233/4. Though lacking any great character, this hotel still offers some of the best rooms in town. The contemporary-styled suites are a tasteful combination of marble and wood throughout, with a sitting area and large, modern bathroom. More spacious than average, the rooms let in plenty of light from balconies with impressive views over Plage Quemado. BB €€

★ **Villa Florido** 40 Pl du Rif ☎ 0539 840847. This 1929 Art Deco dame is easily the city's best value accommodation. While slightly garish in decor, the rooms – most with balcony – are all spacious and sport shiny, modern bathrooms; the corner rooms sleep three adults comfortably. Light sleepers should ask for a room away from the busy Pl du Rif. A street-level restaurant serves up a choice of good-value breakfasts, and day-trips and activities in Al Hoceima National Park can be organized with the English-speaking manager. Single and triple rooms available. €

EATING SEE MAP PAGE 126

Al Hoceima has quite a lot of good, cheap places to eat, but not much nightlife. The restaurants listed here are unlicensed unless mentioned.

Basilic 131 Av Abdelkrim Kattabi. Popular and friendly, with plenty of chairs and tables both streetside (with glass windbreakers) and inside on two a/c levels. The varied menu offers a dozen set breakfasts, a wide range of light dishes, including savoury crêpes, as well as more substantial meat and seafood dishes. For simple tea/coffee and pastry, try their patisserie annexe next door. €€

La Belle Vue 130 Av Mohammed V. One of a number of local cafés sitting side by side by Pl Mohammed VI, this one offers a belle vue indeed of the beach below from a pleasant open-sided terrace. Not renowned for its cuisine and more a place to have an excellent coffee, there is nonetheless a cheap menu of breakfasts and fish and Moroccan standards during the summer months. €€

★ **Club Nautique** In the fishing port (gate 2). Overlooking the port, this restaurant is renowned for huge plates of fresh fish, unloaded daily from the fishing boats just metres away and grilled or fried to your liking. Upstairs is slightly more formal than downstairs, where the bar (licensed) offers plenty of Moroccan wines among other drinks and can get lively with locals. €€

Espace Miramar Rue Moulay Ismail. This popular place sprawls over four terraces that accommodate an indoor-outdoor restaurant, separate pizzeria, small children's play area and plenty of tables on grassy, shaded spots. The menu ranges from soups, salads and omelette, to pizzas, hamburgers and heavier meat and seafood dishes. €€

Jardin Parc Parc Chita, Rue Moulay Idriss. Relaxing spot on the southeast corner of the square with outdoor tables, serving basic but well-cooked tajine and chicken dishes. €

DIRECTORY

Banks & exchange There are many banks on Av Mohammed V; WafaCash bureau de change is on Rue de Tetouan.

Hammam 12 Rue Azzalaga, parallel with Av Hassan II behind the Banque Populaire– a picture hung outside tells you which sex is in occupation.

Post office Rue Moulay Idriss I, opposite Parc Chica.

Nador

Upon independence in 1956, **Nador** was just an ordinary Riffian village, given work and some impetus by the port of the nearby Spanish enclave of Melilla. Its later designation as a provincial capital led to extensive growth based on the cement industry and the legal and illegal traffic passing through its own busy **port** at Beni Nsar. It has

2

steadily grown into an ugly, sprawling town and until recently the future looked grim. However, swept up in the country's ambitious tourism vision, there are lofty plans (endorsed by King Mohammed VI himself) under way to develop **Mar Chica Lagoon**, beside which the city lies, and its outlying spit with tourism developments including hotels and holiday homes, a golf course and a marina.

Perhaps paradoxically, the king has also endorsed a massive new **industrial port complex**, "Nador West Med", expected to serve as a storage platform for petroleum products, to supply not only Morocco but also the surrounding region. For the time being, Nador is primarily a **transport hub** with little to offer other than a pleasant lagoon-side promenade and some birdwatching in the marshes and dunes east of the town (see page 138).

ARRIVAL AND INFORMATION

NADOR

As Nador is a duty-free port, roads between here and Fez are invariably used for smuggling and therefore subject to numerous police and even customs checks and subsequent delays; the best ground transport option is rail.

By plane Nador al Aroui Airport (⊚ onda.ma/en) is situated 23km south of the city. *Grands taxis* are located outside the terminal building and typically charge 200dh for up to six people.

Destination Casablanca (4–7 weekly; 1hr 25min).

By train Nador has two train stations, Nador Sud (South) and Nador Ville; the latter is only 500m north of the city centre. Red *petits taxis* are sometimes waiting in the station car park, otherwise it's usually pretty easy to hail one from the adjoining main road; a fare into town will cost no more than 10dh.

Destinations Beni Nsar Port (4 daily; 25min); Beni Nsar Ville/Melilla border (4 daily; 10min); Casablanca Voyageurs (1 direct & 2 connecting daily; 10hr 30min); Fez (2 direct & 1 connecting daily; 6hr); Oujda (1 connecting daily; 4hr 35min); Rabat (1 direct & 2 connecting daily; 10hr); Taourirt

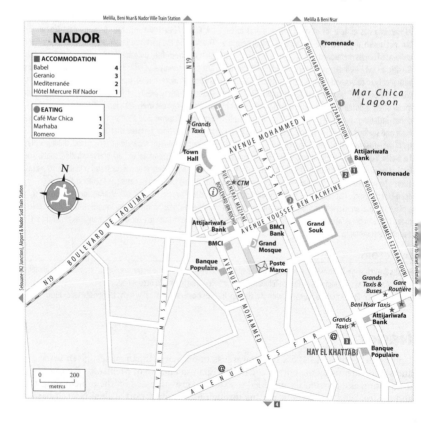

NADOR

ACCOMMODATION
Babel	4
Geranio	3
Mediterranée	2
Hôtel Mercure Rif Nador	1

EATING
Café Mar Chica	1
Marhaba	2
Romero	3

(3 direct daily; 2hr).

By bus The main bus station lies southeast of the city centre, at the southern end of Av des FAR. CTM and a number of long-distance private companies operate from another bus rank near the junction of Av Mohammed V and Rue Général Meziane.

Destinations Aknoul (daily; 3hr 30min); Al Hoceima (2 CTM & 10 others daily; 3hr 15min); Bab Berred (2 CTM & over 10 others daily; 7hr); Beni Nsar (at least hourly; 25min); Berkane (over 10 daily; 1hr 30min); Fez (3 CTM & over 10 others daily; 5hr 30min); Guercif (at least hourly; 3hr); Imzouren (2 CTM & 8 others daily; 2hr); Issaguen/Ketama (2 CTM & over 10 others daily; 6hr); Oujda (over 10 daily; 2hr 30min); Rabat (2 CTM & over 5 others daily; 9hr); Saïdia (over 5 daily; 2hr); Tangier (2 CTM & over 5 others daily; 10–11hr); Taza (3 CTM & over 10 others daily; 3hr 30min); Tetouan (2 CTM & over 5 others daily; 13hr).

By grand taxi The sprawling *grand taxi* rank is opposite the main bus station at the southern end of Av des FAR.

Destinations Al Hoceima (2hr 15min–3hr); Beni Nsar (15min); Berkane (1hr 30min); Oujda (3hr); Taza (2hr).

By ferry Ferries operate from the Gare Maritime Beni Nsar, 8km north of Nador and 1km east of the Melilla border. Shared *grands taxis* constantly ply the route to/from Nador (12dh), arriving and departing from the busy roundabout 300m west of the ferry terminal. It's worth noting that immigration formalities take place on board for all Nador-bound (Beni Nsar) ferries, thus avoiding the often-laborious wait experienced at the Melilla–Morocco land border post with Melilla-bound ferries (see page 135).

Destinations Almería (2–4 daily; 4–5hr); Motril, Granada (3 weekly; 5hr); Sète (1 weekly; 29hr).

Tourist information ONMT tourist office, 88 Bd Ibn Rochid (Mon–Fri 8.30am–4.30pm; ☎0536 330348).

ACCOMMODATION   SEE MAP PAGE 130

Babel Cnr Prince Sidi Mohammed & Bvd Taha Houssiene ☎0536 606901. This functional hotel is in a quiet neighbourhood 1km south of the bus and *grand taxi* stations and they also arrange airport pick-ups. A grand staircase leads to the 44 light en suite tiled rooms on the upper floors, which are small but spotless with good heating and a/c; some have balconies. A café is at ground level, while a licenced restaurant is on the first floor. BB €€

Geranio 16 Rue 20, Hay el Khattabi ☎0536 602828. In the dustier downtown quarter but still cheap and cheerful, offering clean rooms with small bathrooms and plenty of hot water, though ask for a room away from the often-noisy street. There's also a decent ground-floor café. €

Mediterranée 2–4 Av Youssef Ben Tachfine ☎0536 606495. The best mid-range option in town, just one street from the lagoon promenade. A multi-storey block-type hotel, the rooms are pretty bland and functional, but have a/c, TV and balconies - many of them sea-facing. A ground-floor restaurant serves breakfast, plus there's a café next door. Singles and triples are available. €€

★ **Hôtel Mercure Rif Nador** 1 Av Youssef Ben Tachfine ⓦaccorhotels.com.The quality four-star Mercure has 190 rooms of different sizes and standards, with all the mod cons you'd expect and spacious balconies - although avoid the noisier street side and opt for a pool-facing room. Facilities are the best in town with a gym, spa, two restaurants, bar and the vast pool with sunbathing terraces and wonderful lagoon views. As suitable for holidaymakers as it is for business and family-friendly too. BB €€

EATING   SEE MAP PAGE 130

Café Mar Chica Bd Mohammed Ezzeraktouni. Jutting into Mar Chica Lagoon, this dark but cosy café has seashell-embedded walls and is decorated with anchors, antique gas lamps and other paraphernalia. There are plenty of tables outside, with stunning lagoon and promenade views. Besides a pastry and tea/coffee breakfast, the kitchen offers a small menu of unmemorable Moroccan staples. €

★ **Marhaba** Av Ibn Rochd. By far the best restaurant in town, specializing in seafood but with plenty of other offerings including good-value couscous and a variety of tajines, including rabbit. The sparkling kitchen is open for all to see, and the service is professional and friendly. Choose between a table in the large marble-and-stucco interior or under a smaller shaded outdoor patio. No alcohol. €€

Romero Cnr Av Youssef Ben Tachfine & Av Hassan II ☎0536 332777. This stalwart has been around for years and serves up a decent offering of fish and seafood dishes. Located on a busy corner, seating is mostly inside where it's air-conditioned and quieter. €€

Melilla

Spanish-occupied **MELILLA** (Mlilya in Arabic) is a friendly little place, with a pride in its mix of cultures and an interesting selection of early twentieth-century modernist architecture. Pleasures are to be found, too, in an exploration of the walled old town, **Medina Sidonia**, with its stunning views out across the Mediterranean. It's a popular weekend destination for those living in Morocco, and if you're here in August, there's the marvellous, if misleadingly titled **Semana Naútica**, when the port fills with sailing boats from mainland Spain and further afield for a fortnight (*semana* means one week) of maritime extravaganzas and regattas.

Melilla centres on **Plaza de España**, overlooking the port, and **Avenida Juan Carlos I Rey**, leading inland off it. This is the most animated part of town, especially during the evening *paseo*, when everyone promenades up and down, or strolls through the neighbouring **Parque Hernandez**. To the northeast, Medina Sidonia rises up from a promontory, to watch over the town centre and marina.

Bear in mind that Melilla runs on Spanish time and the euro is the accepted currency (see page 136).

Brief history

Together with Ceuta, Melilla is the last of Spain's Moroccan enclaves – a former penal colony that saw its most prosperous days under the protectorate until 1956, when it was the main port for the Riffian mining industry. Between 1956 and 2000, the city's population halved to a little over 65,000, split roughly two to one between Christians and Muslims (mostly Berber), along with minor populations of Jews and Indian Hindus. Since 2000, however, **immigration** from the European mainland has risen, due largely to attractive tax laws and the city's duty-free status. The enclave's various religious and ethnic communities get along reasonably well, despite an episode of rioting in 1986, after the enactment of Spain's first real "**Aliens Law**" threatened to deprive certain Muslim families of their residence rights. There were further **riots** in 1996, when four hundred Spanish Foreign Legionnaires, a tough bunch posted here by the Madrid authorities out of harm's way, went on the rampage after one of their number had been killed in a bar brawl.

Along with Ceuta, Melilla achieved **autonomous status** in 1995 after years of shilly-shallying on the issue by Madrid for fear of offending Morocco. However, the enclave is still staunchly Spanish, highlighted by a 2007 visit by King Juan Carlos and Queen Sofia – the first royal visit in 80 years – seen by some to be almost an act of defiance towards persistent Moroccan calls for re-integration.

Medina Sidonia

Until the beginning of the twentieth century, the walled "Old Town" of **Medina Sidonia**, wedged in above the port, was all there was of Melilla. This was the site of the original Phoenician colony of Rusadir around the tenth century BC, which the Spanish took in 1497, a kind of epilogue to the expulsion of the Moors from Spain after the fall of Granada in 1492. As an enclave, its security was always vulnerable, and at various periods of expansionist Moroccan rule – it was blockaded throughout the reign of Moulay Ismail – the Spanish population was limited to their fortress promontory and its sea approaches. The quarter's streets were laid out along the lines of a Castilian fort, following a major earthquake in the sixteenth century.

Plaza Maestranza

Steps near the fishing port lead up to the quarter's main square, **Plaza Maestranza**, entered by the Gothic **Puerta de Santiago**, a gate flanked by a chapel to St James the Apostle – known to Spaniards as *Matamoros*, "the Moor-Slayer".

La Concepción
Free

Beyond Plaza Maestranza you come to an old barracks and armoury, and, if you follow the fortifications round from here, a small fort, below which is the church of **La Concepción**, crowded with Baroque decoration, including a revered statue of Nuestra Señora de Victoria (**Our Lady of Victory**), the city's patroness.

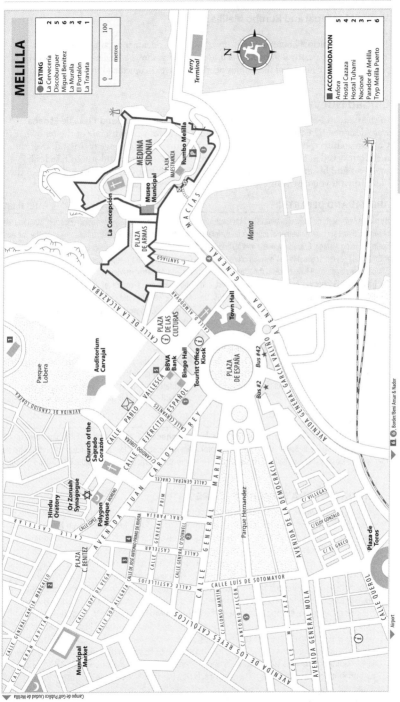

MELILLA

● EATING
La Cervecería 2
Discoburguer 5
Miguel Benítez 6
La Muralla 3
El Portalón 4
La Traviata 1

0 metres 100

■ ACCOMMODATION
Anfora 5
Hostal Cazaza 4
Hostal Tuhami 2
Nacional 3
Parador de Melilla 1
Tryp Melilla Puerto 6

Museo Municipal and Rumbo Melilla

Free

The **Museo Municipal** houses a miscellany of historical documents, coins and ceramics. Also interesting is the nearby **Rumbo Melilla** museum, which shows a fifteen-minute audiovisual projection on the history of the various peoples to have occupied and influenced the town.

Ciudad Nueva

In the Ciudad Nueva (New Town), many of the buildings around **Plaza de España** were designed by **Enrique Nieto**, a *modernista* (Art Nouveau) disciple of the renowned Catalan architect, Antoni Gaudí. Nieto arrived in 1909 at the age of 23 and, over the next four decades, transformed Melilla's architecture. The tile and stucco facades left by Nieto and his imitators – in a style more flowery than Gaudí's – are a delight of the New Town if you cast your eyes above the shops (see page 134).

ARRIVAL AND DEPARTURE
MELILLA

By plane Aeropuerto de Melilla (w aena.es) is 3km southwest of the town and services a number of routes from mainland Spain including Malaga, Granada, Almeria and Madrid. Rent A Car Melilla (w rentacarmelilla.es) have an office here. Air Europa (w aireuropa.com) have offices at the airport.

By bus Bus #43 operates between the border post and Melilla's main square, Plaza de España, and costs €0.90. On the Moroccan side of the border, bus #19 operates between Beni Ansar and Nador.

By grand taxi *Grands taxis* from Nador drop you at the border post of Beni Ansar. Metered taxis are available on the Spanish side. Travelling into Morocco, you can usually pick up collective *grands taxis* for Nador just over the border, or at the informal rank just to the west of the roundabout (100m from the border).

By ferry Melilla's ferry terminal (*Estacíon Maritima de Melilla*; w estacionmaritimamelilla.com) is at the far end of Avda Generál Macías, a short walk from Plaza de España. Offices for Acciona Trasmediterránea (w trasmediterranea. es) and Armas (w naviearmas.com) are in the terminal, and there are a couple of travel agencies just outside. Advance bookings are essential in Aug and at the end of Easter week. It's worth noting that immigration formalities take place on board for all Nador-bound (Beni Ansar) ferries, thus avoiding the often-laborious wait experienced at the Melilla–Spain land border post with Melilla-bound ferries (see page 135). Full details on ferries can be found in "Basics" (see page 30).

Destinations Almería (5–7 weekly; 6hr); Málaga (5–7 weekly; 8–9hr); Motril, Granada (1–2 daily; 4hr 30min).

INFORMATION

Tourist information Oficina de Turismo, Plaza de las Culturas (Mon–Fri 8am–3pm; w melillaturismo.com). There's also a kiosk by the town hall on Plaza de España.

Telephones When phoning Melilla from Morocco (or anywhere else outside Spain), you must prefix numbers with the international code (☏ 00 34). Dialling numbers

CIUDAD NUEVA'S ARCHITECTURE

A short, circular **walk** taking in the highlights of the New Town's *modernista* architecture starts in Plaza de España with Melilla's most famous Art Deco building, the **town hall**, a Nieto building of 1947. Avenida Juan Carlos I Rey, leading away from the Plaza de España, begins with the 1917 **Trasmediterránea** building on the left, followed by another fine piece of Art Nouveau at no. 9, built in 1915. From here head for Calle Ejército Español to have a look at no.16 and continue up Calle Lopez Moreno, checking out the *modernista* buildings on the right-hand side, among them Nieto's **Or Zoruah Synagogue** (Holy Light Synagogue; visits arranged via the tourist office; see opposite), built in 1924, the ground floor of which bizarrely houses a cheap trinket shop. Opposite is the **Polygon Mosque**, also by Nieto, and dating to 1945. Back on Avenida Juan Carlos I Rey, there is quite a selection around Plaza Comandante Benitez and, just down Avenida de los Reyes Católicos, check out those on Calle Sor Alegría, before heading along Avenida General Prim to see the building on the corner of Castelar. The last building, the **bingo hall** on the corner of Comandante Emperador and Ejército Español, just off Plaza de España, has another fine stucco facade, in Art Deco style this time.

THE NADOR–MELILLA BORDER

On a good day you can cross the **Nador–Melilla border** in ten or fifteen minutes. At other times, you may need considerable time and patience. During the summer it's often extremely crowded, with Moroccans returning from (or going to) jobs in Europe, as well as travellers off the ferry. If you want to avoid the queues, it is a good idea to spend a couple of hours in Melilla after arriving off a ferry, to let the main traffic get through. Early mornings are very busy on both sides of the border.

If you are **driving**, be aware that smuggling goes on at the border, with periodic police crackdowns on a trade that includes both drugs and people, with Moroccans and sub-Saharan Africans attempting to cross illegally into mainland Spain. Driving to the border at night, keep an eye out for road checks – not always well lit but usually accompanied by tyre-puncturing blockades. If you've rented a car in Morocco, you can usually take it into Melilla but not into mainland Spain.

The 200m that separates the Moroccan and the Spanish sides of the border is a **no-man's-land** isolating a prosperous European town from an unemployment-ridden African one. In recent years, and like the identical migrant crisis in Ceuta (see page 98), there's been a number of assaults on the heavily-fortified 6m-high double border fence by large groups of sub-Saharan Africans desperate to enter Europe. Most are stopped immediately, but some do manage to break through and run into Spanish territory.

2

within Melilla you must include the local code (☎952) as part of the nine-digit number. To phone Morocco from Melilla, you need to dial ☎00 212, followed by the local code (minus the initial zero) and number.

Time Melilla works to Spanish time, an hour ahead of Morocco (2hr ahead between the times when Europe and Morocco change to daylight saving).

ACCOMMODATION
SEE MAP PAGE 133

Rooms tend to be in short supply in Melilla and are expensive by Moroccan standards. If you have problems, the tourist offices (see above) might be able to help.

Anfora Calle Pablo Vallesca 16 ⓦhotelanfora.net. This functional mid-range option is in a great location, with stunning views from the rooftop terrace. The soft-coloured rooms are a good size with modern bathrooms and private balconies; the fifth-floor breakfast room has great views through floor-to-ceiling windows but the buffet is very basic. BB €€

Hostal Cazaza Calle de José Antonio Primo de Rivera 6 ☎952 684648. Set in a charming Art Deco relic, with rooms which are a little scruffy, *Cazaza* is a friendly, well-maintained place. All rooms have TV and a large bathroom, and there's a small café on the ground floor for breakfast. €

★ **Hostal Tuhami** Calle Generál García Margallo 13 ☎952 686045. Within strolling distance to everything, the friendly staff and good-value rooms make this one of the town's best choices. The modern tiled rooms (family rooms available) all have a/c and satellite TV, but the bathrooms are a bit on the small side. €

Nacional Calle José Antonio Primo de Rivera 10 ☎952 684540133. This quaint and friendly hotel has small but comfortable rooms with modern bathrooms; those facing outwards are brighter and fresher and have Juliette balconies. There's also a quiet street-level restaurant, and car rental is available for day-trips to Morocco. €€

Parador de Melilla Avda de Cándido Lobera – overlooking the Parque Lobera ⓦparador.es. Rather dated but with large rooms and balconies providing fine views over the town, plus a swimming pool (June–Oct), though unfortunately both food and service often leave something to be desired. Its elevated location can challenge tired legs at the end of the day. €€

★ **Tryp Melilla Puerto** Esplanada de San Lorenzo ⓦmelia.com. Popular chain hotel and recently renovated in contemporary style offering a good standard of service. The rooms and suites (including one adapted for wheelchair users) lack a balcony but are bright, spacious and well-equipped and the beachfront location is very appealing, only a short stroll from the town centre. There's a decent in-house restaurant and separate café, a small gym and parking. €€

EATING AND DRINKING
SEE MAP PAGE 133

Melilla has some great **tapas bars**, but not much in the way of **restaurants**; the main concentration lies in the area east of Av Juan Carlos I Rey, between the Plaza de España and the Municipal Market. There is also a cluster of cafés and restaurants in the new marina to the south of the

fishing port. Alcohol is, of course, a lot easier to come by here than in Morocco.

★ **La Cervecería** Calle General O'Donnell 23 ☎952 683427, ⓦcerveceriamelilla.com. In business since 1991, this popular tapas bar-restaurant has whacky all-green *modernista* decor, good food and decent wines available by the glass. Service is very friendly, too. €€

Discoburguer Calle Carlos Ramírez de Arellano 5. A small, but popular and casual bar and burger joint (as the name suggests) with a 1950s US diner-style décor. The menu features dozens of choices of burgers, baguettes and toasties and some main meals like chorizo and chicken tortillas or steak and chips. The sangria and beer are both cold and served quickly. €

Miguel Benitez Paseo Marítimo Mir Berlanga 25 ⓦ restaurantemiguelbenitez.es. Popular family-owned restaurant with three dining salons and a wonderful setting overlooking the seaside promenade. The menu spans the gamut of traditional Spanish cuisine offering everything from basic tortilla, *arroz* (rice) and *huevos* (egg) dishes through to a signature *Paella de Marisco y Pesacdo* (fish and seafood paella), all prepared with great aplomb. €€€€

La Muralla Calle Mirador de Florentina ⓦ restaurante lamuralla.net. This century-old restaurant is built into the Medina wall and oozes history, with many artefacts adorning the walls, while a small outdoor section has fantastic views over the port. While specializing in meat dishes, including a popular *Solomillo con Hojaldre* (Beef Wellington), there are also plenty of seafood options, though not much for vegetarians. €€€

El Portalón Avda Generál Macías 9. Popular café-restaurant across from the fishing port serving tapas, pizza, and average seafood– the coffee is good though. €€

La Traviata Calle Ejército Español 5. Well-run and popular bar-restaurant serving modern gourmet Spanish food, such as *el pulpo con espuma de patata* (grilled squid on a bed of mashed potato) at top-end prices. The portions are huge; try to leave space for dessert. €€€

DIRECTORY

Banks & exchange There are a number of banks on or near Avda Juan Carlos I Rey, all of which have ATMs and will change sterling, dollars or dirhams. It's worth shopping around to get the best exchange rates. Note that, as part of Spain, Melilla only uses euros.

Golf Campo de Golf Público Ciudad de Melilla, Calle de Chile (18 holes; ⓦ golfmelilla.com).

Hospitals Hospital Comarcal, Calle Remonta 2 (☎ 952 670000); Hospital Militar, Calle General Polavieja s/n (☎ 952 674743).

Post office Calle Pablo Vallescá.

The far east coast

The **Mediterranean coastline** stretches east from Nador all the way to the Algerian border. Until recently it was relatively undisturbed, with just a few small villages that burst at the seams in summer but counted more birds than people for the rest of the year. Change has come, however, and the wave of development that continues to wash over much of Morocco has found its way to these shores. Beachfront promenades have been laid and concrete apartment blocks are inevitably following; the most ambitious example of these developments are manifest in the extravagant and ill-conceived tourist enclave of Saïdia Mediterrania (see page 137).

The atmosphere along this coast during **summer** is infectious, and it's a great time to experience modern Morocco, where families play in the shallows and Arabic pop music blares out from mobile phones. Unfortunately, this development comes at an inevitable cost, and the coastline's remarkable **ecosystem** appears to be under siege from the increase in development and the resultant waste issues.

Kariet Arekmane

A bus from Nador runs daily, departing the main bus station at around 10am and heading to Ras el Ma via Kariet Arekmane (1hr) before returning back to Nador at around 2pm; during summer, you'll usually find a few *grands taxis* in Nador departing in the morning for Kariet Arekmane and returning in the late afternoon – or you can charter a *grand taxi* for the day and stop off at Ras el Ma as well

The village of **Kariet Arekmane**, 30km from Nador, gives access to the eastern fringe of Mar Chica Lagoon. This is a desolate area but picturesque in its own way, with salt marshes that provide manifold attractions for birdwatchers. From the village, a tarred road rudely cuts across the marshes to a sandy beach lined with a promenade and a few semi-permanent restaurants. This is a popular weekend spot with Spaniards from Melilla, though there's still no accommodation as yet, just expensive holiday homes. During summer, the beach comes to life with umbrellas for rent, jetskis zipping across the flat waters, and even lifeguards on duty.

Ras el Ma

A bus from Nador runs daily, departing the main bus station at around 10am and heading past Kariet Arekmane to Ras el Ma (2hr 30min) before returning back to Nador at around 2pm, so you'll have to sleep over (see page 137) if you want to spend any time here – or you can charter a *grand taxi* for the day and stop off at Kariet Arekmane as well

Also known as Cap de l'Eau and Ras Kebdana, **Ras el Ma** is a pleasant (if at times scruffy) fishing village, facing another of Spain's offshore island possessions on this coast, the three tiny **Islas Chafarinas**. The village has a brown sandy **beach**, a smattering of decent cafés and restaurants and a little harbour where you can watch the daily catch come in. Be here on a summer Sunday and you'll find the beach packed with people, many of them bussed in from inland villages. Often strewn with rubbish, the condition of the beach gets better the further east (away from the port) you walk.

ACCOMMODATION AND EATING   RAS EL MA

Auberge de Cap de L'eau On the road to Saïdia ✆ 0536 640264. Here you'll find spacious en-suite rooms sleeping up to four people, and there's also a large restaurant serving both Moroccan staples and plenty of seafood. **€**

Capado Next to the port. *Capado* specializes in fresh fish, offering some dishes by the kilo, and also serving wood-fired pizza. A shaded rooftop terrace provides a sweeping coastal panorama, and there's a little playground for toddlers. **€€**

Saïdia

Only a few years ago, **SAÏDIA** was a low-key holiday town, rambling back from the sea in the shadow of a still-occupied nineteenth-century **kasbah**, and fronted by one of the best beaches on the Mediterranean. The past decade, however, has seen massive development along the coast to the west of town. Officially named "**Saïdia Mediterrania**" though signposted along the coast simply as Station Balnéaire ("seaside resort"), the new development functions as a separate resort from Saïdia itself, even though the two almost meet. The growth has been enormous to say the least, with hundreds of apartment blocks, many of them half-finished and already crumbling, stretching along the beach and for a few hundred metres inland. In addition, the resort is home to one of the country's largest marinas, an adjacent outdoor shopping complex, a few sprawling five-star resorts, and an eighteen-hole golf course.

If you prefer birds to beaches, there are rewarding **birdwatching** sites in the marshes and woodland stretching behind the beach towards the Oued Moulouya (see page 138), although in high season you'll have to pick your way through the rubbish. Each year, Saïdia hosts the annual eight-day Festival Saïdia Raggada in May. It's a great opportunity to listen to some indigenous *chaabi*, *raï* and *amazigh* music, or to see *raggada* and *laäoui* folk-dancing ensembles.

ARRIVAL AND DEPARTURE   SAÏDIA

By bus The modern, clean bus station is located just north of the kasbah and market. It's a 5min walk from here to the beach. Destinations Afhir (over 10 daily; 45min); Berkane (5 daily; 45min); Nador (over 5 daily; 2hr); Oujda (1 CTM & over 5 others daily; 1hr 30min–2hr).

By grand taxi *Grands taxis* operate from the eastern edge of the market and the car park lot of the adjacent bus station. Destinations Ahfir (30min); Berkane (30min); Oujda (1hr).

ACCOMMODATION

Be Live Grand Saïdia Saïdia Mediterrania ⓦ belive hotels.com. The closest to town of the mega resorts, and perhaps the best of the lot and well-priced. The attractive rooms are quite large and have all the mod cons you'd expect. There's a number of swimming pools and nine in-house restaurants, as well as a private beach area which can become not-so-private in summer when musicians, souvenir hawkers and camel rides throng the sand. FB **€€€**

Iberostar Saïdia Saïdia Mediterrania ⓦ iberostar. com. Decked out in Mediterranean blue and white, this beachfront chain resort offers almost six hundred large rooms with all the mod cons. There are also three restaurants (with long queues on busy days), a lobby bar, five swimming pools, gym, spa and kids' activities. BB **€€€**

Paco 41 Bd Hassan II ✆ 0536 625110. Although a rather spartan hotel, this is still the town's best budget option. Rooms are en suite with hot water, and there's a friendly, though slightly seedy, ground-floor bar. **€**

2

BIRDS AND DUNES

The coast east of Nador offers compelling sites for **birdwatching** – and plant wildlife – with a series of highly frequented freshwater and saline sites.

At **Kariet Arekmane** a path leads out, opposite the village mosque, past saltpans and a pumping station (right-hand side) to an extensive area of **salt marsh**. This is covered by the fleshy-stemmed marsh glasswort or *salicornia*: a characteristic "salt plant" or *halophyte*, it can survive the saline conditions through the use of glands which excrete the salt. The **insect life** of the salt marsh is abundant, including damselflies, brightly coloured grasshoppers and various ants and sand spiders. The **birds** are even more impressive, with black-winged stilt, greater flamingo, coot, great-crested grebe, and various gulls and terns wheeling overhead.

Further along the coast, a walk east of the resort of **Ras el Ma** demonstrates the means by which plants invade **sand dunes**: a sequential colonization is known as "succession", where one plant community gradually cedes to the next as a result of its own alteration of the environment. Typical early colonizers are marram grass and sea couch, which are eventually ousted by sea holly and sea spurge, then finally by large, "woodier" species such as pistachio, juniper and cistus. Whole sequences can be seen occurring over time along the beach. The area attracts a variety of interesting **sea birds** as well, including the internationally rare slender-billed curlew and **Audouin's gull** (thought to breed on the adjacent offshore Chafarinas Islands; see page 137). Other more familiar birds include dunlin, Kentish plover and oystercatcher.

Even further along the coast is the freshwater lagoon system that marks the mouth of the **Oued Moulouya**. The lagoons here are separated from the sea by a remarkable series of sand spits, no more than fifty metres across, and the **birdlife** is outstanding. Secluded among the reed-beds, it is possible to locate grey heron, white stork and little egret while the water's surface is constantly patrolled by the ever-alert black terns and kingfishers. Other varieties that you should manage to spot, wading in the shallows, are redshank, spotted redshank (in summer) and black-tailed godwit. The mouth and adjacent wetlands are, however, under serious threat from tourism development. In response to local and international pressure, a small parcel of wetland encompassing the mouth has been declared a protected area funded by, among others, the Global Environmental Fund and UNDP. Bird hides and information signboards have been erected along a marked walking path.

The Spanish-owned **Islas Chafarinas**, incidentally, are another important wildlife site, which has been declared a nature reserve. The three small islets support the Mediterranean's largest sea-bird colonies; sadly, the endangered monk seals disappeared from the islands in the 1990s and haven't been seen since.

Picasso Cnr Rue Zerktouni & Av Mohammed V ☎ 0536 625753. This seafront hotel is located above its own popular café-restaurant (open to all 6am-1am), which serves standard fish dishes and good coffees and juices. The sparsely furnished rooms, some with sea-facing balconies, are quite large, airy, and tiled throughout – the reverse a/c helps to warm them up in winter. BB €̄

EATING & DRINKING

La Corniche Av Mohammed V, opposite Pl du 20 Août. This popular restaurant offers plenty of tables both inside and under a covered, wooden-decked terrace overlooking the beach. The menu offers decent light options, such as shawarmas, panini and pizza, as well as delicious savoury crêpes and a few pasta dishes. The service can be a bit slow, but the views make up for it. €̄€̄

De la Paix Bd Hassan II, opposite Pl du 20 Août. This small, well-established restaurant serves up a decent selection of seafood specialities as well as Moroccan staples. The service is usually prompt and cheerful, and there's seating both inside and on the pavement overlooking the square. €̄€̄

Paloma Blanca Av Mohammed V. Slightly more formal than the other beachfront restaurants but also with informal seating, sunbeds and umbrellas on the beach itself, with a menu that focuses on seafood – other choices are tajines, paninis and pizzas and there's good coffees and ice-creams too €̄€̄

Berkane and the Zegzel Gorge

The route east from Nador to Oujda along the N2 is well served by buses and *grands taxis*. It holds little of interest along the way, but if you've got the time (and ideally a car), there's a pleasant detour around **Berkane** into the **Zegzel Gorge**, a dark limestone fault in the Beni Snassen mountains – the last outcrops of the Rif.

Berkane

BERKANE is a strategic market town, French-built and prosperous, set amid an extensive region of orchards and vineyards. If you stay, you're likely to be one of the only tourists – or the only – in town, so there aren't any hustlers. Berkane is surrounded by vast orchards, most of them growing clementines. Many of the town's buildings are painted in shades of orange, and a **festival** is held each May to commemorate the harvest.

Berkane's main square, **Place Mohammed V** is at the western end of town on the N2 road (Boulevard Mohammed V), next to the bridge over the Oued Cherrâa. About 1km further along Boulevard Mohammed V is the main roundabout junction of the Nador–Oujda N2 highway, as well as the offshoot highway to Saïdia and the coast. Almost everything you'll need in Berkane lies between the roundabout and Place Mohammed V.

There isn't much to see in Berkane, but worth a glance is the 1909 **French Church, Église Sainte Agnès**, on Rue Moulay Abdallah, 100m east of Place Mohammed V. Painted in red ochre, with a row of strange grimacing faces picked out in yellow along the top of its facade, the church is no longer in use as a house of prayer, and is now the base for the Association Homme et Environnement (☎0536 610289, ⊕hee.ouvaton. org). A lone voice highlighting both regional and world environmental issues, their staff members can also show you the church's interior.

ARRIVAL AND DEPARTURE   BERKANE

Berkane is a handy transport hub for the far east of the country. Drivers should be wary of buying plastic bottles of cheap petrol from roadside stalls; it's often watered down.

By bus CTM operates from a bus rank on Pl Annasr, Bd Mohammed V, opposite *Hôtel Rosalina*. Other bus companies also operate from Pl Annasr or the adjoining streets.

Destinations Fez (1 CTM and 2–3 others daily; 6hr); Nador (over 10 daily; 1hr 30min); Oujda (1 CTM and over 10 others daily; 1hr 15min); Rabat (1 CTM daily; 9hr); Saïdia (1 CTM and over 5 others daily; 30min); Taforalt (2 daily; 30min).

By grand taxi *Grands taxis* for Nador can be found at the top end of Bd Mohammed V, just before the bridge over the Oued Cherrâa. Those for Saïdia leave from just north of the main Nador–Oujda roundabout on Bd Mohammed V, while those for Oujda and Taforalt gather on Pl Annasr.

Destinations Nador (1hr 30min); Oujda (45min); Saïdia (30min); Taforalt (45min).

ACCOMMODATION AND EATING

Café Le Prince d'Or Cnr Bd Mohammed V & Rue Moulay Abdallah, 100m east of Pl Mohammed V ☎0536 616399. This modern café, popular with a young crowd, offers a menu of light meals including pizzas and paninis. €

Rosalina 82 Bd Mohammed V, 500m west of the main roundabout ☎0536 618992. The town's best hotel, with modern but slightly garish rooms, all with balcony, a/c and TV, although they can suffer from noise from the busy street below. There's a lift and private parking, as well as a lively ground-floor café. BB €

Zaki 27 Bd Mohammed V, 400m east of the main roundabout ☎0536 613460. Looking slightly tired nowadays, this mainstay of the Berkane hotel scene still offers decent, individually decorated and clean rooms with a/c and TV. The in-house restaurant serves up a decent tajine as well as pizzas and panini. BB €€

Taforalt

TAFORALT (Tafoughalt) is a quiet mountain village, 20km southwest of Berkane, active only for the **Wednesday souk**, but serves as a good base for hikers or birdwatchers interested in exploring the gorges and peaks of the nearby Beni Snassen mountains.

Grottes des Pigeons and Grotte du Chameau

Grottes des Pigeons 2km from Taforalt; Grotte du Chameau 10km from Taforalt • Both caves are signed off the Zegzel Gorge road, which is signed off the N2, 10km southwest of Berkane

The **Grottes des Pigeons** is a complex of *grottes* (caves) currently being excavated by a team from Oxford University; some of the earliest human remains in the world have been found here, as well as jewellery – pierced shells which date back a staggering 90,000 years. Information is displayed on a board in the picnic area below the caves, from where a short path brings you to the caves' entrance. While the caves themselves are off-limits, visitors can get quite close to the excavation digs.

A further 8km on is the **Grotte du Chameau**, a cavern of vast stalactites, one of which is remarkably camel-like in shape. This has been closed to visitors for years and now houses a herd of goats. Local boys stationed just before the cave will charge 5dh per vehicle for the use of the car park at the end of the road where you can enjoy the picnic area underneath towering limestone buttresses and dense cedar trees.

Zegzel Gorge

11km from Tarforalt • A limited number of *grands taxis* offer services from Taforalt along the circular gorge route, depending on the condition of the road

A NOTE ON ALGERIA

Throughout the 1990s and into the early 2000s, **Algeria** was effectively off-limits to all foreign visitors. During the **civil war** between 1992 and 1998, over 150,000 people were killed in attacks and reprisals by Islamic fundamentalists and the army; foreigners, as well as Algerian intellectuals, journalists and musicians, were particular targets. After elections in 1999 the situation improved somewhat, although there were still occasional skirmishes with militant Islamic extremists. President Abdelaziz Bouteflika, the military and the powerful State Intelligence Service (DRS) have since kept a tight grip on the country, with Bouteflika winning a fourth term in elections held in 2014. Violence is still a major concern, however, with the militant extremist group **Al-Qaeda in the Islamic Maghreb** (AQIM) implicated in recent attacks and kidnappings. In 2011 three aid workers (two Spaniards and one Italian) were abducted from a refugee camp near the border with Morocco's disputed Western Sahara region, and released over a year later after ransom payments were made. Thirty-nine foreign workers, including six Britons and a UK resident, died in January 2013 after being taken hostage by militants in the In Amenas gas plant, located in the Algerian Sahara close to the Libyan border.

Algeria and Morocco have disputed their **borders** since Algerian independence in 1963. The border was closed in 1975 following Morocco's "Green March" into Spain's former colony of Western Sahara – the Algerians supported Polisario, the Saharan independence movement. The border reopened some years later but was closed again in 1994 when Morocco imposed strict visa restrictions on Algerians following a terrorist attack in Marrakesh.

In 2004, in an attempt to improve relations, Morocco lifted all visa entry requirements for Algerians, a move the Algerians then reciprocated, but the borders remained closed. It's estimated that the border closure costs Morocco $1bn a year in lost trade and tourist revenues. In 2008, citing their "common past and shared destiny", Morocco called on Algeria to normalize relations and reopen the border. There was then a brief breakthrough in the impasse in February 2009 when the border was opened to allow the passage of an aid convoy heading for the Gaza Strip, but in 2014 the two countries marked the twentieth anniversary of the closure of their common border by building a **barbed-wire fence**, starting from the Saïdia beachfront, under the pretext of fighting both terrorism and trafficking. At the time of writing, the fence stretched about 40km along the border. Most political commentators believe that the Western Sahara issue will need to be resolved to Algeria's satisfaction before the border gates open again. It's possible for non-Moroccans to obtain entry visas for Algeria at the embassy in Rabat, but as the situation currently stands, entry to Algeria from Morocco is still only possible **by air**, flying out of Casablanca (see page 261).

The **Zegzel Gorge** is actually a series of gorges, 10km long, which dramatically defines the eastern edge of the Rif mountain range. The gorges offer wonderful **hiking** following the seasonal riverbed of the Oued Zegzel, terraced and cultivated at its wider points with citrus and fruit trees. Three kilometres south from the Grotte du Chameau, a rough track branches off the main dirt road, only suitable for hiking and sturdy 4WD vehicles, and perennially subject to rock avalanches and flash floods. As the track crisscrosses the riverbed, the gorges progressively narrow, drawing your eye to the cedars and dwarf oaks at the summit, until you eventually emerge, 22km from Taforalt, onto the Berkane plain.

2

ARRIVAL AND DEPARTURE
TAFORALT

By bus and grand taxi Two buses daily operate between Berkane and Taforalt (1hr 15min), while *grands taxis* ply the route throughout the day, more frequently on souk days (Wed & Sun).

ACCOMMODATION AND EATING

★ **Auberge de Taforalt** ⓦ taforaltclub.com. Among a smattering of roadside cafés at the northern entrance to town, this very good hotel has quirky cave-like rooms, Berber tents on the roof, and kitchens if you want to self-cater. They also run *Club Taforalt*, across the street, with a pool, children's play area, bar and restaurant. BB. Berber tent €, room €

The Route de L'Unité: Ketama to Fez

At the end of the Spanish Protectorate in 1957, there was no north–south route across the Rif, a marked symbol both of its isolation and of the separateness of the old French and Spanish zones. **The Route de l'Unité**, a road cutting right across the range from **Ketama to Fez** (and an active caravan route from the fourteenth to sixteenth centuries) was planned to provide working contact between the Riffian tribes and the French-colonized Moroccans.

The Route (more prosaically known as the R509), completed in 1963, was built with volunteer labour from all over the country – Hassan II himself worked on it at the outset. It was the brainchild of **Mehdi Ben Barka**, first president of the National Assembly and the most outstanding figure of the nationalist Left before his exile and subsequent "disappearance" in Paris in 1965. Ben Barka's volunteers, fifteen-thousand-strong for much of the project, formed a kind of labour university, working through the mornings and attending lectures in the afternoons.

Today the Route de l'Unité sees relatively little traffic – travelling from Fez to Al Hoceima, it's quicker to go via Taza and the R505; from Fez to Tetouan, via Ouezzane. Nevertheless, it's an impressive and very beautiful road, certainly as dramatic an approach to Fez as you could hope for. However, note the **warning** about driving through here (see page 122).

Taounate

TAOUNATE is a pleasantly bustling little town with sweeping views over the plains to the south. If you can make it for the huge **Friday market**, you should be able to organize a lift out to any number of villages in the region. Numerous cafés and banks, a petrol station and a good daily market line Avenue Mohammed V, the main road through the town.

ARRIVAL AND DEPARTURE
TAOUNATE

By grand taxi *Grands taxis* operate all day between the two major transport hubs of Fez and Issaguen (Ketama). They congregate near the Ziz petrol station on Av Mohammed V. Destinations Fez (1hr 30min); Issaguen/Ketama (1hr 20min).

ACCOMMODATION AND EATING

Du Lac 27 Av Mohammed V ☏ 0535 689367. In the middle of town, up an alley opposite the market entrance, this is a surprisingly good hotel, offering comfortable rooms with a/c. There's also a decent restaurant offering the usual Moroccan standards and a pastry breakfast. €

Tissa

The region around the village of **Tissa** is known for its thoroughbred Hayani horses. Here, in late September/early October, horses and riders from the region gather to compete at the annual **horse fair**. The climax is the competitive **fantasias** judged on speed, discipline and dress. Elsewhere, *fantasias* – traditional cavalry charges culminating in firing of muskets in the air – are put on largely for tourists, but here they are the real thing, for aficionados.

Rafsaï

RAFSAÏ, to the west of Taounate, was the last village of the Rif to be overrun by the Spanish. Vast hectares of **olive groves** surround the village, many of them recently planted thanks to government grants in a bid to offer an alternative to growing *kif* (see page 127). A lively **festival** takes place here every December to celebrate the olive harvest.

If you are into scenic roads and have transport, you might consider taking a 40km dirt road out from Rafsaï to the peak, **Jebel Lalla Outka**, offering a sweeping view of the whole Rif range. The road is reasonable as far as the village of Tamesnite, but thereafter is very rough *piste* and accessible only in summer.

Taza

TAZA was once a place of great importance: the capital of Morocco for periods of the Almohad, Merenid and Alaouite dynasties, and controlling the Taza Gap, the only practicable pass from the east. It forms a wide passage between the Rif and Middle Atlas and was the route to central power taken by Moulay Idriss and the first Moroccan Arabs, as well as the Almohads and Merenids, both of whom successfully invaded Fez from Taza. However, the local Zenatta tribe were always willing to join an attack by outsiders, and in the nineteenth century managed to overrun Taza completely, with centralized control returning only with the French occupation of 1914. Following occupation, Taza was an important centre of the resistance movement; troops fought long and hard in the Rif mountains in skirmishes which occurred sporadically right up to independence.

Modern Taza seems little haunted by this past, its monuments sparse and mostly inaccessible to non-Muslims. The town splits into two parts, the **Medina** (signposted as "Taza-Haut" in reference to its elevated location) and the French-built **Ville Nouvelle**, distinct quarters separated by 2km of road. The Ville Nouvelle is of little interest, though it has the usual facilities, but the Medina, with its magnificent hilltop site, is steeped in history and has a quiet charm.

Aside from offering a pleasant day or two exploring the Medina, Taza is also a good base from which to explore the national park of **Tazzeka**, a treat for drivers and hikers alike (see page 145).

The Medina

The **Medina** is easy enough to navigate, though you may need to ask directions for the few scattered sites. You can get a taste of the town's more recent history at the **Musée du Mechouar** (daily 10am–5pm; free), which houses a small but poignant collection of photos, newspaper cuttings and artefacts. The twelfth-century **Andalous Mosque** is the largest building in the southern section of the Medina – though its courtyards are characteristically well concealed from outside view. The minaret is best viewed from the Mechouar. The **Palais Bou Hamra**, behind the mosque, is the largely ruined and off-limits residence of Bou Hamra, the *Rogui* or pretender to the throne in the early years of the twentieth century (see page 144).

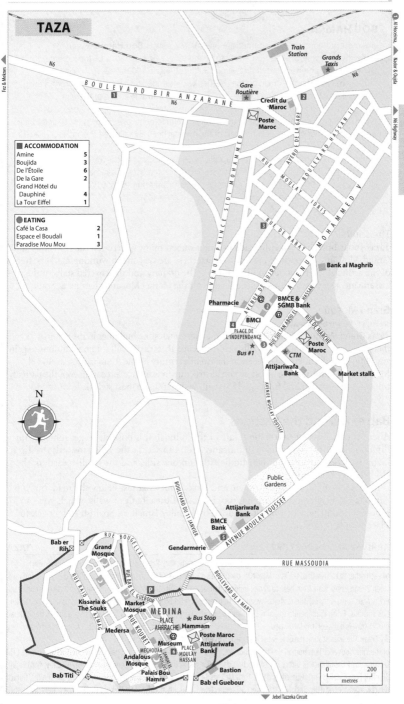

TAZA

N6

BOULEVARD BIR ANZARANE
N6

Fez & Meknes

Train Station

Grands Taxis

Al Hoceima

Nador & Oujda

N6 Highway

Gare Routière

Credit du Maroc

Poste Maroc

2

AVENUE DE LA GARE

RUE MOULAY IDRIS

BOULEVARD HASSAN II

AVENUE PRINCE SIDI MOHAMMED

AVENUE MOHAMMED V

RUE DE RABAT

Bank al Maghrib

AVENUE DE OUJDA

Pharmacie

BMCE & SGMB Bank

BMCI

RUE SULTAN ABOU EL HASSAN

PLACE DE L'INDEPENDANCE

Bus #1

RUE DE MARCHE

Poste Maroc

CTM

Attijariwafa Bank

Market stalls

AVENUE MOULAY YOUSSEF

Public Gardens

BOULEVARD DU 11 JANVIER

Attijariwafa Bank

BMCE Bank

AVENUE MOULAY YOUSSEF

Gendarmerie

RUE MASSOUDIA

BOULEVARD DE 3 MARS

Bab er Rih

Grand Mosque

RUE BOUGELLAL

RUE BAB EL GUEBOUR

RUE BATO

RUE KOUBET

RUE BARHOUNI EL AMAG

Kissaria & The Souks

Market Mosque

MEDINA

PLACE AHRRACHE

P

Medersa

MECHOUAR

Museum

RACHE EL ANDALUS

Andalous Mosque

Palais Bou Hamra

Bab Titi

Bus Stop

Hammam

Poste Maroc

PLACE MOULAY HASSAN

Attijariwafa Bank

Bastion

Bab el Guebour

Jebel Tazzeka Circuit

N

■ **ACCOMMODATION**

Amine	5
Boujida	3
De l'Étoile	6
De la Gare	2
Grand Hôtel du Dauphiné	4
La Tour Eiffel	1

● **EATING**

Café la Casa	2
Espace el Boudali	1
Paradise Mou Mou	3

0 — 200 metres

2

BOU HAMRA

Like most protagonists of the immediate pre-colonial period, **Bou Hamra** was an extraordinary figure, a former forger, conjurer and saint, who claimed to be the legitimate Shereefian heir and had himself proclaimed Sultan at Taza in 1902.

The name Bou Hamra – "man on the she-donkey" – recalled his means of travel round the countryside, where he won his followers by performing "**miracles**". One of these involved talking to the dead, which he perfected by the timely burying of a disciple, who would then communicate through a concealed straw; the pronouncements over, Bou Hamra flattened the straw with his foot (presumably not part of the original deal) and allowed the amazed villagers to dig up the by-then-dead witness.

Bou Hamra's own **death** – after his capture by Sultan Moulay Hafid – was no less melodramatic. He was brought to Fez in a small cage on the back of a camel, fed to the court lions (who refused to eat him), and was eventually shot and burned. Both Walter Harris and Gavin Maxwell give graphic accounts (see pages 145 and 145).

The souks

Taza's **souks** branch off to either side of Rue Koubet, midway between the Andalous and Grand Mosques. Since there are few tourists, these are very much working markets, free of the artificial "craft" goods so often found. The **granary** and the covered stalls of the **kissaria** are also worth a look, in the shadow of the **Market Mosque** (Jemma es Souk).

Grand Mosque

Rue Koubet • No entry for non-Muslims

Taza's **Grand Mosque** is historically one of the most interesting buildings in the country, though, like the Andalous, it is so discreetly screened that it's difficult for non-Muslims to gain any glimpse of the interior. Founded in the twelfth century by the Almohad sultan Abd el Moumen, it is probably the oldest Almohad structure in existence, predating even the partially ruined mosque at Tin Mal (see page 355), with which it shares most stylistic features.

Bab er Rih and the bastions

Above the Medina, at **Bab er Rih** (Gate of the Winds), it is possible to get some feeling for Taza's historic and strategic significance. You can see up the valley towards the Taza Gap: the Jebel Tazzeka and the Middle Atlas on one side, and the reddish earth of the Rif behind on the other.

The actual gate now leads nowhere and looks somewhat lost below the road, but it is Almohad in origin and design. So, too, is most of the circuit of walls, which you can follow round by way of a **bastion** (added by Moulay Ismail, in Spanish style) back to Place Moulay Hassan.

ARRIVAL AND DEPARTURE   TAZA

Most of the transport options are conveniently located close to each other to the north of the Ville Nouvelle, though it's a steep 20min uphill walk from here to Pl de l'Indépendance. *Petits taxis* constantly ply the route between the train and bus stations, Pl de l'Indépendance, and the Medina; local bus #1 travels between the latter two.

By train The train station (Le Gare Taza) is at the north end of the Ville Nouvelle, 1km from Pl de l'Indépendance.

Destinations Casablanca (3 direct & 3 connecting daily; 6hr 30min); Fez (6 daily; 2hr); Guercif (5 daily; 1hr); Meknes (4 direct & 3 connecting daily; 3hr); Nador (2 direct & 2 connecting

daily; 4hr); Rabat (3 direct & 3 connecting daily; 5–6hr).

By bus CTM operates from just off Pl de l'Indépendance, while all other companies operate from a chaotic open rank on Bd Bir Anzarane, about 300m west of the train station. Very few routes originate in Taza, so you should book ahead or arrive early. Most direct services to the coast leave very early in the morning.

Destinations Aknoul (3 daily; 1hr 30min); Al Hoceima (2 CTM & 4 others daily; 3hr 30min); Berkane (2–3 daily; 4hr 15min); Fez (7 CTM daily & others roughly hourly; 1hr 30min); Guercif (roughly hourly; 1hr); Meknes (5 CTM & 4 others daily; 4hr);

Nador (3 CTM & over 10 others daily; 3hr 30min); Oujda (3 CTM daily & others roughly hourly; 3hr); Rabat (5 CTM & over 5 others daily; 6hr); Taourirt (roughly hourly; 2hr).

By grand taxi Grands taxis operate from their own, almost hidden, rank 300m east of the train station. Those heading for Fez run throughout the day. For Al Hoceima and Nador, you

may first have to catch a grand taxi to Aknoul and/or Kassita. From Aknoul you can also catch sporadic grands taxis across the southern slopes of the Rif to Taounate on the Route de l'Unité.

Destinations Aknoul (1hr); Al Hoceima (occasionally; 2hr 45min); Fez (1hr 30min); Guercif (45min); Kassita (2hr); Oujda (3hr).

ACCOMMODATION   SEE MAP PAGE 143

Taza doesn't have a great choice of accommodation but you should find a room any time of year. Don't be shy to ask for a discount during the colder months or if staying more than one night.

Amine 3 Av Moulay Youssef ☎ 0535 672921. Family owned and operated, this is a friendly option with slightly garish, tiled rooms, plus an in-house restaurant that provides the usual bread-and-pastry breakfast. A possible drawback is its location, neither in the Medina nor the Ville Nouvelle. BB €

★ **Boujida** Rue de Rabat ⊕ hotel-boujida.com. Fairly new, this is Taza's best accommodation, offering simple, clean and comfortable tiled rooms including some singles and triples with spacious bathroom, a/c and satellite TV. The service is attentive and pleasant, including in the adjoining café where breakfast is served. Parking available. BB €

De l'Étoile 39 Pl Moulay Hassan ☎ 0535 270179. This is a bargain and the only accommodation within the Medina. A friendly, family-run place with ten decent rooms off a pleasant, tiled courtyard, all with beds, tables and sinks, shared squat toilets, and hot showers (extra charge). There's not much in the way of places to eat round here, but there are kitchen facilities for self-catering. €

De la Gare Cnr Bd bir Anzarane & Av de la Gare ☎ 0535 672448. Handy for transport, as it's opposite the train station, though a long haul from the Medina. Rooms are off a small, shaded courtyard, all have a/c and heating and many have showers and toilets with hot water in the morning and evening. A popular café next door serves a good croissant & coffee breakfast. €

Grand Hôtel du Dauphiné Pl de l'Indépendance ☎ 0535 673567. Not so grand anymore, this old Art Deco hotel in Ville Nouvelle nonetheless offers decent-sized rooms, some with balconies. In the lobby are some interesting photos of French explorers visiting the Friouato Caves (see page 146) back in 1951. There's also a ground-floor café-restaurant, only good for a pastry breakfast or a tajine for supper but it's licensed. €

La Tour Eiffel Bd bir Anzarane ☎ 0535 671562. A slightly overpriced three-star hotel, with a scale model of the Parisian icon above the front door, located a petit-taxi ride from Pl de l'Indépendance. Though lacking any great character, the good-sized carpeted rooms boast all mod cons – ask for a mountain view. There's also a handy lift, and a decent ground-floor restaurant. €€

EATING   SEE MAP PAGE 143

Good street food, such as brochettes, sandwiches and harira soup can be had from stalls in the Medina, as well as the market on Rue de Marché.

★ **Café la Casa** 4–6 Av Mohammed V ☎ 0535 670101. Taza's best dining option, offering a menu of all-day breakfasts as well as mains that encompass pasta, seafood paella, shawarmas and made-to-order couscous and pastilla – but leave room for the chocolate mousse. Pavement tables and the pleasant air-conditioned interior is complemented by a welcome non-smoking policy. €

Espace el Boudali N6 Highway, 2km east of town ☎ 0535 212227. On the edge of town, this large roadside complex includes a restaurant offering the usual Moroccan standards, as well as pizzas, a separate salon de thé and a toddlers' playground. €€

Paradise Mou Mou Av Moulay Youssef ☎ 0535 671111. A popular, compact restaurant off Pl de L'Indépendance, with tables both inside and out, and young, friendly staff. The menu offers a good variety of light meals, including panini, tacos and shawarmas, as well as a few heartier tajines. €€

DIRECTORY

Banks Attijariwafa Bank and BMCE are on Av Moulay Youssef and on Pl Moulay Hassan, in the Medina; Crédit du Maroc is on Av de la Gare.
Hammams Hammam La Medina, Rue Bab el Guebour, just

off Pl Ahrrache in the Medina.
Post office Rue de Marché, Ville Nouvelle; Pl Moulay Hassan, Medina.

Cirque du Jebel Tazzeka

A loop of some 123km around Taza, the **Cirque du Jebel Tazzeka** is a scenic, serpentine circuit through forests of cork, oak and cedar, with sweeping vistas over both the Rif and Middle Atlas ranges. Along the way are the immense **Gouffre du Friouato** (Friouato Caves) and the whole route is fertile ground for birdwatching and other wildlife (see page 146). If you don't have transport, *grand taxi* circuits can be arranged from most accommodation in Taza, starting at 250dh for the day.

Heading in an east–west direction from Taza, the **road** starts out curling around below the Medina before climbing to a narrow valley of almond and cherry orchards. Twelve kilometres out of Taza, the *Café Ras el Ma* is worth a pit stop for the aerial views of the village afforded by its shaded terrace. Beyond here, the road, prone to rock avalanches but generally in good condition, loops towards the first pass (at 1198m), via some great picnic spots and eventually emerging onto the Chiker Plateau. Here, in exceptionally wet years, the **Dayat Chiker** appears as a broad, shallow lake. More often than not, though, it is just a fertile saucer, planted with cereals; geographers will recognize its formation as a classic limestone polje.

Gouffre du Friouato

22km from Taza • ☎ 0666 014790 or 0668 576194 • Torches and waterproofs available for rent

The **Gouffre du Friouato** cave complex, starting 300m below ground level, is said to be the deepest in North Africa – and it feels it, entered by descending into a huge naturally lit "pot", over 30m wide, with over 500 wall-clinging and slippery **steps** down to a scree-filled base. The sense of descending into the entrails of the earth is exhilarating. The entrance fee will get you as far as the base of the first 700 steps at 160m deep – essentially the mouth of the cave – but a more exploratory trip, which takes you 2km into the cave, is available with a number of **guides** who are usually found hanging around near the entrance. Warm, waterproof clothing, sound footwear and a head torch are essential; allow around three hours in total.

Tazzeka National Park

32km from Taza • 🌐 tazekka.com. Shared *grands taxis* run from Taza to Bab Bou Idir in July and August when the campsite is open - the rest of the year you'll have to exclusively hire one

The **Tazzeka National Park**, formed in 1950 and covering some 120 square kilometres, contains some of the most pristine forest remaining in North Africa, and is considered one of the best-managed parks in Morocco. Sitting within the park is the 1980m-high Jebel Tazzeka, whose cedar-topped peak can be accessed by driving 9km up a *piste* that turns off 15km west of Bab Bou Idir, as well as a picnic site, Vallée des Cerfs (Valley of the Stags), set in among moss-covered cork trees and resembling

---

WILDLIFE IN THE TAZZEKA NATIONAL PARK

The **Tazzeka National Park** is one of northern Morocco's most rewarding wildlife sites, positioned, as it is, at the point where the Rif merges with the Middle Atlas. The range's lower slopes are covered in cork oak, the prime commercial crop of this area, and interspersed with areas of mixed woodland containing holm oak, the pink-flowered cistus and the more familiar bracken.

These woodland glades are frequented by a myriad of **butterflies** from late May onwards; common varieties include knapweed, ark green fritillaries and Barbary skippers. The forest floor also provides an ideal habitat for **birds** such as the multicoloured hoopoe, with its identifying crest, and the trees abound with the calls of wood pigeon, nuthatch, short-toed treecreeper and various titmice. The roadside telegraph lines also provide attractive hunting perches for such brightly coloured inhabitants as rollers and shrikes, both woodchat and great grey, who swoop on passing insects and lizards with almost gluttonous frequency.

something out of Tolkien's Middle Earth. **Bab Bou Idir** is a low-key *éstivage* (summer resort), 8.5km west of the Gouffre du Friouato; here you'll find an office, café and campsite (July & Aug only), and several good walks, ranging from twenty-minute rambles to eight-hour hikes.

Taza to Oujda

The route from **Taza to Oujda** is as bare as it looks on the map: a semi-desert plain, broken by little more than the odd roadside town. Nonetheless, if you've got time to spare, and transport, there are a couple of recommendable detours.

Msoun

29km east of Taza, just north of the N6 highway

The village of **MSOUN** sits within a **kasbah** that dates to the reign of Moulay Ismail (1672–1727). Inhabited by a hundred or so members of the semi-nomadic Haoura tribe, the kasbah is still turreted and complete on three sides. You can view its original rainwater cistern and grain silos, alongside the settlement's shop, post office and mosque.

Taourirt

130km from Taza and 220km from Oujda

TAOURIRT, the largest town between Taza and Oujda, was the crossroads between the old north–south caravan route linking Melilla and the ancient kingdom of Sijilmassa (see page 408), and the Taza corridor between Morocco and Algeria. Taourirt itself is of little interest, save for its large **Sunday souk**, but the peaceful **Za Gorges**, about 6km southeast of Taourirt and through which the usually running Oued Za meanders, make a good side trip. The road to the gorges unfortunately isn't signposted – it's best to ask for directions at the *Café Sabrin*, on the town's main roundabout.

ARRIVAL AND DEPARTURE

MSOUN

By bus and grand taxi *Grands taxis* and buses travelling on the N6 highway (rather than the A2 autoroute) can stop at *Motel La Kasbah* (see below), from where the Msoun kasbah is visible 500m north. Services are most frequent (1–2 hourly) during the day.

TAOURIRT

By train Taourirt is a useful transport junction, with trains north to Nador connecting reasonably well with arrivals from Oujda or Fez. The train station is about 1km south of the town's main roundabout.

Destinations Fez (4 daily; 4hr); Nador (3 daily; 2hr); Oujda (3 daily; 2hr).

By bus Buses operate from the *gare routière* on the western edge of town, on the N6.

Destinations Oujda (over 10 daily; 1hr 20min); Fez (over 10 daily; 4hr); Taza (roughly hourly; 2hr).

ACCOMMODATION AND EATING

MSOUN

Motel La Kasbah On the N6, about 100m west of the Msoun turn-off ☎0535 674651. A friendly place for a meal or overnight stop, offering very basic rooms with shared bathrooms (squat toilet). The café-restaurant serves up pretty good tajines and *grillés*, as well as a cheap but tasty omelette and salad lunch. There's also a dusty children's playground. €̄

TAOURIRT

Al Mansour N19 Highway south (Debdou direction), 300m south of the main roundabout ☎0536 694003. A cheapie in a good location and just about adequate for a night's stopover. The large rooms are a bit sparse but have tiled floors, comfortable beds and big windows, and the shared bathrooms are clean, although do not rely on hot water. The street noise usually recedes by 10pm. €̄

Oujda

Open and easy-going, with a large and active university, **OUJDA** has that rare quality in Moroccan cities – nobody makes demands on your instinct for self-preservation. Coming from the Rif, it is a surprise to see women in public again, and to re-enter a Gallic atmosphere, as you move out of what used to be Spanish Morocco into the old French Protectorate zone. Morocco's easternmost town, Oujda was the capital of French Maroc Orient and an important trading centre. A week-long music **festival**, the Festival Internationale du Rai (wfestivaloujdarai.com), takes place each July at various venues around the city.

Brief history

With its strategic location at the crossroads of eastern and southern routes across Morocco and Algeria, Oujda, like Taza, was always vulnerable to invasion and has frequently been the focus of **territorial claims**. Founded in the tenth century by Berber chieftain Ziri Ben Attia, it was occupied for parts of the thirteenth and fourteenth centuries by the **Ziyanids**, whose capital at Tlemcen is today just across the Algerian border. From 1727 until the early nineteenth century Oujda was under Turkish rule – the only town in present-day Morocco to have been part of the **Ottoman Empire**. Following the French defeat of the Ottomans in Algeria, France twice occupied the town prior to its incorporation within the Moroccan Protectorate in 1912, an early and prolonged association that remains tangible in the city's streets and the locals' attitudes.

In more recent years, Oujda's proximity to the **Algerian border** and distance from the government in Rabat led to a reputation for dissidence and unrest. This was particularly evident during the Algerian border war in the early 1960s, and again in the 1980s, in a series of student strikes. Following the restoration of Moroccan–Algerian relations in 1988 the city became truly pan-Maghrebi, with Algerians coming in to shop, and Moroccans sharing in some of the cultural dynamism of western Algeria, particularly Oran, the home of *raï* music. Alas, this is all in the past since the closure of the border in 1994 (see page 140), after which Oujda lost most of its passing trade, including a steady flow of tourists. However, Oujda still holds a big *raï* festival each July – this is the time to see the city at its best.

The Medina and around

The **Medina**, walled on three sides, lies right in the heart of Oujda and is largely a French reconstruction – obvious by the ease with which you can find your way around. It has an enjoyably active air, with **Place du 16 Août**, the city's main square, at its northwest corner.

Entering from **Bab el Ouahab**, the principal gate, you'll be struck by the amazing variety of food – on both café and market stalls. Olives are Oujda specialities, and especially wonderful if you're about after the September harvest. In the old days, more or less up until the French occupation, it was the heads of criminals, rather than olives, that were displayed here. From the gate, the main street leads to **Place el Attarin**, flanked by a *kissaria* (covered market) and a grand *fondouk*. To the northwest of the *kissaria* is **Souk el Ma**, the irrigation souk. This is where the supply of water used to be regulated and sold by the hour. While no longer in use, some of the old irrigation channels can still be seen here.

Running along the outside of the Medina walls, the **Parc Lalla Aïsha** is a pleasant area to seek midday shade. Following it round to the west takes you to the **Bab el Gharbi** from which Rue el Ouahda runs north to the old French **Cathédrale Saint Louis**. The fonts are dry, and the statue niches empty, but there is a beautiful chapel; for admission, ring at the door of the presbytery at the back, on Rue d'Azila.

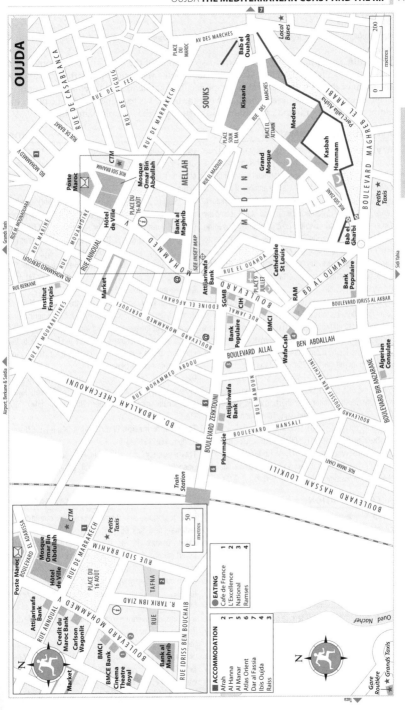

OUJDA

ACCOMMODATION
Afrah 2
Al Hanna 1
Al Manar 5
Atlas Orient 6
Dar al Fassia 7
Ibis Oujda 4
Raiss 3

EATING
Cafe de France 1
L'Excellence 2
National 3
Ramses 4

Sidi Yahia

6km east of Oujda • There are no regular bus services here; take a *grand taxi* and haggle over the price depending on how long you want to stay

SIDI YAHIA, is a rather unimpressive little oasis for most of the year, with only a run-down park area and a few cafés. However, it's a place of some veneration, purportedly housing the tomb of John the Baptist. There are spectacular **moussems** held here in August and September when almost every shrub and tree in the oasis is festooned with little pieces of cloth, a ritual as lavish and extraordinary as anything in the Catholic Church.

ARRIVAL AND INFORMATION

By plane Oujda–Angad Airport (ⓦonda.ma/en) is 12km north of Oujda, and is served by daily flights to Casablanca (1–2 daily; 1hr 10min). Inside the terminal you will find a café, bureaux de change, an ATM, and a number of car rental desks, including Avis (ⓦavis.com), Budget (ⓦbudget.com), Europcar (ⓦeuropcar.com), and local company AirCar (ⓦaircar.ma). *Grands taxis* are usually waiting outside to meet all arrivals and charge around 150dh to take up to six people into the city; other destinations are also possible, including Berkane, Nadorand Saïdia. Royal Air Maroc have an office at the airportand on Bd Mohammed V (ⓦroyalairmaroc.com).

By train Oujda is the end (or beginning) of the east–west route that connects in Fez to the remainder of the national rail network. Directly outside the station building are offices for Budget and Supratours. The city centre is an easy 15min walk straight down Bd Zerktouni, or you can flag down a red *petit taxi* from the junction 75m east of the station.

Destinations Casablanca Voyageurs (2 direct & 2 connecting daily; 11hr); Fez (3 daily; 5hr 30min); Guercif (3 daily; 2hr 30min); Nador (1 connecting daily; 4hr 30min); Rabat (2 direct & 2 connecting daily; 10hr); Tangier (1 direct & 1 connecting daily; 11hr); Taourirt (3 daily; 2hr).

By bus The bus station is 500m southwest of the train station at the junction of the N2, N6 (to Taza) and N17 (to Figuig) highways. It's not very well signposted – look for the large Mohammed VI Mosque next door. *Petits taxis*

ACCOMMODATION

Afrah 15 Rue Tafna ☎0536 686533. Long-established budget hotel located on a busy pedestrianized street, offering comfortable rooms with plenty of hot water all day, and great views across the Medina from the rooftop terrace. Good-value singles. €

★ **Al Hanna** 132 Rue de Marrakech ☎0536 686003. Well located for bus stations, and the best budget option in town, offering neat and clean rooms, some with balconies and some en suite. The vast terrace overlooks Pl du 20 Août and the minaret of the Omar Bin Abdullah mosque. Secure parking available. €

Al Manar 50 Bd Zerktouni ☎0536 688855. Not far from the train station, this functional mid-range hotel offers comfortable rooms, all en suite with a/c and satellite TV. A simple pastry breakfast is served to one side of the hotel's

OUJDA

congregate outside the station and cost around 10dh to the city centre and Medina. CTM operate separately from their office on Rue Sidi Brahim, just off Pl du 16 Août on the edge of the Medina.

Destinations Al Hoceima (3 non-CTM daily; 8hr); Berkane (1 CTM and over 10 others daily; 1hr 15min); Bouarfa/Figuig (1 CTM & 2 others daily; 4hr/6hr); Casablanca (3 CTM daily; 11hr); Fez (4 CTM & over 10 others daily; 5hr); Nador (10 non-CTM daily; 2hr 30min); Rabat (3 CTM & 2–3 others daily; 9hr 30min); Saïdia (1 CTM and over 5 others daily; 1hr 30min–2hr);Tangier (2 CTM daily; 12hr); Taza (3 CTM & others roughly hourly; 3hr).

By grand taxi *Grands taxis* for the airport, Ahfir, Al Hoceima, Berkane, Nador and Saïdia leave from north of the city centre, at the junction of Bd Mohammed Derfouti and Rue Ibn Abdelmalek; those for Taourirt and Taza leave by the main bus station – you'll have to change at Taza for Fez, and there for most points beyond.

Destinations Ahfir (45min); Al Hoceima (occasionally, more in summer; 5hr 30min); Berkane (50min); Nador (occasionally, more in summer; 2hr); Saïdia (1hr); Taza (3hr).

Tourist information Pl du 16 Août (Mon–Fri 8.30am–5.30pm; ☎0536 682036).

Travel agency Carlson Wagonlit, Pl du 16 Août (ⓦcarlson wagonlit.com) deal with general travel arrangements including car rental and flights.

SEE MAP PAGE 149

large reception, and there's a separate café/fast-food restaurant next door. BB €

Atlas Orient Pl de la Gare ⓦhotelsatlas.com. Unfortunately, the management and service of this smart, modern hotel, right by the train station, often fail to match what you'd expect for the price, though the facilities – including a spa, pool and small gym – are of a high standard. The 98 large rooms and suites have all the mod cons, and there are three restaurants and a nightclub. Request an inward-facing non-smoking room, away from the street and club noise. BB €€

★ **Dar al Fassia** 2 Rue Tifelt, Quartier Hay Al Amal ☎0536 686815. Easily spotted overlooking the eastern edge of the Medina, this owner-managed guesthouse trumps all other offerings in town for service and value for money. Facing inwards to a serene courtyard, the four en suite bedrooms are all spacious and comfortable, if slightly sparse, with large flat-screen TVs. Dinner (on request) and breakfast is taken in the warm dining salon or on the pleasant roof terrace. Airport, train and bus pick-ups available. BB €

Ibis Oujda Pl de la Gare ⓦ accorhotels.com. This reliable chain hotel right next to the train station delivers the usual characterless rooms; a few have balconies that overlook the busy Bd Abdallah Chefchaouni. But it's not badly priced and a bar and in-house restaurant look out onto pleasant gardens surrounding the swimming pool. BB €€

Raiss Bd Mohammed V ☎ 0536 703058. A friendly, business-class-style hotel with modern, clean rooms that are a touch on the small side but still comfortable and good value – those at the back are quietest. There's a handy lift, a ground-floor café and parking available. €

2

EATING AND DRINKING

SEE MAP PAGE 149

Oujda has a strong **cultural life** and is one of the most enjoyable Moroccan cities in which to while away an evening. The focus of much evening activity is **Bab el Ouahab**, around which you can get all kinds of grilled food as well as *harira* and boiled snails from stalls. On the other side of the Medina there are plenty of eating places on, or just off, **Bd Mohammed V** and Bd Zerktouni. Those listed here are unlicensed unless mentioned.

Cafe de France 87–89 Bd Mohammed V. One of the fancier places in town, offering a selection of mostly French fish and meat dishes such as *entrecôte* steak and *filet de St. Pierre* (John Dory). It's located upstairs from a café-patisserie, with a nightclub attached. Licensed. €€€

L'Excellence 30 Bd Mohammed V. This popular modern café enjoys a great street-side location. Besides serving possibly the best espresso in town, there's also a great selection of pastries and cakes, as well as more substantial offerings like pizza, panini and omelettes. €

National Cnr Bd Allal Ben Abdallah & Bd Zerktouni. Popular and long-time stalwart of the city's restaurants, with an impressive facade and a spiral staircase of black marble that leads up to an often full and slightly stuffy mezzanine level of tables. An old-fashioned *boucherie* restaurant, you can order your meat by the piece or kilo, and then watch it cooked brochette style or in a tajine. €€

Ramses 2 Bd Mohammed V. The downstairs restaurant serves mainly pizza and panini while the upstairs café and patisserie has a great breakfast menu and fresh juices. €

DIRECTORY

Banks & exchange Banque Populaire, Bd Idriss al Akbar; WafaCash bureau de change, Bd Mohammed V.

Post office Bd Mohammed V, north of Pl du 16 Août.

South to Figuig

In past years, before the eruption of civil war in Algeria, there was a well-established travel route from Oujda, south to the ancient date palm oasis of **Figuig**, and across from there into the Algerian Sahara. While the latter is no longer a possibility, those into isolated journeys might still want to consider the route from **Oujda to Figuig** – and on from here to the southern Moroccan oasis town of **Er Rachidia** (see page 401).

If you're up for the trip, be warned it's a long, hot haul: 369km to Figuig, and a further 393km to Er Rachidia. You can travel by bus or drive: the road is sealed all the way. Whichever way you travel, expect to explain yourself at a number of military checkpoints: this is a sensitive border area (see page 140).

The route

En route between Oujda and Figuig there are just a few roadside settlements and mining towns – for coal, copper, manganese and zinc. If you are driving, **Aïn Benimathar**, 83km from Oujda, is a good point to break the journey: the village has a group of kasbahs, an important (and ancient) **Monday souk**, and some grill-cafés. About 4km to its west is a small oasis, **Ras el Aïn**, with a highly seasonal waterfall. Another possible stop is **Tendrara**, 198km from Oujda, a larger settlement with a **Thursday souk**; it has a traditional marketplace in the centre and sheep and goats corralled on the outskirts. At 241km, you reach **Bouarfa**, the region's administrative centre and transport hub, with buses to Er Rachidia (as well as Figuig and Oujda).

Fez, Meknes and the Middle Atlas

MOUNTAIN LANDSCAPE WITH CEDARS

Fez, Meknes and the Middle Atlas

The undoubted highlight of this region is Fez, the city that has for the past ten centuries stood at the heart of Moroccan history as both an imperial capital and an intellectual as well as spiritual centre. Unique in the Arab world, Fez boasts as many monuments as Morocco's other imperial capitals put together, while the latticework of souks, extending for over a mile, maintain the whole tradition of urban crafts.

Neighbouring **Meknes** has an allure of its own, found throughout the city's pleasant souks and the architecturally rich streets of its sprawling imperial district, a vast system of fortified walls and gates that was largely the creation of Moulay Ismail, the most tyrannical of all Moroccan sultans. Just north of Meknes, the holy mountain town of **Moulay Idriss** and the impressive Roman ruins of **Volubilis** make for a rewarding day-trip.

Though many people heading south from Fez take a bus straight to either Marrakesh or Er Rachidia, it is worth stopping off along the way to explore the cedar-covered slopes and remote hinterlands of the **Middle Atlas**. The most popular route follows the N8 through the Berber market town of **Azrou** to emerge, via the dramatic **Cascades d'Ouzoud**, at Marrakesh. Alternatively, you could cut southeast from Azrou on the N13 towards **Midelt**, before descending through the Ziz Gorges to Er Rachidia and the vast date-palm oases of the Tafilalt that line the route to the Sahara. In between the N8 and the N13, and accessible from both, lies **Imilchil**, home to Morocco's most famous festival and the midway point along a tortuous route across the High Atlas to the Todra Gorge and Tinghir.

Fez

The history of Fez is composed of wars and murders, triumphs of arts and sciences, and a good deal of imagination.
The Land of an African Sultan, Walter Harris

The oldest of Morocco's four imperial capitals and one of the most complete medieval cities of the Arab world, **FEZ** stimulates all the senses: a barrage of haunting and beautiful sounds, infinite visual details and unfiltered odours. It has the French-built **Ville Nouvelle** of other Moroccan cities, but nearly a quarter of Fez's one-million-plus inhabitants continue to live in the extraordinary Medina-city of **Fez el Bali**, which owes little to the West besides electricity and tourists. More than any other city in Morocco, the old town seems suspended in time somewhere between the Middle Ages and the modern world.

Like much of "traditional" Morocco, Fez was "saved" then recreated by the French, under the auspices of **General Lyautey**, the Protectorate's first Resident-General. Lyautey took the philanthropic and startling move of declaring the city a historical monument; philanthropic because he certainly saved Fez el Bali from destruction (albeit from less benevolent Frenchmen), and startling because until then Moroccans were under the impression that Fez was still a living city – the imperial capital of the Moroccan empire rather than a preservable part of the nation's heritage. More conveniently for the French, this paternalistic protection helped to disguise the dismantling of the old culture. By building a new European city nearby – the Ville Nouvelle, now the city's business and commercial centre – then transferring Fez's economic and political functions to Rabat and the west coast, Lyautey ensured the city's eclipse along with its protection.

MOULAY IDRISS

Highlights

❶ Borj Nord and the Merenid tombs The fabled panorama of the Fez Medina is pure magic at sunset, accompanied by the call of muezzins. See pages 159 and 170

❷ Medersa Bou Inania, Fez Delicate zellij, intricate stucco and finely carved cedar wood combine to make this the finest Merenid Islamic college in the country. See page 159

❸ The tanneries Chouwara The hypnotic view of these leather-tanning vats can have barely changed since medieval times. See page 168

❹ Ville Impériale, Meknes Moulay Ismail's immense walled complex contains ceremonial gateways, vast granaries and the venerated mausoleum of the man himself. See page 184

❺ Volubilis and Moulay Idriss Remarkable Roman and Islamic sites that can be combined on an easy day-trip from Meknes. See pages 197 and 201

❻ Cascades d'Ouzoud If you visit only one waterfall in Morocco, if make these spectacular falls. See page 219

❼ Aït Bouguemez While the hordes flock to Toubkal, trekkers in the know hit the peaceful trails of this glorious High Atlas valley. See page 221

❽ Cirque de Jaffar Exciting *piste* circuit that cuts through foreboding badlands scenery, offering standout views of the mountains to the south. See page 225

HIGHLIGHTS ARE MARKED ON THE MAP ON PAGE 156

To appreciate the significance of this demise, you only have to look at the Arab chronicles or old histories of Morocco – in every one, Fez takes centre stage. The city had dominated Moroccan trade, culture and religious life (and usually its politics, too) since the end of the tenth century. It was closely and symbolically linked with the birth of an "Arabic" Moroccan state due to their mutual foundation by **Moulay Idriss I**, and was regarded as one of the holiest cities of the Islamic world after Mecca and Medina. Medieval European travellers described it with a mixture of awe and respect, as a "citadel of fanaticism" yet the most advanced seat of learning in mathematics, philosophy and medicine.

The decline of the city's political position notwithstanding, **Fassis** – the people of Fez – continue to head most government ministries and have a reputation throughout Morocco as successful and sophisticated. What is undeniable is that they have the most

FEZ, MEKNES AND THE MIDDLE ATLAS

HIGHLIGHTS

1. Borj Nord and the Merenid tombs
2. Medersa Bou Inania, Fez
3. The tanneries Chouwara
4. Ville Impériale, Meknes
5. Volubilis and Moulay Idriss
6. Cascades d'Ouzoud
7. Aït Bouguemez
8. Cirque de Jaffar

FEZ ORIENTATION

Even if you felt you were getting to grips with Moroccan cities, Fez is bewildering. The basic layout is simple enough, with a Medina and a French-built **Ville Nouvelle** to its southwest, but here the **Medina** comprises two separate districts: Fez el Bali (Old Fez), in the pear-shaped bowl of the Sebou valley, and Fez el Jedid (New Fez), established on its western edge during the thirteenth century. **Fez el Jedid**, dominated by a vast enclosure of royal palaces and gardens, is relatively straightforward. But **Fez el Bali**, where you'll want to spend most of your time, is an incredibly intricate web of lanes, blind alleys and souks – it takes a couple of days exploration before you even start to feel confident of where you're going. The Medina is vast, and you'll probably find yourself returning from the more far-flung sights in one of the *petits taxis* stationed by the main gates into Fez el Bali (see page 158); while it's easy enough to walk between Fez el Bali and Fez el Jedid, you're better off taking a taxi between the Medina and the Ville Nouvelle (see page 176).

3

developed Moroccan city culture, with an intellectual tradition and their own cuisine, dress and way of life.

Brief history

When the city's founder, Moulay Idriss I, died in 791 AD, Fez was little more than a village on the east bank of the Oued Boukhrareb. It was Moulay's son, **Idriss II**, who really began the city's development, at the beginning of the ninth century, by making it his capital and allowing in refugees from Andalusian Cordoba and from Kairouan in Tunisia – at the time, the two most important cities of western Islam. The impact of these refugees on Fez was immediate and lasting: they established separate, walled towns on either riverbank (still distinct today), and provided the superior craftsmanship and mercantile experience for Fez's industrial and commercial growth. It was at this time, too, that the city gained its intellectual reputation – the tenth-century Pope Sylvester II studied here at the **Kairaouine University**, technically the world's first, where he is said to have learned the Arabic mathematics that he introduced to Europe.

The seat of government shifted south to Marrakesh under the Berber dynasties of the **Almoravids** (1062–1145) and **Almohads** (1145–1248). But with the conquest of Fez by the **Merenids** in 1248, and their subsequent consolidation of power across Morocco, the city regained its pre-eminence and moved into something of a "golden age". Alongside the Medina, the Merenids built a massive royal city – **Fez el Jedid** or New Fez – which reflected both the wealth and confidence of their rule. Continued expansion, once again facilitated by an influx of refugees, this time from the Spanish reconquest of Andalusia, helped to establish the city's reputation as "the Baghdad of the West".

After the fall of the Merenids, Fez became more isolated under the **Saadians** (1554–1669) and the early **Alaouites** (1669–1822), and, although it was here that the French protectorate was formally established in 1912, colonial rule allowed the city little more than a provincial existence. Despite the crucial role the Fassis played in the struggle for **independence** (a time brought electrifyingly to life in Paul Bowles' novel *The Spider's House*; see page 536), Mohammed V retained the French capital of Rabat, condemning the city to further decline. If **UNESCO** had not inscribed it onto their World Heritage list in 1981, it seems likely that much of the old city would have been threatened by extensive physical collapse. Over the last decade or so, continuing efforts to renovate Fez's historical monuments have breathed new life into the Medina and, along with projects to improve working conditions around the tanneries and to restore the Oued Boukhrareb, reinvigorated Fassi pride in their city.

Fez el Bali

With its mosques, medersas and *fondouks*, back alleys crammed with goods-laden donkeys, and a mile-long labyrinth of souks, there are enough sights in **Fez el Bali** (Old Fez) to fill three or four days just trying to locate them. In this – the apparently wilful secretiveness – lies part of Fez's fascination, and there is much to be said for Paul Bowles' somewhat lofty advice to "lose oneself in the crowd – to be pulled along by it – not knowing where to and for how long…to see beauty where it is least likely to appear". Do the same and you must be prepared to get really lost, but then that is half the fun – and it is all the more uplifting to stumble across the magnificent **Medersa Bou Inania**, or to unexpectedly find yourself on Rue Boutouil and realize that the courtyard you are peering into is that of the **Kairaouine Mosque**, the epicentre of religious life in Morocco.

ESSENTIALS

If you want to avoid coinciding with **tour groups**, try visiting the main sights in Fez el Bali between noon and 2pm, when the groups stop for lunch. The flow of life eases considerably on Friday, when much of the Medina takes the day off and crowds thin.

ACCESS

There are four principal entrances and exits to Fez el Bali:

Bab Boujeloud The western gate, the most famous in Fez, easily identified by its brightly coloured tiling and the hotels and cafés grouped on either side. Bus #9 runs from Pl Batha, just to the southeast of Boujeloud, to Pl Atlas in the Ville Nouvelle. There's also a *petit taxi rank* on the square in front of the gate.

Bab er R'cif Central gate by the square and mosque of the same name, and a convenient entrance to Fez el Bali, just a

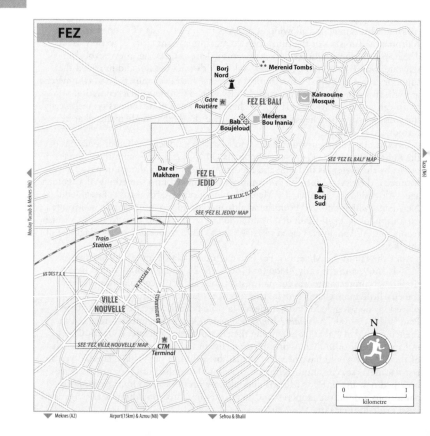

THE BORJ NORD

Like its southern counterpart across the valley, the fortress of **Borj Nord**, perched on the hillside overlooking Bab Boujeloud, was built in the late sixteenth century by the Saadians to *control* the Fassis rather than to defend them. Carefully maintained, the *borj* now houses the country's **Museum of Arms** (Charge; ☎ 0535 645241), full off daggers encrusted with stones, the hefty arsenals of numerous sultans and, occupying pride of place, a cannon 5m long and weighing twelve tonnes, said to be used during the Battle of the Three Kings (see page 500); signage is in Arabic and French only. The main reason for coming up here, though, is for the commanding **views** across the Medina: a spectacular sweep of daily life that, together with the views from the Merenid tombs (a 500m walk round the hillside, along Avenue des Merenides; see page 170), constitute the best panorama of the city.

few blocks below the Kairaouine Mosque. Bus #19 and #29 run between the square and Bd Mohammed V in the Ville Nouvelle; bus #19 runs via Bab el Jedid Nouaïl at the bottom of Fez el Jedid and continues on to the train station, bus #29 continues on to Pl de l'Atlas. Pl er R'cif is also home to a *petit taxi* rank.

Bab Ftouh The southeast gate at the top of El Andalous. There's a *petit taxi* rank here, just outside the gate. See page 171.

Bab Guissa The north gate, a handy exit point for the Merenid tombs. Served by bus #10; *petits taxis* are available by the gate. See page 169.

GETTING AROUND

Routes To help visitors find their way around the Medina, tourism masterminds have scattered star-shaped signs throughout Fez el Bali; the directional markers, positioned at door-top height, correspond with the six colour-coordinated routes in the map produced by the tourist board (see page 177).

Bab Boujeloud

Most people begin their exploration of Fez el Bali at **Bab Boujeloud**, a meeting place with a great concentration of cafés and stalls. With its polychrome-tiled facades – blue (the traditional colour of Fez; "*boujeloud*" means "blue" in Arabic) on the outside and green (the colour of Islam) facing into the Medina – it's a pretty unmistakeable landmark.

From the square just inside the gate, lanes lead down into the Medina: straight ahead for the craft shops of the **Kissaria Serrajine** and for **Talâa Kebira**, the major artery of Fez el Bali (see page 163); or right, via a handful of patisserie stalls, for **Talâa Seghira**, a lane that runs parallel to Kebira for much of its length.

Musée Batha

Pl Batha; entrance on Mahaj el Methab • Charge • Ⓦ fnm.ma

Housed in a late nineteenth-century palace built by Hassan I – in which the agreement for the France-Morocco Protectorate was signed in 1912 – the **Musée Batha** is worth a visit just for its courtyards and gardens, whose cypresses and myrtle trees provide a respite from the exhausting pace of the Medina. The art and crafts collection, one of the finest in the country, concentrates on local artisan traditions, with displays of carved wood, much of it rescued from the city's medersas, and examples of calligraphy and local embroidery, including traditional musicians' costumes. Above all, though, it is the pottery from Fez that stands out – the beautiful pieces, some of them nearly 600 years old, stress the preservation of age-old techniques rather than innovation.

Medersa Bou Inania

Talâa Kebira • Charge

If there is just one building you should seek out in Fez – or, not to put too fine a point on it, in Morocco – the **Medersa Bou Inania** should be it. The most elaborate, extravagant and beautiful of all Merenid monuments, it comes close to perfection in every aspect of its construction: its dark cedar is fabulously carved, the zellij tilework classic, the stucco a revelation. In addition, the medersa is the city's only building still in religious use that non-Muslims are permitted to enter.

Set somewhat apart from the other medersas of Fez, the Bou Inania was the last and grandest built by a Merenid sultan. It shares its name with the one in Meknes, which was completed (though not initiated) by the same patron, **Sultan Abou Inan** (1351–58), but the Fez version is infinitely more splendid. Its cost alone was legendary – Abou

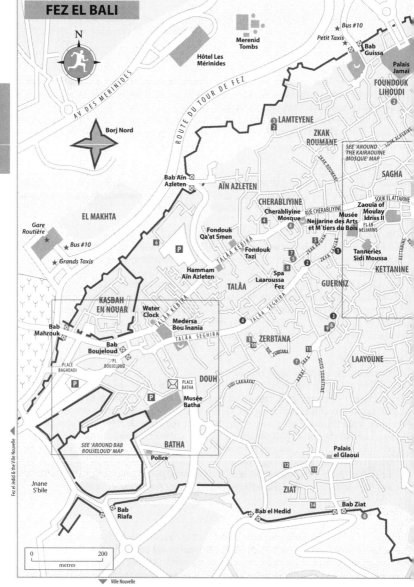

Inan is said to have thrown the accounts into the river on its completion because, "a thing of beauty is beyond reckoning".

At first, Abou Inan doesn't seem the kind of sultan to have wanted a medersa – his mania for building aside, he was more noted for having 325 sons in ten years, deposing his father and committing unusually atrocious murders. The Ulema, the religious leaders of the Kairaouine Mosque, certainly thought him an unlikely candidate and

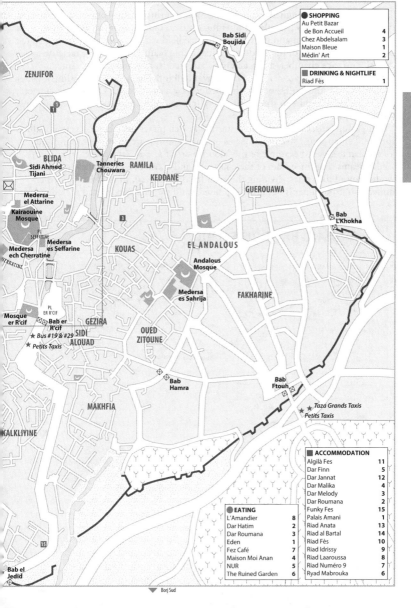

3

● SHOPPING	
Au Petit Bazar	
de Bon Accueil	**4**
Chez Abdelsalam	**3**
Maison Bleue	**1**
Médin' Art	**2**

■ DRINKING & NIGHTLIFE	
Riad Fès	**1**

● EATING	
L'Amandier	**8**
Dar Hatim	**2**
Dar Roumana	**3**
Eden	**1**
Fez Café	**7**
Maison Moi Anan	**4**
NUR	**5**
The Ruined Garden	**6**

■ ACCOMMODATION	
Algilà Fes	**11**
Dar Finn	**5**
Dar Jannat	**12**
Dar Malika	**4**
Dar Melody	**3**
Dar Roumana	**2**
Funky Fes	**15**
Palais Amani	**1**
Riad Anata	**13**
Riad al Bartal	**14**
Riad Fès	**10**
Riad Idrissy	**9**
Riad Laaroussa	**8**
Riad Numéro 9	**7**
Ryad Mabrouka	**6**

advised him to build his medersa on the city's rubbish dump, on the basis that piety and good works can cure anything. Whether it was this or merely the desire for a lasting monument that inspired him, he set up the medersa as a **rival to the Kairaouine** itself (see page 166) and for a while it was the most important religious building in the city, earning the status of a **Grand Mosque** (unique in Morocco) and the right to say the Friday *khotbeh* prayer – which it retains to this day.

The interior

The basic **layout** of the medersa is quite simple – a single large courtyard flanked by two symmetrical halls (*iwan*) and opening onto an oratory. For its effect, it relies on the mass of decoration and the light and space held within. You enter the exquisite onyx marble **courtyard**, the medersa's outstanding feature, through a stalactite-domed entrance chamber, a characteristic adapted from Andalusian architecture. From here, you can gaze across to the **prayer hall** (off-limits to non-Muslims), which is divided from the main body of the medersa by a small canal. Off to each side of the courtyard are stairs to the upper storey (closed to the public), which is lined by **student cells**.

In the courtyard, the **decoration** – startlingly well preserved – covers every possible surface. Perhaps most striking in terms of craftsmanship are the woodcarving and joinery, an unrivalled example of the Moorish art of *laceria*, "the carpentry of knots". Cedar beams ring three sides of the courtyard and a sash of elegant black Kufic script wraps around four sides, dividing the zellij from the stucco, thus adding a further dimension. Abou Inan is bountifully praised amid the inscriptions and is credited

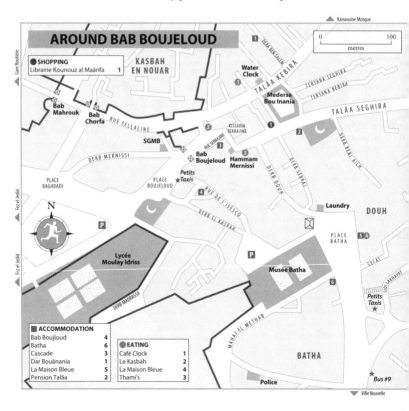

THE FUNCTION OF MEDERSAS

Although Fez is home to many of the finest examples in the Islamic world, **medersas** (student colleges and residence halls) were by no means unique to the city. Indeed, they originated in Khorasan in northeastern Iran and gradually spread west through Baghdad and Cairo, where the Medersa al Azhar was founded in 972 AD and became the most important teaching institution in the Muslim world. They seem to have reached Morocco under the Almohads, although the earliest ones still surviving in Fez are Merenid, dating from the late thirteenth century.

The word medersa means "**place of study**", and there may have been lectures delivered in some of the prayer halls. However, most medersas served as little more than **dormitories**, providing room and board to poor (male) students from the countryside, so that they could attend lessons at the mosques. In Fez, where students might attend the Kairaouine University for ten years or more, rooms were always in great demand and "key money" was often paid by the new occupant. Although medersas had largely disappeared from most of the Islamic world by the late Middle Ages, the majority of those in Fez remained in use right up into the 1950s. Non-Muslims were not allowed into the medersas until the French undertook their repair at the beginning of the Protectorate, and were banned again (this time by the colonial authorities) when the Kairaouine students became active in the struggle for independence.

Since then, **restoration** work, partly funded by UNESCO, has made medersas more accessible. The project is ongoing (see page 169).

3

with the title *caliph* on the foundation stone, a vainglorious claim to leadership of the Islamic world pursued by none of his successors.

The water clock

More or less opposite the medersa entrance, just across Talâa Kebira, Bou Inania's property continues with an extraordinary **water clock** (*magana*), built by the astronomer Abou 'l-Hassan Ali. This was removed for research, and whilst the woodwork has now been restored, the metal parts have yet to be replaced – though the clock is part of a huge renovation project that aims to revamp many of the Medina's long-neglected sites by 2023 (see page 169). An enduring curiosity, it consisted of a row of thirteen windows and platforms, seven of which retained their original brass bowls. Nobody has yet been able to discover exactly how it functioned, though a contemporary account detailed how at every hour one of its windows would open, dropping a weight down into the respective bowl.

Talâa Kebira

Cutting through Fez el Bali and running all the way down to the Kairaouine Mosque (albeit under different names), **Talâa Kebira** (Big Slope) is the Medina's principal thoroughfare, a shop-laden route that's interesting less for specific sights than the accumulation of stimuli that barrage the senses along the way: camel heads advertising the location of the local butchers; vendors bartering in the spice and slipper souks; and donkeys, seemingly everywhere, hauling their heavy loads up and down the rutted lanes.

The fondouks

Along Talâa Kebira's first main stretch, heading down from the Medersa Bou Inania, you pass a number of old **fondouks** – or caravanserais as they were called in the East – that once formed the heart of social life outside the home. They provided rooms for traders and richer students, and frequently became centres of vice, intrigue and entertainment. There were once around two hundred in Fez el Bali, and many of those that survive now serve as small factories or warehouses, often graced with beautiful

THE "PASHA'S PALACE"

Hidden away in the southern district of Ziat, southeast of Place Batha, the intriguing nineteenth-century **Palais el Glaoui** (Charge; ☎0667 366828) served as the Fez residence of T'hami el Glaoui, Pasha of Marrakesh (see page 304). As with all of the Glaoui family's many palaces, it was abandoned after Morocco gained independence in 1956, and is now proudly looked after by Abdou Boukhars, a local artist and one of the few remaining family members.

It's a huge place, taking in seventeen houses, stables, a hammam, a Koranic school and two gardens, though Abdou's interesting tours are usually limited to the main areas, including what was once allegedly the harem. Much is in need of repair, and while the main reason for visiting is the rare chance to poke around an unrestored historical building, the architecture is undoubtedly impressive and the zellij work quite beautiful, particularly in the salons around the central courtyard.

3

fourteenth- and fifteenth-century decorations. The most interesting are **fondouk Tazi**, at no. 54, where drums are made using the leather from adjoining workshops, and, further up, on the opposite side of the street, **fondouk Qa'at Smen**, at no. 89, which was originally a Merenid prison, fitted out with solid colonnades and arches; it's still is use, as a place to buy salted butter (*smen*), olive oil and *khlia*, a kind of beef jerky, though the traditional *jubbana* (lidded jars) that once held the goods were replaced by plastic barrels a long time ago.

Rue Cherabliyine

As Talâa Kebira becomes **Rue Cherabliyine**, so, too, the surroundings change. A district of leather stalls and cobblers, the aptly named "Road of the Slippermakers" is one of the best areas for buying handmade traditional **babouches** (pointy, flat leather slippers). Keep an eye out for the sophisticated-looking grey and black pairs that are unique to Fez; prices vary depending on the quality of the leather (the best type is *ziouani*, or goat skin) and stitching.

Like all neighbourhoods in Fez, Cherabliyine has its focal **mosque** – a fourteenth-century structure with an attractive minaret – but more interesting is the mosque's **washroom**, on the opposite side of the street, open to the elements and clearly neglected but still in its original state, with a horseshoe of toilets surrounding a central ablutions area.

Souk el Attarine

The sweet smell of cinnamon, cumin and cloves wafting around the arched wooden gateway at the end of Rue Tarafine (Talâa Kebira) denotes your entry into the lattice-covered **Souk el Attarine**, or "Spice Market", once the richest and most sophisticated shopping district – but now increasingly home to vendors peddling sunglasses and cheap watches. It was traditionally around the grand mosque of a city that the most expensive commodities were sold and kept, a pattern more or less maintained as you approach the Kairaouine, as the few spice vendors that remain give way to silk traders and shops selling finely embroidered *takchitas* (two-piece wedding garments).

Souk el Henna

Just off Souk el Attarine; accessed through an arch opposite the *Dar Saada* restaurant, or from Derb Fakharine

A quiet, tree-shaded square, **Souk el Henna** adjoins what was once the largest madhouse in the Merenid empire, the Maristane Sidi Frej, said to be the first asylum in the world to implement musical therapy as a method for treating patients. Stalls here continue to sell **henna** and other traditional cosmetics such as *kohl* eyeliner (historically made from antimony but usually now lead sulphide, which is cheaper but also toxic), and lip rouge made from crushed poppy petals. There are plans over the next couple of years to bring the Maristane closer to its roots, with the creation of a healthcare centre, a museum of traditional medicine and a market selling medicinal plants, in which case the souk will move to a nearby fondouk.

Place en Nejjarine and around

Accessed off Souk el Attarine, along Derb Fakharine; or from Derb Dermami, down the steps near the end of Zkak Lahjar (Talâa Seghira)

The beautiful canopied **Nejjarine fountain**, the best known and most beautiful of several mosaic fountains in the Medina, is the focal point of picturesque **Place en Nejjarine**. The square is surrounded by a tangle of workshops making mule saddles or gaudy wedding chairs, and souks filled with the sound and smell of carpenters (the *nejjarine*) – some of Morocco's finest - chiselling away at sweet cedar wood.

Faux guides may try and lead you to the **tanneries** here, but note that these are the smaller tanneries Sidi Moussa and not the more famous tanneries Chouwara, near Place Seffarine (see page 168).

Musée Nejjarine des Arts et Métiers du Bois

Pl en Nejjarine • Charge • Photography prohibited • ☎ 0535 740580

Once a caravanserai for carpenters, the imposing eighteenth-century Nejjarine *fondouk* now houses the delightful **Musée Nejjarine des Arts et Métiers du Bois**, dedicated to showcasing the best of Fez's wooden arts and crafts. Of particular interest are the fourteenth- to eighteenth-century cedar-wood friezes exhibited on the first floor, and, on the floor above, a much more modern *rabab* (string instrument) beautifully inlaid with mother-of-pearl. However, it is the wonderfully restored interior of the building itself that is worth the entrance fee – a small exhibit on the roof terrace covers the renovation, where there's also a **café** offering views over the Medina.

Musée Ryad Belghazi

19 Derb el Ghorba, signed from Pl en Nejjarine, the Karaouine Mosque and Talâa Seghira • Charge • ☎ 0535 741178

Tucked away in a maze of narrow lanes south of Place en Nejjarine, the **Musée Ryad Belghazi** is housed in a traditional riad built in the nineteenth century and now owned by the family of the same name. The museum's few small rooms explain the basic layout and features of this type of architecture, and give you an insight into what a Fassi merchant's house might have contained in the 1800s, with displays of musical instruments, kaftans and Berber jewellery.

Zaouia Moulay Idriss II and around

Accessed from Pl en Nejjarine, along Derb Bab Moulay Ismail; or through the first archway on the right on Souk el Attarine • Closed to non-Muslims

---

THE CULT OF MOULAY IDRISS

There is no particular evidence that **Moulay Idriss II** was a very saintly *marabout*, but as the effective founder of Fez and son of the founder of the Moroccan state he has considerable **baraka**, the magical blessing, or luck, that Moroccans invoke, and his moussem (see page 182) brings the city to a standstill. Originally, it was assumed that Idriss had been buried near Volubilis, like his father, but in 1308 an uncorrupted body was found on the spot where his *zaouia* now stands and the cult was launched. Presumably, it was an immediate success, since in addition to his role as the city's patron saint, Idriss has an impressive roster of **supplicants**. This is the place to visit for: poor strangers arriving in the city, boys before being circumcised and women wanting to facilitate childbirth – and for some long-forgotten reason, Idriss is also the protector of Morocco's sweetmeat vendors.

The major landmark south of Souk el Attarine is the **Zaouia Moulay Idriss II**, one of the holiest buildings in Fez. The shrine has dominated this part of the Medina for over five hundred years but was rebuilt in the eighteenth century by Sultan Moulay Ismail – his only act of pious endowment in the city. The wooden bar that breaches the foot of Derb Bab Moulay Ismail, the lane running off the southeast corner of Place en Nejjarine, marks the beginning of the shrine's *horm*, or **sanctuary precinct**. Until the French occupation of the city in 1911, this was as far as Christians, Jews or mules could go, and any Muslim who went beyond it had the right to claim asylum from prosecution or arrest. These days, non-Muslims are allowed to walk around the outside of the *zaouia*, and although they are not permitted to enter, it is possible to glimpse discreetly inside the shrine and even see the saint's tomb.

Ducking under the bar, head up Derb Bab Moulay Ismail – full of stalls selling silverware, candles, nougat and other devotional offerings – to the women's entrance, where you can look in from the doorway; the fifteenth-century **tomb of Moulay Idriss II** is in the far room on the left amid a scene of intense and apparently High Baroque devotion all around. A curious feature, common to many *zaouias* but rarely visible from the outside, are the numerous European clocks – prestigious gifts and very popular in the nineteenth century, when they were shipped from Manchester by Fassi merchant families (their main export base for the cotton trade).

Kissaria el Kifah

From the end of Derb Bab Moulay Ismail, you can make your way round to the far side of the Zaouia Moulay Idriss II, along the way passing through a tight network of lanes, to the **kissaria al Kifah** (covered market). Founded in 809 AD, it is the oldest souk in the Medina, but what you see today – full of clothes stalls selling *jellabas*, *hendiras* (embroidered wedding shawls) and *babouches* – dates back to the 1950s, when it was renovated following a fire, with a more aesthetic refurbishment in 2017 adding marble floors, zellij fountains and a beautiful berchla-style roof.

Medersa el Attarine

Rue Boutouil • Charge

After the Bou Inania, the **Medersa el Attarine** is the finest of the city's medieval colleges, graced by an incredible profusion and variety of patterning. For all the startling richness of its zellij, wood and stucco, the decoration retains an air of ease, and the building's elegant proportions are never threatened with being overwhelmed. The medersa was completed in 1325 by the Merenid sultan, Abou Said Othman, and is thus one of the earliest in Fez. Its general lightness of feel is achieved by the simple device of using pairs of symmetrical arches to join the marble pillars to a single weight-bearing lintel.

On your way in, stop awhile in the **entrance hall**, whose zellij decoration is perhaps the most complex in the city. Its circular design, based on an interlace of pentagons and five-pointed stars, perfectly demonstrates the intricate science (and philosophy) employed by the craftsmen; the patterns radiate – as Titus Burckhardt notes in *Moorish Art in Spain* – from "a single point as a pure simile for the belief in the oneness of God, manifested as the centre of every form or being".

Around the first floor are **cells** for over sixty students, which operated as an annexe to the Kairaouine University until the 1950s. If you can get onto it (access is erratic), the medersa's roof affords one of the most complete possible **views of the Kairaouine Mosque**.

Kairaouine Mosque

Rue Boutouil • Closed to non-Muslims

The **Kairaouine Mosque** was the largest mosque in Morocco until the construction of the Hassan II Mosque in Casablanca (see page 260) – and vies with Cairo's Al-Azhar for the title of the world's oldest university. Today, it remains the fountainhead of the country's religious life, governing, for example, the timings of Ramadan and the other Islamic festivals.

The mosque was founded in 859 AD by the daughter of a wealthy refugee from the city of Kairouan in Tunisia, but its present **dimensions**, with sixteen aisles and room for twenty thousand worshippers, are essentially the product of tenth- and twelfth-century reconstructions: first by the great Caliph of Cordoba, Abd er Rahman III, and later under the Almoravids.

For non-Muslims, who cannot enter the mosque's courts and prayer halls, the Kairaouine is a rather elusive sight. The building is so thoroughly enmeshed into the surrounding houses and shops that it is impossible to get any clear sense of its shape at close quarters; indeed, the best views of the mosque are actually from the Borj Nord (see page 159) or the Merenid tombs (see page 170). Down in the Medina, at most you can get only partial views of it from the adjoining rooftops or through the four great **entrances** to its main courtyard – at least one of the doors just past *Café Boutouil* are usually open, letting you peek into the mosque's rush-matted and round-arched interior.

Nobody seems to object to tourists gaping through the gates, though inevitably the centrepieces that would give order to all the separate parts – the main aisle and the main mihrab – remain hidden from view. The overall **layout** was inspired by the Mezquita in Cordoba: the courtyard is open to the sky, with a large fountain at its centre and two smaller ones under porticoes at each side, added in the seventeenth century and based on originals in the Alhambra in Granada.

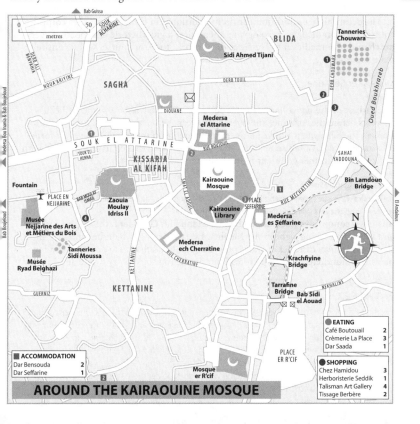

AROUND THE KAIRAOUINE MOSQUE

ACCOMMODATION
Dar Bensouda 2
Dar Seffarine 1

EATING
Café Boutouail 2
Crèmerie La Place 3
Dar Saada 1

SHOPPING
Chez Hamidou 3
Herboristerie Seddik 1
Talisman Art Gallery 4
Tissage Berbère 2

Place Seffarine and around

A wedge-shaped square on the southeastern side of the Kairaouine Mosque, **Place Seffarine** is almost wilfully picturesque, with its metalworkers (*dinandiers*) hammering away at immense copper cauldrons, and a gnarled old tree at its centre. A chance for a breather after the intensity of the central Medina, the square is a good place to stop for a drink (see page 180) and to get your bearings before taking one of a number of onward routes: south, through souks specializing in jewellery and used metal goods, to the **riverside walkway** (see box 180); or north to the **tanners' souk**, on which the city's commercial wealth from the tenth to the nineteenth centuries was founded.

Kairaouine Library

Pl Seffarine

Established by the Kairouan refugees in the ninth century, then stocked by virtually the entire contents of Cordoba's medieval library, the recently restored **Kairaouine Library** once held the greatest collection of Islamic, mathematical and scholarly books outside Baghdad. That much of the library was lost or dissipated in the seventeenth century is a pointed marker of Fez's decline, though it still contains some incredibly rare texts and manuscripts amongst its collection, including a deerskin copy of a Koran dating from the ninth century that is written in gold leaf in an ancient Kufic script.

Despite the studious atmosphere of the library, the **university** here has been largely usurped by modern departments around Fez el Jedid and the Ville Nouvelle, and dispersed throughout Morocco. Until recent decades, though, it was the only source of Moroccan higher education. Entirely traditional in character, studies comprised courses on Koranic law, astrology, mathematics, logic, rhetoric and poetry – very much as at the medieval universities of Europe. Study, of course, was an entirely male preserve.

Medersa es Seffarine

Pl Seffarine

The earliest of the Fez colleges, the **Medersa es Seffarine** was built around 1270 – 35 years before the Attarine, and over eighty years before the construction of Bou Inania. The Seffarine is unlike all the other medersas in that it takes the exact form of a traditional Fassi house, with an arched balcony above its courtyard and still with suggestions of former grandeur in the lofty prayer hall.

Tanneries Chouwara

Rue Chouwara • To view the tanneries, you need to go up into the leather shops that overlook them; a small fee is requested by the *gardiens*, who will give you a sprig of mint to help combat the smell if required

There is a compulsive fascination about the **tanneries Chouwara**, the biggest in Fez and the most striking sight in the Medina. Every morning, when the tanneries are at their most active, cascades of water pour through holes that were once the windows of houses, hundreds of skins lie spread out on the rooftops to dry, while amid the vats

---

THE FEZ

The red cylindrical hat with its black tassel, more correctly known as a Fassi *tarbouche*, is not only worn and manufactured in Fez but as far afield as Egypt and Syria. In the eighteenth and nineteenth centuries, **the fez** became associated with the Ottoman Empire, and in some places it was donned as a mark of support – a gesture that led to it being banned by Kemal Atatürk when he took power in Turkey and abolished the empire. The fez is also going out of fashion in its hometown, and tends to be worn only by older men – most young men now prefer the Tunisian *chechia* or baseball caps.

THE RESTORATION OF FEZ

Unsurprisingly for a city founded over a thousand years ago, Fez has long shown signs of its incredible age. But in the last decade or so, numerous **restoration projects** have been steadily addressing this decline. Rundown **riads** were the first to be renovated, then historical monuments like **medersas** and **fondouks**. More recently, wider-reaching initiatives have sought to tackle problems ranging from urban pollution to workers' rights. The **Dyer's Souk** has been restored, the **Oued Boukhrareb** – once concreted over and reduced to a rubbish-filled trickle – cleaned up and a riverside walkway constructed from the Terrafine Bridge to the Bin Lamdoun Bridge. New viewing areas have been installed around the **tanneries** and conditions improved for the workers below.

---

of dye and pigeon dung (the white ones at the back), an unbelievably Gothic fantasy is enacted as tanners treat the hides. The rotation of colours in the honeycombed **vats** follows a traditional sequence – yellow (supposedly "saffron", in fact turmeric), red (poppy), blue (indigo), green (mint) and black (antimony).

The occasional rinsing machine aside, there can have been little change here since the sixteenth century, when Fez replaced Cordoba as the pre-eminent city of **leather production**. As befits such an ancient system, the ownership is also intricately feudal: the foremen run a hereditary guild and the workers pass down their specific jobs from generation to generation.

For all the stench and voyeurism involved, there is a kind of sensuous beauty about the tanneries. However, it is a guilty pleasure, as one glance across at the gallery of camera-touting foreigners snapping away will testify.

Medersa ech Cherratine

Rue Cherratine • Charge

South of Place Seffarine, a right turn up Rue Cherratine leads to the restored **Medersa ech Cherratine**, a very different proposition to the Seffarine (and indeed all previous medersas). Cherratine dates from 1670 and the reign of Moulay Rachid, founder of the Alaouite dynasty. The design represents a shift in scope and wealth to an essentially functional style, whereby the student cells are grouped around three corner courtyards, and latrines/ablutions around the fourth.

North to Bab Guissa

From Rue Hormis (the first lane on the left just inside the entrance to Souk el Attarine), a network of alleys wend their way northwards through a series of produce markets before emerging at **Bab Guissa**. The sights en route are more curiosities than monuments, and are troubled by few tourists – which, of course, is part of the area's appeal. About halfway between Souk el Attarine and the gate, the route passes the western end of **Souk Achebine**, whose historical function as a traditional-medicine souk survives in the shop on the left-hand side that still sells snakeskins, chameleons and other supposed "cures".

From Bab Guissa, you can take a *petit taxi* back to Bab Boujeloud or up the hill behind the gate to the **Merenid tombs** (see page 170), an astounding spot to watch dusk descend over the Medina.

El Andalous

The eastern quarter of Fez el Bali, across the Oued Boukhrareb from the Kairaouine, is known as **El Andalous**, after the Arab immigrants who settled here after fleeing Cordoba in the early ninth century. For the first three centuries of their existence, El Andalous and the Kairaouine (settled just seven years later) were separate walled cities – the name for the most northerly bridge across the river, Bin Lamdoun, translates as

A TOMB WITH A VIEW

Up above Bab Guissa, the crumbling remnants of the **Merenid tombs** stand vigil over the sprawling Medina, a particularly atmospheric place at dawn or dusk, when the call to prayer sweeps across Fez el Bali. From this superb vantage point you can delineate the more prominent of Fez's reputed 365 mosque minarets. At sunset, the sky swarms with a frenzy of starlings, egrets and alpine swifts adding further spectacle to the scene. All around you are spread the Muslim cemeteries that flank the hills on each side of Fez, while below, the city's major **monuments** protrude from the hubbub of rooftops. The pyramid-shaped roof of the Zaouia of Moulay Idriss II is easily defined. To its left are the two minarets of the Kairaouine Mosque: Burj en Naffara, or the Trumpeter's Tower (the shorter of the two), and the original minaret. The latter, slightly thinner in its silhouette than usual and with an unusual whitewashed dome, is the oldest Islamic monument in the city, built in 956 AD.

The sounds of the city, the stillness and the contained disorder below all seem to make manifest the mystical significance that Islam places on urban life as the most perfect expression of culture and society.

The route to and from the tombs can lead through some unsavoury areas, so it's best to catch a **petit taxi** up here, from either Bab Guissa or Bab Boujeloud.

"The Bridge Between the Cities" – and the intense **rivalry** between them often erupted as factional strife. It still lingers enough to give each area a distinct identity, although since the thirteenth century this has been a somewhat one-sided affair: according to Fassis, the Andalousis had more beautiful women and braver soldiers, but the Kairaouinis have always had the money.

Whatever the truth of the tale, nearly all of the most famous Andalusian scholars and craftsmen lived and worked on the other side of the river, and as a result the atmosphere in the quarter has a somewhat provincial character. Monuments are few and far between and the streets are quieter and predominantly residential.

GETTING TO   EL ANDALOUS

From the Kairaouine Three bridges connect the Kairaouine Mosque and the tanneries quarter with El Andalous: the Bin Lamdoun, reached down the right-hand branch of Rue Mechattine; humpbacked Krachfiyine; and the Tarrafine, north of Pl er R'cif.

From Pl er R'cif The *place* is served by buses #19 and #29

from the Ville Nouvelle, as well as *petits taxis* from across the city.

From Bab Ftouh You can begin your exploration at Bab Ftouh, at the southeastern end of El Andalous, which is served by *petit taxis*.

Medersa es Sahrija

Derb Yasmina • Charge

The quarter's most interesting monument, the beautifully restored **Medersa es Sahrija** is generally rated the third-finest medersa in the city after the Attarine and Bou Inania. Named after the unusual, large pool in its courtyard, the medersa (still functioning as a Koranic school) is worth visiting for the considerable range and variety of its **original decoration**: the zellij is among the oldest in the country, and the palmettes and pine cones of the cedar-wood carving hark back to Almohad and Almoravid motifs. Built around 1321 by Sultan Abou el Hassan, the Sahrija is more or less contemporary with the Attarine and a slightly earlier version of his medersa in Meknes (see page 159), which it resembles in many ways.

Andalous Mosque

Derb Andalous • Closed to non-Muslims

Fronting the square just along the lane from the Medersa es Sahrija and built at the highest point of the valley, the **Andalous Mosque** was founded in the late ninth century (allegedly by the sister of the woman who founded the Kairaouine Mosque) and saw considerable enlargements under the Almoravids and Merenids. There's little to be seen other than the monumental entrance gates, which were a thirteenth-century Almohad addition, designed by artisans from Granada and most notable for their beautifully carved wooden awning.

Bab Ftouh and around

A strange no-man's-land of run-down houses, the region south of the Andalous Mosque and extending beyond **Bab Ftouh** was once a leper colony and is traditionally known as a quarter of necromancers, thieves, madmen and saints. The **cemetery** that covers the hills just outside the gate, the largest in Fez, is home to the whitewashed **koubba of Sidi Ali Ben Harazem**, a twelfth-century mystic who has been adopted as the patron saint of students and the mentally ill; Harazem's *koubba* is the squat, green-roofed building that dominates the skyline. The saint's moussem, held in the spring, is one of the city's most colourful; in past centuries, it was often the cue for riots and popular insurrections.

Fez el Jedid

Unlike Fez el Bali, whose development and growth seems to have been almost organic, **Fez el Jedid** ("New Fez") was a planned city, built by the Merenids at the beginning of their rule, under Sultan Abou Youssef in 1276, as a practical and symbolic seat of government.

The chronicles present the Merenids' decision to site their city some distance from Fez el Bali as a defence strategy, though this would seem less against marauders than to safeguard the new dynasty against the Fassis themselves – and it was only in the nineteenth century that the walls between the old and new cities were finally joined. It was not an extension for the people in any real sense, being occupied largely by the vast royal palace of **Dar el Makhzen** and a series of garrisons. This process continued with the addition of the **Mellah** – the Jewish ghetto – at the beginning of the fourteenth century; forced out of Fez el Bali after one of the periodic pogroms, the Jews provided an extra barrier (and scapegoat) between the sultan and his Muslim faithful.

GETTING TO	**FEZ EL JEDID**
On foot You can walk to Fez el Jedid in 10min from Bab Boujeloud, via the Jnane S'bile; locals advise against walking from the Ville Nouvelle on your own (see page 176).	**By bus** Bus #19 runs from the Ville Nouvelle to Pl er R'cif in Fez el Bali, stopping at Bab el Jedid Nouaïl, the southern entrance to the Mellah.

Jnane S'bile

Entrances on Av Moulay Hassan (Av des Français) and on the side roads that frame the gardens • 8am–7.30pm, closed Mon

The scale shifts as you walk to Fez el Jedid from Bab Boujeloud, the labyrinthine alleyways and souks of the Medina giving way to a stretch of massive walls. Within them spread the rose-filled gardens of **Jnane S'bile** (sometimes called the Jardins de Boujeloud), their pools diverted from the Oued Fez. The gardens are a vital lung for the old city – a stroll along their tree-fringed pathways makes a welcome respite from the bustle of the Medina, and you can spend an hour or two at the tranquil café-restaurant in the southwestern corner (see page 180), adjacent to an old water wheel that once supplied water to the gardens.

Petit Mechouar

At the western end of Avenue des Français lies the enclosed square of the **Petit Mechouar**, once the focus of city life and a stage for the sort of snake charmers, acrobats and storytellers that are still found in Marrakesh's Jemaa el Fna; they were cleared out when the *mechouar* was closed for repairs in the mid-1970s and have never been allowed back.

The gate on the northern side of the square is the monumental **Bab es Seba**, a thirteenth-century Merenid structure that was the main approach to the Dar el Makhzen and Fez el Bali until King Hassan II realigned the site in 1967–71. It also served as a gallows for the Infante Ferdinand of Portugal, who was hanged here, head down, for four days in 1443. He had been captured during an unsuccessful raid on Tangier and was doomed after his country failed to raise the ransom. As a further, salutary warning, his corpse was cut down, stuffed and displayed beside the gate, where it remained for the next three decades.

Less imposing but equally as important is **Bab Mechouar**, the gate to the south, which opens onto the grounds of the Dar el Makhzen. It was through this gate that ordinary citizens would approach the palace to petition the king – the *mechouar* was where they would wait for admission.

Vieux Mechouar

Heading through Bab es Seba from the Petit Mechouar leads into the **Vieux Mechouar**, understandably much larger than its neighbour but surprisingly nowhere near as old, having been laid out at the nineteenth century by Sultan Moulay Hassan (it is also

3

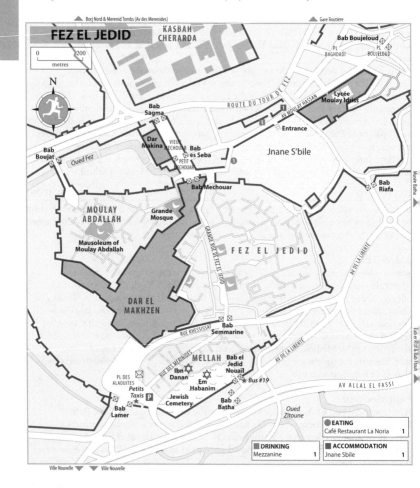

THE JEWS OF FEZ

The enclosed and partly protected position of the Mellah fairly accurately represents the historically ambivalent position of **Moroccan Jews**. Arriving for the most part with compatriot Muslim refugees from Spain and Portugal, they were never fully accepted into the nation's life. Yet nor were they quite rejected as in other Arab countries. Inside the Mellah, they were under the direct protection of the sultan (or the local *caïd*) and maintained their own laws and governors.

Whether the creation of a **ghetto** ensured the actual need for one is debatable. Certainly, it greatly benefited the reigning sultan, who could depend on Jewish loyalties and also manipulate the international trade and finance that they came to dominate in the nineteenth century. But despite their value to the sultan, even the richest Jews led extremely circumscribed lives – in Fez before the French Protectorate, no Jew was allowed to ride or even to wear shoes outside the Mellah, and they were severely restricted in their travels elsewhere.

3

known as Place Moulay Hassan). The square is flanked along the whole of one side by the **Dar Makina**, an arms factory built by Italians in 1886, and is today used as the main venue for the Fez Festival of World Sacred Music (see page 182).

A smaller gate, the nineteenth-century **Bab Sagma**, stands at the far end, forcing you into an immediate turn as you leave Fez el Jedid through the Merenid outer gateway. The huge complex on the opposite side of the road is the **Kasbah Cherarda**, a fort built by Sultan Moulay Rachid in 1670 to house – and keep at a distance – the Berber tribes of his garrison. The partially walled compound is now the site of a hospital, a school and an annexe of the Kairaouine University.

Moulay Abdallah

Heading through the gate on the southwestern corner of the Petit Mechouar brings you to the **Moulay Abdallah** district, an old *quartier reservé* that was once home to cafés, dance halls and brothels – a red-light district established by the French Protectorate. The quarter, focused around a main street that twists around to Fez el Jedid's 1276 **Grand Mosque**, has a slightly forlorn feel about it today.

Mausoleum of Moulay Abdallah

Closed to non-Muslims • To get here from the Grand Mosque, follow the street to the west for 50m onto a small square and take the right fork at the far end; you will see the minaret of the mausoleum shortly after

West of the Grand Mosque, on the way to Bab Boujat, is the **Mausoleum of Moulay Abdallah**, a mosque and medersa complex that also contains the tombs of four sultans of the current Alaouite dynasty, from the eighteenth and twentieth centuries.

The Mellah

South of the Petit Mechouar, souk-speckled Grand Rue de Fez el Jedid leads down to the **Mellah**, once home to the city's Jewish families but now largely resettled by poor Muslim emigrants from the countryside. Although the quarter's name came to be used for Jewish ghettos throughout Morocco, it originally applied only to this one in Fez, christened from the Arabic word for "salt" (*mellah*), perhaps in reference to the Fassi Jews' job of salting the heads of criminals before they were hung on the gates.

In the immediate aftermath of independence in 1956, the Mellah's seventeen-thousand-strong **Jewish population** left for Casablanca, Paris and Israel virtually en masse. Today, just a handful of Jewish families live here and in the Ville Nouvelle, and all that remains of their presence are a scattering of synagogues – you can visit the UNESCO-restored **Ibn Danan Synagogue** (off Rue des Merinides; charge) – and their eighteenth- and nineteenth-century **houses**, conspicuously un-Arabic, with

TAKING THE WATERS OF MOULAY YACOUB

A pleasant day-trip for a swim and a hot bath, the spa village of **Moulay Yacoub**, 21km northwest of Fez, has been offering cures for the afflicted for centuries. Legend relates that the village was named either after Sultan Moulay Yacoub Ben Mansour – cured after his first bath, they say – or is a corruption of Aquae Juba, the spring of a local Berber king, Juba, who was envious of Roman hot baths. Either way, the hillside village's fame is founded on its sulphur-rich spa waters, which are pumped from some 1500m below ground and reach temperatures of around 54°C. Cars and taxis park at the top of the village, leaving you to descend flights of steps past stalls whose bathing goods add a chirpy resort atmosphere.

Buses run hourly from the main bus station in Fez (30min), while *grands taxis* depart from the *gare routière* (20min).

OLD THERMAL BATHS
Charge

The old **thermal baths** (*baignoires* or *anciennes thermes*) are halfway down the hill and have a more medicinal purpose – albeit fairly basic to Western eyes. They're usually busy, but you can enjoy a hot bath on your own (*baignoire individuelle*) or with a friend. Massage and jacuzzi are also available, while the masseurs in the thermal baths can put you through your paces with a hammam-style scrub. Although fairly recently refurbished, beware that both facilities – baths and pool – are only cleaned once a week on Monday evening, so you're probably best not swimming that afternoon.

VICHY THERMALIA SPA
Ⓦ moulay-yacoub-vichy-thermalia-spa-hotel.fr/en • Charge

Much more upmarket than the old thermal baths, the **Vichy Thermalia Spa** is a spa-hotel for serious medical treatment – mostly rheumatism and respiratory problems – and full-on self-indulgence that is as exclusive as it gets in Morocco. The half-day Thermal Spa Pass grants you access to the indoor pool and vaporarium and includes a bathrobe and towel.

their tiny shuttered windows and elaborate ironwork balconies that overhang busy Rue des Merenides.

Jewish cemetery
Entrance along the street off the eastern corner of the car park near Pl des Alaouites • closed Fri evening for Jewish Sabbath and also Sun morning • Charge

On the southern edge of the Mellah, the white, rounded gravestones of the **Jewish cemetery** stretch along the hillside that runs down towards the Ville Nouvelle. The most visited (and most distinctive) tombs are those of eighteenth-century **Rabbi Yehuda Ben Attar**, covered in peppermint and black mosaic tiles, and **Lalla Solica Hatchouel**, its bright green roof topped by three vase-like turrets. Hatchouel, born in 1817, caught the eye of Prince Moulay Abderrahman, who asked her to convert to Islam, so he could marry her; she refused and was promptly imprisoned and executed for the affront, aged just 17, and has since been venerated as a martyr.

Built in 1928 and until fairly recently in regular use for services, the restored **Em Habanim Synagogue** now serves as a museum containing a clutter of bric-a-brac, much of it only tangentially related to Fez's Jewish community (ask the *gardien* to open the door if it's locked).

Dar el Makhzen
Closed to the public

Lording it over Place des Alaouites at the bottom of Fez el Jedid, the **Dar el Makhzen**, or Royal Palace, is one of the most sumptuous complexes in Morocco. Set amid vast gardens, it has constantly been rebuilt and expanded over the centuries, and while the numerous pavilions and guest wings that make up the current complex are strictly off-limits to the public, you can still admire the fabulous ceremonial **gateway** that fronts the square, its different-sized doors each adorned with enormous brass knockers and surrounded by dizzying zellij tilework.

ARRIVAL AND DEPARTURE — FEZ

BY PLANE

Fes-Saïs Airport is 15km south of Fez, off the N8 to Azrou (w onda.ma). There are branches of Banque Populaire and BCME in Arrivals, offering decent exchange rates. *Grands taxis* to the town centre are a fixed fee , whether you're on your own or in a group of up to six; alternatively, bus #16 to

the train station leaves the airport at least every hour. In Fez, the offices of Royal Air Maroc are at 54 Av Hassan II

BY TRAIN

Fez train station is off Av des Almohades in the Ville Nouvelle, a 10min walk from the concentration of hotels

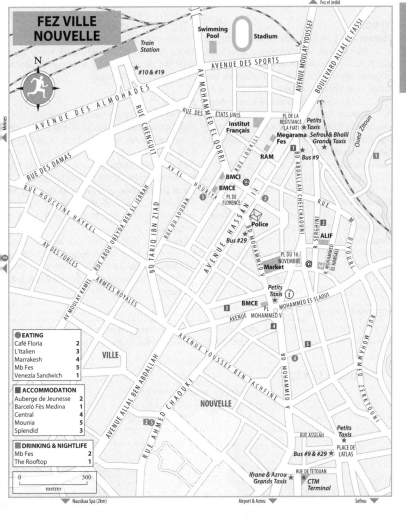

EATING
Café Floria 2
L'Italien 3
Marrakesh 4
Mb Fes 5
Venezia Sandwich 1

ACCOMMODATION
Auberge de Jeunesse 2
Barceló Fès Medina 1
Central 4
Mounia 5
Splendid 3

DRINKING & NIGHTLIFE
Mb Fes 2
The Rooftop 1

around Pl Mohammed V; from the station, the #16 bus runs to the airport roughly every hour. Bus #10 passes the *gare routière* on its way to Bab Guissa, in Fez el Bali; if you walk to Av Hassan II, you can pick up the #9 bus to nearby Pl Batha. Beware of unofficial *petits taxis* drivers (official *petits taxis* in Fez are metered), who charge very unofficial rates for the trip into town; the fare to Bab Boujeloud should be around 12dh.

Destinations Asilah (5 daily; 3hr 45min–4hr 45min); Casablanca (roughly hourly; 3hr 50min–4hr 20min); Kenitra (roughly hourly; 2hr–2hr 25min); Marrakesh (12 daily; 8hr); Meknes (roughly hourly; 30min); Nador (3 daily; 5hr 45min–7hr); Oujda (4 daily; 5hr 30min–6hr 25min); Rabat (roughly hourly; 2hr 50min–3hr 20min); Tangier (6 daily; 5–6hr); Taza (6 daily; 2hr).

BY BUS

Stations Most buses leave from the *gare routière*, just north of Bab Mahrouk, on the western edge of Fez el Bali, though there are also terminals in the Ville Nouvelle and by the various gates to the Medina. CTM has an office here, though its own principal station is on the corner of Rue Tetouan and Bd Mohammed V in the Ville Nouvelle (ⓦctm.ma). Supratours buses (ⓦsupratours.ma) run from the train station in the Ville Nouvelle. Leaving Fez for the south, note that convenient night buses cover most routes – to Marrakesh and Rissani, for example.

Destinations Agadir (4 CTM & 4 others daily; 10hr 45min–12hr); Al Hoceima (2 CTM daily; 5hr); Azrou (3 CTM & 1 Supratours daily, others frequently; 1hr 15min–3hr); Casablanca (16 CTM daily & others hourly; 4hr 30min); Chefchaouen (5 CTM & 7 others daily; 4hr–4hr 30min); Er Rachidia (1 CTM, 1 Supratours & 6 others daily; 7hr 15min–8hr 30min); Erfoud (1 CTM & 1 Supratours daily; 9hr); Ifrane (2 CTM daily, others frequently; 45min); Larache (4 CTM and 3 others daily; 4hr 15min–5hr); Marrakesh (6 CTM & 5 others daily; 7–10hr); Meknes (8 CTM daily, others frequently; 1hr); Midelt (1 CTM, 1 Supratours & 6 others

daily; 5hr –6hr 30min); Moulay Yacoub (roughly hourly; 30min); Nador (3 CTM & 12 others daily; 4hr 30min–5hr 30min); Oujda (6 CTM & 10 others daily; 4hr 30min–5hr); Rabat (17 CTM daily & others hourly; 3hr–3hr 30min); Rissani (1 CTM, 1 Supratours & 6 others daily; 9hr 15min–10hr); Sefrou (roughly hourly; 45min); Tangier (6 CTM & 13 others daily; 6–8hr); Taza (11 CTM daily & others hourly; 1hr 30min–2hr 30min); Tetouan (4 CTM & 12 others daily; 5–6hr).

BY GRAND TAXI

Ranks *Grands taxis* mostly operate from the rank outside the *gare routière* near Bab Mahrouk. Exceptions are those from Ifrane and Azrou, which use a rank opposite the CTM office, 100m west of Pl de l'Atlas; Sefrou and Bhalil, which use a rank 100m southeast of Pl de la Résistance (also called La Fiat); and Taza, which arrive at Bab Ftouh.

Destinations Azrou (1hr); Bhalil (45min); Casablanca (3hr 30min); Ifrane (45min); Marrakesh (8hr); Meknes (1hr); Midelt (3hr); Moulay Yacoub (20min); Rabat (2hr 30min); Sefrou (30min); Taza (1hr 15min).

BY CAR

Parking For Fez el Bali, you can leave your car in car parks around Bab Boujeloud (southwest of the gate, on the waste ground opposite the Lycée Moulay Idriss); in Aïn Azleten, north of Talâa Kebira; by Bab Guissa; and by Bab el Jedid, south of Pl er R'cif. Central options for parking in the Ville Nouvelle include Pl de Florence and Pl du 16 Novembre.

Petrol stations There are several petrol stations in the Ville Nouvelle: around Pl de l'Atlas, near the beginning of the road to Sefrou and Midelt; and off Bd Abdallah Chefchaouni.

Car rental Avis, 50 Bd Abdallah Chefchaouni (ⓦavis.ma); Europcar, 45 Av Hassan II (ⓦeuropcar.ma) and Hertz, Bd Lalla Maryem, 1 Kissariat de la Foire (ⓦhertz.ma), allow return delivery to a different centre; they also all have desks at the airport.

GETTING AROUND

By petit taxi *Petits taxis* in Fez use their meters, so offer good value (note that prices increase fifty percent after 8pm). Useful *petit taxi* ranks include: Pl Boujeloud, just south of Bab Boujeloud; Pl Batha, southeast of Bab

---

SECURITY IN FEZ

Despite what some *faux guides* may say, the **Medina** is not a dangerous place, though it's better to avoid walking around the quieter areas before 8am if you can help it; and note that there have been several reports of daytime muggings by people walking to and from the Merenid tombs, north of Bab Guissa. In the **Ville Nouvelle**, locals warn that robbery is a problem at night on Avenue Allal Fassi, the isolated main road between Place de la Résistance and the Musée Batha; if you must walk it, do so only in groups of at least three people. Avoid, also, the overgrown hillside east of Place de la Résistance, between *McDonald's* and the train track, where muggings have occurred even in daylight.

Boujeloud; Bab Guissa; Pl er R'cif, south of the Kairaouine Mosque; Bab Ftouh, at the top of the El Andalous quarter (all Fez el Bali); and Pl de la Résistance and Pl Mohammed V (both in the Ville Nouvelle).

By bus You're unlikely to need city buses, which are crowded and less convenient but hardly any cheaper than *petits taxis*, though the following can be useful (note that the numbers to look for are marked on the sides of the buses; those on the back are completely different): #9 (Pl de l'Atlas to Pl Batha, via Bd Abdallah Chefchaouni); #10 (train station to Bab Guissa, via the *gare routière*); #19 (train station to Pl er R'cif); #29 (Pl de l'Atlas to Pl er R'cif, via Bd Mohammed V).

INFORMATION

Tourist office On the east side of Pl Mohammed V (Mon–Thurs 9am–1pm & 2–4pm, Sat & Sun 9am–1pm; ⓦ festourism.org).

Useful websites The best blog on Fez is the well-respected and up-to-date ⓦ riadzany.blogspot.co.uk written by expats living in the city and full of interesting articles and wide-ranging news.

Maps *Fès: The Thematic Tourist Circuits* includes a large fold-out map of the Medina and provides information on half a dozen themed itineraries using colour-coded routes that correspond with the star-shaped tourist signs scattered throughout the Medina. It's available from most newsstands and *bureaux de tabac* – check those across from the Museé Batha. *Plan de Fès* is a simple but useful plan detailing both the Medina and the Ville Nouvelle, with a smaller insert of Fez el Jedid.

GUIDES AND TOURS

A tour is a useful introduction to Fez el Bali, but the normal rules apply (see page 54), so whether you get an official or unofficial **guide**, or even one from your hotel or riad, it's essential to work out in advance the main points you want to see and – as elsewhere in Morocco – make it absolutely clear if you are not interested in shopping. Note that most **organized tours** don't run on Fridays.

meant by a "full" day.

Unofficial guides Guides who tout their services (particularly around Bab Boujeloud) are likely to be unofficial and technically illegal. This doesn't necessarily mean they're to be avoided – some who are genuine students (as most claim to be) can be excellent – but you have to choose carefully, ideally drinking a tea together before settling a rate or declaring interest.

GUIDES

Official guides Legitimate guides identify themselves by laminated identity cards around their necks and can be engaged at the tourist office in the Ville Nouvelle or through riads in the Medina. No matter how many people are in your group, there is a set fee for a half-day/ whole day, although it is always a good idea to clarify in advance exactly what is

TOUR COMPANIES

Plan-it Morocco ⓦ plan-it-morocco.com. Well-respected local experts who organize a range of interesting activities, from patisserie classes and food-tasting tours of the Medina to learning to cook with a Moroccan family.

ACCOMMODATION

Staying in Fez used to mean either comfort (and a reliable water supply) in the **Ville Nouvelle** or roughing it in the Medina hotels of Fez el Bali and Fez el Jedid. No longer. While there are still plenty of basic *pensions* in **Fez el Bali**, many of which could do with a makeover and better plumbing, the rise and rise of Fez's **riad** scene means that you can now find real class and character in renovated old-city palaces, if you are prepared to pay for it – though most riads have one smaller room available to suit restricted budgets. The group of backpacker hostels around **Bab Boujeloud**, though, remain an ideal launchpad from which to explore the old city's sights and souks. As an alternative, places in **Fez el Jedid** are within a 15min walk of Fez el Bali and less frequented by tourists (and hustlers). Space is at a premium in all categories, so be prepared for higher prices than other parts of Morocco, and reserve in advance if possible, especially during festival time (see page 182).

FEZ EL BALI, SEE MAPS PAGES 160, 162 AND 167

HOTELS AND HOSTELS

Bab Boujloud 49 Pl Iscesco ☎ 0535 633118. One of the few mid-range options around Bab Boujeloud. Most rooms are en suite with a/c and offer comfort at the expense of character – many have "views" of adjoining buildings, though the incredible Medina panorama from the large terrace makes up for that. BB €€€

Batha Pl Batha ☎ 0535 741077. A tour-group favourite next to the Musée Batha, this three-star is comfy if a little bland, its character concealed in the bar of the older block behind, formerly the British consulate. Also has a small swimming pool. BB €€€

Cascade 26 Rue Serrajine ☎ 0535 638442. Usually full by midday during high season, this busy Boujeloud favourite is frequented by a young international crowd. Offers small,

3

simple and very basic rooms (a few with tiny windows), hot showers and one of the best terraces in Bab Boujeloud (where you can also bed down for the night). En-suite rooms are good value. €€

Dar Bouânania 21 Derb Ben Salem, off Talâa Kebira ☎ 0535 637282. Simple, minimalist and fairly dark rooms (sleeping up to 4; en suite are extra) arranged around an intimate courtyard of painted woodwork and zellij that hints at riad charm at a fraction of the price. €€€

Dar Jannat 89 Derb ahl Tadla, off Talâa Seghira ☎ 0535 636000. Homely B&B offering some of the best-value rooms in Fez, unassuming in style but thoughtfully furnished with Moroccan artefacts and Berber bedspreads. Most are twins or doubles, though there's also a 6-person dorm and a family rooms sleeping up to 4 (from 390dh). The restaurant does a decent range of couscous dishes, tajines and brochettes; cooking classes and day-trips are also available. double €€€

★ **Dar Melody** 18 Rue Laalouj Kebira. In the quieter El Andalous quarter, just across the Oued Boukhrareb from the tanneries, this beautifully renovated old merchant's house has just three (spacious) rooms. All are charmingly designed, and the roof terrace enjoys tremendous views of the Medina, but it is the incredibly helpful hosts, Laurence and Bernard, that set this place apart and ensures that wannabe guests will need to book well in advance. That and the great breakfasts. BB €€€

Funky Fes 60 Arset Lamdelssi ⓦ funkyfes.com. This mellow hostel is on the southern fringes of the Medina but is a firm favourite for backpackers looking for an alternative to the cheapies around Bab Boujeloud. Rooms – a wide range of dorms and en suite doubles – are pretty standard but benefit from a/c, and the communal areas wouldn't look out of place in most riads. They also offer good-value tours of Fez, plus excursions to Meknes, the Middle Atlas and further afield. BB dorm €, double €€€

Palais Amani 12 Derb el Miter ⓦ www.palaisamani. com. Expansive palace bearing the Art Deco hallmarks of its 1930s refurb, with two types of room and a variety of suites (all crisply modern, most with iPods and flat-screen TVs) set around a courtyard garden. Standard rooms are quite subdued, so it's worth paying extra for a bit more character. You can eat here in one of the best hotel restaurants in the city (see page 181), while the on-site spa has its own hammam. BB €€€€

Pension Talâa 14 Talâa Seghira ☎ 0535 633359. A mellower alternative to the *Cascade* (see above), this simple *pension* offers a strip of pleasant doubles that, whilst showing signs of age, should appeal to travellers on a tight budget. Friendly staff and a rooftop terrace are also plus points. €

RIADS

Algilà Fes 17 Derb el Mokri, Akbat Sbaa ⓦ algilafes.com. Set in an increasingly popular area south of Talâa Kebira and a short walk from Pl Batha, this super-smart option has a dozen rooms and suites that frame the courtyards of three

---

HAMMAM A GOOD TIME

With a reputed 250 **hammams** sprinkled across the city, Fez is one of the best places in Morocco to join the locals in a long, relaxing hot bath, with a rigorous scrub-down thrown in for good measure. If you're unfamiliar with the routine (see page 39), it's best, especially for women, to ask someone at your hotel or riad to escort you. Don't forget to take your towel, soap, shampoo (or *ghasoul*, the fine-mud alternative) and swimsuit (or change of underwear). Several upscale **riads** have their own hammams and spas, which are more luxurious and less daunting, but also much pricier – and, at the end of the day, not quite the same experience.

HAMMAMS

Hammam Aïn Azleten Talâa Kebira, 200m south of Bab Aïn Azleten. In a convenient location between the Medersa Bou Inania and the *fondouks* on Talâa Kebira, Aïn Azleten is one of the cleanest hammams in Fez; an exfoliating scrub costs 40dh. Daily: men 6am–noon & 8.30–11pm, women noon–8.30pm.

Hammam Mernissi Derb Serrajine, near Bab Boujeloud. A scrubbed-up traditional hammam

offering public and private (book in advance) scrub downs (150dh/200dh) and massages (100dh extra). Public daily: men 6am–10.30am & 8pm–1am, women 11am–7pm; private daily 11am–10pm.

SPAS

Les Bains Amani Palais Amani, 12 Derb el Miter ⓦ www.palaisamani.com; Stylish, luxurious hotel spa with a full range of hammam services, roof-top massages (from 495dh), and candle-lit treatments.

Nausikaa Spa Av Bahnini, Route Aïn Smen, Ville Nouvelle ⓦ nausikaa.ma. Marble-clad modern spa in the southern Ville Nouvelle, centred round a hammam, steam rooms and sauna, and offering massages, reflexology and various other treatments.

Spa Laaroussa Fez Riad Laaroussa, 3 Derb Bechara, off Talâa Seghira ⓦ riad-laaroussa.com. Detox amid the sublime surroundings of a sympathetically restored seventeenth-century bathhouse (see page 179). Try a hammam and black-soap body scrub or a massage with essential oils.

adjoining eighteenth-century houses. The bedrooms are more contemporary in design than most, and all come with a/c and flat-screen TVs – a rarity in Medina riads. €€€

Dar Bensouda 14 Zkak el Bghel ⓦ riaddarbensouda. com. Hidden down a quiet alleyway south of Pl en Nejjarine, this attractive *dar* makes a big first impression, with its striking central courtyard and tremendous roof terrace. Rooms are (stylishly) pared-back in comparison to the lavish zellij and decoration of the main house itself. BB €€€

Dar Finn 27 Zkak Rouah ☎ 0655 018975. Lovingly restored traditional townhouse with a laidback family vibe – the *dar* is named after the owners' son – and deftly combining striking zellij in its central courtyard with a more modern walled garden, complete with tempting plunge pool. The seven suites (some sleeping up to three, one sleeping up to four) are all grand, though the Pacha Suite, with its intricately carved wooden ceiling, is the pick of the bunch. There are good breakfasts and even better evening meals. BB €€

Dar Malika 22 Rue Ferrane Couicha ⓦ darmalikafez. com. This intimate guesthouse, a tastefully renovated 300-year-old *dar*, offers four comfortable rooms (one a twin) and an instantly homely, sociable atmosphere. Home-cooked meals (on request) are served in the snug courtyard or on the terrace. Minimum 2-night stay. BB €€

★ **Dar Roumana** 30 Derb el Amer ⓦ darroumana.com. Very stylish riad in the north of Fez el Bali, one of the most finely crafted restorations in the whole of the Medina. The five suites (three with lovely baths) are all nicely done, and those on the ground floor are particularly spacious, but if you can push the boat out a bit, it's worth opting for the four-poster Yasmina Suite – a real beauty, with its very own balcony. The split-level terrace boasts one of the best views in Fez, and there's a superb on-site restaurant too (see page 181). BB €€€

★ **Dar Seffarine** 14 Derb Sbaa Louyate, off Pl Seffarine ⓦ darseffarine.com. Slap-bang in the heart of Fez el Bali, with some of the oldest zellij and stucco of the city's riads, and rooms styled in a sort of Moroccan minimalism by its designer-architect owners; the Kobbe suite is a knockout. Add in a community spirit that sees guests breakfast together, and you have one of the most appealing – and well-priced – options in the Medina. BB €€€

La Maison Bleue 2 Pl Batha ⓦ maisonbleue.com. The first riad in Fez and still one of the best, an intimate world of luxury opposite the Musée Batha, where rooms, some with a private terrace, are named after female members of the family who built and still own it; the library once belonged to a professor at the Kairaouine. Style is a mix of Moroccan and classy European pieces, and there's excellent traditional dining in its restaurant (see page 179). BB €€€€

★ **Riad Anata** 16b Derb el Hamia ⓦ riadanata.com. Hip little riad, light, airy and very tranquil, and tastefully done out in a more contemporary style than most. The five

rooms are individually decorated to match their colour-themed names and are spaced around a gorgeous central courtyard or are up on the roof. There's a plunge pool to cool off in, plus hands-on cooking classes. BB €€€

Riad al Bartal 21 Rue Sournas ⓦ riadalbartal.com. Just inside Bab Ziat, so a little further from the action, but an attractive and welcoming choice – the light touch of its French owners abounds, from the arty, pared-down decor in the plant-filled courtyard to individually styled rooms with painted ceilings and *tadelakht* walls. If you can afford it, suites are worth the extra. €€

Riad Fès 5 Derb Ben Slimane ⓦ riadfes.com. A deceptively expansive boutique hotel – architecturally one of the grandest in Fez – this stunning Relais & Châteaux property gives guests the option of staying in a variety of contemporary or more traditionally furnished rooms, some with *tadelakht* bathroms but all exquisitely done out. Public areas are sumptuous and service is immaculate throughout. There's a pool in the grounds, a spa and a stylish bar (see page 183), and a terrace with arguably the finest Medina views in Fez. €€€€

★ **Riad Idrissy** 13 Derb Idrissy ⓦ riadidrissy.com. Beautifully renovated riad full of set-piece furnishings, such as the wooden *makarba* adorning the wall of one suite, and thoughtful styling throughout; the airy suite on the top floor sleeps four and has its own terrace. The charming English host is full of tips about life in Fez, though perhaps the best advice he could give is to dine at some point in the riad's delightful restaurant, *The Ruined Garden* (see page 182). Interesting cooking classes (bread-making, vegetarian dishes and Moroccan sweets) are also available. BB €€€

Riad Laaroussa 3 Derb Bechara, off Talâa Seghira ⓦ riad-laaroussa.com. Housed in a seventeenth-century palace, *Laaroussa* is a popular contender with a modern twist on traditional decor. Rooms enjoy deliciously smooth *tadelakht* bathrooms (coloured depending on their name); large suites come with open fireplaces and beautiful painted wooden ceilings. The large courtyard and spacious furnishings provide a calming retreat from the commotion of the Medina, and there's also a stylish hammam and spa (see page 178). BB €€€€

★ **Riad Numéro 9** 9 Derb Lamsside ⓦ riad9.com. A beautiful riad, lavishly renovated with real attention to detail and bearing the sophisticated touch of an interior designer throughout. The accommodating house manager and her equally helpful staff show a genuine concern for your enjoyment, while breakfast on the terrace is the perfect start to the day. Just 3 rooms, so book well in advance. Prices include airport/train station pick-up. BB €€€

Ryad Mabrouka 25 Derb el Miter ⓦ ryadmabrouka. com. Through a door in an unassuming dead-end alley, Moroccan style is paired with French antiques and European paintings at this very well-established riad, a reflection

3

> ## STREET EATS
>
> Wandering the lanes of Fez el Bali, you'll notice whisps of steam swirling around metal cauldrons and carrying with them the tempting aroma of *bisara*, a thick fava-bean soup; vendors (try those near the start of Talâa Kebira) usually top it with a glug of local olive oil and a sprinkle of cumin. Braver souls may like to tackle the **snail stands** on the corner of Talâa Seghira and Derb el Horra, where safety pins constitute the cutlery – they're used for plucking the little critters out of their softened shells. Another street snack worth trying is *jben*, an acidic white **goat's cheese** that's only vaguely removed from yoghurt; the stall on the corner of Talâa Seghira and Sidi Mohammed Belhaj proudly displays theirs stacked on dark green leaves.

of the eclectic tastes of its friendly owners. There's a welcoming plunge pool in the idyllic garden, and great views of the Medina from the terrace. BB €€€

FEZ EL JEDID, SEE MAP PAGE 172

Jnane Sbile 22 Kasbat Chems ⓦhotel-jnane-sbile. fes-hotels.net. Two-star with a glitzy salon, offering comfortable, if slightly poky, mod-con rooms and pleasant views from the terrace over the gardens across the road. A decent option for those looking for proximity to the Medina without the noise. €

VILLE NOUVELLE, SEE MAP PAGE 175

★ **Auberge de Jeunesse** 18 Rue Abdeslam Seghrini ⓦ hihostels.com/hostels/fes. Set in a small garden in a quiet backwater east of Bd Bdallah Chefchouani, this is one of the best youth hostels in Morocco: easy-going, friendly and with spotless dorms and doubles. There are (free) hot showers in the morning and evening. The enthusiastic Fassi manager is also a mine of local information. Doors close at 9pm. BB dorm €, double €

Barceló Fès Medina 53 Av Hassan II ⓦ barcelo.com. Dominating the northern end of Av Hassan II, this huge

white curve of a building does a lot of things right, despite the confusing name (this being the Ville Nouvelle and all, and some way from the actual Medina). Rooms, whilst well sized, are surprisingly perfunctory, though, and the suites, particularly, are rather bare for the price, but you're paying for service and facilities, which include a swimming pool, gym and spa with hammam, plus a sleek restaurant and an equally modern café overlooking La Fiat. BB €€

Central 50 Rue Brahim Roudani ☎00535 622333. Good-value, popular one-star that's often full thanks to its clean and bright rooms – some with small en-suite shower cubicles – that are heated in winter. €

Mounia 60 Bd Zerktouny ☎0535 624838. This friendly, modern hotel is one of the best mid-range choices in the Ville Nouvelle. Attractive public areas are decorated with zellij, and the smart rooms all come with central heating, a/c and satellite TV. BB €€

Splendid 9 Rue Abdelkrim el Khattabi ☎0535 622148. An efficient hotel, whose Art Deco facade belies the modern en-suite rooms within; there's also a good restaurant, bar and swimming pool. One of the best-value options in the Ville Nouvelle, when it's not booked out by tour groups. BB €

EATING

Fez is the culinary capital of Morocco, and you should try pastilla, the great Fassi delicacy of pigeon pie, at least once during your stay. Eating options in **Fez el Bali** and **Fez el Jedid** have improved greatly in recent years, though outside the riads and the smarter palace restaurants, they are still generally on the basic side; this is a good place, though, to try street-stall snacks such as *bisara* soup (see page 180), while the colourful fruit and veg market near Bab er R'cif (closed Fri) is worth a visit for its mounds of olives, dates and other nibbles. The **Ville Nouvelle** is home to most of Fez's patisseries and modern (licensed) restaurants, as well as (in the Borj Fez shopping centre) a supermarket and food hall. If you want to talk with Fassis on any basis other than guide or tout to tourist, your best chance will be in the new town's numerous modern cafés – as the home of the city's university, it's also more likely

that the students you meet in the Ville Nouvelle will be exactly that.

FEZ EL BALI, SEE MAPS PAGES 160, 162 AND 167

CAFÉS

Café Boutouil Rue Boutouil. At the very heart of the old city, by the Kairaouine Mosque, *Café Boutouil* does a good line in coffee and pastries, but its speciality is *panachi*, a mixture of milk, almond milk and raisins, with a blob of ice cream on top for good measure (a bargain at 10dh).

★ **Café Clock** 7 Derb el Magana, signposted off Talâa Kebira ⓦ cafeclock.com. Housed in a restored *dar*, this café-restaurant-cum-cultural centre is a buzzing hangout for students and tourists alike. The food is inventive and delicious, ranging from chicken *rfissa* (85dh) to fig and blue-cheese salad (65dh) – though few people can resist the camel burger (95dh), fresh off the dromedary stall outside. Check the website for weekly schedules that include music nights and storytelling, plus courses in Arabic, calligraphy and cooking (see page 181).

Crèmerie La Place Pl Seffarine. Relax over an orange juice or a mint tea accompanied by the sound of metalworkers on one of the most diminutive squares in Fez el Bali.

RESTAURANTS

L'Amandier Palais Faraj, Bab Ziat ⓦpalaisfaraj.com. This upmarket hotel restaurant, on the hillside near Bab Ziat, offers a varied menu that includes traditional dishes such as pastilla (pigeon or seafood) and stuffed cockerel, alongside international dishes like pasta with quail. There are great views over the Medina from the window-side tables, but you pay for the privilege: mains start at 160dh, and the *degustacíon* menu will set you back some 750dh. Licensed.

Dar Hatim 19 Derb Ezaouia ☎0666 525323. Tuck into scrumptious, lovingly cooked traditional dishes in this beautiful family home. Meals are from a set menu, but you get a choice of 4 or 5 mains (lamb tajine, fish, turkey brochettes, chicken pastilla) – though it's very easy to fill up on the freshly baked bread and array of tasty Morccan salads to start.

★ **Dar Roumana** 30 Derb el Amer ⓦdarroumana.com. One of the best riad restaurants in the Medina, where creative Franco-Moroccan two- and three-course menus (275/350dh) are served in a pretty candlelit courtyard. Food varies with the season, with market-fresh dishes ranging from braised local rabbit to charcoal-cooked quail with date molasses and pomegranate seeds – a signature dish of sorts (*roumana* means "pomegranate"). Book in advance. Licensed.

Dar Saada 21 Rue el Attarine ⓦrestaurantsaada.com. Tasty Moroccan dishes (brochettes from 80dh, tajines from 90dh) all in vast portions – two people could be satisfied

with one main dish and a plate of vegetables – in a gorgeous century-old palace whose fine carving was renewed after a fire in 1972. Licensed.

Eden Palais Amani 12 Derb el Miter, off Rue Oued Zhoune ⓦpalaisamani.com. This former palace north of the tanneries makes a swish setting for locally sourced Moroccan cuisine, with a choice of á la carte dishes (duck confit, Sephardic slow-cooked beef tajine; mains from 175dh) and seasonal two- or three-course menus (225dh/285dh) that change every month. Make sure you leave room for their sinfully soft home-made lemon mousse. Finish with a nightcap on the terrace bar (open till midnight). Booking essential. Licensed.

Fez Café Le Jardin des Biehn, 13 Akbat Sbaa ☎0535 635031, ⓦjardindesbiehn.com. Laidback restaurant enjoying a tranquil setting in the attractive gardens of the attached *maison d'hôte*. The daily-changing menu (mains from 135dh) is on the short side, but the quality Mediterranean food – along the lines of swordfish *pavé* and a trio of brochettes with roast veg – is certainly a break from the norm. Licensed.

La Maison Bleue 2 Pl Batha ☎0535 741843, ⓦmaisonbleue.com. This beautiful riad (see page 179) makes a romantic setting for generous three- and four-course menus (350dh/550dh) served by attentive slipper-wearing waiters. The choice of mains includes *seffa medfouna*, fluffy couscous cooked to a thirteenth-century recipe, which follows on from a mouthwatering array of Moroccan salads, a meal in itself. An *oued* player and Gnaoua musicians add to the ambience.

Le Kasbah Rue Serrajine ☎0535 741533. One of the most appealing options in Bab Boujeloud due to two terraces with views over the Medina and zellij-covered walls. A la carte brochettes, fish tajines and sausages (mains from 70dh) are a better bet than the fairly uninspiring set menu (100dh), though this is a great place just for a drink.

Maison Moi Anan 30 Zkak Lma, off Talaa Kebira ☎0535

3

FASSI EATERS

It's never going to be easy to replicate the rich and resounding flavours of **Fassi cuisine** in your kitchen back home, but knowing the right blend of spices to put into your tajine will make a real difference to your cooking, while whipping up a sweet pastilla pie should wow even the most discerning of dinner-party guests. Most **cookery classes** focus on a three-course menu and start with a visit to one of the Medina souks to pick up the necessary (fresh) ingredients. All of the places listed below include bread-making workshops and the opportunity to bake your creation in a local *farine* (oven).

Clock Kitchen ⓦcafeclock.com/clock-kitchen. Learn

how to make a variety of starters and mains (choose from couscous, tajines and pastilla) from the team at *Café Clock* (see page 180), or brush up your pastry skills on their patisserie day-course.

Fez Cooking School ⓦfezcookingschool.com. Held on the rooftop of the opulent *Palais Amani* (see page 178), with a choice of trying to master Moroccan and Fassi classics or (more expensive) Sephardic dishes.

Plan-It Morocco ⓦplan-it-morocco.com. Take a Moroccan cookery class with a twist, held in a Fassi home where you can discover the secrets of a good marinade, learn to cook traditional tajines or perfect the art of making a variety of sticky patisseries.

635713. Located down one of the tiniest alleyways in Fez, this stylish bijou Thai restaurant makes a refreshing break from tajines and couscous, with authentic *tom yum* soup, Penang beef, green chicken curry and the like (mains from 90dh). The chef is also a fashion designer – you can check out some of his collection on the way in.

NUR 7 Zkak Rouah ☎0694 277849, ⓦnur.ma. Uber-stylish eatery run by a former *El Bulli* chef, Najat Kaanache. Her creative take on local ingredients results in unusual but superb tasting menus (700dh) that change by the day, depending on what's on offer at the Medina markets. Booking essential. Licensed.

★ **The Ruined Garden** Riad Idrissy, 13 Derb Idrissy ⓦruinedgarden.com. Run by a charming Englishman, this novel setup south of Talâa Seghira occupies a delightful sunken garden that was only discovered while renovating the attached riad (see page 179). Tuck into tasty Moroccan tapas (chickpea cake, smoky *zaalouk*, popcorn *makuda*; 85dh for four) and more unusual mains such as sardine tajine and *daghmira* (onion tart), or push the boat out with a *mechoui* feast (240dh/person; order in advance).

★ **Thami's** 50 Serrajine, Bab Boujeloud ☎070 640130. In an unbeatable location a stone's throw from Bab Boujeloud, you can people-watch to your heart's content over simple but satisfying food, great value at around 50dh for dishes such as egg-topped *kefta* tajine.

FEZ EL JEDID, SEE MAP PAGE 172

CAFÉ

Café Restaurant La Noria Off Av Moulay Hassan ☎0535 654 255. A quiet spot near the water wheel behind the Jnane S'bile gardens, good for breakfast (until 11am) and a bargain cup of a coffee, though you can also grab *harira* soup or a Berber omelette, or tuck into a range of dishes that are big enough to share.

VILLE NOUVELLE, SEE MAP PAGE 175

CAFÉS AND SNACK BARS

Café Floria Av Hassan II, a block north of the main post office ☎0535 650835. A great place for people watching on Av Hassan II, boasting excellent croissants and – almost as important – very clean toilets.

Venezia Sandwich 7 Av el Houria (formerly Av de France). A superior fast-food joint in a row of similar places, with grilled sausages, fried fish and a range of cheap panini (20dh).

PUTTING THE FEZ IN FESTIVALS

Fez is home to several important **festivals** and **moussems**, ranging from annual pilgrimages to week-long celebrations of Fassi cuisine. The focal point of the cultural calendar, though, is the nine-day-long Festival of World Sacred Music, a highly regarded gathering of global musicians that has produced spin-offs in the UK and North America.

FESTIVAL OF WORLD SACRED MUSIC

The **Festival of World Sacred Music** (☎0535 740535, ⓦfesfestival.com), held in May or June, has developed into the country's most interesting and inspiring cultural festival. Recent years have seen Sufi chanters from Azerbaijan, *khora* players from Mali and a Byzantine choir from Greece. Concerts take place throughout the Medina and in the Ville Nouvelle: at the Musée Batha; by Bab Boujeloud and Bab Makina; in the Petit Mechouar; at the Institut Français; and sometimes further afield, such as amid the ruins of Volubilis.

FEZ FESTIVAL OF SUFI CULTURE

The **Fez Festival of Sufi Culture** (☎0535 931822, ⓦfestivalculturesoufie.com) is usually held in the last week of October and comprises a number of performances that take place each night in the courtyard of the Musée Batha (organized discussions are held during the day); it's a rare opportunity to experience the music of the world's most renowned Sufi musicians and vocalists.

MOUSSEM OF MOULAY IDRISS II

The largest moussem held inside a major Moroccan city, the **Moussem of Moulay Idriss II** takes place in Fez each September and involves a long procession to the saint's tomb (see page 166). Fez el Bali is packed out, however, and you will have a better view from Place Batha or Place Boujeloud, before the procession enters the Medina proper.

RESTAURANTS

L'Italien Av Omar Ibn Khattab ☎0535 943384. Well-produced staples such as carpaccio, escalope Milanaise and a dozen or so pastas, but oven-baked pizzas (from 75dh) are the speciality at this slick Italian diner near the train station: stylishly presented thin-crust beauties, from margharitas to the signature truffle-oil-laced L'Italien. There's a select list of Moroccan wines to wash them down with.

Marrakesh 11 Rue Omar el Mokhtar ☎0535 930876. Small and cute, with a fairly limited menu, though the food (tajines, merguez and the like) is well cooked and tasty.

★ **Mb Fes** 12 Rue Ahmed Chaouki ⓦmbrestaurant lounge.com. Ultra-trendy restaurant whose clean-lined interior of granite walls, smoked mirrors and designer Italian furniture sets the scene for beautifully presented French-Moroccan fusion food. Licensed.

DRINKING

As with Medina quarters throughout Morocco, drinking in **Fez el Bali** and **Fez el Jedid** is mostly restricted to hotels and riads; consequently, the area is much quieter at night, except during Ramadan, when shops and stalls stay open until 2 or 3am. The **Ville Nouvelle** has a slightly wider range of bars, though note that not all places will feel comfortable for women.

page 179) offers a slew of contemporarily cool bars, where you can relax by a fountain-filled courtyard or poolside or up on its amazing roof terrace. Choose from beers, cocktails or dozens of fine wines, most from the vineyards of Morocco. A perfect spot to unwind, in a beautiful setting with attentive staff on hand.

FEZ EL BALI AND FEZ EL JEDID, SEE MAPS PAGES 160 AND 172

★ **Mezzanine** 17 Kasbat Chams ☎0611 078336. Super-chic joint, overlooking the Jnane S'bil gardens, that works just as well in the early evening as it does in the early hours. Chill out in the Moroccan-cool lounge bar or head up for al-fresco drinks on the roof terrace; Mediterranean tapas platters are also served.

Riad Fès Derb Ben Slimane ⓦriadfes.com. This riad (see

VILLE NOUVELLE, SEE MAP PAGE 175

Mb Fes 12 Rue Ahmed Chaouki ⓦmbrestaurantlounge. com. The mezzanine lounge bar at this swanky restaurant (see page 183) makes a stylish late-night destination for cocktails and cognacs.

The Rooftop Hotel Sahrai, Bab Lghoul, Dhar el Mehraz ☎0535 940332. One of two bars at this sleek hotel perched on the hillside overlooking the Ville Nouvelle, where you can enjoy pricey cocktails, mocktails and a lengthy list of whiskeys on the designer terrace. Live DJs at the weekend.

ENTERTAINMENT

As the country's cultural capital, there is normally something going on in Fez, whether it's a photography show at the Institut Français or an evening of Gnaoua music at *Café Clock* (see page 180).

Megarama Fes 60 Av Hassan II, near Pl de la Résistance, Ville Nouvelle. One of several cinemas in the Ville Nouvelle

screening foreign films, mainly dubbed into French.

Institut Français 33 Rue Ahmed Loukili, Ville Nouvelle ⓦif-maroc.org/fes. The institute's gallery in the Ville Nouvelle holds art exhibitions and talks, and there are regular traditional-music concerts in the Musée Batha.

SHOPPING

SEE MAPS PAGES 160, 162 AND 167

Fez has a rightful reputation as the centre of Moroccan traditional crafts, but bear in mind that it also sees more tourists than almost anywhere bar Marrakesh. However much you bargain, **rugs** and **carpets** will probably be cheaper in Meknes, Azrou or Midelt, and although the **brass, leather and cloth** here are the best you'll find, you will need plenty of energy, a good sense of humour and a lot of patience to get them at a reasonable price – Fassi dealers are expert hagglers. Note that many shops are closed on Fridays.

Au Petit Bazar de Bon Accueil 35 Talâa Seghira. Fifth-generation Fassi dealers, specializing in antiques, textiles and Berber jewellery – the older, more interesting stuff is in the room upstairs.

Chez Abdelsalam Sidi Mohammed Belhaj, off Derb er Rom. Lovely (but expensive) hand-painted wooden pieces, including *mashrabiyas* (latticework windows), from

a craftsman who worked on objects in the Musée Nejjarine des Arts et Métiers du Bois (see page 165).

★ **Chez Hamidou** 14 Derb Chouwara. Surprisingly overlooked by tour groups, Hamidou's little enterprise is stacked full of *babouches* and cushion covers, the speciality of the shop and reputedly the best in the Medina.

Herboristerie Seddik 15 Derb Chouwara. Just outside the tanneries, this well-laid out shop is worth worth a visit for its wide variety of herbs, oils and spices, plus medicinal plants and hammam essentials such as *ghasoul* and black olive soap.

Librairie Kounouz al Maârifa 11 Talâa Seghira. Decent selection of English-language titles covering Moroccan design, cooking and modern life, as well as novels by Ibn Battutah, Naguib Mahfouz and, of course, Paul Bowles.

Maison Bleue 68 Talâa Seghira. Three rooms in a slender old house crammed with traditional ceramics and pottery from Fez (the distinctive blue-and-white pieces) and Safi (dark green, and the kind most commonly exported from Morocco).

Médin' Art 19 Zkak Lahjar. This trendy boutique is quite unlike any other shop in Fez, selling a range of contemporary paintings, bags and unusual items such as stools made from old tyres – and (unusually for the Medina) at fixed prices.

Talisman Art Gallery 150 Sidi Moussa. Well worth a browse for the gorgeous surroundings – intricate zellij floors and carved cedar doors – even if you can't afford the beautifully presented but (generally) pricey goods on offer.

Tissage Berbère 4 Derb Taouil. Reasonable carpet prices, despite its location on a well-trodden route, and bartering with the informative owner over his beautiful silk and woollen kilims is an enjoyable experience.

DIRECTORY

Banks and exchange As always, the BMCE (branches in the Ville Nouvelle at Pl Mohammed V, Pl Florence and Pl de l'Atlas) is best for exchange and handles Visa/Mastercard transactions. Banque Populaire has two branches in Fez el Bali: halfway down Talâa Seghira; and on Derb Kaid el Khammar, by Bab Ftouh. Others elsewhere include: Banque Populaire opposite the Dar el Makhzen in Fez el Jedid; Crédit du Maroc on Bd Mohammed V; and SGMB by Bab Boujeloud.

Golf The Fes Royal Golf Club, 17km from Fez on the Route d'Ifrane (☎0535 665210), was designed by Cabell B Robinson and has an 18-hole, par-72 course.

Language courses The Arabic Language Institute in Fez (ALIF), 2 Rue Ahmed Hiba (☎0535 624850, ⊚alif-fes.com) is an American initiative offering a range of courses plus private lessons. There are three-week and six-week courses in Modern Standard Arabic or Moroccan Arabic at all levels. ALIF also has its own residence for students, or the option of a homestay with a Moroccan family.

Laundry There's a laundry near Bab Boujeloud at the northern end of Pl Batha, facing the post office.

Left luggage/baggage A deposit is available at the bus station.

Pharmacies There are pharmacies opposite the SGMB bank by Bab Boujeloud, on Pl Batha and on the Grande Rue des Merenides in the Mellah, plus numerous ones throughout the Ville Nouvelle. The Pharmacie du Municipalité, just up from Pl de la Résistance, on Av Moulay Youssef, is open overnight.

Police There are *commissariats* at the Préfecture de Medina around the corner from the Musée Batha, and by the post office on Bd Mohammed V. The police emergency number is ☎19.

Post office The main post office is on the corner of Bd Mohammed V and Av Hassan II in the Ville Nouvelle (Mon–Fri 8am–4.30pm, Sat 8.30am–noon); the poste restante section has a separate side entry to the right of the main building (same hours). There's also a post office on Pl Batha, and branch offices just north of the Medersa el Attarine and on Pl des Alaouites, on the edge of the Mellah.

Swimming The municipal pool is at Av des Sports, just west of the train station (closed mid-Sept to mid-June).

Meknes and around

Cut in two by the wide river valley of the Oued Boufekrane, **MEKNES** is a prosperous city with a notably relaxed and friendly atmosphere, due in part to a large student population. Monuments from its past, particularly the extraordinary creations of Moulay Ismail, justify a day or two's rambling exploration, as do the affable souks of its Medina –a uniquely well-preserved combination that have earned the entire city a place on UNESCO's World Heritage list. Visitors en route to Fez will find Meknes a good introduction to the drama of its more illustrious neighbour, while those coming in the other direction are sure to enjoy the reduced tempo.

An easy excursion from Meknes, **Volubilis** and **Moulay Idriss** embody much of Morocco's early history: Volubilis as its Roman provincial capital, Moulay Idriss in the creation of the country's first Arab dynasty. Their sites stand 4km apart, at either side of a deep and very fertile valley, about 25km north of the city.

Ville Impériale

More than any other town in Morocco, Meknes is associated with a single figure, **Sultan Moulay Ismail** (see page 188). During his 55-year reign, the city was transformed from a forgettable provincial centre into a spectacular capital with twenty gates and over fifty palaces enclosed within 45km of exterior walls. The principal remains of Ismail's creation – the **Ville Impériale** of palaces and gardens, barracks,

---

MEKNES ORIENTATION

Meknes is simpler than it looks on the map. The **Medina** and its neighbouring **Mellah** (the old Jewish quarter) occupy the west bank of the Oued Boufekrane, with the walls of Moulay Ismail's **Ville Impériale** edging away to their south; marking the transition between the Medina and the Ville Impériale – and a focal point for both – is **Place el Hedim**, a good place to fix your bearings. The **Ville Nouvelle** (the modern district constructed by the French) stretches along a slope above the east bank of the river, radiating from the impressive **Place Administrative**.

---

granaries and stables – sprawl below the Medina amid a confusing array of walled enclosures, and it's a long morning's walk to take in everything.

Place el Hedim and around

Seeking a grand approach to his palace quarter, the Dar el Kebira, Moulay Ismail demolished the houses that formed the southwestern corner of the Medina to create **Place el Hedim** ("Square of Demolition and Renewal"). It was remodelled in the 1990s into a pedestrian plaza, and from late afternoon the square takes on a festive air as storytellers and musicians, acrobats and traditional doctors gather until mid-evening, much like Marrakesh's Jemaa el Fna in miniature.

Bab Mansour

Dominating the southern end of Place el Hedim and the centrepiece of the city's ensemble of walls and gateways, the immense **Bab Mansour** (or Bab Mansour Laheej, the "Victorious Renegade") is startlingly rich in its ceremonial decoration and almost perfectly preserved. Its name comes from its architect, one of a number of Christian renegades who converted to Islam and rose to a high position at Moulay Ismail's court. A local tale relates that the sultan inspected the completed gate, then asked El Mansour whether he (Ismail) could do any better, a Catch 22 for the hapless architect, whose response ("yes") led to his immediate execution. That said, the story may be fictional, because the gate was completed under Ismail's son, Moulay Abdallah.

Whatever the truth, the gate is the finest in Meknes, if not in all Morocco, and an interesting adaptation of the classic Almohad **design**, flanked by bastions that are purely decorative and whose marble columns were brought from Volubilis – indeed, they are more impressive than any that remain at the site itself. The patterns on both gate and bastions are elaborations of the Almohad *darj w ktarf* motif (similar to the fleur-de-lys), the space between each motif filled with a brilliant array of zellij created by a layer of cutaway black tiles – just like the ornamental inscription above, which extols the triumph of Ismail and, even more, that of Abdallah, bragging that no gate in Damascus or Alexandria is its equal.

Musée de Meknès

Rue Dar Smen • Charge

The compact **Musée de Meknès** contains various artisanal artefacts, displayed in half a dozen rooms around the central courtyard of what was the city's old Tribunal. Though not as impressive as the nearby Dar Jamaï (see page 189), it is worth a visit if you are on a short trip to Morocco, as the exhibits come from all corners of the country: pottery from Fez, pieces from Taroudant and the Tafilalt, and farming implements from the south.

Habs Kara and the Koubba el Khayatine

Pl Lalla Aouda • Charge (includes entrance to the *koubba*)

Beneath the dusty scrubland southwest of Place Lalla Aouda runs a series of subterranean vaults, lit only by the skyholes that stud the ground above and known, by popular tradition, as the **Habs Kara** or the "Prison of Christian Slaves". They were more likely a storehouse or granary, although there were certainly several thousand Christian captives at Ismail's court. Either way, the huge underground vault, dark and dank, is deeply atmospheric and makes a great venue for the Moroccan art now on display here.

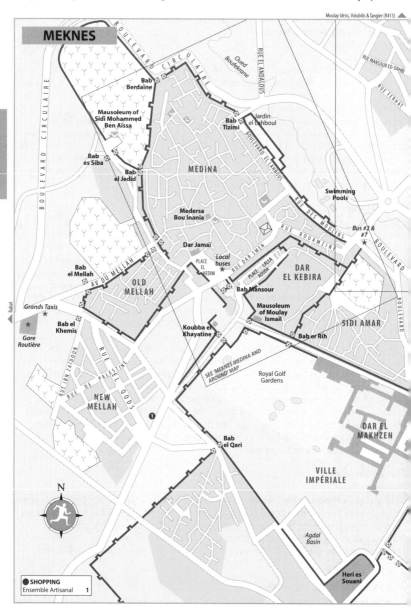

The green-tiled building to the left of the prison's entrance is the seventeenth-century **Koubba el Khayatine**, an anonymous zellij-covered reception hall for ambassadors to the imperial court.

Mausoleum of Moulay Ismail

300m south of Bab Mansour · closed Fri morning; tomb open to Muslims only · Free · Modest dress required for both women and men

3

3

SULTAN MOULAY ISMAIL (1672–1727)

"The **Sultan Moulay Ismail**," wrote his chronicler, Ezziani, "loved Mequinez, and he would have liked never to leave it." But leave it he did, ceaselessly campaigning against the rebel Berber chiefs of the south, and the Europeans entrenched in Tangier, Asilah and Larache, until the entire country lay completely under government control for the first time in five centuries. His reign saw the creation of Morocco's strongest ever – and most coherent – army, which included the Black Guard, a ruthless regiment of sub-Saharan "slave soldiers", and, it is reckoned, a garrison force of one in twenty of the male population. The period was Morocco's last golden age, though the rigid centralization of all decisions, and the fear with which the sultan reigned, led to a slide into anarchy and weak, inward-looking rule.

Ismail's achievements were matched by his **tyrannies**, which were judged extreme even by the standards of the time – and contemporary Europeans were burning their enemies and torturing them on the rack. His reign began with the display of four hundred heads at Fez, most of them of captured chiefs, and over the next five decades it is estimated that he was responsible for over thirty thousand deaths, not including those killed in battle. Many of these deaths were quite arbitrary – mounting a horse, Ismail might slash the head off the eunuch holding his stirrup; inspecting the work on his buildings, he would carry a weighted lance, with which to batter skulls in order to "encourage" the others. "My subjects are like rats in a basket," he used to say, "and if I do not keep shaking the basket they will gnaw their way through."

Yet the sultan was a tireless **builder** throughout Morocco, constructing towns and ports and a multitude of defensive kasbahs, palaces and bridges. By far his greatest efforts were focused on **Meknes**, where he sustained an obsessive building programme, often acting as architect and sometimes even working alongside the slaves and labourers. Ironically, time has not been kind to his constructions in his favoured hometown. Built mainly of *tabia*, a mixture of earth and lime, they were severely damaged by a hurricane even in his lifetime, and were left to decay thereafter, as subsequent Alaouite sultans shifted their capitals back to Fez and then Marrakesh. Walter Harris, writing only 150 years after Ismail's death, found Meknes "a city of the dead…strewn with marble columns and surrounded by great masses of ruin". Thankfully, more recent city authorities have tackled the restoration of the main monuments with more energy.

The **Mausoleum of Moulay Ismail** is one of only five religious sites in Morocco that non-Muslims may visit. The mausoleum has been a point of reverence since Ismail's death (it was constructed in his own lifetime) and is still held in high esteem. Given tales of the ruler's excesses, this might seem puzzling to Westerners, but Ismail (see page 188) is remembered in his homeland for his achievements: bringing peace and prosperity after a period of anarchy, and driving out the Spanish from Larache and the British from Tangier. His extreme observance of orthodox Islamic form and ritual also conferred a kind of magic on him, as, of course, does his part in establishing the ruling Alaouite dynasty – although, technically, the dynasty began with his brother, Moulay Rachid, Ismail is generally honoured as the founder.

From the ornately decorated annexe, you can peer into the **sanctuary** in which the sultan is buried – the two grandfather clocks were gifts from King Louis XIV – but non-Muslims cannot approach the tomb itself. However, even from an outside vantage point you can gain a good idea of the reverence with which the shrine is treated – you will almost invariably see villagers here, especially women seeking *baraka* (charismatic blessing) and intercession from the saintly sultan's remains.

Dar el Kebira

The dilapidated quarter of **Dar el Kebira**, accessed through a gate on the left beyond the Mausoleum of Moulay Ismail, was the sultan's great palace complex. It was destroyed in 1755 by the same earthquake that flattened Lisbon, but you can still make out the imperial structures – there were originally twelve pavilions within the complex – above and between the houses here: ogre-like creations of massive scale compared with the modest dwellings they sit among. They were completed in 1677 and dedicated at a midnight celebration, when the sultan personally slaughtered a wolf so its head could be displayed at the centre of the gateway.

Dar el Makhzen

The buildings that make up Ismail's last and finest palace, the **Dar el Makhzen**, lie partially hidden behind the mile-long corridor running beyond Bab er Rih –the most you can see are a few brief glimpses over the heads of the guards posted by occasional gates in the crumbling 20ft walls. The palace backs onto the landscaped grounds of the **Royal Golf Gardens**, once the sultan's sunken garden but now private and strictly *interdit* unless you play a round on one dedicated section (see page 196).

Unlike the Dar el Kebira, the Makhzen is still a minor royal residence, though Mohammed VI rarely visits Meknes – and prefers to stay with his aunt in Lahboul on the few occasions that he does.

Heri es Souani

Charge

Following the corridor that runs behind the Dar el Makhzen will eventually bring you out by the **Heri es Souani** (or Dar el Ma), the chief sight of the Ville Impériale. The startling series of high-vaulted chambers here were storerooms and granaries, filled with provisions for siege or drought. Each of Moulay Ismail's palaces had underground plumbing (well in advance of Europe), and here you can see a remarkable system of chain-bucket wells built between each of the storerooms – one on the right, near the back, has been restored – giving a powerful impression of the complexity of seventeenth-century Moroccan engineering. The rows of ruined, roofless vaults that stretch off into the distance through the door at the back were once the royal stables, home to some 1200 horses from Ismail's cavalry.

Just as worthwhile is the **view from the roof**, which is accessed through the entrance on the right (though it's frequently closed to visitors). From its **garden**, you can gaze out over the Dar el Makhzen and the placid waters of the Agdal Basin, built as an irrigation reservoir and pleasure lake, and now a popular spot for promenading families.

The Medina

Although taking much of its present form and size under Moulay Ismail, the **Medina** bears far less of his stamp than the Ville Impériale, having grown organically since the time of the Almoravids and been far too congested to accommodate any of his grandiose plans. Its main sights, in addition to the extensive **souks**, are the delicately decorated **Medersa Bou Inania** and the **Dar Jamaï**, a rewarding palace museum on the southern fringes.

Dar Jamaï

Rue Sekkakine, on the northern side of Pl el Hedim · closed Tues · charge · ☎ 0555 530863

One of the finest examples of a late nineteenth-century Moroccan palace, the **Dar Jamaï** was originally built in 1882 by the same family of viziers (high government officials) who erected the Palais Jamaï in Fez. After 1912, it was used as a military hospital, becoming the Museum of Moroccan Art in 1920. Today, it houses one of the best museums in Morocco.

The exhibits are predominantly of the same age as the palace, though several pieces of **Meknes pottery** date back to around Ismail's reign, and some of the beautiful cedar-wood doors were carved in the fourteenth century. A display of Berber jewellery

3

also catches the eye, though the best is that of **Middle Atlas carpets**, in particular the bold geometric designs of the Beni M'Guild tribe. Most of the exhibits are labelled in French and Arabic only, but the friendly guards will often give you an official guided tour to give you a little context to what you're looking at.

Artefacts and antiques aside, the museum is worth a visit as much for the building, looking better than ever after a year-long renovation and boasting a gorgeous upper-

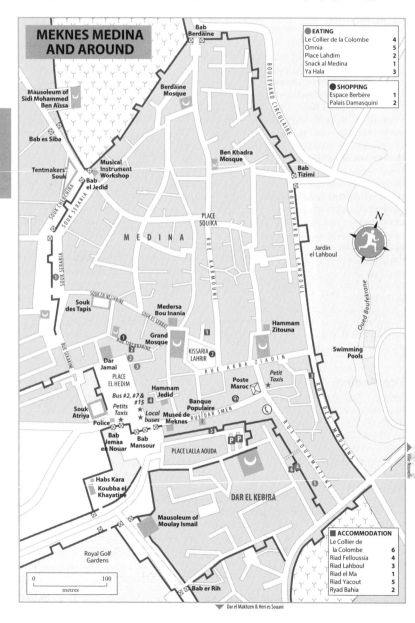

MEKNES MEDINA AND AROUND

EATING
Le Collier de la Colombe	4
Omnia	5
Place Lahdim	2
Snack al Medina	1
Ya Hala	3

SHOPPING
Espace Berbère	1
Palais Damasquini	2

ACCOMMODATION
Le Collier de la Colombe	6
Riad Felloussia	4
Riad Lahboul	3
Riad el Ma	1
Riad Yacout	5
Ryad Bahia	2

floor **reception room** – arguably the museum's highlight – with intricate woodcarvings on the ceiling. The viziers' **Andalusian Garden** has also been preserved, a lush courtyard with palm and fruit trees usually twittering with birds.

The souks

Much more compact than their counterparts in Fez, the **souks** of Meknes are hassle-free and a pleasure to browse. **Souk Atriya**, on Place el Hedim itself, is one of the best produce markets in the country, particularly worth visiting for its spice and sweet stalls; from here, dive into the Medina proper and follow the lanes around **Souk en Nejjarine** and along the city walls to the west. The best times to visit are early in the morning (around 7 or 8am) or late afternoon; note that the shops close on Friday, when the Medina is pretty much deserted.

Souk Atriya

Pl el Hedim

Running along the western side of Place el Hedim, **Souk Atriya** (Covered Market) is usually buzzing with locals doing their shopping for the day. Pick a path between the rows of multicoloured spice stalls, olives piled high into pyramids, butchers doing a brisk trade in sheep heads and fat ox tongues, and sweet stalls so loaded with cakes and patisserie that you can hardly reach the stallholder to pay.

Souk en Nejjarine, Souk des Tapis and Souk es Sebbat

Head through the archway to the left of the Dar Jamaï, and follow the lane (Rue Tiberbarine) north, forking left at the mosque – you've gone too far if you get to Espace Berbère

From Place el Hedim, twisting alleyways lead north to **Souk en Nejjarine**, which together with Souk es Sebbat makes up the Medina's major market street. The carpenters (*nejjarine*) who gave the souk its name have moved out to the city walls, and the first few stalls in this area now trade in modern clothes and football shirts. Turning left, there's an area of textile stalls, behind which a parallel arcade, the Souk Joutiya es Zerabi, or **Souk des Tapis** (Carpet Market) , is crammed with Berber traders from the surrounding countryside proudly displaying their wares. The quality of the carpets and kilims can be very high, as can prices, though because Meknes lacks the constant stream of tourists that swamp Fez or Marrakesh, dealers are more willing to bargain.

Turning right onto Souk en Nejjarine brings you to **Souk es Sebbat** and a classier section of the market – starting off with *babouche* vendors and moving on to the fancier goods aimed at tourists near the medersa.

Kissaria Lahrir

At the eastern end of Souk es Sebbat; keeping the Grand Mosque on your right, follow the lane as it curves east and you'll see the entrance to the *kissaria* opposite one of the doorways (marked no. 20) to the mosque

Most of the work in the **Kissaria Lahrir** is dedicated to textiles, with a throng of bobbin-makers near the entrance using battered old bicycle wheels to spin their threads. But follow the route round to the side and you'll find traditional **silver damascene** being made, a craft brought here from Damascus by Jewish settlers in the late fifteenth century – the hair-thin silver thread is slowly engraved in steel from memory, and the ceramic then burnt in a kiln to produce the striking black colouring. At the Palais Damasquini (see page 196), the family of Essaidi M'Barek has passed on the skills for such delicate work from one generation to the next.

Souk Seraria and Souk Cherchira

Just outside of the tangled alleyways of the Medina proper, the souks that run along the city walls look unpromising at first, but things get more interesting if you follow the inner side of the wall past the flea market of Souk Bezzarine to **Souk Seraria**, an assortment of **craftsworkers**, grouped in trade guilds. There are woodworkers, basketmakers, ironsmiths and saddlers, charcoal-sellers and men chipping away at rocks of salt, and at the top, around **Bab el Jedid**, you'll find **musical-instrument workshops** and a side street off **Souk Cherchira** that's the domain of **tent-makers** – although they rarely sew any traditional tents these days. North of the gate, a **meat market** takes over, dotted with pens of chickens nervously awaiting their fate, before giving way to **fruit and veg stalls** as the road nears Bab Berdaïne.

Medersa Bou Inania
Opposite the Grand Mosque • Charge

Built around 1358, so more or less contemporary with the great medersas of Fez, the **Medersa Bou Inania** would be virtually hidden amid the souks were it not for its imposing bronze doorway. It takes its name from the notorious Sultan Abou Inan, though it was founded by his predecessor, Abou el Hassan, the great Merenid builder behind the Chellah in Rabat and Salé's eponymous medersa. A modest and functional building, the medersa, or Islamic college (see page 163), follows the plan of Hassan's other principal works in that it has a single **courtyard** opening onto a narrow **prayer hall**, and is encircled on both floors by tiny, windowless students' **cells**, with exquisitely carved cedar screens. It has a much lighter feel to it than the Salé medersa, and in its balance of cedar wood, exquisitely carved stucco and zellij, achieves a remarkable combination of intricacy – no area is left uncovered – and restraint.

From the **roof**, you can gaze across to the tiled pyramids of the **Grand Mosque** and its towering minaret, inlaid with green tiles. Its simple decoration is echoed in the minarets beyond, a design that's unique to Meknes – those of Fez or Marrakesh tend to be more elaborate and multicoloured.

The northern Medina

Beyond the Bou Inania Medersa, the Medina is largely residential, dotted with the occasional fruit and vegetable market, and the lone **Ben Khadra Mosque**, which has beautiful polychrome doors and some exquisite coloured stucco. Continuing north along Rue Karmouni, you'll pass the **Berdaïne Mosque**, rebuilt after its minaret tragically collapsed in 2010 (during Friday prayers, the busiest time of the week), killing over forty worshippers. Just beyond here, the narrow lanes end and you emerge into a long, open square, at the far end of which stands the monumental **Bab Berdaïne** (Gate of the Saddlers), another of Ismail's creations; a rugged, genuinely defensive structure, it looks like a more muscular version of the central section of Bab Mansour.

Mausoleum of Sidi Mohammed Ben Aïssa
Closed to non-Muslims

Follow the city walls that extend along the main road northwest of the Medina and you will catch occasional glimpses on your right of an enormous **cemetery** – almost half the size of the Medina in extent, at the heart of which lies the mausoleum of one of the country's most famous and curious saints, **Sidi Mohammed Ben Aïssa** or Cheik el Kamel. Reputedly a contemporary of Moulay Ismail, Ben Aïssa conferred on his followers the power to eat anything, even poison or broken glass, without suffering any ill effects. His cult, the Aissaoua, became one of the most important in Morocco, and certainly the most violent and fanatical. Until prohibited by the French, some fifty thousand devotees regularly attended the saint's annual **moussem** (see page 194).

ARRIVAL AND DEPARTURE   **MEKNES**

By train The town's two train stations are both in the Ville Nouvelle: the main station, the Grande Gare, is 1km east of the centre; the smaller, more convenient Gare el Amir Abdelkader is a couple of blocks away, though not all trains stop here.

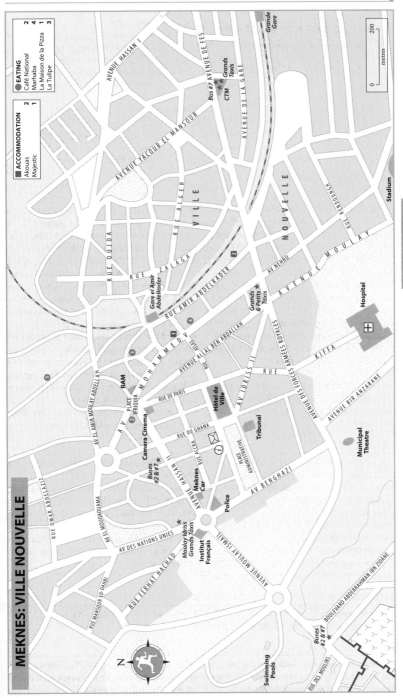

MEKNES: VILLE NOUVELLE

■ ACCOMMODATION	
Akouas	2
Majestic	1

● EATING	
Café National	2
Marhaba	4
La Maison de la Pizza	1
La Tulipe	3

MOUSSEM OF SIDI MOHAMMED BEN AÏSSA

The **Moussem of Sidi Mohammed Ben Aïssa**, held on the eve of Mouloud (see page 45), was once one of the most outrageous spectacles in Morocco. The moussem was the principal gathering of the **Aissaoua** brotherhood and an occasion for them to display their powers of endurance under trance, piercing their tongues and cheeks with daggers, eating snakes and scorpions and devouring live sheep and goats.

While their activities today are more subdued, the event is still a dramatic sight. With enormous conical tents popping up around the *marabout* tomb of Sidi Mohammed Ben Aïssa, and crowds of country people in white *jellabas* gathering beneath the city walls, the modern moussem has the appearance of a medieval tournament, never more so than during the spectacular focal **fantasia** (a charge of horses with riders firing guns at full gallop) that takes place near Place el Hedim.

3

Destinations Asilah (5 daily; 3hr 5min–4hr 15min); Casablanca (roughly hourly; 3hr 15min); Fez (roughly hourly; 30min); Kenitra (roughly hourly; 1hr 30min); Marrakesh (12 daily; 7hr 20min); Oujda (3 daily; 6hr 45min–7hr 30min); Rabat (roughly hourly; 2hr 15min–2hr 45min); Tangier (5 daily; 3hr 55min–5hr 25min); Taza (4 daily; 3hr 15min).

By bus The main bus station is on the north side of the New Mellah, just outside Bab el Khemis, though note that the bus for Moulay idriss (#15) leaves from the stop in front of Bab el Mansour. Arriving by CTM, you'll be dropped at their station (ⓦ ctm.ma) just off Av de FAR, at the eastern end of the Ville Nouvelle; there's a handy central CTM ticket office in a *téléboutique* at 15 Rue Rouamazine.

Destinations Agadir (1 CTM & 5 others daily; 11hr); Al Hoceima (2 CTM daily; 7hr); Azrou (4 CTM & 12 others daily; 1hr 30min–2hr 30min); Casablanca (9 CTM & 12 others daily; 3hr 20min–4hr 15min); Er Rachidia (3 CTM & 1 other daily; 6hr); Fez (8 CTM daily, others frequently; 1hr); Ifrane (2 CTM & 2 others daily; 1hr 15min–2hr); Larache (2 CTM & 3 others daily; 2hr 45min–4hr 35min); Marrakesh (2 CTM & 6 others daily; 7hr–7hr 50min); Midelt (3 CTM & 1 other daily; 4hr); Moulay Idriss (frequent; 35min); Nador (2 CTM & 6 others daily; 5hr 30min–6hr 15min); Oujda (3 CTM & 4 others daily; 5hr 30min–7hr); Rabat (8 CTM & 12 others daily; 1hr 45min–2hr 45min); Rissani (1 CTM & 1 other daily; 8–9hr); Tangier (4 CTM & 7 others daily; 4hr 30min–6hr); Taza (8 CTM & 1 other daily; 2hr 45min–4hr); Tetouan (1 CTM & 4 others daily; 5hr 45min); Tinghir (4 daily; 9hr).

By grand taxi Most services, including those to Fez and Oujda, use a yard alongside the *gare routière*, though there are also ranks next to the CTM bus station and at the junction of Av des FAR and Av Mohammed V. *Grands taxis* for Moulay Idriss leave from Av des Nations Unies, near the Institut Français in the Ville Nouvelle.

Destinations Azrou (1hr); Fez (1hr); Ifrane (1hr); Midelt (3hr); Moulay Idriss (25min); Rabat (1hr 45min).

GETTING AROUND

There are a few useful **local bus** services, but on the whole it's much more convenient to jump in a (blue) *petit taxi*. Further afield, buses serve **Moulay Idriss** (see page 201), while *grands taxis* run to both the town and the nearby ruins of Volubilis (see page 197).

By bus Local buses #2 & #7 run between the Medina (Pl el Hedim) and the Ville Nouvelle, leaving every 30min or so.

By petit taxi There are *petit taxi* ranks in the Medina, on Pl el Hedim and on the corner of Rue Dar Smen and Rue Rouamazine, and in the Ville Nouvelle, at the junction of Av des FAR and Av Mohammed V. Drivers charge fifty percent extra after 8pm.

By calèche Drivers of horse-drawn carriages waiting on the corner of Pl el Hedim will take up to six passengers on a tour of the Ville Impériale; the trip lasts about an hour, depending on stopping time.

By car None of the major car rental companies have offices in Meknes: try Volubilis Car, Ave idrissi passage Mimousa (ⓦ volubiliscar.com).

INFORMATION

Tourist information The town's tourist office is at 27 Pl Administrative in the Ville Nouvelle (Mon–Fri 8.30am– 4.30pm, Sat 8–11.30am; ☎ 0535 525538).

ACCOMMODATION

The ever-growing number of **riads** in the Medina and the Ville Impériale are by far the best places to stay. Meknes' **hotels** are mainly concentrated in the Ville Nouvelle, close to most of the town's restaurants and bars; budget travellers may prefer to stick to the Medina's **pensions**, as cheaper options are few and far between. Booking accommodation is really only a necessity around the time of the Sidi Mohammed Ben Aïssa moussem (see page 194).

THE MEDINA AND THE VILLE IMPÉRIALE, SEE MAP PAGE 190

Le Collier de la Colombe 67 Rue Driba ⓦ lecollierde lacolombe.com. Arguably the best accommodation in Meknes outside the riads, with two very differently styled rooms – one fairly cramped but split over two levels – plus three smart suites with private balconies (€€€) that share the same great views as the restaurant below (see page 195). Fantastic breakfasts to boot. BB €€

★ **Riad Felloussia** 23 Derb Hammam Jedid ☎ 0535 530840. Charming riad in a handy central location, tucked down an alleyway beyond the neighbourhood hammam (see page 196) and accessed through a gateway just up from Bab Mansour. The spacious suites, set around a small garden courtyard, are beautifully furnished, including various objets d'art from the owner's time in West Africa, though they can feel a bit airless at times. The kindly staff are warm and welcoming and cook up consistently delicious dinners. One of the two terraces enjoys good views of the evening antics on Pl el Hedim. BB €€€

Riad Lahboul 6 Derb Aïn Sefli ⓦ riadlahboul.com. A beautiful, homely riad in the quieter eastern fringes of the Medina, overlooking the attractive Jardin el Lahboul on the other side of the road. The half dozen compact en-suite rooms are done out in different regional styles ("Chleuhowi", for example, has a wood-carved four poster; "Berber" has bed covers from the Middle Atlas and kilim wall hangings), while Mouna's home-cooked cuisine (set menu €€€) is worth skimping on lunch for. Cookery and traditional Moroccan music workshops also offered. BB €€

★ **Riad el Ma** 4 Derb Sidi Besri, off Kissaria Lahrir ⓦ riad-el-ma.com. This cute little riad – in the thick of

the action – is focused around its plant-filled courtyard, complete with tranquil tinkling fountain. There are log fires in the lounge in winter and a small roof-terrace pool for the warmer months. The two suites are decent value, though the cheaper Red Room is arguably the nicest in the riad. €€

Riad Yacout 22 Pl Lalla Aouda ⓦ riad-yacout-meknes. com. A slick upscale riad, perhaps the best outside of the Medina proper (it's on the edge of the Ville Impériale), well priced, tastefully decorated and equipped with a hammam, rooftop plunge pool and excellent restaurant. Rooms vary quite wildly in style – some are opulently traditional, others much more modern, with flat-screen TVs – so it pays to check out a few first. BB €€€

Ryad Bahia Rue Tiberbarine ☎ 0535 554541. Charming family-run riad, elegantly restored by local artisans and well located for the souks, on the lane that curves up towards the Medersa Bou Inania. All rooms are en suite and have a/c, and many are furnished with antique painted woodwork. The terrace has good views over the Medina, and there's a small but high-quality restaurant. BB €€€

VILLE NOUVELLE, SEE MAP PAGE 193

Akouas 27 Rue Amir Abdelkader ⓦ hotelakouas. com. All the mod cons – double-glazing, a/c, heating, satellite TV – in an international-standard if fairly bland business hotel near the CTM station. There's a small indoor pool and a decent restaurant, open to non-residents; the *Akouas* also has its own piano bar and nightclub (daily midnight–3am). €€

★ **Majestic** 19 Av Mohammed V ⓦ hotelmajestic meknes.ma. This 1930s Art Deco hotel marries vintage charm with comfortable, clean rooms (most en suite) offering heating and –in some cases – balconies. Add in friendly management and a large roof terrace and you've got the best mid-priced choice in the Ville Nouvelle. €€

EATING AND DRINKING

Eating in the Medina is largely at basic **café-grills** or **traditional houses** where you can tuck into excellent food at a fraction of the price you'd pay in the touristy equivalents in Fez. The Ville Nouvelle is home to the city's finest **patisseries** as well as a dozen or so decent **restaurants**, most serving a daily three-course menu. The Ville Nouvelle's **bars** are boisterous affairs with an all-male clientele that many women will find intimidating. Your best bet for a drink is at one of the area's hotels or at a restaurant in the Medina; all smarter options, and a few of the moderates, are licensed to serve alcohol.

MEDINA, SEE MAP PAGE 190

CAFÉ

Snack al Medina Souk en Nejjarine. Friendly fruit-juice place, virtually in the walls of the Medina, where you can

mix and match your own combinations – anything with pistachio is generally delicious – and take a well-earned breather at the upstairs tables. Simple food also served. €

RESTAURANTS

Le Collier de la Colombe 67 Rue Driba ⓦ lecollier delacolombe.com. This smart restaurant, in the ornate mansion of "Sultan" Lakhal (a non-Alaouite pretender to the throne on the death of Moulay Youssef in 1927), has an interesting menu of decent-value Moroccan dishes (go for the pastilla or beef brochettes; mains around €€€), though many people just come here for a drink – night and day, the views across the valley to the Ville Nouvelle are stunning, especially from the roof terrace. Licensed. €€€

Omnia 8 Derb Aïn el Fouki, signposted from Rue Rouamazine ☎ 0535 533938. Cosy Medina home where you dine in a couple of beautifully decorated alcoves while the family seemingly go about their business. The set menu is succinct but more varied than most places, and what is on there – *kefta* tajine and honey-sweetened beef *kamama* among others – is unfailingly tasty. €̄

Place Lahdim Pl el Hedim. Eating places around Pl el Hedim are notoriously unhygienic, so opt for a drink at this popular café instead and some of the best views in town –the square is great for people watching, especially at sunset. €̄

★**Ya Hala** 10 Rue Sidi Amar Bouaouda ☏0649 988816. Home cooking at its best from a mother-and-son team (she cooks, he serves) in the downstairs of their Medina house. Food, including dishes such as home-made couscous and chicken pastilla, is cooked to order but well worth the wait. €

3

VILLE NOUVELLE, SEE MAP PAGE 193

CAFÉ AND PATISSERIE
Café National 6 Av Mohammed V . Smart, split-level café with attentive service and seating on the outside pavement. It also doubles as a bakery and an excellent little patisserie offering a variety of sticky treats.

La Tulipe Pl Maarakat Lahri. A smart, modern place to while away some time sipping on decent coffee or indulging yourself with expensive ice cream and sticky patisserie, which you can eat in a fondant-hued interior or on a quiet terrace upstairs.

RESTAURANTS
Marhaba 23 Av Mohammed V ☏0535 521632. A no-nonsense, old-school canteen, popular with locals for a budget serving of freshly baked bread and thick *harira* soup, grilled brochettes or rotisserie chicken. €̄

★**La Maison de la Pizza** Complex Moulay Ismail. Easily the best pizza in Meknes, if not all Morocco. The friendly owner, a native New Yorker, takes pride in serving up a dozen varieties of generously topped proper pizza (from 25dh) at this funky little diner. Go hungry if you plan on tackling a 19-incher. €̄€̄

ENTERTAINMENT

Camera Pl Ifriquia, Ville Nouvelle. Ancient cinema showing a varied programme of (mostly French) movies.
Institut Français Rue Ferhat Hachad, Ville Nouvelle

ⓦif-maroc.org/meknes. Comprehensive programme of well-priced shows, including concerts, theatre, dance, cinema and literature events, plus a popular student café.

SHOPPING   SEE MAPS PAGES 186 AND 190

Ensemble Artisanal Above the local bus station on Av Zine el Abidine Riad. A good place to watch young craftsmen at work, and to either shop without the bother of bartering (prices are fixed) or to get a sense of how much you should pay at the souks.
Espace Berbère Rue Tiberbarine. An interesting and eclectic collection of craft items spread across two shops

including lamps, silver tables and, of course, Berber carpets.
★**Palais Damasquini** Kissaria Lahrir. The oldest establishment in Meknes still working with silver damascene, and something of an institution in these parts (King Mohammed V shops here when he's in town), this little workshop turns out exquisite plates, vases and other beautiful items.

DIRECTORY

Banks and exchange There are several banks in the Ville Nouvelle, concentrated around Pl Administrative and along Av Mohammed V. In the Medina, Banque Populaire on Rue Dar Smen, near Bab Mansour, and the BMCE on Rue Rouamazine have ATMs. The BMCI near the Dar Jamaï on Pl el Hedim has a bureau de change.
Golf The Meknes Royal Golf Club at Bab Belkari (ⓦgolf dumaroc.com) has a nine-hole, par-36 course in the landscaped grounds of the Royal Golf Gardens.
Hammams Hammam Zitouna, behind the mosque of the same name, is allegedly the oldest – and many say the nicest – hammam in Meknes (daily: men 6am–noon & 9pm–midnight; women 1–9pm). Hammam Jedid, down an alley opposite the Musée de Meknès (follow signs for *Riad Felloussia*), is an atmospheric traditional neighbourhood

hammam, offering *ghasoul* (clay) scrubs and massages (same hours and prices as Hammam Zitouna).
Medical care Hôpital Militaire Moulay Ismail, Bd El Hansali (☏0535 517397).
Pharmacy The most convenient pharmacy is on Rue Sekakine, just west of the Dar Jamai.
Police The local HQ is on Pl Ferhat Hachad, at the western end of Av Hassan II in the Ville Nouvelle (☏19). There's a smaller station in the Medina, next to Bab Jemaa en Nouar in the southwest corner of Pl el Hedim.
Post office The main post office is in the Ville Nouvelle, on the northern corner of Pl Administrative. There's also a branch in the Medina, on the corner of Rue Dar Smen and Rue Rouamazine.

Volubilis

A striking sight, visible for miles on the bends of the approach roads, the Roman ruins of **VOLUBILIS** occupy the ledge of a long, high plateau, 25km north of Meknes. Below their walls, towards the town of Moulay Idriss, stretches a rich river valley; beyond lie the dark, outlying ridges of the Zerhoune mountains. The drama of this scene – and the scope of the ruins themselves – are undeniably impressive, so much so that Volubilis was inscribed as a UNESCO World Heritage site in 1997 and the ruins were a key location for Martin Scorsese's film *The Last Temptation of Christ*.

3

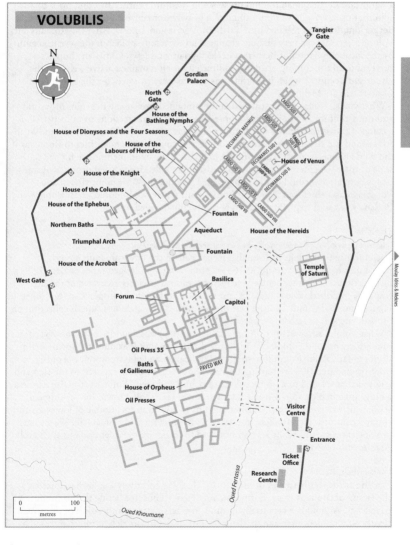

Brief history

Except for a small trading post on an island off Essaouira, Volubilis (a corruption of *oualili*, Arabic for oleander) was the Roman Empire's most remote and far-flung base. It represented – and was, literally – the end of the imperial road, having reached across France and Spain and then down from Tangier, and despite successive emperors' dreams of "penetrating the Atlas", the southern Berber tribes were never effectively subdued.

In fact, direct **Roman rule** here lasted little over two centuries – the garrison withdrew early, in 285 AD, to ease pressure elsewhere. But the town must have taken much of its present form well before the official annexation of the Kingdom of Mauretania by Emperor Claudius in 40 AD. Tablets found on the site, inscribed in Punic, show a significant **Carthaginian trading presence** in the third century BC, and prior to colonization it was the western capital of a heavily Romanized, but semi-autonomous, **Berber kingdom** that reached into northern Algeria and Tunisia. After the Romans left, Volubilis experienced very gradual change. Latin was still spoken in the seventh century by the local population of Berbers, Greeks, Syrians and Jews; Christian churches survived until the coming of Islam; and the city itself remained active well into the seventeenth century, when its marble was carried away by slaves for the building of Moulay Ismail's Meknes.

What you see today, well excavated and maintained, are largely the ruins of second- and third-century AD buildings – impressive and affluent creations from its period as a **colonial provincial capital**. The land around here is some of the most fertile in North Africa, and the city exported wheat and olives in considerable quantities to Rome, as it did wild animals from the surrounding hills. Roman games, memorable for the sheer scale of their slaughter (nine thousand beasts were killed for the dedication of Rome's Colosseum alone), could not have happened without the African provinces, and Volubilis was a chief source of their lions – within just two hundred years, along with Barbary bears and elephants, they were pretty much wiped out.

The site

Charge •The site is exposed and can get very hot –visit early and bring a hat and plenty of water

The **entrance to Volubilis** is through a minor gate in the city wall, built along with a number of outer camps in 168 AD following a prolonged series of Berber insurrections. The **visitor centre** here features various artefacts excavated at the site (capitals, inscribed tablets, mosaics and the like), although the displays are captioned in French and Arabic only and the best of the finds, which include a superb collection of bronzes, are still in Rabat (see page 241).

What Volubilis has retained *in situ*, though, is the great majority of its **mosaics**, some thirty or so, the finest of which line the **Decumanus Maximus**, the town's main thoroughfare. Aside from those subjected to heavy-handed restoration, the once brightly coloured tiles are starting to show the effects of being exposed to the elements and most have faded to a subtle palette of ochres and greys. Similarly, the site requires a bit of imagination to reconstruct a town (or, at least, half a town, for the original settlement was twice the size of what remains today) from the jumble of low walls and stumpy columns. Nevertheless, you leave with a real sense of Roman city life and its provincial prosperity, while it's also not hard to recognize the essentials of a medieval Arab town in the layout.

House of Orpheus

Starting at the southern end of the site, in what was effectively a suburban quarter, the **House of Orpheus** is an enormous complex of rooms just beside the beginning of a paved way. Although substantially in ruins, it offers a strong impression of its former luxury – an opulent mansion, perhaps for one of the town's richest merchants. Each of its two main sections – public and private – have their own separate entrance and interior court. The private rooms, which you come to first, are grouped around a small patio, which is decorated with a more or less intact **dolphin mosaic** (in the southwest corner). You can also make out the furnace and the pipes of the heating system (just to the right of the entrance), the kitchen and the **baths**, an extensive system of hot, cold and steam rooms.

A little further inside, the house's public apartments are dominated by a large atrium – half reception hall, half central court, and again preserve a very fine mosaic, **The Chariot of Amphitrite Drawn by a Seahorse**. The best mosaic here, however, from which the house takes its name, is that of the **Orpheus Myth**, located just behind this in a room that was probably the *tablinium*, or archives.

Oil presses and the Baths of Gallienus

South of the House of Orpheus is a mixed area of housing and industry, each of its buildings containing the remains of at least one **oil press**. The extent and number of these presses (there are 58 dotted across the site in total), built into even the grandest mansions, reflect the olive's central importance to the city and indicate perhaps why Volubilis remained unchanged for so long after the Romans' departure. A significant proportion of its twenty thousand population must have been involved in some capacity in the oil's production and export.

Heading north from the House of Orpheus, you pass first through the remains of the city's main **public baths**, restored by the Emperor Gallienus in the third century AD (the building to the right served as a communal toilet), and then alongside **Oil Press 35**, repaired in 1990 and featuring a reconstruction of the grinding mechanism, including both grinding stones.

The Forum, Capitol and Basilica

Above the House of Orpheus, a broad, paved street leads up towards the **Forum**, the arrangement of which is typical of a major Roman town: built on the highest rise of the city and surrounded by its main political, administrative and religious buildings, the sand-coloured ruins of which dominate the site.

Inscriptions date the **Capitol**, the smaller and lower of the two main buildings, to 218 AD, when this public nucleus seems to have been rebuilt by the African-born Severan emperors. Adjoined by small forum **baths**, it is a simple building with a porticoed court (the porticos themselves now heavily restored) that leads on to a small temple and altar dedicated to the official state cult of Jupiter, Juno and Minerva. The large five-aisled **Basilica** to its side, framed by impressive Corinthian columns, served as the courthouse, while immediately across the Forum were the small court and stalls of the **central market**.

Storks have colonized some columns of the Capitol and Basilica; on a quiet day, you can hear their clacking noises and will almost certainly see a few circling above or standing sentinel over their nests.

The Triumphal Arch and around

The **Triumphal Arch**, right in the middle of the town, had no purpose other than to create a ceremonial proscenium for the principal street, the **Decumanus Maximus**, which was fronted in traditional Roman and Italian fashion by shops built in the tiny cubicles. It was erected in 217 AD to honour the Severan emperor Caracalla and was once topped with a bronze chariot, according to a weathered inscription. The heavily eroded medallions on either side presumably depict Caracalla and his mother, Julia Domna, who is also named in the inscription.

The aqueduct and fountains across from the arch once supplied yet another complex of public baths, the **Northern Baths**. Opposite them is the **House of the Acrobat** (also called House of the Athlete), which retains an impressive **Mosaic of an Acrobat** or "chariot jumper" – depicted receiving the winner's cup for a desultory race, a display of great skill that entailed leaping on and off a horse in full gallop.

3

House of the Ephebus

The first of the great Decumanus Maximus mansions, the **House of the Ephebus** takes its name from the bronze of a youth found in its ruins – and today displayed in Rabat. In general plan, it is very similar to the House of Orpheus, once again containing an olive press in its rear section, though this building is on a far grander scale, with pictorial mosaics in most of its public rooms and an ornamental pool in its central court. Finest of the mosaics is a representation of **Bacchus Being Drawn in a Chariot by Panthers** – a suitable scene for the *cenacula*, or banqueting hall, in which it is placed.

House of the Columns to the House of the Bathing Nymphs

Separated from the House of the Ephebus by a narrow lane is a mosaic-less mansion, known after the pillars that dominate its peristyle as the **House of the Columns**, and adjoining this, the **House of the Knight** with an incomplete mosaic of **Bacchus Discovering Ariadne** asleep on the beach at Naxos; both houses are largely ruins. More illuminating is the large mansion that begins the next block, similar in plan but with a very complete mosaic of the **Labours of Hercules**; almost comic caricatures, these give a good idea of typical provincial Roman mosaics. The next house along, the **House of Dionysos and the Four Seasons**, holds the site's best-preserved mosaic, the tiling of Dionysos and her muses still hinting at the exuberant original colours. In the neighbouring house, the artistic mosaic of the **Bathing Nymphs** is unfortunately severely deteriorated around its central area.

Gordian Palace

North of the House of the Bathing Nymphs, approaching the partially reconstructed **Tangier Gate**, stands the **Gordian Palace**, former residence of the procurators who administered both the city and the province. Despite its size, however, and even with evidence of a huge **bathhouse** and pooled courtyards, it is unmemorable, stripped of its columns and lacking any mosaics. Its grandeur may have made it a target for Ismail's building mania; indeed, how much of Volubilis remained standing before his reign is an open question – Walter Harris, writing at the turn of the twentieth century, found the road between here and Meknes littered with ancient marbles, left as they fell following the announcement of the sultan's death.

House of Venus

On the road running parallel to the Decumanus Maximus, the **House of Venus** features the most exceptional ensemble of mosaics in Volubilis. The villa's most outstanding mosaics lie beyond the central court, in the "public" sections. Straight ahead is the **Cortege of Venus**, in which the Three Graces are depicted rowing the goddess to shore accompanied by a retinue of Nereids and Tritons. Off to the far right are **Diana Bathing** (and surprised by the huntsman Actaeon, whom she turns into a stag) and the **Abduction of Hylas by the Nymphs**. Each of these scenes, especially the last two, is superbly handled in stylized, fluid animation. They date – like that of the mosaic in the **House of the Nereids** (two houses further down, on the opposite side of the road) – from the late second or early third century AD, and were a serious commission. It is not known who commissioned the house itself, but its owner must have been among the city's most successful patrons – magnificent bronze busts of Cato the Younger and Juba II were also found here and currently form the centrepiece of Rabat's Archeological Museum (see page 241).

Temple of Saturn

Leaving the site by the path below the Forum, you pass close by the ruins of a **temple** on the opposite side of the stream, sometimes referred to as Temple B. The Romans dedicated it to Saturn, but it seems to have previously been used for the worship of a Carthaginian god; several hundred votive offerings were discovered during its excavation.

ARRIVAL AND DEPARTURE   VOLUBILIS

By bus From Meknes, you can take one of the frequent #15 city buses from the stop on the southern end of Pl el Hedim to Moulay Idriss and then a regular shuttle bus from there to the ruins.

By grand taxi Taxis run to Moulay Idriss from Meknes, departing from a stop near the Institut Français in the Ville Nouvelle, from where you can charter another *grand taxi* to take you on to the ruins. Alternatively, you could charter your own *grand taxi* from Meknes for a half-day excursion (with 3hr or so at the site).

By car If you're driving to Volubilis from the north, note that after you've turned east after Sidi Kacem the route might be signposted only to Oualili (its Arabic name).

On a tour Most of the riads and hotels in Meknes can organize a car and driver for the trip to both Volubilis and Moulay Idriss.

On foot You can walk between Moulay Idriss and Volubilis; it's a scenic and safe 4km stroll, particularly enjoyable in the early morning when locals will join you on their way to the olive groves.

Moulay Idriss

The holy town of **MOULAY IDRISS**, spread across the foothills of Jebel Zerhoune, 25km north of Meknes and 4km from Volubilis, takes its name from its founder, Morocco's most venerated saint and the creator of its first Arab dynasty. His mausoleum, the reason for its sacred status, is the object of constant pilgrimage, not to mention an important summer **moussem** – a trip to which is worth a fifth of the *hajj* to Mecca. For most Western tourists, there is little specific to see and certainly nothing that may be visited – non-Muslims are barred from the shrine – but you could easily lose a happy half-day exploring the tangled lanes that shimmy between the sugar-cube houses scattered over the hills, enjoying delightful window-views or just absorbing the laidback atmosphere. Few tourists bother to stay overnight, another reason to linger.

Zaouia of Moulay Idriss

Closed to non-Muslims • From the main square, head north, through the archway, and the *zaouia* is directly ahead

Rebuilt by Moulay Ismail, the green-tiled pyramids of Moulay Idriss's **zaouia** (mausoleum) lie right at the heart of town, flanked on either side by the hillside residential quarters of Khiber and Tasga. The shrine itself is cordoned off from the street by a low, wooden bar, to keep out Christians and beasts of burden.

While you can get an idea of its grandeur on the ground, you'll have to climb up to one of the vantage points near the pinnacle of each of the town's quarters for a true sense of the shrine's scale. The terrace near the **Zaouia of Sidi Abdallah el Hajjam**, above Khiber (the taller hill, to the shrine's left) has the best views– take the passageway on your left (facing the shrine) to Rue Drazat and follow the signs for "Slimani", turning left under the archway before *Maison d'Hôte Slimani* and then left again (uphill) at the sign for Rue el Hafa up a flight of steps (all 150 of them) to reach the terrace. Up here, you'll also find souks selling a variety of religious artefacts for Muslim visitors, especially plain white candles for use in the mausoleum.

Merdersa Moulay Idriss

The medersa is quite difficult to find among the narrow streets near the Khiber quarter, but the *gardien* at the Zaouia of Sidi Abdhallah el Hajjam (see above) can show you the way for a small tip

On your way up into the Khiber quarter, aim for the minaret of the **Medersa Moulay Idriss**, now a Koranic school. It was constructed with materials taken from Volubilis, and the cylindrical minaret – the only one of its kind in Morocco – was built in 1939 by a *hadji* who had been inspired by those he had seen in Mecca. A *surah* (chapter) from the Koran is inscribed in Kufic script around it, made out of green mosaics.

MOULAY IDRISS AND THE FOUNDATION OF MOROCCO

Moulay Idriss el Akhbar (The Great) was a great-grandson of the Prophet Mohammed; his grandparents were Mohammed's daughter Fatima, and his cousin and first follower, Ali. Heir to the Caliphate in Damascus, he fled to Morocco around 787 AD, following the Ummayad victory in the great civil war that split the Muslim world into Shia and Sunni sects.

In **Volubilis**, then still the main centre of the north, Idriss seems to have been welcomed as an *imam* (a spiritual and political leader), and within a few years had succeeded in carving out a considerable kingdom nearby. At this new town site, more easily defended than Volubilis, he built his **capital**, and he also began the construction of **Fez**, continued and considerably extended by his son, Moulay Idriss II, that city's patron saint. News of his growing power filtered back to the East, however, and in 791 the Ummayads had Idriss poisoned, doubtless assuming that his kingdom would crumble.

They were mistaken. Alongside the faith of Islam, Idriss had instilled a sense of unity among the region's previously pagan (and sometimes Christian or Jewish) Berber tribes, which had been joined in this prototypical Moroccan state by increasing numbers of **Arab Shiites** loyal to the succession of his *Alid* line. After Moulay Idriss' assassination, Rashid, the servant who had travelled with him to Morocco, took over as regent until 805, when the founder's son was old enough to assume the throne of what was Morocco's first independent kingdom.

ARRIVAL AND INFORMATION

By bus The #15 bus from Meknes drop you at the very base of the town, from where it's a short but steep walk up the stall-lined road to the main square.
Destination Meknes (frequent; 35min).
By grand taxi *Grands taxis* make regular runs from Meknes, leaving from near the Institut Français in the Ville Nouvelle (10dh/*place*).

Destination Meknes (25min).
Guides It's not easy to find your way up through the town's winding streets (most end in abrupt blind alleys), particularly around the Khiber quarter, but unofficial guides can be enlisted. Alternatively, most *maisons d'hôte* can provide half-day tours of Moulay Idriss.

ACCOMMODATION AND EATING

Until 2005, non-Muslims were not permitted to stay overnight in Moulay Idriss – the last place in Morocco to keep this religious prohibition – but today there are a number of family-run **maisons d'hôte**. **Restaurants** are still pretty scarce, as the majority of the town's guesthouses cook up evening meals; for a quick bite, your best bet is the grill cafés on the square by the mausoleum, followed by some excellent local nougat from the Khiber souks.

La Baraka 22 Aïn Smen ☎ 0535 544034. Pleasant lunchtime restaurant on the road that winds out of town above Khiber, serving tasty tajines sprinkled with local olives, accompanied by tremendous views from the terrace. €€

La Colombe Blanche 21 Derb Zouak, Tasga; turn right at the mausoleum, left at the fountain, then follow the green signs ⓦ blanche.xtadia.com. Well-established *maison d'hôte* in an intimate family home, with a dozen mismatched rooms spread around the first floor and the terrace; it's worth paying a few extra euros for a room with your own balcony. Home-cooked menus in the tiled salon are good value (cooking classes are also available). Tour groups sometimes stay here at the weekend, so book

ahead. BB €€
Dar Zerhoune 42 Derb Zouak, Tasga; turn right at the mausoleum, left at the fountain, then follow the green stencil signs ⓦ darzerhoune.com. Tranquil guesthouse with a friendly Kiwi proprietor and some nice traditional touches (including keyhole doors throughout), plus excellent meals (the restaurant is open to non-guests for lunch) and great views of Jebel Zerhoune from the cushion-strewn roof terrace. You can bake your own bread in the local communal oven, and bikes are available to rent for the short ride to Volubilis. BB €€

Scorpion House 54 Drouj el Hafa, Khiber; turn left at the mausoleum and follow the green signs ⓦ scorpio nhouse.com. Stunning property from the team behind Fez's *Café Clock* (see page 180) which sits high up on the Khiber hillside and looking directly over the mausoleum. It's all very chic, and the food, be it *maakouda* (spicy potato cakes), *charmoula* sardines or *kefta* kebab, is top notch, though it is so exclusive that it opens by prior reservation only –which effectively gets you your very own restaurant for a couple of hours. €€€€

The Middle Atlas

Covered in forests of oak, cork and giant cedar, the **Middle Atlas** is a beautiful but relatively little-visited region. The brown tents of nomadic Berber encampments immediately establish a cultural shift away from the European north; the plateaus are pockmarked by dark volcanic lakes; and the towns initially feel different, too, their flat, gabled houses lending an Alpine-resort feel, particularly at the "hill station" resort of **Ifrane**, where the king has a summer palace.

If you just want a day-trip from Fez, the Middle Atlas is most easily accessible at **Sefrou**, a relaxed market town 28km southeast of the city, though **Azrou** should be on most itineraries as well, an interesting Berber settlement with an excellent and authentic souk, and ideally located for forays into the surrounding cedar forests.

At Azrou, the road forks and you can take one of two routes. The N13 heads southeast to the former mining town of **Midelt** and on to Er Rachidia, a journey that traces the old **Trek es Sultan**, or Royal Road, an ancient trading route that once carried salt, slaves and other commodities with caravans of camels across the desert from West Africa. Heading southwest, the N8, the main route to Marrakesh, skirts well clear of the Atlas ranges, and is lined with dusty, functional market centres, though you can cut south from here to **Azilal**, jumping-off point for the magnificent **Cascades d'Ozoud** and the stunning High Atlas valley of **Aït Bouguemez**, or strike out for **Imilchil** and the epic mountain roads that lie beyond.

3

GETTING AROUND

THE MIDDLE ATLAS

By public transport Buses are plentiful on the stretch between Fez and Er Rachidia, but travellers may find a few problems stopping en route between Fez and Marrakesh, where buses are often full when they pull into towns and few people alight along the way. The solution is flexibility: take the occasional *grand taxi* or stop for a night to catch an early bus, and you won't be stuck for long.

By car You'll be able to properly explore the Middle Atlas

if you've got your own wheels, enabling you to venture deeper into the cedar forests around Azrou and up (and down) surfaced mountain roads, to Imilchil and the Aït Bouguemez. A 4WD opens up the network of *pistes* in the southern half of the range, and allows for some pretty adventurous journeys in the High Atlas, particularly in the eastern areas of the Aït Bouguemez.

Sefrou and around

The fate of **SEFROU** is to be just 28km south of Fez. Anywhere else in Morocco, this ancient walled town in the foothills of the Middle Atlas would receive a steady flow of visitors, just as it did when it served as the first stop on the caravan routes to the Tafilalt; until the Protectorate, it marked the mountain limits of the **Bled el Makhzen** – the Governed Lands. Instead, the pull of the larger city leaves Sefrou, once known as the Jardin du Maroc, virtually ignored by most tourists, a source of some local resentment and the reason, perhaps, for the extreme persistence of the few hustlers here.

To add insult to injury, Sefrou actually predates Fez as a city, but while Fez became a playground for the finest medieval craftsmen Morocco had to offer, Sefrou ended up with just a couple of **mosques** to its name. Indeed, there are few sights per se, and nothing that you can actually visit, though a trip here is more about wandering the compact **Medina** and the adjacent **Mellah**, heading off on **walks** into the surrounding hills or to the unusual cave houses in nearby **Bhalil**.

The Medina

In comparison with Fez, the **Medina** of Sefrou inevitably feels rather low-key, although it is equally well preserved on its modest scale – a pocket-size version of Fez el Bali that is far less intimidating for many visitors – and the untouristy atmosphere makes it a pleasant place to explore by instinct. The **Thursday souk**, in particular, remains a largely local affair, drawing Berbers from neighbouring villages to sell garden produce and buy basic goods.

The main entrance into the Medina is through **Bab M'kam**, set into the nineteenth-century ramparts on the eastern side of Place Moulay Hassan. Beyond here, the main street of the old Arab town winds down to the rubbish-strewn **Oued Aggaï**, where it follows the river first past the **Adloun Mosque** and then the **Grand Mosque**, with its domed minaret; both are closed to non-Muslims. Turning left here leads into an area of covered **souks**, where traders set up shop behind uniformly mint-green doorways and chickens amble about among them.

Walking back to the bridge by the Adloun Mosque you can cross the river and head right (southwest) for **Bab Merba** (and the covered market just outside the walls) or left (southeast) to exit the Medina via **Bab Mejles**.

The Mellah

A dark, cramped conglomeration of tall, shuttered houses and tunnel-like streets, Sefrou's **Mellah** is one of the oldest in Morocco. There seems to have been a Jewish-Berber population here long before the coming of Islam and, although most converted, a large number of Jews from the south settled again in the town under the Merenids. As late as the 1950s, at least a third of the population were Jews, but while only a handful remain – most having left for Casablanca, Israel or Paris – the district still seems distinct; the local synagogue (actually just outside the Mellah, through Bab Merba) is consequently in some disrepair but can still be visited if you can track down the gardien (10dh donation). When entering Sefrou via the main road from Fez, look out for the **Kaf el-Moumen** ("Cave of the Faithful"), the burial place of renowned saints

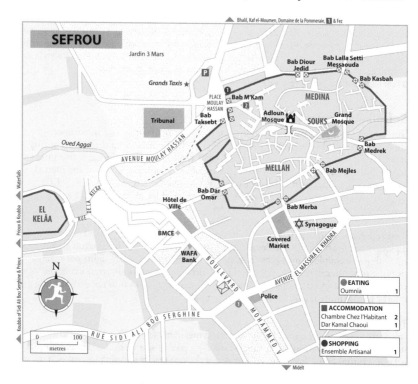

WALKS AROUND SEFROU

High enough into the Middle Atlas to avoid the suffocating dry heat of summer, Sefrou is a good base for some modest **walking**. Dozens of **springs** emerge in the hills above the town and a few waterfalls are active for part of the year.

KOUBBA OF SIDI ALI BOU SERGHINE

For a relatively easy target, take the road up behind the post office on Boulevard Mohammed V (Rue Sidi Ali Bou Serghine), which divides into a fork after about a kilometre. The right-hand branch leads to a small, deserted French fort, known as the **Prioux**, and to the **koubba** of one Sidi Ali Bou Serghine. The views from around here are thrilling: in winter, the snowcapped Mischliffen; in summer, the cedars and holm oaks cresting the ridges to infinity. You can also reach the *koubba* (and fort) by taking the left fork in the road that splits in front of **El Kelâa**, a *ksar* (fortified settlement) that's quite interesting in of itself and reached on Rue de la Kelâa, west of the sharp bend in the main road across the Oued Aggaï.

THE WATERFALLS

Heading up Rue de la Kelâa from the main road and taking the right-hand fork in front of El Kelâa leads instead to a junction signposted *"Cascades"*, from where a single-lane tarmac road follows the river to a small hydroelectric power station; 250m beyond this, below imposing rocky outcrops, are the **waterfalls**, at their best in spring. Flash floods regularly wash away the path here, so repair work may bar your access to a pool beneath for a paddle.

3

of both Islamic and Judaic faith – unique in Morocco. It's now visited and revered by both faiths equally.

Bhalil

5km northwest of Sefrou • No direct buses from Fez; connect in Sefrou (see page 206)

Tumbling down a hillside 5km from Sefrou, the extraordinary village of **Bhalil** is known in Arabic as "the beauty of the night," first named by those in ancient Fez who would come to the region and see the fires at the entrance of the inhabited caves, many of which are still in use as troglodyte dwellings. The **cave houses** are in the old part of the village, a charming network of pink- and yellow-painted buildings connected by innumerable bridges; go through the arch at the bottom of the village (where *grands taxis* drop off) and take any of the narrow lanes that run up the hill to the left.

Bhalil's other quirky claim to fame is as Morocco's "centre" for producing **jellaba buttons** (more like rounded balls of thread used as buttons). You'll see women sitting outside their houses, chatting as they work their way through mounds of thread – a long job, given that there are at least two hundred buttons on every *jellaba*.

FESTIVALS IN SEFROU

Sefrou hosts the **Moussem of Sidi Lahcen el Youssi**, a seventeenth-century saint, in August or September each year (exact date varies depending on the Islamic calendar), but it is the **Fête des Cerises**, the annual cherry festival held each June, that's the big do around these parts. Now on UNESCO's Intagible Cultural Heritage list, it draws sizeable crowds for its music, folklore and *fantasias* (horse-riding displays), climaxing with the crowning of the Cherry Queen on the last evening.

ARRIVAL AND INFORMATION

SEFROU AND AROUND

By bus Buses from Fez (roughly hourly; 45min) leave from Pl de la Résistance (La Fiat) in the Ville Nouvelle, usually dropping off passengers at "Le Jardin", the area around Pl Moulay Hassan in Sefrou.

By grand taxi From Fez, *grands taxis* run from just below La Fiat to Sefrou's Pl Moulay Hassan (30min) and to Bhalil (45min). *Grands taxis* regularly shuttle between Pl Moulay

Hassan and Bhalil (5min). Moving on, you can cross onto the Fez–Marrakesh road by getting a *grand taxi* to Immouzer du Kandar (30min) and picking up another taxi from there to Ifrane (30min) or Azrou (45min).

Services The post office and banks are on Bd Mohammed V in the Ville Nouvelle.

ACCOMMODATION

SEE MAP PAGE 204

Chambre Chez l'Habitant 57 Ibn Toumert Siti Mesaouda, Sefrou ☎0634 473353. Wonderful homestay hidden away in the heart of the Medina. There's just a single double room (en suite shower, with a bathroom just outside the door), with use of a beautifully tiled salon, but the welcoming owners are charm personified (their daughter will probably teach you to write your names in Arabic) and cook up excellent evening meals. BB €€

★ **Dar Kamal Chaoui** 60 Kaf Rhouni, Bhalil (call ahead for directions) ⓦkamalchaoui.com. The family home of

super-friendly Kamal Chaoui is a real gem: lovely bedrooms, sensitively furnished and with *tadelakht* bathrooms, that are even warm in winter, thanks to the ingenious home-made heating system. Kamal is very passionate about Bhalil and takes guests on excellent neighbourhood tours (he speaks exceptional English, French, and German), during which you may get invited into a Berber cave house, plus day-hikes in the region. Tasty Moroccan meals are served up in the evening. BB €€€

EATING

SEE MAP PAGE 204

Oumnia Bd Mohammed V. Cheap, friendly place, whose dark split-level dining room lies beyond a smoky café. Brave

the fumes for simple omelettes or a 3-course menu that includes *kefta*, tajines and the like. €

SHOPPING

SEE MAP PAGE 204

Ensemble Artisanal Pl Moulay Hassan. With just a handful of shops that open in rotation, Sefrou's tiny Ensemble Artisanal is small beer compared with those in

Fez or Marrakesh but still worth a visit – you can usually see woodcarvings, metalwork and *jellabas* being created by hand.

Dayet Aaoua and the Route des Lacs

The gorgeous freshwater lake of **Dayet Aaoua**, 45km south of Fez, makes a good place to break the journey to Ifrane or Azrou, and marks the start of a circuit that runs around a couple of other attractive lakes in the area. Like these, Aaoua can often be dry beyond early spring, but when full its mosaic of habitats supports a wide variety of animals, particularly birds (see page 207). Green frogs take refuge from the summer drought within the lake's protective shallows, and a multitude

DOMAINE DE LA POMMERAIE

Halfway between Fez and Ifrane lies **Domaine de la Pommeraie** (☎0664 904709, ✉domainedelapommeraie@hotmail.fr), a hidden delight for food lovers. With a true passion for increasing sustainable Middle Atlas tourism, farmer Tarik Lechkar grows the area's only truly **organic produce**. A highlight of a visit here is the goat and sheep **cheese tasting**; you can also sample a range of produce that have been cultivated on site, from honey and olive oil to saffron and black truffles. Cooking classes using freshly grown produce can also be arranged.

The farm is signed off the P5012, a poorly maintained, potholed *piste* that runs west from the N8 – the turning is on your right (after 30km) if heading south from Fez, on your left (after 10km) if travelling north from Immouzer du Kandar. Buses and *grands taxis* run between Fez and Ifrane, and you can hop off at the turning; from here it's about a twenty-minute walk to the farm, or you can call ahead and arrange for Tarik to meet you at the N8.

BIRDLIFE ON THE DAYET AAOUA

When the waters of Dayet Aaoua are full, the lake attracts all kinds of waders and wildfowl, and over forty different species winter here, including **cranes** and **flamingos**. Waders include **black-winged stilt**, **green sandpiper** and **avocet** (one of Morocco's most elegant birds), and the deeper waters provide food for flocks of **grebes** (great-crested, black-necked and little varieties) and, in spring, the magnificent **crested coot** (which has spectacular bright red knobs on either side of its white facial shield, when in breeding condition). The reedbeds shelter **grey heron** and **cattle egret** and ring with the songs of well-hidden **reed-** and **fan-tailed warbler**.

The abundance of summer migrants, sand martins especially, proves an irresistible draw for resident and migrant **birds of prey** – there are regular sightings of the acrobatic **red kite** here, and you may also see **Montagu's harrier**, quartering overhead and ever alert for any unsuspecting duck on the lake below.

3

of dragonflies and damselflies of shimmering reds, blues and greens patrol the water's surface.

You can follow the road all the way around Dayet Aaoua, or take the left-hand fork at its northeastern edge to pick up the P5016 and complete the rest of the so-called **Route des Lacs**. This *piste* connects with the P7237 to loop south past **Dayet Ifrah**, one of the largest lakes in the area, before (as the P7231) fringing the drought-ridden lake of **Dayet Hachlaf** on its way. If you're heading on to Ifrane, 16km to the south, you can take the R707 en route (on your right) and rejoin the N8 closer to town.

ACCOMMODATION　　　　　　　　　**DAYET AAOUA AND THE ROUTE DES LACS**

Le Gîte Dayet Aoua Take the left fork at the northeastern end of Dayet Aoua; it's on the left after 200m ⓦ gitedayetaoua.com. An inviting chalet-style house at the far end of the lake, with wood-panelled rooms, a library and a cosy licensed restaurant, plus a good-sized pool for summer. Treks and horse-riding excursions can be arranged, though it's enough just to wander around the farm grounds, complete with peacocks. €€

Gîte de la Montagne Signposted off the southern side of Dayet Aaoua, 3km up a winding track ☏ 0662 586472. Tucked away in the hills above the lake and accessible only with your own transport, this secluded compound offers basic but comfortable (and heated) rooms, home-cooked meals and refreshing walks. BB €€

Ifrane

With its manicured parks, ornamental lakes, and pseudo-Alpine villas set along broad leafy streets, **IFRANE** is something of an anomaly among Moroccan towns: a little prim, even perhaps a little smug. Although the name reveals the site has long been inhabited – "*yfran*" are the "caves" in which local Berbers once lived – the modern town was created by the Protectorate in 1929 as a self-conscious "*poche de France*" (pocket of France), then adopted enthusiastically after independence by Moroccan government ministries and the wealthier bourgeoisie, who own the gleaming top-of-the-range motors parked throughout town during summer. Ifrane has won extra prestige with the addition of a **Royal Palace**, whose characteristic green tiles (a royal prerogative) can be glimpsed through the trees on the descent into the valley.

The stone lion and around

While Ifrane retains an easy-going, affluent air, it rather lacks the human touch of older settlements, and most visitors content themselves with a walk by the **Oued Tizguit**, below the Royal Palace, or maybe a stroll around the **university** (see page 208), before heading further into the Middle Atlas. One "sight" on everyone's

BY ROYAL DEGREE

On January 16, 1995, King Hassan II inaugurated the **Al Akhawayn University** (Ⓦaui.ma) on the northern edge of Ifrane, its chalet-style buildings, cream walls and russet-tiled roofs the design of Michel Pinseau, the architect behind the king's showpiece Hassan II Mosque in Casablanca (see page 260). The name Al Akhawayn ("Brothers" in Arabic) denotes it as the brainchild (and beneficiary) of the Moroccan king and his "brother", King Abdullah Bin Abdulaziz of Saudi Arabia; it has also been funded by the United States and, to a lesser extent, the British Council. The undergraduate and postgraduate curricula are modelled on the American system of higher education, and lectures are in English.

King Hassan was keen to underpin his creation with the religious and cultural values of **Christianity** and **Judaism** as well as of **Islam**. The university is dedicated to "practical tolerance between faiths" and a mosque, church and synagogue are on campus to provide, as the king put it, "a meeting place for the sons of Abraham", a concept endorsed by the Prince of Wales when he visited Ifrane in 1996.

You can arrange **to visit the campus** by contacting the Office of Admissions in advance; try to go on a weekday afternoon when the students are about.

itinerary, though, is Ifrane's landmark **stone lion**, located in a copse fronting *Hôtel Chamonix* just south of the town's squeaky-clean Alpine resort-style centre; a reminder of the lions that once roamed the Atlas, it was allegedly carved by an Italian prisoner of war.

ARRIVAL AND DEPARTURE   IFRANE

By bus The bus station, referred to as *halte routière*, is used by CTM and the majority of local buses but is nearly 2km southwest of Ifrane, near the southwest corner of the Parc des Ombres Noires; *petits taxis* run their from the town centre. Destinations Azrou (frequently; 25min); Casablanca (1 CTM & 1 other daily; 5hr); Er Rachidia (1 CTM & 3 others daily; 5hr), Fez (2 CTM daily & others frequently; 45min); Marrakesh (2 CTM & 4 others daily; 8hr 30min–9hr 10min); Meknes (2 CTM & 2 others daily; 1hr 15min–2hr); Midelt (1 CTM; 2hr 25min); Rabat (1 CTM & 5 others daily; 3hr 25min), Rich (1 CTM daily; 3hr 30min).

By grand taxi *Grands taxis* gather just beside the bus station. Destinations Azrou (20min); Fez (45min); Immouzer du Kandar (30min); Meknes (1hr).

INFORMATION

Tourist information The regional Délégation du Tourisme office is on Pl du Syndicat, on the corner of Av Mohammed V and Av Prince Moulay Abdallah (☎0535 566821), and can provide you with maps of the area, information on local events and contact details for local guides and activities.

ACCOMMODATION

To help maintain its air of exclusivity, Ifrane doesn't do cheap accommodation, nor is it always easy to find a place in summer, when reservations are recommended. That said, you're unlikely to need to stay over, particularly given the proximity of the more interesting town of Azrou (see page 209), and its greater range of options.

Chamonix Av de la Marche Verte ☎0535 566028. Comparatively good-value hotel, whose light, spotless rooms come with heating, a/c and TV. It's a short walk from the restaurants grouped around the town centre – although it also has its own, serving a range of options to a decent standard. €€€

Hotel Relais Ras Elma Bd Mohammed VI ☎0535 567658. A clean and well-maintained option a short way south of town but with good access to walks or cycles in the surrounding forested area (mountain bikes are available for rent). A little on the motel side, but with a contemporary style and pleasant, spacious en-suite rooms with TV and double glazing, keeping it warm in winter. €€

Mischliffen Resort & Golf Av Hassan II Ⓦmichlifen ifrane.com. Exclusive hotel somewhere between luxury Alpine chalet and Scottish hunting lodge. Choose from cosy, wood-panelled "Deluxe" rooms, or much more spacious (and much more expensive) suites – though incredibly, given the price of both, you'll still have to fork out extra for breakfast. Two pools, an ultra-chic spa, four restaurants (see page 209) and a Jack Nicklaus-designed golf course complete the picture. Rates vary considerably from one day to the next; booking online in advance can also lower the cost a little. €€€€

EATING

Forest Hay Riad. Relaxed café-restaurant occupying a chalet-style building in the heart of the pedestrianized town centre, serving soups, salads and comfort food such as Philly cheesesteaks and veggie burgers, plus stylish and intricately crafted gateaux. €

Michlifen Resort & Golf Av Hassan II ⓦ michlifenifrane. com. Fine dining in this luxury hotel (see page 208) comes with a heavy French accent in the Art Deco *Cedray* (reservations recommended), with dishes such as roasted

lamb with pepper-and-honey ice cream. Slightly cheaper Moroccan and Middle Eastern meals are on offer in *L'Oriental*, and lunchtime pasta, carpaccios and (rather aptly) fondue in the more relaxed *Le Chalet*. €€€€

La Paix Av de la Marche Verte ☎ 0535 566675. Upmarket, modern place, where a la carte meals in the restaurant start at 70dh for merguez or rabbit tajine. The attached café-cum-patisserie provides cheaper sandwiches and pizzas. €€€€

DIRECTORY

Post office There's a post office on the main central square, behind the *Hôtel Chamonix*

Banks There are numerous banks with ATMs in the main

central square; Banque Populaire is usually the most reliable option.

Azrou and around

The first real town of the Middle Atlas, **AZROU** makes an attractive "introduction" to the region, an important but welcoming Berber market centre enclosed by wooded slopes on three sides. The town grew at the crossroads of two major routes – north to Meknes and Fez, south to Khenifra and Midelt – and for a long time it held a strategic role in controlling the mountain Berbers. Moulay Ismail built a **kasbah** here, the remains of which survive, while more recently the French established the prestigious **Collège Berbère** – one plank in their policy to split the country's Berbers from the urban Arabs.

South of Azrou lies some of the most remote and beautiful country of the Middle Atlas: a region of dense **cedar forests**, limestone plateaus and polje lakes that is home to some superb wildlife including the Barbary macaque (see page 211). At its heart, and an obvious focus for a trip, are the waterfalls of **Oum er Rbia**, the source of Morocco's largest river.

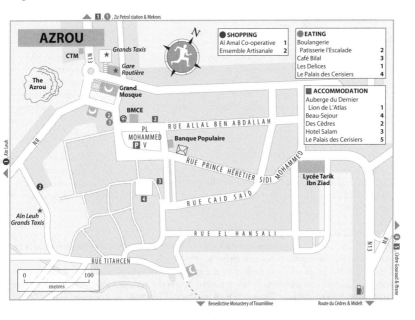

THE MONKS OF TIOUMLILINE

The **monastery of Tioumliline** was built in 1926 by French **Benedictines**, and until the late 1960s played an important role in the life of the local Berber community. The focus of the monastery's life was its *dispensaire* or **clinic**, outside the walls of the complex and by the road to Aïn Leuh. The clinic offered free medical treatment and medicines to any passer-by; Berber families in isolated mountain villages used to bring their sick relatives to be treated and looked after by the monks. As well as free medical care, the monastery supplied the poorest Berber families – and generally anyone whose harvests failed – with basic foodstuffs.

The Istiqlal Party closed the monastery down in 1968, believing that the monks were trying to convert the locals. Most of the Benedictines were relocated to the Abbey of Calcat in France, while their superior, Father Gilbert, went to the Abbey of Saint Benoît de Koubiri, near Ouagadougou in Burkina Faso.

Since then, the monastery has slowly fallen into disrepair, though it did receive a touch of TLC in 2010 when it served as the setting for Xavier Beavouis's French film *Of God and Men*, based on the kidnapping and murder of monks in Algeria in 1996; one of the two survivors of that massacre has since taken up residency at the monastery of Nôtre Dame de l'Atlas near Midelt (see page 225).

The monks themselves may have long gone, but they are still affectionately remembered by many of the locals, including the Boudaoud family, who live in the former dispensary; **Saleh Boudaoud**, a mountain guide (see page 212), can tell you stories about the monastery and show you around the ruins.

The azrou

Azrou's defining feature is the massive knobble of rock on its western edge – the **azrou** ("rock" in Berber) after which it is named. Villagers allegedly used to gather at the rock to trade goods (there's been a Berber market here since the 1840s), though the bigger outcrop to the northeast has a more justifiable claim. Locals clamber to the top of the *azrou*, but you can get just as good a view of the plains that run southwest of town from the **lookout** opposite the impressive Grand Mosque that adjoins the main square, Place Mohammed V.

The souk

One of the most compelling reasons to visit Azrou is its Tuesday **souk**, which is held around 1.5km north of town and draws Berbers from the surrounding mountain villages. At first, it appears to offer little more than fruit and vegetable stalls, but keep going and you'll see a stretch of wasteland where locals strike deals over donkeys, sheep and goats and there are often a few musicians and storytellers performing; beyond this is a smaller section for high-quality **carpets** and textiles.

Lycée Tarik Ibn Ziad

One of the most dominant buildings in town, the **Lycée Tarik Ibn Ziad** is the former home of the **Collège Berbère**, which provided many of the Protectorate's interpreters, local administrators and military officers. As a new French-created elite, Azrou graduates also played a significant role in the pre-independence nationalist movement.

Benedictine Monastery of Tioumliline

3km south of Azrou in the hills above town • Take the road to Midelt (N13), turn right after 2km (signposted "Tioumliline") and follow this road for another 1km; also reached via the backroad to Aïn Leuh, which branches off the N13

One of several good walks to be had in the surrounding hills – lush when watered by seasonal springs and home to Barbary macaque – is the pleasant afternoon stroll to the derelict twentieth-century **Benedictine Monastery of Tioumliline** (see page 210). On your way back to town, you can cut across the hills south of the monastery on any of the footpaths that crisscross the area.

Route des Cèdres

The **cedar forests** that lie to the south of Azrou are a unique habitat in Morocco, their verdant, soaring treetops contrasting starkly with the surrounding aridity and barrenness of the Middle Atlas range and providing dense cover for troupes of **Barbary macaque** (see page 211). You can best appreciate this on the signed, 35km-long **Route des Cèdres**, which dissects large swathes of forest (holm oak as well as cedar) as it wends its way from a junction on the N13 (known locally as the "Moudmane junction"), 8km south of Azrou, towards Aïn Leuh. **Treks** in this region (see page 212) offer very different scenery to the rest of Morocco; the landscape is at its best in spring, when the foliage is greenest and meadow flowers burst into life.

If you're not going all the way to Aïn Leuh, then reaching the roadside **picnic spot** around 10km in is a satisfactory second best, cutting through enough of the forest to give you a good impression of its splendour. With more time, it's worth continuing 11km beyond this to **Lac Afenourir**, the largest lake in the Middle Atlas and home to wigeon, black-necked grebe and significant numbers of regionally rare ruddy shelduck and crested coot.

Cèdre Gouraud

Turning left instead of right at the Moudmane junction leads to more mighty cedars, among them the 130ft-high **Cèdre Gouraud**, singled out by a makeshift sign nailed to the tree – and the fact that, after a life allegedly spanning nine centuries, it is now well and truly dead. The history of its name is a mystery – Colonel Gouraud was General Lyautey's second-in-command from 1912 to 1914, but why a soldier should lend his name to a tree is not clear, the confusion only confounded by a recent authority that claimed Gouraud's cedar was actually felled at the turn of the century.

ARRIVAL AND DEPARTURE   AZROU AND AROUND

Azrou is something of a transport hub, located at the apex of roads heading north **to Fez and Meknes** and at the point where the route south forks: **to Marrakesh** (the N8) or **to Midelt and Er Rachidia** (N13). As most bus services are just passing through, tickets sometimes only go on sale when the bus arrives and the conductor tells the people in the ticket office how many places are available – cue a mad scramble if seats are scarce. Arrive early and set up a place by the ticket window to ensure you'll be at the front of the queue if that happens.

By bus The *gare routière* is just north of the central Grand Mosque; the CTM office is on Bd Hassan II (⦿ ctm.ma).

BARBARY MACAQUES

The cedar forests around Azrou shelter several troupes of **Barbary apes** (*singe margot*), a glimpse of which is one of the wildlife highlights of a visit to Morocco. Despite the name, they are actually members of the **macaque** family (they picked up the "ape" moniker due to their lack of a tail) and roam the forests in troupes of up to a hundred monkeys. The Middle Atlas is home to three-quarters of the world population, though numbers are severely in decline due to a combination of habitat destruction and illegal pet trading, and in 2009 the International Union for Conservation of Nature (IUCN) added them to their Red List of **endangered** species.

Barbary macaque can be found throughout the region, feeding along the forest margins, though you are virtually guaranteed to see them around the **Cèdre Gouraud** and at the **Moudmane junction** (on the N13, 8km southeast of Azrou), where they laze around the picnic area in search of food. Be warned that they are *very* accustomed to humans due to the unfortunate local habit of feeding them for camera-toting tourists.

Destinations Agadir (5 daily, 12hr); Beni Mellal (for Azilal and El Ksiba; 2 CTM & 9 others daily; 4hr 45min); Casablanca (4 CTM & 3 others daily; 4hr 50min–6hr 25min); Er Rachidia (3 CTM, 6 others daily; 4hr 30min–6hr); Essaouira (1 daily, 10hr); Fez (3 CTM & 1 Supratours daily, others frequently; 1hr 15min–2hr 30min); Ifrane (frequently; 25min); Marrakesh (2 CTM & 7 others daily; 8hr–8hr 35min); Meknes (4 CTM & 12 others daily; 1hr 30min–2hr 30min); Midelt (1 CTM, 6 others daily; 2hr 25min–4hr 30min); Rabat (4 CTM & 5 others daily; 3hr 5min–5hr 15min); Rissani (1 CTM , 2 others daily; 6hr 45min–8hr); Tangier (5 daily; 6–7hr); Tetouan (3 daily; 7hr).

By grand taxi There are two *grand taxi* stations in Azrou – the main one is just behind the bus station, whilst *grands taxis* for Aïn Leuh stop just south of the Ensemble Artisanal.

Destinations Aïn Leuh (30min); Fez (1hr); Ifrane (20min); Immouzzer (50min); Meknes (1hr); Midelt (2hr).

ACTIVITIES

Trekking To explore the extensive cedar forests south of Azrou (see page 211) with English-speaking guides, contact Moulay Abdellah Lahrizi (T 0662 190889, E lahrizi37@yahoo.co.uk), president of the local branch of the Association of Mountain Guides, or Boujemâa and Saleh Boudaoud (T 0632 361990, E salehboudaoud@gmail.com), knowledgeable guides who live with their families in the monastery of Tioumliline's old dispensary (see page 210).

Mountain biking Moulay Abdellah Lahrizi (see above) runs mountain-bike day-trips and multi-day trips, including bike rental and guide.

3

ACCOMMODATION

SEE MAP PAGE 209

Bear in mind that the nights around these parts are cold, particularly in winter; central heating is only provided in dearer places (that are further from Azrou).

Auberge du Dernier Lion de L'Atlas 16 Bd Hassan T 0535 561868. Super-friendly place, a 5min *petit taxi* from the *grands taxis* rank, with a hotch-potch of rooms that, though comfortable, could do with a bit of TLC. Owner Aziz is a wealth of information on the region, promoting cultural awareness from his *auberge*/cultural centre. Meals can be arranged and heating is available in winter. €

Beau-Sejour 45 Pl Moulay Hachem Ben Salah T 0535 560692. Rooms are boxy (particularly the triples) but clean, and some have balconies overlooking the square; all have shared bathrooms. The terrace enjoys 360-degree views of the surrounding hills and provides a cheaper sleeping option in summer. €

Des Cèdres Pl Mohammed V T 0535 562326. Perhaps the best value in central Azrou. Spacious, comfortable rooms, though very dark, are enjoyably old-fashioned, all with high ceilings and washbasins; a shared balcony overlooks the square. The restaurant, with outdated decor but decent food, has set menus (€) as well as a la carte options that include Atlas trout. €

Hotel Salam Pl Moulay Hachem Ben Salah T 0669 226402. Despite the uninspiring entrance, this hotel feels a little like a riad, with indoor plants and homely decor. All bathrooms are shared, but the place is clean and well maintained. There's no restaurant, but guests are welcome to buy their own food and enjoy it on the rooftop terrace with panoramic views of the city. €

★ **Le Palais des Cerisiers** Route du Cèdre Gouraud, signed off the N8, 6km northeast of Azrou, W lepalaisdescerisiers.com. The tone at this Alpine-esque lodge is set by the very grand wooden staircase and continues in the large comfortable bedrooms, some with balconies looking out across the surrounding cherry-blossom trees (hence the name) to the hills beyond. Non-guests are welcome to at the refined restaurant or bar (see page 212). There's a swimming pool and spa, and mountain bikes are available for exploring the cedar forest – the Cèdre Gouraud is 7km away. BB €€€€

EATING AND DRINKING

SEE MAP PAGE 209

Basic grills line the roads around the Grand Mosque and prepare the usual brochettes and spit-roast chicken – the stalls towards the *azrou* tend to be better than those towards the bus station, but as ever, double check that the birds were not left on the spit overnight if you choose chicken for lunch.

Boulangerie Patisserie l'Escalade Off the northwest cnr of Pl Mohammed V T 0535 563419. Classy patisserie, perhaps the best of several clustered around Pl Mohammed V, selling a variety of fresh French breads as well as tasty cakes and pastries, some of them savoury. €

Café Bilal Pl Mohammed V T 0535 562233. A café-restaurant serving a range of meals, from simple sandwiches to chicken pastilla, which can be enjoyed either at the sitting area inside or on the small terrace by the road. €

Les Délices 114 Nakhil W lesdelicesrestaurant.weebly.com. Arguably the top place to eat in town, and probably the cleanest too – it was founded by a local pharmacist who places hygiene as a top priority. The restaurant has a contemporary feel and serves generous portions of reasonably priced international and Moroccan food to a high standard. €€

Le Palais des Cerisiers Route du Cèdre Gouraud, signed off the N8, 6km northeast of Azrou W lepalaisdescerisiers.com. The attentive staff at this silver-service restaurant in a lovely lodge (see page 212) proudly serve excellent food that includes warm goat's cheese salad, turkey brochettes, grilled Atlas trout au meunière (a speciality) and chocolate fondant. There's usually a roaring log fire in the wood-panelled British Bar, plus sink-worthy Chesterfields and a good selection of wines (especially reds) and spirits. €€€€

SHOPPING
SEE MAP PAGE 209

In addition to the Tuesday souk, the craft stalls in the old quarter of town around Pl Moulay Hachem Ben Salah and Pl Mohammed V can turn up some beautiful items, fairly priced if not exactly bargains.

Al Amal Co-operative Aït Yahya Ouala, 2km from Azrou. This co-op, in the village of Aït Yahya Ouala (catch a *grand taxi* from the rank by the Ensemble Artisanale) offers a unique shopping experience, selling products that range from black soap to herbal distilled waters. Visitors are advised to ring ahead – and may be able to persuade the women to prepare a traditional couscous lunch for their arrival (100dh per person, cheaper in a group).

Ensemble Artisanale Bd Mohammed V ☎0667 158139. It may feel a bit sleepy compared with cooperatives in Fez and Marrakesh, but this small collection of craft shops produces some decent modern rugs and attractive cedar carvings.

DIRECTORY

Banks and exchange The BMCE and Banque Populaire on Pl Mohammed V have ATMs and (in the former) a *bureau de change*.

Post office The post office is just east of the square, behind the Banque Populaire.

Aïn Leuh

The Berber village of **AÏN LEUH**, 30km southwest of Azrou, is typical of the Middle Atlas, with its flat-roofed houses tiered above the valley. As at Azrou, there are ruins of a kasbah built by Moulay Ismail, and in the hills behind the town there are **springs** and a more or less year-round waterfall – the main reason (for those without their own wheels) for coming here, as the Sources de l'Oum er Rbia, a further 35km along the P7311 (see page 215), are inaccessible on public transport.

Aïn Leuh's **souk** is held on Wednesday (though it can extend a day in either direction) and serves as the weekly gathering of the Beni M'Guild tribes, still semi-nomadic in this region – you may see them camping out with their flocks in heavy, dark tents. As a colonial *zone d'insécurité*, this part of the Atlas was relatively undisturbed by French settlers, and the traditional balance between pasture and forest has remained largely intact.

ARRIVAL AND DEPARTURE
AÏN LEUH

By grand taxi *Grands taxis* run fairly regularly from Azrou to Aïn Leuh (30min), particularly on market days. Trying to go direct to Aïn Leuh from Khenifra may mean a long wait for the taxi to fill up, so your best bet is to get a *grand taxi* to Azrou (1hr) and change there for Aïn Leuh.

By car The most direct route from Azrou is south along the N8, turning left (after 17km) on to the P7311 and following it into Aïn Leuh, though the cross-country Route des Cèdres, which emerges on the N8 just south of Aïn Leuh, is the more scenic option (see page 211). Coming from Khenifra, take the N8 northbound toward Azrou; after around 65km, turn right onto the P7311 and follow for 12km.

ACCOMMODATION AND EATING

Auberge Le Magot de L'Atlas Route Tagounit, signposted just before Aïn Leuh on a backroad to Azrou ☎0661 841084. A dozen neat little rooms, mostly with shared bathroom facilities, in a rambling country house, with an enclosed camping area and a restaurant that serves humble tajines as well as a variety of grills (meals€). Organizes trout-fishing trips to the area's many lakes and rivers and serves as a decent base for walks further afield. Camping/rooms €/€

Ferme d'Hotes La Cascade Ajaabou Signposted just outside of Aïn Leuh (just after the turn for Zaouia d'Ifrane) ☎0678 834991. A farm-villa-turned guesthouse, this hotel has a handful of neat rooms, one lined with local cedar wood (which makes it probably the warmest in the winter). The highlight of this place is its location, tucked outside of town against a backdrop of oak trees; it's a peaceful and removed retreat from the at-times lively village. €€

Zaouia d'Ifrane

Hidden away in what feels like the true heart of the Middle Atlas mountains, **Zaouia d'Ifrane** is well worth a night or two. Incredibly, the village is still untainted by tourism, though it's surely only a matter of time before things change, given the potential for outdoor pursuits in the surrounding hills and the village's magnificent position amidst verdant scenery, backed by waterfalls cascading from a jutting escarpment.

In **town**, you'll find a few small shops and friendly locals who maintain a traditional way of life. Worth a stop is the Anou-certified **women's co-op** (from the car park, walk left and it's on your left; women usually onlocation) where you can buy handmade textiles and rugs of all sizes, plus take a peek at their centre for educating local women.

The falls

The **falls**, which originate from springs and irrigation canals (and thus don't flow when the canals are being used to water the upper fields) are an easy 25-minute **ramble** from town – starting in the centre, head eastwards up alongside the waterfalls and continue for five minutes or so along a well-worn path that leads behind the cliff face and into the ravine of a small stream, from where you climb further up until you reach a mini-plateau overlooking the region. Facing back towards town, cross over the fields here to the waterfall's edge, where you'll emerge to stunning views and a pleasant picnic spot. To return to Zaouia d'Ifrane, walk alongside the falls' edge until you find a trail zigzagging down the western flank to a road that leads back to town.

ARRIVAL AND DEPARTURE ZAOUIA D'IFRANE

By grand taxi If you don't have your own transport, your best bet is to hire an entire *grand taxi* from Aïn Leuh (30min), as no shared ones go this way; you can ask your driver to take the more scenic route (see page 214). A *grand taxi* from Azrou takes around 1hr.

By car The most direct route is from Azrou along the N8,

turning left (east) after around 30min, at the signposted junction. Otherwise, continue on to Mrirt and head northeast on the P7210; after 10km, branch left onto the P7309 to take you through to Zaouia d'Ifrane. However, by far the most scenic route is from Aïn Leuh (see page 214).

ACCOMMODATION AND EATING

Ferme Hachimi 10min walk northwest of town, off the gravel road to Aïn Leuh ☎ 0668 829145. The upstairs of this little farm *auberge* just outside town has been nicely refurbished, and the impressive terrace offers lovely panoramic views. Hot-water showers and Western shared bathrooms are on site. No wi-fi. Hassan, the delightful and knowledgeable owner, also rents out rooms in a little *gîte* in town. HB €€

Gîte Amnay (Chez Fatihi) Down a little alley in the centre of town, off the main road, near the mosque ☎ 0659 546586. The best choice in the village, *Gîte Amnay*

(spelled *Amnaye* on some signs) is set in a comfortable, charming and well-kept family home serving excellent food. The friendly owner can arrange walks in the region and speaks some English. HB €€

Gîte Challal ☎ 0672 063576, ✉ hicham_fakhim@ hotmail.fr. Owned by local Hicham, this little *gîte* has been pleasantly refurbished and, although hobbit-like, has cosy rooms with various sleeping options for individuals or groups. All bathrooms are shared but have good hot-water showers. HB €€

THE ROAD FROM AÏN LEUH

One of the highlights of the entire region is to **drive or cycle** along the 16km gravel backroad that links Aïn Leuh with Zaouia d'Ifrane, the most stunning and scenic route in the Middle Atlas – if not one of the best in Morocco. Exiting Aïn Leuh on the southbound P7311, take the right-hand turn after the road wiggles sharply, about a kilometre from town (look for a slightly dilapidated Zaouia d'Ifrane sign); in the opposite direction, leaving Zaouia d'Ifrane on the road heading northwest out of town, take the sharp right-hand turn after a kilometre or so.

Sources de l'Oum er Rbia and around

40km from Aïn Leuh, 50km from Khenifra • From Aïn Leuh, take the P7311 southbound towards Aguelmane Azigza (50min; signposted); from Khenifra, take the P7306 eastwards, and after 22km turn left (northbound) along the P7311 towards Aguelmane Azigza • Though completely paved, the road to the falls is quite potholed in parts and can become waterlogged and impassable in winter, when you should ask about conditions before you set out; parking is by the concrete bridge over the Rbia, from where it's a 10min walk to the falls

Bubbling along the bottom of a twisting valley, the **Sources de l'Oum er Rbia** are a popular pilgrimage for Moroccans, marking the starting point of the country's longest river – though the back route there from Azrou is equally as interesting, a 35km drive through mountain forest (where you're almost certain to come across Barbary macaques) and open country dotted with grazing sheep and odd pitched-roof farmsteads.

Guides may offer to walk you to the falls, although this is entirely unnecessary given the very clear path that leads up to the gorge. Here, the water comes out in forty or more **springs** (*sources*), many of them marked with café-shelters that are tightly wedged along the banks – a great spot to kick back with a sugary mint tea. You may see locals taking a dip further up the gorge, by a small waterfall, but swimming is not advisable as the currents are extremely strong.

Aguelmane Ouiouane (Wiwane)

13km northeast of Sources de l'Oum er Rbia

There are no accommodation options at Oum er Rbia itself, but you can stay nearby at **Aguelmane Ouiouane** (**Wiwane**), a small lake and scenic resting point, though it is sometimes disturbed by trucks accessing a quarry nearby.

ACCOMMODATION	SOURCES DE L'OUM ER RBIA AND AROUND

Auberge Hbibi Ouiouane Aguelmane Ouiouane (Wiwane) ☎ 0642 206762. Located right along the water's edge of Lake Ouiouane, this immaculate, well-lit guesthouse, run by friendly Khadija, has a handful of quaint rooms (one of which is en suite), plus. an area with facilities for camping. You can grab food here, too (breakfast €, dinner €€). It's possible to walk to l'Oum er Rbia and/ or on to Zaouia d'Ifrane from here – Khadija (who speaks basic English) frequently sets up guided walks for guests. Camping €, double €€

Aguelmane Azigza

35km (around 45min) from Khenifra, 72km (around 1hr 30min) from Aïn Leuh

Beyond the springs at Oum er Rbia, the main road heads off to the west, crossed by a confusing array of *pistes*. After 18km, a turn-off on the left leads 3.5km to the **Aguelmane Azigza**, a dark and deep lake, secluded among the cedar trees. You can camp and swim here, as many Moroccans do, and the area is home to some terrific **wildlife**: the wooded slopes of the lake throng with insects, including the brilliant red and black grasshopper and the small Amanda's blue butterfly, while the forest provides nesting and feeding areas for woodland finches and titmice, including the elusive hawfinch, identified by its heavy bill. There's more birdlife in the waters, too, notably diving duck (mainly grebes and coot), and marbled teal in autumn and winter.

El Ksiba, Imilchil and across the Atlas

Enclosed by apricot, olive and orange groves, the dusty Berber village of **EL KSIBA**, roughly 150 km southwest of Azrou and 4km from the N8, serves primarily as a jumping-off point for the journey to Imilchil and **across the High Atlas**, a dizzying trip that eventually wends its way through the Todra Gorge (see page 397) to Tinghir, at the heart of the great southern oases routes (see page 394).

Aghbala, Ikassene and the Plateau des Lacs

South of El Ksiba, the **R317** (also known here as the Trans-Atlas road) twists through varied forest to cross the Tizi n'Isli pass. At the junction just beyond this, an unnamed road branches eastward to **Aghbala** (65km from El Ksiba), a busy market town with a Wednesday souk, before eventually connecting with the R503 Khenifra–Midelt road – an attractive circuit, surfaced but in a poor state. Staying on the R317, the route south to Imilchil provides a spectacular itinerary, with steep drops off the roadside and constant hairpin climbs and descents. Beyond **Ikassene**, something of a staging post on this route, the road improves as it hauls upwards past Tassent (periodic landslides may block it) to a high valley and a *col*, giving views of the **Plateau des Lacs** – the twin mountain lakes of **Tislit** (near the road) and **Isli** (pristine and much larger, but a 10km walk away), named after a thwarted couple from Berber folklore, whose tears fell to form the two lakes.

Imilchil and beyond

Despite losing some of its striking old buildings, there's still a certain beauty about **IMILCHIL** (115km from El Ksiba), the main draw of the central High Atlas and the destination for many trans-Atlas travellers. The village serves as the regular souk (Friday) for the whole region but is more famous for its September moussem, the so-called **Marriage Market of Aït Haddidou** (see page 217), which attracts streams of tourist traffic up the surfaced road from Rich.

Beyond Imilchil, the R317 runs through fertile land to Bou Azmou, where the R706 heads east to Rich and the Midelt–Er Rachidia road. To fully cross the Atlas, you'll need to press on south to the friendly village of **Agoudal**, at which point the road splits: southwest for the fairly tortuous 6905 *piste* via the Tizi n'Ouano (2750m) to Msemrir and the **Dàdes Gorge** (see page 390); southeast for the paved route via the Tizi n' Tigherhouzine (2706m) to Aït Hani, Tamtatoucht and the **Todra Gorge** (see page 397).

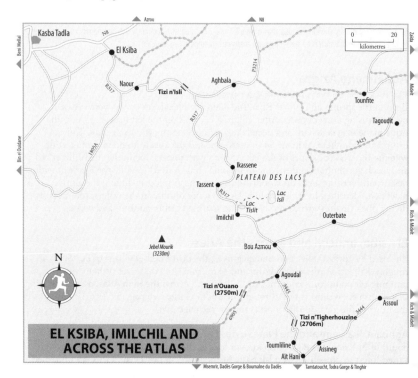

EL KSIBA, IMILCHIL AND ACROSS THE ATLAS

IMILCHIL MOUSSEM: THE MARRIAGE MARKET OF AÏT HADDIDOU

The world-famous **Imilchil Moussem** – the "Fête des Fiancés" or "Marriage Market" – is the mother of all Moroccan mountain souks, a gathering of thirty thousand or more Berbers from the Aït Haddidou, Aït Morghad, Aït Izdeg and Aït Yahia tribes. Over the three days of the September fair (Friday to Sunday), animals are traded; clothes, tools and provisions bought and sold; and distant friends and family members reunited before the first snowfalls isolate their high villages. What makes it especially highly charged, however, is that it is here the region's youngsters come to decide whom they're going to marry.

The tradition derives from colonial times, when the officials from the Bureau des Affaires Indigènes used to insist the Berbers assembled in Agdoul, site of a yearly transhumance fair, to register births, deaths and **marriages**. After independence, the custom was encouraged by the Moroccan tourist office, which the locals blame for propagating the myth that the marriages contracted here were entered into spontaneously. In fact, the matches are nearly all arranged in advance and merely formalized at the moussem.

All the same, the fair provides the perfect opportunity for unmarried Berbers – particularly women trapped at altitude for most of the year – to survey their prospects. Dressed in traditional finery, with hefty jewellery and eyes rimmed with heavy black kohl, the girls parade around in groups, flirting outrageously with the boys as eagle-eyed elder relatives look on. Later, singing, dancing and drumming give both sexes further opportunities to mingle.

Unfortunately, the influx of tourism has seriously compromised the authenticity of the event, and while local life continues with its serious market and marriage elements, a pure **folklore festival** for tourists has been shifted up to Lac Tislit. Neither part is actually at Imilchil, of course, and the date is not always easy to discover – contact the ONMT (see page 58) for details. Rates for beds, food and water (which has to be brought in by lorry) tend to be greatly inflated, so fix prices in advance; it's also advisable to bring plenty of warm clothing as the nights at this altitude (over 2000m) can get bitterly cold by the end of September.

ARRIVAL AND DEPARTURE

By bus You'll need to catch an early bus from Azrou (2 CTM & 9 others daily; 4hr 45min) or Azilal (5 daily; 2hr 30min) to Beni Mellal in order to connect with onward buses from there to El Ksiba (1hr 30min); from El Ksiba, a daily bus runs on to Aghbala (2hr).

By grand taxi *Grands taxis* shuttle from Beni Mellal (see above) to El Ksiba (45min), from where you can connect with other taxis on to Aghbala (1hr 30min) and Imilchil (4hr).

By car Coming from the north, you may prefer to take the

EL KSIBA, IMILCHIL & ACROSS THE ATLAS

P7308, 16.5km south of Khenifra, and the R503 and P3214 to Aghbala, before picking up the R317 – a less tortuous route than the drive from El Ksiba. The road over the Atlas is paved all the way to Tinghir, but you'll need a 4WD for the challenging *piste* between Agoudal and Msemrir, at the northern end of the Dàdes Gorges, plus the proper equipment: a pick and spade for the occasional very rough detour (beware of scorpions when shifting rocks), some warm clothes and a tent for sleeping out at night – Atlas nights are chilly, even in summer.

INFORMATION

Banks and post offices El Ksiba has a bank and a post office (next door to the *Henry IV* hotel), while Imilchil also has a post office in the village centre.

Guides Among the resident guides in Imilchil, the reliable

Bessou Chabou (☎ 0668 564475), who also runs a *pension* in town (see page 218), is qualified both in Morocco and France and can organize local treks and longer trips further afield.

ACCOMMODATION AND EATING

Travelling across the Atlas from El Ksiba can be a time-consuming affair; without your own wheels, you'll probably need to stop for a night along the way. In addition to the

hotels listed below, there are **rooms** to rent in Ikassene and Agoudal, both of which also have a few **cafés** providing simple meals.

EL KSIBA

Henri IV In the Quartier Administrative ☎ 0523 415002. One of the few options in El Ksiba, this small hotel makes a passable place to bed down if you need to stop en route, in attractive surroundings. From opposite the central petrol station, head uphill and bear left after about 300m; if coming by car from the N8, take the left before you enter El Ksiba. €

LAC TISLIT

Auberge Tislite On the west side of Lac Tislit ⓦ auberge-tislite.com. This kasbah-style place is in a marvellously atmospheric spot, with basic rooms, shared showers and excellent home-cooked meals from Malika, the attentive owner. €

IMILCHIL

Auberge Chez Bassou In the centre of the village ☎ 0668 564475, ✉ chezbassou.hotel@com. Budget minimalism with style, this *pension* has spotless bedrooms (most en suite) with just a blanket on the bed by way of decor. Traditional Berber cuisine is served in the sparse restaurant. Bassou himself is a qualified mountain guide, and can organize treks in the area (see page 217). HB €€

Izlane In the centre of the village ⓦ hotelizlane.com. Cheerily decorated little place, with (sporadic) hot showers and a terrace with fine mountain views. The friendly staff can arrange guides and mules for regional treks. HB €€

3

Azilal and around

The perfunctory town of **AZILAL**, just over 60km south of the N8, feels more of an oversized village than provincial capital, yet its loose affiliation of streets have a garrison, banks and hotels, and a Thursday souk. It's a fairly low-key place, and unlikely to feature on anyone's radar were it not conveniently situated for the Cascades d'Ouzoud and the High Atlas villages of the Aït Bouguemez; in addition, the road from Marrakesh that runs north via Azilal is surfaced all the way and makes a far more interesting route north than the N8 across the Tadla plain.

Bin el Ouidane

Grand taxis run to the reservoir from Azilal (25min)

Just under 30km northeast of Azilail lies the **Bin el Ouidane** reservoir, one of the earliest (1948–55) and most ambitious of Morocco's irrigation schemes. The creation of the dam here has changed much of the land – formerly as dry and barren as the phosphate plains to the northwest. Over the last few years, several hotels have cropped up on the lake's shores, offering a scenic chance to get away from it all for a couple of days.

ARRIVAL AND ACTIVITIES

By bus Buses drop off at a patch of waste ground behind the main square in Azilal (backed by a large mosque), near the budget hotels on Av Hassan II. If coming from the north, you'll need to catch an early bus from Azrou (2 CTM & 9 others daily; 4hr 45min) to Beni Mellal in order to connect with onward buses from there to Azilal.

Destinations Beni Mellal (5 daily; 2hr 30min); Demnate (3 daily; 1hr 30min); Marrakesh (3 daily; 3hr 30min); Tabant (daily; 3hr).

By grand taxi Azilal *grands taxis* can be found at a rank beside the bus station; they mostly serve Beni Mellal (see above) and Demnate, but also run to the Cascades d'Ouzoud and to Agouti, Tabant and Zaouia Ahansal in the

AZILAL AND AROUND

Aït Bouguemez.

Destinations Agouti (2hr); Beni Mellal (2hr); Cascades d'Ouzoud (30min); Demnate (1hr); Tabant (3hr); Zaouia Ahansal (3hr 30min).

Trekking Yahya Bouziti (☎ 0666 642183, ⓦ hotel binelouidane.com) is an official trekking guide who runs trips (some with well-known companies) into nearby Aït Bouguemez and the M'Goun Massif.

Watersports In summer, watersports including pontoon boating, jetskiing and kayaking are available at Bin el Ouidane lake; contact *Widiane Suites & Spa* (see page 219) for more information.

ACCOMMODATION AND EATING

Azilal has a couple of decent cheapies, if you need to stop over. With your own wheels (and a bigger budget), the lakeside hotels at **Bin el Ouidane** are an attractive alternative, providing great views of the deep-blue waters.

AZILAL

Assounfou Av Hassan II, 250m east of the town square ☎ 0523 459220. Probably the smartest option in town – the rooms even have carpets and are heated in winter – though still rather shabby. €

Dades Av Hassan II, 300m west (left) of the bus station ☎ 0523 458245. The best of Azilal's budget places, friendly and with a dozen colourful rooms set above a café – though the decor and style in some, particularly the twins, is more hospital-like than hotel. €

Ibnou Ziad Restaurant Av Hassan II, 50m west of the town square. One of the (few) simple café-restaurants that are the only places to eat in Azilal, this down-to-earth spot is fronted by a line of bubbling tajines sold by weight (from €).

BIN EL OUIDANE

Bin el Ouidane Route de Ouaouizeght ☎ 0523 442600, ⓦ hotelbinelouidane.com. Comfortable, fashionably rustic lodge whose wide variety of rooms enjoy lovely views over the reservoir. There's a surprisingly lush little garden with a kidney-shaped pool and a kids' play area. Activities include recommended boat safaris on the Oued Ahansal. BB €€€

L'Eau Vive Route de Ouaouizeght ⓦ dareauvive.com. Modest campsite whose pitches occupy a beautiful grassy

terrace overlooking the river downstream of the dam – an idyllic place to stop for a coffee or lunch at their restaurant (set menu 90dh). There are also homely rooms (some en suite; newer ones are nicer than those in the older house), though the real highlight of a stay is the small wooden rental cabin facing the waterfront. You can also book treks here to nearby Aït Bouguemez and the M'Goun Massif (see above). Camping €, double HB €€, cabin HB €€€

Widiane Suites & Spa Route de Ouaouizeght ⓦ widiane.net. Swish but pricey complex running down the hillside on the reservoir's northern shore. Both the traditional and more modern suites are very spacious; some come with private terraces, all have superb views over Bin el Ouidane. There are three restaurants (one a 20min boat ride away) and a lounge bar, a couple of infinity pools and a plush spa offering Thai and Balinese treatments. The very friendly management can help you organize lots of activities on the *barrage*, from kayaking to jetskiing (see above). BB €€€€

DIRECTORY

Banks The Banque Populaire opposite Azilal's main square has an ATM, and there's a Crédit Agricole 200m to the east.

Post office There's a post office next on Av Hassan II, 300m (west) of the bus station.

Cascades d'Ouzoud

The **Cascades d'Ouzoud** are the most spectacular in Morocco, their amphitheatre of waterfalls falling into pools in a lush valley that remains invisible from the path until the last moment. The wide spread of cataracts at the top isn't entirely natural – water from the river is funnelled through a variety of irrigation channels towards the rim of the falls – but the result is an image that is not too far removed from the Muslim idea of Paradise depicted on gaudy prints throughout the nation. Despite the cascades appearing in every national tourism brochure, the atmosphere remains laidback and relaxing. Throw in the pleasant walks to be had in the locale and, the fact that in late afternoon, arching rainbows appear in the mist around the falls , and you've got even more reason to stay overnight.

The falls

The path to the base of the falls starts from the top of Ouzoud, to the left of the *Dar Essalam*, then zigzags past cafés and souvenir stalls to the great basins below the cascades, where boatmen in rickety rafts row visitors to the **main pool**; the first viewpoint, halfway down the path, is the best place to see the largest rainbows and is close enough to feel the spray on your face. Before you descend, however, take a look at the **lip of the falls**, just past the *Riad Cascades d'Ouzoud* at the top of the village. The little concrete huts here shelter small **watermills**, some still grinding wheat into flour as the river is diverted through the wheels before it plunges over the edge. Although technically forbidden, you can swim in one of the **lower pools** – currents are dangerous in the main pool beneath the falls – and you might spot the occasional Barbary macaque under the oak and pomegranate trees; your best chance is at daybreak or an hour or so before dusk, when they come to drink in the river.

Hikes around the falls

For a memorable short hike (3hr round-trip), head beyond the lower pools to **Tanaghmelt**, the so-called Mexican village (though some guides prefer "Berber village"), a fascinating place connected by semi-underground passages. To get there, follow the path that runs past the lower pools and up to the left, past a farmhouse and on up to the top of the plain; the village is sited on the slopes of the wooded hills to the west, about 1km along the path, which drops to a stream before climbing up towards the houses.

Another path follows the river valley beyond the falls for 3.5km to the **Gramâa Nakrouine**, a series of caves located near the point where the river drops into a tributary flowing from Bin el Ouidane (2hr). Following the path for a further 3.5km beyond here leads to the **Gorges de l'Ouzoud el Abid**, where the valley is at its narrowest and most impressive (5hr round-trip from the caves).

ARRIVAL AND DEPARTURE
CASCADES D'OUZOUD

By bus From Marrakesh, you'll need to get a bus for Azilal and get off at the turning for Ouzoud (3 daily; 3hr to the turn-off), from where it's a 15min *grand taxi* ride. Heading in the other direction, it's easiest to backtrack to Azilal, picking up a bus there to Beni Mellal (5 daily; 2hr 30min) for Azrou (2 CTM & 9 others daily; 4hr 45min) or (if you time it right) direct to Marrakesh (3 daily; 3hr 30min).

By grand taxi There are regular taxis to and from the falls from Azilal (30min).

By car Ouzoud lies 16km down a surfaced road off the R304, a turning 21km southhwest of Azilal. Going to and from Marrakesh, it's quickest to travel along the P3105 via Khemis des Oulad on the N8 (51km of tarred road), though the R304 via Demnate (see page 223) is the more interesting route.

On a tour Several agencies in Marrakesh offer day-trips to the falls, including Toubkal Peaks (✆toubkal-peaks.com), who provide first-rate excursions with a team of local experts.

INFORMATION

When to visit The falls are at their best from March till mid-June (the paths get busy in high summer); they're shrouded in darkness for much of the morning and early afternoon, so aim to visit mid- to late afternoon.

Guides Most of the hotels can organize hikes to Tanaghmelt and the Gorges de l'Ouzoud el Abid, or you can ask at the café at the top of the village, by the turn-off to the *Hôtel Restaurant de France*.

ACCOMMODATION AND EATING

Camping at Ouzoud can be great in spring and early summer: several **campsites** lie at the top of the village, all fairly basic but offering shady spots for tents and motorhomes, while **cafés** on the path downhill have spaces where you can camp for a small fee.

Chellal d'Ouzoud 100m down the path to the falls ☎0523 429180 Nicely renovated kasbah-style hotel, with bright, comfortable rooms and chilled-out communal salons, plus a friendly proprietor who can do the plummiest British accent this side of Eton. The restaurant offers a menu of Moroccan staples from €€. Terrace €, double €€

De France 500m from the top of the village, on the other side of the river ☎0523 429176. Set among olive groves on the opposite side of the river and offering something more tranquil, the *Hôtel de France* has bright rooms, some en suite , and a pleasant garden with a child-friendly swimming pool. €

★ **Riad Cascades d'Ouzoud** Northeast corner of the square at the bottom of the village ✆ouzoud.com. The only upmarket choice in the village, based in a beautifully restored *pisé* house whose rustic chic sits comfortably alongside traditional features. Berber rugs and lovely *tadelakt* bathrooms set off the rooms, which have open fires in the winter. The restaurant (€€ set menu) and reading area are just as cosy. BB €€€

CLIMBING JEBEL M'GOUN

Snowcapped **Jebel M'Goun** (4068m) is Morocco's only summit above 4000m outside the Toubkal massif, and a popular target for trekkers, giving an easy but long ascent from the Tarkeddit plateau, directly south of Agouti. Most guides (see page 222) follow the *piste* southwest out of Tabant, tracing the Oued Arous via the village of Aït Sayd to the shepherd's pastures around **Azib Ikkis** (2hr 30min). The path then climbs up over the **Tizi n'Tarkeddit** (a further 3hr 30min or so), before descending to the refuge at **Tarkeddit**, reached after another 1hr 30min. An early start the next day leads southeast to the pyramid peak of **M'Goun West** (3978m) before curving northeast around the ridge to **Jebel M'Goun** itself (8–10hr return from the refuge).

HELPING HANDS IN THE HAPPY VALLEY

There are over forty **associations** and **cooperatives** in the Aït Bouguemez, more than one for every village in the valley, and each is committed to aiding and enhancing their community, developing the right kind of tourism and maintaining the skills needed to produce traditional crafts. For a valuable insight into valley life that's difficult to otherwise obtain, and the chance to give something back to the local communities, you can visit the cooperatives, a selection of which are listed below.

You can keep supporting the villages of the Aït Bouguemez when you've returned home thanks to the ingenious **Anou** (w theanou.com) project, a community of artisans centred around an online platform that enables artisans, regardless of literacy or education levels, to sell their rugs, jewellery, wooden handicraft and other carefully crafted pieces directly to customers all over the world. Morocco's first "fair trade" movement, it started in the village of Agouti but has since expanded beyond the High Atlas to include artisans from all over the country.

Association Ighrem Agouti w ighrem.e-monsite. com. Principally home to the Atelier de Sculpteur and their beautifully carved boxwood bowls, this very active association (now a part of Anou) is also developing a women's carpet cooperative. Past initiatives include free eye tests for the valley's villagers.

Coopérative Tikniouine Timit ☎ 0678 520880. Small artisan food shop signed down the bottom of a rutted path in Timit, selling locally produced walnut oil, apple jam, honey and cheese.

École Vivante On the road between Timit and the turning to Tabant w ecolevivante.com. Since 2010, this primary school has been providing (free) much-needed formal education for the valley's dispersed villages; you can visit if you reserve ahead of time by emailing info@ecolevivante.com. Donations are appreciated.

Touda Bous-Enna Gîte Azoul, Ighoulene, Aït Bouli w theanou.com/store/76. *Gîte Azoul* (see page 223), in the Aït Bouli Valley, is the home of Touda Bous-Enna, who makes her own stunning Anou-certified carpets and is attempting to teach other local women her trade so they can form an association of their own. Well worth a visit. To get there, take the R302 from just west of Agouti (signed to Aït Bouli) for about 13km; at the second river crossing, you'll enter the village of Ighoulene, where a rough, winding *piste* (signed for *Gîte Azoul*) leads up to the *gîte*.

Aït Bouguemez

The remote and breathtaking **Aït Bouguemez** is second only to Jebel Toubkal in popularity among mountain-lovers, not only for its own unique beauty but also as a base for ascending **Jebel M'Goun**, one of Morocco's highest summits (see page 220). Sometimes referred to as the *Vallée Heureuse* or Happy Valley, this flat, fertile stretch is memorably picturesque, its patchwork of cultivated barley fields spread beneath soaring peaks. Mud-brick villages cling to the lower slopes, which are barren for the best part of the year bar spring, when they are carpeted in wildflowers.

A world away from the well-trodden routes around Jebel Toubkal, the valley has until recently existed in relative isolation – the road in here was only built at the turn of the millennium. This arduous way of life has fostered a remarkable community spirit among the valley's villages and led to the creation of a considerable number of self-help initiatives (see page 221).

Around the valley

Despite the variety of mountainous day hikes on offer, one of the best walks is the simple ramble along the valley floor, dropping in on a few of the villages that dot the landscape between **Agouti**, the westernmost settlement in the valley, and **Tabant**, an administrative centre that's home to the regional Sunday souk.

A track up behind **Timit**, around 5km east of Agouti, leads to the fortified hilltop granary of **Sidi Moussa**, a squat, circular building that doubles as a shrine. Women villagers head up here to receive *baraka* at the tomb of the *marabout* Sidi Moussa, a holy man said to help with infertility – though the 25-minute climb is equally worth it for the spectacular views over the entire valley.

In nearby **Aguerd n'Ouzrou**, faint **dinosaur footprints** can just about be made out on the rocks at the bottom of the slope behind *La Kasbah du M'Goun* (see page 223), the fossilized footfall of 15m-long *Atlasaurus imelakei* (from *imelake*, Arabic for "giant"), which roamed the Aït Bouguemez over 165 million years ago.

Heading along the *piste* that runs past **Imelghas**, the tiny settlement that lies just beyond the turning to Tabant, a side track at Ifrane leads to **Zaouia Oulemsi**, which essentially defines the eastern or upper end of the Aït Bouguemez and is the highest and most remote village in the valley. From here, you can hike down to the seasonal **Lac Izoughar**, dominated by **Jebel Azourki** (3677m) and other big hills, and a favoured pasture for nomads tending their flocks.

Zaouia Ahansal and beyond

Beyond the village of Ifrane, the eastbound *piste* climbs over the **Tizi n'Tirghist** (2629m) to meet up with the backroad from Aït Mohammed (see below) before climbing yet again, over the **Tizi n'Tselli** (2603m), to descend down to **Zaouia Ahansal**. The village was founded in the twelfth century by Sidi Said Ahansal and is home to the *marabout*'s shrine, but its spectacular surrounding landscapes are the real draw: the remarkable tower architecture of **Agoudim**, a village just off the main *piste* to the southeast, is unique north of the Atlas, while **Taghia**, a dozen or so kilometres further south, faces some of the finest gorge and cliff scenery in the country, a rock climber's playground of Dolomitic scope.

The *piste* makes a sharp descent from Zaouia Ahansal to Tamga and the towering limestone walls of **La Cathédrale des Rochers**, a striking rock formation surrounded by Aleppo pines that wouldn't look out of place in Yosemite National Park – a spectacular goat path actually leads to the summit dome. From here, the *piste* continues north to **Tilouguite** (Saturday souk) and ultimately **Ouaouizeght** (100km from Zaouia Ahansal), at the far northeastern end of Bin el Ouidane (see page 218).

ARRIVAL AND DEPARTURE   **AÏT BOUGUEMEZ**

BY CAR

All of these routes are long and slow – make sure you have enough food, petrol and water with you.

By 2WD For now, there's only one way into the Aït Bouguemez. Agouti, the first village in the valley (at its western end), is 69km from Azilal (2hr or so along the R301, depending on your vehicle). Just before the village of Aït Mohammed (50km from Azilal), turn right onto a highly spectacular road that wends its way down to the lower end of the valley; the route is usually passable in a normal car, but it's worth ringing your accommodation in advance to check in early spring or after rain, as "dry" riverbeds cross the road at various parts. You can get as far as Imelghas and Tabant, 8km beyond Agouti, but will need a 4WD to get any further (though note that the passes east of Tabant are often snowbound in winter).

By 4WD With a 4WD, you can continue through Aït Mohammed and follow the (decent) *piste* that drops down to the eastern end of the Aït Bouguemez, turning right for Zaouia Oulemsi (for Lac Izoughar) and Tabant or left for Zaouia Ahansal (85km from Aït Mohammed) and La Cathédrale des Rochers; Zaouia Ahansal can also be reached on a *piste* southeast of Bin el Ouidane via Ouaouizeght and Tilouguite. Alternatively, the R302, a fairly well-maintained *piste* from Demnate, accesses the Aït Bouguemez via Imi n'Ifri and the Aït Bouli.

BY PUBLIC TRANSPORT

By bus A daily minibus service runs from near the mosque in the centre of Azilal to Tabant (3hr).

By grand taxi Taxis from Azilal serve several villages in the Aït Bouguemez, including Agouti (2hr), Tabant (3hr) and Zaouia Ahansal (3hr 30min).

INFORMATION AND GUIDES

Guides Most of the accommodation in the valley can provide guides for treks that range from a 90min walk around the valley's villages to a multi-day ascent of Jebel M'Goun (see page 220), or you can hire one at the Bureau des Guides in Tabant (Mohammed Achari is particularly recommended; ☎0523 459327 or ☎0661 340190) or via the Association Ighrem in Agouti (see page 221). Trekking here can be a serious undertaking, so make sure you are

properly equipped (see page 346).

Guidebooks The best guides to the region (in English) are Des Clark's *Mountaineering in the Moroccan High Atlas* and Michael Peyron's *Great Atlas Traverse*.

Maps West Col's 1:100,000 *Mgoun Massif* ridge map and EWP's 1:160,000 *Azilal - M'Goun* cover the Aït Bouguemez and Jebel M'Goun and are available in the UK.

ACCOMMODATION AND EATING

There are several surprisingly chic places to stay in and around the Aït Bouguemez, and those on cheaper budgets will find dozens of simple *gîtes* spread among the villages, with double rooms from around 150dh.

Dar Ahansal Amazraï, 1km north of Agoudim ⓦ dar ahansal.net. Very comfortable accommodation, particularly given the remote location, in a modern stone-built house set on a lip overlooking the Ahansal valley. Dinners of soups, tajines and the like use garden-fresh produce. The personable owner, a mountain guide himself, can organize treks to Agoudim and Taghia, amongst other places. HB €€€

Dar Itrane Imelghas, ⓦ touda.co.uk. Sensitively constructed guesthouse that blends into the village of Imelghas. Rooms are a bit stark but are comfortable and have duvet-topped beds and heaters in winter – the valley can get *very* cold. Wholesome dinners are served gathered around the log fire in the main salon, and there's a great terrace. *Dar Itrane* is involved in several local projects and contributes a percentage of its profits to the local community. BB €€€

★ **Gîte Azoul** Aït Bouli, ⓦ giteazoul.wordpress.com. This wonderful little rustic lodge is worth venturing into the neighbouring Aït Bouli for the generous hospitality

of its owners, Touda and Lahcen, and sublime views overlooking the valley. The *gîte* offers plenty of rooms (shared bathrooms), a salon with the best vista in the region and a hammam for those who need a solid scrubbing after walking in the region. HB €̄

La Kasbah du M'Goun Aguerd n'Ouzrou ☎ 0662 778148. Set back from the road on a little hillock above the rest of this tiny village and offering traditional rooms with rug-strewn floors (some sleeping up to 5) and six-bed dorms. There's a lovely terrace pool, and the owner, a qualified mountain guide, organizes hikes around the valley and ascents of Jebel M'Goun. Twenty-percent discount when booked through their website. Dorm €̄, double €€€

★ **Touda Ecolodge** Zaouia Oulemsi ⓦ touda.co.uk. Incredibly homely lodge in a remote location at the far eastern end of the Aït Bouguemez, its simple but smart rooms decorated with Berber knick-knacks. Delicious dinners (€€/person) are home-cooked by friendly Naima, whilst breakfast on the terrace is accompanied by superb panoramic views of snowcapped mountains. There's also a library, and a hammam to relax in after a day spent hiking to nearby Lac Izoughar. BB €€€

Demnate

You may have to change buses along the way to Marrakesh at **DEMNATE**, a walled market town 65km or so from Ouzoud and Azilal and 95km from Marrakesh, but there is little incentive to stop unless you can time your visit for the interesting Sunday **souk**, by far the largest in the region, which is held 2km out of town on the Sidi Rahal road. There's also a small daily souk just outside the ramparts, as well as a central market with butchers and bakers, and fruit and vegetable stalls (the area is renowned for its olive oil and almonds), though you could also while away the time between connections poking around the Glaoui-era **kasbah** or the old **Mellah** (until the 1950s, half the population of Demnate were Jews).

Imi n'Ifri

Around 6.5km southeast of Demnate • Take a *grand taxi* from the square 300m beyond Bab el Arabi

The impressive natural bridge of **Imi n'Ifri** spans a yawning gorge, the result of the partial collapse of an underground cave system, and is guaranteed to unnerve anyone of a vertiginous disposition. It's a quiet, untouristed spot, with a seasonal restaurant to sit in and little to do but watch the aerobatic displays of choughs and swifts, or the *sibsib* (ground squirrels) on roadside walls.

ARRIVAL AND DEPARTURE   DEMNATE

By bus Buses drop passengers at a stop 400m to the right of the old town gate, Bab el Arabi.
Destinations Azilal (3 daily; 1hr 30min); Marrakesh (12 daily; 2hr).
By grand taxi *Grands taxis* run from just outside Bab el Arabi to Azilal (1hr) and Marrakesh (1hr 15min)

By car From the Imi n'Ifri bridge, southeast of town, the R307 (the right-hand fork) sets off over the Atlas, emerging eventually on the plains between Ouarzazate and Skoura (see page 386), whilst the R302, the left-hand fork, runs up to the Aït Bouli and the Aït Bouguemez (see page 221).

ACCOMMODATION

★ **Kasbah Timdaf** On the El Attaouia road, 6.5km north of Demnate ⓦ kasbahtimdaf.com. Surrounded

3

CLIMBING JEBEL AYACHI

Seen from a distance, the long wave crest of **Jebel Ayachi** (3747m), 15km southwest of Midelt, appears to curve over the horizon, such is the scale of these dramatic mountains. A guide is recommended (see page 226), but to tackle Ayachi independently you can take a taxi to the springs 2km beyond Tattiouine, from where an easy ascent leads to the many summits of this huge range, long thought to be the highest in Morocco (at 4167m, Toubkal tops it by some 400m).

The only information on this in English is in Des Clark's winter-walking *Mountaineering in the Moroccan High Atlas* and Michael Peyron's *Great Atlas Traverse* guide, which details the whole zone between here and the Toubkal massif; EWP's 1:160,000 *Rich-Midelt* map covers the region.

---

by poppy fields and olive groves, this delightful ecolodge and working farm is far superior to anything in town, an aesthetic blend of stonework and wood ceilings, its spacious, warmly decorated rooms kitted out with Berber blankets and bright wardrobes daubed with Amazigh symbols. The tranquil garden is planted with jasmine and papyrus, and there's a pool and traditional *beldi* hammam.

Village walks, bike rides and cooking lessons are available. They also arrange transfers to and from Marrakesh and surrounding sights. BB €€€

Marrakesh Av Bab el Had ☉ 0523 506996. By far the best option in town itself, the *Marrakesh* has clean, good-value standard rooms, with blanket-clad beds and Western toilets – fairly unusual for Demnate in this price category. €

Midelt and around

At **MIDELT**, reached through a bleak plain of scrub and desert, you have essentially left behind the Middle Atlas. As you approach from the north, the greater peaks of the High Atlas appear suddenly through the haze, rising behind the town to a massive range, the **Jebel Ayachi**, at over 3700m. The sheer drama of the site – tremendous in the clear, cool evenings – is one of the most compelling reasons to stop over. Though the town is comprised of little more than a street with a few cafés and hotels and a small souk, it's a pleasant place to break a journey, partly because so few people do and partly because of its easy-going (and predominantly Berber) atmosphere. Indeed, there is a hint of the frontier town about Midelt, a sense reinforced by the nearby deserted mining settlements of **Mibladene** and **El Ahouli**.

Midelt is so far inland that it has a microclimate of extremes: bitterly cold in winter and oppressively hot in summer. Consequently, one of the best times to visit is autumn, particularly at the start of October, when the town hosts a modest **apple festival**. Year-round, try to arrive for the huge **Sunday souk**, which spreads back along the road towards Azrou and is a fruitful hunting ground for quality carpets.

Souk el Jedid and Souk Tapis

The most interesting section of town is the area around **Souk el Jedid**, a daily fruit and vegetable market located behind the stalls near the bus station. Just to the south of the main souk is the arcaded **Souk Tapis**, or carpet souk, a relaxed place to shop for (superb) rugs – mostly local, geometric designs from tribes of the Middle Atlas. Ask to see the "antique" ones, few of which are actually more than ten or twenty years old, though they are usually the most idiosyncratic and inventive.

Kasbah Myriem

1.5km southwest of Midelt, on the road to Tattiouine

Housed in a former convent building, the *atelier* (workshop) of **Kasbah Myriem** is run by Franciscan nuns, who welcome visitors to see carpets, blankets and beautiful traditional embroidery being made from start to finish by local women. Girls learn techniques from as young as 5 years old (committing them to memory), and women who choose to continue after marriage, rather than focus on domestic duties, are paid for their work. Consequently, the women practise and pass on traditional skills and designs, and also contribute to their own domestic economies. Admittedly, this is not the cheapest place to buy a carpet (though there are also embroidered tablecloths and napkins, handkerchiefs and bags), but your money contributes directly to the local economy and the pieces are of high quality; all "*fait avec amour*", as the nuns put it.

Nôtre Dame de l'Atlas

The convent building itself, **Nôtre Dame de l'Atlas**, is home not to the nuns – who live in a house opposite – but to four elderly Trappist monks, part of the only monastery in North Africa; among their number is Frère Jean-Pierre Schumacher, the only living survivor of the massacre of seven Jesuit monks in Tibhirine, Algeria, in 1996. Visitors are welcome to join in the convent's Mass (times are posted on the metal gate at the entrance but normally held at around 7.15am).

Cirque de Jaffar

The *cirque* loops 79km southwest of Midelt and takes a good half-day to complete

The classic route around Midelt is the **Cirque de Jaffar**, a good *piste* that leaves the Midelt–Tattiouine road, 25km southwest of town, to edge its way through a hollow in the foothills of Jebel Ayachi. The views of the High Atlas mountains are truly dramatic, and the rugged road ensures an element of adventure – this is very different countryside to that immediately around Midelt. Here, eagles soar above the hills and mule tracks lead down to valleys dotted with the occasional kasbah. The route eventually loops back to the Midelt–Azrou road after 34km – turn right, onto the 3426, near the Maison Forestière de Mitkane.

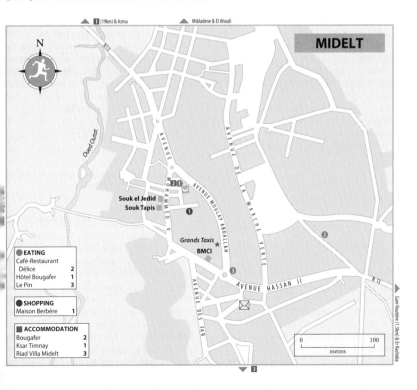

MIDELT

EATING
Café-Restaurant Délice	2
Hôtel Bougafer	1
Le Pin	3

SHOPPING
Maison Berbère	1

ACCOMMODATION
Bougafer	2
Ksar Timnay	1
Riad Villa Midelt	3

El Ahouli and Mibladene

The S317 heads 15km northeast of Midelt to Mibladene, where the road (the 3419) deteriorates and the tarmac virtually disappears as you approach El Ahouli, 11km further on (4WD recommended for this stretch due to risk of flash floods); beyond El Ahouli, a rough track continues downstream to Ksabi from where you can complete the circuit to Midelt by the N15 and N13 • *Grands taxis* charge around 400dh for a return trip to El Ahouli, including a 2hr stopover at the mines (some refuse, though, due to the poor condition of the track)

Less than an hour's drive from Midelt, on the banks of the Oued Moulouya where it emerges from its spectacular gorge, lie the derelict mines of **El Ahouli**. From the turn of the twentieth century, and long before on a more modest scale, the locals extracted silver and lead from the rocky terrain here; in 1979, around three thousand people still worked the mines but all had gone by the mid-1980s. You don't have to be an industrial archeologist to be impressed by the ruins that lie strewn along both sides of the river: tunnels, aqueducts, aerial ropeways, barrack-like living quarters and, above all, the mine buildings themselves, pressed high against the cliff face like a Tibetan monastery. Tracks cut across the sides of the gorge – first used by mules, then a mineral-line railway passing through the tunnels – and everywhere there is rusting machinery.

Modest excavations are still being worked at **Mibladene** (appropriately, "Our Mother Earth" in Berber), around halfway to El Ahouli. In some respects, the desolate rust-red landscape around Mibladene, and the barren and tortuous route onwards from here, are reason enough to do the trip: the bleak plateau where Mibladene is located leads to a narrow and picturesque gorge, negotiated by frequent river crossings on rattling wooden bridges.

ARRIVAL AND INFORMATION   MIDELT

By bus Midelt's *gare routière* is on the road to Er Rachidia. Destinations Azrou (1 CTM & 6 others daily; 2hr 25min–4hr 30min); Er Rachidia (2 CTM daily, others frequent; 2hr–2hr 30min); Erfoud (1 CTM & 1 other daily; 3hr 45min); Fez (1 CTM, 1 Supratours & 6 others daily; 5hr 10min–6hr 30min); Marrakesh (3 daily; 8hr); Meknes (3 CTM & 1 other daily; 4hr); Merzouga (1 daily; 4hr 30min); Ouarzazate (1 daily; 7hr); Rich (1 CTM daily, others frequent; 1hr–1hr 30min); Rissani (1 CTM daily, others frequent; 4hr 15min).

By grand taxi Taxis depart regularly from the rank on Av Moulay Abdallah.
Destinations Azrou (2hr); Er Rachidia (2hr); Fez (3hr);

Meknes (3hr).
By car It's 125km from Azrou to Midelt (the R13/N13), along a magnificent stretch of the Middle Atlas; a possible break on the journey, 50km from Azrou, is the eerily beautiful Aguelmane Sidi Ali, the largest of the region's many mountain lakes (1km from the N13). A *piste* leads southwest from Midelt, beyond the Cirque de Jaffar, all the way to Imilchil, but with a standard car it's easier to push on to Rich, 75km to the south, and take the surfaced road, the R706, west from there.
Services There's a BMCI bank with an ATM on Av Hassan II; the post office is further down the road and a block south (Mon–Fri 8am–4.15pm).

TOURS

Tours *Ksar Timnay* (see page 226) specializes in 4WD excursions to the El Ahouli mines, Jebel Ayachi and around   the Cirque de Jaffar as well as trekking.

ACCOMMODATION   SEE MAP PAGE 225

Midelt has a reasonable spread of accommodation, but hotels are often full by mid-afternoon in peak season, so arrive early or make a reservation in advance.
Bougafer 7 Bd Mohammed V ☎0535 583099. A friendly, modern place above a café (see page 227), with rooms distributed over two floors, some renovated and en suite, others more basic with shared facilities (hot showers cost extra). There are great views from the roof terrace, where a delicious breakfast of homemade pancakes and omelettes is served. €̄
Ksar Timnay On the N13, 19km northwest of Midelt

ⓦ ksar-timnay.com. Very popular (and educational) spot, with friendly management and excellent facilities including a restaurant and seasonal swimming pool. Rooms are in either a motel-style block or a newer luxury faux-kasbah ("*Riad Mimouna*"), all with a/c and satellite TV, and there's a pleasant camping area. There are plenty of cultural activities on offer, and treks and 4WD excursions can also be arranged (see page 226). Camping €̄, double BB €̄€̄, riad BB €̄€̄€̄
Riad Villa Midelt Pl Verte, ⓦ riadvillamidelt.com. On the southern fringes of town, this traditional-style modern "villa" is comparatively pricey but is a cut above anything

else in Midelt – and the pool is a godsend if you're here at any time approaching summer. The spacious en suite rooms enjoy a/c, and some also have a fireplace, while the Moroccan dishes served up in the restaurant are consistently good. The friendly owner can offer plenty of advice on onward routes. BB €€

EATING

SEE MAP PAGE 225

Café-Restaurant Délice 125 Bd Palestine Outhalli. A good choice for a quick snack, this light and airy spot next to Hotel Safari Weekend does salads, pizzas and shawarma kebabs but is best known for its (cheap) paninis, stuffed to the brim with fillings such as merguez sausage. €

Hôtel Bougafer 7 Bd Mohammed V. The restaurant below the hotel of the same name (see page 226) is immensely popular with locals for its tender beef brochettes and rotisserie chicken (both good value), though there's also a reasonable set menu (€€) as well. €

Le Pin Av Hassan II. Part of a tourist complex, with a hall-like dining room and a (more relaxing) bar and café in the gardens – a pleasant spot for breakfast or a light lunch of simple brochettes, chicken tajine or omelettes. €

SHOPPING

SEE MAP PAGE 225

Maison Berbère 15 Rue Mohammed Amraoui. The friendly owners of this carpet boutique (no link to the mini chain that has branches in the south) are happy to talk you through a variety of quality Berber rugs from the Middle and High Atlas (their family is from Imilchil), unfurling plenty of geometrically patterned weaves but with less of the hard-sell than you might be used to at similar shops.

3

The Atlantic coast: Rabat to Essaouira

HASSAN II MOSQUE, CASABLANCA

The Atlantic coast: Rabat to Essaouira

This five-hundred-kilometre stretch of Atlantic coastline takes in Morocco's urban heartland and accounts for close to a fifth of the country's total population. It's an astonishingly recent growth along what was, until the French Protectorate, a neglected strip of coast. The region is dominated by the country's elegant, orderly administrative capital, Rabat and the dynamic commercial capital, Casablanca. Keep heading south, and you'll encounter some delightfully low-key coastal resorts, including El Jadida, Oualidia and Essaouira. This is the most Europeanized part of Morocco, where you'll see middle-class people in particular wearing Western-style clothes and leading what appear, on the surface at least, to be quite European lifestyles.

The fertile plains inland from Rabat (designated *Maroc Utile*, or "Useful Morocco", by the French) have been occupied and cultivated since Paleolithic times, with Neolithic settlements on the coast to the south, notably at present-day **Temara** and **Skhirat**, but today it is French and post-colonial influences that dominate in the main coastal cities. Don't go to Casa – as **Casablanca** is popularly known – expecting some exotic movie location; it's a modern city that looks very much like Marseilles, the French seaport on which it was modelled. **Rabat**, too, which the French developed as a capital in place of the old imperial centres of Fez and Marrakesh, looks markedly European, with its cafés and boulevards, though it also has some of Morocco's finest and oldest monuments, dating from the Almohad and Merenid dynasties. If you're on a first trip to Morocco, Rabat is an ideal place to get to grips with the country. Its Westernized streets make an easy cultural shift and it's an excellent transport hub, well connected by train with Tangier, Fez and Marrakesh. Casa is maybe more interesting after you've spent a while in the country, when you'll appreciate both its differences and its fundamentally Moroccan character.

Along the coast are a large number of **beaches**, but this being the Atlantic rather than the Mediterranean, tides and currents can be strong. **Surfing** is a popular sport along the coast and Essaouira is Morocco's prime resort for **windsurfing**.

The coast to Rabat

Although by no means an idyllic stretch of sand, the coast from **Kenitra to Rabat** still has a few decent beaches and a couple of attractions that are worthy stops along this very busy section of the national highway.

Kenitra

KENITRA was established by the French as Port Lyautey – named after the Resident General – with the intention of channelling trade from Fez and Meknes. It never quite took off, however, losing out in industry and port activities to Casablanca, despite the rich farming areas of its hinterland. Today, it has a population of around 400,000, employed mainly in paper mills and a fish cannery. It's livelier than most Moroccan towns of its size, with a noticeably friendly atmosphere that goes some way to make up for the paucity of sights. There are also several **beaches** within easy reach.

THE BEACH AT ESSAOUIRA

Highlights

❶ Hassan Mosque, Rabat Never completed, the minaret of this Almohad mosque is a masterpiece of Islamic architecture. See page 240

❷ Chellah, Rabat As beautiful a ruin as you could imagine, with Roman remains and royal tombs from the Merenids. See page 242

❸ Colonial architecture, Casablanca Downtown Casa is a living monument to French 1930s Art Deco styles. See page 254

❹ Hassan II Mosque, Casablanca One of the world's largest, Hassan II's great mosque

can (unusually for Morocco) be visited by non-Muslims. See page 260

❺ Cité Portugaise, El Jadida Walk round the ramparts of this unique UNESCO World Heritage Site, and check out the cistern where Orson Welles filmed *Othello*. See page 267

❻ Oualidia oysters North Africa's finest, best eaten fresh at one of this friendly coastal town's lagoonside restaurants. See page 271

❼ Essaouira Morocco's most relaxed seaside town, with a Medina that's easy to explore and a wide bay perfect for kite- and windsurfers. See page 275

HIGHLIGHTS ARE MARKED ON THE MAP ON PAGE 232

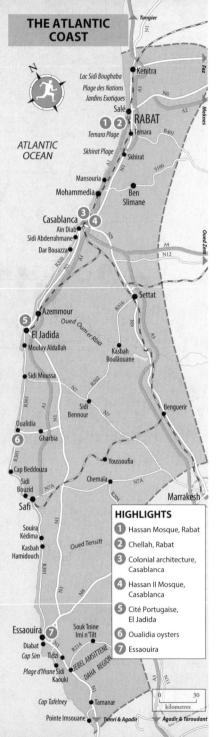

THE ATLANTIC COAST

ATLANTIC OCEAN

HIGHLIGHTS

1. Hassan Mosque, Rabat
2. Chellah, Rabat
3. Colonial architecture, Casablanca
4. Hassan II Mosque, Casablanca
5. Cité Portugaise, El Jadida
6. Oualidia oysters
7. Essaouira

Kenitra has two main streets: **Avenue Mohammed V**, the town's main artery, which runs east to west, and **Avenue Mohammed Diouri**, running north to south. The central square, dominated by the *baladiya* (town hall), is **Place de Municipalité**, two blocks north of Avenue Mohammed V and three blocks east of Avenue Mohammed Diouri.

ARRIVAL AND DEPARTURE   KENITRA

By train There are two train stations: Kenitra station, the most central, at the southern end of Av Mohammed Diouri; and Kenitra Medina, one stop north, off the eastern end of Av Mohammed V and near the bus station.

Destinations Asilah (8 direct & 2 connecting daily; 2hr 30min); Casa Port (roughly hourly 5.50am–10.10pm; 1hr 40min); Casa Voyageurs (1–2 hourly 4.25am–9.20pm; 1hr 40min); Fez (hourly 9.48am–11.50pm; 2hr); Marrakesh (9 daily; 5hr); Mohammedia (1–3 hourly; 1hr 15min); Rabat (1–3 hourly; 35min); Tangier (8 direct & 2 connecting daily; 3hr 15min).

By bus All companies, including CTM, operate from the main *gare routière*, 200m north of Av Mohammed V and three blocks east of Pl de Municipalité.

Destinations Casablanca (10 daily; 2hr 30min); Chefchaouen via Ouezzane (5 daily; 3hr); Larache (15 daily; 1hr 45min); Rabat (roughly hourly; 1hr); Souk el Arba du Rharb (10 daily; 1hr 15min); Tangier (5 daily; 3hr).

By grand taxi *Grands taxis* for Souk el Arba du Rharb (change here for Chefchaouen) operate from the *gare routière*, while those for Rabat leave from Av Mohammed Diouri, one block north of Av Mohammed V.

Destinations Rabat (45min); Souk el Arba du Rharb (1hr).

ACCOMMODATION

Ambassy 20 Av Hassan II ☎ 0537 379978. Basic but central; each room has a little laundry room as well as a bathroom, and some have a/c. There are also two smoky bars (one with a pool table) and a mediocre fish restaurant. BB €€

★ **Mamora** Pl Administrative ☎ 0537 371775, ⓦ mamorakenitra.com. Art Deco-era, business-class hotel with slightly small but good-value, modern rooms. There's a pleasant swimming pool, comfortable bar and reasonable restaurant, albeit with a limited menu. BB €€€

De la Poste 307 Av Mohammed V ☎ 0537 377769. The best of the town's cheapies, this friendly little place is about halfway up the avenue and close to a number of cafés. The tiled rooms (ask for extra blankets in winter) are bright and well kept, and simply furnished with comfortable beds and antique wardrobes. Rooms are en suite. €

Relax Parc d'Activite Commerciale Marjane ⓦ relax maroc.com. Kenitra's newest hotel, part of a chain, with a pool and restaurant, a couple of kilometres south of town near the Marjane hypermarket. €€

EATING, DRINKING AND NIGHTLIFE

Café Metropole Cnr Av Mohammed V & Rue Sebta. Classy, comfortable establishment on the main street, with seating on a street-side wooden deck or inside the non-smoking, female-friendly a/c interior, decorated with pictures of New York. The menu ranges from breakfast and light meals to pizza, pasta dishes and ice creams. €€

River Club Rue el Jahid ⓦ riverclub.ma. True to its name, this popular café-restaurant commands a beautiful, sweeping view over the Oued Sebou. There are plenty of tables both inside and outside, and the menu offers panini, pasta and Moroccan standards. Mosquitoes are sometimes a problem on summer evenings. €€

DIRECTORY

Banks Banks can be found along avenues Mohammed V and Mohammed Diouri; Currency Exchange Point, Rue Al

Mountanabi (opposite *Hôtel la Rotonde*).
Post office Av Hassan II, just off Pl Administrative.

Lac Sidi Boughaba

12km southwest of Kenitra • Free • ☎ 0537 747209 • Bus #15 from Kenitra (35min)

The birdlife-rich but rubbish-strewn **Lac Sidi Boughaba** is a narrow freshwater lake divided by a central causeway that gives access to the lake's southern edge. This is also where you'll find the **National Centre for Environmental Education** (CNEE), focused mainly on environmental education for local schoolchildren. The best viewing points for the lake's birdlife are from the causeway or the viewing deck at the education centre.

Plage des Nations

17km north of Rabat • Bus #28 runs hourly between Plage des Nations and Av Moulay Hassan in Rabat via Bab Khemis in Salé (50min); *grands taxis* operate from Salé during summer (30min)

4

The **Plage des Nations** (also called Sidi Bouknadel) was named after the foreign diplomats and their families who started swimming here in the 1970s – and continue to do so. With a popular corniche promenade and overlooked by a large residential golf estate, it has a very relaxed, friendly and cosmopolitan feel about it and is unusual in that young Moroccan women feel able to come out here for the day. The beach itself is relatively clean, with big, exciting waves but dangerous currents, and is patrolled by lifeguards during the summer months.

Museé Dar Belghazi

N1 Highway, directly opposite the turn-off for Plage des Nations (Sidi Bouknadel) • Charge

The **Museé Dar Belghazi** is home to four rooms of manuscripts, nineteenth-century carpets and textiles, eighteenth- and nineteenth-century ceramics, and examples of woodwork, armour and jewellery. There's not much by way of explanatory text in the museum other than a small booklet in French and Arabic, and it's expensive, but if you have a particular interest in Moroccan or Islamic art, then the trip out here is worthwhile.

ACCOMMODATION AND EATING   PLAGE DES NATIONS

Firdaous Plage des Nations ☎ 0537 822131. A 1970s-style resort hotel that seems to be stuck in a time warp, located right on the beach – all rooms have a sea view, and

you can get a suite for not much more than the price of a room. There's a swimming pool, plus a bar, restaurant and snack bar. BB €€

Les Jardins Exotiques de Bouknadel

N1 Highway, 6km south of Plage des Nations, 13km north of Rabat • Charge • ⓦ jardinsexotiques.com • Bus #9 (to Kenitra) from Bab Chellah and Bab el Had in Rabat (30min)

The **Jardins Exotiques de Bouknadel** are a very pleasant and tranquil respite from the everyday traffic noise and commotion just metres from their walls. A compact botanical haven, the gardens were laid out by French horticulturalist Marcel François in the early

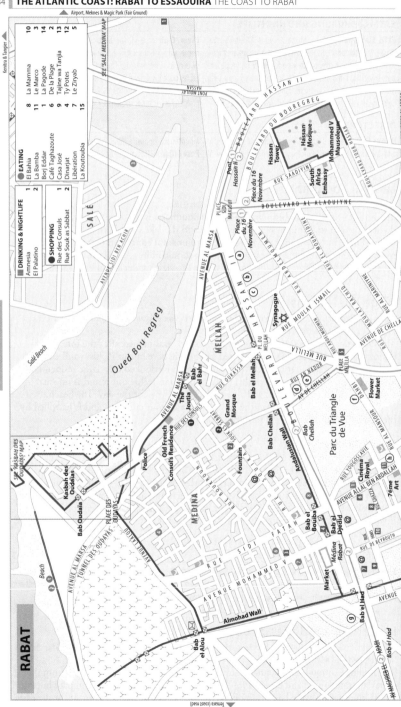

DRINKING & NIGHTLIFE
Amnesia 1
El Palatino 2

SHOPPING
Rue des Consuls 1
Rue Souk as Sabbat 2

EATING
El Bahia 8
La Bamba 11
Borj Eddar 1
Café Taghazoute 6
Casa José 9
Dinarjat 7
Libération 15
La Koutoubia

La Mamma 10
Le Marco 3
La Pagode 14
De la Plage 2
Tajine wa Tanjia 13
Ty Potes 12
Le Ziryab 5

RABAT

PUBLIC TRANSPORT

Bus # 35 (Salé, Magic Park)	h
Bus # 3 (Agdal)	i
Bus # 12, # 13 (Salé)	f
Bus #2, #9, #33	g
Kenitra Grands Taxis	c
Khémisset Grands Taxis	b
Meknes Grands Taxis	d
Sale Grands Taxis	e
Sale Buses	a

ACCOMMODATION

Al Maghrib al Jadid	3	El Mamounia	9
Bélère	15	Malak	5
Caleche d'Or	14	Riad el Maâti	2
Capitol	6	Royal	11
Central	12	Sofitel Rabat	
Le Dawliz	1	Jardin des Roses	16
Dorhmi	4	Splendid	8
Gaulois	10	Velleda	13
Majestic	7		

1950s, fell into decline in the 1980s and were rescued in 2003 by the king's "Fondation Pour la Protection de l'Environnement", being assiduously renovated before a grand reopening in 2005.

Entering the gardens, colour-coded paths direct visitors across a series of bamboo bridges and through a sequence of regional creations. There's a **Brazilian rainforest**, a formal **Japanese garden**, a Mexican cactus garden, and a piece of **French Polynesia**, with palm trees all round and flashes of bright red flowers. The last of the series is an **Andalusian garden** with a fine collection of Moroccan plants. There's also a **terrarium**, and a **museum** detailing the gardens' transformation.

Worth a visit at any time of the year but particularly delightful in spring or early summer, the gardens are popular with school groups during the week and families at weekends.

Rabat

Capital of the nation since 1912, elegant and spacious **RABAT** is the very image of an orderly administrative and diplomatic centre. Lacking the frenetic pace of Morocco's other large cities, Rabat is sometimes harshly referred to as "provincial". Sure enough, there are times when it's hard to find a café open much past ten at night, but there's other times when the city comes out from its conservatism and even makes a little noise, such as during the Festival of Rhythms each May. Befitting its regal status, Rabat – along with neighbouring **Salé** – has some of the most interesting historic and architectural monuments in the country, and the fact that the local economy does not depend on tourist money makes exploring these attractions a great deal more relaxed than cities like Fez and Marrakesh.

Brief history

The Phoenicians established a settlement at Sala, around the citadel known today as **Chellah**. This eventually formed the basis of an independent Berber state, which reached its peak of influence in the eighth century, developing a code of government inspired by the Koran but adapted to Berber customs and needs. It represented a challenge to the Islamic orthodoxy of the **Arab** rulers of the interior, however, and to stamp out the heresy, a *ribat* – the fortified monastery from which the city takes its name – was founded on the site of the present-day kasbah. The *ribat*'s presence led to Chellah's decline – a process hastened in the eleventh century by the founding of a new town, **Salé**, across the estuary.

The **Almohads** rebuilt the kasbah and, in the late twelfth century, **Yacoub el Mansour** ("the Victorious") created a new imperial capital here. His reign lasted almost thirty years, allowing El Mansour to leave a legacy that includes the superb **Oudaïa Gate** of the kasbah, **Bab er Rouah** at the southwest edge of town, and the early stages of the **Hassan Mosque**. He also erected over 5km of fortifications, though it is only in the last sixty years that the city has expanded to fill his circuit of *pisé* walls.

Notoriety and pirates

After Mansour's death, Rabat's significance was dwarfed by the imperial cities of Fez, Meknes and Marrakesh, and the city fell into neglect. Sacked by the Portuguese, it was little more than a village when, as New Salé, it was resettled by seventeenth-century Andalusian refugees. In this revived form, however, it entered into an extraordinary period of international piracy and local autonomy. Its corsair fleets, the **Sallee Rovers**, specialized in the plunder of merchant ships returning to Europe from West Africa and the Spanish Americas, but on occasion raided as far afield as Plymouth and the Irish coast – Daniel Defoe's Robinson Crusoe began his captivity "carry'd prisoner into Sallee, a Moorish port".

The Andalusians, owing no loyalty to the Moorish sultans and practically impregnable within their kasbah perched high on a rocky bluff above the river, established their own pirate state, the **Republic of the Bou Regreg**. They rebuilt the Medina below the kasbah in a style reminiscent of their homes in the Spanish city of Badajoz, dealt in arms with the English and French, and even accepted European consuls, before the town finally reverted to government control under Moulay Rachid, and his heavy-handed successor, Moulay Ismail.

A capital once again

Unofficial piracy continued until 1829 when Austria took revenge for the loss of a ship by shelling Rabat and other coastal towns. From then until the French made it their colonial **capital**, moving it from the more conservative and harder to defend Fez, Rabat-Salé was very much a backwater. Upon independence in 1956, and perhaps also concerned about the influence wielded by Fez, Mohammed V decided to keep Rabat as the country's capital. It's taken a few generations, but the city now seems comfortable with this weighty responsibility and, of late, has begun to promote itself as more than just a residence for the diplomatic and governmental corps. A number of large-scale developments, including a revamped riverside promenade and a new tramway system, were pushed through specifically to benefit the local people.

The Medina

Rabat's **Medina** – all that there was of the city until the French arrived in 1912 – is a compact quarter, wedged on two sides by the sea and the river, on the others by the twelfth-century Almohad and seventeenth-century Andalusian walls. It's open and orderly in comparison to those of Fez or Marrakesh, and still essentially the town created by Muslim refugees from Badajoz in Spain, but with its external features intact, its way of life seems remarkably at odds with the government business and cosmopolitanism of the Ville Nouvelle.

The Medina's plan is typical of others in Morocco, with a main market street – **Rue Souika** and its continuation **Souk es Sebbat** – running beside the Grand Mosque, and behind it a residential area scattered with smaller souks and "parish" mosques. The buildings, characteristically Andalusian, like those of Tetouan or Chefchaouen, are part stone and part whitewash, with splashes of yellow and turquoise and great, dark-wood studded doors.

From **Boulevard Hassan II**, half a dozen gates and a series of streets give access to the Medina, all leading more or less directly through the quarter, to emerge near the kasbah and the hillside cemetery. On the west side, the two main streets – **Avenue Mohammed V** and **Rue Sidi Fatah** – are really continuations of Ville Nouvelle avenues, though, flanked by working-class café-restaurants and cell-like hotels, their character is

THE MARSHAL'S MEDINAS

The existence of so many ancient, walled Medinas in Morocco – intact and still bustling with life – is largely due to **Marshal Hubert Lyautey**, the first of France's Resident Generals, and the most sympathetic to local culture. In colonizing Algeria, the French had destroyed most of the Arab towns, and Lyautey found this already under way when he arrived in Rabat in 1912, but, realizing the aesthetic loss – and the inappropriateness of wholesale Europeanization – he ordered demolition to be halted and had the Ville Nouvelle built outside the walls instead. His precedent was followed throughout the French and Spanish zones of the country, inevitably creating "native quarters", but preserving continuity with the past. Lyautey left Morocco in 1925 but when he died in 1934 he was returned and buried in a Moorish monument in Rabat until 1961, when his body was "repatriated" to Paris.

CARPETS IN RABAT

Rabat **carpets**, woven with very bright dyes (which, if vegetable-based, will fade), are a traditional cottage industry in the Medina, though they're now often made in workshops, one of which you can see on the kasbah's *plateforme* (see page 239). Some of the traditional carpets on sale, particularly in the shops, will have come from further afield. They are officially graded at a special centre just off Rue des Consuls – to the right as you climb towards the kasbah.

The upper, terraced end of Rue des Consuls, in Rabat's Medina, is a centre for **rug and carpet shops**. On Monday and Thursday mornings, a **souk** for carpets new and old takes place here, and on the adjoining street of Souk es Sebbat.

---

immediately different. Entering along either street, past a lively, modern food market and a handful of stalls selling fruit, juice and snacks, you can turn right along **Rue Souika**, which is dominated by textiles and silverware along the initial stretch, giving way to shoe stalls as you approach the Grand Mosque. The shops are all fairly everyday, and not, for the most part, geared to tourists.

Grand Mosque
Souk es Sebbat • Entry to the mosque is forbidden to non-Muslims

There are few buildings of particular interest in the Medina, as most of the medieval city – which predated that of the Andalusians – was destroyed by Portuguese raids in the sixteenth century. The **Grand Mosque**, founded by the Merenids in the fourteenth century, is an exception, though it has been considerably rebuilt – its minaret, for example, was completed in 1939. Opposite, there is a small example of Merenid decoration in the stone facade of a public **fountain**, which now forms the front of an Arabic bookshop.

The Mellah

The **Mellah**, the old Jewish quarter, lies to the east of Rue Oukassa, and remains the poorest and most run-down area of the city. It was only designated a Jewish quarter in 1808 – Jews previously owned several properties on Rue des Consuls, to the north – and no longer has a significant Jewish population. If you can find a local guide, you may be able to look into some of its seventeen former **synagogues**. None of these function: the only active synagogue in the city is a modern building, one block from here, at the northern end of Rue Moulay Ismail.

With its meat and produce markets, the Mellah looks a somewhat uninviting and impenetrable area, but it is worth wandering through towards the river. A daily **joutia**, or **flea market**, spreads out along the streets below Souk es Sebbat, down to Bab el Bahr. There are clothes, pieces of machinery, and general bric-a-brac, with the odd bargain occasionally to be found.

Rue des Consuls

Like the Mellah, **Rue des Consuls** used to be a reserved quarter – the only street of the nineteenth-century city where European consuls were permitted to live. Many of the residency buildings survive, as do a number of impressive merchants' *fondouks* – most in the alleys off to the west (the French consul's residence, now rather run-down, is at the end of an alley called Impasse du Consulat de France). Shopping is pleasantly hassle-free, and there are some good **jewellery shops**, with a mix of Middle Eastern and European designs at good prices.

Kasbah des Oudaïas

The site of the original *ribat* and citadel of the Almohad, Merenid and Andalusian towns, the **Kasbah des Oudaïas** continues to stand sentry over the mouth of the Oued

RABAT **THE ATLANTIC COAST: RABAT TO ESSAOUIRA** 239

Bou Regreg. Only 150 metres from end to end, the kasbah is an evocative, village-like quarter of whitewashed houses with brightly coloured doors and is a delight to explore.

Bab Oudaïa

The kasbah's main gate, **Bab Oudaïa**, is from the Almohad period, like so many of Morocco's great monuments. Built around 1195, it was inserted by Yacoub el Mansour into a line of walls already built by his grandfather, Abd el Moumen. The walls in fact extended well to its west, leading down to the sea at the edge of the Medina (excavations are now revealing some of these), and the gate cannot have been designed for any real defensive purpose – its function and importance must have been ceremonial. It would have been the heart of the kasbah, its chambers acting as a courthouse and staterooms, with everything of importance taking place nearby. The **Souk el Ghezel** – the main commercial centre of the medieval town, including its wool and slave markets – was located just outside the gate, while the original sultanate's palace stood immediately inside.

The interior

The main entrance to the kasbah is through a gateway to the right of Bab Oudaïa itself (which is usually closed except when used for exhibitions). From here, **Rue Jamaa** (Street of the Mosque) runs straight down to a broad terrace commanding views of the river and sea. Along the way, you pass by the **Kasbah Mosque**, the city's oldest, founded in 1050, though rebuilt in the eighteenth century by an English renegade known as Ahmed el Inglisi – one of a number of European pirates who joined up with the Sallee Rovers. El Inglisi was also responsible for several of the forts built below and round the seventeenth-century **plateforme**, originally a semaphore station, on which was built an eighteenth-century warehouse, with views across to Salé.

Access into the kasbah is also possible via a horseshoe arch at the bottom of the stairway, close to the entrance to Musée des Oudaïa (see page 239). This leads (straight ahead) through a door in the palace wall to Rue Bazo, where a right turn will take you down to the *Café Maure* (see page 246), a fine place to retreat, high on a terrace overlooking the river.

Andalusian Garden

Kasbah; access is via a small gateway facing Av al Marsa, or from Rue Bazo within the kasbah • Free

The grounds of the old palace (now the Musée des Oudaïa) contain a formal **Andalusian Garden** constructed by the French in the twentieth century. True to Andalusian tradition, it features deep, sunken beds of shrubs and flowering annuals. Historical authenticity aside, it's a delightful place, full of the scent of fruit trees, daturas, bougainvillea and a multitude of herbs and flowers. It has a modern role too, as a meeting place for women, who gather here in small groups on a Friday or Sunday afternoon. On its north side is a small museum, dedicated in principle to jewellery, but it has been closed for some years for "restoration" and it is not clear when or whether it will reopen.

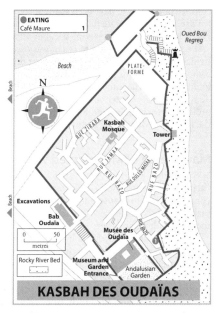

KASBAH DES OUDAÏAS

OUED BOU REGREG'S SANDBANK HANDICAP

The guns of the forts and the *plateforme* in Rabat's **kasbah** once regularly echoed across the estuary in Salé. The **Oued Bou Regreg** ("Father of Reflection River") is quite open at this point and it would appear to have left the corsair fleets vulnerable, harboured a little downstream, where fishing boats today ferry people across to Salé. In fact, a long **sandbank** lies submerged across the mouth of the estuary – a feature much exploited by the shallow-keeled pirate ships, which would draw the merchant ships in pursuit, only to leave them stranded within the sights of the city's cannon. The sandbank proved a handicap in the early twentieth century and diverted commercial trade to the better-endowed Casablanca.

The beach

Accessed from Av al Marsa or via a set of steep steps from the kasbah's *plateforme*

Rabat's local **beach** is crowded throughout the summer, as is the Salé strip across the water, though neither is very inviting, and you'd be better off at the more relaxed (and less testosterone-charged) sands at the Plage des Nations or Temara Plage (see pages 233 and 251). However, there's often a fun wave for bodysurfers, although stand-up surfers also manage to catch a few waves most days.

Hassan Mosque and Tower

Bd Tour Hassan

The most ambitious of all Almohad buildings, the now-ruined **Hassan Mosque** was, in its time, the second largest mosque in the Islamic world, outflanked only by the one in Smarra, Iraq. Though little remains today apart from its vast tower, or minaret, its sheer size still seems a novelty.

The mosque was begun in 1195 – the same period as Marrakesh's Koutoubia and Seville's Giralda – and was designed to be the centrepiece of Yacoub el Mansour's new capital in celebration of his victory over the Spanish Christians at Alarcos, but construction seems to have been abandoned on his death in 1199. Its extent must always have seemed an elaborate folly – Morocco's most important mosque, the **Kairaouine** in Fez, is less than half the Hassan's size, but served a much greater population.

The mosque's **hall**, roofed in cedar, was used until the Great Earthquake of 1755 (which destroyed central Lisbon) brought down its central columns. Never rebuilt, some of the columns have been partially restored and at least offer some sense of the building's size. The imposing **tower** ("le Tour Hassan") has remained standing, and dominates almost every view of the capital. Some 50m tall in its present state, it would probably have been around 80m if finished to normal proportions – a third again of the height of Marrakesh's Koutoubia.

Mausoleum of Mohammed V

Bd Tour Hassan • Free

Facing the Hassan Tower – in an assertion of Morocco's historical independence and continuity – is the **Mausoleum of Mohammed V**, begun on the king's death in 1961 and inaugurated six years later. Hassan II and his brother, Moulay Abdellah, are buried here too, alongside their father.

The mausoleum was designed by Vietnamese architect Vo Toan. With **zellij mosaics** rising from a marble floor to a ceiling of hand-carved cedar wood and gold leaf, its spiralling designs pay homage to traditional Moroccan techniques. Visitors file past fabulously costumed royal guards (who are happy to be photographed) and Fez-topped security agents (who aren't) to an interior balcony; the **tomb** of Mohammed V, carved from white onyx, lies below, an old scholar often squatting beside it, reading from the Koran.

Ville Nouvelle

French in construction, style and feel, the **Ville Nouvelle** provides the main focus of Rabat's life, above all in the cafés and promenades of the broad, tree-lined Avenue Mohammed V. There's a certain grandeur, too, in some of the Mauresque colonial public buildings around the main boulevards, which were built with as much desire to impress as those of any earlier epoch.

Bank al-Maghreb Museum

Rue du Caire; entrance at the side of the Bank al Maghrib • Charge; audio-guide (French and Arabic) available • ☎ 0537 216472

Numismatists will enjoy the modern and interesting **Bank al-Maghreb Museum**; it's quite plush and very well laid out, with **coins** dating back to the Phoenicians and the Berber kingdom of Mauretania arranged in chronological order and accompanied by informative text via touch-screen computers. There's also an exhibit housing over a hundred **paper notes** in slide-out display cases.

Almohad walls and gates

More or less complete sections of Yacoub el Mansour's **Almohad walls** run right down from the kasbah to the Royal Palace and beyond – an extraordinary monument to El Mansour's vision. Along their course four of the original **gates** survive. Three – **Bab el Alou**, **Bab el Had** and **Bab Zaer** – are very modest. The fourth, **Bab er Rouah** (Gate of the Wind), is on an entirely different scale, recalling, and in many ways rivalling, the Oudaïa. If you walk between Bab er Rouah and the much-restored Bab Zaer, you'll pass a series of modern gates leading off to the vast enclosures of the **Royal Palace** – which is really more a collection of palaces, built mainly in the nineteenth century. To enter, you will need to register your passport in the office located through the second door on the left if you're walking alongside the walls on Avenue Moulay Assan.

Bab er Rouah

Av Moulay Hassan • Interior chambers are used for exhibitions • Free

Contained within a massive stone bastion, **Bab er Rouah** achieves the tension of movement – with its sun-like arches contained within a square of Koranic inscription – and a similar balance between simplicity and ornament as the Bab Oudaïa. The west side, approached from outside the walls, is the main facade, and must have been designed as a monumental approach to the city; the shallow-cut, floral relief between arch and square is arguably the finest anywhere in Morocco. Inside, you can appreciate the gate's archetypal defensive structure – the three domed chambers aligned to force a sharp double turn.

Archeological Museum

23 Rue Ifni el Brihi • Charge

Rabat's **Archeological Museum** is the most important in Morocco. Although small – surprisingly so in a country which saw substantial Phoenician and Carthaginian settlement and three centuries of Roman rule – it houses an impressive collection of Roman-era **bronzes**.

The bronzes are displayed in a special annexe with a separate entrance; although included in the entry fee, it's sometimes closed when the pieces are on loan to other museums. The artefacts date from the first and second centuries AD and were found mainly at the provincial capital of **Volubilis** (near Meknes), together with a few pieces from Chellah and the colonies of Banasa and Thamusida. Highlights include superb figures of a **guard dog and a rider**, and two magnificent **portrait heads**, reputedly those of Cato the Younger (Caton d'Utique) and Juba II – the last significant ruler of the Romanized Berber kingdoms of Mauretania and Numidia before the assertion of direct imperial rule. Both of these busts were found in the House of Venus at Volubilis (see page 200).

Back in the main building, there are showcases on two floors; each contains finds from different digs, of little interest unless you have already visited the area – or plan to do so. Captions are in Moroccan Arabic and French only.

Chellah

Cnr Av Yacoub Al Mansour & Bd Moussa Idn Nossair • Charge

The most beautiful of Moroccan ruins, **Chellah** is a startling sight as you emerge from the long avenues of the Ville Nouvelle. Walled and towered, it seems a much larger enclosure than the map suggests. The site has been uninhabited since 1154, when it was abandoned in favour of Salé across the Bou Regreg. But for almost a thousand years prior to that, Chellah (or Sala Colonia, as it was known) had been a thriving city and port, one of the last to sever links with the Roman Empire and the first to proclaim Moulay Idriss founder of Morocco's original Arab dynasty. An apocryphal local tradition maintains that the Prophet himself also prayed at a shrine here.

Under the Almohads, the site was already a royal burial ground, but most of what you see today, including the gates and enclosing wall, is the legacy of "The Black Sultan", **Abou el Hassan** (1331–51), the greatest of the Merenids. The **main gate** has turreted bastions creating an almost Gothic appearance. Its base is recognizably Almohad, but each element has become inflated, and the combination of simplicity and solidity has gone. The Kufic inscription above the gate is from the Koran and begins with the invocation: "I take refuge in Allah, against Satan."

To your left coming from the entrance, signposted "Site Antique", are the main **Roman ruins**. They are of a small trading post dating from 200 BC onwards, are well signposted and include a forum, a triumphal arch, a Temple of Jupiter and a craftsmen's quarter.

The Sanctuary

From the main gate, the **Islamic ruins** are down to the right, within an inner sanctuary approached along a broad path through half-wild gardens. The most prominent feature is a tall stone-and-tile **minaret**, a ludicrously oversized stork's nest usually perched on its top. Indeed, Chellah as a whole is a good spot for **birdwatching**, especially in nesting season.

The **sanctuary** itself appears as a confusing cluster of tombs and ruins, but it's essentially just two buildings: a mosque, commissioned by the second Merenid sultan, Abou Youssef (1258–86), and a *zaouia*, or mosque-monastery, added along with the enclosure walls by Abou el Hassan. You enter directly into the *sahn*, or courtyard, of **Abou Youssef's Mosque**, a small and presumably private structure built as a funerary dedication. It is now in ruins, though you can make out the colonnades of the inner prayer hall with its mihrab to indicate the direction of prayer. To the right is its minaret, now reduced to the level of the mosque's roof.

Behind, both in and outside the sanctuary enclosure, are scattered **royal tombs** – each aligned so that the dead may face Mecca to await the Call of Judgement. Abou Youssef's tomb has not been identified, but you can find those of both Sultan **Abou el Hassan** and his wife **Shams ed Douna** (Morning Sun). El Hassan's is contained within a kind of pavilion whose external wall retains its decoration, the *darj w ktarf* motif set above three small arches in a design very similar to that of the Hassan Tower. Shams ed Douna has only a tombstone – a long, pointed rectangle covered in a mass of verses from the Koran. A convert from Christianity, Shams was the mother of Abou el Hassan's rebel son, Abou Inan, whose uprising led to the sultan's death as a fugitive in the High Atlas during the winter of 1352.

The Zaouia

The **Zaouia** is in a much better state of preservation than the sanctuary, its structure, like Abou el Hassan's medersas, that of a long, central court enclosed by cells, with a smaller oratory or prayer hall at the end. There are fragments of zellij tilework on some of the colonnades and on the minaret, giving an idea of its original brightness, and there are traces, too, of the mihrab's elaborate stucco decoration. Five-sided, the **mihrab** has a narrow passageway (now blocked with brambles) leading to the rear – built so that pilgrims might make seven circuits round it. This was once believed to give the equivalent merit of the *hadj*, the trip to Mecca: a tradition, with that of Mohammed's visit, probably invented and propagated by the *zaouia*'s keepers to increase their revenue.

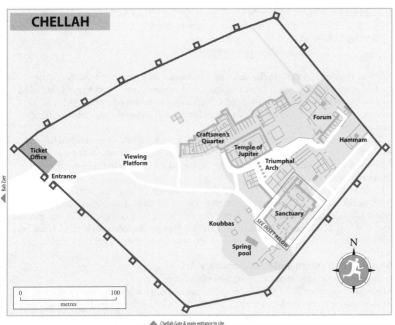

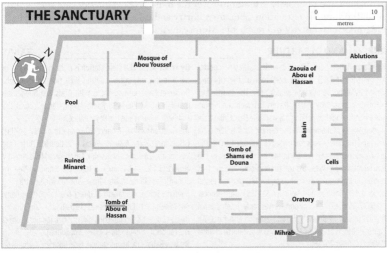

4

RABAT AIRPORT SHUTTLE BUS TIMES

Monday From Rabat noon, 4.05pm & 6.30pm; from airport 2.20pm, 6.55pm & 9.20pm.

Tuesday From Rabat 1.25pm, 2.45pm, 3.45pm, 4.40pm, 5.50pm & 6.40pm; from airport 4.15pm, 5.35pm, 6.05pm, 7.05pm, 7.35pm 8.40pm & 9.30pm.

Wednesday From Rabat 3pm; from airport 5.20pm.

Thursday From Rabat 1pm, 3.40pm, 4.30pm, 5.30pm & 6.15m; from airport 3.20pm, 6.30pm, 7.05pm, 8.40pm & 9.15pm.

Friday From Rabat 11am, 4.05pm & 6.30pm; from airport noon, 1.20pm, 6.55pm & 9.20pm.

Saturday From Rabat 1.25pm, 2.45pm, 3.15pm, 4.20pm, 5.50pm & 6.35pm; from airport 4.15pm, 5.25pm, 5.35pm, 7.05pm, 7.35pm 8.40pm & 9.25pm.

Sunday From Rabat noon; from airport 2.20pm.

Off to the right and above the sanctuary enclosure are a group of **koubbas** – the domed tombs of local saints or *marabouts* – and beyond them a **spring pool**, enclosed by low, vaulted buildings. This is held sacred, along with the eels which swim in its waters, and women bring hard-boiled eggs for the fish to invoke assistance in fertility and childbirth.

At the far end of the sanctuary, you can look down a side valley to the **Bou Regreg estuary**. From here, you can appreciate that this site was destined, from early times, to be settled and fortified. The site was easy to defend and the springs provided water in times of siege.

If you're here in **spring**, you'll see hundreds of flowers in bloom as well as birdlife, with storks nesting and the egrets roosting. The site is rarely busy except on Fridays, when Moroccans are admitted for free – families come to spend the day in the gardens, and children play among the ruins. The annual **Jazz au Chellah festival** takes place here over five days each September, with the 1500-seat capacity often sold out each night.

Museum of Modern and Contemporary Art

Cnr avs Moulay Hassan & Allal Ben Abdallah • Charge • ⓦ museemohammed6.ma

Opened in October 2014 after a decade of planning, with backing from the king himself and at a reported cost of over 200 million dirhams, the strikingly all-white **Museum of Modern and Contemporary Art** is a work of art in itself. A number of permanent and temporary exhibitions cover the multi-levelled interior, and there's also an auditorium, art restoration laboratory, library and café. Information accompanying the works is exclusively in French and Moroccan Arabic.

ARRIVAL AND DEPARTURE   RABAT

By plane Rabat–Salé airport (ⓦ onda.ma/Nos-Aéroports/ Aéroport-Rabat-Salé) is 7km northeast of the city and served by a shuttle bus and *grands taxis*. The shuttle bus (45min), operated by Stareo, travels between the airport and a nondescript bus parking bay opposite Rabat Ville train station, on Av Mohammed V. The current tariff is 20dh one way, and the timetable is somewhat complicated, to say the least (see page 244). A sign in the terminal displays the official rates for *grands taxis* (up to six people) The modern terminal has bureaux de change and ATMs, plus car rental desks, which include Avis (ⓣ 0537 831198) and Europcar (ⓣ 0537 724141). The airport serves only international flights, mainly to Brussels, Madrid, London and Paris. Air France's office is at 281 Av Mohammed V, just north of *Hôtel Balima* (ⓣ 0537 707580).

By train Rabat Ville train station is right in the middle of the Ville Nouvelle, a few minutes' walk from many hotels. On street level are two banks with ATMs and Budget car rental (ⓣ 0537 705789). Rabat Agdal station serves the southern suburbs and the Royal Palace.

Destinations Asilah (8 direct & 2 connecting daily; 3–4hr); Casablanca Port (6.30am–9pm 1–2 hourly; 1hr); Casa Voyageurs (26 daily; 1hr 10min); Casablanca Mohammed V airport (5.15am–7.45pm 1–3 connecting hourly; 2hr–2hr 30min); Fez (19 daily; 2hr 30min–3hr 10min); Kenitra (1–3 hourly; 35min); Marrakesh (9 direct & 3 connecting daily; 4hr 25min–5hr 10min); Meknes (19 daily; 2hr–2hr 30min); Oujda (2 direct & 1 connecting daily; 10hr); Tangier (8 direct & 2 connecting daily; 3hr 35min– 5hr 30min).

By bus Rabat's main bus station, Gare Routière Kamra is on

Bd Hassan II (the N1 highway), 3km southwest of the centre. CTM operates from its own station 400m further southwest along Bd Hassan II. Local buses ply the route between the bus station and Bab el Had (bus #30 picks up right outside the terminal, buses #17 and #41 stop just behind it), or you can get a *petit taxi* (around 20dh). The closest tramway stop is Ibn Rochd (Line 1), on Pl Ibn Iznassen about 1.5km southeast along Av Ibn Rochd.

Destinations Agadir (7 CTM & over 10 others daily; 9–10hr); Al Hoceima (2 CTM daily; 9–10hr); Casablanca (over 20 CTM & very frequent others daily; 1hr 30min); Chefchaouen (1 CTM & 2 others daily; 5hr); Essaouira (over 10 daily; 8hr 30min); Fez (17 CTM daily & others hourly 5am–7pm; 3hr 30min); El Jadida (over 10 daily; 4hr); Marrakesh (10 CTM daily & others hourly; 4hr 30min–6hr); Meknes (14 CTM daily & others hourly; 2hr 30min); Nador (2 CTM & over 5 others daily; 9hr); Ouarzazate (1 CTM & 5 others daily; 9hr 30min); Safi (8 daily; 6hr); Tangier (7 CTM and over 10 others daily; 4–5hr); Oujda (5 CTM & 2 others daily; 9hr 30min); Tetouan (7 CTM & over 10 others daily; 5–6hr).

By grand taxi Shared *grands taxis* between Rabat and Casablanca operate from just outside the main bus station. Those for Fez, Meknes and Salé congregate at the Shell petrol station on Bd Hassan II, next to *Hôtel Bou Regreg* and opposite Bab Chellah.

Destinations Casablanca (1hr 20min); Fez (2hr 30min); Meknes (1hr 50min); Salé (15min).

GETTING AROUND

By bus While the tram is the easiest way to get around Rabat, there are a few local bus services that can still be very useful (see page 245).

By tram A modern, a/c tram system (daily 6am–10pm; ⓦ tram-way.ma) links Rabat and Salé. Line 1 runs east to west via Agdal and both Rabat Ville and Salé train stations, while Line 2 runs northwest to southeast via Bd Hassan II and Salé bus station. Both cross the Oued Bou Regreg and stop near Rabat's Hassan Mosque and Salé's Bab Mrissa. Tickets cost 6dh and can be purchased from ticket vendors at each station or on-board conductors. The ticket allows 1hr travel from the time of your first in-tram validation, provided no two journeys (in either direction) are the same.

By taxi *Petits* and *grands taxis* can be found on Bd Hassan II and by the train station; *petits taxis* are not allowed to run between Rabat and Salé.

By car In addition to the offices at the airport and train station (see above), car rental companies in town include: Avis, 7 Rue Abou Faris al Marini (☎ 0537 721818); Europcar, 25 bis Rue Patrice Lumumba (☎ 0537 722328).

INFORMATION

Tourist information The Conseil Régional du Tourisme have a website at ⓦ visitrabat.com.

ACCOMMODATION   SEE MAP PAGE 234

Hotel space can be tight in midsummer, and especially July, when budget-priced rooms in particular are at a premium, so it's a good idea to book ahead. A couple of cheapies aside, most of the better hotels are in the Ville Nouvelle.

MEDINA AND KASBAH

Al Maghrib al Jadid 2 Rue Sebbahi ☎ 0537 732207. Basic and clean, though the decor is a garish combination of candy-pink and bright blue. Hot showers are available in the morning only (extra charge). The owners also run the *Hôtel Marrakech*, down the street at no.10, with exactly the same prices and colour scheme. €̅

Dorhmi 313 Av Mohammed V ☎ 0537 723898. Family owned and managed, and nicely positioned, just inside Bab el Djedid. The clean and simple first-floor rooms open inwards to a central courtyard, though there's no common sitting area. Separate hot shower (extra charge) and squat toilet. €̅

USEFUL LOCAL BUS ROUTES

Note that the services departing from around **Bab el Had** are heavily used by locals and the ensuing noise and confusion often requires a steady head to both locate your desired service and successfully embark the bus.

#2 from opposite Bab el Had to the intercity bus station.

#3 from just by Rabat Ville train station down Avenue Fal Ould Ouemir in Agdal to Avenue Atlas.

#9 from opposite Bab el Had to Salé, Jardins Exotiques, Museé Dar Belghazi and the Plage des Nations turn-off.

#12 and **#13** from just off Place Melilla to Salé.

#33 from opposite Bab el Had to Temara Plage.

#35 from Avenue Allal Ben Abdallah to Salé and Magic Park.

Riad el Maâti 15 Rue Sidi el Maâti ⓦ riadelmaati.com. Meticulously restored by the French-Moroccan owner-managers, this riad has whitewashed walls throughout and high-ceilinged rooms that are simply but very tastefully furnished, with modern, spacious bathrooms. Meals are served in a dining room with fireplace or on the wide rooftop terrace, accessible (as is one of the rooms) by wheelchair thanks to that Medina rarity – a lift. BB €€€€

VILLE NOUVELLE

Bélère 33 Av Moulay Youssef ⓦ belere-hotels.com. This is a comfortable, well-positioned hotel with impressive management and friendly staff. The rooms exude a touch of luxury with soft, neutral tones throughout, plush carpeted floors, spacious marble bathrooms, and heavy curtains to soften the outside street noise. The larger suites also have a small sitting area and balcony, plus there are a couple of restaurants (the breakfast buffet can often disappoint), a piano bar and a nightclub. BB €€€€
Caleche d'Or 11 Av Moulay Youssef ☎ 0537 701319. Across the road from Rabat Ville station and with a good selection of cafés and restaurants close by, this is one of the city's better two-star options. Accessed from a steep marbled staircase, the tiled rooms are bright and clean with a/c, sparkling modern bathrooms and satellite TV. €€
Capitol 34 Av Allal Ben Abdallah ☎ 0537 731236. One of the more modern two-star options in the city centre and about a 10min walk from Rabat Ville station. Accessed by a handy lift, all rooms are tiled with their own bathroom and satellite TV; those overlooking the busy street offer a balcony, while those at the rear are quieter and better value. A first-floor restaurant offers a menu of Moroccan standards and room service. €€
Central 2 Rue Al Basra ☎ 0537 707356. One of the better cheapies, conveniently located for restaurants, banks and Rabat Ville station. Most rooms have patterned colonial floor tiles and some have showers (otherwise they're 10dh), with hot water mornings and evenings only. €
Gaulois Cnr Rue Hims & Av Mohammed V ☎ 0537 723022. Friendly old hotel with a spacious grand entrance and balustraded stairway. While not exactly ageing graciously, it's still pretty good value for money. There's

guarded parking (30dh) out front. €
Majestic 121 Bd Hassan II ⓦ hotelmajestic.ma. This long-established hotel, accessed by a flight of stairs, offers rather characterless but bright and clean rooms; some overlook the Medina, but these can also be noisy. Limited guarded parking is available. €€
Malak Pl Melilla ⓦ malakhotel.com. One of the better mid-range options, located a short walk from Bab Chellah. The contemporary styled rooms are simply but tastefully furnished, with spacious modern bathrooms – request a room facing away from busy Pl Melilla. A ground-level café-restaurant offers a basic breakfast as well as an all-day menu of Moroccan standards. BB €€
El Mamounia 10 Rue Mamounia ☎ 0537 724479. A three-floor climb but rewarded with a good-value cheapie, homely in a slightly kitsch kind of way. Hot showers (shared) are extra. €
Royal Cnr Rue Amman & Av Allal Ben Abdallah ⓦ royalhotelrabat.morocco-ma.website/fr. A long-standing mid-range hotel with comfortable and reasonable rooms – not huge, but refurbished, clean and well maintained. The best ones overlook the attractive Parc du Triangle de Vue. BB €€
Sofitel Rabat Jardin des Roses Cnr avs Doustour & Imam Malik, Souissi ⓦ sofitel.com. The rooms in this deluxe five-star have a modern designer touch with all the mod cons you'd expect for the price, and all have a balcony overlooking the vast gardens or the city. Located in the suburb of Souissi just beyond the royal palace, it's a 10min petit taxi drive from the Medina. BB €€€€
Splendid 8 Rue Ghazza ☎ 0537 723283. Another budget traveller's favourite, this friendly old hotel centres on a pleasant courtyard with flowers and banana trees. The rooms are high-ceilinged and fairly simple but functional, with firm mattresses and big, old wardrobes; some come with a sink while others have their own showers (hot water evenings only). €
Velleda 106 Av Allal Ben Abdallah ☎ 0537 769531. Located on the fifth floor (fortunately there's a lift), the rooms here are pretty basic but clean, with tiled floors, small bathrooms, TV and a desk. The staff are friendly and the location is good, with a ground-floor café and convenience store. €

EATING
SEE MAPS PAGES 234 AND 239

For a capital city, Rabat is pretty quiet, but it does have some excellent restaurants – many of them moderately priced or inexpensive – plus loads of good cafés. As ever, the cheapest places to eat are in the Medina, just inside the walls on Av Mohammed V.

MEDINA AND KASBAH
El Bahia Bab el Bouiba, 4 Bd Hassan II. Standard Moroccan fare such as tajines, kebabs and salads, in a pleasant courtyard, upstairs or on the pavement outside, though service can be slow. €

Café Maure Rue Bazo, Kasbah. Adjoining the kasbah's Andalusian Garden is this small shaded terrace-café. It's a great spot to take a break and look out over the river mouth and beyond to Salé. Tea and coffee are on offer, and there are cakes too. €
Café Taghazoute 7 Rue Sebbahi. This clean and airy café serves simple dishes, including delicious fried fish, plus decent omelettes which makes it a good option for breakfast. It tends to be busy with office workers at lunchtime. €
Dinarjat 6 Rue Belgnaoui, off Bd el Alou ⓦ dinarjat.ma. This palatial restaurant with fine Moroccan dishes and

musical entertainment, in a seventeenth-century mansion at the northern end of the Medina, makes a good affordable choice if you wish to spoil yourself). Licensed. €€€

Libération 256 Av Mohammed V. One of the city's better budget restaurants, with generous portions of couscous every day. Downstairs offers good people watching while upstairs is quieter and has more seating. €€

Le Ziryab 10 Impasse Ennajar, signposted from Rue des Consuls, ⊚restaurantleziryab.com. Very popular among execs, diplomats and politicians, with good reason: the five-course menu is first-class Moroccan fare. Add the accompaniment of traditional music and the exquisite interior, and this is worth a special treat. Ask for a lantern-led escort from the Medina entrance, and come hungry – each course is almost a meal in itself. Licensed. €€€€

VILLE NOUVELLE

La Bamba 3 Rue Tanta, a small side street behind the Hôtel Balima. Serving up European and Moroccan dishes, as well as good-value three-course set menus, in a pleasant space and accompanied by good service. Licensed. €€

Casa José 279 Bd Mohammed V ⊚www.legrand comptoir.ma. A classy and spacious tapas bar, with a small range of good tapas, mainly seafood-based, to accompany your beer or wine, as well as more substantial courses if you want them. €€

La Koutoubia 10 Rue Pierre Parent, off Rue Moulay Abdelaziz. Home to a bar and, with a separate entrance through a quaint wood-and-glass extension, an old-style 1950s restaurant, serving excellent Moroccan dishes; try the honeyed lamb and almond tajine. The service – watched over by an English-speaking patron who's been there from the beginning – is very good. Licensed. €€

La Mamma 6 Rue Tanta. A typically dark and cosy pizzeria, with a varied menu of Italian classics including wood-fired pizza and char-grilled meats. Next door is *La*

Dolce Vita (same hours), owned by the same patron and offering luscious Italian-style ice cream. Licensed. €

La Pagode 13 Rue Baghdad. *La Pagode* has been around for a while now and remains one of the more popular Asian restaurants in town, with a large menu of mainly Chinese and Vietnamese dishes, and sushi too. They also have a takeaway and delivery service. Licensed. €€

Tajine wa Tanjia 9 Rue Baghdad. Little restaurant with a pleasant atmosphere, accompanied most nights by live *oud* playing. The menu is mainly well-presented Moroccan food of a consistently high standard, with a range of tajines (including vegetarian), tanjia (jugged beef or lamb), and couscous on FriLicensed. €€

★**Ty Potes** 11 Rue Ghafsa ⊚typotes.com. A very popular French deli-bistro with a cosy non-smoking interior (with wi-fi) or leafy, pleasant courtyard, serving up light meals (*galettes*, *crêpes*, *tartines*) as well as items from a daily blackboard menu. The deli offers a wide selection of cheeses, cured meats, jams and sauces, and the drinks menu includes cider. Reservations recommended. Licensed. €€

BEACH AREA

On the beachfront below the Kasbah des Oudaïas are two popular seafood restaurants, accessed via a path from the kasbah's *plateforme* (see page 239) or by a short side road off Av al Marsa. Both are licensed and offer great sea views.

Borj Eddar Plage de Rabat ⊚borjeddar.com. Set within seventeenth-century walls and popular with tour groups, this classy restaurant offers a menu that is surprisingly good value. Besides the expected plethora of seafood dishes, including a tummy-stretching platter for two; there's also a good choice of meat tajines and couscous. €€€€

De la Plage Plage de Rabat. Perhaps the less fancy of the two beach restaurants, though the menu still offers a wide choice of fish, mostly priced by weight and all of it rather average in quality. But the view over the water is astounding. €€€

DRINKING AND NIGHTLIFE SEE MAP PAGE 234

The city's nightlife is pretty sedate. Outside of the main hotels and restaurants, **bars** are few and far between, while many **nightclubs**, notably those around Pl de Melilla, are little more than pick-up joints, though you'll need to dress up to get in.

Amnesia 18 Rue de Monastir, ⊚facebook.com/ AmnesiaRabat. This American-themed club pumps out a

mix of Euro and Arabic pop but rarely gets very full.

El Palatino 133 Av Allal Ben Abdallah. Very popular Spanish-style tapas bar. The in-house DJs know their stuff and there's nightly drink specials as well as regular themed parties, such as Karaoke Mondays. Good fun without too much pretentiousness.

SHOPPING SEE MAP PAGE 234

Limited but rewarding shopping opportunities are on offer in both the **Medina** and **kasbah**, as shops stock all the same handicrafts as those in Marrakesh and Fez. The relative **lack of hassle** and hard bargaining makes shopping here quite pleasant.

Rue des Consuls Medina. The Medina's main tourist street, with shops selling handicrafts from other parts of Morocco, such as leatherwork from Marrakesh and pottery

from Fez, along with some locally made items such as lamps and carpets. Rabat used to be a major producer and seller of carpets, and there's still a carpet auction held on Rue des Consuls every Mon and Thurs morning.

Rue Souk as Sabbat Medina. A covered extension of Rue Souika, this short stretch houses a number of small shops selling jewellery, *jellabas*, *babouches* and musical instruments.

DIRECTORY

Banks & exchange Most are along avs Allal Ben Abdallah and Mohammed V. BMCE, 340 Av Mohammed V has a bureau de change (daily 8am–8pm), and two ATMs. Bureaux de change include Currency Exchange Point, Av Moulay Youssef between hotels *Bélère* and *Caleche d'Or* and WafaCash, cnr Av Mohammed V & Rue Ghaza. CIH bank, 4 Av Maghreb el Arabi, has a foreign exchange ATM.

Doctors and hospitals Dr Youssef Alaoui Belghiti, 6 Pl des Alaouites (☎0537 708029); Dr Mohammed el Kabbaj, 8 Rue Oued Zem (☎0537 764311); Dr Taghride Jamaleddine Harou (Female, English-speaking), 2nd floor, 2 Av Allal Ben Abdallah (☎0537 734739). For emergencies call the Service Médical d'Urgence on ☎0537 737373.

Embassies Algeria, 46 Bd Tariq Ibn Ziad (☎0537 767668); Canada, 66 Av Mehdi Ben Barka, Souissi (☎0537 544949, ⓦmorocco.gc.ca); Mauritania, 6 Rue Thami Lamdouar, Souissi (☎0537 656678); South Africa, 34 Rue des Saadiens (☎0537 689163, ⓦgov.za); UK, 28 Av SAR Sidi Mohammed, Souissi (☎0537 633333, ⓦwww.gov.uk/world/organisations/british-embassy-rabat); US, Km 5.7, Av Mohamed VI, Souissi (☎0537 637200, ⓦusembassy.gov/morocco). Australia is represented by the Canadian embassy. The nearest Irish representation is in Casablanca (see page 265).

Festivals Festival Mawazine ("Festival of Rhythms"; ⓦmawazine.ma) runs over 7–10 days each June in a number of venues around the city, including the Théâtre National Mohammed V, Rabat's riverside promenade, and Salé beach. The nightly performances usually cover a wide range of genres, from classical Andalusian to Arabic pop and Western rock. Jazz au Chellah , a joint effort between the EU and Morocco, takes place over 5 days sometime between June and Sept. Performances take place each evening at the Chellah (see page 242).

Golf The Dar es Salaam Royal Golf Club, 9km out of Rabat on Zaers Rd (ⓦwww.royalgolfdaressalam.com) is one of the country's finest, with two eighteen-hole and one nine-hole courses designed by Robert Trent-Jones.

Pharmacies Renaissance, 352 Av Mohammed V, just north of the post office.

Police The main station is on Av Tripoli, near the cathedral (☎0537 720231), with a police post at Bab Djedid and another on Rue des Consuls, and one in the kasbah.

Post office Cnr avs Mohammed V and Jean Jaurès, opposite the Bank Al Maghrib.

Salé

Though now essentially a suburb of Rabat, **SALÉ** was the pre-eminent of the two right through the Middle Ages, from the decline of the Almohads to the pirate republic of Bou Regreg (see page 237). Under the Merenids, as a port of some stature, it was endowed with monuments such as its superb **Medersa Bou Inan**.

ZAOUIAS, MOUSSEMS AND MARABOUTS

Round Salé's Grand Mosque, and over to the northwest, you can view (but only enter if you are Muslim) a trio of interesting buildings.

The first is the **Zaouia Sidi Ahmed el Tijani**, founder of the Tijaniyya Sufi order and whose elaborate portal faces the Grand Mosque and Medersa. *Zaouias* are a mix of shrine and charitable establishment, maintained by their followers, who once a year or more hold a moussem, a pilgrimage festival, in the saint-founder's honour.

The most important of Salé's moussems is the "**wax moussem**" of its patron saint, Sidi Abdallah Ben Hassoun, whose *zaouia* stands at the end of the Rue de la Grande Mosquée, by the cemetery. His moussem, held on the eve of Mouloud (the Prophet's birthday; see page 45), involves a spectacular procession through the Medina with candle bearers (a hereditary position) carrying huge and elaborate wax candles in the form of lanterns mounted on giant poles, followed by various brotherhoods, dancing and playing music. The procession starts about 3pm and culminates early evening at the *zaouia*; the best place to see it is at Bab Bou Haja.

At the far end of a cemetery (again forbidden to non-Muslims), which spreads down to the river, is a third revered site, the white *koubba* of the **Marabout of Sidi Ben Achir**. Sometimes known as "Al Tabib" (The Doctor), Ben Achir was a fourteenth-century ascetic from Andalusia. His shrine reputedly effects cures for blindness, paralysis and madness. Enclosed by nineteenth-century pilgrim lodgings, it also has a considerable annual moussem on the eve of Mouloud.

In the twentieth century, after the French made Rabat their capital and Casablanca their main port, Salé became a bit of a backwater. The original **Ville Nouvelle** was just a small area around the bus station and the northern gates, but recent developments have changed this, with a major project, Bou Regreg Marina, continuing to take shape on the riverbank.

Salé is a centre for **pottery**, and its plain ceramic tajines are – for practical rather than aesthetic purposes – the best in the country.

The Medina

For the most part, Salé still looks and feels very different from Rabat, particularly within its **Medina** walls, where the souks and life remain surprisingly traditional. Lacking any great "attractions" as such, there are few tourists – all the more reason to visit.

Bab Mrisa

The most interesting point to enter Salé's Medina is through **Bab Mrisa**, near the *grand taxi* terminal. Its name – "of the small harbour" – recalls the marine arsenal that used to be sited within the walls, and explains the gate's unusual height. A channel running here from the Bou Regreg has long silted up, but in medieval times it allowed merchant ships to sail right into town. The gate itself is a very early Merenid structure of the 1270s, its design and motifs (palmettes enclosed by floral decoration, bands of Kufic inscription and *darj w ktarf*) still inherently Almohad in tone.

The souks

Inside Bab Mrisa you'll find yourself in a small square, at the bottom of the old **Mellah** (Jewish quarter). Turning to the left and continuing close to the walls for around 350m, you come to another gate, **Bab Bou Haja**, beside a small park. If you want to explore

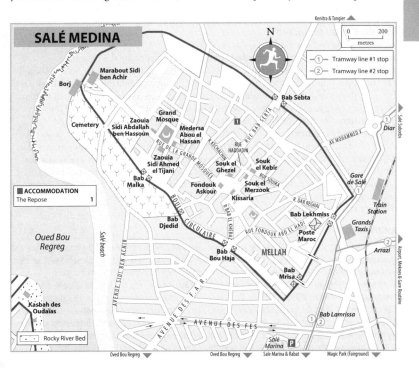

the souks via the route outlined below, veer right and take the road which runs along the left-hand side of the park (Rue Bab el Khebaz). If not, continue on just inside the walls to a long open area; as this starts to narrow into a lane (about 40m further down), veer to your right into the town. This should bring you out more or less at the **Grand Mosque**, opposite which is the **Medersa Abou el Hassan** (see page 250).

The park-side street from Bab Bou Haja is **Rue Bab el Khebaz** (Street of the Bakers' Gate), a busy little lane that emerges at the heart of the **souks** by a small **kissaria** (covered market) devoted mainly to textiles. Most of the alleys here are grouped round specific crafts – a particular speciality is the pattern-weave mats produced for the sides and floors of mosques, which you can find in the **Souk el Merzouk**. There is also a wool souk, the **Souk el Ghezel**, while wood, leather, ironware, carpets and household items are in the **Souk el Kebir** – the grand souk.

Close by the *kissaria* is a fourteenth-century hospice, the **Fondouk Askour**, with a notable gateway (built by Abou Inan), and beyond this, the Medina's main street, **Rue de la Grande Mosquée**, leads uphill through the middle of town to the Grand Mosque. This is the simplest approach, but you can take in more of the souks by following the parallel **Rue Kechachin**. Along here are the carpenters and stone-carvers, as well as other craftsmen. On **Rue Haddadin**, a fairly major intersection which leads off to its right up towards Bab Sebta, you'll come upon gold- and coppersmiths.

Grand Mosque
Rue de la Grande Mosquée • Gateway and minaret open access; prayer hall and mihrab closed to non-Muslims

The area around the **Grand Mosque** is the most interesting part of town, with lanes fronting a concentration of aristocratic mansions and religious *zaouia* foundations. Almohad in origin, the mosque is one of the largest and earliest in Morocco. Unfortunately, non-Muslims can only see the gateway and minaret, which are recent additions, though Muslims can enter to see the prayer hall and mihrab, which are original.

Medersa Abou el Hassan
Rue de la Grande Mosquée • Charge

Everybody can visit the restored **Medersa Abou el Hassan**, opposite the mosque's monumental, stepped main entrance. The medersa was founded in 1341 by Sultan Abou el Hassan, and is thus more or less contemporary with the Bou Inania medersas in Meknes and Fez. Like them (though rather smaller), it is intensely decorated with carved wood, stucco and zellij, leaving hardly an inch of space that doesn't draw the eye into a web of intricacy.

The **patterns**, for the most part, derive from Almohad models, with their stylized geometric and floral motifs, but in the latter there is a much more naturalistic, less abstracted approach. There is also a new stress on **calligraphy**, with monumental inscriptions carved in great bands on the dark cedar wood and incorporated within the stucco and zellij. Almost invariably these are in the elaborate cursive script and are generally passages from the Koran.

Close to its entrance there is a stairway up to the former cells of the students (now partially renovated to look almost liveable) and to the **roof**, where, looking out across the river to Rabat, you sense the enormity of the Hassan Tower.

ARRIVAL AND DEPARTURE — SALÉ

By train The train station is conveniently located just across the N1 highway from the Medina's eastern walls. Destinations Asilah (8 direct & 2 connecting daily; 2hr 45min); Casa Port (1–2 hourly 6.17am–8.40pm; 1hr 20min); Casa Voyageurs (1–2 hourly 4.59am–10.30pm; 1hr 15min); Rabat (1–2 hourly 4.59am–9.47pm; 15min); Tangier (8 direct & 2 connecting daily; 3hr 30min–5hr 30min).
By tram The easiest way to travel between Salé and Rabat is by the tramway (w tram-way.ma). Both lines cross the Oued Bou Regreg, stopping at the Hassan Mosque and Tower in Rabat and opposite Bab Mrisa in Salé. Line 1 also calls at both Rabat Ville and Salé train stations.
By bus The *gare routière* is 1km east of the Medina, a short walk from Hassan II tramway station (Line 2). Long-distance services are restricted to those listed below; CTM buses don't stop in Salé. Regular city buses run between the eastern end of Bd Hassan II in Rabat and the *grand taxi* station in Salé. Destinations Casablanca (over 10 daily; 2hr); Kenitra (over

20 daily; 45min); Tangier (2 daily; 4hr 30min).
By grand taxi Grands taxis from the Shell petrol station on Bd Hassan II in Rabat, opposite Bab Chellah, will usually drop off at Bab Bou Haja or Bab Mrisa on the way to Salé's grand taxi station opposite Bab Lekhmiss.

ACCOMMODATION

SEE MAPS PAGES 234 AND 249

Le Dawliz Av du Bouregreg ⊕ hoteldawlizrabat.ma. To the east of the Medina and overlooking the river, this top-end hotel offers large rooms and suites with all mod cons, plus a complex of bars, restaurants and a nightclub. €€€€

★ **The Repose** 17 Zankat Talaa, Ras Chejra, Medina ⊕ therepose.com. The first and still the best riad in the Medina, with four individually decorated suites, some with a fireplace. The service and attention is impeccable, as are the in-house meals with locally sourced, often organic, ingredients. Traditional experiences can be arranged, such as a visit to the local hammam or henna hand painting. BB €

EATING AND DRINKING

SEE MAP PAGE 234

In the evening, you can eat in the Medina at one of the many snack cafés along Rue Kechachin, but by 10pm the streets are often empty and shops and cafés closed. The opposite is the case at the marina, where there's a selection of café-restaurants that stay open till late.

★ **Le Marco** 2 Av de Fes, Marina ⊕ marco.ma. Opened in 2015, this has rapidly become one of *the* places to dine in Salé. Styled as a French brasserie, the classy interior includes an open-to-view kitchen as well as a children's play corner, while the outdoor terrace offers wonderful river views. The cuisine is largely top-end but there are also some cheaper salads and sandwiches, and the service is genuinely friendly. Licensed. €€€

The coast from Rabat to Casa

4

Between **Rabat and Casablanca** lie a number of sandy **beaches**, popular with locals from both cities, especially during the summer holiday months. Apartment complexes are steadily taking over large tracts of the coastline here, supplying an increasing demand for city workers willing to commute.

Temara

Temara Ville is on the Rabat–Casa Port train line (6.30am–8pm 2 hourly), and *petits taxis* will take you from the train station to the beach for 10dh; the beach is served by bus #17 from outside Bab el Had in Rabat, and in summer *grands taxis* make the journey from Bd Hassan II

Thirteen kilometres south of Rabat, the town of **Temara** is notable primarily for its small kasbah, which dates from Moulay Ismail's reign during the seventeenth and eighteenth centuries. However, most visitors come here for its beach, **Temara Plage**, 4km west of town. Packed in summer and deserted for the rest of the year, it's a pleasant if slightly wild stretch of golden sand. The sea here offers the odd wave for surfers but only confident swimmers should venture out past the breakers.

Mohammedia

Formerly known as Fedala but renamed following the death of Mohammed V in 1961, the port of **MOHAMMEDIA** has a dual identity, as the site of Morocco's main oil refineries and

---

COUP ON THE COAST

The **Royal Palace** at **Skhirat Plage**, between Rabat and Mohammedia, was the site of a **coup** attempt by Moroccan generals during King Hassan II's birthday celebrations in July 1971. The coup was mounted using a force of Berber cadets, who took over the palace, imprisoned the king and killed a number of his guests. It was thwarted by the apparently accidental shooting of the cadets' leader, General Mohammed Medbuh, and by the strength of personality of Hassan, who reasserted control over his captors. Among the guests who survived was Malcolm Forbes (see page 79). The palace still stands, though it has understandably fallen from royal favour.

the base of its petrochemical industry, but also as a holiday playground for Casablanca, with one of the best beaches on the Atlantic, a racecourse and a royal golf club.

With its friendly, easy-going atmosphere, pleasant palm-lined streets and a fine selection of restaurants, Mohammedia makes an enjoyable stopover, or a base for Casablanca. Between the train station and the Ville Nouvelle, there is a small square **kasbah**, built during a period of Portuguese occupation and still preserving its original gateway.

ARRIVAL AND DEPARTURE   MOHAMMEDIA

By train The modern train station is on the southeast edge of the town, just under 2km from the downtown hotels and restaurants. A *petit taxi* to the station from the centre should cost 10dh.

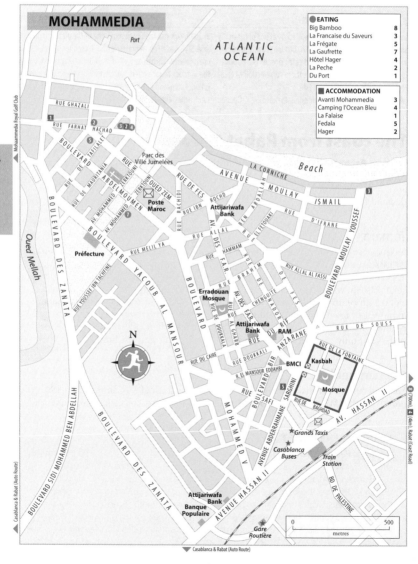

MOHAMMEDIA

Port

ATLANTIC OCEAN

Mohammedia Royal Golf Club

RUE GHAZALI

RUE FARHAT HACHAD

BOULEVARD DE TAFILALET

RUE DE MAURITANIA

RUE ABDEL MOUMEN

AV. MOHAMMED ZERKTOUNI

Parc des Ville Jumelées

Poste Maroc

Préfecture

BOULEVARD DES ZANATA

Oued Mellah

RUE YOUSSEF IBN TACHFINE

BOULEVARD YACOUB AL MANSOUR

RUE MELIL YA

RUE DE FES

RUE RACHIDI

RUE IBN ROCHD

Attijariwafa Bank

AV. DES HAMMAM

RUE ALLAL

RUE FAR

RUE BRAHIM

Erradouan Mosque

RUE DE DOUKKALA

AV. DES FAR

RUE CHENGUITE

RUE DE RIF

RUE DOUKKALI

Attijariwafa Bank

RAM

RUE DU RIF

RUE ANZARANE

RUE DU CAIRE

BMCI

R. EL MANSOUR EDDAHBI

RUE SAFI

BOULEVARD SANGHINI

BOULEVARD ABDERRAHMANE

MOHAMMED V

AVENUE

Casablanca Buses

Grands Taxis

AVENUE HASSAN II

BOULEVARD SIDI MOHAMMED BEN ABDELLAH

BOULEVARD DES ZANATA

Attijariwafa Bank

Banque Populaire

LA CORNICHE

AVENUE MOULAY ISMAIL

Beach

RUE ABDALLAH MOULAY

RUE D'IFRANE

RUE ALLAL AL FASSI

BOULEVARD MOULAY YOUSSEF

RUE DE SOUSS

RUE DE LA FONTAINE

Kasbah

Mosque

RUE DE BAGHDAD

AV. HASSAN II

Train Station

BO DE PALESTINE

Gare Routière

Casablanca & Rabat (Auto Route)

Casablanca & Rabat (Auto Route)

Rabat (Coast Road)

N

● **EATING**
Big Bamboo	8
La Francaise du Saveurs	3
La Frégate	5
La Gaufrette	7
Hôtel Hager	4
La Peche	2
Du Port	1

■ **ACCOMMODATION**
Avanti Mohammedia	3
Camping l'Ocean Bleu	4
La Falaise	1
Fedala	5
Hager	2

0   500
metres

Destinations Casa Port (7.15am–9.37pm 1–2 hourly; 25min); Casa Voyageurs (5.55am–10.39pm 1–3 hourly; 25min); Rabat (6.14am–10,55pm 1–2 hourly; 45min).

By bus Long-distance buses operate from the *gare routière*, just off Av Hassan II and a 10min walk from the train station; CTM buses don't stop in Mohammedia. Local buses travelling the 30km to Casablanca depart from Av Hassan

II, just in front of the train station; the best bus to take is #900, which stops on Av des FAR, near Pl Zellaqa (hourly 8am–7pm).

By grand taxi *Grands taxis* to and from Av des FAR in Casablanca operate from Av Hassan II, opposite the train station.

Destination Casablanca (30min).

ACCOMMODATION   SEE MAP PAGE 252

Avanti Mohammedia Bd Moulay Youssef ⓦavanti mohammedia.com. Formerly known as *L'Amphitrite Beach*, this large top-end complex is on the beachfront, with over 150 rooms and suites, all with balconies but not all with ocean views. There is a choice of restaurants and bars, as well as a decent-sized swimming pool, gym, uber-trendy nightclub and a pretty good spa that usually requires advance booking. BB €€€€

Camping l'Ocean Bleu 4km north of town on the R322 coast road towards Rabat ☎0660 911922. Friendly, family-run beachfront campsite with shaded pitches for tents and camper vans, as well as a few simple bungalows. Basic food provisions are available all year, and there's a restaurant in summer. Limited wi-fi. €

La Falaise Rue Farhat Hachad ☎0523 324828. A basic but clean and friendly little place, with twelve spotless

rooms (only one is en suite but all have a hand basin) facing inwards to a tree-shaded central courtyard. There's a popular, at times noisy, bar next door. Reservations recommended. €

Fedala 6 Av Abderrahmane Sarghini ⓦhotelfedala. com. A busy yet welcoming mid-range hotel across from the kasbah. The rooms are comfortable, despite suffering slightly from a garish over-the-top Moroccan theme, with lots of bright colour, intricate headboards and large, heavy drapes. There's a number of public areas. BB €€

Hager 3 Rue Farhat Hachad ☎0523 325921. Modest and faded hotel, with a rooftop restaurant and a bar. The tiled rooms are a bit spartan but clean and spacious, plus there are a few tired suites that have large sitting rooms. There's a small but welcome lift to cover the three floors. BB €€

EATING AND DRINKING   SEE MAP PAGE 252

For its size, Mohammedia's choice of restaurants is impressive, especially for fish. Breakfast and snacks are available from a number of cafés looking onto the pleasant, grassed Parc des Ville Jumelées or at the eastern end of the beachfront promenade.

Big Bamboo Av Hassan II (1km NW of the train station) ⓦbamboopub.ma. A very popular and unpretentious bar-restaurant with a number of seating areas both inside and out, including an "Irish corner" complete with big-screen TV for live football. The Asian-European menu includes stir-fries and a very good *filet de bœuf*, and there's often live music and salsa dancing. €€

La Francaise des Saveurs 1 Rue Farhat Hachad. Open since 1947 but looking sleek and modern from a twenty-first-century facelift, this classy patisserie also doubles as the downtown bakery. Along with a good selection of breads and pastries (15–28dh), there's always a tempting display of chocolate creations that can be gift-boxed should you wish. €

La Frégate Rue Oued Zem. Come here for rock lobster, prawns and all manner of seafood in generous helpings, particularly with shellfish paella. There's a takeaway and delivery service too. Licensed. €€€

La Gaufrette Av Mohammed Zerktouni. One of the better cafés looking onto Parc de Mohammedia, female-friendly and with a pleasant and shaded pavement area along with more formal seating inside. A choice of

breakfast options is accompanied by a snack menu offering sandwiches and pizza A good spot to while away a few hours of people watching. €€

Hôtel Hager 3 Rue Farhat Hachad. This hotel's two restaurants are both worth a visit. The rooftop one offers a varied menu that leans towards seafood but also offers standards such as a lamb tajine or chicken brochettes, accompanied by ocean glimpses and a welcoming breeze during summer. The ground-floor bar offers beer and tapas. Licensed. €€

La Peche Rue Farhat Hachad. Unpretentious and popular seafood restaurant serving some of the best calamari, fish, oysters and cheap paella in town. There's also a few other options, including pizza. Can get very busy on Sun with well-to-do Casablancans enjoying their weekly seafood feast. €

★ **Du Port** 1 Rue du Port ⓦrestoport.ma. One of the classiest restaurants along the coast, with nautical decor inside and an outdoor upper deck sporting ocean views. Renowned for its charcoal grills, it isn't cheap but the food is inventive and accompanying sauces delicious. Seafood is the obvious menu-filler, with dishes such as roasted monkfish medallions with mushrooms, though meat-fans are also accommodated – there are plenty of steak options. Reservations recommended on weekends. Licensed. €€€€

4

DIRECTORY

Banks Attijariwafa Bank, Banque Populaire & SGMB are all on Av Hassan II, about 500m southwest of the train station. Attijariwafa Bank also has a couple of other branches along Av des FAR. The post office has an ATM.

Golf Mohammedia Royal Golf Club, Bd des Zanata (wrgam.ma).

Post office Av Mohammed Zerktouni, facing Parc des Ville Jumelées, and at Av Hassan II, opposite the train station.

Casablanca

Morocco's biggest city and commercial capital, **CASABLANCA** (Dar el Baïda in Arabic) is the Maghreb's largest port, and busier than Marseilles, on which it was modelled by the French. Its development, from a town of 20,000 in 1906, has been astonishing, but ruthlessly deliberate. When the French landed their forces here in 1907, and established their Protectorate five years later, Fez was Morocco's commercial centre and Tangier its main port. Had Tangier not been in international hands, this probably would have remained the case. However, the demands of an independent colonial administration forced the French to seek an entirely new base. Casa, at the heart of *Maroc Utile*, the country's most fertile zone and centre of its mineral deposits, was a natural choice.

Superficially, with a population of over three million, Casa today is not unlike a large southern European city. Arriving here from the south, or even from Fez or Tangier, most of the preconceptions you've been travelling round with will be happily shattered by the city's cosmopolitan beach clubs or by the almost total absence of the veil. But these "European" images shield what is substantially a first-generation city – and one still attracting considerable immigration from the countryside – and perhaps inevitably some of Morocco's most intense social problems.

Casablanca's most obvious sight is the **Hassan II Mosque**, and it also has the only **Jewish museum** in the Muslim world, but the city's true delight remains the **Mauresque and Art Deco architecture** built during the colonial period, in particular the 1920s and 1930s. Casa can be a bewildering place to arrive, but once you're in the centre, orientation gets a little easier. Its focus is a large public square, **Place Mohammed V**, and most of the places to stay, eat, or (in a rather limited way) see, are located in and around the avenues that radiate from it. A few blocks to the north, still partially walled, is the **Old Medina**, which was all there was of Casablanca until around 1907. Out to the south is the **Habous** quarter – the **New Medina**, created by the French, while to the west, along the Corniche past the Hassan II Mosque, lie the beach suburbs of **Aïn Diab and Anfa**.

CASABLANCA'S COLONIAL ARCHITECTURE

The French-built city centre and its formal, colonial buildings already seem to belong to a different and distant age. The style of the administrative buildings in particular is known as **Mauresque**, or sometimes as "Neo-Moorish", essentially a French idealization and "improvement" on traditional Moroccan styles, with lots of horseshoe arches, and even the odd touch of *darj w ktarf*, originally an Almohad motif. Many private buildings of the early colonial period (from 1912 until the early 1920s) were heavily influenced by the flowery **Art Nouveau** of *fin-de-siècle* Europe. Following the 1925 Exposition des Arts Decoratifs in Paris, a new and bolder style, named **Art Deco** after the Exposition, began to take hold, inspired by many sources, including traditional Moroccan design. A meander along downtown Casa's streets, taking in the city's Deco heritage – be sure to look upwards, since most of the finer features stop short of ground-floor level – can prove very rewarding.

CHURCH OF ST JOHN THE EVANGELIST

The **Church of St John the Evangelist**, on the corner of Avenue Moulay Hassan I and Rue Félix et Max Guedj (ⓦ stjohnscasablanca.org), stood in open fields when it was built in 1906. Within twelve months of its consecration, the church was involved in events that led to the **first French landings**. Some Europeans working on the port were murdered when Shaweea tribesmen from the interior invaded the town and sacked the church. Peace – of a sort – was restored by a French bombardment and subsequent occupation.

In 1942, during **World War II**, the church was filled with Allied troops involved in Operation Torch (see page 264). A member of the congregation at this time was General George Patton, who had led his troops ashore at Safi. He presented the oak pulpit, which still stands in the church, "in memory of the men of all nations who fell in the fighting around Casablanca". After his death in 1945, the carved frontal for the communion table was presented to St John's by his family. The church stands on land still owned by the British Crown, and Sunday services are conducted at 9.30am and 11.30am.

Boulevard Mohammed V and around

Linking the city centre with Casa's eastern suburbs, **Boulevard Mohammed V** became the palette on which the French wished to showcase their Protectorate-era architectural prowess. The **Hôtel Lincoln** is an early example of colonial Mauresque (see page 254), dating from 1916. Though now derelict, partially collapsed and consequently fenced off, its architectural grandness is still plainly visible. Opposite here is the **Marché Central**, built in the 1920s to serve the neighbourhood's European clientele and still the busiest downtown market (see page 265). West of the Lincoln along the south side of **Boulevard Mohammed V**, there's a whole row of splendid facades from the same period, starting with the post office at no. 116, which incorporates a Europeanized version of the Almohad *darj w ktarf* motif. The most striking facade on this strip is the **Maroc Soir/Le Matin du Sahara** newspaper office, one block west, which boasts a wonderful frontage based on a hexagram motif, topped with a green-tiled roof. There are more fine buildings on both sides of the boulevard for a couple of blocks east, but if you turn south up Rue Mohammed el Qorri, you'll see the **Rialto Cinema**, a gorgeous 1930s Art Deco picture palace, both inside and out.

Continuing south along Rue Mohammed el Qorri, you emerge at **Place Aknoul**, in the thick of some of Casa's finest colonial-era buildings. The road straight ahead, **Rue Tahar Sebti**, is full of them, and **Rue Abdelkarim Diouri**, over to your left, has a nice little bunch at its junction with Rue Ibn Batouta (two blocks up), especially the *Bar Lyonnais*. Opposite is the 1919 **Hôtel Volubilis** and behind that, the 1922 **Hôtel Transatlantique**. Beyond here, on Avenue Lalla Yacout, the **Auto Hall** at no. 44 is a very imposing Art Deco edifice.

Rue Prince Moulay Abdallah

Some wonderful architecture can be seen above the street level in the immediate area around **Rue Prince Moulay Abdallah**. Heading west from Place Aknoul, down Rue Idriss Lahrizi towards the post office, there are some great facades along both sides of the street. It's worth making a detour to take the first street on the left, Rue Mohammed Belloul, where the **Hôtel Guynemer** (see page 262), at the first corner on the right, has some Art Deco panels up on its cornerpiece. A right here brings you to the pedestrianized stretch of **Rue Prince Moulay Abdallah**, where there's a whole row of Mauresque and Art Deco facades (see page 254) on both sides, and some lovely little touches too: the Art Deco doorway at no. 48, for example, has a bird of paradise incorporated into the ironwork (as does 25 Rue Mouftakir Abdelkader, in the same block, just round the corner), while no. 72 is topped with some pretty Art Nouveau ironwork. At the northern end of the pedestrianized street is **Place 16 Novembre**, where

CASABLANCA

4

Azemmour, El-Jank, Ain Diab & Anfa

Hassan II Mosque

Minaret

BOULEVARD SOUR DJEDID

BOULEVARD DES ALMOHADES

BOULEVARD MOULAY YOUSSEF

RUE JULES MAURAN

RUE DE GOULMINA

RUE DE GOULMINA

BOULEVARD ZIRAOUI

BOULEVARD TAHAR EL ALAOUI

RUE JEMAA ACHCHLEUH

OLD MEDINA

Chleuh Mosque

Grand Mosque

Casa Port Train Station

RUE DES ANGLAIS

RUE MOHA OU SAID

Bab Marrakesh

RUE CHAKIB ARSALANE

BOULEVARD ZIRAOUI

BOULEVARD DE BORDEAUX

Clocktower

AVENUE DES F.A.R

JILALI

RUE SIDI BELYOUT

Place Nations Unies

AV DES F.A.R.

SEE INSET

RUE LÉON L'AFRICAIN

PLACE OUED EL MAKHAZINE

Bus to Ain Diab

RUE FM GUEDJ

St John Evangelist

PLACE DES NATIONS UNIES

BOULEVARD MOHAMMED V

RUE KARAIB

RUE ALLAL BEN

D'ANFA

BD DE PARIS

PLACE 16 NOVEMBRE

AV HOUMAN

RUE AZIZ BELLAL

RUE EL FKIH EL FOUDI

Synagogue

LUSITANIA

BOULEVARD MOULAY HASSAN

BD D'ALGER

Bank al Maghrib

PLACE AKNOUL

EL KADI ABASSAT

RUE PRINCE MOULAY ABDALLAH

RUE IBN BATOUTA

PLACE DE LA FRATERNITÉ

U.S. Consulate

Poste Maroc

RUE MOUFTAKIR ABDELKADER

RUE DRISS LAHRIZI

RUE AZRELMENK

RUE CHAOUIA

AbderrahmanSlaoui Foundation Museum

AVENUE RACHIDI

PLACE MOHAMMED V

AVENUE LALLA

BOULEVARD HASSAN SOUKTANI

Cathédrale of Sacré Coeur

Law Courts

RUE EL HARRAR

Auto Hall

Prefecture

French Consul

RUE MUSTAPHA EL MAARI

AVENUE HASSAN

AVENUE JEAN JAURES

Place Mohammed V

BD MOULAY YOUSSEF

BOULEVARD DU 11 JANVIER

Acima

BOULEVARD MOHAMMED

RUE MOUSSA BEN NOUSSAIR

RUE BRAHIM ROUDANI

Parc de la Ligue Arabe

PLACE SAINT-EXUPERY

RUE ALLAL AL FASSI

BD RAHAL EL-

RUE OMAR SLAOUI

AVENUE MERS SULTAN

Villa des Arts

Administration de Défense National

MAARIF

BOULEVARD ZERKTOUN

RUE MUSTAPHA EL MAANI

AVENUE NADI

BD A MAR

Grands Taxis for El Jadida Safi and Essaouira & Airport (25km)

Oasis & Museum of Moroccan Judaism

Nôtre Dame de Lourdes

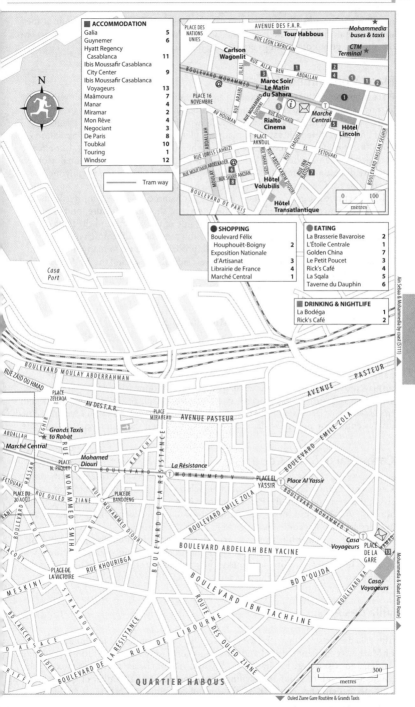

ACCOMMODATION

Galia	5
Guynemer	6
Hyatt Regency Casablanca	11
Ibis Moussafir Casablanca City Center	9
Ibis Moussafir Casablanca Voyageurs	13
Maâmoura	7
Manar	4
Miramar	2
Mon Rêve	4
Negociant	3
De Paris	8
Toubkal	10
Touring	1
Windsor	12

Tram way

SHOPPING

Boulevard Félix Houphouët-Boigny	2
Exposition Nationale d'Artisanat	3
Librairie de France	4
Marché Central	1

EATING

La Brasserie Bavaroise	2
L'Étoile Centrale	1
Golden China	7
Le Petit Poucet	3
Rick's Café	4
La Scala	5
Taverne du Dauphin	6

DRINKING & NIGHTLIFE

La Bodéga	1
Rick's Café	2

no. 19 is the most handsome of a trio of charming Art Deco buildings, while at the southern end, Boulevard de Paris leads west to Place Mohammed V. On the way, check out the fine group of buildings around the junction with Rue Tata.

Place Mohammed V

Place Mohammed V is truly grand in scale. The public buildings around it served as models for administrative architecture throughout Morocco. The square stood at the centre of a network of boulevards drawn up by Resident General Lyautey's chief architect, **d'Henri Prost**, who made his plan based on a projected population of 150,000, considered far too high by many when he proposed it in 1914, but already exceeded by the time he left in 1923. Prost was keen to combine traditional Moroccan forms with current European town planning ideas, and was more than anyone else responsible for Casablanca's shape, and much of its architectural style.

The effect of the central ensemble in Place Mohammed V is very impressive indeed, the only feature out of place being a clock tower in the old **Préfecture**, on the south side of the square. The **law courts** on the east side of the square, and the **Bank al Maghrib** on the north are both solidly imposing too, and unlike much of the city's architecture, barely seem to have aged at all, probably because so many more recent buildings are modelled on them. On the west side of the square, the 1919 **post office** incorporates lots of surprisingly traditional features, in the tilework around the door for example, as well as the ceiling and brass chandelier within.

Abderrahman Slaoui Foundation Museum

12 Rue du Parc • Charge • ☎ 0522 206217

Located in a restored 1940s villa down a quiet, leafy street, the **Abderrahman Slaoui Foundation Museum** showcases a life's worth of "treasure hunting" by the museum's namesake, a well-travelled Moroccan businessman. A number of exhibitions are displayed through the multi-level villa, showcasing antique Moroccan gold jewellery, artworks from early twentieth-century Morocco and vintage *Orientaliste* posters, and *curiosités* and objets d'art from around the world. It's all very classy and well presented (ask reception for an English-language programme), and there's a lovely rooftop **café**.

Cathedral of Sacré Cœur

Rue d'Alger • Not in use for services, but you should still be able to go inside; open from time to time for temporary art exhibitions

Casablanca's most classic piece of colonial architecture, the **Cathedral of Sacré Cœur**, sits at the western end of the **Parc de la Ligue Arabe**. Quite European in style, though adopting some African forms, the cathedral was built to a wonderfully balanced and airy design, paying genuine homage to its Moroccan setting.

Though it no longer functions as a religious building, most days you can still look around. There's not all that much to see inside except the stained-glass windows, which are truly impressive and, if you're lucky, the *gardien* may escort you to the top of the tower for a brilliant view of the city and port (a small tip is appreciated).

Villa des Arts

30 Bd Brahim Roudani • Free • 🌐 villadesarts.ma

The **Villa des Arts**, set in a 1930s Art Deco villa, is part of the ONA Foundation, one of Morocco's eminent cultural and artistic organizations. Accessed through a peaceful garden and past a large fountain, the all-white villa has been lovingly restored by the foundation, and its grand high-ceilinged entrance leads to a number of galleries hosting both permanent and temporary exhibitions of contemporary art.

Old Medina

Just to the west of both the port and Casa's downtown area, the **Old Medina** dates largely from the late nineteenth century. Before that, it was little more than a group of village huts, half-heartedly settled by local tribes after the site was abandoned by the Portuguese in 1755. Casa Branca, the town the Portuguese founded here in the fifteenth century after the expulsion of the pirates, had been virtually levelled by the great earthquake of that year. Only its name ("White House": *Casablanca* in Spanish; *Dar el Baïda* in Arabic) survives.

The Medina has a slightly disreputable air (it's said to be the place to go to look for any stolen goods you might want to buy back) but it isn't sinister, and it can be a good source for cheap snacks, fake watches and general goods. A single main street, which starts from the top end of Boulevard Félix Houphouët Boigny, by a restored clock tower, as **Rue Chakib Arsalane**, becomes **Rue Jemaa Ach Chleuh** halfway along. A small eighteenth-century bastion, the **Skala**, has been restored, with some old cannons and an upmarket café-restaurant (see page 254).

Quartier Habous (New Medina)

About a kilometre southeast of the city centre, at the end of Avenue Mers Sultan, is the **Quartier Habous** – or **New Medina** – which displays a somewhat bizarre extension of Mauresque. Built in the 1930s, it was intended as a model quarter, and it still has a

CASABLANCA'S SLUMS

4

Alongside its wealth and its prestige developments – notably the Hassan II Mosque – Casablanca has had a reputation for extreme poverty, prostitution, crime, social unrest and the **bidonvilles** (shanty towns) which you will see on both sides of the train track as you come into town. In fact, the French word *bidonville* – literally "tin-can town" – was coined in Casablanca in the 1920s, when construction workers on a building project in the Roches Noires district, east of the port area, knocked up some temporary accommodation next to their main quarry. Over the decades, other migrant workers followed suit, and the *bidonvilles* escalated, partly from the sheer number of migrants – over a million in the 1960s – and partly because few of them intended to stay permanently. Most sent back their earnings to their families in the country, meaning to rejoin them as soon as they had raised sufficient funds for a business at home.

The pattern is now much more towards **permanent settlement**, and this, together with a strict control of migration and a limited number of self-help programmes, has eased and cleared many of the worst slums. Additionally, *bidonville* dwellers have been accorded increasing respect during recent years. Officially they cannot be evicted if they have lived in a property over two years (though in practice this continues to happen), and after ten years they acquire title to the land and building, which can be used as collateral at the bank for loans. The dread of every *bidonville* family is to be evicted and put in a high-rise block, regarded as the lowest of the low on the housing ladder.

The problem of a concentrated urban poor, however, is more enduring, and it represents – as it did for the French – an intermittent threat to government stability. Through the 1940s and 1950s Casa was the main centre of anti-French **rioting**, and post-independence it was the city's working class that formed the base of Ben Barka's Socialist Party. There have been strikes here sporadically in subsequent decades, and on several occasions they precipitated rioting, most violently in the food strikes of 1982. More recently, the *bidonvilles* also proved a fertile recruiting ground for *jihadi* extremists – one *bidonville*, **Sidi Moumen**, was home to perpetrators of bomb attacks in Casablanca in 2003 (portrayed in the 2014 movie *Horses of God*), and Madrid the following year, and also to a suicide bomber who blew himself up in a Casablanca internet café in 2007.

kind of Legoland look, with its neat little rows of streets. What's most unreal, perhaps, is the neighbourhood **mosque**, flanked by a tidy stretch of green just as if it were a provincial French church.

South again from the New Medina, at the junction of avenues Mers Sultan and 2 Mars, alongside the Rond-point de l'Europe, the **Church of Notre-Dame de Lourdes** was completed in the 1950s. It's smaller than the Cathedral of Sacré Cœur and still in use. Its beautiful stained-glass windows, the work of Gabriel Loire, a master craftsman from Chartres, are its pride and joy.

Hassan II Mosque

Bd Sidi Mohamed Ben Abdallah • Charge • Ⓦ fmh2.ma •20min walk from downtown along Bd Moulay Youssef, or *petit taxi*, or bus #56 from Bd Félix Houphouët Boigny

Raised on a rocky platform reclaimed from the ocean, the **Hassan II Mosque** was inaugurated on August 30, 1993. Designed by French architect Michel Pinseau, it is open to non-Muslims on accompanied visits that also take in the mosque's huge and elaborate basement hammam.

From the city centre, the mosque's huge size (20,000 square metres) tricks you into thinking it's nearer than it is. The **minaret** is 200m high, making it by far the tallest structure in the country, and the tallest minaret in the world. A laser on its summit projects a beam towards Mecca. It has space for 25,000 worshippers within and 80,000 more in the courtyard. From the street, the mosque seems to float on the ocean below, a reminder of the Koran's statement (11:7), reiterated by Hassan II, that God's throne is upon the water. In order that the faithful can "contemplate God's sky", the enormous roof of the mosque rolls open on occasions.

The facts of the mosque's **construction** are almost as startling as its size. During the early 1990s, when it was being readied for opening, 1400 men worked by day and a further 1100 by night. Most were master-craftsmen, working marble from Agadir, cedar from the Middle Atlas, granite from Tafraoute, and (the only import) glass from Murano in Venice. Its cost is reckoned to have exceeded £500m/US$750m, raised by not entirely voluntary public subscription.

Aïn Diab

3km west of the port and Old Medina • Bus #9 from Bd Félix Houphouët Boigny, tram to Aïn Diab Plage station, *petit taxi* from Pl des Nations Unies or 30–45min walk

A **beach** within Casa may not sound alluring – and it's certainly not the cleanest and clearest stretch of the country's waters – but **Aïn Diab**'s big attraction is not so much the sea, in whose shallow waters Moroccans gather in phalanx formations, as the **beach clubs** along its front, each with one or more pools (usually of filtered sea water), a restaurant and a couple of snack bars. The prices and quality of the clubs vary – most locals have annual membership, and for outsiders a day or weekend ticket can work out expensive – so it's worth wandering round to check out what's available.

Museum of Moroccan Judaism

81 Rue Chasseur Jules Gros, 5km south of town • Charge • Ⓦ jewishmuseumcasa.com • *Petit taxi* from the centre – ask your driver to wait as taxis locally are scarce, or a 15min walk from Oasis tram and train station

The **Museum of Moroccan Judaism**, in the southern suburb of Oasis, is the only Jewish museum to be found in the Islamic world. It is also an important resource of information on Morocco's massive Jewish heritage, one that rather dwarfs the country's five-thousand-strong Jewish population, of whom more than sixty percent live in Casablanca.

The museum, housed in a bright, modern building, exhibits photographs of synagogues, ancient cemeteries and Jewish holy sites nationwide. Also on display are reconstructed synagogue interiors, books and scrolls, traditional costumes – both full- and doll-size – and sacramental items, mostly made of silver and some hailing from Manchester, in the UK. Since **silverwork** was once the preserve of Morocco's Jews – even today, you'll find the jewellery souk in the Mellah (Jewish quarter) of many Moroccan towns – there are exhibits here of Jewish-made silver jewellery, and a reconstructed jeweller's workshop.

ARRIVAL AND DEPARTURE   CASABLANCA

BY PLANE

Casablanca's Mohammed V Airport (ⓦ casablanca-airport. com) is around 25km from downtown Casa. Royal Air Maroc offers a daily service (1hr 45min) between Casablanca and Algiers, which is currently the only way to travel direct between the two countries (see page 140). To get into town from Mohammed V Airport, trains run hourly to and from Casa Port (via Casa Voyageurs, no change required) daily 5.55am–9.55pm, with a further two services at 11.45pm and 3.55am (50min; 40dh 2nd class). The official rate – always current and not "out of date" as some taxi drivers try to persuade – for a *grand taxi* between the airport and the city centre is signposted at the taxi rank just outside the terminal building. Car rental companies with desks at the airport include Avis (ⓦ avis.ma), Hertz (ⓦ hertz.ma) and local company First-Car (ⓦ firstcar.ma). There are bank ATMs and bureaux de change in the main terminal building.

Airlines Air France, 11 Av des FAR (ⓦ airfrance.com); British Airways, Centre Allal Ben Abdallah, 47 Rue Allal Ben Abdallah (ⓦ ba.com); Iberia, 17 Av des FAR (ⓦ iberia.com); Royal Air Maroc, 44 Av des FAR (ⓦ royalairmaroc.com).

Destinations Agadir (4–6 daily; 1hr–1hr 20min); Al Hoceima (1 weekly; 2hr 20min); Dakhla (1–2 daily; 2hr 15min); Fez (7 weekly; 55min); Laayoune (1–2 daily; 1hr 35min); Marrakesh (5–7 daily; 40min–55min); Nador (7 weekly; 1hr 25min); Ouarzazate (6 weekly; 1hr 10min); Oujda (2 daily; 1hr 10min); Tangier (9 weekly; 1hr).

BY TRAIN

The first stage of the country's grand development of a 1500km **high-speed rail** (HSR) network, between Casablanca and Tangier, was inaugurated in late 2018. The line with super-slick trains has cut the journey time between Casablanca and Tangier from nearly 5 hours to just over 2 hours.

CASA PORT

The most convenient of Casablanca's train stations is Casa Port (*Gare du Port*), near the end of Bd Félix Houphouët Boigny, 500m from Pl des Nations Unies. Opened in 2014 after a massive reconstruction, the multistorey building now includes various dining options and an undercover car park. Only local trains from the surrounding region (including the airport) call here, as most intercity trains stop at the less convenient Casa Voyageurs.

Destinations Aéroport Mohammed V (6.08am, 7.17am, 7.50am, then hourly 9.08am–9.08pm; 50min); Casa Voyageurs (1–2 hourly 6.08am–9.08pm, 13min); Aïn Sebaa (1–2 hourly 6.35am–9.40pm; 10min); Kenitra (1–2 hourly 6.35am–9.40pm; 1hr 40min); Mohammedia (1–2 hourly 6.35am–9.40pm; 25min); Rabat (1–2 hourly 6.35am–9.40pm; 1hr).

CASA VOYAGEURS

Belying its status as one of the country's major rail hubs, the nondescript Casa Voyageurs (*Gare des Voyageurs*) station is tucked away some 2km from the city centre, at the far eastern end of Bd Mohammed V. *Petits taxis* are often waiting outside but are renowned for overcharging. Otherwise, catch a connecting train to Casa Port or the tram, which travels along Bd Mohammed V between the station and Pl des Nations Unies, or you can walk (30min).

Destinations Aéroport Mohammed V (5.40am, 6.26am, 7.34am, 8.09am, then hourly 9.26am–9.26pm; 32min); Asilah (8 direct & 2 connecting daily; 4hr–5hr 30min); Casa Port (1–2 hourly 7.11am–11.11pm, 13min); El Jadida (8 daily; 1hr 25min); Fez (hourly 6.05am–10.05pm; 4hr); Kenitra (1–2 hourly 5.50am–9.20pm; 1hr 40min); Marrakesh (9 daily; 3hr 20min); Meknes (hourly 6.05am–10.05pm; 3hr 15min); Mohammedia (5.50am–10.30pm 1–2 hourly; 25min); Nador (1 direct & 2 connecting daily; 10hr 30min–11hr 20min); Oujda (1 direct & 2 connecting daily; 10–11hr); Rabat (1–2 hourly 5.50am–10.30pm; 1hr 30min); Tangier (8 direct; 4hr 40min–6hr 20min & 2 connecting daily; 7–8hr).

BY BUS

CTM buses operate from their conveniently located city-centre terminal on Rue Léon l'Africain. Both *petits* and *grands taxis* are usually parked directly outside. Most private bus firms operate out of the Ouled Ziane *gare routière*, 4km southeast of the city centre and best reached by *petit taxi*; alternatively, bus #10 & #36 operate between Bd Mohammed V (opposite the Marché Central) and the busy Ouled Ziane road. For Mohammedia, local bus #900 (hourly 8am–7pm) operates from Rue Ziad ou Hmad, just west of Pl Zellaca and near Casa Port station.

Destinations Agadir (13 CTM & over 20 others daily; 8–9hr); Beni Mellal (6 CTM daily & others roughly hourly; 4hr); Chefchaouen (1 CTM & 1–2 others daily; 6hr); El Jadida

(8 CTM daily & others hourly; 2hr); Er Rachidia (2 CTM & 2 others daily; 11hr); Essaouira (4 CTM & over 10 others daily; 7–8hr); Fez (14 CTM & over 10 others daily; 4hr 30min); Laayoune (5 CTM daily; 19–20hr); Marrakesh (21 CTM daily & others hourly; 4hr); Meknes (11 CTM & over 10 others daily; 4hr); Ouarzazate (3 CTM daily; 9hr); Oujda (5 CTM daily; 11hr); Rabat (31 CTM daily & others every 15–30min; 1hr 30min); Tangier (5 CTM & over 10 others daily; 5hr 30min–6hr 30min); Tetouan (6 CTM & over 10 others daily; 6–7hr).

BY GRAND TAXI

Most *grands taxis* operate from the Ouled Ziane *gare routière*. The main exceptions include those for Rabat, which operate on Bd Hassan Seghir, very near the CTM terminal; Mohammedia, which operate from Rue Zaid ou Hmad, just west of Pl Zellaca and close to Casa Port train station; and El Jadida, Safi and Essaouira, which operate on Bd Brahim Roudani, by the junction with Bd Bir Anzarane in Maarif, 2km southeast of the city centre (served by local buses; see below). Destinations El Jadida (2hr); Fez (3hr 30min); Mohammedia (30min); Rabat (1hr 20min); Safi (3hr 30min); Tangier (5hr).

GETTING AROUND

By bus The most useful bus routes are those that connect downtown with Casa Voyageurs (#2), Ouled Ziane *gare routière* (#10 or #11), and the Essaouira/El Jadida taxi stand in the suburb of Maarif (#7). The other useful services are #56 from Bd Félix Houphouët Boigny and Pl Oued el Makhzine to Hassan II Mosque, and #9 from the same stops to Aïn Diab. Be warned that traffic is often terrible and buses can get very crowded at rush hours.

By taxi *Petits taxis* are easy to find along the main avenues and are invariably metered – as long as the meter is switched on... There is a fifty-percent surcharge at night.

By tram Casa's modern, a/c tramway network (daily 5.30am–10.30pm; ⊛casatramway.ma) began operating in late 2012 and offers almost fifty stops along some 30km of track, providing access between the city centre and the seaside suburb of Aïn Diab and the Casa Voyageurs train station.

By car Traffic is a nightmare in Casa, and frequently gridlocked. If hiring, it's much easier to pick up a car from the airport at the end of your stay in the city and head out to explore Morocco from there.

INFORMATION

Tourist information Syndicat d'Initiative, 98 Bd Mohammed V (☎0522 221524); central and offers free maps, but not much else. The Conseil Régional du Tourisme have a kiosk just north of Pl Mohammed V, on Av Hassan II, and another next to the Hassan II Mosque (⊛visitcasablanca.ma).

ACCOMMODATION

Although there are a large number of **hotels** in Casa, they operate at near capacity for much of the year and can fill up at short notice for conferences. If possible, **book ahead**, or at least arrive fairly early in the day. Even with a reservation, it's wise to phone ahead the day before to confirm. There are a good number of cheapies located **downtown** between the CTM bus station and Marché Central, though many have definitely seen better days.

DOWNTOWN, SEE MAP PAGE 256

★ **Galia** 19 Rue Ibn Batouta ☎0522 481694. The best budget option in the city, with friendly English-speaking management and in a very handy location next to a tram station and close to CTM. The tiled rooms are functional and clean, with or without bathroom (24hr hot water), and strong wi-fi. €

Guynemer 2 Rue Mohammed Belloul ☎0522 275764. Popular, family-run hotel in the most architecturally interesting part of town, with great Art Deco touches on the exterior. Room sizes vary – the singles and doubles are more modern, whereas the older twins have much larger bathrooms. It has a licensed restaurant and the staff are very friendly, helpful and mostly speak good English. Airport (and sometimes bus & train) pick-ups can be prearranged. €

Hyatt Regency Casablanca Pl des Nations Unies ⊛casablanca.regency.hyatt.com. Casablanca's most prominent and best-managed deluxe hotel, with a range of five-star facilities and three restaurants, as well as a bar and separate nightclub that are both popular with the after-work business crowd. Service is impeccable and the rooms are modern and spacious, including two adapted for wheelchair users. Prices are "dynamic" but the maximum price of a standard double shouldn't exceed €€€€

Ibis Moussafir Casablanca City Center Cnr Rue Zaid ou Hmad & Rue Sidi Belyout ⊛ibis.accorhotels.com. Located across the road from Casa Port, this stock-standard offering holds no surprises. The rooms are comfortable, compact and with just enough mod cons to justify the price; seven are wheelchair-adapted. There's a buffet breakfast and separate restaurant. BB €€€

Ibis Moussafir Casablanca Voyageurs Pl de la Gare ⊛ibis.accorhotels.com. As with other original hotels in this chain, it's situated right beside the train station; in this case it's Casa Voyageurs, so hardly central, though very convenient for a late arrival (book in advance) or early departure. Rooms are small but functional, and there is a restaurant, (sometimes noisy) bar, and car park. €€€

4

OLD AND NEW STREET NAMES

The names of Casa's chief squares – **Place Mohammed V** and **Place des Nations Unies** – are a source of enduring confusion. In 1991, Hassan II declared that the old Place des Nations Unies (around which are grouped the city's main public buildings) be known as Place Mohammed V, while the old Place Mohammed V (the square beside the Medina) was renamed Place des Nations Unies.

As elsewhere in Morocco, many of the old **French street names** have been revised to bear **Moroccan names**, but many people use the old names – as do some street maps. In this edition, we have used the new Moroccan names. Significant conversions include:

- Rue Branly – Rue Sharif Amziane
- Rue Claude – Rue Mohammed el Qorri
- Rue Colbert – Rue Chaouia
- Rue Foucauld – Rue Araibi Jilali
- Rue de l'Horloge – Rue Allal Ben Abdallah
- Rue Jean Jaurès – Rue Mohammed Ben Ali
- Rue Pegoud – Rue Mohammed Belloul
- Rue Poincaré – Rue Tata

Maâmoura 59 Rue Ibn Batouta ⓦhotelmaamoura. com. Owner-managed and one of the city centre's better value options, located on a lively side street on the edge of the Art Deco neighbourhood. The modern, tiled rooms are very spacious if a little bland and soulless – neutral tones of beige and chocolate abound. There's a poky café for breakfast and a grand restaurant. BB €€

Manar 3 Rue Chaouia ☎0522 452751. Close to the CTM station, this dependable cheapie offers simply furnished tiled rooms with satellite TV and spacious bathrooms; those facing inward are quieter. The reception area is rather grand, with a large chandelier and wall mural depicting charging horsemen, and an in-house café on a mezzanine at the rear. €€

Miramar 22 Rue León l'Africain ☎0522 310308. Just 50m from the CTM, this is the cheapest of the little hotels in the city centre. It has an old-fashioned feel, and bathroom facilities are shared (shower costs extra), but the rooms are decent enough for the price. €

Mon Rêve 7 Rue Chaouia ☎0522 311439. A friendly little place, and one that has long been a favourite with budget travellers. All rooms (some en suite) are accessed up a steep spiral staircase, and many of them have been renovated, but still relatively spartan. €

Negociant 116 Rue Allal Ben Abdallah ☎0522 314023. Opposite *Hôtel Touring* (see below), and very similar, though currently priced slightly higher, with clean, comfortable rooms (some en suite); it's a popular choice with Moroccan families. Shared-bathroom singles are available. €

De Paris 2 Rue Sharif Amzian ☎0522 273871. A popular lower end option in the centre of town; rooms facing the street are larger and have balconies but can also be noisy. There's a busy modern café at street level. It's often full, so book ahead or arrive early. €

Toubkal 9 Rue Sidi Belyout ☎0522 311414. Part of the Best Western chain, this hotel's major attributes are its central location and safe street parking, as well as the friendly service. The rooms are comfortable enough but

nothing very special for the price, though sizeable discounts are usually available, especially in the colder months. €€

★ **Touring** 87 Rue Allal Ben Abdallah ☎0522 310216. An excellent-value, friendly old French hotel, with clean, comfortable rooms, some with their own shower (though shared toilets), and hot water most of the day. It's even got its own little mosque. Definitely the first choice of the cheapies on this street. €

Windsor 93 Pl Oued el Makhazine ☎0522 200352. Regal looking hotel with spacious rooms that have either a large bathroom or just a shower. There's also a decent bar, the staff are generally friendly and helpful, and there's a number of cafés close by. BB €

AÏN DIAB

The seaside suburb of Aïn Diab (about 20dh from the centre by *petit taxi*, 8dh by tram, or 5dh on bus #9; see page 262) provides an alternative base to the city. The options for tourists are all in the moderate to luxury price range, as the few cheaper hotels in the area cater exclusively for Moroccan guests.

Azur 41 Bd de la Corniche ⓦwww.azurhotel.ma. Across the road from the beach, equipped with a decent size swimming pool, at times noisy bar, and a pretty good restaurant. The rooms, most sea-facing, are elegantly furnished with a few modern touches and good-sized bathrooms. BB €€€

Bellerive 38 Bd de la Corniche ☎0522 797504. An ageing but friendly family-run hotel overlooking the beach. Rooms are a bit small and dated; request a balcony with a sea view. There's a good pool, small playground, and a restaurant serving burgers, club sandwiches and kebabs. BB €€

Le Littoral Bd de l'Ocean Atlantique ☎0522 797373. Beachfront hotel with friendly management and staff, and large rooms with all the mod cons – most face seawards with a balcony. There's a very good restaurant, swimming pool and nightclub. BB €€

YOU MUST REMEMBER THIS...

One of the best-known facts about the city is that it wasn't the location for Michael Curtiz's **Casablanca** movie, all of which was shot inside the Warner Bros studio in Hollywood. Banking on a major hit and upset by the Marx Brothers filming *A Night in Casablanca*, Warner Bros even wanted to copyright the very name Casablanca – which could have been inconvenient for the city.

The film of course owes its enduring success to the romantic tension between Humphrey Bogart and Ingrid Bergman, but at the time of its release it received a major publicity boost by the appearance of Casablanca and Morocco in the news. As the film was being completed, in November 1942, the Allies launched **Operation Torch**, landing 25,000 troops on the coast north and south of Casablanca, at Kenitra, Mohammedia and Safi. The troops, under General Eisenhower, consisted mainly of Americans, whom Roosevelt believed were less likely than the British to be fired on by the Vichy French colonial authorities. An even more fortunate coincidence took place in the week of the film's première in Los Angeles in January 1943, as Churchill and Roosevelt had arranged an Allied leaders' summit, and the newsreels revealed its location: the **Casablanca Conference**, held in Anfa, out beyond Aïn Diab. Such events – and the movie – are not, it has to be said, evoked by modern-day Casa, though the movie is commemorated in the city at the American-owned *Rick's Café* (see page 264).

CAMPING

Camping Oasis Dar Bouazza, 25km south of Casablanca on the coast road to Azemmour ☎ 0522 290767. Spacious, with modern, clean ablutions (showers cost extra) and plenty of stands for camper vans, but make sure you're near a power source. The beach and restaurants are nearby. €

EATING

SEE MAP PAGE 256

If you can afford the fancier **restaurants**, Casa has the best dining in Morocco. On a budget, your choice is more limited, but there are plenty of chicken **rôtisseries** and **snack joints**, so you won't starve. In addition to the places listed here, there are inexpensive **hole-in-the-wall eateries** in the Old Medina, and if you're putting together a picnic, the Marché Central on Rue Chaouia groans under the weight of the freshest and best produce in Morocco.

La Brasserie Bavaroise 129–131 Rue Allal Ben Abdallah. Rough wooden floors and high ceilings hint at this French-style brasserie's previous life as a German alehouse. Nowadays it's one of Casa's more intimate dining experiences, with an impressive menu of fish and meat dishes as well as a reasonably priced set lunch menu exquisitely prepared and accompanied by an extensive wine list. Worth the splurge. Licensed. €€€

L'Étoile Centrale 107 Rue Allal Ben Abdallah. The most "local" of the restaurants on this street and a worthy introduction to Moroccan cuisine, with a traditional interior and a friendly, easy-going atmosphere. The menu concentrates on couscous, pastillas and tajines and is consistently good. €€

Golden China 12 Rue Araibi Jilali. A welcome if a trifle pricey diversion for those suffering from tajine fatigue. The large menu covers the whole gamut of Chinese-influenced Asian cuisine, with a few vegetarian options. It's rarely full and service is usually attentive. Licensed. €€

Le Petit Poucet 86 Bd Mohammed V ☎ 0522 275420. A slice of old Casablanca, this restaurant is dressed up like a 1920s Parisian salon (which is what it was), where French aviator and writer Saint-Exupéry used to recuperate between his mail flights south to the Sahara – a couple of framed sketches by him grace the walls. It used to be quite a classy restaurant, but nowadays it's more like a bar that serves a few standard Moroccan dishes. Licensed. €

Rick's Café 248 Bd Sour Jdid, off Bd des Almohades ⊛ rickscafe.ma. A varied lunch and dinner menu offers a fusion of Moroccan, French and Californian cuisine – try the goat's cheese and fig salad. The pianist (Issam rather than Sam) creates a Forties and Fifties musical ambience, and apparently never tires of playing the inevitable "As Time Goes By". Touristy, obviously. Licensed (see page 265). €€€

★ **La Sqala** Bd des Almohades ⊛ sqala.ma. An upmarket café-restaurant amid pleasant gardens in an eighteenth-century bastion of the Medina wall, complete with cannons. The menu is vast and inventive, with a tummy-expanding breakfast menu , a number of light and crunchy salads, as well as more substantial dishes such as tajines and grilled steaks. They also serve all-day juices, coffees, teas and cake (but no alcohol). €€

Taverne du Dauphin 115 Bd Félix Houphouët Boigny ☎ 0522 221200, ⊛ taverne-du-dauphin.com. Long-established and very popular fish restaurant, with tables on the pavement as well as a more intimate, classier area at the rear, the two bisected by a lively, smoky bar serving seafood tapas. The menu is almost solely dedicated to the ocean, with just a few *grillés* for non-seafood eaters. The service can be a bit up and down; reservations advisable. Licensed. €€€

DRINKING AND NIGHTLIFE

Casa has a surprisingly elusive nightlife in the city centre, where although **bars** are plentiful, they are almost exclusively the domain of men and prostitutes. This also goes for most of the **clubs** in town, which tend to be tacky cabaret joints at best. There are a few ultra-chic lounge bars out in the suburbs and Aïn Diab – self-conscious and full of self-importance, they don't usually charge admission but the drinks and meals are exorbitantly expensive.

BARS

Of ordinary bars around town, those attached to the restaurants *Le Petit Poucet* and *Taverne du Dauphin* (see above) are quite relaxed and there are also a few by the Rialto Cinema. If you want to check out some typical all-male hard-drinking dens, you'll find a row of them next to *La Bodéga*, along Rue Allal Ben Abdallah behind the Marché Central.

DOWNTOWN, SEE MAP PAGE 256

★ **La Bodéga** 127 Rue Allal Ben Abdallah ⓦ bodega. ma. Lively, rustic taverna-style setting with a street-level Spanish-and-Tex-Mex restaurant where it's OK to just have a drink and watch big screen sports, as well as a downstairs bar and dancefloor (salsa night Tues). It's fun and not too pretentious, and the drinks (including sangria) are reasonably priced.

Rick's Café 248 Bd Sour Jdid, off Bd des Almohades ⓦ rickscafe.ma. Although the ground floor is primarily a restaurant (see page 264), there's a second-floor cigar lounge just perfect for a gin and tonic while watching Bogey & Bergman's *Casablanca* on a big screen. There's also a less formal, tropical-themed rooftop terrace "bar'n'bbq".

CLUBS

There's a high concentration of clubs along Bd de la Corniche out in Aïn Diab. The term in general use for a dancefloor nightclub is "disco", while "nightclub" usually means a place with tables and a cabaret floorshow.

AÏN DIAB

Armstrong Legend 41 Bd de la Corniche. A very popular, though small, club with live music and a great party atmosphere. It can get quite packed at weekends, when it's worth reserving a table.

SHOPPING
SEE MAP PAGE 256

Casablanca lacks any souks or quarters where artisans practise their craft; any traditional **souvenirs** on offer are imported from elsewhere in the country. The quality can therefore be low and prices high, making souvenir shopping only worthwhile if you're about to leave the country.
Boulevard Félix Houphouët Boigny. On both sides of this busy road is a string of souvenir shops, all selling the same stuff and keen to secure your business at the highest negotiable price.
Exposition Nationale d'Artisanat Cnr Av Hassan II & Rue Maarakat Ohoud. Three-storey building stuffed with crafts from all over the country, with fixed prices and largely hassle-free assistance from the salesmen. Popular with large tour groups.
Librairie de France 4 Rue Chenier. This well-established bookshop caters largely for locals, but also offers a quality selection of English-language classics, a few guidebooks and some souvenir coffee table-style books.
Marché Central Bd Mohammed V. Large undercover market selling everyday grocery items, a few souvenirs, spices and argan oil, fresh produce (good olives), fresh seafood and fresh flowers. A hive of activity each day from early morning through evening, there's also a number of cafés and snack restaurants and it's worth a visit even if you're not shopping. Bordered by Bd Mohammed V, Rue Allal Ben Abdallah, Rue Abdallah Almedouini, and Rue Chaouia.

DIRECTORY

Banks & exchange Most banks have main branches with ATMs along Av des FAR, between Pl des Nations Unies and Pl Zellaqa. Attijariwafa Bank, Av Hassan II (off Pl des Nations Unies) has an exchange ATM, and WafaCash bureau de change BMCI, Bd Mohammed V (off Pl des Nations Unies) has an exchange ATM; Attika Bureau de Change, 22–24 Rue Allal Ben Abdallah
Consulates Ireland (Honorary Consul), Résidence Al Hadi (entrance B, 5th floor, #20), 57 Bd Abdelmoumen (ⓣ 0522 272721); UK, 36 Rue de la Loire, Polo (ⓣ 0522 857400); US, 8 Bd Moulay Youssef (ⓦ usembassy.gov/morocco).
Festivals Jazzablanca (ⓦ jazzablanca.com) brings together diverse international and Moroccan performers for five days of fusion Jazz, held each April or May at the Casa-Anfa Hippodrome.

Football Casa is the best place in Morocco to see football; the city's rivals, Raja and Wydad (also known as WAC) both play at the Complexe Mohammed V on Rue Socrate in Maarif; check the local press for fixtures.
Hospitals and doctors Dial ⓣ 15 for emergency services or call SOS Médecin (ⓣ 0522 444444) or SOS Médecins Maroc (ⓣ 0522 989898) for a doctor, or SAMU (ⓣ 0522 252525) for an ambulance. Clinics open round the clock for emergency treatment include: Clinique Badr, 35 Rue el Alloussi Bourgogne (ⓣ 0522 492380–84) and Clinique Yasmine, Bd Sidi Abderrahman Hay el Hana (ⓣ 0522 396960). English-speaking doctors include: Dr Mohammed Bennani, 45 Rue Atlas Maarif (ⓣ 0522 994799); Dr Alain Guidon, 4 Rue Mohammed Ben Ali (Rue Jean Jaurès), Gauthier (ⓣ 0522 267153).

Pharmacies There's an all-night pharmacy in the Préfecture in Pl Mohammed V; details of other pharmacies open out of hours appear in the local press, or on lists displayed by all pharmacies.
Police Bd Brahim Roudani (☎ 0522 989865). For emergencies call ☎ 19.
Post office Pl Mohammed V; 116 Bd Mohammed V, cnr Rue Chaouia.

Swimming pools Complexe Mohammed V (see above) houses an Olympic-size indoor swimming pool open to the public. You can swim at the beach clubs on the Corniche, in the open-air Piscine Océanique in Aïn Sebaa, and the pool at the *Hyatt Regency* (charge for non-guests).
Travel agencies There is a Carlson Wagonlit travel agent on the corber of Rue Allal Ben Abdallah and Rue Araibi Jilali (☎ 0522 203051).

South of Casablanca

The road and train line run side by side from Casablanca, firstly west past Azemmour to El Jadida, and then **south** across the plains to Marrakesh. To the east lies the desolate, dusty and largely unattractive phosphate-mining region, the Plateau des Phosphates.

Azemmour

Despite its strategic site at the mouth of the great Oum er Rbia River, **AZEMMOUR** has always been a backwater, and sees fewer tourists than any other Moroccan coastal town. This makes it a quiet, rather sedate place to visit, and staying at a riad in the whitewashed clifftop Medina is rather an attractive option.

Once in town, getting your bearings is straightforward. The town lies between the N1 Casablanca–El Jadida highway and the El Jadida coastal road, and red *petits taxis* constantly ply the route between the two roads. The main thoroughfare is **Avenue Mohammed V**, which leads to a busy, grassed square, **Place du Souk**, with the **Medina** straight ahead.

The Medina

The Portuguese remained in Azemmour long enough to build a circuit of walls, directly above the banks of the river and dramatically extended by the white **Medina**. The best view of all this – and it is impressive – is from across the river, on the way out of town towards Casablanca.

The kasbah

Entrance gate is 200m north of Pl du Souk • If you wait around, the local *gardien* may arrive, open up and show you round; if he doesn't turn up, try asking at the cafés overlooking Pl du Souk

From Place du Souk, on the landward side of the ramparts, you'll see a sixteenth-century **gate** with an unusual, European-style, semi-circular arch. Through it extends the old **kasbah** – largely in ruins but safe enough to visit. Once inside the ruins, you can follow the parapet wall round the ramparts, with views of the river and the gardens, including henna orchards, along its edge. Also here is **Dar el Baroud** (The House of Powder), a large tower built over the ruins of an old gunpowder store; note also the ruined Gothic window.

The synagogue

Mellah • Private viewings only • Small donation appreciated to see the tomb

The old **Mellah** – Azzemour had a substantial Jewish population until the 1960s – lies beyond the kasbah at the northern end of the Medina. Here, beside ramparts overlooking the Oum er Rbia, is the old town **synagogue** which is still well maintained and visited occasionally by practising Jews from Casablanca and El Jadida. It's cared for by a local family and you can look inside to see the tomb of Rabbi Abrahim Moul Niss, a shrine for Jewish pilgrims and the focus of an August moussem.

Haouzia beach

30min walk or a *petit taxi* ride (5dh) through the eucalyptus trees beyond the town; for personal safety, it's advisable to follow the road (signposted to the "Balnéaire du Haouzia") rather than the riverbank

The river currents at Azemmour are notoriously dangerous, but there's a nice stretch of sand at **Haouzia beach,** where a small complex of company holiday cabins occupy part of the stretch. For **birdwatchers,** the scrub dunes around the mouth of the river should prove rewarding territory.

ARRIVAL AND DEPARTURE
AZEMMOUR

By train The train station (Azemmour Halte) is inconveniently located 2km out of town, on the far side of the N1. You can usually catch a *petit taxi* from the station, though sometimes demand outweighs supply. Aside from El Jadida, services to all other destinations connect through Casa Voyageurs.
Destinations Casa Voyageurs (8 daily; 1hr 10min); El Jadida (8 daily; 20min).

By bus Local bus #101 operates between Azemmour's bus rank at Bd Boujdour, between the N1 & Av Mohammed V, and El Jadida at Pl de France, 200m south of the bus station.
Destination El Jadida (hourly 7am–8pm; 25min).
By grand taxi *Grands taxis* operate all day between the bus rank and El Jadida (Rue Abdelmoumen el Mouahidi, by the bus station).
Destination El Jadida (hourly 7am–7pm; 15min).

ACCOMMODATION AND EATING

Accommodation and dining options are limited. Other than the in-house restaurants of the Medina *maisons d'hôte,* there are a few café-restaurants located around Pl du Souk.
★ **L'Oum Errebia** 25 Derb Chtouka, Medina ⓦ azemmour-hotel.com. Once the kitchen and servant quarters for the town's *caïd, L'Oum Errebia* is now renovated with a distinctly modern touch – bright, abstract paintings adorn almost every spare bit of wall space, while a number of private nooks allow for some quality quiet time. There's a choice of rooms and views; the river view from the terrace

is unequalled. Dinner is a set menu (€€€, open to non-residents) of traditional Moroccan food, sourced locally and often organic. BB €€
Riad 7 2 Derb Chtouka, Medina ⓦ riad7.com. An elegant, almost minimalistic Swiss-owned riad in the heart of the Medina, with contemporary artworks and furniture and decorated in blacks, whites and greys throughout. The five en-suite rooms boast quality fittings and a few mod cons, and the kitchen provides delicious, authentic Moroccan cuisine. BB €€

4

El Jadida and around

EL JADIDA is a stylish and beautiful town, retaining the lanes and ramparts of an old Portuguese Medina, now a UNESCO World Heritage Site. It was known as **Mazagan** under the Portuguese, who held it from 1506 until 1769. The city was taken from the Portuguese by Sultan Sidi Mohammed Ben Abdallah and then in the nineteenth century was renamed El Jadida – "The New" – after being resettled, partly with Jews from Azemmour, by Sultan Abd er Rahman. Under the French, it grew into a quite sizeable administrative centre and a popular beach resort.

Moroccans from Casablanca and Marrakesh, even Tangier or Fez, come down to the beach here in summer; when the bars are crowded, there's an almost frenetic evening promenade and – as in Casa – Moroccan women are visible and active participants.

Cité Portugaise

El Jadida's **Medina** is the most European-looking in Morocco: a quiet, walled and bastioned seaside village, with a handful of churches. It was founded by the Portuguese in 1513, and retained by them until 1769 – it is still popularly known as the **Cité Portugaise**. As they withdrew, the Portuguese blew up several of the churches and other important buildings. The Moors who settled here after the Portuguese withdrawal tended to live outside the walls. As in all the open ports on this coast, there was also an important Jewish community handling the trade with Marrakesh; uniquely, old Mazagan had no separate Jewish Mellah.

Portuguese Cistern

Midway along Rue Mohammed Ali Bahbai; accessed by steps • Charge

The beautiful old **Portuguese Cistern** is a subterranean vault that mirrors its roof and pillars in a shallow film of water covering the floor. It was used to startling effect in Orson Welles's 1952 film of *Othello*; he staged a riot here and filmed it from within and above. It also featured in a Moroccan TV ad for Samar coffee, and locals associate it with that, rather than Welles. Bring your camera.

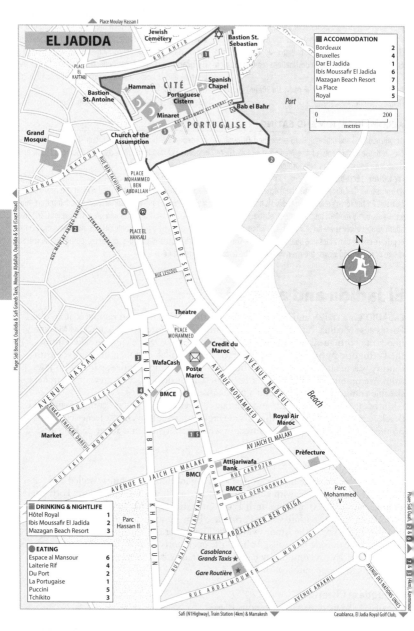

EL JADIDA

ACCOMMODATION
Bordeaux	2
Bruxelles	4
Dar El Jadida	1
Ibis Moussafir El Jadida	6
Mazagan Beach Resort	7
La Place	3
Royal	5

DRINKING & NIGHTLIFE
Hôtel Royal	1
Ibis Moussafir El Jadida	2
Mazagan Beach Resort	3

EATING
Espace al Mansour	6
Laiterie Rif	4
Du Port	2
La Portugaise	1
Puccini	5
Tchikito	3

The ramparts
Free

From the original gate onto the port, **Bab el Bahr** (Sea Gate), you can climb onto the **ramparts** and walk most of the way round (there's an obligatory descent at Bastion St-Antoine), offering a fascinating, almost voyeuristic view of life within the Medina. You can also explore all the bastions; by **Bastion St Sebastian**, the restored former **synagogue** has an interesting crescent and Star of David on its back wall, while from the bastion itself there's a great view looking north over an extensive Jewish cemetery.

Churches and mosques

The Christian **churches** and chapels of the Portuguese City are generally closed; but worth seeking out for its shiny brass spire is the small **Spanish chapel**, located in the heart of the Medina to the north of Rue Mohammed Ali Bahbai and now bricked up bar a small section used as a shop. More impressive is the seventeenth-century Portuguese **Church of the Assumption** by the entrance to the Cité Portugaise, which was once restored and used as a cultural centre, but is now again empty. The minaret of the **Grand Mosque**, immediately north of the Church of Assumption, was once a five-sided watchtower or lighthouse, and is said to be the only pentagonal minaret in Islam.

The beaches

El Jadida's town **beach** spreads southeast from the *cité* and port, well beyond the length of the town. It's a popular strip, though from time to time polluted by the ships in port. Three kilometres further east along the coastal road, past the **Phare Sidi Ouafi** (lighthouse) and towards the *Mazagan Beach Resort*, is a broader strip of sand where Moroccan families set up tents for the summer. Good swimming is to be had, and there are makeshift beach cafés in the summer. **Plage Sidi Bouzid**, 2km southwest of the *cité* (bus #14 from Place Mohammed V), is more developed, with a seaside promenade flanked by some fancy villas and a few café-restaurants.

Moulay Abdallah

11km south of El Jadida on the R301 coast road • Buses and *grands taxis* ply the R301 daily between here and El Jadida (15–30min) and Oualidia (45min–1hr)

MOULAY ABDALLAH (also called Tit) is a tiny fishing village, dominated by a large *zaouia* complex and partially enclosed by a circuit of ruined walls. An important **moussem** here in late August attracts thousands of devotees – and almost as many horses in the parades and *fantasias*.

Ribat Tit-n-Fitr

The village walls span the site of a twelfth-century **ribat**, or fortified monastery, known as **Ribat Tit-n-Fitr**, which was built as a base for Sufi mystics, and to defend the coast from a possible Norman invasion – a real threat at the time, the Normans having launched attacks on Tunisia. Today, there is little to see, though the **minaret** of the modern *zaouia* (prominent and whitewashed) is Almohad; behind it, through the graveyard, a second, isolated minaret is thought to be even older. If so, then it is the only one surviving from the Almoravid era – a claim considerably more impressive than its simple, block-like appearance might suggest.

ARRIVAL AND DEPARTURE **EL JADIDA**

By train The train station is inconveniently located 4km south of town on the Marrakesh road (N1); *petits taxis* are usually available. Services to all major destinations connect through Casa Voyageurs.

Destination Casa Voyageurs (8 daily; 1hr 20min).
By bus All services including CTM call at the bus station on Av Mohammed V, at the southern end of town; from here it's a 15min walk to the Medina or to most hotels. *Petits taxis*

are usually available.

Destinations Casablanca (6 CTM daily & others hourly; 2hr); Marrakesh (over 10 daily; 4hr); Oualidia (over 10 daily; 1hr 30min); Rabat (over 10 daily; 4hr); Safi (8 CTM & over 10 others daily; 2hr 30min).

By grand taxi *Grands taxis* from Casa drop you by the bus station, while those from Oualidia (and sometimes direct to Safi) operate from a station on Av Zerktouni, about 2km west of the Cité Portugaise.

Destinations Casablanca (2hr); Oualidia (1hr); Safi (2hr).

ACCOMMODATION
SEE MAP PAGE 268

It's a good idea to book in advance in summer, when rooms can be very hard to find and prices are higher.

★ **Bordeaux** 47 Rue Moulay Ahmed Tahiri, signposted from Rue Ben Tachfine ☎0523 373921. Down a small side street, this old hotel – the oldest in town, so the patron claims – is spotlessly clean and attractively refurbished, and some rooms are now en suite with a/c. Easily the best of a number of cheapies in this neighbourhood. €

Bruxelles 40 Av Ibn Khaldoun ☎0523 342072. Cheap and cheerful, this hotel is in a handy location just 10min walk from both the beach and Medina. The ageing but large, clean rooms are accessed by a steep stairway – some are en suite and others have balconies. The wi-fi is good, and drivers will appreciate the undercover parking. €

Dar El Jadida 7 Rue Joseph Nahon, Cité Portugaise ☎0523 372807 or ☎0610 266145. One of a number of Medina *maisons d'hôte* that have opened in recent years, this one is more homely than most thanks to the friendly Sicilian owner-manager, a former gondolier. The rooms are pretty compact and have private bathrooms, though not all are en suite. Breakfast on the terrace is accompanied by sweeping city and ocean views, and a delicious authentic Italian dinner is available if pre-booked. BB €

Ibis Moussafir El Jadida Pl Nour el Kamar ⊛ibishotel. com. In a prime location right on the beach. The rooms are the usual Ibis standard – compact, carpeted and with a couple of mod cons, many have sea views (no balconies), and two on the ground floor are wheelchair-friendly. The service is usually good, and there is a restaurant, bar, swimming pool and secure parking. BB €€€

Mazagan Beach Resort Plage Haouzia, 5km north of El Jadida ⊛mazaganbeachresort.com. Sprawling and impressive resort with hundreds of elegantly furnished rooms, all with French balconies offering sea (sometimes only partial) or pool views, and a choice of restaurants & bars, as well as a nightclub and casino. There's private beach access, an eighteen-hole golf course, a good spa and gym, and a free shuttle from Casablanca's Mohammed V Airport. BB €€€€

La Place Av Ibn Khaldoun at Rue Jules Verne ☎0523 373700. A modern three-star that's about the comfiest place to stay in the centre of town, with clean rooms and en-suite facilities. BB €€

Royal 108 Av Mohammed V ☎0523 342839. An ageing yet attractive hotel with large, airy rooms, some en suite with balcony, but no shared facilities for those without their own bathrooms. Noise can be a problem, from both the busy street and the lively beer garden. Convenient for the bus station. €

EATING
SEE MAP PAGE 268

El Jadida's dining scene leaves something to be desired, offering a plethora of snack **fast-food joints** and just a few rare and worthy exceptions.

Espace al Mansour 46 Av Mohammed V. A popular locals' restaurant between the bus station and town centre. Choose from pavement tables, or a colourful a/c interior. The menu offers fast, light options such as pizzas, panini, pastas, shawarma and brochettes, as well as a great selection of fresh juices. €

Laiterie Rif Rue Ben Tachfine. This small juice shop is perfect for a healthy breakfast. Order a bowl of fruit salad, accompanied by a fresh juice or smoothie, and enjoy at one of the simple pavement tables. €

Du Port Northern end of the port. This first-floor restaurant in an unprepossessing building has a lovely view of the sea and serves good and plentiful seafood, including oysters from nearby Oualidia. Licensed. €€

La Portugaise Rue Mohammed Ali Bahbai, Cité Portugaise. A very pleasant little restaurant with red-and-white-checked tablecloths, serving Moroccan rather than Portuguese dishes, including an exceptional beef tajine. €€

Puccini 70 Av Nabeul. Ground floor bar and steak house and a separate upstairs restaurant with an ocean view. Offering a nice break from tajines and couscous, the Mediterranean-inspired menu is varied and good value, with plenty of seafood and meat dishes, as well as pizzas and crunchy salads. Licensed. €€

Tchikito Rue Mohammed Smiha. A hole-in-the-wall fish restaurant that's been serving generous helpings at low prices since 1960. Try the excellent mixed fish platter with chilli sauce. €

DRINKING AND NIGHTLIFE
SEE MAP PAGE 268

Drinking is kept away from the public eye and consists mainly of smoky **hotel bars** – try the *Hôtel Royal* or *Ibis*

Moussafir (see page 270).

Mazagan Beach Resort Plage Haouzia, 5km north of

El Jadida ⓦmazaganbeachresort.com. If funds allow, head out to this resort, with its bars, casino and *Alias*

nightclub, which has hosted big-name "Eastern" live acts such as Cheb Mami.

DIRECTORY

Banks Located mostly south of the town centre between Pl Mohammed V and the bus station; exchange is available from Currency Exchange Point, cnr Pl Mohammed V & Av Mohammed V.

Golf *Mazagan Beach Resort* (18 holes; ⓦmazaganbeach resort.com; see page 270); El Jadida Royal Golf Club, Plage

Haouzia, 6km north of El Jadida (18 holes).

Hammam There's one in the Cité Portugaise at 1 Rue No. 45 – enter the double gate, turn left along Rua do Arco and it's 50m along on your right – with separate entrances for women and men.

Post office Pl Mohammed V.

Oualidia

OUALIDIA, 78km south of El Jadida, is a stunningly picturesque little resort – a fishing port and lagoon beach, flanked by a kasbah and a royal villa. The **kasbah** is seventeenth-century, built under the Saadian sultan El Oualid (after whom the village is named) as a counterweight and alternative to Portuguese-held El Jadida. Until Sultan Sidi Mohammed took El Jadida, the lagoon made an excellent harbour and, as late as 1875, a French geographer thought that "by a little dredging the place would again become the safest shipping station on the whole Moroccan seaboard". The **royal villa**, now empty, was built for Mohammed V, who celebrated many birthdays and other family events here.

Today, most Moroccans know Oualidia for its **Japanese oysters**; Morocco's first oyster farm was launched here in 1957 and nowadays it harvests some two hundred tonnes a year, mostly sold locally. But the town really deserves to be better known as a resort: its beach is excellent for **surfing and windsurfing**, and swimming is safe and easy thanks to the shielded lagoon. The atmosphere for most of the year is very relaxed, aside from August when the place is jam-packed with Moroccan holidaymakers.

ARRIVAL AND DEPARTURE

OUALIDIA

By bus and grand taxi Buses and *grands taxis* ply the route north to El Jadida and south to Safi throughout the day; both depart from Av Hassan II (the El Jadida–Safi

highway).

Destinations El Jadida (1hr–1hr 30min); Safi (1hr).

ACCOMMODATION AND EATING

Oualidia has a limited (though good quality) selection of traditional **hotels**, which invariably also double as **restaurants**, and privately-owned **self-catering villas**. Villas can be booked through Maroc Lagune Location (ⓦmaroc-lagune.com), with rates typically around 800–1200dh/night, depending on the size of the villa and season.

L'Hippocampe Cnr rues Palais Royal & 11 Janvier, Oualidia

Lagoon ⓦhippocampeoualidia.com. A delightful place, halfway up the slope between the lagoon and the village. The simple en-suite rooms are accessed off a pretty garden, while two suites overlook the lagoon. There are steps down to a "private" beach with free kayaks, plus there's a pool and very good restaurant with an outdoor terrace bar. BB €€€€

L'Initiale Oualidia Plage ☎0523 366246. A family-run place that's the last along the beach road, with six smallish

4

BIRD HABITATS AROUND OUALIDIA

The 70km of coast between **Sidi Moussa** (36km south of El Jadida) and **Cap Beddouza** (34km south of Oualidia) is one of the richest **birdlife habitats** in Morocco. The coastal wetlands, sands and saltpans, the jagged reefs, and the lagoons of Sidi Moussa and Oualidia shelter a huge range of species: flamingos, avocets, stilts, godwits, storks, terns, egrets, warblers and many small waders. Numerous countryside species come in, too; golden oriole and hoopoe have been recorded, and flocks of shearwaters are often to be seen not far offshore. The best watching locations are the two lagoons and the rocky headland at Cap Beddouza.

rooms, two with a sea view (book ahead for those). Despite its close proximity to the beach, the restaurant doesn't have any views, but is still pleasant enough and has a leafy garden. Besides a wide choice of seafood, the menu also offers pizza and pastas and a few meat dishes. BB €€

Issa Blanca Bd Tariq Ibn Ziad ⓦfacebook.com/naddiaelkhadri. Owner-managed and friendly hotel-restaurant just a short walk over the dunes to the beach (though a good 15min stroll from the main restaurant-beach area). The colourful, airy rooms, some with sea views, are

tiled and tastefully decorated with modern furnishings, while the stylish ground-floor restaurant offers a varied menu of seafood and Italian-Moroccan dishes, which can be home delivered should you be staying in a rented villa nearby. €€

Motel-Restaurant à l'Araignée Gourmande Opposite Bd Tariq Ibn Ziad Oualidia Lagoon ⓣ0523 366447. Alongside the lagoon beach, offering dated but reasonably well-kept rooms, some with lagoon views. There's also a suitably nautical yet unpretentious restaurant specializing in excellent seafood. BB €

Safi and around

The coastal port city of **SAFI**, halfway between El Jadida and Essaouira, with an old **Medina** in its centre, walled and turreted by the Portuguese, has a strong industrial-artisan tradition, with a whole quarter devoted to **pottery workshops**. These have a virtual monopoly on the green, heavily glazed roof tiles used on palaces and mosques, as well as providing Morocco's main pottery exports, in the form of bowls, plates and garden pots.

Safi has two main squares, **Place de l'Indépendance**, just south of the Medina, and **Place Mohammed V** on the higher ground in the Ville Nouvelle (also known as the *Plateau*).

Dar el Bahar
Pl de l'Indépendance • currently closed for maintenance

The **Dar el Bahar**, or Château de la Mer, is the main remnant of Safi's 1508–41 Portuguese occupation. Built in the Manueline (Portuguese late Gothic) style of the day as the governor's residence, it was later a fortress and a prison. Within, you can see the old prison cells at the foot of a spiral staircase to the ramparts, where a line of Dutch and Spanish cannons are ranged pointing out to sea.

The Kechla
Av Moulay Youssef • free

The old Medina walls climb north, enclosing the Medina, to link with a large fortress known as the **Kechla**, Portuguese in origin, and entered from the east side, outside the Medina walls. Until 1990 it housed the town's prison, and is now the local base of the Ministry of Culture, but they don't mind you popping in and look round. The not-very-exciting **National Ceramics Museum**, previously housed here, has moved down the road to Rue Medina Mounoura.

Cathédrale Portugaise
Off Rue du Socco, Medina • Charge • Head northeast up Rue du Socco for about 100m, until it opens out a little; by the entrance to the Grand Mosque, a sign painted on the wall points the way through a small doorway

A visible relic of the Portuguese occupation is the Medina's **Cathédrale Portugaise**. It's actually just the choir gallery of what was planned to be the cathedral, left uncompleted when the Portuguese withdrew. It's adorned with sixteenth-century Manueline motifs.

Sufi shrines

If you are Muslim, you can enter two important Sufi shrines in the Medina: the **Marabout Sidi Bou Dheb** (at the bottom end of Rue du Socco) and the **Zaouia of Hamidouch** (near the Kechla). Sidi Bou Dheb is perhaps the best-known Sufi saint in

Morocco and both his *marabout* and the Hamdouchia *zaouia* host **moussems** (held in May in recent years) attended by their respective brotherhoods. These feature music, dervish-type dancing and, often, trance-induced self-mutilation with hatchets and knives.

La Colline des Potiers

La Colline des Potiers (potters' quarter) sprawls above the Medina, with its dozens of whitewashed beehive-kilns and chimneys. The processes here remain traditional – electricity and gas have made scarcely an inroad on the tamarisk-fired kilns and the foot-powered pottery wheels – and the quarter is worth at least the time it takes to wander up the new concrete steps and pathways. At the foot of the hillside is a street of

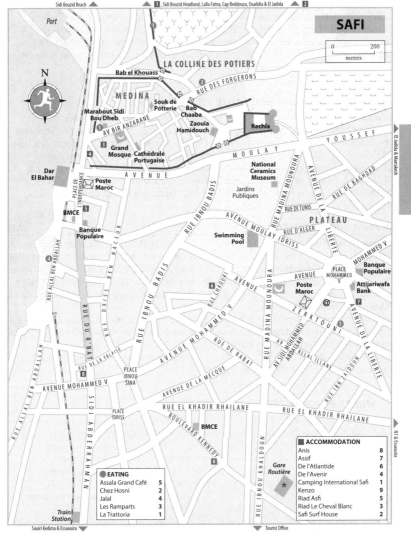

showrooms. The products on display match those on offer in Fez, such as tiles, bowls and other housewares, and can be up to half the price, depending on your bargaining skills. Unofficial guides may hustle for business, and while the kilns are easily located without assistance, some guides may take you to more remote kilns and make it easier to take photographs and ask questions. If you do accept an offer of a guided "tour", agree a price beforehand (perhaps 10dh per person) and don't be intimidated into buying anything.

Sidi Bouzid beach

2km north of Safi · Accessed by walking through Safi port or driving down a hairpin road from Sidi Bouzid

The road north of Safi first rises 2km up to the headland of Sidi Bouzid, where a glorious sweeping view looking back over the city awaits. Down below the headland is **Sidi Bouzid beach** where, on November 8, 1942, American troops under General Patton landed as the southernmost thrust of Operation Torch (see page 264), the Vichy French position offering little resistance. A pleasant 3km stretch of golden sand, the beach is jam-packed with Moroccan holidaymakers during summer and virtually deserted for the rest of the year.

Lalla Fatna and Cap Beddouza

Lalla Fatna 15km north of Safi, Cap Beddouza 23km north of Safi · Local buses #10 and #15 from Pl de l'Indépendance

North of Safi, the rocky headland gives way intermittently to sandy beaches, sheltered by cliffs and with good waves for surfers as well as safe swimming conditions. The best of these cliff-sheltered beaches is **Lalla Fatna**, 15km north of Safi and a steep two-kilometre descent from the road, with a **koubba**, but little else, so bring provisions. If camping, be sure to pitch your tent far enough back from the tides. Another 8km further on from Lalla Fatna is the headland and lighthouse of **Cap Beddouza**, with another very pleasant sandy beach.

ARRIVAL AND INFORMATION   SAFI

By train Safi's small train station is about 1.5km south of the Medina (15min walk); all trains connect via Benguerir. *Petits taxis* can usually be hailed from the street. Destinations Benguerir (2 daily; 2hr), connecting to Casablanca Voyageurs (2hr 20min), Fez (6hr 30min), Marrakesh (1hr) and Rabat (3hr 25min).

By bus All companies including CTM operate from the *gare routière*, around 1.5km and a confusing 20min walk south of the Medina. *Petits taxis* can be hailed from Bd Kennedy just outside the station's entrance.

Destinations Agadir (4 CTM & over 10 others daily; 6hr); Casablanca (9 CTM & over 20 others daily; 4–5hr); El Jadida (6 CTM & over 10 others daily; 2hr 30min); Essaouira (4 CTM & over 20 others daily; 2hr); Marrakesh (1 CTM & 15 others daily; 2hr); Oualidia (2 CTM & over 10 others daily; 45min).

By grand taxi Shared *grands taxis* operate from the bus station.

Destinations Casablanca (3hr 30min); El Jadida (2hr); Essaouira (2hr 30min); Marrakesh (2hr); Oualidia (1hr).

Tourist information Online in French at ⓦ safi-ville.com.

AND THE SARDINES?

Safi's famed **sardines** are caught in the deeper waters of the Atlantic, from Boujdour in the south to Safi in the north. There are around five hundred 18–20m wooden trawlers in the town fleet and you can still see them being made in the boatyards at Safi, Essaouira and Agadir. The fleet lands 350,000 tonnes of sardines annually (seventy percent of the country's total seafood catch) and most of them are canned in Safi. Increasingly, those caught further south are landed at the nearest port and brought to Safi in refrigerated trucks. Most of the tins get sold abroad – Morocco being the **world's largest exporter** of sardines.

ACCOMMODATION SEE MAP PAGE 273

Anis Cnr Rue du R'bat & Rue de la Falaise ☎0524 463078. Cheerless but reasonably central place with a range of room types, some with en-suite facilities. €̄

Assif Av de la Liberté ⓦwww.hotel-assif.ma. An average mid-range hotel, with functional but dated tiled rooms, some (for not very much more) with a/c, heating and balcony, and there's an adequate restaurant. €̄€̄

De l'Atlantide Rue Chaouki ☎0524 462160. Over one hundred years old and once the centre of Safi society. It's well and truly lost her sparkle but still retains a certain old colonial charm, especially in the grand public areas. The rooms are old and tired, but some offer a great view across to the Atlantic. €̄

De l'Avenir 1 Impasse de la Mer ☎0524 131446. The best of a trio of cheap hotels tucked just inside the Medina (hotels *Essaouira* and *Paris* are tolerable fall-backs). Hot showers (extra charge) on the first floor, grand views of the sea from some rooms and a busy café downstairs. €̄

Camping International Safi 2km north of town, signposted to the right off the road to Oualidia ☎0524 463816. Spacious and well shaded, this campsite has a shop and pool, as well as an internet café close by. It offers some great views over the town and towards the sea, and it's 1km from Sidi Bouzid beach. €̄

Kenzo 82 Bd Kennedy ⓦkenzohotel.com. A very good mid-range hotel in a handy location, though on a busy street. Some of the compact rooms boast a balcony. There's also a ground-floor café and patisserie, and a separate restaurant. BB €̄€̄

Riad Asfi 11 Pl de l'Indépendance ⓦhotelriadsafi. com. One of the newer hotels in town, with large modern rooms, most facing inwards but some with a fantastic view over the port and ocean. The fifth-floor restaurant offers the same great views. The management is spot-on, and staff are eager to please. Good-value singles. €̄€̄

★ Riad Le Cheval Blanc 26 Derb el Kaouss ⓦriad-cheval-blanc.com. Great location near the port entrance to the Medina, this attractive riad has been tastefully restored by its French-Moroccan owners. The rooms are typically on the dark side but have decent-sized bathrooms. A sumptuous breakfast is served on the rooftop terrace, accompanied by sweeping Medina views. BB €̄€̄

Safi Surf House 1 Rue de la Crête ⓦsurfsafi.com. Owner-managed by a knowledgeable local who also runs a surf school down on the main beach. The house is styled like a riad, with a large inner courtyard surrounded by a variety of rooms, all en suite and some sleeping up to six. The kitchen offers fresh and wholesome meals, and the vibe is relaxed and friendly. BB €̄€̄

EATING AND DRINKING SEE MAP PAGE 273

Assala Grand Café 19 Av Zerktouni. A large café with a choice of pavement seating or tables inside spread out over two levels, where big-screen TVs show sport, music and news. €̄

★ Chez Hosni 7 bis, Rue des Forgerons. A hole in the wall that just happens to serve the best tajines in town. The charming and friendly multi-lingual owner-chef takes genuine pleasure in serving his patrons, often joining them for a chat. Both the fish and meat tajines are recommended, as is the unique dessert tajine of cooked fruits. €̄€̄

Jalal Rue Allal Ben Abdallah. A café with a large children's play area and a terrace overlooking the sea, serving tea, coffee and cold drinks. €̄

Les Ramparts 1 Av Bir Anzarane. Friendly café with a welcome shaded front porch looking out over the busy entrance to the Medina, as well as plenty of tables inside with large TV screens showing football. €̄

La Trattoria 2 Route de l'Aouinate, near the Délégation des Pêches Maritime de Safi. Upmarket and very pleasant restaurant with a good choice of pizzas, pastas and seafood dishes (try the obvious local speciality of seafood spaghetti), all reasonably priced. A little out of the way, but it's comfortable inside and well managed. Licensed. €̄€̄

DIRECTORY

Banks Banque Populaire, BMCE, BMCI & Crédit du Maroc are all on or close to Pl de l'Indépendance. Attijariwafa Bank, Crédit du Maroc & SGMB are all on Bd Kennedy, next to *Hôtel Abda*.

Post office Av Sidi Mohammed Abdallah, off Pl Mohammed V, and another branch on Pl de l'Indépendance.

Essaouira

ESSAOUIRA, by popular acclaim Morocco's most likeable resort, was once a haven for hippie backpackers, but it's gradually been moving upmarket, and budget travellers may be hard put nowadays to find food or accommodation within their price range. An eighteenth-century town, enclosed by medieval-looking battlements, Essaouira's whitewashed and blue-shuttered houses and colonnades, wood workshops and art galleries, boat-builders and sardine fishermen all provide a colourful and very pleasant backdrop to the beach. The feathery Norfolk Island pines which surround it thrive only in a pollution-free atmosphere. Many of the tourists who come to Essaouira are drawn by the wind, known locally as the *alizee*, which in spring and summer can be a bit remorseless for sunbathing but creates much-sought-after waves for **windsurfing** and, increasingly, **kitesurfing**. The same winds make Essaouira pretty terrible for **surfing** – those in the know head down the coast to Imsouane and Taghazout (see page 285).

Brief history

A series of forts were built here from the fifteenth century but it was only in the 1760s that the town was established and the present circuit of walls constructed. It was known to Europeans as **Mogador**, possibly from the prominent *koubba* of Sidi Mgdoul, used for navigating entry to the bay. Less likely is the legend that the town's patron saint was a Scotsman named McDougal who was shipwrecked here in the fourteenth century. To Moroccans it was known as Seurah, from the Berber "little picture".

The walls were commissioned by sultan **Sidi Mohammed Ben Abdallah**, and carried out by a French military architect, Theodore Cornut, which explains the town's unique blend of Moroccan Medina and French grid layout. The original intention was to provide a military port, as Agadir was in revolt at the time and Sultan Mohammed Ben Abdallah needed a local base. Soon, however, commercial concerns gained pre-eminence. During the nineteenth century, Mogador was the only Moroccan port south of Tangier that was open to European **trade**, and it prospered greatly from the privilege. Drawn by protected trade status, and a harbour free from customs duties, British merchants settled in the kasbah quarter, and a large Jewish community in the Mellah, within the northeast ramparts.

Decline set in during the French Protectorate, with Marshal Lyautey's promotion of Casablanca. Anecdote has it that he arrived in Essaouira on a Saturday when the Jewish community was at prayer; he cast a single glance at the deserted streets and decided to shift to the port of Casablanca further up the coast. The decline was accelerated after independence, by the exodus of the Jewish community. These days, however, the town is very much back on its feet, as a fishing port, market town and ever-more-popular resort. Orson Welles' 1952 film **Othello** was largely shot in Essaouira, and opens with a tremendous panning shot of the Essaouira ramparts, where Welles placed a scene-setting "punishment" of Iago, suspended above the sea and rocks in a metal cage.

The ramparts

The **ramparts** are the obvious place to start a tour of Essaouira. The **Skala de la Ville** (daily sunrise–sunset; free), the great sea bastion that runs along the northern cliffs, has the town's main woodworkers' souk at street level, and on the rampart above that, a collection of European cannons, presented to Sultan Sidi Mohammed Ben Abdallah by nineteenth-century merchants. At its northern end is the circular **North Bastion**, with panoramic views across the Medina and out to sea.

The Mellah

In the northeast corner of the Medina, the Mellah is the former Jewish quarter. The **Jewish community** in the last quarter of the nineteenth century may have comprised as much as half of the town's population. Largely businessmen, traders and jewellers, Essaouira's Jewish population built themselves large mansions within their quarter, some with up to twenty rooms. Alas, most of these residences are now derelict, many

---

ESSAOUIRA ART GALLERIES

Essaouira has become quite a centre for **painting and sculpture**, and many of its artists have made a name for themselves in both Morocco and Europe. Artists with their own distinctive styles tend to have an entourage of second-rate imitators, so it's worth checking that the artist whose works you're looking at really is the one whose work you were interested in (this should be the case in any of the galleries listed here).

Association Tilal 2 Rue du Caire. A gallery exhibiting the work of half a dozen or so local painters with quite distinctive styles. Many of the pieces exhibited here have been knocked up quickly to sell at low prices: to buy some of the artists' better work, you'll have to speak

to them personally and perhaps commission something. The association should be able to put you in touch.

Espace Othello 9 Rue Mohammed Layachi, behind the Hôtel Sahara. Owned by a Belgian, originally as an overflow for the artwork he was exhibiting in his nearby restaurant; it's now a standalone gallery, with paintings and sculptures by local artists.

Galerie d'Art Frederic Damgaard Av Okba Ibn Nafia. Paintings and sculptures by twenty or so locally based artists, in a gallery founded by a Danish furniture designer, who has passed it on to two Belgian art lovers he hand-picked for the job. The gallery also has an *atelier* (workshop) at 2 Rue el Hijalli, just off Pl Chefchaouni.

---

have been flattened with bland new buildings in their place, and the whole quarter lacks the vibe and energy of other parts of the Medina, reflecting the general trend in most of the country's Mellahs.

At the far northeast corner of the Medina, **Bab Doukkala** leads to a small Christian cemetery dating from colonial times (100m on the left), which is not currently open to the public. Some 400m beyond Bab Doukkala there is further evidence of the former Jewish community in the extensive Jewish **cemetery** – two vast grey lanes of tombstones, carefully tended and well ordered, in a site on both sides of the road. The entrance is on the left.

The port

Essaouira is Morocco's third fishing **port** after Agadir and Safi, and the harbour area bustles with life for most of the day, with the local wooden fishing boats either being built or repaired, and the fishing fleet bringing in the day's catch. Some boats also offer rides. The sea bastion by the harbour, the **Skala du Port**, is open to the public (daily 9am–5pm; 60dh), and worth popping in to climb on the ramparts and enjoy the views.

The beaches

The main **town beach**, south of the Medina, extends for miles, much of it backed by dunes, out towards Cap Sim. On its early reaches, the main activity, as ever in Morocco, is football. There's virtually always a game in progress and at weekends a full-scale local league takes place here, with a dozen matches side-by-side and kick-offs timed in line with the tides. If you wish to join them (it's all barefoot), just ask alongside each "pitch" and you'll be welcomed into a game. The weekend games are especially fun even just to watch, and on occasions half the town seems to turn out for the occasion.

The southern end of the beach also has a dozen or so **camel** men, offering rides up and down the sands, or out to the dunes. If you fancy a ride, watch the scene for a while and be sure to pick someone you feel confident about – it's a long way to fall. You'll need to bargain for the best rates.

The **north beach**, known as the **Plage de Safi**, is good in hot weather and with a calm sea, but the water can be dangerous if the wind is up. It's reached from the north end of town by skirting left along scruffy side streets for 100m once outside Bab Doukkala, the reward on arrival being miles of often delightfully empty sand.

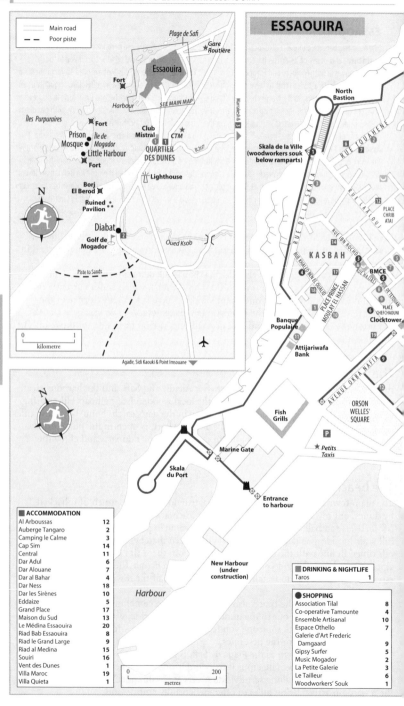

ESSAOUIRA

Main road
Poor piste

Plage de Safi
Gare Routière
Essaouira
Fort
Harbour
SEE MAIN MAP
Marrakesh à 3

Îles Purpuraires
Fort
Prison
Mosque
Île de Mogador
Little Harbour
Fort

Club Mistral
CTM
QUARTIER DES DUNES
R 207

Lighthouse

North Bastion
Skala de la Ville (woodworkers souk below ramparts)
RUE TOUAHENE
RUE DE LA SKALA
RUE TAALOU
PLACE CHRIB ATAI
RUE IBN ROCHD
KASBAH
RUE KHALID BEN EL OUALID
RUE MALIKI
RUE DETTOUR
BMCE
PLACE CHEFCHAOUNI
Clocktower

Borj El Berod
Ruined Pavilion
Diabat
Golf de Mogador
Oued Ksob
Piste to Sands

N
0   1
kilometre

Agadir, Sidi Kaouki & Point Imsouane

Banque Populaire
Attijariwafa Bank
PLACE PRINCE MOULAY EL HASSAN

AVENUE OKBA NAFIA
ORSON WELLES' SQUARE
Petits Taxis
P

Fish Grills

Marine Gate
Skala du Port
Entrance to harbour

New Harbour (under construction)

Harbour

0   200
metres

N

ACCOMMODATION

Al Arboussas	12
Auberge Tangaro	2
Camping le Calme	3
Cap Sim	14
Central	11
Dar Adul	6
Dar Alouane	7
Dar al Bahar	4
Dar Ness	18
Dar les Sirènes	10
Eddaize	5
Grand Place	17
Maison du Sud	13
Le Médina Essaouira	20
Riad Bab Essaouira	8
Riad le Grand Large	9
Riad al Medina	15
Souiri	16
Vent des Dunes	1
Villa Maroc	19
Villa Quieta	1

DRINKING & NIGHTLIFE

Taros	1

SHOPPING

Association Tilal	8
Co-operative Tamounte	4
Ensemble Artisanal	10
Espace Othello	7
Galerie d'Art Frederic Damgaard	9
Gipsy Surfer	5
Music Mogador	2
La Petite Galerie	3
Le Tailleur	6
Woodworkers' Souk	1

▲ Plage de Safi

Gare Routière & Grands Taxis

Bab Doukkala

RUE EL MELLAH

RUE DE KUWAIT

MELLAH

RUE OUIDA

RUE D'OUM RABIA

RUE ABDELAZIZ EL FACHTALY

RUE ABDALLAH

RUE ABDELAZIZ EL FACHTALY

AV MOHAMMED ZERKTOUNI

BOULEVARD MOULAY YOUSSEF

RUE CHBANATE

5

**Marché d'Epices
(Spice Market)**

**Hammam
Mounia 8**

9

RUE IBN KHALDOUN

11 2

RUE SIDI MOHAMMED BEN ABDALLAH

10

13

RUE SIDI ABDELSMIH

**Attijariwafa
Bank**

RUE MENSRA

**Souk des
Bijoutiers
(Jewellers' Souk)**

RUE MOHAMMED EL QORRY

15

AVENUE DE L'ISTIQLAL

RUE MALIK BEN RAHAL

16

RUE EL ATTARIN

@

**Grand
Mosque**

MEDINA

RUE D'AGADIR

7

3 Police

AVENUE DU CAIRE

**@ i Royal Air
Maroc**

Bab es Sebaa

Bab Marrakesh

10

**South
Bastion**

P

13

Supratours

4

AVENUE LALLA AICHA

AVENUE EL MOUKAOUAMA

RUE LAGOUASS

RUE LAGOUASS

Toilets

20

BOULEVARD MOHAMMED V

RUE LALLA AMINA

Beach

Toilets

UCPA

●EATING	
Les Alizes	4
Bab Laâchour	11
Beach & Friends	1
Chalet de la Plage	13
Dar al Baba	5
La Découverte	7
Essalam	10
Laayoune	8
La Licorne	3
Patisserie Chez Driss	6
La Petite Perle	9
Le Table Madada	12
La Triskalla	2

CTM

Quartier des Dunes, Agadir, Marrakesh, Club Mistral, Sidi Kaouki & Point Imsouane ▼

Bordj el Berod

The ruins of an old fort, **Bordj el Berod**, lie sinking into the sand at the far southern end of Essaouira's wide bay. According to local mythology, this was the original "Castle Made of Sand" that inspired the track of that name on **Jimi Hendrix**'s *Axis Bold as Love* album, and it's said that Hendrix played impromptu concerts here for his fellow hippies back in the day. Nice though it would be to believe this, Hendrix stories in Essaouira want taking with a pinch or two of salt. *Axis Bold as Love*, for example, was released in January 1968, but Hendrix didn't visit Morocco until July 1969; he spent a week touring the country, of which a few days at most were in Essaouira.

On the southern side of the Oued Ksob, which is impassable at high tide, the fort is an excellent viewing spot for the Îles Purpuraires, offshore, and their birdlife (see page 280). Inland you can see the ruins of a royal summer pavilion.

ARRIVAL AND DEPARTURE   ESSAOUIRA

By plane Essaouira–Mogador Airport is 15km south of town on the Agadir road. Inside the modern terminal are a bureau de change and desks for the international car rental franchises Avis, Budget and Europcar. While a few *grands taxis* are usually waiting, demand often exceeds supply and it's best to arrange a transfer through your accommodation in advance. Alternatively, if you don't mind a long walk, local bus #2 travels past the airport turn-off, which is 2km from the airport itself (hourly; 30min). Royal Air Maroc have an office at 15 Rue de Caire.

By train Although you can book train tickets to/from Essaouira, the Marrakesh–Essaouira sector is made by bus via the national rail carrier's road subsidiary, Supratours (see below).

By bus Private buses arrive at the *gare routière*, about 500m north and a 10min walk from Bab Doukkala. Especially at night, it's worth taking a *petit taxi* into town. Taxis cannot enter the Medina city walls, but you can hire one of the barrow boys who are usually on hand outside the Medina's gates to wheel your luggage to a hotel for you – bargain for the price. CTM buses terminate at their office in Pl 11 Janvier, 1km south of the Medina (tickets can be booked in the Medina at Internet Club, next to the tourist office on Av du Caire), while Supratours buses operate from their conveniently located office at the end of a short cul-de-sac by the Medina's south bastion (off Av Lalla Aïcha). Supratours tickets are best bought the day before, and you can add connecting tickets for onward rail travel from Marrakesh.

Destinations Agadir (3 CTM, 2 Supratours & over 20 others daily; 3hr 30min); Casablanca (4 CTM & over 20 others daily; 6–8hr); Marrakesh (2 CTM, 6 Supratours & 18 others daily; 3hr); Rabat (15 daily; 8hr 30min); Safi (4 CTM, 1 Supratours & over 20 others daily; 2hr).

By grand taxi Shared *grands taxis* operate from a yard by the *gare routière*. If arriving into Essaouira, request the driver drop you off close to the Medina on the way to the *gare routière*.

Destinations Agadir (2hr 30min); Casablanca (5hr);

THE ÎLE DE MOGADOR

Out across the bay from Essaouira lie the **Îles Purpuraires**, named from the dyes for purple imperial cloth that the Romans once produced on the islands from murex shellfish. Here also, Sir Francis Drake ate his Christmas lunch in 1577, commenting on the "verie ugly fish". The largest of the islands, known as the **Île de Mogador**, is flanked on each side by a fort which, together with the fort on the islet just off the town harbour and the Bord el Berod on the beach, covers all possible approaches to the bay. It also has a small harbour, a mosque, a few rusting cannons and a nineteenth-century prison used for political exiles but long closed. There was a Phoenician settlement on the landward side of the island in the late seventh century BC.

Nowadays the uninhabited island is a nature reserve, and the only non-Mediterranean breeding site of **Eleonora's falcon**, Morocco's most dramatic bird, which is best seen with binoculars from the beach, in the early evening half-light. The falcons are summer visitors to Morocco, staying between May and October before heading south to Madagascar for winter. They are often seen hunting over the dunes south of Oued Ksob. The nearby river course also has many **waders** and **egrets** and occasional rarities such as gull-billed tern and Mediterranean gull.

Inezgane (2hr 30min); Marrakesh (2hr 30min); Safi (2hr 30min).

By car If you're driving, it's worth making use of a guarded car park, in front of the harbour offices, south of Pl Prince Moulay el Hassan, or just east of Bab es Sebaa.

GETTING AROUND

By taxi There is a *petit taxi* rank by the car park at the southern end of Av Okba Ibn Nafia, and taxis also serve the Medina entrances at Bab es Sebaa and Bab Doukkala.

Car rental In addition to the firms at the airport (see above), Avis have a branch at 28 Av Oued el Makhazine.

INFORMATION

Tourist information Av du Caire, opposite the police station (☎0524 783532).

ACCOMMODATION   SEE MAP PAGE 278

MEDINA

Al Arboussas 24 Rue Laâlouj, down a small alley ☎0661 461643. A nineteenth-century former Jewish residence that has been nicely adapted, with soft shades of blue, green and yellow throughout, offering eight small but impeccably clean rooms, all en suite and decorated with local textiles and intricate zellij tiling, spread out over three floors. A delicious breakfast is served at wrought-iron tables on the discreet rooftop terrace, where there are also a few sun loungers. BB €

Cap Sim 11 Rue Ibn Rochd ⌨hotelcapsim.com. Central, clean and popular, with small but comfortable rooms, some en suite and facing outwards. The bathrooms' water is partly solar-heated. BB €

Central 5 Rue Dar Dheb, off Rue Sidi Mohammed Ben Abdallah ☎0524 783623. Cheap and cheerful basic rooms and friendly staff in a nice old house around a patio with a fig tree. Shared hot showers (extra charge). €

Dar Adul 63 Rue Touahene (near the Skala) ⌨daradul. ma. Lashings of whitewash give this place a bright, airy feel, and help keep it cool in summer. It's run by a French artist, with a selection of different-sized rooms, some split level, and the largest with a fireplace to make it cosy in winter. BB €€

Dar Alouane (also called La Maison des Couleurs) 66 Rue Touahene ☎0524 476172. Simple and stylish, done out in very original decor and beautiful colours, with a range of rooms (one single available) and suites at different prices, some with shared bathrooms but still excellent value. €

Dar al Bahar 1 Rue Touahene ⌨daralbahar.com. Wild sea views (especially from the terrace), cool whitewashed rooms, and paintings and window blinds by some of the best local artists make this an excellent choice, though it's a bit tucked away. BB €€

Dar Ness 1 Rue Khalid Ben Oualid ⌨darness-essaouira. com. A very well-located nineteenth-century house turned into an attractive riad by its French owner. There's a variety of room sizes, some with ample and welcome natural light, plus there's a great rooftop terrace. The staff are attentive yet not over friendly. BB €

Dar les Sirènes 59 Rue Chbanate ⌨darlesirenes.com. Essaouira's most elegant riad, set in an old house near Bab Doukkala and transformed into a super-stylish modern space by its Italian architect owner, with smooth *tadelakt* walls in cool, creamy tones. There's a choice of five rooms or suites, and the owner is often on hand to dispense advice. BB €€

Eddaize 109 Av Mohammed Zerktouni ☎0524 473032. Near Bab Doukkala and away from the more touristy parts of the Medina, *Eddaize* is spick and span, with cheap singles rooms. Some doubles are en suite but not all rooms have outside windows. €

Grand Place 4 Pl Prince Moulay el Hassan ☎0524 475925. A budget hotel that's trying to head at least slightly upmarket. It's conveniently located and reasonable value, and the rooms are bright and breezy – the best have balconies, although those overlooking the square can be a bit noisy. There's a popular restaurant down below and a terrace up top with fantastic Medina and sea views. €

Maison du Sud 29 Rue Sidi Mohammed Ben Abdallah ⌨hotelmaisondusud.com. An eighteenth-century house built around a covered patio with a fountain. Most rooms are split-level with a sitting area and bathroom below the sleeping area; ask for one away from the noisy street. BB €€

★ **Riad Bab Essaouira** 35 bis, Bd Moulay Abderrahmane Eddakhil ⌨riad-bab-essaouira.com. Small, stylish and well-managed riad with suites only, decorated throughout in a subtle Afro-Gnaoua theme. Each suite occupies one floor and includes a living room and separate bathroom with individual water heater. There's a communal salon and self-catering kitchen, and the rooftop suite has its own small terrace. €€

Riad le Grand Large 2 Rue Oum Rabii ☎0524 472866. Despite its name, this is a small, cosy place with ten colourful yet smallish rooms, lovely staff, a restaurant and roof-terrace café (and the best room is on the roof). Good value, with reductions off-season. BB €

Riad al Medina 9 Rue el Attarine ⌨riadalmadina.eu. A former palatial mansion built in 1871, which had fallen on hard times by the 1960s and become a budget hotel for

APARTMENTS FOR RENT

If you're looking for a little more space and privacy or plan to stay for more than a couple of nights, it can be worth **renting an apartment** or a suite within Essaouira's Medina. There are a surprising number available, all refurbished and modernized and especially affordable for families or small groups. The pioneer of this type of accommodation in Essaouira has been Karimo (⍵karimo.net) whose office is Jack's Kiosk on Place Prince Moulay el Hassan. You may also be accosted by key-waving local residents either at the bus station or as you enter the town's southern fringe, but always check out what's on offer carefully, and be sure of the price and services you have agreed upon before accepting.

hippies – guests supposedly included Jimi Hendrix, Frank Zappa, Grace Slick and Cat Stevens. Now refurbished, it gets mixed reports: some people love it for its central location, history and character; others hate it, largely because it's quite basic by package-tour standards, and pretty pricey for what you get. BB €€

Souiri 37 Rue el Attarine ⍵hotelsouiri.com. Very central and deservedly popular, with a range of rooms; the cheaper ones have shared bathrooms. Those at the front are larger and have outside windows, though the ones at the back are quieter. €

Villa Maroc 10 Rue Abdallah Ben Yassin, just inside the Medina wall, near the clock tower, ⍵villa-maroc.com. Established long before riads became trendy, with two old houses converted into a score of rooms and suites, heated in winter and decorated with the finest Moroccan materials. It even has its own hammam. Most of the year you will need to book several months ahead, though it's always worth a call on the off chance. Non-residents can dine here if they reserve before 4pm. BB €€€€

NEAR THE BEACH

★**Auberge Tangaro** Diabat village, 4km south of Essaouira, signposted from the main road ⍵auberge tangaro.com. An Italian-owned place opened in 1920 that provides a quiet alternative to staying in Essaouira. There's a main house with an excellent licensed restaurant and a communal lounge flanked by two rows of rooms and suites, all simply furnished. Although electricity arrived in 2011, the candles are still lit every night. It's peaceful, slightly rustic and full of charm. BB €€

Le Médina Essaouira Bd Mohammed V ⍵accor.com. Large, contemporary styled rooms and suites with private balconies, plus interconnecting rooms for families, and one room adapted for wheelchair users. Facilities include a bar, a large pool and a thalassotherapy spa centre (that is, you bathe in sea water in a spa as opposed to just swimming in the sea), and there are two overpriced, underperforming restaurants. They also have a small, guests-only section of beach, with umbrellas and sun loungers. BB €€€€

Vent des Dunes 20 Rue el Bakkay, Quartier des Dunes ⍵ventdesdunes.com. Peaceful, well-managed villa-style hotel that offers a variety of different sized, great-value rooms, including a couple of larger ones for families. There's an in-house restaurant that also provides picnic baskets, or it's a 200m walk to the beach café-restaurants. BB €

Villa Quieta 86 Bd Mohammed V, Quartier des Dunes ⍵villaquietaessaouira.com. A luxurious mansion, some 2km south of town, built in semi-traditional style by the current owner's father in the 1950s. The rooms are tasteful and comfortable, and the place retains the feel of an upscale guesthouse rather than a hotel. There's a sheltered pool and garden, and it's only 150m to the beach. BB €€€€

CAMPSITES

Camping le Calme Ida ou Gourd, 9km east of town, on the Marrakesh road ☎0661 530413. Pleasant site located among the argan trees. Good ablutions, and there's an on-site restaurant, as well as a shop selling basic provisions. Discounts for long stays. €

EATING

SEE MAP PAGE 278

For an informal lunch, or early evening meal, you can't do better than eat at the line of **grills** down at the port, an Essaouira institution, with fish as fresh as can be. You choose from the fish displayed in front of your stall, and have it grilled there and then. Prices are fixed and displayed, but unfortunately some of the stalls have been getting rather hassly of late, and also overcharging (needless to say, it's the same ones that hustle for business who try to pull a fast one), so check prices first, and choose a stall that doesn't try to accost you.

MEDINA

Les Alizes 26 Rue de la Skala. Quiet and intimate, this restaurant has built up a good reputation for Moroccan dishes, both traditional and inventive three-course set menus including dishes such as chicken *sefaa* (sweet couscous with cinnamon). The place is spotless and the service always friendly. Book ahead if possible. Licensed. €€

Bab Laâchour Bab Laâchour, by Pl Prince Moulay el Hassan. A café favoured by locals downstairs, with a more tourist-oriented restaurant on the floor above, overlooking the square, where you can get a selection of fish dishes and tajines, and there's a cheap set menu. Licensed. €

Dar al Baba 1st floor, 2 Rue de Marrakech, cnr Rue Sidi Mohammed Ben Abdallah. This upstairs restaurant has a short but sweet menu of Italian dishes, including mixed antipasti, fish soup and (for dessert) sorbet. It's most celebrated for its own fresh pasta. Licensed. €

La Découverte 8 bis Rue Houmane el Fetaouki ⓦ essaouira-ladecouverte.com. French-Moroccan cuisine is served at this little place run by a French couple (she does the cooking, he greets and serves the customers), with a short but sweet menu of excellent food including fish pastilla, vegetables *au gratin* and a constantly changing choice of daily specials. €€

Essalam 23 Pl Prince Moulay el Hassan. Good, low-priced set menus, though the choice is limited to the usual soup–tajine–fruit combos. Good for breakfast too. €€

Laayoune 4 bis Rue Hajjali. A popular place for Moroccan staples in a warm, relaxed setting with low-lying, candlelit tables and friendly service. €€

La Licorne 26 Rue Skala ⓦ restaurant-lalicorne-essaouira.com. An upmarket Moroccan restaurant serving some of the best traditional French and Moroccan food in town. The tajine of saffron-infused chicken with roasted almonds is particularly recommended, and features on the set menu. €€€

Patisserie Chez Driss 10 Rue Hajjali, just off Pl Prince Moulay el Hassan. One of the town's most popular meeting places, this long-established place serves up delicious fresh pastries and coffee in a quiet leafy courtyard. Ideal for a leisurely breakfast. €

La Petite Perle 2 Rue el Hajjali. A small place with low divan seating, popular among travellers who come for the generous servings of good traditional Moroccan cooking. There's a selection of three- and four-course set menus, all finishing off with a pot of freshly brewed mint tea. €€

Le Table Madada 7 Rue Youssef el Fassi ⓦ latelier madada.com. Housed in a former carob warehouse, this restaurant offers excellent super-fresh seafood, including a fantastic fish platter (variable price), spider crab *au gratin* and lobster pastilla. €€€€

★ **La Triskalla** 58 Rue Touahen. A friendly, chilled-out café-restaurant popular with a younger crowd of both locals and travellers; the dimly lit interior adds to the relaxed atmosphere. The largely pescatarian menu offers healthy, light food and changes daily, plus there's a good selection of fresh juices and herbal teas. Occasionally there are art exhibitions, live music or film nights. €€

NEAR THE BEACH

Beach & Friends Bd Mohammed V, Quartier des Dunes. Worth the walk from the Medina, this beachside restaurant is partly shaded outside, though still susceptible to the wind, with live music on the beach on Fri and Sat evenings. You can recline on sun loungers, couches and comfy wicker chairs, or low-lying loungers inside. The menu offers burgers, salads and pizzas, as well as steaks. Licensed. €€

Chalet de la Plage Bd Mohammed V, on the seafront, just above the high-tide mark ⓦ restaurantchaletdelaplage. com. Originally built of wood by the Ferraud family in 1893, the building is now a little gloomy, and barnacled with marine mementoes, but the seafood and ocean views are truly memorable. Avoid lunchtime, when day-trippers overwhelm the place. Licensed. €€€

DRINKING AND NIGHTLIFE SEE MAP PAGE 278

Taros 2 Rue de la Skala, overlooking Pl Prince Moulay el Hassan. The best evening venue in town, on a rooftop terrace overlooking the main square. Come here for the happy vibe, great views, food, cocktails and a good selection of wines and beer. There's live music some nights, and even the odd mingling musician.

SHOPPING SEE MAP PAGE 278

Despite its size, Essaouira rivals Marrakesh and Fez as a centre for attractive items, and it's relatively hassle-free. The big buy here is marquetry work made from **thuya** (also spelt thuja; *arar* in Arabic), an aromatic mahogany-like hardwood from a local coniferous tree. As usual, beware of tourist emporiums selling *trafika* (simulated antiques and fossils). Tiles with Hebrew lettering, supposedly old tiles from the Mellah, are a favourite scam here, and any shop selling them is probably worth avoiding. Of the souks, worth particular attention are the **Marché d'Epices** (spice market) and **Souk des Bijoutiers** (jewellers' market), on either side of Rue Mohammed Zerktouni.

Co-operative Tamounte Rue Khaled Ben Oualid. This is a good place to buy both thuya marquetry and argan oil. In both cases it comes from cooperative enterprises – a co-

op of fifteen artisans make the thuya products, and a rural women's co-op make the oil. Quality is high, and prices are fixed, marked, and comparatively low, so you're not only contributing to fair-trade democratic enterprise, but also getting a good deal.

Ensemble Artisanal Rue Mohammed el Qorry, just inside Bab Marrakesh. This bright, whitewashed courtyard hosts a handful of thuya carvers, artisan jewellers and a painter. In a courtyard on the right, a Brazilian ombú tree, one of only three in Morocco, was planted when the town was founded in the eighteenth century.

Music Mogador 53 Rue Sidi Mohammed Ben Abdallah. This shop sells CDs of North African music, most notably the official CDs of the annual Gnaoua World Music Festival (see page 284).

4

Woodworkers' souk (Skala de la Ville) Rue de la Skala. Built into the ramparts are a number of marquetry and woodcarving workshops, long established in Essaouira, where artisans produce amazingly painstaking and beautiful thuya work. With total justice, they claim that their produce is the best in the country, and this is the best place to buy it.

DIRECTORY

Banks and money changers There are three banks with ATMs on the plaza between Pl Prince Moulay el Hassan and the port, plus BMCE, 8 Rue Hajjali, and there are money-changers around the Medina including Pro Change by the Great Mosque on Av de l'Istiqlal (daily 8am–10pm) and at 3 Rue I aâlouj.

Golf Golf de Mogador, Diabat (36 holes; ⓦ golf-mogador-essaouira.com); guests at nearby *Auberge Tangaro* (see page 282) get preferential rates.

Hammam Hammam Les Deux Portes, Rue d'Oum Rabia (near *Riad le Grand Large*).

Post office The main office is on Av Lalla Aicha at Av Moukaouama; there's a smaller one on Rue Laâlouj in the Medina, and one by the *gare routière*.

South of Essaouira

The main road **south from Essaouira** offers some pleasant exploration, especially if you have your own transport. There are a number of hamlets and villages dotted along the coast, most of them the domain of wind-, kite- and wave surfers.

Sidi Kaouki and around

Bus #2 runs 9 times daily between Essaouira's Bab Doukkala and Sidi Kaouki (30min)

The beach at **SIDI KAOUKI**, 20km south of Essaouira, attracts **wind- and kitesurfers** virtually year-round, and wind generators have been installed to supply up to 95 percent of the village's electricity. For a village of only 120 or so inhabitants, it has an astonishing amount of **accommodation**, though very little else (no banks, for example). Near the beach is the original **Marabout of Sidi Kaouki**, which is reputed to cure female sterility, and beyond that is **Cap Sim**, backed by long expanses of dunes.

ACCOMMODATION AND EATING   SIDI KAOUKI

There are a couple of **restaurants** at the village's entrance, as well as a few other **café-restaurants** scattered along the beachfront road. Light meals and cold beer are also available at the landmark Sidi Kaouki Surfclub (ⓦ sidi-kaouki.com), which rents out gear for surfers, windsurfers and kitesurfers.

Résidence La Kaouki ⓦ sidikaouki.com. Rustic retreat that oozes simplicity and warmth. Electricity-free, the en suite rooms are candlelit, the water is heated by gas and wood, and the meals are as authentic as they come. BB €

★ **Villa Soleil** ☏ 0670 233097. Wonderful little place set back from the beachfront, with bungalows in a spacious garden as well as a larger villa. The Belgian owner-managers run a tight and happy ship, with spotless rooms and a very good in-house restaurant. €

On towards Agadir

For off-road vehicles, the *pistes* south along the coast from Sidi Kaouki offer a mix of long strands, dunes and scenic headlands, with occasional blue-painted fishing boats. Eventually the main road (N1) is rejoined north of **Smimou**, a one-street town with

GNAOUA AND WORLD MUSIC FESTIVAL

A dozen or so local moussems, fairs and festivals are held in March–Oct. Essaouira's main annual event is the **Gnaoua and World Music Festival** (ⓦ festival-gnaoua.net) in May or June, which focuses on a fusion of Gnaoua and world music. Stages are set up in the plaza between Place Prince Moulay el Hassan and the port, and outside Bab Marrakesh, and performers come from all over Morocco, West Africa and Europe. During the festival, you can expect transport and hotels to be full, so book well ahead.

WATERSPORTS AROUND ESSAOUIRA

Essaouira and its nearby beaches are Morocco's prime **wind- and kitesurfing** destinations, drawing enthusiasts throughout the year. The trade wind at Essaouira is northwesterly and blows year-round; it's stronger in summer – if you're inexperienced, try to get out early in the morning – but the swell is bigger in winter. The winds can be quite strong but the curved shape of Essaouira's bay, along with a gently sloping sandy bottom that creates a wide shallow area along the shoreline, makes it ideal for novices. Even during summer, the water temperature rises only to 20ºC maximum, so a wetsuit is required all year.

There are numerous **surf shops** and schools in Essaouira, as well as one or two further south in Sidi Kaouiki (see page 284) and Imsouane (see page 285). Essaouira's nonstop winds, though great for wind- and kitesurfing, can be a disappointment for board **surfing**, for which you're better off down at Imsouane with its easterly facing bay.

EQUIPMENT AND LESSONS

Ion Bd Mohammed V, Quartier des Dunes ⓦ ocean vagabond.com. Surf school at the far southern end of the beach which offers surfing, windsurfing and kitesurfing lessons, and rents out surfboards, wetsuits, kayaks and equipment for windsurfing or kitesurfing.

Explora Av de l'Istiqlal ⓦ explorawatersports.com. Lessons and equipment rental for surfing, windsurfing and kitesurfing.

UCPA Bd Mohammed V, 500m south of the Medina ⓦ ucpa.com. Windsurfing, kitesurfing, bodyboarding and kayaking, equipment and lessons.

a petrol station and a couple of café-restaurants. A few kilometres before Smimou, a metalled road which soon turns to *piste* leads west to **Plage d'Ifrane**, one of the finest but most isolated beaches on this stretch of coast.

Inland, just south of Smimou, lies the forested whaleback of **Jebel Amsittene** (905m). A challenging *piste* climbs to traverse the crest of this grand viewpoint, and descends not far from **Imi n'Tilt**, a busy Monday souk, and a recommended venture if you have 4WD. A little further south of Smimou, another scenic *piste* leads westward to **Cap Tafelney**, below which lies a curious village and a bay full of fishing boats.

Imsouane

The coast is rockier if approached from **Tamanar** than Smimou, a larger town with a few restaurants. Fifteen kilometres south, a surfaced road leads to **Imsouane**, which used to be a picturesque little harbour with a few fishermen's cottages, but is now gradually being built up. No matter what swell, tide or wind condition prevails, its two bays should offer something for surfers and windsurfers. There's a **surf school**, Planet Surf Morocco (ⓣ 0528 218783) down near the market, with a handful of shops nearby that rent out and repair surf gear.

ARRIVAL AND DEPARTURE   IMSOUANE

By public transport Buses and *grands taxis* running between Essaouira and Agadir can drop you off at the turn-off (the second Imsouane turn-off if coming from Agadir), where you should be able to get a shared *grand taxi* down to Imsouane.

ACCOMMODATION AND EATING

Auberge Tasra Southern entrance to the village ⓦ tasra.info. More a hostel than a hotel, offering rooms and dorms with shared bathrooms, a self-catering kitchen, and a laidback vibe. There's also a bar-restaurant open to non-residents. Dorm €̄, double €̄

Camping Imsouane Opposite Auberge Tasra. Rather neglected but easy-going and rustic, this basic campsite has been upgraded with modern ablutions, water access and trees planted for shade, although it'll be a while before they

give any. Meals are available up the road at *Auberge Tasra*, and the site has glorious, sweeping ocean views. €̄

Kahina l'Auberge Near the market in the centre of the village ⓣ 0528 826032. Formerly a surf school (and they still rent out surfboards), this is now just an auberge, whose basic but comfortable rooms open onto a central courtyard (shared bathrooms; 24hr hot water). There's also a restaurant (open to non-guests) with tasty seafood and great sea views from a shaded terrace. €̄€̄

4

Marrakesh

THE BAHIA PALACE

5

Marrakesh

Marrakesh – "Morocco City", as early foreign travellers called it – has always been something of a marketplace where tribesmen and Berber villagers bring their goods, spend their money and find entertainment. At its heart is the Jemaa el Fna, an open space in the centre of the city, and the stage for a long-established ritual in which shifting circles of onlookers gather round groups of acrobats, drummers, pipe musicians, dancers, storytellers, comedians and fairground acts. The city's architectural attractions are no less compelling: the magnificent ruin of the El Badi Palace, the delicate carving of the Saadian Tombs and, above all, the Koutoubia Minaret, the most perfect Islamic monument in North Africa.

It won't take you long to see why Marrakesh is called the **Red City**. The natural red ochre pigment that bedecks its walls and buildings can at times seem dominant, but there's no shortage of other colours. Like all Moroccan cities, it's a town of two halves: the ancient walled **Medina**, founded by Sultan Youssef Ben Tachfine in the Middle Ages, and the colonial **Ville Nouvelle**, built by the French in the mid-twentieth century. Each has its own delights – the Medina with its ancient palaces and mansions, labyrinthine souks and deeply traditional way of life, and the Ville Nouvelle with its pavement cafés, trendy boutiques, gardens and boulevards.

Marrakesh has become Morocco's **capital of chic**, attracting the rich and famous from Europe and beyond. Though the vast majority of its residents are poor by any European standard, an increasing number of wealthy foreigners are taking up residence and their influence on the tourist experience is evident.

Marrakesh has **Berber** rather than Arab origins, having developed as the metropolis of Atlas tribes. Once upon a time, it was the entrepôt for goods – slaves, gold, ivory and even "Morocco" leather – brought by caravan from the ancient empires of Mali and Songhay via their great desert port of Timbuktu. All of these strands of commerce and population shaped the city's souks and its way of life, and even today, in the crowds and performers of the Jemaa el Fna, the nomadic and West African influence can still seem quite distinct.

Despite its size and the maze of its souks, Marrakesh is not too hard to **navigate**. The broad, open space of the **Jemaa el Fna** is at the heart of the Medina, with the main souks to its north, and most of the main sights within easy walking distance. Just west of the Jemaa el Fna is the unmistakeable landmark of the **Koutoubia** Minaret, and from here, the city's main artery, **Avenue Mohammed V**, leads out through the Medina walls at Bab Nkob and up the length of **Guéliz**, the downtown area of the Ville Nouvelle. You might want to consider hiring a **guide** (see page 316) to explore the Medina, but with a decent map – or the willingness to go with the flow and get delightfully lost – it really isn't necessary.

Brief history

Marrakesh was founded near the beginning of **Almoravid** rule, by the first Almoravid dynasty ruler, **Youssef Ben Tachfine**, around 1062–70. It must at first have taken the form of a camp and market with a *ksour*, or fortified town, gradually developing round it. The first seven-kilometre **circuit of walls** was raised in 1126–27, replacing an earlier stockade of thorn bushes. These, many times rebuilt, are essentially the city's present walls – made of *tabia*, the red mud of the plains, mixed and strengthened with lime.

ALMORAVID KOUBBA

Highlights

❶ Jemaa el Fna The world's most amazing city square: an open-air circus of acrobats, dancers, musicians and storytellers. See page 294

❷ Koutoubia Simple but beautifully proportioned, the Koutoubia Mosque's minaret is the most perfect in North Africa, and a classic piece of Almohad architecture. See page 296

❸ Souks Haggling for crafts in the traditional market area at the heart of Marrakesh's Medina is an archetypal Moroccan experience. See page 298

❹ Almoravid koubba This tiny ablutions building is the last remnant of the original

city, and the only intact Almoravid building in Morocco. See page 301

❺ Ben Youssef Medersa Stucco, zellij tilework, and carved cedar wood mark this beautiful medersa. See page 301

❻ El Badi Palace The "Incomparable Palace", now an incomparable ruin. See page 307

❼ Bahia Palace The ideal of Arabic domestic architecture expressed in a nineteenth-century politician's mansion. See page 309

❽ Majorelle Garden A sublime garden, with cacti, lily ponds, and an Islamic Arts museum housed in a stunning pavilion. See page 312

HIGHLIGHTS ARE MARKED ON THE MAP ON PAGE 290

5

The golden age

Of the rest of the Almoravids' building works, hardly a trace remains. The dynasty that replaced them – the **Almohads** – sacked the city for three days after taking possession of it in 1147, but they kept it as their empire's capital.

With the 1184 accession to the throne of the third Almohad sultan, **Yacoub el Mansour**, the city entered its greatest period. *Kissarias* were constructed for the sale

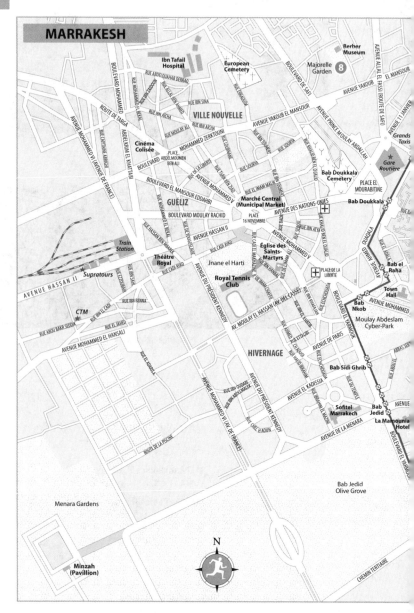

and storage of Italian and Oriental cloth, a new kasbah was begun, and a succession of poets and scholars arrived at the court. Mansour's reign also saw the construction of the great **Koutoubia Mosque and minaret**.

By the 1220s, the empire was beginning to fragment amid a series of factional civil wars, and Marrakesh fell into the familiar pattern of pillage, ruination and rebuilding. In 1269, it lost its status as capital when the Fez-based **Merenids** took power, though

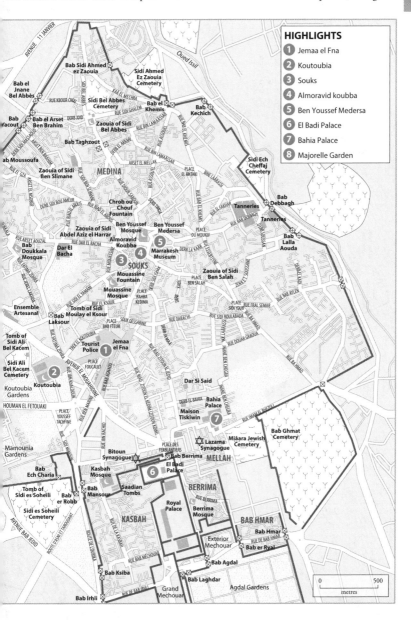

HIGHLIGHTS

1. Jemaa el Fna
2. Koutoubia
3. Souks
4. Almoravid koubba
5. Ben Youssef Medersa
6. El Badi Palace
7. Bahia Palace
8. Majorelle Garden

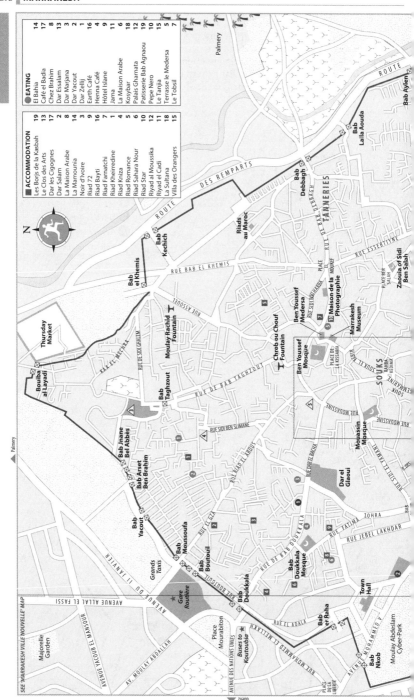

■ ACCOMMODATION	
Les Borjs de la Kasbah	19
Le Clos des Arts	13
Dar les Cigognes	17
Dar Salam	2
La Maison Arabe	8
La Mamounia	14
Noir d'Ivoire	3
Riad 72	9
Riad Bayti	16
Riad Farnatchi	7
Riad Kheirredine	1
Riad Kniza	4
Riad Romance	5
Riad Sahara Nour	6
Riad Star	10
Riyad al Moussika	12
Riyad el Cadi	11
La Sultana	18
Villa des Orangers	15

● EATING	
El Bahia	14
Café el Badia	17
Chez Brahim	8
Dar Essalam	13
Dar Marjana	3
Dar Yacout	2
Dar Zellij	1
Earth Café	16
Henna Café	4
Hôtel Islane	9
Jama	11
La Maison Arabe	6
Kosybar	18
Palais Gharnata	12
Patisserie Bab Agnaou	19
Pepe Nero	10
Le Tanjia	15
Terrasse le Medersa	5
Le Tobsil	7

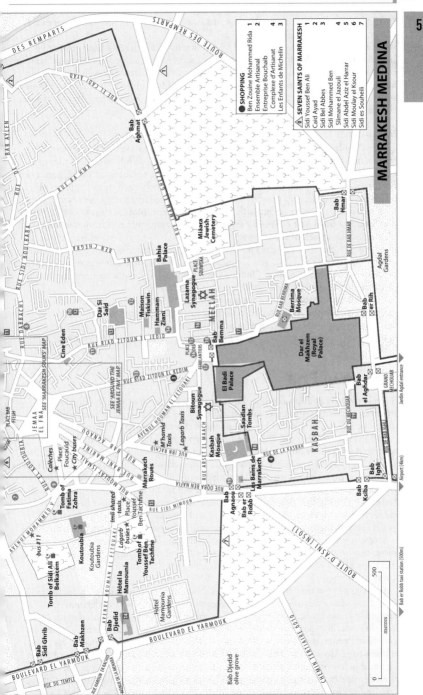

MARRAKESH MEDINA

SHOPPING
Ben Zouine Mohammed Rida	1
Ensemble Artisanal	2
Entreprise Bouchaib	4
Complexe d'Artisanat	
Les Enfants de Michelin	3

SEVEN SAINTS OF MARRAKESH
Sidi Youssef Ben Ali	1
Caïd Ayad	2
Sidi Bel Abbes	3
Sidi Mohammed Ben	4
Slimane el Jazouli	5
Sidi Abdel Aziz el Harrar	6
Sidi Moulay el Ksour	
Sidi es Souheili	7

5

in 1374–86 it did form the basis of a breakaway state under the Merenid pretender Abderrahman Ibn Taflusin.

Taking Marrakesh, then devastated by famine, in 1521, the **Saadians** provided a last burst of imperial splendour. Their dynasty's greatest figure, **Ahmed el Mansour**, having invaded Mali and seized control of the most lucrative caravan routes in Africa, had the **El Badi Palace** – Marrakesh's largest and greatest building project – constructed from the proceeds of this new wealth, and the dynasty also of course bequeathed to Marrakesh their wonderful mausoleum, the **Saadian Tombs**.

Modern times

Under the **Alaouites**, Marrakesh lost its status as capital to Meknes but remained an important imperial city, and the need to maintain a southern base against the tribes ensured the regular presence of its sultans. But from the seventeenth to the nineteenth centuries, it shrank back from its medieval walls and lost much of its former trade.

During the last decades prior to the Protectorate, the city's fortunes revived somewhat as it enjoyed a return to favour with the Sherifian court. **Moulay Hassan** (1873–94) and **Moulay Abd el Aziz** (1894–1908) both ran their governments from here in a bizarre closing epoch of the old ways, accompanied by a final bout of frantic palace building. On the arrival of **the French**, Marrakesh gave rise to a short-lived pretender, the religious leader El Hiba, and for most of the colonial period it was run as a virtual fiefdom of its pasha, **T'hami el Glaoui** – the most powerful, autocratic and extraordinary character of his age (see page 304).

Since **independence**, the city has undergone considerable change, with rural emigration from the Atlas and beyond, new methods of cultivation on the Haouz plain and the development of a sizeable tourist industry. It has a thriving industrial area and is the most important market and administrative centre of southern Morocco.

Jemaa el Fna

There's nowhere in Morocco like the **Jemaa el Fna** – no place that so effortlessly involves you and keeps you coming back for more. By day, most of the square is just a big open space, in which a handful of **snake charmers** play their flutes at cruelly mutilated cobras (see page 297), **medicine men** (especially in the northeast of the square) display cures and nostrums, and **tooth-pullers**, wielding fearsome pliers, offer to pluck the pain from out of the heads of toothache sufferers, trays of extracted molars attesting to their skill. It isn't until late afternoon that the square really gets going. At dusk, as in France and Spain, people come out for an early evening promenade (especially in Rue Bab Agnaou), and the square gradually fills until it becomes a whole carnival of storytellers, acrobats, musicians and entertainers. Come on down and you'll soon be immersed in the ritual: wandering round, squatting amid the circles of onlookers, giving a dirham or two as your contribution. If you want a respite, you can move over to the rooftop terraces, such as the *Grand Balcon du Café Glacier* (see page 321), for a vista over the square, its storytellers and musicians, and the crowds who come to see them.

As a foreigner in the Jemaa, you can feel something of an interloper. Most of the crowd are Moroccan of course (few foreigners, for example, will understand the storytellers' tales), but tourists also make a major contribution to both the atmosphere and the cash flow. Sometimes a storyteller or musician may pick on you to take part or contribute generously to the end-of-show collection and, entering into the spectacle, it's best to go denuded of the usual tourist trappings such as watches, money-belts or too much money; **pickpockets** and scam artists operate (giving a "present" and then demanding payment for it is an old scam to beware of; asking tourists to change counterfeit euro coins is a more recent one). The crowds around performers are sometimes used as an opportunity to grope female foreigners, and by male Moroccans and gay male tourists for cruising.

Sideshow attractions include games of hoop-the-bottle, **fortune-tellers** sitting under umbrellas and women with piping bags full of **henna** paste, ready to paint hands, feet or arms with "tattoos" that will last up to three months. Don't let anyone start painting you until you've agreed a price, and beware of synthetic "black henna", which contains a toxic chemical – only red henna is natural (the *Henna Café* guarantees to use only natural henna; see page 321).

For refreshment, stalls offer orange and grapefruit **juice** (but have it squeezed in front of you if you don't want it adulterated with water and sugar, or even squash), while neighbouring handcarts are piled high with **dates**, dried figs, almonds and walnuts, especially delicious in winter when they are freshly picked in the surrounding

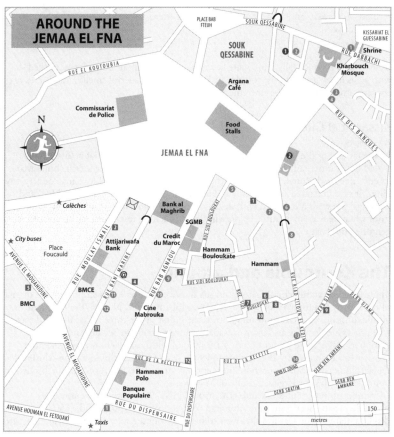

ACCOMMODATION		EATING		Le Grand Balcon		DRINKING	
Aday	10	El Bahja	11	du Café Glacier	5	Grand Hôtel	
Ali	2	Café-Restaurant Toubkal		Kassabine Café	1	Tazi	1
Central Palace	3	Canne à Sucre	9	Marrakchi	4		
CTM	1	Chez Bahia	6	Oscar Progrès	12	SHOPPING	
Essaouira	7	Chez Chegrouni	3	Patisserie des Princes	10	Jemaa el Fna	
De Foucauld	5	Earth Café	14	Les Prémices	7	Market	2
Gallia	12	Henna Art Cafe	13	Tanjia stalls	2	Olive Stalls	1
La Gazelle	11						
Ichbilia	4						
Jnane Mogador	8						
Medina	6						
Sherazade	9						

5

THE DEVELOPMENT OF THE JEMAA EL FNA

Nobody is entirely sure when or how the Jemaa el Fna came into being – nor even what its **name** means. The usual translation is "assembly of the dead", a suitably epic title that may refer to the public display here of the heads of rebels and criminals (the Jemaa was a place of execution until well into the nineteenth century). The name might alternatively mean "the mosque of nothing" (Jemaa means both "mosque" and "assembly" – interchangeable terms in Islamic society), recalling an abandoned Saadian plan to build a new grand mosque on this site.

Either way, as an open area between the original kasbah and the souks, the square has probably played its present role since the city's earliest days. It has often been the focal point for **rioting** and the authorities have plotted before now to close it down and move its activities outside the city walls. This happened briefly after independence in 1956, when the government built a corn market on part of the square and tried to turn the rest into a car park, but the plan lasted barely a year. Tourism was falling off and it was clearly an unpopular move. As novelist Paul Bowles observed, without the Jemaa, Marrakesh would be just another Moroccan city.

---

countryside. As dusk falls, the square becomes a huge open-air **dining area**, packed with stalls lit by gas lanterns, and the air is filled with wonderful smells and plumes of cooking smoke spiralling up into the night (see page 320).

Kissariat el Guessabine

75 Rue Dabbachi • Free

At the far end of the Jemaa el Fna's northeastern branch, the **Kissariat el Guessabine** would be an unremarkable little *kissaria* (covered souk), but for the kitsch **shrine** that its entrance has become, dedicated to the king, Mohammed VI. "I love my country, my king," it says in Arabic and English, and among sea shells, silver-painted pebbles and minerals, the walls are decked with dozens of photographs of the king and his family, from when he was small until the present day, a touching testament to the monarch's genuine popularity.

The Koutoubia and around

The absence of architectural features on the Jemaa el Fna serves to emphasize the drama of the nearby **Koutoubia Minaret**, off Avenue Mohammed V. Nearly 70m high and visible for miles on a clear morning, this is the oldest of the three great Almohad towers (the others are the Hassan Tower in Rabat and the Giralda in Seville) and the most complete. Its pleasing proportions – a 1:5 ratio of width to height – established the classic Moroccan design. The mosque to which it is attached (closed to non-Muslims) replaced an earlier structure whose meagre ruins are just next to it on the north side. At 60m by 80m, it's the largest mosque in Marrakesh.

Completed under **Sultan Yacoub el Mansour** (1184–99), work on the minaret probably began shortly after the Almohad conquest of the city, around 1150. It displays many of the features that were to become widespread in Moroccan architecture – the wide band of ceramic inlay near the top, the pyramid-shaped, castellated merlons (battlements) rising above it, the use of *darj w ktarf* ("cheek and shoulder"; see page 542) and other motifs – and it also established the alternation of patterning on different faces. Here, the top floor is similar on each of the sides but the lower two are almost eccentric in their variety. The semicircle of small lobed arches on the middle niche of the southeast face was to become the dominant decorative feature of Almohad gates. The three great **copper balls** at the top are the subject of numerous legends, mostly of supernatural interventions to keep away thieves. They are thought to have originally been made of gold, the gift of the wife of Yacoub el Mansour, presented as penance for breaking her fast for three hours during Ramadan.

Close to the arches, the stones of the main body of the tower become slightly smaller, which seems odd today, but not originally, when the whole minaret was covered with plaster and painted, like that of the Kasbah Mosque (see page 305). There was talk about restoring this on the Koutoubia, but the authorities settled for a straight clean-up – to stunning effect, especially when it's **floodlit** at night. At the same time, archeologists excavated the original mosque, which predates the tower, confirming that it had had to be rebuilt to correct its alignment with Mecca.

Tomb of Fatima Zohra

Alongside the mosque, and close to Avenue Mohammed V, is the **tomb of Fatima Zohra**, now in a white *koubba*. She was the daughter of a seventeenth-century religious leader and tradition has it that she was a woman by day and a white dove by night; women still dedicate their children to her in the belief that her blessing will protect them.

Koutoubia Gardens

To the south and west of the Koutoubia are the **Koutoubia Gardens**, attractively laid out with pools and fountains, roses, orange trees and palms, very handy for an afternoon stroll, and giving excellent views of the Koutoubia.

Hôtel la Mamounia

Av Bab Jdid • Charge • Dress code enforced: no jeans or trainers, and clothes must be deemed sufficiently "elegant" for entry

The luxurious **Hôtel la Mamounia** (see page 317) has been rebuilt and enlarged since the days when Winston Churchill and Franklin D. Roosevelt stayed here, although the **Winston Churchill suite** (usually open only to hotel guests) is preserved as it was when visited by its namesake. Decoratively, the hotel is of most interest for the 1920s Art

---

ANIMALS IN THE JEMAA

One thing you'll see in the **Jemaa el Fna**, especially in the daytime, before the true performers arrive, are the **snake charmers** and **monkey men**. A lot of tourists pay to have their photographs taken with the snakes and monkeys, unaware of the cruelty, the threat to endangered species, and the criminal gangs they are subsidizing in the process.

The snakes used by the charmers – **cobras and vipers** – are venomous species native to Morocco which often have their fangs removed and usually have their mouths sewn up, leaving just enough space for their tongues to protrude. Thus mutilated and unable to feed, the snakes soon starve to death and are then simply replaced from the wild. Obviously this cruel practice does not encourage their conservation.

Worse still is the position of the **Barbary macaques**, an endangered species (see page 211). The monkey men on the square belong to **criminal gangs** engaged in poaching the primates as infants from the wild. Although they make money from tourists having photographs taken with the animals, they also sell baby monkeys to foreigners and, even more often, Moroccans living abroad, many of whom then abandon the animals when they become too big to cope with. It's illegal to capture or keep Barbary macaques, but the law is not enforced and the monkey men are left free to ply their trade openly. Be aware that if you pay them for photographs, you are subsidizing the criminal poaching gangs and thus also helping to hasten the Barbary macaques' extinction.

5

Deco touches of **Jacques Majorelle** (see page 312), and their enhancements, in 1986, by King Hassan II's then-favourite designer, André Paccard.

The *Mamounia*'s **gardens** were once royal grounds, laid out by the Saadians with a succession of pavilions. Today they're slightly Europeanized in style but have retained the traditional elements of shrubs and walkways. Churchill, who liked to paint in the gardens, described them to Roosevelt, when they were here together in 1943, as the loveliest spot in the world.

The souks

It is spicy in the souks, and cool and colourful. The smell, always pleasant, changes gradually with the nature of the merchandise. There are no names or signs; there is no glass… You find everything – but you always find it many times over.

Elias Canetti: The Voices of Marrakesh

The **souks** north of the Jemaa el Fna seem vast the first time you venture in, and almost impossible to navigate, but in fact the area that they cover is pretty compact. A long, covered street, **Rue Souk Smarine**, runs for half their length and then splits into two lanes – **Souk el Attarin** and **Souk el Kebir**. Off these are virtually all the individual souks: alleys and small squares devoted to specific crafts, where you can often watch part of the production process.

If you are staying for some days, you'll probably return often to the souks – and this is a good way of taking them in, singling out a couple of specific crafts or products to see, rather than being swamped by the whole. To get to grips with the general layout, you might find it useful to walk round the whole area once with a **guide**, but it's certainly not essential: with a reasonable map, (see page 316) you can quite easily navigate the souks on your own, and besides, getting a little bit lost is all part of the fun.

The most interesting **times** to visit are in the early morning (6.30–8am) and late afternoon, at around 4 to 5pm, when some of the souks auction off goods to local traders. Later in the evening, most of the stalls are closed, but you can wander un-harassed to take a look at the elaborate decoration of their doorways and arches; those stalls that stay open, until 7 or 8pm, are often more amenable to bargaining at the end of the day.

The easiest approach to the main souks from the Jemaa el Fna is opposite Rue des Banques (see map, page 299), where a lane to the left of *Terrasses de l'Alhambra* restaurant leads to Souk Ableuh, dominated by stalls selling olives. Continue through here and you will come out opposite the archway that marks the beginning of Rue Souk Smarine.

Souk Smarine

Busy and crowded, **Rue Souk Smarine** is an important thoroughfare, traditionally dominated by textiles and clothing. Today, tourist "bazaars" are moving in, but there are still dozens of shops in the arcades selling and tailoring traditional shirts and kaftans. The street is covered by an iron trellis with slats across it that restrict the sun to shafts of light; this replaces the old rush (*smar*) roofing, which along with many of the souks' more beautiful features was destroyed by a fire in the 1960s.

Rahba Kedima

To the east of Souk Smarine, **Rahba Kedima** is an open square with stalls set up in the middle selling baskets, hats and souvenirs. Around its southwestern corner, **Apothecary**

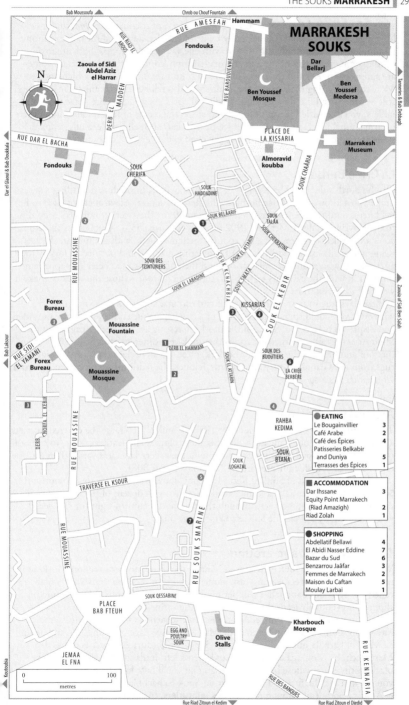

Bab Moussoufa

Chrob ou Chouf Fountain

Hammam

RUE AMESFAH

RUE BHJJRE EL AMOUS

Fondouks

RUE BAROUDIENNE

MARRAKESH SOUKS

N

Zaouia of Sidi Abdel Aziz el Harrar

Dar Bellarj

Ben Youssef Mosque

Ben Youssef Medersa

DERB EL MADDEN

Dar el Glaoui & Bab Doukkala

RUE DAR EL BACHA

PLACE DE LA KISSARIA

Tanneries & Bab Debbagh

Marrakesh Museum

Almoravid koubba

Fondouks

SOUK CHERIFA ❶

SOUK CHAARIA

SOUK HADDADINE

SOUK BELAARIF

❷

SOUK TALAA

SOUK CHERBATINE

❷

RUE MOUASSINE

SOUK DES TEINTURIERS

SOUK EL LABADINE

SOUK EL ATTARIN

SOUK KCHACHBIA

SOUK SMATA

Zaouia of Sidi Ben Salah

Forex Bureau

❸

KISSARIAS

Mouassine Fountain

SOUK EL KEBIR

❸ ❹

Bab Laksour

❺

RUE SIDI EL YAMANI

Forex Bureau

DERB EL HAMMAM

❶

SOUK DES BIJOUTIERS

Mouassine Mosque

❷

SOUK EL ATTARIN

LA CRIÉE BERBÈRE

❻

DERB CHORFA EL KEBIR

❹

RAHBA KEDIMA

❸

RUE MOUASSINE

SOUK BTANA

SOUK LOGHZAL

TRAVERSE EL KSOUR

❺

RUE MOUASSINE

RUE SOUK SMARINE

❼

SHOPPING

PLACE BAB FTEUH

SOUK QESSABINE

Kharbouch Mosque

EGG AND POULTRY SOUK

Olive Stalls

RUE KENNARIA

Koutoubia

JEMAA EL FNA

0   100

metres

Rue Riad Zitoun el Kedim

Rue Riad Zitoun el Djedid

● EATING

Le Bougainvillier	3
Café Arabe	2
Café des Épices	4
Patisseries Belkabir and Duniya	5
Terrasses des Épices	1

■ ACCOMMODATION

Dar Ihssane	3
Equity Point Marrakech (Riad Amazigh)	2
Riad Zolah	1

● SHOPPING

Abdellatif Bellawi	4
El Abidi Nasser Eddine	7
Bazar du Sud	6
Benzarrou Jaâfar	3
Femmes de Marrakech	2
Maison du Caftan	5
Moulay Larbai	1

5

stalls sell traditional cosmetics – earthenware saucers of cochineal (*kashiniah*) for lip-rouge, powdered kohl (traditionally made of stibnite, a mineral form of antimony trisulphide, but commonly substituted with cheaper lead sulphide – both are toxic) for darkening the edges of the eyes, henna (the only cosmetic that unmarried women are supposed to use) and the sticks of *suak* (walnut root or bark) with which you see Moroccans cleaning their teeth. The same stalls also sell herbal and animal ingredients still in widespread use for spells and medicinal cures. As well as aphrodisiac roots and tablets, you'll see dried pieces of lizard and stork, fragments of beaks, talons and other bizarre animal products. Some shops (to be avoided) also sell gazelle skulls, leopard skins and other products from **illegally poached** endangered wild animals.

La Criée Berbère

On the north side of Rahba Kedima, a passageway leads through to a bustling, carpet-draped area known as **La Criée Berbère** (the Berber auction). **Slave auctions** used to be held here, until the French occupied the city in 1912. They were conducted, according to travel writer Budgett Meakin's 1902 account (see page 533), "precisely as those of cows and mules, often on the same spot by the same men…with the human chattels being personally examined in the most disgusting manner, and paraded in lots by the auctioneers, who shout their attractions and the bids". Most had been kidnapped and brought in with the caravans from Mali, travelling on foot – those too weak to make it were left to die en route.

These days, the souk specializes in **rugs and carpets**, and if you have the time and willpower you could spend the best part of a day here while endless stacks are unfolded and displayed before you. Some of the most interesting are the Berber rugs from the High Atlas – bright, geometric designs that look very different after being laid out on the roof and bleached by the sun. The dark, often black, backgrounds usually signify rugs from the Glaoui country, up towards Telouet; the reddish-backed carpets are from Chichaoua (see page 314).

Around the kissarias

The **kissarias**, lying between Souk el Attarin and Souk el Kebir, are the covered markets at the heart of the souks, mostly selling blankets, clothes and leather goods. To the east of Souk el Kebir, **Souk des Bijoutiers** is a modest jewellers' lane, less varied than the one established by Jewish craftsmen in the Mellah (see page 308).

At the northern end of Souk el Kebir is a convoluted web of alleys that comprise the **Souk Cherratine**, essentially a leather workers' souk, with dozens of purse-makers and sandal cobblers. If you bear left through this area and then turn right (or vice versa), you should arrive at Place de la Kissaria (see page 301).

The Dyers' Souk and around

West of the *kissarias*, **Souk el Attarin**, originally the spice and perfume souk, forks at its northern end. The street leading east, along the edge of the *kissarias* is **Souk Smata**, also called the **Souk des Babouches** (slipper market). Lined with shops selling Moroccan slippers, it eventually leads through to Souk Cherratine (see page 300).

The western fork from Souk el Attarin is **Souk Kchachbia**, which contains some interesting shops including Femmes de Marrakech (see page 326) and, directly behind it, Moulay Larbai's mirror shop (see page 327). A right turn just past Femmes de Marrakech, by Moulay Larbai's shop, and then a left, leads to **Souk Haddadine**, the blacksmiths' souk, whose banging and clanging you'll hear long before arriving. Before you get that far, the first and second left off Souk Kchachbia (if coming from Souk el Attarin) both lead through to **Souk des Teinturiers**, the dyers' souk, the area's main attraction, and always colourful, hung with bright skeins of wool or fabric drying in the sun. You can also usually catch some of the dyers at work, pounding cloth in their big vats of coloured liquid.

West of the dyers' souk, the street widens out into a square opposite an elaborate triple-bayed **fountain** adjoining the Mouassine Mosque. Built in the mid-sixteenth century under the prolific Saadian builder, Abdallah el Ghalib, it is one of many such fountains in Marrakesh with a basin for people set next to two larger troughs for animals. Its installation was a pious act, directly sanctioned by the Koran in its charitable provision of water for men and beasts.

Around Place de la Kissaria

Place de la Kissaria, an open space surrounded by important public buildings, sits at the northern end of the souks area. Its north side is dominated by the **Ben Youssef Mosque**, successor to an original put up by the city's Almoravid founders. The mosque was completely rebuilt under the Almohads, and several times since, so that the building you see today dates largely from the nineteenth century.

Marrakesh Museum

East side of Pl de la Kissaria • Charge • ⓦ museedemarrakech.ma

The **Marrakesh Museum** is housed in a magnificent late nineteenth-century palace, **Dar Mnebbi**. The palace was built for Mehdi Mnebbi, defence minister of Moulay Abdelziz (1894–1908), who later became Moroccan ambassador in London. Nearly derelict after years of neglect, the palace was bought up and restored by local arts patron Omar Benjelloun, and opened as a museum in 1997. It houses exhibitions of Moroccan art and sculpture, both traditional and contemporary. It is the **restoration** itself, however, that is most remarkable, especially in what was the hammam, and in the now-covered inner courtyard with its huge brass lamp hung above a central fountain.

Almoravid koubba

South side of Pl de la Kissaria • Charge • ⓦ almoravidkoubba.com

The **Almoravid koubba** (Koubba Ba'adiyn) is just a small, two-storey structure, but as the only Almoravid building to survive intact in Morocco (except possibly a minaret in Tit near El Jadida; see page 269), its style is at the root of all Moroccan architecture. Its **motifs** – such as pine cones, palms and acanthus leaves – appear again in later buildings such as the nearby Ben Youssef Medersa (see below). The **windows** on each of the different sides became the classic shapes of Almohad and Merenid design – as did the **merlons**, the complex "ribs" on the outside of the dome, and the square- and star-shaped octagon on the inside, which is itself repeated at each of its corners. It was probably just a small ablutions annexe to the Ben Youssef Mosque, but its architecture gives us our only clue as to what that mosque might originally have looked like.

Excavated only in 1952, the previously covered-over *koubba* is well below today's ground level, and you have to go down two flights of stairs to get to where it was built. Next to it are attendant facilities including a large **water cistern**, and remains of **latrines** and **fountains** for performing ablutions, much like those you will still find adjacent to many Moroccan mosques.

Ben Youssef Medersa

Derb Zaouiat Lahdar, 30m north of the Marrakesh Museum • Charge • ⓦ medersabenyoussef.ma

5

The **Ben Youssef Medersa** was a Koranic school attached to the Ben Youssef Mosque, where students learnt the Koran by rote, and is the most beautifully decorated building in Marrakesh, with lashings of classic Moroccan decor – zellij tiling, stucco plasterwork, carved cedar wood – all worked to the very highest standards.

Like most of its counterparts up in Fez, the Ben Youssef was a **Merenid** foundation, established by the "Black Sultan" Abou el Hassan (1331–49), but rebuilt in the 1560s under the Saadians. As with the slightly later Saadian Tombs, no surface is left undecorated, and the overall quality of its craftsmanship, whether in carved wood, stuccowork or zellij tilework, is startling.

The **central courtyard**, its carved cedar-wood lintels weathered almost flat on the most exposed side, is unusually large. Along two sides run wide, sturdy, columned arcades, which were probably used to supplement the space for teaching in the neighbouring mosque. Above them are some of the windows of the **dormitory quarters**, from which you can get an interesting perspective – and attempt to fathom how over eight hundred students were once housed in the building. One room is furnished as it would have been when in use. At its far end, the court opens onto a **prayer hall**, where the decoration is at its best preserved and most elaborate, with a predominance of pine-cone and palm motifs.

East of Place de la Kissaria

The main route between the Ben Youssef Medersa and the city gate of Bab Debbagh is marked at its halfway point by **Place el Moukef**, more an intersection than a square, where four routes meet. Westward, Rue Souk des Fassis, the road to the Ben Youssef Medersa, is lined by *fondouks* (see page 303), while in the opposite direction, Rue Bab Debbagh passes through the rather smelly tanneries area on its way to Bab Debbagh. North of Place el Moukef is another city gate, Bab el Khemis (see page), while Rue Essebtiyne, leading south of the *place*, forks after 200m. Bearing right here, you come to Place Ben Salah, where the **Zaouia of Sidi Ben Salah**, with its very fine and prominent minaret, was commissioned by a fourteenth-century Merenid sultan.

Maison de la Photographie

46 Rue Souk des Fassis • Charge • ⓦ maisondelaphotographie.ma

The **Maison de la Photographie** houses a reasonably interesting collection of early twentieth-century (and a few late nineteenth-century) photographs of Morocco, some made from glass negatives. The photographs are exhibited over three floors, with one room dedicated to pictures of the Jemaa el Fna, and the terrace (with café) gives good views over the Medina rooftops.

Bab Debbagh

Though supposedly Almoravid in design, over the years **Bab Debbagh** must have been almost totally rebuilt. Passing through the gate, you become aware of its very real defensive purpose: three internal chicanes are placed in such a manner as to force anyone attempting to storm it to make several turns. Just before the gate, several shops on the left give good **views** over the quarter from their roofs, and shopkeepers will let you up for a small fee – agree it first or you'll be mercilessly overcharged.

The tanneries

Marrakesh's **tanneries**, flanking Rue Bab Debbagh, are more scattered and thus less interesting to look at than those at Fez. They were built at the edge of the city not only because of the smell, but also for access to water: a stream, the Oued Issil, runs just outside the Medina walls. The smell comes largely from the first stage, where the hides are soaked in a vat of pigeon droppings. The natural dyes traditionally used to colour the leather have largely been replaced by chemicals, many of them carcinogenic – a fact to remember when you see people standing waist-deep in them. If you want to take a closer look at the tanning process, come in the morning, when the cooperatives are at work. One tannery that's easy to find is on the north side of the street about 200m before Bab Debbagh, opposite the blue-tiled stand-up fountain, with another one about 200m further west. Ignore hustlers trying to persuade you that you have to pay them for entry, and if they latch onto you, point out that you do not want a guide and will not be paying them for following you. Be aware however that they can be persistent and sometimes physically threatening, and may even try to prevent you leaving if you don't pay them.

Bab el Khemis

Built at an angle in the walls near the Medina's northern end, **Bab el Khemis** is a reconstructed Almoravid gate surrounded by concentric rings of decoration and topped with Christmas-tree-like castellations. Its name means "Thursday Gate", a reference to the **market** held outside, 400m to the north, past a *marabout's* tomb and a former cemetery, now landscaped as a little park. Although the main market is held on a Thursday morning, there are stalls out most days. It's really a local produce market, though handicraft items are also sold.

North of the Ben Youssef Mosque

The area immediately **north of the Ben Youssef Mosque** is cut by two main streets: Rue Assouel and Rue Bab Taghzout. These were, with Bab Doukkala, the principal approaches to the city until the twentieth century and along them you find many of the old **fondouks** used for lodging by merchants visiting the souks (see page 303).

Chrob ou Chouf fountain

Follow Rue Baroudienne north from its junction with Rue Amesfah and turn right at the end to find Marrakesh's most famous drinking **fountain**: a small sixteenth-century

---

FONDOUKS

One of the most characteristic types of building in the Medina is the **fondouk** or caravanserai. Originally inns used by visiting merchants when they were in Marrakesh to trade in its souks, *fondouks* have a courtyard in the middle surrounded by what were originally stables, while the upper level contained rooms for the merchants. Some date back to Saadian times (1520–1669), and some still have fine original woodcarving or stuccowork.

Today, Marrakesh's *fondouks* are in varying states of repair; some have become private residences, others commercial premises. Some are now tourist souvenir shops where visitors are welcome, but even in others, the courtyard doors are often left open, and no one seems to mind if you wander in to have a look.

Interesting *fondouks* include: a group on **Rue Dar el Bacha** by the junction with Rue Mouassine; a couple just south of the junction on **Rue Mouassine** itself; a row on the south side of **Rue Bab Debbagh**, behind the Ben Youssef Medersa; a whole series along **Rue Amesfah**, north of the Ben Youssef Mosque; and one directly opposite the **Chrob ou Chouf fountain**. *Terrasse le Medersa* restaurant (see page 303) is on the terrace of a *fondouk*.

5

EL GLAOUI: THE PASHA OF MARRAKESH

T'hami el Glaoui, Pasha of Marrakesh during the French Protectorate, was the last great southern **tribal leader**, a despot and shrewd supporter of colonial rule (see page 368) – and personal friend of Winston Churchill. Cruel and magnificent in equal measure, he was a spectacular party-giver in an age where rivals were not lacking. At the extraordinary *difas* or banquets held at his palace, the **Dar el Glaoui**, for his Western friends, "nothing", as Gavin Maxwell wrote, "was impossible." Hashish and opium were freely available, and "to his guests T'hami gave whatever they wanted, whether it might be a diamond ring, a present of money in gold, or a Berber girl or boy from the High Atlas".

He was so hated by Marrakshis that, on his death in 1956, a mob ransacked the palace and lynched his henchmen. However, passions have burnt out over the years, and the family has been rehabilitated. One of T'hami's sons, Glaoui Abdelssadak, rose to high rank in the Moroccan civil service and became vice president of Gulf Oil. Dar el Glaoui, west of Ben Youssef Mosque on Rue Dar el Bacha, now houses the offices of the UMT trade union federation but part of it is used as a museum for temporary exhibitions (Charge), and is well worth popping into for a look at the building alone.

recessed fountain known as **Chrob ou Chouf** ("drink and look"), most notable for its finely carved cedar-wood lintel.

Zaouia of Sidi Bel Abbes

Rue Sidi Bel Abbes • No access to the mosque and mausoleums for non-Muslims

The old city gate of **Bab Taghzout** marked the limits of the Medina from Almoravid times until the eighteenth century, when Sultan Mohammed Abdallah extended the walls to enclose the **Zaouia of Sidi Bel Abbes**. The *zaouia* commemorated the most important of Marrakesh's seven saints, who lived in the twelfth century (see page 305), and as a cult centre it often wielded great influence and served as a refuge for political dissidents.

There has been a shrine here since at least the fourteenth century, but the *zaouia* as we see it today was commissioned by the Saadian sultan **Abou Feris** at the beginning of the seventeenth century, and it underwent major restoration in the middle of the eighteenth. Non-Muslims are not allowed to enter the buildings (or even, strictly speaking, the main courtyard), but may see something of the complex and its activities from outside the official boundary. The *zaouia* has always prospered; it still owns much of the quarter to the north and continues its educational and charitable work, distributing food each evening to the blind.

The southern Medina

The area south of Jemaa el Fna is quite different from that to the north of it, generally more open and home to **Dar el Makhzen** (the royal palace), the **kasbah** (old inner citadel), and the **Mellah** (former Jewish quarter). The two obvious focal sights, not to be missed, are the **Saadian Tombs**, preserved in the shadow of the Kasbah Mosque, and **El Badi**, the ruined palace of Ahmed el Mansour. Also worth seeing are the **Bahia Palace** and the nearby **Dar Si Said** and **Maison Tiskiwin museums**.

Bab Agnaou

From the Jemaa el Fna, **Rue Bab Agnaou** and its continuations lead to a square flanked by two gates. Directly ahead is **Bab er Robb**, leading out of the Medina towards the High

Atlas mountains. To its left, somewhat battered and eroded, is **Bab Agnaou**, one of the two original entrances to the kasbah, though the magnificent blue granite gateway which stands here today was built in 1885. The name actually means "black people's gate", a reference to its use by swarthy commoners, while the fair-complexioned aristocracy had their own entrance into the kasbah (now long gone). The gate is surrounded by concentric arches of decoration and topped with an inscription in decorative script, which reads: "Enter with blessing, serene people." The semi-circular frieze above the arch creates a three-dimensional effect without any actual depth of carving.

Kasbah Mosque
On the east side of Bab Agnaou, also directly accessible from Rue Ibn Rachid • No access to non-Muslims

THE SEVEN SAINTS OF MARRAKESH

Some two hundred holy men and women have their tombs in Marrakesh, but the most important are the **Sabatou Rijal**, literally "seven men", though usually translated in English as "**seven saints**". Other than being holy men who are buried in Marrakesh, the seven don't have a lot in common: they lived at different times, came from different places, and didn't even all die in Marrakesh. The circuit of their tombs (marked by yellow triangles on the Medina map; see page 292) was established in the seventeenth century under the Alaouite ruler **Moulay Ismail**, to give the city some religious significance and to attract pilgrims (tourists, in other words). The tombs get their most visitors during a rather low-key week-long annual **moussem** held in their honour in late March, and they are visited in a specific order, travelling anticlockwise round the Medina. In that order, these are the seven:

(1) Sidi Youssef Ben Ali, whose tomb is located just outside Bab Aghmat, at the Medina's southeastern corner, was a Marrakshi leper who spent most of his life in a leper colony just outside the walls here, where he died in 1196 or 1197. If you've got a touch of leprosy, this is the saint to visit for *baraka*.

(2) Caid Ayad was born in Ceuta in 1083 and studied theology in Muslim Spain under Andalusia's greatest teachers before moving to Marrakesh. He was employed in turn by both the Almoravids and the Almohads, and died in 1149. His *zaouia* is just inside Bab Aylen.

(3) Sidi Bel Abbes (see page 304), also originally from Ceuta, died in Marrakesh in 1205 and was known for the strictness of his religious observance (he knew the Koran by heart at the age of sixteen), and for his acts of charity, especially towards blind people. It is said that in his day, a blind person never went hungry in Marrakesh, and the visually impaired still come to him for *baraka*.

(4) Sidi Mohammed Ben Slimane el Jazouli, a descendant of the Prophet, was expelled from Safi around 1460 because the governor feared his Shereefian status and reputation as a holy man made him a potential political rival. He neither lived nor died in Marrakesh, but his body was moved to a series of locations before finally being laid to rest in 1541 in a mausoleum about 200m southwest of Sidi Bel Abbes, and 200m north of Rue Riad el Arous.

(5) Sidi Abdel Aziz el Harrar was born in Marrakesh, but made his name in Fez, where he was based in the Medersa el Attarine (see page 166). He died in 1508 and was buried in a mausoleum on Rue Mouassine, near the junction of Rue Amesfah with Rue Baroudienne.

(6) Sidi Moulay el Ksour was a Berber from the mountains who studied in Fez and Granada before coming to Marrakesh to become a disciple of Sidi Abdel Aziz el Harrar. When Portuguese forces attacked the city in 1514, he led the popular resistance movement that kept them out, and died in 1528, to be buried only 300m northwest of the Jemaa el Fna, not far from Bab Fteuh.

(7) Sidi es Souheili was a great Islamic jurist from Málaga who came to Marrakesh around 1182 at the call of the Almohad sultan Yacoub el Mansour. He died here three years later, and his *zaouia*, in a cemetery just outside Bab er Robb (inaccessible to non-Muslims), hides a former gate in the city wall called Bab ech Charia.

5

The **Kasbah Mosque**, was, as its name suggests, the main Friday mosque for the
Kasbah. Its minaret looks gaudy and modern, but in fact it dates from 1190, making
it contemporary with the Koutoubia (see page 296). It really was painted green and
white back in the day, and was restored to its original state in the 1960s. The rest of
the mosque is not original, however, as it was rebuilt after being destroyed when a
gunpowder store blew up in 1569.

Saadian Tombs

Off Pl des Tombeaux Saadiens, accessed from a passage on the south side of the Kasbah Mosque • Charge

The **Saadian Tombs** are the kasbah's main sight. Housed in a quiet, high-walled
enclosure, shaded with shrubs and palms, they belong to the dynasty that ruled
Morocco from 1554 to 1669. The best time to see them is first thing in the morning,
before the crowds arrive, or late in the afternoon when they, and the heat, have largely
gone.

There was probably a **burial ground** behind the royal palace before the Saadian period,
but the earliest **tomb** here dates from 1557, and the main structures were built under
Sultan Ahmed el Mansour, around the same time as the Ben Youssef Medersa and the
El Badi Palace. A few prominent Marrakshis continued to be buried in the mausoleums
after Saadian times: the last, in 1792, was the "mad sultan", **Moulay Yazid**, whose
22-month reign was one of the most violent and sadistic in the nation's history. Named
as the successor to Sidi Mohammed, Moulay Yazid threw himself into a series of revolts
against his father, waged an inconclusive war with Spain, and brutally suppressed a
Marrakesh-based rebellion in support of his brother. A massacre followed his capture of
the city, though he had little time to celebrate his victory – a bullet in the head during
a rebel counterattack killed him soon after.

The tombs escaped plundering by the rapacious Alaouite sultan **Moulay Ismail**,
probably because he feared bad luck if he desecrated them. Instead, he blocked all
access bar an obscure entrance from the Kasbah Mosque. The tombs lay half-ruined
and half-forgotten until they were rediscovered by a French aerial survey in 1917, and a
passageway was built to give access to them.

Ahmed el Mansour's mausoleum

The finest of the two main **mausoleums** in the enclosure is on the left as you come
in – a beautiful group of three rooms, built to house **Ahmed el Mansour's tomb** and
completed within his lifetime. Continuing round from the courtyard entrance, the first
hall is a **prayer oratory**, a room probably not intended for burial, though now almost
littered with the thin marble stones of Saadian princes. It is here that Moulay Yazid was
laid out, perhaps in purposeful obscurity.

Architecturally, the most important feature of this mausoleum is the **mihrab**, its
pointed horseshoe arch supported by an incredibly delicate arrangement of columns.
Opposite this is another elaborate arch, leading to the domed **central chamber** and
Ahmed el Mansour's tomb itself, which you can glimpse through the next door
in the court. The tomb, slightly larger than those surrounding it, lies right in the
middle, flanked on either side by those of the sultan's sons and successors. The
room is spectacular; faint light filtering onto the tombs from an interior lantern in
a tremendous vaulted roof, the zellij full of colour and motion and the undefined
richness of a third chamber almost hidden from view.

The rest of the site

The **other mausoleum**, older and less impressive, was built by Ahmed in place of an
existing pavilion above the tombs of his mother, Lalla Messaouda, and of Mohammed
ech Sheikh, the founder of the Saadian dynasty. It is again a series of three rooms,
though two are hardly more than loggias.

5

Outside, round the garden and courtyard, are scattered the tombs of over a hundred more Saadian princes and members of the royal household. Like the privileged 66 given space within the mausoleums, their gravestones are brilliantly tiled and often elaborately inscribed.

El Badi Palace

South of Pl des Ferblantiers • Charge

Though substantially in ruins, and reduced throughout to its red *pisé* walls, enough remains of **El Badi Palace** to suggest that its name – "The Incomparable" – was not entirely immodest. The palace was originally commissioned by the Saadian sultan **Ahmed el Mansour** shortly after his accession in 1578. The money for it came from the enormous ransom paid by the Portuguese after the Battle of the Three Kings (see page 500). It took his seventeenth-century successor **Moulay Ismail** over ten years of systematic work to strip the palace of everything valuable, and there's still a lingering sense of luxury and grandeur. What you see today is essentially the ceremonial part of the **palace complex**, planned on a grand scale for the reception of ambassadors, and not meant for everyday living. The scale of the palace, with its sunken gardens and vast 90m pool, is certainly unrivalled, and the odd traces of zellij and plaster evoke a decor that was probably as rich as that of the Saadian Tombs.

Central court

The palace's **entrance** was originally in the southeast corner of the complex, but today you enter from the north, through the Green Pavilion, emerging into a vast **central court**, over 130m long and nearly as wide. In its northeast corner, you can climb up to get an overview from the ramparts, and a closer view of the **storks** that nest atop them. Within the central court are four **sunken gardens**, two on the northern side and two on the southern side. **Pools** separate the two gardens on each side, and there are four smaller pools in the four corners of the court. When the pools are filled – as during the June folklore festival that takes place here – they are an incredibly majestic sight.

Summer pavilions

On each side of the courtyard were **summer pavilions**. Of the **Crystal Pavilion**, to the east, only the foundations survive. On the opposite side, a monumental hall that was used by the sultan on occasions of state was known as the **Koubba el Hamsiniya** (The Fifty Pavilion), after its size in cubits.

Stables and dungeons

South of the courtyard, accessed just to the right of the building housing the *minbar*, are ruins of the palace **stables**, and beyond them, leading towards the intriguing walls of the present royal palace, a series of **dungeons**, used into the last century as a state prison.

Koutoubia Minbar

The original **minbar** (pulpit) from the **Koutoubia Mosque** (see page 296) is housed in a pavilion in the southwest corner of the main courtyard. It may not sound like much, but this *minbar* was in its day one of the most celebrated works of art in the Muslim world. Commissioned from the Andalusian capital Cordoba in 1137 by the last Almoravid sultan, Ali Ben Youssef, it took eight years to complete, and was covered with the most exquisite inlay work, of which, sadly, only patches remain. When the Almohads took power, they installed the *minbar* in their newly built Koutoubia Mosque, where it remained until it was removed for restoration in 1962, and eventually brought here. Unfortunately, members of the public are not usually allowed to walk all the way round it to inspect the surviving inlay work, but the *gardien* may relent if you show a particular interest. Photography is not usually allowed.

5

The Mellah

Marrakesh's **Mellah** (Jewish quarter) was created in 1558, though no record remains of why it was done at this particular time. It may have been to use the Jews as a buffer zone (and scapegoat) between the palace and the populace in times of social unrest, but more likely it was simply to make **taxation** easier. The Jews of Marrakesh were an important financial resource – they controlled most of the Saadian sugar trade, and comprised practically all of the city's bankers, metalworkers, jewellers and tailors. In the sixteenth century, at least, their quarter was almost a town in itself, supervised by rabbis, and with its own souks, gardens, fountains and synagogues.

The present-day Mellah, known officially as **Hay Essalam**, is much smaller in extent and almost entirely Muslim – most Marrakshi Jews left long ago for Casablanca, France or Israel (although the king is actively encouraging the Moroccan Jewish diaspora to return). The few who remain, outwardly distinguishable only by the men's small black skullcaps, are mostly poor, old or both. The quarter, however, is immediately distinct: its houses are taller than elsewhere, the streets are more enclosed, and even the shop cubicles are smaller. Until the Protectorate, Jews were not permitted to own land or property – nor even to ride or walk, except barefoot – outside the Mellah. Today, though not a sought-after neighbourhood, its air of neglect and poverty is probably less than at any time during the past three centuries.

The easiest approach to the Mellah is from **Place des Ferblantiers** – the tinsmiths' square. Formerly called Place du Mellah, this was itself part of the old Jewish souk, now an atmospheric little square, surrounded by the workshops of lantern makers. North of here, off the street leading up to Rue Riad Zitoun el Jedid, is a **jewellers' souk**, where one of the traditional Jewish trades has pretty much been taken over by Muslim craftsmen. The Mellah's main market, **Souk el Mellah**, just across the street, specializes in spices, which are piled up in attractively multicoloured and very photogenic pyramids. Like a lot of the Mellah, the market is currently being given something of a facelift.

Lazama Synagogue

36 Derb L'Azen Nissim • Charge

The main road into the Mellah leads along the southern side of the Bahia Palace. Heading along it from Souk el Mellah, the first left (under a low arch) takes you to **Place Souweka**, a small square at the centre of the Mellah, very much like the goal in a maze. If you ignore that turning, the main road does a twist, and the next left (Derb Ragraga – its entrance surmounted by plaques directing you to various riads) takes you after 100m to the **Lazama Synagogue**. Like all the Mellah's synagogues, it was part of a private house, which you'll notice is decorated with Star of David zellij tiling. The synagogue is still in use, although the interior is modern and not tremendously interesting.

Miâara Jewish cemetery

Av Taoulet el Miaara • Charge

The **Miâara Jewish cemetery** is reckoned to date from the early seventeenth century. More sprawling than the cemetery in Fez (see page 174), it is well tended and boasts eleven shrines belonging to Jewish *marabouts* (*tsadikim* in Hebrew), illustrating an interesting parallel between the Moroccan varieties of Judaism and Islam.

Bitoun Synagogue

Rue Arset el Mâach (Rue de l'Electricité) • Not open to the public

Just outside the Mellah, the first-floor **Bitoun Synagogue** is out of use and its interior is not open for visitors, but it has the most interesting and unusual **exterior** of any synagogue in Morocco, located above a herb shop and painted in mustard yellow with arcaded balconies, and of course a Star of David motif.

Bahia Palace

Rue Riad Zitoun el Jedid • Charge

5

The **Bahia Palace** was originally built in 1866–7 for **Si Moussa**, a former slave who had risen to become Moulay Hassan's chamberlain, and then grand vizier. Moussa's son, **Bou Ahmed**, who himself held the post of chamberlain under Hassan, became kingmaker in 1894 when Hassan died while returning home from a *harka* (tax-collecting expedition). Ahmed concealed news of the sultan's death until he was able to declare Hassan's fourteen-year-old son Moulay Abd el Aziz sultan in his place, with himself as grand vizier and regent (see page 503). He thus gained virtually complete control over the state, which he exercised until his death in 1900. He began enlarging the Bahia (meaning "brilliance") in the same year as his coup, adding a mosque, a hammam and even a vegetable garden. When he died, his servants ransacked the palace, but it was restored and, during the Protectorate, housed the French Resident General.

The small riad

Visitors enter the palace from the west, through an arcaded courtyard which leads to a **small riad** (enclosed garden), part of Bou Ahmed's extension. The riad is decorated with beautiful carved stucco and cedar wood, and salons lead off it on three sides. The eastern salon leads through to the **council room**, and thence through a vestibule – where it's worth pausing to look up at the lovely painted ceiling – to the **great courtyard** of Si Moussa's original palace. The rooms surrounding the courtyard are also all worth checking out for their painted wooden ceilings.

The large riad

North of the great courtyard is the **large riad**, the heart of Si Moussa's palace, fragrant with fruit trees and melodious with birdsong, approaching the very ideal of beauty in Arabic domestic architecture. To its east and west are halls decorated with fine zellij fireplaces and painted wooden ceilings. From here, you leave the palace via the **private apartment** built in 1898 for Ahmed's wife, Lalla Zinab, where again you should look up to check out the painted ceiling, carved stucco, and stained-glass windows.

Maison Tiskiwin

8 Rue de la Bahia • ⓦ tiskiwin.wdro.net • 200m north of Bahia Palace on Rue Riad Zitoun el Jedid – where the street opens out to the left, take a right turn under an arch, and it's 100m ahead on the right; look for the yellow sign

The **Maison Tiskiwin** is an early twentieth-century townhouse built in Spanish-Moroccan style. Within lies a unique collection of Moroccan and Saharan artefacts, billed as "a journey from Marrakesh to Timbuktu and back". They come from the collection of Dutch anthropologist **Bert Flint**, a Moroccan resident since 1957. Each room features carpets, fabrics, clothes and jewellery from a different region of the Sahara, with explanatory notes in French. The exhibition illustrates the long-standing cultural links across the desert, a result of the centuries of caravan trade between Morocco and Mali. At the time of research the museum was closed for renovations, the date of re-opening is unknown.

Dar Si Said

Derb Si Said • Charge

Dar Si Said, a smaller version of the Bahia Palace, was built in the late nineteenth century for a brother of Bou Ahmed, who, though something of a simpleton, nonetheless gained the post of royal chamberlain. It's a lovely building, with beautiful pooled courtyards, scented with lemons and flowers and cooled by palms. The museum now houses an exhibition on weaving and carpets, with examples from around the country, but the building is rather more interesting than the exhibits.

Agdal gardens

Route d'Agdal • Free • Bus #6 from Pl Foucauld

The **Agdal gardens**, adjoining the Medina to the south, sprawl over four square kilometres. They were originally watered by a system of wells and underground channels, known as *khettera*, from the base of the Atlas in the Ourika Valley and dating, in part, from the earliest founding of the city. These fell into disrepair and the gardens were largely abandoned until the nineteenth century, when they were restored. At the heart of the gardens are a series of pools, the largest of which is the **Sahraj el Hana** (Tank of Health – now a green, algae-clogged rectangle of water), which was probably dug by the Almohads and is flanked by a ramshackle old *minzah*, or summer pavilion, where the last few pre-colonial sultans held picnics and boating parties.

The Ville Nouvelle

Marrakesh's **Ville Nouvelle** radiates out from **Guéliz**, its commercial centre. Though it's hardly chock-a-block with attractions, it does have one must-see: the **Majorelle Garden**. South of Guéliz, the **Hivernage** district, built as a garden suburb, is where most of the city's newer tourist hotels are located. Further afield, on the northeastern edge of town, is Marrakesh's **palmery**.

Guéliz

The heart of modern Marrakesh, Guéliz has a certain buzz that the sleepy old Medina rather lacks. Its main thoroughfare, **Avenue Mohammed V**, runs all the way down to the Koutoubia, and it's on and around this boulevard that you'll find the city's main concentration of upmarket shops, restaurants and smart pavement cafés. Its junctions form the Ville Nouvelle's main centres of activity: Place de la Liberté, with its modern fountain; Place 16 Novembre, by the main post office; and Place Abdelmoumen Ben Ali, epicentre of Marrakesh's modern shopping zone. Looking back along Avenue Mohammed V from Guéliz to the Medina, on a clear day at least, you should see the Koutoubia rising in the distance, with the Atlas mountains behind.

L'Église des Saints-Martyrs

Rue de l'Imam Ali • Free

Built in 1930, Marrakesh's little Catholic church, **L'Église des Saints-Martyrs**, could be straight out of rural France but for its distinctly Marrakshi red-ochre hue. The church is dedicated to six Franciscan friars who insisted on preaching Christianity on the city's streets in the year 1220. When the sultan ordered them to either desist or leave, they refused, and were promptly beheaded, to be canonized by the Church in 1481. Proselytizing for religions other than Islam remains illegal in Morocco to this day.

European Cemetery

Rue Erraouda • Free

The **European Cemetery**, opened in 1925, is a peaceful plot with lots of wild flowers, and some quite Poe-esque French family mausoleums. A large white obelisk near the entrance is dedicated to the soldiers who fell fighting in Africa for democracy and Free France during World War II; 333 of these men have their last resting places in the cemetery's section H. Section B is devoted to children who died in infancy, and the oldest section, to the left of the obelisk as you come in, contains the tombs of colonists from the 1920s and 1930s, most of whom seem to have been less than forty years old when they died.

5

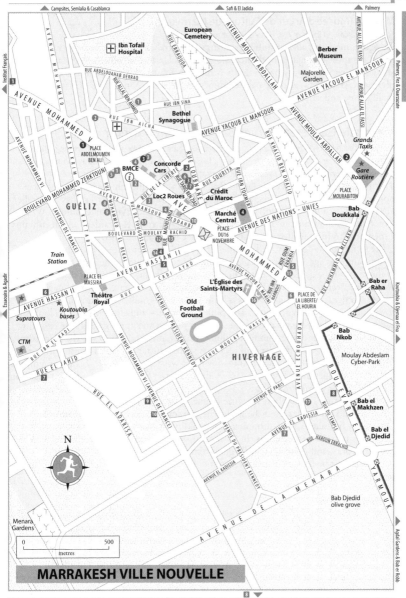

MARRAKESH VILLE NOUVELLE

◼ ACCOMMODATION				● EATING				◼ DRINKING & NIGHTLIFE	
Atlas Asni	9	Toulousain	3	Al Bahriya	12	Grand Café de		555 Famous Club	8
Farouk	4	Youth Hostel	7	Al Fassia	3	la Poste	10	African Chic	5
Fashion	5			Amal Restaurant	1	Katsura	15	Café Atlas	1
Ibis Marrakech		● SHOPPING		Amandine	8	Lunch d'Or	16	Café-Bar de l'Escale	4
Centre Gare	6	Aswak Assalam	2	Café du Livre	6	Rôtisserie de		Chesterfield Pub	2
Du Pacha	2	Librairie Chatr	1	Café des Negociants	4	la Paix	11	Kechmara	3
The Red House	8	Librairie Menzil		Chez Lamine Hadj	2	La Taverne	5	Theatro	7
Ryad Mogador		el Fan	3	Comptoir Darna	17	La Trattoria	9	VIP Club	6
Menara	10	Marché Central		Hôtel Farouk	14	Winoo	13		
Tafoukt	1	(Municipal Market)	4						

5

MACMA (Musée d'Art et de Culture de Marrakech)

34 Passage Ghandouri, 61 Rue Yougoslavie • Free • ⓦ museemacma.com

This cool, modern gallery exhibits paintings of Marrakesh and Morocco by European artists from the colonial period, including Eugène Delacroix and Jacques Majorelle, along with contemporary paintings by Moroccan artists, plus a selection of classic photos of Marrakesh, antique painted doors and chests, ceramics and objets d'art – all in all, a fine collection.

Majorelle Garden and Yves Saint Laurent Museum

Rue Yves Saint Laurent (off Av Yacoub el Mansour) • Charge • No picnics or unaccompanied children allowed • ⓦ jardinmajorelle.com, Wmuseeyslmarrakech.com• When leaving the garden, ignore the taxi drivers waiting outside, who run a cartel and will not take you unless you pay well over the odds; simply walk down to the main road and hail a cab there

The small **Majorelle Garden**, or Jardin Bou Saf, is a meticulously planned twelve-acre botanical garden, created in the 1920s and 1930s by French painter Jacques Majorelle (1886–1962), and subsequently owned by fashion designer **Yves Saint Laurent**. When Yves Saint Laurent died in 2008, his ashes were scattered in the garden, which contains a memorial to him, while the street the entrance is in was renamed after him.

The feeling of tranquillity in the garden is enhanced by verdant groves of bamboo, dwarf palm and agave, the cactus garden and lily-covered pools. The Art Deco pavilion at the heart of the garden is painted in a striking cobalt blue – the colour of French workmen's overalls, so Majorelle claimed, though it seems to have improved in the Moroccan light. This brilliantly offsets both the plants – multicoloured bougainvillea, rows of bright orange nasturtiums and pink geraniums – and also the strong colours of the pergolas and concrete paths – pinks, lemon yellows and apple greens. The enduring sound is the chatter of the common bulbuls, flitting among the leaves of the date palms, and the pools also attract other bird residents such as turtle doves and house buntings. The garden became better known abroad when it was featured by Yves Saint Laurent in a brilliant reproduction at London's 1997 Chelsea Flower Show. Pierre Bergé and Madison Cox's *Majorelle, A Moroccan Oasis* is a superbly photographed coffee-table book on the garden, sometimes available at Librairie Menzil el Fan (see page 326).

Just around the corner from the Majorelle Garden, the new **Yves Saint Laurent Museum** is housed in a jaw-dropping new building and displays fifty of the great designer's most iconic creations. In its auditorium, you can see a short film about YSL's life and works, and there are usually good temporary exhibitions too.

Tickets must be bought in advance online. Be warned that entry fees are pricey eand queues can be long.

Berber Museum

In Majorelle's former studio, housed within the pavilion, the **Berber Museum** kicks off with an exhibition about Morocco's Berbers, their culture and languages, and where in the country they live, before launching (in the next room) into a display of traditional Berber crafts, including textiles and carpet-making, and showing the tools used in making them, as well as the finished articles. There's even a beautiful but slightly rickety wooden *minbar* (mosque pulpit) from the Middle Atlas, decorated with Berber designs. The next room is dedicated to jewellery, all of it silver, as gold is considered unlucky in Berber tradition. The last room contains a display of Berber costumes from different regions of the country.

The palmery

5km northeast of town, between the Route de Fès (N8) and the Route de Casablanca (N9) • The Route de Fès turn-off is served by bus #17 or #26, with plenty of taxis, but the Route de Casablanca end has no public transport, so it's best to take a taxi up to that end to start, and finish at Route de Fès

Marrakesh's **palmery (palmeraie)**, or oasis, is far from being the most spectacular in the country, but it has a certain tranquillity and makes a pleasant change from the urban landscape. Plus, at 5ºC cooler than the Medina, it can be particularly appealing in summer. Supposedly, it sprang from stones spat out by the date-munching troops of Marrakesh's founder, Youssef Ben Tachfine, but in fact the **dates** produced by its fifty thousand-odd palms are not of eating quality. Dotted with the villas of prosperous Marrakshis, the palmery also boasts a golf course and a couple of luxury hotels.

The most popular route through the oasis is the **Circuit de la Palmeraie**, which meanders through the trees and villas from the Route de Fès to the Route de Casablanca. The classic way to see it is by *calèche* (see page 316), and the sightseeing bus, the Marrakech Bus Touristique (see page 316), travels round it too. It's also possible to ride around the palmery on a camel – men by the roadside offer rides – or you could even explore it on foot, though it's quite a long 5km stroll.

Menara Gardens

Gardens • Free • Minzah • Charge • Bus #11 from Av Mohammed V (southbound) or Pl Youssef Tachfine

Southwest of the Hivernage district, the **Menara Gardens** are a popular picnic spot for Marrakshi families, as well as tourists, centred on a rectangular pool providing a classic postcard image beneath a backdrop of the High Atlas. Originally dating from the twelfth century, it was restored and its pavilions rebuilt in the mid-nineteenth century. The poolside *minzah* (pavilion) replaced an earlier Saadian structure. Aside from the pool, the garden is largely filled with olive trees, and there's usually someone by the park entrance offering camel rides.

ARRIVAL AND DEPARTURE   MARRAKESH

BY PLANE

Marrakesh's Menara airport (Ⓦ marrakech.airport-authority. com) is 4km southwest of town, and is connected with Pl Foucauld (by the Koutoubia) by bus #19. The bus runs daily every 30minvia Av Mohammed V and Bd Mohammed VI, and can be joined at any bus stop en route. *Petits taxis* (for up to three passengers) or *grands taxis* (for up to six) have fixed an artificially high fare for journeys between the airport and town which is posted up in the arrivals lounge. It's not advisable to walk to town from the airport (or vice versa), as people regularly get mugged on the road. If you really want to do it cheaply, exit the airport, cross over the main road and take bus #11 or #20 from in front of the first row of shops 200m to your left (the bus stop isn't marked, but buses will stop there) to Av Mohammed V; however, these buses can be very slow and very crowded. From town to the airport, but not the other way (unless a passing one happens to have space, in which case it will stop at the same place as the #11 or #20 bus), you can take a shared *grand taxi* for M'hamid from the north end of Rue Ibn Rachid and ask to be put off at the airport turn-off, leaving you just 300m to walk. Arriving at the airport late at night, you won't always find the exchange kiosks open, but there are ATMs in the arrivals hall; taxis will in any case usually accept euros, and sometimes even dollars or sterling, at more or less the equivalent dirham rate. Most international car rental firms have desks at the airport, or will meet arrivals by arrangement.

BY TRAIN

The train station is on Av Mohammed VI at Av Hassan II, a 10min walk west of Guéliz. Buses #8, #10, #14 and #66 connect the station with Pl Foucauld (by the Koutoubia); they can be picked up across Av Hassan II at the corner of Rue Zoubeir. The most comfortable way to travel to Tangier is to take a couchette on the night train, preferably booking by the morning of your day of travel.

Destinations Casablanca Voyageurs (9 daily; 3hr 20min); Fez (9 daily; 7hr 35min); Kenitra (9 daily; 5hr); Meknes (9 daily; 6hr 45min); Oujda (2 daily changing at Fez; 14–15hr); Rabat (9 daily; 4hr 25min); Safi (2 daily changing at Benguerir; 3hr 20min); Tangier (1 direct & 6 connecting daily; 8hr 30min–10hr 30min).

BY BUS

GARE ROUTIÈRE

Long-distance buses, other than Supratours and most CTM services, depart from the *gare routière* just outside the walls of the Medina by Bab Doukkala, and has left-luggage facilities. You can walk into the centre of Guéliz from the *gare routière* in around 10min by following Av des Nations Unies (to the right as you exit the bus station, then straight on bearing

5

MARRAKESH TO AGADIR AND ESSAOUIRA

The A7 toll **motorway** to Agadir supplements the old **N8** road over the Imi n'Tanoute or Tizi Maachou pass (see map, page 334), which was built in the 1970s, and was something of a hot spot for accidents. Most buses and shared taxis now use the motorway, which cuts around an hour off the journey time, but the old road has its points of interest, and you'll be using the first part of it if heading for Essaouira.

CHICHAOUA

The road on **to Essaouira** (R207) branches off the N8 at **Chichaoua**, a small town and administrative centre, known for its **carpets**. Brightly coloured, often with stylized animal forms, they are sold at the local Centre Coopératif and also at the town's Thursday market. West of Chichaoua, the R207 extends across the drab Chiadma plains, passing **Sidi Mokhtar**, 25km from Chichaoua, which has a Wednesday souk with an attractive array of carpets.

KASBAH MTOUGGI

South from Sidi Mokhtar and west of the N8 and A7, roads lead to the **Kasbah Mtouggi**. This was the old tribal kasbah of the Mtouggi clan, and a ruin almost as impressive as Telouet (see page 365). The Mtouggi were the third of the clans described by Gavin Maxwell (see page 534) as "Lords of the Atlas", alongside the Glaoui (see page 368) and the Goundafi (see page 355), and they dominated this western Atlas pass, just as the Goundafi and Glaoui did the eastern routes.

IMI N'TANOUTE AND TIZI MAACHOU

Heading for Agadir from Chichaoua, the N8 begins a slow climb towards **Imi n'Tanoute**, another administrative centre, with a **Monday souk**, before cutting through the westernmost edge of the High Atlas. A few kilometres further along the N8 from Imi n'Tanoute is the **Tizi Maachou pass** (1700m). The road south of the pass runs by the **dams of Tanizaourt** before descending into the fertile Souss Valley.

ALTERNATIVE ROUTES TO AGADIR

There is also a minor tarred road, the **R212**, which breaks off the N8 just west of a bridge over the Oued Nfis, 23km west of Marrakesh, and goes direct to Imi n'Tanoute. It's no faster than the N8, but pleasantly quiet. If you have 4WD transport, you might alternatively want to consider the **old Tizi Maachou road** (6404), a *piste* that runs east of the N8 and A7, which you can rejoin at **Argana**. As a more scenic alternative south of Argana, you can take the now-surfaced road over the dramatic Tizi Iferd (Tizi Babaoun) pass, which descends into the Souss Valley nearer Taroudant.

---

right). To the Pl Jemaa el Fna the simplest route is around 25min: follow the Medina walls (to your left as you exit the bus station) southwest down to Av Mohammed V, then turn left. You can take a more direct route through Bab Doukkala via Rue Mouassine, though this is easier to follow in the other direction. A *petit taxi* is about 10dh from the *gare routière* to the Jemaa el Fna, less to Guéliz. Alternatively, catch bus #16, from outside the bus station, which runs through the heart of Guéliz, or buses #8, #10, #12, #14, #15, #16, #17 and #66, which stop directly opposite Bab Doukkala itself (although the bus stop displays only the numbers #11 and #11B), and head south to Pl Foucauld. Leaving town, it's worth buying tickets a day in advance for destinations with limited services, such as Tizi n'Test or Zagora.

Destinations Agadir (every 30min 5am–9pm, then hourly till midnight; 3hr 30min); Aoulouz via Tizi n'Test (2 daily; 9hr); Azilal (9 daily; 3hr); Beni Mellal (14 daily; 4hr); Casablanca (every 30min 7am–8pm, plus 4 earlier services; 4hr); Demnate (9 daily; 1hr 30min); El Jadida (15 daily; 4hr); Essaouira (18 daily; 3hr); Fez (8 daily; 10hr); Laayoune (1 daily; 15hr); Meknes (8 daily; 9hr); Ouarzazate (6 daily; 5hr); Rabat (24 daily; 4hr 30min–5hr 30min); Rissani (2 daily; 12hr); Safi (15 daily; 2hr); Tafraoute (4 daily; 10hr); Taliouine (1 daily; 10hr); Tangier (6 daily; 10hr); Taroudant (5 daily; 6hr 30min); Tetouan (3 daily; 11hr 30min); Tiznit (12 daily; 7hr); Zagora (2 daily; 9hr 30min).

SUPRATOURS

Supratours buses (🌐 supratours.ma) terminate on Av Hassan II next to the train station (accessed via platform 1), though they only sell tickets if there is space after the allocation for train passengers from Casablanca/Rabat (as there are no trains south of Marrakesh). *Grands taxis* are often on hand to pick up the overflow at these times, particularly for Agadir.
Destinations: Agadir (13 daily; 3–4hr); Dakhla (2 daily; 24hr); Essaouira (6 daily; 3hr); Laayoune (6 daily; 15hr 30min–18hr 30min); Ouarzazate (4 daily; 4hr 30min–5hr 15min); Zagora (1 daily; 7hr 45min).

CTM

CTM buses terminate at their office on Rue Aboubaker Sedik (🌐 ctm.ma), west of Guéliz and two blocks south of Supratours. They also have an office at the *gare routière*, where you can buy tickets and sometimes board the buses (or board a feeder bus which will take you to them). CTM tickets are best bought in advance.
Destinations: Agadir (17 daily; 3hr 30min); Beni Mellal (3 daily; 3hr); Casablanca (20 daily; 3hr 30min); Dakhla (1 daily; 23hr); Essaouira (2 daily; 2hr 30min); Fez (6 daily; 5hr 30min–8hr 30min); Laayoune (2 daily; 15hr); Meknes (3 daily; 7hr); Ouarzazate (7 daily; 4hr 30min); Rabat (10 daily; 4hr 30min); Tangier (2 daily; 9hr 30min); Taroudant (1 daily; 5hr); Tetouan (2 daily; 10hr); Tiznit (7 daily; 5hr 30min); Zagora (2 daily; 7hr).

BY GRAND TAXI

Shared *grands taxis* for most destinations terminate behind the *gare routière* bus station, though they may drop you off in front of it on Pl Mourabiton. Bab er Robb taxi station – which is actually 1.5km southwest of Bab er Robb, near the junction of Av Mohammed VI and the Route d'Asni – is used by *grands taxis* for some High Atlas destinations. Although you may occasionally find a shared taxi there for Setti Fatma, the best place to pick one up – as well as, in season, minibuses to the ski resort of Oukaïmeden – is Lagarb, which can be reached by shared taxis from the southern end of Rue Ibn Rachid, south of the Jemaa el Fna, or on local bus #25 from Pl Youssef Ben Tachfine. Shared taxis for Asni and Imlil (for which you'll usually have to change at Asni) operate from the other side of Pl Youssef Ben Tachfine, while those for M'hamid (via the airport turn-off) run from the north end of Rue Ibn Rachid.
Destinations from behind the gare routière Azilal (2hr 30min); Casablanca (2hr 30min); Essaouira (2hr 30min); Inezgane (3hr); Moulay Brahim (1hr); Ouarzazate (3hr); Taroudant (4hr).
Destinations from Bab er Robb taxi station Oukaïmeden (winter only; 2hr); Setti Fatma (infrequent; 1hr).
Destinations from Rue Ibn Rachid Lagarb (1hr); M'hamid via airport turn-off (15min).
Destinations from Pl Youssef Ben Tachfine Asni (occasional; 1hr 20min); Imlil (1hr).

GETTING AROUND

By bus There are a number of useful bus routes in the city (see page 315) run by Alsa (🌐 alsa.ma). The most important from a tourist point of view are buses #1 and #16 along Av Mohammed V between Guéliz and the Koutoubia.
By petit taxi It is a fairly long walk between Guéliz and the Medina, but there are plenty of *petits taxis*. There are taxi ranks at most major intersections in Guéliz, and in the Medina, outside the *Grand Hôtel Tazi*, and at the Pl des Ferblantiers at the end of Av Houman el Fetouaki. *Petits* taxis have meters, which they should use. If a taxi driver doesn't want to use the meter, it is because they intend to overcharge you, but you may struggle to find anyone who'll agree to use it, in which case you'll have to haggle to get a reasonable price. Particularly to and from the airport, and from the Hivernage hotels, taxi drivers have agreed an artificially high fixed price among themselves, and won't use the meter. Especially if taking a taxi far afield, such as to one of the campsites or golf courses, and the driver won't

LOCAL BUS ROUTES

The following buses leave from Avenue el Mouahidine alongside Place Foucauld, opposite *Hôtel de Foucauld*:
#1 along Avenue Mohammed V to Guéliz, then up Avenue Mohammed Abdelkrim el Khattabi (Route de Casablanca) to Semlalia.
#8, #10, #14 & #66 all go to Bab Doukkala (for the bus station), then on down Avenue Hassan II past the train station.
#6 to Bab Ighli and the entrance to the Agdal gardens.
#11 M'hamid via the airport turn-off.
#16 to Guéliz via Bab Doukkala.
#17 and #26 to the Route de Fès for the palmery.
#19 circular route from the airport to Place Foucauld, then north up Avenue Mohammed V, south down Avenue Mohammed VI and back to the airport.

5

SIGHTSEEING BUS TOURS

If you don't have much time and you want to scoot around Marrakesh's major sights in a day or two, the **hop-on hop-off Marrakech Tour bus** (Ⓦ alsa.ma) could be for you. Using open-top double-deckers, with a commentary in several languages including English, the tour follows two circular routes: the Medina/Guéliz bus departs from Place Abdelmoumen Ben Ali every 20–30min; the palmery bus leaves from the same place hourly 1–5pm. You can get on and off where you like, and tickets can be bought on board or at Place Abdelmoumen Ben Ali or Place Foucauld.

use the meter but specifies a price, confirm the price using the word "dirhams", or the driver may claim on arrival that the price quoted was in euros. If you get a *petit taxi* out to the city's outskirts and the driver doesn't try to pull any stunts over the fare, get a phone number to call them for the way back.

By grand taxi *Grands taxis* can be chartered for by the day for a reasonable price if split between four people (they fit six, but four is comfortable). Negotiate at the ranks in Jemaa el Fna or by the post office in Guéliz. By law *grands taxis* have to display prices for specified trips; these are per trip, not per person.

By calèche In addition to taxis, *calèches* (horse-drawn cabs) line up on Pl Foucauld near the Koutoubia, and at some of the fancier hotels. These can take up to five people and aren't much more expensive than *petits taxis*, but be sure to fix the price in advance, especially for a tour of the town. The Menara and palmery, and also the Agdal Gardens (see page 310) are perfect destinations for a *calèche* trip.

By bike, motorbike, moped or scooter You can rent bicycles on Pl de la Liberté and a number of roadside locations in Hivernage, but mopeds or scooters from these places are unlikely to be properly insured, so it's better to rent those from a reputable firm with a fixed address. Marrakech Roues, 3 Rue Bani Marine (Ⓦ marrakech-roues. com) rent bicycles, scooters, mopeds and quad bikes. Loc2Roues on the upper floor of Galerie Élite, 212 Av Mohammed V (Ⓦ loc2roues.com) rents scooters, mopeds and motorbikes.

By car Local firms include: First Car, 234 Av Mohammed V (Ⓦ firstcar.ma); Najm Car, shop #9, Galerie Jakar, 61 Av Mohammed V (Ⓦ najmcar.com). International franchises include: Budget, 68 Bd Mohammed Zerktouni (Ⓦ budget. ma); Europcar, 63 Bd Mohammed Zerktouni (Ⓦ europcar. ma); Hertz, 154 Av Mohammed V (Ⓦ hertz.ma). Many hotels can also arrange car rental, often at competitive rates. If returning a car to the airport, be aware you may be stung for a "service charge" unless you get it washed first (best to do it the day before).

INFORMATION

Tourist information The Délégation Régionale de Tourisme, on Pl Abdelmoumen Ben Ali in Guéliz (Mon–Fri 8.30am–4.30pm; ☎ 0524 436239), keeps a dossier with listings of hotels, campsites, car rental firms and other contacts, and staff are generally happy to answer questions

so long as they aren't too difficult.

Maps The *Marrakech Evasions* map (Ⓦ facebook.com/ marrakechevasions), produced by Éditions Bab Sabaa, is available for free at some hotels and riads.

ACCOMMODATION

The Medina has the main concentration of small, **budget hotels**, especially around the Jemaa el Fna. It is also where you'll find most of Marrakesh's **riads**, usually hidden away deep in its backstreets. Guéliz, whose hotels tend to be concentrated in the mid range, is handier for transport, especially for the train station. Hotels in Hivernage and Semlalia are upmarket, but they're pretty soulless. **Advance bookings** are a good idea, especially for the more popular places in the Medina; the busiest times are Easter and Christmas/New Year.

MEDINA, SEE MAPS PAGES 292, 295, 299 AND 311

Most of the Medina's budget accommodation is concentrated in the small area south of the Jemaa el Fna.

Riads and more deluxe hotels tend to be further afield.

HOTELS

Aday 111 Derb Sidi Bouloukat ☎ 0524 441920. This friendly budget hotel is well kept, clean and pleasantly decorated. Rooms with shared facilities, grouped around a central patio, are small and most have only inward-facing windows, but there's also a newer wing with more comfortable, en-suite rooms, or, for those really counting the coins, you can sleep on the roof. €

Ali Rue Moulay Ismail Ⓦ hotel-ali.com. This busy hotel, with en suite a/c rooms, is used by groups heading to the High Atlas, so it's a good source of trekking (and other) information, and staff are always extremely helpful. The place has a general air of business and being right in the middle of things, though that won't appeal to everyone. Book ahead. BB €

Les Borjs de la Kasbah Rue du Mechouar, Kasbah ⓦ lesborjsdelakasbah.com. This cool boutique hotel, created out of seven old houses at the southern end of the kasbah, has much of the style of a riad along with the trappings of a luxury hotel. There are several patio spaces, a pool, a spa and a classy restaurant. The rooms range from small- singles (€€€) and doubles to full-sized deluxe rooms, at good prices for what you get. BB €€€€

Central Palace 59 Derb Sidi Bouloukat ☎ 0524 440235. The rooms here are a cut above those in the other budget hotels in the back alleys south of the Jemaa el Fna, and correspondingly slightly pricier, but what this place also has going for it is its easy-to-find location, just off Rue Bab Agnaou, a stone's throw from the Jemaa. €

CTM Pl Jemaa el Fna ☎ 0524 442325. Situated above the old bus station (hence its name), now used as a car park, and handy if you're driving. There are two categories of rooms: old, unmodernized rooms with shared bathroom, and modernized en suite rooms with a/c in summer, heating in winter. The last category includes rooms 1–4, which overlook the square, though this does of course make them noisy. Breakfast is served on the roof terrace, which also overlooks the square. BB €

Dar les Cigognes 108 Rue de Berrima ⓦ lescigognes. com. A luxury boutique hotel run by a Swiss-American couple in two converted Medina houses that gets consistently good reports. It's done up in traditional fashion around the patio, but with modern decor in the rooms and suites. There's a library, a hammam, a jacuzzi, a salon and a terrace where you can see storks nesting on the walls of the royal palace opposite (hence the name, which means "house of the storks"). BB €€€€

Dar Salam 162 Derb Ben Fayda, off Rue el Gza ☎ 0524 383110. A Moroccan family home which takes in guests, this is a true *maison d'hôte* as opposed to a riad, a place to relax and put your feet up rather than admire the decor. The food is similarly unpretentious – tasty home-style Moroccan cooking, like your mum would make if she were Marrakshi. BB €

Essaouira 3 Derb Sidi Bouloukat ⓦ essaouirahotel marrakech.com. Formerly one of the most popular cheapies in Marrakesh, it's now gone upmarket but is still deservedly popular, with en suite rooms around a central patio, and a roof terrace. €€€

De Foucauld Av el Mouahidine, facing Pl de Foucauld ⓦ foucauld.morocco-ma.website/fr/. Rooms are a little sombre and some on the small side, but they're decent enough, with a/c, heating and constant hot water (with a choice of tub or shower). There's a roof terrace with views of the Koutoubia, and a restaurant with buffet suppers. €

★ **Gallia** 30 Rue de la Recette ⓦ hotellegallia.com. This beautifully kept hotel, founded in 1929, claims to be the second oldest in Marrakesh, after *La Mamounia*. It's housed in a restored Medina mansion with immaculate en suite rooms off two tiled courtyards, one with a fountain, palm tree and caged birds. There's central heating in winter and a/c in summer. Book online, at least a month ahead if possible. It's not strictly wheelchair accessible, but staff are very helpful to chair users. €€

La Gazelle 12 Rue Bani Marine ☎ 0524 441112. Well-kept if slightly dull hotel on a street with food stalls and small grill cafés. Windows in the downstairs rooms open onto a covered patio, while those upstairs face the outside. Some rooms have bathrooms, and there's a discount after three nights' stay. €

Ichbilia 1 Rue Bani Marine ⓦ hotel-ichbilia.com. Sometimes referred to as the *Sevilla* (*Ichbilia* is the Arabic for Seville), this hotel is well placed for shops, banks and cafés, with rooms off a covered gallery, some plain and simple but still clean and comfortable, others with a/c and private bathroom. €

Jnane Mogador Derb Sidi Bouloukat, by 116 Rue Riad Zitoun el Kedim ⓦ jnanemogador.com. Run by the same management as the *Essaouira*, this more upmarket hostelry is extremely homely, and a firm favourite among Marrakesh's mid-range accommodation options. Set in a beautifully restored old house, it boasts charming rooms, in warm tints with modern furnishings, around a lovely fountain patio, plus its own hammam and a roof terrace. €€

★ **La Maison Arabe** 1 Derb Assebbe Bab Doukkala, behind the Doukkala mosque ⓦ lamaisonarabe.com. This is one of Marrakesh's classiest hotels, boasting high standards of service in a gorgeous nineteenth-century mansion restored with fine traditional workmanship – the furnishings are sumptuous, as is the food (see page 322), there are two beautifully kept patios and a selection of rooms and suites, some with private terrace and jacuzzi. There is no pool on the premises, but a free shuttle bus can take you to the hotel's private pool nearby. BB €€€€

La Mamounia Av Bab Jdid ⓦ mamounia.com. Set in palatial grounds, this is Marrakesh's most famous, most expensive and most exclusive hotel (see page 297), though some would say it's more snooty than classy. Decoratively, it's of most interest for the 1920s Art Deco touches by Jacques Majorelle (of Majorelle Garden fame), and their enhancements, in 1986, by the then Moroccan king's favourite designer, André Paccard. The rooms are done out in warm reds and browns, with magnificent marble bathrooms, but some of the simple "classic" rooms can be a bit small, so it's best to pay slightly more for a "superior" or "deluxe" room. €€€€

Medina 1 Derb Sidi Bouloukat ☎ 0524 442997. Located in a street full of good budget hotels, the *Medina*, which has been around seemingly forever, is a perennial favourite among the cheapies, and often full. It's clean, friendly and pretty good value, and there's always hot water in the

5

RIAD-BOOKING AGENCIES

These agencies each manage a stable of riads, with a wide choice available.

Marrakech Médina 102 Rue Dar el Bacha, Northern Medina ⓦmarrakech-medina.com. A firm that's actually in the business of doing up riads as well as renting them out, with a reasonable selection in all price ranges.

Marrakech Riads Dar Cherifa, 8 Derb Chorfa Lakbir, Mouassine, Northern Medina ⓦmarrakech-riads. net. A small agency with only nine riads (plus one in Fez), committed to keeping it chic and authentic.

---

shared showers. The owner – who used to work in Britain – speaks good English. They have a small roof terrace, and in summer there's the option of sleeping up there. €̄

Sherazade 3 Derb Jama, off Rue Riad Zitoun el Kedim ⓦhotelsherazade.com. Before riads took off big time, this place was already on the scene, an old merchant's house, prettily done up, that gets rave reviews from our readers. Besides a lovely roof terrace, the hotel offers a wide variety of well-maintained rooms at different prices, not all en suite. Run very professionally by a German-Moroccan couple, it's extremely popular, so book well ahead. €̄

La Sultana 403 Rue de la Kasbah ⓦlasultanamarrakech. com. This is an extremely stylish blend of accommodation types: riad elegance, boutique personal attention and five-star facilities. The whole place is done out in wonderful carved cedar wood, whose scent infuses the hotel, and liberally sprinkled with antiques and objets d'art; facilities include a hammam, pool, jacuzzi, spa, lounge bar, library, panoramic terraces and excellent restaurant – all just around the corner from Bab Agnaou and the Saadian Tombs. €€€€

Villa des Orangers 6 Rue Sidi Mimoun ⓦvilladesorangers.com. This gorgeous luxury establishment is officially a hotel, but it's a riad in the true sense of the word: an old house around a garden patio – three in fact – with orange trees and lots of lovely carved stucco. There's a range of rooms and suites, many with their own private terrace. Breakfast and lunch included but not supper. €€€€

RIADS

Marrakesh is where the riad craze started, and there are some sumptuous riads here, especially at the top end of the market, with some very friendly and homely places at the lower end too, but some are overpriced and nothing special, so it's worth shopping around. Most places offer low rates in July and Aug. Though not officially classified as riads, *Les Borjs de la Kasbah* (see page 317) and *Dar les Cigognes* (see page 317), and *Hôtel Gallia* (see page 317), *Jnane Mogador* (see page 317), *Hôtel Sherazade* (see page 318) and *Villa des Orangers* (see page 318) are all worth considering too.

Le Clos des Arts 50 Derb Tbib, off Rue Riad Zitoun el Jedid ⓦleclosdesarts.com. Italian-owned riad done out in tasteful cream, white and beige, giving a classic but slightly washed-out look. It's friendly, tranquil and relaxing. BB €€€€

Dar Ihssane 14 Derb Chorfa el Kebir, near Mouassine Mosque ☎0524 387826. A good-value riad in an eighteenth-century mansion with many original features (some of which were only discovered during renovation). It's owned by the nephew of painter Georges Bretegnier, and decorated with some of Bretegnier's original artwork. BB €€€

Equity Point Marrakech (Riad Amazigh) 80 Derb el Hammam Mouassine ☎0524 440793, ⓦequity-point. com. A hostel in a riad, with all the architectural charm of any other riad, but a fun crowd and four- to eight-bed dorms (each with its own bathroom) instead of the usual flowers-on-the-pillow service. There's a pool, bar and restaurant, plus cool spaces to hang out in and a friendly atmosphere rather than an exclusive one. Dorm €̄, double €€

★ **Noir d'Ivoire** 31 Derb Jedid, near Bab Doukkala ⓦnoir-d-ivoire.com. A magnificent riad, impressive from the moment you walk in, owned by an English interior designer, who's done it out in cream, brown and black (the name refers to the colour scheme), with a feel that manages to be classy yet cosy at the same time. There's a spa, two pools and a bar, and service is scrupulous, reflecting the fact that there's almost one staff member per guest. BB €€€€

Riad 72 72 Derb Arset Aouzal, near Bab Doukkala ⓦriad72.com. A very sleek and stylish Italian-owned riad, with sparse but extremely tasteful modern decor, palms and banana trees in the courtyard and its own hammam (but no pool). BB €€€€

Riad Bayti 35 Derb Saka, Bab el Mellah ⓦriad-bayti. com. A great old house, formerly owned by a family of Jewish wine merchants in the Mellah, with that quarter's distinctive high ceilings and wide veranda, giving a spacious feel. Run by a dynamic young French couple, with warm modern decor that perfectly complements the classic architecture. Afternoon tea is included in the rate. BB €€€

Riad Farnatchi 2 Derb Farnatchi, off Rue Souk el Fassi ⓦlefarnatchi.com. The suites (there are no ordinary rooms) at this five-star British-owned riad are extremely spacious, each with either a balcony, a private terrace or its own patio, and the understated decor incorporates some beautiful original features. There are also two common patios, one with a pool, and the spa is excellent (and open to non-guests by appointment). Rates include free airport transfer, fruit and mineral water, and canapés before dinner. They also run an interesting restaurant directly opposite, *Le*

Trou au Mur, which specializes in *mechoui* (pulled lamb) and revived old-school Moroccan recipes. BB €€€€

Riad Kheirredine 2 Derb Chelligui, Sidi Ben Slimane ⓦ riadkheirredine.com. Super-cool and very welcoming Italian-run riad in a residential part of the Medina, very handy for the Majorelle Garden and the bus station. There are two patios and two pools, and the rooms and public spaces are done out in delicious creams and dark-chocolate browns. BB €€€€

★ **Riad Kniza** 34 Derb l'Hotel, near Bab Doukkala ⓦ riadkniza.com. Owned by a top antique dealer and tour guide (whose clients have included US presidents and film stars), this is one classy riad, with beautiful rooms and a state-of-the-art pool, not to mention sauna, hammam and massage room, genuine antiques for decoration and solar panels for ecologically sound hot water – yet it still manages to feel like a real Moroccan family home. The family themselves (all English-speaking) are always on hand to make you feel welcome, the food is excellent and the service absolutely impeccable. They also now have a free museum of antiques directly opposite. BB €€€€

Riad Sahara Nour 118 Derb Dekkak, near Bab Doukkala ☎ 0524 376570. More than just a riad, this is a centre for art, self-development and relaxation. Workshops in music, poetry and painting are held here, self-development programmes in meditation and relaxation techniques are available, and guests who wish to hold artistic happenings are encouraged. And if none of that appeals, you can simply enjoy the calm atmosphere on the patio, shaded by orange, loquat and pomegranate trees. BB €€€

Riad Star 31 Derb Alailich, off Rue de Souk des Fassis ⓦ riadstar.com. Former home of jazz dancer Josephine Baker, who lived here during World War II, when she was a spy for Free France. The riad is themed around Baker's era, with memorabilia and even costumes that you can wear. The rooms are stylish, with black-tiled bathrooms, and there's an in-house hammam and a rooftop sun terrace. BB €€€€

Riad Zolah 26 Derb el Baroud, Hart Essoura ⓦ riad romance.com. Nice for a bit of romance, but welcoming to single travellers and non-couples too, this little riad has a spacious main patio with (for a riad) a large pool, a small roof terrace, and a light, modern feel, with classic touches (the building is seventeenth-century). The English-speaking owners don't live in, but are usually on hand to look after guests and dispense knowledge and information. BB €€€

★ **Riyad al Moussika** 62 Derb Boutouil, near Dar Si Said ⓦ riyad-al-moussika.com. A gem of a riad, formerly owned by T'hami el Glaoui (see page 304), with absolutely gorgeous decor, all designed to exact specifications in traditional Moroccan style by its Italian owner, resulting in a harmonious and beautiful Italian-Moroccan style – like a traditional Marrakshi mansion, but better. The walls are decked with contemporary paintings by local artists, and the riad claims to have the finest cuisine in town (doubling

as the *Pepe Nero* restaurant; see page 322). Rates include afternoon tea. BB €€€€

Riyad el Cadi 86–87 Derb Moulay Abdelkader, off Rue Dabachi ⓦ riyadelcadi.com. The former home of a German diplomat who was ambassador to several Arab countries, and embellished with his wonderful collection of rugs and antiques, this riad incorporates five patios, three salons, a pool, a hammam and excellent standards of service. As well as ordinary guest rooms, there are two wonderful suites, and the "blue house": a patio with two double rooms, which is rented in its entirety. BB €€€€

GUÉLIZ, SEE MAP PAGE 311

Farouk 66 Av Hassan II ☎ 0524 431989. Owned by the same family as the *Ali* in the Medina, and housed in a rather eccentric building, with all sorts of branches and extensions, it offers a variety of rooms – check a few before choosing – all with hot showers. Staff are friendly and welcoming, and there's an excellent-value restaurant (see page 324). €

Fashion 45 Av Hassan II ⓦ fashionhotel.ma. Terracotta tiling, nicely carved black-painted wooden furnishings and large windows grace the rooms at this tastefully designed three-star, where the bathrooms feature reliable hot showers with a strong jet. There's also a rooftop pool and basement hammam. BB €

Ibis Marrakech Centre Gare Av Hassan II/Pl de la Gare ⓦ ibishotel.com. This spick-and-span chain hotel located right by the train station is not the most exciting accommodation in town, but it's good value. It offers efficient service, a swimming pool, a restaurant and a bar in the lobby, and the buffet breakfasts are good. Lunch and dinner also available. BB €€€

Du Pacha 33 Rue de la Liberté ☎ 0524 431327. A 1930s-built hotel with an old-fashioned kind of feel and large if rather drab rooms, most around a central courtyard, with a/c and satellite TV. There's a good restaurant, but no pool. BB €€

Tafoukt 116 Place du Petit Marché, off Route de Targa ☎ 0524 379000. This small hotel is a cut above most of the Ville Nouvelle options, and great value for money. All the rooms are "junior suites" (that is, they have a sitting area as well as a bedroom area, but not as separate rooms), and the place is well-kept and has room service, a spa and a pool. BB €

Toulousain 44 Rue Tariq Ben Ziad ⓦ hoteltoulousain. com. This excellent budget hotel was originally owned by a Frenchman from Toulouse (hence the name). It has a secure car park and a variety of rooms, plainly decorated but always spick and span, some with shower, some with shower and toilet, some with shared facilities, and some with ceiling fans. BB €

HIVERNAGE, SEE MAP PAGE 311

Hivernage's chain four- and five-stars are amateurish in comparison with their equivalents abroad, and far less attractive than similarly priced Medina riads, but most are

5

wheelchair accessible, and are more child-friendly, with large pools.

Atlas Asni Av Moulay el Hassan ☎0524 339999. The Atlas chain's top offering in Marrakesh, set amid extensive gardens and best known for its spa facilities, but service is mediocre, and certainly not five-star by international standards. Three rooms are adapted for wheelchair users. BB €€€

The Red House Bd el Yarmouk ⓦ theredhousemarrakesh. com. A beautiful nineteenth-century mansion (also called *Dar el Ahmar*) full of fine stucco and zellij work downstairs, where the restaurant offers gourmet Moroccan cuisine. Accommodation consists of eight luxurious suites – extremely chic and palatial – though European imperial rather than classic Moroccan in style. BB €€€€

Ryad Mogador Menara Av Mohammed VI (Av de France) ⓦ ryadmogador.com. Five-star (though really more like four-star) whose facilities include a health club and three restaurants. The lobby is done out in classic style, with painted ceilings, chandeliers and a very Moroccan feel. Rooms, on the other hand, are modern, light and airy. Four rooms are adapted for wheelchair users. BB €€€€

CAMPING

Camping Caravanning Ferdaous 13km from the city centre on the Casablanca road (N9, formerly P7) ☎0524 304090. With temperamental plumbing and little shade, this campsite will suffice for an overnight stay if using a car or camper van, but it's not really convenient as a base for exploring Marrakesh on foot. €

Relais de Marrakech 10km from the city centre on the Casablanca road, opposite Grand Stade football ground ⓦ hotel-lerelaisdemarrakech.com. A large, upmarket campsite, with free hot showers, a pool and wi-fi. There are rooms and permanent tents available (worth asking for a discount), or you can pitch your own tent or park a camper van. Camping €, permanent tent €, double €

YOUTH HOSTEL, SEE MAP PAGE 311

Youth Hostel Rue el Jahid, Guéliz ☎0524 447713. Friendly, with quiet, sparkling clean dorms and a small garden. Very near to the train station, and even nearer to the CTM office. €

EATING

Guéliz has most of the city's French-style cafés, bistros and restaurants. In the Medina, there are the Jemaa el Fna food stalls, many inexpensive café-restaurants, and a number of upmarket palace-restaurants.

MEDINA, SEE MAPS PAGES
292, 295, 299 AND 311

Recommendations for the Medina span the range: from a bench in the Jemaa el Fna to the most sumptuous palace setting. Only the more expensive places are licensed to sell alcohol. Among the smarter eating places are palace-restaurants in former mansions with beautiful traditional decor. Many of these are well hidden away, and can be difficult to find, especially at night; if in doubt, phone in advance and ask for directions – sometimes the restaurant will send someone to meet you.

JEMAA EL FNA FOOD STALLS

Even if you don't eat at them, at some stage you should at least wander down the makeshift lane of **food stalls on the Jemaa el Fna**, which look great in the evening, lit by lanterns. As well as couscous and **pastilla**, there are spicy merguez sausages, **harira** soup, salads, fried fish, or, for the more adventurous, **stewed snails** (over towards the eastern side of the square), and sheep's heads complete with eyes. To partake, just take a seat on one of the benches, ask the price of a plate of food and order. It's probably worth avoiding places that try to hustle you, and it's always wise to check the price of a dish before you order, or you're likely to be **overcharged**. Also be aware that if they give you unasked-for bread and olives, you will be charged for them, even if you don't touch them. Stalls patronized by Moroccans are invariably better than those whose only customers are tourists, and you can still enjoy the atmosphere while avoiding all the little tricks (not to mention the very real risk of tummy upset from dubious standards of hygiene) by just having a bowl of *harira* at one of the soup stalls instead of a full meal. If you want a soft drink or mineral water with your meal, the stallholders will send a boy to get it for you. On the southern edge of the food stalls, a row of vendors sell a hot, spicy galangal drink (**khoudenjal**), said to be an aphrodisiac, and usually taken with a portion of nutty cake. Orange and grapefruit **juice stalls** line both sides of the food stall area at all hours of the day, but check the price first, and insist on having the juice pressed in front of you – if they pull out a bottle of ready-pressed juice, it'll most likely be watered down, and quite possibly mixed with squash.

5

THE CHEAPEST MEDINA EATS

Apart from the Jemaa itself (see page 320), there's a concentration of cheap and basic eateries on **Rue Bani Marine**, a narrow street that runs south from the post office and Bank al Maghrib on Jemaa el Fna, between and parallel to Rue Bab Agnaou and Rue Moulay Ismail. Another street of cheap eats, with grills on one side and fried fish on the other, is the small street that runs from **Rue Arset el Maach** alongside **Place des Ferblantiers** to the entrance of the El Badi Palace. There's also a row of places just outside the walls at **Bab Doukkala**, between the bus station and the *grand taxi* stand.

CAFÉS

Le Bougainvillier 33 Rue Mouassine. An upmarket café and quiet retreat in the middle of the Medina: handy for a break after a hard morning's shopping in the souks. Set in a secluded patio, the lack of actual bougainvillea flowers is made up for by bougainvillea-coloured paintwork and chairs. There are salads, sandwiches, cakes, juices, coffee and tea, even tajines, but most of all it's a pleasant space to relax.

Café el Badia Next to Bab Berrima. On a rooftop looking out over Pl des Ferblantiers and towards the Mellah, this is one place to get close to the storks nesting on the walls of the El Badi Palace. It serves a range of hot and cold (non-alcoholic) drinks, and set menus (including one vegetarian) featuring soup, salad, couscous, and Moroccan sweetmeats for afters. €€

Café des Épices Pl Rahba Kedima, north side ⓦ cafedes epices.ma. A small café offering refuge from the hubbub, with orange juice, mint tea, coffee in various permutations, including spiced with cinnamon, plus sandwiches, tajines and views over the Rahba Kedima from the upper floor and the roof terrace. €€

Canne à Sucre 38 Rue Bab Agnaou. This may be a bog-standard coffee and juice bar at the back, but out front they sell wonderful freshly pressed sugar cane juice,along with bite-size pieces of coconut cake. They also have *msimmen* (pancake-like griddle bread) with a variety of sweet and savoury fillings. €

Le Grand Balcon du Café Glacier Jemaa el Fna, south side. This place has the fullest view over the Jemaa, taking it all in from a perfect vantage point. You can come up for just a drink (tea, coffee or soda), but they also do food, including salads, brochettes and tajines. €€

Henna Café 93 Rue Arset Azoual ⓦ hennacafe marrakech.com. As well as tea and coffee, this place, with a roof terrace and downstairs café area, offers salads and snacks that differ from the Marrakesh norm, like falafel and tahina with pitta-type bread. They also have a henna tattoo menu, where you can choose a design, all profits of which are ploughed back into the community, such as for various educational classes provided free to local children. €

PATISSERIES

Patisserie Bab Agnaou Inside Bab Agnaou. Little more than a hole in the wall, actually in the gate itself, this little patisserie serves nothing fancy, just good, traditional Moroccan sticky delights, mostly involving nuts and filo pastry fried in syrup on the premises. Even if you don't want to buy a kilo of them, a triangular *briouat* (filo parcel, in this case with nuts), perfumed with orange blossom water, is irresistible. €

Patisseries Belkabir and Duniya 63–65 Rue Souk Smarine. Two shops, side by side, specializing in traditional Moroccan sweetmeats, stuffed with nuts and drenched in syrup, and particularly popular during the holy month of Ramadan, when of course they are eaten at night. €

Patisserie des Princes 32 Rue Bab Agnaou. A sparkling patisserie with mouthwatering pastries at prices that are a little high by local standards but worth the extra. They also have treats like almond milk and ice cream. The *salon de thé* at the back is a very civilized place to enjoy breakfast, morning coffee or afternoon tea. €

DINERS AND SNACK BARS

El Bahja 24 Rue Bani Marine. This place is popular with locals and tourists alike. It's good value, cheap and generally unexciting, though its *kofta* is highly rated, and don't miss the house yoghurt for afters. €

Café-Restaurant Toubkal Southeast corner of Jemaa el Fna. As well as fruit juices, home-made yoghurts and pastries, they also offer a range of salads, tajines and couscous. It's also a great place for a breakfast of coffee with bread and jam or with *msimmen* and honey. €

Chez Bahia 206 Rue Riad Zitoun el Kedim. A café-diner offering pastilla, low-priced snacks and excellent set breakfasts with pancake-like *msimmen*. For the rest of the day, there are wonderful tajines bubbling away out front to tempt you. €

Oscar Progrès 20 Rue Bani Marine ☏ 0666 937147. One of the best budget restaurants in town, with friendly service, excellent value set menus, and large servings of couscous (go for that or the brochettes in preference to the tajines, which are rather bland). €

RESTAURANTS

Café Arabe 184 Rue Mouassine ⓦ cafearabe.com. A sophisticated bar-restaurant in the heart of the Medina, very handy for the souks, with excellent Moroccan and

5

European cooking and snappy service, plus juices, teas, cocktails and mocktails, served on the terrace, on the patio or in the salon. Licensed. €€€

Chez Brahim 38 Rue Dabbachi. This budget restaurant, just a short walk from the Jemaa el Fna, offers rooftop dining with the usual range of Moroccan staples (salads, brochettes, tajines, couscous), and good value set menus. €€

Chez Chegrouni Jemaa el Fna, east side. Come at a quiet time if you want to bag one of the front seats on the upstairs terrace, as only these have a view over the square. Popular with tourists, this place does decent couscous and good tajines at moderate prices, though the portions are on the small side. €

Earth Café 2 Derb el Zouaq, off Rue Riad Zitoun el Kedim, and 3 Place des Ferblantiers. Marrakesh's first vegetarian restaurant offers a range of dishes including veggie burgers, "warm salad" and filo pastry parcels containing assorted combinations of vegetables and sometimes cheese. The portions are generous, and the food is well prepared and delicious, enough to tempt any carnivore, and a nice change from the usual Moroccan fare. They also serve excellent juices and herbal infusions, and the atmosphere is intimate and relaxed. €€

Henna Art Cafe Rue de la Recette ⓦmarrakech hennaartcafe.com. A restaurant and art gallery offering vegetarian, vegan and gluten-free options as well as burritos, soups and veg tajine, not to mention henna tattoos. €

Hôtel Islane 279 Av Mohammed V ⓣ0524 440081. The main attraction at this rooftop restaurant is its unparalleled view of the Koutoubia rather than its not-very-good-value set menu. That said, its breakfast buffet isn't bad. €

Jama 149 Rue Riad Zitoun el Jedid. A quiet little patio with a large palm tree growing out of it, lit up with candles in the evening, and serving a small selection of well-cooked and modestly priced traditional tajines, including beef with figs or chicken with lemons and olives, followed by their own house yoghurt. €€

Kassabine Café 77 Rue Dabbachi, by Kissariat el Guessabine. The sunny terrace of this bright little café-restaurant has a perfect vista over the busy street below, and you can see all the way down the western branch of the Jemaa el Fna. The tajines are lovingly made and include a wonderful beef with courgettes version, as well as old favourites like chicken with lemon and olives. €€

Kosybar 47 Pl des Ferblantiers ⓦkosybar.com. A slick fusion-food restaurant and bar, with upstairs terraces. At lunchtime there's a set menu or light but exotic dishes such as tofu stir-fry, and in the evening there's a full a la carte menu with offerings such as beef tajine with apricots, or the lighter option of sushi. Licensed. €€€

Marrakchi 52 Rue des Banques ⓦlemarrakchi.com. High up above the square, with imperial but intimate decor,

impeccable service and superb food, including delicious pastilla, and several couscous and tajine options, including vegetarian. In the evenings there's a belly dancer. Licensed. €€€

La Maison Arabe 1 Derb Assebbe Bab Doukkala, behind the Doukkala mosque ⓦlamaisonarabe.com. As well as being Marrakesh's best hotel (see page 317), this is one of the city's top eating places, with two restaurants, of which the Moroccan one offers dishes such as beef tajine with quinces, while the *Three Flavours* restaurant offers Moroccan, European and Asian dishes such as fillet of John Dory with artichokes or Thai-style chicken in coconut milk. They also offer cookery classes (see page 327). Licensed. €€€€

Pepe Nero Riyad al Moussika, 17 Derb Cherkaoui (off Rue Douar Graoua) ⓦpepenero-marrakech.com. The terrace and lounge of the *Riyad al Moussika* make a very elegant venue for this classy restaurant, serving fine Moroccan and Italian food (though the latter is generally best) prepared by a Moroccan-Italian chef and accompanied by Moroccan and Italian wines. Starters include a wonderful salmon tartare in balsamic sauce, which you can follow with house pasta such as celery root ravioli in chive sauce. Mains include *canard à l'orange*, and there's a gluttonous chocolate pudding to finish. €€€

Les Prémices Jemaa el Fna, south side; map p.295. Good Moroccan and European food including well-prepared tajines (chicken with lemon and olives is a good bet), steaks, fish, pizzas and even crème brûlée. It's on the very southeastern corner of the square, but close enough for a view of the action. €€

Le Tanjia 14 Derb Jedid, near Pl des Ferblantiers. Stylish Mellah bar-restaurant in an old mansion done out in modern decor, with belly dancers every night. The menu offers well-cooked Moroccan dishes, including some vegetarian options, and the prices aren't outrageously expensive. Try tajines such as chicken with honey and almond or lamb with apricots, or check out the lunchtime set menus. Licensed. €€€

Terrasse des Épices 15 Souk Cherifa ⓣ0524 375904, ⓦterrassedesepices.com. This terrace restaurant, above the souks, is run by the same people as *Café des Épices* (see page 321). It has separate bays for each table giving diners their own space and a bit of privacy, while still allowing you to enjoy the great views. You can start with a trio of Moroccan salads, followed by monkfish tajine, with crème brûlée for afters. €€€

★ **Terrasse la Medersa** Fondouk Lahbabi, 4 Rue de Souk des Fassis. In a *fondouk* adjoining the Ben Youssef Medersa (originally only on the roof terrace, hence its name), this unassuming little café-restaurant offers a variety of mocktails, juices and inexpensive Moroccan dishes (chicken tajine with lemon and olives), served with a smile. €€

TANJIA

The dish for which Marrakesh is known throughout Morocco is **tanjia**, or jugged meat, usually beef but sometimes lamb. Strictly speaking, the tanjia is the jug itself, and the traditional way to make a tanjia is to go the butcher with your jug (or use one of the butcher's), buy the meat and spices to put in it, and then take it to a hammam and have it cooked slowly in the embers of the bathhouse furnace. When the urn emerges from the embers a few hours later, the meat is tender and ready to eat. Most reasonably upmarket Marrakesh restaurants offer tanjia, as do cheaper tanjia diners such as the **tanjia stalls** opposite the olive souk (see map page 295), where you order it by weight (a quarter kilo is enough for one person).

PALACE RESTAURANTS

El Bahia 1 Rue Riad Zitoun el Jedid, by Bahia Palace. A proper palace restaurant, but with bargain-priced menus in a beautifully restored mansion, all finely carved stucco and painted wooden ceilings. €€

Dar Essalam 170 Rue Riad Zitoun el Kedim ⓦdar essalam.com. This seventeenth-century mansion has five different salons, all beautifully done out and dripping with zellij and stucco. Winston Churchill and Sean Connery are among the past diners here, and Doris Day and James Stewart ate here in Hitchcock's The Man Who Knew Too Much. The foodis good, with pastilla or harira to start, followed by tajine, couscous or chicken m'hammer (with ginger and cumin). The ambience is superb, and in the evening there are musicians, belly dancers and Moroccan Berber dancers. €€€€

Dar Marjana 15 Derb Sidi Ali Tair, off Rue Arset Aouzal ⓦdarmarjanamarrakech.com. This restaurant is housed in a beautiful early nineteenth-century palace. Among the tasty dishes they serve, two classics stand out: poultry pastilla and couscous aux sept légumes. Look for the sign above the entrance to a passageway diagonally across the street from the corner of the Dar el Glaoui; take the passage and look for the green door facing you before a right turn. €€€€

Dar Yacout 79 Sidi Ahmed Soussi ⓦdaryacout.com. Housed in a gorgeous old palace, the Yacout opened as a restaurant in 1987, with columns and fireplaces in super-smooth orange- and blue-striped tadelakt plaster, designed by acclaimed American interior designer Bill Willis, whose use of tadelakt here and elsewhere made it massively trendy in Moroccan interior design. The classic Moroccan tajine of chicken with preserved lemon and olives is a favourite here, but the fish tajine is also excellent. The cuisine has received Michelin plaudits in the past, though standards are beginning to slip as the tour groups move in. €€€€

Dar Zellij 1 Kaa Essour, Sidi Ben Slimane ⓦdarzellij. com. A seventeenth-century riad where you can take lunch (daily except Tue, à lka carte) or dinner on the patio or in one of the lounges, all decked out in red and super-comfortable. Start with Moroccan salad and briouats (filo-pastry parcels), followed by pastilla and then a tajine (vegetarian options available), and round it off with sweet pastilla or orange in cinnamon. €€€€

Palais Gharnata 5–6 Derb el Arsa, off Rue Riad Zitoun el Jedid ☎661 626813. Popular with foreign visitors, though unfortunately the food is merely so-so and individual diners play second fiddle to groups. However, the decor is splendid, as the building is a magnificently decorated sixteenth-century mansion, with an Italian alabaster fountain at its centre; scenes from The Return of the Pink Panther were shot here. Past patrons have included Jacqueline Kennedy and the Aga Khan. €€€€

Le Tobsil 22 Derb Abdellah Ben Hessaien, near Bab Ksour. The Moroccan cuisine is sumptuous at this intimate riad, reached by heading south down a little alley just east of the Bab Ksour junction. It's considered by many to be the finest restaurant in town, with delicious pastilla and the most aromatic couscous you could imagine, though the wine (included in the price) doesn't match the food in quality. Worth booking ahead. €€€

GUÉLIZ, SEE MAP PAGE 311

CAFÉS AND PATISSERIES

Amandine 177 Rue Mohammed el Bekal ⓦamandine marrakech.com. An elegant café-patisserie stuffed full of scrumptious almond-filled Moroccan pastries and French-style cream cakes, where you can relax with a coffee and your choice of sweetmeat.

Café du Livre 44 Rue Tariq Ben Ziad, by Hôtel Toulousain ⓦfacebook.com/cafedulivre. A very elegant space, serving tea and coffee, breakfasts, salads, sandwiches and brochettes, even what they call "tapas" (actually meze) and there's also draught beer. The café has a library of second-hand English books to read or buy, and they often show English and European football.

Café des Negociants Pl Abdelmoumen Ben Ali ☎0524 422345. Slap bang on the busiest corner in Guéliz, this grand café has been going since 1936 and it's the place to sit out on the pavement and really feel that you're in the heart of modern Marrakesh. It's also an excellent venue in which to spend the morning over a coffee, with an omelette or a set breakfast.

5

RESTAURANTS

Al Bahriya 69 Bd Moulay Rachid. Very popular fish restaurant, always crowded out at lunchtimes. For a very reasonable price you get a big plate of fried squid and whiting, plus bread, olives and sauce, or there's prawn piri-piri or fish stew. Unbeatable value. €€

★ **Al Fassia** Résidence Tayeb, 55 Bd Mohammed Zerktouni ⓦ alfassia.com. Truly Moroccan – both in decor and cuisine – specializing in dishes from the country's culinary capital, Fez, and run and staffed almost entirely by women. Start with that great classic, pigeon pastilla, followed by a choice of five different lamb tajines, among other sumptuous Fassi offerings. The ambience and service are superb. €€€

★ **Amal Restaurant** Cnr Rue Allal Ben Ahmed & Rue Ibn Sina ⓦ amalnonprofit.org. A non-profit self-help organization for disadvantaged women where training in the catering trade is put to good use in this lunchtime restaurant. What exactly's on offer changes from day to day, but there's always a tasty tajine, and cakes and pastries too. They also offer cookery workshops (see page 327). €€

Le Catanzaro 50 Rue Tarik Ibn Ziad. One of the city's most popular Italian restaurants, crowded at lunchtime with Marrakshis, expats and tourists. Specialities include *saltimbocca alla romana* and osso bucco alla milanese , and there's crème brûlée or tiramisu to round it off with. You're strongly advised to book, but you can just turn up and queue. Licensed. €€€

Chez Lamine Hadj 19 Résidence Yasmine, Rue Ibn Aïcha. Unpretentious, inexpensive restaurant, very popular with Marrakshis for solid traditional meat dishes. The chicken tajine is popular, or you can go all the way and get a sheep's head or half a kilo of tanjia (see page 323). €

Comptoir Darna Av Echouada, Hivernage ⓦ comptoir marrakech.com. Downstairs it's a restaurant serving reliably good Moroccan and international cuisine, with dishes like lamb tajine with prunes and almonds or "weeping tiger" (steak in ginger sauce), as well as one or two vegetarian options, and there's cabaret entertainment in the evenings. Upstairs it's a chic lounge bar, very popular with Marrakesh's young and rich. €€€€

Hôtel Farouk 66 Av Hassan II. From noon the hotel restaurant offers an excellent-value 50dh set menu with soup, salad, couscous, tajine or brochettes, followed by fruit, ice cream or home-made yogurt. Alternatively, tuck in to one of their excellent wood-oven pizzas. €

Grand Café de la Poste Rue el Imam Malik, just off Av Mohammed V behind the post office ⓦ grandcafedela poste.restaurant. More grand than café, this is in fact quite a posh restaurant (and a seriously good people-watching spot) serving international cuisine. The menu changes regularly, but a typical dish might be spaghetti bolognese or salmon escalope with basmati rice. Wash it down with a cup of Earl Grey, or a choice of rums, tequilas and fine brandies if you prefer something harder. €€€

Katsura 1 Rue Oum Errabia ⓦ katsura.ma. A Thai and Japanese restaurant, with the usual Thai standards including green or red curries (75–90dh), plus Japanese snacks, mainly sushi, and bento lunch boxes. The food's fresh and tasty, and the service is pleasant and efficient; they also deliver. A refreshing change from the usual Moroccan dishes. €€

Lunch d'Or Rue de l'Imam Ali. It can be hard to find an honest-to-goodness cheap Moroccan eatery in the Ville Nouvelle, but this place serves tasty and very cheap tajines, though they'll be gone by 4pm-ish, after which there's just tea and *harira* soup. Great value and very popular with workers on their lunch break. €

Rôtisserie de la Paix 68 Rue de Yougoslavie. An open-air grill, established in 1949, specializing in wood barbecue. It's all served either in a salon with a roaring fire in winter, or in the shaded garden in summer. Couscous served Fri only. Licensed. €€

La Taverne 22 Bd Mohammed Zerktouni. As well as a drinking tavern, this is a pretty decent restaurant – in fact, it claims to be the oldest in town – where you can dine on French and Moroccan food indoors or in a lovely tree-shaded garden. Dishes include *steak au poivre*, and there's a good-value four-course set menu. Licensed. €€

La Trattoria 179 Rue Mohammed el Bekal ⓦ latrattoria marrakech.com. The best Italian food in town, with impeccable service and excellent cooking, set in a 1920s house decorated by Bill Willis (as in *Yacout*; see page 323). As well as freshly made pasta, steaks and escalopes, there are specialities such as beef medallions with parmesan – plus a wonderful tiramisu to squeeze in for dessert. €€€€

★ **Winoo** 77 Bd Moulay Rachid. A justifiably popular café-restaurant where you can stop by for a juice or smoothie, a big salad or a tajine, all freshly made, well presented and very inexpensive. As you might expect, it gets very busy at mealtimes. €

DRINKING AND NIGHTLIFE

SEE MAPS PAGES 295 AND 311

Entertainment and nightlife in the **Medina** revolve around Jemaa el Fna. For a drink in the Medina, choices are limited; apart from the *Tazi* (see page 325), you can get a beer – or more likely a cocktail – in the *Café Arabe* (see page 321), *Kosybar* (see page 322) or *Le Tanjia* (see page 322), all of which double as upmarket bars. In the **Ville Nouvelle**, there's more variety; some of the bars are rather male, but

women should be all right in the *Chesterfield* (see page 325) and also in the bars of hotels such as the *Ibis* (see page 319), as well as the *Comptoir Darna* (see page 324), which is an upmarket bar as well as a restaurant. **Nightclubs** can be fun, though some at the top end of the market are a bit snooty, and may frown, for example, on jeans or trainers; most play a mix of Western and Arabic music, but it's the

5

GAY MARRAKESH

For **gay men**, a certain amount of cruising goes on in the crowds of the Jemaa el Fna in the evening, and along Avenue Mohammed V. The gay male tourist scene in Marrakesh is growing, and a number of riads are run by gay couples, but in 2014 a British man and his Moroccan alleged gay partner were arrested for walking arm in arm along Avenue Mohammed V, and only released after massive international publicity, so discretion is still advised. There is no easily perceptible **lesbian scene** in Marrakesh as yet, and in 2016 two teenage girls were arrested for kissing when the mother of one of them reported her own daughter to the police for it; again, they were eventually released after international outcry, but the incident underlines the need for discretion.

latter that really fills the dancefloor. None of them really gets going until around midnight (in fact, some don't open until then), and they usually stay open until 3 or 4am.

BARS

African Chic 5 Rue Oum Errabia. One of Marrakesh's most congenial bars, informal and relaxed, with cocktails, wines and beers, tapas, salads, pasta, or even meat or fish dishes, not to mention live Latin and Gnaoua music every night.

Café Atlas Pl Abdelmoumen Ben Ali. A pavement café in the very centre of Guéliz, but wander inside, and hey presto, it is magically transformed into a bar, with bottled beer, spirits and plates of bar snacks on the counter. Taking your drink out on the pavement is considered indiscreet; remain within, where respectable passers-by won't notice that you're imbibing.

Café-Bar de l'Escale Rue Mauritanie. A down-at-heel, spit-and-sawdust kind of bar, this place has been going since 1947 and specializes in good bar snacks, such as fried fish or spicy merguez sausages — you could even come here for lunch or dinner (there's a dining area at the back). The interior isn't recommended for unaccompanied women, especially in the evening, but there's a family-friendly (no-booze) terrace out front by day.

Chesterfield Pub 119 Av Mohammed V. Upstairs in the *Nassim Hôtel*, this supposedly English-style pub is one of Marrakesh's more sophisticated watering holes, with a comfortable if rather smoky bar area, all soft seats and muted lighting. There's also a more relaxed, open-air poolside terrace to lounge about on with your draught beer or cocktail of a summer evening.

Grand Hôtel Tazi Cnr Rue Bab Agnaou & Av el Mouahidine, Medina. Once, this was the only place in the Medina where you could get a drink, and it's still the cheapest. There's nothing fancy about the bar area — squeezed in between the restaurant and the lobby, and frequently spilling over into the latter — but it manages to be neither rough nor pretentious (a rare feat among

Marrakesh drinking dens), and you can also drink on the roof terrace. Women should feel comfortable drinking here.

Kechmara 3 Rue de la Liberté ⓦ kechmara.com. Downstairs, *Kechmara* is a cool bar-café with a slightly Japanese feel; upstairs there's an open-air terrace with a contemporary design. It's a hip place, with modern art exhibitions and music (mostly soul, jazz and blues) on the terrace some evenings. It also serves food including burgers or even fish and chips as well as tapas.

NIGHTCLUBS

555 Famous Club Hotel Ushuaïa Clubbing, Bd Mohammed VI, Aguedal ⓦ beachclub555.com. The Marrakesh branch of a famous Tangier beach club. It's pricey — to get in, to get a drink, to use the cloakroom — but most nights are ladies' nights, so ladies go free, and in principle get certain drinks free too, although they may give you the runaround on that. Music is a mix of electronic dance, hip-hop and Arabic hits, and the crowd are also very mixed. There's quite a lot of prostitution, and no photos are allowed, a rule that's rigorously policed.

Theatro Hôtel es Saadi, Av el Kadassia (also spelt Qadassia), Hivernage ⓦ theatromarrakech.com. One of Marrakesh's more interesting nightclubs, located in, as its name suggests, an old theatre. Tuesday is ladies' night, and some other nights are themed. They play the usual mix of house, techno and R'n'B with Algerian *raï* and Middle Eastern pop (except on specific nights, such as Dutch house night), but the special effects and circus-style performers on stage make it a cut above most Marrakesh clubs.

VIP Club Pl de la Liberté ⓦ facebook.com/VIPNightClub. Marrakech. The gullet-like entrance leads down to the first level, where there's a lounge bar. Further down, at the deepest level, and open from midnight only, there's what the French call a *boîte*, meaning a sweaty little nightclub. It's got a circular dancefloor and a small bar area, but despite its diminutive size, the place rarely seems full.

SHOPPING

SEE MAPS PAGES 292, 295, 299 AND 311

There are a massive number of shops in Marrakesh selling all kinds of crafts, but nothing you won't get cheaper elsewhere

5

in Morocco. However, if you're flying home out of Marrakesh, buying your souvenirs here can be very convenient.

FIXED-PRICE CRAFTS

Ensemble Artisanal Av Mohammed V, 200m southeast of Bab Nkob. Before setting off into the souks, it's worth taking a look at this government-run complex of small arts and crafts shops selling a reasonable range of goods, notably leather, textiles and carpets. Shopping here is hassle-free, and the prices, which are supposedly fixed (though actually you can haggle), are a good gauge of the going rate if you intend to bargain elsewhere. At the back are a dozen or so workshops where you can watch young people learning a range of crafts including carpet-weaving.

Entreprise Bouchaib Complexe d'Artisanat 7 Derb Baissi Kasbah, near the Saadian Tombs, ⓦcomplexe artisanal.com. Another place with supposedly fixed prices, which are only slightly higher than what you might pay in the souks, and, though you probably won't be allowed to browse freely, the sales assistants who follow you round are generally quite charming and informative. In particular, it's a good place to check out carpets and get an idea of the maximum prices you should be paying.

CARPETS

Bazar du Sud 14 & 117 Souk des Tapis, off Pl Rahba Kedima, Medina. A huge variety of carpets from all over the south of Morocco. Most claim to be old (if you prefer them spanking new, pop next door to Bazar Jouti at nos. 16 & 119), and are coloured with wonderful natural dyes such as saffron (yellow), cochineal (red) and indigo (blue).

JEWELLERY

Abdellatif Bellawi 56 & 103 Kissariat Lossta, between Souk el Kebir & Souk Attarine, Medina. A great selection of beads and bangles, including Berber bracelets from the Atlas in chunky solid silver, traditional Berber necklaces from the Atlas and Sahara, West African money beads, and necklaces from as far away as Yemen. There are also rings, earrings and woollen Berber belts, with some Cowrie-encrusted Gnaoua caps hanging up outside the door.

El Abidi Nasser Eddine 9 Souk Smarine, Medina. A discreet and rather upmarket shop for antique jewellery or modern designer pieces, all exquisite, all expensive, plus silverware, manuscripts and some very fine objets d'art. A place for those seeking something finer than the usual souk wares.

CLOTHES

Benzarrou Jaâfar 1 Kissariat Drouj (off Souk Smata by no.116), Medina. This trio of shops in a little corner of the *kissaria* is the best place to come for pukka traditional Moroccan *babouches* (slippers), men's and women's, in various colours and traditional styles. There's no pressure or hard sell.

Ben Zouine Mohammed Rida 142 Rue Arset Azoual, Medina. A good place to get a tailor-made local-style shirt or blouse, be it in cotton, linen or wool, though opening hours can be a bit haphazard (morning is the best time to catch them). You choose your cloth, get measured up, specify what buttons or even embroidered design you want on it, and come back a day or two later to collect.

Femmes de Marrakech 67 Souk Kchachbia, Medina. A dress shop run by a women's cooperative, creating their own garments, and also selling – on a fair-trade basis – clothes made at home by other women. The dresses are handmade from pure cotton and linen fabrics in a mix of Moroccan and Western styles. They also sell cosmetics, also made by a women's co-operative on a fair-trade basis.

Maison du Caftan 65 Rue Sidi el Yamani, Medina. Upmarket boutique selling robes, tunics and kaftans, from see-through glittery gowns and sequinned velvet tunics to embroidered silk kaftans that make sumptuous housecoats. Most are for women, but there are also a few men's garments. Past customers include Jean-Paul Gautier, Mick Jagger and Samuel L. Jackson, as photos on the wall testify.

BOOKS

Librairie Chatr 19 Av Mohammed V, Guéliz. The best bookshop in town, selling mainly French titles, with lots of books on Morocco, sometimes including books on trekking and off-roading, plus a small selection of titles in English at the back. The front part of the shop supplies artists' materials, including paint and brushes, as well as a large and varied selection of pens.

Librairie Menzil el Fan Résidence Tayeb, 55 Bd Mohammed Zerktouni, Guéliz. There are lots of full-colour coffee-table books here, including several on Marrakesh and Moroccan interior design. Other subjects covered include architecture, textiles and jewellery, and cooking (though mostly in French).

FOOD

Aswak Assalam Cnr Av 11 Janvier & Av Prince Moulay Abdallah, Guéliz ⓦaswakassalam.com. This is the most central supermarket – certainly not the most colourful shopping in town, but quick and easy. There's a good patisserie section, and grains and spices which you can weigh out yourself. You'll also find a fuller (and probably fresher) range of dairy products than at grocery stores, and there are even consumer goods, including couscous steamers.

Jemaa el Fna Market Jemaa el Fna (east side), Medina. This little covered market is of most interest as a place to get fruit and veg just off the main square, though it also sells meat and even shoes.

Marché Central (Municipal Market) Rue Ibn Toumert, Guéliz. This is the Ville Nouvelle's main market, and it's a far cry from those in the Medina. Expats and better-off Marrakhis come here for their fresh fish, meat, fruit and veg. There are two butchers selling horsemeat, one selling pork, and shops specializing in pickled lemons, perfumed soaps, fossils, ceramics, booze, tourist tat, paintings and fresh flowers.

Olive stalls Souk Ableuh (just off Jemaa el Fna), Medina. This souk consists of rows of stalls piled up with olives. The wrinkled black ones are the typical Moroccan olive, delicious with bread but a bit salty on their own. Of the green olives, the ones flavoured with bits of lemon are among the tastiest. Other delicacies here include spicy red *harissa* sauce and bright yellow lemons preserved in brine, a favourite ingredient in Moroccan cooking.

MISCELLANEOUS
Les Enfants de Michelin 84 Rue Riad Zitoun el Kedim,

Medina. The most imaginative in a group of shops that recycle disused tyres. The oldest of them made hammam supplies such as buckets and flip-flops, then diversified into picture frames and tuffets (try no.97 for those), but this shop makes clothes and accessories, hovering between stylish and fetishy, but certainly interesting.

Moulay Larbai 96 Souk el Kchachbia, Medina. Moulay Larbai's claim to fame is that it was he who first started making mirrors framed with small pieces of mirror or of coloured glass, and that he still makes the best ones in the souk, which indeed he does. His mirrors come in various shapes and sizes, and he uses proper Iraqi-style, stained glass for the colours.

DIRECTORY

Banks and exchange The main area for banks and ATMs in the Medina is off the south side of the Jemaa el Fna on Rue Moulay Ismail. In Guéliz, the main area is along Av Mohammed V between Pl Abdelmoumen Ben Ali and the market. BMCE's branch in the Medina (Rue Moulay Ismail on Pl Foucauld) has a bureau de change. The post office on 16 du Novembre will also change cash, as will the branches at the train station and the Jemaa el Fna. There are also lots of private foreign exchange bureaux around town including one off the Jemaa el Fna on Rue Riad Zitoun el Kedim at Derb Sidi Bouloukat, and one at *Hôtel Farouk* in Guéliz (see page 319). Even when these are closed, the hotels *Ali* (best rates in town; see page 316) and *Central Palace* (see page 317) will change money.

Cinemas Colisée on Bd Mohammed Zerktouni, Guéliz; Cinéma Mabrouka, Rue Bab Agnaou, Medina.

Cookery classes Workshops in Moroccan cooking are offered by *La Maison Arabe* (see page 317;) and *Amal Restaurant Solidaire* (see page 324;). Marrakech Food Tours (w marrakechfoodtours.com) offer 3½hr daytime or evening food tours; book online.

Dentist Dr Abdel Jouad Bennani, 112 Av Mohammed

V (first floor), opposite Délégation de Tourisme, Guéliz (☎ 0524 449136), has been recommended and speaks some English.

Doctors Dr Abdelmajid Ben Tbib, 171 Av Mohammed V, Guéliz (☎ 0524 431030), is recommended and speaks English. Dr Frédéric Reitzer, Immeuble Berdaï (entrance C, 2nd floor), 1 Av Moulay el Hassan (at Pl de la Liberté), Guéliz (☎ 0524 439562), also speaks some English. There's also an emergency call-out service, SOS Médecins (☎ 0524 404040), which charges around 500dh per consultation, but its doctors vary in their competence.

Golf Golf courses have proliferated around Marrakesh in recent years. The oldest is Marrakesh Royal Golf Club (w royal-golf-marrakech.com), 5km southeast of town on the old Ouarzazate road, once played on by Churchill and Eisenhower. Others include: Amelkis Golf Club, southeast of town at Km12 on the Route de Ouarzazate (w golfamelkis. com); Palmeraie Golf Club (w palmgolfclubmarrakech.com), attached to the *Palmeraie Golf Palace* hotel, off the Route de Casablanca, northeast of town; Samanah Country Club, 14km south of town on the Route d'Amizmiz (w samanah.com); Atlas Golf Resort, 5km out on the Route de Fès (w atlas.golf-

FESTIVALS AND EVENTS

The two-week **Festival National des Arts Populaires** held in June or July each year, is the country's biggest and best folklore and music festival, with musicians and dancers coming in from across Morocco and beyond, spanning the range of Moroccan music. Shows start around 9pm and are preceded by a *fantasia* at Bab Jedid, with Berber horsemen at full gallop firing guns into the air. Marrakesh also has an annual **Marathon**, run on the third or fourth Sunday in January (see w marathon-marrakech.com for details), and the **Marrakesh Film Festival** in November or early December (w festivalmarrakech.info), in which the featured movies are shown at cinemas across town and on large screens in the El Badi Palace and the Jemaa el Fna. The Marrakesh Biennale (w marrakechbiennale.org) is a visual arts festival held in even-numbered years in late April or early May, with events held at locations around town, and in March every year, TEDx Marrakesh (w tedxmarrakesh.net) is a series of TED-style talks delivered at the *Es Saadi* hotel in Hivernage.

5

club-marrakech.com); Assoufid (@assoufid.com), 10km southwest of town on the road that goes past the airport; Al Maaden Golf Resort, 5km southeast of town off the P2012 (@al-maaden.golf-club-marrakech.com).

Hammams There are plenty of hammams in the Medina. The three closest to the Jemaa el Fna are Hammam Polo on Rue de la Recette, Hammam Bouloukate on Derb Sidi Bouloukat, and one at the northern end of Rue Riad Zitoun el Kedim. All open for both men and women with separate entrances for each. Hammams specifically for tourists include Hammam Ziani, 14 Rue Riad Zitoun el Jedid (@hammamziani.ma), open for both sexes (separate areas); more expensive is Les Bains de Marrakech, 2 Derb Sedra, down an alley by Bab Agnaou in the kasbah (@lesbainsdemarrakech.com). You won'tbe able to share a steam bath experience with your partner – if you want to do that, you'll have to stay at one of the many riads with their own in-house hammam; *Riad Farnatchi* (see page 318) has a very good one that's open to non-guests.

Hospitals Polyclinique du Sud, at the corner of Rue de Yougoslavie and Rue Ibn Aïcha, Guéliz (☎0524 447619), is a private clinic with a good reputation which is used to settling bills with insurance companies.

Laundry Pressing Oasis, 44 Rue Tarik Ibn Zaid, Guéliz, two doors from *Hôtel Toulousain*.

Pharmacies Several along Av Mohammed V, including Pharmacie de la Liberté, just off Pl de la Liberté, which will call a doctor for you if necessary. In the Medina, try Pharmacie de la Place and Pharmacie du Progrès on Rue Bab Agnaou just by Pl Jemaa el Fna. There's an all-night pharmacy by the Commissariat de Police on Jemaa el Fna and another on Rue Khalid Ben Oualid near the fire station in Guéliz. Other all-night and weekend outlets are listed in pharmacy windows.

Police The tourist police (*brigade touristique*) are on the west side of the Jemaa el Fna (☎0524 384601).

Post office The main post office on Pl 16 du Novembre, midway down Av Mohammed V in Guéliz. The smaller post office on Pl Jemaa el Fna is open similar hours, with a bureau de change round the back.

SPANA Visitors can see how animals are cared for at SPANA's clinic for *calèche* horses, mules and donkeys run by British animal welfare charity SPANA (see page 47) directly north of the Medina in Cité Mohammadi, Daoudiat (@spana.org.ma/contact/centre-de-marrakech.html).

Swimming pools Many hotels allow non-residents to use their pools if you have a meal, or for a fee. In the Medina, the *Grand Hôtel Tazi* (see page 325) is one that allows outside guests for a charge. Also handy, especially if you're with kids, is Oasiria, at Km4, Route du Barrage, on the Asni/Oumnass road (@oasiria.com); it even runs free shuttle buses from town. The *Palmeraie Golf Palace* hotel in the palmery runs a pricier place called Nikki Beach (@palmeraieresorts.com), which gets mixed reports.

The High Atlas

TREKKING IN THE HIGH ATLAS

The High Atlas

The High Atlas, North Africa's greatest mountain range, contains some of the most intriguing and beautiful regions of Morocco. A historical and physical barrier between the northern plains and the pre-Sahara, its Berber-populated valleys feel – and indeed are – very remote from the country's mainstream urban life. The area is North Africa's premier trekking destination; casual day-hikers and serious mountaineers alike will find appealing routes in the region, offering both towering mountains (*jebels*) and spectacular passes (*tizis* or, in French, *cols*). Just a short distance from the hustle and bustle of Marrakesh is Toubkal National Park, home to a number of the most impressive summits, including Jebel Toubkal (4167m), and beautiful, traditional villages that appear locked in time.

Picturesque Berber villages and remote pinnacles, however, aren't the only draws here. The landscape varies from season to season: winter drops metres of snow that lead to gushing river valleys in spring; summer brings an unforgiving sun, while the autumnal sunlight brings the browns and reds of the peaks to life.

One of the benefits of trekking the region is being able to walk unencumbered, since muleteers and their mules are available for hire. Mountain guides are an invaluable resource, and always recommended if you are heading away from the main routes. Other options include mountain biking, which is steadily increasing in popularity on the dirt tracks (*pistes*) and mule paths.

ACTIVITIES AND TOURS   THE HIGH ATLAS

A number of trekking and biking companies operate in the region, though most are based in Marrakesh. The following are all recommended for their qualifications, professionalism, language ability and overall quality.

Argan Xtreme Sports ⓦ argansports.com. Quirky but of sound quality, this outfit has been running bike tours since 2011 (with customers including Richard Branson, and at least one Saudi prince). They also do long-term rental, if you fancy going your own way.

Bike Adventures in Morocco ⓦ bikeadventuresin morocco.com. Esteemed company offering exclusive biking excursions into nearly every region of the country. Itineraries include biking north to south in the Central High Atlas, riding from the High Atlas to the Atlantic, and a number of routes not offered by any others. High-quality bikes and equipment are available for rent. It's best to arrange trips well before your arrival.

Maroc Nature ⓦ maroc-nature.com. Building tailor-made trips for individuals and small groups, Maroc Nature is one of the country's premier trekking and biking operators. The company uses quality equipment and offers fully supported trips in the Atlas Mountains and other areas.

Toubkal Peaks ⓦ toubkal-peaks.com. Unique itineraries involving trekking, skiing and desert expeditions for groups of all sizes can be arranged with this local team of experts offering quality service.

Toubkal Guide ⓦ toubkalguide.com. Offering tailor-made and small group treks and tours, Toubkal Guide has established a deserved first-class reputation through consistently high feedback from clients for providing quality experiences in all areas of the Atlas Mountains.

★ **Yak Travel** ⓦ yaktravel.co.uk. Running small-group treks around the High Atlas – and beyond – under the charge of Alan Parker, who has developed a worldwide reputation for his understanding of the mountains, thanks to decades of trekking experiences in Morocco.

The Ourika Valley

The **Ourika Valley**, cutting deep into the High Atlas, is a popular escape from the summer heat of Marrakesh – particularly the village of **Setti Fatma**, a weekend resort for young Marrakshis, who ride out on their mopeds to lie around and picnic beside the streams

Highlights

❶ Ourika Valley A cool escape from Marrakesh, the valley makes an easy day-trip for a short climb up to its waterfalls, or lunch at a riverside café. See page 332

❷ Atlas Berbers The High Atlas is populated mainly by Berbers, who have a unique culture, dress and traditions – call in at the Berber Museum en route to Setti Fatma to find out more. See page 336

❸ Skiing at Oukaïmeden Want to say you've skied in Morocco? Oukaïmeden is the spot; winter months bring snow and crowds enjoying the manageable peaks. See page 337

❹ Jebel Toubkal North Africa's highest peak is a goal for most Atlas trekkers, offering summer walks and winter mountaineering. See page 339

❺ Imlil and Armed These Toubkal trailhead villages are remote enough to get a taste of Berber mountain life, even if you go no further. See pages 341 and 343

❻ Ouirgane This region in the foothills of the High Atlas offers hidden walks, stunning panoramas and plenty of outdoor activities throughout the year but is best enjoyed in the cooler months. See page 350

❼ Tin Mal This twelfth-century mosque in the heart of the Atlas is one of only three mosques in all Morocco which can be visited by non-Muslims. See page 355

HIGHLIGHTS ARE MARKED ON THE MAP ON PAGE 334

and waterfalls. The village lies at the end of the road, although a difficult but motorable *piste* continues further up the valley to Timichi, with mule **paths** then leading onwards to **Tacheddirt**, (see page 349), **Oukaïmeden** (see page 337), and **Imlil** (see page 341), the latter being the most popular base for those heading to the top of Toubkal.

Tafza and around

Grands taxis from Bab er Robb in Marrakesh (see page 315) at frequent but irregular times (50 mins)

The Ourika Valley proper begins 30km from Marrakesh at **Tnine de l'Ourika** (also sometimes simply referred to as "Ourika"), a small roadside village which hosts a Monday **souk** – worthy of a quick stop if you happen to be passing through. Just beyond, across the river, is **Dar Caid Ouriki**, with a picturesque *zaouia* set back in the rocks, near the ruins of an old *caidal* **kasbah**. However, the area's major sight is a little further down the road in the unimposing village of **TAFZA**, 37km from Marrakech, where the kasbah has been restored and now houses a good **museum**.

La Safranière de l'Ourika

Tnine de l'Ourika • Charge • Ⓦ safran-ourika.com

It's worth popping into **La Safranière de l'Ourika** on your way from Marrakesh to the mountains. Though the bulbs are actually sourced from Taliouine, Morocco's saffron capital (see page 440), good soil allows the precious herb to be grown here; you can buy a packet or two to take away with you, or simply enjoy wandering around the grounds.

Jardin Bio-Aromatique d'Ourika

Tnine de l'Ourika • Charge • Ⓦ jardin-bioaromatique-ourika.com

The botanical gardens of Nectarome, a French-Moroccan company specialising in natural cosmetics, the **Jardin Bio-Aromatique d'Ourika** is a grand spot to relax for a

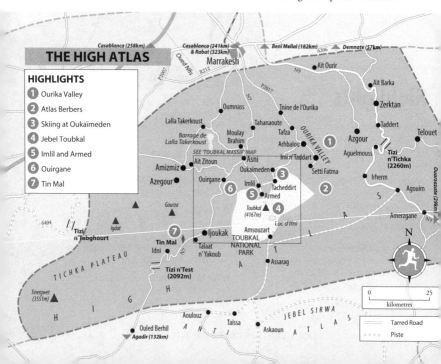

6

> ### WEATHER AND AFFECTED ROUTES
>
> The High Atlas is subject to **snow** from November to April, and even the major passes of Tizi n'Tichka (on the road to Ouarzazate) and Tizi n'Test (on the road to Taroudant) can be closed for periods of a day or more. However, these passes are seldom blocked for long and **snow barriers** on the roads leading up into the mountains will be down if the passes are not open to the public. If blocked, the southern regions can be reached from Marrakesh via the Tizi Maachou pass (the N8, along with A7 toll highway towards Agadir) followed by the N10 through Taroudant and Taliouine.
>
> The spring **thaw** can present problems, too, when snowmelt causes rivers to swell and become dangerous to cross. The possibility of dangerous **flash floods,** which can erupt suddenly and violently (particularly in spring, and again after summer storms), must also be taken seriously. To keep safe, always camp on higher ground while avoiding areas which might become the course of a water torrent, notably dried-up riverbeds.

while on your way up the Ourika Valley. As well as being a veritable feast for your olfactory glands, guests are able to use company products on site – try a footbath, or even splash out on a full foot massage.

ACCOMMODATION   TAFZA AND AROUND

★**Kasbah Bab Ourika** Tnine de l'Ourika ⓦ kasbah babourika.com. This stunning high-end, eco-friendly establishment is worth splurging on before or after any activities in the High Atlas and stands way above other hotels in the area. Picture-perfect panoramic views, first-class food and an on-site garden will entice a long stay. Most arrange a private transfer here from Marrakesh, and

they can pick up or drop off in Setti Fatma too. €€€€
Kasbah Jad Auberge Tnine de l'Ourika ⓣ 0661 324456. Not a bad find, this is exceptional value for the price, you'll get a simple room (all with balconies, some with patio), but of even more appeal are the indoor pool and hammam. There's even a modest on-site library, and a TV lounge if you've really run out of things to do. €̄

Arhbalou

Beyond Tafza, scattered at intervals over the next thirty-odd kilometres are a series of tiny hamlets, interspersed with a few summer homes and the occasional hotel and café-restaurant. The only sizeable settlement of significance along the route is **ARHBALOU** (50km southwest of Marrakesh), where most of the local people on the buses get off. The village sees smaller crowds in the summer months than Setti Fatma (a further 20km along the road) and offers riverside alfresco meals at slightly better prices.

Setti Fatma

SETTI FATMA is a straggly riverside village, substantially rebuilt, expanded and made safer after its devastation by floods in 1995. The setting, with grassy terraces and High Atlas peaks rising to over 3700m, feels like a dreamscape after venturing from the dry plains that surround Marrakesh. In the rocky foothills above the village are a series of six (at times seven) **waterfalls**. The mountains provide a startling backdrop that, to the southwest, includes the main trekking/climbing zone of Toubkal (see page 343), for which Setti Fatma is one possible entry point.

The waterfalls

Guides both real and "faux" will attempt to get you to the main **waterfalls**, but they're easy to get to independently, by crossing the river from the main body of town. Upon crossing, you'll see several cafés where you can order a tajine that should be ready by your return; it's here that the **trail** begins. The first waterfall is a fairly straightforward clamber over the rocks, and is flanked by another café. The higher waterfalls are a lot more strenuous to reach and quite tricky when descending, requiring a head for heights and solid footwear.

ARRIVAL AND DEPARTURE
SETTI FATMA

By grand taxi Occasional shared *grands taxis* from Marrakesh run from the Bab er Robb gate to Setti Fatma (90min). In Setti Fatma, taxis pick up and drop off in the centre of the village.

Guides To hire a guide for the waterfalls of Setti Fatma or beyond, stop by the Bureau des Guides et Accompagnateurs,

the official information point for the region, located near the *Asagour*. Longer excursions, such as the trek to Imlil, or routes through Oukaïmeden and further afield, are best arranged ahead of time if you don't bring your own gear (see page 346 for advice).

ACCOMMODATION

Setti Fatma has an ever-growing number of places to stay. The region gets congested during summer weekends and at festival time (when there'll be nothing going, bar a huge impromptu campsite along the terraced riverside). Outside these periods you should have little problem finding a room.

Asgaour Village centre ☎ 0524 485294. Friendly, spic-and-span operation whose simple, well-lit rooms come with a/c and heating, and often have a small TV and refrigerator; private bathroom and shower also available. Go

for a room in the back, facing away from the road and river, for maximum tranquillity. Food available, but not great. €̄

★ **Au Bord de l'Eau** 2km north, on the road from Marrakesh ✪ obordelo.com. An excellent option, with rooms – all en suite, some with private patio – decorated in a calm, modern style quite at odds with the remote location. The couple who run the place are excellent sources of information, and the garden is a splendid place to chill out after a hike. €̄

HIGH ATLAS BERBERS

Until recent decades, the High Atlas region – and its **Berber inhabitants** – was almost completely isolated. When the French began their "pacification" of Morocco in the 1920s, the way of life here was essentially feudal, based upon the control of the three main passes (*tizis*) by a trio of **"clan" families**, "the Lords of the Atlas". Even after the French negotiated the cooperation of these warrior chiefs, it was not until the spring of 1933 – just over two decades after the establishment of the Protectorate – that they were able to subdue them and control their tribal land. This occurred only with the cooperation of the main feudal chief, **T'hami el Glaoui**, who continued to control the region as Pasha of Marrakesh (see page 304).

These days, the region is under official government control through a system of local *caids*, but in many villages the role of the state remains largely irrelevant, and if you go trekking you soon become aware of the mountains' highly distinctive culture and traditions. The longest established inhabitants of Morocco, the Atlas Berbers never adopted a totally orthodox version of Islam and the Arabic language has, even today, made little impression on their indigenous **Tachelhaït** dialects. Their **music** and **ahouache** dances (in which women and men both take part) are unique, as is the village **architecture**, with stone or clay houses tiered on the rocky slopes, craggy fortified **agadirs** (collective granaries), and **kasbahs**, which continued to serve as feudal castles for the community's defence right into the twentieth century.

Berber women in the Atlas go about unveiled and have a much higher profile than their rural counterparts in the plains and the north. They perform much of the heavy labour – working in the fields, herding and grazing cattle and goats and carrying vast loads of brushwood and provisions. Whether they have any greater status or power within the family and village, however, is questionable. The men retain the "important" tasks of buying and selling goods and the evening/night-time irrigation of the crops, ploughing and doing all the building and craftwork.

As an outsider, you'll be constantly surprised by the friendliness and openness of the Berbers, and by their amazing capacity for languages – there's scarcely a village where you won't find someone who speaks French or English, or both. The only areas where you may feel exploited – and pestered by kids – are the main trekking circuits around Jebel Toubkal, where tourism has become an all-important source of income. Given the harshness of life up here, its presence is hardly surprising.

6

La Perle de l'Ourika 3km north, on the road from Marrakesh ☎ 0524 484477. This little gem of a hotel, a 10min walk from town and with direct access to the river, is superbly run by an English-speaking artist. There are five well-kept rooms (the orange one is particularly nice), some of which overlook the garden; most have private bathrooms. Book well ahead on weekends, and in the summer. €̄

EATING

Azilal Village centre. This hotel-restaurant is a real family affair, and despite the number of tourists they encounter every year, a cheery welcome is guaranteed. It's also about the cheapest place around, though portions are surprisingly large, and the food hearty; as is usually the way in these parts, tajines are your best choice (go for the date one, in season). €̄

Azro Village centre. This quaint restaurant has outdoor terraced seating shaded by willows near the river, and serves good set menus featuring tasty tajines and kebabs. Avoid the soup, however, as it tends to be bland and not freshly made. €€

★ **La Perle de l'Ourika** 3km north, on the road from Marrakesh. As well as offering inviting accommodation (see page 337), this out-of-town place has a renowned restaurant overlooking a garden of fig and quince trees, serving scrumptious couscous and seasonal quince tajine. Reservations advised. €€

Oukaïmeden

Imagine adding Africa to the list of places you've been skiing – the resort of **OUKAÏMEDEN** makes that little cache of travel kudos rather attainable. Though primarily known as a ski centre, the village makes a good target in its own right in warmer months; since it's a calmer and much easier trekking base than Setti Fatma, especially for those setting out towards Toubkal; you can spot Atlas **wildlife** on some attractive day hikes (see page 338), or hunt down some prehistoric **rock carvings** (see page 339).

The ski slopes

The slopes of **Adrar-n-Oukaïmeden** offer the best **skiing** in Morocco, and boast the highest ski lifts on the African continent (3273m). The upper slopes give access to good *piste* and off-*piste* skiing (though given the paucity of visitors and lack of machinery, the former often feels like the latter), while on the lower slopes a few basic drag lifts serve nursery and intermediate runs. For **cross-country skiers**, several crests and *cols* are accessible, and ski mountaineers often head south to Tacheddirt (see page 349).

Snowfall and snow cover can be erratic, but the **season** is regarded as January to the end of March; the lifts close at the end of April, even if there are perfect skiing conditions. **Equipment** can be rented from several shops around the resort; rates are fairly modest, but quality fluctuates so ask around. Daily **ski passes** are cheap, too, and there are modest charges if you want to hire a **ski guide** or instructor – ask at any of the shops, or talk with the staff at *Chez Juju* (see page 338) or the CAF Refuge.

Walks from Oukaïmeden

The **walking trails** from Oukaïmeden are strictly summer only: routes can be heavily snow-covered late into spring. However, weather conditions allowing, the

6

HIGH ATLAS WILDLIFE

The High Atlas has unique flora and fauna, which are accessible even to the most reluctant rambler if you base yourself at **Oukaïmeden**, **Imlil** or **Ouirgane**.

The passes ring to the chorus of the **painted frog** and the North African race of the **green toad** during their spring breeding seasons, while some species of reptile, such as the **Moorish gecko**, have adapted to the stony walls of the area's towns and villages. **Butterflies** that brave these heights include the Moroccan copper and desert orange tip, and painted ladies heading from West Africa to western England. Other inhabitants include the almost invisible **praying mantis**, the scampering **ground squirrel** and the rare **elephant shrew**.

Birds to be found among the sparse vegetation include Moussier's redstart and the crimson-winged finch, which prefers the grassy slopes where it feeds in flocks; both birds are unique to North African ranges. The rocky outcrops provide shelter for both chough and alpine chough and the rivers are frequented by dippers which swim underwater in their search for food. Overhead, darting Lanner falcon or flocks of brilliantly coloured bee-eaters add to the feeling of abundance that permeates the slopes of the High Atlas. In the cultivated valleys, look out for the magpie, which, uniquely, has a sky-blue eye mark; there are also storks galore. Other High Atlas birds, as the snow melts, include shore larks, rock bunting, alpine accentor, redstarts and many species of wheatear.

Local flora is impressive, too. The spring bloom on the lower slopes comprises aromatic thyme and thorny caper, mingling with golden spreads of broom. Higher slopes are covered by more resilient species, such as the blue tussocks of hedgehog broom. The wet meadows produce a fantastic spread of hooped-petticoat daffodils, *romulea* and other bulbs, and Oukaïmeden in May/June has acres of orchids in bloom.

trail to Tacheddirt (3–4hr) is pretty clear even in winter, being a *piste* as far as the pass, **Tizi n'ou Addi** (2954m), reached in about two hours. On the descent, the trail divides in two, with both branches leading down into Tacheddirt, where basic accommodation is available. From here there are several possible onward routes (see page 349).

If you want to get slightly more off the beaten path, it's possible to take the mule path from Tizi n'ou Addi southwest to the settlement of **Ouanesekra** (where you can also find basic accommodation; see page 348). From here, the options are endless. You can either trek northeast via Tacheddirt and Tizi n'Tacheddirt (3172m) towards the Ourika Valley, southwest via Tizi n'Tamatert (2279m) to Imlil, or southeast via Tizi Likemt (3555) to Azib Likemt and then Lac d'Ifni.

ARRIVAL AND DEPARTURE   OUKAÏMEDEN

By grand taxi There is no direct public transport from Marrakech to Oukaïmeden which is best reached by taking a *grand taxi* as far as Lagarb, departing from Bab er Robb in Marrakech (see page 315) at frequent but irregular times, and then taking a local bus onwards from Lagarb.

ACCOMMODATION AND EATING

The hotels cater mainly for the ski season, but most stay open year-round.

Chez Juju Main road, centre of Oukaïmeden ☎ 0524 319005. Although a little pricier than it should be (and prices vary by season), this lodge has the best rooms in the area, making it a great base from which to go skiing or walking; request a room facing south towards the ski hill for the sun and the views. The place also boasts a nice bar-restaurant, with tables inside and out (mains from €€). Summer €, winter €€

Club Alpine Chalet At the beginning of town just before the centre ☎ 0524 319036. Open for both members and non-members, this well-equipped CAF lodge has six dormitories, along with a bar and restaurant, which serves substantial meals (€). Prices vary by season, but are always very affordable. €

The Toubkal Massif

Enclosing the loftiest peaks of the High Atlas, and sitting within **Toubkal National Park**, the **Toubkal Massif** is Morocco's number one trekking destination. You can reach trailhead villages in under two hours from Marrakesh, and the main walking routes are easily followed. Walking just a short distance from the most common starting point, **Imlil**, you are transported to a very different world – mountain villages offer a stark contrast to the previous roadside towns, with Berber houses, stacked one on top of another in apparently organic growth, appearing to sprout from the rocks. The local population is immediately distinct from their city compatriots; the women dress in brilliant attire even when working in the fields.

In summer, **Jebel Toubkal** (4167m), the highest peak in North Africa, is walkable right up to the summit; if you're pushed for time, you could climb it and be back in Marrakesh in two days – though at some risk of altitude sickness. Alternatively, if you feel unable to tackle an ascent of Toubkal, it's possible to have a genuine taste of the mountains by spending time exploring lesser-visited valleys accessible from Imlil.

Aside from the entry points given here, the region can be approached on various treks from Ouirgane (see page 350) or Ijoukak (see page 354), a little further west; the Ourika Valley from the east (see page 332); or the ski resort of Oukaïmeden (see page 337). Trekkers looking for a more unusual approach – and with sufficient time to spend – might enter from the south, through the Tifnoute Valley and Lac d'Ifni (see page 345).

Asni

The end of the line for most buses and *grands taxis*, **ASNI** is little more than a roadside village and marketplace from where you can head straight on to Imlil, a further 17km to the southeast. The most interesting time to be here is for the **Saturday souk**, when the enclosure behind the row of shop cubicles is filled with local produce (this is a big fruit-growing region) and livestock stalls.

ARRIVAL AND DEPARTURE   **ASNI**

From Marrakesh There is one rather unreliable daily bus leaving Marrakech's Bab Doukkala bus station (see page 313) for Taroudant at around 10am, passing through Asni about one hour later. Additionally, minibuses (1hr) and

---

PREHISTORIC ROCK CARVINGS IN THE ATLAS

Some of the Atlas's fascinating **prehistoric rock carvings**, depicting animals, weapons, battle scenes, an apparent game area and various unknown symbols, can be found just before Oukaïmeden's ski area site – follow the sign pointing to "Gravures Rupestres." It's worth contacting **local expert** Hassan Hachouch (☎0678 551527, ✉eagleatlas1@gmail.com) for a trip to the carvings. He speaks French well and leads site visits in passable English. He is a valuable resource to point out some of the lesser-known carvings.

An **eco-museum** near the carvings displays photos of the flora and fauna of Toubkal National Park and surroundings, as well as information about the carvings themselves. If you find it closed, call Hassan Hachouch (see above) or H. Ait Lahaj (☎0676 89 14 08). There is no official entry charge for either the rock carvings or the eco-museum, although a modest tip is expected.

A puzzling, related feature of prehistoric rock sites in the Atlas and elsewhere are **cupmarks** – groups of small circular hollows (Peter Ustinov suggested they were egg cups) with no apparent pattern carved into exposed rock surfaces at ground level. Unlike the usual rock art, they appear in granite (in the western Atlas) and conglomerate (at Tinerhir) as well as sandstone (in the Middle Atlas).

Most of the rock carvings are depicted in the indispensable **guidebook**, *Gravures Rupestres du Haut Atlas* (on sale in the Oukaïmeden Club Alpin Français chalet, and in some Marrakesh bookshops), though it is only available in French.

6

TOUBKAL MASSIF

0 — 5 kilometres

N

Setti Fatma & Ourika Valley

Difficult route to Ourika Valley (Kissaria Gorge)

Imlil & Taliouine

Ourika Valley & Marrakesh

El Makhzen & Tizi n' Ou Ichddane

Taghbart

Marrakesh, Amizmiz, Tameslohtt & Moulay Brahim

Amizmiz

Taroudant (Tizi n'Test)

Timichi

Timiquist

Timguist

Adrar n'Theghmmar (3892m)

Aguoins

Anpour (3616m)

Tizi n'Outhattar

Tizi n'Eddi

Tacheddirt

Tizi n'Tacheddirt

Azib Likemt

Tizi n'Likemt

Tizi n'Ourai (3109m)

Tizi n'Ououraine (3124m)

Amsouzart

Tissaldai

Tagadirt

Timzakane

Imhilene

Ouaneskra

Oukaïmeden (3273m)

Oukaïmeden

Ski Lift

Oukaïmeden (3277m)

Tizi n'Tamatert

Azib Tifni

Tizi n'Terhaline (3247m)

Alsoual (3842m)

Toubkal (4167m)

Tizi n'Ouanoums (3664m)

Asif n'Mouraine

Lac d'Ifni (2312m)

INEMANE VALLEY

Tamatert

Tizi n'Tagharat

Afekoi

Amsakrou

Ikiss

Aguersioual

Imlil

Aït Souka

Armed

Sidi Chamharouch

Azib Imi n'Oussalf

Toubkal Refuges

Tizi n'Ouagane

AIT MIZANE VALLEY

Matat

Mzik

Tizi Mzik

Aguelzim

Ras n'Ouanoukrim

Tadat

Aït Youb

Tizi Melloul

Tamadout

Id Aïssa

Tizi Oussem

Azib Tamsoult

Tazaghart (3845m)

Tazaghart Refuge

T A Z A G H A R T   P L A T E A U

Asni

Marigha

KIK PLATEAU EDGE

Tassa Ouirgane

Tizi n'Ouahou

Tisgui

Tikhfist

Asif Zagrawa

Tizi Ouadou

Agauni

Ouirgane

Nfis Gorge

Gouzra (3280m)

Tizi n'Iguidi

AGOUNDIS VALLEY

P.203

Ijoukak

Talâat n'Yakoub

grands taxis (20dh; 50min) depart from Marrakesh's Bab er Robb gate at frequent but irregular intervals.

On from Asni The 17km to Imlil – where most treks begin – is pretty straightforward, with minibuses and *grand taxis* shuttling back and forth along the winding road. A spot in a *grand taxi* can also be negotiated for the journey to Ouirgane, and even (in stages, and unreliably) over the Tizi n'Test; you may prefer to simply book the whole taxi.

Leaving Asni, buses and *grands taxis* depart from near the main market entrance; for Imlil, Ouirgane, and Ijoukak, minibuses start from the roadside south of the petrol station.

Banks and ATMs Bank Chaabi – with ATM – is located in the centre of town, next to the chemist at the junction of the P2005 (the road to Imlil) and the main R203.

6

ACCOMMODATION AND EATING

As there's limited **accommodation** in Asni, most sensibly head straight on to Imlil or Ouirgane. For **meals**, most of the café-stalls by the souk will fix you a tajine or *harira*.

Kasbah Tamadot 4 km from town on the road to Imlil ⓦ virginlimitededition.com. If you are looking for luxury while in the mountains, look no further than Richard Branson's tastefully and lavishly decorated restored kasbah. Beautiful views can be enjoyed across and up valley towards Toubkal while dining at its beautiful, terraced restaurant, serving both local and international cuisine. €€€€

Vallée Verte 2 km from town on the road to Imlil ⓞ 0662 133731. South of town and boasting an out-of-the-way feel, this is a very decent choice for those heading up to the mountains. Rooms have been lovingly decorated (blueish on the ground floor, reddish on the upper level), and all have balconies – most with a view of the pool, and others with a gorgeous vista of the valley and mountains. Best reached by *petit taxi* from town, if you don't have your own transport; good food available from the on-site restaurant. €€

Imlil

Just past Asni, the road begins to climb; below it the valley of the Oued Rhirhaia unfolds, while above, small villages crowd onto the rocky slopes. Halfway up the valley, at a roadside café, there's a sudden good view of Toubkal. As you emerge at **IMLIL** the air feels quite different – silent and rarefied at 1740m. Paths head off in all directions among the valleys, making this region a walker's paradise.

Imlil itself, while rapidly expanding in recent years, is still little more than a roadside settlement, but with sufficient shops along the main thoroughfare, and plenty of small guesthouses and hotels. It is the most popular **starting point** for those heading for Jebel **Toubkal**, and indeed a good spot to get supplies, hire mountain guides, or spend the night to get your bearings in the region, although it's not worth spending much more than one day here, given the much more appealing villages scattered just beyond.

EDUCATION FOR ALL

A local NGO providing much-needed opportunities for Morocco's next generation, **Education for All** (EFA; ⓦ efamorocco.org), offers educational support and boarding for **girls** from rural communities beyond primary school.

Very few girls from rural communities in the High Atlas Mountains get the chance to further their education beyond the primary level – in rural Morocco, up to 83% of females are illiterate. Most secondary schools are located in larger towns several kilometres away, and parents struggle to afford lodging for their children. Many girls find themselves working or married at a very young age, without a chance to reach their full potential.

Opening its first **boarding house** in **Asni** in 2007, EFA now has five boarding homes in full operation for girls ages 12 to 18 years. Of those girls supported by EFA, over ninety percent pass national secondary school exams (Morocco's national average is just over fifty percent), with a high percentage going on to university.

Although casual visits to the boarding houses aren't normally possible, EFA organizes a number of fundraising events that are open to all, including the **Marrakesh Atlas Etape cycle race** (ⓦ marrakech-atlas-etape.com) each April, a challenging ride taking in one of North Africa's most beautiful and hardest climbs. You can also **donate** via EFA's website.

6

ARRIVAL AND DEPARTURE

IMLIL

By grand taxi The best and most straightforward way to get to Imlil is to take a shared *grand taxi* from Bab er Robb in Marrakesh to Asni (see page 315), from where you can take another *grand taxi* or minibus to Imlil (30min).

ACTIVITIES AND TOURS

A number of trekking, biking and day-tour companies operate in the region, and though most are based in Marrakesh (see page 332, at the top of the chapter), some have walk-in offices in Imlil itself (including *Toubkal Guide*; see page 332).

Mountain Travel Morocco In central Imlil ⓦ mountain-travel-morocco.com. Run by a handful of entrepreneurial local guides, offering treks and walking excursions for all levels of expertise.

ACCOMMODATION

Imlil has various **accommodation** options, ranging from hotels to refuges and *gîtes*. Small provisions shops and cafes line the main road through the village, and guests can have affordable **meals** at all of the local guesthouses. For a more authentic **Berber village** experience, stay in nearby **Tamatert** (2km east of Imlil, towards the Imenane Valley) or Aït **Souka** (midway between Imlil and Tamatert, but off the road, on the opposite side of the river). Another alternative is Armed (see page 343).

IMLIL AND AROUND

Authentic Toubkal 20min walk northwest of Imlil ⓦ authentictoubkallodge.com. The hospitable Berber family who run this place try to make its name ring as true as possible, from the rugs strewn about to couscous cooking demonstrations. All sorts of activities can be planned from here, and the viewing terrace is a grand spot to mull things over; rooms themselves are a mix of en suite and shared-facility. €€

Dar Adrar Douar Achain, 1km from Imlil in the direction of Armed ⓦ daradrar.com. A 15min uphill walk from Imlil (consider a mule if you have heavy luggage), this established trekking base is a charming mountain guesthouse with en suite rooms, great food, nice sitting areas, and family rooms. Meals are prepared on site. €

Gîte Tamsoulte West of centre ⓦ gitetamsoulte.com. As far down the price range as you'll want to go, this is actually quite an attractive little gîte, with three rooms which are small and bare, but acceptably clean. The owners are friendly sorts, and able to whip up breakfast with advance warning. €

Kasbah Du Toubkal A 20min walk from Imlil ⓦ kasbah toubkal.com. An eco retreat, perched up high in a magical setting – after a pick-up at their Imlil office (with luggage transported on mules) it takes a trek through apple orchards and walnut groves to reach the front door. Managed by the local Berber community, with authentic Berber touches, it offers a range of accommodation, topping out with the luxuriant apartment suite whose large bay windows give unparalleled views of the High Atlas. Dinner is available. €€€€

AÏT SOUKA

Atlas Imoula Between Imlil and Aït Souka ⓦ atlas imoula.com. On the right side of the road as you head out of the centre of Imlil, just before reaching Ait Souka, this small guesthouse offers clean, comfortable rooms at a competitive price. BB €

Dar Aimane ⓣ 0662 154189. This guesthouse, located on the Tamatert road, proffers amazing views of the Imlil Valley. Run by long-time mountain guides, it boasts open fires, bathrooms, a/c in all rooms, and heating through the winter. Laundry service possible, and scrumptious dinners available. €

★ **Riad Atlas Chateau** ⓦ riadatlaschateau.com. Owned by Driss Lachguer, a popular Berber mountain guide, this family-run guesthouse provides spacious, pristine rooms with private bathrooms (except some cheaper rooms), plus a/c and heating. Solid breakfasts included. Other meals available (€€). BB €

TAMATERT

★ **Douar Samra Imlil** ⓦ douar-samra.net. An artsy haven tucked into a local Berber village, this little establishment has more pizzazz than you might expect. With a *Swiss Family Robinson*, life-in-the-trees feel, rooms are comfy and inviting; some are lit only by candles, while others have electricity. Mini-suites are recommended, although the grand prize goes to the tree house (HB €€€). HB €€

Imlil Lodge Between Imlil and Tamatert ⓦ imlil-lodge. com. Owned by an English-speaking official mountain guide (the fellow behind *Toubkal Guide* trekking company), this well-designed lodge has quaint, affordable rooms, most with private bathrooms – they're the area's best option at this price level. Private parking and luggage storage while trekking are available, and they offer good-value transfers from Marrakesh. €

Kasbah Imlil ⓣ 0661 417636. This well-established, family-run guesthouse is found at the very top of Tamatert village. It provides smart, clean, comfortable rooms, while the roof-terrace restaurant offers wonderful views right across the Aït Mizane valley towards Tizi Mizzik. BB €

Riad Toubkal Ecolodge ⓦ toubkalecolodge.com. Owned by an official mountain guide, this relatively new guesthouse is found on the northern edge of Tamatert, affording excellent views across the surrounding countryside; with beautifully decorated rooms, it represents an excellent choice within this price bracket. BB €

Armed

The largest village of the Mizane Valley, **ARMED** is an extraordinary-looking place, built on a huge moraine spur above the valley at 1960m. Steep-tiered fields of potatoes, onions, barley and various kinds of fruit line the valley sides, their terraces edged with purple iris. The village is used as a base or overnight stop by a number of trekking companies, and several houses have been converted to well-equipped *gîtes*.

The forty-five-minute **walk from Imlil to Armed** (also called Aroumd, Around or Aremd) follows the banks of the Mizane River southwards, and makes a nice excursion. On the west side there's a well-defined mule track that zigzags above the river for about 2km before dropping to cross a bridge across the valley and heading up into the village. On the east bank, there's a more interesting (though rough) path – much the same distance, and only slightly harder to follow.

ARRIVAL AND DEPARTURE ARMED

By public transport To reach Armed from Marrakesh, you first need to get to Imlil (see page 341) from where it's a relatively short walk to Armed.
With a private vehicle For those accustomed to navigating mountain roads, there's a *piste* connecting Imlil and Armed; however, it can get precarious, especially in the winter, and in general it's much better to park in Imlil and walk.

ACCOMMODATION

There's only one small shop in Armed, so if you're cooking for yourself it's best to bring supplies with you. Otherwise, every guesthouse can provide **meals** at reasonable costs.

★ **Dar Warawte** Village centre ☎ 0670 414623. An impressive yet affordable lodge owned by a renowned local guide (who can set up quality treks with top-notch equipment, food, and support), located right in the centre of the village. With views of the surrounding valleys and Toubkal, it's a superb base to start or end your journey, and offers dormitory, budget and deluxe rooms and a private hammam. The deluxe rooms on the upper floor (€€) have their own bathrooms with shower and a great terrace. Lunch and dinner also available for pre-booked guests (ask ahead for *rfissa* – a wonderful lentil dish). BB dorm €, double €

Dar Bab Toubkal At the trailhead ☎ 0661 873771. Right up where the hikes begin, this is a surprisingly large structure hereabouts – four whole levels, and very sturdy-looking. The agreeable owners have really put some effort in with the furnishings and decoration, and some rooms sleep three or four. BB €

★ **Dar Imperial** East rise of village ⓦ darimperial. com. This rustic lodge a prime location above the village, and simple rooms sleeping one to four. Meals on site are superb) and best ordered in the morning – the done thing is to have breakfast up on the roof, taking in a commanding view of the surrounds, then return there before dusk with a cup of something hot. BB €

Roches Aremd South of village centre ⓦ rochesaremd. com. A popular overnight spot for local trekking companies, this lovely "lodge of rocks" has four clean rooms, all with shared bathrooms and jazzy bedspreads. Meals can also be prepared on site, and eaten on the roof-with-a-view. BB €

Climbing Toubkal

Most trekkers leaving Imlil or Armed are en route for the **ascent of Jebel Toubkal** – a walk rather than a climb after the snows have cleared, but serious business nonetheless. From Imlil, it's three hours to the pilgrimage site of **Sidi Chamharouch**, followed by another three to four hours to the **Toubkal refuges** (3207m; 12km from Imlil; 6–7hr in all), which lie at the foot of Toubkal's final slopes.

The majority of hikers start for the refuges early to mid-morning, in order to stay the night. Then, you'll have a fresh start at first light the next morning for the ascent of Toubkal, which will allow for the clearest panorama from the peak – afternoons can be cloudy and inclement weather can move in fast. Arriving at the Toubkal refuges early in the day also gives you time to acclimatize to the altitude and rest: many people find the hardest part of the trek is the last hour before arriving at the refuges, so it's important to take it easy.

Note that the ascent of Jebel Toubkal is, for some, merely the first (or last) stage of a longer loop route departing Imlil, which takes six days (see page 345 for the remainder).

Armed to Sidi Chamharouch

From Armed, the **Toubkal trail** goes up the flood plain, with unavoidable stream crossings, which are only sometimes problematic in the spring after periods of rain or snowmelt (arrange a mule ride with your guesthouse if so). At the end of the flood plain the track zigzags up to make its way to the gorge high above. If you've been following the main mule trail on the west side of the valley from Imlil (see page 341), you can continue without going into Armed.

The river is crossed by bridge once more just before you arrive at the hamlet of **SIDI CHAMHAROUCH** (1hr 30min–2hr from Armed). Set beside small waterfalls, this is a disordered row of cafes, all built into one another. Its seasonal population of a dozen or so run grocery shops for trekkers and Moroccan pilgrims, who come to the village's *marabout* **shrine** – a boulder sited across the river from the village and reached by a concrete bridge that non-Muslims are strictly forbidden to cross. The shrine is probably a survival of a very ancient nature cult – in these parts often thinly veiled by the trappings of Islam; on the approach to the village you may notice a tree, sacred to local tradition, where Berbers hang strips of cloth and make piles of stones. Although it seems pristine, avoid drinking any untreated water here, or around the Toubkal huts.

Sidi Chamharouch to the Toubkal refuges

Beyond Sidi Chamharouch, the Toubkal trail climbs steeply in zigzags, and then traverses the flank of the valley well above the Mizane. The trail is clear the whole way to the **Toubkal refuges**, which, at 3207m, often mark the spring snow line. In winter the snow line can drop to Sidi Chamharouch, and mules have to be replaced by porters, which should be arranged before your trip in Imlil or Armed.

ACCOMMODATION   **SIDI CHAMHAROUCH TO THE TOUBKAL REFUGES**

After sunset, it feels pretty cold at the two refuges, even in mid-August. Both are open throughout the year, and have hot showers, sitting rooms and kitchens.

Les Mouflons ⊕0524 449767, ⊛refugetoubkal.com. This nicely equipped lodge has a slightly larger community area than the Toubkal Refuge (though it's slightly colder), and has an open, alpine feel. Meals €€. Dorm beds €, doubles €

Toubkal Refuge ⊕0661 695463, ⊛refugedutoubkal. com. This older shelter has a bit more rustic appeal than *Les Mouflons*. The sitting area is kept warm, and there's some mobile phone coverage. Eating areas are shared, and chatting with other trekkers makes for a nice evening; it's always crowded in March/April (ski-touring season) and July–September (trekking season). Meals cost €, and reviews are mixed. Dorm beds €

The Toubkal refuges to the summit

At the Toubkal refuges you're almost bound to meet people who've just come down from **Jebel Toubkal** – and you should certainly take advantage of talking to them and the refuge *gardiens* for an up-to-the-minute description of the routes and the state of the South Cirque (Ikhibi Sud) trail to the summit. If you don't feel too confident about going it alone, take a guide – sometimes they are available at the refuges – Make sure that you take your time, allowing your body to acclimatize slowly to the altitude changes (see page 346).

The South Cirque

The **South Cirque** (Ikhibi Sud) gives the most popular and straightforward ascent of Toubkal: depending on your fitness, it should take between two and a half and four hours to the summit (2–2hr 30min to descend). There is a path, polished in parts, which is easy enough to follow, although it can be quite slippery underfoot. More of a problem is finding the right track down through the upper slopes of loose scree. Take your time coming down, since it can be rough on the knees.

The **trail** begins above the Toubkal Refuge, dropping down to cross the stream and then climbing again to reach the first of Toubkal's innumerable fields of boulders and scree. These are the most tiring (and memorable) features of the trek up, and it can be gruelling for inexperienced walkers. The **summit**, a sloping plateau of stones marked by a large metal tripod, is eventually reached after the serpentine path brings you to the spectacular southern cliffs. It should be stressed that **in winter** even this easiest of routes is a **snow climb**, and best for experienced hikers or those climbing with a guide. Slips can and have had fatal consequences. If you are properly equipped, check out the start the night before, and set off early. Ice axes and crampons are essential in icy conditions, and note that this is also a splendid ski route.

The North Cirque
An alternative ascent – though longer (4hr 30min) and best for more experienced climbers – is the **North Cirque** (Ikhibi Nord). En route you will pass the remains of an aircraft that crashed while flying arms to Biafra; the cairn of Tibherine, the small peak dominating the valley, is actually one of its engines. The final ridge to the summit area calls for some scrambling. You could descend (2hr–2hr 30min) by the South Cirque back down to the refuges.

6

The Grand Toubkal Loop

The **Grand Toubkal Loop** takes six days and makes a satisfying, and very scenic, addition to the ascent of Toubkal. From the Toubkal refuges, the loop heads south to scenic **Lac d'Ifni**, then north to **Azib Likemt and Tacheddirt**, before returning to **Imlil**. The walk is fairly strenuous, but can be done by most fit walkers. Following the route in this direction is recommended, since it means finishing more of the harder portions in the morning and descending – rather than climbing – one of the most gruelling ascents in all of Africa (especially in the heat or snow).

For the first part of the walk, be sure to carry plenty of **water** and enough **food** for up to two to three days, since there are no reliable facilities until you get past Lac d'Ifni; you'll need to bring a tent, too, though with your own mat and sleeping bag it's possible to overnight in shepherds' huts by Lac d'Ifni. The walk is best done from late May to mid-October; in winter the passes of Tizi n'Ouanoums (3664m) and Tizi Likemt (3555m) can be closed with deep snow; in these conditions, those with hefty mountaineering experience and proper equipment – including crampons, ropes and ice axes – can attempt the trek without much issue.

Day 1: Imlil to the Toubkal refuges
The first day of the **trail** heads from Imlil to the Toubkal refuges; the account of this section was covered earlier in this chapter (see page 349).

Day 2: Toubkal refuges to Azib Imi n'Ouassif
From Toubkal refuges, the trail climbs up a rough, stony slope and then winds round to the head of the Mizane Valley towards the imposing **Tizi n'Ouanoums**, a narrow pass which takes around an hour to reach. The path continues onward and downward to **Azib Imi n'Ouassif** (2800m) along the Assif n'Moursaine riverbed, which you'll cross back and forth several times. It usually takes three hours to reach here from the refuges, and it makes a good place to stop (or camp) for the first night, although it's extremely hot in the summer as the river valley absorbs the sun's heat all day long. Alternatively, you might want to push on for a couple more hours to Lac d'Ifni, where you can camp in shepherds' huts (see below).

Day 3: Azib Imi n'Ouassif to Amsouzert via Lac d'Ifni
The walk from **Azib Imi to Lac d'Ifni** is fairly straightforward, though be warned that the path down the valley is steep and scree-filled, and the lake doesn't come back into sight until you're almost there. When you do finally see it, **Lac d'Ifni** is a memorable sight, its only human habitations a few shepherds' huts (*azibs*), and the only sound that of water idly lapping on the shore. Incredibly, a small **café** here (usually closed in winter) offers minimal but welcome refreshments. From the north side of the lake, follow the path east to the valley above Imhilene, and beyond it joins a road to the village of

6

ATLAS TREKKING PRACTICALITIES

EQUIPMENT AND EXPERIENCE

Unless you're undertaking a particularly long or ambitious trek – or are here in winter conditions – there are no technical problems to hold anyone back from trekking in the Toubkal area, or climbing the peak itself. However, the mountain needs to be taken seriously. You must have decent **footwear and clothing** – it's possible to be caught out by summer storms as well as bad winter conditions – and you should be prepared to camp out if you are going on longer treks (or find the Toubkal refuges full). In winter and spring, depending on conditions, you might need an ice axe and crampons; these can be hired in Imlil. It's important to keep to a **gentle pace** until you are properly acclimatized as altitudes of 3000–4000m can be very demanding, especially when combined with the midday heat and walking over long sections of rough boulders or loose scree.

SEASONS

Toubkal is usually under **snow** from November until May, and experienced mountaineers can enjoy some classic climbs, ski ascents and treks in winter, though be cautious of storms. In spring, the best trekking lies below the snow line, and less experienced trekkers should only aim for the summit when the snow has gone. In all cases, take local advice before you climb.

ALTITUDE

Toubkal is 4167m above sea level, and much of the surrounding region stands above 3000m, so **the risk of acute mountain sickness (AMS)**, also referred to as altitude sickness, must be taken seriously. Although rare, the possible outcomes include death. Moving too hurriedly into higher altitudes is its major cause, so it's important to pace your ascent, allowing your body time to **acclimatize**. One of the best ways to do this is to spend at least one night in the Imlil or Armed area before setting off for the Toubkal basecamps; this should give your body time to adjust through the night. If you do develop a bad headache, dizziness, confusion or more than slight breathlessness and feel like vomiting, it is imperative that you descend straight away: descending by a few hundred metres usually brings about immediate relief.

Make sure that you are fully familiar with the signs and symptoms of AMS before you head for the Atlas Mountains (such as by reading a specialist trekking guide book) and be prepared to take appropriate action if you suffer from any of them. Equally, look out for the signs and symptoms in others; often those suffering with AMS cease to think clearly and therefore fail to recognise the signs in themselves; the intervention of others can therefore be critical.

ACCOMMODATION

Official **gîtes** are found at a number of villages in the High Atlas. These are often the homes of mountain guides, who can provide mules and assistance, as well as food, showers, toilets and sometimes hammams. All official *gîtes* are graded by the tourist authorities, who may have lists of them. In villages where there are none, it is usually possible to find a room to rent; just ask around. There are also two CAF **refuge huts** in the heart of the mountains (see page 349), plus designated areas for camping. Bring a tent and warm sleeping bag – nights can be freezing, even in summer, and you must use the toilet facilities provided.

GUIDES, MULES AND COOKS

Official mountain guides can be found in Imlil, as well as at a number of the larger villages in the Toubkal region. Always ask to see their official documentation before engaging anyone as your guide, as there are many active untrained *"faux guides"* in the area. **Mules**, too, can be hired to carry your baggage and camping equipment, usually in association with a muleteer.

Guides' level of expertise and quality can vary greatly. If hiring a mule, one can usually be shared between two/sometimes three people when on shorter treks requiring less baggage. If you're setting out from Imlil, say, for Lac d'Ifni, or the Toubkal or Tazaghart refuges, a mule can be a very worthwhile investment. It is customary to tip the guide and muleteer at the end of your trek; this is entirely discretionary and should not be disproportionate to their wages. You will also need to pay a small fee to the car park supervisor in Imlil if you've left your car there.

A further advantage of hiring a guide is that you can negotiate for them to buy all provisions for your trek, to prepare meals and even to provide a specialist cook (for a charge, of course). A specialist cook will cost you just a little more than a muleteer, although sometimes the guide or muleteer himself will perform both duties for a small additional supplement.

Note that, contrary to often repeated assertions, guides and muleteers are generally very willing to work during the month of **Ramadan** (see page 44), though since most will want to be home with their families in time for the Eid festivities, you may need to work your dates around this.

WATER

Bottled spring water is often available in villages, and sometimes even along the side of main trails in the Toubkal National Park. However, giardiasis **bacteria** is present in many streams and rivers downriver from human habitation (including the Toubkal refuges), so purification tablets (or battery-operated water-treating UV lights, or a quality filter pump) are strongly recommended, along with the additional precaution of boiling the water.

CLOTHES

Even in summer you'll need a warm sweater or jacket and a wind-breaker, as well as waterproofs in case of afternoon storms. Hiking boots are ideal, although you can get by with a decent pair of hiking trainers. The sun is very strong here, making a hat, sunblock and sunglasses essential, while gloves and a warm hat are very useful for evenings. In winter, full mountaineering clothing is always required.

OTHER THINGS TO BRING

You can buy **food** in Asni, Imlil and some of the other villages – or negotiate meals in the places where you overnight – though this becomes increasingly expensive the higher and the more remote you get (one can avoid this problem by hiring a specialist cook; see above). Water purification tablets or filtering systems are worthwhile on longer trips, as are stomach pills, insect repellent and wet wipes (which should be used on hands before meals).

Children often ask for *bonbons, stylos, dirhams* and *cadeaux*, but it's better if you don't oblige since this only increases expectations of future trekkers. A worthwhile contribution that you can make to the local economy is to trade or give away some of your gear at the end of your journey – this is always welcomed by guides and muleteers.

GUIDEBOOKS AND MAPS

There are limitless Atlas trekking routes, only a selection of which are detailed here. For other ideas, engage a professional guide or invest in one of the Atlas Mountain trekking **guidebooks**; *Moroccan Atlas: the Trekking Guide* by Alan Palmer (Trailblazer) is recommended.

Large-scale survey **maps** are available for the region; most are 1:100,000, though Toubkal is also mapped at 1:50,000 and even 1:40,000. These – and the guidebook mentioned above – are best obtained in advance from specialist map/travel shops outside of Morocco, though occasionally guides or shops in Imlil or Oukaïmeden, or *Hôtel Ali* in Marrakesh (see page 316) have some maps to sell.

SKI-TOURING

The Toubkal Massif is popular with **ski-mountaineering** groups from February to April. Most of the *tizis* (passes) – and Jebel Toubkal and other peaks – can be ascended in this manner, and there's an *Haute Route* linking the huts. The descent from Toubkal summit to Sidi Chamharouch is as fine as any. The Toubkal refuges can get pretty crowded at these times; the Tazaghart refuge can make a quieter base for serious winter trekkers.

Amsouzert, reached in around three hours after the lake. This reasonably sized village has decent **accommodation** options (see page 348), which all serve meals, and is your last chance to stock up on **provisions** (or to bail on the hike due to illness or bad weather, since the road here leads out of the mountains to the south).

Day 4: Amsouzert to Azib Likemt

The walk from **Amsouzert to Azib Likemt** takes a solid seven to nine hours, so aim to depart early, with ample food and water supplies. From Amsouzert, the path continues north up the valley to reach **Tagadirt** in just over two hours. From Tagadirt, the path heads northwest towards **Tizi n'Ououraine** (3124m); once you reach the river, known as the **Assif n'Tinzer**, bear north along the well-marked path heading along the majestic river gorge. You'll start out on the west side of the ridge before crossing onto the eastern side. By the time you reach **Azib Likemt**, you'll have crossed the river a handful of times. Some of the precipitous ridge walking isn't for the faint of heart, but the stunning views make it a worthwhile endeavour; take care when camping, as this upper valley is notorious for scorpions. The country east of Azib Likemt, the **Kissaria Gorges**, is wild in the extreme, and too hard even for mules.

Day 5: Azib Likemt to Tacheddirt

Leaving the lush pastureland of Azib Likemt will take some fortitude as you head off on one of the most boulder- and scree-ridden walks in the Atlas; varied scenery makes this six- to seven-hour walk fly by, but the change in altitude (and possible changes in weather) necessitate an early start. From Azib Likemt, the path heads along the west side of the river gorge to the impressive **Tizi Likemt** (3555m) pass, about three hours along. Continue heading along the well-worn path northwest – still along the river – towards **Tacheddirt** (2314m), which takes a further two to three hours to reach. You can spend the night here (see page 350); alternatively, push on for a couple of kilometres to the lesser-visited village of Ouanesekra (see page 348), or use Tacheddirt for side-trips away from the loop described here (see page 349).

Day 6: Tacheddirt to Imlil

More a scenic walk of four to five hours than a trek, day five provides a well-merited respite after the previous, longer days. From Tacheddirt, a road runs to Imlil (and there's some transport, if desired). This is the easiest path to follow, but a more rewarding route (5–6hr) is to walk twenty minutes west to **Ouanesekra**, a pleasant mountain hamlet with some small provision shops. Continue west to Tamguist and then head north to Tinerhourhine, in the direction of Ikiss; just before Ikiss, an easily spotted mule path heads west to Tizi n'Aguersioual (2050m), where you'll need to go southwest to Aguersioual and continue south along the Mizane Valley to Imlil.

ACCOMMODATION   **THE GRAND TOUBKAL LOOP**

The following places offer basic mountain accommodation, and can all provide food as well. Note that rooms are also available in Tacheddirt (see page 350).

AMSOUZERT

Gîte Himmi Omar Offers beds in basic dorms with shared bathroom; to find it, ask at one of the local cafés or shops. Note that it's usually closed in winter, due to passes being blocked by snow. €

OUANESEKRA

Gîte Gressafen ☏ 0667 968617. Trekkers can get to this simple *gîte* during winter without too much issue. There's a fireplace on site, but call ahead to have a supply of firewood stocked up. €

Gîte Ouanesekra A no-frills establishment that makes a passable place to spend the night; has few amenities and no fireplace for the winter. €

West of Imlil

While most trekkers set their sights on Toubkal and its impressive backstage of Lac d'Ifni and lofty summer pastures, the west side of the national park also offers some stunning walks and access to lesser-visited villages. This area of the park contrasts with other regions with its infinite panoramic views – you're not as tucked into the valleys, or in the shadow of Toubkal. In particular, the area **west of Imlil** offers a good acclimatization trek to **Tizi Oussem** village, from where you can continue westbound to **Ourigane**, making this a worthwhile two-day trek. A harder trek from Imlil climbs to the **Tazaghart Refuge** (accessible also in reverse on a yet more difficult trail from the Toubkal refuges and Armed). For both routes, you'll first need to head to **Tizi Mzik**, where the path forks.

6

To Tizi Oussem and Ourigane
Taking the right (southwest) fork at Tizi Mzik will soon bring you to the village of **TIZI OUSSEM**, in the next valley west of Imlil (about four hours in total), which makes a good place to spend the night (see below) before continuing to the Ourigane Valley. The walk from Tizi Oussem to Ourigane is a long day's journey (6–7hr); as you set off, keep initially to the east bank and then drop onto the flood plain to cross to the west bank at a narrowing. The path keeps high then zigzags down to cross the river to gain height again on the east side, passing the walled farm-village of **Azerfsane**, beyond which the path swings west and drops to the river again, where a mule track on the left bank helps guide you to the top. From here, you can choose to follow a *piste* west to **Ourigane** or northwest to **Marigha**. It's easier to get transport back to Marrakesh from Marigha (and saves about 45 minutes of walking); if you continue onward to Ourigane, you can stay in local lodging or head to Marrakesh.

To the Tazaghart and Toubkal refuges
Taking the left fork instead at Tizi Mzik will bring you, via a hillside path and an ascent, to the **Tazaghart Refuge** (also known as *Lépiney*); 5–6 hr from Imlil, this offers stunning views over the national park's western half, and functions as a climbing base for the fine cliffs of **Tazaghart**.

From the Tazaghart Refuge, there are three ways to access the **Toubkal refuges**, each increasing in difficulty the further south you go. The most common and **easiest** route (5hr) is to head east over the **Tizi Aguelzim**, where the well-worn trail continues south to the Toubkal refuges. Alternatively, you can continue southward from the Tazaghart Refuge and then bear east towards the **Tizi n'Tadat**. This trail eventually connects to and heads south on the trail leading to the Toubkal refuges (6hr). The third and **most difficult** path, which should be reserved for experienced and well-geared trekkers (especially in winter), is via **Tizi Melloul** (3–4 hr from the Tazaghart Refuge). Following this, the trail bears east and then north for two to three hours, bringing you to the south end of the Toubkal refuges (see page 349 for the Toubkal ascent).

West of Tizi Melloul is the extraordinary **Tazaghart Plateau** (3843m) with its fine vistas of the entire region. This side trip takes up to five hours round trip, and should also only be attempted by experienced trekkers, especially in winter.

ACCOMMODATION   **WEST OF IMLIL**

★ **Gîte Tizi Oussem** In the centre of Tizi Oussem, off the main gravel thoroughfare through town. This *gîte* may be one of the best you'll stay in on any trek in the High Atlas. Well run and welcoming, you can have meals prepared for you (€) or make your own, and an on-site hammam makes the trek here worthwhile. €

Tazaghart Refuge Also known as the *Lépiney*, this offers basic accommodation in dorms; facilities are minimal, with a shared (non-Western) toilet, no shower or hot water, solar panel electricity for lights only, and no fireplace. To get access, you may have to go back down to Tizi Oussem (a 12km/4hr walk away) to get the hut *gardien* to open it up. €

Tacheddirt
Offering unparalleled views over the Inemane Valley, the expansive scenery around **TACHEDDIRT** (2000m), 8km east of Imlil, is wonderfully photogenic. The village itself is a bustling mix of what was and what is: mud homes meet concrete structures,

somehow working together to keep the place serene, diverse and alive. Tacheddirt makes a delightful base from which to explore the surrounding mountains; the **trek to Setti Fatma** is one of the most scenic, satisfying, and challenging of various options.

Tacheddirt to Setti Fatma

The trek from **Tacheddirt to Setti Fatma** is one of the best routes for anyone contemplating more than a simple day-trip into the hills; taken at a reasonable pace, it takes two days. There's a well-defined mule track, which becomes a *piste* beyond Timichi, all the way so no particular skills are needed; general fitness is required, however, and several sections of the trail are quite exposed and steep. You'll probably want to carry some food supplies with you, although cooking gear and provisions are not essential since meals (and rooms) are offered at the village of **Timichi**.

   Tacheddirt to Timichi is a superb day's walk. The first three hours or so are spent zigzagging up to the **Tizi n'Tacheddirt** (3272m), a route with ever more spectacular views. Green terraced fields give way to rough and craggy mountain slopes, before the path down crosses one of the more barren sections. As you approach Timichi the valley again becomes more cultivated and the area has several *gîtes*, making it a good overnight stop.

Tacheddirt to Asni

There's a long but straightforward *piste* from Tacheddirt down-valley to **Asni**, taking seven to nine hours. It's an enjoyable route through a fine valley – a good (and neglected) exit from the mountains. You could also do this route from Imlil, heading off down from the Tizi n'Tamatert (1hr from Imlil) to the bottom of the valley at Tinhourine. If you want to camp out at night, there are possible places to pitch a tent below Ikiss or Arg, and there are also *gîtes* at Ikiss and Amsakrou (60dh/person). A fine pass rises opposite Ikiss to cross a *tizi* to Aguersioual and so back to Imlil, an excellent round trip.

ARRIVAL AND DEPARTURE
TACHEDDIRT

By public transport From Marrakesh, *grands taxis* to Asni depart from Bab er Robb (see page 315) at frequent but irregular times (90 mins); from Asni, local minibuses connect to Tacheddirt (1hr 30min), but only between 8am and noon, though sometimes it's possible to get one as late as 2pm, and they are especially frequent on Saturday (market day).

On foot You can walk to Tacheddirt from Imlil in 3–4hr (see page 341).

By car It's possible to self-drive the road from Asni to Tacheddirt, via Imlil, but the terrain is rough and steep in places.

ACCOMMODATION

Gite Likemte Village centre ☎0615 906875. Most horizontal surfaces seem to be covered with rugs at this cheery *gîte*, whose colourful rooms (shared facilities only) are very good value. Food isn't included, but cheap meals are available. €̄

Tigmi Tacheddirt Village centre ☎0667 968617. This spacious and comfy lodge seated at the edge of the Imenane Valley offers the best accommodation in the region and was built by a local entrepreneur from Armed. The refuge has plenty of beds available for individuals and small groups, and is often used by trekkers passing through on various circuits. Self-catering apartments available as well. HB dorm €̄, double €̄

Ouirgane

OUIRGANE is an up-and-coming destination due to its proximity to Marrakesh and its stunning greenery, red-earth hills and pine forests, all of which combine to make it worth an overnight stay – or, of course, longer. It's a wonderful spot to rest up after a few days of trekking around Toubkal, and makes a pleasant base in itself for day-walks into the surrounding foothills, mountain-bike forays or horse riding. The village also hosts a small Thursday souk.

Both Ouirgane and the lush Marigha region heat up in the summer due to their indented position among the peaks, which means that while it's cooler than Marrakesh, it's still best to visit (or plan activities) here from February to May and mid-September to December.

Treks around Ouirgane

Day treks in Ouirgane are best done with a guide (see page 352). One recommended walk that you can request from a local expert is to start in **Marigha**, head south to the village of Marigha Izdern (1200m) and on to Imareghan Noufla (1220m), which has some stone olive oil presses still in use. From here, you'll head onward to **Tinzert**; enjoy the view of the Takherkhourte Peak (2500m) in the distance. From Tinzert, continue to Tagadirt n'Ousni and the village of Tamgounssi and down to Asni for transport back to Ouirgane or to Marrakesh. The total walking time is four to five hours.

6

Ouirgane to Imlil

Alternatively, walking from **Ouirgane to Imlil** is an overnight treat full of stunning views and steady climbing, and essentially the reverse of the route given in the Imlil section (see page 341). From Ouirgane (or easily followed on the road connecting Imarira and Tassa Ouirgane), head east towards Tassa Ouirgane, where the well-trodden path will take you along the edge of the beautiful **Azzadene Valley**. When you reach Azerfsane, head south along the major river valley, Assif n'Ouissadene, finally connecting to the town of Aït Aïssa (Id Aissa) after five to six hours, which has a couple of small *gîtes* offering basic accommodation and meals. From Aït Aïssa, continue south to Tizi Oussem where you'll change direction, heading east over Tizi Mzik, through Azib Mzikene, and finally into

---

BIKING THE MARIGHA CIRCUIT

Exploring the area around Ouirgane **by bike** is a great way to see more of this rich region via the backroads. One of the best circuits is the **Marigha Ciruit**, an 18km route that should take about three hours to complete.

Head southwest out of Ouirgane on the paved road to **Taroudant**. At a sign for *Chez Momo II*, take the left turn. Further, the paved entry becomes a gravel road as it heads uphill. Keep right and at the crest of the hill, you'll have a superb view of the Ouirgane barrage.

The views of the Azzadene Valley come into view as you continue uphill and the *piste* finally gives way to flat riding; continue along the same *piste* to the village of **Agouni** (which means hungry in the local dialect). The *piste* opens up at the edge of Agouni to an area once inhabited by a local Jewish population. The buildings are painted white (a rare feature, interpreted locally as holy ground), and the site comes to life every August for a private moussem celebration.

Behind the Jewish village, the *piste* splits – continue straight (slightly left) to stay on course. It's possible here to detour up to the stunning village of **Tikhfirst**, 4km away, by turning right and following the *piste* steeply uphill – sublime views over the countryside await. Local families are known for their tea-making, so this makes a nice point to refresh before heading back downhill.

Continue on the road past the Jewish settlement; within a few minutes you'll reach the village of **Anraz**, where the *piste* becomes a smooth single-track trail. You'll bike for a short distance through shady homesteads as the trail becomes a road again after half a kilometre at the village of **Torrort**. From here, take the *piste* downhill (left) to cross the bridge over the Assif n'Ouissadene. Just after this point, there's an intersection where you'll see a sign for Takhrkhort National Park. Turn left here towards **Tassa Ouirgane**; a right turn will take you, a few minutes later, to some of the best **views** of the entire ride – from here, backtrack to take the parth to Tassa Ouirgane.

From the intersection, head north along the well-maintained road, which connects to the Taroudant and Marrakesh road after about 5km. Here, turn left to return back to Ouigane.

the Mizane Valley and on to Imlil. This second day's walk also takes about five to six hours. From here you can continue up to Toubkal (see page 344).

ARRIVAL AND DEPARTURE	OUIRGANE

By bus There is one rather unreliable daily bus which departs for Taroudant from Marrakech's Bab Doukkala bus station at around 10am, passing through Ouirgane about an hour later.

Alternatively, you can travel to Asni (see page 339) and then take a *grand taxi* to Ouirgane, which is about 17km away.

ACTIVITIES

Bike rental Bikes should be rented from Marrakesh; most companies (see page 316 for recommendations) offer drop-off, experienced guides, other equipment and lunches. **Guides** Hotels often have local guides on hand, otherwise,

it's best to arrange one ahead of time (see page 346). **Horse riding** The equestrian centre at the *Résidence de la Roseraie* (see page 352) offers riding; book well in advance.

ACCOMMODATION AND EATING

All of the **hotels** listed below offer **meals**, which are usually available to both guests and non-guests. It's a good idea to book ahead, and preferably to have a clean pair of clothes to change into if you've been trekking.

Chez Momo A few km past Ouirgane on the main Taroudant road ⓦ aubergemomo.com. An attractive, quiet, garden-set hotel with a small pool. Rooms are clean, though a little basic for the price. The restaurant serves classic Berber dishes. BB €€

★ **Domaine Malika** 4km north of Ouirgane, just west of Maghira ⓦ domainemalika.com. Has been ranked among *Condé Nast Traveler*'s 100 Best Hotels in the World, this is a highly recommended luxury retreat with a two-night minimum stay. The affordable sumptuousness combines with freshly made gourmet meals to create a well-deserved respite after exploring the surrounding peaks and valleys. BB €€€€

★ **Kasbah Africa** Follow directions to Dar Tassa (see page 332), then signs to Kasbah Africa ⓦ kasbahafrica. com. This contemporary African retreat boasts modern decor that blends well into the surrounding landscape. The restaurant and common areas offer stunning views of the Azzadene Valley spreading into the horizon. All of the deluxe stone suites come with full amenities, plus some nice extras such as a telescope and chess set. The whole place is family-

friendly (with an attractive pool) and fun – a highlight is the pet donkey and small tortoise sanctuary on site. BB €€€€

L'Oliveraie de Marigha 4km north of Ouirgane, on the main road ☎ 0524 484281. This little gem, set in natural surrounds, makes a great spot for a retreat from Marrakesh. You can spend the day poolside, eating at their award-winning restaurant, and they can arrange pick-ups (both by car and, for the full VIP experience, helicopter) from Marrakesh. The rooms, suites and spacious bungalows are scattered through the lush gardens, and accessible rooms for the mobility impaired are also available. BB €€€€

Ouirgane Ecolodge Maghira ⓦ ouirgane-ecolodge.com. Owned by experienced mountain guide, Mohamed Aztat, this elegant small hotel has been developed with a firm commitment to ethical tourism. With just seven rooms, it is located in a beautiful setting beside the National Taghrghourte Reserve. BB €

Résidence de la Roseraie Centre of Ouirgane ⓦ laroseraiehotel.com. Once Ouirgane's most luxurious hotel, this place has benefitted from recent renovations (sadly not true of their website, at the time of writing). It has 45 appealing rooms scattered around a rose garden, and facilities include a swimming pool, spa, tennis courts, an equestrian centre and a renowned restaurant. BB €€€€

Amizmiz and around

The small, dusty town of **AMIZMIZ**, 58km from Marrakesh, is the site of a long-established **Tuesday souk** – one of the largest Berber markets of the Atlas, and not a key destination for tourists. The town comprises several quite distinct quarters, including a *zaouia*, kasbah and former Mellah, separated by a small, usually dry, river. Amizmiz makes a good base for mountain biking (see page 353) and trekking in the High Atlas.

From Amizmiz, the nearby village of **Aït Zitoun** is a lesser known yet much better place to start treks than Amizmiz, as you can arrange both mules and supplies here, along with a local guide. Aït Zitoun is a tricky place to find; it's located on a short *piste* veering left off the main road connecting Amizmiz to Ouirgane (look for a small sign for *Gîte Aït Zitoun*). It's possible to arrange a **walk to Ouirgane** from here, which takes three to four days and is best done in the cooler months. The walk is at a relatively low altitude for the mountains, and the surrounding hills are green in the spring months and roasted brown in the summer and autumn. For the most part, it's a steady, easy foray into villages, valleys and foothills, but there are some slightly steep inclines approaching the ridges.

An alternative to both of these villages for an overnight stop is **Lalla Takerkoust**, 22km northeast of Amizmiz. Views from the lake of the surrounding mountains make for wonderful photo opportunities in the winter with the surrounding snowcapped peaks in clear view. A few villages dot the landscape and walking to some of the low-lying hills for views of the region makes a worthwhile day's venture.

6

MOUNTAIN BIKING – AND SOME ROUTES FROM AMIZMIZ

Morocco offers some of the best **adventure riding** in the world with routes suitable for all abilities. The High Atlas has jeep and mule tracks that cover the countryside, and several **adventure companies** offer mountain biking as a pursuit (see page 332). Travelling independently, it's important to be aware of local sensibilities; ride slowly through villages, giving way to people where necessary, especially those on mules and children tending livestock. If **renting a bike**, negotiate essential extras like a pump, puncture repair kit and/or spare inner tube. A helmet is recommended, and carry plenty of water.

Of the **three routes** detailed below, the first two can be done by a novice with a rented bike, while the third is best left to the proficient, preferably on their own bike. All routes begin and end at *Le Source Bleu* (see page 354) in *Irghagn*, above Amizmiz. As few roads are signposted, the Amizmiz 1:100,000 **topographical map** is highly recommended, and best obtained from specialist map shops (see page 332) before you leave home.

ROUTE 1: THE OUED ANOUGAL CIRCUIT

From *Le Source Bleu*, descend to the *piste* road running from Amizmiz to Azegour and then head on uphill past the *Maison Forestière*. About 1.5km beyond, a narrow *piste* branches off left, taking you down the west side of the valley to pass through the village of Aït Ouskri, from where there are tremendous views up the valley, to Jebel Gourza and Jebel Imlit. The *piste* continues, passing the villages of Tizgui, Toug al Kheyr and, after 10km, Imi-n-Isli and Imi-n-Tala ("big spring"), before crossing the Anougal River below **Addouz** to the eastern side of the valley. Care should be taken **in spring**, when the river can become swollen from melted snow. Following the *piste* through Imzayn, and sticking to the lower track, leads to Igourdan and, after about 12km, uphill, to **Aït Hmad**.

Leaving Aït Hmad behind, the road widens to become a full-width *piste* jeep track allowing a fast but safe downhill back into Amizmiz.

ROUTE 2: JEBEL TIMERGHIT CIRCUIT

Follow the Route 1 description to Imi-n-Tala then take a *piste* westwards through the forest to reach **the Oued Erdouz road** from Azegour, with Jebel Timerghit towering above. Turn left and circuit the hill to **Toulkine** and on through the granite landscape towards Azegour. Five hundred metres before Azegour you come to a junction – turn left here, crossing a bridge over the Oued Wadakar, and continue past the remains of a mining site. The route then runs through forest and, after a gentle crest run, descends in numerous bends to Amizmiz, passing the *Maison Forestière*.

ROUTE 3: TOULKINE DESCENT

Begin the route in the same way as those above, but don't break off left as in Route 1. Keep on ahead for the long toil through the forest to gain the gentler crest before descending into the **Erdouz-Wadakar valley** where there are extensive ruins from the mining that once took place here. Cross the bridge and turn right to circuit round to Toulkine. A *piste* heads northwest from the village but instead follow the mule track that heads due north over the crest to circuit the valley heads with Adghous perched in the middle. This then wends through the **Jebel Aborji forest** before a rather brutal descent to the plains at Tiqlit. Note that it's advisable to check the route at Toulkine.

6

This area was badly impacted by the 2023 earthquake, but most buildings have now been repaired.

ARRIVAL AND DEPARTURE

AMIZMIZ
By public transport Amizmiz is best reached either by *grand taxi* from Bab er Robb in Marrakesh (see page 315), or on the Alsa City Bus (#45) from the same place (55min).

AÏT ZITOUN
By public transport Public transport does not go directly to Aït Zitoun – the best way to get here is from Amizmiz (or even Ouirgane) in a public or private-hired *grand taxi*; in Amizmiz, they depart from the centre of town. Whether from here or Ouirgane, ask the driver to stop at the Aït Zitoun sign, from where it's a 5min walk to the village. Coming back, you might be able to flag down a *grand taxi* headed for Amizmiz, but your best bet is to hire one privately.

AMIZMIZ AND AROUND

By car From Amizmiz, head in the direction of Ouirgane for 15km; look carefully for the sign to Aït Zitoun on the left. From Ouirgane, head in the direction of Amizmiz for 21km, and conversely look out for a sign on the right

LALLA TAKERKOUST
By public transport Lalla Takerkoust is most easily reached by *grand taxi* from Bab er Robb in Marrakesh (see page 315) at frequent but irregular times (40min); alternatively, you can take a *grand taxi* from Asni (see page 339).
By car The road (P2024) via the small town of Moulay Brahim along the Kik Plateau with views of the High Atlas is splendid, especially in winter and spring.

ACCOMMODATION

AMIZMIZ
Dar Achorafa 3km from Amizmiz towards Imintanout ⓦ achorafa.com. Comfortable and affordable, this is a peaceful escape dedicating both time and energy to local sustainable projects in the town and surrounding villages. Rooms are spacious and tidy, and the grounds well kept; the restaurant serves up tasty meals using produce grown on site. €€
★ **Maroc Lodge** 1km from Amizmiz towards Tizguine ⓦ maroc-lodge.com. A splendid retreat at any time of year, the four small villas here are great for couples or families. With an outdoor dining area, pool and heavenly gardens, it's a true escape into solitude after a day's trekking, and serves up first-rate meals. BB €€€€
Le Source Bleu Irghagn, 4km southwest of Amizmiz on the P2009 towards Azegour ☎ 0524 454595 or ☎ 0670 105714. A standard *auberge*, offering single, double and family rooms that are great for those on a budget. €

AÏT ZITOUN
Gîte Aït Zitoun 15km east of Amizmiz in the direction of Ouirgane; look for a very small sign on the left pointing down a gravel road to the gîte ☎ 0667 236045 or ☎ 06667 06308. This rustic guesthouse is a good base for arranging treks, through owner Ibrahim Ouahmane, and trekkers are invited to turn up without reservation.

Accommodation is in basic dorms with solid sponge mats serving as beds, and shared bathrooms. Good meals are available. HB €

LALLA TAKERKOUST AND AROUND
Dar Zitoune On the road from Moulay Brahim, 18km before Lalla Takerkoust ☎ 0662 408380. This affordable guesthouse is a diamond in the rough. With seven rooms (sleeping up to four), it's a solid middle-range place, and a great location to base yourself for paragliding and walking (in cooler months). There's a lovely small pool, a superbly manicured garden and great food available. €
Le Flouka Auberge Northwest shore of Lalla Takerkoust ⓦ leflouka-marrakech.com. Meaning "boat", this place has several accommodation options. A private apartment or villa is perfect for families or small groups, while the riad or regular rooms are better for individuals and couples. Great pool, meals and a "pirate ship" bar make it a fun place to stay. €€
Jnane Tihihit Douar Makhfamane, right on the edge of Lalla Takerkoust ⓦ riad-t.com. The former farm is now a relaxing rural guesthouse estate. Animals on site, and large grounds will make you want to stay; as befits the location, rooms are on the large side, and they're all delightful affairs. €€€

Ijoukak and around

IJOUKAK is an important market town where the Agoundis Valley joins the Nfis. Walking from Ijoukak, you can easily explore the **Tin Mal Mosque** and **Talaat n' Yakoub**, with its crumbling kasbah – or try some more prolonged trekking in the **Agoundis Valley**, which offers a two-day route to Toubkal.

Talaat n'Yakoub

2km southwest of Ijoukak

Just 2km southeast of Ijoukak, the village of **TALAAT N'YAKOUB** (which has an interesting mountain **souk** on Wed) is the site of the former **Goundafi kasbah** known locally as **Agadir n'Gouj**. Decaying and partially ruined, the medieval-looking kasbah (which actually dates from 1907) looms over the village from a dramatic hilltop setting – but you'll have to make do with admiring it from afar, as the building is currently **closed** to visitors.

6

Tin Mal Mosque

8km southwest of Ijoukak • Walkable from Ijoukak (around 1hr); alternatively, take a *grand taxi* from town

The Tin Mal Mosque, quite apart from its historic and architectural importance, is a beautiful monument – isolated above a lush reach of river valley, with harsh mountains backing its buff-coloured walls. It has been partially **restored** and is a very worthwhile stop. The mosque is set a little way above the modern village of **Tin Mal** (or Ifouriren) and reached by wandering uphill from the road bridge. The mosque was badly damaged in the 2023 earthquake and is currently closed.

Brief history

The mosque was finished by Abd el Moumen around **1153–54**, partly as a memorial to Ibn Toumert who started constructing it in 1125 as a Koranic school (*tinmil* means "school" in ancient Berber), and also as his own family's mausoleum. Obviously **fortified**, it probably served also as a section of the town's defences, since in the early period of Almohad rule Tin Mal was entrusted with the state treasury. Today, it is the only part of the fortifications – indeed, of the entire Almohad city – that you can make out with any clarity. The Almohad city had been home to twenty thousand Berbers before it was largely destroyed in the Merenid conquest of 1276.

That Tin Mal remained standing for that long, and that its mosque was maintained, says a lot about the power that Ibn Toumert's teaching must have continued to exercise over the local Berbers (see page 356). Even two centuries later the historian Ibn Khaldun found Koranic readers employed at the tombs and, when the French began restoration in the 1930s, they found the site littered with the shrines of *marabouts*.

The interior

Architecturally, Tin Mal presents a unique opportunity for **non-Muslims** to take a look at the interior of a traditional Almohad mosque. It is roofless, for the most part, and two of the corner pavilion towers have disappeared, but the mihrab (or prayer niche) and the complex pattern of internal arches is substantially intact. The arrangement is in a classic Almohad design – the T-shaped plan with a central aisle leading towards the mihrab – and is virtually identical to that of the Koutoubia in Marrakesh (see page 296), more or less its contemporary. The one element of eccentricity is in the placing of the **minaret** over the mihrab: a weakness of engineering design that meant it could never have been much taller than it is today. In terms of decoration, the most striking feature is the variety and intricacy of the **arches** – above all those leading into the mihrab, which have been sculpted with a stalactite vaulting. In the **corner domes** and the **mihrab vault** this technique is extended with impressive effect. Elsewhere, and on the face of the mihrab, it is the slightly austere geometric patterns and familiar motifs (the palmette, rosette, scallop, etc) of Almohad decorative gates that are predominant.

The Agoundis Valley

Aït Youl walkable from Ijoukak (a long all-day round-trip) • Enquire at *Berber Homestay* (see page 356) about the sporadic public transport up the valley

Winding east from Ijoukak, the **Agoundis Valley** offers an alternative access to Toubkal; it takes two days of serious trekking from Ijoukak to reach the Toubkal refuges. On foot, from Ijoukak head out on the Marrakesh road, cross the Oued Agoundis river bottom and turn right onto the up-valley road, passing several *gîtes*. The scenery opens up to distant peaks and there are a surprising number of villages. After an hour's walking you reach the wreck of an old mineral processing plant, a gondola still high in the air on a cable stretched across the valley to mines that closed decades ago. Continue walking to the village of **Taghbart** where there is a fork; take the right branch to cross the river, which makes an impressive ascent to the 2202m **Tizi-n-Ou-Ichddane** on the Atlas watershed. The Agoundis *piste* soon passes **El Makhzen** and a prominent house in wedding-cake style before becoming progressively narrower, exposed and rough, passing perched villages and ending at the village of **Aït Youl**. From here, strong walkers can reach the Toubkal Refuge in a day (see page 344), crossing the **Tizi n'Ougane** (risk of snow on the final slopes from November through May), passing through wild gorges and screes on the way.

ARRIVAL AND DEPARTURE
IJOUKAK AND AROUND

By bus or taxi *Grands taxis* (2hr 15min) or a daily bus, from Bab er Robb, but it's easier to go via Asni (see page 339). To reach Talaat n'Yakoub, you can take a local taxi onwards from the town centre (5min or so).

ACCOMMODATION

There are limited accommodation options in Ijoukak; if you get stuck, consider a room in nearby Talaat n' Yakoub, and there's another option past Tin Mal, on the way to Tizi n'Test. ★ **Auberge Tigmmi n'Tamazirte** 3km south of Ijoukak ⓦ tigmmi-ntmazirte.com. Standing proud like a child-sized fort, this simple auberge has a couple of drawcards – the view from the terrace is just wonderful, and the on-site hammam helps guests to soothe away the day's exertions. All rooms are en suite, and decorated with Berber flourishes. Great meals. They run a number of workshops and classes (including pottery and essential oils), and offer various trekking and mountain-biking opportunities. BB €
Berber Homestay Central Ijoukak ⓦ berberhomestay. com. Just what it says on the tin, the Berber family here delight in teaching guests the ways of their people – if you've ever fancied making your own couscous or tajines, here's your chance. Rooms are well tended, and there are en suite options available. BB €
Dar El Mouahidens Located 8km past Ijoukak on the main road to Taroudant ☎ 0676 253452. The only

IBN TOUMERT AND THE ALMOHADS

Tin Mal's site seems now so remote that it is difficult to imagine a town ever existing in this valley. In some form, though, it did. It was here that **Ibn Toumert** and his lieutenant, **Abd el Moumen**, preached to the Berber tribes and welded them into the **Almohad** ("unitarian") movement; here that they set out on the campaigns which culminated in the conquest of all Morocco and southern Spain; and here, too, a century and a half later, that the Almohads made their last stand against the incoming Merenid dynasty.

Known to his followers as the *Mahdi* – "The Chosen One", whose coming is prophesied in the Hadith (Sayings of The Prophet) – Toumert was born in the High Atlas, a member of the Berber-speaking Masmouda tribe, who held the desert-born Almoravids, the ruling dynasty, in contempt. For Toumert, Almoravid Morocco contained much to disapprove of and, returning from the East – where he formulated the strict Almohad doctrines – with a small group of disciples, he began to preach against all manifestations of luxury and against women mixing in male society.

After being exiled from the Almoravid capital, Marrakesh, in 1124, Ibn Toumert and Abd el Moumen set out to mould the Atlas Berbers into a religious and military force. They also stressed the significance of the "second coming" and Ibn Toumert's role as *Mahdi*. Hesitant tribes were branded "hypocrites" and massacred – most notoriously in the Forty-Day Purge of the mountains – and within eight years none remained outside Almohad control.

TREKKING THE TICHKA PLATEAU

Exploring the **Tichka Plateau** and the **western fringes of the High Atlas**, you move well away from established tour-group routes and pass through Berber villages that scarcely ever see a foreigner. On the approach to the plateau you might be invited to stay in a Berber village home, but otherwise you must be prepared to camp on the plateau itself where there is no permanent settlement. Carry all provisions, and means of purifying your drinking water. Sanitation is often poor in the villages, although eating and drinking in village homes is safe, as the food (mainly tajines) is thoroughly cooked and the drink is invariably mint tea.

However you approach it, the Tichka Plateau is a delight. Grazing is controlled so in spring the meadows are a mass of early daffodils and flowers. **Imaradene** (3351m) and **Amendach** (3382m) are the highest summits, west and east, and both make superlative viewpoints. The plateau is drained through the Oued Nfis gorge, itself fed by numerous side-gorges, first passing below the Tiziatin oak forest then underscoring a series of villages, one of which – called Imlil, but not *that* Imlil – has a shrine to Ibn Toumert, the founder of the Tin Mal/Almohad dynasty.

There are three **approaches** to the Tichka Plateau, from the west (via **Imi n'Tanoute**, at the junction of the N8 and R212 and on the main Marrakesh–Agadir bus route, and **Timesgadiouine**), the south (via **Taroudant and Ouled Berhil**) and the east (via the Tizi n'Test road).

Budget permitting, it is most efficient to hire **4x4 transport with driver** to transfer you, possibly with your guide, to meet a pre-organised muleteer at your chosen trailhead. Hotels in Taliouine (including the *Escale Rando*, see page 441) can make such arrangements. Alternatively, you could organise a bespoke **small group trek** through UK-based *Yak Travel* (w yaktravel.co.uk; see page 332). Lastly, the IGN 1:100,000 maps for the area are *Tizi n'Test* and *Igli*.

accommodation on the road between Tin Mal and the peak of the Tizi n'Test. Pleasant rooms with a superb garden and outdoor dining area make it a decent base for day walks to see the protected mountain goat region of Adrar n'Iger. Buses linking Marrakesh and Taliouine (or Taroudant) will stop here on request. €

The Tizi n'Test

The **Tizi n'Test** (2092m) is an awe-inspiring pass that crosses the Atlas and connects to Taroudant and Taliouine. Cutting right through the heart of the Atlas, the road was blasted out of the mountains by the French from 1926 to 1932 – the first modern route to link Marrakesh with the Souss plain and the desert: an important pass for trade and for the control and subjugation of the south.

The road becomes truly momentous 18km before it connects to the N10 – a rather tortuous stretch filled with hairpin bends. A lovely, yet challenging drive, it's one of the more scenic jaunts in the whole country, giving way to unmatched panoramas that serve as a splendid gateway to the Souss region of the country. Over the Tizi n'Test pass, the descent towards the **Taroudant–Taliouine road** is dramatic: a drop of some 1600m in little over 30km. Throughout, there are fabulous vistas of the mountains jutting out around the Nfis Valley with clusters of villages hundreds of feet below.

ARRIVAL AND DEPARTURE   THE TIZI N'TEST

From November to the end of April the pass can be blocked with snow. When this occurs, a sign is put up on the roadside where the Asni–Test road leaves Marrakesh, and also on the roadside past Tahanaoute. The nearest accommodation to the pass is *Dar El Mouahidines* (see page 356), near Tin Mal.

By bus There are daily buses from Marrakesh to Taliouine (TR Kham, departing Bab er Robb at 9pm) and Taroudant (CTM, departing at 2am); the journey takes 7–8 hr.

By grand taxi Given the unsociable hour of the arrival of these buses at Tizi n'Test, you might consider a *grand taxi* from Marrakesh or Asni if coming from the north, or from Taliouine or Taroudant from the south, though from the latter two you may have to change in Ouled Berhil.

By car Experience of mountain roads is advisable. The route is well paved, but between the pass and the intersection with the N10 it has almost continuous hairpin bends.

The southern oases routes

AÏT BENHADDOU

The southern oases routes

The Moroccan pre-Sahara begins as soon as you cross the Atlas to the south. It is not sand for the most part – more a wasteland of rock and scrub, which the Berbers call *hammada* – but it is powerfully impressive. There is, too, an irresistible sense of wonder as you catch your first glimpse of the great southern river valleys: the Drâa, Dadès, Todra and Ziz. Lush belts of date-palm oases, scattered with the fabulous mud architecture of kasbahs and fortified *ksour* villages, these are the old caravan routes that reached back to Marrakesh and Fez and out across the Sahara to Timbuktu, Niger and old Sudan, carrying gold, slaves and salt well into the nineteenth century.

7

Most travellers' first taste of the region is the **Tizi n'Tichka**, the dizzying pass up from Marrakesh, and the iconic kasbashs at **Telouet** and **Aït Benhaddou** – an introduction that is hard to beat. Benhaddou is less than an hour's drive from **Ouarzazate**, a modern town created by the French to "pacify" the south and one of the area's few urban centres of any significance, buoyed in recent years by its association with the film industry. From here, you can follow the old **trading routes**: south through the Drâa to **Zagora** and the fringes of the desert at **M'Hamid**; or east through the Dadès to the towering **Todra Gorge** and, ultimately, the dunes at **Erg Chebbi** near Merzouga. These are beautiful journeys, the roads rolling through crumbling mud-brick villages and past long ribbons of deep green palmeries as they stretch out towards the Sahara.

The southern oases were long a mainstay of the pre-colonial economy. Their wealth, and the arrival of tribes from the desert, provided the impetus for two of the great **royal dynasties**: the Saadians (1554–1669) from the Drâa Valley, and the current ruling family, the Alaouites (1669–present) from the Tafilalt. By the nineteenth century, however, the advance of the Sahara and the uncertain upkeep of the channels that watered the oases had reduced life to bare subsistence, even in the most fertile strips. Under the French, with the creation of modern industry in the north and the exploitation of phosphates and minerals, they became less and less significant, while the old caravan routes were dealt a final death blow by the closure of the Algerian border in 1994.

Although the date harvests in October, centred on **Erfoud**, still give employment to the *ksour* communities, the rest of the year sees only the modest production of a handful of crops – henna, barley, citrus fruits and, uniquely, roses, developed by the French around **El Kelâa M'Gouna** for the production of rose-water and perfume. Severe drought in the 1990s had a devastating effect on crops, including dates, and forced much of the male population to seek work further north, but since 2007 the water levels have greatly improved and the palmeries are returning to their picture-book lushness once more.

GETTING AROUND   THE SOUTHERN OASES ROUTES

The south is a vast region, stretching some 675km from Ouarzazate to Figuig, though the area can be broken down nicely into more manageable **circuits**. The simplest – Marrakesh to Zagora and back, or the return from Marrakesh to Tinghir – can be covered in around five days, though to do them any degree of justice you'll need a lot longer. With ten days or more, the loop from Ouarzazate to Merzouga (via Tinghir), and thence southwest to Zagora and M'Hamid, becomes a possibility, stringing together the region's main highlights via good roads and dependable transport connections.

BY BUS

All the main routes in this chapter are covered by regular buses; the road from Ouarzazate to Tinghir and on to Erfoud (for Merzouga) is particularly well served. Travelling by bus in the desert in summer can be physically exhausting, though: most trips tend to begin at dawn to avoid the worst of the heat and, for the rest of the day, it can be difficult to summon up the energy to do anything.

KASBAH TELOUET

Highlights

1 Telouet The abandoned feudal kasbah of the "Lords of the Atlas" is hugely evocative. See page 365

2 Aït Benhaddou The cream of the south's desert architecture, used as a striking location for numerous movies. See page 366

3 Palmeries Fed by ancient water courses, the great palmeries of Morocco's southern oases form an astounding contrast with the desert. See pages 385, 394 and 403

4 Kasbah stays You should try to spend at least a night in one of these iconic buildings, hand-crafted with mud and straw and providing welcome respite from the desert heat. See pages 377, 387 and 414

5 Dadès Gorge Outlandish rock formations and ruined kasbahs at the head of a valley winding deep into the Atlas watershed. See page 390

6 Todra Gorge This dramatic cleft in the High Atlas is one of the country's finest natural spectacles. See page 397

7 Erg Chebbi Morocco's most impressive sand dunes, stretching out to the border with Algeria, are best explored on camel back. See page 409

HIGHLIGHTS ARE MARKED ON THE MAP ON PAGE 362

BY CAR

If you can afford to rent a car, even for just two or three days, you'll be able to take in a lot more, with a lot less frustration, in a reasonably short period of time – there are numerous rental outlets in Ouarzazate (see page 372), some of which allow you to return their vehicles to Marrakesh, Fez, Agadir or Casablanca.

Services Petrol stations can be found along all the main routes. Local mechanics are generally excellent, and most minor problems can be quickly (and often cheaply) dealt with.

Equipment It's wise to carry water, in case of overheating, and, above all, be sure you've got a good spare tyre – punctures tend to be frequent on southern roads.

Driving on pistes Many of the *pistes* in the south are navigable in a rental car, but be aware that the insurance is invalid when you drive on them. In reality, 4WDs are a better bet for *pistes*, even more so in winter and early spring (they're essential for the Dadès route across the Atlas, for which you should also be able to do basic mechanical repairs).

Scams The practice known as "fake breakdowns" is prevalent throughout the south but particularly refined along the road from Ouarzazate to Zagora. People standing next to stationary cars will flag you down, ostensibly for help getting to a garage; but when you arrive at the next town, they'll insist on returning the favour by offering you a "special price" on items from their handicraft shop. As difficult as it may sound, don't stop to "help".

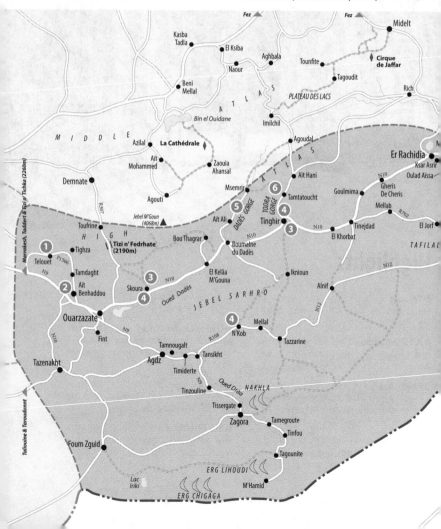

BY TRUCK

On many of the minor routes, local Berber lorries (*camions*) or pick-ups (*camionettes*) run a bus-type service, charging standard fares for their trips, which are usually timed to coincide with the network of souks or markets in villages en route. The trucks cover a number of adventurous desert *pistes* as well as the very rough road over the Atlas from the Dadès Gorge.

INFORMATION

When to visit Spring is by far the most enjoyable time to travel, particularly if you're heading for Zagora, reckoned to be the hottest town in the country, or Merzouga – though the Drâa, in particular, is subject to flash floods at this time of year, and passes across the Atlas can be difficult or impossible. Autumn, with the date harvests, is also good. Temperatures can climb well above 50ºC in midsummer, while in winter the days remain hot but it can get very cold at night.

Health Some rivers in the south, including the Asif Ounila flowing past Aït Benhaddou, contain bilharzia, a parasite that can enter your skin, including the soles of your feet; when walking by streams in the oases, take care to avoid contact with water. Travellers are advised to drink only bottled mineral water in southern Morocco.

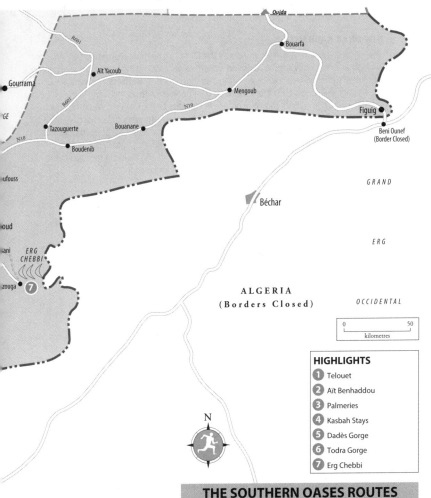

HIGHLIGHTS

1. Telouet
2. Aït Benhaddou
3. Palmeries
4. Kasbah Stays
5. Dadès Gorge
6. Todra Gorge
7. Erg Chebbi

THE SOUTHERN OASES ROUTES

KSOUR AND KASBAHS

Arguably *the* defining image of the south, **ksour** (**ksar** in the singular) and **kasbahs** are found throughout the region, peeking out of palmeries and edging the roads that cut through the great river valleys, most notably the Dadès, the so-called Route of a Thousand Kasbahs, and the Drâa.

A *ksar* (or *ighrem* in Berber) is essentially a **fortified tribal village**, while a kasbah (or *tighremt*) is a **fortified home** made for the ruling family. Both *ksour* and kasbahs are imposing structures, built – in the absence of other available materials – out of the mud-clay **pisé** of the riverbanks. A unique and probably indigenous development of the Berber populations, they are often monumental in design and fabulously decorated, with bold geometric patterns incised into exterior walls and slanted towers. Seasonal rains wash off some of the mud, so the buildings require constant upkeep – once a kasbah has been left unmaintained, it declines very fast, with twenty years enough to produce a ruinous state if the walls are not renewed.

Agadirs, also variants of the *ksar* structure, used to serve as a combination of tribal fortress and communal granary or storehouse for the villages.

THE DRÂA KASBAHS

Few of the *ksour* and kasbahs that shadow **the Drâa** can be more than a hundred years old, though you frequently see the ruins and walls of earlier *ksour* abandoned just a short distance from their more modern counterparts. Most are populated by **Berbers**, but there are also Arab villages here, and even a few scattered communities of **Jews**, still living in their Mellahs. All of the southern valleys, too, have groups of **Haratin**, descendants of West African slaves brought into Morocco along the caravan routes. Inevitably, these populations have mixed to some extent – and the Jews here are almost certainly converted Berbers – though it is interesting to see just how distinct many of the *ksour* still appear, both in their architecture and customs. There is, for example, a great difference from one village in the Drâa to the next as regards women's costumes, above all in the wearing and extent of veils.

THE DADÈS KASBAHS

Though several of the Skoura kasbahs date, at least in part, from the seventeenth and eighteenth centuries, the majority of kasbahs in **the Dadès** oases are relatively modern. Most of the older fortifications were destroyed in a vicious tribal war in 1893, and many that survived were pulled down in the French pacification of the 1920s and 30s. The kasbah walls in the Dadès, higher and flatter than in the Drâa, often seem un-scaleable, but in the course of a siege or war there were always other methods of conquest – a favourite means of attack in the 1890s, according to the writer Walter Harris, who journeyed here in disguise, was to divert the water channels of the oasis round a kasbah and simply wait for its foundations to dissolve.

Telouet and the Tizi n'Tichka

The direct route between Marrakesh and Ouarzazate, the **Tizi n'Tichka** (N9) is a spectacular piece of engineering, its pulse-racing series of switchbacks providing ever more jaw-dropping views until it eventually crests the central High Atlas at its eponymous pass. It was built to replace the old caravan route to the Drâa and the south, which was controlled during the nineteenth century and much of the twentieth by the legendary **Glaoui family**, the greatest and most ambitious of all the Berber tribal leaders – their kasbah-headquarters, a vast complex of buildings abandoned only in 1956, still stands at **TELOUET**, less than an hour from the main road.

Arrow-straight as it runs out from Marrakesh across the Haouz Plain, the Tizi n'Tichka soon contours forest slopes high above the Oued Ghdat valley, twisting past small villages and fields as it heads to **Taddert**, the last significant village on the north side of the pass – though most traffic now stops a kilometre beyond the centre, where all the roadside cafés and restaurants are located. The road thereafter climbs in an amazing array of hairpin bends to reach pastureland (*tichka* means "high pasture") before a final pull up to the **Tichka pass** itself (2260m), marked by cafés and the obligatory souvenir stall or two; not far down on the south side of the pass is the turning to Telouet and the Ounila Valley. The main road south winds down through **Igherm**, 10km further on and home to a well-restored *agadir* (to find someone to unlock it, ask at the roadside hotel, *Chez Mimi*), gradually flattening out until it reaches the turn-off to Aït Benhaddou (see page 366), just 19km before Ouarzazate.

Kasbah Telouet

Signed 500m down a track, north of Telouet village (the other side of the village if approaching from the Tizi n'Tichka) • Charge

The bizarre **Kasbah Telouet** is one of the most extraordinary sights of the Atlas – fast crumbling into the dark red earth, but still offering, in parts, a peculiar glimpse of the style and melodrama of Moroccan political government and power still within living memory. There's little of aesthetic value – many of the rooms have fallen into complete ruin – but nevertheless, even after over a half-century of decay, there's still vast drama in this weird and remote site, and in the decorated salon walls, often roofless and open to the wind.

The main halls and reception rooms

The kasbah is an unbelievable labyrinth of locked doors and connecting passages – it is said that no single person ever fully knew their way around the entire complex – though these days you can only access the **main halls** and **reception rooms**. The latter, remarkably intact, given the crumbling exterior, at least give a sense of the quantity and style of the decoration, still in progress when the pasha died and the old regime came to a sudden halt. "The outward and visible signs of ultimate physical ambition", as Gavin Maxwell put it in *Lords of the Atlas* (see page 534), they have delicate iron window grilles and fine carved ceilings, though the overall result is once again the late nineteenth- and early twentieth-century combination of sensitive imitation of the past and out-and-out vulgarity.

The roof

There's a tremendous scale of affectation, too, perfectly demonstrated by the use of green Salé tiles for the **roof** – usually reserved for mosques and royal palaces. From up here, you can look down upon some of the courts and chambers, the bright zellij and stucco enclosing great gaping holes in the stone and plaster. The really enduring impression, though, is the wonder of how and why it ever came to be built at all.

ARRIVAL AND DEPARTURE   **TELOUET AND THE TIZI N'TICHKA**

By bus The daily bus from Marrakesh (bound for Anemiter, 12km beyond Telouet) departs from Bab Rhemat at 3pm (4hr), returning from Telouet at 7am; the daily bus from Ouarzazate leaves at noon (3hr), returning from Telouet at around sunset.

By grand taxi *Grands taxis* run from Marrakesh to Anemiter (see page 367) via Telouet (3hr), and from Ouarzazate direct to Telouet (2hr).

By car It takes around 4–5hr to drive the Tizi n'Tichka from Marrakesh to Ouarzazate, with the pass itself roughly halfway along the route. Like all High Atlas passes, the road is seasonal and can be snowbound in winter and early spring, when barriers at either end will block your way. The Kasbah Telouet is an easy but slow-going 20km drive (about 40min) from the main road, along the paved but potholed 6802; alternatively, it's 45km (around 1hr 15min) along the recently paved road from Tamdaght, just north of Aït Benhaddou (see page 367), offering drivers a scenic short cut between two of the finest kasbahs in the south.

ACCOMMODATION

It's unlikely you'll need to stop on the way south to Ouarzazate, but there are a couple of places on the Tizi n'Tichka that are useful for drivers looking for a place to stay before hitting Marrakesh or heading to the airport – *I Rocha*, in particular, would make a very pleasant end to any Moroccan adventure.

7

THE TIZI N'TICHKA

★ **I Rocha** Tisselday, 145km from Marrakesh ⓦirocha. com. Charming guesthouse up in the hills overlooking a quiet stretch of the Tizi n'Tichka, with lovely views from its terrace and a sheltered little pool. The en suite rooms are on the small side but are light-filled, thoughtfully decorated and come with a/c; good meals are served in the social salon – often accompanied by a roaring log fire – and there's a funky adjoining bar. BB €€

TELOUET

Auberge Telouet 500m north of the village, opposite the turn-off to the Kasbah Telouet ⓦtelouet.com. Accommodation in an ersatz kasbah, with nicely kept rooms and views over Telouet from the panoramic terrace. There are a few cheaper rooms in an older inn across the road, including a large living space that can sleep eight with shared bathrooms. The food in the restaurant is good and the owner can also arrange evening meals in a trio of village houses. BB €

Maison d'hôtes Dar Aissa In the centre of the village ⓦdaraissatelouet.onlc.eu. Sparsely decorated but good-value rooms around a courtyard full of flowers in the home of Almodhik Aissa, with mix-and-match beds, shared bathrooms, a simple rug-strewn salon and a good view of the kasbah from the roof. Meals are available, usually cooked by a family member. €

7 Aït Benhaddou and around

The first thing you hear from the guides on arrival at **AÏT BENHADDOU**, 190km from Marrakesh and just 34km from Ouarzazate, is a list of its **film credits**. Though this is a feature of much of the Moroccan south, the Benhaddou *ksar* has a definite edge over the competition. *Lawrence of Arabia* was filmed here, of course; Orson Welles used it as a location for *Sodom and Gomorrah*; and for *Jesus of Nazareth* the whole lower part of the village was rebuilt. More recently, Russell Crowe's character received his combat training here in *Gladiator*, and it's been featured in some episodes of *Game of Thrones*. It was declared a UNESCO World Heritage Site in 1987 and finally, between 2007 and 2012, using as much wood and earthen techniques as possible to keep the site as historically preserved as possible, some controlled **restoration** was carried out.

With its souvenir shops and constant stream of tour groups, Aït Benhaddou is not really the place to catch a glimpse of fading *ksar* life, but it is one of the most spectacular sights of the Atlas, piled upon a low hillock above a shallow, reed-strewn river. Its buildings are among the most elaborately decorated and best preserved in the south; they are less fortified than is usually the case along the Drâa or the Dadès, but, towered and crenellated, and with high, sheer walls of dark red *pisé*, they must have been near impregnable in this remote, hillside site.

The ksar

As ever, it's impossible to determine exactly how old **the ksar** of Aït Benhaddou is, although the maze of narrow alleyways and crenulated towers you see these days are mainly from the 17th century, but there could have been buildings here since at least the eleventh century. The importance of the site, which commands the area for miles around, was its position on the trans-Saharan trade route from Marrakesh to Ouarzazate and the south. In the twentieth century, the significance of this route disappeared with the creation of the Tizi n'Tichka, which has led to severe depopulation – there are now only ten resilient families inhabiting the **kasbahs**, earning a sparse living from the valley's agriculture and rather more from the tourists who pass through.

It contains a mosque, two cemeteries (Jewish and Muslim), a public square, and by following the network of lanes uphill, you'll eventually arrive at the ruins of a vast and imposing **agadir**, or fortified granary, from where there are great views over the surrounding desert.

Tamdaght

Spread across a platform above a bend in the river, its fringes hemmed in by canyon walls, **TAMDAGHT**, 6km further up the valley from Aït Benhaddou, has a more

A WALK THROUGH THE OUNILA VALLEY

As hard as it is to imagine today, the tranquil **Ounila Valley**, set amid high, parched hillsides and edged in by remarkably coloured scree slopes, served as the main route over the Atlas until the French constructed the Tizi n'Tichka to the west. The paved road (the P1506) sees relatively little traffic and makes for a fine **two-day walk from Telouet** following the Oued Ounila as it snakes south **to Aït Benhaddou**.

The scattered communities here make abundant use of the narrow but fertile valley, which slowly unveils a wealth of dark red and crumbling kasbahs and *agadirs*, cliff dwellings, terraced orchards and olive trees – and everywhere children calling to each other from the fields, the river or the roadside. The first stop, after 12km, is Anemiter (2hr 30min walk from Telouet), one of the best-preserved fortified villages in Morocco and well worth a visit, even if you go no further. Leaving the village, the main track clings to the valley side, alternately climbing and descending, but with a general downhill trend as you make your way south. After 3km, you cross a sturdy bridge, beyond which the road follows the left bank of the river to the hamlet of Assako (2hr 30min from Anemiter), where it climbs to the left round some spectacular gorges before dropping steeply; walkers should aim to get beyond this exposed high ground before camping. The trail passes the little village of Tourhat (around 3hr 30min from Assako) before bringing you to Tamdaght (another 3hr), a scattered collection of buildings with a classic kasbah (see page 367). Just 6km from Tamdaght (1hr 15min), along a lush river valley, lies Aït Benhaddou.

If you only wanted to walk **part of the way**, you could take a *grand taxi* from Telouet to **Anemiter** (the daily bus that runs between the two doesn't leave Telouet until 5pm). You'll need to take your own provisions, but **mules** can be hired in both Telouet and Anemiter.

ACCOMMODATION

Gîte d'étape de Tighza Tighza, 10km from Anemiter towards Telouet ⓦ telouet-anmiter.gitemaroc.net. A fine *gîte*, overlooking terraced fields in the village of Tighza and run by the Bouchahoud brothers, both mountain guides – they can arrange camping trips to turquoise Lake Tamda or walks into the mountains and on to Telouet, Tamdaght or Aït Benhaddou. Most rooms are en suite, some with balconies, and there are more basic cheaper rooms in the older section of the house with shared facilities. Set dinners (€€€) and guests are invited to help out in the kitchen. BB dorm €, double €

Kasbah Tigmi N'Oufella Anguelz, 12.5km from Telouet towards Aït Benhaddou ☏ 0661 235953. Just three en-suite rooms in a restored *pisé* home – one of which takes over the entire top floor and sleeps four comfortably. They are beautifully decorated with traditional Moroccan furnishings and semi-exposed Tatouine-style ceilings, and have views of the garden. Laoucine is a gracious host, who can cook a mean tajine. BB €€

authentic Berber feel than its neighbour. The village, which formerly flourished with the caravan route over the Tizi n'Tichka, is dominated by the remnants of a **Glaoui kasbah**. Few of the day-trippers that pass through Aït Benhaddou make it this far, but the landscape en route is worth the journey as it passes through some spectacular scenery featured by Ridley Scott in *Gladiator* and Oliver Stone in *Alexander*. Following the riverbank **on foot**, you've the added bonus of crossing the lush, terraced gardens below the kasbah: the walk takes 1hr 15min each way from Aït Benhaddou (from where the path can be reached below *Defat Kasbah*).

Beyond Tamdaght, the road leads 40km northwest to Telouet and the Tizi n'Tichka pass – a beautiful route, particularly on foot, the increasingly magnificent landscape punctuated at regular intervals by villages (see page 367).

Kasbah Tamdaght

Village centre • Knock at the main door (facing the road) • Charge

Quietly crumbling into the valley floor, the relatively little-visited **Kasbah Tamdaght** – its towers crowned by gigantic storks' nests – makes an interesting counterpoint to its more illustrious neighbour down the road. One or two wings are on the verge of collapse, but you can visit the only section of the building still inhabited, which was used as a set in both the films *Gladiator* and *The Mummy*.

ARRIVAL AND INFORMATION

By public transport You can catch a bus (between Ouarzazate and Marrakesh) or a *grand taxi* from Ouarzazate to the turn-off to Benhaddou (20min), where you can pick up another taxi for the remaining 9km to the village (about 25dh for the whole journey). Leaving town at the end of the day can be tricky: local traffic tends to dry up by 4pm, allowing taxis to charge what they think they can get away with. Back at the turnoff, you can get another *grand taxi* to Ouarzazate or try your luck flagging down a bus to Marrakesh (they stop if they have seats

AÏT BENHADDOU AND AROUND

available). Alternatively negotiate a private hire *grand taxi* in Ouarzazate.

By car Aït Benhaddou is 9km off the main Tizi n'Tichka pass road, but it has only one lane and is not in great condition, requiring careful driving if you're arriving by rental car.

Guides Enthusiastic (but entirely unnecessary) guides hang around the parking area in the "new village", on the west bank of the river, hoping to escort visitors across the bridge (or stepping stones) to the *ksar*.

ACCOMMODATION AND EATING

Given how difficult it can sometimes be to find transport out of Aït Benhaddou, you may well end up deciding to **spend the night** here; if you do, get up at dawn to see the *ksar* at its best. There's no shortage of options (though note that the best places are actually outside of Aït Benhaddou itself). **Cafés** and **restaurants** are somewhat thinner on the ground, with most people opting to eat at their hotel or guesthouse.

★ **Auberge Ayouze** Asfalou, 3km north of Aït Benhaddou ☎ 0524 883757 or ☎ 0671 191706. This little

mud-brick *auberge* is full of atmosphere and has fostered quite a loyal following thanks to its friendly French-Moroccan hosts and their likeable staff – with just six attractive rooms, all except one with private terrace, you'll often need to book in advance. Good food (dinner €€, book a half board rate or tell them before 5pm), good music and a welcoming pool and bar complete the picture. BB €€

Kasbah Ellouze On the southern edge of Tamdaght ⓦ kasbah-ellouze.com. Stylish place run by a couple from

THE GLAOUI

The extent and speed of **Madani** (1866–1918) and **T'hami el Glaoui**'s (1879–1956) rise to power is remarkable. In the mid-nineteenth century, their family were simply local clan leaders, controlling an important Atlas pass between Marrakesh and the south but lacking influence beyond it. Their entrance into national politics began dramatically in 1893. In that year's terrible winter, **Sultan Moulay Hassan**, on returning from a disastrous *harka* (subjugation or burning raid) of the Tafilalt, found himself at the mercy of the brothers. With shrewd political judgement, they rode out to meet the sultan, feting him with every detail of protocol and, miraculously, producing enough food to feed the entire three-thousand-strong force for the duration of their stay.

The extravagance was well rewarded. By the time Moulay Hassan began his return to Marrakesh, he had given *caid*-ship of all the lands between the High Atlas and the Sahara to the Glaoui and, most important of all, was forced to abandon vast amounts of the royal armoury (including the first cannon to be seen in the Atlas) in Telouet. By 1901, the brothers had eliminated all opposition in the region, and when the **French** arrived in Morocco in 1912, they were able to dictate the form of government for virtually all the south, putting down the attempted nationalist rebellion of El Hiba, pledging loyalty throughout World War I and having themselves appointed **pashas of Marrakesh**, with their family becoming *caids* in all the main Atlas and desert cities. The French were content to concur, arming them, as Gavin Maxwell wrote, "to rule as despots, [and] perpetuating the corruption and oppression that the Europeans had nominally come to purge".

The Glaoui's controversial alliance with the Protectorate continued over the next few decades, and in 1953 T'hami again played an influential part in the dethroning of a sultan, conspiring with the French to **overthrow Mohammed V**. It was his last act of betrayal. Within a few months of Mohammed V's return to Morocco in 1955, T'hami was dead, his properties seized by the state and ultimately abandoned to the ravages of time.

LIGHTS, CAMERA, ACTION! OUARZAZATE ON THE SILVER SCREEN

Ever since David Lean shot **Lawrence of Arabia** at nearby Aït Benhaddou in 1962, film directors have been drawn to Ouarzazate, and the area has, over the years, stood in for Afghanistan, Jerusalem, Persia, Somalia, Ancient Egypt and even Tibet. Bernardo Bertolucci came here in 1990 to film Paul Bowles's novel, **The Sheltering Sky**, while Martin Scorsese based much of **The Last Temptation of Christ** (1998) and **Kundun** (1996) in the surrounding *hammada* – as a tottering Tibetan temple at the Atlas Corporation Studios just outside of town (see page 371) can testify to. Oliver Stone shot **Alexander** here in 2004, while Ridley Scott can't seem to get enough of the place, choosing the region for **Gladiator** (1999), **Black Hawk Down** (2001), **Kingdom of Heaven** (2005) and **Prometheus** (2012). Proving that Ouarzazate has still got what it takes, Clint Eastwood used it in **American Sniper** (2015), and it's the backdrop to several scenes in the TV series **Game of Thrones** (2011–2020). However, Covid-19, travel restrictions forced film producers to look for backdrops closer to home or to create digital worlds, and once restrictions were finally lifted, the film industry never really returned to this area of southern Morocco to the same extent.

7

Nîmes in France – modern, but following traditional lines, with a range of cavernous rooms that combine authentic Moroccan design with mod cons such as a/c and heaters in winter. There's a small, heated swimming pool and plenty of roof areas for relaxing; beautifully cooked meals are served on a breezy rear terrace overlooking the village orchard (*ellouze* means "almond" in Arabic). Closed Ramadan and early Jan. HB €€

★ **Riad Caravane** 3km north of Aït Benhaddou ⓦ riad-caravane.com. Attractive, newly built riad featuring *tadelakt* walls and spacious, minimalist rooms. The rooftop terrace provides a beautiful view over the oasis, there's a heated swimming pool, and the food is a superb blend of Moroccan, French and Swiss (set dinner menu €€). There are only eight rooms, all come with private bathrooms and a/c, and one sleeps three and another four – book ahead. BB €€

Riad Ksar Ighnda 2.5km north of Aït Benhaddou ⓦ ksar.ighnda.net. Classy hotel, oozing luxury chic and beautifully lit at night. Rooms offer the best of both worlds, where wonderful mattresses and DVD players meet smoothly traditional *tadelakt* bathrooms. Lounge about the

immaculate gardens, take a dip in the sleek pool or unwind with an argan-oil treatment in the spa. The classy restaurant welcomes visitors with a reservation and is top-notch, too. HB €€€

Riad Maktoub On the main road in the centre of Aït Benhaddou ⓦ riadmaktoub.com. Attractive *pisé*-style building with small but cool rooms and a handful of more elaborate suites, enclosing a courtyard pool. International or Moroccan meals are served in the salon (€€€ set menu), around the pool or on either of the elegant terraces overlooking the kasbah. Hammam and massages are available. BB €€

La Rose du Sable On the main road in the centre of Aït Benhaddou ⓦ hotellarosedusable.com. Arguably the best value in town, this family-run hotel has eighteen comfy rooms (some sleeping up to six), a decent restaurant (set menus from €€), lovely terrace and a big pool, one end of which is perfect for toddlers. The cheapest rooms without bathrooms are in the basement, and bargain-hunters may enjoy sleeping on a mattress and stargazing on the roof terrace. €̄

Ouarzazate

At some stage, you're likely to spend a night in **OUARZAZATE**, (pronounced *waz-are-zat*) the main access point and crossroads of the south, and it can be a useful if functional base from which to visit the *ksour* and kasbahs of Aït Benhaddou or Skoura. Although lacking the architectural charm of other local settlements, the town nevertheless has a buzzy, almost cosmopolitan feel, contrasting sharply with the sleepier places elsewhere in the region.

Like most of the new Saharan towns, Ouarzazate was created as a Foreign Legion garrison and administrative centre by the French in the late 1920s. During the 1980s, it became something of a boom town, as the tourist industry embarked on a wildly optimistic building programme of luxury hotels, based on Ouarzazate's marketability as a staging point for the "Saharan Adventure", and the town was given an additional boost from the attentions of **film-makers** (see page 369).

Ouarzazate holds a mystic attraction for Moroccans, too – similar to the resonance of Timbuktu for Europeans – and recent years have seen renewed expansion. Vast residential complexes are springing up in response to the growing demand from young people unwilling to live with their parents, as well as an influx from rural areas. An ill-fated golf course development to the north of the city was, unsurprisingly, abandoned, although the hotel itself is open, and there are plans to build yet more five-star hotels. Whether the region will attract enough visitors in the future to sustain all this development remains to be seen. The city recently completed a huge solar power station, which, alongside hydro and wind plants, is providing half of Morocco's energy and has generated a large number of jobs.

Kasbah Taourirt

Off Av Mohammed V, at the eastern (Tinghir) end of town • Charge • A 20min walk from the centre of town

Although built by the Glaoui, the **Kasbah Taourirt** was never an actual residence of its chiefs, though its location, at this strategic junction of the southern trading routes, meant that it was always controlled by a close relative. In the 1930s, when the Glaoui were the undisputed masters of the south, it was perhaps the largest of all Moroccan kasbahs – an enormous family domain housing numerous sons and cousins of the dynasty, along with several hundred of their servants and labourers, builders and craftsmen, including Jewish tailors, jewellers and moneylenders.

After being taken over by the government following independence, the kasbah fell into drastic **decline**. Work carried out in the 1990s was only partially successful, with parts of the structure washed away by heavy rains. What you can see – the main reception courtyard and a handful of principal rooms – are lavishly decorated but not especially significant or representative of the old order of things. A small section of the original, a kind of village within the kasbah, remains occupied today, though, and makes for interesting wandering.

Musée du Cinema

Av Mohammed V, opposite Kasbah Taourirt at the eastern end of town • Charge • A 20min walk from the centre of town

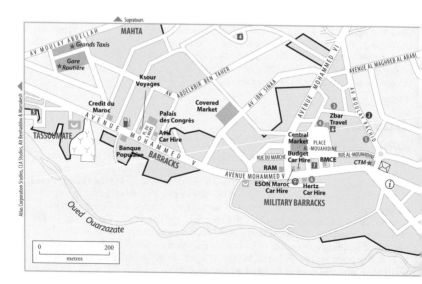

Housed in a former studio, the **Musée du Cinema** is a neat introduction to Ouarzazate's movie-making history and worth a nose around if you're unable to get out to the bigger studios on the edge of town: you can wander among dusty props and sets used in international films such as *The Mummy* and *Asterix and Obelix: Mission Cleopatra*, as well as an interesting collection of cinematic paraphernalia.

Atlas Corporation Studios

Just off Av Mohammed V, on the western outskirts of town • ⓦ studiosatlas.com • Charge • Catch the regular yellow bus from Av Mohammed V, or take a *petit taxi* from the centre of town

Established in 1983 for the production of *The Jewel in the Nile*, the **Atlas Corporation Studios** put Ouarzazate on the movie map. Blockbusters such as *Gladiator* were shot here, while Timothy Dalton's James Bond bounded about a Moroccan "Afghanistan" in *The Living Daylights* at Atlas. It's still a popular studio with the TV networks, and film crews are often on site, in an endless cycle of constructing sets and taking them down again.

Several of the bigger pieces have been kept for posterity, and a few minutes' wandering will take you from a Buddhist temple (Martin Scorsese's *Kundun*) to the pyramids (ABC's *Cleopatra*), via a Middle Eastern street scene or two. Many are on the brink of collapse, though, and look like a strong gust could finish them off at any moment – which is strangely part of their appeal.

CLA Studios

Just off Av Mohammed V, on the western outskirts of town • Charge • ⓦ cla-studios.com • Catch the regular yellow bus from Av Mohammed V, or take a *petit taxi* from the centre of town

The gated **CLA Studios**, just along the road from the Atlas Corporation Studios, is slicker than its predecessor, but not necessarily more enjoyable. A small museum displays various props from various films, including *Body of Lies* and *Prince of Persia*, and there are a couple of large sets some 2km from the studios and visited by car – the settlement you can see in the distance served as Ridley Scott's "Jerusalem" in *Kingdom of Heaven*.

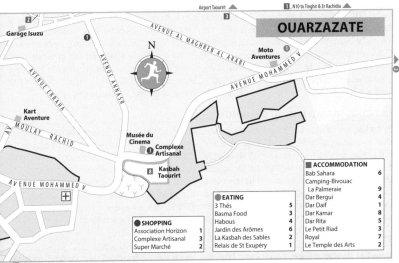

OUARZAZATE

● SHOPPING	
Association Horizon	1
Complexe Artisanal	3
Super Marché	2

● EATING	
3 Thés	5
Basma Food	3
Habous	4
Jardin des Arômes	6
La Kasbah des Sables	2
Relais de St Exupéry	1

■ ACCOMMODATION	
Bab Sahara	6
Camping-Bivouac La Palmeraie	9
Dar Bergui	4
Dar Daif	1
Dar Kamar	8
Dar Rita	5
Le Petit Riad	3
Royal	7
Le Temple des Arts	2

7

FINT OASES

From the main road it would be easy to miss the oases of Fint, 20km southwest of Ouarzazate. This entire lush, green secret world is squeezed down in-between soaring canyon walls and from the plateau across which the main road runs there's almost nothing visible that gives away the presence of this wonderful place. Follow the dirt road sharp downward though and you'll find yourself in one of the most enjoyable oases in southern Morocco. Thousands of palm trees line a small river and on the edge of this Saharan forest are a number of traditional villages of mud-brick buildings. There's not much to actually do here aside from gentle walks through the palm groves or clambering up onto the plateau for views down onto the oases. Despite its proximity to Ouarzazate, Fint remains fairly unknown among tourists and the people are exceptionally welcoming. This is definitely the kind of place you could come for a day and stay for a week. There are a couple of places to stay including the excellent Hotel Oasis Fint/La Terrasse des Délices (wterrassesdelices.com), which offers a range of nicely decked out rooms, superb views from the terrace and good meals that, in the evening, are often accompanied by live music. Guides are on-hand to help you explore the confusing web of walkways in the oases.

ARRIVAL AND DEPARTURE

OUARZAZATE

By plane Ouarzazate Aéroport (wonda.ma) is 2km north of town, and served by flights from Casablanca (6 weekly; 1hr 5min) and Marrakesh (3 weekly; 40min); *petits taxis* make the short run into town (30dh). There's a café, a BMCE Bank exchange counter and car rental desks - all open when flights arrive and depart. RAM has an office at 1 Av Mohammed V (w royalairmaroc.com).

By bus Private long-distance buses operate from the *gare routière* at Mahta, 1km from the centre; it's a 15min walk into town, or take a *petit taxi*. If possible, book your ticket at least one day in advance. The CTM office is on Av Mohammed V. It's worth taking a taxi to the Supratours office, which is out on the western edge of town, near the *gare routière*.

Destinations Agadir (2 CTM & 14 others daily; 7hr 30min); Agdz (3 CTM, 2 Supratours, 3 others daily; 1hr); Boumalne du Dadès (1 CTM, 3 Supratours & 12 others daily; 1hr 45min–2hr 15min); Beni Mellal (4 daily; 8hr); Casablanca (4 CTM, others hourly; 8hr 15min); El Kelâat M'Gouna (1 CTM, 3 Supratours & 14 others daily; 1hr 35min); Er Rachidia (1 CTM, 1 Supratours & 10 others daily; 5hr–5hr 30min); Erfoud (1 Supratours & 2 others daily; 6hr 30min); Fez (transfer in Er

Rachidia with Supratours, 5 others daily; 12hr); Foum Zguid (2 daily; 5hr 30min); M'Hamid (1 CTM, 5 others daily; 5hr); Marrakesh (4 CTM, 3 Supratours & others hourly; 4hr–5hr 30min); Meknes (5 daily; 11–12hr, but better to connect in Azrou or Fez); Merzouga (1 Supratours daily; 8hr); Rabat (several daily; 10hr); Rissani (1 Supratours daily; 7hr); Skoura (1 CTM & 2 others daily; 45min); Taliouine (1 CTM & 5 others daily; 3hr); Taroudant (1 CTM & 8 others daily; 5hr); Tata (3 daily; 5hr); Tazenakht (1 CTM & 2 others daily; 1hr 30min); Tinejdad (1 Supratours & 6 others daily; 4hr); Tinghir (1 CTM, 3 Supratours & others hourly; 3hr 30min); Tiznit (1 daily; 9hr 30min); Zagora (3 CTM, 2 Supratours & 7 others daily; 2hr 30min–4hr).

By grand taxi Most *grands taxis* arrive/collect outside the *gare routière* in Maha. There are regular runs to Agdz (1hr 30min), Boumalne du Dadès (1hr 30min; for connections to Tinghir 2hr 15min), El Kelâat M'Gouna (1hr 30min), Marrakesh (4hr) and Zagora (2hr 30min). They also go westward toward Tazenakht (2hr), Taliouine (4hr) and Taroudant (5hr). Departures are negotiable for Casablanca (7hr 30min; but better to connect in Marrakesh), Skoura (45min) and Aït Benhaddou (1 hr, but an expensive private trip).

GETTING AROUND AND INFORMATION

By car Dozens of car rental agencies operate in Ouarzazate, most from the airport or offices on Av Mohammed V or Pl du 3 Mars. Best of the local firms is ESON Maroc, on Av Mohammed V on the same side of the road and opposite the RAM office across Av Mohammed VI (w eson-maroc. com), which has helpful staff and new cars. International companies are more expensive: Avis, Pl du 3 Mars (w avis. ma); Budget, 4 Av Mohammed V, next door to ESON Maroc

(above) (w budget.com); Europcar, airport (w europcar. com); Hertz, 35 Av Mohammed V, diagonally opposite the RAM office (w hertz.ma). Garage Isuzu on Av Al Maghreb al Arabi is recommended for any necessary repairs.

Tourist office The region's principal tourist office, on Av Mohammed V, just across from the post office (t 0524 882485), has a few brochures, but you're better off asking advice from your (or any other) hotel.

TOURS

Désert et Montagne Maroc Kasbah Douar Talmasla,   signed 3km off Route de Zagora w desert-montagne.

ma. Run by French-qualified mountain guides Jean-Pierre and Zineb Datcharry, and the best option for arranging tailor-made adventure trips into the High Atlas, including trekking and mountaineering, as well as multi-day trips into the Erg Chebbi.

Kart Aventure Av Moulay Rachid ⓦ kartaventure.com. Runs buggy and 4WD trips and circuits to the desert, gorges and mountains, from a few hours to a week-long adventure.

Ksour Voyages Pl du 3 Mars ⓦ ksour-voyages.com. Bespoke tours of repute, which range from day trips to the desert near Zagora to three-day tours from Ouarzazate to

Fez via Todra Gorge and the Erg Chebbi dunes.

Travel Exploration Lot 24, Al Hassania ⓦ travel-exploration.com. Winner of the 2014 World Travel awards, Travel Exploration specialize in private tours, offering mid-range to luxury trips into the desert, 4WD and camel excursions, as well as tours all over Morocco to see the imperial cities and more. Pricing can be given via email.

Zbar Travel Pl Al-Mouahidine ⓦ zbartravel.com. Recommended agency offering tours to the dunes near M'Hamid, where they have another office (see page 383).

ACCOMMODATION   SEE MAP PAGE 370

Most of the cheaper and unclassified places in Ouarzazate are grouped in the centre of town; the more upmarket chain hotels are mainly set back on the plateau to the north. A more picturesque alternative would be to stay out at Aït Benhaddou (see page 368).

Bab Sahara Pl Al-Mouahidine ☎ 0524 884722. Central place on a quiet square, well located for the market and the restaurants along Av Mohammed V. Rooms are available with showers and some come with a/c. Those that face the square have small balconies. Breakfast and other meals are available in the sunny café (set menu €€). BB €

★ **Dar Bergui** Sidi H'ssain Ben Nacer ⓦ darbergui.com. Hard to find but heavenly when you do. Run by a delightful French couple, *Dar Bergui* has five airy *pisé* rooms set around a tremendous pool, and a lovely terrace with stunning Atlas views. There are three double and two family rooms, all en suite with a/c. Fine French Berber fusion cuisine is on offer too (€€€ set menu; reservations required). Can organize guides for day trips to the film studios and desert. BB €€

★ **Dar Daif** Douar Talsmasla, 9km east of the city centre on the edge of the palm groves ⓦ dardaif.ma. Popular with European travellers as they also organize local activities such as mountain-biking and canoeing as well as desert tours (ⓦ desert-montagne.ma). Beautifully decorated with mosaic tiles and carpets, the inside and outdoor lounges, terraces and cosy nooks are tranquil and peaceful, and facilities include a hammam and restaurant (set dinner from €€€). The standard rooms sleep up to three, and the particularly small doubles are a lower price. BB €€

★ **Dar Kamar** Kasbah Taourirt ⓦ darkamar.com. Wonderfully romantic hotel hidden in the heart of the kasbah, with stylishly rustic African adobe rooms, wall-to-wall candles, a deluxe hammam, massage and a dreamy terrace (which provides beautiful views over the city and Lake Al Mansore Dahabi). The alcohol-licensed restaurant serves set menus for €€€. Manager Mohammed speaks excellent English and French. Quite pricey, but worth the splurge. BB €€€

Dar Rita 39 Rue de la Mosquée, Tassoumate ⓦ darrita.com. A great find, tucked down the back alleys of one of Ouarzazate's oldest neighbourhoods and run with pride by

its charming Portuguese owner, Rita, and her indefatigable brother. Seven brightly painted rooms are spread across two floors and decorated with lanterns, clay pots and carved wooden doors that the owners have picked up during their time in Morocco. Dinner is a social affair (set menu €€€), and a good forum for honest local sightseeing advice. BB €€

Le Petit Riad Av Moulay Abdallah, Hay Al Wahda ⓦ lepetitriad.com. A charming and tranquil *maison d'hôte* run on the eastern outskirts of town, looking out towards the snowcapped Atlas mountains. Six chic rooms, a small pool and fabulous meals cooked by friendly owner Fatima Agoujil, the first officially trained female guide in the region — you can help her out in the kitchen and learn some authentic recipes (with no charge if staying more than one night) and also gain valuable local information. A multi-course menu is reasonably priced at €€€. All rooms come with a/c. BB €€

Royal 24 Av Mohammed V ☎ 0524 882258. Clean, well maintained and decent value, fronted by its own pizzeria and with a variety of rooms, priced according to size and if they are en suite and/or have a/c. Cell-like singles with shared bathrooms are cheap. It's central but can be noisy until about midnight. €

Le Temple des Arts 173–174 Hay Al Wahda ⓦ templedesarts-ouarzazate.com. Lavish five-star just north of the city centre, bedecked in marble, scattered with sculptures and dedicated to the city's movie industry, with most of the grand public areas looking like they're straight off a movie set themselves. Rooms have all mod cons and there's two restaurants and a swimming pool. BB €€€€

CAMPING

Camping-Bivouac La Palmeraie Route de Zagora, 3km south of town ⓦ camping-ouarzazate.com. Pitch your tent amid fruit trees in a palmery just outside of town. All the usual facilities (hot showers cost a little extra), plus a few simple en-suite rooms, Berber tent mud huts and a wonderfully camp pink dining room where produce from the garden is served and music is occasionally laid on. Free wi-fi and washing machines (extra charge) are available. Camping for two and car €, BB double €, BB Berber tent €

EATING AND DRINKING

Ouarzazate is one of the few places in the south where you can eat well outside your hotel, with several very good **restaurants** indeed, and the top-end ones have wine lists. The best bets for cheap eats are the **café-grills** grouped around the central market at Pl Al-Mouahidine, Rue Al-Mouahidine and along nearby Rue du Marché, where you'll find the usual brochettes, tajines and *kefta*, but also traditional dishes like tanjia – and for the more adventurous, braised cow hooves with chickpeas. For **breakfast**, the sunnier north side of Av Mohammed V is the area to head for, with a row of terrace cafés serving French baguettes, pastries and coffee.

3 Thés Av Moulay Rachid ⓦouarzazate.com/restaurant-3thes. Generous portions of classic Moroccan dishes – follow one of eight salads with a tasty tajine (a week's worth to choose from) – as well as lighter snacks available all day. Popular with locals and expats alike. €

★ **Basma Food** Hay El Hassani. Perhaps the best deal in town, but just far enough back from Av Mohammed V to remain off the radar of most visitors. The brochette and chips is great value, but try and drop by here on a Tuesday or a Saturday (fresh-fish days in Ouarzazate), when you can tuck into fish tajine or a fried-fish meal. €

Habous Pl Al-Mouahidine. Ouarzazate's top spot for a coffee, serving several kinds of delicious Moroccan bread, in addition to crusty baguettes, croissants and *pains au chocolat*; they also do the full gamut of sticky local patisserie

(sold by weight). The lengthy menu of the adjoining grill features pasta, pizza and various steaks. €

Jardin des Arômes 69 Av Mohamed V. The excellent Moroccan cuisine, intimate lounge areas, tasteful décor, pretty garden (as the name suggests) make this restaurant one of the best spots in town for a romantic evening. The interesting menu includes tajines, couscous and specialities like lamb shank with mushrooms and olives or pastilla with milk and almonds. €€€

★ **La Kasbah des Sables** 195 Hay Aït Kasif ⓦlakasbah dessables.com. Arguably the finest dining in Ouarzazate, in a rambling refurbished kasbah on the eastern fringes of the city. The half-dozen salons leading off the sprawling central courtyard are full of paintings, sculptures and antiques, making a rather grand setting for dishes that include confit of rabbit with peach nectar and fillet of sea bass with fig *en papillote*. No wonder film crews celebrate here after wrapping up. Closed July. €€€€

Relais de St Exupéry 13 Av Moulay Abdallah, just off the main Tinghir road ⓦrelais-ouarzazate.com. Excellent Moroccan and French cuisine cooked by Jean-Pierre, the indomitable Bordelais chef-proprietor. Memorabilia from the *Aéropostale* days of *Little Prince* author Antoine de Saint-Exupéry adorns the walls, but the food is the real attraction: try the wonderful pigeon pastilla, camel with "Mali" sauce or saffron ice cream. €

SHOPPING

The **central market** (daily) on Rue du Marché is great for spices and souvenir trinkets, while the **covered market** (daily) on Av Ibn Sinaa sells fruit and veg. **Souk days** are Saturday, in Tabounte, and Sunday, out by the Zone Industrielle.

Association Horizon Av Ammasr, ⓦassociation-horizon. org. Self-help scheme whose less able-bodied workers craft attractive pottery, weaving and metalwork. You can also visit workshops to watch them in action.

Complexe Artisanal Av Mohammed V, opposite the Kasbah Taourirt. This group of shops sells stone carvings, pottery, metal lamps, embroidered linen and a couple of local specialities such as geometrically patterned, silky woollen carpets and silver necklaces and earrings incorporating *tazras* (chunky orange copal beads).

Super Marché Av Mohammed V next to BMCE bank. Small supermarket selling beer and wine in addition to the usual groceries. Open until 10pm.

DIRECTORY

Banks Banks and ATMs are plentiful, with a BMCE, Banque Populaire and a Crédit du Maroc, among others, along Av Mohammed V.

Hospital Hôpital Bougafer, Av Mohammed V (☎0524 882444), between the tourist office and Kasbah Taourirt.

Post office The post office is on Av Mohammed V.

The Drâa

South of Ouarzazate, on the other side of a tremendous ridge of the Anti-Atlas, begins the **Drâa Valley** – a 125km belt of date-palm oases that eventually merges into the Sahara near the village of **M'Hamid**. It is possible to complete a circuit through and out from the Drâa, heading from the valley's main town, **Zagora**, west through Foum Zguid and Tata to the Anti-Atlas, or east to the Jebel Saghro or Rissani and Merzouga. However, most visitors content themselves with a return trip along the N9 between Ouarzazate and Zagora: a great route, with plenty of signposted lookout points, taking you well south of anywhere in the Tafilalt, and flanked by an amazing series of turreted and creamy pink *ksour* and kasbahs (see page 364); most of the larger and older ones are grouped a little way from the road, up above the terraces of date palms.

GETTING AROUND

By car The road from Ouarzazate to Zagora is well maintained and, for the most part, broad enough for two vehicles, though it narrows beyond Tamegroute, south of Zagora. Be wary of "fake breakdowns", a scam prevalent throughout the south but refined along this road (see page 362).

THE DRÂA

By public transport If you're taking the bus south from Ouarzazate, get yourself a seat on the left-hand side for the most spectacular views. You could hire a *grand taxi* for the day from Ouarzazate, stopping to explore some of the kasbahs en route; be very clear to the driver about your plans and agree on a fee before setting off.

Agdz and the road to Zagora

You descend into the Drâa Valley at **AGDZ** (pronounced "Ag-dèz"), 70km from Ouarzazate and a minor administrative centre for the region. *Agdz* means "Place of Rest", and it's certainly worth taking a break here: there are several well-preserved **kasbahs** in the original town (reached by turning north from the main square), including the seventeenth-century former home of Agdz's *caïd*, or chieftain. Just to the north of the village begins a beautiful **palmery**, and if the river here is low enough (take care to avoid the bilharzia-infested water), you can get across to view a few kasbahs on the far side, in the shadow of Jebel Kissane. A souk is held on Thursdays just outside of town on the road towards Zagora.

Tamnougalt

A first, magnificent sign of the architecture to come, the *ksar* at **TAMNOUGALT**, perched on a hill 6km south of Agdz, is one of the oldest in Morocco and perhaps the most dramatic and extravagant of any in the locality. The village was once the capital of the region, and its assembly of families (the *jemaa*) administered what was virtually an independent republic. Today, it's a wild cluster of buildings, each fabulously decorated with pockmarked walls and tapering towers, and populated by Mezguita Berbers. The **museum** and **kasbah** of the local *caïd* next door to *Chez Jacob* (charge) is worth a look.

Timiderte

Some 15km south of Tamnougalt, on the opposite side of the river, is the Glaoui kasbah of **TIMIDERTE**, now operating as a guesthouse (see page 377) but also giving travellers the chance to poke around a refurbished mud-brick palace for the price of a lunchtime tajine.

You'll have to ford the river again, this time on foot – ideally with some local assistance as the best crossing place isn't all that obvious – to reach another superb kasbah, the **Aït Hammou-Sa'd**.

BIRDING AT THE EL MANSOUR EDDAHBI BARRAGE

Some 15km of bleak, stony *hammada* from Ouarzazate, a side road leads 11km down to the **El Mansour Eddahbi Barrage**, an essential stop on any birdwatcher's itinerary. Throughout the year (especially March–May & late July to Nov), the area attracts a variety of **migrants**, **waterfowl** and **waders**. There have also been sightings of various desert-dwelling species such as blackbellied sandgrouse, thick-billed lark and raptors including lanner falcon. Over the last few decades, freak rains have occasionally flooded the reservoir, and the Drâa has, for the first time in recent memory, run its course to the sea beyond Tan Tan.

7

LIFE IN THE PALMERIES

The vast **palmeries** that carpet the **Drâa**, **Dadès** and **Ziz valleys** are the historical lifeblood of the Moroccan south – indeed, oases down here are traditionally measured by the number of their palms, rather than in terms of area or population – and they still play a vital role for their communities. Families continue to toil over individual plots that have been handed down through the generations, growing apricots, pomegranates, figs and almonds among the palms, and tomatoes, carrots, barley and mint in the shaded earth below.

Irrigation methods have barely changed in centuries, either. The fields are watered by a combination of communal wells and *khettara*, underground channels that can run for large distances across the *hammada*. Water is funnelled off to each plot in turn, with every family receiving the same amount of time to replenish its crop.

The greatest threat to this traditional way of life is **Bayoud disease**, a fungus that attacks the roots of palms, killing them off within a year and leaving a gap in the protective wedge of trees through which the wind (and destructive sand) blows through. First detected in the Drâa in the second half of the nineteenth century, Bayoud disease is reckoned to have infected two-thirds of Moroccan palmeries, wiping out nearly twelve million trees over the last century or so. Recent years, however, have seen the successful introduction of disease-resistant hybrids, which, together with increased rainfall, has led to much-improved health in the majority of the region's palmeries – in addition to the palmery at Agdz, there are fine examples at Skoura (see page 385), Tinghir (see page 394) and in the Ziz Valley (see page 403).

Tinzouline

Beyond Timiderte, and after the junction with the R108 to Rissani and Merzouga, a striking group of *ksour*, dominated by a beautiful and imposing *caïd's* kasbah, stands back from the road at **TINZOULINE**. The village hosts a large Monday souk, and with some guidance you can follow a *piste* 7km west of the village to see a group of three-thousand-year-old **rock carvings** at Foum Chenna.

ARRIVAL AND DEPARTURE

By bus Buses call in at the Grande Place in Agdz, and pull up next to the Banque Populaire; the CTM office is on the northeast corner of the square, directly opposite the mosque. The Supratours office is around 500m from the Grand Place on the road towards Ouarzazate.

Destinations Agadir (2 CTM; 6hr 30min); Casablanca (1 daily, 9hr); M'Hamid (1 CTM & 1 other daily; 3hr); Marrakesh (3 CTM, 2 Supratours & 2 others daily; 6hr); Ouarzazate (4

CTM, 2 Supratours & 3 others daily; 1hr); Rabat (1 daily; 10hr 30min); Tamegroute (1 CTM; 2hr); Taroudant (2 CTM; 5hr); Zagora (3 CTM, 2 Supratours & 1 other daily; 1hr 55min–3hr).

By grand taxi *Grands taxis* are also located in the centre of the Grand Place and will frequently run to Tamnougalt (15min), Timiderte (20min), Tinzouline (45min), Ouarzazate (1hr30min), Zagora (1hr 30min) and M'Hamid (2hr 30min).

ACCOMMODATION AND EATING

If you stop in Agdz, travelling on public transport in either direction, you'll probably have to **stay** overnight to get a place on the Zagora/Ouarzazate bus; having your own vehicle brings Tamnougalt and Timiderte into play. As befits the *ksar*-studded Drâa, many of the best choices around here are converted historical kasbahs.

AGDZ

Café Restaurant Sables d'Or Northern side of the Grande Place. Nice little place on the edge of the square, airy inside and with a few tables set back on the outside pavement. Simple menu of omelette breakfasts with coffee

and juice turkey and chicken kebabs, slowly roasting on a spit by the entrance. €

Dar Jnane 1.5km along the road north of the Grande Place ☎ 0524 843947 or ☎ 0673 181314. In a great location, nestled in the palmery north of town in the shadow of meringue-topped Jebel Kissane, this hundred-year-old Kasbah has been restored and sits in a lovely garden full of almond and fruit trees. It offers three a/c en suite rooms, one can sleep four, and with advance notice can organize mattresses in a Berber tent (€). Set dinners available. The owners also operate a two-bedroomed apartment on the main square in the centre of the village. BB €€

AGDZ AND THE ROAD TO ZAGORA

★ **Dar Qamar** 1.8km along the road north of the Grande Place ⊛ dar-qamar.com. One of the nicest hotels in the region, run by a charming French couple. Carefully restored rooms (some with four-posters; all with a/c) feature *tataoui* ceilings and *tadelakt* baths and are clustered around a pretty garden with a decent-sized pool, which is heated during winter. Relax in the hammam, the library, the jacuzzi or in the cosy firelit salon, and tuck into delicious Moroccan/Mediterranean dishes (three courses €€€€) served under stars on the terrace. BB €€

TAMNOUGALT

★ **Bab el Oued** 1km off the N9 ☎ 0660 188484 or ☎ 0619 402832, ⊛ ecolodgemaroc.com. Set at the foot of Tamnougalt *ksar* and not far from the gurgling Drâa, this friendly French-Moroccan-run eco-lodge – the only green-key certified establishment in Agdz – is a veritable oasis, with several stylish mud-brick "huts" dotted around a serene and colourful garden with an inviting pool. Delicious home-made jams and organic produce straight from the garden are used in the restaurant (set menus for lunch and three-course dinner). BB €€€

Chez Yacob 2km off the N9 ☎ 0524 843394 or ☎ 0666 104305. Perennially popular place offering eight simple but gorgeously cool rooms in a refurbished kasbah and a large roof terrace where you can bed down for the night. Mohammed, the manager, speaks good English and will give you the lowdown on the area. HB terrace €, double €€

TIMIDERTE

Kasbah Timidarte 800m from the N9 ⊛ kasbah timidarte.com. Restored by local craftsmen, accommodation at this *ksar in the heart of the palm grove* is simple, even sparse in parts, but the rooms, en suite and with shared bathrooms, look good in a minimalist sort of way, and the friendly staff can help you meet locals keen to share their experiences of life in Timiderte. Dinner €. BB €

DIRECTORY

Bank There's a Banque Populaire on the western side of Agdz's Grande Place.

Post office Agdz's post office is 100m along the road that leads north off the Grand Place.

Zagora

ZAGORA seems unpromising at first sight: a drawn-out modern market town with a big crop of hotels and government buildings and few sights of specific interest. As the region's main staging post for trips to the fringes of the Sahara, it attracts more tourist attention than it deserves in itself, yet still manages to make a pretty agreeable rest stop, particularly if you're staying in the **Amazrou palmery** south of town. The Drâa River, Morocco's longest, passes through Zagora, though it's not always full of water as a dam in Ouarzazate halts the river's flow. But in summer, it is often full when it's typical to see children swimming and local people strolling along the boardwalk. Additionally, an obligatory photo must be taken at the 'Timbuktu, 52 Days' road sign in town. The original sign has been replaced by successive copies throughout the years, and today's mural depicts camels and nomads.

Aside from its relative proximity to the desert, another draw are Zagora's festivals. The Drâa's big event, the **Moussem of Moulay Abdelkader Jilali**, is celebrated here during the Mouloud, and like other national festivals in the town, such as the **Fête du Trône** in July, is always entertaining.

Amazrou

Across the river to the southeast, 2km from the centre of Zagora, the hamlet and **palmery** of **Amazrou** is a great place to spend the afternoon, wandering amid the shade of its gardens and *ksour*. The village is, inevitably, wise to the ways of tourism – children try to drag you into their houses for tea and will hassle you to adopt them as guides – but, for all that, the traditional ways of oasis life remain largely unaffected.

The local sight, which any of the kids will lead you to, is the old Jewish kasbah, **La Kasbah des Juifs**. The Jewish community here was active in the silver jewellery trade – a craft continued by Muslim Berbers after their exodus, as a visit to the workshops lining the road to Tamegroute will testify.

Jebel Zagora

Coming by car, turn left at the roundabout just beyond the river in Amazrou and, after 2km, take the rough track opposite *Camping de la Montagne*; if you're coming on foot, consider taking a taxi to the trailhead on hot days

Watching the sunset from the slopes of **Jebel Zagora**, the bulkier of the two mountains southeast of town, is something of a tradition. Strictly speaking, Zagora is the one with a military post on top, though the name is also used for the smaller, sugarloaf hill nearby.

The track up the mountain leads to a pass between the two peaks, then curves back, rising across the hillside to a popular **viewpoint**; unless you've got a 4WD, you'll need to walk the last few hundred metres. Alternatively, you can walk up the mountain following a zigzag **footpath** (around 45min) that starts opposite the *Palais Asmâa* (the grand, kasbah-style hotel on the Route de M'Hamid in Amazrou).

Just below the track are the remnants of a colossal eleventh-century **Almoravid fort**, built as an outpost against the powerful rulers of the Tafilalt and later used to protect the Timbuktu-bound caravans passing below. The track subsequently goes on to the military fort on the summit (entry forbidden) but the view gains little; from the viewpoint, a footpath runs across the hillside and can be followed back down to the road.

Musée des Arts et Traditions de la Vallée du Drâa

Located down a covered alleyway in the Ksar Tissergate, abutting the palmery 5km north of Zagora • Charge • *Petits taxis* run to Tissergate from Zagora

The excellent **Museé des Arts et Traditions de la Vallée du Drâa** is a dusty old museum in the nicest of senses. Housed in a mud-brick kasbah, its three well-worn floors offer a charming insight into life in the Drâa, from a motley ensemble of agricultural implements to collections of colourful marriage costumes and the forty of so medicinal herbs used by a *fakir*, or Islamic holy man. The proud gardien is on hand to answer questions (in French), though all the displays are (refreshingly) labelled in English.

ZAGORA

● SHOPPING
Cavern du Troc	2
Maison Berbère	1

■ ACCOMMODATION
Azalai Desert Lodge	2
Camping Oasis Palmier	8
Chez Ali	4
Ma Villa au Sahara (Villa Zagora)	7
La Petite Kasbah	6
Prends ton Temps	1
Riad Dar Sofian	9
Riad Lamane	5
La Rose des Sables	3

● EATING
Chez Ali	3
Dromadaire Gourmand	1
Hôtel La Rose des Sables	2

DESERT TRIPS FROM ZAGORA

Nearly every tourist in town is here for the Sahara, and yet Zagora is still some way from the **desert** proper, so make sure you know exactly where your trip is headed. The closest **dunes** are at **Nakhla**, northeast of town, and **Tinfou**, about 25km south along the N9 (see page 382), which are easy to get to but not particularly impressive. Closer to M'Hamid lie the **Erg Lihoudi** (see page 382) and the **Erg Ezahar**, though the latter – also known as the Screaming Dunes due to the incredible sound they make (the noise is actually caused by vibrating sand grains) – are usually only offered on trips out of M'Hamid (see page 383). Finally, around 60km southwest of M'Hamid (and a good 3hr from Zagora), is the unforgettable **Erg Chigaga** (see page 382), the real deal, offering relative isolation and a sea of golden sand ebbing out into the distance – though getting here involves a much longer (and expensive) journey.

Virtually all the hotels and campsites in Zagora have tie-ins with **camel-riding** outfits, and there are numerous agencies just itching to get you onto the back of a dromedary. **Rates**, as ever, are negotiable, so it pays to shop around. Recommended **agencies** include Amazing Journeys Morocco on Bv Mohammed V north of the post office (ⓦ morocco-desert-camp.com), Caravane du Sud, on the roundabout just over the Oued Drâa in Amazrou (ⓦ caravanesud.com), and Zagora Desert Travel on Hay Drâa in the northeast of town (ⓦ zagoradeserttravel.com).

7

ARRIVAL AND DEPARTURE
ZAGORA

By plane Aéroport Zagora is 7km southwest of Zagora, on the left-hand side of the N12 when travelling towards Foum Ziguid. It currently offers one weekly flight to Ouarzazate (40min) and two weekly flights to Casablanca (1hr 35min). Check RAM's website for more details (ⓦ royalairmaroc.com).

By bus CTM buses depart from the company's office on Bd Mohammed V; Supratours are based 200m further north along Mohammed V, near the Banque Populaire. Private buses leave from the *gare routière* on the northern outskirts of town.

Destinations Agadir (1 CTM & 2 others daily; 11hr); Agdz (3 CTM & 3 others daily; 1hr 55min–3hr); Casablanca (2 CTM & 6 others daily; 12hr); Foum Zguid (2 daily; 3–4hr); Inezgane (2 daily); M'Hamid (1 CTM daily & others hourly; 1hr 40min–2hr); Marrakesh (2 CTM & 6 others daily; 7hr 30min–9hr 30min); Ouarzazate (3 CTM, 2 Supratours & 9 others daily; 2hr 30min–4hr); Rabat (4 daily); Salé (2 daily); Tagounite (1 daily); Taliouine (1 CTM & 1 other daily; 5hr 10min–6hr); Tamegroute (1 CTM daily & others hourly; 25min); Taroudant (2 CTM & 1 other daily; 7hr 40min); Tazenakht (2 CTM & 2 others daily; 3–4hr).

By grand taxi *Grands taxis* run regularly to Tamegroute (20min), Tinfou (30min), Tagounite (1hr), Agdz (1hr 30min), M'Hamid (1hr 30min), Ouarzazate (3hr) and occasionally to Marrakesh (7hr) from the rank on Bd Mohammed V, a 15-minute walk from the newer bus station.

By truck Lorries make the daily haul to Rissani (10hr) and, in the other direction, along the rough road to Foum Zguid (5hr), with more leaving on Mondays (souk day in Foum Zguid, and also a good day for onward travel).

GETTING AROUND AND INFORMATION

By taxi *Petits taxis* run throughout Zagora and are easily flagged down along the main streets. They will only do runs inside of town and to places just outside like Amazrou, Tissergate and the airport; to get further afield, you'll need a *grand taxi* (see above).

Tourist information Zagora's Provincial Tourist Office is in a rather grand-looking building on the roundabout at the far western end of Av Atlas Zaouit el Baraka (ⓣ 0524 848686), and is a friendly source of information.

ACCOMMODATION
SEE MAP PAGE 378

There's a wide range of **hotels** – in both Zagora and Amazrou, an excellent, fast-growing alternative base – and some nicely located campsites, especially for those with transport. Travellers on tight budgets should also note that many mid-scale hotels will let you bed down on roof terraces or in nomad **tents**; most hotels are also happy for non-residents to use their pools, bars and restaurants.

Azalai Desert Lodge Near Ksar Tissergate, 7km north of Zagora ⓣ 0661 164394, ⓦ azalailifeexperience.com. An African lodge offering eight stylish and contemporary rooms, where huge bay windows lining the back face out to palm groves, which are dotted with hammocks and private dining areas within the oasis. A swimming pool, free bike rental, library, hammam and spa (extra charge) make this

7

lodge a true retreat. The owners also have a luxury desert camp in the dunes. HB €€€

★ **Chez Ali** Av Atlas Zaouit el Baraka ⓦ chezali.net. A haven of greenery on the edge of town, offering clean, secure and relaxing accommodation in 24 comfortable rooms (en suite, and with a/c), and two cheaper bungalows sharing a bathroom in the back garden. The family owners here have provided genuinely hospitable service and have, over more than two decades, created a lovely space filled with flowers, fruit trees and peacocks, while a swimming pool is enclosed by the garden (open to non-guests for a small fee). Altogether the nicest, best-value option in Zagora itself (and with a recommended restaurant to boot), but far from a secret, so book ahead. BB bungalow € room €

Ma Villa au Sahara (Villa Zagora) Route de Nakhla, Amazrou, 100m north of the roundabout ⓦ mavilla ausahara.com. A lovely little place south of the Drâa, with understated *pisé*-pastel rooms, some with balconies; the luxuriant garden is drenched in bougainvillea and cut through by lantern-lit walkways. The chunky fireplace will keep you warm in the colder months, and there's a *petit* pool for hotter days. A comfortable rooftop Berber tent with six beds offers a cheaper option. BB Berber tent/per person €, double €€

La Petite Kasbah Route de M'Hamid, Amazrou ⓦ hotel zagora.com. A lovely *auberge* bordering the fringe of the Amezrou palmery. Owner Brahim is a welcoming host and places an emphasis on catering well for small groups. Traditional *pisé* rooms come with *tadelakt* bathrooms, a/c and eco-showers. A swimming pool, restaurant and rooftop terrace with views of the palmeries completes the picture. BB €

Prends ton Temps Signed off Bd Mohammed V 1km north of the junction with Av Allal Ben Abdallah ☎ 0524 846543 or ☎ 0661 466945. "Take Your Time" pretty much sums up this laidback and slightly eccentric joint: a courtyard ringed by funkily decorated little cabins and Berber tents (some en suite and a/c) and a couple of salons. The irrepressible owner Belaid comes from a nomadic tribe and is an accomplished player of the Arabian lute, so expect long evenings of music and folk stories. Set menus are from

€€. BB Cabin/tent with shared toilet €, en-suite cabin €

★ **Riad Dar Sofian** Route de Nakhla, Amazrou, 700m north of the roundabout ⓦ riaddarsofian.com. Arguably the most stylish guesthouse in Zagora, set on the fringes of the palmery. Constructed in traditional *pisé*, the interior is much more contemporary, with a sleek lounge, lightly decorated rooms with embroidered linen and rain showers, and a striking set-piece fountain that cuts through the floors. The charming manager can help arrange tours, though most guests are happy to lounge by the lovely swimming pool, edged with towering palms. Superb food and an alcohol licence, with set menus from 160dh. BB €€

Riad Lamane Route de M'Hamid, Amazrou ⓦ riad lamane.com378. Swish hotel hidden behind high walls in the heart of the palmery. Rooms are beautifully appointed, with decor looking towards sub-Saharan Africa, *tadelakt* en-suite bathrooms and private balconies; deceptively grand villas frame the garden, or you can bed down in cosy Berber tents. A library, pool and well-stocked bar add to the charm. Bicycles can be rented to explore the palmeries and guided walks of the Jewish Quarter and an old *ksar* can be arranged. BB €€€

La Rose des Sables Av Allal Ben Abdallah ☎ 0524 847274. This deceptively large budget hotel has a range of clean and comfortable rooms – some with shared bathrooms, others with balconies – and a very friendly owner. The ground-floor restaurant is simple but has some of the best food in town (see below). Rooms with a/c are available. €

CAMPING

Camping Oasis Palmier Route de Nakhla, Amazrou, 400m north of the roundabout ☎ 0524 846724 or ☎ 0613 985231. Set at the foot of Jebel Zagora, on the far side of the river, this simple campsite has a pleasant mix of well-shaded pitches and Berber tents, with clean toilet blocks (showers cost extra), a relaxing café and friendly management. Two en-suite rooms and a family apartment offer an alternative to camping. Wi-fi connects at the reception and a laundry service is available. Camping € room €

EATING AND DRINKING

SEE MAP PAGE 378

Most people eat in their hotels, particularly if they're based in the Amazrou palmery, with many places offering competitive half- or full-board deals, though the cafés clustered around the intersection of Bd Mohammed V and Av Allal Ben Abdallah are a good bet for cheaper eats.

Chez Ali Av Atlas Zaouit el Baraka ⓦ chezali.xtadia.com. For a delightful evening meal, it's hard to beat the restaurant here: dining is communal, at candlelit tables in the lush grounds, and most of the food – *chakchouka* salad, *makfoul* tajine – comes straight from his walled vegetable garden. €€

Dromadaire Gourmand Bd Mohammed V, 2km north of the junction with Av Allal Ben Abdallah. It's quite a

way along the Agdz road from the centre of Zagora, but the "Gourmet Camel" is one of the better places to eat in town, with a pleasant traditional salon and pavement tables. The menu is classic Moroccan, including a "Marriage" tajine; you can ask in advance for *mechoui* (groups only) and, of course, camel. €€

Hôtel La Rose des Sables Av Allal Ben Abdallah. Good-value Moroccan staples attract locals and tourists alike to this popular hotel restaurant. Choose from tajines with apricots and prunes or push the boat out for a comparatively keenly priced pastilla or *mechoui*; there are filling brochettes and tasty soups too. €€

SHOPPING

Caverne du Troc Route de M'Hamid, Amazrou. A treasure-trove of carpets and the usual trinket boxes and crafts, offering a great shopping experience. Carpets are divided into sections according to age and serious buyers may even be taken up to the antique section of the shop, which offers some truly authentic treats.

Maison Berbère Av Hassan II. The Zagora branch of the Alaoui family chain, which has a reputation for its rugs, is one of the best-quality outlets in the south, fairly hassle-free and likely to draw you in for an hour or so's mint tea-assisted browsing.

DIRECTORY

Banks BMCE, Banque Populaire and Credit Agricolé on Bd Mohammed V have ATMs and will advance cash against Visa cards.

Post office The Post Office is located on Bd Mohammed V around 50m from the CTM office, towards Agdz.

South to M'Hamid and the Erg Chigaga

The Zagora oasis stretches for some 30km south of town, where the Drâa dries up for a while, to resurface in a final fertile belt before the desert. With a car, it's a fine journey, with the interesting village of **Tamegroute** a worthwhile stop on the way down to **M'Hamid**, the climax of this trip and the gateway to the towering dunes of the **Erg Chigaga**.

Tamegroute

Despite appearances, **TAMEGROUTE**, 18km from Zagora, was once the most important settlement in the Drâa Valley. It's an unusual place, a group of *ksour* and kasbahs wedged tightly together and linked by low, covered passageways. Here, uniquely, the narrow alleys extend beneath the village (locals refer to it as the "**underground kasbah**"), though you'll need a guide to venture into the darkness.

Tamegroute's standout sight is the **Zaouia Naciri**, but the village is also known for its pottery, which bears the green glaze reminiscent of ceramics from Fez. Wanting to develop Tamegroute, the founders of the Naciri Brotherhood invited merchants and craftsmen from Fez to settle in the village – two families still working in the small **potters' cooperative** (Mon–Fri 8am–6pm), on the left as you leave Tamegroute travelling towards Tinfou, claim Fez forebears.

Zaouia Naciri

Faux guides will try to show you the way to the *zaouia*, but it's easy enough to find unaided: look for the tall white minaret through the archway at the back of the main square (the library is through the other archway, on the square's northeast corner) • Donations expected • No photography allowed in the library

Tamegroute owes its importance to its ancient and highly prestigious **Zaouia Naciri**, which was a seat of learning from the eleventh century and, from the seventeenth century, the base of the Naciri Brotherhood. Founded by Abou Abdallah Mohammed Ben Naceur (an inveterate traveller and revered scholar), the *zaouia* exercised great influence over the Drâa tribes until recent decades. Its sheikhs (or holy leaders) were

A DATE TO REMEMBER

The **dates** of the Zagora oasis are reputedly some of the finest in the country, they are harvested from September to November, a claim you can put to the test at the twice-weekly souk (Wed & Sun), where stallholders sell several dozens of Morocco's 220 or so different date varieties – look out for **mejhoul**, **bouskri**, **jihel** and, particularly, the sweet **boufeggous**, which will last for up to four years if stored properly. If you're not in town for the market, never fear: you can't get too far along the Drâa's roads before being accosted by kids brandishing boxes of the sugary snacks, often encouraging you to make a purchase by leaping out in front of your car.

known as the "peacemakers of the desert", and it was they who settled disputes among the *ksour* and between the caravan traders converging on Zagora from the Sudan. They were missionaries, too, and as late as the 1750s sent envoys to convert the wilder, animist-minded Berber tribes of the Atlas and Rif.

As in centuries past, the *zaouia* is today a refuge for the sick and mentally ill, whom you'll see sitting around the courtyard; they come in the hope of miraculous cures and/or to be supported by the charity of the brotherhood and other benevolent visitors. The complex consists of a *marabout* (the tomb of Naceur), a medersa (still used by up to eighty students, preparing for university) and, in a nearby building, a small but very interesting library that was once the richest in Morocco, containing forty thousand volumes on history, languages, mathematics, astronomy and, above all, Islam. All but about 4,000 of these have now been stolen or dispersed to Koranic schools and other museums around the country, but Tamegroute preserves a number of very early editions of the Koran printed on gazelle hide – the English-speaking curator can point out one dating from 1063 – and some rare ancient books, including a thirteenth-century algebra primer featuring Western Arabic numerals, which, although subsequently dropped in the Arab world, formed the basis of the West's numbers, through the influence of the universities of Moorish Spain.

Tinfou

You'll get your first glimpse of the Sahara at **TINFOU**, 7km on from Tamegroute – though in reality it is little more than that. Abruptly rising from the blackened *hammada*, the dunes ("dune" would be a more accurate description) are a national monument; it is thought that they cover the ruins of the kasbah of Tiguida, which was once used as a bank for the trans-Saharan nomad traders, and rumour has it that there is still gold hidden beneath the sand.

M'Hamid and the dunes

A small administrative centre built around a café-lined square, **M'HAMID** (also known as M'Hamid el Ghizlane) was once an important marketplace for nomadic and trans-Saharan trade, but of this role only a rather mundane Monday souk remains. Although M'Hamid is still more low-key than Zagora, you might be forgiven for thinking the village's main *raison d'être* these days is getting tourists onto camels – there are any number of operators, official and unofficial, who offer **camel trips** into the desert proper.

Erg Lehoudi

The most easily accessible of the dunes around M'Hamid are those at **Erg Lehoudi** ("Dunes of the Jews"), 8km north of town, which can be reached, with guidance, in a normal car via a *piste* just outside the village. They see more than their share of day-trippers (and their rubbish) and hustlers, and despite reaching a height of over 100m, somehow feel rather mundane.

Erg Chigaga

The most dramatic dunes in the entire Zagora region lie some 60km southwest of M'Hamid, where the 300m-high crescents of the **Erg Chigaga** ripple away into the horizon. The expense and time involved in getting here – a return trip by camel takes around five days; by costly 4WD, you can get there in less than two hours – is well worth it, and with quieter dunes and more spaced-out camps, the desert experience is much more akin to how you might imagine it.

ARRIVAL AND DEPARTURE	**SOUTH TO M'HAMID AND THE ERG CHIGAGA**

By bus The timing of the daily CTM bus from Zagora to Tamegroute and M'Hamid is inconvenient (it leaves Zagora at 7pm, arriving in Tamegroute 15min later and in M'Hamid after a further 1hr 25min), though local minibuses leave every hour or so. The daily CTM service to Casablanca (13hr 30min) leaves M'Hamid's main square at 6am, stopping en route at Zagora (1hr 20min), Agdz (3hr 30min), Ouarzazate (4hr 45min) and Marrakesh (9hr 45min); private services run twice daily on the same route.

By grand taxi Taxis leave throughout the day from Zagora to Tamegroute (20min) and M'Hamid (1hr 30min), depending on demand; alternatively, chartering one for an early morning trip to Tamegroute and the sand dunes near Tinfou can be easily arranged.

By car The 94km road from Zagora to M'Hamid is surfaced so the village can be reached in any car. Note that the old road south of Zagora to Anagam, on the south bank of the Drâa (the 6965, still marked on some maps), is now out of use.

TOURS

A lot of travellers organize their desert trips from Zagora, but there's no shortage of opportunities in M'Hamid to arrange a (usually cheaper) **camel safari** – including at most of the hotels. **Prices** are pretty standard, and should include a guide, camel, all meals and a tent; if you want a longer trip, the day-rate quoted may rise dramatically.

Amazing Journeys Morocco Tagounite centre ⓦ morocco-desert-camp.com. Owned by professional guide Lahsen Alkouch, who also runs a superb desert camp in a beautiful area of the Erg Chigaga dunes. Able to organize camel and 4WD excursions, treks into the mountains and customized trips.

Iguidi Tours M'Hamid, near the car park just beyond the end of the tarmac ☎ 0672 385395. Run by a local Saharwi nomad family, offering trekking as well as overnights in the Erg Lehoudi and multi-day trips into the Erg Chigaga.

Sahara Services At the Hotel Mhamid Kasbah Sahara (below), M'Hamid ⓦ saharaservices.info. Overnight camel trips to a variety of desert camps, from mobile tents to luxury setups, plus Arabic and cooking courses. They can arrange trips around M'Hamid's Nomad Festival in mid-March.

Zbar Travel At Hotel Elgizlane in the centre of the village, M'Hamid ⓦ zbartravel.com. Camel and 4WD excursions, including trips to Erg Ezahar (Screaming Dunes), the nearest big dunes to M'Hamid; Zbar's trips usually include sandboarding.

ACCOMMODATION

TAMEGROUTE

Jnane-Dar Diafa Opposite the Zaouia Naciri ☎ 0524 840622 or ☎ 0661 348149. Homely place run by a good-humoured Moroccan-Swiss couple, with accommodation spread between the kasbah-style main house (nine rooms, some with shared bathrooms) and the well-tended garden (Berber tents). Traditional meals are available. One of the best-value options in the region and also has room for camper vans. BB tent €, double €

TINFOU

★ **Kasbah Hotel SaharaSky** Tinfou ⓦ saharasky.net. Just 500m from Tinfou's large dune, this specialist hotel, run by German astronomer Fritz Gerd Koring, is the first private observatory in North Africa, the rooftop astro-observatory attracting astro-photographers and astronomers from all over the world. Guests can gaze at the dark Sahara sky through one of eight high-tech GPS telescopes – one with enough power to view galaxies ten billion light years away – and read up about their discoveries in the astronomy library; non-guests can enjoy dinner with guided stargazing (book in advance). The rooms themselves are very comfortable, with fantastic sunset views, the traditional Berber food is good, and a spa with a jacuzzi and sauna completes the experience. Closed during Ramadan. HB €€

M'HAMID

Dar Azawad Near Oulad Driss, 4km north of M'Hamid ⓦ darazawad.com. The most upmarket digs in town: opt for one of the "Saharan" rooms or a slightly bigger and more attractively furnished "Sultan" room – both are in the shady garden and share the same careful craftsmanship, particularly in their Tataouine-style ceilings. There is also cheaper accommodation in Berber tents (€€) Guests can enjoy a heated pool and a swanky hammam and spa, and tuck into dinners created with produce from the hotel's vegetable garden. Their range of desert bivouacs includes the most luxurious option in M'Hamid, a private camp with king-size beds in a tent with its own bathroom (€€€€). BB €€€

★ **Dar Sidi Bounou** Bounou, 4km north of M'Hamid, ⓦ darsidibounou.com. Run by a delightful Canadian-British artist and her Moroccan musician partner, *Sidi Bounou* is a real find, with just three comfortable rooms in the main house, magical Berber tents and *nwala* huts in the garden, and sleeping on the roof can be arranged. Guests are treated as part of the family, meaning excellent food (lunch and dinner €€), local gossip and impromptu music sessions most nights. BB tent or hut €, double €€

Hamada du Drâa 500m south of M'Hamid, on the opposite side of the riverbed ⓦ hamada-sahara.com. Pitching a tent on the orange earth at *Hamada* is by far the cheapest option in M'Hamid, though they also have box-shaped mud-brick "nomad tents", and a/c standard rooms inside the main building. The pool and restaurant are open to everyone, as well as a hammam. Camping €, double €€

★ **Mhamid Kasbah Sahara Services** On the main N9 approach road 1km before the centre of the village,

☎0661 164394. This attractive kasbah hotel is affiliated with Sahara Services for desert trips – they run four dune camps of varying standards. The 12 comfortable and traditionally furnished a/c rooms have excellent gushy hot showers, and are complimented by lovely terraces opening onto an orange orchard and the palmery and a swimming pool. Guests can accompany staff to the market to buy provisions for meals. BB €

West of the Drâa

There's little to detain you in the towns lying **west of the Drâa**, though they can be useful stopovers on the way to the Anti-Atlas or the coast. From Zagora, a rough road (upgraded from a *piste* but still in poor condition) heads west to tiny **FOUM ZGUID**, where it joins up with the R111 to Tazenakht and the N12 to Tissint and Tata. The journey is rather monotonous, though the onward roads are quite scenic in parts, the latter charting a wide river valley through some startlingly barren backdrops. The town itself is slowly becoming a base for (much-touted) tours to **Lac Iriki**, a saltpan 65km south of Foum Zguid.

North of Foum Zguid, the carpet-weaving town of **TAZENAKHT** stands at the junction of the Agadir and Ouarzazate roads, at the centre of a wonderfully remote route. If you're going to buy a rug, this is probably the best place to do so – there are numerous shops on Avenue Hassan II, where attractive weaves are made by women from nearby villages.

ARRIVAL AND INFORMATION
WEST OF THE DRÂA

FOUM ZGUID
By bus Buses run from the centre of Foum Zguid to Tazenakht (3 daily; 1hr 30min), Tata (2 daily; 2hr 30min) and Zagora (2 daily; 3–4hr), among other destinations.
By truck Pick-ups serve Zagora (5hr), with more on Mondays (souk day in Foum Zguid) and Wednesdays and Sundays (souk days in Zagora).

TAZENAKHT
By bus Tazenakht is quite a transport hub, with buses heading off in all directions.

Destinations Agadir (1 CTM & 3 others daily; 6hr); Foum Zguid (3 daily; 1hr 30min); Marrakesh (3 daily; 6hr 30min); Ouarzazate (1 CTM & 10 others daily; 1hr 35min); Taliouine (1 CTM & 5 others daily; 25min–1hr).
By grand taxi There are regular *grands taxis* to Ouarzazate (1hr) and (less so) Taliouine (1hr).
Services Tazenakht has a Banque Populaire with an ATM and a couple of petrol stations.

ACCOMMODATION AND EATING
You're unlikely to need to **spend the night** in Tazenakht – and some people find the late evening atmosphere in town can be a little edgy – though stopping off in Foum Zguid can be useful if you're taking a trip out to Lac Iriki. For cheap **meals** in Tazenakht, the cafés opposite the bus station turn out grilled kebabs and lentil stews.

Auberge Iriki Hay Alhalawane, Foum Zguid ☎0528 806568 or ☎0672 757610. Candy-striped building at the far end of Foum Zguid (on the way out to Tata), with simple but clean and bright rooms and views over Jebel Bani. There's a car park where camping can be negotiated, and decent food in the restaurant. BB €

The Dadès and Todra

Stretching northeast from Ouarzazate, the **Dadès Valley** is at times harsh and desolate, but there's a bleak beauty on the plain between the parallel ranges of the High Atlas and the Jebel Saghro. Along much of its length, the river is barely visible above ground, making the sudden appearance of its vast oases all the more astonishing. Littered with half-hidden mud-brick houses – the Dadès is also known as the **Route of a Thousand Kasbahs**, for obvious reasons – the palmeries lie along the N10 from Ouarzazate to Erfoud, offering an excellent and easy opportunity for a close look at a working oasis and, in **Skoura**, a startling range of imposing kasbahs.

THE MARATHON DES SABLES

A gruelling slog across 250km of barren *hammada* and scorching desert, the Marathon des Sables is generally acknowledged as the toughest foot race in the world. Runners are required to carry all their own equipment, including GPS (in 1994, Italian runner Mauro Prosperi spent nine days lost in the desert after getting caught in a sandstorm – he survived by drinking bats' blood and was eventually found in Algeria, 300km off track) and the dozen litres of water they'll consume during each of the six days it takes to complete the course.

Founded by a Frenchman, Patrick Bauer, in 1986, the race takes place in March or April, and today attracts around nine hundred runners each year, 250 or so from the UK, from a surprisingly broad range of demographics; in 2012, the French runner Joseph Le Louarn completed his sixth Marathon des Sables at the ripe old age of 78. The constantly changing route has recently included places such as Foum Zguid and Merzouga, although competitors stay overnight in bivouac villages. For further information, see ⓦ marathondessables.com; UK runners interested in competing should visit ⓦ marathondessables.co.uk).

7

Impressive though these are, however, it is the two gorges that cut from the valley into the High Atlas that steal the show: the **Dadès Gorge** itself, carving up a fertile strip of land behind **Boumalne du Dadès**, and, to the east, the **Todra Gorge**, a narrowing cleft in high rock walls north of **Tinghir**. Beyond both, roads run into the heart of the Atlas, a wonderful (and, from Tinghir, fairly easy) trip that emerges near Beni Mellal in the Middle Atlas.

To the south of the Dadès, the volcanic rock and limestone pinnacles of the Jebel Saghro offers exciting options, either on foot or on its network of rough *piste* roads in a 4WD.

Skoura oasis

The **Skoura oasis** begins quite suddenly, around 30km east of Ouarzazate, along a tributary of the Drâa, the Oued Ameridil. It's an extraordinary sight even from the road, which for the most part follows its southern edge – a very extensive, very dense palmery, with an incredibly confusing network of tracks winding across fords and through palms to scattered groups of *ksour* and kasbahs.

Kasbah Ameridil

2km west of Skoura village • Charge• To get there, follow the footpath behind *Kasbah Aït Ben Moro* (see page 387), across the (usually dry) Oued Ameridil; the kasbah can also be reached along a short but bumpy "road" (actually the riverbed; may be flooded in winter) signed right (west) off the road to Ouarzazate, 2km from Skoura village – the kasbah is around 700m along this side road

The grandest and most extravagantly decorated kasbah in the oasis, **Kasbah Ameridil** may well look familiar: it's eminently photogenic and features in travel brochures, coffee-table books, and it once graced the back of the fifty-dirham note (Cascades d'Ouzoud, page 219 does that today).

Ameridil was built in the seventeenth century for the *caïd* of Skoura, and various implements from the original building line one wall of the courtyard, including some ingenious little locks whose keys doubled as toothbrushes. You can poke around a variety of rooms that once served as kitchens – one still retains the ovens used to cook *tafarnoute* (bread baked over stones on the ground) and *tanourte* (bread baked on the the side of the oven) – a Koranic school and a mosque, and bedrooms used by the chief and his four wives.

Dar Aït Sous, Dar Lahsoune and Kasbah Aït Abou

Follow signs (green triangles painted on trees) to Dar Lorkham up the main *piste* at the eastern end of Skoura village, crossing the (dry) riverbed en route; you can also reach *Aït Abou* by turning left off the road to Toundant

There are several impressive kasbahs in the palmery to the north of Skoura village. After about 4km, you'll come to a pair of kasbahs, **Dar Aït Sous** and **Dar Lahsoune**; the former, small but once very grand, is in a ruinous state, used only for animals; the latter, once a Glaoui residence, is state-owned, and private. A further 2km drive takes you to the magnificent **Kasbah Aït Abou**, the tallest in the palmery and second in Skoura only to Kasbah Ameridil. It lies on well-farmed land and is still inhabited; you can pop in for a drink or a meal (it's now a restaurant and there are six rooms in the garden ☎0614 332429, €€) and soak up the views from its terrace.

Marabout Sidi M'Barek

Beyond *Kasbah Aït Abou*, on the edge of the palmery, you can follow a trail to the imposing **Marabout Sidi M'Barek**, one of seven in the Skoura oasis. A high wall, broken only by a door, encloses the *marabout*, which doubles as a grain store – a powerful twofold protection on both spiritual and military levels.

ARRIVAL AND DEPARTURE   SKOURA OASIS

By bus Buses stop in tiny Skoura village, which lies off the main road, at the eastern end of the oasis, with services from Ouarzazate (1 CTM & 4 others daily; 45min), Boumalne du Dadès (1 CTM & 6 others daily; 1hr 15min), El Kelâa M'Gouna (hourly; 35min) and Tinghir (1 CTM & 11 others daily; 2hr 35min); *Restaurant La Kasbah (aka Café Jabran)*, at the junction where the main street peels off the N10, doubles as the CTM office.

Services There's a post office, a branch of Banque Populaire with an ATM, and a couple of petrol stations on Skoura's single main street.

Guides Navigating the tiny palmery roads can be confusing, so hiring a guide is definitely worth considering, particularly for the kasbahs north of Skoura, which can otherwise be hard to find; most hotels provide their own guides and run their own excursions and can also organize transfers from Ouarzazate for up to four.

ACCOMMODATION AND EATING

The choice of **accommodation** around Skoura runs the full gamut, from basic *auberges* to luxurious hideaways; many places rent bikes for exploring the palmery. Most people dine at their hotels, though the no-frills **restaurants** ranged around the main junction in Skoura village are handy for a bite to eat if you're passing through, serving cheap omelettes, salads, tajines and brochettes.

Chez Slimani Signed off the N10 700m west of the village; follow the orange-painted rocks along a piste for 1.5km ☎0524 852359 ☎0610 229103. Hidden in the palmery beyond Kasbah Ameridil, this is the best budget option: a handful of basic rooms and (clean) shared washrooms surrounding a dusty courtyard, with a sunny roof terrace overlooking the palmery and a pleasant garden. You'll have livestock for neighbours, but what *Slimani* lacks in comforts it more than makes up for with atmosphere. HB €

THE R307: TRANS ATLAS TO DEMNATE

The spectacular **R307** is an attractive alternative to the Tizi n'Tichka, serving as an adventurous short cut through the heart of the Atlas for drivers bound for Fez. Paved, it is normally passable in a normal car and receives a fair amount of regular maintenance. However, in winter there can be heavy snowfall and mudslicks and rockslides are not uncommon when it is more comfortable in a 4WD; ask oncoming traffic what the road conditions are like ahead.

About 15km east of Ouarzazate and 26km west of Skoura, the road heads north from the N10 towards the mountains, making a dramatic ascent through extremely barren country to reach the **Tizi n'Fedrhate** (2191m). The road loses this height in the descent to the **Vallée de Tessaout** and the village of **Toufrine**, after which there is a long climb, with some tremendous views of vast landscapes and remote villages all round, before the road heads down to **Demnate** (see page 223), some 135km (around 3hr 30min in good weather, up to 6hr in bad) after leaving the N10 behind.

Dar Ahlam ⓦdarahlam.com. Set amid an oasis that was once the local ruler's private falconry ground, this beautiful Small Luxury Hotels of the World property is so exclusive that there aren't any signs to it: arrange to be met in the centre of Skoura village to be shown the way. Once there, you'll find it's as well appointed as you'd expect for the (extortionate) price, which includes as many Moroccan clay scrubs and Thai massages as your body can handle. Rates are fully inclusive (BB and HB available in low season only). €€€€

Dar Lorkam 7km up the main piste at the eastern end of Skoura village; follow the green triangles painted on trees ⓦdar-lorkam.com. Tucked away deep in the palmery, *Dar Lorkam* has six lovely double rooms and one family suite around a courtyard with a child-friendly swimming pool at its centre. The restaurant serves a fusion of French and Moroccan cuisines. Closed Jan. HB €€

★ **Les Jardins de Skoura** Signed off the N10 700m west of Skoura village; follow the orange arrows along a piste for 4km ⓦlesjardinsdeskoura.com. A real oasis within the oasis. The eight lovely rooms at this beautifully renovated farmhouse show great attention to detail, the

staff are friendly and attentive, and the tranquil gardens that give its name are the perfect place to unwind, ending in an inviting little pool. Dinner (€€€) is recommended because the Moroccan and Mediterranean food is superb. Guided walks are on offer in the palmery. BB €€

Kasbah Aït Ben Moro On the N10, 1.5km west of Skoura village ☎0524 852116, ⓦkasbahaitbenmoro.com. An eighteenth-century kasbah beautifully renovated by its Spanish expat owner and comprising a dozen or so doubles (plus several triples from €100), furnished and decorated in traditional style. The swimming pool, set in a stone terrace at the back, affords good views over the palmery, and the food is top-notch, too (dinner 150dh). BB €

Kasbah Les Nomades 600m up the main piste at the eastern end of Skoura village ☎0661 896329. Rather grand for the price, this family affair has eight colourful en suite and a/c rooms, four are in turrets that overlook the palmery, and traditional meals are served in the restaurant. Also runs a well-stocked craft shop next to Ben Moro (above), that among other trinkets sells excellent Berber rugs and jewellery. HB €

El Kelâa M'Gouna

Travelling through the Dadès in spring, you'll find the fields around **EL KELÂA M'GOUNA**, 45km east of Skoura, laced with the bloom of thousands of small pink **roses**, cultivated into hedgerows dividing the plots. The roses – *Rosa damascena*, probably brought here from Persia by the Phoenicians – are harvested by local women, who start very early in the morning before the heat dries the bloom. Trucks ferry the petals to Kelâa's two factories, where they're distilled into the rose oil that forms the basis of all the moisturizers, hand creams and other rose-related products that you'll see in the region's shops. The size of the factories reflects the task at hand: there are an estimated 4200km of rose hedges around Kelâa, with each metre yielding around a kilogram of petals, and ten tonnes of petals are needed to produce just two or three litres of rose oil.

In late May (sometimes early June), a **rose festival** is held in the village to celebrate the new year's crops – a good time to visit, with villagers coming down from the mountains for the market, music and dancing.

Cooperative Artisanale des Poignards Azlag

On the N10 on the eastern edge of town

Kelâa's tradition of dagger-making is still going strong at the **Azlag Dagger Cooperative**, a one-stop knife shop that provides work for one hundred artisans and their families. It's laid out with a large showroom in the front, and a series of small workshops in a U-shape around the sides and back. There's usually someone working away hammering intricate designs into curved (synonymous with the Berber town of Azlag) and straight (Taureg) blades in pretty much the same way that Berber craftsman have for the last seven hundred years.

Vallée des Roses

North of El Kelâa M'Gouna begins one of the most scenic but least explored regions of the central High Atlas. Tourist literature likes to refer to it as the "**Vallée des Roses**", but in fact the famous roses are grown not so much in a single valley as a tangle of different ones. A spectacular 35km road runs here from El Kelâa, weaving up the Hdida Valley and traversing the Imi n'Louh plateau (where Berber nomads still pass the winter in little caves) to cross the Jebel Ta'Louit. From the pass (2084m), you can survey the full glory of the M'Goun massif to the north; turn back here unless you have a 4WD, in which case you can drop steeply via some hair-raising switchbacks to **Bou Thaghrar** (pronounced "Boot-Ag-*ra*"), a trio of villages on the valley floor that hold some impressive ruined kasbahs.

ARRIVAL AND INFORMATION   **EL KELÂA M'GOUNA**

By public transport Buses and *grands taxis* pull into a strip at the centre of El Kelâa outside the post office, with buses running from and to Ouarzazate (hourly; 1hr 35min), Skoura (hourly; 35min), Boumalne du Dadès (hourly; 35min) and Tinghir (hourly; 1hr 30min–1hr 55min) among others. Regular minibuses run from El Kelâa to Bou Thaghrar

for the Vallée des Roses (30min).

Services Crédit Agricole in the centre of town has an ATM, and 200m southwest is the post office and a petrol station. The small supermarket next to Crédit Agricole has a good stock (daily 8am–8pm), and the Weds souk sells food.

ACCOMMODATION

Kasbah Assafar 1km off the road that runs to Bou Thaghrar, 5km north of El Kelâa ⓦkasbahassafar.com. Skilfully restored *pisé* kasbah in the village of Aït Khyar, with a terrace that makes the most of its lofty position (1400m altitude) – there are eight rooms (two en suite) but make sure you ask for one with valley views. Also operates *Assafar Cottage* nearby, which has seven dorm rooms with three–ten beds, shared bathrooms and a self-catering kitchen – or eat at the main restaurant. Cooking (€€€, set menus) centres around honest Berber food (cooking classes are available). Owner Boullouz Aziz is a very experienced mountain guide who can organize walking and mountain biking in the Vallée des Roses and the Jebel Saghro. BB dorm €, shared bathroom €, en suite room €€

★ **Kasbah Itran** 3.5km north of El Kelâa on road to Bou Thaghrar ⓦkasbahitran.com. Run by the hospitable Taghda brothers (all seven of them), the enchanting *Kasbah Itran* is set high on an escarpment overlooking the mouth of the M'Goun river valley, with its spectacular ruined kasbah, *ksour* and irrigated gardens. The nine stylishly decorated rooms (two can sleep up to five) make the most of the views, which extend across the Dadès to the distant Jebel Saghro and snow-covered Jebel M'Goun. Breakfasts are served on a magnificent terrace, dinner indoors in a candlelit Moroccan salon (set menu €€). They also run excellent walking trips in the Vallée des Roses and into the M'Goun massif. HB shared bathroom €, en suite room €€

Boumalne du Dadès

The perfunctory town of **BOUMALNE DU DADÈS**, 50km east of El Kelâa M'Gouna, holds little of interest – it's not much more than a straggle of shops and cafés and

---

TREKKING IN THE VALLÉE DES ROSES

Beyond Bou Thaghrar, at the northern end of the **Vallée des Roses** (see page 387), the *pistes* degenerate or disappear altogether, making this prime **trekking territory**, which for the most part remains blissfully beyond the reach of most 4WDs. Depending on the amount of time you have, a typical route in the region could range from a day hike through the **satellite villages of Bou Thaghrar** to a ten-day trek north through the magnificent **Gorges du M'Goun**, a real adventure involving hours of wading waist-deep through meltwater. With three days to spare, the varied (and mostly dry) walk to **Ameskar**, via Alemdoun and Amejgag – the conventional approach route for mountaineers bound for M'Goun – would be an ideal sampler, passing through a series of pretty villages and some superb gorges.

PRACTICALITIES

April and May, while the roses are being harvested, are the **best months** to walk here, but the routes are practicable in all but the height of summer. **Guides** are essential, not just to show the way but also to help relate to local Berber people, few of whom see many trekkers; contact *Kasbah Itran* or *Kasbah Assafar* (see page 388), both of which organize highly recommended trips around the region, or El Kelâa's Bureau des Guides, 500m west of town (☎0661 796101 or ☎0662 132192).

a large market square where farmers trade their livestock and produce on busy Wednesday and Sunday mornings. That said, there's a likeable commercial buzz about the place, and as the main gateway to the Dadès Gorge, which starts just a few kilometres to the northwest of town, and the Jebel Saghro, it can serve as a useful base. Boumalne also offers bird-watching possibilities in the expanse of hammada, or desert fringe, to the south of town where red-rumped wheatear, lanner falcon and the elusive Houbara bustard may be spotted by keen twitchers.

ARRIVAL AND DEPARTURE BOUMALNE DU DADÈS

By bus Buses drop and pick up from outside the covered market; note that the CTM ticket office is north of the market square near *Hôtel-Restaurant Bougafer*. Minibuses head off throughout the day to the Dadès Gorge and Msemrir (2hr), departing from a stop just in front of the covered market.

Destinations Agadir (1 daily; 8hr); Casablanca (2 daily; 10hr); El Kelâa M'Gouna (hourly; 35min); Er Rachidia (1 CTM & 1 other daily; 3hr 30min); Erfoud (2 daily; 5hr); Fez (2 daily; 12hr); Goulmim (1 daily; 11hr); Goulmima (1 daily; 2hr); Marrakesh (1 CTM, 1 Supratours & 5 others daily;

7hr); Meknes (2 daily; 11hr); Merzouga (1 Supratours; 6hr); Ouarzazate (hourly; 1hr 45min–2hr 15min); Skoura (hourly; 1hr 15min); Tantan (1 daily; 16hr); Taroudant (1 daily; 7hr); Tinejdad (1 daily; 1hr 30min); Tinghir (hourly; 45min); Tiznit (1 daily; 9hr); Zagora (1 daily; 6hr).

By grand taxi Taxis make regular runs from the rank outside the covered market to El Kelâa (30min), Ouarzazate (1hr 20min), Tinghir (40min), Tinejdad (1hr 30min), with several daily services to Msemrir (1hr 30min). Taxis to the Dadès Gorge (20min) can also be negotiated.

INFORMATION AND TOURS

Services There's a Banque Populaire with an ATM on the main street, but the post office is a little harder to find, hidden down a bumpy track at the top end of town. Petrol stations bookend Boumalne.

Guides All the below speak English and French and prices can be negotiated by email. Ilyas Tamlalte runs Berber Nomad Trekking, (w berbernomadtrekking.com) and is an expert young and enthusiastic guide who is local to the Dadès region. He can organize walks in the Vallée des Roses, treks (1–3 days) in the Jebel Saghro,

and treks between Dadès Gorge and Todra Gorge (3 days). Alternatively, Lhoussain Oufkir (w moroccotrekkingguides. wordpress.com) is a Boumalne Du Dadès resident and has been guiding for more than 20 years and can take you on hikes through the Dadès Gorge, or on multi-day trekking trips to Jebel Saghro (he also speaks Dutch). Also, Hamou Aït Lhou, at the Bureau des Guides at the western end of town (t 0667 593292, e hamou57@voila.fr), runs similar trips including a day trip to the Dadès Gorge with lunch with a Berber family.

ACCOMMODATION

Bougafer Near the market square, just off the main road t 0612 212278 or t 0668 167757. Best of a mediocre bunch of cheapies, with small rooms (private and shared bathroom options) set off a bare-bones salon, but it's clean enough and some sleep four making it good value for friends or a family. Breakfast on the little terrace overlooking central Boumalne is a good start to any day. There's also a popular café on the ground floor serving tajines, couscous and brochettes (mains €€). BB €

Kasbah La Jeanne Clearly signed off the N10 north of town, on the eastern side of the river t 0524 830072 or t 0667 415697. A beautiful family-run eco-kasbah, built from scratch over five years by environment enthusiast Moha Mansoub. With walls 70cm thick, the kasbah demonstrates how effective *pisé* builds are during winter. Rooms are spacious and homely, with handmade juniper doors and *tadelakt* bathrooms. Moha is an authorized guide and can organize treks and excursions into the Vallée des Roses and Jebel Saghro. Dinner €€€. BB €€

★ **La Perle du Dadès** 500m down a piste off the N10 (crossing the Oued Dadès en route), 6.5km west of

Boumalne; if the river's too deep, follow blue markers for 6km along a piste signed off the main road at the top of Boumalne itself w perledudades.com. A little out of town, but hugely popular with families, as it's big on room size and even bigger on things to do, including ping pong, billiards, table football, a swimming pool and hammam. There's a variety of rooms at a variety of prices (including some troglodyte cave rooms), all decorated with mementoes from the French owners' time in West Africa. BB €€

Riad Soleil Bleu At the end of a piste 500m beyond the Xaluca Dadès t 0524 830163 or t 0650 499876. Appealing place, with sweeping views of the valley, psychedelic decor and two kinds of room: "standard" on the ground floor and more luxurious ones upstairs with a/c and balconies. There's space for parking and camping with hot showers. Also serves delicious, inventive meals. Camping €, BB double €

Xaluca Dadès Signed off the N10, near the Shell station w xaluca.com. Popular tour-group hotel with 106 nicely designed rooms but the personal touch of a much smaller operation thanks to great staff. There's a gym, tennis court and a funky bar, and a varied (and tasty) buffet spread each night. Non-residents are welcome to lounge around the beautiful pool drinking beer or wine and enjoying the fine views. BB €€€

EATING AND DRINKING

Atlas Dadès Bd Mohammed V. Agreeable café covering the seasonal bases with two terraces, a small garden and a fire-heated salon for winter, where you can enjoy a coffee or an orange juice, or tuck into grilled sausages, brochettes, a sandwich or a vegetable tajine. Free wi-fi is available. €€

Oussikis Place de Souk, on the eastern side of the market square ☎ 0524 831829. An established spot for local traders and great for people watching over lunch, with a well-kept open kitchen and a menu of traditional Moroccan dishes that change regularly. €€

Dadès Gorge

The 45-km-long **Dadès Gorge**, with its high cliffs of limestone and weirdly shaped erosions, begins almost immediately north of Boumalne du Dadès. A mixture of modern houses and older *ksour* edge the road, with fields fronting gentle slopes at first but giving way to increasingly precipitous drop-offs as the road nears Msemrir. Most travellers get as far as **Aït Oufi**, 25km or so into the gorge, before turning back. It's a fine day-trip, but it would be a shame not to explore the area further – pushing on, the gorge closes to its narrowest point just 9km further along, while a couple of days' walking in and around the gorge from one of its many hotels will reward you with superb scenery, with plenty of kasbahs and *pisé* architecture to admire.

Boumalne to Aït Oudinar

About 8km along the road into the gorge, you pass the old, rust-red Glaoui kasbah of **Aït Youl**, shortly after which the road climbs over a little pass, flanked by the *Hotel-Restaurant Meguirne*, a fine place to stop for lunch (see page 392); its owner takes a proprietary interest in a hidden side-valley nearby, organizing enjoyable one and half to two hour hikes (with or without guide), or rent a mountain bike for a day (80dh).

The most impressive **rock formations** in this area lie another few kilometres along the road at **Tamlalt**, just after the *Hôtel Tamlalte*, where an extraordinary cliff known as the "**Monkey's Fingers**" rises from the far side of the valley. The rock, a weathered conglomerate of pebbles thought to have settled where a huge river entered a primordial sea, is a startling sight, looming over the villagers who toil in the fields below; a gorge, in places only a few feet wide, can be followed right through the rocks (ask locally).

Beyond Tamlalt, the valley floor is less fertile and the hills gentler. The road continues through the hamlet of Aït Ali to **Aït Oudinar** (around 23km from Boumalne), where a bridge spans the river and the gorge narrows quite dramatically.

Aït Oudinar to Msemrir

After passing *Les Vieux Chateaux*, the road climbs by a coil of hairpin bends before squeezing through the tight, narrow mouth of the gorge to reach **Taghia n'Dadès**. From here, you can scramble east up the hill to a **cave** with stalactites, or walk north to a small but impressive gorge (the "**Petit Gorge**"), with views down over the Dadès Valley.

For a distance beyond Taghia, the east side of the gorge is dominated by the Isk n'Isladene cliffs. Emerging from their shadow, the road follows a canyon to Tidrit where it snakes up and crosses the face of one of the huge canyon loops before the final run to Msemrir; the rock face all along this route is run through with incredible swirling patterns. Two kilometres before Msemrir, the Oussikis valley can be visited by an even rougher *piste* that runs off to the left, accessing a scenic walk along the Barrage d'Oussikis (2hr return).

Msemrir

Little more than a scattering of dusty government buildings and cafés, **Msemrir**, 60km from Boumalne, has a desultory, frontier feel to it. The lively Saturday souk provides the only real incentive to stop, but you may want to use the village as a staging post in a longer journey across the mountains – north of Msemrir, *pistes* run east to join the Todra Gorge at Tamtatoucht and north across the High Atlas.

ARRIVAL AND DEPARTURE

By public transport *Grands taxis*, minibuses and Berber pick-ups leave regularly from outside the covered market in Boumalne du Dadès for Aït Ali (45min) and Msemrir (1hr 30min by *grand taxi*, 2hr by minibus).

By car The road up the Dadès Gorge is surfaced all the way to Msemrir and is accessible – spring floods permitting – throughout the year.

TO THE TODRA GORGE

By car With a 4WD, you could tackle the *piste* that runs from Msemrir to Tamtatoucht, north of the Todra Gorge (see map, page 216). The route (passable May–Sept) runs northeast off the Msemrir–Agoudal *piste* (which starts at Tilmi, 15km north of Msemrir) to the Tizi n'Uguent Zegsaoun (2639m), before dropping down through a long valley and across wobbly limestone strata to emerge just north of Tamtatoucht. Note, however, that it's a long, uphill haul from the Dadès, and the seventy-odd kilometres of *piste*, often in a shocking state, can take a full day to travel. It's much easier (and quicker) to backtrack down the Dadès and

DADÈS GORGE

access the Todra Gorge/Tamtatoucht via Boumalne, the N10 and Tinghir – Boumalne to Tinghir is only about an hour's drive.

On a tour Ilyas Tamlalte of Berber Nomad Trekking (see page 389), is one of several guides who runs three-day treks along the *piste* connecting the Dadès and Todra gorges; he can also organize 4WDs and prices can be arranged by email.

ACROSS THE ATLAS

By truck Pick-up trucks run daily up the *piste* from Msemrir to Agoudal, where you can connect with trucks to Imilchil (see page 216).

By car With a 4WD, you can drive to Agoudal yourself (passable May–Sept), picking up the *piste* at Tilmi: allow 4hr to Agoudal – it's 60km or so of very rough driving, cresting the Tizi n'Ouano (2750m) along the way – and a further 2hr 30min along the paved road to Imilchil. Most people, however, cross the Atlas on the paved road from Tamtatoucht (see page 397).

TOURS

Most of the hotels in the gorge offer **guided walks**, either within the gorge itself, to the Petit Gorge or to other hidden canyons; alternatively, several guides in **Boumalne** run trips in and around the gorge (see page 389).

ACCOMMODATION

The first 10km of the route is speckled with **auberges** and **restaurants**, though the gorge's largest concentration of **hotels** lies 27km from Boumalne, hemmed in by slabs of cliff. In winter, temperatures in the gorge plummet at night, so check what sort of **heating** your hotel has if visiting at this time of year. The accommodation below is listed in the order you encounter it coming **from Boumalne**.

Agdal Msemrir, 60km from Boumalne ☎ 0671 532052. This simple hotel-cum-café on Msemrir's main drag is only of interest if you're looking for somewhere to stop on a longer journey across the Atlas. It's the best choice in town, though, thanks to its gregarious owner, who oversees eight en-suite rooms set around a small Berber salon. BB €

★ **Auberge Chez Pierre** 25km from Boumalne ⓦ chez pierre.org. The eponymous Pierre might no longer be in charge, but the current owners of this hospitable *auberge* have kept the family feel. Twelve tastefully decorated rooms (four luxury suites) occupy a traditional-style *pisé* building, with its own pool (the only one in the valley) and well-kept gardens, but the main event here is the tremendous food: duck, quail and goat-cheese dishes feature regularly on a locally sourced set menu (priced separately) that combines the best of Moroccan and French cooking. Organized

activities include walks to the Gorge of Sidi Boubker. Heated by radiators during winter. BB €€

Auberge Tissadrine 27km from Boumalne ☎ 0524 831745 or ☎ 0670 233418. Light and airy hotel run by two brothers, whose en suite rooms have been nicely refurbished in authentic style; some come with balconies. Take dinner in the attractive salon or out on the riverside terrace. There's heating from open fires and electric heaters during the winter. Varied guided walks explore a nearby canyon. HB €

Berbère de la Montagne 34km from Boumalne ⓦ berbere-montagne.com. One of the best-value mid-price places in the area – with ten tastefully furnished and heated en suite double, triple and quad rooms (wherever you lay your head it's the same price per person) that have the feel of a Mediterranean villa about them, and carefully prepared Berber meals served on a lovely streamside terrace. The hotel also has a pleasant, wooded campsite (with electricity) and makes a good base for short walks in and around the gorge. Camping €, HB double €€

Riad des Vieilles Charrues 24km from Boumalne ⓦ riadvieillescharrues.com. Skilfully restored riad in the village of Aït Oudinar, run by the welcoming Naïm family, offering ten spacious rooms (three with a/c), good home

7

cooking set dinner menu for an additional fee) and central heating to help keep you warm in winter. Relax on the suntrap of a terrace or head off into the hills on guided walks. BB €€ **Source de Dadès** 33km from Boumalne ⓦ hotel-jardin-source-dades.com. A traditional building that catches the

sun in winter, with only three double and one triple rooms, all impeccably clean; charm is derived from its striking location, just before the gorge narrows, and hospitable service. The friendly owners organize numerous walks in the area, including gorge-top hikes and trips to nearby caves. HB €

EATING AND DRINKING

Hotel Restaurant Meguirne 14km from Boumalne ⓦ auberge-miguirne-dades.com. The views make this a fine place to stop for lunch (as tour groups do); the food, such as brochette and chips is prepared by Ali, the unfailingly cheerful owner. In summer, the breakfast terrace is the first in the valley to catch the sun. Nine en-suite rooms are available (€€ HB).

Hôtel Café Timzzillite 29km from Boumalne. Worth a coffee stop at least, with stupendous views from a blustery terrace on the edge of the cliffs down over the Dadès' much-photographed section of switchback turns – though they also do vegetable kebabs and an unusual spaghetti-based menu. Simple en-suite rooms are available with hot water, heaters and extra blankets (€€ BB).

The Jebel Saghro

The brooding mountain range looming to the south of the N9 is the **Jebel Saghro**, a starkly beautiful jumble of volcanic peaks and weirdly eroded tabletop mesas. Dramatically barren ("*jebel saghro*" means "dry mountain" in Berber), it is quite unlike the High Atlas or Anti-Atlas, and is increasingly attracting trekkers keen to explore its gorges, ruined kasbahs and occasional villages. The austere landscape is punctuated by the black tents of the semi-nomadic **Aït Atta tribe** – fiercely independent through the centuries, and never subdued by any sultan, the Aït Atta were the last bulwark of resistance against the French, making their final stand on the slopes of Jebel Bou Gafer (see page 394).

The traverse

The classic **Saghro trek** cuts through the heart of the range, from **Tagdilt to N'Kob**, on the other side of the mountains (three days). Following the *piste* south out of Tagdilt, you can pick up a path that wends past the **Isk n'Alla** (2569m) and then up towards the **Tizi n'Ouarg**, an area of high meadows and a good spot to camp. A side trip up **Jebel Kouaouch** (2592m) is rewarded with fine views back towards snowcapped M'Goun and south towards N'Kob; or you can push on, past some extraordinary rock formations: the spires of **Tassigdelt Tamajgalt** and the **Tête de Chameau**, near Igli, a striking conglomerate that, in the right light, doesn't look too unlike a camel's head. From Igli, you can then either follow a path south over the **Tizi n'Taggourt** or divert east to take in **Bab n'Ali**, the Saghro's most notable feature and a spectacular sight at dawn or dusk. The routes converge near the village of **Ighazoun n'Imlas**, from where a *piste* heads south down a remarkably green valley before climbing out to wander a barren waste to N'Kob (see page 413).

An alternative **route from Iknioun** (five days) heads east, under the shadow of **Amalou n'Mansour** – at 2712m, the highest summit in the Saghro – to Maddou, from where you can make a side trip north to **Jebel Bou Gafer** (see page 394); you'll probably need to camp here overnight to make the most of a visit to the battlefield. Backtracking to Maddou, the route continues via **Tizilit** and **Imi n'Site** to emerge near some rock carvings at the R108, 8km east of N'Kob.

The circuit

The much longer anticlockwise **loop from El Kelâa M'Gouna** and back (ten days) follows part of the traverse but also takes in the more diverse scenery of the Saghro's northern and southern foothills. From El Kelâa (you could also hike a similar circuit to and from Boumalne), the path crosses a plain to the villages of **Aït Youl** (also reachable in a taxi) and, much further on, **Afoughal**, at the foot of **Jebel Afoughal** (2196m). The route continues south over the **Tizi n'Tagmoute** before heading east along dry river valleys and through chiselled gorges, with views to **Tine Ouaiyour** (2129m), in the centre of the range.

At Ighazoun n'Imlas, the path picks up the northern section of the "traverse" route, following it to the **Tizi n'Ouarg** before turning back west to crest both the **Tizi n'Tmighcht** and the **Tizi n'Irhioui**, steep mountain passes with breathtaking views as far as the High Atlas. From here on, it's a downwards hike back to Aït Youl and, ultimately, El Kelâa again.

ARRIVAL AND INFORMATION   JEBEL SAGHRO

When **planning a trek** in the Saghro, bear in mind the harshness of the terrain and the considerable distances involved. With the exception of the Vallée des Oiseaux, off the Boumalne–Iknioun road, which is a feasible destination for day-trips (see page 389), this is not an area for short treks, nor does it have much infrastructure. **Accommodation** camping, *gîtes* and village homes.

By pick-up, taxi or car There's a daily pick-up truck from Boumalne du Dadès to Tagdilt, off the R6907, and taxis run most days from Tinghir and Boumalne to Iknioun, further along the road. The N'Kob souk is on a Sunday, so you may also be able to pick up a ride south on the Saturday. You can also access Iknioun on a *piste* from Tinghir, a very beautiful road but one that's only passable in a 4WD.

When to visit The Jebel Saghro is a popular trekking destination between October and April, when the High Atlas is too cold and snow-covered for walking; in the summer, it's too hot and exposed and water is impossible to find.

Guides Hiring a guide is recommended for trekking and for exploring by (4WD) vehicle – road signs are rare and navigating isn't easy, while flash floods often lead to diversions or worse. There are *bureau des guides* and/or independent guides in Boumalne du Dadès (see page 389), Tinghir (see page 396), El Kelâa M'Gouna (see page 388) and, to the south, N'Kob (see page 414); you might hire guides and muleteers in the villages at the northern base of the mountains.

Tours Pathfinders Treks in Marrakech (🌐 pathfinderstreks. com), or adventure tour companies abroad, including Explore (🌐 explore.co.uk), Walks Worldwide (🌐 walksworldwide. com) and On The Go Tours (🌐 onthegotours.com).

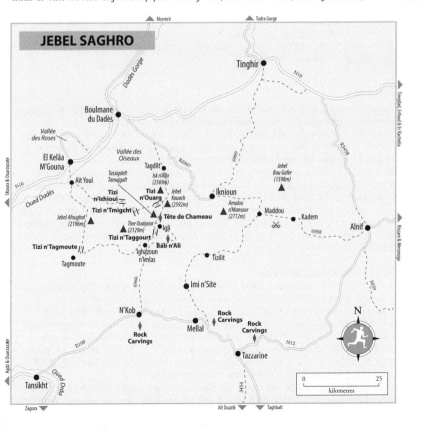

THE BATTLE FOR BOU GAFER

For three centuries or more, the **Aït Atta** tribe were the great **warriors** of the south, dominating the Jebel Saghro and its eastern extension, the Jebel Ougnat. As guerrilla fighters, they resisted the French occupation from the outset, finally retreating in early 1933 to the rocky stronghold of the **Jebel Bou Gafer**, a chaos of gorges and pinnacles. Despite the Aït Atta being vastly outnumbered by superior French forces, what followed was, according to David Hart in *The Aït 'Atta of Southern Morocco*, "the hardest single battle which the French had ever had to fight in the course of their 'pacification' of Morocco".

The French first attacked the stronghold on February 21, after which they launched almost daily attacks on the ground and from the air – the French are believed to have used four air squadrons at the battle, in addition to some 83,000 troops (the Aït Atta, in comparison, numbered around a thousand fighting men). Many died on both sides, but the Aït Atta, under the command of **Hassou Ba Salem**, did not surrender for over a month, by which time they were reduced to half their strength and had run short of ammunition.

Ba Salem's **conditions on surrender** included a promise that the Aït Atta could maintain their tribal structures and customs, and that they would not be "ruled" by the infamous T'hami el Glaoui, the pasha of Marrakesh, whom they regarded as a traitor to their homeland (see page 304). The French were content to accept, the battle meaning that their "pacification" was virtually complete, and giving them access to the valuable silver and copper mines at Moudou.

Ba Salem died in 1960 and was buried at Taghia, his birthplace, 5km from Tinghir (see page 395). Ali, his son, succeeded him as leader of the tribe, and took part in the 1975 Green March into the Western Sahara; he died in 1992 and is also buried at Taghia. As for the **battlefield** itself, local guides will show you the sites, including ruins of the stronghold. It is still littered with spent bullets, which are covered in spring by colourful clumps of thyme, rockroses and broom.

Tinghir

Despite serving largely as a base for the trip up into the Todra Gorge, **TINGHIR** is a more interesting place than other administrative centres along the N10: overlooked by an abandoned but ornamental Glaoui kasbah and flanked by extensive **palmeries** that feel a world apart, with their groups of *ksour* built at intervals into the rocky hills above. Tinghir's own **ksar** has been extensively restored in parts (one of its mosques has even been rebuilt in pink concrete), but the Aït el Haj Ali district, in the south, retains an appealing air of authenticity. The Monday **souk**, just west of town, is one of the largest in the south and a good place to pick up pottery from the palmery village of El Hart.

The lushness of Tinghir's palmeries seems all the more special after the journey from Boumalne, a bleak 53km drive across desolate plains with only the hazy **Jebel Saghro** for company, the barren outlines of its mountains looming to the south like something from the steppes of Central Asia.

Tinghir and Todra palmeries

You can access the Tinghir palmery through the town's *ksar*, or by heading east (right) off the N10 just beyond the Todra Gorge turning; for the Todra palmery, catch a taxi to the entrance to the Todra Gorge and head south into the palmery on foot from there

Lining both sides of the Oued Todra to the north of town, the **Tinghir and Todra palmeries** are major attractions in themselves, dotted with picturesque villages whose *ksour* and kasbahs are incised with extraordinarily complex patterns. Walk or ride on the west side of the valley for the best panoramas of the Todra palmery, a blanket of palms shielding olives, figs, almonds and alfalfa; the *Hôtel Saghro* (see page 397) enjoys fine views of the Tinghir palmery from its terrace bar.

The small village of **Afanour** makes a pleasant destination for an afternoon ramble around the Tinghir palmery, with its restored *pisé* mosque. Consider though a longer walk which means you could also take in **Souk el Khemis** (Thursday souk) and **El Hart**, 15km southeast of Tinghir and comprising El Hart n'Igourramen, with a *marabout* that is the focus of a June/July moussem, and the larger El Hart n'Iaamine, famous for its earthenware pottery; note that the potters can be difficult to find without a guide (see page 396), as they work out of their (unmarked) homes. The tombs of the Aït Atta chief, Hassou Ba Salem (see page 394), and his son, Ali Ba Salem can also be visited at nearby **Taghia**.

Ikelane Mosque

Signed off the N10, just north of the turning to the Todra Gorge; follow the white arrows for 300m • Charge

Despite its ancient appearance, the nineteenth-century **Ikelane Mosque** was a fully functioning focus of the community until a decade or so ago, until which time it

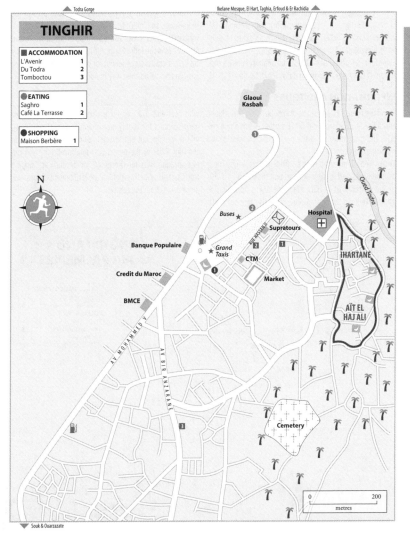

served as both mosque and medersa for the people of Afanour – the *ksar* itself was abandoned in 2002.

The whole complex has been lovingly restored, and you can wander around the mud-brick ablutions room (complete with well) and peek into the prayer hall, with its characterfully cockeyed supporting pillars. The reward for climbing up on to the roof – once the Koranic school's "classroom" – is far-reaching views across the palmery.

ARRIVAL AND DEPARTURE
TINGHIR

By bus All buses arrive at and depart from the main road, Av Mohammed V (the N10), next to the Pl Principale. Both the CTM and Supratours offices are located on Rue Hassan II. Destinations Agadir (3 daily; 14hr); Boumalne du Dadès (1 CTM daily & others hourly; 45min); Casablanca (3 daily; 11hr); Er Rachidia (1 Supratours & 4 others daily; 4 hr); Erfoud (1 daily; 3hr 30min); Fez (3 daily; 15hr); Marrakesh (1 CTM, 2 Supratours & 5 others daily; 7hr 30min); Meknes (4 daily; 9hr); Merzouga (1 Supratours daily; 5hr); Ouarzazate (2 Supratours & 9 others daily; 2hr 30min); Rabat (3 daily; 12hr); Rissani (1 daily; 4hr); Tangier (1 daily; 16hr); Tinejdad (1 CTM, 1 Supratours & 10 others daily; 1hr); Zagora (2 daily; 6hr).

By grand taxi Taxis run regularly from Pl Principale to Boumalne du Dadès (40min), Kelaa M'Gouna (1hr 30min), Ouarzazate (2hr), Tinejdad (45min) and Er Rachidia (2hr), and occasionally to Erfoud (best to connect in Tinejdad) and Rissani (2hr 15min). It is possible to negotiate taxis to the Todra Gorge and Imilchil.

By truck Berber lorries also leave from Pl Principale, bound for villages in the Todra Gorge and beyond; after the Monday souk, numerous lorries set out for villages in the High Atlas, passing Imilchil on their way to Aghbala.

INFORMATION AND TOURS

Services There's a Banque Populaire opposite Pl Principale, and a Crédit du Maroc and BMCE further south along the N10. The post office is on the northeastern corner of the municipal gardens.

Tours *Hôtel Tomboctou* runs a variety of local trips. These include walks and donkey rides around the palmery, a visit to the potteries at El Hart n'laamine 15km from Tinghir, and 4hr treks in the Todra Gorge. They also hire out 4WDs

with fuel and a driver for a circuit of Todra and Dades gorgescontact the highly recommended SupraTeam Travel, which operates out of the hotel, for multi-day packages in the High Atlas or the desert (ⓦsupratravel.com). You can also arrange trips for the gorge (or beyond) at *Camping Ourti*, near the Shell station on the N10 towards Boumalne, around 1km from the centre.

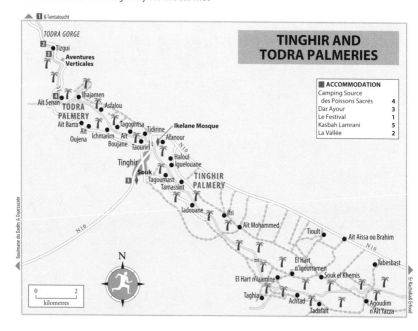

TINGHIR AND TODRA PALMERIES

■ **ACCOMMODATION**
Camping Source des Poissons Sacrés	4
Dar Ayour	3
Le Festival	1
Kasbah Lamrani	5
La Vallée	2

ACCOMMODATION   SEE MAPS PAGES 395 AND 396

L'Avenir In the pedestrian zone near the central market ☎ 0672 521389. A very decent little budget hotel above a cluster of shops, with good-value rooms and a great roof terrace – its very central location means possible noise; try to get rooms in the rear, facing quieter streets. An excellent source of information on climbing in the gorge. HB €

Kasbah Lamrani On the N10, 1km west of the centre ⓦ kasbahlamrani.com. A large, upscale hotel in ersatz kasbah style, though the 22 well-equipped rooms have been smartly done and there are plenty of facilities, including a big pool, huge terraces, a bar and two decent restaurants. Bike rental is available too. HB €€€

Du Todra Av Hassan II ☎ 0524 834249. Open since 1935,

this place has seen better days and is in need of some TLC. Rooms are somewhat basic but its comfortable communal area, interesting decor and central location make it a passable and affordable overnight stop. €

★ **Tomboctou** Av Bir Anzarane ⓦ hoteltomboctou. com. A kasbah built for Sheikh Bassou in 1944, tastefully converted by Moroccophile Spaniard Roger Mimó, *Tomboctou* is one of the country's memorable small hotels. There's a range of tasteful and cosy rooms (all cool in summer and heated in winter) and friendly staff on hand to help with exploring the local area. There's also a pool in the courtyard, a good restaurant (set menus €€€) and a small bar. BB €€

EATING AND DRINKING   SEE MAP PAGE 395

Tinghir isn't a place for fancy dining, though you can get tasty **meals** at the *Hôtel Tomboctou* (see page 397). There are plenty of cheap cafés and grills around the centre, where you can fill up at any time of day; stock up at the market on trekking and picnic food for trips up the gorge.

Saghro On the hill north of the centre. It's worth venturing up to the *Hôtel Saghro* to enjoy a drink at the

bar, or more accurately the bar's panoramic *terrasse*, which enjoys superb views across the Tinghir palmery. €€

Café La Terrasse On the N10, at the eastern end of the municipal gardens. A good blend of tourists and locals, all tucking into above-average tajines and brochettes and the like, either at pavement tables or on the eponymous terrace. €€

SHOPPING   SEE MAP PAGE 395

Maison Berbère Next to the mosque, near Pl Principale. Well-stocked branch of the excellent crafts

chain, heaving with high-quality rugs, carpets and silver.

The Todra Gorge

Few people visit the south without taking in the **Todra Gorge**, and with good reason. At its deepest and narrowest point, only 15km from Tinghir, this trench through the High Atlas presents an arresting spectacle, its gigantic rock walls changing colour to magical effect as the day unfolds. *Faux* guides hang around the gorge, but the hassle is generally low-key, and at weekends and holidays there's a cheerfully laidback vibe – locals more than outnumber tourists, and families come to picnic by the river.

En route to the gorge proper, the road climbs along the west flank of the **Todra palmery** (see page 394), a last, fertile shaft of land, narrowing at points to a ribbon of palms between the cliffs. The really enclosed section of the gorge itself extends for just a few hundred metres and should certainly be walked, even if you're not going any further, for the drama of the scenery. However, if you do press on a little further, after a kilometre or so you'll reach the beautiful family-run guesthouse and truly welcoming Berber hospitality of *Dar Ayour* (see page 398).

Tamtatoucht and beyond

The road up the Todra Gorge grows gradually less spectacular as you progress uphill, but with your own vehicle it's worth pressing on to **TAMTATOUCHT**, 18km beyond the gorge, for a taste of the high mountains. A sizeable sprawl with a growing number of attractive hotels and cafés, the village is situated beneath a ring of beautiful peaks, and with local guidance you can head off for rewarding day-walks in the area.

Just beyond Tamtatoucht, a rough *piste* heads west to the **Dadès Gorge**, scaling huge slabs of unstable limestone (this is 4WD-only territory) on its way (see page 391). Staying on the main route will bring you to **Aït Hani**, 15km further on and set in a high and barren landscape. From here, surfaced roads lead east to Rich (for Midelt) and

---

WALKING IN THE TODRA GORGE

Most of the guides hanging around the gorge try to lead visitors on walks, but the following **route** (1hr 30min–2hr) can be hiked without assistance. Once through the cliffs that mark the narrowest section of the gorge, look for a **side valley** leading quite steeply left (south) from the roadside to a pronounced saddle between two peaks – you'll be able to make out the **path** climbing on the left flank of the hillside. An easy ascent takes you to the pass (around 45min), from where you could head for the peaks for splendid views over the gorge, or follow the path dropping downhill to your left, keeping to a line of silvery-grey rocks that fringe a dry riverbed. After around thirty minutes, the path then climbs briefly to a second pass, from where it descends to **Tizgui**, a well-preserved *ksar* on the edge of the Todra palmery.

---

north **across the High Atlas** to Imilchil and Aghbala – a superb journey, offering a real experience of Berber mountain life and some of the most exciting scenery in Morocco, in a succession of passes, mountains, rivers and gorges.

ARRIVAL AND DEPARTURE   THE TODRA GORGE

By bus Minibuses run regularly from Tinghir to Tamtatoucht (45min), beyond the gorge itself, and on to Aït Hani, 35km north of Tinghir.

By petit taxi Taxis ferry back and forth between Tinghir and the group of hotels just before the narrowing of the gorge, as well as further on to Tamtatoucht.

ACROSS THE ATLAS

By car The road north from Aït Hani was paved in 2011, shortening the journey to Agoudal dramatically and opening up the route to normal tourist cars. At Agoudal (see page 216), you can join the surfaced road to Imilchil and Aghbala, which eventually seesaws down to Kasba Tadla and the N8 (the Beni Mellal–Fez road).

By grand taxi *Grands taxis* run from Tinghir to Imilchil (2hr 30min), where you can connect with other taxis heading further north.

By truck Not so long ago, travelling on a succession of Berber lorries was the only real way of negotiating this stretch of the Atlas, and without your own transport they can still provide a useful (and memorable) service. The lorries are timed to coincide with local village souks: promising days to start out are Wednesday (for Aït Hani's Thursday souk) and Friday (for Imilchil's Saturday souk), but there's usually at least one lorry heading north each day. Setting out from Todra, the managers of the hotels at the mouth of the gorge usually have an idea of when the next one will pass through – and will help arrange your first ride.

INFORMATION

Money There are no banks between Tinghir and Kasba Tadla, so you'll need to carry enough money for the journey. Don't underestimate the expense of buying food in the mountains (up to twice the normal rate), nor the prices

charged for rides in Berber lorries.
Police There are police stations at Aït Hani and Imilchil if you need serious help or advice on the state of the area's *pistes*.

ACCOMMODATION

Given the traffic and crowds of tourists and hustlers who mill around them through the day, the cluster of small **hotels** at the foot of the cliffs are far from peaceful, and in winter can be very cold as the sun only reaches them at noon. However, things calm down considerably in the evening after the day-trippers have left, and their rooftops make ideal vantage points from which to admire the escarpments. The accommodation below is listed in the order you encounter it **from Tinghir**.

EN ROUTE TO THE GORGE, SEE MAP PAGE 396

Camping Source des Poissons Sacrés 9km from

Tinghir ☎ 0629 889729. Flanking a particularly luxuriant stretch of the palmery, this is the best choice of a string of well-established campsites, with simple rooms and the option of rooftop sleeping or shady tent camping. It also boasts a spring flowing into a pool where a shoal of supposed sacred fish swim. Terrace €, Berber tent €, camping €, double €

★ **Dar Ayour** 15km from Tinghir ☎ 0524 895271, ⓦ dar ayour.com. A little gem, this brightly furnished guesthouse in the village of Tizgui has a range of individually designed rooms (it's worth looking at a couple first, as they are very different), some with lovely little balconies. The cushion-strewn lounge is a great place to relax, as is the swimming pool and garden that runs down to the Oued Todra. Breakfast and Moroccan/French set menu dinners are served on a gorgeous terrace. The gorge is just a 10min walk away. HB €€

La Vallée 15.5km from Tinghir ☎ 0524 895126 or ☎ 0667 050810. Pick of the budget places just before the entrance to the gorge, offering simple en-suite rooms (and a few cheaper ones with shared facilities) that are generally cleaner than the competition. Popular with climbers, thanks to its logbook with useful route descriptions (climbing gear also available to rent). HB €

IN THE GORGE, SEE MAP PAGE 396

★ **Le Festival** 5km from the mouth of the gorge, 22km from Tinghir ⓦ aubergelefestival-todragorge. com. This intimate solar-powered eco-*auberge*, the only accommodation between the mouth of the gorge and Tamtatoucht, has a truly rustic feel and provides an excellent base for climbers and trekkers. There are two "tower" rooms in a castle-like building that sleep up to four, and five inventive double/twin en-suite "cave rooms" built into the rock below. The resident chef presents excellent meals from an open kitchen using produce from the garden (€€€ set

dinner menu), and climbing gear and bikes can be hired. A different and atmospheric place to spend the night. BB €€

TAMTATOUCHT

Les Amis At the entrance to the village ☎ 0670 234374. The nicest of the group of hotels that has sprung up at the entrance to town, with 15 clean and spacious rooms, hearty food and impromptu music sessions. Guests are welcome to sleep on the terrace during summer (€), which provides a stunning view of the wind-eroded landscape, and there's also a campsite with bathrooms and electric points. Mohammed is the oldest of seven brothers that run the place and speaks multiple languages fluently and enjoys sitting with his guests and talking about the region. Camping €, HB double €€

Baddou Near the entrance to the village ⓦ auberge-baddou-todra.com. Just up the road from Les Amis, this friendly place has 16 rooms of varying sizes, en suite or sharing bathrooms, plus a good campsite enclosed by a stone wall with some shade, hot showers and electricity. The sunny terrace with kidney-shaped pool equipped with little fountain is a lovely place to relax, and in warm weather dinner is served in a semi-open Berber tent. Camping €, HB double €

East to the Tafilalt

After the comparatively populous area around the gorges, the run east to Er Rachidia, Erfoud and the great palmeries of the Tafilalt is a desolate one. The N10 to Er Rachidia (for Midelt and the road to Fez) is a fast but dull highway through barren country that's broken only by the long, straggling oasis of Goulmima. The more attractive R702 to Erfoud (for Merzouga) is, in parts, eerily impressive, with sections of the road occasionally submerged in sand.

The R702 branches off the N10 3km east of **Tinejdad**, from where it follows a course of lush oases – populated by the Aït Atta tribe, traditional warriors of the south who once controlled land and exacted tribute as far afield as the Drâa (see page 394). After leaving the oasis at **Mellab**, which has a fine *ksar*, it is more or less continuous desert *hammada* until the beginning of the vast palmery of **El Jorf**, the Tafilalt's largest *ksar*, on

---

CLIMBING IN THE TODRA GORGE

Climbers have been scaling the Todra Gorge's craggy cliffs since 1977, when a group of Frenchmen opened the West Pillar way, and there are now over four hundred **routes** spread across forty different sectors. The routes are fairly technical, with most ranging from French Grades 5 to 8 and varying in length from 25m to 300m, so tend to suit experienced climbers more – though the Plage Mansour has several easy climbing routes and is ideal for those relatively new to rock climbing.

A number of hotels and guides in and around the gorge rent equipment and run **climbing trips**. Aventures Verticales have a small shop in Tizgui village, 400m before the entrance to the gorge (ⓦ climbing-in-morocco.com). They offer guided climbing and instruction, equipment rental, sell maps and guides, and also do lots of work in the upkeep of the fixed equipment in the gorge. If you're climbing on your own, it's worth consulting the **logbooks** at various hotels in the gorge first, which will alert you to any problems on the rock – over the past few years, kids have been known to tamper with several access bolts, and even fixtures for top ropes.

> ## BERBER CEMETERIES
> The long fields of pointed stones that you'll see thrust into the ground, both here and elsewhere along the oasis routes are **Berber cemeteries**. Otherwise unidentified, they are usually walled off from the desert at the edge of the *ksour*: a wholly practical measure to prevent jackals from unearthing bodies – and in so doing, frustrating the dead's entry to paradise.

the approach to Erfoud. Over much of the journey from Mellab to Erfoud, the land is pockmarked by parallel lines of strange, volcanic-shaped humps – actually man-made entries to the old underground **irrigation channels** or *khettara* (see page 376).

Tinejdad

TINEJDAD itself is one long street, but the town is distinguished by having two of the best **museums** in the region just a few kilometres to the west along the N10. There are further impressive kasbahs and *ksour* in the Ferkla oasis, which spreads to the north and west of Tinejdad: ask directions to **Ksar Asrir**, the one-time capital of the oasis, in the palmery north of the main road; or head to **El Khorbat**, an immaculate nineteenth-century *ksar* further towards Tinghir that is also home to the Musée des Oasis.

Musée Sources Lalla Mimouna

9km west of Tinejdad • Charge

The extraordinary Musée Sources Lalla Mimouna achieves that rare combination of inspirational setting and absorbing content. Its owner, Zaid, has spent the last thirty years collecting artefacts including eighteenth- and nineteenth-century agricultural tools, pottery from Fez and Tamegroute, Berber jewellery and textiles, all displayed here in a beautiful complex of *pisé* buildings set around exposed underground springs. Don't miss the wooden Koran tablets in the last room, or Zaid's demonstration of a *tanassa*, an ancient Berber water clock that ensured every plot within the palmery received its equal share.

Musée des Oasis

800m off the N10, 2km west of Tinejdad • Charge

Spread over three beautifully restored buildings in the heart of El Khorbat, the informative **Musée des Oasis** houses a collection of artefacts and photos showcasing rural life, from local festivals to the economy of the Salt Road. It's all been thoughtfully put together by Spanish writer and architectural conservationist Roger Mimó, though the displays on the tribal system and the *pisé* construction underlying the region's many kasbahs and *ksour* are particularly pertinent for travelling in the south.

ARRIVAL AND INFORMATION

By public transport Most buses heading east from Tinghir stop in the centre of Tinejdad (hourly; 1hr). *Grands taxis* pull into the eastern end of Tinejdad.

EAST TO THE TAFILALT

Services Banque Populaire and Crédit Agricole banks with ATMs are in the centre on the main street (N10), as is the post office.

ACCOMMODATION AND EATING

TINEJDAD

★ **Gite El Khorbat** 800m off the N10, 2km west of Tinejdad ⓦelkhorbat.com. A handful of rooms stylishly converted, with en suite bathrooms and Berber textiles. You can also eat here at a swish little restaurant, with tasty local (including camel tajine) and Mediterranean dishes, as well as vegetarian options (set diners €€-€€€). The owner, Spanish writer and hotelier Roger Mimó, restored the adjacent kasbah

that houses an impressive museum that depicts the region's Berber, Jewish, and agricultural history (see page 400). BB €€

Panorama On the main street (N10) in the centre of town. Pleasant daytime café popular with passing trade with a wicker-shaded roadside terrace shaded by palms, offering a decent range of Moroccan staples including tajines, plus salads and pastas, and there are clean bathrooms and sometimes wi-fi. €

The Ziz and the Tafilalt

The great date-palm oases of the **Oued Ziz** and the **Tafilalt** come as near as anywhere in Morocco to fulfilling Western fantasies about the Sahara. They do so by occupying the last desert stretches of the **Ziz Valley**: a route shot through with lush, cinematic scenes, from the river's fertile beginnings at the **Source Bleue**, the spring water pool that is the oasis meeting point of **Meski**, to a climax amid the rolling sand dunes of **Merzouga**. Along the way, once again, are an impressive succession of *ksour*, and an extraordinarily rich palmery – historically the most important territory this side of the Atlas.

Strictly speaking, the **Tafilalt** (or Tafilalet) comprises the oases south of **Erfoud**, its principal town and gateway. Nowadays, however, the provincial capital is the French-built garrison town and administrative centre of **Er Rachidia**, a convenient pitstop heading north, through the great canyon of the Ziz Gorges, to Midelt and Fez.

Er Rachidia and around

7

ER RACHIDIA was established by the French as a regional capital – when it was known as Ksar es Souk, after their Foreign Legion fort. Today, it represents more than anywhere else the new face of the Moroccan south: a shift away from the old desert markets and trading routes to a modern, urban centre. The town's role as a military outpost, originally against tribal dissidence, particularly from the **Aït Atta** (see page 394), was maintained after independence by the threat of territorial claims from Algeria, and there is still a significant garrison here – not that you'd ever really know that from the relaxed air that pervades its orderly grid of tidy streets.

Meski and the Source Bleue

Signed off the N13 17km south of Er Rachidia • Charge • Coming by bus, ask to get out by the turn-off, from where it's a 400m walk down to the pool (note, though, that going on to Erfoud or back to Er Rachidia can be tricky, since most of the buses pass by full and don't stop)

The small palm grove of **Meski** is watered by a natural spring water pool: the famous **Source Bleue**, extended by the French Foreign Legion and long a postcard image

7

THE TALE OF THE TAFILALT

The **Tafilalt** was for centuries the main Moroccan terminus of the **caravan routes** – the famous **Salt Road** across the Sahara to West Africa, by way of Timbuktu. Merchants travelling south carried weapons, cloth and spices, part of which they traded en route at Taghaza (in modern-day Mali) for local **salt**, the most sought-after commodity in West Africa. They would continue south, and then make the return trip from the old Kingdom of Ghana, to the west of Timbuktu, loaded with **gold** (one ounce of gold was exchanged for one pound of salt at the beginning of the nineteenth century) and, until European colonists brought an end to the trade, **slaves**.

These were long journeys: Taghaza was twenty days by camel from the Tafilalt, Timbuktu sixty, and merchants might be away for more than a year if they made a circuit via southern Libya (where slaves were still sold up until the Italian occupation in 1911). They also, of course, brought an unusual degree of contact with other cultures, which ensured the Tafilalt a reputation as one of the most unstable parts of the Moroccan empire, frequently riven by religious dissent and separatism.

Dissent began when the *Filalis*, as the Tafilalt's predominantly Berber population is known, adopted the **Kharijite heresy**, a movement that used a Berber version of the Koran (orthodox Islam forbids any translation of God's direct Arabic revelation to Mohammed). Separatist tendencies date back much further though, to the eighth century, when the region prospered as the independent kingdom of **Sijilmassa** (see page 408).

In the fifteenth century, the region again emerged as a centre of trouble, fostering the *marabout* uprising that toppled the Wattasid dynasty, but it is with the establishment of the **Alaouite** (or, after their birthplace, *Filali*) dynasty that the Tafilalt is most closely associated. Mounted from a *zaouia* in Rissani by Moulay Rachid (see page 408), and secured by his successor Moulay Ismail, this is the dynasty that still holds power in Morocco, through Mohammed VI. The Tafilalt also proved a major centre of resistance to the French, who were limited to their garrison at Erfoud and an outpost of the Foreign Legion at Ouled Zohra until 1931.

THE TAFILALT TODAY

Deprived of its contacts to the south, the Tafilalt today is something of a backwater, with a population estimated at around eighty thousand and declining, as the effects of drought and **Bayoud disease** have taken hold on the palms (see page 376). Most of the population are smallholding farmers, with thirty or so palms for each family, from which they could hope to produce around a thousand kilos of dates in a reasonable year – with the market price of hybrid dates around 15dh a kilo, there are certainly no fortunes to be made.

and favourite campsite for travellers (see page 403). It's set on the riverbank, below a huge ruined *ksar* on the opposite bank and with several of the springs channelled into a naturally heated **swimming pool**. The fish-frequented pool is perfectly safe to swim in, though as it's a popular hangout for local boys, women bathers may feel self-conscious; be warned, though, that the river is likely infected with bilharzia (see page 363).

Outside midsummer, you might also consider walking part of the way downstream in the valley bottom, southeast of Meski. The superb four-hour **trek** along the Oued Ziz will bring you to **Oulad Aïssa**, a *ksar* with fabulous views over the upper Tafilalt.

ARRIVAL AND DEPARTURE   ER RACHIDIA AND AROUND

By plane Er Rachidia's Aéroport de Errachidia Moulay Ali Cherif is 4km northeast of the city and is served by flights   from Casablanca (4 weekly; 1hr 10min); *petits taxis* make the short run into town.

By bus The bus station is on Pl Principale, just south of Av Moulay Ali Cherif, the main street that runs all the way through town.
Destinations Casablanca (1 CTM & 2 others daily; 10hr); Erfoud (1 CTM, 2 Supratours & 12 others daily; 1hr–1hr 30min); Fez (1 CTM, 1 Supratours & 10 others daily; 7hr 15min–8hr); Figuig (2 daily, via Bouarfa; 7hr); Marrakesh (1 CTM & 1 Supratours daily; 10hr); Meknes (1 CTM & 5 others daily; 5hr 30min); Merzouga (1 Supratours daily; 2hr 15min); Midelt (3 CTM, 1 Supratours & 7 others daily;

2hr); Ouarzazate (1 CTM, 1 Supratours & 5 others daily; 5hr 30min); Rich (8 daily; 1hr 15min); Rissani (1 CTM & 5 others daily; 2hr); Tinejdad (2 daily; 1hr 30min); Tinghir (1 CTM & 8 others daily; 2–3hr).
By grand taxi There's a large rank southeast of the bus station, from where *grands taxis* make fairly frequent runs to Rissani (1hr 30min), Erfoud (1hr; you can get dropped off at the Meski turning, for the same price), Merzouga (2hr), Tinejdad (1hr 30min), Tinghir (2hr) and Midelt (2hr). Taxis will go to Fez and beyond, but best to negotiate price with a group.

ACCOMMODATION AND EATING
SEE MAP PAGE 401

Despite its size, Er Rachidia has a limited choice of decent **hotels** within the city centre and if you want to camp, the *Source Bleue* at Meski is the nearest possibility. A couple of the hotels listed below host decent **restaurants**, and there are also many good grills and cafés clustered around the centre. The **covered market** is a reliable source of fresh fruit and vegetables.
Auberge Tinit 3km west of the city centre on the N10 to Tinejdad ⓦ auberge-tinit.info. Squat kasbah-style modern complex with spotless en-suite rooms around a central courtyard garden, an on-site restaurant (*menus* from €€) and a refreshing swimming pool. BB €€
Le Riad 4km west of the city centre on the N10 to Tinejdad ⓦ hotelleriad.com. The most upscale option in town (or at least near it), with 30 comfortable rooms – each with a small sitting area and fitted with all mod cons – facing into a courtyard with a huge swimming pool, restaurant and bar. It's a little dated though so pricey for what you get, and service can be half-hearted at times. BB €€

★ **Vallée Ziz** 3 Rue El Houria, off Av Moulay Ali Cherif ⓦ hotelvalleeziz.com. A spotless three-star hotel with a light and modern (if business-like) feel and very centrally located within walking distance to restaurants, buses etc. All 21 rooms come with en-suite bathrooms, a/c and satellite TVs; reliably good value and a perfect overnight stopoff. BB €€
Zerda Boucherie & Restaurant 47 Av Moulay Ali Cherif. Popular restaurant with outside tables on the main street diagonally opposite the covered market, attracting savvy travellers with its delicious brochettes and bargain omelettes. €

CAMPING
Source Bleue Meski, 17km south of Er Rachidia ☎ 0671 560144. Shaded by bamboo, palms and tamarisks, the famous *Source Bleue* campsite is run by the local commune of M'Daghra, with a pool, shower block (extra charge), electric points, and the inevitable souvenir shops, although the traders can be pushy. At times a simple restaurant has operated, but if not, bread, dates, and basic provisions can be bought. €

The Ziz Valley

Trailing the final section of the **Oued Ziz**, the road south of Er Rachidia (the N13) is one of the most pleasing of all the southern routes – a dry red belt of desert just beyond Meski, it suddenly drops into the great **Ziz Valley**, a massive **palmery** and a prelude of the Tafilalt, leading into Erfoud. Away from the road, *ksour* are almost continuous, glimpsed through the trees and high walls enclosing gardens and plots of cultivated land.

If you want to stop and take a closer look, the *ksar* at **AOUFOUSS**, 40km from Er Rachidia and the site of a Thursday souk, is perhaps the most accessible, offering a lovely glimpse of life within the palmeries. Drivers can follow a scenic "Circuit Touristique" through the area around the village, while a stunning viewpoint off the N13 overlooks the green river of palm trees running through the valley, dotted with crumbling kasbahs. Alternatively, **Maadid**, off to the left of the N13 as you approach Erfoud, is also interesting – a really massive *ksar*, which is considered to be the start of the Tafilalt proper.

TOURS
THE ZIZ VALLEY

Guides Abdel Karim ☎ 0662 294386 or ☎ 0667 768907, or arrange through Ifrane-based Journey Beyond Travel ⓦ journeybeyondtravel.com. Known locally as Tata, Abdel leads treks into the surrounding kasbah-filled valley and palm groves, and can arrange desert trips into Erg Chebbi alongside 4WD excursions into nomadic areas. He is president of a tourism association in Aoufouss, and also has a background as a farmer with a degree in animal husbandry.

ACCOMMODATION

The following places are all in or around **Aoufouss**: some are on the main road through the valley (the **N13**), and some are on (or reached via) the **byroad** through the village itself, clearly signed from a turning on the N13. Directions below assume you're driving **southbound** along the N13, towards Erfoud.

★ **Gîte Dar UI** From the N13 take the right turn for Aoufouss, then the second right turn (signposted) in the village over a small bridge – then keep looking for signs ☎ 0668 158553 or ☎ 0634 564242. This clean, well-managed gîte offers four simple but charming rooms in a peaceful location. Owner Hassan's friendly hospitality makes for a comfortable stay, and the family farms organically and serves up delightfully fresh meals in the restaurant (meals €-€€). A little tricky to find, but if you call ahead Hassan will come and meet you at the turning into Aoufouss. €

★ **Maison d'Hôtes Sahara** Aoufouss byroad, 5km from the turning off the N13 ☎ maisondhotessahara.com. Perched up against the side of the valley, this Berber family-run guesthouse provides welcoming hospitality alongside amazing views over the palm groves. A small

carpet weaving cooperative works from inside the hotel and walks to the kasbahs can be arranged, as well as harvesting fruit and vegetables in the oasis with locals. All rooms are en suite with a/c. HB €€

Maison d'Hôte Zouala N13, 30km south of Er Rachidia and 15km before Aoufouss ☎ 0535 578182 or ☎ 0672 144633. Pleasant little guesthouse in a Berber farmhouse with traditional en-suite rooms and hot showers – and delicious evening meals served in a vast salon. Trickier to find than the *Gîte dans la Palmerie*, but worth seeking out for the warm welcome and tranquil location. HB €€

CAMPING

Camping Tissirt Ziz Aoufouss byroad, on the right-hand side shortly before it rejoins the N13 ☎ 0662 141378. Tucked into the heart of the palm grove and immersed by fig, olive, almond and palm trees, this campsite is well run and has all the usual amenities. Two simple rooms and a Berber tent offer an alternative to camping. The owners can provide meals; breakfast €, tajines for dinner €€. Camping €, double room and Berber tents BB €

Erfoud

ERFOUD, like Er Rachidia, is largely a French-built administrative centre, and its desultory frontier-town atmosphere fulfils little of the promise of the Tafilalt. Arriving from Er Rachidia, however, you get a first, powerful sense of proximity to the desert, with frequent sandblasts ripping through the streets, and total darkness in the event of a (not uncommon) electrical blackout. Erfoud once functioned as a launchpad for trips to the dunes at Merzouga, but has been left high and dry with the surfacing of the Rissani–Merzouga road. Now, unless they're here for the date festival (see page 406), it tends to be bypassed by travellers who arrive early enough in the day to pick up onward transport.

Fossils D'Erfoud

500m out of town on the road towards Er Rachidia • Free • ⓦ fossilserfoudmorocco.com

Erfoud's only point of (minor) interest is the local marble industry, which produces the attractive black marble that adorns every bar top and reception desk in town. Uniquely, the high-quality stone contains hundreds of little fossils – mostly ammonites and cone-shaped orthoceras – which you can see being slowly revealed in 3D at the **Fossils D'Erfoud**. It takes an hour for hefty-looking saws to cut the huge blocks into workable chunks, which are then carved, and polished up at smaller hand-held machines. Small decorative products are for sale, such as jewellery boxes and paperweights, though you'd be hard pushed to transport a bathroom basin home.

ARRIVAL AND INFORMATION   ERFOUD

By bus CTM and Supratours buses depart from Pl des FAR near their offices on Blvd Mohammed V; others, including local buses and minibuses for Merzouga (you may have to change at Rissani), leave from the *gare routière* which lies just outside of Erfoud on the road towards Tinghir.
Destinations Er Rachidia (1 CTM, 2 Supratours & 12 others daily; 1hr–1hr 30min); Fez (1 CTM & 3 Supratours daily via Er Rachidia; 8hr 30min); Marrakesh (1 Supratours daily; 11hr);

Meknes (1 CTM & 1 Supratours daily; 7hr 30min); Merzouga (2 Supratours & 4 others daily; 1hr–1hr 30min); Midelt (1 CTM & 1 Supratours daily; 3hr–3hr 20min); Ouarzazate (3 Supratours & 4 others daily; 6hr 30min); Rissani (1 CTM, 1 Supratours & 5 others daily; 30min–1hr); Tinghir (2 daily; 3hr 30min).
By grand taxi *Grands taxis* leave from opposite the post office on Av Moulay Ismail, making fairly frequent runs to

Er Rachidia (1hr 30min), Rissani (30min), Merzouga (1hr).
Services Most of what you may need – banks, internet,

post office, the hospital and a little supermarket – can be found along Av Moulay Ismail.

ACCOMMODATION SEE MAP PAGE 405

Canne 85 Av Moulay Hassan ⓦhotelrestaurantcannes.com. Good value, if noisy, central spot run by a team of efficient women, the dated *Canne* has spotlessly clean a/c rooms, most are triples, as well as a lively café below. Breakfast €€

Kasbah Tizimi 2km west of town on the R702 to Tinghir ⓦkasbah-tizimi.com. A modern *pisé* building featuring traditional wood beams, ironwork and immaculate tiling. The rooms are attractively decorated and ranged around patios and a flower-filled garden, and there's a large pool, tea room, bar and spacious terrace. Meals are a la carte or buffet depending on occupancy. BB €€

Merzouga 114 Blvd Mohammed V ☎0535 576532. Best of the rock-bottom options, this hotel has reasonably clean en-suite rooms with hot showers, or you can sleep on the terrace for next to nothing. Breakfast is decent value. Terrace €, double €

Xaluca Arfoud 7km north of town on the N13 to Er

Rachidia ⓦxaluca.com. Smart *pisé* hotel complex, part of a small Spanish-owned chain, offering good value at this level. Swish rooms, opening onto small courtyards, are dominated by pastel colours, and the furniture, decor and fittings make use of regional arts and crafts – all the bathrooms are made from the local fossil-filled marble. The poolside bar is open to non-residents, as is the restaurant for the decent buffet lunch and dinner (€€€€). BB €€€

CAMPING

Camping Tifina 8km south of town, on the N13 to Rissani ⓦtifina-maroc.com. Far more appealing than Erfoud's shabby municipal campsite is this well-appointed complex spread across several acres, with camping, Berber tents or West African-style bungalows. Facilities include a nice pool, jacuzzi, hammam, BBQ area and bar. Set dinners €€€. Camping €, Berber tent €, bungalow €

EATING AND DRINKING SEE MAP PAGE 405

Most cafés and restaurants are found on Blvd Av Mohammed V and around Pl des FAR. Try to sample the

local specialities: *khalia*, a spicy stew of mutton or kid, flavoured with over forty spices and served in a tajine with

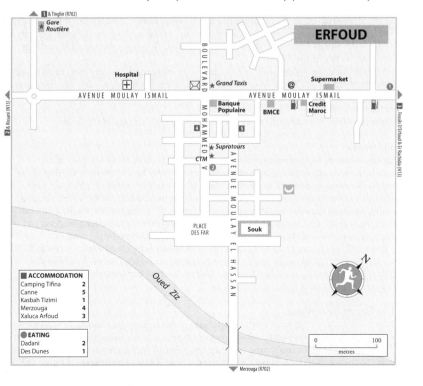

ERFOUD

ACCOMMODATION
Camping Tifina	2
Canne	5
Kasbah Tizimi	1
Merzouga	4
Xaluca Arfoud	3

EATING
| Dadani | 2 |
| Des Dunes | 1 |

7

THE FESTIVAL OF DATES

As with all such events, Erfoud's lively **Festival of Dates**, held over three days in early October, is a mixture of symbolism, sacred rites and entertainment – traditionally, dates bring good luck, whether tied to a baby's arm (to ensure a sweet nature), thrown at a bride (to encourage fertility) or offered to strangers (to signify friendship).

On the first morning of the festival, prayers are said at the *zaouia* of Moulay Ali Shereef at Rissani (see page 408), followed in the evening by a fashion show of traditional costumes: a pride of embroidered silk, silver and gold headdresses, sequins and elaborate jewellery. Then there are processions, camel races and, on the last night, traditional music and spiritual songs.

---

vegetables, egg and parsley; or *madfouna*, a wheat-flour base topped with onions, tomatoes, olives, minced lamb and cheese that is southern Morocco's answer to pizza.

★ **Dadani** Cnr Rue Allal Ben Abdellah and Blvd Mohammed V. Grab a drink and some patisserie at this congenial corner café with a large terrace, or head to the upstairs restaurant for Moroccan staples (including *khalia*) prepared with fresh ingredients and served in huge portions.

Good coffee, too. €

Des Dunes Av Moulay Ismail ⓦ restaurantdesdunes. com. Smart little restaurant with a welcome greeting: the mouthwatering waft of pizza freshly baked in a wood-fired oven. Moroccan is also on the menu, but it's difficult to look past their speciality, with eight varieties to choose from – though given the surroundings you should probably go for heart of palm. €€

Rissani

RISSANI stands at the last visible point of the Oued Ziz; beyond it, steadily encroaching on the present town and its ancient **ksour ruins**, begins the desert. From the eighth to the fourteenth centuries, this was the site of the first independent kingdom of the south, **Sijilmassa**, traces of which survive to the west of town. Much later, it became the first capital of the Tafilalt, and served for centuries as the last stop on the great caravan routes – the British journalist Walter Harris reported thriving gold and slave auctions in Rissani as late as the 1890s.

A quarter of today's population still live in a large seventeenth-century **ksar**, in addition to which there is just Place al Massira and a single street, lined by the usual administrative buildings you'll see across the country. It's a pretty quiet town, coming to life only for its famous weekly **souk** (Tues, Thurs & Sun), which can often turn up a fine selection of Berber jewellery, including the crude, almost iconographic designs of the desert.

Sijilmassa

Clearly visible at the beginning of the last century, the ruins of Sijilmassa have all but vanished, its crumbling buildings methodically worn away by the relentless shifting of the sands. The most accessible and visible remains of this once-powerful kingdom (see page 408) are to be found a little to the west of Rissani, on the east bank of the Oued Ziz, and within the right angle formed by the N13 as it turns east to run into town – here you can trace the walls of a mosque with an early mihrab facing south, an adjoining medersa and the waffle-like walls of the citadel, topped by towers on the length by the river.

Just south of El Mansouriya, again on the east bank of the Oued Ziz, you can still see the gate that marked the ancient city's northern extremity. Known locally as the **Bab er Rih**, it is thought to date from the Merenid period but has certainly undergone restoration since then.

The Circuit Touristique

The circuit is signed off the N13 1.5km west of Rissani but is better driven in a clockwise direction, starting at Ksar Akbar and the Zaouia of Moulay Ali Shereef; from Pl al Massira in Rissani, head towards Merzouga and turn right at the first roundabout (about 1.5km from the square)

The local tourist office has strung together a number of well-preserved medieval *ksour* to the south of Rissani on a waymarked 21km "**Circuit Touristique**" through the palmeries. While no longer the bustling communities they once were, the *ksour* make an interesting and thought-provoking side excursion – it is especially beautiful in the golden light of sunset.

Ksar Akbar

Heading clockwise around the circuit, the first *ksar* you'll encounter, about 2.5km southeast of Rissani, is the still impressive, nineteenth-century **Ksar Akbar**. The *ksar* is an awesomely grandiose yellow-hued stone ruin that was once a palace in exile, housing the unwanted members of the Alaouite family and the wives of the dead sultans. Most of the structure, which still bears considerable traces of its former decoration, including some tilework, dates from the beginning of the nineteenth century.

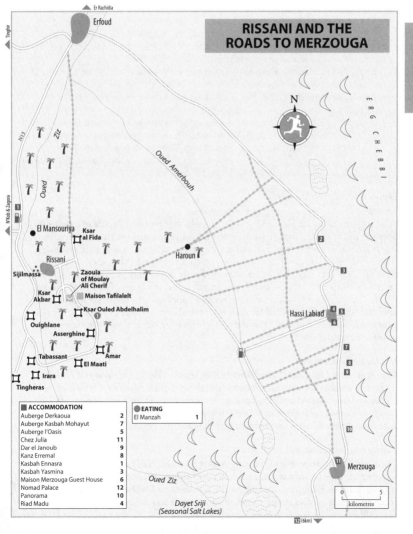

RISSANI AND THE ROADS TO MERZOUGA

7

■ ACCOMMODATION	
Auberge Derkaoua	2
Auberge Kasbah Mohayut	7
Auberge l'Oasis	5
Chez Julia	11
Dar el Janoub	9
Kanz Erremal	8
Kasbah Ennasra	1
Kasbah Yasmina	3
Maison Merzouga Guest House	6
Nomad Palace	12
Panorama	10
Riad Madu	4

● EATING	
El Manzah	1

THE BERBER KINGDOM

The ancient city of **Sijilmassa** was founded in 757 AD by **Berber dissidents**, who had broken away from orthodox Islam, and until its collapse under civil unrest in 1393, dominated southern Morocco. The kingdom's wealth was built on the fertility of the **oases** south of Erfoud, a string of lush palmeries that are watered by the Oued Gheris and Oued Ziz, which led to Sijilmassa's description as the "Mesopotamia of Morocco". Harvests were further improved by diverting the Ziz, just south of modern-day Erfoud, to the west of its natural channel, thus bringing it closer to the Gheris and raising the water table. Such natural wealth was reinforced by Sijilmassa's trading role on the **Salt Road** to West Africa (see page 402), which persisted until the coast was opened up to sea trade, particularly by the Portuguese, in the fifteenth century – coins from Sijilmassa in this period have been found as far afield as Aqaba in Jordan.

Most historians agree that Sijilmassa stretched for 14km, from just south of El Mansouriya to a point near the *ksar* of Gaouz, on the "Circuit Touristique" (see page 406), though opinion is still divided over its plan: some see it as a fragmented city, comprising several dispersed *ksour*, much as it was after the civil war at the end of the fourteenth century, others as a single, elongated city, spread along the banks of the rivers.

The garrison underwent a major restoration by the Alaouites, who brought Sijilmassa to renewed prominence as the provincial capital of the Tafilalt in the seventeenth century, but it was **destroyed** – this time for good – by the Aït Atta in the early part of the nineteenth century.

In the mid-1990s, the ruins were on the radar of the World Monuments Fund as an endangered site. But despite a decade of excavation, no further preservation work has been carried out since 1998, and the ruins continue to erode into the dry earth of the Tafilalt.

With thanks to Dr Ron Messier

Zaouia of Moulay Ali Shereef

2km southeast of Rissani • Mosque and tomb closed to non-Muslims • Free

Standing proud beside Ksar Akbar is the popular but peaceful **Zaouia of Moulay Ali Shereef**, the original Alaouite stronghold and mausoleum of the dynasty's founder. It was from this *zaouia* (which is still an important national shrine) that the ruling Alaouite dynasty launched its bid for power, conquering first the oases of the south, then the vital Taza Gap, before triumphing finally in Fez and Marrakesh. It has had several face-lifts in its time – most significantly when it was rebuilt in 1965 following the flooding of the Ziz – and owes its modern appearance to the latest round of aesthetic tweaking, in 1997. Although you're unable to venture beyond the central courtyard, you can still make out the tomb from the entrance, and peer into the mosque next door.

Ksar Oualed Abdelhalim

A second royal *ksar*, **Ksar Oualed Abdelhalim,** stands 2km further down the road. Although notable for its huge ramparts and the elaborate decorative effects of its blind arches and unplastered brick patterning, it's unfortunately in a pretty poor state of repair. A *ksar* was first built here in the fourteenth century, though the current ruins date from 1846, when it was constructed to house the governor of the Tafilalt.

Asserghine, Tabassant and Tingheras

The circuit continues round, passing **Asserghine** and half a dozen or so other *ksour* on its way to **Tabassant**, to the left and some distance from the road. On the way back up to Rissani, a turning to the left leads to **Tingheras**, perhaps the most interesting *ksar* on the entire route, set on a knoll and enjoying fine views over the Tafilalt.

Ksar al Fida

2km northeast of Rissani• Donation expected • Coming by car, follow signs from the N13 towards Mezguida

The nineteenth-century **Ksar al Fida** served as the *caïd*'s palace until 1965. Today, the welcoming owner is normally on hand to give you a whistle-stop tour of the building in a mixture of French and Arabic; even if you speak neither language, you'll get his drift. Unfortunately, most of its antique items have been moved to Er Rachidia, but it's still well worth a visit.

ARRIVAL AND DEPARTURE

By bus CTM services run from their office in busy Pl al Massira; private buses pull into the bus station 500m to the north. Minibus vans leave for Merzouga hourly from the square. All northbound services go via Erfoud and Er Rachidia.

Destinations Er Rachidia (1 CTM, 1 Supratours & 5 others daily; 1hr 45min); Erfoud (1 CTM, 1 Supratours & 4 others daily; 30–45min); Fez (1 CTM & 1 Supratours daily; 8hr 15min–9hr); Marrakesh (1 Supratours & 3 others daily;

RISSANI

12hr); Meknes (1 CTM & 1 Supratours daily; 8–9hr); Merzouga (2 Supratours daily; 30min); Midelt (1 CTM & 1 Supratours daily; 4hr); Ouarzazate (1 Supratours; 7hr 30min); Tinghir (1 Supratours daily; 4hr 30min); Zagora (1 daily; 6hr).

By grand taxi Taxis to and from Erfoud (30min) use a rank opposite *Hôtel Sijilmassa*, just north of Pl al Massira; taxis for Merzouga (30min) leave from opposite the pharmacy on the corner of the square.

INFORMATION AND TOURS

Money Both the Banque Populaire and Crédit Agricole on Pl al Massira have ATMs (the last chance to get money out before the Sahara, as there are no ATMs in Merzouga).

ACCOMMODATION AND EATING

SEE MAP PAGE 407

With the dunes just down the road, few travellers spend the night in Rissani, instead visiting on a day-trip from Merzouga (or Erfoud) or taking in the *ksour* en route elsewhere. Those that do stop over tend to stay at places just **outside of town**, on the N13 to Erfoud – the small hotels **in the centre** are generally grubby and overpriced. Eating options are equally limited: head for the area around the souk for standard café food.

El Manzah Opposite the Ksar Ouled Abdelhalim, along the Circuit Touristique. A peaceful place to stop off for lunch when touring the Circuit Touristique, conveniently sited next to one of its main highlights. The brochettes are tasty, but of course the *madfouna* is a speciality. €̄

Kasbah Ennasra Next to the Ziz petrol station 3km north of town, on the N13 to Erfoud ⍵ ennasra.com. Rissani's best luxury option: highlights include four-poster beds (in spacious rooms), an attractive patio and swimming pool, hammam, and a first-class restaurant (set menus from €̄€̄€̄). Non-residents can drop by for lunch or dinner (mains €̄€̄-€̄€̄€̄) and a dip in the pool. BB €̄€̄

Merzouga and the Erg Chebbi

No one who has stayed in the Sahara for awhile is quite the same as when he came… Once a man has been under the spell of the vast, luminous, silent country, no other place is quite strong enough for him, no other surroundings can provide the supremely satisfying sensation of existing in the midst of something that is absolute.

Their Heads are Green and their Hands are Blue, Paul Bowles

The Erg Chebbi dunes at **MERZOUGA** are indisputably one of the great sights of Morocco. Rising to 150m in places, these giant sand hills lining the Algerian border may not be as imposing nor as extensive as some in North Africa, but they come closer than anywhere else in the country (at least, anywhere else that's relatively accessible) to fulfilling most people's expectations of what a true desert should be. The result, though, is that Merzouga can sometimes feel less like the *désert profond* than a Saharan circus, with groups of luxuriously turbaned tourists posing for photographs with *hommes bleus* under the acacia trees or astride camels.

To stand any chance of experiencing the scenery in its essential state, you should aim to come here out of season (Jan & Feb are the quietest months) and choose your spot very carefully. At the height of summer, the few visitors who brave the fierce heat to reach Merzouga are mostly Moroccans, attracted by the reputed power of the sands to cure rheumatism. Sufferers are buried up to the neck for a few minutes in the afternoon – any longer (and earlier) than that can be fatal.

The dunes

Rising dramatically from a plain of blackened *hammada*, the **dunes** of the **Erg Chebbi** stretch 28km from north to south and are 7km across at their widest point – a relatively modest sea of sand compared with the great Erg Occidental of southern Algeria but still an impressive taste of the Sahara's grandeur. The highest dunes are those near, or just south of, Merzouga itself, peaking with the aptly named **Grande Dune de Merzouga**, a golden mountain recognizable – in addition to being the tallest dune around – by the distinctive tamarisk tree at its base. The dunes are spectacular at any time of day, but early morning and late afternoon are the best times to view them; to find a relatively peaceful ridge free of footprints, however, you'll have to be prepared to walk for an hour, or else arrange a camel trip (see page 410).

7

ARRIVAL AND DEPARTURE   MERZOUGA AND THE ERG CHEBBI

Thanks to the paved road from Rissani, getting to Merzouga is easy, though getting to your hotel isn't quite so smooth. *Pistes* – marked with posts – peel east off the main road at regular intervals (at junctions flagged by signboards); if you're **driving** in a standard rental car, don't be tempted to improvise, as there are many patches of soft sand where you might easily get stuck. To avoid the **faux guides** who greet buses and *grands taxis*, book your accommodation in advance and try to get your hotel to meet you on arrival.

By bus Both CTM and Supratours make the long journey down from Marrakech to Merzouga, stopping in *Ouarzazate*, Tinghir, Erfoud and Rissani. Supratours also has a direct service down from Fez, stopping in most of the major towns including Er Rachidia and Rissani. There are also local buses from Erfoud and Rissani.

Destinations Er Rachidia (1 Supratours daily: 2hr 15min); Erfoud (1 CTM, 2 Supratours & 4 others daily; 1hr–1hr 30min); Fez (1 Supratours daily; 10hr 45min); Marrakesh (1 CTM & 1 Supratours daily; 12hr 30min); Ouarzazate (1 CTM & 1 Supratours daily; 8hr); Rissani (1 CTM & 2 Supratours

CAMEL RIDES AROUND MERZOUGA

Having crossed Morocco to stand at the edge of the Sahara, you can hardly leave without hopping onto a **camel** and heading off into the dunes. **Rides** range from a one- to two-hour lollop over the crescents to catch the sunrise or sunset to a fifteen-night expedition deep into the desert; most people opt for an overnight stay at a Berber camp where you'll enjoy the clearest of night skies and a memorable sunrise the following day. A cameleer, meals, tea and blankets are included in the price, but it's advisable to bring extra clothes and a sleeping bag, as nights can get excruciatingly cold. If you've never been to the desert before, think about starting with a short trip before signing up for longer journeys – the feeling of pure isolation, surrounded by a seemingly never-ending sea of sand, is an incredible experience (described as a "baptism of solitude" by Paul Bowles), but it's not to everyone's taste.

You can **arrange a trip** through your hotel or at one of the other *auberges* around Merzouga (see page 411); *Kasbah Mohayut* and *Nomad Palace* are particularly recommended, or you could contact Trips in Morocco (🐫tripsinmorocco.com), a local operator who also specializes in longer trips and tours from Marrakech and Fez. Whatever company you chose to go through, each is likely to use its own jealously guarded routes and **camps** – the smaller, more expensive setups (usually no more than six people) are more atmospheric but less comfortable than the permanent camps – but it can be a matter of luck whether you hit a crowded section of the dunes or not. Generally, the further from the main group of *auberges* you go, the more chance you have of avoiding other camel trains and (even more importantly) 4WD drivers and quad bikers, though their noisy antics have been more limited in recent years. Note, too, that the longer multi-day trips stop operating after February, after which time it just gets too hot.

daily; 30–45min); Tinghir (1 CTM & 1 Supratours daily; 5hr). **By grand taxi** *Grands taxis* regularly ply the route from Rissani to Merzouga village (30min), leaving from the corner of Pl al Massira.

ACTIVITIES AND TOURS

Camel rides The most popular activity in Merzouga can be arranged at hotels and *auberges*, or with tour companies Best of Merzouga or Trips in Morocco (see page 410).

Sandboarding Most operaters that organize overnight stays at Berber camps offer sandboarding as part of the itinerary and you can go sandboarding on the dunes south of the village; Le Grand Dépôt de Merzouga, 300m down the street from *Café des Amis*, on the corner of the main road through Merzouga village, rents boards.

Guided tours Several hotels run guided tours of the oasis at the end of Hassi Labiad or to nearby villages to listen to Gnaoua music. Additionally, you can contact Abdel Karim (see page 403) who can set up guided and driving tours of the region.

ACCOMMODATION AND EATING   SEE MAP PAGE 407

Merzouga's **accommodation** is strung out over a wide area, nestled at the foot of the dunes in a straggling line; much of it is actually around **Hassi Labiad**, the small village north of Merzouga proper. It helps to know where your chosen hotel actually is before you arrive, as the final leg off the N13 from Rissani is across rough *hammada* and can be a long one if you stay at the northernmost group of hotels, some of which lie a considerable way from the tarmac. Outside high season, rates are surprisingly low, mainly because most places make their real money on camel trips. With just a few unremarkable **café-restaurants** to choose from, you'll get a much better deal if you eat at your hotel, paying an inclusive half- or full-board rate. The accommodation below is listed in the order you encounter it **from Rissani**.

★ **Auberge Derkaoua** 23km north of Merzouga village; 5km from the main road ☎ 0535 577140 or ☎ 0661 343677. Beautiful *pisé* complex in traditional style, set amid olive, almond and fruit orchards on the northern fringes of Erg Chebbi. The traditionally decorated en-suite rooms are very comfortable, but you'll probably want to spend more time lazing in the lovely garden, which has a pool and a pretty terrace restaurant. Closed Jan, July & Aug. BB €€

Auberge Kasbah Mohayut 4.5km north of Merzouga village; 2km from the main road ⓦ hotelmohayut.com. Welcoming duneside kasbah, run with a smile by Moha and his cousin, whose cheerily decorated rooms flank shady corridors or are dotted around a pleasant pool. You can tuck into tasty meals in an attractive tree-dappled courtyard; there's a good buffet breakfast, too. Organizes a variety of camel rides as well as more unusual trips, such as a mule-back tour of the Hassi Labiad oasis. BB €€

Auberge l'Oasis 6.5km north of Merzouga village, at Hassi Labiad; 2.5km from the main road ⓦ auberge oasismerzouga.com. Previously a Koran school, this jolly little setup has simple en-suite rooms around a central garden and swimming pool, and the option of bunking down on the roof terrace or pitching a tent (with light, water and power). Bargain dinner menu. Terrace €, camping €, BB double €

★ **Chez Julia** 100m behind the mosque in Merzouga village ⓦ chezjulia.xtadia.com. In a traditional desert house in Merzouga itself, this perennial favourite is defined by an appealing combination of comfort and authenticity. Owned and run by Austrian painter Julia Günther, the *auberge* has half a dozen uniquely decorated colour-themed rooms, sharing three bathrooms between them. The good menu features a freshly prepared combination of Moroccan and Austrian dishes (from Schnitzel to pastilla) and set dinners are decent value. BB €€

Dar el Janoub 3.5km north of Merzouga village; 2km from the main road ⓦ dareljanoub.com. One of the better top-end places, with large, minimalist rooms, a shady courtyard, a lovely pool that's softly lit at night, and a perfect terrace for sundowners, right by the desert's edge. If you really want to push the boat out, take one of the two suites that enjoy their own lounge and private terrace overlooking the dunes (€€€€). HB €€€

★ **Kanz Erremal** 4km north of Merzouga village; 2km from the main road ☎ 0535 578482. Stylish kasbah with variety of lantern-lit rooms adorned with hand-crafted local knick-knacks – some come with private terrace and dune views, and all have swish little bathrooms. The large public areas leading off the central atrium make a pleasant retreat from the sun, though the highlights lie outside: a chic terrace at the edge of the sand and a superb infinity pool that gives the impression you're actually taking a dip in the Sahara. BB €€

Kasbah Yasmina 18km north of Merzouga village; 11km from the main road ⓦ merzougayasminahotel. com. Established *auberge* right on the dunes, beside a seasonal lake where you might see flamingos – the location is spectacular, the views from the sunny rear terrace superb and there's also a nice pool. The cool rooms and suites vary widely in price depending on the view and size, and there's also a large grouping of cheaper Berber tents at the edge of the sand. HB Berber tent €, double €€

Maison Merzouga Guest House 6.5km north of Merzouga village, at Hassi Labiad; 2.5km from the main road ⓦ merzouga-guesthouse.com. Ten doubles and triples in the *pisé* guesthouse of the Seggaoui family, set

7

7

DESERT WILDLIFE

At first glance, the desert seems harsh and inhospitable, a scorched habitat devoid of life bar the occasional scarab beetle leaving tiny tracks across the sand. But there are acacias, tamarisk and calotropis here, and lichens and algae that survive on the dew that clings to the undersides of rocks and stones.

Such modest pickings provide sustenance for the many **birds** that pass through on their spring and autumn migrations, as well as native desert-dwelling species. Spotted sandgrouse, white-crowned wheatears, Egyptian nightjars, eagle owls and Houbara bustards are just a few of the magnificent species that can be seen, while, incredibly, greater flamingos can sometimes be found at Dayet Sriji and other lakes near Merzouga – but bear in mind that these can disappear to nothing in dry years.

The desert and *hammada* also house **reptiles** such as Berber skink, Montpellier snake and fringe-toed lizard, whose feet are perfectly adapted for their desert environment, as well as nocturnal **mammals**; you're less likely to see them, but jerboa, desert hedgehogs and fennec (desert fox) make their presence felt by leaving footprints in the morning sand.

---

back from the dunes but with cosy rooms, a keyhole pool and plenty of good old-fashioned hospitality. Sandboarding and Berber cooking classes can be arranged as well as the usual desert tours. BB €€

Nomad Palace 7km south of Merzouga village, at Ksar Mezguida ⓦ hotelnomadpalace.com. The dunes aren't as high at this far southern end of the Erg Chebbi, but the area's much more peaceful as a result. The *auberge* boasts a huge Moroccan salon with an open fire, and well-furnished rooms opening onto a quiet courtyard garden and swimming pool. The owner also runs excellent camel trips to a less frequented area on the far, east side of Erg Chebbi, via a more varied route than normal. HB €€

Panorama 2km north of Merzouga village; 1km from the main road ☎ 0668 967625. Run by the hospitable Aït Bahaddou family, this budget *auberge* stands further from the sand than most, at the top of a hill outside Merzouga, but the views are stupendous: the sunset terrace enjoys arguably the best panorama this side of the Atlas. The rooms (some sleeping three or four) are well aired and the restaurant serves tasty tajines and *madfouna* ("Berber pizza"). They run various tours including visits to hear Gnaoua music at a nearby village. HB €

★ **Riad Madu** 4.5km north of Merzouga village; 2km from the main road ⓦ riadmadu.com. A very stylish and contemporary option with an original feel. Ten rooms (four luxury suites and six standard) come with their own unique decor centred around a particular colour. The open-view kitchen serves delightful Moroccan and Berber food with a modern twist (fixed price set menu). A swimming pool and roof terrace complete the picture. The riad also owns its own luxury camp in the dunes for the same rates. HB €€€

DIRECTORY

Money Note that there are no ATMs in Merzouga, so you'll need to get cash out in Rissani if necessary.

Post office There's a post office at the northern end of Merzouga village, just beyond the turn-off to *Nomad Palace*.

West to the Drâa

Around 3km north of Rissani, the N12 branches west off the main Erfoud road **towards Alnif**, **Tazzarine**, **N'Kob** and, ultimately, Zagora. The route sees little tourist traffic but provides a scenic link between the Tafilalt and the Drâa Valley, with the barren majesty of the Jebel Saghro shadowing the road for much of its length. Aside from the landscape, **fossils** are this region's main attraction – the stretch between Alnif and Tazzarine, in particular, has become the centre of a low-scale mining industry whose principal export is large trilobites (see page 413), sold from dozens of roadside stalls.

Alnif

Trilobites and potatoes are the stock in trade of **ALNIF**, 90km west of Rissani – the former scraped from ancient canyon walls around the town, the latter grown in the palmery winding northwards into the hills. It's along the line of this old watercourse that a well-frequented *piste* cuts across a saddle dividing the Jebel Saghro and Jebel Ougnat ranges to join the N10, the main Dadès highway, 21km southeast of Tinghir. In town, the **Ihmadi Trilobites Centre** (on the main road) sells genuine fossils with fixed pricing – the owner, Mohand, spent time mapping the area for the British Geological Survey and runs short trips to local **fossil sites** (☎0666 221593, ✉alnifearth@gmail.com).

Tazzarine and around

Beyond Alnif, the scenery grows wilder as you approach **TAZZARINE**, 66km to the west and set in a grassy oasis surrounded by bare mountains. There's a straggling row of shops but little you'd really want to stop for in town. Further afield, though, at **Tiouririne** (7km away) and **Aït Ouazik** (26km), you can find some vivid **prehistoric rock carvings** (*gravures rupestres*), the six-thousand-year-old drawings depicting giraffes, ostriches, buffalo, antelope and other animals from a time when the surrounding area was grassy steppe – ask at *Camping Amasttou*, 800m down a track to the left at the Taghbalte/N'Kob junction just west of town.

N'Kob

The rambling *ksar* of **N'KOB**, 190km west of Rissani and only 40km from the junction with the Drâa Valley road, dominates the most spectacular stretch of the N12, its kasbah-studded old quarter looking north from the rim of an escarpment across a large palmery to the peaks of the Jebel Saghro. The number of grand houses in N'Kob testify to its former prominence as a market hub for the region, but today the town is a refreshingly off-track destination – other than a couple of **prehistoric rock-carving** sites across the valley (which you'll need help from your hotel or guesthouse to find), there's

---

PRECIOUS STONES? BUYING ROCKS AND FOSSILS IN THE SOUTH

Throughout the south, boys bound into the paths of oncoming cars to offer crystalline mementoes of Morocco, and **rocks** and **fossils** fill most tourist shops across the region. But before you part with your hard-earned dirhams, it's worth knowing what to look out for: tennis-ball-sized crystals in a hollow **geode** can cost more on the Moroccan hard-shoulder than they would in Britain or the US, while brilliant orange and red geodes look attractive but are unknown to natural science, as are the rock crystal (quartz) given an iridescent metal coating by vendors.

Attractive spirals of **ammonites** (Carboniferous to Jurassic) are common in limestone areas of Britain, but in Morocco they can be bought sliced and polished as well as "raw". Don't rely on the names you're given by the shopkeeper – look at the centre spiral of the ammonite and the ridge around its shell to check how far features have been "enhanced" by a chisel.

Slightly older than ammonites, **trilobites** appear in shops as identical beige-coloured fossils on grey slate. In nature, they are rarely so perfect – beware plaster casts. The early trilobite *Paradoxides* is about the size of a hand, with long whisker-like spines. A deep-sea inhabitant, it is often found looking rather squashed sideways, where the silts on which it lived have been sheared by pressure. The *Calymene* and *Phacops* types of trilobites are about 200 million years younger than *Paradoxides*, and measure about two inches long, with a crab-like outer skeleton. The half-rounded shield-like skull, often found separated from the exo-skeleton, can appear in a shop with the skeleton carved around it as a tribute to modern Moroccan craftsmanship.

In the black limestone regions near Erfoud, the white crystalline shapes of **nautilus** and **orthoceras** are cross-sectioned and polished to emphasize their internal structure before being formed into ashtrays and coffee tables (see page 404). They can of course be transported for you at a cost – though they never quite seem to look so good back home.

nothing much to see, but the traditional *pisé* architecture and fine views from the roof terraces tempt many visitors into staying longer than they intended.

Into the Jebel Saghro

For trekkers, N'Kob serves as an important staging post for trips across the **Jebel Saghro** (see page 392), though you can also explore the mountains from a spectacular *piste* that heads north of town to crest the Saghro via the **Tazi n' Tazazert**, eventually dropping into the Dadès Valley at Iknioun, near Boumalne du Dadès. Winding through dramatic rock formations and gorges, the route rivals the crossing of the High Atlas, with superb views from the pass. An added incentive is the spectacular pinnacles of **Bab n'Ali**, which you can reach in a half-day's walk from a pleasant, conveniently situated *gîte*, 8km along the road from N'Kob.

ARRIVAL AND INFORMATION   WEST TO THE DRÂA

By public transport Buses cover the route between Rissani and Zagora (1 daily; 6hr), leaving Rissani's *gare routière* at 10am; *grands taxis* depart from the rank near *Hôtel Sijilmassa* (1hr) for Alnif, where you can pick up another taxi for the next onwards leg.

By car It's a long haul to the Drâa (295km from Rissani to Zagora), but the road is good; there are petrol stations in Mecissi, Alnif and Tazzarine. Leaving Tazzarine, make sure you turn right to stay on the N12/R108 for Zagora – the

road that heads straight on, to Zagora via Taghbalte, is a rough *piste* that, despite being much shorter, will actually take you a lot longer.

Guides The Bureau des Guides in N'Kob (☎0667 487509) arrange various treks into the Jebel Saghro, including a reverse of the classic three-day Tagdilt–N'Kob crossing (see page 392); alternatively any of the hotels in N'Kob can arrange excursions into the range.

ACCOMMODATION AND EATING

Most people cover the road between Rissani and the Drâa in one go, but given the distance, you may want to break the journey in two; if so, it's worth pushing on to **N'Kob**, by far the most appealing place to stay along this route, with a good choice of accommodation.

ALNIF

Etoile du Sud In the centre of town, on the left as you head towards Tazzarine The best place for a quick meal if you're just passing through, this simple café has friendly staff and reasonably priced traditional food – the menu includes tasty beef skewers, brochette and good chips. €̄

La Gazelle du Sud At the top end of town ☎0670 233942.There's no denying this place is bright: done out in pink, with the handful of small and simple rooms (three en suite) a contrasting shade of mint green. The clean bathrooms are spiked with incense, and there's also an on-site restaurant open to all (mains €). €̄

N'KOB

Auberge Ouadjou 500m west of town ☎auberge ouadjou.com. The best camping option in the area with

very good facilities, though you can also sleep in Berber tents or in one of the seven compact but clean rooms in a *pisé* kasbah complex. There's a swimming pool and a cheerful restaurant and Berber cooking classes can be arranged. Camping €̄, HB Berber tent €̄, HB double €̄

★ **Kasbah Baha Baha** The old quarter ☎kasbahabaha. com. This splendidly renovated kasbah is owned by an ethnographer from Marrakesh, with a library of interesting academic papers, a small museum and some lovely rooms in the square towers on the upper floors, decorated with plush Moroccan textiles and carpets. Outside, the garden features a couple of mock-Berber encampments flanking a pool, and the whole site enjoys a wonderful panorama over the valley. Mule trips into the Jebel Saghro and camel rides into the *hammada* can be arranged. BB €̄

Ksar Jenna 2km west of town ☎0524 839790. Owned and run by an Italian-Moroccan couple, this self-consciously chic place has just seven rooms, all stylishly furnished with ceramics and expensive textiles – though the highlight is a lush garden filled with flowers, fruit trees and water features. Lunch and dinner (open to non-residents) is a daily-changing affair. HB €̄€̄

Figuig

Hard up against the Algerian border, in the far southeast of the country, and once a stop on the route between Tangier and Timbuktu across the Sahara, the charming oasis town of **FIGUIG** (pronounced "F'geeg") today is literally the end of the road.

The border has been closed since 1994, turning Figuig into an isolated outpost, and so the long slog to get here from Er Rachidia is a somewhat perverse route to take – a lot of travelling in order to complete a loop **via Bouarfa** to Oujda in northern Morocco (see page 148). For those that do make the trip (and not many do), the journey is half the fun: spectacular in its isolation and scenically extraordinary, dominated by huge empty landscapes, blank red mountains, mining settlements and military garrisons.

The other half is the town itself, nestled in its oasis of possibly 200,000 date palms, and studded with seven strange, archaic shapeed, pink-tinged *ksour*, their watchtowers having evolved as much from internal tension within the *ksour* as from any need to protect themselves from the nomadic tribes of the desert. It's a laidback place, where life ticks by at an addictively slower rhythm, and the simple pleasure of wandering its shady alleys never seems to fade.

ARRIVAL AND DEPARTURE
FIGUIG

By bus Buses stop at the *gare routière* on Blvd Hassan II, the main road through the new town, with services to Oujda (2 daily; 6–7hr) via Bouarfa (2hr), where you can connect to Er Rachidia (2 daily; 5hr).

By car It's a very long journey from both Er Rachidia (378km) and Oujda (386km) but easy enough in a normal tourist car, the only diversion being the roadside *gendarmerie* who pass the time collecting car numbers and your mother's maiden name (the "undefined boundary" with Algeria runs parallel to the road).

INFORMATION

Guides It can be worth hiring a guide through your hotel to help you navigate the the palm groves and the confusing network of alleyways that make up Figuig's various *ksour*.

Services A petrol station and Crédit Agricole and Banques Populaires, with ATMs, are on Blvd Hassan II in the new town.

ACCOMMODATION AND EATING

Figuig Blvd Hassan II ☏ 0536 899309. Friendly place with slightly shabby but spacious and spotless en suite rooms in the modern part of town, with stunning views down the valley to the closed border, and Algeria beyond. There's also a secure area for camping and a café that benefits from the same memorable vista (tajines or couscous but order in advance), though the pool can sometimes lack its essential ingredient. Guides can be arranged here to help you navigate the confusing network of alleyways in town. Camping €, double €

Maison Nana Rue Ouled Sellam Ksar Zenaga ☏ 0536 897570 or ☏ 0658 579573. The hotch-potch of seven en suite rooms may lack character, but the warmth of hosts Sylvie and Mostapha more than makes up for it, as does the food, made with vegetables from their own garden. Great views and stargazing are to be had on the panoramic terrace. HB €€

Agadir, the Souss and Anti-Atlas

PAINTED ROCKS, TAFRAOUTE

Agadir, the Souss and Anti-Atlas

Few travellers to Morocco head south of Marrakesh, bar the sun-seekers flying directly to – and then, precisely two weeks later, directly out of – Agadir, a winter beach resort for Europeans that counts as the area's major tourist destination. It's an agreeable place which makes a good starting point for trips around the area, including a series of beaches lining the coast to north and south, and the sometimes delightful towns and villages dotted around the Anti-Atlas Mountains to the east and the desert beyond. While there are few bona fide tourist sights in this area, the scenery is often spectacular, and perfect road-trip fodder – head down the right roads and you'll find Spanish Art Deco architecture, remote oases, fascinating rock formations, ancient rock carvings and vista after superlative vista, the landscapes often dotted by the argan trees that the area is famed for.

Agadir's beaches can often be packed, but those to its north are less developed, including the one at **Taghazout**, Morocco's number-one surfing resort. A short way inland from here is **Paradise Valley**, a beautiful and exotic palm gorge, from which a mountain road trails up to the seasonal waterfalls of **Immouzer**. East of here is **Taroudant**, capital of the wide and fertile Souss valley, and boasting massive walls, animated souks and good hotels as its calling-cards. Further south, into the Anti-Atlas mountains, **Tafraoute** and its valley are even more compelling – the stone-built villages and villas set amid a stunning landscape of pink granite and vast rock formations. To the south of Agadir, the beaches are scarcely developed, ranging from solitary campsites at **Sidi Rbat** – one of Morocco's best locations for birdwatching – and **Aglou Plage**, down to the old port of **Sidi Ifni** – only relinquished by Spain in 1969 and full of splendid Art Deco colonial architecture.

Agadir

Many independent travellers turn their noses up at the very mention of **AGADIR**, a beachside city whose economy is heavily dependent upon pre-packaged Euro-tourism. While its *raison d'être* will be immediately apparent to even a casual visitor, if you look past the souvenir stands and lobster-skinned beach-goers, you'll see a calm, pleasant place arranged along a wide, scenic bay. Swathes of park and garden break up the hotel and residential zones, and the magnificent **beach** is untrammelled by Spanish Costa-style high-rise building. It may sometimes feel that the city is a little soulless, but this relative lack of bustle has novelty value if you're arriving from any other Moroccan town.

Agadir is, in fact, the core of the country's fifth-biggest urban conglomeration; its population is now almost 800,000 and rising each year, as the city slowly crawls uphill. This number swells further on weekends, when the nouveau riche from Casablanca and Rabat head down the coast en masse. The slew of **cosmopolitan restaurants** catering to both local and international tourists may also come as blessed relief from couscous, tajines and brochettes to those who've been on the road in Morocco for a while, as will the chance to cut loose at one of the city's many **bars** and clubs.

Downtown Agadir is centred on the junction of Boulevard Hassan II and Avenue Prince Moulay Abdallah, with Avenue du Prince Sidi Mohammed. Rebuilt in 1960s "modernist" style, it has all the trappings of a town centre, with office blocks, a post office, town hall (Hôtel de Ville), municipal market and banks. Just to the northeast

SANDY SHORES IN AGADIR

Highlights

❶ Agadir beach Golden sand, top-class hotels and sun pretty much year-round make this the country's number one seaside resort. See page 421

❷ Surfing at Taghazout Morocco's top surfing spot, a village beach resort with a whole series of excellent right hand point breaks attracting both local and foreign surfers. See page 432

❸ Taroudant Once the nation's capital, this delightful walled town with two markets and bags of character is nowadays being dubbed "mini Marrakesh" by the tourist industry. See page 434

❹ The Tata circuit Head on a spectacular loop through and beyond the Anti-Atlas mountains, passing through the frontier-style town of Tata – and, if you can track them down, a whole series of ancient rock carvings. See page 443

❺ Tafraoute Tucked away in the Anti-Atlas mountains amid a landscape of strange rock formations, this friendly little town makes a great base for exploring them. See page 450

❻ Sidi Ifni A former Spanish enclave built from scratch in the 1930s with an Art Deco town hall, an Art Deco mosque and even an Art Deco lighthouse. See page 463

HIGHLIGHTS ARE MARKED ON THE MAP ON PAGE 420

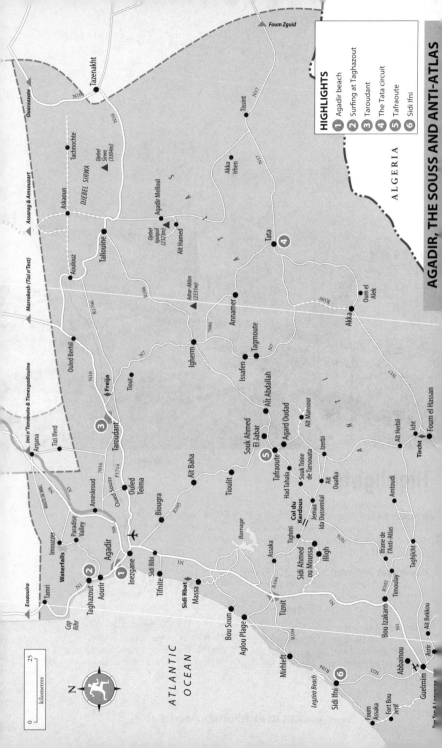

HIGHLIGHTS

1 Agadir beach
2 Surfing at Taghazout
3 Taroudant
4 The Tata circuit
5 Tafraoute
6 Sidi Ifni

ALGERIA

ATLANTIC OCEAN

N

0 ————— 25
kilometres

is an area known as **Talborjt**, with a concentration of budget hotels and small café-restaurants. To the west is the **beach**, and following the sand to the north you'll eventually hit the pleasing, relatively modern **marina** area, now a favourite coffee spot with young locals.

Brief history

Agadir's **history** closely parallels that of Morocco's other Atlantic ports. It was colonized first by the Portuguese in the fifteenth century, then, recaptured by the Saadians in the sixteenth, carried on its trading with intermittent prosperity, overshadowed, more often than not, by the activities of Mogador (Essaouira) and Mazagan (El Jadida). Abroad, Agadir's name was once known mainly for the **Agadir Crisis** of 1911, when, during the run-up to World War I, Germany sent a warship to Agadir bay to support Moroccan independence against French designs. Germany's real motive – to undermine a Franco-British alliance by using Britain and France's conflicting interests in Morocco – failed when Britain cut a deal with France, allowing the French to split Morocco with Spain while the British got a free hand in Egypt and Cyprus.

The really big event in Agadir's history was the devastating **earthquake** of February 29, 1960: a tremor that killed 15,000 and left most of the remaining 50,000 population homeless. Just four years into independence, the earthquake was an especially traumatic event, and in its aftermath, the whole city had to be rebuilt from scratch. Little over half a century on, the result is quite impressive; the mammoth reconstruction effort shows modern Morocco at its best.

8

The beach

Lifeguards on duty north end of the beach mid-June to mid-Sept daily

Agadir's **beach** is pretty good: a wide expanse of fine sand, which extends an impressive distance to the south of the town, is swept each morning and patrolled by mounted police. Along its course are a number of cafés, some of which rent out sunbeds and umbrellas. The ocean – it should be stressed – has a **very strong Atlantic undertow** and is definitely not suitable for children unless closely supervised. Even adults are advised not to go out swimming alone. The northern end of the beach has lifeguards on duty in summer, and a system of flags to tell you how dangerous it is to swim; the big beach hotels also have guarded sections for their residents, and you can rent a sunbed with a parasol at neighbouring restaurants. Lastly, the beach is also a good place for **watersports** (see page 424).

The beach empties when the sun goes down, and the pleasant **promenade** that abuts much of the beach's central section takes over as the city's focal point. Lined with restaurants and licked by a sea breeze, it's a thoroughly pleasant place, a fact made evident by its popularity with local families padding along on their evening constitutional, occasionally purchasing Chinese-made novelty toys from the many hawkers.

Valley of the Birds

Between Bd Hassan II & Bd du 20 Août • Charge

As a break from the beach, and especially if you have children to amuse, you might wander into the **Valley of the Birds**, a narrow strip of parkland, with a little aviary of exotic birds, a small herd of Barbary sheep and some other mammals, a waterfall and a children's playground. It's all very pleasant, and the lush vegetation draws a rich variety of birds throughout the year, but inevitably, some of the animal enclosures are distressingly small. Children might enjoy a ride on the "**tourist train**", which goes on a journey around town, starting from Boulevard du 20 Août, at the bottom of the valley.

▲ Aourir (13km), Aghazoute (20km) & Essaouira (N1; 172km)

AGADIR

MARINA

Fishing Port

Club Royale de Jet-Ski

Agadir Bowling Lounge

DHL (Post)

Délégation de Tourisme

ANCIENNE TALBORJT

Car Rental Booths

RAM

CTM

New Mosque

Rialto Cinema

Municipal Market

Basma

Exposition Memoire d'Agadir

Jardim de Olhão

Supratours

TALBORJT

Hammam

Ensemble Artisanal

PLACE DE L'ESPERANCE

Hôtel de Ville

of the Birds Valley

Tourist Train

Theatre

Amazigh Heritage Museum

Synagogue

Conseil Régional du Tourisme

Municipal Stadium

Jardin Talborjt

Prefecture de Police

WC

Atlantic Palace

Royal Palace

Grands Taxis

PLACE SALAM (PL. DE L'ABATTOIR)

City buses

Catholic Church

Souk el Had

Beach

EATING

L'Ardoise Gourmande	6
Les Blancs	3
Bollywood	4
Chiche Kabab	11
Cote Court	12
Daffy	9
Daily's	8
Fishing port stalls	1
Jour et Nuit	5/7
Patisserie Tafarnout	13
La Scala	14
Senso	2
Talborjt Mini	10

ACCOMMODATION

Aferni	2
Argana	13
Atlantic	10
El Bahia	6
Diaf	5
Massa	4
Petite Suède	1
Résidence Sacha	8
Résidence Yasmina	11
Royal Atlas	12
Sindibad	3
Sofitel Thalassa	15
Tiznine	7
La Tour du Sud	9
Thimoulay	14

SHOPPING

Argan Naturel	6
Boras	5
Ensemble Artisanal	4
Fromital	3
Souk Tarik el Kheir	1
Uniprix	2

DRINKING & NIGHTLIFE

1001 Nuits	4
Actor's	3
Casa de España	1
English Pub	2
Flamingo	5

0   300
metres

▶ Marrakech (N8; 256km)

▶ Gare Routière

Inezgane (8km), Airport (22km), Taroudant (N1; 85km) & Tiznit (90km)

Gare Routière (1km)

▼ 14 (800m), 15 (1.2km)

AVENUE AL MOUN
RUE CHOUHADA
RUE DE MARRAKECH
RUE DE PARIS
RUE MADRID
RUE DES NATIONS UNIES
RUE DU CAIRE
AVENUE DU GÉNÉRAL KETTANI
AVENUE DES FORCES ARMÉES ROYALES (F.A.R.)
RUE TARFAYA
RUE CHANGUIT
AVENUE DU 29 FEVRIER
AVENUE KENNEDY
RUE DE LA FOIRE
RUE 18 NOVEMBRE
AVENUE MOUQAOUAMA
AVENUE ESSAOUIRA
BOULEVARD DU 20 AOUT
RUE CHAIR AL HAMRA MOHAMMED BEN BRAHIM
ROUTE DE L'OUED SOUSS
BOULEVARD MOHAMMED V
AVENUE MOHAMMED V
RUE DE FES
RUE DE MEKNES
RUE HASSAN II
RUE DE MARRAKECH
AVENUE PRINCE MOULAY ABDALLAH

Amazigh Heritage Museum

Rue de la Foire • Charge

Towards the southern end of the city centre is an outdoor theatre – built along Roman odeon lines – and a pedestrian precinct of tourist shops and restaurants, where the small **Amazigh Heritage Museum** has a collection of Berber cultural artefacts, including a few old manuscripts (in Arabic, not Berber), some wooden doors and bowls, and quite a lot of silver jewellery. Unless you have a particular fascination for Berber jewellery, there's nothing of much excitement here, and you can see the lot in fifteen minutes; the rotating exhibitions are less local in focus, but often more diverting.

Jardim de Olhão

Av du President Kennedy; entrance on west side of compound • Free

The **Jardim de Olhão** is a very pleasant outdoor space. A landscaped garden with a café-restaurant and children's playground, it was created to celebrate Agadir's twinning with the town of Olhão in southern Portugal. The walls and buildings in the garden are constructed in a traditional Berber style which some claim was inspired by Portuguese architecture, though the influence is hard to see, and could just as easily have been the other way round anyway.

Exposition Mémoire d'Agadir

Av du President Kennedy • Charge

Just next to the Jardim de Olhão (see above), the two little wings of the **Exposition Mémoire d'Agadir** have some interesting photographs of Agadir as it was before and immediately after the 1960 earthquake – it's only really worth popping by if you're already in the Talborjt area.

Ancienne Talborjt

Entrance from road running uphill from Rue Mokhtar Soussi, opposite *Camping International Agadir* (see page 427) • Free

The raised plateau of **Ancienne Talborjt**, which entombs the town demolished in the 1960 earthquake, stands to the west of the city centre. Many of the dead were left *in situ* here, sprayed with lime in order to prevent the spread of disease, then covered up with a large mound of earth. It's marked by a small mosque and unfinished memorial garden, though there's very little to see; however, relatives of the fifteen thousand dead occasionally come to this park area to walk, remember and pray: a moving scene, even after so many years.

The old kasbah

On the hill north of the port • Free

The city's **old kasbah** is an eight-kilometre round trip from the centre, but worth making if you have transport, or by *petit taxi*, for a marvellous view of Agadir and the coast. You can see the kasbah from central Agadir, with a vast Arabic "Allah–King–Nation" slogan on the slope below, in white stones, illuminated at night.

Although it survived the quake, the kasbah is little more than rubble encircled by a bare outline of walls and an **entrance arch** – the latter with an inscription in Dutch and Arabic recording that the Netherlands began trading here in 1746, capitalizing on the rich sugar plantations of the Souss plain. It's not much, but it is one of the few reminders that the city has any past at all, so complete was the destruction of the 1960 earthquake. The touts scrounging for tourist money up here will do their best to haul your thoughts back to present-day Morocco, and they can be annoyingly persistent with their offers of jewellery for sale, photographic opportunities with snakes and

ACTIVITIES IN AND AROUND AGADIR

As you'd expect from a tourist-oriented city, there's plenty to do in the Agadir area – even once you've exhausted the culinary and alcoholic possibilities.

Bowling and billiards Knock down skittles or work on your cue skills at the Agadir Bowling Lounge, facing the northern end of the beach on Rue de la Plage (🅦 bowlingloungeagadir. com). They also have air hockey, billiards and basketball shooting.

Casino There are a few casinos around town; a good one can be found in the Atlantic Palace resort (see map page 422; 🅦 casinoagadir.com), on the Route de l'Oued Souss.

Golf Agadir has several golf clubs to the southeast of town. Royal Golf, an 18-hole course 12km out on the Route d'Aït Melloul 🅦 royalgolfagadir.com, is generally considered the finest. The others are off the Inezgane road at Km7: Golf des Dunes (🅦 golflesdunesagadir.com), with three nine-hole courses; Golf du Soleil (🅦 golfdusoleil.com), with two recently revamped 18-hole courses; and Golf de l'Ocean (☎ 0528 824146), with an ocean view, and 27 holes amid dunes and trees.

Hammam and spa therapy To sweat out the grime in Talborjt, the Bain Maure Essalama, just off Rue Mahdi Ibn Toumert, is open daily. Of more modern extraction is the Basma wellness and beauty centre (🅦 centrebasma.ma), open to females only, and providing facials, massage and the like; there's a salon and hammam on site too.

Surfing There are good waves up the coast from Agadir, especially in the surfer haven of Taghazout (see page 432).

Watersports Jetskiing is available at the northern end of the beach at Club Royale de Jet-Ski ; the same outfit also offers flyboarding, which essentially turns you into a water-jet version of Iron Man.

camels, or insisting you pay a nonexistent entry fee. There are also a few unguarded steep drops from the kasbah walls – pay heed if travelling with children.

ARRIVAL AND DEPARTURE   AGADIR

BY PLANE

Al Massira Airport (🅦 agadir-airport.com) is 25km east of Agadir. There are several ATMs here, and taxis will usually accept euros. Holiday companies' buses meet flights and shuttle passengers to their hotels, and if you've bought a flight-only deal you could try tagging along with fellow passengers. Otherwise, *grands taxis* are always waiting outside. There is no direct bus to downtown Agadir, but you can reach it on local buses via Inezgane (see page 425), which is also the way to go if you're planning to head from the airport to destinations other than Agadir. Heading back *to* Al Massira, it's usually easier to get a *grand taxi* from Inezgane to Ikhourbane, a little village just to the north of the airport; drivers will drop you on the main road, just outside the gate.

Airlines Royal Air Maroc have an office in Agadir on Av Général Kettani, opposite the junction with Bd Hassan II.

Car rental Avis (🅦 avis.ma); Budget (🅦 budget.ma); Europcar (🅦 europcar.ma); First Car (🅦 firstcar.ma); Hertz (🅦 hertz.ma).

Destinations Casablanca (4–6 daily; 1hr 15min); Dakhla (2 weekly; 1hr 40min); Laayoune (2 weekly; 1hr).

BY BUS

All buses serving Agadir operate from the bleak concrete *gare routière* at the eastern edge of town, 3km from Talborjt on Rue Chair el Hamra (aka Bd Abderrahim Bouabid); it's around 10–12dh by *petit taxi*, or 3.5dh on bus #4 from Bd Mohammed V. The best and most convenient bus services from Agadir (though not the cheapest) are operated by Supratours (10 Rue des Oranges) and CTM (Rue Yacoub el Mansour), and can be booked at their offices in town. More buses will take you to Inezgane than to Agadir itself (see page 425), but since Agadir's *gare routière* is fairly far out of the centre anyway, it doesn't actually make much difference. From Inezgane or the *gare routière*, the bus stop on Bd Mohammed V, just before Av Prince Sidi Mohammed, is the most convenient for Talborjt.

Destinations Beni Mellal (5 daily; 7hr 30min); Casablanca (1–2 hourly; 5hr 30min–8hr); Dakhla (10 daily; 18–20hr); Essaouira (hourly; 3hr 30min); Fez (9 daily; 10–12hr); Guelmim (2–3 hourly; 4–5hr); Laayoune (16 daily; 11–12hr); Marrakesh (3–4 hourly; 3–4hr); Meknes (7 daily; 11hr); Ouarzazate (3 daily; 7hr); Rabat (hourly; 8–11hr); Safi (hourly; 5–6hr); Tafraoute (7 daily; 4–6hr); Tangier (3–4 daily; 14hr); Tan Tan (2–3 hourly; 6–7hr); Taroudant (3 daily; 1hr 45min); Tata (6 daily; 7hr); Tiznit (2–3 hourly; 2–3hr).

BY GRAND TAXI

Shared *grands taxis* use a rank a block south of the local bus station at Pl Salam (aka Pl de l'Abattoir), a longish walk or short taxi ride from Talborjt. For farther-flung destinations you'll have to head to Inezgane (see page 425) and get a connection there.

Destinations from Agadir: Aourir (20min); Inezgane (20min); Taghazout (25min); Taroudant (1hr 15min); Tiznit (1hr 45min).

Destinations from Inezgane: Essaouira (2hr 30min); Guelmim (4hr 30min); Laayoune (9hr); Marrakesh (3hr); Massa (45min); Ouled Berhil (2hr); Ouled Teima (40min); Sidi Ifni (3hr 30min); Tan Tan (6hr 15min); Taroudant (1hr) and Tiznit (1hr 30min).

GETTING AROUND

Agadir is for the most part a walkable city, though you may want to use **petits taxis** for transport between the bus or taxi stations and Talborjt or the beach hotels. Alternatively, you can rent **scooters** or **motorbikes**, which would also allow you to explore the beaches north and south of town.

By bus The main city bus terminal is at Pl Salam (Pl de l'Abbatoir), a couple of blocks north of the *grand taxi* station, but the most useful routes (see page 426) run along Bd Mohammed V.

By bike and motorbike Various operators rent out motorbikes, scooters, and bicycles along Bd du 20 Août, south of Route de l'Oued Souss, but many are cowboys. A reliable firm will rent for 24hr rather than just until nightfall, and will show full paperwork proving that the insurance, minimal though it might be, covers you (and passenger if necessary) and detailing help in the event of a breakdown.

Car rental Bungalow Marhaba on Bd Mohammed V houses numerous rental agencies, including Budget, Hertz, Lotus Cars (☎ 661 531386), and local operator Youness Cars (🌐 younesscars.com). There are also agencies at the airport (see page 424).

INFORMATION AND TOURS

Tourist information The Délégation de Tourisme (☎ 0528 846377) is in Immeuble Iguenwane, on Bd Mohammed V, northwest of town towards the port. Staff are helpful and generally happy to answer questions. There is also a Conseil Régional du Tourisme (☎ 0528 842629) in the Chamber of Commerce building on Bd Hassan II near the Amazigh Heritage Museum – not strictly speaking a tourist information office, but staff are usually happy to give out information.

Tours Some of the best sights in this chapter are visitable on day-trips from Agadir – your hotel will probably have pamphlets.

Festivals July's Timitar Festival (🌐 festivaltimitar.ma), dedicated to nomadic music, is not on a par with Essaouira's (see page 284), but draws musicians from all over southern Morocco, as well as North and West Africa, France, Spain and even Latin America. Agadir also has a small film festival in Feb (🌐 fidadoc.org), at the Rialto cinema behind the municipal market.

ACCOMMODATION SEE MAP PAGE 422

Most of the budget hotels are in Talborjt, which has the advantage of local-oriented shops, cafés and street life. More upmarket places are worth booking ahead in high season, but may offer large discounts off-season; most of the package-style establishments are south of central Agadir, though there are some good options closer to the city proper. Note that there are also plenty of appealing places to stay in the area surrounding Agadir, including Taghazout (see page 431), Paradise Valley (see page 433) and Immouzer (see page 434).

THE INEZGANE SHUFFLE

Some 13km south of **Agadir** lies the city of Inezgane – almost a suburb of Agadir, but completely different to its more illustrious brother in almost every way. There's nothing to see here bar "regular" Moroccan life spooling along (there are plenty of places to stay, if you so desire), but for travellers it's useful in two main ways. One is for those unwilling to shell out on a *grand taxi* from the **airport** to Agadir – from the airport you can get to Inezgane on local bus #37 from outside the airport building, and from there take bus #97 or #98 or shared *grand taxi* to Agadir. It's also handy when leaving Agadir, or for those looking to head somewhere else immediately after arrival at the airport. It has just as many bus departures as Agadir (see page 424), and far more choice for *grands taxis* (see page 425). From the airport, bus #37 drops you off right next to the *grand taxi* station in Inezgane; for the bus station, just walk across to the other side of the *grand taxi* stands; buses to Agadir stop around the corner on the Agadir road. From Agadir, Inezgane can be reached by *grand taxi* from Place Salam, or on bus #97 or #98 from Avenue Mohammed V.

8

8

USEFUL BUS ROUTES

#04 Anza – Avenue Mohammed V – Avenue Mouqaouama – Gare Routière
#31 Place Salam – Avenue Mohammed V – Aourir
#32 Place Salam – Avenue Mohammed V – Aourir – Taghazout
#33 Place Salam – Avenue Mohammed V – Aourir – Taghazout – Tamri
#37 Inezgane (ALSA bus station) – Agadir airport
#42 Inezgane (Agadir road) – Massa
#97 & #98 Port – Avenue Mohammed V – Inezgane

HIGH-END HOTELS

Argana Bd Mohammed V ⓦhotel-argana.com. Large, well-equipped hotel priced a wee bit lower than the heavier hitters nearer the beach. The rooms are large and easy on the eye, but the USP here is the gigantic swimming pool – a pity that the buffet breakfasts don't quite cut the mustard. On the pool's fringe, you'll find *1001 Nuits*, the best shisha bar in town (see page 428). BB €€

Royal Atlas Bd du 20 Août ⓣ0528 294040. A five-star hotel which actually tries quite hard to meet that standard. It's very grand, with well-appointed rooms, friendly but laidback staff, three restaurants, three bars and a spa, plus it backs right onto the beach. It claims to be wheelchair accessible, although it doesn't have any specially adapted rooms. Promotional rates are often available. BB €€€€

Sofitel Thalassa Baie des Palmiers ⓦsofitel.accor hotels.com. The prettier and better located (and, yes, the pricier) of two nearby *Sofitel* properties, this is a real gem, decorated in neo-Arabic style, largely black-and-white though with splashes of colour where appropriate. You can splash about yourself in two swimming pools (including a heated indoor one), and the rooms provide what you'd expect at this price level. BB €€€€

Thimoulay Baie des Palmiers ⓦtimoulayhotel.com. Gentler and less package-oriented than most hotels at this price level, its design apparently taking cues from Art Deco (a little hard to spot) and Berber motifs. The rooms themselves vary widely in style and value for money, so try to look at a few before booking; on site you'll find a spa, swimming pool and small fitness centre. BB €€€

MID-RANGE HOTELS

Aferni Av du Général Kettani ⓣ0528 840730. It's worth asking for a room with a bathtub and balcony in this pleasingly old-fashioned three-star hotel, which boasts a pool – heated in winter – and terrace, plus TVs and safes in each room. The hotel also lacks a bar, which you may consider a plus or minus. BB €€

★ **Atlantic** Bd Hassan II ⓦatlantichotelagadir.com. A super little addition to the area, this small hotel manages to feel like an oasis of calm despite its central location. Guests tend to walk around with a deservedly smug look on their faces, no doubt partly due to the on-site hammam and

wonderfully photogenic pool, while the bar has happy-hour discounts. Rooms are modern affairs with Arabic design motifs – a bit of a winner, really. €€

★ **Résidence Sacha** Pl de la Jeunesse ⓦagadir-maroc. com. Just off the town centre in a quiet square. Calm and artistically decorated, this French-managed establishment is one of Agadir's most pleasing places to stay. Some of its range of good-sized self-catering studios and apartments come with private gardens, and there's a small swimming pool surrounded by funky yellow sunbeds. Rates drop heavily if you're here for blocks of a week; otherwise, online booking engines have the best deals. €€

Résidence Yasmina Rue de la Jeunesse ⓦresidence-yasmina.com. Self-catering apartments with small bedrooms but large sitting rooms and decent-sized kitchens, plus a lobby and salon done out in traditional zellij tilework, and a swimming pool and children's pool. There's often a discounted rate of one sort or another available. €€

Sindibad Pl Lahcen Tamri ⓣ0528 823477. Set on Talborjt square, this is a deservedly popular two-star hotel with a restaurant and bar, spotless a/c rooms, a plunge pool on the roof – and Sindbab prints in the lobby. They normally offer rack-rate discounts if you're staying three nights or more, even in high season. €

BUDGET HOTELS AND GUESTHOUSES

★ **El Bahia** Rue el Mahdi Ibn Toumert ⓣ0528 822724. A fine little two-star hotel, beautifully modernized with three categories of room (with shared facilities, with shower, and with shower and toilet), all with satellite TV, but not all with outside windows. The terrace is beautifully sunny, with an interestingly kitsch fountain. All in all, Agadir's best place at this price level. €

Diaf Rue Allal Ben Abdallah ⓣ0528 825852. The rooms here are small, but everything's neat and clean; some have en-suite bathrooms, and beds are a decent size (even in the twins). Rooms on the first floor are a lot nicer than those on the roof, however, which are a bit poky. There's a handy café downstairs, and the road outside was being prettied up at the time of writing. €

Massa Pl Lahcen Tamri ⓣ0528 826362. Facing Talborjt's pretty main square, here you'll find rooms that are simple but clean and well looked after, set around an upstairs

courtyard decorated with murals. There are some drearier rooms downstairs, with shared bathroom facilities but 24hr hot water. A very cheap option for lone travellers. €
Petite Suède Bd Hassan II ⓦ petitesuede.com. One of the first hotels built after the earthquake, this amiable place is not too far from the beach, and remains consistently popular with foreign travellers. All rooms have en-suite showers, though most have shared toilets. Some also have a balcony, and there's also a sun terrace. BB €
Tiznine 3 Rue Drarga ⓦ hoteltiznine.com. Tucked away up a charmingly run-down side street, this little hotel is bright and gleaming, with pleasant rooms decorated with curtains and bedding in various shades of green. It's slightly pricier than the other Talborjt cheapies, but well worth the difference. €
La Tour du Sud Av Kennedy ☎ 0528 822694. A small but immaculate hotel whose en-suite rooms have smoked-glass windows and little balconies, built around two courtyards with large trees growing out of them. It's worth avoiding the ground-floor rooms, however, especially on the side facing the street. €

EATING
SEE MAP PAGE 422

Agadir has **cafés** and **restaurants** to suit all budgets, and its array of international food is by far the largest in the Moroccan south. Inexpensive café-restaurants are concentrated in Talborjt, some with bargain set menus, and good for brekky if it's not provided at your accommodation; most of the restaurants lining the beach and the boulevards are tourist traps, with waiters outside trying to hustle in any passing foreigner who shows an interest, or merely happens to glance in their direction, and some throw hidden service fees onto the bill.

RESTAURANTS
★ **L'Ardoise Gourmande** Bd Hassan II. This modern French bistro is the best such operation in town, with all manner of selections available from the obligatory blackboard menu. Entrees include yummy eggs Florentine, snails and oysters, while for mains you can plump for things like canard confit or porc filet mignon. The desserts can be excellent (try the chocolate soufflé), and there's a lengthy wine selection. €€
Les Blancs Marina. One of the most upmarket restaurants in town, with chairs overlooking (and basically on) the beach, a loungey vibe, and excellent Spanish food doled out to relaxed-looking diners. Try Iberian-ham croquettes for starters, a chorizo omelette, or plump for a paella (two-person min). As befits a Spanish restaurant, they've a decent selection of wine. €€
Bollywood Bd Tawada, off Rue de la Plage. Reliable curry house in a winning location off the boardwalk, with a good mix of tasty, affordable dishes – usually served to the accompaniment of Lata Mangeshkar Bollywood classics. The *paneer masala* is particularly good or there's chicken lamb and beef curries, or the local option – camel curry. It's licensed, too, but note that a service charge will be added to your bill. €€
Chiche Kabab Bd Hassan II. This snack shack is full to bursting most nights – a bit like most customers' arteries. Try the shawarma, the "Biggy Biggy Burger", or all manner of paninis and pizzas; they rather unfairly plonk a set of five dips on your table, making it rather tempting to order chips too. €
Cote Court Bd Hassan II. Forming part of a members-only tennis club, though open to anyone, this is one of the snazziest-looking places in Agadir, with the regular ping of wine glasses an inadvertent soundtrack each evening. However, it's not that pricey. €
Daffy Rue des Oranges. A long-time favourite offering pavement dining or seats around the tables inside, with reasonable set menus and plenty of tajines, including veggie and lots of fish options, plus dishes like pastilla, *mechoui* or tanjia for two if ordered in advance. €
★ **Fishing port stalls** Outside Port d'Agadir. Not on a par with their equivalents in Essaouira, but the stalls here will do you freshly caught fish grilled over charcoal for not very much money. It's a fair way out, but an authentically local experience; go to the inner area to escape the traffic, and get your own drinks at the shops, or you'll pay a lot more to have them brought to your table. €
Jour et Nuit Bd Tawada (on the beach off Rue de la Plage). This restaurant serves international-style dishes such as lamb chops, steaks and roast chicken; Moroccan staples including a good mixed grill (feeds two); and snacks including assorted sandwiches and a range of salads. There's also a bar. A slightly posher branch – without a bar, but with a large balcony overlooking the sea – is set in a 1930s-style building just 50m to the north (same hours). €€
La Scala Bd de l'Oued Souss. This well-regarded upmarket restaurant specializes in Mediterranean cuisine, including modern dishes such as duck with ginger and orange, or salmon *paupiette* (rolled up and stuffed with dill), all served on a large terrace surrounded by trees. €€€

CAFÉS AND TEAROOMS
Daily's Bd Hassan II. Modern cafe which, rarely for Morocco, usually has more female than male customers – this can be a nice change of pace, whatever your gender. Breakfast sets are great value and the price includes good coffee, and light meals are available, as well as colourful macaroons. €
Patisserie Tafarnout Cnr Bd Hassan II & Rue de la Foire. Agadir's poshest patisserie, a place in which to indulge yourself with utterly sinful pastries such as delectable lemon tarts. It's a decent breakfast option, too, with their morning deal (actually available until 2pm) giving you three small pastries and a hot drink or juice – a

8

pity that the coffees here aren't terribly good. €̄

Senso Marina ☎ 0528 848060. The best of the litter of cafés fronting the marina, all of which are predictably popular with local youngsters. As well as coffees and teas it lso has decent ice creams – some of the flavours here are a little unusual, including date (tasty), Snickers (exactly what you'd expect) and the electric-blue "Strump" (meaning Smurf, and therefore made from goodness-knows what). €̄

★ **Talborjt Mini** Av du 29 Fevrier. For something extremely local, hunt down this bustling, unsigned corner spot, which sells little bar mint tea, harira soup, and freshly made doughnuts. €̄

DRINKING AND NIGHTLIFE
SEE MAP PAGE 422

For an international resort, Agadir has surprisingly few bars, clubs or discos outside of the large hotels, though many restaurants are licensed. Locals tend to leave the beach venues to the tourists, and many chaps drink at the several simple, smoky bars in the crusty complex around the Souk Tarik el Kheir (see page 428). **Nightclubs** get going around 11pm or midnight and stay open till 3 or 4am, or later, depending on how many people are still there. Prostitution is rife but illegal – girls and punters usually travel in separate taxis to avoid police attention, and clampdowns are not unknown.

legit recommendation in the area. Exuding a loungey vibe, and often pulsing with reggaeton, beers aren't cheap, but if you want cheaper, there's plenty of choice nearby.

English Pub Bd du 20 Août. Full English breakfast served all day, live English footie on the telly, and karaoke every night make this a home from home for English tourists determined not to go native; on weekends, however, DJ sets see it packed out with trendy local sorts. Downsides are that the beer selection has nothing English whatsoever – it's mainly Moroccan brands you can get for half the price elsewhere, so cocktails are bettervalue.

BARS

1001 Nuits Bd Mohammed V. Located by the *Hotel Argana* pool (see page 426), this is the most attractive shisha spot in town, with cushions for lounging in various Berber-like tents. Service, however, can be painfully slow.

Casa de España Off Av Prince Moulay Abdallah. The smoky, male-only bars around the Souk Tarik el Kheir are usually avoided by tourists, but this tapas bar is the sole

CLUBS

Actor's Royal Atlas Hotel, Bd du 20 Août. One of Agadir's top nightclubs, with guest DJs, a variety of sounds and a mixed crowd. Entry, which includes one drink can be pricey.

Flamingo Agadir Beach Club, Bd du 20 Août. Lively if rather seedy nightclub attached to one of the bigger beach package hotels, and very popular with Moroccans as well as foreigners. Music is usually ear-splittingly loud house.

SHOPPING
SEE MAP PAGE 422

Argan Naturel 129 Rue Marrakech. Sells various kinds of honey (from 65dh/jar), as well as olive- and argan-oil shampoo.

Boras Bd du 20 Août. This shop has a wide selection of alcohol, and is well located near the beach.

Ensemble Artisanal 30 Av du 29 Février. Just up the road from Talborjt, this is an attractive souvenir complex, and incredibly quiet unless group tours are visiting. Prices at most shops are fixed.

Fromital 6 Rue Fal Ould Omair. Talborjt shop purveying

its own excellent, locally produced cheeses, which are also available at big supermarkets elsewhere in the country.

Souk Tarik el Kheir Off Av Prince Moulay Abdallah. A good first stop for crafts and souvenirs, with many of the small stores in this complex offering fixed, marked prices.

Uniprix Cnr Bd Hassan II & Av Prince Sidi Mohammed. Sells crafts and souvenirs at fixed prices, as well as a wide range of alcohol – and bottles of tabasco, if you'd like to zing up your couscous a tad.

AGADIR'S MARKETS

Agadir has plenty of touristy shops, but its markets offer more of a Moroccan feel. The **Municipal Market** (daily 9am–8pm) is a two-storey concrete block in the centre of town between Avenue des FAR and Avenue Prince Sidi Mohammed, with a display of wet fish downstairs cheek by jowl with fossils and handicrafts. Upstairs, it's mostly souvenir shops with rather high prices. **Talborjt** has a plain and simple little food market (daily 8am–6pm) on Rue Mahdi Ibn Toumert just northwest of Place Lahcen Tamri, selling mostly fruit and veg.

Agadir's most impressive market, however, is the **Souk el Had**, in a massive walled enclosure on Rue Chair al Hamra (Tues–Sun 8am–6pm), selling fruit, vegetables, household goods and clothes, with a few tourist stalls thrown in. Sunday is the big day, when it spreads out over the neighbouring streets, as people come from all over the region to buy and sell their wares.

Banks There are many banks with ATMs on Av Général Kettani between Bd Hassan II and Bd Mohammed V, plus BMCE and Banque Populaire on Av Kennedy near the junction of Av du 29 Février in Talborjt.

Cinema Cinema Rialto is very cheap and specializes in Bollywood epics and martial-arts action films.

Consulates Ireland, *Hôtel Kenzi Europa*, Bd du 20 Août; UK, *English Pub*, Bd du 20 Août.

Doctors and clinics Most of the big hotels can provide addresses for English-speaking doctors. Clinique al Massira,

on Av Prince Moulay Abdallah at the junction of Av du 29 Février (☎ 0528 380840) has 24hr emergency service.

Pharmacies There's a night pharmacy at the town hall behind the main post office, and a list of *pharmacies de garde* (all-night chemists) posted in the windows of most town pharmacies.

Post offices The main post office is right at the top of Av de Prince Sidi Mohammed. There's also a DHL office on Av Mohammed V.

Around Agadir

There are a few enchanting places within easy day-trip reach of Agadir, and some are worth an overnight stay at least. To the south is the **Massa lagoon**, which forms part of a national park and functions as an important breeding ground for birds. Heading north instead, the coastal road passes first through the industrial suburb of **Anza**, though beyond that is a great swathe of **beach**, interrupted here and there by headlands and for the most part deserted. Charming **Taghazout** is the best spot around here, though some choose to stay in the uglier communes of **Aourir** and **Tamraght** just to its south. North of Taghazout, **25km Plage** (its distance from Agadir) is an attractive beach backed by a rocky headland, with good surfing. From here on to Cap Rhir, a stretch also known as **Paradis Plage**, are many little beaches, with caves on the rocky outcrops, including a really superb strand at Amesnaz, 33km from Agadir. Even further on is **Cap Rhir** (41km north of Agadir), a good surf-spot (see page 432).

8

To the northeast is the tiny hamlet of **Immouzer**, famed for a waterfall with a highly scenic plunge pool. The 7002 road here leaves the N1 coast road at Aourir, 12km north of Agadir; on the way up you'll pass **Paradise Valley**, a beautiful palm-lined gorge with a number of *auberges* and camping opportunities. Lastly, a surfaced road – mountainous, but incredibly scenic – connects Immouzer with the N8 Agadir–Marrakesh road, allowing easy access from Ameskroud, Taroudant or Marrakesh.

Souss-Massa National Park

The **Massa lagoon**, on the coast around 40km south of Agadir, is part of the **Souss–Massa National Park**, and is one of Morocco's most important **bird habitats** (see page 430), attracting unusual desert visitors and often packed with flamingos, avocets and ducks. The best times to visit are March to April and October to November. Most transport takes you to Massa village, from which you can walk along the *oued*, an area rich in birdlife, and to the beach at **Sidi Rbat**. It was here in 682 AD, according to legend, that the Arab general Okba Ibn Nafi (see page 496), after sweeping westward with his armies to take North Africa for Islam, famously rode his horse into the ocean, declaring before God that only the sea prevented him from going further. The beach itself is often misty and overcast – even when Agadir is basking in the sun – but on a clear day, it's as good as anywhere else and the walks are enjoyable.

ARRIVAL AND DEPARTURE   SOUSS-MASSA NATIONAL PARK

By car Transport of your own is a considerable advantage for getting to, and exploring, the lagoon area; the closest rental agencies are in Agadir (see page 424).

By taxi You could charter a taxi in Agadir for the day, though you'll save money by heading first to Inezgane (see page 425), then taking a *grand taxi* from there.

BIRDWATCHING AROUND AGADIR

The **Oued Massa** has a rich mix of habitats and draws a fabulous array of birds. The **sandbars** are visited in the early morning by flocks of sandgrouse (black-bellied and spotted) and often shelter large numbers of cranes; the **ponds** and **reedbed** margins conceal various waders, such as black-tailed godwit, turnstone, dunlin and snipe, as well as the black-headed bush shrike (*tschagra*) and little crake; the deeper **open waters** provide feeding grounds for greater flamingo, spoonbill, white stork and black-winged stilt; and overhead the skies are patrolled by marsh harrier and osprey. The surrounding **scrubby areas** also hold black-headed bush shrike and a variety of nocturnal mammals such as Egyptian mongoose, cape hare and jackal, while **Sidi Rbat** has a local population of Mauritanian toads. Twenty kilometres inland, the **Barrage Youssef Ben Tachfine** is an enormous freshwater reservoir where possible sightings include black wheatear and rock dove.

If the Oued Souss is flowing (it often dries out), the **Souss estuary** is also of interest to **birdwatchers**. The northern banks of the river have good views of a variety of waders and wildfowl including greater flamingo (most evident in Aug and Sept), spoonbill, ruddy shelduck, avocet, greenshank and curlew, while the surrounding scrubby banks also have large numbers of migrant warblers and Barbary partridge. The **Royal Palace**, built in the 1980s in an imaginative blend of traditional and modern forms, can be glimpsed from the riverbank, but is not open to visitors. To reach the estuary by road, take the Inezgane road out of Agadir (bus #21 or #23 from Avenue Mohammed V), to the junction 7km out of town, where a sign announces the beginning of Inezgane's city limits; turn right here, opposite a military base, but be warned if wandering around the woods here that there have been reports of robberies, sometimes at knifepoint, so leave your valuables behind, and don't go alone.

Lastly, the area around **Cap Rhir** (41km north of Agadir), together with **Tamri village and lagoon** (3km further north), is good for birdwatching – including the rare bald ibis, Madeiran and Bulwer's petrels, Cory's and Manx shearwaters, gannets, common scoter and Audouin's gulls. There have been reports of birdwatchers being menaced here by youths, so – again – it's best not to come alone.

By bus The #42 runs from Inezgane, just south of Agadir (see page 425) every 30min till 7pm.

On a tour It's possible to hop on a group tour in Agadir (see page 425); Tours often include a visit to Tiznit (see page 458).

ACCOMMODATION

★ **La Dune** ⓦladune.de. Painted in shocking pink, this hotel features seven elegant guest rooms, all with terraces boasting superlative beach views, as well as seven Berber-style tents that are arguably even more pleasant to stay in. Excellent value, all in all, and the food's good. Tent €, double BB €

Ksar Massa ⓦksarmassahotel.com. A gorgeous and isolated kasbah-style resort with a swimming pool, hammam, restaurant and beach, not to mention sumptuous rooms done out with different colours and materials in each, mostly inspired by different parts of Morocco. BB €€€€

Aourir

Twelve kilometres north of Agadir, the coastal road hits the small, bustling, pleasantly ugly town of **AOURIR**. Together with its sister village of **Tamraght**, a kilometre beyond and slowly being shut off from the beach by large-scale development, they're often jointly known as "Banana Village" after the banana groves that divide them; the roadside stalls sell local bananas in season. It's only really worth staying if you plan to **surf**, or see somewhere both coastal and genuinely "local" in feel; otherwise, Taghazout to the north (see page 432) is far more attractive, and almost as close to the breaks in any case.

Aourir and Tamraght share **Banana Beach**, a sandy strip broken by the Oued Tamraght, the dividing line between the two villages. Banana Beach is especially good for less experienced surfers, with slower, fatter breaks than those at points to the north.

Around 2km north of Tamraght, a prominent rocky headland, **Les Roches du Diable**, is flanked by further good beaches, including **Cro Cro Beach** to its north, where surfboards can be rented (see page 432).

ARRIVAL, ACTIVITIES AND INFORMATION   AOURIR

By bus Buses #31, #32 and #33 from Agadir stop here roughly every 20min between them (20min), with the latter two continuing on to Taghazout.

By grand taxi You can take a *grand taxi* here from the main rank in Agadir (see page 425), though given the frequency of the buses it's only worth doing if you want to charter a cab for yourself (handy if you have a surfboard, for example). There are also shared taxis from Aourir to Paradise Valley and Immouzer; as usual, it's best to try early in the

day, though there are still quite a few in the afternoon.

Treks and rental vehicles Just north of Tamraght, Amodou Cheval (ⓦ amodoucheval.com) offers horse and camel treks into the mountains behind the coast, as well as buggies and quad bikes for hire.

Money There's an ATM next door to the *Hotel Littoral* (see page 431), and though it's fairly reliable, you're advised to bring along enough money to last a day or two, at least.

ACCOMMODATION AND EATING

There are a few cheap eateries in the market-like area heading inland from the crossroads. Aourir is dry, too, so bring your own alcohol from Agadir, if you want any.

Camping Atlantica Km14 ⓦ atlanticaparc.com. A huge, relatively new campsite a little north of Aourir, full of retired Europeans in large camper vans, on little plots divided by hedges, giving it the air of a prim small-town suburb on the Continent – there are even prefab bungalows. It has a large pool and direct access to Cro Cro Beach, and a little shade provided by the trees between the plots. Camping €̄, chalet €€

Littoral Km12, by the roundabout in the centre of Aourir ⓞ 0528 314726. This two-star is Aourir's best hotel,

just north of the Immouzer turn-off, on the inland side of the road, with spotless, peach-coloured rooms, tiled blue floors, self-catering suites and a pool. A bargain compared to Agadir's hostelries. The restaurant offers a variety of fish and pasta dishes, including pesto or Napolitana for vegetarians, or richer dishes such as lamb with dried plums. €̄

★ **Tajine Aourir** Km12, opposite the Afriquia petrol station. With splendid views across the river to Tamraght from its cheery upper-floor terrace, this is the best of a short line of restaurants in the area just north of the roundabout, all of which are hugely popular with weekenders from Agadir. There are also various brochettes; get here by mid-afternoon, before they start to run out of ingredients. €€

Taghazout

At one time, the fishing village of **TAGHAZOUT** – six kilometres north of Aourir, and eighteen from Agadir – was Morocco's hippy resort par excellence; with its pleasing curl of sand broken up by large rocks, and surrounded by an amphitheatre-like parade of buildings fringed with baby blue, you can see why. The clientele has changed somewhat, since Taghazout is now the country's main surf resort instead (see page 432), but the laidback vibe and friendly relationship between villagers and tourists remain; few travellers stay for less than a week.

ARRIVAL AND INFORMATION   TAGHAZOUT

By bus Buses #32 and #33 head here from Agadir, via Aourir, running every 30min or so between them (25min).

By grand taxi *Grands taxis* come here from the main rank in Agadir (see page 425), or you can charter a cab for yourself (good for those with a surfboard).

Money There are no ATMs in Taghazout – the closest one is 6km away in Aourir – so bring as much cash as you need from Agadir or elsewhere. You can usually pay for accommodation online or in person by card.

ACCOMMODATION

Local firms rent out apartments, but you may be able to find a cheaper deal by renting a room from a local family. You'll need to haggle and the longer you stay the less you'll pay.

★ **Amouage** Main road at north end of town ⓦ surfmaroc.co.uk. Part of the *Surf Maroc* stable is this eye-poppingly gorgeous affair, and one not squarely

aimed – this may be a Taghazout first – at the surfer set. Poke around the super-relaxed compound and you'll find an on-site spa, bar and infinity pool; their dorm beds are overpriced, yes, but still better value than any others in town. BB dorm €̄, double €€€

L'Auberge Taghazout main beach ⓦ surfmaroc.co.uk.

8

SURFING AROUND TAGHAZOUT

There are absolutely loads of surf spots along the coast both north and south of Taghazout. The huge majority are long right-hand point breaks. Most of the waves are long tapering walls – hollow sections are the exception rather than the norm. **Killers**, 6km north of the village and named after the killer whales which are often seen here, has one of the most consistent breaks, a powerful, perfectly peeling charger which breaks over a rock shelf. **Source**, just south of Killers, is so called for the fresh water bubbling up underneath it. **Anchor Point**, just north of Taghazout, is the most famous wave in the country. It can hold solid swell which peels for hundreds of metres down the point. At the north end of the village beach itself, **Hash Point** is supposedly used by those too stoned to make it to the others, but otherwise is a reasonable enough wave.

Another surf haven is **Cap Rhir**, 41km from Agadir and distinguished by its 1926 French-built lighthouse. A prime surfing spot is **Boilers**, a powerful right break named after the relic of a shipwreck that's perched on an island: the paddle-out between the wreck and the shore demands good duckdiving or immaculate timing to avoid being washed up by sets. **Draculas** is another longright named after its pincushion of sea urchins, breaks just inshore of Boilers. There are also good surf spots north and south of Taghazout, notably at **Banana Beach** between Aourir and Tamraght (see page 430), and **Cro Cro Beach** just north of Tamraght (see page 431).

PRACTICALITIES

If you're not bringing surfing gear along, there are plenty of **rental spots** in and around Taghazout – several dedicated surf shops rent out, sell or repair boards, and sell surfing accoutrements. The main movers and shakers on the surfing scene are British firm Surf Maroc (ⓦsurfmaroc.co.uk), who rent out equipment from their office at *Taghazout Villa* (see above), and offer surf guiding and tuition along with accommodation in Taghazout. They offer special surf-and-stay packages at their two hotels, and rent out apartments at surfing spots further north. Also worth checking out is Surf Berbere (ⓦsurfberbere.com), who have a guesthouse just off the main road (see above) and a café on the beachfront; their week-long surf-and-stay packages are good value, and there are yoga options available too. Almugar Surf Shop, by the bus stop in Taghazout, also rent and repair surfing equipment.

Once a beach guesthouse for hippies, this place just grows and grows, with new facilities all the time, but still manages to be easy-going, informal and friendly. It's a delightful place to stay, with small but pleasant rooms, hot-water showers, a roof terrace, movie room (often as not showing surfing films) and a restaurant downstairs (see page 432). BB €€

Surf Berbere Just off the main road in the centre of town ⓦsurfberbere.com. Though the simple rooms in this guesthouse are usually rented by the week as part of surf packages (see page 432), it's also possible to take them by the day. Breakfast is served at a beachside café with grand views of the Atlantic bashing in. BB dorm €, double €€

EATING AND DRINKING

The eating scene here has become far more traveller-oriented in recent years, with "surf" used as a menu-item prefix with monotonous regularity, but poke around and you'll still find simple places serving up grilled fresh fish and fish tajines, as well as those doling out smoothies and granola breakfasts. Note that the place is Sahara-dry as far as alcohol goes – staff at the various *Surf Maroc* locations organize occasional booze-runs to Agadir.

Dar Joséphine Main road near south end of town. The most attractive restaurant on the main road by far, though be sure to nab a table on the elegant outdoor terrace for the full effect. The food on the blackboard changes by the day, and is

usually an interesting mix of local and European – expect to see goodies such as grated carrot in orange and cinnamon, pastilla or calamari in spicy sauce; the set meals are decent value, and there are always lots of veggie options. €€

Surf It Above the beach. Good spot for local staples, with cous-cous, tajines and grilled fish, and a choice of indoor or beach-view outdoor seating. €

World Of Waves Above the beach. Usually busy from morning through to night, and with its speakers pulsing with music for much of the day, this is where to head for an open-air smoothie or espresso; they also have pasta dishes, salads, omelettes and the like at reasonable prices. €€

Paradise Valley

Free

Paradise Valley begins around 10km east of Aourir – a deep, palm-lined gorge, with a river snaking along the base. There's a well-marked 2.7km walking trail at around 28km from Aourir, heading uphill most of the way to rejoin the road – it's also pleasant to delve down into the ravine and try to figure your own way back out. With more time in hand, you can hire a mule to explore the valley's **Berber villages** (ask at the hotels), and it's a glorious place to **camp**, though pitch your tent well away from the riverbed in case of flash floods.

ARRIVAL AND DEPARTURE   PARADISE VALLEY

By public transport Trucks, minibuses and shared taxis between Aourir and Immouzer will set you down at Paradise Valley on request, and will pick you up if not full.

By car and motorbike It's a lovely ride up from Aourir,

though be sure to take the right-hand fork after the main body of the village – the left-hand one looks like the main road, but leads to a dead-end.

ACCOMMODATION AND EATING

Auberge Bab Immouzer 2.5km above Paradise Valley, ⓦ aubergebabimouzer.com. Not quite such good value as the other *auberges*, nor as well kept, though it benefits from a large swimming pool surrounded by a spacious sun terrace, well hidden away from the road. There are good views from the restaurant, but the small windows in the rooms mean that they don't share it, and the cheaper rooms don't really have a view at all. €

★ **Auberge le Panoramic** 3.5km above Paradise Valley ☎ 0528 216709. Run by a charming family, this place certainly lives up to its name, with impressive views down the valley and a panoramic terrace where you can

take lunch. There's another panoramic terrace on the roof of its accommodation wing, which is just across the road, boasting a swimming pool and its own little fruit orchard. It's worth taking half-board here, unless you plan to eat at one of the other *auberges*. €

Tifrit 3km above Paradise Valley (500m below Auberge le Panoramic) ☎ 0528 216708. Run by the same family as the *Panoramic* (see above), and set among palms and olives, this small *auberge* has cool rooms, a swimming pool, and fine Moroccan meals on its terrace; they also sell locally made honey and argan oil. HB €€

Immouzer

Heading east from Paradise Valley, a further 25km of winding mountain road takes you to the village of **IMMOUZER**, a small regional and market centre of the Ida Outanane tribe, tucked away in a westerly outcrop of the Atlas and renowned for a lofty **waterfall**,

ARGAN TREES

One of the stranger sights of the Souss and surrounding coastal region is goats browsing among the branches of spiny, knotted **argan** trees, a species similar to the olive that is found only in this region. Though some younger goatherds seem to have a sideline in charging tourists to take photographs, the actual object of the exercise is to let the goats eat the outer, fleshy part of the argan fruit. The hard, inner nut is then cracked open and the kernel crushed to extract the expensive oil.

Argan **oil** is sweet and rich, and is used in many Moroccan dishes and in salads, or for dunking bread. It is also used to make **amalou**, a delicious dip of honey and almond paste. An expensive delicacy, argan oil is not easily extracted: while one olive tree provides around five litres of olive oil, it takes the nuts from thirty argan trees to make just one litre of argan oil. Plastic **bottles** of argan oil are occasionally sold at the roadside in the Oued Souss area, but are very often adulterated with cheaper oils. It is therefore better to buy argan oil or *amalou* from a trustworthy source such as Argan Naturel in Agadir (see page 428), *Hôtel Tifrit* in Paradise Valley (see page 433), or specialist shops in Marrakesh or Essaouira. Argan oil is also sometimes sold in larger supermarkets.

whose base is within walking distance down the slopes. Bar the waterfall and a refreshing, rarified air, there's not too much else of tourist interest here, bar a **souk** held every Thursday. The local speciality is **honey**, made by bees that browse on wild thyme, lavender and other mountain herbs. There's also a five-day honey moussem in late July or early to mid-August. Note if you are considering buying honey here that it may well be illegal for you to import it into your home country.

Waterfalls

4km from Immouzer • Free • 1hr on foot from Immouzer

The spectacular **waterfalls** for which Immouzer has long been renowned are best seen at their foot, 4km downhill to the northwest of the village and flanked by a clutch of souvenir stalls. The falls have been very adversely affected by drought of late; tight control of irrigation now reduces the cascade on most occasions to a trickle, with the villagers "turning on" the falls for special events only. However, the petrified canopy of the falls is of interest in its own right, and there's a full **plunge pool**, one that's rather chilly even at the height of summer.

A surfaced road twists down to the foot of the falls, though it's far more pleasant for pedestrians to take the footpath which branches off the road just after it starts heading downhill. Additionally, and even more thrillingly, a path from the lowest point in the garden of the *Hôtel des Cascades* follows a water channel across cliffs; it's then possible to scramble down into the olive groves, but it isn't a route for the timid or unfit (or those in flip-flops), and ascending again is harder still.

ARRIVAL AND DEPARTURE   IMMOUZER

By public transport From Agadir, take a *grand taxi* or city bus to Aourir (see page 425), from where there are shared *grands taxis* and minibuses to Immouzer. The most frequent services are on Thurs, when the weekly souk is held, but on other days you shouldn't have too long to wait.

ACCOMMODATION AND EATING

Amalou At the end of the waterfall road, near the foot of the falls ☎ 0528 846966. More-than-acceptable budget option with simple rooms, a swimming pool (summer only), and a restaurant serving surprisingly good food – try the chicken-and-lemon tajines. €

★ **Des Cascades** Signposted from the main square ☎ 0528 826016. A delightful place, set amid gardens of vines, apple and olive trees, roses and hollyhocks, with a panorama of the mountains rolling down to the coast (all rooms have a balcony and a share of the view), and a spectacular path down to the foot of the falls. The food, too, is memorable, and there's a swimming pool (summer only) and tennis court. The hotel can organize trekking on foot or by donkey, maintains *gîtes* to overnight in, and has arrangements with families further afield to put up guests. €€

Le Miel Near the end of the waterfall road. When visiting the falls, eat at *Hotel Amalou* (see above), but grab your coffee here – it's the best you'll find for miles around. They do other simple snacks and drinks as well. €

Taroudant and around

With its majestic, tawny-brown and honey-gold circuit of walls, **TAROUDANT** is one of the most elegant towns in Morocco. Its position at the heart of the fertile Souss valley has always given it a commercial and political importance, and the Saadians briefly made it their capital in the sixteenth century before moving on to Marrakesh. Taroudant is a friendly, laidback sort of place, with a population of around 70,000 and the good-natured bustle of a Berber market town. While on your walk around, note the distinctive, highly beautiful blue veils that many of the older local ladies wear. It's a good base for **trekking** into the Western High Atlas or the Jebel Sirwa as well as for two superb road routes – north over the **Tizi n'Test** to Marrakesh (see page 357), and south to **Tata** (see page 443), **Foum el Hassan** (see page 447) and beyond.

Despite its extensive ramparts and large tracts of open space, the town is quite compact. Within the walled "inner city" there are just two main squares – **Place Assarag** (officially renamed Place Alaouyine) and **Place Talmoklate** (officially Place en Nasr) – and these mark the centre of town, with the main **souk** area between them to the north. The pedestrianized area of **Place Assarag** is the centre of activity and comes alive in late afternoon as the sun's heat eases off and people come out to promenade. Lately it has seen the return of performers such as storytellers, snake charmers and musicians – as in Marrakesh's Jemaa el Fna, but on a smaller scale, of course.

East of Taroudant, the spectacular kasbah in **Freija** is worth a stop, set in a lovely village which makes a good overnight layover. Further down the road, the oasis and kasbah of **Tioute** is also close enough to explore in a half-day's trip by car, or an energetic day by rented bike.

The walls

7km walking circuit around the exterior; also possible to tour by bicycle (see page 437), or take a *calèche* from just inside Bab el Kasbah (see page 437)

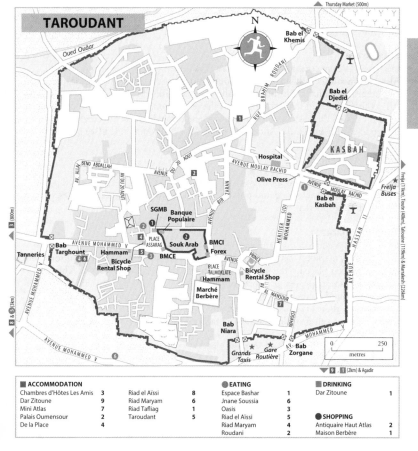

The town's **walls** and bastions, now restored in many places, make an enjoyable 7km circuit, which is best undertaken in the late afternoon in order to witness the ramparts getting fired up by the sunset. Unfortunately, there are no paths atop the walls, meaning that you'll have to go around the outside, though there are stairs up onto them at the **Bab el Kasbah**, a triple-arched structure that's the most imposing of the city's several gates. The finest stretch, in architectural terms, runs south from there to Bab Zorgane, though the setting sun often plays fancy tricks on the north-facing sections around Bab el Khemis and Bab el Djedid.

The kasbah

Just to the north of Bab el Kasbah, the **kasbah** was originally a Saadian winter palace complex, and contains the ruins of a fortress built by Moulay Ismail. You won't see much these days – the kasbah is now home to the city jail, a fire station and a law court, and isn't at all photogenic.

The souks

Aside from its ramparts, Taroudant's main attractions are its two daily souks: the **Souk Arab**, immediately east of Place Assarag (and north of Place Talmoklate), and the **Marché Berbère**, south of Place Talmoklate. There's also a diverting **Thursday market** a little way north of the walls.

Souk Arab

Many entrances, but easiest approached along the lane by the BMCE bank, or from Pl Assarag • Free

Also known as the "belt" market, the **Souk Arab** is good for rugs, carpets, leather goods and other traditional crafts, but especially jewellery. This comes mainly from the Anti-Atlas villages (little of it is as "antique" as the sellers would have you believe), though until the 1960s there was an artisan quarter here of predominantly Jewish craftsmen. For good-quality wares, the Antiquaire Haut Atlas is recommended (see page 439).

Marché Municipal

Easiest access is via Pl Talmoklate • Free

The **Marché Municipal** has more everyday items than the Arab souk, with spices and vegetables as well as clothing and pottery, and again jewellery and carpets. Parts of it are rather atmospheric.

Thursday market

1km north of Bab el Khemis, then easily visible on the left • Free

The **Thursday market**, where Berbers from the villages sell farm produce and sometimes craftwork, takes place up the road from the northeast gate, **Bab el Khemis**. This market once took place in an area just north of the gate, but in 2014 was moved to a "proper" gated compound by the local government, ostensibly to facilitate tax collection. Nevertheless, there are usually far too many tradespeople to fit into the place, and the large yard out front provides additional market space (tax-free, presumably).

The tanneries

Turn left outside Bab Targhount, then right after 100m • Free

The leather **tanneries** are outside the town walls on account of their smell – leather is cured in cattle urine and pigeon droppings – and for the proximity to a ready supply of water. Compared with those in Marrakesh or Fez, they are small, but tidy; your presence is likely to be noticed immediately, but the resultant pestering is usually small-scale. Sheep, cow and goat leather articles are all on sale, but don't buy skins of rare or

TREKKING FROM TAROUDANT

From Taroudant's rooftop terraces, the fang-like **peaks** of Awlim (3482m) and Tinerghwet (3551m) look temptingly close on the rugged northern skyline. The area is easily reached from Taroudant, as is the Tichka Plateau (see page 357). The Jebel Sirwa (see page 441) is also within practical reach of the town; you should really allow at least a week for a cursory visit, more if possible. One of the very best **trekking routes** in Morocco, nicknamed "The Wonder Walk", is a two-week trip up to the plateau and on to Jebel Toubkal (see page 339), Morocco's highest peak.

If you are interested in a **guided trek**, contact El Aouad Ali through the hotels **Roudani** (see page 438) or **Taroudant** (see page 438). He is a highly knowledgeable, English-speaking mountain expert, and can organize treks at short notice if need be. It is best to avoid other agencies as there have been some unpleasant rip-offs by cowboy operators.

endangered species, which are also unfortunately on sale: their importation is banned in most Western countries, and buying them, or indeed patronizing shops which sell them, encourages illegal poaching of rare animals.

ARRIVAL AND DEPARTURE TAROUDANT

By bus Buses use Taroudant's *gare routière*, which is a yard just outside the walls by Bab Zorgane; you can buy tickets on the buses, or in advance from a clutch of agencies just inside the walls. Buses to Freija use a stop outside the town hall at the beginning of the Ouarzazate road. There are buses to Marrakesh via the thrilling road of Tizi n'Test each Sat morning; otherwise, get a minivan from the *gare routière* to Tin Mal (see page 355), and onward transport from there.
Destinations: Agadir (3 daily; 1hr 45min); Casablanca (13 daily; 8–10hr); Igherm (3 daily; 2hr 30min); Marrakesh (6 daily; 4hr); Ouarzazate (6 daily; 5hr); Rabat (3 daily; 13hr); Taliouine (5 daily; 2hr); Tata (3 daily; 4hr 30min).

By grand taxi *Grands taxis* use a yard immediately west of the one used by buses. To Tata, there are rarely direct shared *grands taxis*; set off early in the day to avoid getting stranded at Igherm.
Destinations: Agadir (1hr 15min); Aoulouz (1hr); Freija (20min); Igherm (1hr 30min); Inezgane (1hr 15min); Marrakesh (4hr); Ouled Berhil (40min); Taliouine (1hr 30min).

GETTING AROUND

By petit taxi There are plenty of *petits taxis* for short journeys (usually to be found in Pl Assarag).
By bicycle and scooter You can rent bicycles by the hour, half- or full-day from a little shop on Av Mohammed V just off Pl Assarag between Crédit du Maroc and Bank Attijaraiwafa. Alternatively, you can rent velo-scooters or motos from *Location 2 Roues*, opposite the mosque.
By car Many choose to rent a car here to chalk off the sights around town and some of the surrounding countryside; it's also a good start-finish point for those tackling the Tata circuit (see page 443). There are several rental spots dotted around town – ask your hotel for details of the one closest to you.
By calèche You'll see a fair few horse-drawn *calèches* angling for business around town, particularly around Bab el Kasbah.

ACCOMMODATION SEE MAP PAGE 435

WITHIN THE WALLS
Mini Atlas Av el Mansour Eddahbi ☎ 0528 551880. The staff here are very friendly and the rooms are small but sparkling, with en-suite showers, though hot water only runs at certain times of day. Breakfast costs extra. €
Palais Oumensour Borj Oumensour ⓦ palaisoumensour. com. A charming, if overpriced, hotel tucked away at the end of a calm side street in the city centre. The pool is small but certainly does the trick after a long day of walking, and the rooms are beautifully appointed, with huge bathrooms (though the toilet cubicles can be tricky to get into). BB €€

De la Place Pl Assarag ☎ 0528 852623. Though it's in a good location, on the main square (enter through the tearoom), the rooms are a bit grubby and very basic, with shared bathroom facilities and no hot water. If you can negotiate a reduced rate, however, its low price might make it worthwhile for tight budgets. €
Riad Maryam 40 Derb Maalem Mohammed, signposted off Av Mohammed V ⓦ riadmaryam.com. Taroudant's original riad, with six rooms and a suite around a lovely patio garden. The decor is interesting (a double-edged sword), but it has a certain charm, as do the family

who run the place, and the food is wonderful. It's a little hard to find – ask directions when you're in the area. BB €€
★ **Riad Tafliag** Derb Taffelaght ⓦ riad-tafliag.com. Enduringly popular riad hotel whose nine traditionally-decorated rooms are simply dreamy places to stay for a few days. There are bicycles for hire, and also a small pool, while the rooftop provides lovely views of the sun's rising and setting. BB €€
Taroudant Pl Assarag ⓣ 0528 852416. A Taroudant institution and the oldest hotel in town, this was run by a grand old French *patronne* up until her death in 1988, and retains her influence – and some of her old poster collection. Very good value, with a patio garden, and charmingly tiled rooms. €

OUTSIDE THE WALLS
★ **Chambres d'Hôtes Les Amis** 800m west of Bab Targhount ⓣ 0667 601686. A stay at this guesthouse is more like being in a Moroccan family home than a hotel, with clean and pleasant rooms, constant hot water, a roof terrace, and use of the kitchen. BB €

★ **Dar Zitoune** 2km south of town, on the Agadir road ⓦ darzitoune.com. The best upmarket choice in town, with fourteen a/c bungalows and eight suites all set in a magnificent garden (one which smells absolutely wonderful in the evening), and a "Berber village" of stylish tents out back. There are two large pools, and a smaller one featuring a jacuzzi. It's a little way out of town, though mercifully the food is also excellent if you'd rather not move too far for dinner. There's also a bar (see page 438). BB €€€
Riad el Aïssi Nouayl el Homr, on the Ameskroud road ⓣ 0661 173089, ⓦ riadelaissi.ma. A beautifully restful place in a little village 3km southeast of town, set amid nineteen hectares of orange, lemon and banana trees in a 1930 pasha's mansion, and both owned and managed by a local lady (unusual, in these parts). The rooms are enormous, and each comes with an individual terrace; rounding out the picture are a pool with beautiful views of the mountains to the north, and a restaurant serving excellent Moroccan and Italian food (see page 438). It's a short way from the centre, though call and the staff may pick you up. BB €€

EATING SEE MAP PAGE 435
It has to be said that Taroudant's culinary scene has failed to keep pace with its accommodation choices – there are very few places of note to eat. For real budget food, there are stands selling small **sandwiches** filled with merguez or sardine balls, though for tax reasons most have, sadly, gone the way of the dodo. If you're in luck, you'll find one on Av Bir Zaran, and another opposite western exit of the Marché Municipal. **Juice shops** around town sell all kinds of concoctions, and there's a stand on Av Bir Zaran doling out freshly-pressed sugar cane juice with ginger and lime.

WITHIN THE WALLS
Espace Bashar Av Moulay Rachid. Simple place for coffee and tea, though with one major string to its bow – come by just before sunset, climb on up to the terrace, and pick out birdsong while Taroudant's prettiest town gate fires up with the final rays of the day. €
Oasis Pl Assarag. The most popular of the many cafés around the city's colourful main square, selling so-so pizza and spaghetti to those in need of something non-native to tickle their tastebuds, but far more notable for its tea and espresso (avoid the overmilky *café au lait*), and *crêpes à l'orange*. Often crowded with local gents watching international football games on the telly. €
Riad Maryam 40 Derb Maalem Mohammed, signposted off Av Mohammed V ⓣ 0528 551112. The Moroccan home

cooking here is so good that it has featured more than once in the French gourmet magazine *Saveurs*. Non-residents can eat here, but must book at least two hours ahead. €€€
Roudani Pl Assarag. Simple Moroccan dishes such as tajines and couscous are on offer at this hotel restaurant; nothing too special, but all tasty, fresh and well prepared. Food is served at tables on the square – a great place to take in the evening atmosphere or daytime bustle. €€

OUTSIDE THE WALLS
Jnane Soussia Av Mohammed V. Moroccan cuisine served in a relaxed, open-air restaurant just south of the walls, set around a star-shaped pool, with views of orange trees and music stirring the air. There's veal tajine with prunes, chicken tajine with lemon and olives or, if ordered in advance, *mechoui* (roast lamb) or pigeon tajine with raisins. It's mostly pretty good, but you can also just drop in for a mint tea or mango juice. €€€
★ **Riad el Aïssi** Nouayl el Homr ⓦ riadelaissi.com. This excellent, out-of-the-way hotel (see page 438) churns out some great food, as much as possible of which is made with ingredients culled from their own gardens. Interestingly, Jacques Chirac once stopped by for a snack. They're proudest of their goat tajine (feeds two), but couscous and other cheaper staples are available; the salad items and fruit juices are super fresh. You'll need to take a taxi from the centre. €€€

DRINKING SEE MAP PAGE 435
Dar Zitoune 2km south of town, on the Agadir road ⓦ darzitoune.com. This excellent hotel (see page 438) has a well-stocked bar, and it's not that pricey at all. Enjoy

your glass of wine out by the pool, or in their eye-catching bar area. It's a little far from town, though staff will find a cab to get you home.

SHOPPING SEE MAP PAGE 435

Antiquaire Haut Atlas Souk Arab. A lovely, and lovely-looking, antique shop in the Arab souk; to find it, entering the souk from Pl Assarag by the BMCE bank, continue roughly straight ahead, and it's on the right after 200m.

Maison Berbère Off Pl Assarag. On a side street just north of the main square (look out for the signs), this sells elaborate tajines and vases, amid the regular touristy stuff. The owner speaks English, too.

DIRECTORY

Banks Several banks on and around Pl Assarag have ATMs and exchange facilities, as do a trio east of Bab el Kasbah on Av Hassan II.

Car repairs There are garages and spares shops just inside and outside Bab Targhount, and inside Bab Zorgane.

Hammams Hammam Tunsi, 30 Av Mohammed V. There's also a hammam with an entrance for men just next to the *Hôtel el Warda* and an entrance for women round the back in an alley between 177 and 162 Av Mohammed V.

Freija

11km east of Taroudant • Hourly buses from just east of the kasbah in Taroudant; shared *grands taxis* from the Taroudant *gare routière*

The ancient, fortified village of **Freija** stands atop a hill rising above the Oued Souss. The *oued* is quite wide here, and usually dry, but when it does flood, the hill keeps the *pisé* (mud-brick) houses safely high and dry. As well as being quite picturesque, and a good spot for birdwatching, Freija affords sweeping views of the river, the fertile plains beyond, and the High Atlas.

ACCOMMODATION

Riad Freija 3.5km west of of Freija ⓦriadanma.com. The best place to stay in the Freija area (avoid the riad converted from the kasbah by the main road), with a series of modern, pleasingly decorated rooms – all named after

8

THE ROAD FROM TAROUDANT TO TALIOUINE

The main road linking **Taroudant and Taliouine** (N10), has a few notable spots in which to stop, whether or not you've got your own vehicle; a couple of them also make great places to hunker down for the night.

Heading east from Taroudant, you'll first come across tiny **Freija** (see page 439), which is worth a little wander around, though it's a little tricky to get eastward transport from here. It's easier to visit with your own wheels, which will also allow you to make a side-trip to the old kasbah in **Tiout** (see page 440).

Next comes **Ouled Berhil**, 43km east of Taroudant; it's a non-entity of a town but of note for its old kasbah, 800m south of the main road (signposted from the centre of the village), which has been turned into a sumptuous hotel-restaurant, the Riad Hida (see below). Buses along the N10 stop in Ouled Berhil, and there are shared taxis to Taroudant and Aoulouz.

Lastly, there's the town of **Aoulouz**, 34km east of Ouled Berhil; it has quite a lively little market, at its busiest on Wednesdays and Sundays, but for travellers it's more notable for the two daily **buses** to Marrakesh via **Tizi n'Test**, one of the most exciting mountain roads in Morocco: a series of hairpin bends cutting across the High Atlas (see page 357). There are shared taxis from the centre of the village to Taroudant (1hr), Inezgane (2hr 15min), Ouled Berhil (30min) and Taliouine (40min).

ACCOMMODATION AND EATING EN ROUTE

Riad Hida Ouled Berhil ⓦpalaisriadhida.com. This nineteenth-century palace was bought in the 1950s by Danish millionaire Börg Kastberg, who spent thirty years restoring it to its former glory. It now has deluxe rooms and suites, spacious grounds, a magnificent garden and a great restaurant. HB €€€

Sahara Aoulouz ☎0672 674948. A surprisingly nice place in this little town, with nice, fresh rooms and shared – but, importantly, clean – bathroom facilities. €

other Moroccan cities famed for riad accommodation – arrayed around a swimming pool. Given the slightly remote location, you'll most likely be dining at the riad, too, which is no bad thing. BB €€

Tiout

25km southeast of Taroudant • No public access • Infrequent *grands taxis* from Taroudant (mainly mornings and late afternoons)

The stone-built Glaoui kasbah at **TIOUT** is one of the grandest in the south, and is still owned by the local *caid*. Profiled against the first foothills of the Anti-Atlas, it is a wonderfully romantic sight, and was used as a location in Jacques Becker's 1954 French film *Ali Baba and the Forty Thieves*. You can't go in, but from near its ramparts you'll be able to take in fabulous views over the luxuriant palmery, with the High Atlas peaks beyond.

ACCOMMODATION AND EATING   TIOUT

Igrane By the main road below the kasbah ☎ 0618 790365. Villa in a great location, set off the main road just by the palmery. There are only three rooms, all with delightful straw-and-*pisé* walls, so call ahead to make sure they've got space. HB €€

Kasbah Tiout Inside the kasbah ☎ 0668 747243. Head on up the road leading to the kasbah, and you'll eventually have to stop at this restaurant-with-a-view. There's a great value set menu (there will be no other options, though they could perhaps rustle up an omelette), but even if you're not hungry, it's a delightful place for coffee or tea. €€

8 | Taliouine and around

More village than town, there's a palpable end-of-the-road feeling once you've reached **TALIOUINE** – the roads do continue, however, and thanks to good accommodation options and some superlative vistas, the place makes a logical stopover point en route to Taroudant, Ouarzazate or Tata. The aforementioned views are mostly made up of various shades of gold and brown, often sculpted into comb-patterns by varying forces, such as the page-like rocks making up the surrounding mountains, grooves made by the hooves of goats which peck at the local scrubland, ploughed furrows on brown fields which seem dry year-round, and tyre-tracks on the dusty roads winding their lonely courses out of town. All in all, it's a study in understated beauty.

Taliouine is most famed for its **saffron** (harvest season usually runs Sept–Oct) and one-gram packets are sold at shops in town – note that saffron is damaged by light, so it's best not to buy if it has been left out in glass jars for any length of time. The town also has a Monday **souk**, held across the valley behind the kasbah.

Within swiping range of town are the peaks of the **Jebel Sirwa**; Taliouine makes a good base for this trekker's paradise, though to reap maximum reward you'll have to stay in the mountains for at least a few days.

The kasbah

Just off the main road, across the river

The magnificent **kasbah**, visible across the river to the east of the village, was built by the Glaoui after the French evicted the original landowners to make way for it. However, the Glaoui regained the land after independence, and although large parts of the kasbah are derelict, one member of the family, together with his French wife, has restored part of it and opened a *maison d'hôte* in it (see page 441). There are more kasbahs in the hills round the village, if you have time to explore them.

ARRIVAL AND DEPARTURE   TALIOUINE

By bus The main bus stop is on the main road, towards the west end of the village. Buses can be picked up elsewhere, but won't stop if they're full.

Destinations Agadir (5 daily; 3hr 30min); Casablanca (2

daily; 12hr); Er Rachidia (1 daily; 11hr); Marrakesh (1 daily via Tizi n'Test; 7hr); Ouarzazate (6 daily; 3hr); Rabat (1 daily; 14hr); Taroudant (6 daily; 2hr); Tazenakht (6 daily; 1hr 30 min); Tinerhir (1 daily; 8hr); Zagora (1 daily; 8hr).
By grand taxi *Grands taxis* leave just along from the bus stop.
Destinations Aoulouz (40min); Taroudant (1hr 30min);

Tazenakht (less frequently; 1hr).
By car or motorbike If heading to or from Tata, you're best advised to take the scenic P1743 (see page 444).
Banks There are branches of Banque Populaire and Attijawiwafa on the main road, both with foreign card-friendly ATMs.

INFORMATION AND ACTIVITIES

Trekking A few trekking specialist operators are located in and around Taliouine, with Zafrani (ⓦzafrani.ch) particularly recommended for tours of Jebel Sirwa.

Banks There are branches of Banque Populaire and Attijawiwafa on the main road, both with foreign card-friendly ATMs.

ACCOMMODATION SEE MAP PAGE 442

Atlas Bordeaux By the bus stop ☎0666 752292. The best of the handful of ultra-cheapies on the main drag in the centre of the village. The rooms are simple, but clean and fresh, with hot showers (usually). Though the neighbouring small hotels may be slightly cheaper, they are also dirtier. €
Auberge Le Safran On the main road near the eastern edge of town ⓦauberge-safran-taliouine-sud-maroc.com. This good-value place has become a default option in its price category, with rooms that are simple but colourfully decorated. They now have a pool, though like the rooms themselves, it could often do with a little more cleaning. They also have a restaurant downstairs (see page 441). €

Camping Toubkal 3.5km east of town ☎0528 534343. This campsite has passable bungalow rooms, including some a/c and two adapted for wheelchairs, a small grocery store, a cheap restaurant, and a swimming pool. Wi-fi near the reception only. Camping €, bungalow €€
★ **Escale Rando** In the kasbah ☎0528 534600. A member of the family who owned the land before the kasbah was built has now established this *maison d'hôte* in part of it which has been restored from its ruinous state. Most rooms have shared bathroom facilities, though a few are en suite. BB €€

EATING SEE MAP PAGE 442

Taliouine is no gourmand's paradise, and there are few actual restaurants to speak of. However, there are plenty of informal grill-spots near the bus stop.
Auberge Le Safran On the main road near the eastern edge of town ⓦauberge-safran-taliouine-sud-maroc.com. If you're not eating at your accommodation, this hotel (see page 441) is your best in central Taliouine. Most items on the menu involve saffron somewhere along the line. Go

for the brochettes, rice and veggies, all with a hint of the magic herb. €€
Laiterie Freres Assounfou On the main road in the centre of town. There are a fair few little cafés on the main drag, but this little shop – interestingly decorated with mauve paint, purple tables and a pink-metal staircase inside – makes the most pleasant drinking spot. €

SHOPPING

★ **Calligraphie Tifinaghe** South of the main road, eastern side of town. Shop-gallery in which a cheery local gent, Moulid Nid Ouissadan, creates some cool-looking Berber-text calligraphy, with the aid of saffron, rose-water, and "magic" (the latter element otherwise known as a blowtorch). Good for souvenirs including T-shirts and bags, too, and every visitor gets a blowtorched Berber version of

their name for free. A great little place.
Cooperative Souktana de Safran On the main road, eastern side of town. Ostensibly a museum, with one attractive exhibition room that teaches nobody anything at all, this is the most reliable place in town in which to buy saffron (30dh or so for a bag). You may be offered a cup of saffron tea if you call by at the right time.

Jebel Sirwa

The **Jebel Sirwa** (sometimes spelled Djebel Siroua) is an isolated volcanic peak, rising from a high area (3000m-plus, so take it easy) to the south of the High Atlas. It offers good trekking, rewarded by magnificent views, a cliff village and dramatic gorges. It's best in spring; winter is extremely cold. For those with 4WD, one of the great scenic *pistes* of Morocco circles north of Sirwa, a two- to three-day trip from Taliouine via **Askaoun** and **Tachnocht**, rejoining the N10 north of Tazenakht.

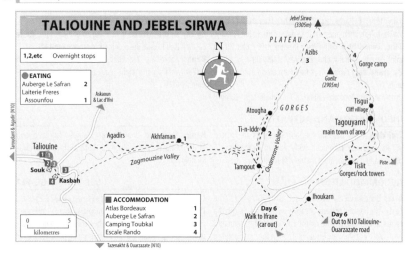

A week-long **walking circuit** taking in Jebel Sirwa is outlined on the map (see page 442), where the numbers represent the overnight halts.

The route

The circuit begins on day one with a gentle valley ascent from Taliouine to **Akhfaman** where there are rooms and a kasbah. The *piste* actually reaches west of here as far as Atougha but, souk days apart, transport is non-existent and the walk is a pleasant introduction to the trek. Beyond Akhfaman the *piste* climbs over a pass to another valley at **Tagmout** and up it to **Atougha**, before contouring round into the upper valley, where you can stay at *azibs* (goat shelters) or bivouacs.

Jebel Sirwa (3304m) can be climbed from Atougha in five to six hours: a pull up from the southern cirque onto a plateau, crowned with rock towers; the nervous may want to be roped for one section of the final scramble. The sub-peak of **Guliz** is worth ascending, too, and a bivouac in the gorge below is recommended.

Beyond Guliz, you should keep to the lower paths to reach **Tisgui**, where there are rooms available. In Tisgui, don't fail to visit the unique **cliff village**, whose houses, ranked like swallows' nests on a 300m precipice, are now used as grain stores. Continuing the circuit, past fields of saffron, you reach **Tagouyamt**, the biggest village of the Sirwa area, where rooms are available, and which is connected by *piste* to the Taliouine road. Trails leave it to pass through a couple of villages before reaching the river, which is followed to the extraordinary conglomerate features of the **Tislit gorges**. This natural sculpture park is amazing; you can camp or get rooms at the village.

A road now runs from Tislit back to wider civilisation, following the valley to **Ihoukarn** and then to **Ifrane**. You can get a vehicle out from Tislit, or alternatively trek over the rather barren rise back to Tagmout, and spend a couple of days retreading your steps back to Taliouine.

INFORMATION   **JEBEL SIRWA**

Tours Mules to carry gear, as well as tent rental, can be arranged by various hotels in Taliouine (the *Escale Rando*, see page 441, is recommended), or by staff at the *Kasbah* restaurant in Taroudant (see page 441), though they don't operate in the Sirwa in winter. Trips can also be organised remotely.

Maps If you are going it alone, the relevant survey maps are the 1:100,000 *Taliwine* and 1:50,000 *Sirwa*.

The Tata circuit

Heading **south** across the **Anti-Atlas** from Taroudant, or east from Tiznit, you can drive, or travel by bus or a combination of *grands taxis* and trucks, to the desert oases of **Tata**, **Akka** and **Foum el Hassan** to the west, or **Foum Zguid** to the east. This is one of the great Moroccan routes, still very much a world apart, with its camel herds and lonely, weather-beaten villages. As throughout southern Morocco, **bilharzia** is prevalent in the oases, so avoid contact with pool and river water.

GETTING AROUND   THE TATA CIRCUIT

By public transport Transport can be sparse, which means you'll have to think ahead if you want to stop off at various places en route and be somewhere with a reasonable hotel by the time transport dries up. The other problem is that smaller places like Oum el Alek and Aït Herbil have nowhere for visitors to stay, and are not served by *grands taxis* – they'll drop you off, but are unlikely to be passing with a free seat for you. Buses are more frequent than they used to be, but it can be a long wait. Hitching is not advisable in this area.

By car The easiest way to see the area is to rent a car. Agadir has the best choice (see page 424), though Tafraoute gets you closer to the loop.

Tata

The small garrison town of **TATA** is a pretty long way from anywhere, and from whichever direction you're arriving, it'll be something of a relief to see its orderly array of pink-coloured buildings, flanking a large oasis below a steep-sided hill known as **La Montagne**, largely occupied by the military. The town is resplendent under an azure sky governed by an unblinking sun – temperatures often sail into the forties, though humidity is next to zero. Tata is a leisurely place with a friendly (if early-to-bed) air, and distinct desert influences in the dark complexion of the people, the black turbans of the men and the colourful sari-like coverings of the women.

There's not too much of tourist import in town – its attraction is a palpable feeling of remoteness, and simply the reward of getting here in the first place. One of the nicest things to do here is go **walking** in the palmery, which is at its best in the morning or early evening, before the sun hits its zenith. There's also a Sunday market in town, and a very lively Thursday **souk** held at an enclosure – or, more accurately, a series of *pisé* courtyards known as El Khemis, 6km out on the Akka road (N12); dates are the mainstay at both.

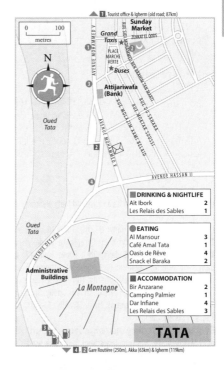

ARRIVAL AND DEPARTURE
TATA

By bus Buses use the *gare routière*, located south of town on the Akka road, around 300m south of the *Relais des Sables*. You'll pay around 7dh for a taxi to

ROUTES TO TATA

FROM TAROUDANT

Leaving the N10 Taroudant–Taliouine road after 8km at Aït Iazza, the R109 passes **Freija** (see page 439) and the turning to **Tiout** (see page 440), before winding its way up into the stark Anti-Atlas mountains. Transport is scarce – only four buses a day in each direction. Direct shared *grands taxis* are also rare: most terminate at **Igherm** (also spelt Irherm; 93km from Taroudant), where there's a **Wednesday souk**. If you get stranded here, basic rooms are available at a couple of café-restaurants.

Igherm is also a crossroads, with scenic, surfaced roads to Taliouine (see page 440) and Tafraoute (see page 450), as well as the old R109 road to Tata via Issafen. Though buses still continue south on the R109, it has now been superseded by the spectacular route 7086, climbing over the ragged mountain strata before dropping down into a valley, which it follows to Tata. On this road, at **Annamer** – a blaze of almond blossom in March – you can visit one of the best-preserved *agadirs* in Morocco, a huge walled courtyard with tiers of minute storerooms reached by ladders made of notched tree trunks. If you want to see inside, ask around for the *gardien*, who will, of course, expect a tip for his trouble. If you want to enquire about trucks from Igherm to Taliouine or Tafraoute, try asking around the petrol station in the middle of town, or the cafés around it, where the truck drivers hang out and play cards.

FROM FOUM ZGUID

From **Foum Zguid** (see page 384), there is a surfaced road, two daily buses, and occasional *grands taxis* to Tata; most buses start in Tazenakht (see page 384) and Ouarzazate (see page 372). The route runs through a wide valley, following the course of a seasonal river, amid an extremely bleak landscape, which is now and then punctuated by the occasional oasis and *ksar*, with the wave-like range of the Jebel Bani to the south. At **Tissint**, halfway from Foum Zguid, there's a gorge and waterfall, whose best vantage point is 2km west of town on the road to Tata. Tissint is also a good base for scenic walks into the desert.

FROM TALIOUINE

If heading from **Taliouine**, you're best advised to take the P1743, which splits off from the N10 around 15km to the east on the Tazenakht road. This is one of the most scenic drives in this whole part of Morocco, and there's a good road the whole way – you'll have most of it to yourself. It heads south via **Agadir Melloul** and **Akka-Irhen** (25km east of Tata, with a Thurs souk); the latter is your best and most scenic pit stop for coffee, in either direction. Heading to Tata, you'll then join the N12 for the final westward stretch.

or from central Tata, though it's an easy and fairly pleasant twenty-minute walk.

Destinations: Agadir (3 daily; 6–7hr); Akka (6 daily; 1hr); Bou Izakarn (6 daily; 4hr); Casablanca (2 daily; 13hr); Foum el Hassan (6 daily; 2hr); Foum Zguid (2 daily; 2hr 30min); Guelmim (2 daily; 5hr); Igherm (3 daily; 2hr 30min); Marrakesh (3 daily; 10hr); Ouarzazate (2 daily; 5hr); Rabat (1 daily; 17hr); Tan Tan (2 daily; 8hr); Taroudant (2 daily; 4hr 30min); Tiznit (4 daily; 5–6hr); Zagora (1 daily; 8hr).

By grand taxi Collective *grands taxis* leave from just north of Pl Marche Verte, and sometimes from the square itself.

It can take some time for them to get together enough passengers to set off, and services are extremely sparse – you're better off going by bus. However, there are occasional departures (especially in the morning) to the destinations below, as well as taxi-trucks to Foum Zguid (especially Sun night and Mon morning for the Monday souk).

Destinations Akka (1hr); Bou Izakarn (3hr 30min); Foum el Hassan (2hr); Foum Zguid (2hr 30min).

By car There are some lovely scenic routes to Tata (see page 444). It's always a good idea to fill your tank before leaving or when arriving here, since the only two petrol stations for dozens of miles either way are, nonsensically, staring at each other across the road to the south of town, just past the *Relais des Sables*. If driving westward, the only fuel stop before Bou Izakarn is the Ziz station at Aït Herbil (see page 447).

INFORMATION

Tourist information The Délégation de Tourisme (☎ 0528 802075) is on the old Igherm road, 500m north of *Hôtel Tigmmi*. For guides, you could do worse than asking at the *Oasis de Rêve* restaurant (see page 445).

Bike rental Bicycles can be rented from the campsite on Av Mohammed V.

Bank and post office There's an Attijariwafa, with ATM, on Av Mohammed V; the post office is on the same road.

ACCOMMODATION
SEE MAP PAGE 443

Bir Anzarane Off Av Mohammed V, by the market ☎ 0667 099842. This bare-bones ultra-cheapy is at least cleaner, and also slightly cheaper, than the others on the same road, and unlike those, this one at least has a shared shower, albeit in the same room as the shared toilet. €

Camping Palmier Off Av Mohammed V, overlooking the oued ☎ 0528 802810. A far better option than the town's barren *Camping Municipal*, this campsite has adequate space and at least a little shade. Its mosque-side location means that you'll also most likely get a nice early start to the day. Camping €

Dar Infiane Off the Akka road, in the palmery ⓦ dar infiane.com. Upmarket boutique hotel with six rooms and several terraces and patios, in a 500-year-old converted kasbah with palm-frond furnishings and traditional palm-wood ceilings. Overpriced, for sure, but the most upmarket option hereabouts. BB €€

★ **Les Relais des Sables** Av des FAR ⓦ hotelrelaisdes sables.com. The best-value place to stay in town is this three-star hotel with a bar, restaurant and small – though photogenic – swimming pool. Rooms here are small but colourful and comfy, with en-suite showers and toilets; alternatively, there are mini-suites with a sitting area and complete bathroom. To eat in the restaurant, you need to order two or three hours ahead. €€

EATING
SEE MAP PAGE 443

Most guests choose to dine at their accommodation, though there are a few little restaurants on and around Av Mohammed V.

Al Mansour Av Mohammed V. The best of the small restaurants on the main street, though there's no guarantee what they'll have at any particular time. They can at least usually whip up a tajine for you. €

Café Amal Tata Av Mohammed V. This café-restaurant is usually devoid of a chef, but its dryish garden is a pleasant spot for coffee or fresh orange juice. €

★ **Oasis de Rêve** Av Mohammed V. This tiny outfit is the nicest place to eat in Tata by far – try the mixed grill of *kefta*, turkey and the best merguez in town, served by an English-speaking chap who's a good source of local knowledge. €

Snack el Baraka Rue Sidi Mohammed Ben Brahim Tan Marti. Cheery sandwich shop with a couple of outdoor tables and ingredients that always seem fresher than the nearby competition. If you fancy something a little unusual – the staff will look at you strangely – ask for a sandwich featuring the delicious local merguez sausages mixed up with omelette. €

DRINKING AND NIGHTLIFE
SEE MAP PAGE 443

★ **Aït Ibork** On the Akka road south of town, just past the bus station turn-off. For a fun local experience, head to this café for an evening shisha). In keeping with Moroccan norms, the smoking is done out back, out of sight; the light is so dim that you'll be able to see the stars in between exhalations. Unlicensed.

Les Relais des Sables Av des FAR ⓦ relaisdessables. com. This hotel has missed a trick: it's the only bar for miles and miles around, but they've forgotten to mark up their beer prices. Sit back and enjoy swigging a beer by the pool, overlooking the wadi.

Akka and around

Fifty kilometres southwest of Tata, the N12 passes through **AKKA**, a flyblown roadside town abutted, to its north, by a large **palmery**. With less military investment, the place as a whole is not nearly as orderly as Tata; like its sibling, there's little else to see bar the oasis itself, though it's one of the most pleasant in the area, and lends itself to aimless wandering. There's also a weekly **souk** on Thursdays, where the oasis dates (Akka means "dates" in Teshalhit) are much in evidence. There's a smaller souk on Sundays.

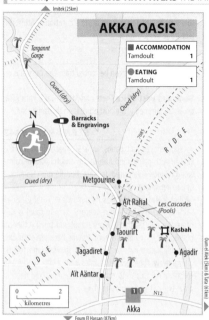

8

The oasis

It's worth taking a morning to explore Akka's **oasis**. Local sights include a **kasbah** and **agadir** (granary) southeast of the village of Aït Rahal, and **Les Cascades** – a series of shallow, dammed irrigation pools, enclosed by palms. Local people bathe in these pools, but they are reputed to harbour **bilharzia**, so avoid contact with the water – both here and in the irrigation canals. To reach Les Cascades by road, turn right after crossing the dry riverbed west of Akka, then head through the almost contiguous palmery villages of Aït Aäntar, Tagadiret and Taouriret; on foot, and with a keen sense of direction, it's more fun to head through the palmerie.

Targannt Gorge

A scorching three-hour trek to the northwest of Aït Rahal (don't forget to carry plenty of water) is the **Targannt Gorge**, in which a cluster of oases are tucked between the cliffs. There are ruins of houses, though the place is deserted nowadays, save for the occasional nomadic camel herder. En route is a small hill on which the French built a barracks. There are **rock engravings** of oxen at the eastern end of the hill – some modern, others perhaps up to two thousand years old. Approaching the gorge, a lone palm tempts you to its mouth. A **guide** from the village would be helpful when looking for the carvings.

Oum el Alek

7km southeast of Akka, off the Tata road

There are more **rock carvings**, said to be prehistoric, near the village of **OUM EL ALEK** (or Oum el Aälague). Anyone with a particular interest is best advised to get in touch with the *gardien* – the *Café-Hôtel Tamdoult* (see page 446) in Akka should be able to put you in touch.

ARRIVAL AND DEPARTURE   AKKA AND AROUND

By bus Buses run to and from the main road in the middle of the village.

Destinations Agadir (6 daily; 6hr); Bou Izakarn (8 daily; 3hr); Guelmim (2 daily; 3hr); Tata (9 daily; 1hr); Tiznit (6 daily; 4hr 30min).

By grand taxi There are sparse shared *grands taxis* to Tata

and Bou Izakarn. Don't leave it too late if you want onward transport – as at Tata, it dries up early.

Destinations Bou Izakarn (2hr 30min); Tata (45min).

By car or motorbike Note that there's nowhere to fill up on petrol in Akka – the closest places are in Tata to the east, and Aït Herbil to the west.

ACCOMMODATION AND EATING   SEE MAP PAGE 446

Tamdoult On the main road, in the middle of the village ☎ 0528 808030. This café-hotel is the only place to stay in Akka, and pretty much the only reliable place to eat as well. The rooms are very basic, though they'll do if

you have to overnight here, and the food's decent enough, though nothing spectacular. Even if you're not staying, it's a good pit stop for coffee and a game of pool. €

AKKA OASIS

Imitek (25km)

N

ACCOMMODATION
Tamdoult   1

EATING
Tamdoult   1

Targannt Gorge

Oued (dry)

Oued (dry)

Barracks & Engravings

RIDGE

Oued (dry)   Metgourine

Aït Rahal   Les Cascades (Pools)

Taourirt   Kasbah

RIDGE   Tagadiret   Agadir

Aït Aäntar

Oum el Alek (5km) & Tata (61km)

0   2
kilometres

N12

Akka

Foum El Hassan (87km)

Foum el Hassan and around

FOUM EL HASSAN (also spelt Fam el Hisn), 90km southwest of Akka, and 4km off the main road (N12), is basically a military post on the edge of an oasis where there was some fighting with Polisario in the early 1980s. There isn't much in Foum el Hassan itself aside from a few shops and a couple of cafés, but there are countless **prehistoric rock carvings** in this region. The only decent accommodation in the area is in nearby **Icht** (pronounced "Isht"), where there's also an interesting old-town area to poke around.

Tircht

5km from Foum el Hassan • Free, though you'll need the services of a guide (see page 448) • On foot from Foum el Hassan, follow the *oued* through the "V" in the mountains north of town; bear right after 2km where it splits

The **rock carvings** at **Tircht** (pronounced "Tirsht") , a peaked mountain about 5km from Foum el Hassan, are worth a look. However, neither the mount nor the carvings are easy to find: you are best advised to employ someone from town as a **guide** (see page 448). The best carvings require a little climbing to get to, but they are among the finest in Morocco – elephants and rhinoceroses, 15cm to 30cm high, dating roughly from 2000–500 BC, a time when the Sahara was full of lakes and swamps.

Ancienne Icht

Icht, around 10km from Foum el Hassan • Free, though a guide is required (see page 448)

Icht town's main point of interest are some old cave-style dwellings, now generally referred to as **Ancienne Icht**. Built to provide shade and cool air by day and protection and warmth by night, the partly **subterranean complex** is wonderfully atmospheric, almost like a clutch of ancient riads hewn out of the rock, and joined together with a network of tunnels. Amazingly, you'll need to navigate some stretches by torch, even at noontime. Even more incredible is the fact that a couple of families are still living troglodyte-style existences here, devoid of light for much of the day, their wooden door shut to the outside world. There's even a little mosque here, though to find this you're best off enlisting the services of a guide (see page 448).

8

Aït Herbil

Off the N12, 15km northwest of Foum el Hassan – the junction is right opposite a filling station • Free • *Grands taxis* from Foum el Hassan, Akka, Tata or Bou Izakarn; for onward travel, however, you'll be lucky to find a passing *grand taxi* with places free, so short of hitching you'll have to depend on infrequent buses (8 daily in each direction)

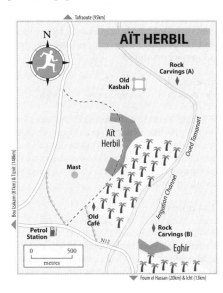

Less renowned than the rock carvings at Tircht are those at the village of **Aït Herbil**, a homely oasis where there's plenty of greenery providing welcome shade for inhabitants – or the very, very few foreigners who venture this way looking for rock carvings. There are two series, marked as "A" and "B" on the map (see page 447); both are easily accessible on foot, though you may have to ask locals for directions, and most of them will have no idea what you're on about.

"**A**", overlooking Oued Tamanart, consists of as many as a hundred small carvings, depicting gazelles, bison, a giraffe and a bird or two, in a steep rock-fall, and to the right of a patch of distinctively lighter grey rocks (indicating several deep and dangerous wells). The rock-fall looks recent but clearly, with the carvings all in the same place, it has not shifted for centuries, even millennia. "**B**", north of the partly deserted village of Eghir, can be found by following the irrigation channel for 800m from the main road, where a signpost points the way. There are fewer carvings here but they are larger and more impressive.

ARRIVAL AND INFORMATION
FOUM EL HASSAN AND AROUND

By bus Buses between Tata and Bou Izakarn (4 – 5 daily) make the four-kilometre detour to stop at Foum el Hassan; they'll also drop off at Icht or Aït Herbil, though it's hard to pick up a bus at the former.

By grand taxi Infrequent *grands taxis* run to Bou Izakarn and Tata.

Destinations Bou Izakarn (1hr 30min); Tata (2hr).

Guides You'll need to sequester the services of a guide to

see most of the local engravings. Mouloud (☎ 0661 660587) is the expert for just about everything between here and Tata, though since he doesn't live locally you'll have to call well in advance; Hassan (☎ 0668 065754) will get you to the Tircht carvings; and Abdellah (☎ 0650 684659, or contactable through *Borj Birmane*) or his French-speaking cohort can take you around Icht village.

ACCOMMODATION AND EATING

★ **Borj Biramane** Icht ⊕ borj-biramane.com. Just off the main road at Icht, this French-run place is the only genuine accommodation in the area, and it's a real beaut. There are shared Berber tents, a/c rooms (one of which has been converted very effectively for wheelchair users) and camping

facilities, all arrayed around a pool that's small but highly inviting, thanks to the chunky mountains surrounding the complex. The food is top notch too (a good job, since there's nothing else around), and they've a nice selection of wines and spirits. Camping €, Berber tent € per person, double €€

Amtoudi

If you have your own wheels, it's worth making an excursion from the N12 Bou Izakarn –Tata road to visit **AMTOUDI** (or Id Aïssa, as it appears on most maps), a very scenic little village surrounded by soaring red cliffs straight out of *Road Runner*, and tucked away into a frond-filled ravine at the end of the P1315 from Aday. Presided over by one of Morocco's most spectacularly located **agadirs**, it's a likeable, extremely quiet little hamlet, and by far the best place to stay the night between Tata and Tiznit. Staying on here will also give you the chance to benefit from some good hiking opportunities.

The agadir
Allow at least 2hr for the round trip up and down • Open whenever the *gardien* is around; call him from one of the *auberges* (see page 449) • Charge

Boasting formidable towers and ramparts, Amtoudi's **agadir** (fortified granary) sits on an eyrie-like setting atop the spur of a hill, reached up a steep zigzag path. There is a small collection of antiquities dotted around the place, and parts of the walls and towers have been restored. Make sure the *gardien* is available before tackling the climb, as the *agadir* is kept locked; it's also a good idea to bring a torch, which will come in handy in some sections.

The gorges
Organize excursions though Amtoudi's *auberges* (see page 449)

A walk up the substantial **gorge** at the end of the village leads to another *agadir*, with huge curtain walls, perched high above a cliff. 3km on and you will arrive at a spring and waterfall. You can climb – or ride a mule – up a winding track and walk around the site, providing the *gardien* is there. If by chance you find the place overrun by visitors, you can escape the crowds with a walk down the palm-filled gorge; here another imposing but decaying *agadir* is perched on top of the cliff and, after about 3km, you'll come to a spring and waterfall.

ARRIVAL AND DEPARTURE   AMTOUDI

By car Amtoudi can be reached on a *piste* which leaves the N12 at the village of Taghjicht, or on a surfaced road (signposted to Amtoudi) which leaves the N12 14km east of Taghjicht. The two roads join at Souk Tnine D'Adaï, a village known for its decorative doors; from here the P1315 makes the quick trip east to the ravine that Amtoudi calls home. Unfortunately, there are no public transport links here.

ACCOMMODATION

Amtoudi On the western approach to the village ⓦ hotel amtoudi.com. This is one of the first sets of buildings you'll see when approaching Amtoudi from the west, a friendly *auberge* with simple rooms, hot water, a restaurant and a camping area. As well as food and accommodation, they offer half-day walking tours. Camping €, BB double €

Auberge l'Ombre d'Arganier Inside the village ☎ 0668 398675. The only place to stay in town at the time of writing, its simple rooms livened up with splashes of colourful paint, and occasional artistic frills. It's also the best place to eat in Amtoudi, whether you're staying here or not – anything complicated (ie grills or tajines) will have to be ordered in advance, but you can hold them to an omelette or coffee at any time. Dorm/shared tent €, double €

Bou Izakarn

The village of **BOU IZAKARN** – set where the roads from Tata, Tiznit and Guelmim meet, and strung out to a certain extent along all three of them – is mostly of interest to people needing to change buses or shared taxis here. It's a lazy kind of place, where not much happens, except during its Friday **souk**; you might as well stay the night in Tiznit, which isn't too far to the north (see below), or Guelmim, even closer to the southwest (see page 466).

ARRIVAL AND DEPARTURE   BOU IZAKARN

By bus All buses stop in the centre of the village, usually at the start of the road they'll be taking.
Destinations Guelmim (hourly; 30min); Tata (8 daily; 4hr); Tiznit (hourly; 1hr 15min–1hr 30min).
By grand taxi Shared *grands taxis* leave from the Tiznit road, by the main roundabout in the centre of town, for Tiznit and Inezgane. Across the square, at the start of the Tata road, they run to Timoulay (14km east of Bou Izakarn), Ifrane de l'Anti-Atlas and occasionally Foum el Hassan. For Guelmim, they leave from a rank on the Guelmim road at the south end of the village, 500m off the main square.
Destinations Foum el Hassan (1hr 30min); Guelmim (30min); Ifrane de l'Anti-Atlas (20min); Inezgane (2hr); Timoulay (10min); Tiznit (1hr).
Banks and post office You'll find a post office and Banque Populaire near the roundabout at the centre of town.

ACCOMMODATION

Anti-Atlas Tiznit road, by the main roundabout ☎ 0528 788134. As far as cheapies go, this is a much better place to make for than the grubby offerings at the same price in Akka. The rooms are decent enough, grouped around a little courtyard with flowers and citrus trees, and there are shared bathroom facilities. €

THE BLUE SULTAN

Tiznit itself was used as a base by **El Hiba** (also known as Ma el Aïnin), the ruler of Smara in the Western Sahara, who declared himself sultan of Morocco here in 1912 after learning of Moulay Hafid's surrender to the French under the Treaty of Fez. El Hiba was known as the **Blue Sultan** on account of his blue desert robes. He led a considerable force of Berbers to Marrakesh, which acknowledged his authority, before advancing on Fez in the spring of 1913. Here his forces were defeated, but El Hiba continued his resistance. Basing himself at Taroudant, and then in the Anti-Atlas mountains, he fought on until his death, near Tafraoute, in 1919. Despite his defeat, the Berbers of the Anti-Atlas mountains still remained outside of French control, and only suffered their first true occupation with the bitter French "pacification" of the early 1930s.

Tafraoute and around

Locked in a muscular, red-granite mountain embrace, and charming in a dusty, windswept sort of way, **Tafraoute** is worth all the effort and time it takes to reach – "like the badlands of South Dakota", as Paul Bowles put it, "writ on a grand scale". Created as an administrative centre by the French, yet still only home to around five thousand hardy souls, Tafraoute is one of the most relaxed destinations in Morocco, though a few *faux guides* may still make a nuisance of themselves. The best time to visit is early spring, when the almond trees are in full blossom, or in autumn, after the intense heat has subdued; in midsummer, it can be debilitatingly hot.

There's not too much to see in the city itself, bar some **rock carvings** in **Tazka**, just to the south, and as such its biggest appeal lies in exploring the surrounding area – north to the beautiful villages of the **Ameln Valley**, nestled under an awesome escarpment; or south to gorges, palmeries, and curious rock formations such as **Napoleon's Hat**, or the "**Pierres Peints**", painted blue and pink by a Belgian artist. South again and over a mountain pass is the **Gorge Aït Mansour**, where several villages are strung out along a highly picturesque palmery. However, the adventure can start before you even enter Tafraoute, since the town is approached by scenic roads through the Anti-Atlas from Tiznit or Agadir (see page 454).

Tazka

About 2km southwest of Tafraoute

It's an easy walk from Tafraoute to the village of **Tazka**, a pleasing, super-quiet little place in which many houses – some of them hundreds of years old – have incorporated the surrounding cliffsides and boulders into their design. Most people are here to hunt ancient gazelle – two **rock carvings**, hidden away on the western periphery of the village. Far easier to spot than the engravings are the remains of an old kasbah, and a **Maison Traditionelle**.

The carvings

Free • Off the road behind the small mosque; turn right on the dirt path, which will veer you around to the left then between two buildings – the carvings are on and below a granite bluff visible just after the path veers to the left

Modest in size and appearance they may be, but Tazka's **carvings** make for an enjoyable hunt. An incongruous white dot on the granite bluff indicates the more modern of two gazelle carvings; the older one is on the upward-facing edge of a fallen boulder, behind the tree in front of the newer one.

Maison Traditionelle

Abutting the kasbah, behind the mosque • Charge

TAFRAOUTE: VILLAGE ECONOMICS

Among Tafraoute villagers, **emigration** to work in the grocery and hotel trade – all over Morocco and France – is a determining aspect of life. The men return home to retire, however, building European-looking villas amid the rocks, and most of the younger ones manage to come back for a month's holiday each year – whether it be from Casablanca, Tangier, Paris or Marseille.

But for much of the year, the **women** run things in the valley, and the only men to be found are the old, the family-supported or the affluent. It is a system that seems to work well enough: enormously industrious, and very community-minded, the Tafrauteis have managed to maintain their villages in spite of adverse economic conditions, importing all their foodstuffs except for a little barley, the famed Tafraoute almonds and the sweet oil of the argan tree.

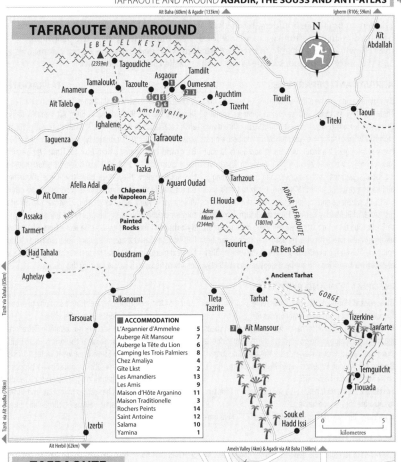

TAFRAOUTE AND AROUND

Aït Baha (60km) & Agadir (133km) ▲

Igherm (R106; 59km) ▲

N

Aït Abdallah

J E B E L   E L   K E S T

(2359m)   Tagoudiche

Tamaloukt   Tazoulte   Asgaour   Tamdilt

Anameur   Oumesnat

Aït Taleb   *Ameln Valley*   Aguchtim

Tioulit

Ighalene   Tizerht

Titeki

Taouli

Taguenza   **Tafraoute**

Adaï   Tazka

Afella Adaï   Aguard Oudad   Tarhzout

Châpeau de Napoleon

Aït Omar   El Houda

ADRAR TAFRAOUTE

Assaka   Painted Rocks   *Adrar Mkorn (2344m)*   (1801m)

Tarmert

Had Tahala   Taourirt   Aït Ben Saïd

Aghelay   Dousdram   **Ancient Tarhat**

GORGE

Talkanount   Tleta Tazrite   Tarhat   Tizerkine

Tarsouat   Tanfarte

Aït Mansour   Temguilcht

Tiouada

Izerbi   Souk el Hadd Issi

0   5   kilometres

▇ ACCOMMODATION

L'Argannier d'Ammelne	5
Auberge Aït Mansour	7
Auberge la Tête du Lion	6
Camping les Trois Palmiers	8
Chez Amaliya	4
Gîte Lkst	2
Les Amandiers	13
Les Amis	9
Maison d'Hôte Arganino	11
Maison Traditionelle	3
Rochers Peints	14
Saint Antoine	12
Salama	10
Yamina	1

Tiznit via Tahala (65km) ◄

Tiznit via Aït Ouafka (78km) ◄

8

Aït Herbil (62km) ▼

Ameln Valley (4km) & Agadir via Aït Baha (168km) ▲

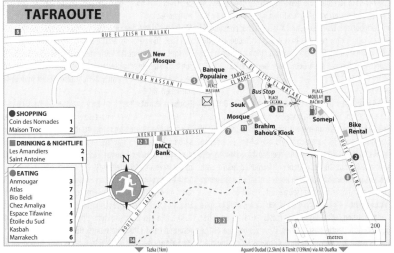

TAFRAOUTE

RUE EL JEISH EL MALAKI

New Mosque

RUE EL JEISH EL MALAKI

Banque Populaire

AVENUE HASSAN II   TARIQ EL NAHJI

Bus Stop

PLACE MASSIRA   PLACE DU SALAMA   PLACE MOULAY RACHID

Souk   Somepi

Mosque   Bike Rental

AVENUE MOKTAR SOUSSIV   Brahim Bahou's Kiosk

BMCE Bank

ROUTE D'AMELNE

N

● SHOPPING

Coin des Nomades	1
Maison Troc	2

▇ DRINKING & NIGHTLIFE

Les Amandiers	2
Saint Antoine	1

● EATING

Anmougar	3
Atlas	7
Bio Beldi	2
Chez Amaliya	1
Espace Tifawine	4
Étoile du Sud	5
Kasbah	8
Marrakech	6

0   200   metres

Tazka (1km) ▼

Aguard Oudad (2.5km) & Tiznit (139km) via Aït Ouafka ▼

Hidden among huge boulders, by the kasbah, is a four-floor **Maison Traditionelle**. It's best used as an opportunity to see how locals live, though these days the proprietor lives elsewhere; he'll be able to organize small musical performances or tea ceremonies, and the entry fee includes a side-jaunt to the gazelle carvings (see above).

ARRIVAL AND DEPARTURE   TAFRAOUTE

By bus Tafraoute can be a little frustrating to reach by bus. There are few services, and several companies running them, but for advice you'll have to hunt each office down individually, since there's no *gare routiere*. In addition, almost every service goes via Tiznit, which can add hours to your journey; only two daily services go directly to Agadir via Aït Baha (saving only an hour or so), and there's nothing at all heading east. The only CTM service (daily to Casablanca via Tiznit, Inezgane and Agadir) starts from the CTM office, just south of Pl Moulay Rachid. There are hourly Lux buses to Tiznit, but these are city-style vehicles, making for an uncomfortable ride across the mountains – choose another company. The unnumbered Lux services to the Ameln Valley and south to Agard Oudad leave from stops around Pl Moulay

Rachid; most other services start from Rue el Jeish el Malaki. Destinations Agadir (6 daily; 4–5hr); Aït Baha (3 daily; 2hr); Casablanca (5 daily; 14hr); Marrakesh (4 daily; 10hr); Rabat (2 daily; 16hr); Tiznit (hourly; 3hr).

By grand taxi Shared *grands taxis* for Tiznit (2hr 30min) leave from Rue el Jeish el Malaki; for the short hop to the Ameln Valley, they leave from the Route d'Amelne. Unfortunately, there are no regular services in any other directions – you'd have to charter a whole cab to get somewhere like Igherm, or the direct road to Agadir.

By minibus Minibuses to Tiouada leave from Pl Moulay Rachid Mon–Sat at around 11.30am, returning at 5.30am the next morning; don't treat these times as gospel, and ask for advice from locals before tackling this route.

INFORMATION AND ACTIVITIES

Bike rental Maison de Vacances, more or less opposite the *Kasbah* restaurant, has well-kept bicycles for.

Mechanics You'll find a few mechanics and tyre repair shops north of the bus stop in the crook where the main road does a sharp bend, and also down towards the Afriquia filling station.

Banks The Banque Populaire on Pl Massira and the BMCE on Av Moktar Soussi have ATMs.

Festival A moussem is held in the second week of February to celebrate the almond harvest.

Trekking Brahim Bahou (☎0661 822677, ✉brahim-

izanzaren@hotmail.com) operates from a kiosk by the souk mosque, and offers two-day treks to Jebel el Kest.

Climbing A look at the scenery surrounding Tafraoute will make rock-climbers go weak at the knees. Try to hunt down *Climb Tafraoute* by Steve Broadbent, a meticulous compendium of information about almost every possible climb in the area, and a handy crag selector; the *Kasbah* restaurant (see page 453) has copies to look at, and some info can be found on a related website (⎗climb-Tafraoute. com)

ACCOMMODATION   SEE MAP PAGE 451

The hotels in Tafraoute are generally pretty good value. At the top end, the arrival of competition has made prices even more negotiable than usual, and it's worth shopping around to see who'll give you the best deal (all frequently offer promotional rates). Further accommodation options can be found 4km north in the Ameln Valley (see page 455).

HOTELS

Les Amandiers On the hill above town ☎0528 800008. Located up a hill and with views out over town, this is Tafraoute's top hotel in more ways than one – as attested by photos here, Mohammed V laid one of the foundation stones. It has, to a certain extent, been upstaged by the new kids in town, but still has a lot of old-fashioned charm, with a wood-panelled lobby, great views, and large, airy rooms. There's also a cosy little bar (see page 453). BB €€

★ **Les Amis** Pl Moulay Rachid ☎0528 801921. Solid budget option, with airy rooms (costs extra for en suite) decorated in gentle pastel tones. It overlooks one of the town's main junctions, and though rooms facing the road

aren't all that noisy, light sleepers are advised to get one further back. €

Maison d'Hôte Arganino Near the old mosque ☎0670 661105. Tucked away at the end of a small alley by the mosque, this delightful little pension-style guesthouse is run by the family who used to live in it, and it still very much retains an old family atmosphere. It also has its own little hammam. BB €

Rochers Peints Route de Tazka ⎗hotelrocherspeints-Tafraoute.com. A very impressive hotel, tastefully done. The first-floor rooms are more attractive than those on the second floor, with straw-and-pisé-covered walls, coloured glass windows, and carved wooden doors from Mali. All rooms have a/c and satellite TV. €€

Saint Antoine Av Moktar Soussi ☎0528 801497. A slick, modern if somewhat overpriced hotel, with efficient, English-speaking staff, cool, spacious rooms, a bar (see page 453) and a nice big swimming pool. There's also a decent restaurant and 24hr room service. BB €

★ **Salama** By the river ⎗hotelsalama.com. A good-value

hotel, originally dating from 1966, but refurbished, with quite large rooms in warm, earthy colours, en-suite bathrooms, a roof terrace, a fire in winter and a reputable restaurant. €̄

CAMPING
Camping les Trois Palmiers Off the Tiznit road ☎ 0662

405870. The most central campsite, a 10min walk from the centre, is set in a small secure enclosure with hot showers and three small rooms. It tends to overflow out of its enclosure and onto the surrounding land in winter and spring, when Tafraoute plays host to a swarm of camper vans driven by sun-seeking retired Europeans. Camping €̄, double €̄

EATING SEE MAP PAGE 451

Atlas Route de Tazka. Basic but well-presented Moroccan nosh – chicken or lamb brochettes, liver, steak, sandwiches and breakfasts – in café surroundings complete with blaring TV. Dishes include chicken or veal brochettes. €̄
★ **Espace Tifawine** Route d'Ameln. If you've made it this far, you may be crying out for something other than the Moroccan culinary tricolore of couscous, brochettes and tajines. You can eat all three of those here, too, but even more tempting are the tasty wood-fired pizzas, which you can eat outside around the swimming pool. In addition, with wi-fi and good coffee, it's a good place in which to plot your day, or onward trip. €̄
Étoile du Sud Av Hassan II. A set-menu restaurant serving delicious Moroccan food, either indoors or outside in a Bedouin-style tent, with an occasional cabaret and floor show for tour groups. You can order separate items from the

menu, but they'll most likely attempt to give you a "free" dessert and charge for the set anyway. €̄€̄
★ **Kasbah** Route d'Aguard Oudad ☎ 0660 954269. Pine-panelled and hung about with carpets, this is an appealingly decorated salon where much of the menu revolves around tajines – options available include beef with almonds and prunes, a veggie option, and a rather unique – and very tasty – tajinified omelette with onions, tomatoes and olives. Moroccan wine and saffron tea are available, and the owner is a very, very useful source of local information, especially for trekking and rock-climbing (see page 452). €̄€̄
Marrakech Tariq el Nahzi. An unpretentious family-run place overlooking the road, with excellent-value meals (60dh set menu) and friendly service. The couscous here is particularly tasty, though the omelette breakfast set is also a good shout. €̄

DRINKING SEE MAP PAGE 451

Les Amandiers On the hill above town. This hilltop hotel has a bar which is, in theory, open to residents only – in practice, anyone can drink here. The bar itself is an atmospheric little cubby-hole behind reception, though they usually allow people to drink in the fancy dining hall; they've a surprisingly large range of spirits, including gin

and Martini, as well as cheap beer.
Saint Antoine Av Moktar Soussi. This hotel (see page 452) recently moved its bar to the basement, and made it far larger and louder – disco ball, pumping music, but despite the effort, it's usually only home to two or three local chaps having a bottle of Flag.

SHOPPING SEE MAP PAGE 451

Tafraoute is well known for its *babouches* (slippers), and a narrow street of *cordonniers* sells quality slipperwear just north of the Coin des Nomades. In addition, there's a Wed souk, held by the river in the centre of town.
Coin des Nomades Just west of the Salama. Also signed as the "Meeting Place of Nomads", this is a pleasant little space (oddly full of posters of Rafael Nadal) in which to shop without pressure to buy – you may even have to get the

proprietor's attention.
Maison Troc Route d'Aguard Oudad. The most reliable carpet shop in town, with a range of styles from nearby areas – mostly Anti-Atlas but also some High Atlas variants (and they'll happily explain the difference, as well as arrange postage if necessary). They also have some silver implements, and old Jewish money.

Ameln Valley

Around 4km north of Tafraoute at its closest point • 45min on foot from Tafraoute, though little shade on the road • Lux buses (unnumbered) from Tafraoute every 30min, running past most settlements • Grands taxis from Tafraoute

You could spend days, if not weeks, wandering round the 26 villages of the **Ameln Valley**, north of Tafraoute. Set against the backdrop of the Jebel el Kest's rock face, they are all beautiful both from afar and close up – with springs, irrigation systems, brightly painted houses and mosques.

The **Ameln villages** are built on the lower slopes of the Jebel el Kest, between the "spring line" and the valley floor, allowing gravity to take the water through the village and on to the arable land below.

ROUTES TO TAFRAOUTE

Tafraoute is a bit of a long way from anywhere, but the various **routes** into town are all stunners. These include the "main" roads from **Tiznit** and **Agadir** – both are beautiful and involve plenty of mountain zigzagging, but the Tiznit approach has the edge, winding through a succession of gorges and a grand mountain valley.

FROM TIZNIT

The **Tiznit–Tafraoute** R104 passes a succession of villages, most named after their souk day (see page 50). In winter and spring the road is sometimes crossed by streams but it is generally passable enough; the drive takes around two hours, but leave plenty of time to see, and navigate, the mountains before dusk.

At **Assaka** (20km from Tiznit), a bridge crosses the Oued Tazeroualt – the river that causes most difficulty in winter and spring. Nineteen kilometres further on, a side road heads 10km south to the *zaouia* of **Sidi Ahmed ou Moussa**, which in the seventeenth century controlled its own state, the Tazeroualt, its capital at nearby (and now deserted) **Illigh**. The *zaouia* hosts a **moussem** in the second or third week of August, which is worth trying to attend. Sidi Ahmed is the patron saint of Morocco's acrobats, most of whom come from this region – and return to perform.

Just beyond **Tighmi**, 42km from Tiznit, the road begins its ascent of the **Col du Kerdous** (1100m), with the kasbah-like *Hôtel Kerdous* (see below) marking the top of the pass. The area is good for paragliding, though there isn't much activity these days.

At the end of the descent, entering the village of **Jemaa Ida Oussemlal** (64km from Tiznit), the road divides. The left fork, which runs downhill through the village, is the direct road to Tafraoute, a picturesque route that drops into the Ameln Valley at Tahala, once a Jewish village. The right fork, a newer road, which skirts round Jemaa Ida Oussemlal, is longer but well surfaced, flatter and faster going, arriving in Tafraoute through a grand spectacle of mountains and the lunar landscape around Agard Oudad (see page 456). Just after Aït Ouafka, it splits again – take the right-hand fork for **Izerbi**, where an ex-housing minister has built a Disney-style chateau.

Lastly, along the road from Tiznit to Tafraoute, you may occasionally see children holding little furry animals for sale – live, on a piece of string – by the roadside. These are **ground squirrels**, which are known locally as *anzid* or *sibsib*, and are destined for the **tajine** dish, in which they are considered quite a delicacy, their flesh being sweet since they subsist mainly on a diet of almonds and argan nuts. You will not get *anzid* tajine in any restaurant, however, unless perhaps you provide the squirrels yourself.

FROM AGADIR

The R105 road **from Agadir to Tafraoute** is a bit drab until you reach the village of **Aït Baha**, which is a lively shopping centre on Wednesday, its souk day, and you can also stay overnight here. From Aït Baha, the road south to Tafraoute is a highly scenic, though slow and winding mountains ride, past a series of fortified kasbah-villages. The most spectacular fortified village in the region, **Tioulit**, is to the west of the road, around 35km south of Aït Baha, with the best views of it from the south (so looking back, if you're coming from Agadir). Another 13km on, you'll easily discern the *Kasbah de Tizourgan* (see below).

ACCOMMODATION AND EATING EN ROUTE

★**Kasbah de Tizourgan** Tioulit ⓦtizourgane-kasbah.com. This is one of Morocco's most distinctive guesthouses, located in a thirteenth-century kasbah. Rooms are small but immaculate, with shared bathroom facilities, and there's a very good restaurant – a good job, since you have to take half-board. HB €€

Hôtel Kerdous KM 54, Route de Tiznit Tafraoute ⓦhotel-kerdous.com. At the top of the Col du Kerdous pass, this hotel is set in an old fort with well-turned-out a/c rooms and a pool. It deserves at least a stop for a tea, and the breathtaking views. €

Oumesnat

Oumesnat, like most Ameln settlements, emerges out of a startling green and purple rockscape, crouched against the steep rock walls of the valley. Its houses are often bizarre constructions, some built on top of older houses deserted when they had become too small or decrepit; a few of them, with rooms jutting out over the cliffs, are held up by enormous stilts and have raised doorways entered by short (and retractable) ladders.

La Maison Traditionelle

Charge

One of Oumesnat's houses, known as **La Maison Traditionelle**, is owned by a blind Berber and his family, who show visitors round. They give an interesting **tour**, explaining the domestic equipment – grindstones, water-holders, cooking equipment – and the layout of the house with its guest room with separate entrance, animals' quarters, and summer terrace for sleeping out. To get the most from a visit, you may need to engage an interpreter, such as one of the guides recommended in Tafraoute (see page 450).

Jebel el Kest

Trekking along the valley is no great hardship (see page 456), but more serious hikers might consider making the ascent of the **Jebel el Kest** (2359m). A striking feature on it is the **Lion's Face** at Asgaour – a rock formation which really does look like the face of a lion in the afternoon light when seen from Tafraoute. Getting up is a rough and rocky scramble – there's no actual climbing involved – over a mountain of amethyst quartzite from **Tagoudiche**, the Almen's highest village (spelt Tagdichte on the road sign). There is a black igneous dyke below the summit pyramid, and the summit itself, being a pilgrimage site, has shelters on the top, as well as hooped petticoat daffodils blooming in spring. The easiest route is not obvious, and a **guide** is advisable. In addition, many other areas scattered on both the southern and northern slopes of the Jebel el Kest offer excellent rock climbing, usually on sound quartzite.

8

ACCOMMODATION

THE AMELN VALLEY, SEE MAP PAGE 451

There are some great places to stay around the Ameln Valley, especially around the junction with the road from Tafraoute. Sadly the old *gîte* once used by hikers tackling the Jebel el Kest has closed down – hiking operators will find you somewhere to stay if necessary.

AROUND THE AMELN VALLEY JUNCTION

L'Argannier d'Ammelne 500m east of the junction ⓦ arganierammelne.com. This hotel offers small but sweet rooms with smooth, polished walls, each in a different colour, set around a small garden. There are also camping facilities and dorm beds. Camping €, BB double €

Auberge la Tête du Lion 600m east of the junction ☎ 0528 801165. A scenic spot, located directly opposite the Lion's Face (hence the name). The spacious a/c rooms are arranged around a lush garden, and there's a panoramic roof terrace and a restaurant. €

★ **Chez Amaliya** Just west of the junction ⓦ chez amaliya.com. Boasting perhaps the best pool view of any hotel in Morocco, this is a cool place with an elegant lobby and well-appointed rooms, all presided over by an enthusiastic Dutch woman. There's wi-fi in the lobby area, and it reaches most of the rooms. The food is top-notch, too, and the place is licensed. BB €€

OUMESNAT

Gîte Lkst ☎ 0661 718678. A tranquil setting and beautiful scenery are the plus points here, while hard mattresses and darkish rooms are the minus points. It isn't the most traditional Berber experience (note the old-school payphone and Kodak sign), but it's a decent place to stay, at a very reasonable price. €

Maison Traditionelle ☎ 0661 513793. The owners of this grand house (see page 450) also offer bed and breakfast or half-board in a nearby village home, with a/c rooms – heated in winter – and a little garden. The website hasn't been updated in years, but gives you the picture; rooms are bookable on some major online accommodation engines. BB €

WALKS AROUND THE AMELN VALLEY

With 26 villages strung out like pearls along a straightish river bed, beneath a curtain of granite to the north, it's easy to get your bearings in the Ameln Valley, and the main bone of contention is where to start and finish your **walk**. Many villages have basic shops where you can buy drinks, if little else. Getting around, you can use a combination of taxis and walking, or rent bicycles. However, the paths between the villages are sometimes hard to find, or even nonexistent, so especially on a bike you may have to head back towards the main road from time to time. It's not too far a stretch though – Oumesnat to Anameur, for example, is around 12km.

Most choose to start their walk in **Oumesnat** (see page 455), one of the prettiest valley villages. From here, you can walk through or above a series of villages to **Anameur**, where there is a *source bleue*, or natural springwater pool (for looking at, not for swimming in), a meandering hike of around three hours in total. Along the way is **Tazoulte**, one of four local villages with Jewish cemeteries, remnants of a community now completely departed, though Jewish symbols are still inscribed on the region's silverware, which was traditionally made by Jews. On your way, you'll also pass the starting point for a hike up the Jebel el Kest (see page 455).

If you don't want to re-tread the same route when returning to Tafraoute, you can walk over a **pass** back from the R104 road near Ighalene in around three hours. The path isn't particularly easy to find, but it's a lovely walk, taking you past flocks of sheep and goats tended by their child-shepherds. The route begins as a *piste* (east of the one to Tagoudiche); you follow a dry riverbed off to the right, up a side valley, where the zigzags of an old track can be seen. Cross to go up here (not straight on) and, once over the pass, keep circling left till you can see Tafraoute below.

EATING

SEE MAP PAGE 451

There aren't many places to eat in this whole area. Most people eat an evening meal at their **hotel** (all offer good half-board rates), and perhaps grab lunch in Tafraoute.

Anmougar By the junction. Simple rooftop cafe with pictures of all sorts of tempting food – and never, ever any food. Still, it's a great place to sit and drain a coffee or mint tea with a spectacular view of the valley. €

★ **Bio Beldi** Aït Omgas ☎ 0697 820288, 🐦 facebook. com/RestaurantBioBeldi. Presided over by a friendly English-speaker, this is a wonderful place which sources almost all of its ingredients from the area – including eggs from the chickens running around the charming garden out back, where you'll mostly likely end up eating. Veggies will be in their element with things like the spicy zaalouk salad or cous-cous, while meat-eaters can try a tajine; there are plenty of juices available too, including yummy beetroot. Quite a superb place, and in the middle of nowhere to boot. €

Chez Amaliya Just west of the junction 🐦 chezamaliya. com. This hotel (see page 455) is a great place to drop in for a simple meal if you're in the area and don't feel like going back to town for lunch. They have the usual range of Moroccan dishes (shout out to their meatball-and-egg tajine, and there's wine available in the adjacent bar. €€

Agard Oudad

3km south of Tafraoute

Head south from Tafraoute for a short but enjoyable walk or cycle to **AGARD OUDAD**, a dramatic-looking village built under a particularly bizarre outcrop of granite. Like many of the rocks in this region, this has been given a name; most of the others are named after animals – people will point out their shapes to you – but this one is known, in good French-colonial tradition, as **Le Chapeau de Napoléon** (**Napoleon's Hat**). There's little else to do in the village, which seems to muddle through the day on permanent siesta, though your presence will certainly pique the interest of its locals.

Painted rocks

1.5km southwest of Agard Oudad • Free • Accessible by bicycle (see page 452) or car; follow road past Agard Oudad until the sign for "Rochers Peints" pointing right, then follow *piste* 2km or so – loop trip possible by following *piste* further out west, eventually emerging onto the R104 in Afella Adaï • On foot, you can take a short cut away from the main road by following the flat *piste* round to the right behind the Chapeau de Napoléon, and you'll see the rocks on your left after a couple of km

The **Painted Rocks** (also known as the Pierres Bleues, or Rochers Peints) were executed in 1984 by Belgian artist **Jean Verame** and a team of Moroccan firemen, who hosed some eighteen tons of paint over a large area of rocks; Verame had previously executed a similar project in Sinai. The rocks had lost some of their colour over the years so a local man decided to refresh them in 2010, to mixed reactions from local people, many of whom disliked the project, especially after pieces of the paint started washing off into the local streams. Now, however, budding modern artists – mostly younger travellers from elsewhere in Morocco – are adding their own hues to the mix on nearby rocks. Controversy aside, it's an absorbing spectacle, especially when the setting sun imbues its own take on proceedings.

Gorge Aït Mansour

Just over 30km southeast of Tafraoute • Minibuses leave Tafraoute for Tiouada and Souk el Hadd Issi around 11.30am–noon, returning around 5.30am the following day; unless you fancy hitching back, you'll have to stay the night • The area is far better tackled by car

For a beautiful day-trip from Tafraoute, drive southeast towards the **Gorge Aït Mansour**, a route that first rises into beautiful Anti-Atlas mountain scenery, then descends into some fabulous gorges and palmeries. It's possible to make a loop of the route in a sturdy vehicle.

Leaving Tafraoute, the road here climbs over the hills, with superb panoramas back across Tafraoute and the Ameln Valley, before reaching reach **Tleta Tazrite** (15km from Tafraoute), which has a souk on Friday. From Tleta Tazrite, the road heads south then descends rapidly into **Aït Mansour**, where many people like to park up and stroll through the massive palmery, which is beautifully cool in the heat of the day. The palmery stretches a good 6km along the floor of a valley, while the route itself rises above it, giving amazingly beautiful vistas – especially from the fine *agadir* (fortified granary) at the crest, a little behind which you can see a yellow mosque backed by sumptuous-looking rock formations. Just south of this, at **Souk El Hadd Issi**, the palmery ends.

To the south, a *piste* (for which really you need 4WD) heads off to Aït Herbil (see page 447), passing a number of ancient **rock carvings**, though they are not easy to find and a guide would be advisable. The first and least difficult group of carvings to find are some 700m east of the road, about 6.4km south of the junction, and feature long-horned cattle and elephants, which lived in this part of Africa when the carvings were made. To the east, you can make the loop back to Tleta Tazrite via the villages of Tiouada, Temguilcht and Tarhat – though none are especially beautiful.

8

ACCOMMODATION AND EATING

GORGE AÏT MANSOUR, SEE MAP PAGE 451

GORGE AÏT MANSOUR

Auberge Aït Mansour Near the north end of the palmery ☏ 0528 735198. This friendly guesthouse in the palmery has simple rooms, but the surrounding area is enchanting, and they'll be able to whip you up a simple meal. Call ahead, or there may be nobody there to greet you. HB €

Tiznit and around

Many of Morocco's walled cities creak under the weight of tourist hordes, but little **TIZNIT** is pleasingly "real". While it may lack the heady atmosphere of Taroudant, Fez and the like, it perhaps makes for a more genuinely local experience. Despite its solid circuit of huge *pisé* walls, the city was only founded in 1882, when Sultan Moulay Hassan (Hassan I) was undertaking a *harka* – a subjugation or (literally) "burning" raid – in the Souss and Anti-Atlas. These days, the few travellers who make it to southern Morocco are extremely likely to hit Tiznit at some point; clean, neat and tidy, the city makes a good staging point en route to Tafraoute, Sidi Ifni or Tata, and is worth at least a day of your time, especially if you're interested in **jewellery**, for which the city has achieved national renown (see page 460). As an added bonus, there's a nice beach not far away at **Aglou Plage**, 17km west of Tiznit – a nice place to stay, too and another reason to extend your stay in the area (see page 460).

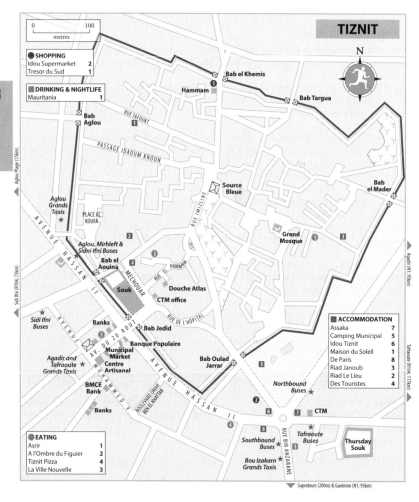

8

● SHOPPING
Idou Supermarket 2
Tresor du Sud 1

■ DRINKING & NIGHTLIFE
Mauritania 1

● EATING
Asrir 1
A l'Ombre du Figuier 2
Tiznit Pizza 4
La Ville Nouvelle 3

■ ACCOMMODATION
Assaka 7
Camping Municipal 5
Idou Tiznit 6
Maison du Soleil 1
De Paris 8
Riad Janoub 3
Riad Le Lieu 2
Des Touristes 4

The Medina

Tiznit has five kilometres of **walls** and seven major **gates**, the most important of which are **Bab Ouled Jarrar** and **Bab Jedid**. The second of these was a French addition, as its name ("New Gate") indicates; it is also called Les Trois Portes ("the three gates"), though in fact it consists of four gateways. The Medina also contains a number of *ksour* which were there before the walls were built.

The walled town's main square, the **Mechouar**, was once a miltary parade ground; it's now rather ugly, and essentially used as a car park. Far prettier is the **Grand Mosque** in the centre of the Medina, which has an unusual minaret, punctuated by a series of perches; these are said to be an aid to the dead in climbing up to paradise, and are more commonly found south of the Sahara in Mali and Niger. Around the corner from the mosque is the **Source Bleue**; recently renovated, and occasionally home to a family of geese, this spring is dedicated to the town's patroness, Lalla Tiznit, a saint and former prostitute martyred on this spot, whereupon water miraculously appeared.

ARRIVAL AND DEPARTURE

TIZNIT

By bus Most buses pick up and drop off near the main roundabout, where the Tafraoute road meets the Guelmim road (Rue Bir Anzarane); you're best advised to head here and ask for the best place to stand for any particular location. CTM buses stop outside their office on Rue Mohammed Hafidi, less than 100m east of the main roundabout, though you can buy tickets more centrally at their Mechouar office; Supratours buses stop outside their office on Rue Bir Anzarane, about 300m south of the main roundabout. City-style Lux buses head to surrounding areas, including the #1 to Aglou Plage, and the #18 to Mirhleft and Sidi Ifni (every second one goes via Aglou Plage too); they arrive at and depart from a yard just outside Bab el Aouina. Destinations: Agadir (2–3 hourly; 2hr); Bou Izakarn (2 hourly; 1hr–1hr 30min); Casablanca (1–2 hourly; 10–11hr); Dakhla (9 daily; 17–18hr); Guelmim (2–3 hourly;

1hr 30min–2hr 30min); Laayoune (16 daily; 9–10hr); Marrakesh (2–3 hourly; 5–8hr); Mirhleft (hourly; 45min); Ouarzazate (1 daily; 9hr 30min); Rabat (8 daily; 11–13hr); Sidi Ifni (hourly; 1hr 30min); Smara (3 daily; 7–8hr); Tafraoute (hourly; 3hr); Tan Tan (2–3 hourly; 4hr 30min); Tata (6 daily; 7hr).

By grand taxi Collective *grands taxis* for most destinations use a yard opposite the post office, where you'll find vehicles serving Agadir, Inezgane, Mirhleft, Sidi Ifni and Tafraoute. Vehicles for Bou Izakarn and Guelmim have a station on Rue Bir Anzarane, just south of the main roundabout. Shared *grands taxis* for Aglou Plage can be found on Av Hassan II, by the southwestern corner of the city wall. Destinations Agadir (1hr 15min); Aglou Plage (15min); Bou Izakarn (1hr); Guelmim (1hr 30min); Inezgane (1hr); Mirhleft (45min); Sidi Ifni (1hr 30min); Tafraoute (2hr).

INFORMATION

Banks and exchange There are plenty of banks in town, as well as a couple of bureaux de change.

Hammam There's a traditional hammam just inside the walls at Bab el Khemis, open for men and women.

ACCOMMODATION

SEE MAP PAGE 458

Budget hotels in the Medina cannot all guarantee hot water, but there's a public showerhouse, Douche Atlas (both sexes), in a cul-de-sac off Rue du Bain Maure.

HOTELS

Assaka Rue Bir Anzarane, on main roundabout ☎0528 602286. Quite a bargain, this place, since it's effectively a two-star hotel at backpacker prices. The rooms are impeccable, with a/c, heating, balcony, TV and good en-suite bathrooms. **€**
Idou Tiznit Av Hassan II, by main roundabout ☎0528 600333. Tiznit's only real "hotel" option, a four-star forming part of a small nationwide chain, with spacious rooms, a/c, satellite TV, a pool and professional staff – but it's a little bit soulless, especially the "bar", for which there are still signs everywhere, even though it has been mothballed for years.

There's usually some kind of promotional rate on offer. BB **€€**
Maison du Soleil 470 Rue Tafoukt ☎0676 663175. A small, prettily done out little *maison d'hôte* in a residential area of the Medina, near Bab Aglou and away from the main tourist zone, with just five rooms (two en suite) and a sunny patio, not to mention very reasonably priced home-cooked meals. BB **€**
De Paris Av Hassan II, by main roundabout ☎0528 862865. A friendly and modestly priced hotel, with cosy rooms (en suite, with a/c, heating and TV) and a popular restaurant. Consistently popular with foreign backpackers. **€**
★ **Riad Janoub** Rue de la Grand Mosque ☎riadjanoub. com. Run by an affable couple, this is now top dog in town, its splendidly decorated rooms set around a delightful pool. The place really comes into its own in the evening – clamber

8

up to the rooftop for a look at the sunset, then come back down for the delectable dinners. BB €€
Riad Le Lieu Rue Imzilen Issaoui ⊛ riadlelieu.ellohaweb.com. Hidden away in the alleys northeast of Bab el Aouina, this is a super little place, set around a courtyard painted a French colonial lemon, and shaded from the sun by a ceiling of flowers. It's here that their excellent breakfasts are served – and dinner too, if you so desire. Rooms are a little small, and most have shared facilities, though these are kept spotless. BB €
★ **Des Touristes** 80 Pl Mechouar ✆ 0528 862018. A

deservedly popular backpacker hotel, with hot showers, friendly staff and old-fashioned iron bedsteads. The communal areas are decorated with pictures of Paris in the 1950s and an impressive collection of banknotes, and it's by far the best budget option in town. €

CAMPING

Camping Municipal Right up against the walls by Bab Ouled Jarrar ✆ 0528 601354. Tiznit's campsite is secure and has more shade than most Moroccan campsites. It's popular with retired Europeans in camper vans, especially in winter. €

EATING SEE MAP PAGE 458

★ **Asrir** Pl Rue Id Ali Oubihi. A surprising find in the Medina area, this pleasing little hidey-hole wouldn't look out of place in the trendier parts of Marrakesh – a calm, covered courtyard centred around a couple of trees. Unfortunately, they've stopped serving food and shisha, and removed the Saharan record sleeves that once lined the walls, but every hipster-type in town seems to end up here (there's even a power socket at each seat), and it's a great spot for coffee or tea. €
A l'Ombre du Figuier Psge Akchouch ⊛ facebook.com/OmbreDuFiguier. A good find, this friendly courtyard restaurant is about your best bet in town for local food, with regular staples augmented by interesting additions such as camel culet or horse tajine. It doesn't quite live up to the

surprisingly substantial amount of hype it has generated online, but worth tracking down regardless. €€
Tiznit Pizza Bd Hassan II. The pizzas here are not going to satisfy any serious cognoscenti, but they're reasonable enough as Moroccan pizzas go, and the place is full most evenings. €
★ **La Ville Nouvelle** Av du 20 Août ✆ 0528 600963. Just outside the walls, this popular place has a little bit of everything. It's good for bargain breakfasts of juice, hot drink and pain au chocolat; the top floor has a "panoramic terrace", with a non-smoking saloon on the middle floor, plus there's free wi-fi. Food on offer includes spag bol, brochettes and tajines and the excellent "cous-cous royale", made with chicken, beef and spicy sausage. It's also good for cheap baked goods and an espresso or avocado juice. €

DRINKING SEE MAP PAGE 458

Mauritania Rue Bir Anzarane. There's a small restaurant in this hotel, but most are here for the booze – the several halls out back are often filled with tradespeople and colourful local fellows, knocking back cheap beer. It's also

possible to get yours to take away, the shame hidden by an old newspaper, or fetching black plastic bag. Very atmospheric, but not a place for lone females, or anyone who likes washing their hands after using the loo.

SHOPPING SEE MAP PAGE 458

The **jewellery souk** (Souk des Bijoutiers) is still an active crafts centre despite the loss to Israel of the town's large number of Jewish craftsmen; the jewellers occupy the northern part of the **main souk**, which can be entered from the Mechouar. Over to the south, outside the walls, off Avenue du 20 Août, there's a **municipal market** selling meat, fruit, veg and household goods.
Idou Supermarket Off Av Hassan II. Well-stocked

supermarket, which may come in handy if you're using Tiznit as a springboard to somewhere more remote. Open round the clock, too.
Tresor du Sud Just in from Bab el Khemis. The most popular shop in town with tourists, a friendly spot with a visually appealing collection of silver bangles, filigree work, and earrings, as well as some very dangerous-looking daggers.

Aglou Plage

The beach at **AGLOU PLAGE** (**Sidi Moussa d'aglou**), 17km west of Tiznit, sits by a barren, scrub-lined road; it's an isolated expanse of sand with body-breaking Atlantic surf. It has a dangerous undertow, and is watched over in summer by military police coastguards, who only allow swimming if conditions are safe. **Surfing** can be good, but you have to pick the right spots; it's also popular with **paragliders** from September to April, though most people doing these activities actually hole up in Mirhleft, down the coast (see page 461). Quite a few Moroccans (including migrant workers from

France) come down in summer, with a trickle of Europeans in winter. Otherwise, the place is very quiet.

There are a couple of *marabout* tombs on the beach and, about 1.5km to the north, a tiny (and rather pretty) **troglodyte fishing village**, with a hundred or so primitive cave huts dug into the rocks. These are slowly being bought up by expats and trendies from up the coast – this place could, in time, become a backpacker magnet.

ARRIVAL AND DEPARTURE AGLOU PLAGE

By bus Take bus #1 from Tiznit (see page 459) – some of the #18s head here too on their way to Mirhleft and Sidi Ifni. **By grand taxi** *Grands taxis* run frequently from Tiznit though some only go to Aglou village, 3km short of the beach, so try to take one that goes all the way.

ACCOMMODATION AND EATING

Camping Aglou Plage On the main road ☎0528 613234. Popular and deservedly so, this municipal campsite is about 500m up from the beach, on the right if coming from Tiznit. Guests get 50 percent discount at the adjacent water park – and yes, it does have water slides. €̄

Tay Fad d'Laz Overlooking the beach ☎0528 613755. The most presentable of the several restaurants and cafés facing the beach – grab an outdoor seat and some couscous, calamari, or just a coffee or tea. €̄

Mirhleft

MIRHLEFT is a friendly, bustling village about halfway between Tiznit and Sidi Ifni, set a kilometre back from a series of good beaches with crashing waves and strong currents, which particularly attract **surfers**. The town has little of tourist interest bar the old **French fort** overlooking it to the east and a Monday **souk** (devoted mainly to secondhand items), but it's a nice little place to hole up for a few days, walking the dusty streets and enjoying a carefree atmosphere – the latter perhaps the biggest contributing factor behind the surprisingly substantial expat population, mostly made up of French and Belgian retirees.

The beaches

There are four main **beaches** around Mirhleft, each with their own particular vibe and appeal. Furthest north is **Imintourga Beach**, also known as the "main" beach; 1km from central Mirhleft, this wide curl of sand is the most popular in the area, and can get packed out on weekends. Next comes **Aftas Beach**, a tiny, secluded spot directly below town, and also home to *Aftas Beach House* (see page 462). Next comes **Marabout Beach**, 1.5km to the south and so named because of the tomb (and mosque) just off its centre; it's also home to the *Dar Najmat* hotel (see page 462), and famed for the intriguing – and highly photogenic – rock formation sticking straight up from the beach like a miniature mountain. Last, but by no means least, is the **Plage Sauvage**, a wide beach with the most protection of all four, and therefore the best place for swimming; there are also surf spots in the vicinity.

French fort

Walk up Bd Legzira and just keep going • Free

An old military **French fort**, built by the Foreign Legion in 1936 and underscored by Arabic text, overlooks the village from the hill above, which you can climb for beautiful views over the surrounding countryside. It's a popular sunset-watching spot, especially with young local couples seeking a bit of privacy.

ARRIVAL AND DEPARTURE

By bus Mirhleft is on the #18 Lux bus route linking Tiznit and Sidi Ifni; buses stop on the main road in the centre of town. Half of them take a detour to swing by Aglou Plage (see page 460) on their way to and from Tiznit.

Destinations Aglou Plage (roughly every 2hr; 45min); Inezgane (daily; 3hr) Sidi Ifni (hourly; 45min); Tiznit (hourly; 1hr).

By grand taxi Mirhleft is served by *grands taxis* from Sidi Ifni (30min) and Tiznit (45min), but they can be sparse, especially around lunchtime – they run from the main road in the middle of the village.

INFORMATION AND ACTIVITIES

Banks There's an Attijariwafa Bank, with an ATM, on the main road.

Excursions Staff at the *Abertih* (see page 462) can organize all sorts, including quad-bike trips, donkey rides, and paragliding.

Surfing For board and suit rental, there are innumerable small-scale operators in town. For lessons, ask at *Café Aftas* (☎0670 729583), next door to *Aftas Beach House* (see page 462).

Paragliding This has become a very popular activity here in recent years; the *Abertih* (see page 462) is a great source of info and can organise trips.

ACCOMMODATION

TOWN CENTRE

The town-centre options below are all on the same road, which runs parallel to the main road 100m to the east; it's easy to find, even if you're not looking for it, since all roads seem to converge here.

★ **Abertih** On the corner of the main street with the Tiznit–Ifni road ☎0528 719304. The best hotel in the village, run by an amiable Frenchman and tastefully decorated, with a good restaurant (see page 462), constant hot water and some en-suite rooms (extra charge). There's a hammam around the side, too. BB €̄

Atlas Opposite the souk ☎0528 719309. A bog-standard Moroccan hotel revamped for tourists; rooms are but small and simple, some en suite, and most without outside windows. There's a roof terrace giving views of the fort, the showers and toilets are impressively clean, and they supply towels, soap and shampoo. €̄

Tafoukt Next to the souk ☎0528 719077. This simple, no-nonsense hotel charges ordinary Moroccan rates, and makes no particular concessions to tourists, but it's clean and decent, and frankly just as good as pricier places nearby. Most of the rooms have windows facing inward, and those at the top get a lot more light than the first floor. €̄

OUT OF TOWN

Aftas Beach House Aftas beach ☎0675 164271. A small guesthouse run by an Englishwoman, in a great location, right on its own little beach, with almost nothing else there. The rooms are small, and slightly pricier ones have ocean views. Food is available (for guests only), and *Café Aftas* next door (see page 462) offers surfing lessons. Note that there's often a two-night minimum. €̄

★ **Auberge des Trois Chameaux** On the hill above town, just below the fort ⌨3chameaux.com. Classy *maison d'hôte* housed in what used to be the officers' quarters of the French army fort. There's a choice of rooms (which are actually more like junior suites) and, for not much more money, suites with private terraces and wonderful views. There's also a heated swimming pool, parking facilities, an in-house hammam, good food and great vistas over the countryside. HB €̄€̄€̄€̄

★ **Dar Najmat** Marabout Plage, 2km south of town ⌨darnajmat.com. A beautiful *auberge* with bright, modern a/c rooms and a scenic infinity-style pool. Standing on its own at the end of a small, picturesque beach, hotel is dominated by an impressively large rock and overlooked by a mosque and a row of small shops, with just one beach café. The beach is not suitable for surfing, which keeps most of the Mirhleft crowd away. HB €̄€̄€̄€̄

Sally's B&B Overlooking Imintourga Beach, just west of town ⌨sallymirleft.com. A nice option close to town, in a quiet neighbourhood, this B&B is a great place to chill out, with picture-perfect views from the rooftop. Though there's no pool, the beach is right below, and the studio room here is absolutely huge. HB €̄€̄

EATING AND DRINKING

All options listed here are on the same road in the town centre – aim for the souk.

Abertih The menu at this hotel (see page 462) changes daily, but the food is always good, and you can have beer or wine with your meal. There's usually fish cooked *a la plancha* and couscous on offer, but keep your fingers crossed and they may have spider crab or camel. A pity that it's only open in the evenings. €̄€̄

La Bonne Franquette Hôtel du Sud. On the same road as the city-centre accommodation, the *Hôtel du Sud's* restaurant cooks up some tasty grub, including grilled fish and camel tajine. It's also licensed. €̄€̄

Chourouk ☎0662 739658. Popular with locals (always a good sign), this is the place to head for cheap local staples:

think tajines, couscous, and a fried fish platter. Head on up to the rooftop for pleasant views over the town's focal-point road. €

★ **Tifawin Cafe**. This tiny place has been a breath of fresh air in dusty Mirhleft, and every foreigner in town seems to pop by for breakfast – all-day options include muesli and avocado on toast), as well as omelettes and toasted sandwiches. Coffee's good, they serve avocado juices in myriad ways, or try the "jus vert" with apple, cucumber, mint, parsley and lemon. €

Sidi Ifni and around

Known as "Ifni" to its friends, **SIDI IFNI** is the most attractive town in southern Morocco, and uniquely interesting: built in the 1930s, on a clifftop site, it is surely the finest and most romantic Art Deco military town ever built. Many buildings from that era have been the victims of neglect, but with a realization by the authorities that they attract tourists, steps have been taken to conserve the town's heritage. In addition, there's the colonial aspect – this enclave was relinquished by Spain only in 1969, after the Moroccan government closed off landward access, and many locals still speak Spanish.

The site, then known as Santa Cruz del Mar Pequeño ("Holy Cross of the Small Sea"), was held by Spain from 1476 to 1524, when the Saadians threw them out. In 1860, the Treaty of Tetouan (see page 502) gave it back to them, though they didn't reoccupy it until 1934, after they – or rather, the French – had "pacified" the interior.

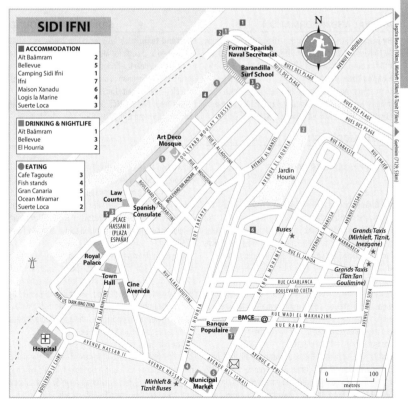

Sidi Ifni's main attractions are its Spanish feel and **Art Deco architecture** (see page 465), and a relaxed atmosphere – you'll spy dreadlocked local chaps ambling around, and a few local girls wear outfits which most likely make their parents furious, while it's the only place this side of Agadir where one could go on a bar crawl (there are *three* bars!). The beach, with a *marabout* tomb at its northern end, is not that great (the beaches at Legzira and Mirhleft are better; see pages 464 and 461) and is prone to long sea mists; it can be surprisingly cloudy in summer, when warm Saharan winds mix with cool ones from the Altantic, though the sun often burns through after noon. On Sundays a large **souk** takes place just east of the abandoned airfield, and each June 30 the city hosts a **festival** to celebrate its 1969 reincorporation into Morocco.

Legzira Beach

10km north of Sidi Ifni • Walkable along the coast from Sidi Ifni (see page 466) • On the #18 Lux bus line from Sidi Ifni (hourly), which continues to Mirhleft and Tiznit • Surfboards and gear can be rented here (see page 467), as well as quad bikes

Wide and handsome, **Legzira Beach** is flanked by natural sea-worn rock archways and overlooked by an old Spanish fort from the hills above, whose thermal currents attract **hang-gliding and paragliding** enthusiasts (see page 467). A rather horrible vacation village has unfortunately now been built directly above the beach, but that doesn't detract from the beauty of the place – something best experienced on the long walk along the coast from Sidi Ifni. Given the fact that the bus stop is both some way uphill from the beach and unsheltered, it makes most sense to bus here from Sidi Ifni (when departures are on the hour) and walk back to town, so long as the tides agree.

ARRIVAL AND INFORMATION

By bus All buses arriving or departing Sidni Ifni stop on Av Mohammed V. To and from Tiznit, your best bet are the #18 Lux buses, which head via Mirhleft; half of them also hit Aglou Plage.

Destinations Agadir (4 daily; 4hr–4hr 30min); Aglou Plage (roughly every 2hr; 45min); Casablanca (2 daily; 12hr); Marrakesh (3 daily; 7hr 45min); Mirhleft (45min); Tiznit (hourly; 2hr)

By grand taxi *Grands taxis* leave four blocks east of Av Mohammed V, though for Mirhleft and Tiznit they're also easy to pick up near the bridge just north of town.

Destinations Guelmim (1hr); Inezgane (3hr 30min); Mirhleft (45min); Tiznit (1hr 30min).

Banks You'll find a BMCE and Banque Populaire on Av Mohammed V, both with ATMs.

ACCOMMODATION

SIDI IFNI, SEE MAP PAGE 463

HOTELS

Aït Baâmram Rue de la Plage ☎0528 780217. By the beach, and with a restaurant and bar (see page 466), this hotel looks dodgy from the outside but has immaculate tiled walls and floors in its public areas. The rooms themselves are a bit chipped and scuffed, though all are en suite. $\overline{\in}$

Bellevue Pl Hassan II ☎0528 875072. Housed in an original Ifni Art Deco building, right on Plaza de España, and next to the law courts, this well-kept hotel has sweeping views over the beach, a good restaurant, and a bar (see page 466). Some rooms are en suite (which doubles the price), but the shared bathroom facilities for those that aren't have hot water from 7–11am only. $\overline{\in}$

Ifni Av Mohammed V. There's a smattering of small, basic hotels very close to each other in the centre, all catering mainly for a Moroccan clientele. Rooms here, as at the rest, are very basic, but at the time of writing, this was the only

one with working hot showers. $\overline{\in}$

Maison Xanadu 5 Rue el Jadida (look for the Ψ symbol on the door) ⓦmaisonxanadu.com. Bright, cheerful, French-owned *maison d'hôte* with lots of jolly pastel colours and breezy, modern, en-suite rooms, plus great views from the roof terrace. The owner is a good source of local advice. BB $\overline{\in\in}$

★**Logis la Marine** Av Moulay Abdellah ⓦlogisla marine.com. Sidi Ifni's fanciest choice, with a small selection of charming rooms, many looking directly onto the ocean; the views are so good here that most passers-by end up taking photos, yet somehow the hotel hides in plain sight. Staff here are switched on, and a lovely breakfast is served in the garden out back. BB $\overline{\in\in}$

★**Suerte Loca** Rue Moulay Youssef ☎0528 87535. Going for years, this is a characterful place– the name (meaning "Crazy Luck") and a bodega-style bar, which is sadly not licensed, reveal its small-town Spanish origins – run by a very welcoming English-speaking family. It has

SPANISH COLONIAL ARCHITECTURE IN SIDI IFNI

The best place in which to start a tour of Sidi Ifni's **old Spanish buildings** is **Plaza de España** (now officially rechristened Place Hassan II), a quiet square whose centrepiece is an Andalusian garden with Spanish tiled benches and a Moroccan tiled fountain. A plinth in the middle once bore the statue of General Capaz, who took Ifni for Spain in 1934. At the northern end of the square, the now-empty **Spanish consulate**, a building straight out of García Márquez, stands next to a Moorish Art Deco building, which used to be the church, and is now the **law court**. At the other end of the plaza, the blue-and-white-striped **town hall**, complete with its town clock, stands next to the former governor-general's residence, now the **royal palace**; here you'll also spy the **Cine Avenida**, a real beaut which was in regular use in colonial times, but now only sparingly for special events.

Nearer the sea, there's a magnificent Art Deco **lighthouse** (to which you can't get too close), while heading north down Rue Moulay Youssef, you'll find what must be the world's only **Art Deco mosque**, small and rather pretty, with blue piping up the sides of the minaret. At the street's northern end is a building in the shape of a ship, which once housed the **Spanish naval secretariat**. It was the first large building to go up in Sidi Ifni, and its two forward portholes were the windows of cells where miscreant sailors were held.

Lastly, old Spanish street signs on **Avenue Mohammed V** still identify it as Calle Seis de Abril, and several of its buildings are original Ifni Art Deco. The **post office** was much more splendid before the top storey was demolished, and under Spanish rule it used to issue its own stamps, featuring wildlife, traditional costumes and even the town's buildings.

8

cheap rooms in the old Spanish wing, slightly pricier en-suite ones in a new wing, and is deservedly popular; try for one of the rooms splendid views of the sea, way down below. It also has an excellent café-restaurant (see page 465), a roof terrace, and a surf shop next door (see page 467). €̄

CAMPSITES
Camping Sidi Ifni Rue de la Plage ☎ 0528 876734. The best campsite in town, though it has absolutely no shade at all; however, it does have a swimming pool in summer

(open to all), high walls for security, and sunshine most of the day. Rooms are also available; oh, and there's a bar (see page 465). Camping €̄, double €̄

LEGZIRA BEACH
Legzira Beach Club On the beach ☎ 0670 522800. The best choice on the "strip", with tidy rooms, some with bathrooms and terraces (a massive plus point, considering the view), plus a decent restaurant downstairs. Single rooms are good value. €̄

EATING

SIDI IFNI, SEE MAP PAGE 463
Cafe Tagoute Av Moulay Abdellah. Given the superlative views, it's amazing how crappy the eateries on the pedestrianised clifftop walk are; this is the better of two adjacent cafes, with very good coffee and fruit juice, and old Ifni stamps and black-and-white photos on the walls. €̄
Fish stands By the market. These hole-in-the-wall market eateries always have excellent fish tajines on the go, and they can also whip up fried sardines, or a mixed *friture* of squid, sole, prawns and whiting. It's unfair to single out a stall, but the first one on the left as you enter is very reliable. €̄
Gran Canaria Av Mohammed V. This modern, upper-floor spot bills itself as a seafood place, but is in reality quite Italian – it's far better for pasta (including home-made lasagne) and wood-fired pizzas, while tiramisu and panacottaare on the dessert list. €̄€̄

Ocean Miramar 3 Av Moulay Abdallah. Better for the views than the food, this restaurant has a scenic terrace; they specialize in fish, including a good seafood gratin, while there's chocolate mousse or banana split for afters. They also do breakfasts. €̄
★ **Suerte Loca** Rue Moulay Youssef. This cool hotel (see page 464) is also one of the best options for food in Sidi Ifni – many places in town advertise Spanish-style dishes, but this is often the only place actually serving paella, Spanish tortillas and the like, making for a nice break from the norm. Also consider the yummy almond milkshake, or the non-alcoholic crepe suzette. €̄

LEGZIRA BEACH
★ **Abouis** On the beach. Good food overlooking the beach, with tasty cheese omelettes, couscous through the

week, large paella that's enough for two, grilled fish, and good coffee. The yummy sauces that they'll plonk on your table with most meals are *mojo* – a speciality from the Canary Islands, a few hundred kilometres to the west, these really should have greater worldwide renown, and you may well end up making your own back home. €€

DRINKING AND NIGHTLIFE

SIDI IFNI, SEE MAP PAGE 463

★ **Aït Baâmram** Rue de la Plage. This hotel (see page 464) is where locals come to drink, an atmospheric place with a pleasingly seedy-looking interior and a clutch of outdoor tables gazing straight at the sea; these are wonderful sunset roosts, and after that they're illuminated only by ambient light. As well as beer there's a decent selection of spirits for somewhere so remote. Bring your mosquito repellent, if you want to sit in the outdoor area.

Bellevue Pl Hassan II ☎ 0528 875072. This Art Deco hotel (see page 464) has a cool little bar up on top, overlooking the sea; sadly you're not allowed to consume alcohol on the outdoor terrace. It's pricer than the other places, but more relaxed, and with free olives to munch on.

El Hourria Av el Houria. Once a restaurant, this is now a lovely shisha bar; apple and mint are your two flavour choices, while they replace your charcoals with alarming frequency and theatrical tong-clacks. No alcohol.

Guelmim and around

Surrounded by some impressively bleak scenery, **GUELMIM** (also Romanized as Goulimine or Gulimime) is an administrative town with a distinctly frontier feel and a couple of small, fairly animated **souks**, including two **evening markets**. One of these runs off the Route d'Agadir (now officially renamed Boulevard Mohammed VI), mainly selling food, and one off Avenue des FAR, mainly selling clothes.

You may meet local hustlers here indulging in theatrical cons, usually involving invitations to see "genuine *hommes bleus*" (supposedly desert nomads, clad in blue) in tents outside town, inevitably just an excuse to relieve tourists of some money.

Caid Dahman Takni's palace

On a side street off Av Mohammed V • Free

The nearest thing that Guelmim has to a tourist sight is the remains of **Caid Dahman Takni's palace**, hidden in the backstreets behind the *Hôtel la Jeunesse*, and ruined now but barely a hundred years old. Just a corner and the back survive in any substantial form, but the views from here are pretty good – just watch out for the shards of bottle-glass which blanket the ground.

THE LEGZIRA WALK

Make no bones about it – the 10km shoreside **trek** (lasting 2–3hr) from **Sidi Ifni to Legzira beach** is, quite simply, one of southern Morocco's most enjoyable walking routes. Many locals will try to convince you that you need a guide; this is not true, and as long as you bear a few simple things in mind, it's quite easy. The main thing that you'll need to take note of is the **tide**: the route is only possible at low tide, and the daily times are very easy to find online. Secondly, you'll need to head up the cliff and away from the beach at one point, just before the first rock arch you'll come across on the way up from Sidi Ifni. The uphill path is easy to spot, as is the downwards counterpart, which slides gently down a wide crevasse a few hundred metres further north. After that, you'll pass through more spectacular arches on your way to Legzira. You'll be able to do this route in flip-flops, though do note that at various points you'll have to walk across large, slippery stones, some of which are covered in moss and algae.

SURFING AND PARAGLIDING AROUND SIDI IFNI

In recent years, Sidi Ifni has become something of a base for **surfing and paragliding**. Favourite surfing spots are the main beach, just in front of the tennis courts, and another beach 100m south of the new port. There are a few places offering surf lessons and equipment in town, but by far the best is *Barandilla Surf School*, adjoining the **Suerte Loca**. There are other small operators on Legzira beach, including *Legzira Surf School*. Favourite paragliding spots are the hills behind Ifni, and at Legzira Beach; your best sources of information are the **Abertih** in Mirhleft (see page 462),.

Camel market

1km out of town on the Tan Tan road

Guelmim's Saturday morning souk, known as the **camel market**, is rather a sham. It has the usual Moroccan goods (grain, vegetables, meat, clothes, silver, jewellery, sheep and goats), but what it doesn't have many of is camels, which have fallen from favour over the years in the wake of lorries and transit vehicles, and the caravan routes are more or less extinct. Those you do see have been brought in for show, or to be sold for meat.

ARRIVAL AND DEPARTURE

By plane The airport is 5km out of town, off the Sidi Ifni road; there's no public transport so you'll have to charter a *grand taxi* to get there. Note that it's a military airfield, too – you'll have to show documents at the entrance, and printed tickets help. Arriving by air, you may need to call your hotel to send a taxi.

Destinations Casablanca (5 weekly via Tan Tan; 2hr 50min); Tan Tan (5 weekly; 30min).

By bus Most buses use the *gare routière* on the Bou Izakarn road. The CTM and Supratours offices are just north of the *gare routière*, on Av Abaynou.

Destinations: Agadir (2–3 hourly; 4hr 30min); Akka (2 daily; 8hr); Casablanca (1–2 hourly; 14hr); Dakhla (9 daily; 16hr); Foum el Hassan (2 daily; 6hr); Laayoune (1–2 hourly; 7hr); Marrakesh (2–3 hourly; 9hr 30min); Ouarzazate (2 daily; 15hr); Rabat (9 daily; 16hr); Sidi Ifni (2 daily; 1hr); Smara (4 daily; 6hr); Tan Tan (2–3 hourly; 2hr); Tata (2 daily; 9hr 30min); Tiznit (2–3 hourly; 2hr 30min).

By grand taxi *Grands taxis* for most destinations leave from next to the *gare routière*. For Assaka, they leave from a station on Av Hassan II at the junction of Av el Moukouama, where Land Rover taxis can also be

GUELMIM AND AROUND

found. For Asrir, they use a station southeast of the centre, on the new Asrir road.

Destinations Agadir (4hr 45min); Asrir (15min); Assaka (1hr 30min); Bou Izakarn (1hr); Inezgane (4hr 30min); Laayoune (5hr); Sidi Ifni (1hr); Tiznit (2hr 30min); Tan Tan (1hr 30min).

INFORMATION

Banks There are plenty of banks with ATMs. The BMCE is on Av Hassan II, 100m west of *Hôtel Salam*.
Hammam Next to the post office, with showers as well as steam rooms. Men's and women's entrances are either side of a café.

ACCOMMODATION
SEE MAP PAGE 467

★ **Carrefour** 31 Av Mohammed V ☎ 0528 771510.

8

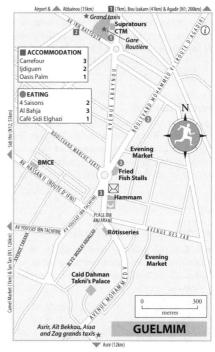

GUELMIM

Airport & Abbainou (15km) ★ Grand taxis (7km), Bou Izakarn (41km) & Agadir (N1; 200km)

Supratours
CTM
Gare Routière

■ **ACCOMMODATION**
Carrefour 3
Ijdiguen 2
Oasis Palm 1

● **EATING**
4 Saisons 2
Al Bahja 3
Café Sidi Elghazi 1

AV IBN BATTOUTA
AVENUE ABAYNOU
BOULEVARD MOHAMMED VI (ROUTE D'AGADIR)
BOULEVARD MARCHE VERTE
AV HASSAN II (ROUTE D'IFNI)
AV YOUSSEF IBN TACHFINE   AV YOUSSEF IBN TACHFINE
AVENUE ZERKTOUNI
BD LT MOURAT ABDALLAH
AVENUE MOHAMMED V
Sidi Ifni (N12; 53km)
Camel Market (1km) & Tan Tan (N1; 126km)

Evening Market
BMCE
Fried Fish Stalls
Hammam
PLACE BIR ANZARANE
Rôtisseries
AVENUE DES FAR
Evening Market
Caid Dahman Takni's Palace

0   300
metres

Asrir, Aït Bekkou, Assa and Zag grands taxis ★
Asrir (12km)

N

ASRIR MOUSSEM

A large **moussem** is held annually in early June at **Asrir**, 10km southeast along the Asrir road. Traditionally a camel traders' fair, there are still many humped beasts present at the festival today. There's also usually **Guedra dancing**, a seductive women's dance of the desert, performed from a kneeling position (developed for the low tents) to a slow, repetitive rhythm.

The nicest place in the centre, with rooms that'll make you forget you're in Guelmim for a while – all are en suite with wooden furnishings and clean, spacious bathrooms, and the service is by far the most professional in town. Located right above a petrol station, though thankfully the sounds and smells don't carry into the rooms. €̄
Ijdiguen 194 Av Ibn Battouta ☏ 0528 771453. Bright, clean and right opposite the bus station, with shared hot showers and friendly staff. Great if you've just arrived on a late bus, or need to catch an early one. €̄
Oasis Palm Route d'Agadir ⓦ oasispalmhotel.com. A middle-of-nowhere experience is on offer at this hotel 7km to the northeast of town, part of (and actually the *only* part of) a "new" village which may never be completed. There's a pool, the rooms are good, the views are sweeping, and there's food available on site. BB €̄

EATING
SEE MAP PAGE 467

For cheap eating, try the clutch of **rôtisseries** (spit-roast chicken joints) on Av Mohammed V by Pl Bir Anzarane.
4 Saisons Bd Mohammed VI. Juice and dessert cafe that's cheap, cheesy and colourful. Ice cream and fruit shakes are cheap and tasty; there's no English menu, but it's easy to point at what you want. €̄
Al Bahja Bd Mohammed VI. Cheap local place for fried fish, or beans served with offal, bread and side-salad. €̄
Café Sidi Elghazi Av Ibn Battouta. Very handy café-restaurant by the *gare routière*, with a bit of everything: tajines, couscous, pizzas, sandwiches, juices, coffee and cakes. Just what you need if arriving or leaving by bus at a silly hour. €̄

Abbainou

15km north of Guelmim • Head up the Sidi Ifni road, and it's signed to the right after the airport

There are several spring baths in the Guelmim area, but easiest to reach are those in **Abbainou**, a tiny oasis reachable by *grand taxi*. The hot springs – gender-segregated, of course, and on cool mornings steam can be seen coming off the palmery irrigation channels. There's a basic campsite, and a café and bakery in the village centre.

Fort Bou-Jerif

35km from Guelmim • Paved road to Tisséguemane branches left off Sidi Ifni road 1km outside Guelmim, then there's 20km of *piste*

Fort Bou-Jerif is a truly romantic spot, set 13km from the sea beside the Oued Assaka, with a wonderful **auberge-campsite** in an old French Foreign Legion camp – and all in the middle of nowhere. From here, you can go on some superb four-wheel-drive excursions in the area, including trips to the **Plage Blanche** – the "White Beach" that stretches for sixty or so kilometres along the coast southwest of Guelmim. Travellers heading for Mauritania and Senegal should also be able to pick up information here as a lot of overlanders stop over at the fort on their way down.

ACCOMMODATION AND EATING
FORT BOU-JERIF

Fort Bou-Jerif Auberge ⓦ fortboujerif.com. This wonderful place offers accommodation in a "motel", a "little hotel" and a "hotel"; alternatively you can camp, with a nomadic tent on offer if you don't have your own. Most people take half-board, which is a good idea as the food is good (camel tajine the speciality) and there's nowhere else to eat. Camping per person €̄, nomadic tent per person €̄, double €̄

8

The Tarfaya Strip and Western Sahara

DUNES NEAR LAAYOUNE

9 The Tarfaya Strip and Western Sahara

Few travellers venture south of Guelmim, unless bound for Mauritania or Senegal. Certainly, the dead-end administrative town of Tan Tan has few attractions, though surfers in particular may want to check out the rather more appetizing beach resort of Tan Tan Plage. The last town in Morocco proper, Tarfaya, is really just a sleepy little fishing village that sometimes gives the impression of having been all but forgotten, but it has a charmingly lazy air about it. Once over the demarcation line into the Western Sahara, things change, and the cities of Laayoune and Dakhla are bright, modern places by comparison, settled by pioneering Moroccans enticed with state subsidies. However, of more interest to many travellers is the surrounding landscape, and you are sure to spend much of your time here travelling across vast, bleak tracts of stony desert known as *hammada* – there's certainly no mistaking that you've reached the Sahara proper.

Back in the days of empire, the Oued Drâa (see map, page 474) formed the border between the French and Spanish protectorates. As such, the entire area covered by this chapter came under Spanish, rather than French, colonial rule. You'll still see a few remnants from those days here and there – particularly in Tarfaya, Laayoune and Dakhla – and occasionally have locals speaking to you in Spanish, though French has now almost entirely replaced it as the dominant **second language** throughout the region. Today, the region is also of some **economic importance** to Morocco, centring on the phosphate mines at Boukra, southeast of Laayoune, and rich deep-water fishing grounds offshore; the latter's potential is gradually being realized with the development of fishing ports at Laayoune, Dakhla and Boujdour, together with industrial plants for fish storage and processing.

The approach from Guelmim to **Tan Tan** runs along 125km of straight desert road, across a bleak area of scrub and *hammada*; the town is rather dull despite the fun-sounding name, though its eponymous beach area is a pleasant place to stay. The N1 road hugs the coast south, passing over dramatic river mouths and through sand dunes; the only towns of note are **Akhfenir** and, 3km off the main road, **Tarfaya**. The Western Sahara starts at the village of **Tah**, where a red granite monument flanking the road commemorates the 1975 Green March (see page 488). Once south of the border, you begin to traverse real sand desert – the **Erg Lakhbayta** – before crossing the Seguiat al-Hamra (a wide, and usually dry, river) to enter **Laayoune**, a surprisingly large city considering its distance from "regular" Morocco, and a good place to hole up for a day or two. From here you can head inland to **Smara**, a great little desert town also accessible from Tan Tan – a good loop route. Finally, the road is reasonably good from Laayoune to **Dakhla**, with cliffs plunging down to the sea on the western side of the road, and plain desert on the inland side. Drivers should beware of occasional sand-drifts, and camels grazing by or on the road – the done thing is to stop your car and shoo the beasts away for their own protection (and, of course, that of other road users), though you'd be forgiven for taking a few photos too.

Returning, if you don't fancy a repeat of the journey, there are flights from Dakhla and Laayoune to Agadir or the Canary Islands (see pages 482 and 490).

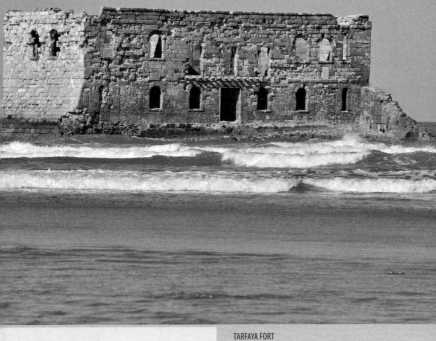

TARFAYA FORT

Highlights

❶ Tarfaya A sleepy fishing village with an offshore fort, which you can wade over to at low tide, and a museum dedicated to Antoine de Saint-Exupéry. See page 478

❷ Laayoune A pioneering boom town built on subsidies and determination, with just a ghost, in its oldest quarters, of a Spanish colonial past. See page 479

❸ Nothingness Western Sahara is one of the least densely populated places on earth – on some stretches, such as those heading to Smara, you'll be amazed by the sparseness of human habitation, and the sheer amount of, well, nothing that there is to see. See page 484

❹ Smara This out-of-the-way desert town was once the seat of the "Blue Sultan", whose palace and great mosque constitute the main sights. See page 484

❺ Dakhla The furthest south you can go by land from Europe without a visa – 22km from the tropics (but certainly no tropical paradise), sun all year round, a laidback vibe, and some lovely beaches within spitting distance of town. See page 487

❻ Fish Some places here have some really fabulous fish and seafood on offer, locally caught, fresh as can be, and – especially in Dakhla – often served up in the form of Spanish dishes such as paella or *pulpo alla gallega*. See page 492

HIGHLIGHTS ARE MARKED ON THE MAP ON PAGE 474

9

And once you've reached Dakhla, Dakar and Banjul are actually just as close as Marrakesh and Casablanca, though to hit them overland you'll need a pricey Mauritanian visa (see page 491).

Tan Tan and around

The first stop on the long road south to Mauritania is **Tan Tan**, a drab administrative centre of just over seventy thousand inhabitants. Its streets bustle with simple commerce, and you'll see plenty of mules hauling goods around in metal carts; given the inhospitable surroundings, the herbal aromas pervading over many streets may also come as a pleasant surprise. Aside from its moussem (see page 477), Tan Tan's one claim to fame is that it was a departure point for Hassan II's famous **Green March** to occupy the Western Sahara (*La Marche Verte*, or *el Massira el Khadra*; see page 488). Other than that, there are basically no sights of any note – in fact, you're better off

9

staying out west at **Tan Tan Plage** (see page 477), a relatively pleasant place which also has the sea bashing in.

If you do end up staying or stopping off in Tan Tan, you'll find a town whose bulk is strung out along the modest **Avenue Mohammed V**, and the slightly busier **Boulevard Hassan II**; the latter also doubles as the main national road. On the way south of the crossroads you'll spot a small hill, though this is off-limits to the public; you'll still have nice views over the **Oued Ben Khalil** from the adjacent stretch of Avenue Mohammed V, and the oued itself is good strolling territory. Just to the south is a square ringed with super-cheap guesthouses and featuring a tiny **park** – about the most attractive spot in a generally ugly, if occasionally atmospheric, town.

ARRIVAL AND DEPARTURE   TAN TAN AND AROUND

By plane The airport (ⓦonda.ma/en) is located on a rise to the west, 7km out of town on the road to Laayoune and Smara.

Destinations Casablanca (5 weekly; 1hr 40min); Guelmim (5 weekly; 30min).

By bus All buses except Supratours and CTM leave from Pl de la Marche Verte. Supratours buses stop outside their office at 118 Bd Hassan II, while the CTM stop and office is 1km further west, over the Oued Ben Khalil. Southbound services with these two operators are often full by the time they get to Tan Tan, so you may not get a seat – it's advisable to book in advance.

Destinations Agadir (2–3 hourly; 6–7hr); Casablanca (15 daily; 14–16hrs); Dakhla (12 daily; 12hr); Guelmim (2–3 hourly; 1hr 30min–2hr); Laayoune (1–2 hourly; 4hr–5hr

30min); Marrakesh (1–2 hourly; 9–12hr); Smara (4 daily; 3–4hr); Tarfaya (2–6 daily; 3–4hr); Tiznit (2–3 hourly; 3hr 30min–4hr 30min).

By grand taxi Most shared *grands taxis* leave from Pl de la Marche Verte. Shared taxis for Tan Tan Plage (12dh/place) run from a block just east of Bd Mohammed V, a little way north of the *Rôtisserie Abi Anass* restaurant (see page 476).

Destinations Dakhla (10hr); Guelmim (1hr 30 min); Inezgane (6hr); Laayoune (3hr 30min); Smara (3hr); Tan Tan Plage (30min); Tarfaya (infrequent, usually early morning; 2hr 30min); Tiznit (infrequent, usually early morning; 3hr 15min).

By car For drivers, note that there are plenty of mechanics around Pl de la Marche Verte, and a few around the Tan Tan Plage taxi stand.

INFORMATION AND ACTIVITIES

Banks There are a few banks on Bd Hassan II (including two branches of BMCE within 100m of each other), as well as the Banque Populaire on Bd Mohammed V, all with ATMs.

Hammam The Hammam Oued Ibn Khalil occupies a small triangle of land at the northern end of Av Chaab.

ACCOMMODATION   SEE MAP PAGE 476

There are a large number of **unclassified hotels** on and around Pl de la Marche Verte and La Poste de la Police, most of them very grotty but very cheap. Grubby and insalubrious as they are, many of these places will balk at letting unmarried couples share a room. There's more choice in **Tan Tan Plage**, which makes a more pleasant place to stay (see page 477).

Bir Anzarane 154 Bd Hassan II ☎ 0528 877834. The best deal in town, carpeted throughout, with shared bathrooms and very reasonable prices, though not all rooms have outside windows, and it's a bit of a haul from Pl de la Marche Verte. €

El Hagounia 1 Rue Sidi Ahmed Rguibi ☎ 0528 878561. A cut above the other hotels in this part of town (and unlike many competitors, they even have wi-fi), with bare but large and generally clean rooms and shared hot showers. As in a lot of very cheap hotels here, it charges per person, so the cost of a single is exactly half that of a double. €

Sable d'Or Bd Hassan II ☎ 0528 878069. This is the best hotel in Tan Tan, a two-star with large and immaculate en-suite rooms, some of which have a balcony; try to get one away from the noise of the main road. Also on site is a decent restaurant, selling Moroccan staples at Moroccan prices. €

EATING   SEE MAP PAGE 476

Food is not one of Tan Tan's high points, and most eating places are grubby and unappetizing; there are plenty of cafés, which fill up whenever there's a big football game on telly, especially if it involves Barça or Real Madrid. As for **bars**, forget it, since Tan Tan is dry.

Café Restaurant Bouchaab 111 Av Chaab, by Pl de la

Marche Verte ☎ 0528 878416. This three-floor café claims to serve tajines and *harira* at any time of the day or night. However, just like their purported free wi-fi, this is not a claim to be relied on, but you can at least hold them to a coffee or juice at any time. Women may find the upper floors a bit all-male for their liking, but downstairs is fine. €

9

PARALLELS AND DEMARCATION LINES

In colonial times, the Oued Drâa was the border between the French and Spanish protectorates. The land to the south, the **Tarfaya strip**, was part of the Spanish Protectorate in Morocco, along with the area around Tetouan and Al Hoceima in the north. It was not considered part of Spain's two Saharan colonies (together known as the **Spanish Sahara**), of which the northernmost, **Seguiat el Hamra**, began at the 27°40′ N line just south of Tarfaya, while the southern one, **Rio de Oro**, began at the 26th parallel, just south of Boujdour. In 1958, two years after the rest of Morocco gained independence, the Spanish gave back the Tarfaya strip, but they kept the Spanish Sahara until November 1975 (see page 488).

Espace Rahab Off Rue Issam. Overlooking a minute park, this café is the nicest sit-and-chill spot in Tan Tan. Coffees are pretty good; there's also free wi-fi.

★ **Rôtisserie Abi Anass** Off Rue Issam. By far the most pleasant and salubrious of the little eating places around the small, park-like square that functions as Tan Tan's centre of activity. A plate of spit-roast chicken with chips and salad here certainly won't break the bank; you can wolf down your bargain meal outside, if either of the tables are free, or on the pleasant upper level. €

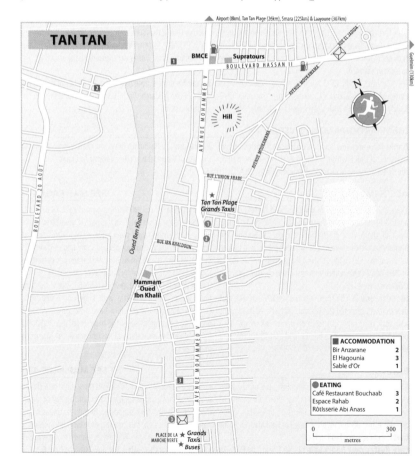

TAN TAN

Airport (8km), Tan Tan Plage (26km), Smara (225km) & Laayoune (307km)

Guelmim (130km)

BMCE
Supratours
BOULEVARD HASSAN II
RUE EL JADIDA
AVENUE MOUKAWAMA

AVENUE MOHAMMED V

Hill

AVENUE MOUKAWAMA

RUE L'UNION ARABE

Tan Tan Plage
Grands Taxis

RUE IBN KHALDOUN

Oued Ben Khalil

Hammam
Oued
Ibn Khalil

AVENUE MOHAMMED V

BOULEVARD 20 AOÛT

PLACE DE LA
MARCHE VERTE
★ Grands
Taxis
★ Buses

■ ACCOMMODATION	
Bir Anzarane	2
El Hagounia	3
Sable d'Or	1

● EATING	
Café Restaurant Bouchaab	3
Espace Rahab	2
Rôtisserie Abi Anass	1

0 — 300
metres

Tan Tan Plage

9

Twenty-six kilometres from Tan Tan proper, and just off the coastal route to Laayoune, **TAN TAN PLAGE** has become popular with Morocco's small surfing fraternity – while not quite on the already-modest scale of Sidi Ifni up the coast (see page 463), you'll most likely spot a few dreadlocked, Marley-shirted chaps gazing at the waves from the recently renovated beachfront promenade. Though not very good for casual bathing due to its large breakers and strong currents, the exposed, often windswept **beach** gets quite busy in summer, and the crowd is almost entirely local – a lovely sight, though one which comes to a sudden halt heading south, thanks to a surprisingly major **fishing port** responsible for a large percentage of Morocco's sardine exports. With a decent little selection of small hotels and restaurants, Tan Tan Plage is a far more attractive place to stay than Tan Tan town itself.

ARRIVAL AND DEPARTURE
TAN TAN PLAGE

By bus Many of the buses heading between Tan Tan and points further south now stop at Tan Tan Plage, though it's far easier to get off one than on. Supratours has an office in town, near the mosque, though it's next to useless unless a departure is imminent – infuriatingly, they won't sell you a ticket in advance. Otherwise, you may be able to pick up buses for Akhfenir, Tarfaya (or the Tarfaya *croisement*) and Laayoune at the junction (Rond Point des Poissons) with

the Laayoune road, 3km from the beach, but don't count on them stopping for you. It's often best just to head into Tan Tan by grand taxi (see below) – even if you're heading south and will therefore have to double back on yourself, it generally saves time and effort, and often money too.
By grand taxi It's easiest to come here by *grand taxi* from Tan Tan (20min). These drop off in the town's de facto main square; likewise, head here when going back to Tan Tan.

ACCOMMODATION

Camping Equinox Av Al Wahda ☎0661 170510. The best of a string of campsites strung along the beach west of town, this is a popular stop-off for overlanders heading to West Africa. There's space for tents and camper vans, or guests can stay in Bedouin tents or pleasant rooms. There are plenty of hot shower facilities, but it's usually open in summer only. Camping €, Bedouin tent €, double €
★ **Castillo Dalilah** Bd Moulay Rachid ☎0528 879685. A little inland from the beach at the very northern edge of town, this small, castle-shaped hotel is excellent value, with rooms that are lovingly designed, clean and en suite.

It also looks very pretty at night, when the lights come on – a small thing, maybe, but such touches make you look forward to returning to your room after a prom along the beachfront. €
Kasba Av Mohammed V, by the beach ☎0528 879898. There are a few hotels and guesthouses lining the beachside in the town centre, and this is the best and most attractive of the bunch. The reception area and downstairs restaurant (see page 477) are pretty enough, but the rooms are nicer still, even if some of the bathrooms feel poky. Four rooms have balconies overlooking the beach – grab one if you can. BB €€

EATING AND DRINKING

For cheap eats, try the clutch of grilled meat spots around the grand taxi ranks – unfortunately you'll see plenty of flies dining on the meat before it's grilled, and they'll most likely pop by for dessert while you're eating.
Kasba Av Mohammed V, by the beach. The restaurant at

this beachside hotel (see page 477) specializes in tajines; some have to be ordered in advance, but others can be requested on the spot, including an excellent squid option. Brochettes, salads and fried fish fill the rest of the menu, and it's also a good place to pop by for coffee or juice. €

TAN TAN'S MOUSSEM

The **moussem of Sidi Mohammed Ma el Aïnin** is a tribal gathering featuring a camel fair and the sacrifice of a female camel. Originally a device used to facilitate trade and animal husbandry in this punishing region, it has become popular with domestic tourists, most of whom are here to watch the camel races. The moussem was traditionally held in June, but the provincial government keeps moving it (most recently it was in May), sotry and contact a local hotel in advance to see if they can give you the latest info on dates.

9

Korea House Rond Point des Poissons, 3km from town on the main road ☎0661 479789. Perhaps the weirdest restaurant in Morocco, run by a Korean family who have – bizarrely – been living on this remote crossroads since the last millennium. They serve a modest selection of Korean dishes, including *mandu-guk* (dumplings in broth), sautéed octopus, and *gyeranmari* (a sort of rolled omelette), but you need to order at least an hour in advance. In fact, the place is more popular with local gents ordering takeaway beer or wine. Ring the bell to enter. €€

La Scala Just west of grand taxi rank ☎0528 879324. This spot adds a little brightness to the town's very modest culinary scene. They serve all sorts of tasty seafood dishes under a suitably fitting blue ceiling, and occasionally paella too. €

Akhfenir

AKHFENIR, 140km south of Tan Tan, is little more than a flyblown roadside settlement with a couple of 24-hour petrol stations and a handful of cafés serving fried fish or tajines – indeed, the town has developed something of a reputation for seafood among Moroccans. While it will always be more of a staging post than a destination in its own right, there are a few things to encourage a stay – there's a pretty stretch of beach (usually too rough for casual bathing), while **flamingos** and migratory birds can sometimes be seen in the lagoons and saltpans along the coast to the south, or in the mouths of the oued to the north.

ARRIVAL AND DEPARTURE   AKHFENIR

By bus and grand taxi All buses between Tan Tan and Laayoune pass through Akhfenir, though you'll most likely have to beg to be let off. To get back on one, you'll need even more luck – a driver willing to stop, and an empty seat to plonk yourself into. The latter advice also goes for *grands taxis*, which shave 20–30min from the bus times each way. Destinations Laayoune (2hr 30min); Tan Tan (2hr).

ACCOMMODATION AND EATING

Akhfenir On the main road, in the centre of the village A small, no-frills, Moroccan hotel, friendly and clean, with large, fresh rooms, shared showers with hot water round the clock, and a kitchen. €

Chez Eric By the beach ☎0672 898722. Facing the ocean, this sweet little guesthouse feels a thoroughly appropriate to stay in little Akhfenir. Rooms have been decorated with an attention rare at this price level, and you'll be able to enjoy breakfast overlooking the beach. They also have 24hr hot water. BB €

La Courbine d'Argent By the beach, 1km west of the village ☎0671 422377. Mostly a centre for sports fishing, this pleasing place also offers good accommodation, birdwatching excursions, and arranges jaunts into the desert on 4WDs, bikes and quad bikes. BB €€

Tarfaya

A laidback, do-nothing place bleached by sunshine and home to a mere six thousand inhabitants, **TARFAYA** is a quiet little fishing town that's probably not far different from its years as a staging post for the Aéropostale Service – when aviators such as **Antoine de Saint-Exupéry** (author of *Night Flight* and *The Little Prince*) used to rest up here on their way down to West Africa, a service commemorated each October (see page 479). In addition, a **monument to Saint-Exupéry** in the form of a plane stands at the northern end of the beach. This formed part of beautification of the beachfront which had been paused halfway for years at the time of writing, though the area still makes a lovely place for an evening stroll; poke a little inland and you'll see a few buildings which have survived since colonial times, like the decrepit Art Deco cinema just north of the museum.

The main street, Bd Ahmed el Haydar, runs roughly east–west through the town centre, and features banks with ATMs, as well as a post office. Elsewhere, there's a cute little souk just west of the *El Bahja* hotel (see page 479).

Casa Mar

9

Just offshore from the beach • Accessible at low tide

Tarfaya was founded at the end of the nineteenth century by a Scottish trader named Donald Mackenzie, and was originally christened Port Victoria after the British queen. Mackenzie had a fort built, now known as **Casa Mar**, the ruins of which are just offshore – a few metres' swim at low tide, and great photograph-fodder during the sunrise.

Musée Antoine de Saint-Exupéry

Av Mohammed V, a block back from the beach road • Nominally free, but you'll be expected to make a purchase from the small shop

The **Musée Antoine de Saint-Exupéry** has exhibits on the airmail service that the *Little Prince* author pioneered. Despite being in the formerly Spanish zone of an Arabic-speaking country, it has explanations in French only. It's just inland from the plane-statue dedicated to Saint-Exupéry – look behind the remains of the yellow fort.

ARRIVAL AND DEPARTURE
TARFAYA

By bus The most reliable operator to use when visiting Tarfaya is Supratours, whose buses to Agadir and Dakhla (via Laayoune) stop outside their office on Bd Ahmed el Hayar. That's the easy bit – of the half-dozen buses which pass daily each way, only one is guaranteed to hit Tarfaya (stops at around 11am or so heading south, and 6.30pm on the way north); the office might be able to tell you the time if another will be coming. Green Sahara Express has a daily bus to and from Agadir; it leaves Tarfaya daily at 10pm. Other companies may set down passengers at the junction (*croisement*) for Tarfaya on the N1, 3km out

of town, but they won't usually pick passengers up there. Officially, at any rate, CTM won't even set you down. Destinations Agadir (2–6 daily; 10hr); Dakhla (1–5 daily; 9hr); Laayoune (1–6 daily; 1hr 30min); Tan Tan (2–6 daily; 3–4hr).

By grand taxi Shared *grands taxis* make the run to and from both Tan Tan and Laayoune, if they can find the passengers – as always, mornings are best. They collect from a small yard by the post office, more or less opposite the Supratours office (see above). If all else fails, locals head to the junction and try hitching.

INFORMATION

Festivals The Aéropostale air service is commemorated annually in October by a "**Rallye Aérien**" (Wrallye toulousesaintlouis.com), with small planes stopping here

on their way south from Toulouse to Senegal – still one hell of a sight, even if biplanes and suchlike are heavily outnumbered by more modern vehicles.

ACCOMMODATION AND EATING

Tarfaya's culinary scene isn't terribly interesting, though cafés along Av Ahmed el Haydar have excellent and very cheap fresh fried fish, or fish tajines.

★ **Aoudate Tarfaya** Eastern end of Bd Ahmed el Haydar ☎ 0528 895868. A choice of very large en suite rooms, or smaller (but still ample) ones with shared bathroom, located at the entrance into town from the main road. Balconies run around two sides of the building, so try to nab a suitable room, and the management speak English. €

El Bahja Bd Bir Anzarane, between Bd Ahmed el Haydar and the museum ☎ 0528 895506. This small, very welcoming hotel offers poky rooms and a terrace with a view over the town, plus a self-catering apartment in a house just up the street. €

Cafe Atlas Bd Ahmed el Haydar, no phone. Brazenly sat opposite the grand taxi rank that you may spend an unhealthy amount of time waiting at, this is a great little breakfast spot where you can pass the time munching on a breakfast of bread, cheese, jam, argan oil and an egg, as well as a good coffee. €

Casamar By the port entrance on Bd Ahmed el Haydar Whotel-casamar-tarfaya.com. Both the rooms and the apartments here are bright and modern, with snatches of sea views. The en-suite toilets can be a bit basic, but all come with a sit-down loo and a shower; you can often lop the rack rates in two. The smoky restaurant by the lobby is also one of the most reliable places to eat in town, selling pizzas and tasty fried fish. €€

Laayoune and around

The largest city in the Western Sahara, **LAAYOUNE** (also known as Al Ayoun or El Aaiun) exudes a rather unique vibe. Though only founded in 1940, and little more

9

than a village when the Moroccans took over, its population has swollen to over two hundred thousand, aided by massive **subsidies** – which apply throughout the Western Sahara – and an agreement that settlers should initially pay no taxes. With most of its residents here by choice (only a minority of families living here actually hail from the area), and both settlers and funding pushed this way by the central government, this middle-of-nowhere city comes across as surprisingly dynamic. Soldiers, billeted here for the conflict with the Polisario (see page 488), have been employed in many construction projects: witness the many fountains, the wide boulevards, and a huge main square suitable for military parades. Recent years have seen a few fancy-ish buildings popping up, as well as modern-day accoutrements such as clothing boutiques, upscale hair salons, and night-time neon. The old **lower town**, built by the Spanish, lies on the southern slope of the steep-sided valley of the **Seguiat el Hamra**; it's quite a delightful place to walk around (see page 482). The new **upper town**, developed since the Green March, sits on the high plateau beyond; these areas are more prosperous, stretching along **Avenue Mecka el Mokarrama**, and radiating outwards from **Place Dchira**.

The cathedral

Plaza de Africa

Sitting pretty on the city's original main square, Laayoune's old **cathedral** sports a yellow tube-roof which may well have been an elongated nod to the domed tops of the city's older houses (see page 482). It's open for weekend Mass, and the

---

TRAVELLING IN THE WESTERN SAHARA

Tourists can travel freely in most Moroccan-controlled parts of what are called the **Saharan Provinces** (an administrative area created to include the **former Spanish Sahara**, while not coinciding with its boundaries), but do check first on the political situation. There have been fierce clashes between Saharawis and Moroccan police in the past (see page 488), and you should be aware that protests often involve violence, and should be avoided. Government advisories (see page 58) will have up-to-date information if any subsequent problems have arisen. Apart from this, the only obstacle would be for visitors who admit to being a writer or journalist: a profession not welcome in the region, unless under the aegis of an official press tour.

Otherwise, visiting Laayoune, Smara, Boujdour and Dakhla is now pretty routine, though it can involve answering a series of questions at numerous **police checkpoints** along the way. This is all usually very amicable, but can be time-consuming. To save time, it's a good idea to print out or photocopy several copies of a sheet with the following information listed, preferably in French (as given here in brackets): family name (*nom*), given names (*prénoms*), date of birth (*date de naissance*), place of birth (*lieu de naissance*), marital status (*situation familiale*), father's name (*nom de père*), mother's name (*nom de mère*), nationality (*nationalité*), occupation (*profession*), address (*addresse*, given in full), passport number (*numéro de passeport*), date of issue (*date de délivrance*), place of issue (*lieu de délivrance*), expiry date (*date d'expiration*), purpose of visit (*motif du voyage* – *tourisme*, for example), make of vehicle (*marque du véhicule* – you may of course have to leave this one blank), vehicle registration number (*matriculation* – ditto), date of entry into Morocco (*date d'entrée en Maroc*), place of entry (*ville d'entrée*) and police number (*numéro de police* – the number stamped in your passport alongside your first entry stamp into Morocco, typically six digits and two letters). For marital status, you could be single (*célibataire*), married (*marié* if male, *mariée* if female), divorced (*divorcé/divorcée*) or widowed (*veuf/veuve*). Armed with this, you can then give your details to police at every checkpoint, which will save them having to ask you for the information point by point, which can be awkward on long bus rides.

9

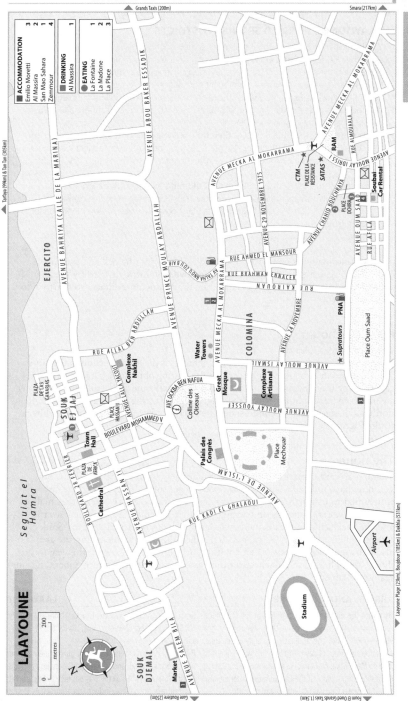

LAAYOUNE

0 200
metres

ACCOMMODATION	
Emilio Moretti	3
Al Massira	2
San Mao Sahara	1
Zemmour	4

DRINKING	
Al Massira	1

EATING	
La Fontaine	1
La Madone	2
La Place	3

Seguiat el Hamra

EJERCITO

SOUK DJEMAL

SOUK EJTAJ

COLOMINA

9

LAAYOUNE'S FORMER SPANISH DISTRICTS

You'll find Spanish colonial echoes aplenty on a stroll around certain parts of Laayoune. These are at their loudest in **Souk ej Jaj** (Glass Market), the district stretching east from Plaza de Africa; this is the oldest part of Laayoune, and many of its residents have been here since Spanish days – as have a number of the street signs. It's very run-down, but it's undoubtedly Laayoune's most atmospheric quarter, and many of the houses here still have the **eggshell-domed roofs** typical of the Western Sahara. You'll see more of these beauties opposite the new bus station, out west in Souk Djemal.

Heading east instead, the district of **Ejercito** (meaning army in Spanish) houses Moroccan troops as it did their Spanish predecessors. South of Avenue Baharia, some of the tubular barracks are now private houses, hemmed in by more modern, box-like, blocks of flats.

The other district left from Spanish times is **Colomina**, to the south of Avenue Mecka al Mokarrama. It is nicknamed Colomina Tarduss ("Kick") because, when the Spanish left, Moroccan settlers kicked in the doors to squat their houses. Nowadays, most of the quarter has been rebuilt.

---

priest will normally let you have a look inside if you ring the bell at a reasonable hour. On the other side of the square is the **town hall**, formerly used by the Spanish administration and now largely occupied by the Moroccan military (so don't try to photograph it).

Place Mechouar

Western end of Av Mecka al Mokarrama

Most striking of Laayoune's modern developments is the **Place Mechouar**, the city's "new" square, and one seemingly ideal for the hosting of military parades. Tent-like canopies line three sides of the square and provide welcome shade, and at each corner are towers to floodlight the whole shebang at night. Peering into the square from its north end is the **Palais des Congrès**, designed by King Hassan II's favourite architect, André Paccard.

The dunes

Walking around central Laayoune, the Sahara may seem a long way away, but you only have to head a short distance out to get some desert kicks. The city is hemmed to its north by a dammed river and a modest oasis fed by the small amount of water that ends up trickling through. You'll get a grand view over it, and the spectacular **dunes** rising beyond, from the northern edge of the Souk el Jaj area – best in the very early morning, when the birdlife inhabiting the area is also at its most loquacious. There's nothing to stop you walking all the way to the dunes, though as with anywhere off the beaten track in the Western Sahara, it's not really advisable.

ARRIVAL AND DEPARTURE   **LAAYOUNE**

By plane The airport (ⓦ onda.ma/en) is about a kilometre southwest of the town centre – think about getting a window seat, since the approach is simply spectacular, and at certain times of day it can look like you're about to land on Mars. Royal Air Maroc (ⓦ royalairmaroc.com) serve domestic destinations and the Canaries; the latter are also served by Binter Canarias (ⓦ bintercanarias.com).

Destinations Agadir (2 weekly; 1hr); Casablanca (1–2 daily; 1hr 35min); Dakhla (2 weekly; 1hr); Las Palmas (1–2 daily; 45min).

By bus The town's large, fairly new *gare routière* lies out west in Souk Djemal, and is home to the major operators. You don't have to head all the way out here to buy a ticket; city-centre booking offices include Supratours on Av Moulay

Ismail, CTM at 198 Av Mecka al Mokarrama, and SATAS at 208 Av Mecka al Mokarrama.
Destinations Agadir (18 daily; 10–12hr); Boujdour (12 daily; 2hr 45min–4hr); Casablanca (9 daily; 19hr); Dakhla (9 daily; 8hr); Guelmim (1–2 hourly; 6–7hr); Marrakesh (14 daily; 15hr); Smara (1 daily; 3hr); Tan Tan (1–2 hourly; 4hr–5hr 30min); Tarfaya (1–6 daily; 1hr 30min); Tiznit (1–2 hourly; 8–9hr).

By grand taxi Shared *grands taxis* leave from a single stand located at the end of Av Abou Baker Essadik, about 2km east of the town centre. Those to Foum el Oued and Laayoune Plage use a station at the far western end of town, right at the end of the road past the stadium.
Destinations Dakhla (7hr); Foum el Oued (15min); Guelmim (5hr 30min); Inezgane (9hr); Laayoune Plage (20min); Smara (3hr); Tan Tan (3hr 30min); Tarfaya (1hr).

GETTING AROUND

On foot Though there are buses heading around Laayoune, it's rarely worth hunting them down, since almost everything of note – including the airport – is within walking distance.
Petit taxis Taxis charge a set rate to get basically anywhere in town; shysters operate at the bus station, where you

should walk a little down the road to find a standard fare.
Car rental One long-established car rental firm is Soubai, on Rue Assila just behind *Hôtel Zemmour* (ⓦ soubaicar.com), but there are plenty around – ask for recommendations at your accommodation.

INFORMATION

Banks and exchange There are plenty of banks in town with ATMs and exchange facilities. One group is at the foot of Bd Mohammed V, near Pl Hassan II, and another is in Pl Dchira. There are also ATMs around the corner from the bus station, but nothing in the airport.

Festivals The Rawafid Azawan festival in Oct hosts musicians from across the Arab world and beyond.
Hammam The surprisingly large Complexe Nakhil, at the eastern end of Av Lalla Yacout, has hammams or showers for both sexes, as well as massage facilities and even a hairdresser.

ACCOMMODATION SEE MAP PAGE 481

Unclassified hotels are concentrated in the Souk ej Jaj and Souk Djemal districts, but they can be very basic indeed, and none too clean. Note that there are also good options at Foum el Oued and Laayoune Plage (see page 484) not far from town.
Emilio Moretti Place Oum Saad ☏ 0528 997101. Part of Laayoune's recent turn towards the snazzy (its night-time neon fringes provide good evidence), this modern affair looks onto the large Place Oum Saad. Not all rooms have views – of anything, not just the park – so choose wisely. There's a cafe-restaurant in the lobby, and service is good. €€
Al Massira 12 Av Mecka al Mokarrama ☏ 0528 894225. Apparently a four-star hotel, though you'd never guess from the dreary lobby, this is still top dog in Laayoune – rooms

are a bit small for the price, but they're tidy enough. Oh, and there's a bar (see page 483). €€€
San Mao Sahara Rue Jaber ☏ 0528 894789. Excellent low-ish budget option, right next to the new bus terminal, and just across the road from some of Laayoune's most attractive domed houses. Rooms are a little plain but the hot water is reliable, the beds are comfy, and wi-fi reaches most parts of the building. €
Zemmour 1 Av Oum Saad ☏ 0528 892323. Better, cleaner and brighter than any of the other budget options by a long way, with pretty little apple-green and cream rooms, some with a balcony. Bathroom facilities are shared but spotless, and showers are hot. It costs slightly more than the rock-bottom options, but it's well worth the difference. €

EATING SEE MAP PAGE 481

You'll be hard pressed to find anywhere outstanding to eat in Laayoune. A new McDonald's now occupies the whole of Place Dchira (formerly home to a lovely restaurant); on the square's northern flank you'll find several identikit cheapies selling grilled meat, with *melaoui* (Moroccan pancakes) and *harsha* (fried semolina flatbread).
★ **La Fontaine** Souk El Jaj, no phone. Look very, very closely and you'll find a delightful little pedestrianised area just east of the Town Hall. This is the best of a slew of cafes that basically all bleed into each other around the fountain

– 7dh will get you what may well be the best espresso in the Western Sahara (and ain't that a claim!). €
La Madone Av 24 du Novembre. A small pizzeria whose pasta dishes are pretty good (try the *spaghetti aux fruits de mer*), and they also do reasonable tajines and pizzas. €
La Place West side of Pl Dchira ☏ 0528 891704. Old-fashioned café where two can have a breakfast coffee and pastry – note that the latter are rather tasty, so you may find yourself heading back to the counter for another pop. €

DRINKING SEE MAP PAGE 481

Al Massira 12 Av Mecka al Mokarrama. Swagger through the lobby of this large-ish hotel (see page 483), and you'll

find a small bar hidden away in the naughty corner to the right.

9

(see page 485)
(see page 484)

A LOOP THROUGH SMARA

It's possible to make a **loop** from Tan Tan along the R101, to Smara, returning by way of the N1 to Laayoune, and from there across to Tan Tan via Tarfaya – a circuit of some 800km. There are **buses** along each section, but they aren't very frequent. If driving, be sure to carry water supplies. The R101 between Tan Tan and Smara is almost devoid of habitation and features, though you will see some hills and valleys on either side of the road, starting around 7km out of Tan Tan, just after the airport. After 91km more, you enter the Saharan Provinces, and a gaggle of petrol stations allow you to take advantage of the lower fuel prices.

Heading from Smara towards Laayoune, the desert is blackish from basalt for the first 5km, before resuming a lighter hue. At **El Asli**, 15km out of Smara, there are prehistoric rock carvings (see page 485). South of the new road, 30km from Smara, stands a large brown flat-topped hill called **Gor el Bered** (Hill of the Wind). At the foot of its west side, just north of the road, a small brown cupola-domed building resembling a *marabout* is in fact a structure built by the Spanish in the 1930s to extract chalk from the calcium-rich rock of the hill. A genuine *marabout* is to be found at **Sidi Khatari**, south of the road some 90km from Smara.

After around 220km, you reach the turn-off to **Boukra**, a phosphate mining town 25km to the southeast. The café at the junction serves bowlfuls of sweetened camel's milk. Boukra and the vast region to its south is a restricted military zone, inaccessible to casual visitors, but continuing north from the junction you'll see the **Boukra–Laayoune conveyor belt** snaking its way south of the road, bearing phosphates seaward for export.

For the last 50km before Laayoune, the canyon of the **Seguiat el Hamra** comes into view on the western side of the road. Seguiat el Hamra means "Red River" and, though there is no water in it for most of the year, the local clay turns it red when it does flow. The canyon is pretty impressive, but if you stop to take a snapshot ensure that you're out of range of anything military. The oasis of **Lemseyed**, 12km before Laayoune, offers fine views over the canyon.

Laayoune Plage

20km southwest of Laayoune • *Grands taxis* from Laayoune (20min) leave from a station 2km west of town

Despite its name, **Laayoune Plage** isn't really a beach, but Laayoune's commercial and fishing port. Aside from being a huge centre for processing sardines, this is also where the phosphate conveyor from Boukra (see page 484) ends up – huge piles of phosphates sit at the southern end of the port, waiting for export.

Laayoune Plage is a sizeable town, much more developed than Foum el Oued, with facilities such as banks and a post office, but although there's plenty of sand, it's in a **harbour**, and you wouldn't want to sit on it or go for a paddle. If driving from Foum el Oued, you'll usually see a lot of camels on the road – picturesque they may be, but they're a hazard to motorists, especially at night.

Smara and around

Once an important caravan stop, **SMARA** (also written as Es Semara) is today a garrison town occupied by the Moroccan army – be careful where you point your camera. Otherwise, it's a small, dry, sleepy old place with not a lot going on, though there's a **souk** every Thursday, and a **festival** every April featuring musical and other entertainments. Because accommodation options are so dire, it's wise to avoid spending the night here, by making an early start from Tan Tan or Laayoune to get here and heading off before transport dries up.

The part of town built under Spanish rule lies between Rue de l'Hôpital, Avenue Hassan II and the oued. The **old mosque** on the corner of Avenue Mohammed V and Rue de l'Hôpital is made of local basalt, with a rather pretty stone minaret, as is the **El Hajra Mosque** to its southwest, which is the main mosque actually used for worship nowadays. A distinctive aspect of the houses here (and elsewhere in the Western Sahara) is the **eggshell-like dome** that serves as a roof. The domes are said to keep the interior cooler by means of convection currents, but a more likely story is that the Spanish built them like this to prevent build-ups of wind-blown sand on the roofs. The domes are certainly not traditional Saharawi structures, as the Saharawis were always nomads and their traditional homes were tents.

The palace and Great Mosque of Ma el Aïnin

On the western fringe of town, off Bd Hassan II • Palace daily 24hr; *zaouia* officially Fri only (daylight hours), but on other days someone should open up and show you around if you knock on the door • Free, though tip of a few dirham appreciated for the *zaouia*

Smara's only link with its past is the remains of the **palace and Great Mosque of Ma el Aïnin**, the "Blue Sultan", a local ruler who tried to oust the French colonialists at the beginning of the twentieth century (see page 449). The palace, near the oued, contains the homes of Ma el Aïnin's four main wives; one of the residencies is now occupied by the *gardien* and his family. The attached **zaouia** is well maintained but usually closed, except on Fridays. Though plastered over like the rest of the palace, the *zaouia* is built of black basalt from the local hills. What's left of the Great Mosque, a separate building further away from the river, is less well preserved, but you can still see the mihrab and rows of basalt arches.

El Asli rock carvings

10km west of Smara • Free, though tips appreciated

At **El Asli**, west of Smara and just south of the Laayoune road, there are a few prehistoric **rock carvings** to look at on your way to or from town. They're located on a 200m-long stretch of black rocks which extend south of the new visitor centre, a castle-like building which is easy to spot from the main road since it's the only thing

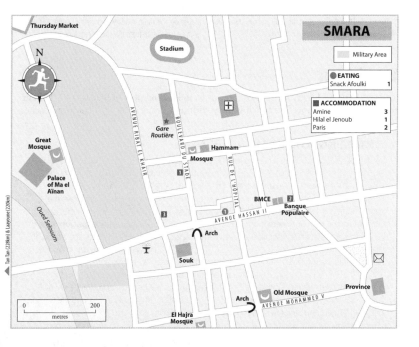

9

for miles around. The carved ostriches, antelopes and suchlike would take ages to find by yourself, but staff from the visitor centre will walk you to them. The centre itself has little of interest inside; instead, take the chance to strike off on foot into this particularly pretty part of the Western Sahara.

ARRIVAL AND INFORMATION   SMARA

By bus All buses leave from the *gare routière*, a yard on Bd de Stade near the stadium, where you'll find the offices of Supratours, SATAS and CTM, the only firms that serve Smara. **Destinations** Agadir (4 daily; 8hr); Guelmim (4 daily; 4hr 30min); Laayoune (1 Supratours service daily; 3hr); Marrakesh (2 daily; 13hr 15min); Tan Tan (4 daily; 3hr).
By grand taxi Shared *grands taxis* leave from the *gare*

routière.
Destinations Guelmim (4hr 30min); Laayoune (3hr); Tan Tan (2hr 30min).
Banks The BMCE and Banque Populaire on Av Hassan II both have ATMs.
Hammam The town hammam is just off Bd de Stade. The left-hand entrance is for women, the right-hand one is for men.

ACCOMMODATION   SEE MAP PAGE 485

Smara has a dismal array of around a dozen small, very cheap hotels, and the only place with anything approaching comfort is hardly a bargain.
Amine 97 Av Ribat el Khair ☏0528 887368. The most upmarket option in town – which isn't saying much at all. Rooms are acceptably clean and have satellite TV, though they're pretty run-down. Some rooms are en suite, but the purported hot water is unreliable, as are the shared shower facilities. €
Hilal el Jenoub 64 Bd du Stade, no phone. This is the

newest of the little ultra-cheap hotels, with small and very basic rooms, but an acceptable level of cleanliness. Although no rooms have showers, there are public ones across the street and a hammam (see page 486) just round the corner. €
Paris 156 Av Hassan II ☏0610 780988. Marginally better than the rock-bottom options – and so it should be, given the price. The rooms are cell-like but clean, though most lack windows, and there are working hot showers. There's a nice little cafe downstairs, too. €

EATING   SEE MAP PAGE 485

There isn't much in the way of restaurants, though places along Av Hassan II serve basic snacks, and there are open-air grills and fried fish stalls around the souk and on Bd de Stade.
★ **Snack Afoulki** Av Hassan II ☏0653 293831. By

far the best place to eat in Smara – and, by extension, for hundreds of kilometres around. It's also one of the only places on the main road with a visible name. For dessert, grab an ice-cream from the shop next door. €

Boujdour

The sea is guarded by cliffs most of the way to the fishing port of **BOUJDOUR**, 188km southwest of Laayoune. The beach is dirty with dangerous rocks – the nearest beaches

SIMMERING TENSIONS IN DAKHLA

While Dakhla is generally quiet and peaceful, deep **tensions** underlie this apparent tranquillity, and occasionally they surface. The Saharawi neighbourhood of **Oum Tounsi** hit the news in February 2011 when it came under attack by Moroccan settlers during the now-abolished annual Dakhla festival. One factor behind the attacks was the resentment of settlers at the subsidies given to returnees from the **Polisario camps** in Algeria if they accept Moroccan citizenship, but the continued opposition of Saharawis to the **Moroccan occupation** remains the most serious issue. Further clashes between settlers and Saharawis erupted after a football match in September 2011, leaving eight dead. The Moroccan news agency Morocco World News, calling Oum Tounsi "a stronghold of smugglers", blamed "ex-convicts" for the trouble, adding that unnamed foreigners had taken advantage of the violence to carry out "activities of subversion". For all that, Dakhla is generally peaceful, but the periodic appearance of SADR flags in Saharawi neighbourhoods invariably leads to raids by Moroccan forces, and the tension between settlers and Saharawis does not look like going away any time soon.

suitable for **swimming** (if you have the transport to reach them) are 20km south, below the cliffs, and 40km north, just beyond a military checkpoint and fishing settlement. The nearest thing to a sight in town is the **lighthouse**, though it's not open to the public, and the soldiers guarding it won't be happy if you try to photograph it.

ARRIVAL AND DEPARTURE
BOUJDOUR

By public transport Buses pass through Boujdour on their way between Laayoune and Dakhla (each 3hr 30min away), and shared taxis run to and from both destinations. The gare routière is on the eastern side of town, about 700m from the very centre.

ACCOMMODATION AND EATING

Av Mohammed V, which runs from the *grand taxi* stand down to the campsite comes alive in the evening with restaurants frying up freshly caught fish, and stalls selling charcoal-grilled brochettes and sausages. There are also café-restaurants on the main road, especially around the SATAS and Supratours offices.

Camping Sahara Line Av Mohammed V ☎ 0528 896893. Bleak, shadeless but well-equipped campsite set 200m from the shore, with cheerful rooms and quite luxurious bungalows, as well as car-wash facilities. Camping €, double €, bungalow €€

Al Qods Av Hassan II ☎ 0528 896573. One of a handful of small hotels in town, this little place on the main drag is neat, tidy and cheap. Bathroom facilities are shared but clean, and there's constant hot water. €

Dakhla

While the mighty Atlantic starts to assume a more tropical hue around **DAKHLA** – no great surprise, since this highly likeable city is just 22km north of the Tropic of Cancer – this is still no Maldives On the subject of distances, here you're also some 544km from Laayoune (Mauritania is closer), and a whopping 2088km from Tangier – you're nearer to Dakar, Bissau and Conakry. However, for a place so far from anywhere, it's remarkably pretty,

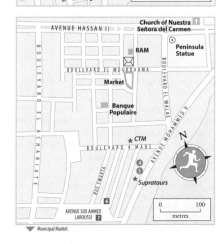

9

orderly and easy-going – add some lovely restaurants and an actual selection of places to drink, and you've got by far the most pleasant place in the Western Sahara. This is a grand spot to start or finish a trip through Morocco.

WESTERN SAHARAN HISTORY

The **Saharawi people** who live in the Western Sahara are largely descended from Arab tribes who moved into the area in the fifteenth century, and established themselves definitively with victory over the indigenous Sanhaja Berbers in the 1644–74 Char Bouba war. They speak an Arabic dialect called Hassania, which is much the same as that spoken in Mauritania, and somewhat different from the dialect spoken in most of Morocco. Their food and music are also more like those of Mauritania than of Morocco. However, Hassania-speaking Saharawis are not confined to the Western Sahara, and many live in southern Morocco too.

SPANISH COLONIAL RULE

Spain held part of the Saharan coast in the early sixteenth century, but the **Saadians** drove them out in 1524, establishing **Moroccan control** over the coastline. In 1884, while European powers, such as Britain, France and Portugal, were carving up the rest of Africa, **Spain** got in on the act and declared the coast between Boujdour and the Nouadibhou peninsula to be a Spanish **"protectorate"**, gradually extending its boundaries inland and northward by agreement with other European powers. The Spanish didn't actually have much control over the area in practice, but built ports at La Gouera and Villa Cisneros (Dakhla), with occasional forays into the interior to "pacify" the Saharawi tribes. Full colonial rule was only introduced after the Spanish Civil War, when the territory was split into two colonies: **Rio de Oro**, with its capital at Villa Cisneros, and **Seguiat el Hamra**, with a new, purpose-built capital at Laayoune.

Following Moroccan independence and the 1958 return of the Tarfaya strip (see page 476), Spain merged its two colonies to form the **Spanish Sahara**, which was considered a province of Spain itself, much like Ifni, Ceuta and Melilla. But it was only in the 1960s, after the discovery of **phosphates at Boukra**, that Spain actually started to develop the territory.

By that time colonialism was out of fashion. Britain and France had pulled out of most of Africa, and only the Fascist-ruled Iberian states of Spain and Portugal still held onto their African colonies, with international pressure mounting on them to quit. In 1966 for example, the **UN** passed a resolution calling on Spain to organize a referendum on independence in the Sahara. Meanwhile, as education became more widespread, the Spaniards were confronted with the same problem that they and the French had faced in Morocco thirty years earlier – the rise of nationalism. **The Movement for the Liberation of the Sahara** was formed in 1967, and in 1970 organized a protest in Laayoune against Spanish rule. This was brutally put down, and the Movement was banned, but Spanish repression only succeeded in radicalizing opposition. In 1973, a group of militants formed the Frente para la Liberación de Seguiat el Hamra y Rio de Oro (**Polisario**), and began a guerrilla campaign for independence.

THE GREEN MARCH, AND WAR

Under pressure from Polisario, and with its dictator General Franco on his last legs, Spain began to consider pulling out of the Sahara, but Morocco's King **Hassan II** now claimed sovereignty over the territory on the basis that it had been under Moroccan rule before Spanish colonization. The case went to the **International Court of Justice** in the Hague, which ruled that, though some Saharawi tribes had indeed paid allegiance to the Moroccan sultan, the territory had not been substantially Moroccan before colonization, and its people were entitled to self-determination. In accordance with this ruling, Spain reluctantly agreed to hold a referendum on independence. Under pressure at home over domestic issues, however (see page 507), Hassan saw advantages in waving the nationalist flag as a distraction, and the next month led a "**Green March**" (*Massira el Khadra*) of 350,000 Moroccan civilians (subsequently replaced by soldiers) across the border to claim the territory. At the same time a secret

Sitting pretty on a long spit of land, Dakhla was known as Villa Cisneros during Spanish rule. During its stint as capital of the Rio de Oro colony, only the colonists and people working for them were allowed into town – the Saharawi nomads who lived

9

agreement was hatched in Madrid to divide the territory between Morocco and Mauritania as soon as Spanish troops had withdrawn.

The Madrid signatories had, however, underestimated the Saharawis' determination to fight for their independence. In February 1976, when Spanish forces left, Polisario proclaimed the **Saharawi Arab Democratic Republic (SADR)**, and fought back against Moroccan and Mauritanian occupation, backed by Algeria, and sometimes Libya, who saw the Sahara as a stick with which to beat their regional rival. Thousands of refugees fled into Algeria, where they settled into increasingly unhygienic Polisario-run refugee camps rather than submit to Moroccan or Mauritanian rule. Algeria ceded the territory around the camps to the SADR; 200,000 people still live in them today.

Polisario's early military successes were impressive, and Mauritania in particular did not have the resources to beat them. In 1978, the war's destabilization of the Mauritanian economy brought down the government. The new regime made peace with Polisario and pulled out of the Sahara (apart from La Gouera and the western side of the Nouadibhou peninsula, which Mauritania still occupies). The Moroccans moved in to replace them, but by the early 1980s they had been pushed into a small area around Laayoune and Dakhla, and the phosphate mines lay idle. Polisario guerillas even managed to infiltrate into Morocco itself. But the Moroccans fought back and, beginning in 1981, built a series of heavily defended **desert walls** (*berm*) that excluded Polisario forces from successively larger areas. The sixth wall, built in 1987, established Moroccan control over two-thirds of the territory, including all its economically important parts and the whole of the coastline. Polisario, now confined to areas behind the *berm*, particularly the region around Bir Lahlou and Tifariti, increasingly turned to diplomacy to gather support, with some success. In 1985, the OAU (now the African Union) admitted the SADR to full membership; Morocco left the organization in protest.

CEASEFIRE AND FUTURE PROSPECTS

In 1988 a UN plan for a **referendum**, to choose between incorporation or independence, was accepted in principle by both sides, and 1991 saw a ceasefire, with the deployment of a UN peacekeeping force called MINURSO, but the years since have seen the UN aims frustrated, with arguments over the voting list leading to repeated postponement of the referendum; Morocco in particular has brought in large numbers of supporters to vote its way, should the promised referendum ever be held. In theory, it will still take place, but observers are sceptical. Having invested so much in the territory – not only in military terms, as subsidies, tax concessions and infrastructure building have all been a heavy drain on the Moroccan economy – it seems inconceivable that Morocco will relinquish its claims. In 2002, Morocco's King Mohammed VI stated that he would never give up any part of the territory, but the king has tried to be conciliatory, granting a royal pardon to hundreds of Saharawi political prisoners, and inviting refugees to come home. In 2007 he proposed a new settlement based on limited autonomy under Moroccan sovereignty, which Polisario inevitably rejected. In 2010, Saharawi residents set up a protest camp at **Gdim Izik** near Laayoune, at first to protest against discrimination, but with calls for independence soon added; Moroccan police dispersed the camp by force, killing a number of people and sparking **riots** across the territory. Protests continued into 2011, and in Dakhla, Moroccan settlers and Saharawis came to blows. There were similar skirmishes with police in 2014. Meanwhile, Morocco has started building little villages along the coast to establish "facts on the ground", and, as an important strategic ally of the West, is unlikely to face much international pressure on the issue. The truth is that prospects for independence are bleak, and limited autonomy is probably the best the Saharawis can hope for.

9

in the desert were excluded. In 1975, the Spanish left and the Mauritanians moved in, to be replaced four years later by the Moroccans. Since then, Dakhla has grown somewhat, but it retains a lazy, sun-bleached atmosphere. Europeans in camper vans head down in winter, drawn by the **deserted beaches** and year-round sunshine – even in January it's hot, and from Europe this is the furthest south you can get by land without needing a pricey visa.

Lastly, Dakhla has also been developing a small **surfing** scene, with windsurfing and kitesurfing increasingly popular pursuits at the northern end of the lagoon, and a couple of surfing supply shops in town.

The town centre

In the **town centre**, the 1953 **Church of Nuestra Señora del Carmen** is about the only thing surviving from Spanish times. Across Avenue Hassan II, a large **statue of the Dakhla peninsula** is reflected in the paving stones of the big, open square. **Avenue Sidi Ahmed Laroussi**, which is really more a square than an avenue, comes into its own in the evenings, when it is transformed into an open-air market for anything from Senegalese woodcarvings to second-hand electronic equipment – though these days, you're more likely to see cheap socks and shoes.

Beaches

Four kilometres west of town, a pencil-like, black-and-white-striped **lighthouse** stands next to an old **Spanish fort**. The fort is inside the lighthouse compound, and neither is open to the public. Directly to their north, however, is a wide sweep of Atlantic **beach**. Strong currents make it dangerous to swim, but the beach is beautiful, and all but deserted.

For bathing, the beaches north of town on the east side of the peninsula are more suitable, starting with a small one by the campsite (see page 492), but with others further north, though you'd need your own transport to reach them. **Trouk** beach, at the very northern end of the lagoon, 26km north of Dakhla, is very popular with kitesurfers.

ARRIVAL AND DEPARTURE | DAKHLA

By plane Dakhla's airport terminal (🌐 onda.ma/en) is 1km to the north of the town centre, off Av de Walae. Royal Air Maroc serve domestic destinations, while Binter Canarias (🌐 bintercanarias.com) fly to Gran Canaria.
Destinations Agadir (2 weekly; 1hr 30min); Casablanca (1–2 daily; 2hr 10min); Laayoune (2 weekly; 1hr); Las Palmas (1–2 weekly; 1hr 15min).
By bus Arriving by bus, you'll be dropped off at the *gare routière*, a 20min walk or 12dh taxi ride west of the centre. You can buy tickets at more central offices: Supratours, Av Mohammed V; CTM, Bd 4 Mars; or SATAS, Bd de Walae. Buses sometimes collect from these spots too, but check at the time of purchase. There are also ticket offices at the

southern end of town (see map page 487).
Destinations Agadir (9 daily; 20hr); Casablanca (3 daily; 28hr); Guerguarat (1 daily; 5hr 30min); Laayoune (9 daily; 8hr); Marrakesh (3 daily; 24hr); Tarfaya (1–5 daily; 9hr 30min).
By grand taxi The *grand taxi* station is at the southern end of town, southwest of the market and the stadium. You'll likely only want to use them for Boujdour, or Laayoune at a push. Some also head all the way into Mauritania (see page 491).
Destinations Boujdour (3hr 30min); Laayoune (7hr).
By rental car Laargoub Car (☎0528930447) allow customers to pick up and drop off at several of their agencies around Morocco, which means that you can use Dakhla as a start or finish line without needing to loop back.

INFORMATION AND ACTIVITIES

Banks There are stacks of banks with ATMs, including the BMCE off Av Hassan II, and the Banque Populaire, a block south of the post office.
Watersports For your kitesurfing and windsurfing needs, contact *Dakhla Attitude* (see page 492), who rent kites. It's a fair bit cheaper at the *Auberge des Nomades du Sahara* (see

page 492). British-run *Sahara Sailing* (🌐 saharasailing. com) offer lagoon trips.
Wildlife watching Italian-run *Dakhla Rovers* (🌐 dakhla-rovers.com) can organise and advise on all sorts, but they specialise in desert trips (often overnighting in the wild), spotting desert foxes, reptiles and birdlife on the way.

9

THE ROAD TO MAURITANIA

Unless you have your own transport, getting from **Dakhla to Mauritania** is best done in a single *grand-taxi* hop. The *Hôtel Sahara* (see page 492) can arrange a ride for good rates. Otherwise, touts around town can put you in contact with Mauritanian drivers, but you'll need to bargain hard to get a good price – try to find out the current rate from the *Sahara* or *Al Baraka* hotels (see page 491). It's also possible to get to the **border** on the 8.30am Supratours bus from Dakhla to Gueguerat (5hr 30min), 370km away; unless there are big delays (and sometimes there are), it should have you by the border long before it closes, but there's accommodation if you get stuck. Mauritanian vehicles will take you from the border to Nouadhibou, so when factoring in the bus ticket you're saving little over taking a *grand taxi*.

ACCOMMODATION

In addition to the hotels below, you can usually **camp** for the night on the Moroccan side if you claim it as your only option.

Barbas Bir Gandouz, 300km south of Dakhla, 80km north of Guerguerat ☎ 0528 897961. This is the last stop for decent accommodation in Moroccan-held territory – a welcome sight on the long road, and with good food to boot. €̄

Border's Gueguerat, 30m from the first border post. The only accommodation around the Moroccan border itself, this is unfortunately run-down, uglier and pricier than *Barbas*. €̄

CROSSING THE BORDER

Formalities are simple enough on the Moroccan side of the border, though you'll need to show documents at least a couple of times. It's rough going on the 5km run between the two border posts – all the more reason to be in the same vehicle throughout. If you've seen *Mad Max*, you'll know what to expect – all sorts of vehicle shells, used televisions, and goodness knows what else (including land mines). It's possible to go on foot, if you tread exactly where the vehicles go, but it's best avoided, all things considered. However you arrive, you'll be accosted by would-be guides at the **Mauritanian border post** – you won't need their assistance, as long as you can track down the **visa room**, which is unmarked and manned by staff who are usually too busy to open the door (so just try to force your way in whenever someone leaves). However, to be prudent, try calling the **Rabat embassy** (see page 248) for the latest information, and bring along hotel bookings, a passport photo or two plus printouts of your flight out of Mauritania (or another West African nation).

MAURITANIA

Most travellers have one of two destinations in mind when hitting Mauritania – **Nouadhibou**, set on a peninsula just under 60km south of the border, or **Nouakchott**, the national capital much further south. The former is smaller and much more likeable, and the start of the famed **iron-ore trains** to Choum (the longest trains in the world, according to some); you can withdraw ouguiya (Mauritanian money) at the Société Général Bank, near the northern end of town, and some restaurants will accept or exchange Moroccan cash (try the Chinese restaurant, which doubles as a brothel). From here to Nouakchott, buses take around 7hr, and the affordable evening flights just 30min.

Coming from Mauritania, if you have a vehicle, you will need to get a **permit** from the Moroccan embassy in Nouakchott (see page 58); you can sometimes get it from the consulate in Nouadhibou, though it's not worth taking the risk. If you don't have a vehicle, **arrange transport** at the *auberges* and campsites in Nouadhibou, or in Nouakchott.

ACCOMMODATION

SEE MAP PAGE 487

TOWN CENTRE

Al Baraka Av Allal Ben Abdellah ⓦ hotelalbaraka.com. A delightful addition to town, this is by far the best choice in its price category, with engaging staff and charming, modern rooms. Given the prime seaside location, it's usually worth splashing out on a room with a sea-view balcony. €̄€̄

9

★ **Dar Rio Oro** Av Ahmed Belafrij, southern end of town, opposite the new mosque ☎0668 969309. Excellent mid-market choice, set into a quiet neighbourhood across the road from the seafront. Rooms are large and comfortable, and though the cheapest use shared facilities, you'll only ever share with one other room, and everything is kept spotless. Breakfast is served with splendid views over the sea. BB €

Sahara Av Sidi Ahmed Laroussi ☎0528 897773. Not to be confused with the *Sahara Regency*, this budget hotel is friendly and central, and can arrange transport to Mauritania. It isn't always super clean, and the shared showers have hot water 6–9pm only. €

Tires Av Sidi Ahmed Laroussi ☎0528 930818. The nicest of the clutch of budget hotels on this road. Each of its floors is set out almost like a three-floor apartment with no living room; the communal showers are clean, and there are sit-down toilets. €

OUT OF TOWN

Auberge des Nomades du Sahara Off the peninsular road, 28km north of town ⌖auberge-des-nomades-du-sahara.com. The cheapest kitesurfing base in the area, for both rental and accommodation. They've two guarded compounds – "Les Dauphins", a small group of octagonal pine-wood bungalows, and "Les Nomades", a slightly smarter collection of bungalows and tents. Transfers included. FB €

★ **Dakhla Attitude** Off the peninsular road, 30km north of town ⌖dakhla-attitude.ma. Tucked into the dunes north of town, this attractive, eco-friendly guesthouse remains Dakhla's best choice for kite- or windsurfing, despite strong competition. It's not cheap, but includes transfers from the airport or bus terminal, and you're right next to the water. FB €€

CAMPING

Camping Moussafir Off the peninsular road, 7km north of town ☎0528 898279. Right by the beach, but far from town, this campsite is friendly and popular with overlanders heading for Mauritania. It has some bare but reasonably large rooms, as well as hot showers (extra charge). Camping €

EATING SEE MAP PAGE 487

In addition to the places listed here, you'll find a handful of cheap places to eat at the southern end of town on Bd Ahmed Ben Chaqroun around the junction with Bd Abderrahim Bouabide. Several restaurants here are licensed.

Bahia 12 Av Mohammed V. Located in Dakhla's oldest hotel, *Bahia* offers good Moroccan food and local fish dishes, including shellfish and *pulpo alla gallega* (fresh boiled octopus drizzled with olive oil and sprinkled with paprika). €

Casa Luis 14 Av Mohammed V ☎0528 898193. Tasty Spanish food including hearty fish platters and a tasty paella. The green and orange-red sauces you may have served with your meal are *mojo*, a product of the Canary Islands which should, by rights, be better known around the world. Licensed. €€

★ **La Maison du Thé** 101 Av Mohammed V ☎0673 224110. Elegant, Frenchified spot with selections made from a blackboard menu. Try the seafood pastilla, or perhaps grilled fish from the sea lapping outside. €€

★ **Samarkand** Av Mohammed V 487. This rambling affair features a beautiful terrace by the sea and is a one-stop shop for meals, snacks and drinks. Grab pastries from the shop out front and enjoy them with coffee; go for a tajine or other Moroccan main in the upstairs restaurant area; grab a fruit juice; or try something more adventurous, such as turkey escalopes or the surprisingly good veggie tempura. All this, plus killer views of the turquoise waters and the dunes of mainland Morocco beyond. €€

Villa Dakhla Av Mohammed V. A sleek and rather posh restaurant, with stylish decor, a carpetted salon and a sea terrace. The menu changes daily, but typical dishes might include half a dozen local oysters followed by pan-fried swordfish steak. €€

DRINKING SEE MAP PAGE 487

La Maison du Thé 101 Av Mohammed V. This snazzy restaurant has the widest selection of alcoholic drinks in the Western Sahara, including beer, wine, and even – feel free to gasp – a choice of spirits.

GOATS IN AN ARGAN TREE

Contexts

History

Morocco's emergence as a nation-state is astonishingly recent, dating from the occupation of the country by the French and Spanish at the turn of the twentieth century, and its independence in 1956. Prior to this, it is best seen as a kind of patchwork of tribal groups, whose shifting alliances and sporadic bids for power defined the nature of government. With a handful of exceptions, the country's ruling sultans controlled only the plains, the coastal ports and the regions around the imperial capitals of Fez, Marrakesh, Rabat and Meknes. These were known as Bled el Makhzen – the governed lands, or, more literally, "Lands of the Storehouse". The rest of the Moroccan territories – the Rif, the three Atlas ranges and the outlying deserts – comprised Bled es Siba, "Lands of the Dissidents". Populated almost exclusively by Berbers, the region's original (pre-Arab) inhabitants, they were rarely recognized as being under anything more than local tribal authority.

The balance between government control and tribal independence is one of the two enduring themes of Moroccan history. The other is the emergence, expansion and eventual replacement of the various **sultanate dynasties**. These at first seem dauntingly complicated – a succession of short-lived tribal movements and confusingly similar-named sultans – but there are actually just seven main groups. The first of them, the **Idrissids**, became the model by founding the city of Fez towards the end of the eighth century and bringing a coalition of Berber and Arab forces under a central *makhzen* (government) authority. The last, the **Alaouites**, emerged in the mid-seventeenth century from the great palm oasis of Tafilalt and, continuing with the current king, Mohammed VI, still hold constitutional power.

Prehistory

Morocco is part of the **Maghreb**, an island of fertile land between the Sahara and the Mediterranean that also includes Algeria and Tunisia. Until around 3000 BC, the Sahara was savannah, fertile enough to support elephants, zebras and a whole range of other wildlife. It seems likely that there were groups of hunter-and-gatherer hominids here as early as a million years ago. Around 15,000 BC there seem to have been **Paleolithic** settlements, and before the Sahara became desert, primitive pastoral and agricultural systems had begun to develop. It is possible also to trace the arrival of two independent Stone Age cultures in the Maghreb: the **Oranian** or **Mouillian Culture** (from around 12,000 BC), and **Capsian Culture** (from around 8000 BC). These are the people who made the cave and rock drawings of the pre-Sahara and High Atlas, Morocco's oldest archeological sites.

c.15,000 BC	c.3000 BC	c.1100 BC
First Paleolithic settlements	Desertification of the Sahara	Arrival of Phoenicians

Phoenicians and Carthaginians

Morocco's recorded history begins around 1100 BC with the arrival of the **Phoenicians**, a seafaring people from what is now Lebanon. By the seventh century BC, they had established settlements along the coast, including Rusadir (Melilla), Tingis (Tangier), Zila (Asilah), Lixis (Larache), Chellah (Rabat), and even Mogador (Essaouira) – of all their colonies, the furthest from their homeland – where they maintained a dye factory on the Îles Purpuraires (see page 280). The settlements were small, isolated colonies, most built on defensible headlands round the coast, and there was probably little initial contact between them and the inhabitants of the interior (known to the Greeks as, *Barbaroi*, or as we now say, **Berbers**). By the fifth century BC, one Phoenician colony, **Carthage** (in Tunisia), had become pre-eminent and gained dominance over the rest. Under Carthaginian leadership, some of the Moroccan colonies grew into considerable cities, exporting grain and grapes, and minting their own coins.

After Carthage's defeat and destruction by Rome in 146 BC, Morocco's Punic colonies grew in prosperity, taking in hundreds of Carthaginian refugees. Even after Rome had annexed and then abandoned the country, Phoenician was still widely spoken along the coast.

Berber kingdoms and Roman rule

Before Rome imposed direct imperial rule in 40 AD, the "civilized" Moroccan territories for a while formed the Berber **Kingdom of Mauretania**, probably little more than a confederation of local tribes, centred round **Volubilis** (near Meknes) and **Tangier**, which gained a certain influence through alliance and occasional joint rule with the adjoining Berber state of **Numidia** (essentially modern Algeria).

The kingdom's most important rulers, and the only ones of whom any substantial records survive, were **Juba II** (25 BC–23 AD) and his son **Ptolemy** (23–40 AD). Juba, an Algerian Berber by birth, was brought up and educated in Rome, where he married the daughter of Antony and Cleopatra. His reign, if limited in its extent, seems to have been orderly and prosperous, and the pattern might have continued under his son, but in 40 AD, Emperor Caligula summoned Ptolemy to an audience in Lyons and had him assassinated – so the story goes, for appearing in a more brilliant cloak than his own. Four years later, the new emperor Claudius imposed direct rule, dividing Rome's North African domains into two provinces: Mauritania Caesarensis (the old Numidia) and **Mauritania Tingitana** (essentially, Morocco). Tingis (Tangier) was the capital of Tingitana, while Volubilis became the seat of the provincial governor.

Roman rule

The early years of Rome's new imperial province were taken up with near-constant **rebellions** – the first one alone needing three years and over twenty thousand troops to subdue.

Perhaps discouraged by this unexpected resistance, the **Romans** never attempted to colonize Morocco–Mauretania beyond its old limits, and the Rif and Atlas mountains were left unpenetrated, establishing an enduring precedent. But Tingitana had a considerable Roman presence: the second-century AD geographer Ptolemy listed more than thirty Roman cities in the province, which provided exotic animals for Roman games, as well as grains, wines, fish sauce (*garum*), olive oil, copper and purple murex

146 BC	44 AD	429 AD
Fall of Carthage marks start of Roman domination	Claudius imposes direct Roman rule	Vandals occupy Morocco

dye. **Volubilis**, the most extensive surviving Roman site in Morocco, was a significant city, at the heart of the north's fertile vineyards and grain fields.

However, as Roman power waned, and Berber uprisings became more frequent, administration was moved from Volubilis to Tingis. Meanwhile, as the Roman Empire crumbled, Germanic tribes from the east moved in to take over its territories. One of these tribes, the Vandals under King Gaiseric, invaded Roman Mauretania in 429 AD, and remained its rulers until 533, when the Byzantine general **Belisarius** defeated them and laid claim to the Maghreb for Byzantium's Emperor Justinian. Since the Byzantine Empire was a continuation of the Roman Empire in the east, this marked a kind of return to Roman rule.

The arrival of Islam

Within thirty years of its foundation (in 622 AD, when the Prophet Mohammed moved with his followers from Mecca to Medina), **Islam** had established itself in the Maghreb at Kairouan in present-day Tunisia, but westward expansion was slowed by Algeria's Berbers – mainly pagans but including communities of Christians and Jews – who put up a strong and unusually unified resistance to Arab control. It was only in 680 that the governor of Kairouan, **Oqba Ibn Nafi**, made an initial foray into Morocco, taking in the process the territory's last Byzantine stronghold at Ceuta. The story goes that Oqba then embarked on a 5000km march through Morocco, all the way to the Atlantic Ocean, but whether this expedition had any real Islamicizing influence on the Moroccan Berbers is questionable. Oqba left no garrison forces and was himself killed in Algeria on his way back to Kairouan.

Islam may, however, have taken root among some of the tribes. In the early part of the eighth century the new Arab governor of the west, **Moussa Ibn Noussar**, returned to Morocco and managed to establish Arab control (and carry out mass conversions to Islam) in both the northern plains and the pre-Sahara, but his main thrust was towards **Spain**. In 711, the first Muslim forces crossed over from Tangier to Tarifa and defeated the Visigoths in a single battle; within a decade the Moors had taken control of all but the remote Spanish mountains in northern Asturias; and their advance into Europe was only halted at the Pyrenees by the victory of Charles Martel at Poitiers in 732.

The bulk of this invading and occupying force were almost certainly **Berber converts** to Islam, and the sheer scale of their military success must have had enormous influence in turning Morocco itself into a largely Muslim nation. It was not at this stage, however, an Arab one. The extent of the Islamic Empire – from Persia to Spain – was simply too great for Arab numbers. Early attempts to impose taxes on the Moroccan Berbers led to a rebellion and, once again outside the political mainstream, the Maghreb fragmented into a series of small, independent **principalities**.

The Idrissids (eighth–eleventh centuries)

Meanwhile the Muslim world was split by the schism between **Sunnis** and **Shi'ites**; when the Islamic empire came under the control of Sunni caliphs, the Shi'ites dispersed, seeking refuge both east and west. One of them, arriving in Morocco around 787, was **Moulay Idriss**, an evidently charismatic leader and a great-grandson

533 AD	622 AD	680 AD
Belisarius takes Morocco for the Byzantines	Mohammed's flight to Medina marks start of Islamic era	Oqba Ibn Nafi brings Islam to Morocco

of the Prophet (see page 165). He seems to have been adopted almost at once by the citizens of Volubilis – then still a vaguely Romanized city – and by the Aouraba Berber tribe. He was poisoned two years later, possibly by order of caliph Harun al-Rashid (of *Arabian Nights* fame), but had managed to set up the infrastructure of an essentially Arab court and kingdom – the basis of what was to become Morocco – and his successors, the **Idrissids**, became the first recognizable Moroccan dynasty. His son **Moulay Idriss II**, born posthumously to a Berber woman, was declared sultan in 807, after an apparently orderly regency, and ruled for just over twenty years – something of a golden age for the emerging Moroccan state, with the extension of a central authority throughout the north and even to the oases beyond the Atlas.

Moulay Idriss II's most important achievement was the development of the city planned (and possibly actually started) by his father: **Fez**. Here, he set up the apparatus of court government, and here he also welcomed large contingents of Shi'ite **refugees**, particularly from Western Islam's two great cities, Cordoba and Kairouan. In incorporating them, Fez (and, by extension, Morocco) became increasingly Arabized, and was transformed into a major Arab centre. The **Kairaouine University** was established, becoming one of the three most important in Islam (and far ahead of those in Europe), and Fez became a vital link in the trade between Spain and the East, and between the Maghreb and Africa south of the Sahara.

After Moulay Idriss's death, the kingdom split into nine different **principalities**. In the ninth century, the dissident Kharijite sect (a movement to the left of Shi'ism) gained the support of many Berbers because it denied any need for the leader of Islam to be an Arab. The desert caravan port of **Sijilmassa** (see page 406) became an important Kharijite stronghold, and remained so until it was attacked in 909 AD by the Shi'ite Fatimids, whose leader the Sijilmassans had imprisoned. The Fatimids went on to conquer Egypt, leaving Morocco in the hands of their Berber allies, the Zirids, but when the Zirids declared their allegiance to the Sunni caliphs in Baghdad, the Fatimids invited an Arabian tribe, the Banu Hilal, to invade and plunder the Maghreb.

The Almoravids (1062–1145)

The **Banu Hilal** did most of their plundering in Tunisia, and by the time they reached Morocco (where they settled in some of the southern oases), the worst effects of their invasion was over, but they shattered the infrastructure and created a power vacuum, which was filled by the two great Berber dynasties of the Middle Ages – the **Almoravids** and the **Almohads**. Both emerged from the south, and in each case their motivating force was religious: a purifying zeal to **reform** or destroy the decadent ways that had reached Morocco from the wealthy Andalusian Muslims of Spain. The two dynasties together lasted only a century and a half, but in this period Morocco was the pre-eminent power of western Islam, maintaining an **empire** that at its peak reached from Spain down to West Africa.

The **Almoravids** began as a reforming movement among the Sanhaja Berbers of what is now Mauritania. A nomadic desert tribe like today's Touaregs, they converted to Islam in the ninth century, but the founders of the Almoravid movement, a local sheikh who had returned from the pilgrimage to Mecca and a *fakir* from the Souss plain, found widespread abuse of orthodox practice. In particular, they preached

711 AD	732 AD	787 AD
Muslims under Tariq Ibn Ziad invade Spain	Battle of Poitiers marks furthest Islamic expansion	Moulay Idriss I arrives in Morocco

against drinking palm wine, playing licentious music and taking more than four wives, and their movement rapidly took hold among this already ascetic, tent-dwelling people.

Founding a *ribat* – a kind of warrior monastery similar to the Templar castles of Europe – the Almoravids soon became a considerable military force. In 1054, they set out from the *ribat* (from which the word Almoravids derives) to spread the message through a *jihad* (holy war), and within four years they had destroyed the empire of ancient Ghana (mostly in what is now Mali) and captured its capital Koumbi Saleh (now in Mauritania). Turning towards Morocco, they founded a new capital at Marrakesh in 1062, and under the leadership of **Youssef Ben Tachfine** went on to extend their rule throughout the north of Morocco and, to the east, as far as Algiers.

Spanish expeditions

In 1085, Youssef undertook his first expedition to **Spain**, invited by the princes of Muslim Spain (Andalusia) after the fall of Toledo to the Christians. He crossed over the Straits again in 1090, this time to take control of Spain himself. Before his death in 1107, he restored Muslim control to Valencia and other territories lost in the first wave of the Christian Reconquest. The new Spanish territories reoriented Moroccan culture towards the far more affluent and sophisticated Andalusian civilization, and also stretched the Almoravid forces too thinly. Youssef, disgusted by Andalusian decadence, had ruled largely from **Marrakesh**, leaving governors in Seville and other cities. After his death, the Andalusians proved disinclined to accept these foreign overlords, while the Moroccans themselves became vulnerable to charges of being corrupt and departing from their puritan ideals.

Youssef's son **Ali** was not interested in ceaseless military activity, and in Spain used Christian mercenaries to maintain control. His reign, and that of the Almoravids, was supplanted in the early 1140s by a new movement, the Almohads.

The Almohads (1145–1248)

Ironically, the **Almohads** shared much in common with their predecessors. Again, they were forged from the Berber tribes – this time in the High Atlas – and again, they based their bid for power on an intense Puritanism. Their founder **Ibn Toumert** attacked the Almoravids for allowing their women to ride horses (a tradition in the desert), for wearing extravagant clothes, and for being subject to Andalusian corruptions such as listening to music and drinking wine. He also claimed that the Almoravids did not recognize the unitary nature of God, the basis of Almohad belief, and the source of their name – the "unitarians". Banished from Marrakesh by Ali, Ibn Toumert set up a *ribat* in the Atlas at **Tin Mal** in 1124, waging war on local tribes until they accepted his authority, and he eventually claimed to be the Mahdi, the final prophet promised in the Koran.

Ibn Toumert was aided by a shrewd assistant and brilliant military leader, **Abd el Moumen**, who took over the movement after his death. In 1145, he was strong enough to displace the Almoravids from Fez, and two years later he drove them from their capital, Marrakesh, making him effectively sultan.

The third Almohad sultan, **Yacoub el Mansour** (The Victorious), defeated the Christians at Alarcos in Spain in 1195 and pushed the frontiers of the empire east to Tripoli. For the

808 AD	828 AD	909 AD
Moulay Idriss II orders construction of Fez	Death of Moulay Idriss II and fragmentation of Morocco	Fatimids take Sijilmassa

first time, there was one single rule across the entire Maghreb and most of Spain, though it did not stretch as far south as under the Almoravids. With the ensuing wealth and prestige, El Mansour launched a great building programme, including a new capital in **Rabat** and magnificent gateways and minarets in Marrakesh and Seville.

Once more though, imperial expansion precipitated disintegration. In 1212, Yacoub's successor, **Mohammed en Nasr**, attempting to drive the Spanish Christians back to the Pyrenees, was decisively defeated at the Battle of **Las Navas de Tolosa**; the balance of power in Spain was changing, and within four decades only the kingdom of Granada remained in Muslim hands. In the Maghreb, the eastern provinces declared independence from Almohad rule and Morocco itself was returning to the authority of local tribes. In 1248, one of these, the **Merenids** (or Beni Merin), took the northern capital of Fez and turned towards Marrakesh.

Merenids and Wattasids (1248–1554)

The last three centuries of Berber rule in Morocco were marked by increasing domestic **instability** and economic stagnation. The last Andalusian kingdom, Granada, fell to Ferdinand and Isabella in 1492. The Portuguese established footholds on Morocco's Atlantic and Mediterranean coasts, while, to the east, the rest of the Maghreb fell under the domination of the Ottoman Empire. New shipping technology allowing Europeans to navigate beyond the Western Sahara also meant the eventual end of the trans-Sahara caravan route.

In Morocco, the main development was a centralized administrative system – the **Makhzen** – maintained without tribal support by standing armies of Arab and Christian mercenaries. It is to this age that the real distinction of Bled el Makhzen and Bled es Siba belongs – the latter coming to mean everything outside the immediate vicinities of the imperial cities.

The Merenids

Perhaps with this background it is not surprising that few of the 21 **Merenid sultans** – or their cousins and successors, the Wattasids – made any great impression. The early sultans were occupied mainly with Spain, at first in trying to regain a foothold on the coast, later with shoring up the kingdom of Granada. There were minor successes in the fourteenth century under the "Black Sultan", **Abou el Hassan**, who for a time occupied Tunis, but he was to die before being able to launch a planned major invasion of Andalusia, and his son, **Abou Inan**, himself fell victim to the power struggles within the mercenary army.

The thirteenth and fourteenth centuries, however, did leave a considerable **legacy of building**, perhaps in defiance of the lack of political progress (and certainly a product of the move towards government by forced taxation). In 1279, the garrison town of **Fez el Jedid** was established, to be followed by a series of brilliantly endowed colleges, or **medersas**, which are among the finest surviving Moorish monuments. Culture, too, saw a final flourish. The historians **Ibn Khaldun** and **Leo Africanus**, and the travelling chronicler **Ibn Battuta**, all studied in Fez under Merenid patronage.

The Wattasids

The **Wattasids**, who usurped Merenid power in 1465, had ruled in effect for 45 years previously as a line of hereditary viziers. After their coup, they maintained a semblance

1062	1124	1147
Marrakesh founded by the Almoravids	Ibn Toumert founds Almohad *ribat* at Tin Mal	Almohads take Marrakesh

of control for a little under a century, though the extent of the Makhzen lands was by now minimal.

The **Portuguese** had annexed and colonized the seaports of Ceuta, Tangier, Asilah, Agadir and Safi, while large tracts of the interior lay in the hands of religious warrior brotherhoods, or **marabouts**, on whose alliances the sultans had increasingly to depend.

The Saadians and civil war (1554–1669)

The Saadians, the first **Arab dynasty** since the Idrissids, were the most important family to emerge in the early years of the sixteenth century, rising to power on the strength of their religious positions (they were Shereefs – descendants of the Prophet). They began by setting up a small principality in the **Souss**, where they established their first capital at Tagmadert in the Draa Valley (exact location uncertain) before moving it to **Taroudant**. Normally, this would have formed a regular part of Bled el Makhzen, but the absence of government in the south allowed them to extend their power to **Marrakesh** around 1524, with the Wattasids for a time retaining Fez and ruling the north.

In the following decades the Saadians made breakthroughs along the coast, capturing Agadir in 1541 and driving the Portuguese from Safi and Essaouira. When the Wattasids fell into bankruptcy and invited the Turks into Fez, the Saadians were ready to consolidate their power. This proved harder, and more confusing, than anyone might have expected. **Mohammed esh Sheikh**, the first Saadian sultan to control both the south and north, was himself soon using Turkish troops, and was subsequently assassinated by a group of them in 1557. His death unleashed an incredibly convoluted sequence of factional murder and power politics, which was only resolved, somewhat fortuitously, by a battle with the Portuguese twenty years later.

Battle of the Three Kings

This event, the 1578 **Battle of the Three Kings**, was essentially a Portuguese crusade, led by the youthful King Sebastião I on the nominal behalf of a deposed Saadian king against his uncle and rival. At the end of the day all three were to perish on the battlefield, the Portuguese having suffered one of the most disastrous defeats in Christian medieval history, and a little-known Saadian prince emerged as the sole acknowledged ruler of Morocco.

His name was **Ahmed "El Mansour"** (The Victorious, following this momentous victory), and he was easily the most impressive sultan of the dynasty. Not only did he begin his reign clear of the intrigue and rivalry that had dogged his predecessors, but he was immensely wealthy as well. Ransoms paid for the remnants of their nobility after the battle reduced Portugal to bankruptcy, and the country, with its Moroccan enclaves, even fell, for a time under the control of Habsburg Spain.

Breaking with tradition, Ahmed himself became actively involved in European politics, generally supporting the Protestant north against the Spanish and encouraging Dutch and English trade. Within Morocco he was able to maintain a reasonable level of order and peace, and diverted criticism of his use of Turkish troops (and his own Turkish-educated ways) by embarking on an **invasion of Mali**. This secured control of the Saharan salt mines and the gold and slave routes from Senegal, all sources of phenomenal wealth, which won him the additional epithet of El Dhahabi (The

1195	1212	1248
Yacoub el Mansour defeats Castilians at Battle of Alarcos	Christians defeat Muslims at Battle of Las Navas de Tolosa	Merenids take Fez

Golden One) and reduced his need to tax Moroccans, making him a popular man. His reign was the most prosperous period in the country's history since the time of the Almohads – a cultural and political renaissance reflected in the coining of a new title, the **Shereefian Empire**, the country's official name until independence in 1956.

Civil war and piracy

Ahmed's death in 1603 caused abrupt and lasting chaos. He left three sons, none of whom could gain authority, and, split by **civil war**, the country once again broke into a number of principalities. A succession of **Saadian rulers** retained power in the Souss and in Marrakesh (where their tombs remain testimony to the opulence and turbulence of the age); another *marabout* force, the **Jila**, gained control of Fez; while around Salé and Rabat arose the pirate **Republic of the Bou Regreg** (see page 237).

Moulay Ismail and the early Alaouites (1669–1822)

Like the Saadians, the **Alaouites** were Shereefs, first establishing themselves as religious leaders – this time in Rissani in the **Tafilalt**. Their struggle to establish power also followed a similar pattern, spreading first to Taza and Fez and finally, under Sultan **Moulay Rachid**, reaching Marrakesh in 1669. Rashid, however, was unable to enjoy the fruits of his labour, since he was assassinated in a particularly bloody palace coup in 1672. It was only with Moulay Ismail, the ablest of his rival sons, that an Alaouite leader gained real control over the country.

Moulay Ismail

The 55-year reign of **Moulay Ismail** (see page 188) was the country's last stab at imperial glory. In Morocco, where his shrine in Meknes is still a place of pilgrimage, he is remembered as a great and just, if unusually ruthless, ruler; to contemporary Europeans – and in subsequent historical accounts – he is noted for extravagant cruelty (though he was not much worse than the European rulers of his day). He stands out for the grandness of the scale on which he acted. At **Meknes**, his new imperial capital, he garrisoned a permanent army of some 140,000 African troops, a legendary guard he had built up personally through slaving expeditions in Mauritania and Mali, as well as by starting a human breeding programme. The army kept order throughout the kingdom – Morocco is today still littered with their kasbah garrisons – and were able to raise taxes as required. The Bou Regreg pirates were brought under the control of the state in 1668, along with their increasingly lucrative revenues.

With all this, Ismail was able to build a palace in Meknes that was the rival of its contemporary, Versailles, and he negotiated on equal terms with European rulers. Indeed, it was probably the reputation he established for Morocco that allowed the country to remain free for another century and a half before the European colonial powers began carving it up.

Mohammed III and Moulay Slimane

Like all the great, long-reigning Moroccan sultans, Moulay Ismail left innumerable sons and a terminal dispute for the throne, with the powerful standing army supporting and dropping heirs at will.

1415	1471	1465
Portuguese take Ceuta	Portuguese take Tangier	Wattasid viziers seize power from Merenids

Remarkably, a capable ruler emerged fairly soon – Sultan **Mohammed III** – and for a while it appeared that the Shereefian Empire was moving back into the mainstream of world events. Mohammed recaptured El Jadida from the Portuguese, founded the port of Essaouira, traded and conducted treaties with the Europeans, and was the first ruler to recognize the **United States of America**.

At his death in 1790, the state collapsed once more into civil war, Fez and Marrakesh in turn promoting claimants to the throne. When this period drew to some kind of a close, with **Moulay Slimane** (1792–1822) asserting his authority in both cities, there was little left to govern. The army had dispersed; the Bled es Siba reasserted its old limits; and in Europe, with the ending of the Napoleonic Wars, Britain, France, Spain and Germany were all looking to establish themselves in Africa.

Moulay Slimane's rule was increasingly isolated from the new realities outside Morocco. An intensely orthodox Muslim, he concentrated the efforts of government on eliminating the power and influence of the **Sufi brotherhoods** – a power he underestimated. In 1818 Berber tribes loyal to the Derakaoui brotherhood rebelled and, temporarily, captured the sultan. Subsequently, the sultans had no choice but to govern with the cooperation of local sheikhs and brotherhood leaders.

Even more serious, at least in its long-term effects, was Moulay Slimane's isolationist attitude towards **Europe**, and in particular to Napoleonic France. Exports were banned, European consuls banished to Tangier, and contacts that might have helped maintain Moroccan independence were lost.

European domination

European powers had from time to time occupied Moroccan ports such as Ceuta, Tangier, El Jadida and Essaouira, but European encroachment in earnest got under way in the nineteenth century. The Moroccan state, still medieval in form, virtually bankrupt and with armies press-ganged from the tribes to secure taxes, was unable to do much about it.

When the **French** occupied Algiers after a victory over the Ottomans in 1830, Sultan **Abd Er Rahman** (1822–59) mustered a force to defend his fellow Muslims but was severely defeated at Isly in 1843. In 1859, the **Spanish** occupied Tetouan, restored to Morocco only after payment of massive indemnities using money borrowed from Britain (for which the sultan had to surrender control of customs administration). The sultan also had to provide Spain with an Atlantic port, which the Spanish later claimed in Sidi Ifni.

Moulay Hassan

By the end of the nineteenth century, both France and Spain had learned to use every opportunity to step in and "protect" their nationals in Morocco. Complaints by **Moulay Hassan** (Hassan I), the last pre-colonial sultan to have any real power, actually led to a debate on this issue at the 1880 **Madrid Conference**, but the effect was only to regularize the practice on a wider scale, beginning with the setting up of an "international administration" in Tangier.

Moulay Hassan could, in other circumstances, have proved an effective and possibly inspired sultan. Acceding to the throne in 1873, he embarked on an ambitious series of modernizing **reforms**, including attempts to stabilize the currency by minting the rial

1492	1506	1509
Fall of Granada: end of Muslim Andalusia	Portuguese take Mogador (Essaouira)	Foundation of Saadian kingdom at Tagmadert

in Paris, to bring in more rational forms of taxation, and to retrain the army under the instruction of Turkish and Egyptian officers. But his social and monetary reforms were obstructed by foreign merchants and local *caids*, while the European powers forced him to abandon plans for other Muslim states' involvement in the army.

Moulay Hassan played off the Europeans as best he could, employing a British military chief of staff, **Caid MacClean**, a French military mission and German arms manufacturers. On the frontiers, he built kasbahs to strengthen the defences at Tiznit, Saïdia and Selouane. But the government had few modern means of raising money to pay for these developments. Moulay Hassan was thrown back on the traditional means of taxation, the *harka*, setting out across the country to subdue the tribes and to collect tribute. In 1894, returning across the Atlas on just such a campaign, he fell ill and died.

The last sultans

Hassan's son **Abd el Aziz** (1894–1907) was a boy of fourteen at his accession, but for the first six years of his rule the country was kept in at least a semblance of order by his father's chamberlain, **Bou Ahmed**. In 1900, however, Bou Ahmed died, and Abd el Aziz was left to govern alone – surrounded by an assembly of Europeans, preying on the remaining wealth of the court. In the Atlas mountains, the tribal chiefs asserted their freedom from government control, and in the Rif, a pretender to the throne, **Bou Hamra**, led a five-year revolt.

European manipulation during this period was remorselessly cynical. In 1904, the French negotiated agreements on "spheres of influence" with the British (who were to hold Egypt and Cyprus), and with the Italians (who got Tripolitania, or Libya). The following year saw the German kaiser Wilhelm visiting Tangier and swearing to protect Morocco's integrity, but he was later bought off with the chance to "develop" the Congo. France and Spain, meanwhile, reached a secret arrangement on dividing Morocco and simply awaited a pretext to execute it.

In 1907, the French moved troops into **Oujda**, on the Algerian border, and, after a mob attack on French construction workers, into Casablanca. Abd el Aziz was deposed by his brother, **Moulay Hafid** (1907–12), in a last attempt to resist the European advance. His reign began with a coalition with the principal Atlas chieftain, **Madani el Glaoui**, and intentions to take military action against the French, but the new sultan first had to put down the revolt of Bou Hamra – who was finally captured in 1909. Meanwhile, supposedly to protect their nationals in Rif mineral mines, the Spanish brought over ninety thousand troops to Melilla. Colonial occupation, in effect, had begun.

The Treaty of Fez

Dissidence at home finally drove Moulay Hafid into the hands of the Europeans. With Berber tribesmen at the walls of his capital in Fez supporting a pretender to the throne (one of a number who arose at the time), the sultan went for help to the French, and was forced to accept their terms.

These were ratified and signed as the **Treaty of Fez** in 1912, which gave the French the right to defend Morocco, represent it abroad and conquer the Bled es Siba. A similar document was also signed with the Spanish, who were to take control of a strip of territory along the northern coast, with its capital in Tetouan and another thinner strip of land in the south, running eastwards from Tarfaya. In between, with the

1524	**1541**	**1554**
Saadians take Marrakesh	Saadians expel Portuguese from Agadir, Safi and Mogador	Saadians take Fez

exception of a small Spanish enclave in Sidi Ifni, was to be French Morocco. A separate agreement gave Spain colonial rights to the Sahara, stretching south from Tarfaya to the borders of French Mauritania.

The French and Spanish Protectorates (1912–56)

The fates of **Spanish and French Morocco** under colonial rule were to be very different. When **France** signed its Protectorate agreement with the sultan in 1912, its sense of **colonial mission** was running high. The colonial lobby in France argued that the colonies were vital not only as markets for French goods but because they fulfilled France's *mission civilisatrice* – to bring the benefits of French culture and language to all corners of the globe. The Spanish saw themselves more as conquerors than colonists and did little to develop their sector, whose government was described by one contemporary as a mixture of "battlefield, tavern and brothel".

Lyautey and "pacification"

France's first Resident General in Morocco was **General Hubert Lyautey**, often held up as the ideal of French colonialism with his stated policy: "Do not offend a single tradition, do not change a single habit". Lyautey recommended respect for the terms of the Protectorate agreement, which placed strict limits on French interference in Moroccan affairs. He recognized the existence of a functioning Moroccan bureaucracy based on the sultan's court with which the French could cooperate – a hierarchy of officials, with diplomatic representation abroad, and with its own social institutions.

But there were other forces at work: French soldiers were busy unifying the country, ending tribal rebellion; in their wake came a system of roads and railways that opened the country to further colonial exploitation. For the first time in Moroccan history, the central government exerted permanent control over the mountain regions. The "**pacification**" of the country brought a flood of French settlers and administrators.

In France, these developments were presented as echoing the history of the opening up of the American Wild West. Innumerable articles celebrated "the transformation taking place, the stupendous development of Casablanca port, the birth of new towns, the construction of roads and dams…The image of the virgin lands in Morocco is contrasted often with metropolitan France, wrapped up in its history and its routines…"

Naturally, the interests of the natives were submerged in this rapid economic development, and the restrictions of the Protectorate agreement were increasingly ignored.

Spain and revolt in the Rif

The early history of the **Spanish zone** was strikingly different. Before 1920, Spanish influence outside the main cities of Ceuta, Melilla and Tetouan was minimal. When the Spanish tried to extend their control into the Rif mountains of the interior, they ran into the fiercely independent Berber tribes of the region.

Normally, the various tribes remained divided, but faced with the Spanish troops they united under the leadership of **Abd el Krim el Khattabi**. In the summer of 1921, he inflicted a series of crushing defeats on the Spanish army, culminating in the massacre of at least thirteen thousand soldiers at **Annoual**. The scale of the defeat, at the hands of tribal fighters armed only with rifles, outraged the Spanish public and worried the

1578	1603	1627
Battle of the Three Kings puts Ahmed el Mansour on throne	Ahmed el Mansour's death leads to political fragmentation	Republic of Bou Regreg founded at Salé

French, who had Berber tribes of their own to deal with in the Atlas mountains. As the war began to spread into the French zone, the two colonial powers combined to crush the rebellion. It took a combined force of around 360,000 colonial troops to do so.

It was the last of the great tribal rebellions. Abd el Krim had fought for an independent **Rifian state**. An educated man, he had seen the potential wealth that could result from exploiting the mineral deposits of the Rif. After the rebellion was crushed, the route to Moroccan independence changed from armed revolt to middle-class campaigning.

French colonial strategies backfire

The French tried but failed to cultivate support from groups within the Moroccan population. Initially they hoped that by educating a middle-class elite, they would find native allies who would favour binding Morocco permanently to France. In fact, the opposite happened: the educated classes of Rabat and Fez were the first to demand **reforms** from the French that would give greater rights to the Moroccans. When the government failed to respond, the demand for reforms escalated into demands for total independence.

The other French tactic for heading off opposition to their rule was to try and play off Berbers against Arabs. It was a classic attempt to "divide and rule", but it failed dismally. The French hoped that by spreading Christianity and setting up French schools in Berber areas, the Berbers would become more Europeanized, and thus allies for them against the Muslim Arabs, but the Berber–Arab division they tried to encourage was largely of their own creation, and had little resonance among Moroccans. Nor were the Berbers especially interested in becoming Christian or European. In 1930, the French tried to bring in a **Berber dahir** – a law setting up a separate legal system for the Berber areas. This was an obvious breach of the Protectorate agreement, which prevented the French from changing the Islamic nature of government, and the depth of feeling against it took the French by surprise and forced them to back down.

The rise and decline of the Istiqlal Party

Until World War II, Morocco's **nationalists** were weak and their demands were for reform of the existing system, not independence. After riots in 1937, the government was able to round up and arrest the entire executive committee of the small nationalist party. But with French capitulation in the war, the climate changed. In 1943, the party took the name of **Istiqlal** (Independence); the call for complete separation from France grew more insistent.

The loyal performance of Moroccan troops during the war had raised hopes of a fairer treatment for nationalist demands, but postwar France continued to ignore Istiqlal, exiling its leaders and banning its publications. During the postwar period, it steadily developed into a mass party – growing from 10,000 members in 1947 to 100,000 by 1951.

To some extent, the developments of the 1950s, culminating in Moroccan independence in 1956, resemble events in Algeria and Tunisia. The French first underestimated the strength of local independence movements, then tried to resist them and finally had to concede defeat. In Algeria and Tunisia, the independence parties gained power and consolidated their positions once the French had left. But in Morocco, Istiqlal was never uncontested after 1956 and the party soon began to fragment – becoming, by the 1970s, a marginal force in politics.

1661	1666	1672
British occupy Tangier, introduce tea to Morocco	Moulay Rachid takes Fez for Alaouites	Moulay Ismail becomes sultan, makes Meknes his capital

Mohammed V leads Morocco to independence

The decline and fall of Istiqlal was due mainly to the astute way in which Sultan (later King) **Mohammed V** associated himself with the independence movement. Despite threats from the French government, Mohammed became more and more outspoken in his support for independence, paralysing government operations by refusing to sign legislation. Serious rioting in 1951 persuaded the French to act: after a period of house arrest, the sultan was sent into exile in 1953 and a puppet, **Ben Arfa**, installed in his place.

This only increased Mohammed V's popularity. Seeing no way out of the spiralling violence of nationalist guerrillas and French settlers, and unable to simultaneously defend three North African colonies (with economic interests dictating that they concentrate on holding Algeria), France let Mohammed V return in 1955, and the following year, 1956, Morocco gained **independence**. Mohammed V then changed his title from sultan to **king**.

Morocco under Mohammed V

Unlike his ancestor sultans, **Mohammed V** had inherited a united country with a well-developed industrial sector, an extensive system of irrigation and a network of roads and railways. But years of French administration had left little legacy of trained Moroccan administrators. As leader of the Muslim faith in Morocco and the figurehead of independence, the king commanded huge support and influence. Istiqlal party members held key posts in his first **government**, which established schools and universities, introduced a level of regional government, and launched ambitious public works schemes. There were moves against the Sufi brotherhoods, and also against European "decadence", with a wholesale clean-up of Tangier. But the king did not perceive the Istiqlal as natural allies and instead built links with the army – with the help of **Crown Prince Hassan**, whose period as commander-in-chief was a defining moment in his political development – and with the police.

Mohammed's influence on the army would prove a decisive factor in the Moroccan state withstanding a series of **rebellions** against its authority. The most serious of these were in the Rif, in 1958–59, but there were challenges, too, in the Middle Atlas and Sahara. The king's standing and the army's efficiency stood the test. In party politics, Mohammed's principal act was to lend his support to the **Mouvement Populaire** (MP), a moderate party set up to represent the Berbers, and for the king a useful counterweight to Istiqlal. In 1959, the strategy paid its first dividend. Istiqlal was seriously weakened by a split which hived off the more left-wing members into a separate party, the **Union Nationale des Forces Populaires** (UNFP) under Mehdi Ben Barka. There had always been a certain tension within Istiqlal between the moderates and those favouring a more radical policy, in association with the unions. A tendency towards parties dividing within and among themselves has been apparent in Moroccan politics ever since, helping to maintain the palace's leading role in the political arena.

Hassan II (1961–99)

Mohammed V's death in 1961 brought to the throne his son **Hassan II**, whose **autocratic rule** had a very thin veneer of parliamentary politics.

1727	1757	1792
Moulay Ismail's death leads to political fragmentation	Mohammed III becomes sultan	Moulay Slimane becomes sultan

Even before independence, in a 1955 speech, Mohammed V had promised to set up "democratic institutions resulting from the holding of free elections". But it was only in 1962 that the country's first **constitution** was put to, and approved by, a referendum. The constitution was drafted in such a way as to favour the pro-monarchy parties, setting the pattern that was to prevail up until the end of Hassan's reign.

The 1960s were marked by the fragility of Morocco's political party structure and the authorities' greater enthusiasm for using bullets and torture chamber rather than the ballot box to handle opposition. This mood was reflected in the **Ben Barka affair**, when Mehdi Ben Barka, leader of the socialist opposition party UNFP, was assassinated in Paris, with apparent connivance between the governments of Morocco and France.

The opposition subsequently split, with the largest element of the UNFP going on to form the **Union Socialiste des Forces Populaires** (USFP). These parties were largely ineffectual, especially after Hassan announced a new constitution in 1970, following a period of emergency rule. Events in 1971–72 showed where the real threat to the monarchy lay.

In July 1971, a group of soldiers broke into the royal palace in Skhirat in an attempt to stage a **coup**; more than one hundred people were killed, but in the confusion Hassan escaped. The following year another attempt was launched, as the king's private jet was attacked by fighters of the Moroccan Air Force. Again, Hassan had a very narrow escape – his pilot was able to convince the attacking aircraft by radio that the king had already died. The former interior minister, General Mohamed Oufkir disappeared soon after (apparently murdered in custody) and the armed forces were restructured.

The Saharan conflict and the UMA

Hassan wanted a cause similar to the struggle for independence that had brought such prestige to his father. That cause was provided in 1975, when the Spanish finally decided to pull out of their colony in the **Western Sahara** (see page 488).

In the 1950s the nationalist Istiqlal party had laid claim to the Spanish Sahara, as well as to Mauritania and parts of Algeria and Mali, as part of its quest for a "Greater Morocco". By 1975, Hassan had patched up the border dispute with Algeria and recognized the independent government in Mauritania, but he retained a more realistic design – Moroccan control of the Spanish Sahara.

Spanish withdrawal from the Western Sahara in 1975 coincided with General Franco's final illness and Hassan timed his move perfectly, sending some 350,000 Moroccan civilians southwards on **El Massira** – the "**Green March**" – to the Sahara. Spain could either go to war with Morocco by attacking the advancing Moroccans or withdraw without holding a referendum on independence, which they had agreed to call after UN pressure. Hassan's bluff worked, and the popular unrest of the 1960s and the coup attempts of 1971–72 were forgotten under a wave of patriotism. But the Polisario guerrillas who had led the fight against Spanish rule (see page 488) now began a campaign against Moroccan occupation. Despite early Polisario successes, the Moroccans managed to assert control over most of the territory, and all of its economically important areas, but in 1988 the two sides agreed a ceasefire under UN auspices, on the principle that a **referendum** would be held on the territory's future.

That promised referendum has yet to take place, but the dispute has damaged Morocco diplomatically; in particular it has left her isolated in African politics since the

1859	1873	1880
Spanish occupy Tetouan	Moulay Hassan (Hassan I) becomes sultan	Madrid Conference confirms Europeans' "protection" rights

African Union recognized the Polisario-declared Saharawi Arab Democratic Republic, prompting Morocco to leave. Algeria strongly backed Polisario, and the resulting friction between Morocco and Algeria has hampered efforts towards regional unity. In 1989, Algeria, Libya, Mauritania, Morocco and Tunisia formed an **Arab Maghreb Union**, known by its evocative acronym UMA (from the French Union du Maghreb Arabe, but sounding like the Arabic word *'umma*, or community), but the Union has been stymied by Moroccan–Algerian hostility arising largely from the Saharan question. In 1994 this sparked the closure of the Algerian–Moroccan border, which has not reopened since.

Economic and social problems

The Saharan war proved to be only a temporary distraction from discontent in Morocco itself. Moreover, the occupation of the Western Sahara and its demands on the economy added to the very problems it was designed to divert attention from. By 1981, some sixty percent of the population were living below the poverty level, **unemployment** ran at approximately twenty percent (forty percent among the young) and a fifth of the urban population lived in shantytowns, or *bidonvilles*.

Popular unrest erupted in the 1984 "**bread riots**" in cities across the country, most notably in Marrakesh, Oujda, Nador and Tetouan. The riots were triggered when the government raised the prices of staple foods following pressure from the International Monetary Fund (IMF) to repay its **burgeoning debt** while phosphate prices were depressed and the country was suffering one of its regular **droughts**. King Hassan had to intervene personally to reverse the decision and, in the opinion of many analysts, save his monarchy from a populist rising.

Dissatisfaction with Hassan's regime in the 1980s and 1990s surfaced in the form of protests by unemployed graduates (despite the dangers of political protest in Hassan's police state), and sometimes violent incidents in the kingdom's universities. In 1990, a general strike called by the CDT trade union federation led to riots in Fez and Tangier, and the decade that followed saw Morocco embark on one of Africa's biggest **privatization** drives.

Change and elections

The opposition, which had been quiet through much of the 1980s, started to reassert itself in the 1990s, as traditional opposition parties showed revived enthusiasm for challenging the government – though not the king. In 1992, a leading dissident, Abraham Serfaty, was one of many well-known figures in a **release of political prisoners** that included many soldiers held, since the 1972 failed coup, in a dungeon prison at Tazmamart in the High Atlas. Several former student radicals who survived imprisonment and torture in the 1960s, '70s and '80s went on to hold positions of responsibility in the local press, universities and even government departments.

In 1996, Hassan held a referendum on constitutional reforms, opening the way for a new bicameral parliamentary system. Local and national elections in 1997 seemed to offer the prospect of genuine power for opposition politicians. Disappointingly, the elections produced a lacklustre campaign and much voter apathy, as a three-way split gave right-wing, centrist and left-wing/nationalist groupings a similar number of seats in the lower house of parliament. Hassan appointed as prime minister the USFP leader

1900	1907	1912
Death of Bou Ahmed leaves Morocco without effective ruler	French occupy Oujda	Treaty of Fez splits Morocco between France and Spain

Abderrahmane Youssoufi at the head of a coalition government that included both USFP and Istiqlal ministers.

One notable factor in the 1997 general election was that Islamist deputies were voted into parliament for the first time, under the Mouvement Populaire Constitutionnel et Démocratique (**MPCD**) banner, but many saw the administration's acceptance of the **MPCD**, who stand at the moderate end of the Islamist spectrum, as a classic piece of Moroccan divide-and-rule, aimed at splitting the Islamist movement.

Mohammed VI (1999–)

On Hassan's death in 1999, his son **Mohammed VI** quickly emerged from his father's shadow, ushering in a new style of rule with widespread popular support. From the very start he made clear his more inclusive agenda by visiting the **troubled north** (long ignored by Hassan), restoring **civil rights** to those remaining political prisoners not covered by previous amnesties (with over eight thousand released in first-year amnesties), and promising a more **relaxed and consensual** form of rule. He sacked Hassan's powerful but unpopular right-hand man, Minister of State for the Interior **Driss Basri**, and allowed a number of high-profile dissidents to return to Morocco, most notably leftist **Abraham Serfaty**, whom he appointed as a personal adviser. In May 2000, he made headlines by freeing his father's most implacable critic, **Abdessalam Yassine**, leader of the banned **Al-Adl wal Ihsane** (Justice and Charity) movement. Dissent is not always tolerated, however, and the king's forces have on occasion clamped down rather harshly on street protests, notably a protest by unemployed graduates in Rabat in June 2000, while newspapers are still prosecuted under laws against "undermining" the monarchy or Morocco's "territorial integrity". Nonetheless, the tenor of Mohammed's reign has been to extend democracy, human rights and free speech, albeit in a cautious fashion.

Legal reforms

In March 2000, the king announced a **National Action Plan**, whose main feature was a Family Law that radically improved the **position of women** under Moroccan law, banning polygamy and introducing more equal family rights. The proposal sparked a backlash by Islamists, who mustered around a quarter of a million supporters at a march in Casablanca to protest the proposals, and the government responded by setting up a consultative commission to consider the question more carefully. After due consideration, parliament decided to go ahead with the proposals, which came into force in 2004, giving women greater legal rights in Morocco than anywhere else in the Muslim world, and more on a par with those of women in Europe.

The birth of a son and heir, Prince Moulay Hassan, in 2003, gave the king an excuse to release some nine thousand prisoners and remit the sentences of thousands more. The same year also saw a major extension of **rights for Berber speakers**, whose languages were taught for the first time in schools in the 2003–4 academic year. Programmes in Berber are also now broadcast on TV.

Terrorism

The Moroccan government was swift to condemn the September 2001 **attacks by al-Qaeda** on the Pentagon and the New York World Trade Center, but the apparent

1921	1942	1943
Abd el Krim launches Rif revolt against colonial rule	Operation Torch – American troops land at Mehdiya, Mohammedia and Safi	Istiqlal Party founded

MOROCCAN STREET NAMES

Moroccan streets are often named after well-known historical figures, events and dates. Transliteration from Arabic into the Roman alphabet means that there are often many variations of the same name.

Abd el Krim el Khattabi Leader of the 1921–27 Rif war against the Spanish (see page 124).

Al Jamia al Arabi The Arab League, founded in Egypt in 1945.

Allal Ben Abdallah House-painter from Guercif shot down in 1953 after driving an open-topped car into a royal procession and attacking France's puppet sultan Ben Arfa with a kitchen knife.

Al Massira al Khadra/La Marche Verte The Green March of November 1975 to occupy the Western Sahara (see page 488).

Bir Anzarane Town in the Western Sahara and site of fierce 1979 battle between Morocco and the Polisario.

El Farabi Islamic philosopher (870–950) from Farab in Uzbekistan who tried to harmonize Greek philosophy with Islamic thinking.

El Houria Freedom.

El Mansour Eddahbi Saadian sultan 1578–1603.

F.A.R. (Forces Armées Royales) The armed forces.

Ferhat Hachad Tunisian trade union leader and Arab nationalist murdered in 1952 by extremist French settlers.

Hassan II King 1975–99, who ordered that all the country's main streets be named after him.

Ibn Batouta Fourteenth-century Tanjawi traveller who visited China, India and most of the Islamic world.

Ibn Khaldoun Tunisian historian (1332–1406), who first proposed a cyclical view of history.

Ibn Rochd One of Islam's greatest philosophers (1126–98), also known as Averroes, who was based in Marrakesh and doctor to Yacoub el Mansour.

Ibn Toumert/Mehdi Ibn Toumert Founder of the Almohads (see page 356).

Ibn Zaidoun Eleventh-century Andalusian poet.

Istiqlal Independence; also the name of Morocco's first political party (see page 505).

Mohammed Ben Abdallah/Sidi Mohammed Ben Abdallah Grandson of Moulay Ismail, sultan 1757–90.

Mohammed V Sultan and subsequently king 1927–53 and 1955–61 (see page 506).

Mohammed VI King since 1999.

Mohammed Zerktouni Armed resistance leader, accused of killing twenty people in a 1953 bomb attack on Casablanca's central market, who took cyanide to avoid giving information under torture.

---

involvement of pro-Islamist Moroccans in those attacks and in the train bombs that killed over two hundred people in Madrid in March 2004 severely embarrassed the Moroccan authorities. In Morocco itself, May 2003 saw attacks on Jewish and Western targets by **suicide bombers** in Casablanca, which resulted in the deaths of 33 people (plus the bombers). The attack severely dented fundamentalist appeal, but a hardcore of support for such actions continues to exist. The authorities reacted to the bombings by rounding up over 1500 people suspected of involvement with militant groups, of whom several hundred were given prison sentences ranging from three months to thirty years. 2011 saw another bomb attack, this time on

1956	1961	1973	1975
Morocco gains independence under Mohammed V	Hassan II becomes king	Polisario founded in Spanish (Western) Sahara	Green March: occupation of Western Sahara

Mokhtar Soussi Poet and intellectual who inspired the nationalist movement during the French occupation.
Moulay Abdallah/Prince Moulay Abdallah Younger son of Mohammed V, brother of Hassan II.
Moulay el Cherif/Moulay Rachid First Alaouite sultan, ruled 1666–72 (see page 501.
Moulay Hassan/Hassan I Sultan 1873–94 (see page 502).
Moulay Idriss Moulay Idriss I (788–91) or Moulay Idriss II (804–28), Morocco's first Arab rulers (see page 496).
Moulay Ismail Second Alaouite sultan (1672–1727; see page 501).
Moulay Youssef French-appointed sultan (1912–27), brother of Moulay Hafid, father of Mohammed V and great-grandfather of Mohammed VI.
Moussa Ibn Noussar General who consolidated the Arab conquest of Morocco in the eighth century (see page 496).
Oqba Ibn Nafi Arab general who brought Islam to Morocco (see page 496).
Oued el Makhazine Site of the Battle of the Three Kings (see page 500).
Salah Eddine el Ayoubi Kurdish-born Islamic leader, known in English as Saladin, who ruled Egypt and Syria 1171–93, and recaptured Jerusalem from the Crusaders in 1187.
Tarik Ibn Ziad Berber chieftain who led the 711 Islamic invasion of Spain and gave his name to Gibraltar – Jebel (mount) Tarik.
Yacoub el Mansour Third Almohad sultan (1184–99; see page 498).
Youssef Ben Tachfine First Almoravid sultan (1062–1106; see page 498).

DATES

January 11, 1944 The Istiqlal party issued a manifesto demanding independence.
February 29, 1960 The Agadir earthquake (see page 421).
March 2, 1956 French recognition of Moroccan independence.
August 16, 1953 Anti-French riots in Casablanca, Rabat, Marrakesh and Oujda.
August 20, 1953 Mohammed V was deposed by the French and exiled on the eve of Aïd el Kebir.
November 6, 1975 The Green March (see page 507).
November 16, 1955 Mohammed V's return from exile.
November 18, 1927 Mohammed V's accession to the throne.
November 18, 1955 Officially considered independence day (though full independence was achieved the following year).

the *Argana Café* in Marrakesh, a tourist favourite, in which seventeen people were killed.

Elections
In the **2002 elections**, the moderate Islamist MPCD, now renamed the PJD (**Parti de la Justice et du Développement**), took thirteen percent of the vote and emerged as Morocco's third biggest political party after the USFP and Istiqlal, which formed an administration together with representatives of four other parties, all essentially organizations for the distribution of patronage, whose ministries were largely staffed

1984	1989	1999	2004
Bread riots break out	Arab Maghreb Union founded	Mohammed VI becomes king	Family Law extends women's legal rights

by their own people. The same pattern continued after the **2007 elections**, in which Istiqlal regained its position as the largest party in parliament – the fact that it could do so with just over a tenth of the vote shows just how fragmented the party system was. Istiqlal leader Abbas el Fassi took over as prime minister at the head of a four-party coalition that included the USFP.

In 2011, the **Arab Spring**, which evolved out of revolutions in Tunisia and Egypt, sparked large demonstrations for jobs and democracy across Morocco. On 20 February, a large pro-democracy **demonstration** in Rabat quickly spread nationwide, with protests in all major cities and many minor ones. The king responded on 9 March by announcing a commission on the constitution, which swiftly reported in June, proposing that elections should be binding, with the king obliged to appoint as prime minister the leader of the largest party. Women's rights were also entrenched in the constitution, and Berber joined Arabic as an official language. The constitution was approved by referendum in July. When **elections under the new constitution** were held in November 2011, turnout rose from 37 percent to 45 percent, and the victors were the PJD, who took 107 of the 395 seats in parliament. As specified in the new constitution – their leader, **Abdelilah Benkirane**, became prime minister, forming a coalition with Istiqlal and two smaller parties. Istiqlal withdrew in 2013, but the coalition was patched up with a few smaller parties. The PJD entrenched its position in the **2016 election**, taking 125 seats, with the royalist Party of Authenticity and Modernity (PAM) forming the main opposition. Saadeddine Othmani took over as prime minister at the head of a PJD-led opposition.

The PJD suffered a complete reversal of fortunes in the 2021 election when they lost a whopping 90 per cent of their seats and became just a minor party. The Naional Rally of Independents won the majority of the seats and Aziz Akhannouch became the prime minister.

On the 8th September 2023 a large earthquake of magnitude 6.8 struck southern Morocco (the epicentre was 70km southwest of Marrakesh) killing more than 2,800 people, injuring many thousands more and leaving a trail of destruction across the remote mountainous areas it struck, as well as parts of Marrakesh.

Prospects

Mohammed VI seems to have done enough to head off any movement for radical change, although many issues remain **unresolved**. The king still has huge powers which he has not surrendered to elected politicians: he still runs the army, the security forces and the religious establishment, and control of the economy and the country's wealth remains in the hands of a small elite strongly linked to the palace. The Western Sahara question is still unsolved, and many people remain extremely cynical about the political systemwhile there are still massive problems of poverty, unemployment and unequal wealth distribution to deal with. However, while many would like to see the pace of reform stepped up, they can now generally voice their demands legally, and peaceful demonstrations have become a regular part of the political landscape. True, people are still arrested if they cross the line – calling for abolition of the monarchy, for example, or, in the Western Sahara, for independence – and press freedom is still heavily restricted, but despite this, the system has become just about inclusive enough to allow supporters of reform to campaign within it rather than being a threat to it.

2010	2016	2021	2023
Tamazight TV, first Berber-language Moroccan TV channel, goes on air	PJD wins second election in a row	PJD decimated in elections. National Rally of Independents forms government	Major earthquake hits southern Morocco resulting in widespread destruction and loss of life

Islam in Morocco

It's difficult to get any grasp of Morocco, and even more so of Moroccan history, without first knowing something of **Islam**. What follows is a very basic background: some theory, some history and an idea of Morocco's place in the modern Islamic world.

Practice and belief

Islam was founded by **Mohammed** (also spelt Muhammad), a merchant from the wealthy city of Mecca, now in Saudi Arabia. In about 609 AD, he began to receive divine messages, and continued to do so for the rest of his life. After his death, these were collated, and form the **Koran** (*Qur'an*). Muslims consider Mohammed to be the final prophet of the same God who is worshipped by Jews and Christians, and Islam recognizes all the prophets of the biblical Old Testament as his predecessors, and also regards Jesus (*Aïssa* in Arabic) as a prophet, but not as the Son of God.

The distinctive feature of Islam is its directness – there is no intermediary between man and God in the form of an institutionalized priesthood or complicated liturgy, as in Christianity; and worship, in the form of prayer, is a direct and personal communication with God.

The Pillars of Faith

Islam has five essential requirements, called "**Pillars of faith**": prayer (*salat*); the pilgrimage to Mecca (*hadj*); the Ramadan fast (*sanm*); almsgiving (*zakat*); and, most fundamental of all, the acceptance that "There is no God but God and Mohammed is His Prophet" (*shahada*). The Pillars of Faith are central to Muslim life, articulating and informing daily existence. **Prayers** are performed five times daily, at sunset (when the Islamic day begins), nightfall, dawn, noon and afternoon, and can be performed anywhere, but preferably in a mosque (*jemaa* in Arabic). In the past, and even today in some places, a *muezzin* would climb his minaret each time and summon the faithful. Nowadays, the call is likely to be pre-recorded, but this most distinctive of Islamic sounds has a beauty all its own, especially when neighbouring *muezzins* are audible simultaneously. Their message is simplicity itself: "God is most great (*Allah o Akhbar*). I testify that there is no God but Allah. I testify that Mohammed is His Prophet. Come to prayer, come to security. God is most great." Another phrase is added in the morning: "Prayer is better than sleep".

Prayers are preceded by ritual washing. The worshipper then removes their shoes and, facing Mecca (the direction indicated in a mosque by the mihrab), recites the Fatina, the first chapter of the Koran: "Praise be to God, Lord of the worlds, the Compassionate, the Merciful, King of the Day of Judgement. We worship you and seek your aid. Guide us on the straight path, the path of those on whom you have bestowed your Grace, not the path of those who incur your anger nor of those who go astray." The same words are then repeated twice in the prostrate position, with some interjections of *Allah o Akhbar*. The prostrate position symbolizes the worshipper's submission to God (Islam literally means "submission"), and the sight of thousands of people going through the same motions simultaneously in a mosque is a powerful one. On Friday, believers try to attend prayers in their local grand mosque, where the whole community comes together in worship, led by an *imam* (much like a Protestant pastor), who may also deliver the *khutba*, or sermon.

Ramadan is the name of the ninth month in the lunar Islamic calendar, during which believers must fast between sunrise and sundown, abstaining from food, drink, cigarettes and sex. Only children, pregnant women and warriors engaged in a *jihad* (holy war) are exempt. Though the day is thus hard, nights are a time of celebration.

The pilgrimage, or **hadj**, to Mecca is an annual event, with millions flocking to Mohammed's birthplace from all over the world. Here they go through several days of rituals, the central one being a sevenfold circumambulation of the Kaba, before kissing a black stone set in its wall. Islam requires that all believers go on a *hadj* as often as is practically possible, but for the poor it may be a once-in-a-lifetime occasion, and is sometimes replaced by a series of visits to lesser, local shrines – in Morocco, for instance, to Fez and Moulay Idriss.

Islam's development in Morocco

Morocco was virtually untouched by the **Sunni–Shia conflict** that split the Muslim world – but the country's unusual geographical and social circumstances have conspired to tip the balance away from official orthodoxy. In the eighth century, many Berbers were attracted to the dissident **Kharijite** strain of Islam, which rejected the Sunni and Shi'ite argument that the leader of the faithful had to be an Arab, and Sijilmasa (Rissani) became the capital of a powerful Kharijite kingdom. Subsequently, Moroccans have in principle been almost universally Sunni, but Sufism and maraboutism became very strong within the religion.

Marabouts

Sufism is the idea that, in addition to following religious rules, people can personally get closer to God by leading a spiritual rather than a materialistic lifestyle, and even by chanting and meditating to achieve a trance-like state. Everywhere in Morocco, as well as elsewhere in North Africa, the countryside is dotted with small domed **koubbas** – the tombs of **marabouts**, Sufi holy men (though the term is also used for the *koubba*) – which became centres of worship and pilgrimage. This elevation of individuals goes against strict Islamic teaching, but probably derives from the Berbers' pre-Islamic tendency to focus worship round individual holy men.

More prosperous cults would also endow educational institutions attached to the *koubba*, known as **zaouias**, which provided an alternative to the official education given in urban medersas (Koranic schools). These inevitably posed a threat to the authority of the urban hierarchy, and as rural cults extended their influence, some became so popular that they endowed their saints with genealogies traced back to the Prophet. The title accorded to these men and their descendants was **Shereef**, and many grew into strong political forces. The classic example in Morocco is the tomb of Moulay Idriss – in the eighth century just a local *marabout*, but eventually the base of the **Idrissid clan**, a centre of enormous influence that reached far beyond its rural origins.

The most influential *marabouts* spawned Sufi **brotherhoods**, whose members meet to chant, play music, meditate, and thus seek personal union with God. This is particularly an important part of the **moussem**, an annual festival associated with each *marabout*. The most famous and flamboyant Moroccan Sufi brotherhood is that of **Sidi Mohammed Ben Aïssa**. Born in Souss in the fifteenth century, he travelled in northern Morocco before settling down as a teacher in Meknes and founding a *zaouia*. His powers of mystical healing became famous there, and he provoked enough official suspicion to be exiled briefly to the desert – where he again revealed his exceptional powers by proving himself immune to scorpions, snakes, live flames and other hostile manifestations. His followers tried to achieve the same state of grace. The Aissaoua brotherhood made itself notorious with displays of eating scorpions, walking on hot coals and other ecstatic practices designed to bring union with God.

Towards crisis

With all its different forms, Islam permeated every aspect of the country's pre-twentieth-century life. Unlike Christianity, at least Protestant Christianity, which to some extent has accepted the separation of church and state, Islam sees no such distinction. **Civil law** was provided by the *sharia*, the religious law contained in the Koran, and **intellectual life** by the *msids* (Koranic primary schools where the 6200 verses were learned by heart) and by the great medieval mosque universities, of which the Kairaouine in Fez (together with the Zitoura in Tunis and the Al Azhar in Cairo) was the most important in the Arab world.

At first, Islam brought a great scientific revolution, uniting the traditions of Greece and Rome with those of India and Iran, and then developing them while Christian Europe rejected the sciences of pagan philosophers. As Europe went through its Renaissance, however, it was Islam that started to atrophy, as the religious authorities became increasingly suspicious of any challenge to established belief, and actively discouraged innovation. At first this did not matter in political terms, but as the Islamic world fell behind in science and learning, Europe was able to take advantage of its now superior technology. Napoleon's expedition to Egypt in 1798 marked the beginning of a century in which virtually every Islamic country came under the control of a **European power**. Because East–West rivalry had always been viewed in religious terms, the nineteenth and twentieth centuries saw something of a **crisis in religious confidence**. Why had Islam's former power now passed to infidel foreigners?

Fundamentalism

Reactions and answers veered between those who felt that Islam should try to incorporate some of the West's materialism, and those who held that Islam should turn its back on the West, purify itself of all corrupt additions and thus rediscover its former power. As colonies of European powers, Muslim nations had little chance of putting any such ideas into effective practice. But **decolonization**, and the discovery of oil in the Middle East, brought the Islamic world face to face with the question of its own spiritual identity. How should it deal with Western values and influence, now that it could afford – both politically and economically – almost total rejection? A return to the totality of Islam – **fundamentalism** – is one option. It has a reactionary side, harking back to an imagined time of perfection under the Prophet and the early caliphs, but it is also radical in its rejection of colonialism and materialism, and its most vehement adherents tend to be young rather than old.

Islam in Modern Morocco

In Morocco today, Islam is the official state religion, and King Mohammed's secular status is interwoven with his role as "commander of the faithful". Internationally too, he plays a leading role. Meetings of the Islamic Conference Organization are frequently held in Morocco and students from as far afield as Central Asia come to study Islam at Fez University. For all these indications of Islamic solidarity, though, **state policy** remains distinctly moderate – sometimes in the face of fundamentalist pressure. The 2004 law on the status of women is a good example of this: 100,000 people marched in Rabat to support the new law, and over 200,000 marched in Casablanca against it, a sign of increasing **polarization** on religious questions, not unlike that in the United States.

In the cities, there has long been tension between those for and against secularization, as well as a large body of urban poor, for whom Islamic fundamentalism can seem to offer solutions. In some circles, Islam is becoming very relaxed; in Casablanca, Rabat, El Jadida and Marrakesh, young people of both sexes can be seen socializing together, young women no longer wear the veil, and have exchanged their frumpy cover-alls for flattering, and even sexy clothes, while young couples go to nightclubs and even drink socially. But against this, the number of people going to pray at mosques is on the up, and among the poor especially, Islam is becoming a mark of pride and respectability. That this is reflected in politics is not surprising, and the moderate Islamist PJD (founded in 1998) has gradually developed into a mainstream party, winning the 2011 and 2016 elections, although any programme involving enforcement of religious strictures would be strongly resented by secular Moroccans.

In the **countryside**, religious attitudes have changed less over the past two generations. Religious brotherhoods such as the Aissaoua have declined since the beginning of the century, when they were still very powerful, and the influence of mystics generally has fallen. As the official histories put it, popular credulity in Morocco provided an ideal setting for charlatans as well as saviours, and much of this has now passed. All the same, the rhythms of rural life still revolve around local *marabouts*, and the annual moussems, or festivals-cum-pilgrimages, are still vital and impressive displays.

Moroccan architecture

As befits a Muslim country, Morocco's architecture is dominated by Islamic religious buildings, most particularly mosques, but also *zaouias* (the shrines of local saints) and medersas (religious schools). Many features of Moroccan architecture – such as the familiar pointed horseshoe arches of doorways and city gates – come from the Middle East and arrived with the Arabs. Though the style has been refined, and decorative details added over the centuries, the country's architectural traditions have changed little since then. The colonial period did, however, make its mark, and there are some particularly fine examples of Art Deco and Art Nouveau styles to be found, though they are confined to the French-built Villes Nouvelles, leaving the traditional Medinas often remarkably untouched.

Brief history

As far as we can tell from their only surviving building of note – the Koubba Ba'adiyn in Marrakesh – it was the **Almoravids** who first used many of the decorative elements that have become so typical of the country's architecture, including merlons (battlement-like castellations), a ribbed dome, and stylized plant-inspired designs resembling pine cones and palm fronds. The **Almohads** introduced the classic Moroccan square minaret, as seen in the Koutoubia at Marrakesh, the Hassan Tower in Rabat, and the Giralda at Seville in Spain. Architectural styles were refined but not radically altered under the **Merenids** and the **Saadians**, who brought in techniques of zellij tilework and carved stucco and cedar wood.

The next big change came with the **colonial period**, when European styles – and the Europeanized North African style known as **Mauresque** – began to appear in the Villes Nouvelles of larger cities, most notably in Casablanca. **Art Nouveau** made a major impact on the Spanish enclave of Melilla, and **Art Deco** similarly dominates the former Spanish enclave of Sidi Ifni, as well as having had a major impact on downtown Casa.

Concrete-and-glass modern architecture has not made many inroads in Morocco, though you'll see it on the outskirts of Casablanca if you're coming in from the south. Nor has post-World War II European architecture especially impressed Moroccans – one of Le Corbusier's brutalist blocks was demolished in the centre of Meknes in 2004 without much comment. Morocco's most impressive modern building, the Mosquée Hassan II in Casablanca, was built using completely traditional styles and techniques.

Mosques

Mosques follow the same basic plan regardless of their age or size. All mosques face Mecca, the birthplace of Islam and the direction in which all Muslims pray. This direction is indicated by an alcove called the **mihrab**, set in the Mecca-facing *qibla* wall. Next to the mihrab in larger mosques is a pulpit, usually wooden, called the **minbar**. Larger mosques will also have a **courtyard**, often with a fountain for ablutions, but the *qibla* end is taken up by a covered **prayer hall**. The **minaret** is a tower from which, back in the day, the *muezzin* would climb to call the faithful to prayer. Moroccan mosques invariably have only one minaret, and since the days of the Almohads in the twelfth century, almost all Moroccan minarets have been square in shape, with a ratio of 5:1 height to width.

A **zaouia** is a shrine or Sufi retreat built around the tomb of a *marabout*, or Islamic saint. It is typically a small, whitewashed building with a small dome or *koubba*, often found among the ordinary tombs in a graveyard. A larger *zaouia* may have a prayer hall attached, and function like a mosque. It will certainly have a mihrab, though not usually a minaret.

Morocco's most important mosque architecture includes the Koutoubia in Marrakesh, the Kairaouine Mosque and the Zaouia of Moulay Idriss in Fez, the Hassan Tower in Rabat, and the Mosquée Hassan II in Casablanca. Non-Muslims, unfortunately, are not allowed inside most mosques.

Medersas

A **medersa** (or madrasa) is a religious school where students come to study Islam, and unlike mosques, medersas are open to non-Muslims. Typically they consist of a large courtyard, with rooms around it for teaching, and rooms upstairs where the students sleep. The medersas of Fez in particular, such as Bou Inania and the Attarin, are richly decorated with carved stucco and cedar wood, and zellij mosaic tilework. Because Islam is suspicious of representational art (lest it lead to idol worship), religious buildings such as medersas are decorated with geometric designs and calligraphy, the latter almost always consisting of quotations from the Koran. Other architecturally interesting medersas include the Abou el Hassan in Salé, and the Ben Youssef in Marrakesh.

Traditional homes

People's **houses** in Morocco do not look outward, like a Western home, but rather inward, to an enclosed patio, an arrangement that guards privacy, particularly for women, who traditionally observed purdah and did not allow men outside the family to see them. Rooms are arranged around the **patio**, usually on two floors with a roof terrace. At one time, most homes would have had a well in the middle of the patio to supply drinking water. A grand house or mansion might have a whole garden in the patio, typically with orange trees, and sometimes a second patio too. The ceilings would be wooden and often beautifully painted.

The very best way to take in Moroccan domestic architecture is to stay in an old riad, particularly in a city such as Marrakesh or Fez. Second best is to visit one of the palatial restaurants in those two cities. In Marrakesh, the Bahia Palace and Dar el Glaoui are also worth a visit.

Kasbahs

A **kasbah** can be a walled residential district (as in Fez), or the citadel of a walled city (as in Tangier and Marrakesh), but in southern Morocco, most impressively in Telouet, Tamdaght and the Skoura Oasis, a kasbah is a fortified citadel, something like a castle, where everyone in a village could take refuge in times of trouble (see page 364). Built of mud-bricks, these kasbahs are rectangular structures with turrets at each corner, usually decorated with Berber motifs.

Wildlife and the environment

Few countries in the Mediterranean region can match the variety and quality of the wildlife habitats to be found in Morocco. The three bands of mountains – Rif, Middle Atlas and High Atlas – with the Mediterranean coastal strip to the north, and the desert to the south, provide a wide variety of habitat types, from coastal cliffs, sand dunes and estuarine marshlands to subalpine forests and grasslands, to the semi-arid Sahel and true desert areas of the south. The climate is similarly diverse: warm and humid along the coastal zones, relatively cooler at altitude within the Atlas ranges and distinctly hotter and drier south of the High Atlas. Not surprisingly, the plant and animal life in Morocco is accordingly parochial, species distributions being closely related to the habitat and climate types to which they are adapted.

Birds

In addition to a unique range of **resident bird species**, distributed throughout the country on the basis of vegetation and climatic zonation, the periods of late March/April and September/October provide the additional sight of vast **bird migrations**.

Large numbers of birds which have overwintered south of the Sahara migrate northwards in the spring to breed in Europe, completing their return passage through Morocco in the autumn, and some north European species choose Morocco to avoid the harshness of the northern winter. These movements can form a dramatic spectacle in the skies, dense flocks of birds moving in procession through bottleneck areas such as Tangier and Ceuta where sea crossings are at their shortest.

Among **field guides** to Moroccan birdlife, the definitive tome – though not easy to find – is Michael Thévenot, Rae Vernon and Patrick Bergier's *The Birds of Morocco* (British Ornithologists' Union, UK), while Patrick and Fédora Bergier's *A Birdwatcher's Guide to Morocco* (Prion Press, UK) is an excellent practical guidebook that includes site maps and species lists. Dave Gosney's two *Finding Birds in Morocco* booklets (Easybirder, UK) – one on the desert, the other on coastal and *mountain* sites – contains much detailed information on where to spot different birds, complete with maps and GPS co-ordinates, but unless you can recognize the species yourself, it would need to be used in conjunction with a field guide.

Resident species

Coastal and marine species include the familiar moorhen and less familiar crested coot, an incongruous bird which, when breeding, resembles its northern European relation but with an additional pair of bright red knobs on either side of its white facial shield. Other species include the diminutive little ringed plover and rock dove.

South of the High Atlas are **desert species**, such as the sandgrouse (spotted, crowned, pin-tailed and black-bellied varieties), stone curlew, cream-coloured courser and Houbara bustard – the latter standing over two feet in height. Other well-represented groups include wheatears (four varieties), larks (seven varieties) and finches, buntings, warblers, corvids, jays, magpies, choughs and ravens (crow family), tits (primarily blue, great and coal) and owls (barn, eagle, tawny and little).

Raptors (birds of prey) provide an enticing roll call of resident species, including red- and black-shouldered kite, long-legged buzzard, Bonelli's, golden and tawny eagles, Barbary, lanner and peregrine falcons and the more familiar kestrel.

KEY WILDLIFE SITES

Features on key Moroccan wildlife, and especially bird habitats are to be found throughout the Guide. They include:

Agadir/Oued Souss Riverbank that attracts waders and wildfowl, migrant warblers and Barbary partridge. See page 430

Aguelmane Azigza Middle Atlas occasional inland lake and forest: hawfinch, diving duck and marbled teal in autumn/winter. See page 215

Boulmane: Desert Hammada Atlas agama and fringe-toed lizard; specialist bird species such as cream-coloured courser, red-rumped wheatear and thick-billed lark; houbara bustard. See page 522

Cedar forests south of Azrou Species include green-eyed lizard and chameleon; butterflies from April onwards; Barbary apes; Moroccan woodpecker and booted eagle. See page 211

Dayet Aaoua Another Middle Atlas occasional lake: flocks of grebes, crested coot, grey heron and cattle egret; migrant birds of prey include red kite. See page 207

Essaouira Coastal dunes, river and offshore islands attract waders and egrets; also Eleonora's Falcon between May and October. See page 280

Fez Evening roost of egret and alpine swift; white stork on rooftop nests of walls. See page 154

Jebel Tazzeka National Park Where the Rif merges with the Middle Atlas: slopes covered in cork oak and woodland; butterflies from late May/early June, and birds such as the hoopoe. See page 146

Jebel Toubkal National Park High Atlas mountains: sights include Moorish gecko, rare butterflies; Moussier's redstart and crimson-winged finch, both unique to North African mountains; hooped-petticoat daffodils, *romulea* and various other bulbs in spring. See page 339

Merja Zerga Large wetland area that guarantees good bird numbers at all times of year, especially gulls and terns (including the Caspian tern). See page 96

Merzouga Sandy (or "true") desert: all-too-brief spring bloom of pink asphodels and mauve statice; Algerian sand lizard and Berber skink; birds include fulvous babbler, blue-cheeked bee-eater, the rare desert sparrow and even Arabian bustard. See page 412

Nador/Kariet Arkmane/Ras el Ma Salt marshes and coastal sand dunes, good for waders and gulls. See page 138

Oualidia Mix of ragged, rocky coast, sands, lagoon, marshes and saltpans. Good for small waders. See page 271

Oued Massa Important inland lagoon and reserve that is perhaps the country's number one bird habitat. See page 430

Oued Moulouya Lagoons and sand spits, with outstanding birds. See page 138

Todra Gorge Marsh frog and green toad; ground squirrel; common bulbul, black wheatear, blue rock thrush and rock dove. Bonelli's eagles nest in the gorge. See page 397

Migrant species

Summer visitors include, among marine and coastal types, Manx shearwater, Eleonora's falcon and the bald ibis – for whom Tamri (see page 430) has one of its few remaining breeding colonies in the world. Mountain species include the small Egyptian vulture and several of the hirundines (swallows and martins) and their close relatives, the swifts, such as little swift, red-rumped swallow and the more familiar house martin. A particularly colourful summer visitor in the Sahel regions is the blue-cheeked bee-eater, a vibrant blend of red, yellow, blue and green, unmistakeable if seen close up.

The list of **winter visitors** is more extensive but composed primarily of marine or coastal species. The most common of the truly marine (*pelagic*) flocks include Cory's shearwater, storm petrel, gannet, razorbill and puffin. These are often found congregated on the sea surface, along with any combination of skuas (great, arctic and pomarine varieties), terns (predominantly sandwich) and gulls (including black-headed, Mediterranean, little, herring and the rarer Audouin's) flying overhead. A variety of coastal and estuarine species also arrive during this period, forming large mixed flocks of grebes (great-crested, little and black-necked), avocet, cattle egret, spoonbill, greater flamingo, and wildfowl such as shelduck, wigeon, teal, pintail, shoveler, tufted duck, pochard and coot. Migrant birds of prey during the winter months include the common buzzard (actually a rarity in Morocco), dashing merlin and both marsh and hen harriers.

Many **passage migrants** pass through Morocco en route to other areas. Well-represented groups include petrels (five varieties) and terns (six varieties) along coastal areas, and herons (four varieties), bitterns, cranes, white and black stork and crake (spotted, little, Baillon's and corncrake) in the marshland/estuarine habitats. Further inland, flocks of multicoloured roller, bee-eater and hoopoe mix with various larks, wagtails and warblers (thirteen varieties), forming large "windfall" flocks when climatic conditions worsen abruptly. Individual species of note include the aptly named black-winged stilt, an elegant black and white wader, with long, vibrant red legs, often found among the disused saltpans; and the nocturnal nightjars (both common and red-necked), which are most easily seen by the reflection of their eyes in the headlamps of passing cars. Birds of prey can also form dense passage flocks, often mixed and including large numbers of black kite, short-toed eagle and honey buzzard. Over open-water spaces, the majestic osprey may be seen demonstrating its mastery of the art of fishing.

Finally, Morocco has its share of occasional or **"vagrant" species**, so classified on the unusual or rare nature of their appearances, including such exotic varieties as glossy ibis, pale-chanting goshawk, Arabian bustard and lappet-faced vulture, but they provide few, if any, opportunities for viewing.

Amphibians and reptiles

Morocco's few remaining **amphibians** are restricted to scarce watery havens, and are more apparent by sound than sight. One of the more common is the green frog, typically immersed up to its eyes in water, releasing the odd giveaway croak. Toads are represented by the Berber toad, another nocturnal baritone, and the Mauritanian toad whose large size and characteristic yellow-and-brown-spotted colouration make it quite unmistakeable. The painted frog is a common participant in the chorus that emanates from the *oueds* (creeks) of the High Atlas, while the wide-ranging whistle of the North African race of the green toad, famed for its ability to change its colour with the surrounding environment, can be heard at altitudes in excess of 2000m.

Reptiles extend from the Mediterranean to the desert. Tortoises are now sadly depleted through "craft items" sold to the tourist trade. The blue and green-eyed lizard and the chameleon frequent the **Middle Atlas**, while the Spanish wall lizard is a common basker on the stony **walls** of towns and villages, as is the Moorish gecko.

Further south, the drier, scrub-covered slopes form an ideal habitat for the horseshoe snake (which can exceed 2m in length) and the Montpelier snake, which feeds on birds and rats, as well as the Atlas agama and fringe-toed lizard.

Desert species include the Algerian sand lizard and the Berber skink, also known as the "sand fish", which inhabits the *ergs* and appears to "swim" through the sand. Morocco's one really poisonous reptile is the horned viper, only half a metre in length, which spends its days buried just below the surface of the sand and feeds by night on jerboas and lizards.

Mammals

Larger animal life in Morocco is dominated by the extensive nomadic herds of goats, sheep and camels which use the most inaccessible and barren patches of wilderness as seasonal grazing areas. One of the most impressive of the wild mammals, however, is the **Barbary ape** – not really an ape in fact, but a macaque monkey (see page 211). These frequent the cedar forests south of Azrou in the Middle Atlas and can be seen on the ground foraging for food in the glades. Other inhabitants of the cedar forest include **wild boar** and **red fox**. A speciality of the Oued Souss, outside Agadir, is the **common otter**; this is now a rare species in Morocco and can only be seen with considerable patience and some good fortune.

The majority of the smaller mammals in Morocco live south of the Atlas ranges in the *hammada*, where the ever-present problem of water conservation plays a major role in the lifestyle of its inhabitants. Larger herbivores include the **Edmi gazelle** and the smaller, and rarer, **Addax antelope,** which graze the thorn bushes and dried grasses to obtain their moisture. Many of the desert varieties reduce the problems of body temperature regulation by adopting a nocturnal lifestyle. Typical exponents of this strategy are the **desert hedgehog** and numerous small rodents such as the **jerboa**. A common predator of the jerboa is the **fennec** (desert fox), whose characteristic large ears are used for both directional hearing (invaluable as a nocturnal hunter) and heat radiation to aid body cooling.

An oddity, found in the Jebel Toubkal area of the High Atlas, is the African **elephant shrew** – a fascinating, mouse-like creature with an elephantine trunk.

Insects and arachnids

Over a hundred species of **butterflies** have been recorded, predominantly in the Middle and High Atlas ranges and are seen from April until September. The Atlas also witnesses one of the world's most extraordinary butterfly migrations in spring, when waves of painted ladies and Bath whites pass through, having crossed the Sahara from West Africa, en route across the Bay of Biscay to the west of England. Other common groups include **grasshoppers**, **crickets** and **locusts**. In the High Atlas, **praying mantis** may be seen.

There are three main groups of **arachnids** in Morocco – scorpions, camel spiders and spiders. Scorpions are nocturnal, hiding under suitable covered depressions during the day such as rocks and boulders (or rucksacks and shoes). Some Moroccan species are poisonous (see page 58) but most are harmless and unlikely to sting unless provoked. Camel spiders (or wind-scorpions) lack a poisonous tail but possess huge jaws with which they catch their main source of prey – scorpions. In the Atlas it is possible to see several small species of tarantula (not the hairy South American variety) and the white orb-web spider *Argiope lobata*.

Flora

Morocco's **flora** is remarkably diverse; the plants here vary enormously with the type of habitat, which ranges from Mediterranean lowlands through to harsher mountains and desert.

Plant species have adapted strategies to cope with the Moroccan climate, becoming either specifically adapted to one particular part of the environment (a habitat type), or evolving multiple structural and/or biochemical means of surviving the more demanding seasons. Others have adopted the proverbial "ostrich" philosophy of burying their heads (or rather their seeds in this case) in the sand and waiting for climatic conditions to become favourable – often an extremely patient process. Oleg Polunin and Anthony Huxley's *Flowers of the Mediterranean* (Chatto & Windus, UK; out of print, but easy to find second hand) is the leading field guide.

The type of flowers that you see will obviously depend entirely on where and when you decide to visit. Some parts of the country have very short flowering seasons because of high temperatures or lack of available water, but generally the best times of year for flowering plants are either just before or just after the main temperature extremes of the

North African summer. The very best time to visit is **spring** (late March to mid-May), when most flowers are in bloom. Typical spring flowers include purple barbary nut iris, deep blue germander and the aromatic claret thyme, all of which frequent the slopes of the Atlas ranges. Among the woodland flora at this time of year are the red pheasant's eye, pink viburnum, violet calamint and purple campanula, which form a resplendent carpet beneath the cedar forests. By late spring, huge tracts of the High Atlas slopes are aglow with the golden hues of broom and, secluded among the lowland cereal crops, splashes of magenta reveal the presence of wild gladioli.

By **midsummer** the climate is at its most extreme and the main concern of plants is to avoid desiccation in the hot, arid conditions. Two areas of exception to these conditions are the **Atlantic coastal zones**, where sea mists produce a slightly more humid environment, and the upper reaches of the **Atlas ranges**, which remain cool and moist at altitude throughout the year. Spring comes later in these loftier places and one can find many of the more familiar garden rock plants, such as the saxifrages and anemones, in flower well into late July and August. Once the hottest part of the summer is past (September onwards), a second, autumn bloom begins with later varieties such as cyclamens and autumn crocus.

Seashores

Seashores have a variety of sand-tolerant species, with their adaptations for coping with water loss, such as sea holly and sea stocks. The dune areas contrast starkly with the Salicornia-dominated salt marshes – monotonous landscapes broken only by the occasional dead tamarisk tree.

Farmland

Arable land is often dominated by cereal crops – particularly in the more humid Atlantic and Mediterranean coastal belts – or olive and eucalyptus groves, which extend over large areas. On the coast around Essaouira and Agadir the indigenous argan tree (see page 433) is common. The general lack of use of herbicides allows the coexistence of many "wild flowers", especially in the fallow hay meadows which are ablaze with the colours of wild poppy, ox-eye daisy, muscali (borage) and various yellow composites.

Lowland hills

Lowland hills form a fascinating mosaic of dense, shrubby species, known as *maquis*, lower-lying, more grazed areas, known as *garrigue*, and more open areas with abundant aromatic herbs and shrubs. *Maquis* vegetation is dominated by cistaceae (rockroses) and the endemic argan tree. The lower-lying *garrigue* is more typically composed of aromatic herbs such as rosemary, thyme and golden milfoil. Among these shrubs, within the more open areas, you may find an abundance of other species such as anemones, grape hyacinths and orchids. The orchids are particularly outstanding, including several of the *Ophrys* group, which use the strategy of insect imitation to entice pollinators and as such have an intricate arrangement of flowers.

Mountains

Flowering later in the year, the slopes of the **Atlas ranges** are dominated by the blue-mauve pitch trefoil and golden drifts of broom. As you travel south through the **Middle Atlas**, the verdant ash, oak, Atlantic cedar and juniper forest dominates the landscape. Watered by the depressions that sweep across from the Atlantic, these slopes form a luxurious spectacle, ablaze with colour in spring. Among the glades beneath the giant cedars of the Middle Atlas, a unique flora may be found, dominated by the vibrant pink peony. Other plants which form this spectacular carpet include geranium, anchusa, pink viburnum, saffron mulleins, mauve cupidanes, violet calamint, purple campanula, the diminutive scarlet dianthus and a wealth of golden composites and orchids.

Further south, in the **High Atlas**, the Toubkal National Park boasts its own varieties and spring bloom; the thyme and thorny caper are interspersed with the blue-mauve pit trefoil, pink convulvulus, the silver-blue and pinks of everlasting flowers of cupidane and phagnalon and golden spreads of broom. At the highest altitudes, the limestone Atlas slopes form a bleak environment, either covered by winter snows or scorched by the summer sun. However, some species are capable of surviving even under these conditions, the most conspicuous of these being the widespread purple tussocks of the hedgehog broom.

Steppe

In the **steppe land** south of the Atlas, temperatures rise sharply and the effect on flora is dramatic; the extensive cedar forests and their multicoloured carpets are replaced by sparse grass plains where the horizon is broken only by the occasional stunted holm oak, juniper or acacia. Commonly known as wattle trees, the acacia were introduced into North Africa from Australia and their large yellow flowers add a welcome splash of colour to this barren landscape. One of the few crop plants grown in this area is the date palm, which is particularly resistant to drought. The steppe land is characterized by the presence of esparto (halfa) grass, which exudes toxins to prevent the growth of competing species. These halfa grass plains are only broken by the flowering of broom in May. Within rocky outcrops, this spring bloom can become a mini-explosion of colour, blending the hues of cistus and chrysanthemum with the pink of rockrose, yellow of milfoil and mauve of rosemary.

Desert

Even **desert areas** provide short-lived blooms of colour during the infrequent spring showers; dwarf varieties such as pink asphodels, yellow daisies and mauve statice thrive briefly while conditions are favourable. Under the flat stones of the *hammada* (stony desert), colonies of lichens and microscopic algae eke out an existence; their shade tolerance and ability to obtain sufficient water from the occasional condensation which takes place under these stones allows them to survive in this harshest of environments. No matter how inhospitable the environment or extreme the climate, somewhere, somehow, there are plants surviving – if you take time to look for them.

Moroccan music

Traditional music, both folk and classical, remains very much a part of life in Morocco, evident at every celebration. Every popular or religious festival involves musicians, and the larger moussems (see page 45) are always good. Keep an eye out for cultural festivals, too, in particular the summer Asilah Festival (see page 89), the Essaouira Gnaoua Festival (see page 284), the Marrakesh Festival of Popular Arts (see page 327), and the Festival of World Sacred Music in Fez (see page 182).

Berber music

Berber music predates the arrival of the Arabs in Morocco, and comes in three main categories: village music, ritual music and the music of professional musicians.

Village music is performed when men and women of a village assemble on festive occasions to dance and sing together. The best-known dances are the **ahouache**, in the western High Atlas, and the **ahidus**, performed by Chleuh Berbers in the eastern High Atlas. In each, drums (*bendirs*) and flute (*nai*) are the only instruments used. The dance begins with a chanted prayer, to which the dancers respond in chorus, the men and women gathered in a large ring in the open air, round the musicians. The *ahouache* is normally performed at night in the patio of the kasbah; the dance is so complicated that the musicians meet to prepare for it in a group called a *laamt* set up specially for the purpose. In the **bumzdi**, a variation on the *ahouache*, one or more soloists perform a series of poetic improvisations. Some of these soloists, such as **Raïs Ajmaa Lahcen** and **Raïs Ihya**, have a national reputation.

Ritual music is rarely absent from celebrations such as moussems or marriages. It may also be called upon to help deal with *jinn*, or evil spirits, or to encourage rainfall. Flutes and drums are usually the sole instruments, along with much rhythmic hand clapping, although people may engage professional musicians for certain events.

The **professional musicians**, or *imdyazn*, of the Atlas mountains are itinerant, travelling during the summer, usually in groups of four. The leader of the group is called the *amydaz* or poet. He presents his poems, which are usually improvised and give news of national or world affairs, in the village square. The poet may be accompanied by one or two members of the group on drums and *rabab*, a single-string fiddle, and by a fourth player, known as the *bou oughanim*. This latter is the reed player, throwing out melodies on a double clarinet, and also acting as the group's clown. *Imdyazn* are found in many weekly souks in the Atlas.

Rwais

Groups of **Chleuh Berber** musicians, from the Souss Valley, are known as **rwais**. A *rwai* worthy of the name will not only know all the music for any particular celebration, but have its own repertoire of songs – commenting on current events – and be able to improvise. A *rwai* ensemble can be made up of a single-string *rabab*, one or two *lotars* (lutes) and sometimes *nakous* (cymbals), together with a number of singers. The leader of the group, the **raïs**, is in charge of the poetry, music and choreography of the performance. Fine clothes, jewels and elaborate gestures also have an important part to play in this ancient rural form of musical theatre.

A **rwai performance** will start with the *astara*, an instrumental prelude, played on *rabab*, giving the basic notes of the melodies that follow (this also makes it possible for the other instruments to tune to the *rabab*). Then comes the *amarg*, the sung poetry which forms the heart of the piece. This is followed by the *ammussu*, which is a sort of choreographed overture; the *tamssust*, a lively song; the *aberdag*, or dance; and finally the *tabbayt*, a finale characterized by an acceleration in rhythm and an abrupt end. Apart from the *astara* and *tabbayt*, the elements of a performance may appear in a different order.

Andalous music

Morocco's classical music evolved in Muslim Spain (Andalusia) though its invention is usually credited to an outstanding musician from Baghdad called **Zyriab**. One of his greatest innovations was the founding of the classical suite called **nuba**, which forms what is now known as **Andalous music**, or **al-âla**. There are, in addition, two other classical traditions, **milhûn** and **gharnati**, each with a distinctive style and form. Andalous music is very popular and greatly loved; during Ramadan, nightly programmes of Andalous classics are broadcast on TV, and people without their own sets gather in cafés to watch them.

The nuba

Originally there were twenty-four **nuba** linked with the hours in the day, but only four full and seven fragmentary *nuba* have been preserved in the Moroccan tradition. Complete *nuba* last between six and seven hours and so are rarely performed in one sitting. Each *nuba* is divided into five main parts, or *mizan*, of differing durations. These five parts correspond to the five different rhythms used within a suite. If a whole *nuba* were being performed then these five rhythms would be used in order: the *basît* rhythm (6/4); *qaum wa nusf* rhythm (8/4); *darj* rhythm (4/4); *btâyhi* rhythm (8/4); and *quddâm* rhythm (3/4 or 6/8).

Traditionally each *mizan* begins with instrumental preludes – *bughya*, *m'shaliya* and *tuashia* – followed by a number of songs, the *sana'a*. There can be as many as twenty *sana'a* within a given *mizan*, although for shorter performances an orchestra may only play three or four before going on to the next rhythm.

The words to many *sana'a* deal, though often obliquely, with subjects generally considered taboo in Islamic society like alcohol and sex – perhaps signifying archaic, pre-Islamic and nomadic roots – although others are religious, glorifying the Prophet and divine laws.

When the Arabs were driven out of Spain, the different Andalusian musical schools were dispersed across Morocco. The school of Valencia was re-established in Fez, that of Granada in Toua and Chefchaouen. Today, the most famous **orchestras** are those of Fez (led by Mohammed Briouel), Rabat (led by Haj Mohamed Toud) and Tetouan. Many fans of Andalous music mourn the passing of the "golden age" in the 1970s and 1980s, when a trio of much lamented masters – **Abdelkrim Rais**, **Abdesadak Chekara** and **Moulay Ahmed Loukili** – led the Fez, Tetouan and Rabat orchestras.

A typical Andalous orchestra uses the following instruments: *rabab* (fiddle), *oud* (lute), *kamenjah* (violin-style instrument played vertically on the knee), *kanun* (zither), *darabouka* (metal or pottery goblet drums), and *taarija* (tambourine). Each orchestra has featured unusual instruments from time to time. Clarinets, flutes, banjos and pianos have all been used with varying degrees of success.

Milhûn

Milhûn is a semi-classical form of sung poetry. Musically it has many links with Andalous music, having adopted the same modes as *al-âla* orchestras, and, like them, it uses string instruments and percussion, though the result can be quite wild and danceable. Unlike Andalous music, which has always been the province of an educated elite, *milhûn* was originally the poetic expression of artisans and traders. Indeed, many of the great *milhûn* singers of the twentieth century began their lives as cobblers, tanners, bakers or doughnut sellers. The greatest *milhûn* composer was **Al-Thami Lamdaghri**, who died in 1856.

The *milhûn* suite comprises two parts: the *taqsim* (overture) and the *qassida* (sung poems). The *taqsim* is played on the *oud* or violin in free rhythm, and introduces the mode in which the piece is set. The *qassida* is divided into three parts: *al-aqsâm*, verses sung solo; *al-harba*, refrains sung by the chorus; and *al-drídka*, a chorus where the rhythm gathers speed and eventually announces the end of the piece. The words of the *qassida* can be taken from anywhere – folk poetry, mystical poems or nonsense lines used for rhythm.

A **milhûn orchestra** generally consists of *oud*, *kamenjah*, *swisen* (a small, high-pitched folk lute related to the *ginbri*), the *hadjouj* (a bass version of the *swisen*), *taarija*, *darabouka* and *handqa* (small brass cymbals), plus a number of **singers**. The most renowned *milhûn* singer of recent times was **Hadj Lhocine Toulali**, who dominated the vibrant *milhûn* scene in Meknes for many decades before his death in 1999. Contemporary singers of note include **Abdelkrim and Saïd Guennoun** of Fez, **Haj Husseïn** and **Abdallah Ramdani** of Meknes, **Muhammad Berrahal** and **Muhammad Bensaïd** of Salé, and the brothers **Mohammed and Ahmed Amenzou** from Marrakesh. In the past ten or so years, some female singers have become stars, including Touria Hadraoui (who is also a novelist) and Sanaa Marahati, whom many consider the future of *milhûn*.

Gharnati

Gharnati, the third music of Arab–Andalusian tradition, derives from the Arabic name of the Andaluisan city of Granada. It is mainly played in Algeria, but Rabat and Oujda are centres for it in Morocco. As with *al-âla*, it is arranged in suites or *nuba*, of which there are twelve complete and four unfinished suites. The *gharnati* orchestra consists of plucked and bowed instruments together with percussion: the usual *ouds* and *kamenjahs* supplemented by the addition of banjo, mandolin and Algerian lute or *kwîtra*.

Sufi music

Among the **Sufi brotherhoods**, music is seen as a means of getting closer to Allah by reaching a trance-like state of mystical ecstasy. In a private nocturnal ceremony called the *hadra*, Sufis may attain this by chanting the name of Allah or dancing in a ring holding hands. The songs and music are irregular in rhythm, and quicken to an abrupt end. Some brotherhoods play for alms in households that want to gain the favour of their patron saint.

The best-known Moroccan brotherhood is the **Gnaoua** – whose members are descendants of slaves from across the Sahara. They claim spiritual descent from **Sidi Bilal**, an Ethiopian who was the Prophet's first *muezzin*. Gnaoua ceremonies are often held to placate spirits, good and evil, who are inhabiting a person or place. They are often called in cases of mental disturbance or to help treat someone stung by a scorpion. These rites have their origins in sub-Saharan Africa, and African influence is evident in the music. The main instrument, the *ginbri* or *sentir*, is a long-necked lute almost identical to instruments from West Africa. The other characteristic sound of Gnaoua music is the *garagab*, a pair of metal castanets. Each Gnaoua troupe is lead by a *ma'alem*, or "master", who plays the *ginbri* and sings the lead vocal parts. The ceremonial part of the proceedings is usually led by a female *mogadema*, or "medium", who is mistress of the arcane spiritual knowledge and huge gallery of saints and spirits, both good and evil, that underpin and influence Gnaoui ritual. In recent decades Gnaoua music has been blended with jazz, rock, funk, hip-hop and even drum 'n' bass. Essaouira holds an annual festival dedicated to Gnaoua music (see page 284).

Jilala are another brotherhood – the devotees of **Moulay Abdelkader Jilal**. Their music is perhaps even more hypnotic and mysterious than that of the Gnaoua and sometimes seems to come from a different plane of existence. The plaintive cycling flute (*qsbah*) and mesmeric beats of the *bendir* (frame drums) carry you forward unconsciously. While in a trance, Jilala devotees can withstand the touch of burning coals or the deep slashes of a Moroccan dagger, afterwards showing no injury or pain.

Other Sufi brotherhoods still practising their own brand of psychic-musical healing in various parts of Morocco include the **Hamadja**, followers of Sidi Ben Ali Hamduj

FOLK INSTRUMENTS

The most common **stringed instrument** is the **ginbri**, an African lute whose soundbox is covered in front by a piece of hide. The rounded, fretless stem has two or three strings. The body of the smaller treble *ginbri* is pear-shaped, that of the bass *ginbri* (*hadjuj* or *sentir*) rectangular. The Gnaoui often put a resonator at the end of the stem to produce the buzz typical of Black African music. The **lotar** is another type of lute, used by Chleuh Berbers. It has a circular body, also closed with a piece of skin, and three or four strings which are plucked with a plectrum. The classic Arab lute, the **oud**, is used in classical orchestras and the traditional Arab orchestras known as *takhts*. Its pear-shaped body is covered by a piece of wood with two or three rosette-shaped openings. It has a short, fretless stem and six strings, five double and one single. The most popular stringed instruments played with a bow are the **kamanjeh** and the **rabab**. The former is an Iranian violin which was adopted by the Arabs. Its present Moroccan character owes a lot to the Western violin, though it is held vertically, supported on the knees. The *rabab* is a spike fiddle, rather like a viol. The bottom half of its long, curved body is covered in hide, the top in wood with a rosette-shaped opening. It has two strings. The Chleuh Berbers use an archaic single-stringed *rabab* with a square stem and soundbox covered entirely in skin. Lastly, there is the **kanum**, a trapezoidal Arab zither with over seventy strings, grouped in threes and plucked with plectra attached to the fingernails. It is used almost exclusively in classical music.

Rapid handclapping and the clashes of bells and cymbals are only part of the vast repertoire of Moroccan **percussion**. Like most Moroccan drums the **darbuka** is made of clay, shaped into a cylinder swelling out slightly at the top. The single skin is beaten with both hands. It is used in both folk and classical music. The **taarija**, a smaller version of the *darbuka*, is held in one hand and beaten with the other. Then there are treble and bass **tan-tan** bongos, and the Moorish **guedra**, a large drum that rests on the ground. There is also a round wooden drum with skins on both sides called a **tabl**, which is beaten with a stick on one side and by hand on the other. This is used only in folk music. As for **tambourines**, the ever popular **bendir** is round and wooden, 40 or 50cm across, with two strings stretched under its single skin to produce a buzzing sound. The **tar** is smaller, with two rings of metal discs round the frame and no strings under its skin. The **duff** is a double-sided tambourine, often square in shape, which has to be supported so that it can be beaten with both hands. Only two percussion instruments are made of metal: **karkabat**, also known as *krakesh* or *karakab*, double castanets used by the Gnaoui, and the **nakous**, a small cymbal played with two rods.

The **Arab flute**, known by different tribes as the *nai, talawat, nira* or *gasba*, is made of a straight piece of cane open at both ends, with no mouthpiece and between five and seven holes, one at the back. It requires a great deal of skill to play it properly, by blowing at a slight angle. The **ghaita** or *rhaita*, a type of oboe popular under various names throughout the Muslim world, is a conical pipe made of hardwood, ending in a bell often made of metal. Its double-reeded mouthpiece is encircled by a broad ring on which the player rests his lips in order to produce the circular breathing needed to obtain a continuous note. It has between seven and nine holes, one at the back. The **aghanin** is a double clarinet, identical to the Arab *arghoul*. It consists of two parallel pipes of wood or cane, each with a single-reed mouthpiece, five holes and a horn at the end for amplification.

and Sidi Ahmed Dghughi, two saints who lived at the end of the eighteenth century, and the **Aïssaoua** from Meknes, who venerate the sixteenth-century holy man Sidi Mohamed Ben Aïssa. The boundaries between these different brotherhoods are often quite blurred, and they tend to hold a common veneration for many saints and spirits, prominent among whom is the fiendish female *jinn* Aisha Kandisha.

Chaabi – Morocco's pop music

Chaabi simply means "popular" music – which covers a huge mix of styles, just as it does in the West. More or less since the advent of radio, the whole Arab world has listened to **Egyptian popular songs**. The tradition is epitomized by Umm Kulthum (Oum Khalsoum) and Mohammed Abdalwahab, but Morocco has added names of its own to the tradition, in particular **Houcine Slaoui** (in the 1940s), and in the following decades, **Ahmed Bidaoui**, **Abdelhadi Belkhayat** and **Abdelwahab Doukkali**. These stars tended to record in Cairo or Beirut, and their music – and language – is essentially Egyptian.

Al'aïta

The oldest of Morocco's own *chaabi* styles is **al'aïta**, the music of the Arabic-speaking rural populations of Morocco's Atlantic coast. It is performed at private and public celebrations, as well as in concert, and is usually sung in Darija (Moroccan colloquial Arabic). Its songs tell of love, loss, lust and the realities of daily life. They begin with a *lafrash*, a slow instrumental prelude (usually played on the violin), then move into free rhythm verses before shifting gear for the finale or *leseb*, which is often twice the speed of the song and forms a background for syncopated clapping, shouting and dancing. An *al'aïta* ensemble usually consists of a male or female vocalist, a violinist, and several percussionists and backing singers, though some groups add a *lotar*. Stars over the years have included the singers **Bouchaïb el Bidaoui** and **Fatna bent Lhoucine**, and the (literally) six-fingered violinist, **Abdelaziz Staati**. In the 1990s, an electric style of *al'aïta* developed, adding keyboards, electric guitars and drum machines. This is still very popular and is the music you most often hear blasting out of stalls in Casablanca or Rabat. Top artists include **Orchestre Jedouane**, **Orchestre Senhaji**, **Khalid Bennani** and **Moustapha Bourgogne**.

Chaabi groups

During the 1970s, a more sophisticated Moroccan *chaabi* began to emerge, using *hadjuj* (bass *ginbri*), lute and *bendir* percussion, along with bouzoukis and electric guitars, to combine Berber music with elements of Arab *milhûn*, Sufi and Gnaoua ritual music, Western rock, reggae and, more recently, rap. The songs were often political, carrying messages that got their authors into trouble with the authorities – even jailed. The leading lights in this movement were **Nass el Ghiwane**, **Jil Jilala** and **Lemchaheb**. The music was hugely influential in the development of **raï music** in neighbouring Algeria, where *raï* singers like Khaled, Cheb Mami, Chaba Fadela and Chaba Sahraoui emerged in the 1980s.

In the 1980s, another wave of *chaabi* groups emerged, based in Marrakesh and employing Gnaoua rhythms. One of the most successful of these has been **Muluk el Hwa** (Demon of Love), a group of Berbers who used to play in Marrakesh's Jemaa el Fna. By far the most popular of the Berber *chaabi* singers, however, is singer **Najat Aatabou**, whose sensational debut, *J'en ai marre* ("I am sick of it"), sold 450,000 copies – many of them in France.

Moroccan raï

Raï – meaning "opinion", "outlook" or "point of view" – originated in the western Algerian region around the port of Oran. It has traditional roots in Bedouin music,

JEWISH MOROCCAN MUSIC

Moroccan Jews, many of whom have now emigrated to Israel, left an important legacy in the north of the country, where their songs and ballads continued to be sung in Haketia, the medieval Spanish spoken at the time of their expulsion from Spain five centuries ago. Apart from the narrative ballads, these were mainly songs of courtly love, as well as lullabies and biblical songs, usually accompanied on a tar. Rounder Records released *Sacred Music of the Moroccan Jews*, a two-CD set of Paul Bowles' 1959 recordings of Moroccan Jewish liturgy, which transport you into the heart of what was once a vibrant subculture but is now, sadly, almost extinct in Morocco.

From Morocco's Jewish community came Zohra el Fassia, the grande dame of Moroccan music in the 1950s, who was from Fez. Moroccan Jewry also produced a great classical Arabic singer, **Samy el Maghribi**, who was born in Safi in 1922. Inspired by the Algerian singer Say el Hilali, he was one of the most appreciated Arabic singers of the 1950s. In 1960 he moved to Canada and in later years devoted himself to a liturgical repertoire. Moroccan Sephardic traditions and music continue to thrive in Israel, the best-known names including Albert Bouhadanna and Rabat-born Emil Zrihan, whose music mixes Arab and Andalusian influences with the Hebrew liturgy.

For anyone interested in Jewish Moroccan music, Chris Silver's blog at ⓦjewishmorocco. blogspot.com is an invaluable resource.

with its distinctive refrain (*ha-ya-rai*), but as a modern phenomenon has more in common with Western music. The backing is now solidly electric, with rhythm guitars, synthesizers and usually a rock drum kit as well as traditional drums. Its lyrics reflect highly contemporary concerns – cars, sex, sometimes alcohol – which have created some friction with the authorities.

Moroccans have taken easily to the music, especially in the northeastern part of the country around the towns of Oujda and Al Hoceima, an area that shares the same cultural roots as the province of Oran over the border in Algeria, where *raï* was born. Home-grown *raï* stars include **Cheb Khader**, **Cheb Mimoun** and the superb **Cheb Jellal**, a pop-*raï* legend from Oujda whose recordings are well worth seeking out. *Raï* influence can also be heard in the sound of folk artists like **Rachid Briha** and **Hamid M'Rabati**, from the Oujda region.

Fusion and Moroccan hip-hop

Morocco was the starting point for all kinds of fusion experiments, with such disparate figures as Brian Jones, Ornette Coleman, Jimi Hendrix, Robin Williamson, John Renbourn and Pharaoh Sanders attracted by its rhythms. One of the earliest attempts to combine Moroccan music with European electronic sounds was made by the German group **Dissidenten** in the 1980s, and since then all manner of Moroccan sounds have been successfully blended with reggae, funk, hip-hop, house and drum 'n' bass.

Hip-hop in particular has become immensely popular in Morocco, as throughout Africa, and accounts for some of the most dynamic Moroccan music of the twenty-first century so far, having taken over from *raï* in the 1990s as Morocco's popular musical genre. Breaking out of a largely localized underground scene, bands like **Fnaïre** from Marrakesh, **H-Kayne** from Meknes and **Fez City Clan** from Fez have galvanized the Moroccan pop scene, singing about social and political issues with a hard-edged lyric. They are joined by rock-influenced Casa band **Hoba Hoba Spirit**, who owe more to punk than to heavy metal, despite their track "El Caïd Mötorhead". They reacted to the 2003 Casablanca bomb attacks with "Ma Tkich Bladi" ("Don't touch my country"), a play on the French anti-racist slogan "*touche pas mon pot*", and put themselves in the forefront of the pro-democracy movement, with their 2011 single "La Volonté de Vivre".

All this is more daring than foreigners might realize: musicians are not as free in Morocco as they are in the West, a fact brought home in 2003, when the authorities imprisoned members of the heavy metal bands **Nekros**, **Infected Brain** and **Reborn**, along with five of their fans, on charges of moral depravity and playing "anti-Islamic" music. Moroccan rapper **L7a9d** (pronounced "El Haqed") was imprisoned for two years in 2011 for criticizing the monarchy in his records, and has been subject to constant harassment ever since. Following the release of his album *Walou* in 2014, he was arrested at a football match and imprisoned for four months, supposedly for ticket touting and assaulting police. He now lives in Belgium.

Discography

Most **music shops** in Britain and the US with a decent world music section should yield at least a few discs of ethnic, folk and Andalous music, or fusion with European groups. In Morocco itself, **cassettes** are still common.

COMPILATIONS

Various Morocco: Crossroads of Time (Ellipsis Arts, US). An excellent introduction to Moroccan music that comes with a well-designed and informative book. The disc includes everything from ambient sounds in the Fez Medina, to powerful Jilala and Gnaoua music, Andalous, **rwai**, Berber, and some good contemporary pop from Nouamane Lahlou.

★ **Various The Rough Guide to the Music of Morocco** (World Music Network, UK). This Rough Guide's release

focuses on contemporary Moroccan sounds, featuring selections from the Amenzou Ensemble, Nass el Ghiwane, Nass Marrakech, Jil Jilala, Mustapha Bourgogne, Bnet Marrakech and U-cef. It is backed up by fulsome liner notes.

Various Anthologie de la Musique Marocaine (Ministère de la Culture, Morocco). These four box sets (with a total of 31 CDs) cover most bases in Moroccan folk and traditional music. All include liner notes in French and Arabic and can be purchased at the Ministry of Culture in Rabat.

BERBER MUSIC

Compagnies musicales du Tafilalet The Call of the Oasis (Institut du Monde Arabe, France). Sublime recordings from the edge of the Sahara, showcasing four groups recorded live at a festival in Erfoud.

Hmaoui Abd El-Hamid La Flûte de l'Atlas (Arion, France). Hypnotic and haunting flute-like *ney*, backed by

percussion, **oud** and zither.

Les Imazighen Chants du Moyen-Atlas (Institut du Monde Arabe, France). A fantastic live recording of musicians from the Middle Atlas, full of power and extravagant emotion.

CLASSICAL/ANDALOUS

Ensemble Amenzou Le Malhûn à Marrakech (Institut du Monde Arabe, France). The Amenzou brothers belong to a revered dynasty of **milhûn** singers and their energetic, youthful approach to the genre is much admired.

El Hadj Houcine Toulali Le Milhûn de Meknes (Institut du Monde Arabe, France). A fine live recording of the great **milhûn** master on top form.

Ustad Massano Tazi Musique Classique Andalouse de Fès (Ocora, France). Again, beautifully recorded and presented. Includes Nuba Hijaz Al-Kabir and Nuba Istihilal.

Various Maroc: Anthologie d'Al-Melhûn (Maison des Cultures du Monde, France). A three-CD set containing performances from many of Morocco's finest **milhûn** singers. An excellent introduction.

SUFI MUSIC

Les Aissawa de Fès Trance Ritual (L'Institut du Monde Arabe, France). Entrancing and intricate music from the Aissawa brotherhood of Fez.

Ihsan Rmiki Al-Samâa: Ecstatic Spiritual Audition (Institut du Monde Arabe, France). Rmiki is the new voice of Andalous music – and this is a moving set, her voice leading a six-person ensemble.

The Master Musicians of Jajouka Apocalypse Across the Sky (Axiom, UK). The power and clarity of these remarkable performers stands out on this Bill Laswell production.

★ **Various Gnawa Night – Music of the Marrakesh Spirit Masters** (Axiom, UK). Gnaoua music at its evocative best, again recorded by Bill Laswell.

JEWISH MOROCCAN MUSIC

Samy El Maghribi Samy el Maghribi (Club du Disque Arabe, France) A collection of old recordings by this legendary Jewish musician whose pride of place in the annals of Moroccan music proves what a big influence Jews once had on urban music.

CHAABI

Najat Aatabou The Voice of the Atlas (GlobeStyle, UK). A superb collection of some of Najat's best-loved songs, including "Shouffi Rhirou" which has been covered brilliantly by the 3Mustaphas3.

Jil Jilala Chama'a (Blue Silver, France). A classic early recording of the seminal **chaabi** rockers. The title track "Chama'a" ("Candle") is an old **milhûn** song which is given a very moody and edgy modern makeover.

Nass el Ghiwane Maroc: Chants d'Espoir (Créon Music, France). Many recordings by the "Rolling Stones of North Africa" are marred by atrocious sound quality; however, this set captures them razor-sharp and passionate.

FUSION

★ **Aisha Kandisha's Jarring Effects El Buya** (Barbarity, Switzerland). An intoxicating mix of Moroccan melodies and traditional string instruments with scratching reverb and rushes of industrial noise.

Hoba Hoba Spirit Blad Skizo (Platinum Music, UK). Hoba Hoba's second album, released in 2005, contains some of their strongest Morocc'n-roll tunes, most notably the title track ("Schizophrenic Country") and the more Gnaoua-flavoured "Ma Ajebtinich".

MoMo The Birth Of Dar (Apartment 22, UK). House-flavoured Moroccan madness with a heavy dance beat. **Dar** means "house" in Arabic... you get the picture.

U-cef Halalium (Apartment 22, UK). A Moroccan producer based in London who fuses the roughneck sounds of the English capital with traditional **chaabi** and Gnaoua, often to wondrous effect.

MOROCCAN HIP-HOP

Fez City Clan Fès. Slicker, more tuneful and more electronic than Morocco's other hip-hop bands, the Clan have taken their very underground Fassi sound nationwide and beyond. This is their first album, and like all really worthwhile pleasures, it leaves you craving for more.

Fnaire Yed el Henna. Fnaire's amazing mix of hip-hop with a wide assortment of traditional Moroccan music makes a richly sweet combination. Tunes like the title track and the percussive "Lalla Mennana" are a truly masterful combination of rap and trad.

H-Kayne HK 1426. The Meknes rappers' sound is deeper, darker and purer than most Moroccan hip-hop. This album, named after the Islamic year in which it was recorded (2005), contains their biggest hit, "Issawa Style".

L7a9d Walou. The music is surprisingly mellow on this latest album from the controversial Casa rapper, human rights activist and Arab Spring supporter, especially considering the hard-hitting nature of his lyrics. Unless you speak Arabic, you probably won't register much of the political message, but English translations of some of his tracks are available online, and the sound is lovely anyway.

Books

There is a wealth of books about Morocco, set in Morocco, or by Moroccans, and you won't regret having one or two along on a trip. The main online bookshops are likely to yield the highest returns on the more esoteric recommendations below. Otherwise, you might want to try the UK-based Maghreb Bookshop, 45 Burton St, London WC1 (☎020 7388 1840, ⓦmaghrebbookshop.com), which supplies current, out-of-print and rare books on all aspects of North Africa, and will ship worldwide.

GENERAL AND TRAVEL

Margaret and Robin Bidwell *Morocco: the Traveller's Companion*. The name's a bit misleading: this isn't so much a traveller's companion as a compendium of titbits from travellers of the past, mainly in the eighteenth and nineteenth centuries, but including everyone from Samuel Pepys and Leo Africanus to Mark Twain and George Orwell, giving their impressions of the people, the land, government and local customs. There are even a few Moroccan recipes.

Paul Bowles *Points in Time*, *Their Heads Are Green*. Novelist, poet and composer Paul Bowles (1910–99) lived in Tangier for half a century and, more or less single-handedly, brought translations of local writers to Western attention (see page 535). These two books of his own are superb. *Points* is a series of tales and short pieces inspired by episodes and sources from earliest times to the present day. *Heads* includes a couple of travel essays on Morocco and a terrific piece on the psychology of desert travel.

★ **Hamish Brown** *The Mountains Look On Marrakech: A Trek Along the Atlas Mountains*. Hamish Brown has been to Morocco every year since 1965 to visit his beloved Atlas mountains, and his love for the country, its people, its landscapes and its wildlife shines through in this inspirational account of a nine-hundred-mile trek right across the High Atlas range.

Hamish Brown *The High Atlas: Treks and Climbs on Morocco's Biggest and Best Mountains*. The best and most important trekking guide to the High Atlas mountains, where to go and how to get there. This is as much about the people as the landscapes, and is as insightful as it's practical.

Elias Canetti *The Voices of Marrakesh*. A small, compelling volume of impressions of Marrakesh in the last years of French rule, by the Nobel Prize-winning author. The atmosphere of many pieces still holds.

★ **Walter Harris** *Morocco That Was*. Harris, **Times** correspondent in Tangier from the 1890s until his death in 1933, saw the country at probably the strangest ever stage in its history – the last years of "Old Morocco" in its feudal isolation and the first of French occupation. *Morocco That Was*, first published in 1921, is a masterpiece – alternately sharp, melodramatic and very funny. It incorporates, to

some extent, the anecdotes in his earlier *Land of an African Sultan* (1889) and *Tafilet* (1895, o/p).

Orin Hargraves *Culture Shock! Morocco*. Hargraves worked in Morocco in the 1980s as a Peace Corps volunteer and this valuable paperback, revised in 2007, is a distillation of his experience, supported by an impressive range of research and, clearly, a lot of conversations throughout the country. He offers perceptive accounts of almost every aspect of contemporary Moroccan life, along with a good overview of history and religion, and an instructive section of dos and don'ts.

John Hopkins *The Tangier Diaries*. Highly entertaining journals of Tangier life – and travels across Morocco – from an American novelist, resident in Tangier during the 1960s and 1970s. Paul and Jane Bowles and William Burroughs all figure large in the diary entries.

Peter Mayne *A Year in Marrakesh*. Mayne went to Marrakesh in the early 1950s, found a house in an ordinary district of the Medina, and tried to live like a Moroccan. He couldn't, but wrote an unusually perceptive account explaining why.

★ **Budgett Meakin** *The Land of the Moors*, *The Moors: A Comprehensive Description* (1902). Out of print but available online (ⓦarchive.org/details/landofmoorscompr00meak), these wonderful encyclopedic volumes were the first really detailed books on Morocco and Moroccan life.

Barnaby Rogerson (ed.) *Marrakech Through Writers' Eyes*. A feast of an anthology, ranging from the earliest accounts, through eighteenth- and nineteenth-century explorers and envoys, to contemporary writers such as Esther Freud and Juan Goytisolo.

Tahir Shah *The Caliph's House*. This is a terrific read: a funny, eccentric and insightful look at Casablanca, and Morocco as a whole, through the narrative of buying and restoring a house in the city.

Josh Shoemake *Tangier: a Literary Guide for Travellers*. An exploration of Tangier as seen through the eyes of foreign writers – everyone from Samuel Pepys to William Burroughs and Mark Twain to Patricia Highsmith – well written and a great companion when you're there.

Jeffrey Tayler *Valley of the Casbahs*. Tayler set out, in 2001, on a journey to trace the Drâa Valley from source to sea, on foot and by camel. His chief objective was to try to meet and understand the "Ruhhal" – the remaining desert nomads.

The journey – one of the most compelling of modern accounts – left him by turns appalled and inspired.

HISTORY

J.M. Abun-Nasr *History of the Maghreb in the Islamic Period*. Morocco in the wider context of North Africa by a distinguished Arab historian.

Marvine Howe *Morocco: The Islamist Awakening and Other Challenges*. A former *New York Times* correspondent who had known the country since the 1950s, returns to live there in 1999. Her return coincides with the new king, Mohammed VI, and the rise of Islamic radicalism in the Arab world. She takes the story through to 2005.

★ **Gavin Maxwell** *Lords of the Atlas*. Drawing heavily on Walter Harris's accounts of the Moorish court (see opposite), this is the story of the Glaoui family – literally the "Lords" of the High Atlas, where they exercised almost complete control from the turn of the nineteenth century right through to Moroccan independence in 1956. Not an attractive tale but a compelling one, and superbly told. Originally published in 1966, it was republished in a superbly illustrated edition in 2000.

C.R. Pennell *Morocco from Empire to Independence*. This is the first general history of modern Morocco. It covers the major strands of power but also the social and cultural life of ordinary Moroccans and is strong on the country's pressing contemporary concerns of poverty, drought and worsening agricultural land.

Douglas Porch *The Conquest of Morocco*. Accessible and fascinating account of the extraordinary manoeuvrings and characters in Morocco at the turn of the twentieth century.

Susan Raven *Rome in Africa*. A well-illustrated survey of Roman (and Carthaginian) North Africa.

Barnaby Rogerson *A Traveller's History of North Africa*. A good, up-to-date, general history, authoritative but very readable, covering not just Morocco, but also Tunisia, Algeria and Libya, which Rogerson sees as a kind of island, isolated by sea and desert, and thus set apart from Europe and sub-Saharan Africa.

David Woolman *Rebels in the Rif*. An academic but fascinating study of the Riffian war in the 1920s and of the tribes' uprising against the Moroccan government in 1956, unfortunately no longer in print.

ANTHROPOLOGY

Michael Brett and Elizabeth Fentress *The Berbers*. An overview of the Berber peoples of Morocco, Algeria and beyond, ranging through anthropology, history and literature.

Elizabeth Fernea *A Street in Marrakech*. A nicely written account of a woman anthropologist's study of and experiences in Marrakesh in the 1980s.

David Hart *Tribe and Society in Rural Morocco*. A collection of essays, dating from 1985 to 2000, around the themes of tribalism and Berber identity in Morocco. More accessible than it sounds, with titles such as *Scratch a Moroccan, Find a Berber*.

Fatima Mernissi *Doing Daily Battle: Interviews with Moroccan Women*. Eleven women – carpet weavers, rural and factory workers, teachers – talk about all aspects of their lives, from work and housing to marriage. A fascinating insight into a normally very private world.

ISLAM

The Koran (translated by Arthur J. Arberry, Oxford University Press; translated by J.M Rodwell, o/p but online at ⓦgutenberg.org/etext/2800). The word of God as proclaimed by Mohammed is notoriously untranslatable. Arberry's version attempts to preserve its poetic beauty and retains the traditional arrangement of suras (according to their length). Rodwell's 1861 translation is a little dated, but provides analytical footnotes, and was originally arranged, as far as possible, in the order in which the suras were composed, making it easier to follow the development of ideas; unfortunately most modern editions of Rodwell's translation revert to the traditional order.

Seyyed Hossein Nasr *Ideals and Realities of Islam*. A good general introduction to the Islamic faith by an Iranian-born American academic, told from the point of view of a believer, explaining his faith for the benefit of non-Muslim Westerners.

ART, ARCHITECTURE AND CRAFTS

James F. Jereb *Arts and Crafts of Morocco*. A fine introduction, with over 150 colour photographs.

Lisa Lovatt-Smith *Moroccan Interiors*. A coffee-table tome aimed at the interior design market, but goes beyond that in its coverage of traditional crafts, and traditional and modern architecture, with lots of gorgeous colour photographs.

Brooke Pickering et al *Moroccan Carpets*. Edited by a New York collector and dealer, this is the best book on Moroccan carpets – a large format, fully illustrated guide, showing examples region by region.

Herbert Ypma *Morocco Modern*. A superbly illustrated book that traces the origins of the great artisan traditions of Morocco (weavers, woodworkers, potters, zellij-makers) and looks at the way contemporary designers and architects reinterpret these influences to create surprisingly modern work.

FOOD

Paula Wolfert *The Food of Morocco*. This is rather lavishly illustrated for a cookbook, but its rich mix of recipes, photographs and general discussion on the basics, principles and defining ingredients of Moroccan cooking, make it an excellent all-round primer. Wolfert's earlier and simpler *Couscous and Other Good Food from Morocco*, originally published in 1973, was the first Moroccan cookbook available in English, and remains among the best, with an emphasis on ordinary, rural cooking.

MOROCCAN FICTION/BIOGRAPHY

TRANSLATIONS BY PAUL BOWLES

By far the largest (and finest) body of Moroccan fiction published in English are the translations by the American writer Paul Bowles, who lived in Tangier from the 1940s until his death in 1999, and also translated the first part of Mohammed Choukri's autobiography (see below). The short stories share a common fixation with intrigue and unexpected narrative twists, and are often punctuated by episodes of violence. None have particular characterization, though this hardly seems relevant as they have such a strong, vigorous narrative style – brilliantly matched by Bowles' sharp, economic language.

Driss Ben Hamed Charhadi *A Life Full of Holes*. Bowles' first Moroccan translation – in 1964 – a direct narrative of street life in Tangier. It was published under a pseudonym, the author being Larbi Layachi who, two decades later, published *Yesterday and Today*, a kind of sequel, describing in semi-fictionalized (and not very sympathetic) form his time with Paul and Jane Bowles.

★ **Mohammed Mrabet** *Love with a Few Hairs; The Boy Who Set the Fire & Other Stories; The Lemon; M'Hashish; The Chest; Marriage With Papers; The Big Mirror; Harmless Poisons***,** *Blameless Sins; The Beach Café and The Voice; Look and Move On: An Autobiography*. Mohammed Mrabet's stories – *The Beach Café* is perhaps his best – are often **kif**-inspired, which gives them a slightly paranoid quality, as Mrabet himself explained: "Give me twenty or thirty pipes…and an empty room can fill up with wonderful things, or terrible things. And the stories come from these things."

OTHER TRANSLATIONS

Abdelkader Benali *Wedding by the Sea*. Moroccan magical realism, and an impressive debut novel by a Moroccan-born author living in the Netherlands since childhood. The story is about a young man who returns (from Holland) to his seaside village in Morocco for his sister's wedding, and during the festivities finds the bridegroom has made off to the local brothel. Sweet revenge lies in store from his sister.

Tahar Ben Jelloun *The Sand Child* and *Corruption*. The best of around a dozen books by Ben Jelloun that have been translated into English. *The Sand Child*, which won the prestigious Prix Goncourt, is the tale of a girl brought up in southern Morocco as a boy in order to thwart Morocco's inheritance laws. *Corruption*, as its title suggests, explores the endemic corruption in contemporary Morocco, through the story of Mourad, the last honest man in the country, who attempts to stay clear of brown envelopes in Casablanca and Tangier.

Mahi Binebine *Welcome to Paradise*. Binebine grew up in Morocco, lived in America and has now settled in France. This is his first book to be published in English and it is utterly engaging: a tale of life in the poorest areas of contemporary Morocco and the motivations that drive people to hand over all their savings to a trafficker to cross the Straits of Gibraltar and take their chances as illegals in Europe. Superbly translated and hugely evocative.

★ **Mohamed Choukri** For *Bread Alone* and *Streetwise*. Choukri's two-part autobiography (the first volume translated by Paul Bowles, the second by Ed Emery) ranks among the best works of contemporary Arabic literature. Born in the Rif, he moved with his family to Tangier at a time of great famine, spending his childhood in abject poverty. During his adolescence he worked for a time for a French family. He then returned to Tangier, where he experienced the violence of the 1952 independence riots. Throughout his adversities, two things shine through: Choukri's determination to use literacy to surmount his desperate circumstances; and his compassion for the normally despised human beings who share this life of "the lowest of the low".

Driss Chraibi *Heirs to the Past*. A benchmark novel, which takes the crisis of Moroccans' post-colonial identity as its theme. It is semi-autobiographical as the author-narrator (who has lived in France since the war) returns to Morocco for the funeral of his father. A number of other Chraibi novels are also available in translation.

Richard Hamilton *The Last Storytellers*. A selection of typically bittersweet tales from what may well be the last generation of traditional storytellers in Marrakesh's Jemaa el Fna, collected, translated and introduced by a sometime BBC Morocco correspondent keen to preserve some remnant of this great Arabic – and in particular Moroccan – tradition.

Fatima Mernissi *Dreams of Trespass: Tales of a Harem Girlhood*. Part fairy tale, part feminist manifesto, a mix of biographical narrative, stories and fantasies by a renowned Moroccan sociologist (author of *Doing Daily Battle*; see page 534), who was born in a Fez harem in 1940.

Brick Ousaïd *Mountains Forgotten by God*. Autobiographical narrative of an Atlas Berber family, which gives an impressive sense of the harshness of mountain life. As the author describes it, it is "not an exercise in literary style [but] a cry from the bottom of my heart, of despair and revolt".

FOREIGN FICTION & BIOGRAPHY SET IN MOROCCO

Once again, Paul Bowles is the outstanding figure in American and European fiction set in Morocco.

PAUL BOWLES

★ **NOVELS**: *The Sheltering Sky; Let It Come Down; The Spider's House*. **STORIES**: *Collected Stories of Paul Bowles 1939–76; Collected Stories; Midnight Mass; Unwelcome Words*. *Collected Stories of Paul Bowles 1939–76* gathers together work from numerous editions, as does the more selective *Collected Stories*. Post-1976 collections include *Midnight Mass* and *Unwelcome Words*. Bowles is the most interesting and the most prolific foreign writer using North African themes, and many of his stories are similar in vein to those of Mohammed Mrabet (see opposite), employing the same sparse forms, bizarre twists and interjections of violence. The novels are different, exploring both Morocco and how Westerners react to it. If you read nothing else on the country, at least try *The Spider's House* – one of the best political novels ever written, its backdrop the traditional daily life of Fez, its theme the conflicts and transformation at the last stages of the French occupation of Morocco.

BIOGRAPHIES AND MEMOIRS: The best of the biographies and memoirs of Bowles and his literary friends and acquaintances in Tangier are:

Michelle Green *The Dream at the End of the World: Paul Bowles and the Literary Renegades of Tangier*. A strong narrative, compulsively peopled: the best read if you're looking for one book on Tangier literary life.

Paul Bowles *Without Stopping*. Bowles' autobiography is of interest for its Moroccan episodes (though William Burroughs wryly dubbed it "Without Telling"), as is his *Two Years Beside the Strait* (published in US as *Days: A Tangier Journal, 1987–89*).

OTHER FICTION

William Burroughs *Naked Lunch*. This iconic Beat novel written in a Tangier hotel room (Villa Muniria) in 1954–57 consists of a series of nightmarish sex-and-drugs-obsessed tableaux. It isn't especially about Morocco, but Tangier features as the "Interzone", and is undoubtedly the place to read it.

Rafael Chirbes *Mimoun*. Compelling tale of a Spanish teacher, based south of Fez, adrift amid sexual adventures and bizarre local life and antagonisms.

Esther Freud *Hideous Kinky*. An English hippy takes her two daughters to Marrakesh, where they live simply, as locals. The narrative – funny, sad, and full of informed insights – is narrated by the 5-year-old.

John Haylock *Body of Contention*. An enjoyable romp set amid the expat community of Tangier in the months following independence in 1957.

John Hopkins *All I Wanted Was Company*. A gossipy tale about an American in Tangier and his lovers, one of whom disappears to the Sahara. The author's *Tangier Diaries* (see page 533) document his time as an expat in Morocco's edgiest city.

Jane Kramer *Honor to the Bride*. A fictional narrative based on a true story about a bride-to-be who is kidnapped, and her family's desperate struggle to get her respectably married off after such a disgrace.

Umberto Pasti *Age of Flowers*. An Italian novel set in Tangier at the end of the 1990s, with a decadent scene of writers and artists counterpoised by the growing influence of Islamists in the streets.

Moroccan Arabic

Few people who come to Morocco learn to speak any Arabic, let alone anything of the country's three Berber languages, but you'll be treated very differently if you make even a small effort to master basic phrases. If you can speak French, you'll be able to get by almost anywhere. Spanish is also useful, especially among older people in the former Spanish colonial zones around Tetouan and the Rif, and in Ifni, Tarfaya and the Western Sahara. People who have significant dealings with tourists will know some English, but that is still a minority.

Moroccan Arabic

Moroccan Arabic, the country's official language, is substantially different from classical Arabic, or from the modern Arabic spoken in Egypt or the Gulf. If you speak any form of Arabic, however, you should be able to make yourself understood. Egyptian Arabic, in particular, is familiar to most Moroccans from TV soaps. If you want to **learn Arabic** in Morocco, ALIF in Fez (see page 184) offer classes.

ARABIC/BERBER PHRASEBOOKS & LEARNING MATERIALS

**ARABIC PHRASEBOOKS
AND DICTIONARIES**
Richard S. Harrell, Harvey Sobelman and Thomas Fox, *A Dictionary of Moroccan Arabic* (Georgetown UP). Two-way Arabic–English dictionary.

ARABIC COURSEBOOKS
Abdellah Chekayri, *An Introduction to Moroccan Arabic and Culture* (Georgetown UP). A textbook and multimedia DVD which does pretty much what it says on the cover. It teaches you not only to speak, but also to read and write Arabic.

Aaron Sakulich, *Moroccan Arabic* (Collaborative Media International). Witty and engaging introduction to Moroccan Arabic with an emphasis on making learning fun.

BERBER COURSEBOOKS
Ernest T. Abdel Massih, *A Course in Spoken Tamazight* (Michigan UP). A coursebook with seven cassettes, out of print but can be found at a price. The same author's *A Reference Grammar of Tamazight* provides backup.

PRONUNCIATION

There are no silent letters – you pronounce everything that's written including double vowels. Letters and syllables in bold should be stressed. Here are some keys to follow:
kh like the "ch" in Scottish lo*ch*
gh like the French "r" (a slight gargling sound)

ai as in "*eye*"
ay as in "*say*"
ou/oua w/wa (Essaouira is pronounced Essa-weera)
q like "k" but further back in throat
j like "s" in pleasure

ARABIC AND FRENCH GLOSSARY

English *Arabic* French

BASICS AND EVERYDAY PHRASES

yes *eyeh*, *naam* oui
no *la* non
I *ena* moi
you (m/f) *enta*/*entee* vous
he *hoo*wa lui
she *hee*ya elle
we *neh*noo nous
they *hoom* ils/elles

(very) good mez*yen* (*bzef*) (très) bon
big *kebeer* grand
small *segheer* petit
old *kedeem* vieux
new *jedeed* nouveau
a little *shwee*ya un peu
a lot *bzef* beaucoup
open *mahlul* ouvert
closed *masdud* fermé
hello/how's it going? *le bes?* ça va?
good morning *sbah* l'*kheer* bonjour

good evening *msa l'kheer* bon soir
good night *leila saeeda* bonne nuit
goodbye *biselama* au revoir
who...? *shkoon...?* qui...?
when...? *imta...?* quand...?
why...? *alash...?* pourquoi...?
how...? *kifesh...?* comment...?
which/what...? *shnoo...?* quel...?
is there...? *kayn...?* est-ce qu'il y a...?
do you have...? *andak...?/kayn...* avez-vous...?
please *afak/minfadlak* to a man or *afik* s'il vous plaît / *minfadlik* to a woman
thank you *shukran* merci
ok/agreed *wakha* d'accord
that's enough/that's all *safee* ça suffit
excuse me *ismahlee* excusez-moi
sorry/ I'm very sorry *ismahlee/ana asif* pardon/je suis désolé
let's go *nimsheeyoo* on y va
go away *imshee* va t'en
I (m/f) don't understand *mafahemsh/mafahmash* je ne comprends pas
do you (m/f) speak English? *takelem/takelmna ingleesi?* parlez-vous anglais?

DIRECTIONS

where's...? *fayn...?* où est...?
the airport *el matar* l'aeroport
the train station *mahattat el tren* la gare de train
bus station *mahattat el car* la gare routière
the bank *el bank* le banque
the hospital *el mostashfa* l'hôpital
near/far (from here) *qurayab/baeed (min huna)* près/ loin (d'ici)
left *liseer* à gauche
right *limeen* à droit
straight ahead *neeshan* tout droit
here *hina* ici
there *hinak* là

ACCOMMODATION

hotel *funduq* hôtel
do you have a room? *kayn beet?* avez-vous une chambre?
two beds *jooj tlik* deux lits
one big bed *wahad tlik kebir* un grand lit
shower *doosh* douche
hot water *maa skhoona* eau chaud
can I see? *Mumkin ashoofha?* je peux le voir?
key *sarut* clé

SHOPPING

I (don't) want... *ena (mish) bgheet...* je (ne) veux (pas)...

how much (money)? *shahal (flooss)?* combien (d'argent)?
(that's) expensive *(hada) ghalee* (c'est) cher

NUMBERS

0 *sifr* zéro
1 *wahad* un
2 *jooj* deux
3 *tlata* trois
4 *arbaa* quatre
5 *khamsa* cinq
6 *sitta* six
7 *sebaa* sept
8 *temanya* huit
9 *tisaoud* neuf
10 *ashra* dix
11 *hadashar* onze
12 *etnashar* douze
13 *talatashar* treize
14 *arbatashar* quatorze
15 *khamstashar* quinze
16 *sittashar* seize
17 *sebatashar* dix-sept
18 *tamantashar* dix-huit
19 *tisatashar* dix-neuf
20 *ashreen* vingt
21 *wahad wa ashreen* vingt-et-un
22 *jooj wa ashreen* vingt-deux
30 *talateen* trente
40 *arbaeen* quarante
50 *khamseen* cinqante
60 *sitteen* soixante
70 *abaeen* soixante-dix
80 *tamaneen* quatre vingts
90 *tisaeen* quatre-vingt-dix
100 *mia* cent
121 *mia wa wahad wa ashreen* cent vingt-et-un
200 *miateen* deux cents
300 *tolta mia* trois cents
1000 *alf* mille
a half *nuss* demi
a quarter *roba* quart

DAYS AND TIMES

Monday *nahar el it neen* lundi
Tuesday *nahar et telat* mardi
Wednesday *nahar el arbaa* mercredi
Thursday *nahar el khemis* jeudi
Friday *nahar el jemaa* vendredi
Saturday *nahar es sabt* samedi
Sunday *nahar el had* dimanche
yesterday *imbarih* hier
today *el yoom* aujourd'hui
tomorrow *gheda* demain

what time is it? *shahal fisa'a?* quelle heure est-il?
one o'clock *sa'a wahda* une heure
2.15 *jooj wa roba* deux heures et quart
3.30 *tlata wa nuss* trois heures et demi
4.45 *arbaa ila roba* cinq heures moins quart

FOOD AND DRINK

BASICS

restaurant *mataam* restaurant
breakfast *iftar* petit déjeuner
egg *beyd* ouef
butter *zibda* beurre
jam *marmalad* confiture
cheese *jibna* fromage
yoghurt *rayeb* yaourt
salad *salata* salade
olives *zitoun* olives
oil *zit* huile
bread *khobz* pain
salt *melha* sel
pepper *haroor* piment
without *bilesh* sans
sugar *sukkar* sucre
the bill *el hisaab* l'addition
fork *forshaat* fourchette
knife *mooss* couteau
spoon *malka* cuillère
plate *tabseel* assiete
glass *kess* verre
What do you have … *Ashnoo kane…* Qu'est ce que vous avez…
…to eat? *…f'l-makla?* …pour manger?
…to drink? *…f'l-mucharoubat?* …pour boire?
What is this? *Shnoo hada?* Qu'est ce que c'est?
I (m/f) am a vegetarian *ana nabati/nabatiya wa la* Je suis vegetarien/ *akulu lehoum wala hout* vegetarienne
This is not what I asked for! *Hedee meshee heea li tlubt!* Ceci n'est pas ce que j'ai demandé
The bill, please. *El hisaab, minfadlik* L'addition s'il vous plaît
Please write it down. *Minfadlik, k'tib'h* Est-ce que vous pouvez l'écrite s'il vous plaît?

MEAT, POULTRY AND FISH

meat *lahem* viande
beef *baqri* boeuf
chicken *jaj* poulet
lamb *houli* mouton
liver *kibda* foie
pigeon *hamam* pigeon
fish *hout* poisson
prawns *qambri* crevettes

VEGETABLES

vegetables *khadrawat* légumes
artichoke *qoq* artichaut
aubergine *badinjan* aubergine
beans *loobia* haricots
onion *basal* oignon
potato *batata* patate
tomato *mateesha* tomate

FRUITS AND NUTS

almond *looz* amande
apple *tufah* pomme
banana *banan* banane
date *tmer* datte
fig *kermooss* figue
grape *ainab* raisin
lemon *limoon* limon
melon *battikh* melon
orange *limoon* orange
pomegranate *rooman* granade
prickly pear (cactus fruit) *hendiya* figue de Barbarie
strawberry *frowla* fraise
watermelon *dellah* pastèque

BEVERAGES

water *lmaa* de l'eau
mineral water *Sidi Ali/Sidi Harazem* (brand names) eau minérale
ice *jeleedi* glace
ice cream *glace* glace
milk *haleeb* lait
coffee *qahwa* café
coffee with a little milk *nuss nuss* café cassé
coffee with plenty of milk *qahwa bi haleeb* café au lait/ café crème
tea (with mint/with wormwood) *atay (bi nana bi sheeba)* thé (à la menthe/à l'absinthe)
juice *aseer* jus
beer *birra* bière
wine *sharab* vin
almond milk *aseer looz* jus d'amande
apple milk shake *aseer tufah* jus de pomme
banana milk shake *aseer banan* jus des bananes
orange juice *aseer limoon* jus d'orange
mixed fruit milk shake jus panaché

COMMON DISHES AND FOODS

bisara thick pea soup, usually served with olive oil and cumin
chakchouka a vegetable stew not unlike ratatouille, though sometimes containing meat or eggs
couscous aux sept seven-vegetable **légumes** couscous (sometimes vegetarian, though often made with meat stock)

harira bean soup, usually also containing pasta and meat

kefta minced meat (usually lamb)

loobia bean stew

mechoui roast lamb

merguez small, spicy dark red sausages – typically lamb, though sometimes beef – usually grilled over charcoal

pastilla sweet pigeon or chicken pie with cinnamon and filo pastry; a speciality of Fez

(pommes) frites French fries

salade Marocaine salad of tomato and cucumber, finely chopped

tajine a Moroccan casserole cooked over charcoal in a thick ceramic bowl (which is what the word really refers to) with a conical lid

tajine aux olives et citron tajine of chicken with olive and preserved lemon

tanjia a Marrakshi speciality, jugged beef – the term in fact refers to the jug

BREADS AND PASTRIES

briouats/doits sweet filo pastry with a **de Fatima** savoury filling, a bit like a miniature pastilla

briouats au miel sweet filo pastry envelopes filed with nuts and honey

cornes de gazelles marzipan-filled, banana-**(Fr.)/ kab l-ghazl (Ar.)** shaped pastry horns

harsha flat, leavened griddle bread with a gritty crust, served at cafés for breakast

m'hencha almond-filled pastry coils, often covered in honey or syrup

millefeuille custard slice

msimmen flat griddle bread made from dough sprinkled with oil, rolled out and folded over several times, rather like an Indian paratha

Berber words and phrases in Tashelhaït

There are three Moroccan Berber languages, based on geographical areas, and to a certain extent mutually intelligible. They are known by several names, of which these are the most common:

Tarfit, Riffi – The Rif mountains (Northern Morocco)

Tamazight, Zaian – The Middle and High Atlas (Central Morocco)

Tashelhaït, Soussi, Chleuh – The Anti-Atlas and Souss Valley (southern Morocco)

A standard written version of Berber, equivalent to Modern Standard Arabic, has now been introduced and is used for official purposes. The following is a very brief guide to **Tashelhaït words and phrases**.

BASICS

Yes, no Eyeh, oho

Thank you, please Barakalaufik

Good Eefulkee/Eeshwa

Bad Khaib

Today Ghasad

Tomorrow Sbah

Yesterday Eegdam

Excuse me Semhee

Berbers Shleuh

GREETINGS AND FAREWELLS (ALL ARABIC GREETINGS UNDERSTOOD)

Hello La bes darik (man); La bes darim (woman) (response – la bes)

How are you? Meneek antgeet? (response – la bes lmamdulah)

See you later Akrawes dah inshallah

Goodbye Akayaoon Arbee

Say hello to your family Sellum flfamilenik

DIRECTIONS AND NAMES ON MAPS

Where is...? Mani heela...?

...the road to... ...aghares s...

...the village... ...doowar...

...the river... ...aseet...

...the mountain... ...adrar...

...the pass... ...tizee...

...your house ...teegimeenik

Is it far/close? Ees yagoog/eeqareb?

Straight Neeshan

To the right/left Fofaseenik/fozelmad

Where are you going? Manee treet? (s.)/Manee drem? (pl.)

I want to go to... Reeh...(literally, "I want")

ON SURVEY MAPS YOU'LL FIND THESE NAMES:

Mountain Adrar, Jebel

River Assif, Oued

Pass (of) Tizi (n.)
Shepherd's hut Azib
Hill, small mountain Aourir

Ravine Talat
Rock Azrou
("n" between words indicates the possessive, "of")

BUYING AND NUMBERS

1 yen
2 seen
3 krad
4 koz
5 smoos
6 sddes
7 sa
8 tem
9 tza
10 mrawet
11 yen d mrawet
12 seen d mrawet
20 ashreent
21 ashreent d yen d mrawet
22 ashreent d seen d mrawet
30 ashreent d mrawet
40 snet id ashreent
50 snet id ashreent d mrawet
100 smoost id ashreent/ meeya
How much is it? Minshk aysker?

No good Oor eefulkee
Too expensive Eeghula bzef
Come down a Nuqs emeek**little (in price)**
Give me… Feeyee…
I want … Reeh…
Big/Small Mqorn/Eemzee
A lot/little Bzef/eemeek
Do you have…? Ees daroon…?
Is there…? Ees eela…?
…food …teeremt
…a mule …aserdon
…a place to sleep …kra lblast mahengwen
…water …amen

IMPERATIVES YOU MAY HEAR

Gawer, Skoos Sit
Soo Drink
Shta Eat
Rede (when handing something to someone) Here

Glossary

Adhan The call to prayer

Agadir Fortified granary, where grain, dates, gunpowder and other valuables were kept safe during times of inter-clan conflict

Agdal Garden or park containing a pool

Aguelmane Lake

Aïn Spring

Aït Tribe (literally, "sons of")

Alaouite Ruling Moroccan dynasty from the -seventeenth century to the present king, -Mohammed VI

Almohad The greatest of the medieval dynasties, ruled Morocco (and much of Spain) from c.1147 until the rise to power of the Merenids c.1224

Almoravids Dynasty that preceded the Almohads, from c.1060 to c.1147

Amazigh Berber

Andalous Muslim Spain (a territory that centred on modern Andalusia)

Arabesque Geometrical decoration or calligraphy

Assif River (often seasonal) in Berber

Bab Gate or door

Babouches Slippers

Baladiya Town hall or local council

Bali Old

Baraka Sanctity or blessing, obtained through saints or *marabouts*

Barbary European term for North Africa in the sixteenth to nineteenth centuries

Beni Tribe (literally, "sons of")

Berbers Original inhabitants of Morocco and their descendants, particularly those whose first language is Berber (though most Moroccans claim to be at least partly Berber)

Bildi Country-style (of the *bled*)

Bled Countryside, or, literally "land"; **Bled es Makhzen** – governed lands; **Bled es Siba** – land outside government control

Borj Fort

Cadi Islamic judge

Caid District administrator

Chleuh Tashelhaït-speaking Atlas and Souss Valley Berbers

Col Mountain pass (French)

Dar House or palace; **Dar el Makhzen**, royal palace

Darj w ktarf Literally "cheek and shoulder", an Almohad architectural motif resembling a fleur-de-lis

Daya, Deyet Lake

Erg Sand dune

Fakir Koranic schoolteacher or lawyer, or just an educated man

Fantasia Display of horsemanship performed at larger festivals or moussems

Fassi Inhabitant of Fez

Filali Alternative name for the Alaouite dynasty – from the southern Tafilalt region

Firdaous Paradise

Fondouk Inn and storehouse, known as a caravanserai in the eastern part of the Arab world

Gandoura Man's cotton garment (male equivalent of a kaftan); also known as a *fokia*

Gharb Coastal plain between Larache and Kenitra

Gnaoua Itinerant musician belonging to a brotherhood of West African origin (the name is from the same root as "Guinea")

Habbous Religious foundation or bequest of property for religious charities

Hadj Pilgrimage to Mecca

Hammada Stony desert of the sub-Sahara

Hammam Turkish-style steam bath

Harka "Burning" raid undertaken by sultans in order to raise taxes and assert authority

Idrissid First Arab dynasty of Morocco – named after its founder, Moulay Idriss

Imam Prayer leader and elder of mosque

Istiqlal Nationalist party founded during the struggle for independence

Jebel Mountain peak or ridge; a **Jebali** is someone from the mountains; the **Jebala** are the main tribe of the Western Rif

Jedid New

Jellaba Wool or cotton hooded outer garment

Jemaa, Jamaa Mosque, or Friday (the main day of worship)

Jinn Nature spirits (genies)

Joutia Flea market

Kasbah Palace centre and/or fortress of an Arab town; also used to mean a walled residential quarter around the Medina (eg Fez), or the citadel (eg Tangier and in Tunisia), or the whole Medina (eg Algiers). In the south of Morocco, it is a feudal family castle – and it's the root of the Spanish *alcazar*

Kedim Old

Khettara Underground irrigation canal

Kif Marijuana, cannabis

Koubba Dome; small *marabout* tomb

Ksar, Ksour (pl.) Village or tribal stronghold in the south

Lalla "Madam", also a saint

Litham Veil

Maghreb "West" in Arabic, used for Morocco and the North African countries

Maison d'hôte Guesthouse, usually upmarket

Makhzen Government

Marabout Holy man, and by extension his place of burial. These tombs, usually whitewashed domes, play an important (and heterodox) role in the religion of country areas

Mechouar Assembly place, court of judgment

Medersa Student residence and, in part, a teaching annexe, for the old mosque universities

Medina Literally, "city", now used for the original Arab part of any Moroccan town

Mellah Jewish quarter

Merenids Dynasty from eastern plains who ruled from the thirteenth to fifteenth centuries

Mihrab Niche indicating the direction of Mecca (and for prayer)

Minaret Tower attached to a mosque, used for call to prayer

Minbar The pulpit, usually placed next to the mihrab, from which the *imam* delivers his sermon at the midday Friday service in the mosque

Minzah Pavilion in a (usually palace) garden

Moulay Descendant of the Prophet Mohammed, a claim and title adopted by most Moroccan sultans

Mouloud Festival and birthday of the Prophet

Moussem Pilgrimage festival

Msalla Prayer area

Muezzin, Mueddin Singer who calls the faithful to prayer

Nazarene, Nsrani Christian, or, more loosely, a European

Oued (wadi in its anglicized form) River, but particularly a seasonal river or creek

Pisé Mud and rubble building material

Piste Unsurfaced road or track

PJD (Parti de la Justice et du Développement) Moderate Islamist political party, the largest party in Parliament

Protectorate period of French and Spanish colonial occupation (1912–56)

Qahouaji Café *patron*

Qahwa Coffee or café

Ramadan Month of fasting (see page 44)

Ras (literally "head") coastal headland; top or source

Ras el Ma Water source

Riad Patio garden, and by extension a house built around a patio garden; now also used to signify an upmarket guesthouse

Ribat Monastic fortress

Romi Urban, sophisticated – the opposite of *bildi* (see page 542)

Saadian Southern dynasty from Drâa Valley, who ruled Morocco during the fifteenth century

Sebgha Lake or lagoon

Sebsi Pipe for smoking *kif*

Seguia Irrigation canal

Sheikh Leader of religious brotherhood

Shereef Descendant of the Prophet

Sidi, Si Respectful title like "Sir"; also a saint

Souk Market, or market quarter

Sufi Religious mystic; philosophy behind most of the religious brotherhoods

Tabia Mud building material, as *pisé*

Tighremt Similar to an agadir – fortified Berber home and storage place

Tizi Mountain pass

Touareg Nomadic Berber tribesmen of the disputed Western Sahara, fancifully known as "Blue Men" because of the blue dye of their cloaks (which gives a slight tinge to their skin)

UMA (Union du Maghreb Arabe) Regional association of Morocco, Algeria, Tunisia, Libya and Mauritania

Wattasid Fifteenth-century dynasty who replaced their cousins, the Merenids

Zaouia Sanctuary established around a *marabout* tomb; seminary-type base for religious brotherhood

Zellij Geometrical mosaic tilework

Small print and index

A ROUGH GUIDE TO ROUGH GUIDES

Published in 1982, the first Rough Guide – to Greece – was a student scheme that became a publishing phenomenon. Mark Ellingham, a recent graduate in English from Bristol University, had been travelling in Greece the previous summer and couldn't find the right guidebook. With a small group of friends he wrote his own guide, combining a contemporary, journalistic style with a thoroughly practical approach to travellers' needs.

The immediate success of the book spawned a series that rapidly covered dozens of destinations. And, in addition to impecunious backpackers, Rough Guides soon acquired a much broader readership that relished the guides' wit and inquisitiveness as much as their enthusiastic, critical approach and value-for-money ethos. These days, Rough Guides include recommendations from budget to luxury and cover more than 120 destinations around the globe, from Amsterdam to Zanzibar, all regularly updated by our team of roaming writers.

Browse all our latest guides, read inspirational features and book your trip at **roughguides.com**.

Rough Guide credits

Editor: Kate Drynan
Cartography: Carte
Picture Manager: Tom Smyth

Layout: Grzegorz Madejak
Head of DTP and Pre-Press: Rebeka Davies
Head of Publishing: Sarah Clark

Publishing information

Thirteenth edition 2024

Distribution

UK, Ireland and Europe
Apa Publications (UK) Ltd; sales@roughguides.com
United States and Canada
Ingram Publisher Services; ips@ingramcontent.com
Australia and New Zealand
Booktopia; retailer@booktopia.com.au
Worldwide
Apa Publications (UK) Ltd; sales@roughguides.com

Special Sales, Content Licensing and CoPublishing
Rough Guides can be purchased in bulk quantities
at discounted prices. We can create special editions,
personalised jackets and corporate imprints tailored to
your needs. sales@roughguides.com.
roughguides.com

Printed in Czech Republic

This book was produced using **Typefi** automated
publishing software.

Help us update

We've gone to a lot of effort to ensure that this edition of
The Rough Guide to Morocco is accurate and up-to-date.
However, things change – places get "discovered", transport
routes are altered, restaurants and hotels raise prices or lower
standards, and businesses cease trading. If you feel we've got
it wrong or left something out, we'd like to know, and if you
can direct us to the web address, so much the better.
    Please send your comments with the subject
line "**Rough Guide Morocco Update**" to mail@
uk.roughguides.com. We'll acknowledge all contributions
and send a copy of the next edition (or any other Rough
Guide if you prefer) for the very best emails.

ABOUT THE AUTHOR

Stuart Butler is a guidebook author, writer and award-winning photographer who has
written multiple guidebooks on France. He also writes about Spain, East Africa (where he is
the tourism manager of a wildlife conservancy), the Himalayas and South Asia. He lives with
his wife and children in the far southwest of France and when not working can be found
surfing on the beautiful beaches of Les Landes or hiking in the gorgeous Pyrenees. Richard
Trillo has been visiting Kenya since the 1980s, when he first researched this Rough Guide. He
went on to write Rough Guides to many African countries and was Rough Guides' director of
communications. He is the East Africa manager of safari Operator ⓦexpertafrica.com, creating
tailor-made safari itineraries for travellers from all over the world.

Index

YOUR TAILOR-MADE TRIP
STARTS HERE

Tailor-made trips and unique adventures crafted by local experts

Rough Guides has been inspiring travellers with lively and thought-provoking guidebooks for more than 35 years. Now we're linking you up with selected local experts to craft your dream trip. They will put together your perfect itinerary and book it at local rates.

Don't follow the crowd – find your own path.

HOW ROUGHGUIDES.COM/TRIPS WORKS

STEP 1

Pick your dream destination, tell us what you want and submit an enquiry.

STEP 2

Fill in a short form to tell your local expert about your dream trip and preferences.

STEP 3

Our local expert will craft your tailor-made itinerary. You'll be able to tweak and refine it until you're completely satisfied.

STEP 4

Book online with ease, pack your bags and enjoy the trip! Our local expert will be on hand 24/7 while you're on the road.

BENEFITS OF PLANNING AND BOOKING AT ROUGHGUIDES.COM/TRIPS

PLAN YOUR ADVENTURE WITH LOCAL EXPERTS

Rough Guides' English-speaking local experts are hand-picked, based on their experience in the travel industry and their impeccable standards of customer service.

SAVE TIME AND GET ACCESS TO LOCAL KNOWLEDGE

When a local expert plans your trip, you save time and money when you book, even during high season. You won't be charged for using a credit card either.

MAKE TRAVEL A BREEZE: BOOK WITH PEACE OF MIND

Enjoy stress-free travel when you use Rough Guides' secure online booking platform. All bookings come with a money-back guarantee.

WHAT DO OTHER TRAVELLERS THINK ABOUT ROUGH GUIDES TRIPS?

Trip to Spain

This Spain tour company did a fantastic job to make our dream trip perfect. We gave them our travel budget, told them where we would like to go, and they did all of the planning. Our drivers and tour guides were always on time and very knowledgable. The hotel accommodations were better than we would have found on our own. Only one time did we end up in a location that we had not intended to be in. We called the 24 hour phone number, and they immediately fixed the situation.

Don A, USA ★★★★★

Trip to Morocco

Our trip was fantastic! Transportation, accommodations, guides – all were well chosen! The hotels were well situated, well appointed and had helpful, friendly staff. All of the guides we had were very knowledgeable, patient, and flexible with our varied interests in the different sites. We particularly enjoyed the side trip to Tangier! Well done! The itinerary you arranged for us allowed maximum coverage of the country with time in each city for seeing the important places.

Sharon, USA ★★★★★

PLAN AND BOOK YOUR TRIP AT ROUGHGUIDES.COM/TRIPS

Map symbols

The symbols below are used on maps throughout the book

——	International boundary	★	Transport stop	〰	Mountain range	✡	Synagogue
– – –	Chapter boundary	P	Parking	▲	Peak	☦	Tomb
	Motorway	♦	Point of interest	Gorge	Gorge	▨	Mosque
——	Main road	@	Internet access	◖	Dune	⊞	Church
——	Minor road	ⓘ	Tourist office	◗	Cave	▽	Mosque
	Pedestrian road	✉	Post office	⦂	Ruins	▢	Market
= = =	Unpaved road	©	Telephone	🏠	Refuge hut	◯	Stadium
•–•–•	4WD	⊞	Hospital	↑	Rooms	▨	Building
⊓⊓⊓⊓	Steps	⊤	Gardens/fountain	//	Mountain pass	▢	Park
═══	Railway	⊙	Statue	⚘	Waterfall	▢	Beach
– – – –	Ski lift	⛽	Fuel station	⊤	Oasis	⊡	Christian cemetery
— -	Ferry route	⛳	Golf course	⚲	Viewpoint	⊡	Jewish cemetery
– – – –	Footpath	∩	Arch	⊤	Lighthouse	⊡	Muslim cemetery
——	Wall	♟✖	Fort/fortress	▮	Tower	⊡	Saltpan
✈	International airport	⊠-⊠	Gate	⊓	Ksar	▨	Dried river
✈	Domestic airport	🚻	Toilets	✂	Battle site		

Listings key

■	Accommodation
●	Eating
■	Drinking/nightlife
●	Shopping